MW01611800

GREENBOOK

New York
Surrogate's Court

2022 Edition

Surrogate's Court Procedure Act

Estates, Powers and Trusts Law

Related Materials:

**Uniform Rules for Surrogate's Court and Related Rules • Official
Forms for Use in Surrogate's Court • Tax Law Article 26 • General
Obligations Law Article 5 Title 15 • Mental Hygiene Law Articles 81
and 83 • Public Health Law Articles 25-B, 29-B, 29-C, 29-CC, 29-
CCC, 42, 43 & 43-A• Domestic Relations Law Articles 2 and 7**

As amended by the 2021 Regular Legislative Session thru Chapter 480

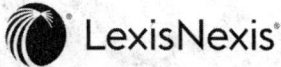

QUESTIONS ABOUT THIS PUBLICATION?

For questions about the **Editorial Content** appearing in these volumes or reprint permission, please call:

Cathy J. Seidenberg, J. D. at .... Direct Dial: (908) 673-3379
Email: .... Cathy.J.Seidenberg@lexisnexis.com
Outside the United States and Canada, please call . . . . (973) 820-2000

For assistance with replacement pages, shipments, billing or other customer service matters, please call:

Customer Services Department at . . . . (800) 833-9844
Outside the United States and Canada, please call . . . . (518) 487-3385
Fax Number . . . . (800) 828-8341
Customer Service Website . . . . http://www.lexisnexis.com/custserv/

For information on other Matthew Bender publications, please call
Your account manager or . . . . (800) 223-1940
Outside the United States and Canada, please call . . . . (937) 247-0293

ISBN: 978-1-6633-2904-2 (print)

Editorial Office
230 Park Ave., 7th Floor, New York, NY 10169 (800) 543-6862
www.lexisnexis.com

MATTHEW◆BENDER

TABLE OF CONTENTS

TABLES OF LEGISLATIVE AMENDMENTS

SURROGATE'S COURT PROCEDURE ACT

ESTATES, POWERS AND TRUSTS LAW

UNIFORM RULES FOR SURROGATE'S COURT (22 NYCRR PART 207)

RULES OF THE CHIEF JUDGE (22 NYCRR PART 36)

ESTATE TAX RULES (20 NYCRR Parts 360–363)

RULES FOR TRUSTS AND ESTATES WITH A CHARITABLE INTEREST (13 NYCRR Part 92)

TABLE OF CONTENTS

OFFICIAL FORMS

Official Forms for Use in Surrogate's Court

Surrogate's Court Checklists

Official Forms Prescribed by Surrogate's Court Procedure Act for Use in Adoptions

NEW YORK STATE TAX LAW ART. 26, Estate Tax

GENERAL OBLIGATIONS LAW ART. 5, TITLE 15, Statutory Short Form Power of Attorney

MENTAL HYGIENE LAW

PUBLIC HEALTH LAW

DOMESTIC RELATIONS LAW

TABLE OF CONTENTS

COURT DIRECTORY

INTEGRATED INDEX

TABLE OF AMENDMENTS

TABLE I
Table of 2021 SCPA Amendments

SCPA Section	Amendment	Effective Date
2222-a	Amended the heading and the section to replace "inmate" with "incarcerated person"	8/2/2021

TABLE II
Table of 2021 EPTL Amendments

EPTL Section	Amendment	Effective Date
	There were no 2021 amendments to the EPTL	

TABLE III
Table of 2021 Tax Law Amendments

Tax Law Section	Amendment	Effective Date
	There were no 2021 amendments to the Estate Tax law	

TABLE IV
Table of 2021 General Obligations Law Amendments

GOL Section	Amendment	Effective Date
5-1501B	Amended subd. 1(b) to add a requirement that two disinterested witnesses sign the power of attorney form	6/13/2021
5-1504	Amended the heading and subd. 1 to add a requirement that two disinterested witnesses sign the power of attorney form; amended subd. 3 to exempt the Department of Health, including social services districts, in the administration of the Medicaid program or other public health insurance programs from the requirement that third parties honor or reject a statutory short form power of attorney within ten business days	6/13/2021
5-1513	Amended the form to make technical changes to the statutory short form sections relating to the designation of multiple agents and add witnessing requirements	6/13/2021

TABLE V
Table of 2021 Mental Hygiene Law Amendments

Mental Hygiene Law Section	Amendment	Effective Date
	There were no 2021 amendments to Mental Hygiene Law Arts 81 or 83	

TABLE VI
Table of 2021 Public Health Law Amendments

Public Health Law Section	Amendment	Effective Date
	There were no 2021 amendments to the Public Health Law articles included in this volume	

TABLE VI
Table of 2021 Domestic Relations Law Amendments

Domestic Relations Law Section	Amendment	Effective Date
111–d	New section, Consideration of blindness during adoption proceedings, added	1/6/2022

SURROGATE'S COURT PROCEDURE ACT

Table of Contents

SCPA

ARTICLE 1
GENERAL
SUMMARY OF ARTICLE

SCPA

§ 101. Short title; how cited

This act shall be known as the surrogate's court procedure act and may be cited as "SCPA". A provision of this act may be cited by its number without being preceded either by the word "section" or the symbol "§". Reference to an article or section without reference to another law shall be deemed to refer to an article or section of this act.

History: Add, L 1966, ch 953, eff Sept 1, 1967 from Sur. Ct. Act § 1 and CPLR § 101.

§ 102. Application of CPLR and other laws

The CPLR and other laws applicable to practice and procedure apply in the surrogate's court except where other procedure is provided by this act.

History: Add, L 1966, ch 953, eff Sept 1, 1967 from Sur. Ct. Act § 316.

§ 103. Definitions

When used in this act, unless otherwise required by the context, or unless a contrary intent is expressly declared in the provision to be construed, the words, phrases or clauses hereafter shall be construed as follows:

1. Acknowledged. Acknowledged or proved in the same manner as a deed is required to be acknowledged or proved and authenticated to be recorded in that county, except that when executed within the state, no certificate of the county clerk shall be required.

2. Administrator. Any person to whom letters of administration have been issued.

3. Administrator c. t. a. Any person to whom letters of administration with the will annexed have been issued.

4. Administrator d. b. n. Any person to whom letters of administration have been issued as a successor to an administrator.

5. Ancillary administrator. Any person to whom ancillary letters of administration have been issued.

6. Ancillary executor or administrator c. t. a. Any person to whom ancillary letters testamentary or ancillary letters of administration c. t. a. have been issued.

7. Ancillary guardian. Any person to whom ancillary letters of guardianship, whether of the person, property, or both, of an infant have been issued.

8. Beneficiary. Any person entitled to any part or all of an estate.

9. Bequest or legacy. A transfer of personal property by will.

9-a. Corporate trustee. Any trust company, any bank authorized to exercise fiduciary powers and any national bank having a principal, branch or trust office in this state and duly authorized to exercise fiduciary powers.

10. Court. The surrogate's court, including any judge or surrogate assigned, elected or appointed to serve as judge of the court.

11. Creditor. Any person having a claim against a decedent or an estate.

12. Devise. When used as a noun, a transfer of real property by will. When used as a verb, to transfer real property by will.

13. Devisee. Any person to whom real property is transferred by will.

14. Distributee. Any person entitled to take or share in the property of a decedent under the statutes governing descent and distribution.

15. Domicile. A fixed, permanent and principal home to which a person wherever temporarily located always intends to return.

16. Domiciliary. A person whose domicile is within the state of New York.

17. Donee of a power during minority. Any person granted or deemed to have the power during minority to manage property vested in an infant.

18. Eligible to receive letters. Not disqualified on any of the grounds described in 707.

19. Estate. All of the property of a decedent, trust, absentee, internee or person for whom a guardian has been appointed as originally constituted, and as it from time to time exists during administration.

20. Executor. Any person to whom letters testamentary have been issued.

21. Fiduciary. An administrator, administrator c.t.a., administrator d.b.n., ancillary administrator, ancillary administrator c.t.a., ancillary executor, ancillary guardian, executor, guardian, preliminary executor, temporary administrator, testamentary trustee, to any of whom letters have been issued, and also the donee of a power during minority and a voluntary administrator and a public administrator acting as administrator or a public administrator or county treasurer to whom letters have been issued, and a lifetime trustee.

22. Funeral expense. Includes reasonable expense of a funeral, suitable church or other services as an integral part thereof, expense of interment or other disposition of the body, a burial lot and suitable monumental work thereon and a reasonable expenditure for perpetual care of a burial lot of the decedent. For the purpose of subdivision one of section eighteen hundred eleven of this act, funeral expense shall also include burial expenses awarded pursuant to article twenty-two of the executive law.

23. Grantor. The creator of a lifetime trust.

24. Guardian. Any person to whom letters of guardianship have been issued by a court of this state, pursuant to this act, the family court act or article 81 of the mental hygiene law.

25. Incapacitated person. Any person who for any cause is incapable adequately to protect his or her rights, including a person for whom a guardian has been appointed

pursuant to article 81 of the mental hygiene law.

26. Incompetent. Any person judicially declared incompetent to manage his affairs.

26-a. Individual trustee. Any trustee who is not a corporate trustee.

27. Infant. Any person under the age of eighteen years; provided, however, that for purposes of appointment of a guardian of an infant, the term infant also shall include a person who is under the age of twenty-one years who consents to the appointment of a guardian after the age of eighteen. It is further provided that such definition shall not be applicable to any provision relating to the New York Uniform Transfers to Minors Act, nor to section 1716 of this act.

28. Intestate. A person who dies without leaving a valid will. Where it is used with respect to particular property, a person who dies without effectively disposing of that property by will. When used as an adjective, to property not effectively disposed of by will.

29. Judicial settlement. A proceeding whereby the account of a fiduciary is settled and adjudicated by decree of the court.

30. Legal life tenant. Any person entitled for his life or for the life of another to the possession and use of real or personal property.

31. Lifetime trust. An express trust, including all amendments thereto, created during the grantor's lifetime other than a trust for the benefit of creditors, a resulting or constructive trust, a business trust where certificates of beneficial interest are issued to the beneficiary, an investment trust, voting trust, a security instrument such as a deed of trust and a mortgage, a trust created by the judgment or decree of a court, a liquidation or reorganization trust, a trust for the sole purpose of paying dividends, interest, interest coupons, salaries, wages, pensions or profits, instruments wherein persons are mere nominees for others, or a trust created in deposits in any banking institution or savings and loan institution.

32. Lifetime trustee. A trustee acting under a lifetime trust.

33. Legatee. Any person designated to receive a transfer by will of personal property.

34. Letters. Includes letters of administration, letters of administration c. t. a., letters of administration d. b. n., limited letters of administration, ancillary letters of administration, ancillary letters of guardianship, ancillary letters testamentary, letters of guardianship, letters of temporary administration, letters testamentary, preliminary letters testamentary and letters of trusteeship. A testamentary trustee who has qualified without the issuance of letters shall be deemed for the purposes of this act to have received letters of trusteeship.

35. Mailing or mail. A direction to mail or for mailing of process, notice or other paper requires deposit of such process, notice or other paper enclosed in a sealed postpaid envelope, directed to the person to be served or notified, in any post office or other depositary under the exclusive care and custody of the United States Postal Service.

35-a. Mailing by express mail. Mailing in conformity with the requirements of the United States Postal Service respecting express mail.

36. Mailing by registered or certified mail. A direction for mailing of process, notice or

other paper by registered or certified mail requires mailing in conformity with the requirements of the United States Postal Service respecting registered or certified mail, as the case may be.

37. Mailing by registered or certified mail; return receipt requested. Mailing in conformity with the requirements of the United States Postal Service respecting registered mail with return receipt requested or certified mail with return receipt requested, as the case may be.

37-a. Mailing by special mail service. A direction for mailing of process, notice or other paper by special mail service requires mailing by express mail or use of any designated delivery service within the meaning of § 7502(f)(2) of the United States Internal Revenue Code of 1986, as from time to time amended.

38. May. When used in this act, in relation to an act to be performed by the court, means in the discretion of the court.

39. Person interested. Any person entitled or allegedly entitled to share as beneficiary in the estate or the trustee in bankruptcy or receiver of such person. A creditor shall not be deemed a person interested. Where this act provides that a "person interested" may apply for relief, a verified allegation of an interest in fact, suffices for the purpose of the application, although the interest may be disputed, unless or until the fact of interest has been judicially determined and no appeal is pending therefrom.

40. Person under disability. Any person who is (a) an infant, (b) an incompetent, (c) an incapacitated person, (d) unknown or whose whereabouts are unknown or (e) confined as a prisoner who fails to appear under circumstances which the court finds are due to confinement in a penal institution.

40-a. Petition. A verified application in the manner provided in CPLR 3020, requesting action upon a matter or relief provided for in the estates, powers and trusts law or this act.

41. Preliminary executor. Any person to whom preliminary letters testamentary have been issued.

42. Presumptive distributee. Any person who would be a distributee as defined in this act, if the person alleged to be deceased, absentee or internee were dead.

43. Process. Citation, order to show cause, subpoena and any other mandate of the surrogate's court by which jurisdiction is obtained of a party.

44. Property. Anything that may be the subject of ownership and is real or personal property, or is a chose in action.

45. Respondent. Every party to a proceeding except a petitioner.

46. Safe deposit company. Any corporation authorized under the banking law to let out receptacles for safe deposit of personal property.

47. Temporary administrator. Any person to whom letters of temporary administration have been issued.

48. Testamentary trust. A trust created by will.

49. Testamentary trustee. Any person to whom letters of trusteeship have been issued.

50. Trust. A testamentary trust or a lifetime trust.

51. Upon the return of process. The time and place for the return of any process and any adjournment thereof, and implies that due proof has been made that the court has jurisdiction over all parties who appeared, have waived or been duly served.

52. Will. A last will, including all the codicils thereto.

Derivation: Add, L 1966, ch 953, eff Sept 1, 1967; amd, L 1967, ch 685, § 2, eff Sept 1, 1967. See below.

Subd. (1): New. Derived Sur. Ct. Act § 314(14).

Subd. (2): New. Derived Sur. Ct. Act §§ 136, 217-a.

Subd. (3): New. Derived Sur. Ct. Act § 133.

Subd. (4): New. Derived Sur. Ct. Act § 136.

Subd. (5): New. Derived Sur. Ct. Act § 159.

Subd. (6): New. Derived Sur. Ct. Act § 159.

Subd. (7): New. Derived Sur. Ct. Act §§ 159, 172, 184, 314(13).

Subd. (8): New. Added by L 1966, ch 953, eff Sept 1, 1967.

Subd. (9): New. Added by L 1966, ch 953, eff Sept 1, 1967.

Subd. (10): New. Const., Art. 6.

Subd. (11): New. Derived Sur. Ct. Act § 314(3); Debtor & Cred. § 270.

Subd. (12): New. Added by L 1966, ch 953, eff Sept 1, 1967.

Subd. (13): New. Added by L 1966, ch 953, eff Sept 1, 1967.

Subd. (14): New. Added by L 1966, ch 953, eff Sept 1, 1967.

Subd. (15): New. Added by L 1966, ch 953, eff Sept 1, 1967.

Subd. (16): New. Added by L 1966, ch 953, eff Sept 1, 1967.

Subd. (17): New. Derived RPL Art. 5.

Subd. (18): New. Added by L 1966, ch 953, eff Sept 1, 1967.

Subd. (19): New. Added by L 1966, ch 953, eff Sept 1, 1967.

Subd. (20): New. Added by L 1966, ch 953, eff Sept 1, 1967.

Subd. (21): New. Derived Sur. Ct. Act § 215-a.

Subd. (22): Added from Sur. Ct. Act § 314(3).

Subd. (23): New. Derived Sur. Ct. Act §§ 172, 314(13).

Subd. (24): New. Derived Sur. Ct. Act §§ 60, 64.

Subd. (25): New. Derived Sur. Ct. Act §§ 59, 63, 64.

Subd. (26): New. Derived Dom. Rel. § 2.

Subd. (27): New. Derived Sur. Ct. Act § 341(1).

Subd. (28): Added from Sur. Ct. Act § 314(8).

Subd. (29): New. Added by L 1966, ch 953, eff Sept 1, 1967.

Subd. (30): New. Added by L 1966, ch 953, eff Sept 1, 1967.

Subd. (31): New. Added by L 1966, ch 953, eff Sept 1, 1967.

Subd. (32): Added from Sur. Ct. Act §§ 59, 314(7).

Subd. (33): New. Derived Sur. Ct. Act §§ 125-c, 136-aa.

Subd. (34): New. Derived Sur. Ct. Act §§ 125-c, 136-aa.

Subd. (35): New. Added by L 1966, ch 953, eff Sept 1, 1967.

Subd. (36): Added from Sur. Ct. Act § 314(10).

Subd. (37): New. Added by L 1966, ch 953, eff Sept 1, 1967.

Subd. (38): New. Added by L 1966, ch 953, eff Sept 1, 1967.

SCPA

Subd. (39):   New. Added by L 1966, ch 953, eff Sept 1, 1967.

Subd. (40):   New. Derived Sur. Ct. Act § 52.

Subd. (41):   Added from Sur. Ct. Act § 314(12) and Gen. Const. § 39.

Subd. (42):   Added from Sur. Ct. Act § 314(15).

Subd. (43):   Added from Banking Law.

Subd. (44):   New. Derived Sur. Ct. Act § 126.

Subd. (45):   Added from Sur. Ct. Act § 314(6).

Subd. (46):   Added from Sur. Ct. Act § 314(9).

Subd. (47):   Added from Sur. Ct. Act § 314(4).

History: Amd, L 1967, ch 685, § 2, eff Sept 1, 1967; L 1968, ch 259 § 1, eff May 14, 1968; L 1968, ch 259, § 1, eff May 14, 1968; L 1974, ch 904, eff Sept 1, 1974, but shall not be construed so as to impair or render ineffectual any proceedings commenced pursuant to law prior to the time the act takes effect; L 1980, ch 135, § 1; L 1980, ch 501, § 1, eff June 24, 1980; L 1980, ch 503, § 1, eff June 24, 1980; L 1981, ch 115, § 110; L 1984, ch 936, § 1, eff Aug 6, 1984, applying to any trust in existence on or after Aug 6, 1984; L 1993, ch 514, §§ 1, 2, eff Jan 1, 1994; L 1999, ch 231, § 7, eff July 13, 1999; L 2000, ch 355, §§ 1, 2, eff Nov 1, 2000; L 2002, ch 134, § 5, eff July 23, 2002; L 2006, ch 518, § 3, eff Aug 16, 2006; L 2018, ch 494, § 5, eff June 26, 2019.

§ 104. Application of act; confirmation of previous acts

Each provision of this act relating to the jurisdiction of the surrogate's court over lifetime trusts or to take the proof of a will and to grant letters or appoint trustees or regulating the mode of procedure in any manner concerning a lifetime trust or an estate of a decedent applies unless otherwise expressly declared therein, whether the estate, if a lifetime trust, was created, or the will was made or the decedent died before or after this act takes effect. All acts hitherto of surrogates and officers acting as such by completing and certifying in their own names any uncertified wills, and by signing and certifying in their own names any uncertified records of wills, and of other proofs and examinations taken in the proceedings of probate thereof before their predecessors in office, are hereby confirmed and declared to be valid and in full compliance with the pre-existing statutory requirements.

History: Add, L 1966, ch 953, eff Sept 1, 1967 from Sur. Ct. Act § 315; amd, L 1980, ch 503, § 2, eff June 24, 1980.

§ 105. Rules for surrogates' courts

The court in each county may make such rules for the conduct of business in its court as it may deem necessary, not inconsistent with statute, and subject to the rules and orders of the administrative board and appellate division applicable thereto.

History: Add, L 1966, ch 953, eff Sept 1, 1967 from RCP § 2 and Jud. Law § 7-a.

§ 106. Appendix of official forms

The state administrator of the state of New York shall have the power to adopt, amend and rescind an appendix of forms. Forms adopted pursuant to this section shall be sufficient under the surrogate's court procedure act and shall be accepted for filing in all of the surrogate's courts. Any judge of the surrogate's court may provide forms other than the official forms for use in his county, provided, however, that the use of such forms shall not be required instead of the official forms.

History: Add, L 1975, ch 157, § 1, eff Sept 1, 1975.

§ 107. Use of electronic filing authorized

1. Notwithstanding any other provision of law, the chief administrator of the courts may authorize a program in the use of electronic means in the surrogate's court as provided in article twenty-one-A of the civil practice law and rules.

2. For purposes of this section, "electronic means" shall be as defined in subdivision (f) of rule twenty-one hundred three of the civil practice law and rules.

History: Add, L 2015, ch 237, § 9, eff Aug 31, 2015.

ARTICLE 2
JURISDICTION AND POWERS

SUMMARY OF ARTICLE

§ 201. General jurisdiction of the surrogate's court

1. The court has, is granted and shall continue to be vested with all the jurisdiction conferred upon it by the Constitution of the State of New York, and all other authority and jurisdiction now or hereafter conferred upon the court by any general or special statute or provision of law, including this act.

2. This and any grant of jurisdiction to the court shall be deemed an affirmative exercise of the legislative power under § 12 (e) of article VI of the Constitution and shall in all instances be deemed to include and confer upon the court full equity jurisdiction as to any action, proceeding or other matter over which jurisdiction is or may be conferred.

3. The court shall continue to exercise full and complete general jurisdiction in law and in equity to administer justice in all matters relating to estates and the affairs of decedents, and upon the return of any process to try and determine all questions, legal or equitable, arising between any or all of the parties to any action or proceeding, or between any party and any other person having any claim or interest therein, over whom jurisdiction has been obtained as to any and all matters necessary to be determined in order to make a full, equitable and complete disposition of the matter by such order or decree as justice requires.

> **History:** Add, L 1966, ch 953, eff Sept 1, 1967 from Sur. Ct. Act §§ 20, 40, 173, 174 and Const. Art. VI § 12; amd, L 1980, ch 503, § 3, eff June 24, 1980.

§ 202. Enumerated proceedings not exclusive

The proceedings enumerated in this act shall not be deemed exclusive and the court is empowered in any proceeding, whether or not specifically provided for, to exercise any of the jurisdiction granted to it by this act or other provisions of law, notwithstanding that the jurisdiction sought to be exercised in the proceeding is or may be exercised in or incidental to a different proceeding.

> **History:** Add, L 1966, ch 953, eff Sept 1, 1967.

§ 203. Jurisdiction of parties and subject matter

The court obtains jurisdiction in every case to make a decree or other determination by the existence of the jurisdictional facts prescribed by statute.

The jurisdiction of the court is exercised by the commencement of a proceeding in the court. All proceedings are special proceedings and are commenced by filing a petition. Personal jurisdiction of parties is obtained by service of process upon the parties or by submission to the jurisdiction of the court by waiver of issuance and service of process, appearance of an adult competent party in person or by attorney or by pleading.

> **History:** Add, L 1966, ch 953, eff Sept 1, 1967 derived in part from Sur. Ct. Act §§ 41, 42, and part from § 48 and CPLR § 304; amd, L 1968, ch 259, § 2, eff May 14, 1968.

§ 204. Presumption of jurisdiction

Where the jurisdiction of the court to make a decree or other determination is drawn in question collaterally, the jurisdiction is presumptively and in the absence of fraud or collusion, conclusively established by an allegation of the jurisdictional facts contained in a verified pleading. Jurisdiction of the parties is presumptively proved by a recital to that effect in the decree.

> **History:** Add, L 1966, ch 953, eff Sept 1, 1967 from Sur. Ct. Act § 43.

§ 205. Domiciliaries; jurisdiction and venue

1. The surrogate's court of any county has jurisdiction over the estate of a decedent who was a domiciliary of the state at the time of his death, disappearance or internment. The proper venue for proceedings relating to such estates is the county of the decedent's domicile at the time of his death, disappearance or internment.

2. A surrogate shall transfer any proceeding to the surrogate's court of the proper county either on his own motion or on the motion of any party.

3. Notwithstanding the foregoing provisions of this section, the surrogate's court of any county has jurisdiction over, and is a proper venue for, the proceedings of any decedent who was a domiciliary of the state at the time of his or her death and who died as a result of wounds or injury incurred as a result of the terrorist attacks on September eleventh, two thousand one.

> **History:** Add, L 1984, ch 128, § 1, eff June 21, 1984, repealing former section 205 entitled, "Effect of exercise of jurisdiction"; amd, L 2002, ch 73, § 5, eff May 21, 2002.

§ 206. Non-domiciliaries; jurisdiction and venue

1. The surrogate's court of any county has jurisdiction over the estate of any non-domiciliary decedent who leaves property in the state, or a cause of action for wrongful death against a domiciliary of the state. The proper venue for proceedings relating to such estates is the county (a) where the non-domiciliary decedent left property, or (b) where personal property belonging to the non-domiciliary decedent has since his death, disappearance or internment come into and remains unadministered, or (c) of the domicile of the person against whom a non-domiciliary left a cause of action for wrongful death.

2. Where venue may lie in more than one county under the provisions of subdivision one, the court where a proceeding is first commenced with proper venue shall retain jurisdiction, and matters relating to the estate of the non-domiciliary decedent pending in the surrogate's courts of other counties shall be transferred to it.

3. A surrogate shall transfer any proceeding to the surrogate's court of the proper county either on his own motion or on the motion of any party.

History: Add, L 1984, ch 128, § 1, eff June 21, 1984, repealing former section 206 entitled, "Exclusive jurisdiction".

§ 207. Lifetime trusts; jurisdiction and venue

1. The surrogate's court of any county has jurisdiction over the estate of any lifetime trust which has assets in the state, or of which the grantor was a domiciliary of the state at the time of the commencement of a proceeding concerning the trust, or of which a trustee then acting resides in the state or, if other than a natural person, has its principal office in the state. The proper venue for proceedings relating to such lifetime trusts is the county where (a) assets of the trust estate are located, or (b) the grantor was domiciled at the time of the commencement of a proceeding concerning the trust, or (c) a trustee then acting resides, or, if other than a natural person, has its principal office.

2. Where venue may lie in more than one county under the provisions of subdivision one, the court where a proceeding is first commenced with proper venue shall retain jurisdiction, and matters relating to the estate of the lifetime trust pending in the surrogate's courts of other counties shall be transferred to it.

3. A surrogate shall transfer any proceeding to the surrogate's court of the proper county either on his own motion or on the motion of any party.

History: Add, L 1984, ch 128, § 1, eff June 21, 1984, repealing former section 207 entitled, "Concurrent jurisdiction of two or more courts over estate of non-domiciliary".

§ 208. Jurisdiction; how affected by locality of certain assets

For the purpose of conferring jurisdiction upon the court:

1. A debt or a cause of action for wrongful death, in favor of a non-domiciliary against a domiciliary, is deemed personal property in the county where the domiciliary, or either of two or more such domiciliaries resides, or if other than a natural person, such domiciliary has its principal office, except that a debt evidenced by a negotiable instrument is deemed for jurisdictional purposes personal property in the county of the situs of the instrument.

2. An insurance policy upon the life of a non-domiciliary decedent shall have the situs of the principal office in this state of the company or corporation issuing the policy of insurance.

3. A share of stock of a corporation of this state owned by a non-domiciliary is deemed personal property in the county where the corporation has its principal office.

4. A life insurance policy or share of stock owned by a non-domiciliary is deemed personal property in the county where the policy or share of stock is situated, the provisions of subdivisions 2 and 3 notwithstanding.

History: Add, L 1966, ch 953, eff Sept 1, 1967 from Sur. Ct. Act § 47 in part; amd, L 1967, ch 685, §§ 4, 5, eff Sept 1, 1967.

§ 209. Powers incidental to jurisdiction of the court

The court has power:

1. To open, vacate, modify or set aside any decree or order of the court directing distribution of the property of an estate which was made prior to the probate of and without knowledge of a will which affects such distribution, and in the same or a different

proceeding, and on notice to the persons or the fiduciaries of the persons to whom the property has been distributed, to make such further and different direction as to such distribution as justice may require, and as an incident thereto, order the refund of any property theretofore distributed erroneously.

2. To sign any decision, decree or order, with its usual signature or initials, and all decisions, decrees or orders heretofore or hereafter so signed shall be valid and binding.

3. To transfer for trial in the surrogate's court having jurisdiction any action or proceeding pending in any court other than the supreme court, which affects or relates to the administration of an estate and to receive for trial any such action or proceeding pending in the supreme court which may by order of the latter court be transferred to the surrogate's court on the prior order of that court and to transfer any action or proceeding other than one which has been previously transferred to it or which affects or relates to the administration of an estate, to any other court, except the supreme court, having jurisdiction of the subject matter in any other judicial district or county provided such other court has jurisdiction over the classes of persons named as parties.

4. To determine a decedent's interest in any property claimed to constitute a part of his gross estate subject to estate tax, or to be property available for distribution under his will or in intestacy or for payment of claims, and to determine the rights of any persons claiming an interest therein, as against the decedent, or as between themselves, and to construe any instruments made by him affecting such property.

5. To settle the account of a fiduciary of a common trust fund as provided in the banking law.

6. To determine any and all matters relating to lifetime trusts.

7. To entertain a proceeding under EPTL 8-1.1.

8. To dismiss any proceeding which the petitioner has neglected to prosecute diligently.

9. To determine any unfinished business pending before its predecessor in office and to sign or certify papers or records left uncompleted or unsigned by its predecessor.

10. In the exercise of its jurisdiction, the court shall have all of the powers that the supreme court would have in like actions and proceedings including, but not limited to, such incidental powers as are necessary to carry into effect all powers expressly conferred herein.

11. The enumeration of powers herein shall not be deemed exclusive.

History: Add, L 1966, ch 953, eff Sept 1, 1967, derived in part from Sur. Ct. Act and in part new, as indicated below. Subd. (1): Added from Sur. Ct. Act § 20(6-a). Subd. (2): Added from Sur. Ct. Act § 20(13). Subd. (3): Added from Sur. Ct. Act § 40(9). Subd. (4): Added from Sur. Ct. Act §§ 20, 49, 145 and Tax Law. Subd. (5): Added from Sur. Ct. Act § 40(10). Subd. (6): New. Added by 1966 N.Y. Laws 953, in effect Sept 1, 1967. Subd. (7): New. Added by 1966 N.Y. Laws 953, in effect Sept 1, 1967. Subd. (8): Added from Sur. Ct. Act § 20(11). Subd. (9): New. Added by 1966 N.Y. Laws 953, in effect Sept 1, 1967. Amd, L 1980, ch 503, § 5, eff June 24, 1980; L 1990, ch 190, § 118, eff May 25, 1990, provided, with respect to estates of decedents dying on or before May 25 1990, the statute as it existed prior to this amendment will apply; L 1995, ch 468, § 1, eff Sept 1, 1995.

§ 210. Jurisdictional predicate

1. Traditional bases. The court shall exercise jurisdiction over persons and property as heretofore or hereafter permitted by law.

2. Additional bases.

(a) The court may exercise personal jurisdiction over any non-domiciliary, or his fiduciary, as to any matter within the subject matter jurisdiction of the court arising from any act or omission of the non-domiciliary within the state, either in person or through an agent and the court may exercise personal jurisdiction over any non-domiciliary, or his fiduciary, as to any matter arising from any act or omission of the non-domiciliary without the state affecting the real property in this state which was in the name of the domiciliary decedent of an estate or personal property which was on deposit in this state in a savings bank, savings and loan institution, commercial bank, lending institution or a brokerage account, stocks, bonds or other marketable securities registered in the name of the domiciliary decedent or with another within one year of the date of death of the domiciliary decedent.

(b) The receipt and acceptance of any property paid or distributed out of and as part of the administration of an estate subject to the jurisdiction of the court, other than the payment of taxes under article 26 of the tax law to the commissioner of taxation and finance, shall constitute a submission by such recipient to the jurisdiction of the court as to any matter concerning the payment or distribution, including proceedings for the recovery thereof.

History: Add, L 1966, ch 953, eff Sept 1, 1967 from CPLR §§ 301, 302; amd, L 1990, ch 190, § 119, eff May 25, 1990, provided, with respect to estates of decedents dying on or before May 25, 1990, the statute as it existed prior to this amendment will apply; L 1993, ch 514, § 3, eff Jan 1, 1994.

§ 211. When jurisdiction in personam obtained

The court may exercise personal jurisdiction over any person as to any matter within the subject matter jurisdiction of the court, if, on analogous facts in an action in the supreme court, such person would be subject to the personal jurisdiction of that court.

History: Add, L 1966, ch 953, eff Sept 1, 1967.

§ 212. Service of process

All processes of the court may be served and executed in any part of the state and without the state when authorized by law.

History: New. Add, L 1966, ch 953, eff Sept 1, 1967; amd, L 1967, ch 685, § 6, eff Sept 1, 1967 from Const. Art. VI § 1(c).

ARTICLE 3
PROCEEDINGS, PLEADINGS AND PROCESS
SUMMARY OF ARTICLE

§ 301. Statute of limitations

(a) For the purpose of computing the period of limitation under article two of the civil practice law and rules, a proceeding is commenced upon the filing of a petition, provided process is issued and service made upon any respondent within one hundred twenty days after the date of the filing of the petition, except that when process is served by publication, the first publication be made within one hundred twenty days of the filing of the petition.

(b) If a proceeding is dismissed for failure to effect proper service, the petitioner may commence a new proceeding, despite the expiration of the statute of limitations after the commencement of the original proceeding, based upon the same instrument, transaction or occurrence or transactions or occurrences within one hundred twenty days of such dismissal provided that service is effected within such one hundred twenty day period.

> **History:** Add, L 1995, ch 379, § 1, eff Oct 1, 1995, applicable to actions commenced on or after such date. Former section 301 was repealed by L 1992, ch 216, effective July 1, 1992.

§ 302. Pleadings

1. Unless otherwise provided in this act

(a) Pleadings shall consist of the petition, answer or objections and account.

(b) There shall be no other pleading unless directed by the court.

(c) An answer or objection shall be served upon the return of process or at such later date as directed by the court.

2. Statements in a pleading shall be sufficiently particular to give the court and parties notice of the claim, objection or defense and shall contain a demand for the relief sought.

3. Copies of all pleadings, except an account, shall be served upon any party who has appeared in the proceeding and demanded a copy of all papers be served upon him, and upon all parties upon whom the court by order or oral direction entered in the minutes directs that service be made. A party who fails to comply with this requirement may be treated as a party in default.

History: Add, L 1966, ch 953, eff Sept 1, 1967 from Sur. Ct. Act § 49 and CPLR §§ 402, 3013, 3014.

§ 303. Verification

All pleadings shall be verified in the manner provided by CPLR 3020.

History: Add, L 1966, ch 953, eff Sept 1, 1967 from Sur. Ct. Act § 50 and CPLR § 3020.

§ 304. Contents of petition

In addition to such other requirements as may be applicable to the petition in a particular proceeding, a petition must substantially set forth:

1. The title of the proceeding, the name and domicile of the person to whose estate or person the proceeding relates and of the petitioner.

2. The facts upon which the jurisdiction of the court depends in the particular proceeding.

3. So far as they can be ascertained with due diligence, the names and addresses of all the persons interested upon whom service of process is required or concerning whom the court is required to have information; and in addition there shall be shown by petition or affidavit in form satisfactory to the court, the following:

(a) If any person be an infant, his age, the date of his birth, whether he has a guardian, whether his father, or if he be dead, his mother, is living, his connection with the estate, and the names and addresses of such persons and the person with whom the infant resides.

(b) If any person be an incompetent, the name and address of his committee, if any, and of the person or institution having his care and custody and if there be no committee, the name and address of an adult relative or friend having an interest in his welfare.

(c) If any person be an incapacitated person, the facts regarding his incapacity and if confined, the name and address of the institution having his care and custody and the name and address of an adult relative or friend having an interest in his welfare, and if a conservatee as designated in section 77.01 of the mental hygiene law, the name and address of his conservator.

(d) If any person be unknown or his name or whereabouts be unknown, a general description of such person, showing his connection with the estate and his interest in the proceeding and the facts showing what effort has been made to ascertain his name or whereabouts.

(e) If any person be a prisoner confined in this state or elsewhere, the name and address of the institution in which he is confined, and the name and address of an adult relative or friend having an interest in his welfare.

(f) If any person be included in a class, and his name be unknown, the names and addresses of those persons of the class who are known, and a general description of all other persons belonging to the class, their connection with the estate, and their interest in the proceeding.

4. That there are no other persons than those mentioned interested in the application or proceeding.

5. A request for the relief sought.

History: Add, L 1966, ch 953, eff Sept 1, 1967 from Sur. Ct. Act § 51; amd, L 1967, ch 685, § 8, eff Sept 1, 1967; L 1981, ch 115, § 111, eff May 18, 1981.

§ 305. Process, where returnable

The process of a surrogate's court, except where otherwise prescribed by law, must be made returnable before the court from which it was issued.

History: Add, L 1966, ch 953, eff Sept 1, 1967 from Sur. Ct. Act § 52 and Jud. Law § 757 and Const. Art. VI § 1(c).

§ 306. Citation

1. A citation must substantially set forth:

(a) The name and domicile of the person to whose estate or person the proceeding relates and of the petitioner.

(b) The names of all persons to be served who have not waived issuance and service of process, or have not appeared. Where the number of persons of any class to be served exceeds 50, it need not specify the name of any person of the class but may be directed to the class by such appropriate designation as the court deems adequate.

(c) The time when and the place where the citation is returnable, which time must be not more than 4 months after the date of issuance.

(d) The object of the proceeding and the relief sought in the petition.

(e) The date when issued.

(f) The name, address and telephone number of the petitioner's attorney.

2. In addition it must substantially set forth:

(a) Where the names of some persons to be served comprising a class are unknown, the names of those persons of the class who are known and a general description of all other persons belonging to the class, showing their interest in the proceeding.

(b) Where the persons to be served are unknown, a general description of such persons, showing their interest in the proceeding.

In either of such cases, where the petitioner is ignorant of the name of a person to be served, he may designate that person in the citation by a fictitious name or so much of his name and identity as is known.

3. The citation shall be in substantially such form as may be provided by the Official Forms appended to this act.

4. The citation shall be attested in the name of the judge of the court and by the seal of the

court, the original shall be filed by the clerk and a copy thereof shall be furnished to the petitioner.

History: Add, L 1966, ch 953, eff Sept 1, 1967 from Sur. Ct. Act §§ 53, 54 in part and CPLR § 1024; amd, L 1967, ch 685, § 9, eff Sept 1, 1967; L 1969, ch 983, § 1, eff Sept 1, 1969; L 1993, ch 514, § 4, eff Jan 1, 1994.

§ 307. Service of process

1. Service by personal delivery. Service of the process may be made on any person by personal delivery to him of a copy of the process either within or without the state.

2. Service by registered or certified mail, return receipt requested, or by special mail service, upon non-domiciliaries. Service of the process may be made by registered or certified mail, return receipt requested, or by special mail service, upon non-domiciliaries, whether or not they be natural persons.

3. Service by court order. As an alternative to service under subdivisions 1 and 2, service may be made in the manner directed by the court; but such service, except as provided by subdivision 6, shall not be ordered upon a domiciliary natural person unless it be shown that, with due diligence, service by personal delivery within the state cannot be effected, or where for good cause shown, personal service within the state would be impracticable. Any proof necessary hereunder may be submitted in the petition or by affidavit. The court may take into account the size of the estate and the remoteness of kinship of any person to be cited in determining the appropriate due diligence necessary to permit alternate service under this section. The court may direct service by any one or more of the following methods, which shall not, however, be exclusive:

(a) service by publication, such as is provided by CPLR 316, subject to 308 and 309, and to such variations of CPLR 316 as the court may provide, except that

(i) where persons are to be served by publication, publication in only 1 newspaper shall be required, or

(ii) where a person is alleged to be within a country with which the United States of America is at war or a place with which the United States of America does not maintain postal communication, the court may direct that a copy of the process shall be mailed on behalf of such person to the officer who may have been appointed to take possession of the property of alien enemies, or

(iii) where the person to be served is an absentee or alleged to be deceased, the court may direct that in addition to the foregoing requirements, the process be published in a newspaper published at or near the place where the absentee was last known to be, or

(iv) in an adoption proceeding under article seven of the domestic relations law or in a proceeding under section three hundred eighty-four-b of the social services law, a single publication in only one newspaper shall be sufficient.

(b) service by mail, by registered or certified mail with or without return receipt requested, or by any manner of special mail service, as the court may direct;

(c) substituted service such as is provided by CPLR 308 (2) and (4), within or without the state, subject to 308 and 309, and to such variations of CPLR 308 as the court may provide;

(d) service within or without the state, by personal delivery to a person duly designated by respondent to receive process in his behalf, or to a person whose relationship, whatever its character, and by blood or otherwise to the respondent, indicates in the circumstances the probability that actual notice will reach the latter through him;

(e) if the interest of a non-domiciliary alien in the estate is less than $2,500 or his address is unknown or such estate's gross assets are less than $25,000, by delivery of a copy of the process to a consular official of the alien's nation.

4. Service upon an infant. Service upon an infant requires that service of process be made upon any one of the following, unless any such one of them is the petitioner, in which case no such service shall be required: his father, his mother, his guardian, any adult person having the care and control of him or with whom he resides, or such person interested in his welfare or education as the court shall by order direct, where it appears to the satisfaction of the court that need for such order exists; and if the infant be of the age of 14 years or over, also upon the infant in person.

5. Service upon an incompetent, conservatee and persons other than natural persons. Unless this act otherwise provides or the court in a given proceeding otherwise directs, CPLR 307, 309 (b), 309 (c), 310, 310-a, 311, 311-a, 312 and 1025 are applicable to service under the foregoing subdivisions of this section.

6. Service upon creditors. Process may be served upon creditors, regardless of the number thereof, by mailing a copy of the process to each of them whether or not they be natural domiciliaries.

History: Add, L 1966, ch 953, eff Sept 1, 1967 from Sur. Ct. Act §§ 55, 56, 56-a, 57, 58, 58-a and CPLR §§ 307-312, 1025; amd, L 1967, ch 685, eff Sept 1, 1967; L 1971, ch 147, eff April 1, 1971; L 1975, ch 215, eff Sept 1, 1975; L 1976, ch 666, eff Jan 1, 1977; L 1980, ch 90, eff Sept 1, 1980; L 1983, ch 12, eff March 15, 1983; L 1993, ch 514, eff Jan 1, 1994; L 1995, ch 355, eff July 29, 1995; L 1995, ch 481, eff Sept 1, 1995; L 2000, ch 355, § 3, eff Nov 1, 2000; L 2016, ch 47, § 1, eff June 1, 2016.

§ 308. Return day of citation

1. Based on place of service. Except as otherwise provided in subdivisions 2 and 3, the time of the return of a citation shall be governed by the following paragraphs:

(a) The citation shall be served at least the following number of days before the return day:

(i) 10 days if the person is served within the state;

(ii) 20 days if the person is served without the state but within the United States, the District of Columbia, the Commonwealth of Puerto Rico or the possessions or territories of the United States; and

(iii) 30 days in all other cases.

(b) The time periods set forth under paragraph (a) of this subdivision shall commence to run from the time that service is complete as provided in 309.

2. Service by publication. If served by publication, the return day shall not be earlier than the day service is completed, as provided in 309.

3. Service on consular official. If served upon a consular official pursuant to 307, subdivision 3 (e), it shall be served at least 30 days prior to the return day.

4. For the purpose of fixing the time within which a process must be served, service upon the clerk of the court, pursuant to designation, is personal service upon the fiduciary within the county where the letters of the fiduciary were issued.

History: Add, L 1966, ch 953, eff Sept 1, 1967 from Sur. Ct. Act as indicated below. Subd. (1)(a): Added from Sur. Ct. Act §§ 59(2), (3). Subd. (1)(b): New. Added by 1966 N.Y. Laws 953, in effect Sept 1, 1967. Subd. (2): Added from Sur. Ct. Act § 50(4).* Subd. (3): Added from Sur. Ct. Act § 56-a. Subd. (4): Added from Sur. Ct. Act § 59(5). *** Ed. Note.** So in the enacted Distribution Tables. Probably should be Sur. Ct. Act § 59(4). Amd, L 1967, ch 685, § 11, eff Sept 1, 1967; L 1968, ch 259, § 5, eff May 14, 1968; L 2000, ch 355, § 4, eff Nov 1, 2000.

§ 309. When service of process complete

1. Service by personal delivery. The service of process is complete immediately upon personal delivery to the respondent when service is so made.

2. Service by other means. Unless the court directs otherwise, the service of the process shall be complete when served by:

(a) mailing or by registered or certified mail, with or without return receipt requested, upon the mailing thereof;

(b) special mail service, upon receipt of the envelope containing the process by the United States Postal Service in the case of express mail or upon receipt of the envelope containing the process by the designated delivery service in the case of any other special mail service;

(c) substituted service, upon the delivery or affixing and the mailing thereof, whichever is done last;

(d) personal delivery to a person duly designated by the respondent, or to a person or consular official designated by the court by order to be served in respondent's behalf, upon such personal delivery;

(e) publication, on the 28th day after the first publication; or

(f) any other means, as the court directs.

3. Service upon an infant. Where service of process upon an infant pursuant to subdivision 4 of section 307 does not require service upon the infant because the infant is under the age of 14 years and does not require service upon one of the other persons listed therein because such other person is the petitioner, service of process upon such infant shall be deemed complete upon the filing of the petition.

History: Add, L 1966, ch 953, eff Sept 1, 1967 from CPLR and Sur. Ct. Act as indicated below. Subd. (2)(a)-(2)(c): Statement of case law. Subd. (2)(d): Sur. Ct. Act § 58. Subd. (2)(e): CPLR 313. Amd, L 1969, ch 772, § 1; L 1995, ch 355, § 2; L 2000, ch 355, § 5, eff Nov 1, 2000.

§ 310. Who may serve process

1. Any person over the age of 18 years, although a party, may serve process of the court within the state.

2. Personal service of process without the state may be made in the same manner as within the state by any of the persons authorized by CPLR 313 even though a party to the proceeding.

History: Add, L 1966, ch 953, eff Sept 1, 1967; amd, L 1969, ch 772, § 2, eff Sept 1, 1969.

§ 311. Designee for person under disability

Whenever the person to be served is a person under disability, whether or not a party so requests, the court may in the interest of such person, require by order or direction in the minutes that a copy of the process issued be delivered to a person designated, in the manner and within the time specified. The person so designated shall have with respect to the proceeding while so designated, in behalf of such person, until the return of process and such further time as directed by the court, the same powers and duties as a guardian ad litem and is authorized to admit service of such process.

History: Add, L 1966, ch 953, eff Sept 1, 1967 from Sur. Ct. Act as indicated below. Subd.
(1): Added from Sur. Ct. Act § 60. Subd. (2): Added from Sur. Ct. Act § 54(3). Amd, L 1967,
ch 685, § 12; L 1974, ch 272, eff Sept 1, 1974.

§ 312. Additional parties; supplemental process

The court may issue a supplemental process at any time and require any party to procure it and cause it to be served in conformity with the provisions of 307 and 308 on any person in any proceeding, so that any person necessary or proper to a final determination therein may be made a party thereto.

History: Add, L 1966, ch 953, eff Sept 1, 1967.

§ 313. Manner of giving notice when not otherwise prescribed

Whenever the manner of giving notice is not otherwise prescribed, the court may direct both as to the form of notice and the manner and time of service thereof. Such direction may be indicated on the process or endorsed upon the application with the same force and effect as if incorporated in an order.

History: Add, L 1966, ch 953, eff Sept 1, 1967.

§ 314. Proof of service of subpoena or process

Proof of service of a subpoena or process shall be made in the manner and form prescribed by CPLR 306 and 4532, provided, however, that a writing admitting service shall not be sufficient if made by an infant under the age of 16 years or an incompetent. Any person of the age of 16 years or over required to be served may in writing admit service of process.

History: Add, L 1966, ch 953, eff Sept 1, 1967 from Sur. Ct. Act § 61 in part and CPLR
§§ 306, 4532.

§ 315. Joinder and representation of persons interested in estates

1. The provisions of this section shall apply in any proceeding in which all persons interested in the estate are required to be served with process. For the purposes of this section, the term "an interest in the estate" includes both interests in income and interests in principal.

2. Representation of class interests.

    (a) Where an interest in the estate has been limited as follows, it shall not be necessary to serve process on any other person than as herein provided:

(i) In any contingency to the persons who shall compose a certain class upon the happening of a future event, the persons in being who would constitute the class if such event had happened immediately before the commencement of the proceeding.

(ii) To a person who is a party to the proceeding and the same interest has been further limited upon the happening of a future event to a class of persons described in terms of their relationship to such party, the party to the proceeding.

(iii) To unborn or unascertained persons, none of such persons, but if it appears that there is no person in being or ascertained, having the same interest, the court shall appoint a guardian ad litem to represent or protect the persons who eventually may become entitled to the interest.

(b) Where a party to the proceeding has a power of appointment it shall not be necessary to serve the potential appointees and if it is a general power of appointment it shall not be necessary to serve the takers in default of the exercise thereof.

3. Representation of contingent interests. Where an interest in the estate has been limited to a person who is a party to the proceeding and the same interest has been further limited upon the happening of a future event to any other person it shall not be necessary to serve such other person.

4. Representation in probate proceeding. In a proceeding for probate of a testamentary instrument the interests of the respective persons specified in subdivisions 2 (a) (ii) and 3 of this section shall be deemed to be the same interest, whether or not their respective interests are in income or in principal or in both, provided that they are beneficiaries of the same trust or fund, that they have a common interest in proving or disproving the instrument offered for probate and that the person who is a party under subdivision 2 (a) (ii) or the person to whom the interest has been limited under subdivision 3 would not receive greater financial benefit if such instrument were denied probate (in the case where such beneficiaries have a common interest in proving such instrument) or admitted to probate, (in the case where such beneficiaries have a common interest in disproving such instrument).

5. Representation of persons under a disability. If the instrument expressly so provides, where a party to the proceeding has the same interest as a person under a disability, it shall not be necessary to serve the person under a disability.

6. The decree or order entered in any such proceeding shall be binding and conclusive on all persons upon whom service of process is not required.

7. In any proceeding in which service of process upon persons interested in the estate may be dispensed with pursuant to the provisions of this section or section twenty-two hundred ten, in addition to such other requirements as may be applicable to the petition in the particular proceeding, the petition shall (i) set forth in a form satisfactory to the court the information required by subdivision three of section three hundred four with respect to the persons interested in the estate upon whom service of process may be dispensed with, the nature of the interests of such persons and the basis upon which service of process may be dispensed with, and (ii) state whether the fiduciary or any other person has discretion to affect the present or future beneficial enjoyment of the estate and, if so, set forth the discretion possessed and, if exercised, the manner in which it has been exercised. Notwithstanding the foregoing provisions of this section and any provisions of the instrument to the contrary, if the court finds that the representation of a person's interest is or may be inadequate it may require

that he be served. The basis for such finding shall be set forth specifically in the order.

8. Nonjudicial settlements of accounts of fiduciaries. Unless the instrument expressly provides otherwise, an instrument settling an account, executed by all the persons upon whom service of process would be required in a proceeding for the judicial settlement of the account, shall be binding and conclusive on all persons upon whom service of process would not be required to the same extent as that instrument binds the persons who executed it.

History: Add, L 1967, ch 739, § 1; amd, L 1973, ch 70, § 2, eff Sept 1, 1973; L 1981, ch 178, § 1, eff June 2, 1981, applying to estates of deceased persons and trusts in existence on or after June 2, 1981.

§ 316. Process to attorney general where persons unknown

In every case where it appears that there is no distributee or beneficiary or that it is not known whether or not there be such, the process shall be issued to the attorney general of the state.

History: Add, L 1974, ch 272, § 2; amd, L 1980, ch 503, § 6, eff June 24, 1980.

SCPA

ARTICLE 4
APPEARANCE; PROTECTION OF PERSONS UNDER DISABILITY; COUNSEL FOR INDIGENT ADULTS IN SURROGATE'S COURT PROCEEDINGS*

SUMMARY OF ARTICLE

§ 401. Appearance of parties

1. Who may appear. A party other than an infant, incompetent or conservatee may appear and prosecute or defend a special proceeding in person or by attorney, except that a corporation or voluntary association shall appear by attorney. An infant by the guardian of his property, an incompetent by the committee of his property and a conservatee by his conservator may appear and prosecute or defend a special proceeding in person or by attorney as provided in 402.

2. How made. An appearance is made by pleading, by waiver, by serving upon the attorney for the petitioner and filing with the clerk a signed notice of appearance or by appearance in person noted upon the record in open court. The notice may be signed by any person authorized under subdivision 1 to appear for the party.

3. Evidence of attorney's authority. Where a party is a non-domiciliary or has not been served personally with process within the state the court may require

(a) that any person appearing for the party furnish acknowledged evidence of authority so to appear and

(b) the authorization to set forth whether there has been executed previously by the party

(i) any power of attorney or similar instrument relating to the party's interest in the estate and

(ii) any assignment of the interest.

4. Appearance by waiver of process. Any adult competent party may also appear by an acknowledged waiver of issuance and service of process which upon filing with the clerk is equivalent to the filing of an acknowledged notice of appearance under subdivision 2. In a probate proceeding the waiver shall state the date of the will to which it relates and that a copy has been furnished or examined.

---

*   Amd, L 1977, ch 82, eff Jan 1, 1978.

5. Termination of appearance of consul. When a consular official shall have appeared in behalf of an alien, a subsequent appearance by the attorney in fact of the alien pursuant to recorded power of attorney or appearance by an authorized attorney shall terminate the appearance of the consul.

History: Add, L 1966, ch 953, eff Sept 1, 1967 from Sur. Ct. Act § 63 and CPLR §§ 321, 322; amd, L 1967, ch 685, § 13; L 1981, ch 115, § 112; L 1984, ch 14, § 1, eff March 6, 1984; L 1993, ch 514, § 6, eff Jan 1, 1994.

§ 402. Appearance for infant, incompetent, conservatee or person under disability

1. An infant may appear by the guardian of his property, an incompetent by the committee of his property, and a conservatee by his conservator. The appointment of a guardian ad litem does not bar the guardian, committee or conservator from appearing as a party. The person so appearing and his attorney shall each file on or before the return day of process an affidavit showing

(a) that he is qualified to protect their rights,

(b) whether he is related to or connected in business with any party to the proceeding or the attorney for any party,

(c) whether he is entitled to share in the estate in which the infant, incompetent or conservatee is interested or is in any way interested therein,

(d) whether he has any interest adverse to or in conflict with that of the infant, incompetent or conservatee and

(e) such additional facts as may be required by the court.

2. A person under disability shall appear by a guardian ad litem where no appearance is made as provided in subdivision one or where the court so directs because of possible adversity or conflict of interest or for other cause.

History: Add, L 1966, ch 953, eff Sept 1, 1967 from Sur. Ct. Act proposed § 62-b and § 64 in part; amd, L 1971, ch 609, eff Sept 1, 1971; L 1981, ch 115, § 113, eff May 18, 1981.

§ 403. Appointment of guardian ad litem

1. By nomination.

(a) An infant over the age 14 years or his parent or guardian may petition the court on or before the return day of process for the appointment of a named attorney as his guardian ad litem. There shall be filed with the petition the affidavit of the attorney showing

(i) that he is qualified to protect the rights of the infant and has no interest adverse to him and

(ii) the circumstances which led to his nomination.

(b) There shall also be filed with the petition the affidavit of the parent with whom the infant resides, or if not residing with a parent, by the person having his legal custody or an adult person with whom he resides, showing that the affiant

(i) consents to the appointment of the nominated attorney,

(ii) has no interest adverse to that of the infant and if he has an adverse interest, whether he has influenced the infant in the nomination and

(iii) such additional facts as may be required by the court.

(c) The court may appoint the nominated attorney guardian ad litem unless because of adversity or conflict of interest or for other cause a different appointment is required.

2. By the court. A person under disability who does not appear by his guardian, committee or conservator pursuant to 402 shall except as otherwise expressly provided appear by a guardian ad litem appointed by the court on nomination or on its own initiative whenever such person is a necessary party or for other reason the court deems it necessary to appoint a guardian ad litem to protect the interests of such party.

3. An appearance for a person under disability by a guardian ad litem is not required and the court may dispense with the same whenever

(a) in an uncontested probate proceeding such person will receive a share equal to or greater than the share to which he would be entitled if decedent had died intestate,

(b) in an accounting proceeding such person receives a specific bequest or a specific devise or a general legacy of a stated sum of money and the accounting party shows to the satisfaction of the court that such person has received his legacy or devise or will receive same in full under the decree to be made in the proceeding,

(c) in any proceeding the public administrator receives process or notice in behalf of the person under disability.

(d) in a probate proceeding the decedent is survived by a spouse who receives the entire estate under the propounded instrument and the petition alleges that probate assets do not exceed $50,000. In such case, letters testamentary should limit the executor to the collection of assets which, in the aggregate, do not exceed $50,000.

History: Add, L 1966, ch 953, eff Sept 1, 1967 from Sur. Ct. Act proposed §§ 62(d-e) and § 64 in part; amd, L 1967, ch 685, § 14, eff Sept 1, 1967; L 1971, ch 609, § 2, eff Sept 1, 1971; L 1974, ch 904, § 2, eff Sept 1, 1974, but shall not be construed so as to impair or render ineffectual any proceedings commenced pursuant to law prior to the time the act takes effect; L 1981, ch 115, § 114, eff May 18, 1981; L 1993, ch 514, eff Jan 1, 1994; L 1995, ch 354, § 1, eff July 28, 1995.

§ 403-a. Proceedings for the commitment of the guardianships and custody of infants; appointment of guardians ad litem

1. The court shall appoint a guardian ad litem to represent an infant in a proceeding for the commitment of the guardianship and custody of such infant brought pursuant to section three hundred eighty-four-b of the social services law or in a proceeding where a revocation of an adoption consent is opposed under section one hundred fifteen-b of the domestic relations law.

2. As used in this section, "guardian ad litem" refers to an attorney admitted to practice law in the state of New York and designated under this section to represent infants in proceedings for the commitment of the guardianship and custody of such infant brought pursuant to section three hundred eighty-four-b of the social services law.

3. (a) The office of court administration may enter into an agreement with a legal aid society for the society to provide guardians ad litem for the surrogate's court in proceedings brought pursuant to section three hundred eighty-four-b of the social services law in a county having a legal aid society.

(b) The appellate division of the supreme court for the judicial department in which a county is located may enter into an agreement, subject to regulations as may be promulgated by the administrative board of the judicial conference, with any qualified attorney or attorneys to serve as guardian ad litem for the surrogate's court in that county in proceedings brought pursuant to section three hundred eighty-four-b of the social services law.

(c) The appellate division of the supreme court for the judicial department in which a county is located may designate a panel of guardians ad litem for the surrogate's court in that county in proceedings brought pursuant to section three hundred eighty-four-b of the social services law, subject to the approval of the administrative board of the judicial conference. For this purpose, it may invite a bar association to recommend qualified persons for consideration by such appellate division in making its designation, subject to standards as may be promulgated by such administrative board.

4. (a) An agreement pursuant to paragraph (a) of subdivision three of this section may be terminated by the office of court administration by serving a notice on the society sixty days prior to the effective date of the termination.

(b) No designations pursuant to paragraph (c) of subdivision three of this section may be for a term of more than one year, but successive designations may be made. The appellate division proceeding pursuant to such paragraph (c) may at any time increase or decrease the number of guardians ad litem designated in any county and may rescind any designation at any time, subject to the approval of the office of court administration.

5. (a) If the office of court administration proceeds pursuant to paragraph (a) of subdivision three of this section, the agreement shall provide that the society shall be reimbursed on a cost basis for services rendered under the agreement. The agreement shall contain a general plan for the organization and operation of the providing of guardians ad litem by the respective legal aid society, approved by the administrative board, and the office of court administration may require such reports as it deems necessary from the society.

(b) If an appellate division proceeds pursuant to paragraph (b) or (c) of subdivision three of this section, guardians ad litem shall be compensated and allowed expenses and disbursements in the same amounts established by section seven hundred twenty-two-b of the county law.

6. The administrative board of the judicial conference may prescribe standards for the exercise of the powers granted to the appellate divisions under this section and may require such reports as it deems desirable.

7. The cost of guardians ad litem under this section shall be payable by the state of New York within the amounts appropriated therefor.

8. Upon an appeal in a proceeding brought pursuant to section three hundred eighty-four-b of the social services law, the court to which such appeal is taken, or is to be taken, shall appoint a guardian ad litem to represent the infant, in accordance with the provisions of this section.

History: Add, L 1977, ch 859, § 2, eff April 1, 1978; amd, L 1986, ch 817, § 5, eff Sept 1, 1986, and applicable to consents to adoptions executed or acknowledged on or after Sept 1, 1986

SCPA

§ 404. Qualification and duties of guardian ad litem

1. A guardian ad litem shall be an attorney admitted to practice in New York.

2. Before entering upon his duties he shall file a consent to act and unless he has previously done so, a statement of no interest adverse to or in conflict with the person under disability.

3. He shall file an appearance and take such steps with diligence as deemed necessary to represent and protect the interests of the person under disability, and file a report of his activities together with his recommendation upon the termination of his duties or at such other time as directed by the court.

> **History:** Add, L 1966, ch 953, eff Sept 1, 1967 from Sur. Ct. Act proposed §§ 62-c and f;
> amd, L 1968, ch 259, § 6, eff May 14, 1968.

§ 405. Compensation of guardian ad litem

1. For services rendered a guardian ad litem shall receive reasonable compensation to be allowed by the court payable from any or all of the following, in such proportion as directed by the court:

(a) the estate,

(b) the interest of the person under disability, or

(c) for good cause shown, any other party.

2. The court may direct that the fixation of the amount of compensation be reserved for future determination.

3. If an infant, incompetent or conservatee appears by his guardian, committee or conservator pursuant to 402 the court may allow the guardian, committee or conservator such sum as the court deems reasonable for his counsel fees and other expenses incurred in protection of the infant's, incompetent's, or conservatee's interest subject to the same requirements in the case of a guardian ad litem of the provisions of the preceding subdivisions of this section.

4. The provisions of this section shall not apply to guardians ad litem appointed by the court pursuant to section four hundred three-a of this chapter.

> **History:** Add, L 1966, ch 953, eff Sept 1, 1967 from Sur. Ct. Act proposed §§ 62-g and
> 62-b and § 280; amd, L 1967, ch 685, § 15; L 1977, ch 859, § 3, eff April 1, 1978; L 1981,
> ch 115, § 115, eff May 18, 1981; L 1993, ch 514, § 8, eff Jan 1, 1994.

§ 406. Person under disability bound by proceeding

Whenever a guardian ad litem shall be appointed for a person under disability as defined in this act or an infant, incompetent or conservatee shall appear by his guardian, committee, or conservator, respectively, or where such appointment is not required under or is dispensed with pursuant to power conferred by this act the proceeding shall be binding upon such person to the same extent as if such person was under no disability.

> **History:** Add, L 1966, ch 953, eff Sept 1, 1967 from Sur. Ct. Act proposed § 62-j; amd,
> L 1969, ch 772, eff Sept 1, 1969; L 1981, ch 115, § 116, eff May 18, 1981.

§ 407. Assignment of counsel for indigent persons

1. (a) Each of the persons described below in this subdivision has the right to the assistance of counsel. When such person first appears in court, the surrogate shall advise such person

before proceeding that he has the right to be represented by counsel of his own choosing, of his right to have an adjournment to confer with counsel, and of his right to have counsel assigned by the court in any case where he is financially unable to obtain the same;

(i) the respondent in any proceeding under section three hundred eighty-four-b of the social services law;

(ii) the respondent in any proceeding for the approval of a surrender instrument under section three hundred eighty-four of the social services law;

(iii) the parent of a child in any adoption proceeding who opposes the adoption of such child;

(iv) the parent of any child seeking custody or contesting the substantial infringement of his or her right to custody of such child, in any proceeding before the court in which the court has jurisdiction to determine such custody;

(v) any of the above persons upon an appeal in any of the above proceedings.

(b) In addition to the cases listed in paragraph (a) of this subdivision, a judge may assign counsel to represent any adult in a proceeding under this act if he determines that such assignment of counsel is mandated by the constitution of this state or of the United States, and includes such determination in the order assigning counsel.

2. Any order for the assignment of counsel issued under this section shall be implemented as provided in article eighteen-B of the county law.

History: Add, L 1977, ch 682, § 3, eff Jan 1, 1978; amd, L 1986, ch 817, § 4, eff Sept 1, 1986.

ARTICLE 5
TRIALS AND HEARINGS
SUMMARY OF ARTICLE

§ 501. Transfer, consolidation and severance

1. The court may upon motion by any party:

(a) Transfer for trial to the surrogate's court having jurisdiction over an estate any action or proceeding pending in any court other than the supreme court which affects or relates to the administration of an estate and transfer any action or proceeding other than one which has been previously transferred to it or which affects or relates to the administration of an estate, to any other court, except the supreme court, having jurisdiction of the subject matter in any other judicial district or county provided such other court has jurisdiction over the classes of persons named as parties.

(b) Consent to receive for trial any action pending in the supreme court which affects or relates to the administration of a decedent's estate.

2. Consolidation and severance

(a) Consolidation. When proceedings pending before the court, including actions transferred under subdivision 1, involve a common question of law or fact, the court upon the motion of any party or on its own initiative may order a joint trial of any or all of the matters in issue or order that the proceedings be consolidated or make such other orders concerning proceedings therein as may tend to avoid unnecessary cost or delay.

(b) Severance and separate trials. In furtherance of convenience or to avoid prejudice, the court upon the motion of any party or on its own initiative may order a severance of any or all of the matters in issue or may order a separate trial of any one or all of the matters in issue and upon determination thereof render an appropriate intermediate or final order.

History: Add, L 1966, ch 953, eff Sept 1, 1967 from Sur. Ct. Act §§ 40(9), 65, 316 and CPLR §§ 325(d), 4011, 602, 603; amd, L 1967, ch 685, § 16, eff Sept 1, 1967; L 1980, ch 503, eff June 24, 1980; L 1995, ch 468, § 2, eff Sept 1, 1995.

§ 502. Trial by jury; waiver or withdrawal

1. Right to jury trial. A party is entitled to trial by jury, if duly demanded, in any proceeding in which any controverted question of fact arises as to which any party has a constitutional right of trial by jury, in any proceeding for the probate of a will in which a controverted

S-33

question of fact arises, and in any proceeding commenced after the death of the creator of a revocable lifetime trust to contest the validity of such trust in which a controverted question of fact arises.

2. Demand for jury.

(a) Cases initiated in the court. Each respondent demanding a jury trial must do so in his answer or objections. A petitioner who desires a jury trial must, without regard to whether or not an answering or objecting respondent has made such demand, serve and file in his own behalf a demand for jury trial within 6 days after the service upon him of an answer or objections.

(b) Cases transferred to the court. In an action transferred to the court under 501, subdivision 1, a party who has duly demanded a trial by jury in the court from which the case is transferred shall be deemed to have duly demanded it in this court. If the party moving such transfer has not so demanded a trial by jury and shall not have waived such right or his time to make such demand has not expired he shall do so in his moving papers. Any other party to the transferred action who has not demanded a trial by jury in the court from which the case is transferred and shall not have waived such right or his time to make such demand has not expired must serve and file with this court a demand for a trial by jury within 10 days after the service upon him of a copy of the order of transfer with notice of entry thereof.

3. Jury fee. The jury fee shall be paid by each party who demands a trial by jury.

4. Order framing issues. After joinder of issue an order framing the issues to be tried shall be submitted on notice by any party. The court may direct any party to submit an order framing issues. The court shall make an appropriate order, a copy of which shall be served by the party submitting it on all parties who have appeared and pleaded.

5. Waiver or withdrawal.

(a) Waiver. A party waives the right to a trial by jury by:

(i) failing to make a demand under subdivision 2;

(ii) failing to appear at the trial;

(iii) filing a waiver signed by him or his attorney with the clerk of the court; or

(iv) orally waiving a trial by jury in open court or at any pre-trial conference, if entered in the minutes taken at the time.

(b) Withdrawal. A party may withdraw a demand for a trial by jury without the consent of the other parties.

6. Advisory jury. The court may submit any issue of fact to an advisory jury as provided in the CPLR. Upon the motion of any party or on its own initiative the court may confirm or reject in whole or in part the verdict of an advisory jury; may make new findings with or without taking additional testimony and may order a new trial. The motion shall be made within 15 days after the verdict. Where no issues remain to be tried the court shall file its decision in writing.

7. The court may direct that any jury trial be had before it or at a trial term of the supreme

court to be held within the county or if there be a county court in such county, in that court. The verdict if not set aside by the court before which the question is tried, shall be certified to the surrogate's court by the clerk of the court in which the trial took place and shall be conclusive except upon appeal.

History: Add, L 1966, ch 953, eff Sept 1, 1967 from Sur. Ct. Act §§ 67, 68; amd, L 1967, ch 685, § 17; L 2003, ch 631, § 1, eff Sept 30, 2003, applying to proceedings to contest the validity of a revocable lifetime trust pending on or commenced on or after its effective date.

§ 503. Proceedings upon jury trial

1. At any time during trial the court upon motion of any party or on its own initiative may direct judgment on one or more issues whenever it determines as a matter of law that the evidence is insufficient to create an issue of fact for a jury on such issue. Whenever judgment is so directed the issue shall thereupon be deemed withdrawn from the jury and it shall render no verdict or finding thereon. The direction of the court shall be entered in the minutes.

2. On consent of the parties any issue may be likewise withdrawn from a jury and judgment directed thereon.

3. The verdict and any order or decision of the court shall be entered in the minutes and if the trial was not held in the surrogate's court the verdict, order or decision shall be certified by the clerk of the court to the surrogate's court, whereupon that court shall enter a final decree accordingly.

History: Add, L 1966, ch 953, eff Sept 1, 1967 from Sur. Ct. Act § 149 in part.

§ 504. Jurors

Jurors shall be selected from any panel in attendance at any trial term of the supreme court or county court of the county.

History: Add, L 1966, ch 953, eff Sept 1, 1967 from Sur. Ct. Act § 70.

§ 505. Trial by the court

1. The court shall decide all issues not required to be tried by a jury.

2. Upon a trial by the court without a jury:

(a) the court shall render a decision directing the order or decree to be entered which, except for such direction, need not contain either the facts found or the conclusions of law.

(b) the decision may be rendered orally and entered in the minutes by the court reporter and transcribed and filed, or may be made and filed by the court in writing.

History: Add, L 1966, ch 953, eff Sept 1, 1967 from Sur. Ct. Act §§ 71, 119 and CPLR § 4211.

§ 506. Reference to hear and report

1. In any proceeding other than one instituted for probate of a will or where a constitutional right to trial by jury exists and is demanded, the court may appoint a referee to report to the court upon the facts or upon a specific question of fact or upon the law and the facts. The report of the referee shall be filed and contain the facts found and the conclusions of law. No exceptions need be filed to the report.

2. No referee to examine an account rendered or to report questions arising upon the

settlement of the account shall be appointed where the estate does not exceed $1,000 in value or in any case where the item or items in such account to which objections have been made do not aggregate more than $200, except that in any such proceeding the court may appoint a referee to serve without compensation.

3. A referee shall have the powers granted by CPLR 4201 and shall conduct the reference in the same manner as a court trying an issue without a jury. The referee shall file his report within 30 days after the matter has been finally submitted. Unless otherwise stipulated a transcript of the testimony together with the exhibits or copies thereof shall be filed with the report.

4. Upon the motion of any party or on its own initiative the court may confirm or reject in whole or in part the report of the referee; may make new findings with or without taking additional testimony or may order a new reference. Any party to the proceeding may serve notice of the filing of the report. Unless the motion be made within 60 days after service of notice of the filing of the report, it shall be deemed confirmed. Where no issues remain to be tried the court shall file its decision in writing.

5. The compensation and expenses of such a referee shall be fixed and allowed as provided by CPLR 8003 (a) and 4321, except as limited by subdivision 2.

6. (a) Upon the consent of the attorneys for all parties who have appeared at the hearing, the court may designate the chief clerk, one of the other clerks, a court attorney or any assistant to take the testimony in any proceeding other than one where a right to trial by jury exists and to report to the court upon the facts or upon a specific question of fact or upon the law and the facts. The report shall be in writing and shall be filed. It shall state the facts deemed to be essential, but need not make findings of fact. No exceptions need be filed to the report. The person so designated must be an attorney at law and shall have all the powers granted by CPLR 4201 and shall conduct the reference in the same manner as a court trying an issue without a jury. A copy of the report shall be sent to the attorney for each party who appeared at the hearing together with a notice that the report shall be deemed confirmed as of course unless within ten days from the date of mailing the report any party shall file with the court, a notice of motion to modify or overrule the report. Upon motion of any party or upon its own initiative the court may confirm, modify or reject the report in whole or in part, may make new findings with or without taking additional testimony or may order a new hearing.

(b) It shall not be necessary to file a transcript of the testimony with such report but on a motion to modify or overrule the report any party may file a copy of the transcript.

(c) Upon the consent of the attorneys for all parties who have appeared at the hearing, the necessity of the preparation of the report by the person so designated may be waived and the matter decided by the court based upon the transcript of the hearing. In such event the expense of the transcript shall be a charge against the estate, or where appropriate, as otherwise directed by the court.

(d) The person so designated as referee shall not receive any compensation from the estate or from any party for his services and shall be reimbursed for his necessary expenses only as provided in 2609 (3) (a).

History: Add, L 1966, ch 953, eff Sept 1, 1967 from Sur. Ct. Act §§ 66, 74 in part and CPLR §§ 4201, 4320, 4403; amd, L 1968, ch 259, § 7, eff May 14, 1968; L 1971, ch 361, eff

Sept 1, 1971; L 1985, ch 8, eff March 19, 1985; L 1993, ch 514, § 9, eff Jan 1, 1994.

§ 507. Testimony of witness

1. The testimony of a witness may be taken at any place the court directs. The party applying therefor shall give such notice of the time and place of taking the examination as the court prescribes and shall pay the court its actual and necessary expenses incurred in taking testimony at a place other than the court.

2. In any uncontested proceeding where an attesting or a material witness who is in another county of the state cannot conveniently attend before the court it may make an order directing that the witness be examined in the surrogate's court of another county and specifying the nature and manner of the examination. A copy of the order must be transmitted to the surrogate so designated, together with the original will or court certified reproduction thereof, where the testimony relates to the execution of a will. The examination may be taken by one of the clerks of the court. After the examination is reduced to writing and subscribed by the witness or otherwise duly authenticated, it, together with a statement of the proceeding upon the execution of the order, must be certified by the surrogate or clerk taking the examination, attested by the seal of his court and returned with the original will or court certified reproduction thereof, if any, to the court which directed the examination, which must file the same in its office.

> **History:** Add, L 1966, ch 953, eff Sept 1, 1967 from Sur. Ct. Act §§ 31, 73, 74 in part; amd, L 1967, ch 685, § 18, eff Sept 1, 1967.

§ 508. Before whom testimony may be taken; issuance of commission

1. Testimony may be taken within or without the state or in a foreign country by an attorney in addition to the persons enumerated in CPLR 3113 (a).

2. The court may issue a commission to a person authorized to take a commission under CPLR 3113 or to an attorney of this state or of the jurisdiction in which the commission is to be taken.

> **History:** Add, L 1966, ch 953, eff Sept 1, 1967; amd, L 1967, ch 685, § 19, eff Sept 1, 1967.

§ 509. Effect of uncontroverted allegations of fact

Except as otherwise prescribed by law, a petition, or account filed in a proceeding, unless denied by answer, objection or other proof, is due proof of the facts therein stated.

> **History:** Add, L 1966, ch 953, eff Sept 1, 1967 from Sur. Ct. Act § 76.

§ 510. Pretrial conference

At any time after issue has been joined, the court, in its discretion, may require the attendance of all parties and counsel at one or more pretrial conferences. The conferences shall be held for the purpose of settlement negotiation, or, in the alternative, to narrow the issues for trial, seek agreement among the parties and counsel as to the admissibility of evidence, seek agreement as to the order in which witnesses will be called, and otherwise provide for the speedy and orderly conduct of trial. Absent objection placed on the record, during a pretrial conference the court may confer with any party or parties and their counsel outside of the presence of any other party or parties and their respective counsel.

> **History:** Add, L 1993, ch 514, § 10, eff Jan 1, 1994.

ARTICLE 6
ORDERS AND DECREES
SUMMARY OF ARTICLE

§ 601. Definition of decree and order; how order enforced

The determination of the rights of the parties to a special proceeding in the court is a decree.

A direction of the court made or entered in writing and not included in a decree is an order.

A decree or order has the same effect and may be enforced in like manner as a similar judgment, decree or order made by the supreme court in an action.

> **History:** Add, L 1966, ch 953, eff Sept 1, 1967 from Sur. Ct. Act § 78; amd, L 1967, ch 685, § 21, eff Sept 1, 1967.

§ 602. Decree or order, when evidence of assets

A decree directing payment by a fiduciary to a creditor of, or a person interested in, the estate, or an order permitting a judgment creditor to issue an execution against a fiduciary is, except upon an appeal therefrom, presumptive evidence that there are sufficient assets in his hands to satisfy the sum which the decree directs him to pay or for which the order permits the execution to issue. A decree charging a deceased fiduciary with assets upon an accounting under 2207, is not evidence of assets in the hands of the accounting fiduciary.

> **History:** Add, L 1966, ch 95 from Sur. Ct. Act § 79; amd, L 1967, ch 685, § 22, eff Sept 1, 1967.

§ 603. Transcript of decree or order

1. Clerk to furnish transcript. Upon the application of any person, the clerk must furnish to him a transcript of any decree or order. If it be for other than money only, the clerk shall insert in the transcript a brief statement of the nature of the relief awarded. Such statement may be inserted under "remarks" as contained in the form set forth in section 255-c of the judiciary law.

2. Docketing with county clerk. A transcript of a decree or order of the court may be filed in the office of the clerk of the county in which the court is located and upon such filing the clerk shall docket the decree or order in like manner and with like effect as a judgment entered in the supreme court within the county. The filing and docketing and any subsequent filing and docketing with any other county clerk shall be governed by the CPLR.

> **History:** Add, L 1966, ch 953, eff Sept 1, 1967 from Sur. Ct. Act § 81; amd, L 1967, ch 685, § 23; L 1968, ch 259, § 8, eff May 14, 1968.

§ 604. Decree; instruments of satisfaction

Upon the request of any person interested, there may be recorded with the court any instrument acknowledging payment of moneys pursuant to a decree or order of the court. Every such instrument to be recorded shall be acknowledged and the record thereof, or a certified copy of such record, shall be presumptive evidence of the contents of such instrument and its due execution and of any payment of money or delivery of property therein acknowledged.

The foregoing shall be in addition to such procedure for satisfaction and the recording thereof as may be provided by the CPLR.

History: Add, L 1966, ch 953, eff Sept 1, 1967 from Sur. Ct. Act § 82 and CPLR §§ 5020, 5021; amd, L 1967, ch 685, § 24, eff Sept 1, 1967.

§ 605. Enforcement of decree by execution

An execution shall not issue out of the court. The enforcement by execution of any decree or order of the court shall take place only after the docketing of a transcript as set forth in 603 of this act, whereupon the decree or order shall be enforceable by execution as if it were a judgment of the supreme court.

History: Add, L 1966, ch 953, eff Sept 1, 1967 from Sur. Ct. Act § 83.

§ 606. Enforcement of decree or order by punishment for contempt; when

1. In any of the following cases, a decree or order of the court, directing the payment of money or requiring the performance of any act, may be enforced by serving a certified copy thereof upon the party against whom it is directed, and if he refuses or wilfully negelects* to obey it, by punishing him for a contempt of court:

(a) Where it cannot be enforced by execution.

(b) Where part of it cannot be enforced by execution; in which case the part or parts which cannot be so enforced may be enforced as prescribed in this section.

(c) Where an execution as prescribed in the preceding section has been returned wholly or partly unsatisfied.

(d) Where the delinquent is a fiduciary and the decree relates to the estate, in which case the court may enforce the decree or order as prescribed in this section, either with or without requiring the issuance of an execution, or after the return of an execution, as it deems proper.

2. For the purpose of enforcement of a decree or order by means of punishment for contempt of court, the proceeding which terminated in such decree or order is deemed continued.

3. The court may refuse to punish any person for contempt of court as authorized in this section, in an instance in which facts are demonstrated to its satisfaction which would justify a release of such person from imprisonment, in accordance with the provisions of section 775 of the judiciary law.

4. No proceedings taken to enforce a decree or order of the court, either by execution, punishment for contempt or otherwise, shall preclude or affect in any manner an action or

---

* So in original. Should be "neglects".

proceeding on a bond given by the person against whom the decree or order was directed.

History: Add, L 1966, ch 953, eff Sept 1, 1967 from Sur. Ct. Act § 84 in part; amd, L 1967, ch 685, § 25, eff Sept 1, 1967.

§ 607. Enforcement of decree or order by punishment for contempt; manner

A person interested in the compliance with a decree or order, directing the payment of a sum of money or the performance of any act, may present to the court a petition showing:

1. One of the grounds prescribed in the preceding section,

2. That a certified copy of the decree or order sought to be enforced has been personally served upon the person against whom it was entered, which service shall be equivalent to a personal demand upon the respondent for the payment of the sum directed to be paid, or the performance of the act directed by the decree or order to be performed,

3. That the respondent has refused or wilfully neglected to obey such order or decree, and

4. Praying that the respondent be directed to show cause why he should not be punished for contempt.

The court may direct that a warrant of commitment issue against the respondent, pursuant to section 757 of the judiciary law, or that the respondent show cause why he should not be punished for contempt. The order to show cause may be served upon the respondent personally or upon his attorney.

Upon the return thereof, if the court is satisfied that the respondent has refused or wilfully neglected to obey the decree or order, it may direct that a warrant of commitment issue against the respondent pursuant to section 757 of the judiciary law or punish the respondent under the provisions of the judiciary law.

History: Add, L 1966, ch 953, eff Sept 1, 1967 from Sur. Ct. Act § 84 in part; amd, L 1967, ch 685, § 26, eff Sept 1, 1967; L 1993, ch 514, § 11, eff Jan 1, 1994.

ARTICLE 7
GENERAL PROVISIONS RELATING TO LETTERS
SUMMARY OF ARTICLE

§ 701. Requisites of letters

1. Letters granted by any court to a fiduciary shall be issued in the name of the people of the state, attested in the name of the judge of the court, sealed with the seal of the court and signed by the court or the chief clerk of the court or such other officer as the chief clerk shall have authorized or deputized for the purpose.

2. To all letters of guardianship of the property of an infant, the court must cause a copy of 1719 and 1720 to be annexed or printed thereon.

3. No court except the court which issues letters shall have power to suspend, modify or revoke them, so long as the court issuing them has jurisdiction of the estate or matter in which the letters were issued.

> **History:** Add, L 1966, ch 953, eff Sept 1, 1967 from Sur. Ct. Act § 88; amd, L 1967, ch 685, § 28, eff Sept 1, 1967.

§ 702. Limited and restrictive letters

Letters may be granted limiting and restricting the powers and rights of the holder thereof:

1. To the enforcement or prosecution of a cause of action in favor of the decedent or his fiduciary under general or special provisions of law, to the defense of any claim or cause of action against a decedent or his fiduciary, and restraining the fiduciary from compromise of the action or the enforcement of a judgment recovered therein until the further order of the court and the filing of satisfactory security if required.

2. Where it is impracticable to give a bond in the full amount required by statute, to receiving and administering only the property which the court may specify, and restraining him from receiving or administering other property until further order of the court.

3. To the adjustment, settlement, satisfaction or discharge of any claim in favor of or against the decedent or his fiduciary.

4. To the performance of any act required in order to discharge the estate of a decedent from liability.

5. To an account in behalf of the decedent for the performance by him of any trust or other responsibility.

6. To the completion of any transfer made by a decedent or his fiduciary and to the execution of any instruments confirming any transfer so made.

7. To the appearance in and conduct of an action in which a decedent or his fiduciary is a necessary or proper party.

8. In the discretion of the court, to represent the estate in a transaction in which the acting fiduciary could not or should not act in his or her fiduciary capacity because of conflict of interest.

9. To commence and maintain any action or proceeding against the fiduciary, in his or her individual capacity, or against anyone else against whom the fiduciary fails or refuses to bring such a proceeding.

10. To any other purpose or act deemed by the court to be appropriate or necessary in respect of the affairs of the estate, the protection thereof or to the proper administration thereof.

In any case where limited and restrictive letters are granted the court may reduce the amount of security otherwise required or dispense therewith according to the circumstances.

Any letters may contain appropriate recitals restraining the holder from doing any such acts or exercising any such powers as may be specified therein until the further order of the court and upon the filing, if ordered, of satisfactory security. The issuance of limited or restrictive letters under this section may be in addition to the issuance of general letters or other, limited or restrictive letters.

History: Add, L 1966, ch 953, eff Sept 1, 196 from Sur. Ct. Act §§ 89, 122, 181 in part; amd, L 1967, ch 685, § 29, eff Sept 1, 1967; L 1993, ch 514, § 12, eff Jan 1, 1994.

§ 703. Letters evidence of authority; effect of appeal

1. Subject to the provisions of the succeeding section, letters granted by the court are conclusive evidence of the authority of the persons to whom they are granted until the decree granting them is reversed or modified upon appeal or the letters are suspended, modified or revoked by the court granting them.

2. A certificate of letters testamentary or of administration duly issued by the clerk of the court shall be sufficient evidence, subject to the provisions of subdivision one hereof, of the existence of such letters and the identity of the fiduciary for all purposes for six months after the date of such issuance.

History: Add, L 1966, ch 953, eff Sept 1, 1967 from Sur. Ct. Act § 90; amd, L 1979, ch 581, § 1, eff July 10, 1979.

§ 704. Priority among different letters

A person who applies in good faith therefor, and to whom letters are first issued from a court having jurisdiction to issue them, has exclusive authority under the letters until they are revoked. He is entitled to demand and recover from any person to whom letters are afterwards issued by any other surrogate's court the property in his hands belonging to the estate. But the acts of a person to whom letters were afterwards issued, done in good faith before notice of the letters first issued are valid and an action or special proceeding commenced by him may be continued by and in the name of the person or persons to whom the letters were first issued.

History: Add, L 1966, ch 953, eff Sept 1, 1967 from Sur. Ct. Act § 91.

§ 705. Time, how reckoned upon successive letters

Where it is prescribed by law that an act must or may be done within a specified time after letters are issued and successive or supplementary letters are issued upon the same estate, the time so specified must be reckoned from the issuing of the first letters, except where it is otherwise specially prescribed by law or where the first or any subsequent letters are revoked as provided in 1413.

History: Add, L 1966, ch 953, eff Sept 1, 1967 from Sur. Ct. Act § 92.

§ 706. When surviving or remaining fiduciary may act; when successor must be appointed

1. Where one of two or more fiduciaries dies or is removed or where letters issued to one of them are revoked, a successor to the deceased fiduciary or to the one who has been removed or whose letters have been revoked shall not be appointed, except where such appointment is necessary in order to comply with the express terms of a will or lifetime trust instrument; but the others may proceed and complete the administration of the estate pursuant to the letters or lifetime trust instrument and may continue any action or special proceeding brought by or against all.

2. When all the persons to whom letters have been issued die or where letters issued to all of them have been revoked by a decree of the surrogate's court, or, in the case of a lifetime trust, when all persons serving as trustee die or are removed, without any successor trustee having been effectively appointed pursuant to the terms of the lifetime trust instrument, that court has, except in a case where it is otherwise specially prescribed by law, the same power

to appoint a successor to the person or persons whose powers have ceased as if the letters had not been issued or as if no appointment had been made. The successor may complete the administration of the estate committed to his predecessor, he may continue in his own name a civil action or proceeding pending in favor of his predecessor and he may enforce a judgment, order or decree in favor of the latter.

History: Add, L 1966, ch 953, eff Sept 1, 1967 from Sur. Ct. Act § 93; amd, L 1980, ch 503, § 8, eff June 24, 1980.

§ 707. Eligibility to receive letters

Letters may issue to a natural person or to a person authorized by law to be a fiduciary except as follows:

1. Persons ineligible

(a) an infant

(b) an incompetent

(c) a non-domiciliary alien except one who is a foreign guardian as provided in subdivision four of section one thousand seven hundred sixteen of this chapter, or one who shall serve with one or more co-fiduciaries, at least one of whom is resident in this state. Any appointment of a non-domiciliary alien fiduciary or a New York resident fiduciary hereunder shall be made by the court in its discretion

(d) a felon

(e) one who does not possess the qualifications required of a fiduciary by reason of substance abuse, dishonesty, improvidence, want of understanding, or who is otherwise unfit for the execution of the office.

2. Persons ineligible in court's discretion. The court may declare ineligible to act as fiduciary a person unable to read and write the English language.

History: Add, L 1966, ch 953, eff Sept 1, 1967 from Sur. Ct. Act §§ 94, 95; amd, L 1967, ch 685, §§ 30, 31, eff Sept 1, 1967; L 1986, ch 780, eff Aug 8, 1986; L 1993, ch 514, § 13, eff Jan 1, 1994; L 1995, ch 469, § 1, eff Aug 2, 1995.

§ 708. Qualification of fiduciaries

Before letters are granted to a fiduciary, the fiduciary shall file in the surrogate's court or family court:

1. An acknowledged instrument stating the fiduciary's domiciliary address and designating the clerk of the court to receive service of any process issuing from the court in like manner and with like effect as if it were served personally upon the fiduciary, whenever the person so receiving letters cannot be found and served within the state after due diligence, which designation shall be irrevocable and shall continue in effect so long as the fiduciary remains in office and until full compliance by the fiduciary with the terms of a decree providing for his or her final discharge. If the fiduciary shall change his or her address so stated the fiduciary shall promptly notify the court of the new address.

2. Unless exempted, an official oath taken before any officer authorized to administer oaths, to the effect that the fiduciary will well, faithfully and honestly discharge the duties of the office and the trust reposed in him or her and duly account for all moneys or other property which may come into his or her hands. The oath shall also describe the office, and

state that the fiduciary is not ineligible to receive letters.

3. Such bond as may be required by law or by order of the court.

4. In the case of a trust company or other fiduciary exempted by law from taking an oath of office and filing a bond, an acknowledged consent to accept its appointment.

5. In the case of a foreign banking corporation or trust company organized under the laws of another state, compliance with subdivision 3 of section 131 of the banking law is required.

> **History:** Add, L 1966, ch 953, eff Sept 1, 1967 from Sur. Ct. Act §§ 95, 98, 182; amd, L 1967, ch 685, § 32; L 1968, ch 259, eff May 14, 1968; L 1988, ch 232, § 3, eff July 8, 1988; L 1993, ch 514, § 14, eff Jan 1, 1994.

§ 709. Objection to grant of letters or appointment of lifetime trustee

Any person interested, including a nominated fiduciary, before letters are granted to another fiduciary or the surrogate's court appoints a trustee of a lifetime trust, may file objections showing his or her interest in the estate and stating one or more of the legal objections set forth in 707 to granting the letters to or the appointment of one or more of the persons about to receive them or to be appointed. Where such objections are filed the court may stay the granting of letters to or the appointment of the person against whom the objection is made until the matter is determined.

> **History:** Add, L 1966, ch 953, eff Sept 1, 1967 from Sur. Ct. Act § 96; amd, L 1980, ch 503, § 9, eff June 24, 1980; L 1993, ch 514, eff Jan 1, 1994; L 2003, ch 612, § 1, eff Sept 30, 2003.

§ 710. Objections which require bond from fiduciary not otherwise required to file bond

1. No bond shall be required of an executor unless required by the will or by 806 or by this section.

2. A person named as executor or a testamentary guardian or trustee who is not required by the will to give a bond, shall be entitled to letters by giving a bond as prescribed by law, although an objection has been established to the satisfaction of the court that the person is a non-domiciliary.

3. If after the issuance of letters, a fiduciary not required by will to give a bond, who is a citizen of the United States, has become a non-domiciliary, he may be required to give a bond in an amount to be fixed by the court, upon objection filed and proof taken.

4. No fiduciary shall remove property of the estate without the state without the prior approval of the court and upon filing a bond if required by the court.

> **History:** Add, L 1966, ch 953, eff Sept 1, 1967 from Sur. Ct. Act § 97; amd, L 1967, ch 685, § 33, eff Sept 1, 1967; L 1969, ch 772, § 4, eff Sept 1, 1969; L 1993, ch 514, § 16, eff Jan 1, 1994.

§ 711. Suspension, modification or revocation of letters or removal for disqualification or misconduct

In any of the following cases a co-fiduciary, creditor, person interested, any person on behalf of an infant or any surety on a bond of a fiduciary may present to the court having jurisdiction a petition praying for a decree suspending, modifying or revoking those letters and that the fiduciary may be cited to show cause why a decree should not be made accordingly:

1. Where the respondent was, when letters were issued to him, or has since become ineligible or disqualified to act as fiduciary and the grounds of the objection did not exist or the objection was not taken by the petitioner or a person whom he represents before the letters were granted.

2. Where by reason of his having wasted or improperly applied the assets of the estate, or made investments unauthorized by law or otherwise improvidently managed or injured the property committed to his charge, including by failing to comply with paragraph (c) of section 8-1.9 of the estates, powers and trusts law, or by reason of other misconduct in the execution of his office or dishonesty, drunkenness, improvidence or want of understanding, he is unfit for the execution of his office.

3. Where he has wilfully refused or without good cause neglected to obey any lawful direction of the court contained in any decree or order or any provision of law relating to the discharge of his duty.

4. Where the grant of his letters was obtained by a false suggestion of a material fact.

5. Where by the terms of a will, deed or order, his office was to cease upon a contingency which has happened.

6. Where he has failed without sufficient reason to notify the court of his change of address within 30 days after such change.

7. Where he has removed property of the estate without the state without prior approval of the court.

8. Where he or she does not possess the qualifications required of a fiduciary by reason of substance abuse, dishonesty, improvidence, want of understanding, or who is otherwise unfit for the execution of the office.

9. In the case of a guardian, where he has removed or is about to remove from the state or where the interests of the infant will be promoted by the appointment of another person as guardian.

10. In the case of a testamentary trustee, where he has violated or threatens to violate his trust or is insolvent or his insolvenvy* is apprehended or is for any other cause deemed an unsuitable person to execute the trust.

11. In the case of a lifetime trustee, a creditor or a person interested, any person in behalf of an infant or any surety on a bond of the trustee may present to the court having jurisdiction a petition praying for a decree removing the trustee or suspending or modifying his appointment and that the trustee may be cited to show cause why a decree should not be made accordingly where the supreme court, if it had jurisdiction, would have cause to remove the trustee or to suspend or modify his appointment.

12. In the case of any fiduciary who fails to file an account within such time and in such manner as directed by the court.

History: Add, L 1966, ch 953, eff Sept 1, 1967 from Sur. Ct. Act §§ 99(1)-(7), (9); amd, L 1967, ch 685, § 34; L 1980, ch 503, § 10, eff June 24, 1980; L 1993, ch 514, § 17, eff Jan

---

* So in original. Should be "insolvency".

1, 1994; L 1995, ch 477, § 1, eff Aug 2, 1995; L 2002, ch 457, § 1, eff Nov 1, 2002; L 2013, ch 549, § 28, eff July 1, 2014.

§ 712. Petition; process thereupon; suspension

A petition as prescribed in the preceding section must show that the case is one therein specified and, if entertained, process must be issued according to the prayer thereof to the fiduciary against whom relief is sought and to such other persons as the court may direct.

Upon the issuance of process the court may by order suspend the respondent wholly or partly from the exercise of his powers and authority during the pendency of the proceeding. A certified copy of the order so made must be served with the process, but from the time it is made, the order is binding upon the respondent and upon all other persons, without service thereof, subject to the exceptions and limitations prescribed in 720 and 721.

History: Add, L 1966, ch 953, eff Sept 1, 1967 from Sur. Ct. Act § 100; amd, L 1973, ch 731, eff Sept 1, 1973.

§ 713. Hearing; decree

Upon the return of process issued as prescribed in the preceding section the court may make a decree suspending, modifying or revoking the letters issued to or removing the respondent or modifying the terms of his appointment or may dismiss the proceeding upon such terms as justice requires.

History: Add, L 1966, ch 953, eff Sept 1, 1967 from Sur. Ct. Act § 101; amd, L 1980, ch 503, § 11, eff June 24, 1980.

§ 714. Certain orders or decrees of other courts to be filed in the surrogate's court

Whenever the supreme court shall suspend or remove or accept the resignation of a guardian of an infant's person or property or both, or of a testamentary trustee appointed by it, a certified copy of the order or decree shall be filed in the surrogate's court of the county having jurisdiction of the infant's person or estate or of the testamentary trust and a minute thereof shall be made and indexed in the book or books kept by the surrogate in which similar orders or decrees made in each surrogate's court are entered.

The county clerk of the county in whose office the order or decree of the supreme court is entered, shall give written notice to the clerk of the proper surrogate's court of the filing of such order or decree.

History: Add, L 1966, ch 953, eff Sept 1, 1967 from Sur. Ct. Act § 101-a; amd, L 1988, ch 232, § 4, eff July 8, 1988.

§ 715. Application by fiduciary for permission to resign

A fiduciary may present to the court at any time a petition praying that he or she be permitted to resign, that his or her letters be revoked and that he or she be permitted to settle his or her account judicially or informally as such fiduciary, and that notice of the application be given to the persons and in the manner directed by the court. The petition shall show the facts upon which the application is founded.

History: Add, L 1966, ch 953, eff Sept 1, 1967 from Sur. Ct. Act § 102; amd, L 2013, ch 483, § 1, eff Nov 13, 2013.

§ 716. Proceedings thereupon

If it shall be determined that the petition should be granted, an intermediate order may be entered forthwith or at any time during the pendency of the proceeding, permitting the petitioner to resign, revoking his or her letters, or removing him or her, appointing a successor, and directing the resigning fiduciary to turn over all assets in his or her hands to his or her successor and settle his or her account judicially or informally. The proceedings thereupon, whether or not the letters of the petitioner be revoked or he or she be removed, must be the same as upon a petition for the judicial settlement of the petitioner's account, except that the successor fiduciary, if one shall have been appointed, shall be a necessary party to it. Upon the resigning fiduciary fully accounting and paying over all money which is found to be due from him or her and delivering over all books, papers and other property in his or her hands to his or her successor, or in such manner as the court directs, a decree may be made discharging him or her accordingly.

History: Add, L 1966, ch 953, eff Sept 1, 1967 from Sur. Ct. Act § 103; amd, L 1980, ch 503, § 12, eff June 24, 1980; L 2013, ch 483, § 2, eff Nov 13, 2013.

§ 717. Suspension of powers of fiduciaries in war service

1. Whenever a fiduciary is engaged in war service, as defined in this section, such fiduciary or any person interested, may present a petition to the court having jurisdiction, praying for a decree suspending the powers of such fiduciary while he is engaged in war service and until the further order of the court and if his suspension will leave no person acting as fiduciary or leave the sole beneficiary of a trust as the only acting trustee thereof, the petition must pray for the appointment of a successor unless a successor has been named in the will or lifetime trust instrument and such successor is not engaged in war service or is not for other reasons unable or unwilling to act as a fiduciary.

2. For the purposes of this section, a fiduciary is deemed to be engaged in war service if he is

(a) a member of the military or naval forces of the United States or any of its allies or if he has been accepted for such service and is awaiting induction therein, or

(b) engaged in any work abroad in connection with a governmental agency of the United States or with the American Red Cross Society or any other body with similar objects, or

(c) interned in an enemy country or is in a foreign country or a possession, dependency or protectorate of the United States and is unable to return to this state, or

(d) a member of the merchant marine service or other similar service.

3. Where the application is made by a fiduciary engaged in war service notice shall be given to the persons and in the manner directed by the court. Where the application is made by any other person notice shall be given to the fiduciary and such other persons and in the manner directed by the court.

4. Upon filing of the petition and proof of service of the notice prescribed, the court may, notwithstanding any other provision of law, suspend the fiduciary engaged in war service from the exercise of all his powers and duties while he remains engaged in war service and until the further order of the court. The decree may further provide that the remaining fiduciary, or if there be none, the successor named in the will or lifetime trust instrument or appointed by the court, is possessed of and may exercise all the powers and be subject to all the duties incidental to his office as fiduciary.

5. The compensation of the successor shall be limited to commissions as computed under 2307, 2308 or 2309, whichever section is applicable to the fiduciary, upon income received and disbursed, and upon principal disbursed. Commissions may be allowed also to his

successor under the provisions of those sections, whichever section is applicable to the successor, if he is entitled to or required to collect the rents of and manage real property. In the event of the resignation or removal of the suspended fiduciary under any other section of this act or in the event of the death of the suspended fiduciary, the foregoing limitations on the computation of the commissions of his successor shall cease to apply and the commissions of the successor shall be computed in the same manner as any other fiduciary.

6. When the suspended fiduciary ceases to be engaged in war service, he may be reinstated as fiduciary if any of the duties of his office remain unexecuted, upon application to the court, and upon such notice as it directs. If the suspended fiduciary is reinstated the court shall remove his successor and revoke his letters and make such other order or decree as justice requires, but such removal and revocation of letters shall not bar the successor from subsequently qualifying as a fiduciary in accordance with the provisions of the will or lifetime trust instrument if for any reason thereafter it becomes necessary that a fiduciary be appointed.

> **History:** Add, L 1966, ch 953, eff Sept 1, 1967 from Sur. Ct. Act § 103-a; amd, L 1967, ch 685, § 35, eff Sept 1, 1967; L 1980, ch 503, § 13, eff June 24, 1980.

§ 718. Nominated fiduciaries in war service

1. Whenever a person nominated in a will or lifetime trust instrument as executor, guardian or trustee is engaged in war service as defined in the preceding section and is unable to qualify as fiduciary because of such service, his failure to so qualify shall not be deemed a final renunciation but a temporary one which shall become final 6 months after such nominated fiduciary ceases to be engaged in war service. If the will or lifetime trust instrument does not name a co-fiduciary or successor fiduciary or if the co-fiduciary or successor fiduciary is unwilling or unable to act and the failure of the nominated fiduciary in war service to qualify leaves no person acting as fiduciary or will leave the sole beneficiary of a trust as the only active trustee thereof, any person interested may file a petition praying for the appointment of a successor to the nominated fiduciary in war service. Notice of the application shall be given to the persons and in the manner directed by the court. Within 6 months from the date the nominated fiduciary ceases to be engaged in war service, and if any of the duties of his office remain unexecuted, he may file a petition praying that he be appointed executor, guardian or trustee, as the case may be, in accordance with the terms of the will or lifetime trust instrument. Notice of the application shall be given to the persons and in the manner directed by the court. The court may grant the application and direct the issuance of letters to or appoint the petitioner jointly with the fiduciary acting or may remove or revoke the letters of the successor appointed to take the place of the nominated fiduciary or may make such other order or decree as justice requires. The removal and revocation of the letters of the original successor to the nominated fiduciary shall not bar the successor from subsequently qualifying as fiduciary if for any reason thereafter it becomes necessary that a fiduciary be appointed.

2. The commissions of a successor appointed under this section shall be computed in accordance with the provisions of 2307, 2308 or 2309, whichever section is applicable to the fiduciary, except that where the successor is removed or his letters revoked he shall not be entitled to commissions for paying or delivering the estate to the nominated fiduciary upon his qualification.

> **History:** Add, L 1966, ch 953, eff Sept 1, 1967 from Sur. Ct. Act § 103-b; amd, L 1967, ch 685, § 36, eff Sept 1, 1967; L 1980, ch 503, § 14, eff June 24, 1980.

§ 719. In what cases letters may be suspended, modified or revoked, or a lifetime trustee removed or his powers suspended or modified, without process

In any of the following cases, the court may make a decree suspending, modifying or revoking letters issued to a fiduciary from the court or removing a lifetime trustee or modifying or suspending the powers of a lifetime trustee without a petition or the issuance of process:

1. Where the fiduciary being duly cited to account neglects to appear upon the return of process without showing a satisfactory excuse therefor and the court has sufficient reason to believe that no valid excuse can be made, or having been ordered to account, fails to file an account within such time and in such manner as directed by the court.

2. Where process issued to a fiduciary in a case prescribed by law cannot be personally served upon him by reason of his having absconded or concealed himself.

3. Where he has defaulted in supplying information concerning assets or affairs of the estate as ordered by the court, pursuant to 2102, or has neglected or refused to obey the order.

4. Where by the judgment of another court of competent jurisdiction the will or lifetime trust instrument under which letters have been issued or the fiduciary appointed is declared to be invalid or ineffective.

5. Where an administrator has failed to give the bond required to sell or to receive the proceeds of a sale of real property or to give a new bond or a new surety when required to do so by an order or decree of the court.

6. Where he has been convicted of a felony or has been judicially committed or has been declared an incompetent.

7. Where he mingles the funds of the estate with his own or deposits them with any person, association or corporation authorized to do business under the banking law in an account other than as fiduciary.

8. In any case in which ancillary letters have been issued where the original letters in the domiciliary jurisdiction have been revoked.

9. Where a temporary administrator has been appointed of the estate of an absentee, and it is shown that the absentee has returned or that he is living and capable of resuming the management of his affairs or that an executor or administrator has been appointed of his estate or that a committee of his property has been duly appointed in this state.

10. Where any of the facts provided in 711 are brought to the attention of the court.

History: Add, L 1966, ch 953, eff Sept 1, 1967 from Sur. Ct. Act §§ 99, 104; amd, L 1967, ch 685, §§ 37, 38, eff Sept 1, 1967; L 1978, ch 550, § 54, eff July 24, 1978; L 1980, ch 503, § 15, eff June 24, 1980; L 2002, ch 457, § 2, eff Nov 1, 2002.

§ 720. Effect and contents of decree suspending, modifying or revoking letters or removing a lifetime trustee or suspending or modifying his powers

Upon the entry of a decree made as prescribed in this act, removing a fiduciary or suspending, modifying or revoking his letters issued to a fiduciary, his powers are suspended, modified or cease, as the case may be. The decree may require him to account for all money and other property received by him and to pay over and deliver all money and other property in his hands, to the court or to his successor or to such other person as is authorized by law to receive it, or it may be made without prejudice to an action or special proceeding for that purpose then pending or thereafter to be brought. The removal* suspension, modification or revocation does not affect the validity of any act within the powers of the fiduciary done by him before his removal or the suspension, modification or revocation of his letters or the service of process, where the other party acted in good faith, or done after the service of process and before entry of the decree where his powers with respect thereto were not suspended or modified by service of process or where the court in a case prescribed by law, permitted him to do the same, notwithstanding the pendency of the special proceeding against him and he is not liable for such an act done by him in good faith.

Where an executor or administrator is also a testamentary trustee of the same estate, a decree revoking his letters as executor or administrator does not affect his power or authority as testamentary trustee, except in the case specially prescribed for that purpose in 1505.

History: Add, L 1966, ch 953, eff Sept 1, 1967, from Sur. Ct. Act §§ 85, 101; amd, L 1967, ch 685, § 39, eff Sept 1, 1967; L 1980, ch 503, § 16, eff June 24, 1980.

§ 721. Preceding section qualified

The preceding section does not affect the liability of a person to whom money or other property has been delivered as distributee or legatee to respond to the person lawfully entitled thereto, where letters are revoked because a supposed decedent is living or because a will is discovered after administration has been granted, in a case of supposed intestacy or a prior will is revoked upon which letters were granted.

History: Add, L 1966, ch 953, eff Sept 1, 1967 from Sur. Ct. Act § 86.

§ 722. Deposit of securities may be ordered on revocation of letters or removal

When upon the revocation of letters or removal of a fiduciary a decree is made in which such fiduciary is personally charged with or directed to pay a sum of money upon a finding that he has made an unlawful investment or disposition of the estate in his hands and the security or other instrument by which such investment or disposition is evidenced or the property in the purchase of which such investment or disposition has been made shall not be a part of the assets which his successor may be required legally to receive, the decree may direct that such security or other instrument or such property, if practicably capable of delivery under such direction, be forthwith deposited with a safe deposit company in such manner as to prevent the withdrawal of the property except upon the order of the court.

History: Add, L 1966, ch 953, eff Sept 1, 1967 from Sur. Ct. Act § 230; amd, L 1980, ch 503, § 17, eff June 24, 1980.

§ 723. Copy of letters issued to chief fiscal officer of county to be transmitted to comptroller

Within ten days after granting letters to the chief fiscal officer of the county the court must transmit to the state comptroller a certified copy thereof.

History: Add, L 1966, ch 953, eff, Sept 1, 1967 from Sur. Ct. Act § 19 in part; amd, L 1971, ch 344, § 1, eff June 1, 1971; L 1971, ch 344, eff June 1, 1971.

§ 724. Inapplicability to lifetime trustees

---

* **Ed. Note.** So in original. Probably should be: "The removal, suspension . . ."

Except as otherwise expressly provided or required by context, this article shall not be applicable to lifetime trustees.

History: Add, L 1980, ch 503, § 18, eff June 24, 1980.

§ 725. Rules relating to estate valuation after letters

The chief administrator of the courts shall promulgate rules to insure that, after letters have been granted to a fiduciary and the fee based on the initial value of the estate has been paid, the court is notified of the actual value of the estate as subsequently shown by a tax return filed under article twenty-six of the tax law, by a proceeding under such article, by any proceeding in surrogate's court involving such estate, or by the filing with the court of such other papers or documents as such rules shall prescribe.

History: Add, L 1984, ch 77, § 2, eff Apr 17, 1984, applying to all estates for which letters have been issued, whether prior to, on, or after the effective date; amd, L 1990, ch 190, § 120, eff May 25, 1990, provided, with respect to estates of decedents dying on or before May 25, 1990, the statute as it existed prior to this amendment will apply.

ARTICLE 8
GENERAL PROVISIONS RELATING TO BONDS
SUMMARY OF ARTICLE

§ 801. Amount; condition; number of sureties; obligees

1. Amount. Whenever a fiduciary or legal life tenant shall be required to file a bond, the amount thereof, except where the court has reduced it or dispensed therewith, shall be fixed as follows:

(a) Executor, administrator, administrator c. t. a., administrator d. b. n., and temporary administrator.

(a) Not Less Than:

i. Value of all personal property receivable by the fiduciary.

ii. Estimated gross rents of real property receivable by the fiduciary for 18 months.

iii. Probable recovery in any cause of action prosecuted by the fiduciary.

In fixing the amount of a bond under this paragraph the court must also take into consideration in the case of a successor executor, administrator, administrator c. t. a., or administrator d. b. n., how much of the estate, if any, has already been administered.

No bond shall be required of any of the above mentioned fiduciaries if the value of the assets to be administered does not exceed the monetary amount defined as a small estate pursuant to subdivision one of section 1301 of this act.

(b) Guardian of the property of an infant

(b) Not less than:

i. Value of all personal property receivable by the guardian.

ii. Estimated gross rents of real property receivable by the guardian for three years.

iii. Estimated gross income for three years from sources other than moneys or other assets committed to the guardian for administration.

(c) i. Testamentary trustee, or executor required to hold, manage or invest property for the benefit of another,

ii. ancillary fiduciaries,

iii. guardian of the person of an infant,

iv. legal life tenant, or

v. any case not provided for in this article where the filing of a bond is required.

(c) In such amount as the court directs.

(d) In granting limited and restrictive letters pursuant to the provisions of 702 the court may dispense with a bond altogether or fix the amount at such sum as it may deem sufficient.

(e) In addition to such powers as are conferred by CPLR 2508, the court may at any time increase or decrease the bond of a fiduciary or legal life tenant when good reason therefor appears.

(f) In fixing the amount of a bond, the court may require evidence as to the character and value of the assets to be committed to the fiduciary and may examine the applicant or any other person under oath or take such other steps as it deems necessary.

2. Condition. Unless the court directs otherwise the condition of the bond shall be that the fiduciary will faithfully discharge his trust, obey all lawful decrees and orders touching the administration of the assets committed to him including but not limited to decrees or orders directing repayment of amounts allowed as advances on commissions and render a verified account of his administration whenever required to do so by the court. In the case of a legal life tenant the condition shall be that the principal account for and deliver to his successors in interest the property held as life tenant.

3. Sureties. The court may authorize or direct the execution and filing of a bond with a sole surety or with two or more sureties or it may dispense with sureties altogether when good reason therefor appears.

4. Obligees of bond. The bond of a fiduciary shall run to the people of the state for the security and benefit of the persons then or thereafter interested in the estate.

History: Add, L 1966, ch 953, eff Sept 1, 1967 from Sur. Ct. Act §§ 121, 122, 135, 136, 163, 169, 169-a, 180, 182, 185, 188; amd, L 1980, ch 17, § 1; L 1982, ch 519, eff Sept 1, 1982; L 1999, ch 168, § 1, eff July 6, 1999, applying to the estate of any person dying on or after the effective date.

§ 802. Approval and filing of bonds; designation of clerk

1. All bonds must be approved by the court. The court may by order authorize one or more clerks or law assistants to approve bonds. Approval of a bond must be endorsed thereon and when so endorsed the bond must be filed in the court.

2. Each surety on a bond shall file an acknowledged instrument stating his domiciliary address and designating the chief clerk of court and his successors in office as a person upon

whom any process of any court of the state may be served in any action or proceeding relating to the bond with like effect as if served personally upon the surety whenever the surety after due diligence cannot be found and served within the state of New York.

3. A corporate surety licensed to transact business in the state shall be deemed to have complied with the requirements of this section if it has filed or does file one acknowledged instrument which applies to all bonds of the corporate surety filed and approved after the date of the filing and which by its term is of indefinite duration and irrevocable.

4. The filing of a designation by a corporate surety shall have the same effect as if a separate designation had been filed with each bond to which it is a party.

History: Add, L 1966, ch 953, eff Sept 1, 1967 from Sur. Ct. Act § 105.

§ 803. Deposit of assets to reduce bond

1. Whenever a bond or new surety may be required, if the value of the estate is so great or for other sufficient reasons the court deems it inexpedient to require security in the full amount prescribed by law it may direct that all or part of the assets of the estate be delivered subject to further order of the court to the county treasurer or other proper fiscal officer, the clerk of the court or a trust company, bank or safe deposit company or otherwise restrict the authority of the fiduciary. The court may thereupon fix the amount of the bond taking into consideration the value of the remainder only of the estate.

2. The assets so deposited shall not be withdrawn from the custody of the depositary and no person other than the proper fiscal officer of such county, city or depositary shall receive or collect any principal or income or other benefits derived from such assets without order of the court.

History: Add, L 1966, ch 953, eff Sept 1, 1967 from Sur. Ct. Act § 106; amd, L 1969, ch 772, eff Sept 1, 1969; L 1993, ch 514, § 18, eff Jan 1, 1994.

§ 804. Bond required when assets deposited with bank or trust company serving as co-fiduciary

When a bank or trust company is a fiduciary and is nominated to serve or is serving with one or more individual fiduciaries the court may make an order directing the deposit of assets with the bank or trust company upon such terms and upon the giving of such bond by the individual fiduciaries as it deems advisable.

History: Add, L 1966, ch 953, eff Sept 1, 1967 from Sur. Ct. Act § 106-a.

§ 805. Bond of administrator, temporary administrator or administrator c. t. a.

1. Before letters are issued to an administrator, temporary administrator or administrator c. t. a. he shall execute and file a bond provided, however, that where the person or persons about to be appointed is or are entitled to the whole estate or where acknowledged consents that a bond be dispensed with or fixed at a reduced amount are executed and filed by all persons interested in the estate the court may dispense with a bond or fix the amount at such sum as will adequately protect the right of all creditors. If such consent be filed by some but not all of the persons interested in the estate, such consent must also specifically release any claim under the bond required and the court may fix the amount at such sum as will adequately protect the rights of all creditors and of the non-consenting persons interested.

2. The court may require that the amount of creditors' claims be ascertained by a notice to creditors which shall be published once a week for 4 consecutive weeks in such newspapers

as the court may select and which shall direct the creditors to file their claims in writing with the clerk of court on or before a day fixed therein, which shall be at least 30 days after the day of first publication.

3. Before an administrator shall receive the proceeds of a disposition of real property pursuant to the provisions of EPTL 11-1.1 he shall file a further bond in the amount of the proceeds unless it be dispensed with as above provided or unless his existing bond is sufficient to cover the proceeds.

History: Add, L 1966, ch 953, eff Sept 1, 1967 from Sur. Ct. Act §§ 121, 126, 135 in part.

§ 806. Bond of a testamentary trustee or executor acting as trustee

Whenever a testamentary trustee is appointed by will or order of the court or an executor is appointed who is required to hold, manage or invest real or personal property for the benefit of another, he shall unless the will provides otherwise, execute and file a bond.

History: Add, L 1966, ch 953, eff Sept 1, 1967 from Sur. Ct. Act § 169 in part; amd, L 1980, ch 503, § 19, eff June 24, 1980.

§ 807. Bond of a legal life tenant

Whenever a legal life tenant is entitled to the possession or control of property under a will, he shall if the court so directs execute and file a bond unless the will expressly provides otherwise.

History: Add, L 1966, ch 953, eff Sept 1, 1967 from Sur. Ct. Act § 169-a.

§ 808. Liability of surety for assets received by principal in another fiduciary capacity

1. A fiduciary is liable for money or other personal property of the estate which was in his hands or under his control when his letters were issued or when he began to serve as lifetime trustee in whatever capacity it was received by him or came under his control.

2. Where the money or property was received by him or came under his control by virtue of letters previously issued to him or his previous appointment as lifetime trustee in the same or another capacity an action to recover the money or damages for failure to deliver the property may be maintained upon both bonds, but as between the sureties upon the bond given upon the issue of the prior letters or upon his prior appointment and those upon the bond given upon the issue of the subsequent letters or upon his subsequent appointment the latter are liable over to the former.

History: Add, L 1966, ch 953, eff Sept 1, 1967 from Sur. Ct. Act § 112; amd, L 1980, ch 503, § 20, eff June 24, 1980.

§ 809. Action or proceeding on bond; disposition of proceeds; summary determination in certain cases

1. When permitted. An action or proceeding on a fiduciary's bond may be brought in either of the following cases if leave of the court by motion on notice to the surety is granted:

   (a) by a person having a judgment or decree against the fiduciary which remains unsatisfied after the expiration of 10 days from date of entry;

   (b) by the fiduciary's successor or if the fiduciary has died, been removed, or his letters have been revoked and if no successor has been appointed, by any aggrieved person, for the recovery of any money or property received by the fiduciary and not duly administered by him or for an injury to the estate caused by his act or omission.

2. Disposition of proceeds. The decree or judgment in the action or proceeding on the bond shall provide for the disposition of any proceeds that may be recovered in the action or proceeding.

3. Summary determination in certain cases. Where a decree has been made directing payment by a fiduciary and payment has not been made within 10 days after date of entry, any person in whose favor the decree was rendered may as an alternative to an action or proceeding on the bond as provided in subdivision 1 seek a summary determination of the surety's liability in the court making the decree. Process shall issue to the surety and such other persons as the court may direct. Upon the return of process the court may conduct such proceedings and make such decree or order as justice shall require.

> **History:** Add, L 1966, ch 953, eff Sept 1, 1967 from Sur. Ct. Act §§ 113, 114, 115, 115-a;
> amd, L 1980, ch 503, § 21, eff June 24, 1980.

§ 810. Application of article to fiduciaries heretofore appointed

The provisions of this article shall apply to fiduciaries heretofore appointed and to trusts created before this act takes effect except that its provisions shall not affect in any manner the liability of sureties on bonds theretofore executed.

> **History:** Add, L 1966, ch 953, eff Sept 1, 1967 from Sur. Ct. Act § 117.

§ 811. General conformity of bonds to CPLR

The provisions of this article shall govern bonds in this court but to the extent consistent with such provisions and as to matters of detail not provided for herein the provisions of CPLR article 25 shall also apply.

> **History:** Add, L 1966, ch 953, eff Sept 1, 1967.

SCPA

ARTICLE 9
TEMPORARY ADMINISTRATION–ABSENTEES AND INTERNEES
SUMMARY OF ARTICLE

§ 901. When temporary administration may be granted

Temporary administration may be granted if the court finds it is in the best interests of the estate in the following cases:

1. When for any cause delay occurs in the grant of letters on the estate of a decedent or a person alleged to be deceased or in the probate of his or her will.

2. When a person having an interest in property in this state has disappeared and is absent from his or her place of abode without being heard of after diligent inquiry. Such person shall be referred to as an absentee.

3. When a person having an interest in property in this state has been made a prisoner of war or has been detained or interned by an enemy country or in an enemy-occupied country or by force, or imprisoned in this country, a foreign country, whether legal or illegal, and who is thereby unable to safeguard and care for his property in this state. Such person shall be referred to as an internee.

> **History:** Add, L 1966, ch 953, eff Sept 1, 1967 from Sur. Ct. Act § 126; amd, L 1993, ch 514, § 19, eff Jan 1, 1994.

§ 902. Procedure for appointment of temporary administrator

1. If a proceeding is pending for probate of a will or for letters of administration, process shall issue to such persons and in such manner as directed by the court.

2. If no proceeding is pending and the alleged delay is in a proceeding for

(a) letters of administration on the estate of a decedent or a person alleged to be deceased, process shall issue to the persons who would be entitled to receive process on an application for such letters;

(b) probate of a will, process shall issue to the executor named in the last will on file in the court of a decedent or a person alleged to be deceased and to such beneficiaries named in such will and to such other persons as directed by the court.

3. In the case of an absentee, process shall issue to the absentee and to the persons who would be his or her distributees if he or she had died on the date of filing the petition. Upon

return of process the court after hearing shall fix and determine the date when the absentee was last seen or heard of.

4. In the case of an internee, process shall issue to the persons who would be his or her distributees if he or she had died on the date of filing the petition.

5. In all cases under subdivisions 1, 2 and 4, the court may dispense with process if it finds that the best interests of the estate so require.

6. After a citation has been issued by the court in a case under subdivision 3 and it is established to the satisfaction of the court that the best interests of the estate of an absentee require immediate supervision or action by a fiduciary, the court may forthwith appoint the temporary administrator to serve during the pendency of the proceeding or for such shorter period of time as the court directs. In no event shall such appointment be for a longer period than six months from the date of issuance of the citation. During the pendency of the proceeding, the court may at any time revoke such letters of temporary administration. The temporary administrator shall not be entitled to commissions under 2307 for services rendered prior to the date of the decree finally appointing the temporary administrator and containing the finding required by subdivision 3, but the court may award such compensation for such services as shall be just, reasonable and proper, not to exceed a full commission for all services rendered by such person as fiduciary during the entire administration of the estate.

7. A petition for letters of temporary administration may be presented by any person interested in the estate of a decedent or a person alleged to be deceased, any beneficiary or nominated executor under the last will of a decedent or a person alleged to be deceased on file in the court, any person who would have an interest in the property of an absentee or internee if he or she were dead, a public administrator, county treasurer, creditor or by a person interested in an action brought or about to be brought in which the decedent, absentee or internee would be a proper party.

History: Add, L 1966, ch 953, eff Sept 1, 1967 from Sur. Ct. Act § 126; amd, L 1967, ch 685, § 40; L 1970, ch 94, §§ 1, 2, eff March 24, 1970; L 1993, ch 514, § 20, eff Jan 1, 1994.

§ 903. General powers of temporary administrator

1. Letters of temporary administration shall confer upon the person named therein, subject to any limitation contained in an instrument offered for probate, all the powers and authority with respect to all real and personal property of a decedent, absentee or internee, and subject him or her to all the duties and liabilities of an administrator with respect thereto except that they do not confer any authority to pay or to satisfy any testamentary disposition or intestate share.

2. Where a temporary administrator is appointed upon the estate of an absentee or internee and the estate includes an interest as a tenant in common, joint tenant or tenant by the entirety of real property in the same or another county, the court may by order authorize the temporary administrator to join with the other tenants or tenant in a sale, mortgage or lease of the real property or in a conveyance to the other tenants or tenant upon such terms as may be approved by the court and assented to by the other tenants or tenant. The sale, mortgage or lease may be authorized without limitation by the purposes, conditions and restrictions stated in article 19. The proceeds of a sale and the rents received upon any lease made pursuant to this subdivision shall be apportioned according to the interest of the parties.

SCPA

3. A temporary administrator appointed upon the estate of an absentee or internee has all the powers and authority enumerated in the preceding subdivisions of this section with respect to the real and personal property of the absentee or internee. The temporary administrator's acts done in pursuance of that authority are binding upon the absentee or internee, if living, or his or her distributees or devisees, if he or she be dead.

4. (a) The court may, in the order directing the issuance of temporary letters of administration or in one or more subsequent orders, limit such letters to the receipt of assets specified in such order or orders and may prohibit the collection of any other assets of the decedent, or may limit, restrict or authorize the person named in such letters in any manner that the court deems advisable for the effective protection of the rights of all persons who may have an interest in the estate of the decedent, absentee or internee.

(b) In such order or orders, the court may make such directions as it deems proper and necessary with respect to the custody and preservation of all papers and records of the decedent, absentee or internee. Discovery and production of such papers and records shall be governed by article 31 of the civil practice law and rules.

History: Add, L 1966, ch 953, eff Sept 1, 1967 from Sur. Ct. Act §§ 127, 129 in part; amd, L 1967, ch 685, § 41, eff Sept 1, 1967; L 1968, ch 259, eff May 14, 1968; L 1993, ch 514, § 21, eff Jan 1, 1994.

§ 905. Actions and proceedings maintainable by or against a temporary administrator

1. A temporary administrator may maintain any action or proceeding for the purpose of taking into his possession, securing and preserving all property of a decedent, absentee or internee or for determining the ownership of property.

2. Any action or proceeding may be maintained against a temporary administrator upon a debt of the decedent, absentee or internee or upon any cause of action to which the decedent, absentee or internee would have been a party in like manner and with like effect as if he were an administrator.

History: Add, L 1966, ch 953, eff Sept 1, 1967 from Sur. Ct. Act § 127 in part; amd, L 1975, ch 280, § 1, eff Sept 1, 1975.

§ 906. Payment of claims by temporary administrator

At any time after the issuance of letters of temporary administration, process may issue to a temporary administrator requiring him to show cause why he should not pay the petitioner's claim. The court may dismiss the petition or direct payment or satisfaction of the claim in whole or in part and may require a refunding bond.

History: Add, L 1966, ch 953, eff Sept 1, 1967 from Sur. Ct. Act § 129 in part.

§ 907. Special powers of temporary administrator in estates of absentees or internees

1. Where it appears to the satisfaction of the court that the spouse, a child or a dependent presumptive distributee of an absentee or internee or the internee himself or herself requires provision out of the estate for his or her benefit, health, maintenance, clothing or education, the court may make such orders from time to time empowering the temporary administrator to make such provision therefor out of all property in his or her hands not needed for the payment of claims as the court deems proper.

2. The court may by order empower the temporary administrator from time to time to conduct any inquiry and to expend funds of the estate therefor to ascertain the whereabouts

or condition of an absentee or internee. The expenditures so made shall be deemed administration expenses.

History: Add, L 1966, ch 953, eff Sept 1, 1967 from Sur. Ct. Act § 131; amd, L 1993, ch 514, § 23, eff Jan 1, 1994.

§ 908. Settlement of temporary administrator's account of a decedent's estate

1. When the time for presentation of claims as fixed by notice duly published has expired or when 7 months have elapsed since the issuance of letters of temporary administration on the estate of a decedent the court may direct a temporary administrator to account upon the application of the temporary administrator. The court upon its own initiative or upon the petition of a person interested, a public administrator, county treasurer or creditor, may direct a temporary administrator to account at any time.

2. Upon the settlement of his account the court may direct the temporary administrator of a decedent's estate to pay the decedent's funeral and administration expenses and direct the ratable distribution of the remaining assets in payment of the claims allowed or established as valid claims against the decedent. The court may direct the payment into court or the retention by the temporary administrator of whatever may remain of the assets of the personal estate of such decedent.

History: Add, L 1966, ch 953, eff Sept 1, 1967 from Sur. Ct. Act § 129 in part; amd, L 1968, ch 259, § 11, eff May 14, 1968.

§ 910. Annual account of internee's estate

1. Except as provided in subdivision 2 a temporary administrator of an internee's property must annually within 30 days after the anniversary of his or her appointment, as long as any of the internee's property or of the proceeds thereof remains under his or her control, file in the court an account in similar manner and form as provided in 1719 and the same shall be verified and examined as provided in 1720 and 1721.

2. Where the temporary administrator omits to file an account as required under subdivision 1 or where it appears that the account is defective, proceedings may be taken as prescribed in 1722.

3. When an internee or another duly appointed representative appears and claims his or her property the temporary administrator shall account for, deliver and pay over the remainder thereof, after making such deductions as are allowable by law.

History: Add, L 1966, ch 953, eff Sept 1, 1967; amd, L 1968, ch 259, eff May 14, 1968; L 1970, ch 396, eff Sept 1, 1970; L 1993, ch 514, § 25, eff Jan 1, 1994.

§ 911. Final determination and distribution of an absentee's estate

1. If it appears at any time during the administration of the estate that the absentee is in fact dead the temporary administrator or a person interested may petition for the probate of his or her will or the grant of full letters of administration and for a judicial determination of the fact of death and if the court finds that it is in the best interests of the estate an accounting and distribution may be directed without the issuance of permanent letters.

2. If before any decree of distribution has been made, an absentee or his duly appointed fiduciary appears and claims his or her property the temporary administrator shall account for, deliver and pay over to the absentee or such fiduciary the remainder thereof after making such deductions as are allowable by law.

3. If the absentee has not appeared or been heard of after the lapse of 5 years from the date of the finding required by 902, subdivision 3 or in case the temporary administrator is not appointed within 4 years after said date, upon the expiration of 1 year after the date of the appointment of the temporary administrator and if the remainder of the property has not been accounted for, delivered or paid over to the absentee or his or her fiduciary under the preceding subdivision of this section the court shall direct an accounting, require the absentee to show cause why his or her assets should not be distributed according to law and thereafter make a decree determining that all interest of the absentee in his or her property has ceased and terminated and directing that all his or her property be distributed to such persons as would be entitled thereto, by will or as in an intestacy, as if such absentee died at the expiration of such 5 year period. Such decree may include a determination of the rights of the absentee or any other person in any contractual or property rights contingent upon the death of the absentee in the same manner as section 2-1.7 of the estates, powers and trusts law. No action shall be brought by an absentee to recover any portion of his or her property after the determination and decree.

History: Add, L 1966, ch 953, eff Sept 1, 1967; amd, L 1967, ch 685, § 43; L 1968, ch 259, eff May 14, 1968; L 1993, ch 514, § 26, eff Jan 1, 1994.

ARTICLE 10
INTESTATE ADMINISTRATION
SUMMARY OF ARTICLE

§ 1001. Order of priority for granting letters of administration

1. Letters of administration must be granted to the persons who are distributees of an intestate and who are eligible and qualify, in the following order:

(a) the surviving spouse,

(b) the children,

(c) the grandchildren,

(d) either parent,

(e) the brothers or sisters,

(f) any other persons who are distributees and who are eligible and qualify, preference being given to the person entitled to the largest share in the estate, except as hereinafter provided:

(i) Where there are eligible distributees equally entitled to administer the court may grant letters of administration to one or more of such persons.

(ii) If the distributees are issue of grandparents, other than aunts or uncles, on only one side, then letters of administration shall issue to the public administrator or chief financial officer of the county.

2. If the sole distributee has died or is an infant, incompetent or conservatee, his fiduciary, committee or conservator, if he is eligible and qualifies shall be granted letters of administration. The court may deny letters to a guardian or committee of the person only.

3. (a) Where all the distributees have died or are infants, incompetents or conservatees the court may grant letters of administration to a fiduciary, committee or conservator of a deceased distributee or infant, incompetent or conservatee distributee, if he is eligible and qualifies. If the court exercises its discretion preference shall be given to the fiduciary, committee or conservator of the distributee entitled to the largest share in the estate.

(b) Where all such distributees are equally entitled to share in the estate the court may grant letters of administration to one or more of their fiduciaries, committees or conservators, if they are eligible and qualify.

4. (a) Where a distributee who has died or is an infant, incompetent or conservatee would

have had a prior right to letters of administration except for his death or disability the court may grant letters to his fiduciary, committee or conservator, if he is eligible and qualifies.

(b) Where no eligible distributee having a prior or equal right to letters of administration will accept the same and there are distributees who have died or are infants, incompetents or conservatees the court may grant letters to a fiduciary, committee or conservator of a deceased distributee, infant, incompetent or conservatee distributee, if he is eligible and qualifies. If the court exercises its discretion preference shall be given to the fiduciary, committee or conservator of the distributee entitled to the largest share in the estate.

(c) Where all such distributees who have died or are infants, incompetents or conservatees in the circumstances of subdivision 4 (b) are equally entitled to share in the estate the court may grant letters of administration to one or more of their fiduciaries, committees or conservators, if they are eligible and qualify.

5. Upon the petition of a distributee having a prior or equal right to letters of administration the court may grant letters jointly to an eligible distributee or distributees and to one or more eligible persons whether distributees or not, including a trust company or other corporation authorized to act as fiduciary. Such joint fiduciaries shall be entitled to commissions as authorized by 2307.

6. Letters of administration may be granted to an eligible distributee or to an eligible person who is not a distributee upon the acknowledged and filed consents of all eligible distributees, or if there are no eligible distributees, then on the consents of all distributees, except that the guardian of the property of an infant distributee, the committee of the property of an incompetent distributee or the conservator of property of a conservatee appointed within the State of New York may so consent on behalf of his ward. For purposes of this subdivision, a distributee is eligible if letters of administration could be issued to him or her alone or acting together with the person or persons so nominated.

7. Letters of administration may be granted to a trust company or other corporation authorized to act as fiduciary upon the acknowledged and filed consents of all eligible distributees, or if there are no eligible distributees, then on consents of all distributees, except that the guardian of the property of an infant distributee, the committee of the property of an incompetent distributee or the conservator of property of a conservatee appointed within the state of New York may so consent on behalf of his ward. For purposes of this subdivision, a distributee is eligible if letters of administration could be issued to him or her alone or acting together with the trust company or other corporation so nominated.

8. When letters are not granted under the foregoing provisions and an appointment is not made by consent as hereinbefore provided then letters of administration shall be granted in the following order:

(a) to the public administrator, or the chief fiscal officer of the county, or

(b) to the petitioner, in the discretion of the court, or

(c) to any other person or persons.

9. Letters of administration may be granted by the court in any case in which a paper writing purporting to be a will has been filed in the court and proceedings for its probate have not been instituted within a reasonable time or have not been diligently prosecuted.

History: Add, L 1966, ch 953, eff Sept 1, 1967 from Sur. Ct. Act § 118 and Banking Law 100-a(2)(a); amd, L 1967, ch 685, § 45, eff Sept 1, 1967; L 1968, ch 267, eff Sept 1, 1968; L 1969, ch 772, eff Sept 1, 1969; L 1971, ch 344, § 2, eff June 1, 1971; L 1981, ch 115, §§ 117–120, eff May 18, 1981; L 1992, ch 595, § 22, eff Sept 1, 1992; L 1993, ch 514, § 27, eff Jan 1, 1994; L 2019, ch 319, § 1, eff Oct 3, 2019; L 2019, ch 420, § 3, eff Oct 29, 2019.

§ 1002. Petition; persons entitled to petition for appointment of an administrator

1. Any person interested in the estate of an intestate or of a person alleged to be deceased or any person to whose appointment as administrator all distributees consent pursuant to 1001 or a public administrator, the chief fiscal officer of the county, creditor or a person interested in an action brought or about to be brought in which the intestate or the person alleged to be deceased, if living, would be a proper party may present a petition to the court having jurisdiction praying for a decree granting letters of administration to him or to another person upon the estate of the intestate or the person alleged to be deceased.

2. The petition must allege the citizenship of the petitioner and the decedent or person alleged to be deceased, that the decedent or person alleged to be deceased left no will, or that the case is within 1001, subdivision 9 and must state whether or not the intestate or person alleged to be deceased left any

(a) personal property and its estimated value and

(b) real property, whether it is improved or unimproved, a brief description thereof, the estimated value of the real property and improvements, if any, and the estimated gross rents for the period of 18 months.

History: Add, L 1966, ch 953, eff Sept 1, 1967 from Sur. Ct. Act § 119; amd, L 1967, ch 685, § 46, eff Sept 1, 1967; L 1975, ch 120, § 1, eff Sept 1, 1975.

§ 1003. Persons who must be served with process; waiver of process; dispensation with service of process

1. In a proceeding for letters of administration upon the estate of a person alleged to be deceased process shall issue directed to such person and to all his presumptive distributees.

2. Every eligible person who has a right to administration prior or equal to that of the petitioner and who has not renounced must be served with process upon an application for letters of administration. When the petitioner is a creditor or a person interested in an action brought or about to be brought in which the intestate, if living, would be a party, process shall also issue to all incompetents, conservatees and infants for whom a committee, conservator or guardian of the property has been appointed who are domiciliary distributees. When the petitioner is a public administrator or county treasurer process shall issue only to such incompetent or conservatee domiciliary distributees whose names and addresses are known to him. The court may dispense with the issuance and service of process upon non-domiciliaries.

3. Any person who has a right to administration prior or equal to that of the petitioner may renounce his right and waive the issuance and service of process by an acknowledged instrument which must be filed in the office of the clerk of the court, except that a public administrator or the chief fiscal officer of the county may not renounce his right and may only be excused from acting, upon his motion duly made and an order made and entered thereupon by the court.

4. The court may dispense with service of process upon a person who has a right to

administration prior or equal to that of the petitioner where it appears that the name or whereabouts of such person is unknown and cannot be ascertained after diligent inquiry, subject to the requirement that the decree granting the letters shall contain a provision directing that in the proceeding for the judicial settlement of the account of the administrator process shall issue and be served upon such person.

5. If an application for letters of administration be made under the circumstances provided in 1001, subdivision 9, process shall also issue to the persons named in the paper writing referred to in that section and the persons to whom process would be required to issue in a proceeding for the probate of such paper writing.

History: Add, L 1966, ch 953, eff Sept 1, 1967 from Sur. Ct. Act §§ 119, 120; amd, L 1967, ch 685, § 47, eff Sept 1, 1967; L 1969, ch 772, eff Sept 1, 1969; L 1971, ch 344, § 3, eff June 1, 1971; L 1971, ch 805 § 1, eff Sept 1, 1971; L 1981, ch 115, § 121, eff May 18, 1981.

§ 1004. Proceedings upon return of process; decree

1. Upon the return of process in a proceeding for letters of administration upon the estate of a person alleged to be deceased the court must inquire into the facts and take proof thereof and if it appears that he is dead the court may make a decree so determining and directing the issuance of letters of administration upon his estate as prayed for in the petition or to such other person who may appear entitled thereto.

2. When process has issued and been returned with proof of due service thereof and no objections have been interposed to the appointment of the petitioner the court may make a decree granting letters of administration as prayed for in the petition or to such other person who may appear entitled thereto.

3. When the issuance and service of process is not necessary or has been dispensed with the court may make a decree granting letters of administration as prayed for in the petition or to such other person who may appear entitled thereto upon presentation of the petition.

History: Add, L 1966, ch 953, eff Sept 1, 1967 from Sur. Ct. Act §§ 119, 120.

§ 1005. Notice of application for letters of administration

1. Before making a decree granting letters of administration on any application therefor the court may require the petitioner or any other person seeking such letters to serve by mail a written notice of the application upon every distributee of the intestate who has not been required to be served with process and who has not appeared in the proceeding or waived service of process therein.

2. The notice shall be entitled in the proceeding and shall state:

(a) each and every name of the intestate known to the person giving the notice,

(b) the fact that letters of administration on the estate have been applied for by petitioner,

(c) that a decree will be made granting letters and to whom,

(d) the names and post-office addresses of petitioner and of each and every distributee set forth in the petition,

(e) that no other distributees are known to exist,

(f) that letters will issue on or after the date fixed in the notice.

3. The original notice shall be filed with proof by affidavit of the mailing of copies thereof.

History: Add, L 1966, ch 953, eff Sept 1, 1967 from Sur. Ct. Act § 121-a; amd, L 1967, ch 685, § 48, eff Sept 1, 1967.

§ 1006. Failure to qualify

The court must upon application of any person interested, a public administrator, the chief fiscal officer of the county, or creditor require an administrator designated by it to receive letters to qualify within a time specified and direct that in default thereof he be deemed to have renounced his appointment.

History: Add, L 1966, ch 953, eff Sept 1, 1967; amd, L 1971, ch 344, § 4, eff June 1, 1971.

§ 1007. Administration de bonis non

1. When the office of administrator becomes vacant for any reason the court may grant letters of administration de bonis non to one or more eligible persons and the proceedings to procure such letters shall be the same as upon an application for original letters of administration.

2. Where the estate has been partially administered by the former fiduciary the court may fix the penalty of the bond in a sum not less than the value of the assets of the estate remaining unadministered.

3. The court may refuse to issue letters of administration de bonis non where distribution of the estate is possible pursuant to the provisions of 2207.

History: Add, L 1966, ch 953, eff Sept 1, 1967 from Sur. Ct. Act § 136; amd, L 1967, ch 685, § 49, eff Sept 1, 1967.

SCPA

ARTICLE 11
PUBLIC ADMINISTRATORS OF THE COUNTIES WITHIN THE CITY OF NEW YORK

SUMMARY OF ARTICLE

§ 1101. Incumbents

The office of public administrator within the counties of the city of New York hereby is continued. The public administrators of the counties within the city of New York in office when this act takes effect shall continue in office until the end of their respective terms or until a vacancy occurs.

> **History:** Add, L 1966, ch 953, eff Sept 1, 1967 from Sur. Ct. Act § 136-a; amd, L 1968, ch 259, § 14, eff May 14, 1968.

§ 1102. Appointment and removal; terms of office

Notwithstanding the provisions of any other law, appointment and removal shall be made as follows:

1. The public administrators of Kings, Richmond, New York, Bronx and Queens counties shall be appointed by and may be removed by the judge or judges of the court of their respective counties and shall continue in office until removed.

2. Each appointment shall be in writing and shall be filed in the office of the county clerk in the county for which the appointment is made.

History: Add, L 1966, ch 953, eff Sept 1, 1967 from Sur. Ct. Act §§ 136-b, 136-c; amd, L 1967, ch 685, § 51; L 1993, ch 655, § 1, eff Sept 3, 1993, applying to all estates pending as of that date, provided, however, the provisions of section one of this act [amending SCPA 1102] shall not take effect until the current public administrator's term expires.

§ 1103. Deputy public administrator

1. The deputy public administrators of the counties of New York City shall be appointed by the surrogate court judge of the county in which they shall serve.

2. The deputy public administrators of any county where the office exists or may be established shall perform the services and shall possess the powers as may be prescribed for and vested in him by the respective public administrators and shall possess every power and perform every duty belonging to the office of public administrator in the circumstances specified by section nine of the public officers law.

3. The deputy public administrator of any county where the office exists or may be established shall continue in office until removed by the surrogate court judge or judges of that county.

4. Each appointment shall be in writing and shall be filed in the office of the county clerk in the county for which the appointment is made.

History: Add, L 1993, ch 655, § 2, eff Sept 3, 1993, applying to all estates pending as of that date, and repealing and replacing former 1103.

§ 1104. Oath and bond

Each person appointed to the office of public administrator or deputy public administrator in any of the counties within the city of New York before entering upon the duties of his office shall take and file the constitutional oath of office and execute a bond in the sum of $50,000 to the city of New York with such sureties as shall be approved by the judge or judges of the court of the county conditioned for the faithful discharge of all duties enjoined on him by law.

History: Add, L 1966, ch 953, eff Sept 1, 1967 from Sur. Ct. Act § 136-d.

§ 1105. Compensation

1. The public administrators of the counties comprising the city of New York shall receive at least two-thirds of the amount paid to the judges of the surrogate's court of the counties within the city of New York.

2. Each of the deputy public administrators of the counties comprising the city of New York shall receive as compensation two-thirds of the amount paid or hereafter paid to the public administrators of each such county, respectively.

3. The public administrators shall not receive to their own use any fees or emoluments in addition to their salaries except as provided in section 1106, subdivision 3.

The above annual salaries shall be included annually in the expense budget of the city of New York.

History: Add, L 1966, ch 953, eff Sept 1, 1967 from Sur. Ct. Act § 136-e; amd L 1966, ch 871, § 1, eff Sept 1, 1967; 1967, ch. 780, eff Jan 1, 1968; L 1967, ch 685, § 52, eff Sept 1, 1967; L 1968, ch 259, § 16, eff May 14, 1968; L 1968, ch 579, §§ 1–4, eff June 16, 1968; L 1969, ch 246, §§ 1, 2 eff April 25, 1969; L 1974, ch 1019, §§ 1-3, eff Jan 1, 1975; L 1980, ch 579, §§ 1, 3, eff July 26, 1980; L 1983, ch 724, § 1, eff Aug 26, 1983; L 2004, ch 751, § 1, eff Feb 27, 2005.

§ 1106. Commissions

1. The public administrators of Bronx, Kings, New York, Queens and Richmond counties shall each retain over and above all necessary expenses upon all moneys which shall come into their respective hands the same commissions as are now or may hereafter be allowed by law to fiduciaries under section 2307.

2. The value of any real or personal property and the increment thereof received, disbursed or delivered shall be considered as money in computing commissions, except where the real or personal property has been specifically devised or bequeathed.

3. On the settlement of the account of the public administrator in each instance, notwithstanding the provisions of subdivisions 1 and 2, the court may allow his reasonable and necessary expenses and disbursements and in addition, a reasonable amount for the expenses of his office, to be fixed by the court, and not to exceed the sum allowed in the respective offices of the public administrators as of December 31, 1992 unless prior to the proposed increase the public administrator has notified the administrative board in writing of the amount of the proposed increase and the reason therefor. Unless the administrative board notifies the public administrator in writing that the proposed increase has been approved by the board, the public administrator shall not implement such increase. The board must pass upon the proposed increase within sixty days of receipt of the request from the public administrator.

4. The commissions and allowances provided for by this section may be retained by the respective public administrators in preference to any debts or claims except funeral expenses.

5. The public administrators of Bronx, Kings, New York, Queens and Richmond counties shall not receive to their own use any fees or emoluments in addition to their salaries.

History: Add, L 1966, ch 953, eff Sept 1, 1967 from Sur. Ct. Act §§ 136-f, 136-g in part; amd, L 1967, ch 780, eff Jan 1, 1968; L 1981, ch 803, § 1, eff July 27, 1981; L 1983, ch 636, § 2, eff July 25, 1983; L 1993, ch 655, § 3, eff Sept 3, 1993, applying to all estates pending as of that date.

§ 1107. Deposit of funds

1. The public administrators shall pay into the treasury of the city of New York all commissions and costs received by them from any source. Such payments shall be made monthly and shall be accompanied by a sworn statement in the form prescribed by the comptroller of the city of New York showing in detail the costs and commissions received and allowed to them.

2. The public administrators shall deposit to their respective credit all moneys by them severally collected and received within 5 days after receipt in demand, time, thrift or other accounts in one or more banks or trust companies designated by the mayor, comptroller and commissioner of finance for the deposit of moneys of the city of New York or in such accounts in savings banks or savings and loan associations located in their respective counties. All interest received on such deposits shall be credited to the respective estates. In

SCPA

case of the insolvency or involuntary liquidation of the depository all money so deposited shall be entitled to equal priority of payment with that given by law to deposits of money by the state superintendent of financial services.

3. Each public administrator shall whenever required exhibit to the city comptroller and the surrogate of the county where appointed the bank books or statements and all other vouchers and documents relating to his office. The comptroller and surrogate shall examine the bank books and statements showing the deposits and the vouchers on which the check is required to be drawn and shall satisfy himself fully as to the correctness thereof and in case of doubt or difficulty he shall report the case to the mayor for his direction.

History: Add, L 1966, ch 953, eff Sept 1, 1967 from Sur. Ct. Act § 136-g in part; amd, L 1967, ch 780, § 5, eff Jan 1, 1968; L 1968, ch 259, § 17, eff May 14, 1968; L 1978, ch 655, § 132, eff July 25, 1978; L 1993, ch 655, §§ 4, 5, eff Sept 3, 1993, applying to all estates pending as of that date; L 2011, ch 62, § 104 (Part A), eff Oct 3, 2011.

§ 1108. Staff; salaries; offices

Notwithstanding the provisions of any other law, appointment and removal shall be made as follows:

1. Assistants and employees.

(a) The public administrators of the counties of the city of New York are hereby vested with the power to appoint and remove such other employees as may be allowed annually in the budget of the city of New York.

(b) The salaries above provided shall be included annually in the budget of the city of New York.

2. Counsel.

(a) In the counties of the city of New York, the court may appoint one or more counsels to the public administrator.

(b) The reasonable compensation of counsel so appointed shall be paid from the respective estates in which legal services are rendered and may be paid as provided in EPTL 11-1.1(b) (22) and the city of New York shall not be required to include in its expense budget any compensation for such counsel.

(c) Any legal fees allowed by the court pursuant to paragraph (b) of this subdivision shall be supported by an affidavit of legal services setting forth in detail the services rendered, the time spent, and the method or basis by which requested compensation was determined. In fixing the legal fees, the court shall consider the time and labor required, the difficulty of the questions involved, the skill required to handle the problems presented, the lawyer's experience, ability and reputation, the amount involved and benefit resulting to the estate from the services, the customary fee charged by the bar for similar services, the contingency or certainty of compensation, the results obtained, and the responsibility involved.

3. Offices.

(a) Suitable offices for the public administrators of Bronx, Kings, Queens and Richmond counties shall be provided by the appropriate fiscal authority in one of the county buildings of such counties, respectively, provided however that in Richmond county such office may be provided in buildings other than a county building.

4. The office of public administrator of Bronx county shall be deemed a civil division within the meaning of section 45 of the civil service law.

History: Add, L 1966, ch 953, eff Sept 1, 1967 from Sur. Ct. Act § 136-h; renumbered from 1008, L 1967, ch 685, eff Sept 1, 1967; amd, L 1967, ch 780, § 6, eff Jan 1, 1968; L 1968, ch 259, § 18, eff May 14, 1968; L 1993, ch 655, § 6, eff Sept 3, 1993, applying to all estates pending as of that date.

§ 1109. Monthly reports to court, mayor and comptroller; annual audit

Each public administrator shall file monthly with the surrogate of the county where appointed, mayor and the comptroller of the city of New York a statement of such of his accounts as have been closed or finally settled in such form as the comptroller may prescribe.

Each public administrator shall file every six months with the surrogate of the county where appointed a report of every estate administered by the public administrator which has not been fully distributed within two years from the date when the first permanent letters of administration or letters testamentary were issued. Such report shall include the name of the decedent, file number, date of issuance of first permanent letters, approximate amount of gross estate, approximate amount that has been distributed to beneficiaries, approximate amount remaining in fiduciary's hands, reason that estate has not yet been fully distributed, date of report, address and phone of public administrator, and address and phone of attorney for the public administrator. Copies of such reports shall be provided, upon request to the attorney general and the state comptroller.

Each public administrator shall conduct annually an audit of his office by an independent certified public accountant and such a report based on such audit shall be filed with the surrogate of the county where appointed, the mayor and the comptroller of the city of New York, the attorney general of the state of New York and the comptroller of the state of New York. Within six months of receipt of the audit, the attorney general and the state comptroller shall report to the appropriate surrogate and public administrator their comments concerning the audit and any suggested recommendations they may have concerning the performance and operation of the public administrator's office. The audit shall be conducted in compliance with generally accepted government audit standards, and shall include a review of the performance of the office with respect to the guidelines and uniform fee schedules established by the administrative board. The costs of such audit and report shall be included annually in the budget of the city of New York.

History: Add, L 1966, ch 953, eff Sept 1, 1967 from Sur. Ct. Act § 136-k; amd, L 1993, ch 655, § 7, eff Sept 3, 1993, applying to all estates pending as of that date.

§ 1110. Responsibility of the city

1. The city of New York shall be answerable for the faithful execution by the public administrator of all the duties of his office and for the application by him of all moneys and property received by him and for all moneys and securities and the interest, earnings and dividends thereon actually received by him or which he should have collected or received.

2. From all such sums paid into the city treasury the city may deduct any charges or commissions thereon which are now or may hereafter be authorized by law.

3. Any person aggrieved by any act or omission of a public administrator and any person entitled to receive any money or property for which the public administrator may be held to

account, shall have each and every remedy against the city of New York as would be available against a fiduciary in like case and may initiate in the surrogate's court having jurisdiction a proceeding for the enforcement of his claim or right and shall serve process thereon on the comptroller of the city. The public administrator then in office shall be a necessary party in such proceeding.

History: Add, L 1966, ch 953, eff Sept 1, 1967 from Sur. Ct. Act § 136-l.

§ 1111. Vacancy in office; delivery of money, papers and effects

1. Whenever a public administrator shall resign or be removed from his office he shall immediately deliver over to his successor all papers, moneys and effects in his hands.

2. In case of the death of a public administrator the persons into whose custody or possession any such papers, money or effects may come shall deliver them on demand to his successor.

3. Delivery may be enforced in the manner provided by law in relation to public officers.

4. The successor upon qualifying shall succeed at once to all the rights, duties and powers of his predecessor in office without the reissuance of letters to him.

History: Add, L 1966, ch 953, eff Sept 1, 1967 from Sur. Ct. Act § 136-m.

§ 1112. Authority to act

The public administrator in his proper county shall have authority to take possession of, manage and collect the rents of the real property and take charge of the personal property of an intestate:

1. Whenever any person not known to have left him surviving a person eligible to receive letters shall die intestate either within this state or elsewhere leaving any real or personal property within the county and

2. Whenever any personal property of such intestate shall arrive within the county after his death.

3. Whenever all of the surviving relatives are not known the public administrator shall conduct a search for all living distributees of the decedent by reference to bank, postal, and telephone records and inquiry of neighbors, and other reasonable steps under the circumstances. The public administrator shall maintain records of all responses to such notices.

History: Add, L 1966, ch 953, eff Sept 1, 1967 from Sur. Ct. Act § 136-n; amd, L 1993, ch 655, § 8, eff Sept 3, 1993, applying to all estates pending as of that date.

§ 1113. Reports of deaths and burials

1. Every person keeping a hotel, boarding or rooming house in any of the counties to which this article applies shall report in writing to the public administrator of his county information concerning every person not a member of his family who shall die in his hotel or house within 12 hours after such death.

2. The chief medical examiner or such similar public officer of each county to which this article applies within 12 hours after an inquest shall report in writing to the public administrator of his county, such information regarding the decedent which he may have.

3. Every undertaker shall file a report in writing with the public administrator of his county

within 12 hours after receiving an order for the burial by him of any decedent having no known distributees or having been survived only by cousins or relatives by marriage, such information regarding the decedent which he may have.

History: Add, L 1966, ch 953, eff Sept 1, 1967 from Sur. Ct. Act § 136-o.

§ 1114. Inquiry and subpoena

1. The public administrator may institute an inquiry in any case in which he is authorized to act as to any matter affecting the estate of the decedent.

2. For that purpose he may issue a subpoena or subpoena duces tecum either before or after the issuance of letters in the name of the court with the same effect as if either were issued by the court.

3. Failure to comply with the directions of the subpoena or subpoena duces tecum shall be punishable as a contempt of court.

History: Add, L 1966, ch 953, eff Sept 1, 1967 from Sur. Ct. Act § 136-q.

§ 1115. Letters not required for small estates

1. Without the issuance of letters the public administrator by virtue of his office shall have all the powers of a fiduciary of a decedent's estate whenever the gross assets of the estate do not exceed the monetary amount defined as a small estate pursuant to subdivision 1 of section 1301 of this act.

2. In the event the aggregate sum of the assets of an estate in which the public administrator commences to act pursuant to subdivision 1 shall exceed the monetary amount defined as a small estate pursuant to subdivision 1 of section 1301 of this act the public administrator shall forthwith apply for letters.

3. The delivery by the public administrator to a debtor, transfer agent or person holding personal property of the decedent of a certificate evidencing his authority to act under this section, his receipt and the surrender of any evidentiary document shall constitute a complete release and discharge for any payment of money or delivery of property made pursuant to the certificate without such person being required to see to the application thereof and with the same effect as if made to any other fiduciary.

History: Add, L 1966, ch 953, eff Sept 1, 1967 from Sur. Ct. Act §§ 136-r, 137-e; amd, L 1977, ch 221, eff June 7, 1977; L 1982, ch 519, § 2, eff Sept 1, 1982; L 1993, ch 655, § 9, eff Sept 3, 1993, applying to all estates pending as of that date.

§ 1116. Application for letters; when court may direct probate

1. The public administrator is authorized to apply for and receive letters as defined in this act.

2. The court may direct the public administration* to present a petition for probate of a will at any time after it is filed.

History: Add, L 1966, ch 953, eff Sept 1, 1967.

§ 1117. No separate bond or oath

The public administrators within the counties of the city of New York shall not be required

---

* So in original. Should probably be "administrator".

to file the designation, separate bond or oath required by 708 before the issuance of letters to him.

History: Add, L 1966, ch 953, eff Sept 1, 1967 from Sur. Ct. Act § 136-s.

§ 1118. Powers before issuance of letters

Before letters are issued to him and subject to the provisions of section 1128 of this article the public administrator is authorized to:

1. Take possession of, collect and secure the personal property within his county of any person who shall die intestate or testate within this state or elsewhere or whose property shall arrive with* the county after his death whenever there is no person eligible to act as fiduciary of an intestate or of a testator, if the executor named in the will refuses or neglects to act or is dead or his whereabouts are unknown or if he is not eligible to receive letters.

2. Take possession of, manage and collect the rents of the real property of an intestate whose distributees are unknown or, whose distributees if known, are non-domiciliaries or of a testator if the executor named in the will refuses or neglects to act or is dead or his whereabouts are unknown or if he is not eligible to receive letters.

3. Pay the funeral expenses of the decedent.

4. Sell as and when authorized by the court perishable property or such other property of the decedent as the preservation of the estate requires.

5. Sell at public auction all property delivered to him as the effects of persons whose deaths have been reported to him by the department of hospitals, the police department or any other department or person.

6. Defray the expenses of the foregoing activities and the expenses incidental to his application for letters.

History: Add, L 1966, ch 953, eff Sept 1, 1967 from Sur. Ct. Act §§ 125(c)(11), 136-t; amd, L 1993, ch 655, § 10, eff Sept 3, 1993, applying to all estates pending as of that date.

§ 1119. Notice to consuls

When the estate is that of an alien it shall be the duty of the public administrator when making application for letters to mail a notice to the consular representative of the nation of which the decedent was a citizen or subject if any there be in the city of New York.

History: Add, L 1966, ch 953, eff Sept 1, 1967 from Sur. Ct. Act § 136-u.

§ 1120. Appearance by consuls

1. In any action or proceeding brought by or against a public administrator in which a non-domiciliary alien is a necessary or proper party the consular representative of the country of which the alien is a citizen or subject may appear in person or by attorney in behalf of the alien if the latter shall default in appearance.

2. No power of attorney or other specific authority from the alien shall be required as a condition to such appearance.

---

* So in original. Should probably be "within".

3. Service upon an alien pursuant to 307, subdivision 3, paragraph (e) may be made without prior service of process personally or otherwise upon the alien.

4. The interests of alien persons under disability shall, however, be represented in all such proceedings by their guardians of the property, committee of the property or conservators of the property, or by guardians ad litem appointed by the court.

> **History:** Add, L 1966, ch 953, eff Sept 1, 1967 from Sur. Ct. Act § 136-v; amd, L 1968, ch 259, § 19, eff May 14, 1968; L 1981, ch 115, § 122, eff May 18, 1981; L 2000, ch 355, § 6, eff Nov 1, 2000.

§ 1121. Grant of letters to others

If any eligible distributee of the decedent shall petition to supersede the public administrator within 4 months after the public administrator has become vested with the powers of a fiduciary on the estate letters shall be granted to him upon proof that the petitioner did not receive notice of the application by the public administrator and upon the further showing that all persons prior or equal in right have been served and have defaulted or waived; but the court may refuse to supersede the public administrator if 6 months have elapsed since he became vested with the powers of a fiduciary.

> **History:** Add, L 1966, ch 953, eff Sept 1, 1967 from Sur. Ct. Act § 136-x.

§ 1122. Delivery of estate assets to fiduciary; expenses, costs and commissions

When the public administrator has been superseded he shall account and deliver to the fiduciary superseding him all the personal property belonging to the estate which he has in his possession or control after deducting his expenses, costs and commissions as provided by law.

> **History:** Add, L 1966, ch 953, eff Sept 1, 1967 from Sur. Ct. Act § 136-y.

§ 1123. General powers of public administrator

1. Every public administrator shall have all the powers specifically granted herein and also the powers given by law to a fiduciary of a decedent's estate.

2. In addition to the foregoing grant of powers and without limitation thereon each public administrator is authorized to:

(a) Sell personal property of the decedent at public auction pursuant to notice appearing for 3 successive days prior to the sale in a newspaper published in the county pursuant to the provisions of section 1128 of this article.

(b) Retain marketable securities beyond 4 months after letters have been granted to him provided that the court has so permitted by order.

(c) Serve process on creditors, legatees or other persons interested, distributees, domiciled outside the city of New York by certified mail, return receipt requested, whenever directed by the court by order in any proceeding, the provisions of section 308 notwithstanding. Such service shall be valid if made at least 30 days before the return day thereof.

(d) Distribute without an accounting proceeding the assets of any estate defined as a small estate in subdivision 1 of section 1301 of this act and upon distribution to take the costs and commissions ordinarily allowed by the court upon the entry of a decree upon final accounting.

(e) File in the court an informatory account in a form prescribed by rule where the gross value of the assets of the estate accounted for does not exceed the monetary amount defined as a small estate in subdivision 1 of section 1301 of this act and shall serve a copy of such informatory accounting by certified mail on all interested parties at least 30 days prior to filing with the court.

(f) Pay for the use and benefit of an infant distributee or legatee who has no guardian of the property the share or legacy due the infant if not exceeding $5,000 by payment thereof in the discretion of the public administrator to a parent or to an adult competent person with whom the infant resides.

(g) Pay or deliver to the commissioner of finance of the city of New York the balance of any moneys or other assets in his hands remaining after settlement of his account or the filing of an informatory account, where payable to persons under disability or whose shares are to be deposited pursuant to section 2218 of this act.

(h) Apply ex parte or upon such notice as directed by the court for an order or decree in any appropriate proceeding requiring the city of New York to return to the public administrator any money or unliquidated assets theretofore deposited by the public administrator and remaining in the treasury of the city of New York and upon further order of the court to make distribution of such recovered funds to the persons entitled thereto.

(i) Receive process or other notice as a necessary party in the following proceedings:

(1) Any proceeding pending in the court where service of process or notice in behalf of any known or unknown person is directed by the court or where the court by order directs the public administrator to appear therein.

(2) Every proceeding for the appointment of an administrator or for the probate of a will where it does not appear that the persons applying or named in the petition are all the distributees of the decedent or where it appears that such persons are related to the decedent in the fourth degree of consanguinity or are more remotely related.

(3) Every proceeding to effect distribution of moneys or property deposited for the account of unknown persons or of infants or incompetents, or of known persons whose shares were deposited pursuant to section 2218. In any such proceeding the public administrator shall be deemed a person interested.

(4) In all such proceedings the public administrator, in his discretion, may take any action in behalf of such person or persons as a person interested might.

(5) Whenever a public administrator acts pursuant to this subparagraph he shall be allowed by the court his proper expenses and his counsel shall be allowed his reasonable fee. Such expenses and fee shall be payable either from the estate generally or from the shares or interests of the respective persons represented by the public administrator, as may be directed by the court.

History: Add, L 1966, ch 953, eff Sept 1, 1967 from Sur. Ct. Act §§ 136-z, 136-aa, 136-dd in part; amd, L 1967, ch 685, § 54; L 1968, ch 259, §§ 20, 21, eff May 14, 1968; L 1969, ch 407, eff May 9, 1969; L 1978, ch 655, eff July 24, 1978; L 1980, ch 89, eff Sept 1, 1980; L 1982, ch 519, eff Sept 1, 1982; L 1993, ch 655, § 11, eff Sept 3, 1993, applying to all estates pending as of that date; L 2012, ch 142, § 1, eff July 18, 2012, applying only to the estates of decedents who shall have died on or after such effective date.

§ 1124.. Appeal; bond

1. The public administrator is authorized to appeal from any order, decree or judgment affecting an estate in his charge or in which he is a party.

2. On such an appeal no bond on his part shall be required to stay execution of the order, decree or judgment appealed from.

> **History:** Add, L 1966, ch 953, eff Sept 1, 1967 from Sur. Ct. Act §§ 136-z in part, 136-bb.

§ 1125. Notification to corporation counsel

1. In any proceeding under 1123, subdivision 2, subparagraph (j) (iii) service upon the public administrator having jurisdiction shall be sufficient and service upon any officer of the city of New York shall not be required.

2. In such proceeding neither the comptroller nor the corporation counsel of the city of New York shall be charged with any duty in respect of the proceedings or with any responsibility for the distribution of the funds made pursuant to the order or decree therein.

3. The public administrator shall in each such proceeding give notice to the corporation counsel of the city of New York of the pendency of the proceeding and shall file a copy of the notice with proof of service thereof as part of the record of the proceeding before entry of an order or decree therein.

> **History:** Add, L 1966, ch 953, eff Sept 1, 1967 from Sur. Ct. Act § 136-cc; amd, L 1967, ch 685, § 55, eff Sept 1, 1967; L 1968, ch 259, § 22, eff May 14, 1968.

§ 1126. Property without value where no administration had

Whenever the public administrator shall receive papers or property of a decedent upon whose estate no letters have been issued or whose property is not sufficient to require administration under 1116, the public administrator is authorized to abandon or destroy all such papers and property in his possession after 5 years have elapsed from the death of the decedent and upon proof satisfactory to him that they are without value. The public administrator and the city of New York shall not be liable or held to account for such property.

> **History:** Add, L 1966, ch 953, eff Sept 1, 1967.

§ 1127. Disposition of records after 10 years

The public administrator is authorized to destroy the file and all of the papers relating to a decedent after the lapse of 10 years from the completion of the administration of his estate. The public administrator and the city of New York shall not be liable or held to account for such action.

> **History:** Add, L 1966, ch 953, eff Sept 1, 1967.

§ 1128. Administrative board for the offices of the public administrators

1. An administrative board for the offices of the public administrators of the state of New York is hereby created. The board shall consist of thirteen members of whom five shall be surrogate court judges, one each selected by the presiding justice of the appellate divisions of the first, third and fourth departments and two selected by the presiding justice of the appellate division of the second department of whom one shall be a surrogate from a county within the city of New York and one shall be a surrogate from a county outside the city of New York, three members shall be selected by the chief administrative judge of the state of New York, two members shall be selected by the president of the New York state bar association of whom one shall be a resident of the city of New York and one member each

shall be selected by the state comptroller, the attorney general and the president of the New York state surrogates' association. The three members selected by the chief administrative judge of the state of New York, and the members selected by the state comptroller, the attorney general, and the president of the New York state bar association, shall not be surrogate court judges or employees of the surrogates court. Each member shall serve without compensation but shall be reimbursed for expenses actually and necessarily incurred in the performance of his or her official duties for the board from the moneys appropriated to the office of court administration. Notwithstanding any inconsistent provisions of this or any other law, general, special or local, no officer or employee of the state or any public corporation, as defined in article two-A of the general construction law, shall be deemed to have forfeited or shall forfeit his or her office or employment or any benefits provided under the retirement and social security law or under any public retirement system maintained by the state or any of its subdivisions by reason of his or her being a member of the board.

2. The board shall establish guidelines and uniform fee schedules for the operation of the offices of public administrators. These guidelines shall include but are not limited to rules for the initial inspection of the decedent's premises and guidelines for the selection and compensation of investigators, appraisers, accountants, warehouses, auctioneers and procedures for the disposal of personal property. With respect to real property the board shall be responsible for preparing uniform procedures for sale; fixing a schedule of approved expenses attendant to such a sale; appraisals, title fees and broker's commissions. This section shall apply to article twelve of this act.

History: Add, L 1993, ch 655, § 12, eff Sept 3, 1993 and applying to all estates pending as of that date.

ARTICLE 12
PUBLIC ADMINISTRATORS IN THE COUNTIES OF ERIE, MONROE, NASSAU, ONONDAGA, SUFFOLK AND WESTCHESTER AND COUNTY TREASURERS APPOINTED ADMINISTRATORS*

SUMMARY OF ARTICLE

§ 1201. Definitions

Whenever used in this article the term public administrator, unless otherwise required by the context or unless a contrary intent is expressly declared, shall mean the public administrators of the counties of Erie, Monroe, Nassau, Onondaga, Suffolk and Westchester.

History: Add, L 1966, ch 953, eff Sept 1, 1967 from Sur. Ct. Act §§ 124, 125, 125-a, b, c; amd, L 1967, ch 685, § 56; L 1979, ch 602, § 1, eff July 10, 1979.

§ 1202. Office established; appointment of successor

The office of public administrator hereby is continued. The public administrator shall continue in office unless removed by the court. Vacancy in such office for any reason shall be filled by the court of the county by appointing a public administrator for the county immediately. In the counties of Westchester, Nassau and Suffolk, the court may appoint a deputy public administrator who shall act generally for and in place of the public administrator whenever required.

History: Add, L 1966, ch 953, eff Sept 1, 2967 from Sur. Ct. Act §§ 124, 125, 125-a, b, c; amd, L 1967, ch 685, eff Sept 1, 1967; L 1973, ch 966, eff June 22, 1973; L 1979, ch 542, eff July 10, 1979; L 1993, ch 655, § 13, eff Sept 3, 1993, applying to all estates pending as of that date.

---

* Amd, L 1993 ch 655, eff Sept 3, 1993.

§ 1203. General bond

Except in the counties of Erie, Monroe and Onondaga the person so appointed shall execute a bond with sureties to be approved by the court to the county in a penal sum to be fixed by the board of supervisors on recommendation of the court and conditioned for the faithful discharge of the duties of his office and that he will fully and correctly account for and pay over all moneys and property which may come into his hands as public administrator according to law, which bond shall be filed with the clerk of the county and the premium thereon shall be a county charge. The bond in the counties of Erie, Monroe and Onondaga shall be in a penal sum fixed by the court and the premium shall be borne personally by the public administrator.

> **History:** Add, L 1966, ch 953. eff Sept 1, 1967 from Sur. Ct. Act §§ 124, 125, 125-a, b,
> c; amd, L 1967, ch 685, eff Sept 1, 1967; L 1997, ch 638, § 1, eff Sept 24, 1997.

§ 1204. Separate bonds

Except in the counties of Erie and Onondaga the public administrator upon entering upon his duties in every estate the gross assets of which exceed the monetary amount defined as a small estate pursuant to subdivision 1 of section 1301 of this act, shall file a bond in a penal sum to be fixed by the court not less than the value of the personal property and the estimated gross rents for 18 months of the real property of which the decedent died seized or possessed and of the probable amount to be received by reason of any right of action granted to a fiduciary for damages for the wrongful death of the decedent. The public administrator in the counties of Erie and Onondaga shall file a bond in every estate in which he shall be appointed or be entitled to act pursuant to section 1211 of this article after the effective date of this act in a penal sum fixed by the court to be determined by such proof as the court deems proper. The bond must be conditioned that the public administrator or his successor will faithfully discharge the trust reposed in him as such and obey all lawful decrees and orders of the court touching the administration of the estate committed to him. The cost of the bond shall be borne by the estate in each instance.

> **History:** Add, L 1966, ch 953, eff Sept 1, 1967 from Sur. Ct. Act §§ 124, 125, 125-a, b,
> c; amd, L 1967, ch 685, eff Sept 1, 1967; L 1980, ch 18, eff Sept 1, 1980; L 1982, ch 519, eff
> Sept 1, 1982; L 1993, ch 655, eff Sept 3, 1993, applying to all estates pending as of that date;
> L 1997, ch 638, § 2, eff Sept 24, 1997.

§ 1205. Vacancy in office; delivery of money, papers and effects; discharge

1. Whenever the public administrator shall resign or be removed, he shall immediately deliver over to his successor all papers, moneys and effects in his hands.

2. In case of the death of a public administrator the persons into whose custody or possession any such papers, moneys or effects shall come, shall deliver them on demand to the successor. Upon the resignation, removal or death of any public administrator, if there be no deputy public administrator, the clerk of the surrogate's court of his county shall immediately take possession for custodial purposes only of all papers, moneys and effects which were in the hands of the public administrator. Delivery in either of the above cases may be enforced in the manner provided by law in relation to public officers. Upon the appointment of a duly qualified successor the clerk shall immediately deliver over to the successor all such papers, moneys and effects so held by him and such successor upon duly qualifying shall succeed at once to all the rights, duties and powers of his predecessor without the reissuance of formal letters to him.

3. In any final accounting by a public administrator the court shall discharge the acting administrator and any prior public administrator who may have acted in the estate.

History: Add, L 1966, ch 953, eff Sept 1, 1967 from Sur. Ct. Act §§ 124, 125, 125-a, b, c; amd, L 1993, ch 655, § 15, eff Sept 3, 1993, applying to all estates pending as of that date.

§ 1206. Staff; offices; counsel

1. Each public administrator, except in the counties of Erie and Onondaga, shall appoint such assistants and employees at such compensation as may be provided by the board of supervisors of his county.

2. Each such county except Erie, Monroe and Onondaga shall provide suitable office space, accommodations and storage space for its public administrator which shall be located conveniently to the court. The board of supervisors of the counties of Monroe and Onondaga may allow the public administrator a reasonable amount for the operation of his office and any allowance presently provided by the board shall continue unless modified or altered by it.

3. Each public administrator may employ counsel in any estate, whose fees and expenses therein shall be approved by the court of his county and shall be charged against the estate.

4. The court may deputize any assistant or employee in the office of the public administrator or other suitable person to hold the title of deputy public administrator who shall perform in the absence of the public administrator such services and shall possess such powers as may be prescribed and vested in him by the court. The deputy public administrator so appointed shall continue in office until removed by the court. In case of vacancy in office for any cause the court may fill it by appointing a suitable assistant or employee as deputy public administrator to take office immediately upon his appointment and qualification. The appointment shall be in writing and shall be filed in the office of the court. Except in the counties of Erie and Onondaga such deputy public administrator shall not receive any extra compensation for acting unless authorized by the board of supervisors.

History: Add, L 1966, ch 953, eff Sept 1, 1967 from Sur. Ct. Act §§ 124, 125, 125-a, b, c; amd, L 1993, ch 655, eff Sept 3, 1993, applying to all estates pending as of that date; L 1997, ch 638, § 3, eff Sept 24, 1997.

§ 1207. Salary; commissions; retention of commissions

1. Except as herein provided the public administrator shall receive an annual salary to be fixed by the board of supervisors of his county for the administration of all estates.

2. The public administrator of the counties of Erie and Onondaga shall be entitled to retain from all moneys or property which come into his hands, after deducting all reasonable and necessary expenses, the same commissions as are now allowed by law to a fiduciary other than a trustee. If he be a licensed attorney-at-law he shall receive as his compensation, in addition to his commissions, the legal fees as attorney for the estate as may be allowed by the court together with his reasonable and necessary expenses and disbursements which shall be a charge against the estate in each instance.

3. The public administrator of the county of Monroe, if he be a duly licensed attorney-at-law shall receive no salary and may act as his own counsel and shall receive as his compensation such legal fees as the attorney of the estate as may be allowed by the court together with his reasonable and necessary expenses and disbursements which shall be a charge against the estate in each instance. If he shall not be an attorney-at-law he shall be

compensated as is provided for in subdivision 1.

4. On the settlement of the account of the public administrator in each instance, except as provided in subdivisions 2 and 3 the court may allow his reasonable and necessary expenses and disbursements and in addition, in the counties of Erie, Monroe, Nassau, Onondaga, Suffolk and Westchester, a reasonable amount for the expenses of his office, to be fixed by the court. In addition thereto he shall be entitled to receive commissions on all moneys or property of any decedent or the proceeds of a cause of action for wrongful death which may come into his hands as provided for a fiduciary other than a trustee.

5. Except as hereinabove provided the public administrator shall not receive to his own use any remuneration in addition to his salary for his services and he shall pay to the treasurer of his county all commissions and costs received by him. Such payments shall be made monthly and shall be accompanied by a sworn statement in such form as the comptroller of his county shall prescribe showing in detail the commissions and costs received and allowed to him.

> **History:** Add, L 1966, ch 953, eff Sept 1, 1967 from Sur. Ct. Act §§ 124, 125, 125-a, b, c; amd, L 1967, ch 685, § 60, eff Sept 1, 1967; L 1983, ch 636, § 1, eff July 25, 1983; L 1997, ch 638, § 4, eff Sept 24, 1997.

§ 1208. Deposit of funds; report to court; annual audit

1. All moneys collected shall be deposited by the public administrator in a state or national bank, savings bank, savings and loan association or trust company and shall, in case of the insolvency or voluntary or involuntary liquidation of the depositary be entitled to equal priority of payment with that given by law to deposits of moneys by the state superintendent of financial services.

2. The public administrator or chief fiscal officer of a county appointed administrator of an estate shall file monthly with the surrogate of the county where appointed a statement of such of his accounts as have been closed or finally settled in such form as the surrogate may prescribe. Each public administrator or chief fiscal officer of a county appointed administrator of an estate shall file every six months with the surrogate of the county where appointed all estate accounts that are unsettled, stating the date the estate was opened, the gross assets of the estate and a list of current charges and disbursements of the estate.

3. Each public administrator shall conduct an annual audit of his office by an independent certified public accountant and such a report based on such audit shall be filed with the surrogate of the county where appointed, the attorney general of the state of New York and the comptroller of the state of New York. The audit shall be conducted in compliance with generally accepted government audit standards, and shall include a review of the performance of the office with respect to the guidelines and uniform fee schedules established by the administrative board. The costs of such annual audit and report shall be included annually in the budget of the county of appointment; provided however that any expenses of the public administrator's office permitted pursuant to section 1106 of this act may be used to pay the costs of such audit.

> **History:** Add, L 1966, ch 953, eff Sept 1, 1967 from Sur. Ct. Act §§ 124, 125, 125-a, b, c; amd, L 1993, ch 655, § 17, eff Sept 3, 1993, applying to all estates pending as of that date; L 2011, ch 62, § 104 (Part A), eff Oct 3, 2011.

§ 1209. Reports of deaths and burials

1. Every person keeping a hotel, boarding or rooming house in any of the counties to which

this article applies shall report to the public administrator of his county information concerning every person not a member of his family who shall die in his hotel, boarding or rooming house, within 12 hours after such death.

2. The chief medical examiner or such similar public officer of each county to which this article applies within 12 hours after an inquest shall report in writing to the public administrator of his county, information, if known, regarding the decedent.

3. Every undertaker shall file a report in writing with the public administrator of his county upon the form provided by him, within 12 hours after receiving an order for the burial by him of any decedent having no known distributees or having been survived only by cousins or relatives by marriage, such information regarding the decedent which he may have.

> **History:** Add, L 1966, ch 953, eff Sept 1, 1967 from Sur. Ct. Act §§ 124, 125, 125-a, b, c; amd, L 1967, ch 685, § 61, eff Sept 1, 1967.

§ 1210. Application for letters; when court may direct probate

1. The public administrator shall have the power to apply for and receive letters as defined in this act.

2. The court may, pursuant to 1402, direct the public administrator to present a petition for the probate of a will at any time after it is filed.

> **History:** Add, L 1966, ch 953, eff Sept 1, 1967 from Sur. Ct. Act §§ 124, 125, 125-a, b, c.

§ 1211. Letters not required; notice to be filed

1. Without the issuance of letters the public administrator in virtue of his office shall have all powers of a fiduciary of a decedent's estate whenever the gross assets of an estate do not exceed in value the monetary amount defined as a small estate pursuant to section 1301 of this act.

2. Upon commencing to act pursuant to this section the public administrator shall file with the court a statement showing the name and domicile of the decedent, the date and place of death and the names, addresses and relationship of any known distributees. The filing of such notice shall have the same effect as the issuance of formal letters.

3. In the event the aggregate sum of the assets of an estate in which the public administrator commences to act pursuant to subdivision 1 shall exceed the monetary amount defined as a small estate pursuant to section 1301 of this act the public administrator shall forthwith apply for letters and file separate bond in the estate.

4. In the event the public administrator acting in any estate pursuant to subdivision 1 shall ascertain the names and whereabouts of persons believed to be distributees in the estate, then and in that event he shall forthwith file a supplemental statement pursuant to subdivision 2.

> **History:** Add, L 1966, ch 953, eff Sept 1, 1967 from Sur. Ct. Act §§ 124, 125, 125-a, b, c; amd, L 1967, ch 685, § 62, eff Sept 1, 1967; L 1977, ch 217, eff June 7, 1977; L 1982, ch 519, § 5, eff Sept 1, 1982; L 1993, ch 655, § 18, eff Sept 3, 1993, applying to all estates pending as of that date.

§ 1212. Powers before issuance of letters

Before letters are issued to him and subject to the provisions of section 1128 of this act the public administrator is authorized to

SCPA

1. Take possession of, collect and secure the personal property within his county of any person who shall die intestate or testate either within this state or elsewhere or whose property shall arrive within the county after his death whenever there is no person eligible to act as fiduciary of an intestate or of a testator if the executor named in the will refuses or neglects to act or is dead or if his whereabouts are unknown or if he is not eligible to receive letters.

2. Take possession of, manage and collect the rents of the real property of an intestate whose distributees are unknown or whose distributees, if known, are non-domiciliaries, or of a testator, if the executor named in the will refuses or neglects to act or is dead or if his whereabouts are unknown or if he is not eligible to receive letters.

3. Make necessary funeral arrangements for the decedent and to pay the reasonable charges therefor.

4. Institute an inquiry as provided by 1216.

5. Sell, as and when authorized by the court, perishable property or such other property of the decedent as the preservation of the estate requires.

6. Defray the expenses of the foregoing activities and the expenses incidental to his application for letters.

History: Add, L 1966, ch 953, eff Sept 1, 1967 from Sur. Ct. Act §§ 124, 125, 125-a, b, c; amd, L 1993, ch 655, § 19, eff Sept 3, 1993, applying to all estates pending as of that date.

§ 1213. General powers

1. The public administrator shall have all the powers specifically granted herein and also the powers given by law to a fiduciary of a decedent's estate.

2. In addition to the foregoing grant of powers and without limitation thereon and subject to the provisions of section 1128 of this act he is authorized to

(a) Sell at public auction the personal property of the decedent delivered to him by any county officer or department, but such sale shall not be had until notice of the public auction shall be published once a week for two consecutive weeks in a newspaper published in the county, the first publication to be not less than 20 days prior to the public auction.

(b) Retain marketable securities beyond 4 months after he has commenced to act as fiduciary of the estate when authorized to do so by order of the court.

(c) File in the court after the expiration of 7 months from the time he or she commences to act as fiduciary of the estate an informatory account in estates in which the gross value of the assets accounted for does not exceed the monetary amount defined as a small estate pursuant to subdivision 1 of section 1301 of this act and a copy of such account shall be mailed by certified mail, return receipt requested, to each of the persons entitled to receive process upon an accounting proceeding provided the names and addresses of such persons be known to him or her. Unless objection or claim be properly filed in the court within 30 days from mailing such account a final decree settling his or her account may be entered without further notice or proceedings and with the same effect as in an accounting proceeding and he or she shall be entitled to the commissions, costs and allowances allowed him or her by the court in the decree.

(d) Pay for the use and benefit of an infant distributee or legatee who has no guardian the share or legacy due him if not exceeding $5,000 by payment thereof in his discretion to a parent or to an adult, competent person with whom the infant resides.

(e) Pay to the comptroller of the state of New York the balance of any moneys or other assets in his hands remaining after settlement of his accounts, formally or informally, where payable to unknown persons or to known persons whose residences are unknown.

(f) Apply ex parte or upon such notice as directed by the court for an order or decree in any appropriate proceeding requiring the county treasurer to return to the public administrator any money or unliquidated assets theretofore deposited by him and remaining in the treasury of the county for the account of unknown persons or of known persons whose domiciles are unknown and upon further order of the court to make distribution of such recovered funds to the persons entitled thereto.

> **History:** Add, L 1966, ch 953, eff Sept 1, 1967 from Sur. Ct. Act §§ 124, 125, 125-a, b, c; amd, L 1967, ch 685, eff Sept 1, 1967; L 1980, ch 19, eff Sept 1, 1980; L 1993, ch 655, § 20, eff Sept 3, 1993, applying to all estates pending as of that date; L 2012, ch 142, § 2, eff July 18, 2012, applying only to the estates of decedents who shall have died on or after such effective date.

§ 1214. Service of process

The public administrator is authorized to make service of process on creditors, legatees or distributees who are non-domiciliaries of his county by certified mail, return receipt requested, whenever the court by order made in any proceeding shall direct. The provisions of 308 notwithstanding, process so served shall be valid if made at least 30 days before the return date thereof.

> **History:** Add, L 1966, ch 953, eff Sept 1, 1967 from Sur. Ct. Act §§ 124, 125, 125-a, b, c.

§ 1215. When authorized to receive process or appear

1. The public administrator may be authorized by the court to receive process or other notice as a necessary party in the following proceedings:

(a) Any proceeding pending in the court where service of process or notice of or in behalf of any known or unknown persons is directed by the court or where the court by order directs the public administrator to appear therein.

(b) Every proceeding for the appointment of an administrator or for the probate of a will where it appears that the persons applying or named in the petition are not all of the distributees of the decedent or where it appears that such persons are related to the decedent in the fourth degree of consanguinity or are more remotely related.

(c) Every proceeding to effect distribution of moneys or property to be deposited or deposited for the account of unknown persons or of infants or incompetents, of known persons whose residences are unknown or of known persons whose shares were deposited pursuant to 2218. In any such proceeding when so authorized the public administrator shall be deemed an interested party.

2. In all such proceedings the public administrator, in his discretion, may take any action in behalf of such person or persons as a party interested might.

3. Whenever a public administrator acts pursuant to this section he shall be allowed by the court his proper expenses and his counsel shall be allowed his reasonable fee. Such expenses and fee shall be payable either from the estate generally or from the shares or interests of the respective persons represented by the public administrator, as may be directed by the court.

> **History:** Add, L 1966, ch 953, eff Sept 1, 1967 from Sur. Ct. Act §§ 124, 125, 125-a, b,
> c; amd, L 1967, ch 685, § 64, eff Sept 1, 1967.

§ 1216. Inquiry and subpoena

The public administrator may institute an inquiry in any case in which he is authorized to act as to any matter affecting the estate of the decedent. For that purpose he may issue a subpoena or subpoena duces tecum in the name of the court either before or after the issuance of letters. Failure to comply with the directions of the subpoena or subpoena duces tecum shall be punishable as a contempt of court.

> **History:** Add, L 1966, ch 953, eff Sept 1, 1967 from Sur. Ct. Act §§ 124, 125, 125-a, b,
> c.

§ 1217. When superseded; accounting authorized

1. When the public administrator in virtue of his office has been superseded he shall deliver to the fiduciary who has superseded him all the personal property belonging to the estate which he has in his possession after deducting therefrom his expenses, costs and commissions as ordinarily allowed by the court upon the entry of a decree upon final accounting.

2. When letters issued to the public administrator have been revoked he shall institute a proceeding for the judicial settlement of his account.

> **History:** Add, L 1966, ch 953, eff Sept 1, 1967 from Sur. Ct. Act §§ 124, 125, 125-a, b,
> c.

§ 1218. Appeal; bond

The public administrator is authorized to appeal from any decree, order or judgment affecting an estate in his charge or in which he is a party. No bond on his part shall be required to stay execution of the order, decree or judgment from which an appeal is taken.

> **History:** Add, L 1966, ch 953, eff Sept 1, 1967 from Sur. Ct. Act §§ 124, 125, 125-a, b,
> c.

§ 1219. Chief fiscal officer of county appointed administrator; qualifications; fees

A chief fiscal officer of a county appointed administrator of an estate shall qualify in the manner prescribed in 708 of this act, shall be vested with all the powers and rights of an administrator and be subject to the same duties and obligations and shall be allowed the same commissions as an administrator, which commissions shall be in addition to the salary and fees now allowed by law to such chief fiscal officer. He may employ an attorney to act for him as such administrator other than the one, if any, appointed to act as the county attorney or the official attorney of such chief fiscal officer.

Where the administrator appointed as above provided leaves office, resigns or is removed from office, or dies, his successor in office, with respect to each of the estates of which his predecessor in office was appointed administrator, shall apply to be appointed administrator de bonis non, within one hundred twenty days after assuming office.

The chief fiscal officer shall be subject to the provisions of section 1128 as it pertains to his administrator's duties.

> **History:** Add, L 1966, ch 953, eff Sept 1, 1967 from Sur. Ct. Act § 123; amd, L 1971, ch

344, eff June 1, 1971; L 1977, ch 259, § 1, eff June 14, 1977; L 1993, ch 655, § 21, eff Sept 3, 1993, applying to all estates pending as of that date.

ARTICLE 13
SETTLEMENT OF SMALL ESTATES WITHOUT COURT ADMINISTRATION

SUMMARY OF ARTICLE

SCPA

§ 1301. Definitions

In this article:

1. A small estate is the estate of a domiciliary or a non-domiciliary who dies leaving personal property having a gross value of $50,000 or less exclusive of property required to be set off under EPTL 5-3.1(a).

2. A voluntary administrator is a person who qualifies and undertakes to settle the estate of the decedent without the formality of court administration as hereinafter provided.

History: Add, L 1966, ch 953, eff Sept 1, 1967 from Sur. Ct. Act § 137-a; amd, L 1970, ch 998, eff May 20, 1970; L 1973, ch 285, eff Sept 1, 1973; L 1975, ch 276, eff June 24, 1975; L 1981, ch 221, eff June 15, 1981; L 1985, ch 9, eff March 19, 1985; L 1996, ch 373, § 1, eff Aug 29, 1996, and applying apply to estates of decedents dying on and after such date; L 2008, ch 300, § 1, eff Jan 1, 2009; L 2012, ch 281, § 1, eff Aug 1, 2012, deemed eff on and after Jan 1, 2011; L 2019, ch 557, § 1, eff Nov 25, 2019.

§ 1302. Kinds of property

This article is not applicable to any interest in real property in this state owned by a decedent, but his owner ship* of an interest in real property shall not prevent the use of this article in administering his personal property.

History: Add, L 1966, ch 953 from Sur. Ct. Act § 137-b, eff Sept 1, 1967; amd, L 1971, ch 312, § 1, eff May 25, 1971.

§ 1303. Persons who may become a voluntary administrator

(a) If the deceased dies intestate, the right to act as a voluntary administrator is hereby given first to the surviving adult spouse, if any, of the decedent and if there be none or if the

---

* In original. Should be "ownership".

spouse renounce, then in order to a competent adult who is a child or grandchild, parent, brother or sister, niece or nephew or aunt or uncle of the decedent, or if there be no such person who will act, then to the guardian of the property of an infant, the committee of the property of any incompetent person or the conservator of the property of a conservatee who is a distributee and if none of the foregoing named persons will act or if there are no known distributees within the categories listed above, then to the chief fiscal officer of the county except in those counties in which a public administrator has been appointed under articles eleven and twelve of this act. After the surviving spouse, the first distributee within the class of persons entitled or if no distributee will act or there are no known distributees within the class of persons entitled, then the chief fiscal officer of the county as above who makes and files the required affidavit, is authorized to act as voluntary administrator, or as successor voluntary administrator in the event of the death or resignation of the voluntary administrator before the completion of the settlement of the estate.

(b) If the deceased dies testate, the named executor or alternate executor shall have the first right to act as voluntary administrator, upon filing the last will and testament with the surrogate's court. If the named executor or alternate executor renounces or fails to qualify by filing the required affidavit within thirty days after the last will and testament has been filed in the surrogate's court, then any adult person who would be entitled to petition for letters of administration with will annexed under section 1418 of this chapter may file the required affidavit and have the right to act as voluntary administrator.

(c) No person other than one hereinbefore mentioned can become a voluntary administrator.

History: Add, L 1966, ch 953, eff Sept 1, 1067 from Sur. Ct. Act § 137-c; amd, L 1967, ch 685, § 66; L 1970, ch 396, eff Sept 1, 1970; L 1970, ch 998, eff May 20, 1970; L 1971, ch 312, eff May 25, 1971; L 1973, ch 741, § 1, eff Sept 1, 1973; L 1976, ch 263, § 1, eff Sept 1, 1976; L 1981, ch 115, eff May 18, 1981; L 1984, ch 224, eff June 19, 1984; L 1990, ch 448, § 1, eff Sept 1, 1990; L 1995, ch 281, § 1, eff July 26, 1995.

§ 1304. Summary procedure

1. When available. No waiting period after the death of the decedent is required.

The procedure prescribed in this article may be used after the decedent's death.

2. Bond. The voluntary administrator need not give a bond.

3. Affidavit. A person may qualify as a voluntary administrator by making and filing with the clerk of the court of the decedent's domicile, or in the case of a non-domiciliary, of the county in which his personal property is located, an affidavit in the form provided by the Official Forms appended to this act, and also a certified copy of the death certificate of the decedent.

4. Record. The clerk shall file the affidavit and assign it a number. The clerk shall enter each such proceeding in the records and indexes of the court. The clerk shall charge a fee of $1 for filing the affidavit. No order of the court or other proceeding shall be necessary. The clerk shall mail to each distributee who has not renounced his or her right to act and to each beneficiary mentioned in the affidavit other than the affiant, a letter or postcard notice of the proceeding under this article. The giving of such notice is not jurisdictional.

5. Furnishing evidence of qualification and authority. A short certificate of the court showing the filing by the voluntary administrator of the required affidavit, shall evidence his, her or its qualification and authority to act. The clerk may indicate on the certificate that it is

valid only for a transfer or transaction as specified thereon. The voluntary administrator shall deliver a certificate to each debtor, transfer agent, safe deposit company, bank, trust company or other person holding or having custody, possession or control of any personal property of the decedent which the voluntary administrator seeks to reduce to possession or otherwise affect the title thereof.

History: Add, L 1966, ch 953, eff Sept 1, 1967 from Sur. Ct. Act § 137-d; amd, L 1967, ch 685, eff Sept 1, 1967; L 1971, ch 312, eff May 25, 1971; L 1993, ch 514, eff Jan 1, 1994; L 1999, ch 168, § 2, eff July 6, 1999, and applying to the estate of any person dying on or after the effective date.

§ 1305. Discharge of debtor, transfer agent, safe deposit company, bank, trust company or other person

The delivery by a voluntary administrator to a debtor, transfer agent, safe deposit company, bank, trust company or other person holding or having custody or possession or control of any personal property of the decedent, of the short form certificate of the court, the receipt of the administrator, and the surrender of any evidentiary document, shall constitute a complete release and discharge for any payment of money or delivery of personal property made pursuant to the certificate, without such person being required to see to the application thereof and with the same effect as if made to any duly appointed fiduciary.

History: Add, L 1966, ch 953, eff Sept 1, 1967 from Sur. Ct. Act § 137-e; amd, L 1967, ch 685, eff Sept 1, 1967; L 1993, ch 514, § 29, eff Jan 1, 1994.

§ 1306. Powers

1. If any person to whom a certificate and receipt are presented by a voluntary administrator refuses to pay, deliver, transfer or issue to the voluntary administrator any personal property of the decedent, the voluntary administrator may maintain an action or proceeding to recover or compel the delivery of the property, or to enforce a contractual or quasi contractual claim owned by decedent, provided the amount claimed, together with all other assets of the estate to be administered under this article, does not exceed the monetary amount defined as a small estate pursuant to subdivision one of section 1301 of this article. In such action or proceeding, a certified copy of the affidavit shall be prima facie proof of the facts therein stated.

2. A voluntary administrator may sell for its reasonable value in cash any personal property of the decedent coming into the voluntary administrator's possession.

3. For the purpose of this article, a voluntary administrator shall be deemed to be the fiduciary of the estate until another fiduciary is appointed, and except as hereinafter provided, the voluntary administrator shall have the rights, powers and duties with respect to personal property of an administrator duly appointed for the estate. The voluntary administrator shall have no power to enforce a claim for the wrongful death of or a claim for personal injuries to the decedent.

Upon the appointment and qualification of another fiduciary of the estate, the powers of the voluntary administrator shall cease.

History: Add, L 1966, ch 953, eff Sept 1, 1967 from Sur. Ct. Act § 137-f; amd, L 1976, ch 111, eff April 6, 1976; L 1982, ch 519, eff Sept 1, 1982; L 1999, ch 168, § 3, eff July 6, 1999, and applying to the estate of any person dying on or after the effective date.

§ 1307. Duties

A voluntary administrator shall

1. Deposit in an estate bank account to be opened by him in a bank, trust company, savings bank, savings and loan association or federal savings and loan association in this state, credit union or federal credit union in this state all money received. He shall sign all checks drawn on or withdrawals from the account in the name of the estate by himself as voluntary administrator. Without compensation for his services, he shall pay so far as possible out of the decedent's assets coming into his possession, the necessary expenses of administration, the reasonable funeral expenses of the decedent and the decedent's debts in the order provided by law. He shall then distribute the balance to the person or persons entitled and in the amount or amounts provided by EPTL 4-1.1 if decedent died intestate or if a will is filed which is valid on its face, he shall distribute to the persons named in such will, subject to the right of any person affected to contest such will at any time.

2. Account for all personal property of the decedent received and disbursed by him by filing with the clerk of the court a statement of all assets collected and of all payments and distributions made by him and receipts for or cancelled checks evidencing such payments and distributions. No fee shall be charged for the filing of such account.

History: Add, L 1966, ch 953, eff Sept 1, 1967 from Sur. Ct. Act § 137-g; amd, L 1969, ch 772, eff Sept 1, 1969; L 1971, ch 312, eff May 25, 1971; L 1995, ch 464, § 3, eff Aug 2, 1995; L 1995, ch 470, § 1, eff Sept 1, 1995.

§ 1308. Liability of voluntary administrator collecting assets

1. A voluntary administrator shall be answerable and accountable to all persons including creditors and distributees of the decedent, beneficiaries named in the will filed with the affidavit and to any fiduciary thereafter appointed, aggrieved by his administration of the decedent's estate under this article, in the same manner as now provided by this act concerning a fiduciary.

2. A voluntary administrator or other person who wilfully and knowingly makes a false affidavit in order to obtain personal property of the decedent as provided in this article, is subject to prosecution for perjury and upon conviction shall be punishable as provided by law in relation to such crime.

History: Add, L 1966, ch 953, eff Sept 1, 1967 from Sur. Ct. Act § 137-h; amd, L 1967, ch 685, eff Sept 1, 1967; L 1971, ch 312, § 5, eff May 25, 1971.

§ 1309. General provisions

1. The use of this article in the settlement of a small estate without the formality of court administration is permissive and not mandatory.

2. As a matter of comity a debtor, transfer agent, safe deposit company, bank, trust company or person in this state holding personal property of a non-domiciliary decedent, may recognize a certified copy of an affidavit or of a short certificate of a judge or clerk of a probate court made under a statute of another state, providing for the settlement of small estates without administration, for the purpose of collecting or obtaining possession of an asset of a decedent in his state, provided that debtors, transfer agents, safe deposit companies, banks, trust companies or persons in such other state holding personal property of a domiciliary decedent shall, whether pursuant to statute or otherwise, recognize and pay or transfer his personal property pursuant to a short certificate of the court made under this article.

3. A debtor, transfer agent, safe deposit company, bank, trust company or person of another

state, shall not be liable to any person in respect of any payment, transfer or delivery of personal property made to a voluntary administrator pursuant to such short certificate.

4. As used in this section, the word "state" means any state of the United States, the District of Columbia, the Commonwealth of Puerto Rico, and the territories and possessions of the United States.

History: Add, L 1966, ch 953, eff Sept 1, 1967 from Sur. Ct. Act § 137-i; amd, L 1967, ch 685, §§ 70, 71, eff Sept 1, 1967.

§ 1310. Payment of certain debts without administration

1. As used in this section

(a) "Debt" means

(i) money or securities payable on account of a deposit in a bank, national bank, trust company, branch of a foreign banking corporation, savings bank, industrial bank, state or federal savings and loan association or state or federal credit union or with a private banker, or funds or securities invested with, held by or deposited with a broker-dealer or with, by or in securities of a management type investment company or trust payable or returnable to, or to the estate of, or to a beneficiary designated by, the depositor or

(ii) money payable by a state or federal savings and loan association or state or federal credit union to, or to the estate of, or to a beneficiary designated by, a member on account of the withdrawal value of his shares or

(iii) money payable by an insurance company or a savings bank authorized to conduct the business of life insurance under an annuity or pure endowment contract or a policy of life, group life, industrial life or accident and health insurance or a contract made by such an insurer, relating to the payment of proceeds or avails thereof, to, or to the estate of, or to a beneficiary designated by, the owner or the person purchasing the annuity or the person insured or the person effecting the insurance or the person effecting the supplemental contract or

(iv) money payable by a public corporation, a state or the federal government or an agency thereof, to, or to the estate of, or to a beneficiary designated by, any natural person or

(v) a pension or retirement or death benefit, profit share, earnings, wages, salary or bonus payable by an employer or by a pension, retirement or profit-sharing plan or system to, or to the estate of, or to a beneficiary designated by, an employee, or

(vi) a balance of money due on an accepted claim or account payable, on account of dividends payable by the superintendent of financial services in liquidation of bank assets, to, or to the estate of, or to a beneficiary designated by, a depositor or

(vii) any personal property deposited with a county treasurer by a coroner or county medical examiner pursuant to sections 785 and 786 of the code of criminal procedure, or

(viii) any personal property on deposit with a hospital, nursing home, residential health care facility or out-patient lodge described in section twenty-eight hundred one of the public health law at the time of the death of a decedent that is payable or returnable to the estate of the decedent;

(b) "Debtor" means the person or persons, partnership, corporation, government or government agency by whom a debt defined in this section is to be paid,

(c) "Creditor" means the employee, depositor, member, or other person, to whom, or to whose estate, or to a beneficiary designated by whom, a debt defined in this section is to be paid and shall include any beneficiary validly designated by such a creditor,

(d) A "designation of a beneficiary" means any writing, signed by the creditor and delivered to the debtor purporting to designate the person to whom a debt shall be paid on death of the creditor or any transaction which operates pursuant to statute as such a designation.

2. Upon the death of a creditor, unless otherwise provided by a designation of a beneficiary which is then in effect, it shall be lawful for the debtor forthwith to pay to the surviving spouse of the decedent not more than thirty thousand dollars of the debt, upon an affidavit made by the spouse showing that the payment and all other payments received by the spouse under this subdivision do not in the aggregate exceed thirty thousand dollars.

3. Not less than thirty days after the death of a creditor, unless otherwise provided by a designation of a beneficiary which is then in effect, it shall be lawful for the debtor to pay not more than fifteen thousand dollars of the debt to

(a) the surviving spouse,

(b) one or more of the children eighteen years of age or older,

(c) either parent,

(d) the brother or sister,

(e) the niece or nephew of the decedent, preference being given in the order named if request for payment shall have been made by more than one such person,

(f) a creditor of the decedent or to a person who has paid or incurred the funeral expense of the decedent, upon the request of the surviving spouse or of one of such relatives.

Payment under this subdivision may be made upon an affidavit by the surviving spouse or relative to whom or at whose request the payment is made, showing

(i) the date of the death of the decedent,

(ii) the relationship of the affiant to the decedent,

(iii) that no fiduciary has qualified or been appointed,

(iv) the names and addresses of the persons entitled to and who will receive the money paid, and

(v) that such payment and all other payments made under this section by all debtors, known to the affiant, after diligent inquiry do not in the aggregate exceed fifteen thousand dollars. This subdivision does not limit the right of a debtor to make payment to a surviving spouse within less than thirty days after the death of the creditor as provided in subdivision two.

4. Not less than 6 months after the death of a creditor, unless otherwise provided by a designation of a beneficiary which is then in effect, it shall be lawful for the debtor to pay a

debt which does not exceed $5,000, or any part of such debt, to a distributee or, to the extent that the funds are not exempt from claims of creditors, to a creditor or to a person who has paid or incurred the funeral expenses upon an affidavit made by the person paid showing

(a) the date of the death of the decedent,

(b) that no fiduciary has qualified or been appointed,

(c) that the decedent was not survived by a spouse or minor child,

(d) that the affiant is entitled to the payment, and

(e) that such payment and all other payments made under this section by all debtors, known to the affiant, after diligent inquiry, do not in the aggregate exceed $5,000.

5. A payment made in good faith under this section shall be a complete discharge to the debtor to the extent of the payment, even though the affidavit on which payment is made be false, and even though payment pursuant to subdivision 3 was not made in the order of preference indicated in that subdivision, provided only that the creditor be dead and that the required number of days elapse between death and payment and, in the case of a payment under subdivision 2 or subdivision 3 that the affiant in fact bear the stated relationship to the decedent and in the case of a payment under subdivision 4 that the affiant be in fact a distributee or creditor or have paid or incurred the funeral expenses.

6. Any person receiving payment pursuant to this section is accountable therefor to the fiduciary of the decedent if one be appointed or to the public administrator of the county having authority to take possession of the money or property constituting the debt except that a surviving spouse entitled to have property set aside to him or to her pursuant to EPTL 5-3.1 need not account for such payments to the extent of the exemption provided therein, and the amount so received shall be credited to such exemption.

7. Nothing in this section shall deprive any person of any right which he would otherwise have to receive payment of a debt, except as against a debtor who has made a payment which is a discharge under subdivision 5, nor shall anything in this section deprive any debtor of any right to make or refuse payment which it would otherwise have. This section does not limit article 26 of the tax law.

8. It shall be lawful for the debtor to pay a debt which does not exceed five thousand dollars or any part of such debt, under subdivision four of this section, to the department of social services or a social services district where the debt is money payable on account of a deposit with the debtor for the personal needs of the deceased creditor while residing in a medical institution or other facility, or otherwise, and the deceased creditor is indebted to the department or district on account of medical assistance furnished to or on behalf of the deceased creditor.

9. This section applies only to creditors who die on or after September 1, 1952.

History: Add, L 1966, ch 953, eff Sept 1, 1967 from Dec. Est. Law § 103-a; amd, L 1967, ch 685, § 72; L 1968, ch 260, eff Sept 1, 1968; L 1969, ch 772, eff Sept 1, 1969; L 1977, ch 109, eff Sept 1, 1977; L 1982, ch 105, eff Sept 1, 1982; L 1982, ch 519, eff Sept 1, 1982; L 1984, ch 224, eff June 19, 1984; L 1986, ch 81, eff May 19, 1986; L 1990, ch 190, § 121, eff May 25, 1990, provided that, with respect to estates of decedents dying on or before May 25, 1990, the statute as it existed prior to this amendment will apply; L 1992, ch 41, § 87, eff April 2, 1992; L 1993, ch 514, § 30, eff Jan 1, 1994; L 1998, ch 69, § 1, eff May 21, 1998, and applying to the estate of any person dying before or after the effective date; L 2011, ch 62, §

SCPA

104 (Part A), eff Oct 3, 2011; L 2019, ch 420, § 4, eff Oct 29, 2019.

§ 1311. Administration of funds payable under social security act of the United States, the unemployment insurance law and the workmen's compensation law

1. In virtue of his office and without issuance of letters each public administrator, and in counties having no public administrator, each county treasurer is authorized to receive from the social security board of the United States or the unemployment insurance fund of the state or from any person making payment under the workmen's compensation law, for application according to law in the payment of administration expenses, funeral expenses and for distribution to the distributees of the deceased any moneys not exceeding $500 payable pursuant to title II of the social security act of the United States or pursuant to the unemployment insurance law, or pursuant to the workmen's compensation law, as the case may be, to the estate of any person dying intestate a resident of his county.

2. The moneys so received by the public administrator or county treasurer shall be applicable to the payment of the expenses of administration, to the payment of reasonable funeral expenses not otherwise provided for and any balance may be distributed without prior accounting decree to the persons entitled thereto as distributees of the decedent.

3. In the case of an infant or incompetent his share, if not exceeding $1,000, may be paid for the use and benefit of the infant to a parent or to some competent person with whom the infant or incompetent resides or who has an interest in his welfare.

4. If the sum payable to a patient in an institution in the state department of mental hygiene is not in excess of the amount which the director of the institution is authorized to receive pursuant to section 29.23 of the mental hygiene law, it may be paid to such director for use as provided in that section.

History: Add, L 1966, ch 953, eff Sept 1, 1967 from Dec. Est. Law § 103-b; amd, L 1969, ch 772, § 10, eff Sept 1, 1969; L 1973, ch 195 § 22, eff April 25, 1973.

§ 1312. Construction

This article is remedial and shall be given a liberal construction.

History: Add, L 1967, ch 685, § 65, eff Sept 1, 1967 from Sur. Ct. Act § 137-i.

ARTICLE 14
PROBATE PROCEEDINGS; CONSTRUCTION OF WILLS; RIGHT OF ELECTION

SUMMARY OF ARTICLE

§ 1401. Proceeding to compel production of will

Whenever it shall appear to the court, sua sponte, or by the petition of a person authorized under the succeeding section of this act to present a petition for the probate of a will, that there is reasonable ground to believe that any person has knowledge of the whereabouts or destruction of a will of a decedent the court may make an order requiring the person or persons named therein to attend and be examined in the premises. Service of the order must be made by delivery of a certified copy thereof to the person or persons named therein either personally or in such manner as the court shall direct. The court may either in the order or otherwise in the proceeding require the production and filing in court of any will of the decedent which it finds is in the possession or under the control of the respondent. The court may impose the reasonable attorneys fees of the petitioner in such a proceeding against a respondent when the court determines the respondent did not have good cause to withhold production of such will or codicil.

History: Add, L 1966, ch 953, eff Sept 1, 1967 from Sur. Ct. Act § 138; amd, L 1993, ch 514, § 31, eff Jan 1, 1994.

§ 1402. Who may propound will; contents of petition; direction of court

1. Who may petition. A petition for the probate of a will may be presented by

(a) any person designated in the will as legatee, devisee, fiduciary or guardian or by the guardian of an infant legatee or devisee or the committee of an incompetent legatee or devisee, or the conservator of a legatee or devisee who has been designated a conservatee pursuant to article seventy-seven of the mental hygiene law;

(b) a creditor or any person interested or any person entitled to letters of administration with the will annexed under 1418;

(c) any party to an action brought or about to be brought in which action the decedent, if living, would be a party;

(d) the Public Administrator or County Treasurer on order of the court, where a will has been filed in the court and proceedings for its probate have not been instituted or diligently prosecuted.

2. Contents of petition. The petition for probate shall allege the citizenship of the petitioner and the testator and shall describe the will being offered for probate and any other will of the same testator on file in the court and shall set forth the names and post-office addresses so far as they can be ascertained with due diligence of all of the persons required to be cited and all of the legatees, devisees and fiduciaries named in the will or any other will so filed.

3. Direction of court.

(a) Where a petition for probate has been filed and the proceeding has not been diligently prosecuted the court may direct the Public Administrator or County Treasurer or authorize any party to take such steps as may be required to bring the proceeding to a decree.

(b) Where necessary, the court shall determine the text or tenor of the will as admitted to probate and may incorporate the will or any part thereof in the decree.

History: Add, L 1966, ch 953, eff Sept 1, 1967 from Sur. Ct. Act §§ 139, 146 in part; amd, L 1967, ch 685, § 73, eff Sept 1, 1967; L 1970, ch 396, § 3, eff Sept 1, 1970; L 1981, ch 115, § 124, eff May 18, 1981.

§ 1403. Persons to be served; content of process

1. In a proceeding for the probate of a will process must issue to the following persons if not petitioners:

(a) The distributees of the testator.

(b) The person or persons designated in the will as executor except that a person designated in the will as substitute or successor executor in the event the designated executor cannot act or fails to qualify need not be served where the designated executor is under no disability.

(c) Any person designated in the will as beneficiary, executor, trustee or guardian, whose rights or interests are adversely affected by any other instrument offered for probate that is later in date of execution or which amends or modifies an instrument offered for probate.

(d) Any person designated as beneficiary, executor, trustee or guardian in any other will of the same testator filed in the surrogate's court of the county in which the propounded will is filed whose rights or interests are adversely affected by the instrument offered for probate.

(e) If the propounded will expressly refers to an instrument which created a power of appointment and purports to exercise such power of appointment, any persons designated in the instrument that created such power of appointment whose rights or interests are adversely affected by the instrument offered for probate.

(f) The testator in any case where the petition alleges that the testator is believed to be dead.

(g) The state tax commission in the case of a non-domiciliary testator.

(h) Where any person to whom process is required to be issued has died, process shall issue to his fiduciary and if none has been appointed, to all persons interested as distributees, nominated fiduciaries or named as legatees or devisees under any will of the deceased filed in the court.

(i) The provisions of section three hundred fifteen shall apply to a proceeding under this section.

2. The process must set forth the name of the proponent and if the will is nuncupative, that fact.

> **History:** Add, L 1966, ch 953, eff Sept 1, 1967 from Sur. Ct. Act § 140; amd, L 1967, ch 685, eff Sept 1, 1967; L 1967, ch 739, § 2; L 1968, ch 259, eff May 14, 1968; L 1984, ch 223, § 1, eff June 19, 1984; L 1997, ch 64, § 1, eff May 20, 1997.

§ 1404. Witnesses to be examined; proof required

1. Except as otherwise provided in this article, 2 at least, of the attesting witnesses must be produced before the court and examined before a written will is admitted to probate if so many of the witnesses are within the state and competent and able to testify.

2. Where the will offered for probate is on file in a court or public office under the laws of which jurisdiction the will cannot be removed the court may issue a commission to a person authorized to take a commission under CPLR 3113 or to an attorney and counsellor-at-law of the state or of the jurisdiction in which the commission is to be taken, to take the testimony and may admit the will to probate upon proof of its provisions, of its existence at the time of the death of the testator and of its due execution. Where the will offered for probate is brought to the surrogate's court by a representative of a public office of another jurisdiction, the court may take proof of the will and permit the representative to return the will to such other jurisdiction. The decree admitting the will to probate shall set forth the full text of the will. The proof so taken and the decree admitting the will to probate shall have the same force and effect as though the will had been filed or had remained in the court.

3. Before a nuncupative will executed under the provisions of EPTL 3-2.2 is admitted to probate its execution and the tenor thereof must be proved by at least two witnesses. Before a holographic will made under the provisions of that section is admitted to probate its execution and the handwriting of the testator must be proved.

4. In all cases the proofs must be reduced to writing. Any party to the proceeding, before or after filing objections to the probate of the will, may examine any or all of the attesting

witnesses, the person who prepared the will, and if the will contains a provision designed to prevent a disposition or distribution from taking effect in case the will, or any part thereof, is contested, the nominated executors in the will and the proponents and, upon application to the court based upon special circumstances, any person whose examination the court determines may provide information with respect to the validity of the will that is of substantial importance or relevance to a decision to file objections to the will. No person who has been examined as a witness under this section shall be examined in the same proceeding under any other provision of law except by direction of the court. The attesting witnesses, the person who prepared the will, the nominated executors in the will and the proponents may be examined as to all relevant matters which may be the basis of objections to the probate of the propounded instrument. There shall be made available to the party conducting such examination, all rights granted under article 31 of the civil practice law and rules with respect to document discovery.

5. Unless the court directs otherwise for good cause shown, the costs of the examinations conducted pursuant to subdivision 4 of this section shall be paid as follows:

(a) in the case of examinations conducted before objections are filed, the testator's estate shall pay the costs of:

(1) the initial production or commission and the examination of (A) the first two attesting witnesses within the state who are competent and able to testify who are produced by the proponent, or (B) if no witness is within the state and competent and able to testify, the witness without the state who resides closest to the county in which the probate proceedings are pending and who is competent and able to testify; and

(2) the stenographer and one copy of the transcripts of such examinations for the court and any guardians ad litem.

The costs of all other examinations, including subsequent examinations of the witnesses described in subparagraph (1) of this paragraph, shall be governed by article 31 of the civil practice law and rules.

(b) In the case of examinations conducted after objections are filed, all costs of such examinations shall be governed by article 31 of the civil practice law and rules.

(c) All costs of document discovery in connection with such examinations shall be governed by article 31 of the civil practice law and rules.

6. Unless the court directs otherwise for good cause shown, if more than one person shall have been involved in the preparation of the will, the term "person who prepared the will" shall mean the person so involved to whom the testator's instructions for preparing the will were communicated by the testator.

History: Add, L 1966, ch 953, eff Sept 1, 1967 from Sur. Ct. Act § 141; amd, L 1992, ch 127, eff Jan 1, 1993; L 1993, ch 514, eff Jan 1, 1994; L 1996, ch 576, § 1, eff Aug 8, 1996; L 1999, ch 460, § 1, eff Sept 7, 1999, and applying to the estates of decedents dying on or after such effective date; L 2011, ch 286, § 2, eff Aug 3, 2011, and applying only to estates of decedents who shall have died on and after such effective date.

§ 1405. When court may dispense with testimony of witness

1. The death, absence from the state or incompetency of an attesting witness required to be examined as prescribed in this or the preceding section or the fact that the witness cannot with

due diligence be found within the state or cannot be examined as an attesting witness by reason of his physical or mental condition may be shown by affidavit or by any competent evidence and when so shown to its satisfaction, the court may by the decree on probate or by order either in writing or entered in the minutes dispense with the testimony of such attesting witness. Where the testimony of an attesting witness has been dispensed with as provided in this section and 1 attesting witness has been examined the will may be admitted to probate upon the testimony of the attesting witness who has been examined without further or additional proof.

2. Where an attesting witness is absent from the state and it is shown that his testimony can be obtained with reasonable diligence the court may and shall upon the demand of any party require his testimony be taken by commission.

3. Where an attesting witness has forgotten the occurrence or testifies against the execution of the will and at least 1 other attesting witness has been examined the will may be admitted to probate upon the testimony of the other witness or witnesses and such other facts as would be sufficient to prove the will.

4. If all of the attesting witnesses are dead or incompetent or unable to testify by reason of physical or mental condition or are absent from the state and their testimony has been dispensed with as provided in this section the will may nevertheless be admitted to probate upon proof of the handwriting of the testator and of at least one of the attesting witnesses and such other facts as would be sufficient to prove the will.

History: Add, L 1966, ch 953, eff Sept 1, 1967 from Sur. Ct. Act § 142; amd, L 1969, ch 221, § 1, eff April 25, 1969.

§ 1406. Proof of will by affidavit of attesting witness out of court

1. In addition to other procedures prescribed for the proof of wills, any or all of the attesting witnesses to a will may at the request of the testator or after his death, at the request of the executor named in the will or of the proponent or the attorney for the proponent or of any person interested, make an affidavit before any officer authorized to administer oaths stating such facts as would if uncontradicted establish the genuineness of the will, the validity of its execution and that the testator at the time of execution was in all respects competent to make a will and not under any restraint. The sworn statement of a witness so taken shall be accepted by the court as though it had been taken before the court, unless:

(a) a party entitled to process in the proceeding raises objection thereto or

(b) for any other reason the court may require that the witness or witnesses be produced and examined.

2. For the purposes of making the affidavit referred to in this section, after the death of the testator, the exhibition to the witnesses of a court-certified photographic reproduction of the will shall be deemed equivalent to the exhibition to them of the original will.

History: Add, L 1966, ch 953, eff Sept 1, 1967 from Sur. Ct. Act § 142-a; amd, L 1967, ch 685, § 76, eff Sept 1, 1967.

§ 1407. Proof of lost or destroyed will

A lost or destroyed will may be admitted to probate only if

1. It is established that the will has not been revoked, and

2. Execution of the will is proved in the manner required for the probate of an existing will, and

3. All of the provisions of the will are clearly and distinctly proved by each of at least two credible witnesses or by a copy or draft of the will proved to be true and complete.

History: Add, L 1966, ch 953, eff Sept 1, 1967 from Sur. Ct. Act § 143; amd, L 1983, ch 672, § 1, eff July 25, 1983, but inapplicable to estates with respect to which a decree of probate or administration became final prior to such date.

§ 1408. Probate not allowed unless court satisfied

1. Before admitting a will to probate the court must inquire particularly into all the facts and must be satisfied with the genuineness of the will and the validity of its execution. The court may, however, accept an affidavit of an attesting witness in the manner and under the circumstances prescribed in this article.

2. If it appears that the will was duly executed and that the testator at the time of executing it was in all respects competent to make a will and not under restraint it must be admitted to probate as a will valid to pass real and personal property, unless otherwise provided by the decree and the will and decree shall be recorded.

3. Where the petition alleges that the testator has disappeared under circumstances sufficient to justify the belief he is dead the court shall take proof of the facts. If it appears that the testator is dead the court may make a decree determining such fact and admitting the will to probate. The decree shall be binding in its effect upon the interests in the estate of persons under disability and of future contingent interests of persons not in being as well as the interests of adult competent persons.

History: Add, L 1966, ch 953, eff Sept 1, 1967 from Sur. Ct. Act § 144; amd, L 1967, ch 685, § 77, eff Sept 1, 1967.

§ 1409. Notice of probate

1. Before letters are issued there shall be filed in the court a notice entitled in the proceeding stating the name of the testator, the name and address of the proponent, and that the will of the testator has been offered for probate or probated, as the case may be. The notice shall further set forth the name and post-office address of each person named or referred to in the petition who has not been served or has not appeared or waived service of process and shall state whether such person is named or referred to in the will as legatee, devisee, trustee, guardian or substitute or successor executor, trustee or guardian. The notice shall further set forth the name and post-office address of the attorney general of the state of New York if the will that has been offered for probate contains a charitable bequest which is either to an unnamed charitable organization or is in an unspecified amount, including but not limited to, a bequest of all or part of the residuary estate.

(a) Where by the terms of the will an interest in a trust or other fund or property has been limited in any contingency to the persons who shall compose a certain class upon the happening of a future event it shall be sufficient to name only the persons in being at the death of the decedent who would constitute the class if such event had happened immediately before the date of such notice, and who have not been served or appeared or waived service of process.

(b) Where by the terms of the will an interest in a trust or other fund or property has been limited to a person who is named in such notice or who has been served or has appeared or waived notice of process, and has been further limited upon the happening of a future event to a class of persons described in terms of their relationship to such person it shall not be necessary to name such class of persons.

2. There shall be filed with the notice proof by affidavit of the mailing of a copy thereof to each of the persons required by the preceding subdivision to be named in such notice, and if any person is an infant or an incompetent, of the mailing of a copy thereof to the person or persons upon whom personal service of process is required to be made with respect to the infant or incompetent. When it appears by the petition for probate that the name or address of any person referred to in this section is unknown mailing to such person of the notice herein described shall not be required.

3. Upon the probate of an estate and distribution of its assets, if any, under this chapter, if an undistributed asset is subsequently found by the estate, the surrogate's court that granted such probate petition shall maintain jurisdiction and shall not require any additional service of the notice required by this section to be served again by the estate, unless such previously undiscovered asset has an estimated value of more than five thousand dollars or it has been more than seven years since the distribution of the assets pursuant to the original probate.

History: Add, L 1966, ch 953, eff Sept 1, 1967 from Sur. Ct. Act § 146; amd, L 1967, ch 685, eff Sept 1, 1967; L 1975, ch 89, § 1, eff Sept 1, 1975; L 1976, ch 250, § 1, eff Sept 1, 1976; L 1997, ch 291, § 1, eff Oct 27, 1997; L 2007, ch 636, § 1, eff Jan 1, 2008.

§ 1410. Who may file objections to probate of an alleged will

Any person whose interest in property or in the estate of the testator would be adversely affected by the admission of the will to probate may file objections to the probate of the will or of any portion thereof except that one whose only financial interest would be in the commissions to which he would have been entitled if his appointment as fiduciary were not revoked by a later instrument shall not be entitled to file objections to the probate of such instrument unless authorized by the court for good cause shown. The objections must be filed on or before the return day of the process or on such subsequent day as directed by the court; provided however that if an examination is requested pursuant to 1404, objections must be filed within 10 days after the completion of such examinations, or within such other time as is fixed by stipulation of the parties or by the court.

History: Add, L 1966, ch 953, eff Sept 1, 1967 from Sur. Ct. Act § 147; amd, L 1971, ch 362, eff Sept 1, 1971; L 1993, ch 514, § 33, eff Jan 1, 1994.

§ 1411. Citation upon filing of objections

1. Whenever objections are filed to the probate of a will, the proponent shall submit to the court for issuance a citation returnable at a motion term of the court (a) reciting that objections have been filed to the will offered for probate and that such objections may be determined at a trial or at a hearing or conference on the return date or on a date to be fixed by the court, and (b) reciting the consequences of failing to appear set forth in the provisions of subdivision six of this section.

2. The citation shall be submitted by the proponent to the court within thirty days after the filing of objections. If the proponent fails to submit the citation, the citation may be submitted by an objectant or any other interested person.

3. The citation shall be issued to (a) each person named or referred to in the propounded

instrument who has not appeared in the proceeding and whose interests would be affected by the outcome of the proceeding, and (b) such other persons as directed by the court.

4. The citation shall be served in accordance with the requirements of sections 307 and 308, except that service may be made by mail as therein provided upon any person whether or not a resident of this state. Proof of the service of the citation shall be made and filed in the court at least two days before the return date of the citation.

5. Each person to whom the citation must be issued, as provided in subdivision three of this section, may waive service of the citation. Each person who has waived or has been served under this section may appear personally or by filing a notice of appearance.

6. Any person who has waived or has been served under this section and who does not appear will not be entitled to further notice, and each objection filed may be determined at a trial or at a hearing or conference on the return date or on a date to be fixed by the court. If a settlement is entered into and agreed to by all parties appearing at the trial, hearing or conference, such settlement and any final determination by the court will be binding on all persons who have waived or have been served with process and who have failed to appear. Any person so failing to appear may be required to contribute to such settlement an amount which bears the same proportion to the total amount of the settlement as his or her interest in the estate bears to the aggregate of the interests in the estate of all persons required to contribute to the settlement.

> **History:** Add, L 1997, ch 87, § 1, eff Jan 1, 1998, and applying to any probate proceedings commenced on or after that date; amd, L 2001, ch 393, § 1, eff Oct 31, 2001.

§ 1412. Preliminary letters testamentary

1. Whenever a petition for probate of a will (other than a lost or destroyed will) has been filed and process has issued thereon, an executor named in the will may file with the court a written request for the issuance to him of preliminary letters testamentary. In its discretion the court may accept a written request for such letters prior to the issuance of process upon such proof as the court shall deem necessary. Where the request is made by one of several nominated executors, notice shall be given to all persons who under the terms of the will have a right to letters testamentary equal to that of the petitioner. Where there is another will of the same testator on file in the court that is later in date than the propounded instrument, notice shall be given to all persons who under the terms of the later will would have the right to letters testamentary immediately upon probate of such later will.

2. (a) Notice hereunder shall be given at the time and in the manner directed by the court and may be given either before or after issuance of preliminary letters. Any person having a right to letters testamentary equal to that of an applicant for preliminary letters testamentary may join in the application for such letters and may request that they issue to him or after the issue of such letters may request that the letters heretofore issued be extended to him. A person named in the will to act as executor upon the occurrence of any contingency may in like manner request issuance of such letters, provided that the contingency has occurred which would entitle him to be appointed executor. A person named as executor in a will later in date than that in which the first applicant is appointed may file a written cross-request for preliminary letters testamentary after he has filed a petition for probate of such later will and process has been issued thereon. Unless, for good cause shown, the court shall otherwise direct, the person named as executor in the latest such will shall have a prior right to preliminary letters testamentary.

(b) When preliminary letters testamentary have been issued and thereafter a will later in date has been filed with a petition for its probate, and process has been issued thereon, an executor named in the later will may request the revocation of the prior letters and the issuance of preliminary letters to him, and upon such notice as the court may direct, the court shall have discretion to revoke the letters theretofore issued and grant preliminary letters testamentary to the executor named in the later will, to grant preliminary letters testamentary jointly to the executors named in both wills, to confirm the grant of letters theretofore issued, or to take such other action as the court deems to be for the best interests of the estate and of the persons interested therein.

3. (a) Upon due qualification as provided in subdivision 5 and upon the issuance of process, and whether before or after the return day of said process, preliminary letters testamentary must thereupon be issued to the person or persons who appear to the court to be entitled thereto, and where the court has accepted a request for such letters prior to the issuance of process, preliminary letters testamentary may be issued in the discretion of the court upon due qualification as provided in subdivision 5. The letters shall confer upon the person named therein, subject to any limitations contained in the instrument offered for probate, all the powers and authority and shall subject him to all the duties and liabilities of an administrator except that they do not confer any power to pay or to satisfy a legacy or distributive share. Unless the court or the instrument offered for probate directs otherwise, a preliminary executor is also authorized to take possession of, manage and sell any real property devised by and any personal property specifically bequeathed by the instrument offered for probate and to allocate the expenses of managing such property in accordance with what is reasonable and equitable in view of the interests of those persons interested in such property and in the estate, except that any such property specifically devised or bequeathed may only be sold or otherwise disposed of with the written consent of the specific devisee or legatee or by court order. This authority shall not prevent the preliminary executor from permitting the devisee or legatee of such property to have possession of such property.

(b) A preliminary executor shall give notice to all parties who have appeared of his or her appointment within ten days of such appointment.

4. (a) The court may in the order directing the issuance of preliminary letters testamentary or in one or more subsequent orders limit preliminary letters testamentary to the receipt of assets specified in such order or orders and may prohibit the collection of any other assets of the decedent, or may limit or authorize the person named in such letters in any manner that the court deems advisable for the effective protection of the rights of all persons who may have an interest in the estate of the decedent.

(b) In such order or orders, the court may make such directions as it deems proper and necessary with respect to the custody and preservation of all papers and records of the decedent. Discovery and production of such papers and records shall be governed by article thirty-one of the civil practice law and rules.

5. Before preliminary letters testamentary are issued to a named executor he shall qualify as provided in 708. If the will offered for probate shall require the filing of a bond by the executor the person requesting preliminary letters testamentary must file his bond in accordance with the requirements of the will. In addition the court shall have full and complete discretion to require him to file such additional bond as it deems advisable under the

circumstances of the particular case. Where the will is silent in respect of the filing of a bond or where it explicitly dispenses with the filing of a bond the court shall nevertheless have full and complete discretion at any time and from time to time to require the person seeking such letters to file a bond in such amount as the court deems advisable under the circumstances of the particular case or it may grant such letters without bond. Where the will explicitly dispenses with the filing of a bond, the court shall grant such letters without bond, unless it determines there are extraordinary circumstances in the particular case to warrant filing of a bond, in which case the court shall have discretion to require the person seeking such letters to file a bond in such amount as the court deems advisable.

6. A decree denying probate to a propounded instrument shall revoke any preliminary letters testamentary issued upon such instrument unless the court shall direct that such letters continue until the termination of any appeal and in such case the court may make such limitations, restrictions or conditions on such letters as justice may require. The court may revoke preliminary letters testamentary at any time

  (a) if it shall appear that the preliminary executor is guilty of unreasonable delay in the probate proceeding or

  (b) for any cause that would justify the revocation of letters under 719 or

  (c) for any other reason deemed by the court to be in the best interests of the estate.

7. A preliminary executor shall not be entitled to the commissions provided for a fiduciary in this act unless the will be admitted to probate and letters testamentary are issued to him, in which event he shall be entitled to commissions as provided in this act for a case where successive letters are issued to the same person on the estate of the same decedent. If the will be denied probate or his letters are revoked for any reason during the pendency of the probate proceeding he shall be entitled for such service to receive only such compensation, if any, as the court shall determine to be reasonable and just for the services rendered by him to the estate, not to exceed the commissions to which an executor would be entitled. For purpose of the fixation of such commissions or compensation any real property or specifically devised personal property of which a preliminary executor took possession and then distributed or otherwise disposed of shall be treated as property received, distributed or delivered.

> **History:** Add, L 1966, ch 953, eff Sept 1, 1967 from Sur. Ct. Act § 153-a; amd, L 1967, ch 685, eff Sept 1, 1967; L 1968, ch 259, § 25, eff May 14, 1968; L 1971, ch 883, eff Sept 1, 1971; L 1973, ch 662, § 1, eff Sept 1, 1973; L 1990, ch 185, § 1, eff May 24, 1990; L 1992, ch 127, § 2, eff Jan 1, 1993; L 1993, ch 514, § 35, eff Jan 1, 1994.

§ 1413. Revocation of letters upon proof of will

Where temporary letters of administration, preliminary letters testamentary or letters of administration on the ground of intestacy have been granted and a will is thereafter admitted to probate and letters issued thereupon or where a subsequent will is admitted to probate and letters issued thereupon, the decree granting probate must revoke the former letters.

> **History:** Add, L 1966, ch 953, eff Sept 1, 1967 from Sur. Ct. Act § 154.

§ 1414. When letters testamentary may be issued

1. After a will has been admitted to probate any person entitled to letters thereunder who is eligible and who appears and qualifies is entitled to letters testamentary.

2. Where a judgment has been rendered in an action establishing a will the surrogate must

record the will and issue letters as directed by the judgment.

3. A person entitled to letters upon a contingency may appear and show that the contingency has happened by which he is entitled to such letters.

4. A person named as an executor by a person other than the testator under a valid power contained in a will must appear and file an acknowledged selection of himself as an executor.

> **History:** Add, L 1966, ch 953, eff Sept 1, 1967 from Sur. Ct. Act § 155; amd, L 1970, ch 396, § 4, eff Sept 1, 1970.

§ 1415. Supplementary letters, executors not named in letters not to act

If the disability of an infant or an alien named as an executor in a will be removed before the administration of the estate is completed he shall be entitled on petition showing the facts to supplementary letters testamentary to be issued in the same manner as the original letters to join in the completion of the administration of the estate with the person or persons previously appointed. A person named in a will as executor shall be deemed to be superseded by the issue to another person of letters testamentary and shall have no power or authority as executor until he appears and qualifies and letters testamentary are issued to him.

> **History:** Add, L 1966, ch 953, eff Sept 1, 1967 from Sur. Ct. Act § 156.

§ 1416. Executor failing to qualify or renounce; how excluded

1. Upon the application of a fiduciary, a person interested or a creditor, the court shall direct an executor named in a will to qualify within a time specified by the court or in default of so doing to be deemed to have renounced the appointment in any case where

(a) a person named as executor in a will does not qualify or renounce within 15 days after probate thereof or

(b) a person chosen by virtue of a power in a will does not qualify or renounce within 15 days after the filing of the instrument designating him or

(c) objections are filed to the grant of letters to a person named as executor in a will or chosen by virtue of a power therein contained and such person does not qualify or renounce within 5 days after the objections have been determined in his favor or, in a case specified in 710, within 5 days after an objection to letters has been established.

2. Where it appears by affidavit or other written proof to the satisfaction of the court that such an order cannot with due diligence be served personally within the state upon the person therein named the court may prescribe the manner in which it must be served.

3. If the person so designated executor does not qualify within the time fixed or within such further time as the court may allow for that purpose an order shall be made declaring that he has renounced his appointment as executor. Such an order may be revoked by the court and letters testamentary issued to the person so failing to renounce or qualify upon his application in a case where he might have retracted an express renunciation as prescribed in the succeeding section.

> **History:** Add, L 1966, ch 953, eff Sept 1, 1967 from Sur. Ct. Act § 157.

§ 1417. Renunciation by nominated executor; retraction thereof

1. A person named as executor in a will may renounce his right to letters testamentary by an acknowledged instrument.

2. A renunciation may be retracted by an instrument executed in like manner as required for the execution of a renunciation at any time before letters testamentary or letters of administration with will annexed have been issued to any other person in his place or after they have been so issued, if such letters have been revoked or the person to whom they were issued has died or become an incompetent and there is no other acting executor or administrator.

3. Where a retraction is so made letters testamentary may be issued to the person making it upon such notice as directed by the court.

4. An instrument specified in this section must be filed in the court having jurisdiction over the estate.

History: Add, L 1966, ch 953, eff Sept 1, 1967 from Sur. Ct. Act § 158.

§ 1418. Letters of administration with will annexed; when and to whom granted

1. If no person is named as executor in the will or selected by virtue of a power contained therein or if at any time there is no executor or administrator with will annexed qualified to act, upon the application of any person who may petition for the probate of the will under 1402 the court must issue letters of administration with will annexed in the following order of priority:

(a) to a sole beneficiary or if he be dead to his fiduciary;

(b) to one or more of the residuary beneficiaries or, if any be dead, to his fiduciary;

(c) if there is no eligible person entitled to letters under subparagraphs (a) and (b) of this subdivision who will accept, the court may issue letters to one or more of the persons interested in the estate or, if any be dead, to his fiduciary.

2. If there is no eligible person entitled to letters under the foregoing subdivision who will accept or an appointment is not made by consent as provided in subdivision 6, letters shall issue to the public administrator or, if there be none for the county, to the treasurer of the county.

3. If none of the persons mentioned in subdivisions 1 and 2 will accept letters the court may issue them to the petitioner or upon petitioner's refusal to accept the same to any person designated by the court.

4. A corporation incorporated within the territorial limits of the United States which is a sole or residuary legatee may act as administrator with will annexed although not specifically so authorized by its charter or by any provision of law.

5. If any person otherwise entitled to letters under subdivision 1 is an infant, incompetent or conservatee the court may issue letters with will annexed to the guardian of the property of the infant, the committee of the property of the incompetent, or the conservator of the property of the conservatee with the same priority as if the infant, incompetent or conservatee had himself been eligible to take letters.

6. Administration may be granted to an eligible person or persons not entitled as beneficiaries upon the acknowledged and filed consent of all of the eligible beneficiaries, or if there are no eligible beneficiaries, then on the consent of all of the beneficiaries, except that the guardian of the property of an infant beneficiary, the committee of the property of an

incompetent beneficiary or the conservator of the property of a conservatee beneficiary appointed within the state of New York, may so consent on behalf of his or her ward. For purposes of this subdivision, a beneficiary is eligible if letters of administration with will annexed could be issued to him or her alone or acting together with the person or persons or so nominated.

7. Administration may be granted to a trust company or other corporation authorized to act as fiduciary upon the acknowledged and filed consents of all the eligible beneficiaries, or if there are no eligible beneficiaries, then on the consent of all beneficiaries, except that the guardian of the property of an infant beneficiary, the committee of the property of an incompetent beneficiary, or the conservator of the property of a conservatee beneficiary appointed within the state of New York, may so consent on behalf of his or her ward. For purposes of this subdivision, a beneficiary is eligible if letters of administration with will annexed could be issued to him or her alone or acting together with the trust company or other corporation so nominated.

8. The court may refuse to issue letters of administration with will annexed where distribution of the estate is possible pursuant to the provisions of this act.

> **History:** Add, L 1966, ch 953, eff Sept 1, 1967 from Sur. Ct. Act § 133; amd, L 1967, ch 685, § 83, eff Sept 1, 1967; L 1968, ch 1067, §§ 1, 2, eff June 22, 1968; L 1981, ch 115, §§ 125, 126, eff May 18, 1981; L 1985, ch 536, § 1, eff July 24, 1985; L 1992, ch 19, § 1, eff March 20, 1992; L 2019, ch 319, § 2, eff Oct 3, 2019.

§ 1419. Process; renunciation or exclusion of persons having prior or equal right

Every eligible person having a right to letters of administration with the will annexed prior or equal to that of the petitioner including an infant, incompetent or conservatee whose guardian, committee or conservator would be entitled to letters, and who has not renounced, must be served. The proceedings upon the application are the same as upon an application for administration upon the estate of an intestate. The court may dispense with the issuance and service of process upon non-domiciliaries.

> **History:** Add, L 1966, ch 953, eff Sept 1, 1967 from Sur. Ct. Act § 134; amd, L 1981, ch 115, § 127, eff May 18, 1981.

§ 1420. Proceeding for construction of will; effect of decree

1. A fiduciary or a person interested in obtaining a determination as to the validity, construction or effect of any provision of a will may present to the court in which the will was probated a petition showing the interest of the petitioner, the names and post-office addresses of the other persons interested, the particular portion of the will concerning which petitioner requests the determination of the court and the necessity for construction. If the application be entertained process shall issue to all persons interested in the question to be presented to show cause why the determination should not be made. On the return of process the court shall take such proof and shall make such decree as justice requires.

2. If in any proceeding for the judicial settlement of an account of a fiduciary any question is presented by any party to the proceeding respecting the propriety of any debit or credit in the account, the determination of which involves the validity, construction or effect of any portion of the will which requires such construction the presentation of the question shall have the same effect as if the petition had expressly requested a construction of the particular portion of the will involved in such determination.

3. If a party in a proceeding for the probate of a will requests a determination of the validity, construction or effect of any provision contained in the will process shall issue to all persons interested in the determination who have not appeared in the proceeding and notice shall be given in such manner as directed by the court to all those persons who have so appeared therein. Upon the entry of a decree admitting the will to probate the court may determine the question of construction or in its discretion may admit the will to probate and reserve the question for future consideration and decree.

4. A decree in any proceeding authorized in this section or a decree settling an account of a fiduciary or a decree on probate which construes or interprets any portion of a will, unless reversed or modified on appeal, shall thereafter be binding and conclusive in all courts upon all parties to the proceeding and upon their successors in interest as to all questions of construction or interpretation of the will therein or thereby determined and of all rights and obligations of the parties involved in the construction, depending thereon, or resulting therefrom.

5. The provisions of section three hundred fifteen shall apply to a proceeding under this section.

> **History:** Add, L 1966, ch 953, eff Sept 1, 1967 from Sur. Ct. Act § 145. Subdivision 5 added by L 1967 ch 739, eff Sept 1, 1967.

§ 1421. Election by surviving spouse

1. Any person interested in obtaining a determination as to the validity or effect of an election to take a share under EPTL 5-1.1 or EPTL 5-1.1-A may present to the court in which the will was probated or from which letters of administration were issued, a petition showing his interest, the names and post-office addresses of the other persons interested and the particular question concerning which he requests the determination of the court.

2. If the application be entertained process shall issue to all persons interested in the question to be presented to show cause why the determination should not be made. On the return of process the court may take proof and shall make such decree as justice requires.

3. The validity or effect of any such election may also be determined in a proceeding for the judicial settlement of the accounts of a fiduciary.

4. For the purpose of determining the validity or effect of any election made pursuant to EPTL 5-1.1 or EPTL 5-1.1-A, either under this section or in a proceeding for the judicial settlement of the accounts of the fiduciary, a person interested shall include any person who has an interest in any of the transactions described in EPTL 5-1.1 or EPTL 5-1.1-A. Where any such person has an interest as trustee of an express trust it shall be sufficient to name and serve the trustee.

5. Whenever it shall appear that a fund or property required to be included in the net estate under EPTL 5-1.1 or EPTL 5-1.1-A has not come into the possession of the fiduciary of the decedent as such, the court shall fix the liability of any person who has any interest in the fund or property or who has possession thereof, whether as trustee or otherwise.

> **History:** Add, L 1966, ch 953, eff Sept 1, 1967 from Sur. Ct. Act § 145-a; amd, L 1968, ch 259, eff May 14, 1968; L 1992, ch 595, § 24, eff Sept 1, 1992.

§ 1422. Record of wills; evidence

A certified copy of the record of the decree admitting a will to probate and of the record of the will so admitted to probate shall be received in evidence in any court in any action or proceeding with the same force and effect as if the original will had been produced and proved in such action or proceeding. The recording of a will in the court shall be evidence that it was duly admitted to probate.

History: Add, L 1966, ch 953, eff Sept 1, 1967 from Sur. Ct. Act § 151 in part.

§ 1423. Record of wills in former courts of probate; evidence

The exemplification of the record of a will proved before the judge of the former court of probate and recorded in his office before January 1, 1785, certified under the seal of the officer having custody of the record, shall be admitted in evidence in any case after it has been made to appear that diligent and fruitless search has been made for the original will.

History: Add, L 1966, ch 953, eff Sept 1, 1967 from Sur. Ct. Act § 153 in part.

§ 1424. Foreign wills; evidence after lapse of time

The exemplification of the record of a will which has been duly proved before a court or officer of competent jurisdiction in any other state, shall, when certified by the officer having by law custody of the record at the time the certificate was made, be admitted in evidence as if the original will was produced and proved when 20 years have elapsed since the will was so proved.

History: Add, L 1966, ch 953, eff Sept 1, 1967 from Sur. Ct. Act § 153 in part.

ARTICLE 15
TRUSTS AND TRUSTEES

SUMMARY OF ARTICLE

§ 1501. Application of act to trusts

1. The provisions of this act apply to any of the following trusts without regard to the domicile of the trustee or to the time of the execution of the will or of the creation of the lifetime trust:

(a) A trust created by the will of a domiciliary.

(b) A trust relating to real or personal property, without regard to the domicile of the testator or the grantor, where if a testamentary trust the will creating the trust was admitted to probate in any surrogate's court of this state or where the situs of the trust or any real property held by the trust is within this state and if a testamentary trust the will creating the trust was duly proved or established or admitted to probate within a foreign country or state, the District of Columbia, the Commonwealth of Puerto Rico, a territory or possession of the United States where it was executed or where the testator was domiciled at the time of his death.

(c) A lifetime trust of which the supreme court would also have jurisdiction.

2. The situs of a trust of personal property created by the will or lifetime trust instrument of a non-domiciliary shall be deemed to be in this state if the personal property is in this state at the date of the testator's death with respect to a testamentary trust or at the time of the creation of the lifetime trust with respect to a lifetime trust and is held and administered in this state in accordance with the will or lifetime instrument or, except where the will or lifetime trust instrument or the laws of the domicile of the testator or the domicile at the time the trust was created of the grantor expressly provide otherwise, if such property is brought into this state for administration.

3. If original probate of the will of a non-domiciliary has been had in any county of this state jurisdiction of the trust created under the will shall be vested in the surrogate's court of that county. If ancillary proceedings in respect of any phase of the estate of a non-domiciliary have been had in any county of the state, jurisdiction of the trust shall be vested in the surrogate's court of that county. If neither an original nor ancillary proceedings has been had in any county of the state, and in all cases involving lifetime trusts, jurisdiction shall be vested in the surrogate's court of any county in which real property subject to the trust is situated,

or if there is no such real property subject to the trust, in the surrogate's court of the county in which any trustee has his residence or its principal place of business: provided that in case the surrogate's court in more than one county might be entitled to entertain jurisdiction over any such trust jurisdiction shall be vested in the surrogate's court first entertaining a proceeding in relation to the trust.

4. Any surrogate may decline to entertain jurisdiction over the administration of a trust of personal property created by the will of or lifetime trust instrument created by a non-domiciliary. Every application to the court to entertain jurisdiction over such a trust shall state whether any previous application for such relief has been made in this state and shall state the disposition thereof and be accompanied by a copy of the will and of the foreign letters, if any have been issued, authenticated as prescribed in 1614, or of the lifetime trust instrument creating the trust, with proof of its authenticity. If the application be entertained the court shall record the will or such instrument in its office.

History: Add, L 1966, ch 953, eff Sept 1, 1967 from Sur. Ct. Act § 171; amd, L 1967, ch 685, § 84, eff Sept 1, 1967; L 1980, ch 503, § 22, eff June 24, 1980.

§ 1502. Appointment of trustee

1. The court may appoint a trustee or successor or successors or co-trustee or co-trustees whenever there is no trustee able to act or all or one of the trustees is unable to act and a successor or co-trustee in his or their place is necessary in order to execute the trust or execute any power created by a will or lifetime trust instrument creating a trust, the execution of which has devolved upon the court or upon the supreme court.

2. The court shall not appoint a trustee, successor or co-trustee if the appointment would contravene the express terms of the will or lifetime trust instrument or if a trustee may be or has been named in the will or lifetime trust instrument as successor, substitute or co-trustee and is not disqualified to act.

3. Until a successor or co-trustee is appointed the remaining trustee or trustees may execute the trust.

4. A trustee, successor or co-trustee may be appointed upon the application of any person interested and upon notice to such persons as the court may designate.

5. The court may appoint a successor trustee for any purposes deemed necessary to complete administration or distribution of a trust which has terminated by the occurrence of the event measuring its duration when there is no person in office able to execute it.

6. A successor trustee shall be subject to the same duties, as to accounting and trust administration, as are imposed by law on trustees and, in addition to the reasonable expenses incurred in the course of trust administration, shall be entitled to commissions as may be fixed by any court having jurisdiction to pass upon the trustee's final account, which shall in no case exceed the commissions allowable by law to trustees.

History: Add, L 1966, ch 953, eff Sept 1, 1967 from Sur. Ct. Act § 168, PPL § 20 and RPL § 111 in part; amd, L 1967, ch 685, § 85, eff Sept 1; L 1980, ch 503, § 23, eff June 24, 1980.

§ 1503. Qualification of trustee appointed by another court

When the supreme court appoints a testamentary trustee a certified copy of the order or decree of appointment and of the bond given by the trustee shall be filed in the surrogate's court of the county having jurisdiction of the trust and a minute thereof shall be made and indexed in the book kept by the court in which orders or decrees appointing trustees are entered. The trustee shall file in such surrogate's court the oath or consent and the instrument of designation required of such fiduciary and letters shall thereupon issue to him from such court. He shall be subject to all the duties and liabilities of a testamentary trustee appointed by the surrogate's court.

> **History:** Add, L 1966, ch 953, eff Sept 1, 1967 from Sur. Ct. Act § 167 in part; amd, L 1967, ch 685, § 86, eff Sept 1, 1967.

§ 1504. Renunciation of appointment: retraction thereof

1. A testamentary trustee may renounce his appointment by a duly acknowledged instrument.

2. By like instrument the renunciation may be retracted at any time before letters have been issued to another in his place or after such letters have been issued, if they have been revoked or the person to whom they have been issued has become unable to act or disqualified. The court may issue letters to the person so retracting upon such notice as it may require.

3. The instrument of renunciation and the instrument of retraction authorized by this section must be filed in the office of the court having jurisdiction of the trust.

> **History:** Add, L 1966, ch 953, eff Sept 1, 1967 from Sur. Ct. Act § 167 in part.

§ 1505. Proceeding when testamentary trustee is also executor or administrator

1. Where the same person is a testamentary trustee and also the executor of the will or the administrator upon the same estate, proceedings taken by or against him as trustee, as prescribed in this act, do not affect him as executor or administrator or persons interested in the general estate, except in one of the following cases:

(a) Where he presents a petition praying for the revocation of his letters, he may in the same petition show that he is entitled to resign as testamentary trustee and may thereupon pray for a decree allowing him to resign and for process accordingly.

(b) Where a person presents a petition praying for the revocation of letters issued to an executor or administrator and any of the facts in the petition are made, by the provisions of this act, sufficient to entitle the same person to present a petition praying for the removal of a testamentary trustee, the petitioner may pray for a decree removing the person complained of in both capacities, and for process accordingly.

2. In either case proceedings upon the petition for resignation or removal, as the case requires, of the testamentary trustee, and for the judicial settlement of his account, may be taken as prescribed in this act, in connection with or separately from the like proceedings upon the petition for the revocation of the letters, as directed by the court.

> **History:** Add, L 1966, ch 953, eff Sept 1, 1967 from Sur. Ct. Act § 170; amd, L 1967, ch 685, § 87, eff Sept 1, 1967.

§ 1506. Nonliability for acts of predecessor executor

A trustee who was not an executor of the estate of the same decedent shall not be liable for breach of trust committed by the executor in any of the following cases:

1. He received the assets of the trust pursuant to a final decree of the court.

2. He did not know of a situation constituting a breach of trust committed by the executor, and does not improperly permit it to continue.

3. He does not neglect to take proper steps to compel the executor to deliver trust property to him.

4. He does not neglect to take proper steps to redress a breach of trust committed by the executor.

History: Add, L 1966, ch 953, eff Sept 1, 1967.

§ 1507. Authority to mortgage, sell, lease or exchange

1. In any case in which the power to mortgage, sell, lease or exchange real property does not exist under the provisions of EPTL 11-1.1 or for other reasons it is for the best interests of the trust, the court of the county having jurisdiction of the trust may on such terms and conditions as seem just and proper authorize any testamentary trustee to mortgage, sell, lease or exchange real property or any part thereof belonging to the trust.

2. If the application be entertained process shall issue to all persons interested in the trust to show cause why the relief requested in the petition should not be granted.

3. On the return of process the court shall make such order as justice requires. Such order and the mortgage, sale, lease or exchange executed in conformity therewith shall be binding and conclusive on the remainders and reversions as well as the immediate or future trust interests in the real property and shall be valid and effectual against all persons under disability as defined in this act and persons not in being, having estates or interests vested or contingent, for life or in trust or in reversion or remainder in such real property or in the proceeds of the sale thereof and shall bind and be conclusive against all other persons so interested or having such estates or interests who shall by acknowledged instrument consent to such order or who have been made parties to the proceeding.

History: Add, L 1966, ch 953, eff Sept 1, 1967 from Sur. Ct. Act § 250-a; amd, L 1967, ch 685, § 88, eff Sept 1, 1967; L 1968, ch 259, § 27, eff May 14, 1968.

§ 1508. Authority to release claims against the state by reason of appropriation of trust property not subject to power of sale

1. The surrogate of any county having jurisdiction of the trust may, by order, authorize any testamentary trustee to release a claim against the state for compensation on account of the appropriation by the state of any real property or any right, interest or easement therein belonging to the trust, and for legal damages caused by the appropriation and for damages sustained by any entry upon, use or occupation of, or injury to the real property by the state prior to completion of the appropriation.

2. Application for the order may be entertained by the court in all cases where the will does not contain a valid power of sale with regard to such property or a sale is not authorized under the provisions of EPTL 11-1.1.

3. Notice of the application shall be given to such persons and in such manner as directed by the court. Prior to the application and irrespective of when the appropriation was effected, the trustee may enter into an agreement with the state, subject to the approval of the court, for the payment of such compensation, a copy of which agreement shall be presented to the court together with the petition.

4. Upon consideration by the court of the petition, the allegations and proofs of the parties and upon the testimony of the petitioner and of at least 2 disinterested persons acquainted with the facts, presented orally or by affidavit, as to the value of the interest of the trust in the property so appropriated, including the legal damage caused by the appropriation and the damages, if any, sustained by the entry upon, use or occupation of, or injury to the real property by the state prior to completion of appropriation and upon inquiring into the facts and circumstances, if it shall appear to the satisfaction of the court that the amount of compensation offered by the state represents the fair market value of the property appropriated and just compensation for the legal damages caused by the appropriation and the damages, if any, sustained by the entry upon, use or occupation of or injury to the property by the state prior to completion of appropriation, the court may by order confirm the agreement and authorize and direct the trustee to execute and deliver to the state a release of such claim and any documents or instruments required by the state to give full effect to the release, for the amount of consideration so offered by the state for such release in full payment of such claim for compensation for the use and benefit of the trust.

5. The order made pursuant to this section and the release and attendant documents and instruments executed and delivered in conformity therewith shall be binding and conclusive on the remainders and reversions as well as the immediate or future trust interests in the real property so held under the trust and shall bind and be conclusive against all persons under disability as defined in this act and persons not in being and all other persons having estates or interests vested or contingent, for life or in trust, or in reversion or remainder in the trust property or in the proceeds of the appropriation thereof by the state.

History: Add, L 1966, ch 953, eff Sept 1, 1967 from Sur. Ct. Act § 250-b; amd, L 1967, ch 685, § 89, eff Sept 1, 1967.

§ 1509. Power over lifetime trusts

Except to the extent inconsistent with other provisions of this act, the surrogate having jurisdiction of a lifetime trust shall have such power over the lifetime trust and its trustee as a justice of the supreme court having jurisdiction over the trust would have.

History: Add, L 1980, ch 503, § 24, eff June 24, 1980.

ARTICLE 16
FOREIGN ESTATES

SUMMARY OF ARTICLE

§ 1601. Legislative declaration of purpose

It is the intent and purpose of this article that ancillary administration shall be granted in this state only when there is an actual administration in the domiciliary jurisdiction. If the law of such jurisdiction does not provide for the appointment of a fiduciary but vests the property of a decedent in a person or persons subject to the obligation to pay the decedent's debts and expenses and the legacies bequeathed in his will or the distributive shares provided by law, such a person shall be recognized as the person acting therein to administer the decedent's estate in accordance with the law thereof, but only if such person has complied with all the requirements of such jurisdiction to entitle him to receive the property of the decedent and is acting or will act there to administer the estate.

> **History:** Add, L 1966, ch 953, eff Sept 1, 1967; amd, L 1967, ch 685, § 90, eff Sept 1, 1967.

§ 1602. Ancillary probate based upon domiciliary probate

1. A written will which upon probate may operate upon any property in this state shall be admitted to probate by the surrogate's court having jurisdiction over the property upon proof that it has been admitted to probate at the testator's domicile or has been established in accordance with the law of such jurisdiction, and if its probate or establishment remains subject to contest under the law of his domicile, upon proof that it is not being contested thereat. A will so admitted to probate under this section is sufficient to operate on any property within the terms of the will, subject to any limitations upon its operation imposed by the law of the testator's domicile in respect of legal capacity. Rights granted by the law of the domicile to take against the will are not affected by this section.

2. A will offered for probate under this section may be contested only upon the ground that the conditions prescribed herein have not been satisfied or that the will has been denied probate in this state.

History: Add, L 1966, ch 953, eff Sept 1, 1967, replacing Sur. Ct. Act § 159; amd, L 1967, ch 685, § 91, eff Sept 1, 1967.

§ 1603. Effect of right to contest or of revocation

1. If under the law of the testator's domicile the probate or establishment of his will therein is subject to contest within a time specified after probate or establishment, no property shall be transmitted to the domicile or distributed to beneficiaries under the will during such period of time unless the court which granted ancillary probate authorizes such transmission or distribution upon proof that

(a) 7 months have elapsed since the issuance of ancillary letters in this state,

(b) a contest of the will is not pending in the testator's domicile and

(c) either the time provided in the domicile for the institution of a contest has expired or one year has expired since the will was admitted to ancillary probate under this article.

2. An ancillary fiduciary who transmits assets to the domicile or distributes to beneficiaries in good faith and pursuant to an order or decree under subdivision 1 shall be discharged from any liability even if the probate or establishment of the will at the domicile is thereafter set aside or revoked for any cause whatever.

History: Add, L 1966, ch 953, eff Sept 1, 1967; amd, L 1967, ch 685, § 92, eff Sept 1, 1967; L 1975, ch 194, § 1, eff Sept 1, 1975.

§ 1604. Ancillary letters on foreign will

1. Upon admission of a will to probate under 1602 the court shall issue, if such be requested, ancillary letters to the following persons in the following order:

(a) The person expressly appointed in the will as executor with respect to property located within this state.

(b) The person to whom domiciliary letters have been issued or if domiciliary letters are not issued, the person appointed in the will to administer all property wherever located.

(c) The person acting in the domiciliary jurisdiction to administer and distribute the testator's estate.

(d) A person entitled under this act to letters of administration c.t.a.

2. If no person named in any subparagraph of subdivision 1 is willing to qualify or to designate a person eligible to receive ancillary letters they shall issue to a person in the succeeding subparagraph of such subdivision who will qualify or to a person designated by him who is eligible to receive letters.

History: Add, L 1966, ch 953, eff Sept 1, 1967 from Sur. Ct. Act § 161 in part; amd, L 1968, ch 259, § 28, eff May 14, 1968.

§ 1605. Original probate

1. A will of a non-domiciliary which upon probate may operate upon any property in this state and is deemed by the laws of this state to have been validly executed for probate in this state, may be admitted to probate in the same manner as any other will may be admitted to probate under this act, except as herein otherwise prescribed.

2. A will which has been admitted to probate or established in the testator's domicile shall

not thereafter be admitted to original probate in this state except

(a) in a case where the court is satisfied that ancillary probate would be unduly expensive, inconvenient or impossible under the circumstances,

(b) where the testator has directed in such will that it shall be offered for probate in this state or

(c) where the laws of testator's domicile discriminate against domiciliaries of New York either as a beneficiary or a fiduciary.

3. A will which by judgment or decree of a competent court in the testator's domicile has been denied probate or establishment shall not be admitted to probate in this state except where the denial of probate or establishment is solely for a cause which is not ground for rejection of a will of a domiciliary testator.

History: Add, L 1966, ch 953, eff Sept 1, 1967; amd, L 1967, ch 685, § 93, eff Sept 1, 1967.

§ 1606. Proof of will by probate in non-domiciliary jurisdiction

In the case of original probate of the will of a non-domiciliary testator an authenticated copy of the will and of its probate or establishment in the jurisdiction in which the will was executed shall be sufficient proof of its contents and of compliance with the law of the place of execution, if no objection is made thereto. If objection to the probate of such a will is filed this section shall not relieve proponent from offering competent proof of the contents and legal sufficiency of the will except that the original will need not be produced unless directed by a court.

History: Add, L 1966, ch 953, eff Sept 1, 1967.

§ 1607. Ancillary letters of administration

1. Upon petition as provided in 1609 and upon proof that letters of administration of the estate of a decedent have been issued by a competent court in the decedent's domicile or upon proof that under the law of that jurisdiction letters of administration are not granted but that a person is acting in that jurisdiction to administer the decedent's estate in accordance with the law thereof, the court may issue ancillary letters of administration. In a case where the court has theretofore issued original or ancillary letters or there is pending before the court an application therefor, the court shall take such proceedings as justice requires.

2. The court shall issue ancillary letters of administration to the following persons in the following order:

(a) The person appointed administrator in the domiciliary jurisdiction or the person acting in that jurisdiction to administer the decedent's estate in accordance with the law thereof.

(b) A person entitled to original letters of administration under this act.

3. If no person named in any subparagraph of subdivision 2 is willing to qualify or to designate a person eligible to receive ancillary letters they shall issue to a person in the succeeding subparagraph of such subdivision who will qualify or to a person designated by him who is eligible to receive letters.

History: Add, L 1966, ch 953, eff Sept 1, 1967 from Sur. Ct. Act §§ 160, 161 in part.

§ 1608. Ancillary letters generally

1. A person acting in the decedent's domicile as executor or administrator or to administer the decedent's estate in accordance with the law thereof may by an acknowledged instrument designate and authorize the appointment of a person eligible to receive letters to act as ancillary administrator or ancillary administrator c.t.a. If conflicting designations or joint plural designations are made or if two or more persons are entitled jointly to letters under this article the court may appoint one or more of the persons so designated or one or more of the persons so entitled.

2. A person to whom ancillary letters are issued must qualify in the same manner as prescribed in this act for the qualification of a fiduciary except that the penalty of the bond may be in such sum as to the court seems just, unless the will dispenses with the filing of a bond by the fiduciary named therein, in which case the court may dispense with the filing of a bond by the fiduciary so named.

3. In any case where the court is satisfied that there is no creditor of the decedent who is a domiciliary of this state and that no estate tax is assessable in this state, ancillary letters may issue without bond. Before issuing such letters without bond, however, the court may require that supplemental process issue, directed generally to all creditors or persons claiming to be creditors who are domiciled in this state and that it be served by publication unless such process had theretofore been served in the proceeding.

4. All of the provisions of this act relating to eligibility to receive letters shall be applicable to appointments made under this article.

5. Before granting ancillary letters on any application therefor the court may require the petitioner or any other person seeking such letters to serve by mail a written notice of the application upon every domiciliary beneficiary who has not been served with process or has not appeared in the proceeding for ancillary letters or waived service of process therein. Such notice shall be in the form prescribed in 1005 if the application be for ancillary letters of administration or in the form prescribed in 1409 if the application be for ancillary letters testamentary or ancillary letters of administration c.t.a. and shall be served in accordance with the applicable section.

6. Any corporate banking institution of any state of the United States, the Commonwealth of Puerto Rico, territory or possession of the United States not entitled of right under the banking law to receive such letters may nevertheless be authorized by the court to receive such letters upon filing such bond as the court may require.

History: Add, L 1966, ch 953, eff Sept 1, 1967 from Sur. Ct. Act §§ 164 in part, 163; amd, L 1967, ch 685, § 94, eff Sept 1, 1967; L 1968, ch 157, §§ 1, 2, eff Sept 1, 1968.

§ 1609. Petition; process

1. A petition for ancillary probate or for ancillary letters of any kind may be made by any creditor, public administrator, county treasurer or person interested or to whom letters may issue under this article. The petition shall state all of the decedent's property in this state and the value thereof, the amount of the security given on the original appointment, the name and post-office address of each domiciliary creditor or each domiciliary claiming to be a creditor and the amount of each claim so far as it is ascertainable.

2. If ancillary letters be requested, process shall issue to the state tax commission, to all

domiciliary creditors or domiciliaries claiming to be creditors and to such other persons entitled to letters or to designate an appointee as the court by order directs. The court may issue process generally to all creditors or persons claiming to be creditors who reside within the state, who shall be served in such manner as directed by the court.

3. If petitioner prays for ancillary probate of a will but does not ask that ancillary letters be issued, it shall be unnecessary to issue any process except to the state tax commission.

History: Add, L 1966, ch 953, eff Sept 1, 1967 from Sur. Ct. Act § 162(1); amd, L 1967, ch 685, § 95; L 1968, ch 157, § 3, eff Sept 1, 1968; L 1968, ch 157, eff Sept 1, 1968; L 1968, ch 259, § 29, eff May 14, 1968; L 1973, ch 72, § 1, eff Sept 1, 1973.

§ 1610. General powers and duties of ancillary fiduciary

1. The provisions of law governing the rights, powers, duties and liabilities of a fiduciary apply to a person to whom ancillary letters are granted under this article except where a special provision is otherwise made or where a contrary intent is expressed in or plainly to be inferred from the context.

2. The court or any court of this state having jurisdiction may direct a person to whom ancillary letters have been issued to pay from the assets received by him in this state the debts of the decedent due to creditors who reside in this state. If the amount of all the decedent's debts here and elsewhere exceeds the amount of all the decedent's property applicable thereto the court may direct the ancillary fiduciary to pay such sum to each resident creditor as equals that creditor's share of all distributable assets.

3. The court or any court of the state having jurisdiction may direct the ancillary fiduciary to distribute the remaining assets after the payment of creditors and expenses to those entitled thereto or to otherwise dispose of the assets as justice requires.

4. Unless a court shall direct the ancillary fiduciary to distribute the assets as provided in the preceding subdivisions he is required to transmit the remaining assets to the state or country where domiciliary letters were granted to be disposed of pursuant to the law thereof.

History: Add, L 1966, ch 953, eff Sept 1, 1967 from Sur. Ct. Act §§ 164, 165, 166.

§ 1611. Ancillary administration of estate of absentee

If it appears that the foreign probate or the grant of foreign administration was based upon the disappearance or absence of the person on whose property ancillary letters are sought under circumstances as to afford reasonable ground to believe that he is dead process shall issue to the disappeared or absent person and shall be served upon him by publication. It shall also be served upon the public administrator of the county or if there be none, upon the county treasurer. If it appears to the satisfaction of the court from the foreign probate or grant of administration or from such other proof as it may require, that such person be dead, it may make a decree determining that fact and granting ancillary administration as prescribed in this article.

History: Add, L 1966, ch 953, eff Sept 1, 1967 from Sur. Ct. Act § 162(2), (3).

§ 1612. Effect of adjudication for or against fiduciary

A prior adjudication rendered by a court of competent jurisdiction for or against an estate fiduciary shall be as conclusive as to the ancillary fiduciary in this state as if he were a party to the adjudication unless it resulted from fraud or collusion of the fiduciary to the prejudice

SCPA

of the estate. This section shall not apply to an adjudication in another jurisdiction admitting or refusing to admit a will to probate.

History: Add, L 1966, ch 953, eff Sept 1, 1967.

§ 1613. Application of general law

Except where special provision is made otherwise, the law of this state relating to wills and to the probate, contest and effect thereof shall apply in the case of a non-domiciliary testator and the law and procedure of this state relating generally to administration and to fiduciaries shall apply to ancillary administration and ancillary fiduciaries.

History: Add, L 1966, ch 953, eff Sept 1, 1967 from Sur. Ct. Act § 166.

§ 1614. Authentication of foreign will or letters

In any case in which a foreign will or letters are required to be proved under this article, the will or letters shall be authenticated in the manner prescribed by the CPLR.

History: Add, L 1966, ch 953, eff Sept 1, 1967.

§ 1615. Record of wills and letters recorded under former law

The record in the court or an authenticated copy of the record of any will recorded pursuant to section 44 of the decedent estate law prior to the effective date of this act shall be presumptive evidence of the will, of the execution thereof and of the letters granted thereon in any action or special proceeding relating to real property. The record in the court or an authenticated copy thereof shall be presumptive evidence of a petition for letters of administration and of the letters granted thereon recorded pursuant to section 44 of the decedent estate law prior to the effective date of this act.

History: Add, L 1966, ch 953, eff Sept 1, 1967.

§ 1616. Application of article

This article shall apply only to the wills and estates of non-domiciliaries.

History: Add, L 1966, ch 953, eff Sept 1, 1967.

ARTICLE 17
GUARDIANS AND CUSTODIANS
SUMMARY OF ARTICLE

§ 1701. Power of court

The court has power over the property of an infant and is authorized and empowered to appoint a guardian of the person or of the property or of both of an infant whether or not the parent or parents of the infant or child are living. Where the guardianship and custody of a child have been committed to an authorized agency pursuant to section six hundred thirty-one of the family court act, or section three hundred eighty-three-c, section three hundred eighty-four or section three hundred eighty-four-b of the social services law, or where both parents of the child whose consent to the adoption of the child would have been required pursuant to section one hundred eleven-a of the domestic relations law are dead, the court may appoint a permanent guardian of a child if the court finds that such appointment is in the best interests of the child.

History: Add, L 1966, ch 953, eff Sept 1, 1967 from Sur. Ct. Act § 173; amd, L 1976, ch 167, § 1, eff Sept 1, 1976; L 2008, ch 404, § 4, eff Nov 3, 2008.

§ 1702. Jurisdiction

1. Where an infant has no guardian the court may appoint a guardian of his person or property, or of both, in the following cases:

(a) Where the infant is domiciled in that county or has sojourned therein immediately preceding the application.

(b) Where the infant is a non-domiciliary of the state but has property situate in that county.

2. Where an infant or child has no guardian, the court may appoint a permanent guardian for the child in accordance with the provisions of section seventeen hundred one of this article where the infant is domiciled in that county or where such child is in the care or custody of an authorized agency, as defined in subdivision ten of section three hundred seventy-one of the social services law, and such authorized agency has its principal office in that county.

3. Where the permanency goal for a foster child who is the subject of a proceeding under article ten or ten-A of the family court act is referral for legal guardianship, a petition filed under this article by a fit and willing relative or other suitable person shall be filed with the court before whom the most recent proceeding under article ten or ten-A of the family court act is pending.

> **History:** Add, L 1966, ch 953, eff Sept 1, 1967 from Sur. Ct. Act § 174; amd, L 1973, ch 286, § 1, eff Sept 1, 1973; L 2008, ch 404, § 5, eff Nov 3, 2008; L 2010, ch 58, § 9 (Part F), eff April 1, 2011.

§ 1703. Petition for appointment; by whom made

A petition for the appointment of a guardian of the person or property, or both, of an infant may be made by any person on behalf of the infant or if the infant be over the age of fourteen years, it may be made by the infant. A petition for appointment as a guardian of the property of an infant may also be made by the public administrator of the county in which the infant resides where no one else is available to serve as guardian. The court may grant such a petition of the public administrator upon its certification that all other efforts to appoint a guardian have been exhausted. A petition for appointment as a permanent guardian of an infant or child may be brought by any person on behalf of the infant or child.

> **History:** Add, L 1966, ch 953, eff Sept 1, 1967 from Sur. Ct. Act § 175; amd, L 1993, ch 514, § 36, eff Jan 1, 1994; L 2008, ch 404, § 6, eff Nov 3, 2008.

§ 1704. Petition for appointment; contents

A petition for the appointment of a guardian of an infant must show:

1. The full name, domicile and date of birth of the infant.

2. The names of the parents whose consent to the adoption of a child would have been required pursuant to section one hundred eleven of the domestic relations law or who was entitled to notice of an adoption proceeding pursuant to section one hundred eleven-a of the domestic relations law, and whether or not they are living or have had their parental rights terminated pursuant to section three hundred eighty-three-c, section three hundred eighty-four or section three hundred eighty-four-b of the social services law or section six hundred thirty-one of the family court act, and if living, their domiciles, the name and address of the person with whom the infant resides and the names and addresses of the nearest distributees of full age who are domiciliaries, if both parents are dead.

3. Whether the infant has had at any time a guardian appointed by will or deed or an acting guardian in socage or guardianship and custody committed pursuant to section three hundred eighty-three-c, three hundred eighty-four or three hundred eighty-four-b of the social services law or section six hundred thirty-one of the family court act.

4. The estimated value of the real and personal property and of the annual income therefrom to which the infant is entitled.

5. If the infant is a non-domiciliary married person and the petition relates to personal property only, that the property is not subject to the control or disposition of the person's spouse by the law of his or her domicile, and the name and domicile of his or her spouse.

6. Whether the petitioner has knowledge that a person nominated to be a guardian therein, or any individual eighteen years of age or over who resides in the home of the proposed guardian is a subject of an indicated report, as such terms are defined in section four hundred twelve of the social services law, filed with the statewide central register of child abuse and maltreatment pursuant to title six of article six of the social services law, or has been the subject of or the respondent in a child protective proceeding commenced under article ten of the family court act, which proceeding resulted in an order finding that the child is an abused or neglected child.

7. The petition may state the reasons why a person nominated would be a suitable guardian and if either parent be living why either of them should not be appointed guardian.

8. In addition, the petition for appointment of a permanent guardian of an infant or child shall include:

(a) an assessment to be performed by the local social services district, which shall contain:

(i) the full name and address of the person seeking to become the guardian;

(ii) the ability of the guardian to assume permanent care of the child;

(iii) the child's property and assets, if known;

(iv) the wishes of the child, if appropriate;

(v) the results of the criminal history record check with the division of criminal justice services of the guardian and any person eighteen years of age or older residing in the guardian's household conducted by the office of children and family services pursuant to subdivision two of section three hundred seventy-eight-a of the social services law if such a criminal history record check has been completed;

(vi) the results of a search of the statewide central register of child abuse and maltreatment records regarding the guardian and any person eighteen years of age or older residing in the guardian's household, including whether such person has been the subject of an indicated report conducted pursuant to subparagraph (e) of paragraph (A) of subdivision four of section four hundred twenty-two of the social services law, if such a search has been conducted; and

(vii) the results of all inspections and assessments of the guardian's home and the child's progress while placed in the home, if any;

(b) a certified copy of the order or orders terminating the parental rights of the child's parents or approving the surrender of the child or the death certificates of the child's parents, as applicable;

(c) the recommendation of the authorized agency involved, if any; and

(d) the suitability, ability and commitment of the permanent guardian to assume full legal responsibility for the child and raise the child to adulthood.

History: Add, L 1966, ch 953, eff Sept 1, 1967 from Sur. Ct. Act § 176; amd, L 1976, ch 167, § 2, eff Sept 1, 1976; L 1976, ch 666, § 33, eff Jan 1, 1977; L 1987, ch 636, § 1, eff Aug 3, 1987; L 1991, ch 164, eff Jan 1, 1992; L 1998, ch 423, § 1, eff July 22, 1998; L 2008, ch 404, § 7, eff Nov 3, 2008; L. 2019, ch 420, § 5, eff Oct 29, 2019.

§ 1705. Persons to be served

1. Upon presentation of the petition process shall issue:

(a) To the parent or parents, and if the infant is married, to the spouse, if such persons are within the state and their residences therein are known, or if there be none, to the grandparents who are within the county.

(b) To the person having the care and custody of the infant or with whom he resides.

(c) If the application is made in behalf of an infant over the age of 14 years by any person, to the infant.

2. No process shall be necessary to a parent who has abandoned the infant or is deprived of civil rights or divorced from the parent having legal custody of the infant or an incompetent or who is otherwise judicially deprived of the custody of the infant or in case the infant is married to a spouse who has abandoned the infant or is deprived of civil rights or divorced or an incompetent.

3. The court shall ascertain so far as practicable what relatives of the infant are domiciled in its county or elsewhere and with whom the infant resides and it may issue process to any relative or class of relatives to show cause why the appointment should not be made.

History: Add, L 1966, ch 953, eff Sept 1, 1967 from Sur. Ct. Act § 177; amd, L 1967, ch 685, § 96, eff Sept 1, 1967; L 1974, ch 904, eff Sept 1, 1974, but shall not be construed so as to impair or render ineffectual any proceedings commenced pursuant to law prior to the time the act takes effect; L 1976, ch 167, §§ 3–5, eff Sept 1, 1976; L 1976, ch 666, § 34, eff Jan 1, 1977, provided, however, that nothing therein contained shall be construed so as to alter, affect, impair, defeat or restore any rights, obligations, duties or interests accrued, incurred, conferred or terminated prior to the effective date of the act; L 1979, ch 199, eff July 5, 1979; L 1985, ch 789, eff April 1, 1986, with authority given to the presiding justice of the appellate division to take actions necessary and proper to effectuate the purposes of the act prior to the effective date; L 1989, ch 675, § 1, eff Jan 1, 1990.

§ 1706. Proceedings thereupon

1. Where process is not issued or upon the return of process, the court shall ascertain the age of the infant, the amount of his or her personal property, the gross amount of the rents and profits of his or her real estate during his or her minority and the sufficiency of the security offered by the proposed guardian. With respect to applications for appointment as a guardian of a child, the guardian shall have the right and responsibility to make decisions, including issuing any necessary consents, regarding the child's protection, education, care and control, health and medical needs, and the physical custody of the person of the child. A permanent

guardian may consent to the adoption of the child. Provided, however, that nothing in this subdivision shall be construed to limit the ability of a child to consent to his or her own medical care as may be otherwise provided by law. If the youth is over the age of fourteen years, the court shall ascertain his or her preference for a suitable guardian. Notwithstanding any other section of law, where the youth is over the age of eighteen, he or she shall consent to the appointment of a suitable guardian.

2. The court shall inquire of the office of children and family services and such office shall inform the court whether or not a person nominated to be a guardian of such infant, or any individual eighteen years of age or over who resides in the home of the proposed guardian is a subject of an indicated report or in a report which is under investigation at the time of the inquiry, as such terms are defined in section four hundred twelve of the social services law, filed with the statewide central register of child abuse and maltreatment pursuant to title six of article six of the social services law. The office shall, upon completion of the investigation, inform the court as to the outcome of such investigation.

History: Add, L 1966, ch 953, eff Sept 1, 1967 from CPLR § 1210(b); amd, L 1967, ch 685, § 97, eff Sept 1, 1967; L 1987, ch 636, § 2, eff Aug 3, 1987; L 1991, ch 164, eff Jan 1, 1992; L 1998, ch 423, § 2, eff July 22, 1998; L 2006, ch 518, § 4, eff Aug 16, 2006; L 2007, ch 525, § 1, eff Aug 15, 2007; L 2008, ch 404, § 8, eff Nov 3, 2008; L 2010, ch 58, § 10 (Part F), eff April 1, 2011.

§ 1707. Decree appointing guardian; term of office

1. If the court be satisfied that the interests of the infant will be promoted by the appointment of a guardian or by the issuance of temporary letters of guardianship of his or her person or of his or her property, or of both, it must make a decree accordingly. If the court determines that appointment of a permanent guardian is in the best interests of the infant or child, the court shall issue a decree appointing such guardian. The same person may be appointed guardian of both the person and the property of the infant or the guardianship of the person and of the property may be committed to different persons. The court may appoint a person other than the parent of the infant or the person nominated by the petitioner. When the court is informed that the infant, a person nominated to be a guardian of such infant, the petitioner, or any individual eighteen years of age or over who resides in the home of the proposed guardian is a subject of or another person named in an indicated report, as such terms are defined in section four hundred twelve of the social services law, filed with the statewide register of child abuse and maltreatment pursuant to title six of article six of the social services law or is or has been the subject of or the respondent in or a party to a child protective proceeding commenced under article ten of the family court act which resulted in an order finding that the child is an abused or neglected child the court shall obtain such records regarding such report or proceeding as it deems appropriate and shall give the information contained therein due consideration in its determination. The court shall provide in its order appointing a guardian of a child for whom the guardian and a local department of social services have entered into an agreement under title ten of article six of the social services law: (a) if the guardian would meet the definition of relative guardian as such term is defined in section four hundred fifty-eight-a of the social services law, the compelling reasons that exist for determining that the return home of the child and the adoption of the child are not in the best interests of the child and are, therefore, not appropriate permanency options for the child; and (b) that the local department of social services and the attorney for the child must receive notice of, and be made parties to, any subsequent proceeding to vacate or modify the order of guardianship.

2. The term of office of a guardian of the person or property so appointed expires when the infant attains majority, unless the infant consents to the continuation of or appointment of a guardian after his or her eighteenth birthday, in which case such term of office expires on his or her twenty-first birthday, or after such other shorter period as the court establishes upon good cause shown; except that the term of office of a guardian of the person of an infant expires upon the infant's marriage prior to attaining majority. The appointment of a guardian of a child shall expire when the infant or child reaches the age of eighteen years, unless the infant or child consents to the continuation of a guardian after his or her eighteenth birthday, in which case such term of office expires on his or her twenty-first birthday, or unless vacated by the court prior to the infant or child's eighteenth or twenty-first birthday if the court finds that, based upon clear and convincing evidence, the guardian failed to or is unable, unavailable or unwilling to provide proper care and custody of the infant or child, or that the guardianship is no longer in the best interests of the infant or child.

> **History:** Add, L 1966, ch 953, eff Sept 1, 1967 from Sur. Ct. Act § 179; amd, L 1976, ch 167, eff Sept 1, 1967; L 1981, ch 287, § 1, eff June 22, 1981; L 1987, ch 636, Aug 3, 1987; L 1998, ch 423, eff July 22, 1998; L 2000, ch 477, § 5, eff Nov 19, 2000; L 2006, ch 518, § 5, eff Aug 16, 2006; L 2008, ch 404, § 9, eff Nov 3, 2008; L 2010, ch 58, § 11 (Part F), eff April 1, 2011; L 2015, ch 56, § 15 (Part L), eff April 13, 2015.

§ 1708. Bonding requirements; investment of guardianship funds

1. Except as provided in this section, all property of the infant shall be secured by bond as provided in this act.

2. (a) The court may dispense with a bond wholly or partly and direct that the guardian jointly with a person or depositary designated collect and receive the moneys and other property of the infant as directed by order and that such moneys and property as it directs be deposited in the name of the guardian, subject to the order of the court, with a bank, savings bank, trust company, safe deposit company, or state or federal credit union designated in the order or invested in the name of the guardian, subject to the order of the court, in the shares of a savings and loan association or the savings account of a federal savings and loan association designated in the order, provided that no deposit or investment of the funds of any one infant in any single bank, savings bank, trust company, savings and loan association, federal savings and loan association, or state or federal credit union shall exceed the maximum amount insured by the federal deposit insurance corporation or the national credit union share insurance fund.

   (b) The court may also dispense with a bond wholly or partly when it authorizes the guardian to purchase and invest in United States savings bonds, treasury bills, treasury notes, treasury bonds, or bonds of the state of New York or bonds or other obligations of any county, city, town, village or school district of the state of New York for the benefit of the infant and directs the guardian to deposit such bonds, bills, notes or other municipal obligations in joint custody with a bank, savings bank, trust company, safe deposit company, or state or federal credit union invested in the name of the guardian, subject to the order of the court. The guardian shall collect and receive all interest and income from such United States savings bonds, treasury notes, treasury bonds or bonds of the state of New York or bonds or other obligations of any county, city, town, village or school district of the state of New York and deposit such interest and income in an account in the name of the guardian, subject to the order of the court, as authorized pursuant to this section with the bank, savings bank, trust company, safe deposit company, or state or federal credit union having joint custody with the guardian of such United States savings bonds, treasury bills, treasury notes, treasury bonds, or bonds of the state of New York or bonds or other obligations of any county, city, town, village or school district of the state of New York.

(c) The court may also dispense with a bond wholly or partly when it authorizes the guardian to invest the guardianship funds pursuant to an investment advisory agreement with a bank, trust company, brokerage house, or other financial services entity acceptable to the court. The investment advisory agreement shall provide that the guardianship funds will be invested in accordance with the provisions of section 11-2.3 of the estates, powers, and trusts law and that the funds so invested shall not be released from the custody of the custodian identified therein except on order of the court. The petition to invest the guardianship funds pursuant to this subdivision shall be accompanied by a copy of the proposed investment advisory agreement. If the custodian of the funds is not the same person or entity providing the investment advice, a separate custodial agreement shall also accompany the petition to invest the guardianship* pursuant to this subdivision. Such custodial agreement shall be with an institution acceptable to the court for the purpose of retaining control of the guardianship funds and shall also provide that the funds under the control of the custodian shall not be released from custody except on order of the court.

(d) Such deposit or investment shall be withdrawn or removed only on the order of the court, except that no court order shall be required to pay over to the infant who has attained the age of eighteen years all the moneys so held unless the depository is in receipt of an order from a court of competent jurisdiction directing it to withhold such payment beyond the infant's eighteenth birthday.

3. Where an infant is a beneficiary of a contract of life insurance under which moneys are payable to the infant or under which rights may accrue to the infant pursuant to election made by his guardian under the terms of the contract, the court may by order dispense wholly or partly with a bond and direct that the insurance company and the guardian shall make no withdrawal of the funds due to the infant under the contract except by joint check to the order of the guardian and a person designated by the court to receive such moneys.

4. The letters issued shall contain the substance of the order.

History: Add, L 1966, ch 953, eff Sept 1, 1967 from Sur. Ct. Act § 180 in part; amd, L 1967, ch 685, eff Sept 1, 1967; L 1975, ch 228, eff Sept 1, 1975, provided, however, the act shall not affect, impair or render ineffectual any order issued pursuant to law prior to the time this act takes effect, except insofar as an order issued pursuant to subdivision (c) of section 1206 of the civil practice law and rules, or its predecessor, designates the age of twenty-one as the age at which the infant may obtain from the depository the money held for the infant upon his demand therefor without further court order; L 1990, ch 330, eff June 30, 1990; L 1993, ch 514, eff Jan 1, 1994; L 1994, ch 300, eff July 20, 1994; L 1995, ch 464, § 4, eff Aug 2, 1995; L 2000, ch 43, § 1, eff June 6, 2000.

§ 1709. Appointment of guardian by supreme court

1. Where the supreme court appoints a guardian of an infant's person or property, or both, a certified copy of the order or decree appointing the guardian and of the bond given by the guardian shall be filed in the surrogate's court of the county in which the infant is domiciled, or if the infant be a non-domiciliary of the state, in the county in which the infant has property

---

* **Ed. Note:** Should probably read "guardianship funds."

and a minute thereof made and indexed in the book kept by the court in which orders or decrees appointing guardians are entered.

2. Letters shall thereupon issue to the guardian from such court upon qualifying as provided in section 708.

3. A guardian so appointed shall be subject to all the duties and liabilities of a guardian specified in this article.

History: Add, L 1966, ch 953, eff Sept 1, 1967 from Sur. Ct. Act § 183; amd, L 1970, ch 396, eff Sept 1, 1970; L 1988, ch 232, § 5, eff July 8, 1988.

§ 1710. Will or deed containing appointment to be proved

A person shall not exercise within the state any power or authority as guardian of the person or property of an infant by virtue of the appointment by the will of an infant's parent, being a domiciliary and dying after this act takes effect, unless the will has been duly admitted to probate and recorded in the proper court and letters of guardianship have been issued thereon; or by virtue of an appointment contained in a deed of the infant's parent, being a domiciliary, executed after this act takes effect, unless the deed has been acknowledged so as to entitle it to be recorded and has been recorded in the office for recording deeds in the county of domicile of the person making the appointment at the time of execution thereof.

History: Add, L 1966, ch 953, eff Sept 1, 1967 from Sur. Ct. Act § 187 in part.

§ 1711. Guardian by will or deed; qualification; renunciation

1. Where a deed containing the appointment of a guardian is not recorded within 3 months after the death of the grantor, the person appointed is presumed to have renounced the appointment and if a guardian is thereafter appointed by the court the presumption is conclusive.

2. Where a will containing the appointment of a guardian is admitted to probate or a deed is recorded as prescribed in the preceding section, the person appointed guardian must within 3 months thereafter qualify as provided by 708 unless contrary to the express provisions of the will or deed and by filing a petition showing the facts which entitle him to qualify and receive letters; otherwise he is deemed to have renounced the appointment.

3. No guardian by will or deed shall receive any property other than the property derived under the instrument of appointment without first giving a bond in a penalty to be fixed by the court.

4. Either before or after the expiration of 3 months the court may extend the time so to qualify for such time as it deems reasonable, upon good cause shown.

5. A person appointed guardian by will or deed may at any time before he qualifies renounce the appointment by an acknowledged instrument filed in the office of the court.

History: Add, L 1966, ch 953, eff Sept 1, 1967 from Sur. Ct. Act §§ 187 in part, 188 in part.

§ 1712. Appointment of successor

When no guardian by will or deed remains in office a guardian may be appointed by the court with all the powers conferred by the will or deed and with the effect prescribed in 706 of this act unless such appointment would be contrary to the express provisions of the will or deed.

History: Add, L 1966, ch 953, eff Sept 1, 1967 from Sur. Ct. Act § 189.

SCPA

§ 1713. Administration of infant's property

1. Upon the petition of the guardian or of the infant or of any person in his behalf, the court, upon notice to such persons, if any, it deems proper, may by order direct the application by the guardian of the infant's property to

    (a) the support and education of the infant;

    (b) the cost of the funeral of a parent of the infant;

    (c) the cost of the funeral of any other person who had no other assets available for funeral expenses and who had named the infant as beneficiary of a policy of insurance upon his life or as beneficiary or donee of any other property, to the extent that the guardian shall have collected such proceeds or property.

2. In all cases the court may determine the amount of expenditure of the infant's funds that is reasonable, proper and just under the circumstances, taking into consideration the liability, if any, of any other person to pay such expenses, his financial ability to pay and all other relevant facts. The payment may be made from income or principal. No payment for the funeral expense of any person shall be authorized unless the court finds that the estate of such person is insufficient to pay it.

3. Notwithstanding the provisions of subdivision 1 a guardian is authorized to apply social security payments received for the benefit of the infant to his education and support without order of the court.

4. Any infant over 14 years of age or any person in behalf of any infant may petition the court having jurisdiction over the infant's estate for the appointment of a guardian ad litem to initiate in behalf of the infant a proceeding for the protection of the infant's financial or other interests and in such proceeding authorize the guardian ad litem to take such action as the court deems proper. The court may entertain the petition if in its judgment the interests of the guardian of the infant are adverse to those of the infant or if in its opinion other valid reasons exist for the initiation of such a proceeding by another than his guardian. It may in similar case appoint a guardian ad litem for such purpose whenever facts have come to its attention showing the necessity for protecting the interests of the infant.

History: Add, L 1966, ch 953, eff Sept 1, 1967 from Sur. Ct. Act § 194; amd, L 1971, ch 805, § 2, eff Sept 1, 1971.

§ 1714. Power to manage during minority property vested in an infant

The donee of a power to manage during minority property vested in an infant resulting from an ineffectual attempt by will or deed to appoint the donee as guardian shall be subject to the provisions of this article. In respect of such property he shall have all the rights and duties of a guardian and shall be entitled to receive the commissions allowed to a guardian.

History: Add, L 1966, ch 953, eff Sept 1, 1967 from Sur. Ct. Act § 194-a.

§ 1715. Authority of guardian to sell, lease, exchange or mortgage

1. The surrogate's court of the county from which letters were issued to the guardian of the property of an infant may, in accordance with this section, authorize the guardian in the name of the infant to sell, lease, exchange or mortgage any interest of the infant in real property.

2. A proceeding therefor may be commenced by the guardian by filing a petition in which the infant, if over the age of 14 years, may join. It must show the facts as to the real property, the interest of the infant therein, the other property of the infant, his financial circumstances and such other facts showing that it is for the best interest of the infant to sell, lease, exchange or mortgage all or a portion of the infant's interest in the real property.

3. If the petition be entertained process shall issue to the infant if he has not joined therein, to the parent or parents, or if there be none, to an adult person with whom the infant resides, the person having his care and custody, and if the infant be married, to the infant's spouse. If the guardian show* to the satisfaction of the court either by the petition or affidavit that he lacks knowledge of the existence, identity, name, residence or location of any person to be served or shows that with due diligence any such person cannot be personally served with process within any state of the United States, the District of Columbia, the Commonwealth of Puerto Rico or a territory or possession of the United States, the court may dispense with such service or make such direction as it deems appropriate for the protection of the infant.

4. On the return of process the court shall take such proof as it deems necessary and make such order as justice and the best interests of the infant require.

5. Any instrument executed by the guardian in the name of the infant in conformity with the provisions of this section shall have the same effect as if the infant being of full age had executed it.

6. The court shall have jurisdiction on like application to ratify and confirm any lease or leases made by the guardian in behalf of the infant and not theretofore authorized, ratified or confirmed by a court of competent jurisdiction.

7. Nothing in this section shall be deemed to authorize a guardian appointed by will or deed to sell, lease, exchange or mortgage the infant's real property contrary to the express provisions of the will or deed.

    History: Add, L 1966, ch 953, eff Sept 1, 1967 from Sur. Ct. Act § 194-b in part; amd, L 1967, ch 685, § 99, eff Sept 1, 1967.

§ 1716. Application for ancillary letters to foreign guardians

1. Where an infant is domiciled within a state of the United States other than this state, or the District of Columbia, the Commonwealth of Puerto Rico or a territory or possession of the United States and is entitled to property within the state or to maintain an action or special proceeding in any court thereof, a guardian of his property to whom letters have been issued by a court of competent jurisdiction within the foreign state, the District of Columbia, the Commonwealth of Puerto Rico, or a territory or possession of the United States where the infant is domiciled, and has there given security in at least the value of the personal property and of the rents and profits of the real property of the infant, may present to the surrogate's court having jurisdiction, a petition showing the facts and particularly whether or not there are any debts due or to become due from the infant to a domiciliary and that the security given is sufficient to cover the property sought to be obtained through such letters and that the court has jurisdiction of the infant and praying for ancillary letters of guardianship accordingly.

2. The petition must be accompanied with exemplified copies of the records and other

---

* So in original. Should probably be "shows".

papers showing that he has been so appointed and has given the security required in this section, which must be authenticated in the manner prescribed by the CPLR. The petition and authenticated records and papers shall be conclusive evidence of the facts therein set forth in any court of this state.

3. Any corporate banking institution in any state, the District of Columbia, the Commonwealth of Puerto Rico or a territory or possession of the United States not entitled of right under section 131 of the banking law to receive such letters may nevertheless be authorized to receive them upon giving the bond which the court may require.

4. Where a non-domiciliary infant resides in a foreign country and is entitled to property within the state or to maintain an action or special proceeding in any court thereof respecting such property, a guardian of his property authorized to act as such within the domicile of the infant may apply to the surrogate's court of the county where the property or any part thereof is situate, for ancillary letters of guardianship on the estate of the infant and the person so authorized must present a petition showing the facts and the additional allegations regarding debts and security required by subdivision 1 and praying for ancillary letters. The petition must be accompanied with the authenticated copies of the records and other papers showing the appointment of the petitioner or where the foreign guardian has not been appointed by any court, with other proof of his authority to act as guardian within the foreign country and also with proof that pursuant to the laws of the foreign country he is entitled to the possession of the infant's personal estate. Authenticated copies of the records where used pursuant to this subdivision must be authenticated by the seal of the court or officer by which or by whom he was appointed or by the officer having the custody of the seal or the record thereof and the signature of a judge of such court or the signature of such officer and of the clerk of such court, if any, and must be further authenticated by the certificate under the principal seal of the department of foreign affairs or of the department of justice of such country, attested by the signature or seal of a United States consul. The petition and authenticated records and papers shall be conclusive evidence of the facts therein set forth in any court of this state.

History: Add, L 1966, ch 953, eff Sept 1, 1967 from Sur. Ct. Act § 184 in part; amd, L 1967, ch 685, § 100, eff Sept 1, 1967.

§ 1717. Proceedings thereupon

1. Where the court is satisfied upon the papers presented as prescribed in the preceding section that the case is within that section and that it will be for the infant's interest that ancillary letters issue to the petitioner, it may make a decree accordingly.

2. The decree may be made without process or process may issue to such persons as the court deems proper, to show cause why the prayer of the petition should not be granted.

3. Before ancillary letters are issued the court may direct that any debts appearing to be due or owing from the infant to domiciliaries be paid or security given therefor.

History: Add, L 1966, ch 953, eff Sept 1, 1967 from Sur. Ct. Act § 185 in part.

§ 1718. Effect of such letters

1. Ancillary letters of guardianship shall be issued as prescribed in the preceding section, without security, except as provided in that section.

2. They authorize the person to whom they are issued to demand and receive the personal property and the rents and profits of the real property of the infant and the proceeds of the

sale, mortgage or lease of the real property of the infant, to dispose of them in like manner as a guardian of the property appointed as prescribed in this article, to remove them from the state and to maintain any action or special proceeding in the infant's behalf.

3. Letters so issued do not authorize the ancillary guardian to receive from a domiciliary fiduciary subject to the jurisdiction of the court, money or other property belonging to the infant, in a case where domiciliary letters have been issued in this state to a guardian of the infant's property, except by special direction made for good cause shown of the court from which the domiciliary letters were issued or unless the domiciliary letters have been revoked.

History: Add, L 1966, ch 953, eff Sept 1, 1967 from Sur. Ct. Act § 186 in part; amd, L 1967, ch 685, § 101, eff Sept 1, 1967.

§ 1719. Annual account

A guardian of an infant's property must within the counties within the city of New York and within the counties of Nassau, Orange, Suffolk and Westchester annually within 30 days after the anniversary of his appointment and within every other county in the month of January of each year, as long as any of the infant's property or the proceeds thereof remains under his control, file in the court the following papers:

1. An account containing a true statement and description of each item of personal property of the infant received by him since his appointment or since the filing of his last annual account, as the case requires, the value of each item so received, a list of the items remaining in his hands, a statement of the manner in which he has disposed of each item not remaining in his hands and a description of the amount and nature of each investment of money made by him.

2. A true account in form of debtor and creditor of all his receipts and disbursements of money during the preceding year, charging himself with any balance remaining in his hands when the last account was rendered and stating the balance remaining in his hands at the conclusion of the year to be charged to him in the next year's account.

3. The names and addresses of the sureties on his bond; if natural persons whether they are living and whether the security of the bond has become impaired.

4. The guardian of an infant's property may be required by the court to produce for examination by it all securities or evidences of deposit or investment which he has relating to the estate of the infant.

5. When the property of an infant has been deposited under the provisions of 1708, and the clerk or guardian clerk of the court shall keep in his office, or the depositary furnishes to the court, an accurate record of receipts of deposits of principal and income of the infant's estate and of withdrawals therefrom, the guardian shall not be required to file an annual account unless the court direct the filing of an account for any year or years.

History: Add, L 1966, ch 953, eff Sept 1, 1967 from Sur. Ct. Act § 190 in part.

§ 1720. Affidavit to be annexed thereto

To each account as prescribed in the preceding section must be appended the affidavit of the guardian to the effect that the account is a true statement according to the best of his knowledge and belief.

History: Add, L 1966, ch 953, eff Sept 1, 1967 from Sur. Ct. Act § 191.

§ 1721. Annual examination of guardian's accounts

In the month of February of each year and thereafter until completed or at such other time as the court deems proper, the court must for the purposes specified in the succeeding section, examine or cause to be examined under its direction all accounts filed within the preceding year. The examination may be made by the clerk of the court or by a special examiner appointed by the court, who must before he enters upon the examination subscribe and take before the court and file with the clerk an oath faithfully to execute his duties and to make a true report to the court.

> **History:** Add, L 1966, ch 953, eff Sept 1, 1967 from Sur. Ct. Act § 192; amd, L 1967, ch 685, § 102, eff Sept 1, 1967.

§ 1722. Proceedings where account defective

1. If it appears to the court upon an examination made as prescribed in the preceding section or by the report of the special examiner that a guardian of an infant's property has omitted to file his annual account or the affidavit relating thereto as prescribed in this article or if the court deems that the interest of the infant requires that the guardian render a more full or satisfactory account or where the court has reason to believe that sufficient cause exists for the guardian's removal, it may appoint a guardian ad litem for the infant for the purpose of filing a petition in his behalf for the removal of the guardian and prosecuting the proceeding for that purpose.

2. In a case specified in subdivision 1 where a special examiner has been appointed the court may appoint such examiner guardian ad litem for the infant and authorize him to procure the filing of an amended or proper account and to prosecute a proceeding for the removal of the guardian when necessary.

3. In all cases of examination or prosecution as provided in this section the court shall fix the compensation of the special examiner and guardian ad litem and may make an order charging it in whole or in part upon the guardian personally, the funds in his hands or upon the county, in which latter case it shall certify the items thereof to the treasurer of the county or the chief fiscal officer thereof or in the city of New York to the proper officers and they shall be audited and paid as other county or city charges.

> **History:** Add, L 1966, ch 953, eff Sept 1, 1967 from Sur. Ct. Act § 193; amd, L 1967, ch 685, § 103, eff Sept 1, 1967.

§ 1723. Powers of a guardian of the property

1. A guardian of the property of an infant shall protect, preserve and manage the property of the infant. He shall have the power to sell the personal property of the infant for any purpose connected with the faithful discharge of his trust, including investing such property or the proceeds thereof, changing investments and disposing of investments, except where his authority is otherwise limited by court order or decree, or in the case of a testamentary guardian, by the terms of the will which appointed him.

> **History:** Add, L 1971, ch 311, § 1, eff Sept 1, 1971. **Ed. Note:** Although there is no subdivision 2, the numeral "1" appears in the statute as passed.

§ 1724. Custodians

An infant or a custodian acting under part six of article seven of the estates, powers and trusts law shall be subject to the jurisdiction of the court in accordance with the provisions of such law.

History: Formerly § 1723, add, L 1966, ch 953, eff Sept 1, 1967; L 1967, ch 685, eff Sept 1, 1967; renumbered § 1724, L 1971, ch 311, § 1, eff Sept 1, 1971; amd, L 2014, ch 112, § 1, eff July 22, 2014.

§ 1725. Temporary guardianship by adoptive parent prior to adoption

1. Upon the filing of a petition for temporary guardianship, as described in section one hundred fifteen-c of the domestic relations law, or upon the filing of a petition for adoption when no prior application has been made for an order of temporary guardianship, the court shall determine promptly whether or not to grant temporary guardianship.

2. A petition for temporary guardianship of the person of an infant to be adopted shall contain at least the following:

(a) The first and last name of the infant, the anticipated surname of the infant subsequent to the completion of the adoption, the anticipated residence of the infant and the infant's date of birth;

(b) The full names, addresses and telephone numbers of the petitioners;

(c) Proof of the consent to the adoption of the infant as required by section one hundred fifteen-b of the domestic relations law; and

(d) A verified statement that the infant will be residing with the petitioners and that the petitioners intend to file a petition for adoption of such infant within forty-five days of the execution of the consent to the adoption of the infant.

3. (a) The court shall inquire of the statewide central register of child abuse and maltreatment and the register shall inform the court whether the petitioner is a subject of an indicated report, as such terms are defined in section four hundred twelve of the social services law, filed with such register. When the court is informed that the petitioner is a subject of an indicated report, as such terms are defined in section four hundred twelve of the social services law, filed with the statewide central register of child abuse and maltreatment, the court shall give such information contained therein due consideration in its determination.

(b) The court shall make an order based upon the best interests of the child. Such order shall:

(i) appoint the petitioner temporary guardian of the person of the child; or

(ii) continue the proceeding for further investigation; or

(iii) if there is apparent cause to remove the child from the petitioners, follow the procedure set forth in subdivision two of section one hundred sixteen of the domestic relations law.

(c) Any decree or order of temporary guardianship issued pursuant to this section shall expire no later than nine months following the date of its issuance or entry of a final order of adoption, whichever is sooner. Such decree or order may be extended for periods of up to three months, upon application to the court, for good cause shown.

(d) Any decree or order issued pursuant to this section shall terminate upon the withdrawal or denial of the petition to adopt the infant named therein, unless the court orders the continuation thereof during the pendency of an appeal from an order denying the adoption petition.

4. If the court denies an application for temporary guardianship, or removes a child from the physical custody of the petitioners, or an order of temporary guardianship expires without the entry of a final order of adoption, or if the petition for adoption is withdrawn or denied, the court:

(a) if such withdrawal, denial or removal is within forty-five days of the execution of the consent to adoption by the birth parent, shall promptly inform the birth parent who consented to the adoption of such withdrawal, denial or removal;

(b) if such withdrawal, denial or removal is subsequent to forty-five days of the execution of the consent to adoption by the birth parent, may inform the birth parent who consented to the adoption of such withdrawal, denial or removal where the court determines that such notice will be in the best interests of the child; and

(c) in any case, shall direct the child protective service to conduct an investigation to assess the condition of the infant and to report its findings to the court within the time specified in the order. If the court has reason to believe that a crime was committed, it shall report such belief to the appropriate district attorney.

5. Rules of court shall provide for the monitoring by the court of filing of an adoption petition within forty-five days of the execution of a consent to adoption, when an application for temporary guardianship has been filed.

History: Add, L 1988, ch 557, § 3, eff Oct 1, 1988; amd, L 1991, ch 164, § 7, eff Jan 1, 1992; L 2002, ch 312, § 11, eff Aug 6, 2002; L 2008, ch 305, § 20, eff July 21, 2008.

§ 1726. Standby guardians

1. For the purpose of this section:

(a) "Standby guardian" means (i) a person judicially appointed pursuant to subdivision three of this section as standby guardian of the person and/or property of an infant whose authority becomes effective upon the incapacity, administrative separation, or death of the infant's parent, legal guardian, legal custodian or primary caretaker or upon the consent of the parent, legal guardian, legal custodian or primary caretaker; and (ii) a person designated pursuant to subdivision four of this section as standby guardian whose authority becomes effective upon the death, administrative separation, or incapacity of the infant's parent, legal guardian, legal custodian or primary caretaker or upon the debilitation and consent of the parent, legal guardian, legal custodian or primary caretaker.

(b) "Legal guardian" means the court-appointed guardian of the infant's person and/or property.

(c) "Attending physician" means the physician who has primary responsibility for the treatment and care of the infant's parent, legal guardian, legal custodian or primary caretaker. Where more than one physician shares such responsibility, or where a physician is acting on the attending physician's behalf, any such physician may act as the attending physician pursuant to this section. Where no physician has such responsibility, any physician who is familiar with the parent's, legal guardian's, legal custodian's or primary caretaker's medical condition may act as the attending physician pursuant to this section.

(d) "Debilitation" means a chronic and substantial inability to care for one's dependent infant, as a result of (i) a progressively chronic or irreversibly fatal illness, or (ii) a physically debilitating illness, disease or injury. "Debilitated" means the state of having a debilitation.

(e) "Incapacity" means a chronic and substantial inability, as a result of mental impairment, to understand the nature and consequences of decisions concerning the care of one's dependent infant, and a consequent inability to care for such infant. "Incapacitated" means the state of having an incapacity.

(f) "Administrative separation" means a parent, legal guardian, legal custodian or primary caretaker's (i) in connection with a federal immigration matter: arrest, detention, incarceration, removal and/or deportation; or (ii) receipt of official communication by federal, state, or local authorities regarding immigration enforcement which gives reasonable notice that care and supervision of the child by the parent, legal guardian, legal custodian, or primary caretaker will be interrupted or cannot be provided.

2. The provisions of this article relating to guardians shall apply to standby guardians, except insofar as this section provides otherwise.

3. (a) A petition for the judicial appointment of a standby guardian of the person and/or property of an infant pursuant to this subdivision may be made only by a parent, a legal guardian of the infant or a legal custodian of the infant; or where the infant is not residing with a parent, legal guardian or legal custodian and, to the satisfaction of the court, such parent, legal guardian or legal custodian cannot be located with due diligence, the primary caretaker of such infant may petition for a judicial appointment of such standby guardian. Application for standing to petition as a primary caretaker shall be upon motion to the court upon notice to such parties as the court may direct.

(b) A petition for the judicial appointment of a standby guardian of an infant shall, in addition to meeting the requirements of section seventeen hundred four of this article:

(i) State whether the authority of the standby guardian is to become effective upon the petitioner's incapacity, upon the petitioner's death, upon the petitioner's consent, or upon the petitioner's administrative separation accompanied by his or her consent required pursuant to the provisions of subdivision seven of this section, or upon whichever occurs first;

(ii) State that the petitioner suffers from (A) a progressively chronic illness; (B) an irreversibly fatal illness and the basis for such statement, such as the date and source of a medical diagnosis, without requiring the identification of the illness in question, or (C) state that the petitioner may become subject to administrative separation and the basis for such statement.

(c) Upon a petition for the judicial appointment of a standby guardian of an infant pursuant to paragraph (a) of this subdivision or for the judicial appointment of a guardian pursuant to paragraph (d) of subdivision four of this section, the court shall conduct a hearing. The court may in its discretion dispense with a hearing for the appointment of a standby guardian, and may in its discretion appoint a guardian ad litem or an attorney for the infant to recommend whether the appointment of a standby guardian as proposed in the application is in the best interest of the infant.

(d) (i) If the court finds that the petitioner suffers from a progressively chronic illness or an irreversibly fatal illness, or finds that the petitioner may become subject to administrative separation, and that the interests of the infant will be promoted by the appointment of a standby guardian of the person and/or property it must make a decree accordingly.

(ii) Such decree shall specify whether the authority of the standby guardian is effective upon the receipt of a determination of the petitioner's incapacity, upon the receipt of the certificate of the petitioner's death, or other such evidence of death that may be satisfactory to the court, or upon the receipt of documentation of the petitioner's administrative separation, and receipt of the petitioner's consent to the commencement of the standby guardian's authority required pursuant to the provisions of subdivision seven of this section, or upon whichever occurs first. The decree shall also provide that the authority of the standby guardian may earlier become effective upon written consent of the parent pursuant to subparagraph (iv) of paragraph (e) of this subdivision.

(iii) If at any time prior to the commencement of the authority of the standby guardian the court finds that the requirements of subparagraph (i) of this paragraph are no longer satisfied, it may rescind such decree.

(e) (i) Where the decree provides that the authority of the standby guardian is effective upon receipt of a determination of the petitioner's incapacity, the standby guardian's authority shall commence upon the standby guardian's receipt of a copy of a determination of incapacity made pursuant to subdivision six of this section. The standby guardian shall file a copy of the determination of incapacity with the court that issued the decree within ninety days of the date of receipt of such determination or the standby guardian's authority may be rescinded by the court.

(ii) Where the decree provides that the authority of the standby guardian is effective upon receipt of a certificate of the petitioner's death, or other such evidence of death that may be satisfactory to the court, the standby guardian's authority shall commence upon the standby guardian's receipt of a certificate of death, or other such evidence of death as may be specified in the decree. The standby guardian shall file the certificate of death, or other such evidence of death, with the court that issued the decree within ninety days of the date of the petitioner's death or the standby guardian's authority may be rescinded by the court.

(iii) Where the decree provides that the authority of the standby guardian is effective upon the standby guardian's receipt of documentation of the petitioner's administrative separation, the standby guardian's authority shall commence upon the standby guardian's receipt of documentation of the petitioner's administrative separation pursuant to subdivision seven of this section, and receipt of the petitioner's consent to the commencement of the standby guardian's authority as required pursuant to the provisions of subdivision seven of this section. The standby guardian shall file the documentation of administrative separation with the court that issued the decree within sixty days of the date of the standby guardian's receipt of documentation of the petitioner's administrative separation or the standby guardian's authority may be rescinded by the court.

(iv) Notwithstanding subparagraphs (i) and (ii) of this paragraph, a standby guardian's authority shall commence upon the standby guardian's receipt of the petitioner's written consent to such commencement, signed by the petitioner in the presence of two witnesses at least eighteen years of age, other than the standby guardian, who shall also sign the writing. Another person may sign the written consent on the petitioner's behalf and at the petitioner's direction if the petitioner is physically unable to do so, provided such consent is signed in the presence of the petitioner and the witnesses. The standby guardian shall file the written consent with the court that issued the decree within ninety days of the date of receipt of such written consent or the standby guardian's authority may be rescinded by the court.

(f) The petitioner may revoke a standby guardianship created under this subdivision by executing a written revocation, filing it with the court that issued the decree, and promptly notifying the standby guardian of the revocation.

(g) A person judicially appointed standby guardian pursuant to this subdivision may at any time before the commencement of his or her authority renounce the appointment by executing a written renunciation and filing it with the court that issued the decree, and promptly notifying the petitioner of the revocation.

4. (a) A parent, a legal guardian, a legal custodian, or primary caretaker under the circumstances described in paragraph (a) of subdivision three of this section or under circumstances described in subparagraph (i) of paragraph (b) of this subdivision may designate a standby guardian by means of a written designation, signed by the parent, legal guardian, legal custodian or primary caretaker in the presence of two witnesses at least eighteen years of age, other than the standby guardian, who shall also sign the writing. Another person may sign the written designation on the parent's, legal guardian's, legal custodian's or primary caretaker's behalf and at the parent's, legal guardian's, legal custodian's or primary caretaker's direction if the parent, legal guardian, legal custodian or primary caretaker is physically unable to do so, provided the designation is signed in the presence of the parent, legal guardian, legal custodian or primary caretaker and the witnesses.

(b) (i) A designation of a standby guardian shall identify the parent, legal guardian, legal custodian or primary caretaker, the infant and the person designated to be the standby guardian, and shall indicate that the parent, legal guardian, legal custodian or primary caretaker intends for the standby guardian to become the infant's guardian in the event the parent, legal guardian, legal custodian or primary caretaker either: (A) becomes incapacitated; (B) becomes debilitated and consents to the commencement of the standby guardian's authority; (C) becomes subject to an administrative separation and consents to the commencement of the standby guardian's authority as required pursuant to the provisions of subdivision seven of this section; or (D) dies prior to the commencement of a judicial proceeding to appoint a guardian of the person and/or property of an infant.

(ii) A parent, legal guardian, legal custodian or primary caretaker may designate an alternate standby guardian in the same writing, and by the same manner, as the designation of a standby guardian.

(iii) A designation may, but need not, be in the following form:

Designation of Standby Guardian

(NOTE: As used in this form, the term "parent" shall include a parent, a court-appointed guardian of an infant's person or property, a legal custodian, or a primary caretaker, and the term "child(ren)" shall include the dependant infant of a parent, court-appointed guardian, legal custodian or primary caretaker

I (name of parent) hereby designate (name, home address and telephone number of standby guardian) as standby guardian of the person and property of my child(ren) (name of child(ren)).

(You may, if you wish, provide that the standby guardian's authority shall extend only to the person, or only to the property, of your child, by crossing out "person" or "property", whichever is inapplicable, above.)

The appointment of _____ as the standby guardian of the person and property of my child(ren) would be in the best interests of my child(ren) because: (Insert justification for appointment of this person as the standby guardian)_____

_____

_____

The standby guardian's authority shall take effect: (1) if my doctor concludes in writing that I am mentally incapacitated, and thus unable to care for my child(ren); (2) if my doctor concludes in writing that I am physically debilitated, and thus unable to care for my child(ren) and I consent in writing, before two witnesses, to the standby guardian's authority taking effect; (3) If I become subject to an administrative separation such that care and supervision of the child will be interrupted or cannot be provided; or (4) upon my death.

In the event the person I designate above is unable or unwilling to act as guardian for my child(ren), I hereby designate (name, home address and telephone number of alternate standby guardian), as standby guardian of my child(ren).

I also understand that my standby guardian's authority will cease sixty days after commencing unless by such date he or she petitions the court for appointment as guardian.

I understand that I retain full parental, guardianship, custodial or caretaker rights even after the commencement of the standby guardian's authority, and may revoke the standby guardianship at any time.

Signature: _____

Address: _____

Date: _____

I declare that the person whose name appears above signed this document in my presence, or was physically unable to sign and asked another to sign this document, who did so in my presence. I further declare that I am at least eighteen years old and am not the person designated as standby guardian.

Witness' Signature: _____

Address: _____

Date: _____

Witness' Signature: _____

Address: _____

Date: _____

(iv) Notwithstanding paragraphs (a) and (b) of this subdivision, a designation of standby guardian shall be effective as if made in accordance with the requirements of this subdivision if it was validly made: (a) where the parent, legal guardian, legal custodian or primary caretaker was domiciled at the time it was executed; (b) in the jurisdiction where it was executed or (c) where the parent, legal guardian, legal custodian or primary caretaker is domiciled at the time the designation becomes effective.

(c) The authority of the standby guardian under a designation shall commence upon either: (i) the standby guardian's receipt of a copy of a determination of incapacity made pursuant to subdivision six of this section; (ii) the standby guardian's receipt of (A) a copy of a determination of debilitation made pursuant to subdivision six of this section and (B) a copy of the parent's, legal guardian's, legal custodian's or primary caretaker's written consent to such commencement, signed by the parent, legal guardian, legal custodian or primary caretaker in the presence of two witnesses at least eighteen years of age, other than the standby guardian, who shall also sign the writing. Another person may sign the written consent on the parent's, legal guardian's, legal custodian's or primary caretaker's behalf and at the parent's, legal guardian's, legal custodian's or primary caretaker's direction if the parent, legal guardian, legal custodian or primary caretaker is physically unable to do so, provided such consent is signed in the presence of the parent, legal guardian, legal custodian or primary caretaker and the witnesses; (iii) an administrative separation and consent as required pursuant to the provisions of subdivision seven of this section or (iv) the standby guardian's receipt of a certificate of death, funeral home receipt or other such document indicating that the parent, legal guardian, legal custodian or primary caretaker has died. The standby guardian shall file a petition pursuant to paragraph (d) of this subdivision within sixty days of the date of its commencement pursuant to this paragraph or such standby guardian's authority shall cease after such date, but shall recommence upon such filing.

(d) The standby guardian may file a petition for appointment as guardian after receipt of either: (i) a copy of a determination of incapacity made pursuant to subdivision six of this section; or (ii) (A) a copy of a determination of debilitation made pursuant to subdivision six of this section and (B) a copy of the parent's, legal guardian's, legal custodian's or primary caretaker's written consent, pursuant to paragraph (c) of this subdivision; (iii) documentation of an administrative separation and consent as required pursuant to the provisions of subdivision seven of this section; or (iv) a certificate of death, or other such evidence of death that may be satisfactory to the court. Such petition must, in addition to meeting the requirements of section seventeen hundred four of this article:

(i) append the written designation of such person as standby guardian; and

(ii) append a copy of: (A) the determination of incapacity of the parent, legal guardian, legal custodian or primary caretaker; or (B) the determination of debilitation and the parental, guardian's, custodian's or caretaker's consent; (C) documentation of an administrative separation and consent as required pursuant to the provisions of subdivision seven of this section; or (D) a copy of the parent's, legal guardian's, legal custodian's or primary caretaker's death certificate, or other such evidence of death that may be satisfactory to the court; and

(iii) if the petition is by a person designated as alternate standby guardian, state that the person designated as standby guardian is unwilling or unable to act as standby guardian, and the basis for such statement.

(e) Subject to the provisions of paragraph (c) of subdivision three of this section, if the court finds that the petitioner was duly designated as standby guardian, that the parent, legal guardian, legal custodian or primary caretaker of the infant is (i) incapacitated, (ii) debilitated and consents, (iii) has become subject to an administrative separation and consents as required pursuant to the provisions of subdivision seven of this section, or (iv) has died, as established by a copy of a death certificate or other such evidence of death as may be satisfactory to the court, that the interests of the infant will be promoted by the appointment of a standby guardian of the person and/or property, and that, if the petition is by a person designated as alternate standby guardian, the person designated as standby guardian is unwilling or unable to act as standby guardian, it must make a decree accordingly. Prior to making its finding, the court may, in its discretion, appoint an attorney for the infant to recommend whether the appointment of the standby guardian as proposed in the petition is in the best interests of the infant.

(f) The parent, legal guardian, legal custodian or primary caretaker may revoke a standby guardianship created under this subdivision: (i) by executing a subsequent designation of guardianship pursuant to paragraphs (a) and (b) of this subdivision, or (ii) notwithstanding the provisions of sections seventeen hundred ten and seventeen hundred eleven of this article, in the case of a standby guardian whose authority becomes effective upon the death of the parent, legal guardian, legal custodian or primary caretaker of the infant, by a subsequent designation of standby guardian set forth in a will of the parent, legal guardian, legal custodian or primary caretaker, or (iii) by notifying the standby guardian verbally or in writing or by any other act evidencing a specific intent to revoke the standby guardianship prior to the filing of a petition. Where the petition has already been filed, by executing a written revocation, filing it with the court where the petition was filed, and promptly notifying the standby guardian of the revocation.

5. The standby guardian may also file a petition for appointment as guardian in any other manner permitted by this article or article six of the family court act, on notice to the parent, legal guardian, legal custodian or primary caretaker and may append a designation of standby guardian to the petition for consideration by the court in the determination of such petition.

6. (a) A determination of incapacity or debilitation must: (i) be made by the attending physician to a reasonable degree of medical certainty; (ii) be in writing; and (iii) contain the attending physician's opinion regarding the cause and nature of the parent's, legal guardian's, legal custodian's or primary caretaker's incapacity or debilitation as well as its extent and probable duration. The attending physician shall provide a copy of the determination of incapacity or debilitation to the standby guardian, if the standby guardian's identity is known to the physician.

(b) If requested by the standby guardian, an attending physician shall make a determination regarding the parent's, legal guardian's, legal custodian's or primary caretaker's incapacity or debilitation for purposes of this section.

(c) The standby guardian shall ensure that the parent, legal guardian, legal custodian or primary caretaker is informed of the commencement of the standby guardian's authority as a result of a determination of incapacity and of the parent's, legal guardian's, legal custodian's or primary caretaker's right to revoke such authority promptly after receipt of the determination of incapacity, provided there is any indication of the person's ability to comprehend such information.

7. Documentation of an administrative separation (a) shall consist of an administrative

order, judicial order, affidavit or affirmation indicating the parent, legal guardian, legal custodian or primary caretaker's administrative separation as defined in this section and (b) shall be accompanied by written consent of the parent, legal guardian, legal custodian, or primary caretaker, signed by the parent, legal guardian, legal custodian, or primary caretaker in the presence of two witnesses at least eighteen years of age, other than the standby guardian, who shall also sign the writing. Consent contained in the formal petition submitted pursuant to subdivision three of this section or the written designation made pursuant to subdivision four of this section shall be sufficient to satisfy the requirement for consent set forth in this subdivision.

8. The commencement of the standby guardian's authority pursuant to a determination of incapacity, determination of debilitation, administrative separation, or consent shall not, itself, divest the parent, legal guardian, legal custodian or primary caretaker of any parental, guardianship, custodial or caretaker rights, but shall confer upon the standby guardian concurrent authority with respect to the infant.

9. (a) The clerk of any county upon being paid the fees allowed therefor by law shall receive for filing any instrument appointing or designating a standby guardian pursuant to this section made by a domiciliary of the county, and shall give a written receipt therefor to the person delivering it. The filing of an appointment or designation of standby guardian shall be for the sole purpose of safekeeping and shall not affect the validity of the appointment or designation.

(b) The appointment or designation shall be delivered only to: (i) the parent, legal guardian, legal custodian or primary caretaker who appointed or designated the standby guardian; (ii) the standby guardian or alternate standby guardian; (iii) the person designated as standby guardian or alternate standby guardian; or (iv) any other person directed by the court.

History: Add, L 1992, ch 290, § 1, eff June 30, 1992; amd, L 1994, ch 478, eff July 20, 1994; L 2000, ch 477, §§ 7–9, eff Nov 19, 2000; L 2003, ch 632, § 1, eff Jan 1, 2004; L 2007, ch 71, §§ 1, 2, eff June 4, 2007; L 2018, ch 79, § 1, eff June 27, 2018.

§ 1727. Petition for termination of account of guardian, committee, or conservator

Where a guardian, committee or conservator is presently maintaining an account on behalf of an infant, incompetent, conservatee or person under disability in an amount not exceeding $10,000.00, which account was established prior to the effective date of this section, the guardian, committee or conservator may petition the court in the county having jurisdiction over said account for an order authorizing the termination of the account and payment of the balance of the account to a parent of such person or to some competent adult with whom such person resides or who has some interest in such person's welfare for the use and benefit of such person.

History: Add, L 1993, ch 514, § 38, eff Jan 1, 1994.

ARTICLE 17-A
GUARDIANS OF PERSONS WHO ARE INTELLECTUALLY DISABLED AND DEVELOPMENTALLY DISABLED*

SUMMARY OF ARTICLE

§ 1750. Guardianship of persons who are intellectually disabled

When it shall appear to the satisfaction of the court that a person is a person who is intellectually disabled, the court is authorized to appoint a guardian of the person or of the property or of both if such appointment of a guardian or guardians is in the best interest of the person who is intellectually disabled. Such appointment shall be made pursuant to the provisions of this article, provided however that the provisions of section seventeen hundred fifty-a of this article shall not apply to the appointment of a guardian or guardians of a person who is intellectually disabled.

     1. For the purposes of this article, a person who is intellectually disabled is a person who has been certified by one licensed physician and one licensed psychologist, or by two licensed physicians at least one of whom is familiar with or has professional knowledge in the care and treatment of persons with an intellectual disability, having qualifications to make such certification, as being incapable to manage him or herself and/or his or her affairs by reason of intellectual disability and that such condition is permanent in nature or likely to continue indefinitely.

     2. Every such certification pursuant to subdivision one of this section, made on or after the effective date of this subdivision, shall include a specific determination by such physician and psychologist, or by such physicians, as to whether the person who is intellectually disabled has the capacity to make health care decisions, as defined by subdivision three of section twenty-nine hundred eighty of the public health law, for himself or herself. A determination that the person who is intellectually disabled has the capacity to make health care decisions shall not preclude the appointment of a guardian pursuant to this section to make other decisions on behalf of the person who is

---

* Amd, L 2016, ch 198, eff July 21, 2016.

intellectually disabled. The absence of this determination in the case of guardians appointed prior to the effective date of this subdivision shall not preclude such guardians from making health care decisions.

History: Add, L 1989, ch 675, § 2; amd, L 2002, ch 500, § 2, eff March 16, 2003, applying to certifications of mental retardation and the capacity to make health care decisions occurring on or after such effective date; L 2016, ch 198, § 2, eff July 21, 2016.

§ 1750-a. Guardianship of persons who are developmentally disabled

1. When it shall appear to the satisfaction of the court that a person is a person who is developmentally disabled, the court is authorized to appoint a guardian of the person or of the property or of both if such appointment of a guardian or guardians is in the best interest of the person who is developmentally disabled. Such appointments shall be made pursuant to the provisions of this article, provided however that the provisions of section seventeen hundred fifty of this article shall not apply to the appointment of a guardian or guardians of a person who is developmentally disabled. For the purposes of this article, a person who is developmentally disabled is a person who has been certified by one licensed physician and one licensed psychologist, or by two licensed physicians at least one of whom is familiar with or has professional knowledge in the care and treatment of persons with developmental disabilities, having qualifications to make such certification, as having an impaired ability to understand and appreciate the nature and consequences of decisions which result in such person being incapable of managing himself or herself and/or his or her affairs by reason of developmental disability and that such condition is permanent in nature or likely to continue indefinitely, and whose disability:

(a) is attributable to cerebral palsy, epilepsy, neurological impairment, autism or traumatic head injury;

(b) is attributable to any other condition of a person found to be closely related to intellectual disability because such condition results in similar impairment of general intellectual functioning or adaptive behavior to that of persons with intellectual disabilities; or

(c) is attributable to dyslexia resulting from a disability described in subdivision one or two of this section or from intellectual disability; and

(d) originates before such person attains age twenty-two, provided, however, that no such age of origination shall apply for the purposes of this article to a person with traumatic head injury.

2. Notwithstanding any provision of law to the contrary, for the purposes of subdivision two of section seventeen hundred fifty and section seventeen hundred fifty-b of this article, "a person who is intellectually disabled and his or her guardian" shall also mean a person and his or her guardian appointed pursuant to this section; provided that such person has been certified by the physicians and/or psychologists, specified in subdivision one of this section, as (i) having an intellectual disability, or (ii) having a developmental disability, as defined in section 1.03 of the mental hygiene law, which (A) includes intellectual disability, or (B) results in a similar impairment of general intellectual functioning or adaptive behavior so that such person is incapable of managing himself or herself, and/or his or her affairs by reason of such developmental disability.

History: Add, L 1989, ch 675, § 2; amd, L 1990, ch 269, eff June 24, 1990; L 2005, ch

744, § 1, eff Oct 18, 2005; L 2016, ch 198, § 3, eff July 21, 2016.

§ 1750-b. Health care decisions for persons who are intellectually disabled

1. Scope of authority. Unless specifically prohibited by the court after consideration of the determination, if any, regarding a person who is intellectually disabled's capacity to make health care decisions, which is required by section seventeen hundred fifty of this article, the guardian of such person appointed pursuant to section seventeen hundred fifty of this article shall have the authority to make any and all health care decisions, as defined by subdivision six of section twenty-nine hundred eighty of the public health law, on behalf of the person who is intellectually disabled that such person could make if such person had capacity. Such decisions may include decisions to withhold or withdraw life-sustaining treatment. For purposes of this section, "life-sustaining treatment" means medical treatment, including cardiopulmonary resuscitation and nutrition and hydration provided by means of medical treatment, which is sustaining life functions and without which, according to reasonable medical judgment, the patient will die within a relatively short time period. Cardiopulmonary resuscitation is presumed to be life-sustaining treatment without the necessity of a medical judgment by an attending physician. The provisions of this article are not intended to permit or promote suicide, assisted suicide or euthanasia; accordingly, nothing in this section shall be construed to permit a guardian to consent to any act or omission to which the person who is intellectually disabled could not consent if such person had capacity.

(a) For the purposes of making a decision to withhold or withdraw life-sustaining treatment pursuant to this section, in the case of a person for whom no guardian has been appointed pursuant to section seventeen hundred fifty or seventeen hundred fifty-a of this article, a "guardian" shall also mean a family member of a person who (i) has intellectual disability, or (ii) has a developmental disability, as defined in section 1.03 of the mental hygiene law, which (A) includes intellectual disability, or (B) results in a similar impairment of general intellectual functioning or adaptive behavior so that such person is incapable of managing himself or herself, and/or his or her affairs by reason of such developmental disability. Qualified family members shall be included in a prioritized list of said family members pursuant to regulations established by the commissioner of the office for people with developmental disabilities. Such family members must have a significant and ongoing involvement in a person's life so as to have sufficient knowledge of their needs and, when reasonably known or ascertainable, the person's wishes, including moral and religious beliefs. In the case of a person who was a resident of the former Willowbrook state school on March seventeenth, nineteen hundred seventy-two and those individuals who were in community care status on that date and subsequently returned to Willowbrook or a related facility, who are fully represented by the consumer advisory board and who have no guardians appointed pursuant to this article or have no qualified family members to make such a decision, then a "guardian" shall also mean the Willowbrook consumer advisory board. A decision of such family member or the Willowbrook consumer advisory board to withhold or withdraw life-sustaining treatment shall be subject to all of the protections, procedures and safeguards which apply to the decision of a guardian to withhold or withdraw life-sustaining treatment pursuant to this section.

In the case of a person for whom no guardian has been appointed pursuant to this article or for whom there is no qualified family member or the Willowbrook consumer advisory board available to make such a decision, a "guardian" shall also mean, notwithstanding the definitions in section 80.03 of the mental hygiene law, a surrogate decision-making committee, as defined in article eighty of the mental hygiene law. All declarations and procedures, including expedited procedures, to comply with this section shall be established by regulations promulgated by the commission on quality of care and advocacy for persons with disabilities.

(b) Regulations establishing the prioritized list of qualified family members required by paragraph (a) of this subdivision shall be developed by the commissioner of the office for people with developmental disabilities in conjunction with parents, advocates and family members of persons who are intellectually disabled. Regulations to implement the authority of the Willowbrook consumer advisory board pursuant to paragraph (a) of this subdivision may be promulgated by the commissioner of the office for people with developmental disabilities with advice from the Willowbrook consumer advisory board.

(c) Notwithstanding any provision of law to the contrary, the formal determinations required pursuant to section seventeen hundred fifty of this article shall only apply to guardians appointed pursuant to section seventeen hundred fifty or seventeen hundred fifty-a of this article.

2. Decision-making standard. (a) The guardian shall base all advocacy and health care decision-making solely and exclusively on the best interests of the person who is intellectually disabled and, when reasonably known or ascertainable with reasonable diligence, on the person who is intellectually disabled's wishes, including moral and religious beliefs.

(b) An assessment of the person who is intellectually disabled's best interests shall include consideration of:

(i) the dignity and uniqueness of every person;

(ii) the preservation, improvement or restoration of the person who is intellectually disabled's health;

(iii) the relief of the person who is intellectually disabled's suffering by means of palliative care and pain management;

(iv) the unique nature of artificially provided nutrition or hydration, and the effect it may have on the person who is intellectually disabled; and

(v) the entire medical condition of the person.

(c) No health care decision shall be influenced in any way by:

(i) a presumption that persons who are intellectually disabled are not entitled to the full and equal rights, equal protection, respect, medical care and dignity afforded to persons without an intellectual disability or a developmental disability; or

(ii) financial considerations of the guardian, as such considerations affect the guardian, a health care provider or any other party.

3. Right to receive information. Subject to the provisions of sections 33.13 and 33.16 of the mental hygiene law, the guardian shall have the right to receive all medical information and medical and clinical records necessary to make informed decisions regarding the person who is intellectually disabled's health care.

4. Life-sustaining treatment. The guardian shall have the affirmative obligation to advocate for the full and efficacious provision of health care, including life-sustaining treatment. In the event that a guardian makes a decision to withdraw or withhold life-sustaining treatment from a person who is intellectually disabled:

(a) The attending physician, as defined in subdivision two of section twenty-nine hundred eighty of the public health law, must confirm to a reasonable degree of medical certainty that the person who is intellectually disabled lacks capacity to make health care decisions. The determination thereof shall be included in the person who is intellectually disabled's medical record, and shall contain such attending physician's opinion regarding the cause and nature of the person who is intellectually disabled's incapacity as well as its extent and probable duration. The attending physician who makes the confirmation shall consult with another physician, or a licensed psychologist, to further confirm the person who is intellectually disabled's lack of capacity. The attending physician who makes the confirmation, or the physician or licensed psychologist with whom the attending physician consults, must (i) be employed by a developmental disabilities services office named in section 13.17 of the mental hygiene law or employed by the office for people with developmental disabilities to provide treatment and care to people with developmental disabilities, or (ii) have been employed for a minimum of two years to render care and service in a facility or program operated, licensed or authorized by the office for people with developmental disabilities, or (iii) have been approved by the commissioner of the office for people with developmental disabilities in accordance with regulations promulgated by such commissioner. Such regulations shall require that a physician or licensed psychologist possess specialized training or three years experience in treating intellectual disability. A record of such consultation shall be included in the person who is intellectually disabled's medical record.

(b) The attending physician, as defined in subdivision two of section twenty-nine hundred eighty of the public health law, with the concurrence of another physician with whom such attending physician shall consult, must determine to a reasonable degree of medical certainty and note on the person who is intellectually disabled's chart that:

(i) the person who is intellectually disabled has a medical condition as follows:

A. a terminal condition, as defined in subdivision twenty-three of section twenty-nine hundred sixty-one of the public health law; or

B. permanent unconsciousness; or

C. a medical condition other than such person's intellectual disability which requires life-sustaining treatment, is irreversible and which will continue indefinitely; and

(ii) the life-sustaining treatment would impose an extraordinary burden on such person, in light of:

A. such person's medical condition, other than such person's intellectual disability; and

B. the expected outcome of the life-sustaining treatment, notwithstanding such person's intellectual disability; and

(iii) in the case of a decision to withdraw or withhold artificially provided nutrition or hydration:

    A. there is no reasonable hope of maintaining life; or

    B. the artificially provided nutrition or hydration poses an extraordinary burden.

(c) The guardian shall express a decision to withhold or withdraw life-sustaining treatment either:

    (i) in writing, dated and signed in the presence of one witness eighteen years of age or older who shall sign the decision, and presented to the attending physician, as defined in subdivision two of section twenty-nine hundred eighty of the public health law; or

    (ii) orally, to two persons eighteen years of age or older, at least one of whom is the person who is intellectually disabled's attending physician, as defined in subdivision two of section twenty-nine hundred eighty of the public health law.

(d) The attending physician, as defined in subdivision two of section twenty-nine hundred eighty of the public health law, who is provided with the decision of a guardian shall include the decision in the person who is intellectually disabled's medical chart, and shall either:

    (i) promptly issue an order to withhold or withdraw life-sustaining treatment from the person who is intellectually disabled, and inform the staff responsible for such person's care, if any, of the order; or

    (ii) promptly object to such decision, in accordance with subdivision five of this section.

(e) At least forty-eight hours prior to the implementation of a decision to withdraw life-sustaining treatment, or at the earliest possible time prior to the implementation of a decision to withhold life-sustaining treatment, the attending physician shall notify:

    (i) the person who is intellectually disabled, except if the attending physician determines, in writing and in consultation with another physician or a licensed psychologist, that, to a reasonable degree of medical certainty, the person would suffer immediate and severe injury from such notification. The attending physician who makes the confirmation, or the physician or licensed psychologist with whom the attending physician consults, shall:

    A. be employed by a developmental disabilities services office named in section 13.17 of the mental hygiene law or employed by the office for people with developmental disabilities to provide treatment and care to people with developmental disabilities, or

    B. have been employed for a minimum of two years to render care and service in a facility operated, licensed or authorized by the office for people with developmental disabilities, or

    C. have been approved by the commissioner of the office for people with developmental disabilities in accordance with regulations promulgated by such commissioner. Such regulations shall require that a physician or licensed psychologist possess specialized training or three years experience in treating intellectual disability. A record of such consultation shall be included in the person who is intellectually disabled's medical record;

(ii) if the person is in or was transferred from a residential facility operated, licensed or authorized by the office for people with developmental disabilities, the chief executive officer of the agency or organization operating such facility and the mental hygiene legal service; and

(iii) if the person is not in and was not transferred from such a facility or program, the commissioner of the office for people with developmental disabilities, or his or her designee.

5. Objection to health care decision. (a) Suspension. A health care decision made pursuant to subdivision four of this section shall be suspended, pending judicial review, except if the suspension would in reasonable medical judgment be likely to result in the death of the person who is intellectually disabled, in the event of an objection to that decision at any time by:

(i) the person who is intellectually disabled on whose behalf such decision was made; or

(ii) a parent or adult sibling who either resides with or has maintained substantial and continuous contact with the person who is intellectually disabled; or

(iii) the attending physician, as defined in subdivision two of section twenty-nine hundred eighty of the public health law; or

(iv) any other health care practitioner providing services to the person who is intellectually disabled, who is licensed pursuant to article one hundred thirty-one, one hundred thirty-one-B, one hundred thirty-two, one hundred thirty-three, one hundred thirty-six, one hundred thirty-nine, one hundred forty-one, one hundred forty-three, one hundred forty-four, one hundred fifty-three, one hundred fifty-four, one hundred fifty-six, one hundred fifty-nine or one hundred sixty-four of the education law; or

(v) the chief executive officer identified in subparagraph (ii) of paragraph (e) of subdivision four of this section; or

(vi) if the person is in or was transferred from a residential facility or program operated, approved or licensed by the office for people with developmental disabilities, the mental hygiene legal service; or

(vii) if the person is not in and was not transferred from such a facility or program, the commissioner of the office for people with developmental disabilities, or his or her designee.

(b) Form of objection. Such objection shall occur orally or in writing.

(c) Notification. In the event of the suspension of a health care decision pursuant to this subdivision, the objecting party shall promptly notify the guardian and the other parties identified in paragraph (a) of this subdivision, and the attending physician shall record such suspension in the person who is intellectually disabled's medical chart.

(d) Dispute mediation. In the event of an objection pursuant to this subdivision, at the request of the objecting party or person or entity authorized to act as a guardian under this section, except a surrogate decision making committee established pursuant to article eighty of the mental hygiene law, such objection shall be referred to a dispute mediation system, established pursuant to section two thousand nine hundred seventy-two of the public health law or similar entity for mediating disputes in a hospice, such as a patient's advocate's office, hospital chaplain's office or ethics committee, as described in writing and adopted by the governing authority of such hospice, for non-binding mediation. In the event that such dispute cannot be resolved within seventy-two hours or no such mediation entity exists or is reasonably available for mediation of a dispute, the objection shall proceed to judicial review pursuant to this subdivision. The party requesting mediation shall provide notification to those parties entitled to notice pursuant to paragraph (a) of this subdivision.

6. Special proceeding authorized. The guardian, the attending physician, as defined in subdivision two of section twenty-nine hundred eighty of the public health law, the chief executive officer identified in subparagraph (ii) of paragraph (e) of subdivision four of this section, the mental hygiene legal service (if the person is in or was transferred from a residential facility or program operated, approved or licensed by the office for people with developmental disabilities) or the commissioner of the office for people with developmental disabilities or his or her designee (if the person is not in and was not transferred from such a facility or program) may commence a special proceeding in a court of competent jurisdiction with respect to any dispute arising under this section, including objecting to the withdrawal or withholding of life-sustaining treatment because such withdrawal or withholding is not in accord with the criteria set forth in this section.

7. Provider's obligations. (a) A health care provider shall comply with the health care decisions made by a guardian in good faith pursuant to this section, to the same extent as if such decisions had been made by the person who is intellectually disabled, if such person had capacity.

(b) Notwithstanding paragraph (a) of this subdivision, nothing in this section shall be construed to require a private hospital to honor a guardian's health care decision that the hospital would not honor if the decision had been made by the person who is intellectually disabled, if such person had capacity, because the decision is contrary to a formally adopted written policy of the hospital expressly based on religious beliefs or sincerely held moral convictions central to the hospital's operating principles, and the hospital would be permitted by law to refuse to honor the decision if made by such person, provided:

(i) the hospital has informed the guardian of such policy prior to or upon admission, if reasonably possible; and

(ii) the person who is intellectually disabled is transferred promptly to another hospital that is reasonably accessible under the circumstances and is willing to honor the guardian's decision. If the guardian is unable or unwilling to arrange such a transfer, the hospital's refusal to honor the decision of the guardian shall constitute an objection pursuant to subdivision five of this section.

(c) Notwithstanding paragraph (a) of this subdivision, nothing in this section shall be construed to require an individual health care provider to honor a guardian's health care decision that the individual would not honor if the decision had been made by the person who is intellectually disabled, if such person had capacity, because the decision is contrary to the individual's religious beliefs or sincerely held moral convictions, provided the individual health care provider promptly informs the guardian and the facility, if any, of his or her refusal to honor the guardian's decision. In such event, the facility shall promptly transfer responsibility for the person who is intellectually disabled to another individual health care provider willing to honor the guardian's decision. The individual health care provider shall cooperate in facilitating such transfer of the patient.

(d) Notwithstanding the provisions of any other paragraph of this subdivision, if a guardian directs the provision of life-sustaining treatment, the denial of which in reasonable medical judgment would be likely to result in the death of the person who is intellectually disabled, a hospital or individual health care provider that does not wish to provide such treatment shall nonetheless comply with the guardian's decision pending either transfer of the person who is intellectually disabled to a willing hospital or individual health care provider, or judicial review.

(e) Nothing in this section shall affect or diminish the authority of a surrogate decision-making panel to render decisions regarding major medical treatment pursuant to article eighty of the mental hygiene law.

8. Immunity. (a) Provider immunity. No health care provider or employee thereof shall be subjected to criminal or civil liability, or be deemed to have engaged in unprofessional conduct, for honoring reasonably and in good faith a health care decision by a guardian, or for other actions taken reasonably and in good faith pursuant to this section.

(b) Guardian immunity. No guardian shall be subjected to criminal or civil liability for making a health care decision reasonably and in good faith pursuant to this section.

History: Add, L 2002, ch 500, § 3, eff March 16, 2003; amd, L 2003, ch 232, § 1, eff July 29, 2003; L 2007, ch 105, § 1, eff Dec 30, 2007; L 2008, ch 262, § 1, eff Jan 3, 2009; L 2009, ch 12, § 1, eff April 7, 2009; L 2010, ch 8, § 27, eff March 16, 2010; L 2012, ch 56, § 18 (Part J), eff March 30, 2012; L 2016, ch 198, § 4, eff July 21, 2016.

§ 1751. Petition for appointment; by whom made

A petition for the appointment of a guardian of the person or property, or both, of a person who is intellectually disabled or a person who is developmentally disabled may be made by a parent, any interested person eighteen years of age or older on behalf of the person who is intellectually disabled or a person who is developmentally disabled including a corporation authorized to serve as a guardian as provided for by this article, or by the person who is intellectually disabled or a person who is developmentally disabled when such person is eighteen years of age or older.

History: Add, L 1989, ch 675, § 2, eff Jan 1, 1990; amd, L 2016, ch 198, § 5, eff July 21, 2016.

§ 1752. Petition for appointment; contents

The petition for the appointment of a guardian shall be filed with the court on forms to be prescribed by the state chief administrator of the courts. Such petition for a guardian of a person who is intellectually disabled or a person who is developmentally disabled shall include, but not be limited to, the following information:

1. the full name, date of birth and residence of the person who is intellectually disabled or a person who is developmentally disabled;

2. the name, age, address and relationship or interest of the petitioner to the person who is intellectually disabled or a person who is developmentally disabled;

3. the names of the parents, children, adult siblings if eighteen years of age or older, the spouse and primary care physician if other than a physician having submitted a certification with the petition, if any, of the person who is intellectually disabled or a person who is developmentally disabled and whether or not they are living, and if living, their addresses and the names and addresses of the nearest distributees of full age who are domiciliaries, if both parents are dead;

4. the name and address of the person with whom the person who is intellectually disabled or a person who is developmentally disabled resides if other than the parents or spouse;

5. the name, age, address, education and other qualifications, and consent of the proposed guardian, standby and alternate guardian, if other than the parent, spouse, adult child if eighteen years of age or older or adult sibling if eighteen years of age or older, and if such parent, spouse or adult child be living, why any of them should not be appointed guardian;

6. the estimated value of real and personal property and the annual income therefrom and any other income including governmental entitlements to which the person who is intellectually disabled or person who is developmentally disabled is entitled; and

7. any circumstances which the court should consider in determining whether it is in the best interests of the person who is intellectually disabled or person who is developmentally disabled to not be present at the hearing if conducted.

History: Add, L 1989, ch 675, § 2, eff Jan 1, 1990; amd, L 2016, ch 198, § 6, eff July 21, 2016; L 2019, ch 420, § 6, eff Oct 29, 2019.

§ 1753. Persons to be served

1. Upon presentation of the petition, process shall issue to:

(a) the parent or parents, adult children, if the petitioner is other than a parent, adult siblings, if the petitioner is other than a parent, and if the person who is intellectually disabled or person who is developmentally disabled is married, to the spouse, if their residences are known;

(b) the person having care and custody of the person who is intellectually disabled or person who is developmentally disabled, or with whom such person resides if other than the parents or spouse; and

(c) the person who is intellectually disabled or person who is developmentally disabled if fourteen years of age or older for whom an application has been made in such person's behalf.

2. Upon presentation of the petition, notice of such petition shall be served by certified mail to:

(a) the adult siblings if the petitioner is a parent, and adult children if the petitioner is a parent;

(b) the mental hygiene legal service in the judicial department where the facility, as defined in subdivision (a) of section 47.01 of the mental hygiene law, is located if the person who is intellectually disabled or person who is developmentally disabled resides in such a facility;

(c) in all cases, to the director in charge of a facility licensed or operated by an agency of the state of New York, if the person who is intellectually disabled or person who is developmentally disabled resides in such facility;

(d) one other person if designated in writing by the person who is intellectually disabled or person who is developmentally disabled; and

(e) such other persons as the court may deem proper.

3. No process or notice shall be necessary to a parent, adult child, adult sibling, or spouse of the person who is intellectually disabled or person who is developmentally disabled who has been declared by a court as being incompetent. In addition, no process or notice shall be necessary to a spouse who is divorced from the person who is intellectually disabled or person who is developmentally disabled, and to a parent, adult child, adult sibling when it shall appear to the satisfaction of the court that such person or persons have abandoned the person who is intellectually disabled or person who is developmentally disabled.

> **History:** Add, L 1989, ch 675, § 2, eff Jan 1, 1990; amd, L 2016, ch 198, § 7, eff July 21, 2016.

§ 1754. Hearing and trial

1. Upon a petition for the appointment of a guardian of a person who is intellectually disabled or person who is developmentally disabled eighteen years of age or older, the court shall conduct a hearing at which such person shall have the right to jury trial. The right to a jury trial shall be deemed waived by failure to make a demand therefor. The court may in its discretion dispense with a hearing for the appointment of a guardian, and may in its discretion appoint a guardian ad litem, or the mental hygiene legal service if such person is a resident of a mental hygiene facility as defined in subdivision (a) of section 47.01 of the mental hygiene law, to recommend whether the appointment of a guardian as proposed in the application is in the best interest of the person who is intellectually disabled or person who is developmentally disabled, provided however, that such application has been made by:

(a) both parents or the survivor; or

(b) one parent and the consent of the other parent; or

(c) any interested party and the consent of each parent.

2. When it shall appear to the satisfaction of the court that a parent or parents not joining in or consenting to the application have abandoned the person who is intellectually disabled or person who is developmentally disabled or are not otherwise required to receive notice, the court may dispense with such parent's consent in determining the need to conduct a hearing for a person under the age of eighteen. However, if the consent of both parents or the surviving parent is dispensed with by the court, a hearing shall be held on the application.

3. If a hearing is conducted, the person who is intellectually disabled or person who is developmentally disabled shall be present unless it shall appear to the satisfaction of the court on the certification of the certifying physician that the person who is intellectually disabled or person who is developmentally disabled is medically incapable of being present to the extent that attendance is likely to result in physical harm to such person who is intellectually disabled or person who is developmentally disabled, or under such other circumstances which the court finds would not be in the best interest of the person who is intellectually disabled or person who is developmentally disabled.

4. If either a hearing is dispensed with pursuant to subdivisions one and two of this section or the person who is intellectually disabled or person who is developmentally disabled is not present at the hearing pursuant to subdivision three of this section, the court may appoint a guardian ad litem if no mental hygiene legal service attorney is authorized to act on behalf of the person who is intellectually disabled or person who is developmentally disabled. The guardian ad litem or mental hygiene legal service attorney, if appointed, shall personally interview the person who is intellectually disabled or person who is developmentally disabled and shall submit a written report to the court.

5. If, upon conclusion of such hearing or jury trial or if none be held upon the application, the court is satisfied that the best interests of the person who is intellectually disabled or person who is developmentally disabled will be promoted by the appointment of a guardian of the person or property, or both, it shall make a decree naming such person or persons to serve as such guardians.

> **History:** Add, L 1989, ch 675, § 2, eff Jan 1, 1990; amd, L 2016, ch 198, § 8, eff July 21, 2016.

§ 1755. Modification order

Any person who is intellectually disabled or person who is developmentally disabled eighteen years of age or older, or any person on behalf of any person who is intellectually disabled or person who is developmental* disabled for whom a guardian has been appointed, may apply to the court having jurisdiction over the guardianship order requesting modification of such order in order to protect the person who is intellectually disabled's, or person who is developmentally disabled's financial situation and/or his or her personal interests. The court may, upon receipt of any such request to modify the guardianship order, appoint a guardian ad litem. The court shall so modify the guardianship order if in its judgment the interests of the guardian are adverse to those of the person who is intellectually disabled or person who is developmentally disabled or if the interests of justice will be best served including, but not limited to, facts showing the necessity for protecting the personal and/or financial interests of the person who is intellectually disabled or person who is developmentally disabled.

> **History:** Add, L 1989, ch 675, § 2, eff Jan 1, 1990; amd, L 2016, ch 198, § 9, eff July 21, 2016.

§ 1756. Limited guardian of the property

When it shall appear to the satisfaction of the court that such person who is intellectually disabled or person who is developmentally disabled for whom an application for guardianship is made is eighteen years of age or older and is wholly or substantially self-supporting by means of his or her wages or earnings from employment, the court is authorized and empowered to appoint a limited guardian of the property of such person who is intellectually disabled or person who is developmentally disabled who shall receive, manage, disburse and account for only such property of said person who is intellectually disabled or person who is developmentally disabled as shall be received from other than the wages or earnings of said person.

The person who is intellectually disabled or person who is developmentally disabled for whom a limited guardian of the property has been appointed shall have the right to receive and expend any and all wages or other earnings of his or her employment and shall have the

---

* So in original. Should probably be "developmentally".

power to contract or legally bind himself or herself for such sum of money not exceeding one month's wages or earnings from such employment or three hundred dollars, whichever is greater, or as otherwise authorized by the court.

History: Add, L 1989, ch 675, § 2, eff Jan 1, 1990; amd, L 2016, ch 198, § 10, eff July 21, 2016.

§ 1757. Standby guardian of a person who is intellectually disabled or person who is developmentally disabled

1. Upon application, a standby guardian of the person or property or both of a person who is intellectually disabled or person who is developmentally disabled may be appointed by the court. The court may also, upon application, appoint an alternate and/or successive alternates to such standby guardian, to act if such standby guardian shall die, or become incapacitated, or shall renounce. Such appointments by the court shall be made in accordance with the provisions of this article.

2. Such standby guardian, or alternate in the event of such standby guardian's death, incapacity or renunciation, shall without further proceedings be empowered to assume the duties of his or her office immediately upon death, renunciation or adjudication of incompetency of the guardian or standby guardian appointed pursuant to this article, subject only to confirmation of his or her appointment by the court within one hundred eighty days following assumption of his or her duties of such office. Before confirming the appointment of the standby guardian or alternate guardian, the court may conduct a hearing pursuant to section seventeen hundred fifty-four of this article upon petition by anyone on behalf of the person who is intellectually disabled or person who is developmentally disabled or the person who is intellectually disabled or person who is developmentally disabled if such person is eighteen years of age or older, or upon its discretion.

3. Failure of a standby or alternate standby guardian to assume the duties of guardian, seek court confirmation or to renounce the guardianship within sixty days of written notice by certified mail or personal delivery given by or on behalf of the person who is intellectually disabled or person who is developmentally disabled of a prior guardian's inability to serve and the standby or alternate standby guardian's duty to serve, seek court confirmation or renounce such role shall allow the court to:

  (a) deem the failure an implied renunciation of guardianship, and

  (b) authorize, notwithstanding the time period provided for in subdivision two of this section to seek court confirmation, any remaining standby or alternate standby guardian to serve in such capacity provided (i) an application for confirmation and appropriate notices pursuant to subdivision one of section seventeen hundred fifty-three of this article are filed, or (ii) an application for modification of the guardianship order pursuant to section seventeen hundred fifty-five of this article is filed.

History: Add, L 1989, ch 675, § 2, eff Jan 1, 1990; amd, L 1992, ch 290, § 2, eff June 30, 1992; L 2009, ch 260, § 1, eff July 28, 2009; L 2012, ch 294, § 1, eff Aug 1, 2012; L 2016, ch 198, § 11, eff July 21, 2016.

§ 1758. Court jurisdiction

1. The jurisdiction of the court to hear proceedings pursuant to this article shall be subject to article eighty-three of the mental hygiene law.

2. After the appointment of a guardian, standby guardian or alternate guardians, the court shall have and retain general jurisdiction over the person who is intellectually disabled or person who is developmentally disabled for whom such guardian shall have been appointed, to take of its own motion or to entertain and adjudicate such steps and proceedings relating to such guardian, standby, or alternate guardianship as may be deemed necessary or proper for the welfare of such person who is intellectually disabled or person who is developmentally disabled.

> **History:** Add, L 1989, ch 675, § 2, eff Jan 1, 1990; amd, L 2013, ch 427, § 2, eff April 21, 2014; L 2016, ch 198, § 12, eff July 21, 2016.

§ 1759. Duration of guardianship

1. Such guardianship shall not terminate at the age of majority or marriage of such person who is intellectually disabled or person who is developmentally disabled but shall continue during the life of such person, or until terminated by the court.

2. A person eighteen years or older for whom such a guardian has been previously appointed or anyone, including the guardian, on behalf of a person who is intellectually disabled or person who is developmentally disabled for whom a guardian has been appointed may petition the court which made such appointment or the court in his or her county of residence to have the guardian discharged and a successor appointed, or to have the guardian of the property designated as a limited guardian of the property, or to have the guardianship order modified, dissolved or otherwise amended. Upon such a petition for review, the court shall conduct a hearing pursuant to section seventeen hundred fifty-four of this article.

3. Upon marriage of such person who is intellectually disabled or person who is developmentally disabled for whom such a guardian has been appointed, the court shall, upon request of the person who is intellectually disabled or person who is developmentally disabled, spouse, or any other person acting on behalf of the person who is intellectually disabled or person who is developmentally disabled, review the need, if any, to modify, dissolve or otherwise amend the guardianship order including, but not limited to, the appointment of the spouse as standby guardian. The court, in its discretion, may conduct such review pursuant to section seventeen hundred fifty-four of this article.

> **History:** Add, L 1989, ch 675, § 2, eff Jan 1, 1990; amd, L 2016, ch 198, § 13, eff July 21, 2016.

§ 1760. Corporate guardianship

No corporation may be appointed guardian of the person under the provisions of this article, except that a non-profit corporation organized and existing under the laws of the state of New York and having the corporate power to act as guardian of a person who is intellectually disabled or person who is developmentally disabled may be appointed as the guardian of the person only of such person who is intellectually disabled or person who is developmentally disabled.

> **History:** Add, L 1989, ch 675, § 2, eff Jan 1, 1990; amd, L 2016, ch 198, § 14, eff July 21, 2016.

§ 1761. Application of other provisions

To the extent that the context thereof shall admit, the provisions of article seventeen of this act shall apply to all proceedings under this article with the same force and effect as if an "infant", as therein referred to, were a "person who is intellectually disabled" or "person who is developmentally disabled" as herein defined, and a "guardian" as therein referred to were a "guardian of the person who is intellectually disabled" or a "guardian of a person who is developmentally disabled" as herein provided for.

History: Add, L 1989, ch 675, § 2, eff Jan 1, 1990; amd, L 2016, ch 198, § 15, eff July 21, 2016.

ARTICLE 18
CLAIMS; PAYMENT OF DEBTS AND FUNERAL EXPENSES

SUMMARY OF ARTICLE

§ 1802. Effect of failure to present claim

If any claim is not presented within 7 months from the date of issue of letters, the fiduciary shall not be chargeable for any assets or moneys that he may have paid in good faith in satisfaction of any lawful claims or of any legacies or distributions to the legatees or distributees of the decedent before such claim was presented. Such 7 month period shall begin on the date letters were first issued to any fiduciary, including a temporary administrator or a preliminary executor, and shall not be interrupted by any subsequent issue of letters, except that the time during which there is no fiduciary in office shall not be counted as part of such period.

History: Add, L 1966, ch 953; amd, L 1967, ch 685, § 105 from Sur. Ct. Act § 208; amd, L 1970, ch 15, § 1, eff Sept 1, 1970; L 2019, ch 520, § 1, eff Nov 20, 2020.

§ 1803. Form and verification of claims; service of notice

1. Every claim against the estate of a decedent other than claims for expenses of administration and claims of the United States or the state of New York must be in writing, contain a statement of the facts upon which it is based and the amount thereof. In addition the fiduciary may require the claimant to present proof by affidavit that the amount of the claim is justly due, that all payments thereon, if any, have been credited, that the claimant knows of no offsets and no evidence of indebtedness and holds no security, except as specifically described in the affidavit.

2. The notice of claim required by this section shall be presented by delivering a copy thereof to a fiduciary personally or by certified mail return receipt requested addressed to the fiduciary at the place of residence stated in the designation required by 708 or upon the clerk of the court pursuant to the designation required under 708 whenever the fiduciary cannot be found or served within the state after due diligence.

3. No claimant shall be entitled to enforce payment of a claim in any proceeding in the court unless the claim be presented in accordance with the provisions of this section or unless it shall be based upon a decree or order of the court or a valid judgment rendered by a court of competent jurisdiction.

History: Add, L 1966, ch 953, eff Sept 1, 1967 from Sur. Ct. Act § 208-a; amd, L 1993, ch 514, § 40, eff Jan 1, 1994; L 2019, ch 520, § 2, eff Nov 20, 2020.

§ 1804. Contingent or unliquidated claims; retention of assets for estate taxes

1. Whenever at the death of any person there shall be a contingent or unliquidated claim against the decedent's estate or an outstanding bond, recognizance or undertaking upon which the decedent was principal, surety, or indemnitor and on which at the time of the decedent's death the liability is still contingent or unliquidated, a claimant or a surety shall have the right to file with the fiduciary an affidavit showing the facts upon which the contingent or unliquidated liability is based and the probable amount thereof, and there shall be no distribution without reservation of such estate assets as the court, by a special proceeding or upon the final accounting, shall determine to be adequate to pay the contingent or unliquidated claim when the amount thereof shall become due and payable. In fixing the amount to be reserved for payment of the claim the court may determine the value of any security or collateral to which the creditor may resort for payment of the debt and may thereafter direct the reservation if necessary of sufficient estate assets to make up the difference between the value of such security or collateral and the amount necessary to pay the contingent or unliquidated claim.

2. If before a final judicial accounting and decree the contingent or unliquidated claim or liability shall have become fixed and liquidated, then evidence thereof shall be filed with the fiduciary in accordance with the provisions of 1803. If the contingent or unliquidated claim has not become so fixed and liquidated the decree on a final accounting shall direct that the assets found sufficient to satisfy the claim or the proportion to which it is entitled be retained in the hands of the accounting party for such period or periods as the court may deem proper for the purpose of being applied to the payment of the claim when fixed and liquidated and that so much of the assets as are not needed for that purpose be afterwards distributed according to law.

3. Where the state estate tax is or may be due and the amount thereof has not been finally determined or such tax cannot for any reason be paid at the time of final judicial accounting and decree thereon, the decree on a final accounting shall direct that assets found sufficient to satisfy the tax or possible tax be retained in the hands of the accounting party for such period as the court may deem proper for the purpose of being applied to the payment of the tax. In that event the commissioner of taxation and finance shall be among those served upon the final accounting. Such portion of the assets as are not needed for that purpose shall be distributed according to law.

History: Add, L 1966, ch 953, eff Sept 1, 1967 from Sur. Ct. Act § 208-b; amd, L 1967, ch 685, § 107, eff Sept 1, 1967; L 1990, ch 190, § 122, eff May 25, 1990, provided, with respect to estates of decedents dying on or before May 25, 1990, the statute as it existed prior to this amendment will apply; L 1993, ch 514, § 41, eff Jan 1, 1994.

§ 1805. Determination of issues arising between representative and the estate; suspension of statute of limitations in certain cases

1. A fiduciary shall not pay out of the property of the decedent any debt alleged to be owing

to him by the decedent until proved and allowed by the court in the proceeding for the judicial settlement of his account. Where a contest arises between the accounting party and any of the other parties respecting property alleged to belong to the estate which the accounting party claims individually or respecting a debt alleged to be due by the accounting party to the decedent or by the decedent to the accounting party, the contest must be tried and determined in the same manner as any other issue arising in the court.

2. Notwithstanding the provisions of the preceding subdivision a fiduciary at any time may present a petition for permission to pay a debt alleged to be owing to him by the decedent. The court may authorize such payment by ex parte order upon such protection to the estate as it deems proper or may require notice of the application to be given to such persons and in such manner as it directs.

3. From the death of the decedent until the first judicial settlement of the account of the fiduciary, the running of the statute of limitations against a debt owing to him from the decedent or any other cause of action in his favor against the decedent is suspended, unless the fiduciary was appointed on the revocation of former letters issued to another person, in which case the running of the statute is so suspended from the issuance of letters to him until the first judicial settlement of his account. After the first judicial settlement of the account of a fiduciary the statute of limitations begins to run again against a debt due to him from the decedent or any other cause of action in his favor against the decedent.

History: Add, L 1966, ch 953, eff Sept 1, 1967 from Sur. Ct. Act § 209; amd, L 1967, ch 685, § 108, eff Sept 1, 1967.

§ 1806. Allowance or rejection of claims

1. Every fiduciary shall promptly give notice in writing to the claimant of the allowance of the claim or of its rejection or of the rejection of some part thereof which he specifies.

2. A notice rejecting a claim in whole or in part shall state the reasons therefor.

3. If the fiduciary shall fail to allow the claim within 90 days from the date that it has been presented to him, the claim shall be deemed to have been rejected.

4. If a claim has been allowed pursuant to the terms of this section, process may issue to the fiduciary requiring the fiduciary to show cause why the petitioner's claim should not be paid. The court may dismiss the petition or direct payment or satisfaction of the claim in whole or in part and may require a refunding bond.

History: Add, L 1966, ch 953, eff Sept 1, 2967 from Sur. Ct. Act § 210; amd, L 1970, ch 396, § 6, eff Sept 1, 1970; L 1993, ch 514, § 42, eff Jan 1, 1994.

§ 1807. Effect of allowance of claim by fiduciary

1. Whenever a fiduciary shall allow a claim other than the fiduciary's own the validity of the claim shall thereby be established, but if it shall appear that the claim was improperly allowed or was fraudulently or negligently paid, any party adversely affected thereby may file objections thereto in any proceeding for the judicial settlement of the account of the fiduciary. A copy of the objections shall be served upon all parties who have appeared and if the claimant has not appeared a copy shall be served upon the claimant personally or by mail. If the court sustains the objections the claim shall thereupon be dismissed if it has not been paid. If it has been paid, in whole or in part, and an amended petition or objections request a direction that the claimant repay to the fiduciary of the estate any amount of the estate assets

determined on the settlement of the account to have been paid to a claimant as a result of fraud, negligence or collusion and if a supplemental citation to this effect was issued and served upon the claimant, then the court, is authorized in the accounting decree to direct repayment by the creditor of the excess to the fiduciary of the estate and may, in addition, impose a surcharge against the fiduciary or otherwise as justice shall require. If there is no amended petition or answer requesting a direction that the claimant repay the amount of estate assets determined to have been paid as a result of fraud, negligence or collusion then a surcharge shall be imposed against the fiduciary in the amount the estate has been damaged by such fraud, negligence or collusion.

2. In such accounting proceeding a party adversely affected may show that a judgment on a claim against a fiduciary was obtained by fraud, negligence or collusion. If the court determines that the judgment was so obtained, a surcharge shall be imposed against the fiduciary in the amount the estate has been damaged by such fraud, negligence or collusion.

History: Add, L 1966, ch 953, eff Sept 1, 1967 from Sur. Ct. Act § 211; amd, L 1993, ch 514, § 43, eff Jan 1, 1994.

§ 1808. Effect of rejection of claim by fiduciary

1. Except as otherwise provided in 1810, whenever a fiduciary rejects a claim in whole or in part all issues relating to the validity and enforceability of the claim shall be tried and determined upon the judicial settlement of his account.

2. The account of the fiduciary shall list all claims rejected by him in whole or in part and the reason for their rejection.

3. Service of the notice required by 1806 shall be completed prior to the filing of any account reporting a rejected claim.

4. Any claimant adversely affected may within 8 days from the return of process serve and file objections to the account together with a copy of his notice of claim and any supporting affidavit filed with the fiduciary. If the fiduciary shall raise any affirmative defense to the claim that is not set forth in his account, he shall within 5 days from the service upon him of a copy of the objections serve and file a reply to the objections setting forth the affirmative defense. Any person whose interests in the estate may be adversely affected by the allowance of the claim may within 8 days from the filing of objections by a claimant serve and file a reply to the objections setting forth any defense to the claim not set forth in the account.

5. Where one whose claim has been rejected by the fiduciary has petitioned for a compulsory judicial settlement of his account the fiduciary may in his answer to the petition show the condition of the estate and all facts relating to the rejection of the claim and pray for a judicial determination of the validity and enforceability of the claim as a preliminary step in the accounting proceeding. The court may thereupon determine the claim and all issues relating thereto and make such direction for its payment as justice shall require.

6. With respect to any limitation of time within which an action or proceeding may be brought and with respect to examinations before trial, bills of particulars and disclosure generally, the presentation of a claim as provided in 1803 shall be deemed the institution of a special proceeding for the collection of the claim.

History: Add, L 1966, ch 953, eff Sept 1, 1967 from Sur. Ct. Act § 211-a.

§ 1809. Proceeding to determine validity and enforceability of claims

1. Whenever a fiduciary has knowledge or notice that a claim may be asserted and no written notice of claim has been presented to him or if a fiduciary has reason to question the validity of any claim, whether such notice has been presented to him or not, and no action or proceeding to enforce the claim has been instituted, the fiduciary may present a petition to the court showing the facts and praying that the claimant or possible claimant be required to show cause why his claim, if any, should not be disallowed. Similarly, any claimant whose claim is made in compliance with 1803, and whose claim has not been allowed in whole pursuant to 1806 may petition the court showing the facts and praying that the fiduciary be required to show cause why the claim should not be allowed.

2. If the petition be entertained process shall issue to the claimant or possible claimant or fiduciary, as the case may be, and, whenever the claim sought is in excess of ten thousand dollars or constitutes twenty-five percent or more of the estimated gross probate estate, whichever is the lesser, to any person whose rights or interests will be affected by allowance of the claim and the person cited may within 8 days from the return day, serve and file an answer. The answer, if filed by the claimant, shall be accompanied by a copy of any notice of claim, supporting affidavit or other evidence of the claim, if any, filed with the fiduciary. If the fiduciary deems it necessary he may, within 5 days from the service upon him of a copy of the answer, serve and file a reply thereto. The claimant may also file a reply to an answer served by the fiduciary.

3. The court may determine the claim and all issues relating thereto as a preliminary step in the accounting proceeding and make such direction as justice shall require.

History: Add, L 1966, ch 953, eff Sept 1, 1967 from Sur. Ct. Act § 211-b; amd, L 1981, ch 135, effective Aug 24, 1981; L 1993, ch 514, § 44, eff Jan 1, 1994.

§ 1810. Claimant's right to action at law or in equity

Nothing in this article shall prevent a claimant from commencing an action on his claim at law or in equity, provided that where a claim has been presented and rejected or deemed rejected pursuant to 1806 in whole or in part the action must be commenced within 60 days after such rejection. Failure to bring such action within 60 days shall not, however, be deemed a waiver of claimant's right to a jury trial.

History: Add, L 1966, ch 953, eff Sept 1, 1967 from Sur. Ct. Act § 211-c; amd, L 1993, ch 514, eff Jan 1, 1994; L 1995, ch 413, § 1, eff Aug 2, 1995.

§ 1811. Payment of debts and funeral expenses

1. The reasonable funeral expenses of the decedent subject to the payment of expenses of administration shall be preferred to all debts and claims against his estate and shall be paid out of the first moneys received by his fiduciary.

2. Every fiduciary must proceed with diligence to pay the debts of the decedent according to the following order:

(a) Debts entitled to a preference under the laws of the United States and the state of New York.

(b) Taxes assessed on property of the deceased previous to his death. Any taxes so paid by a fiduciary on real property which descends to a distributee or passes to a devisee shall be a charge thereon for which the beneficiary must reimburse the estate unless in the case of wills the testator has indicated expressly or by necessary implication that such taxes be otherwise paid.

SCPA

(c) Judgments docketed and decrees entered against the decedent according to the priority thereof respectively.

(d) All recognizances, bonds, sealed instruments, notes, bills and unliquidated demands and accounts.

3. Preference shall not be given in the payment of a debt over other debts of the same class, except those specified in subparagraph (c) of subdivision 2. A debt due and payable shall not be entitled to a preference over debts not due. The commencement of a suit for the recovery of a debt or the obtaining of a judgment thereon against the fiduciary shall not entitle this debt to preference over others of the same class. Debts not due may be paid according to the class to which they belong, after deducting a rebate of legal interest on the sum paid for the unexpired term of credit without interest. A debt or claim of the fiduciary shall not have preference over others of the same class, except that if the claim of the fiduciary is secured by collateral the fiduciary may apply to the court for leave to surrender the collateral and make payment of the claim upon such conditions as directed by the court. Preference may be given to rents due or accruing on leases held by the decedent at the time of his death over other debts specified in subdivision 2 (d) if it appears to the court's satisfaction that such preference will benefit the estate of the decedent.

4. Dividends payable to secured creditors in insolvent estates shall be computed only upon the difference between the face amount of the claim without security and the value of the security itself as of a date to be determined by the court for the fixation of the rights of creditors, unless the creditor shall surrender his security to the fiduciary, in which event the dividend upon such claim when established as valid shall be computed on the full face amount thereof.

History: Add, L 1966, ch 953, eff Sept 1, 1967 from Sur. Ct. Act §§ 212, 216 in part.

§ 1812. Leave to issue execution against decedent's real property

For the purpose of procuring a decree granting leave to issue execution against a decedent's real property a judgment creditor shall present to the court a verified petition showing the facts and praying for such decree and that the person whose interest in the property will be affected by a sale by virtue of the execution and the fiduciary of the judgment debtor may be required to show cause why it should not be granted. Upon the presentation of the petition the court must issue process accordingly. The process must be served either personally or in such manner as directed by the court and upon the return thereof the court may make such decree as justice shall require.

History: Add, L 1966, ch 953, eff Sept 1, 1967 from Sur. Ct. Act § 212-a.

§ 1813. Disputed or unsettled debt or claim may be compromised, compounded or sold; compromise of infant's claim or action in supreme court

1. Upon the application of a fiduciary or any person (other than a claimant) whose rights or interests will be affected by allowance of the claim, the court may for good cause shown either ex parte or upon notice to such persons and in such manner as it directs authorize the compromising or compounding of any debt, claim or demand, due or to become due, which is necessary to be settled, adjusted or liquidated in connection with the settlement of an estate and the sale at public auction on such notice as directed by the court of any uncollectible, stale or doubtful debt or claim belonging to the estate, but any party interested in the final settlement who has not received notice may show on the settlement that the debt or claim was

fraudulently compromised or compounded.

2. In addition to the foregoing powers, the surrogate of any county in which there is no resident justice of the supreme court qualified to act and in which there is then no term of supreme court in session may act pursuant to the provisions of the CPLR with respect to an application for the approval of a settlement of an infant's claim or of a cause of action belonging to an infant, pending in the supreme court in that county, to the same extent and with the same power and jurisdiction as though he were a justice of the supreme court.

History: Add, L 1966, ch 953, eff Sept 1, 1967 from Sur. Ct. Act § 213; amd, L 1967, ch 685, eff Sept 1, 1967; L 2001, ch 234, § 1, eff Sept 4, 2001.

§ 1814. Application

The provisions of this article are not applicable to trusts or the administration thereof.

History: Add, L 1980, ch 503, § 25, eff June 24, 1980.

SCPA

ARTICLE 19
DISPOSITION OF REAL PROPERTY
SUMMARY OF ARTICLE

§ 1901. Real property subject to disposition; "disposition" and "fiduciary" defined

1. The court may authorize or direct the disposition of a decedent's real property or any interest therein for any of the purposes set forth in the succeeding section. The court may entertain an application for disposition under this article even if the proposed disposition is or appears to be authorized by the will or by a statute.

2. Disposition of the real property of a decedent within the meaning of this article includes:

(a) Sale,

(b) Mortgage,

(c) Exchange,

(d) Lease,

(e) Confirmation of a prior lease made without court approval,

(f) Release of the right to an award for the taking of real property by eminent domain, and

(g) Transfer to a spouse or other beneficiary in full or partial satisfaction of the interest or share of such person in the decedent's estate.

(h) Enter into possession of any real property, receive the rents thereof and apply them as directed by the court.

(i) In the event the estate of a decedent is the owner of an estate in common in real property, the executor or administrator may bring a partition action or intervene in a pending partition action on behalf of the estate, if, upon application duly made, the surrogate approves.

3. The term "fiduciary" as used in this article does not include a trustee, guardian, donee of a power to manage during minority property vested in an infant or a voluntary administrator.

History: Add, L 1966, ch 953, eff Sept 1, 1967 from Sur. Ct. Act § 233 in part; amd, L 1968, ch 280, § 1, eff Sept 1, 1968; L 1975, ch 283, § 1, eff June 24, 1975.

§ 1902. For what purposes real property is subject to disposition

The real property may be disposed of for any or all of the following purposes:

1. For the payment of the expenses of administration.

2. For the payment of funeral expenses.

3. For the payment of the debts of the decedent, including judgment or other liens, excepting mortgage liens, existing thereon at the time of his death.

4. For the payment of any transfer, estate or other death tax.

5. For the payment of any debt or legacy charged thereupon.

6. For the payment and distribution of their respective shares to the persons entitled thereto.

7. For any other purpose the court deems necessary.

History: Add, L 1966, ch 953, eff Sept 1, 1967 from Sur. Ct. Act § 234.

§ 1903. Limitations

1. Unless a proceeding under this article to satisfy a debt of the decedent is brought within 18 months from the date when letters were issued to the original fiduciary and unless such letters were granted within 2 years after the date of the death of the decedent the title of a purchaser or mortgagee from the distributee or devisee of the decedent which was acquired before the proceeding was instituted cannot be affected in any way by the proceeding.

2. A proceeding under this article to satisfy any debt cannot be maintained when the real property is exempt by law from levy and sale by virtue of an execution.

3. A proceeding under this article to satisfy a legacy expressly or impliedly charged on the

real property must be instituted within 10 years from the date of the death of the decedent.

History: Add, L 1966, ch 953, eff Sept 1, 1967 from Sur. Ct. Act §§ 233, 245 in part.

§ 1904. Petition and process

1. A proceeding under this article may be instituted by filing of a verified petition by a fiduciary or any person interested. The petition shall include facts showing the condition of the estate.

2. If the petition be entertained process shall issue to all persons interested and also to the creditors if the court so directs.

3. Upon judicial settlement of the accounts of a fiduciary any party to the proceeding may show facts which make a disposition of the real property left by the decedent desirable. When such relief is sought upon an accounting notice thereof shall be given in the process.

4. If any part of the reversion or remainder in the real property or in proceeds of sale thereof is limited in any contingency to the persons who shall compose a certain class upon the termination of any trust or legal life estate, the process shall issue to and be served upon those persons who would be entitled to the reversion, remainder or proceeds if the event upon which the termination of the trust or legal life estate depended had happened immediately before the application was made.

5. No person shall be entitled to process under this section solely by reason of the fact that he has been or may be designated as appointee of said property or proceeds or of any interest therein, under a power of appointment or disposition.

6. The disposition may be authorized whether any persons who may eventually become entitled to the remainders in the real property or to the proceeds of the sale thereof are in being or not, and whether at the time of the disposition the reversion is in the life tenant or in some other person.

7. The state of New York may be made a party in the same manner as a private person where it appears that the property may have escheated or where the state has a lien of record on the interest of any beneficiary. The petition in that case shall show the nature of the interest of the state and the reason or reasons for making the state a party to the proceedings. Upon failure to state such facts, the proceeding shall be dismissed as to the state.

8. The provisions of section three hundred fifteen shall apply to a proceeding under this section.

History: Add, L 1966, ch 953, eff Sept 1, 1967 from Sur. Ct. Act § 236; amd, L 1967, ch 685, § 111, eff Sept 1, 1967; L 1967, ch 739, § 4, eff Sept 1, 1967 added subd 8.

§ 1905. When disposition may be refused or delayed

1. The court may deny the application upon such terms and conditions as justice shall require.

2. If the disposition affects real property and it appears that the net income thereof may be sufficient to make the disposition unnecessary within a reasonable time, the court may postpone the application from time to time and authorize the fiduciary to enter into possession of the property, to receive the rents thereof and to apply the net rents as directed by the court.

History: Add, L 1966, ch 953, eff Sept 1, 2967 from Sur. Ct. Act §§ 235, 232; amd, L 1967, ch 685, § 112, eff Sept 1, 1967; L 1968, ch 280, § 2, eff Sept 1, 1968.

§ 1906. Trial and determination of debts, claims and expenses; statute of limitations

1. If any claim, debt, demand, charge, or expense set forth in the petition presented prior to an application for judicial settlement, or set forth in the account or presented on the judicial settlement is objected to by any party to the proceeding whose interest will be affected by its allowance or disallowance the claim, debt, demand, charge or expense shall be determined, notwithstanding its admission or allowance by the fiduciary.

2. Where a defense arises under the statute of limitations as to any item so admitted or allowed it shall be deemed to be rejected by the fiduciary at the time of the objection and the time between its presentation or the commencement of an action where it was not presented and the time of such objection shall not be a part of the time limited in this act for commencing an action thereon.

History: Add, L 1966, ch 953, eff Sept 1, 1967 from Sur. Ct. Act § 237.

§ 1907. Order determining disposition of real property

1. Upon the return of process the court shall inquire into the facts, the value of the property and the best manner and time of disposition.

2. The court may direct the disposition of all or part of the real property, describing it.

3. The order may determine whether the property shall be sold at public or private sale and may fix the manner, terms and conditions thereof.

4. Where a contract for the disposition of the property accompanies the petition, the order may direct disposition in accordance with its terms or any modification thereof.

5. If the court finds that it is not necessary to dispose of the real property or of any part thereof it may nevertheless determine the rights and interests of the parties and direct a conveyance to them in confirmation of their title or transferring the property to them in full or partial satisfaction of their distributive share.

6. If the order is made in the course of an accounting proceeding, the court shall adjourn a judicial settlement to await the proceedings taken under the order.

History: Add, L 1966, ch 953, eff Sept 1, 1967 from Sur. Ct. Act §§ 238, 242.

§ 1908. Order in which parcels shall be sold

If the sale of real property is necessary for the purposes set forth in 1902, subdivisions 1, 2, 3 or 4 and the decedent dies seized of more than one distinct parcel, the following rules must be observed in determining the order of sale:

1. Property of which the decedent died intestate shall be sold before property which the decedent devised.

2. Property of which the decedent died intestate and which has not been conveyed by the distributees shall be sold before property which has been conveyed by them.

3. Property devised by the residuary clause in the will shall be sold before property which has been specifically devised.

4. When two or more parcels have been devised to the same person or group of persons, parcels which have not been conveyed by the devisees shall be sold before property which

has been conveyed by them.

5. When one parcel has been devised to one person or group and another parcel has been devised to another person or group both parcels shall be equally subject to sale notwithstanding that one parcel may have been conveyed.

History: Add, L 1966, ch 953, eff Sept 1, 1967 from Sur. Ct. Act § 238.

§ 1909. Rights of the parties to be determined; unknowns

1. Where an order is made directing the sale of the real property for distribution or directing the transfer thereof to a spouse or beneficiary the court may fix and determine the rights and interests of the respective parties in the order, or may postpone the determination until the final judicial settlement of the accounts of the fiduciary.

2. If a party entitled to an estate or interest in the property is made a party as a person unknown the court must provide for the protection of his rights, as far as may be, as if he were known and had appeared.

History: Add, L 1966, ch 953, eff Sept 1, 1967 from Sur. Ct. Act § 238 in part.

§ 1910. Bond of fiduciary

1. In any case where the court directs disposition of the property it may direct the fiduciary to furnish such bond as it may require to insure the execution of the order and the accounting by the fiduciary of all moneys received.

2. The court may require a bond notwithstanding that the will authorized an executor to serve without bond.

3. The court may dispense with a bond or require a bond in a reduced amount on condition that the proceeds of the disposition be deposited with a specified bank or trust company, subject to the further order of the court.

History: Add, L 1966, ch 953, eff Sept 1, 1967 from Sur. Ct. Act § 239.

§ 1911. Order to be executed and report made

1. The fiduciary shall thereupon execute the order, subject to the approval of the court, and make a report of his proceedings thereunder.

2. The court may confirm or reject the disposition, extend the order to other parcels or require a re-execution of the order upon such terms and on such conditions as it may direct and it may relieve a purchaser from his purchase or compel specific performance of the agreement by both the purchaser or the fiduciary in any case where such relief might be granted by the supreme court, on such terms as justice shall require.

3. If the contract for the disposition of the property was annexed to the petition and approved by the order, the fiduciary may execute a deed without further order and no confirmation of the sale is required.

4. No decree of distribution or payment of the proceeds of the disposition shall be made in a proceeding commenced within 3 months from the grant of letters until the time for the presentation of claims as fixed by a published notice has expired or 7 months have expired since letters were issued to the original fiduciary and until all known creditors and persons interested who are not parties to the proceeding have been brought in or have appeared.

History: Add, L 1966, ch 953, eff Sept 1, 1967 from Sur. Ct. Act §§ 240, 242; amd, L 1983, ch 457, § 1, eff July 15, 1983.

§ 1912. Effect of death of fiduciary

1. In the event of the death, removal or disqualification of all of the fiduciaries before the granting of an order directing disposition of the real property their successor must be substituted and the proceeding shall continue by or against the successor.

2. In the event of such death, removal or disqualification after the granting of the order but before the complete execution thereof the successor must proceed without further order to complete all unfinished matters as were required of his predecessors.

3. The successor must give such security for the performance of his duties as the court may require.

4. If no successor is appointed the court may make an order authorizing the fiduciary of the last surviving fiduciary, on giving such security as the court may require, to continue the proceeding or to complete all unfinished matters as were required of the fiduciary.

History: Add, L 1966, ch 953, eff Sept 1, 1967 from Sur. Ct. Act § 241.

§ 1913. Conclusiveness of mortgage, lease, conveyance or release executed pursuant to order

The mortgage, lease, conveyance or release made pursuant to an order granted as provided in this article shall bind the remainders and reversions as well as the immediate or future or trust interests in the real property and shall be valid and effectual against all persons under disability, absentees, internees and persons not in being having estates or interests vested or contingent for life or in trust or in reversion or remainder in said real property or in the proceeds of the sale thereof and against all other persons so interested or having such estates or interests who shall by acknowledged instrument consent to such order or who have been made parties to such proceedings or who are not entitled to notice thereof as provided in this article.

History: Add, L 1966, ch 953, eff Sept 1, 1967 from Sur. Ct. Act § 245-a; amd, L 1968, ch 259, §§ 31, 32, eff May 14, 1968.

§ 1914. Execution of the order; decree of judicial settlement

1. When the order has been fully executed the fiduciary shall file, on or before the adjourned day of the judicial settlement, a supplemental account setting forth his proceedings under the order, the amount of the proceeds of the disposition and his expenses incurred thereunder.

2. The court shall thereupon continue and complete the judicial settlement and make such disposition of the funds in the hands of the fiduciary as justice shall require.

History: Add, L 1966, ch 953, eff Sept 1, 1967 from Sur. Ct. Act § 242.

§ 1915. Allowance on bid to spouse, beneficiary or creditor purchasing

1. If upon a sale a spouse, beneficiary or creditor of the decedent becomes the purchaser of any of the decedent's real property the court may, upon his application, direct the amount of his elective share, legacy, distributive share or claim, as the case may be, to be allowed, in the first instance, upon the purchase price and such purchaser shall be required to pay only the balance at the time of the sale.

2. If the proceeds of the decedent's real property shall be insufficient to satisfy the cost and expenses of administration and the debts and funeral expenses of the decedent, the purchasing spouse, beneficiary or creditor shall be allowed and credited upon the judicial settlement of the accounts of the fiduciary only the amount he may be entitled to receive upon his elective share, legacy, distributive share or claim and shall then pay the difference between the amount originally allowed and amount he is entitled to receive.

3. If any purchaser has credit on his bid as above provided no deed shall be delivered to him until the judicial settlement of the accounts of the fiduciary and not until he shall have paid the entire amount required under the provisions of this section.

History: Add, L 1966, ch 953, eff Sept 1, 1967 from Sur. Ct. Act § 243.

§ 1916. Provision for payment of undetermined claims and debts not yet due

If any claim remains undetermined at the making of the decree or any debt is not yet due and the person holding it does not consent to its present payment, the decree shall direct that sufficient funds be retained by the fiduciary to meet the claim or demand when determined or when payable and provide for the distribution of any surplus of the amount so retained.

History: Add, L 1966, ch 953, eff Sept 1, 1967 from Sur. Ct. Act § 244.

§ 1917. Effect of conveyance of decedent's interest under contract

1. A conveyance of the decedent's interest in all the real property held by him under a contract for the purchase thereof operates as an assignment of the contract to the purchaser and vests in him, his distributees and assigns, all the right, title and interest of all the persons entitled at the time of the sale in and to the decedent's interest in the real property.

2. A conveyance of the decedent's interest in a part only of the real property held under such a contract transfers to the purchaser, his distributees and assigns all the decedent's right, title and interest in and to the part so sold.

3. Upon fully complying with the contract the purchaser, his distributees or assigns has the same right to enforce performance thereof with respect to the part conveyed to him and the fiduciary or his assignee has the same right to enforce performance with respect to the residue as the decedent would have had if he were living.

4. Any title acquired by the fiduciary, or his assignee, with respect to the part not sold must be held in trust for the use of the persons entitled to the decedent's interest, subject to the dower or curtesy, if any, of the spouse.

History: Add, L 1966, ch 953, eff Sept 1, 1967 from Sur. Ct. Act § 246.

§ 1918. Right of life tenant to be considered in disposition; distribution of moneys realized

1. Where any party to the proceeding has an existing or inchoate right of dower or curtesy or where any party to the proceeding has a tendancy* by dower or curtesy or an estate for life or for years in the real property the court must determine whether the interests of all the parties will be better protected or a more advantageous disposition can be made of the real property by including the disposition of such right or interest and if the court shall so determine there may be included in the order a direction that such right or interest be included

---

* So in original. Should probably be "tenancy".

in the disposition.

2. The provisions of law in relation to the right of dower, curtesy and estates for life, or for years or future or other interests in actions for the partition of real estate, so far as the same may be applicable, shall govern and control the distribution of moneys realized on such disposition which shall belong to the owner of such right of dower or curtesy, or tenant for life, or for years or future or other interests.

> **History:** Add, L 1966, ch 953, eff Sept 1, 1967 from Sur. Ct. Act § 248; amd, L 1967, ch 685, eff Sept 1, 1967; L 1971, ch 805, § 3, eff Sept 1, 1971.

§ 1919. Restitution from assets subsequently discovered

Where a decree has been made for the application of the proceeds of real property as prescribed in this article and assets which should have been applied thereto are afterward discovered or for any other reason money or other personal property of the decedent, which should have been applied thereto, afterward comes to the hands of the fiduciary, legatee or distributee, the devisee or other person aggrieved may maintain a proceeding in the court to procure reimbursement therefrom.

> **History:** Add, L 1966, ch 953, eff Sept 1, 1967 from Sur. Ct. Act § 249.

§ 1920. Disposition of surplus in action to enforce mortgage or other lien

1. Where real property liable to be disposed of as prescribed in this act is sold in an action or special proceeding, or otherwise, to enforce a mortgage or other lien thereon which accrued during the decedent's lifetime the surplus money must be paid into the surrogate's court having jurisdiction to issue letters upon the estate of the decedent, in the following cases:

(a) Where 18 months have not elapsed since the date when letters were issued to the original fiduciary.

(b) Where a proceeding for the disposition of the real property of the decedent or for a judicial settlement of the accounts of the fiduciary has been commenced within 18 months from the date of the issuance of such letters and is still pending.

(c) Where no such letters have been issued and 2 years have not elapsed since the death of the decedent.

2. Money paid into the surrogate's court as herein provided, pursuant to any direction of another court may be paid out to the fiduciary of the decedent, as directed by an order of the surrogate's court, to be accounted for by him upon the judicial settlement of his accounts or in a special proceeding brought for that purpose in the surrogate's court an order may be entered directing distribution to the persons entitled thereto if 18 months have elapsed since letters were issued to the original fiduciary upon the estate of the decedent or if no such letters have been issued 2 years have elapsed since the death of the decedent.

> **History:** Add, L 1966, ch 953, eff Sept 1, 1967 from Sur. Ct. Act § 250.

§ 1921. Conveyance of real property by fiduciary to vendee of contract of sale made by decedent

1. Where a decedent dies seized of real property after he has made a contract for the conveyance thereof remaining unexecuted at his death his fiduciary or successor may make a deed reciting the contract and conveying the real property.

2. The vendor's fiduciary, distributees, devisees or assigns may file a petition praying for

the confirmation of the conveyance, or the vendee, his fiduciary, distributees, devisees or assigns, for a decree that it be made or delivered, or the vendor's fiduciary may pray for like relief in a petition for the judicial settlement of his account, but no proceeding pursuant to this section shall be required in any case for the sole purpose of perfecting title to real property and any such conveyance heretofore made by a fiduciary of a decedent is ratified and confirmed.

3. In a proceeding pursuant to this section the court shall have jurisdiction to adjudicate the amount remaining payable under the terms of any such contract and the respective rights of the parties.

4. In any case process shall issue to all persons interested and the court shall make such decree or order as justice shall require.

History: Add, L 1966, ch 953, eff Sept 1, 1967 from Sur. Ct. Act § 227; amd, L 1967, ch 685, § 115, eff Sept 1, 1967; L 1968, ch 259, § 33, eff May 14, 1968.

§ 1922. Conclusive presumption after 10 years

An action or proceeding to set aside any disposition of the real property of a decedent pursuant to an order granted under this article or under article 13 of the surrogate's court act by reason of lack of jurisdiction over any person interested in the estate or by reason of any other defect in the procedure must be brought within 10 years after the date of the order or within 1 year after the effective date of this article, whichever date is later. After the lapse of such period the presumption that the order was regular in all respects and that the court had jurisdiction of all persons interested in the estate becomes conclusive.

History: Add, L 1966, ch 953, eff Sept 1, 1967.

§ 1923. Fiduciary of a decedent to notify local assessor of disposition

Whenever the fiduciary of a decedent or his successor shall direct, or take part in or discover that his decedent's real property or any interest therein has been transferred at or following such decedent's death, he shall forthwith investigate and discover the nature of such transfer and file a written notice of such disposition or transfer with the local assessing officer and the local tax office of the locality wherein such property is located. Such notice shall contain the name and last known legal address of the decedent, the location and legal description of the property, if known, and the name and address of the transferee.

History: Add, L 1988, ch 116, § 1, eff July 13, 1988.

SCPA

ARTICLE 20
PROCEEDING TO OPEN SAFE DEPOSIT BOX*

SUMMARY OF ARTICLE

§ 2001.　　　　　　　　Definition

§ 2003.　　　　　　　　Opening safe deposit box

§ 2001. Definition

When used in this article the term fiduciary includes, where no fiduciary has been appointed, any person in actual or constructive possession of any property required to be included in the gross estate or the New York gross estate of the decedent as determined under article 10-c or article 26 of the tax law.

History: Add, L 1966, ch 953, eff Sept 1, 1967 from Sur. Ct. Act § 117-h.

§ 2003. Opening safe deposit box

1. When it appears to the court by petition that a person, firm or corporation has in its possession or under its control papers of a decedent of whose estate the court has jurisdiction or that the decedent has leased from them a safe deposit box and that such papers or safe deposit box may contain a will of the decedent, a deed to a burial plot in which the decedent is to be interred or a policy of insurance issued in the name of the decedent and payable to a designated beneficiary, it may make an order ex parte directing such person, firm or corporation to permit a person named in the order to examine the papers or safe deposit box and to make an inventory of the papers or of the contents of the safe deposit box in the presence of an authorized employee or agent of such person, firm or corporation, and if a paper purporting to be a will of the decedent, a deed to the burial plot or a policy of insurance be found to deliver the will to the clerk of the court, personally or by registered mail as directed by the court or the deed to the person designated in the order or the policy of insurance to the beneficiary named therein. The clerk shall furnish a receipt upon delivery to him of the will.

2. Notwithstanding any provisions of subdivision one of this section, a safe deposit company, trust company, bank, corporation, firm or other person, having in its possession, or under its control one or more safe deposit boxes shall permit an individual or individuals each of whom being a joint lessee with the decedent of said safe deposit box or boxes, or a deputy authorized by the decedent to have access to said safe deposit box or boxes, to examine and make copies of, in the presence and under the supervision of an officer of the company, bank, corporation or firm, any paper or papers found in said safe deposit box or boxes bearing upon the desire of the deceased as to the disposal of his remains, or deed to a cemetery plot, or proof of membership in a burial society. For purposes of this subdivision, the term "deputy" shall mean the person who had access to the decedent's safe deposit box or boxes and to the contents thereof on the last day of decedent's life. After copies have been made of the paper or papers described in this subdivision, the original paper or papers shall be resealed in the safe deposit box or boxes and such officer shall certify that such papers have been resealed and file such certification with the surrogate's court.

History: Add, L 1966, ch 953, eff Sept 1, 1967 from Sur. Ct. Act § 117-b; amd, L 1991, ch 166, eff June 12, 1991; L 1993, ch 536, § 1, eff July 28, 1993.

---

*　Amd, L 1991 ch 190, eff May 25, 1990. SCPA 2002, 2004–2008 were repealed.

ARTICLE 21
MISCELLANEOUS PROCEEDINGS
SUMMARY OF ARTICLE

§ 2101. General provisions

Unless otherwise indicated

1. All proceedings under this article and all proceedings within the jurisdiction of the court under 202

(a) May be commenced by a fiduciary, creditor or person interested.

(b) May be entertained by the court or may be reserved for determination in an accounting or other proceeding or the court may decline to entertain the proceeding. All proceedings shall be deemed entertained unless rejected by the court in writing within 15 days of submission.

(c) Shall be commenced by petition, or any other pleading directed by the court, stating the jurisdictional facts and the facts applicable to the particular relief sought.

2. The jurisdiction of the court over the proceeding shall be deemed to continue until a decree or order therein is fully satisfied.

3. If the petition or other pleading is entertained service of process shall be made upon all persons interested in the proceeding and upon such other persons as directed by the court except that in any proceeding against a fiduciary under 2102 service shall be made only upon the fiduciary unless the court otherwise directs.

4. In any such proceeding the court may grant appropriate relief, grant or deny the relief in whole or in part upon such terms as it deems proper and make such decree or order as justice shall require and may require a refunding bond.

History: Add, L 1966, ch 953, eff Sept 1, 1967 from Sur. Ct. Act §§ 199, 201, 216, 217, 219, 220, 221, 228 in part; amd, L 1967, ch 685, § 118, eff Sept 1, 1967; L 1970, ch 396, eff Sept 1, 1970; L 1993, ch 514, § 46, eff Jan 1, 1994.

§ 2102. Proceedings for relief against a fiduciary

A proceeding may be commenced to require a fiduciary:

1. To supply information concerning the assets or affairs of an estate relevant to the interest of the petitioner when the fiduciary has failed after request made upon him in writing therefor.

2. To set apart and turn over exempt property to which a spouse or child is entitled or if it has been lost, injured or disposed of to pay the value thereof or the amount of injury thereto.

3. After reservation for the payment of the expenses of administration to pay the reasonable funeral expenses of a decedent if there are funds available for such payment.

4. To pay a claim which has been allowed, to deliver a specific bequest or property to a person entitled thereto or to pay a legacy, distributive share, interest in a trust or a claim for an administration expense, and when a trustee is unable to deliver personal property to the person entitled, to pay the value thereof.

5. To pay in advance to any beneficiary of an estate all or part of any beneficial interest to which he is entitled when the property of the estate applicable to the payment of debts, legacies and expenses exceeds by at least one-third the amount of all known claims, legacies having priority and beneficial interests of the same class and the beneficiary needs such payment for his support or education or of his family.

6. To comply with such directions as the court may make whenever two or more fiduciaries disagree with respect to any issue affecting the estate.

History: Add, L 1966, ch 953, eff Sept 1, 1967 from Sur. Ct. Act §§ 199, 201, 216, 217, 219, 220, 221, 228 in part; amd, L 1967, ch 685, § 119, eff Sept 1, 1967; L 1968, ch 259, eff May 14, 1968; L 1980, ch 503, § 26, eff June 24, 1980; L 1985, ch 634, § 3, eff July 28, 1985, applying to the estate of any person dying on or after that date; L 1993, ch 514, § 47, eff Jan 1, 1994; L 2014, ch 404, § 3, eff Dec 20, 2014, applying to the estates of decedents who shall have died on or after such date.

§ 2103. Proceeding by fiduciary to discover property withheld or obtain information

1. A fiduciary may present to the court which has jurisdiction over the estate a petition showing on knowledge or information and belief that any property as defined in 103 or the proceeds or value thereof which should be paid or delivered to him is

(a) in the possession or control of a person who withholds it from him, whether possession or control was obtained prior to creation of the estate or subsequent thereto or

(b) within the knowledge or information of a person who refuses to impart knowledge or information he may have concerning it or to disclose any other fact which will aid the petitioner in making discovery of the property or

(c) he has reason to believe, in the possession or control of a person described in subparagraph (a) of this subdivision or within the knowledge or information of a person described in subparagraph (b) of this subdivision and praying that an inquiry be had respecting it and that the respondent be ordered to attend and be examined accordingly and to deliver the property if in his control.

The petition may be accompanied by an affidavit or other written evidence to support it.

2. "Property" as used in this section shall include any and all personal or real property in which decedent had any interest, including choses in action, money deposited and all property rights of the depositor consequent on the deposit of money by a decedent, grantor or fiduciary or for his account with any authorized banking organization in respect of which the depositary claims no beneficial interest other than its proper costs, fees or expenses.

3. If the court be satisfied there are reasonable grounds for the examination it must make an order accordingly. If the petition does not pray for an inquiry or examination, the court may issue a citation to the person alleged to be in possession or control of the property to show cause why he should not deliver such property or its proceeds or value.

4. If it appear* at any time that a person other than the respondent claims any interest in the property or the proceeds or value thereof the court may issue a citation to such person to show cause why he should not deliver the property if in his control or the proceeds or value thereof and why the court should not determine ownership and right to possession of such property.

5. Service of any order for attendance and examination of any person must be made by delivery of a certified copy thereof to the person or persons therein named and the payment or tender to each of the sum required to be paid to a witness as a subpoena fee.

History: Add, L 1966, ch 953, eff Sept 1, 1967 from Sur. Ct. Act § 205; amd, L 1970, ch 27, eff Sept 1, 1970; L 1980, ch 503, eff June 24, 1980; L 1993, ch 514, § 48, eff Jan 1, 1994; L 1995, ch 576, § 1, eff Aug 8, 1995.

§ 2104. Inquiry; trial and decree

1. Upon the return of the order, whether or not the respondent answers, the petitioner may examine him with respect to the allegations of the petition. If it appears thereon that an issue of title to any property as defined in 103 or the proceeds or value thereof is raised, if he has not theretofore done so, the respondent shall be directed to serve and file an answer accordingly, but the examination, if directed by the court, shall continue. When an issue of title is raised that issue shall be tried as a litigated issue.

2. Any claim of title to or the right to the possession of any property of the decedent or the estate must be made by verified answer.

3. If the possession of the property be denied, proof of that issue may be presented by any party. The court may in an appropriate case make an interim decree directing the delivery of property not claimed by verified answer and continue the proceeding for determination of any litigated issue.

4. If it appears that the petitioner is entitled to the possession of any property the decree

---

* So in original. Should probably be "appears".

shall direct delivery thereof to him or if the property shall have been disposed of or diverted the decree may direct the payment of the proceeds or the value of the property or may impress a trust upon the proceeds or make any determination which the supreme court might decree in following trust property or funds.

5. If it be determined that the petitioner is not entitled to the property or the proceeds or value thereof the court may determine the respective interests of the other claimants thereto.

6. If during the proceeding, other than a trial of issues raised by answer, a respondent is examined concerning any personal communication or transaction between himself and the decedent such examination shall not be deemed to be a waiver of the provisions of CPLR 4519.

History: Add, L 1966, ch 953, eff Sept 1, 1967 from Sur. Ct. Act § 206; amd, L 1967, ch 685, § 120, eff Sept 1, 1967; L 1993, ch 514, § 49, eff Jan 1, 1994.

§ 2105. Proceeding to compel delivery of property by a fiduciary which is claimed by another or others

1. A person having a claim to property as defined in 103 or the proceeds thereof alleged to be in the possession of or under the control of a fiduciary may present to the court which has jurisdiction over the estate a petition showing the facts and praying that the fiduciary be required to show cause why he should not be required to deliver the property or the proceeds thereof.

2. Process shall issue accordingly to the fiduciary.

3. Upon return of process the court must hear the proofs of the parties, determine the issues, and if claim shall have been made to the property or the proceeds thereof by a person or persons other than the fiduciary, the court shall determine the respective interests of the parties in the property or the proceeds or value thereof and make a decree accordingly.

History: Add, L 1966, ch 953, eff Sept 1, 1967 from Sur. Ct. Act § 206-a; amd, L 1980, ch 503, eff June 24, 1980; L 1993, ch 514, § 50, eff Jan 1, 1994.

§ 2106. Proceeding for compromise of controversies between claimants to property or estates where interests of persons under disability or not in being are affected

1. Where the interests of persons under disability or not in being are or may be affected

    (a) A fiduciary may petition for authorization to compromise any controversy between different claimants to the estate or property or portions thereof under administration in accordance with an agreement to which all parties in being claiming an interest in the estate affected by the agreement shall be parties in person or by guardian or committee.

    (b) The proponent or any party to a probate proceeding may petition to adjust by compromise any controversy existing or which may arise between the persons claiming under any will alleged to have been made by the decedent and any persons claiming as distributees of decedent or claiming to be entitled to a right of election or claiming pursuant to an agreement with the decedent or otherwise, in accordance with an agreement to which all such persons as are interested shall be parties, provided that persons named as executors to whom letters have not issued and persons whose interests are not affected by the proposed compromise are not required to be made parties.

2. A person under disability or a person not in being who has a future contingent interest

is a necessary party and shall be represented by a guardian ad litem unless in the case of a person under disability his guardian, committee or conservator shall appear in his behalf. The guardian, committee or conservator so appearing or the guardian ad litem may execute in behalf of the person for whom he appears all proper instruments necessary to effect any compromise approved by the court.

3. If by the terms of the compromise money or property is directed to be held for the benefit of a person under disability or a person not in being it may in a proper case be deposited in court subject to the order of the court.

4. An agreement of compromise made as herein provided if found by the court to be just and reasonable shall be valid and binding upon the interests of persons under disability, persons not in being and all parties to the agreement.

5. An application for the approval of a compromise hereunder must be made by verified petition or, if made in a pending proceeding, by verified supplemental petition, which shall show the provisions of any instruments or documents under which claim is made to the property or estate in controversy, all facts concerning the identity and claims of the parties to the controversy, the possible contingent interests of persons not in being and the necessity for the approval of the compromise.

6. The court may entertain the application prior to the execution of the proposed compromise agreement by all the parties required to execute it and may permit its execution after the commencement of the proceeding by any person interested.

7. The court shall inquire into the facts and make such order or decree as justice shall require in any proceeding.

History: Add, L 1966, ch 953, eff Sept 1, 1967 from Dec. Est. Law § 19; amd, L 1967, ch 685, § 121, eff Sept 1, 1967; L 1979, ch 388, § 1, eff Sept 1, 1979; L 1981, ch 115, § 128, eff May 18, 1981.

§ 2107. Court may direct as to value, manner and time of sale of property and give advice and direction in extraordinary circumstances

1. Whenever the value of property of an estate is uncertain or dependent upon the time and manner of sale thereof a fiduciary may apply by petition to the court for advice and direction as to the propriety, price, manner and time of sale thereof.

2. The court may entertain applications by a fiduciary to advise and direct in other extraordinary circumstances such as complex valuation issues, or tax elections, or where there is conflict among interested parties, but need not entertain jurisdiction if to do so would be merely to substitute the court's judgment for that of the fiduciary.

3. A substantial compliance with the authorization so given shall relieve the fiduciary from any objection that the estate suffered a loss on account of the action taken under court advice and direction.

History: Add, L 1966, ch 953, eff Sept 1, 1967 from Sur. Ct. Act § 215; amd, L 1993, ch 514, § 51, eff Jan 1, 1994.

§ 2108. Proceeding by fiduciary for continuation of a business

A fiduciary may petition for the continuation of a business other than a profession, of which decedent or the person whose estate is being administered was sole owner and it is desired to continue it for the best interests of the estate; provided, however, that a fiduciary may petition for the continuation of a deceased dentist's practice for a period not to exceed eight months, if such practice is continued by a person licensed to practice dentistry in this state. In such proceeding:

1. If the petition be entertained the court may make an intermediate order without notice authorizing continuance of the business pending the return of process and final decree.

2. Any respondent may serve and file an answer within 8 days after the return of process or such further time as the court directs. After inquiring into the facts and hearing the parties, if the court is satisfied the best interests of the estate require the continuation of the business, it may make a decree accordingly.

3. The decree may provide such restrictions, conditions or requirements and such incidental relief, including a direction or permission for incorporation of the business, as the court may order.

4. Whenever a fiduciary shall be authorized under this section to continue a business in other than corporate form the decree shall provide for the extent of the liability of the assets of the business and the assets of the estate apart from the assets of the business for debts and other liabilities arising out of its continuance. The court may make such directions in this regard as it deems advisable in the circumstances. The decree shall further provide for the period of time for continuance.

5. If under a decree granted under this section a fiduciary shall continue and carry on a business other than in corporate form he shall file a certificate of doing business under an assumed name pursuant to the provisions of section one hundred thirty of the general business law. The certificate shall include in addition to the other matters required by that section a statement showing the fiduciary capacity in which he is conducting and carrying on the business and the extent to which the debts and other liabilities incurred in the continuance are to be chargeable to the assets of the estate as provided in the decree. The fiduciary shall be relieved of personal liability if acting within the authority granted and having filed the certificate above provided, but shall be liable only in a fiduciary capacity. Any person having a claim, demand or cause of action arising out of or in connection with the conduct of the business after the filing of the certificate above provided shall thereafter be limited in the payment or satisfaction of such claim, demand or cause of action to such assets as are made available for the payment or satisfaction of debts and liabilities in the decree, provided, however, that nothing herein contained shall relieve the fiduciary from personal liability for the consequences of his own wrongful act or negligence in the continuance of the business and provided further that nothing herein contained shall render ineffectual any provision in a will or other instrument directing or permitting the continuance of a business.

6. Unless otherwise provided in the decree all funds collected and received in continuing and carrying on the business of a decedent shall at all times be kept separate and apart from the funds in the hands of the fiduciary forming part of the general assets of the estate as a whole.

7. Notwithstanding the foregoing provisions, any creditor or person interested may at any time apply to the court for an order requiring the fiduciary to discontinue and wind up the business and the court may thereupon make such order as to it appears for the best interests of the estate, the creditors and all persons interested.

History: Add, L 1966, ch 953, eff Sept 1, 1967 from Sur. Ct. Act § 215-a; amd, L 1967, ch 685, eff Sept 1, 1967; L 1971, ch 805, § 4, eff Sept 1, 1971; L 1997, ch 475, § 1, eff Aug 26, 1997.

§ 2109. Money paid into court and securities taken; how disposed of

The provisions of CPLR 2601 to 2608 inclusive shall be applicable to property paid into court pursuant to an order or decree of this court.

History: Add, L 1966, ch 953, eff Sept 1, 1967 from Sur. Ct. Act § 229 omitted and CPLR § 2609.

§ 2110. Compensation of attorneys

1. At any time during the administration of an estate and irrespective of the pendency of a particular proceeding, the court is authorized to fix and determine the compensation of an attorney for services rendered to a fiduciary or to a devisee, legatee, distributee or any person interested or of an attorney who has rendered legal services in connection with the performance of his duties as a fiduciary or in proceedings to compel the delivery of papers or funds in the hands of an attorney.

2. The proceeding shall be instituted by petition of a fiduciary of the estate or a person interested or an attorney who has rendered services. The court may direct payment therefor from the estate generally or from the funds in the hands of the fiduciary belonging to any legatee, devisee, distributee or person interested.

3. In any event that any such attorney has already received or been paid an amount in excess of the fair value of his services as thus determined the court is authorized to direct him to refund the excess.

4. In any proceeding under this act or the estates, powers and trusts law in which the court determines the compensation of an attorney, the court shall consider the time and value of services performed by a person who is not an attorney, provided such services are performed under the supervision of an attorney and would, if performed by an attorney, be considered by the court in determining the attorney's compensation.

History: Add, L 1966, ch 953, eff Sept 1, 1967 from Sur. Ct. Act § 231-a; amd, L 1990, ch 684, § 1, eff July 22, 1990, applying to all determinations of attorney's compensation, irrespective of when the services were performed or when the proceeding was commenced.

§ 2111. Ex parte application for advance payment of fees of an attorney-fiduciary or guardian ad litem

1. At any time during the administration of an estate and irrespective of the pendency of a particular proceeding an attorney of this state who is a fiduciary, or guardian ad litem may present to the court from which his or her letters or appointment issued a petition praying that he or she be permitted to receive a sum on account of his or her compensation for legal services theretofore rendered to the estate or to the person under disability. No notice of the application shall be required, except that in the case of a guardian ad litem notice shall be given to any attorney or person who has appeared in the proceeding for which the guardian ad litem seeks an allowance. If the application be entertained, the court may award a sum on account of compensation or make such other order, if any, as justice shall require. The total expenses of the application shall be borne by the petitioner personally.

2. An attorney who is a fiduciary may take advances on account of compensation for legal

services rendered to the estate, without application to the court if he shall have at least one co-fiduciary who is not rendering legal services to the estate and all co-fiduciaries have consented to such payment on account or if the instrument under which the attorney is acting permits him to take such payments on account in advance of the settlement of the account.

3. In all cases where any such payment on account of legal services has been taken by an attorney his or her account must disclose the fact and the amount of such payment.

4. The compensation of an attorney for legal services awarded or taken under this section may include compensation for the time and value of services performed by a person who is not an attorney, provided such services are performed under the supervision of an attorney and would, if performed by an attorney, be compensable under this section.

> **History:** Add, L 1966, ch 953, eff Sept 1, 1967 from Sur. Ct. Act § 231-b; amd, L 1967, ch 685, eff Sept 1, 1967; L 1990, ch 684, § 2, eff July 22, 1990, applying to all determinations of attorney's compensation, irrespective of when the services were performed or when the proceeding was commenced; L 1993, ch 514, § 52, eff Jan 1, 1994; L 1997, ch 100, § 2, eff June 11, 1997.

§ 2112. Compensation of persons acting under powers of attorney or other instruments

1. At any time during the administration of an estate and irrespective of the pendency of a particular proceeding the court is authorized either on its own initiative or on application by the fiduciary or a person interested to fix and determine the compensation, charges and expenses of a person acting under a power of attorney or other instrument described in EPTL 13-2.3 for services rendered to his principal, and to review and determine the validity and reasonableness of any such compensation, charge or expense, whether or not it has been fixed previously by agreement.

2. In the event any such person has already received or been paid a sum in excess of the fair and reasonable value of his services, charges and expenses as determined by the court the latter is authorized to direct him to refund the excess. A proceeding therefor may be commenced by the court on its own initiative or by the petition of a person interested.

3. Nothing contained herein shall be deemed to authorize the practice of law by an attorney in fact or other person acting under an instrument described in EPTL 13-2.3 who is not an attorney of this state.

> **History:** Add, L 1966, ch 953, eff Sept 1, 1967 from Sur. Ct. Act § 231-c.

§ 2113. Proof or probate of heirship

1. Where a person seized in fee of real property within the state dies intestate or without devising his real property, his distributees or any of them or any person deriving title from or through such distributees or any of them may present either to the court which has jurisdiction of the estate or to the court of a county where the real property or any part thereof is situated, a petition describing the property and showing the interest or share of the petitioner and of each distributee of the decedent in the property and praying for a decree establishing the right of inheritance thereto and that all the distributees of the decedent be required to show cause why the prayer of the petition should not be granted. Process must issue accordingly.

2. Upon the return of process the court must hear the allegations and proofs of the parties and determine the issues raised. The petitioner must establish

(a) The fact of the decedent's death.

(b) His domicile at the time thereof.

(c) His intestacy, either generally or as to the real property.

(d) His distributees entitled to inherit the property.

(e) The name, age, domicile and relationship to the decedent, of each, and

(f) the interest or share of each in the property.

3. The decree determining the issues shall be recorded by the petitioner in the office of the county clerk or the register, as the case may be, of each county in which the real property is situate, as prescribed by law for recording a deed.

> **History:** Add, L 1966, ch 953, eff Sept 1, 1967 from Sur. Ct. Act §§ 311, 312; amd, L 1993, ch 514, § 53, eff Jan 1, 1994.

§ 2114. Review of compensation of corporate trustee

1. At any time during the administration of a testamentary or lifetime trust and irrespective of the pendency of a particular proceeding, the court may review the reasonableness of the compensation determined by the corporate trustee for the trustee's own services. Any corporate trustee who has received excessive compensation from a trust may be ordered to make appropriate refunds.

2. A proceeding may be instituted by petition of a corporate trustee of the trust or any person interested in the trust. No accounting shall be required in such proceeding.

3. No trustee shall be liable or accountable for any commissions paid to another trustee hereunder which a court orders to be refunded to the trust or any person interested in the trust.

> **History:** Add, L 1984, ch 936, § 9, eff Aug 6, 1984.

§ 2115. Review of costs of delegation by trustee

1. At any time during the administration of a trust and irrespective of the pendency of a particular proceeding, the court with jurisdiction of the trust may review the reasonableness of the costs of a delegation by the trustee under section 11-2.3 of the estates, powers and trusts law and under section 554 of the not-for-profit corporation law.

2. A proceeding may be instituted by petition of the trustee or any person interested in the trust. No accounting shall be required in such proceeding.

3. The court shall grant such relief as it deems appropriate under the circumstances.

4. The terms "trust" and "trustee" as used in this section are defined in section 11-2.3 of the estates, powers and trusts law.

> **History:** dd, L 1994, ch 609, § 4, eff Jan 1, 1995; amd, L 2010, ch 490, § 13, eff Sept 17, 2010.

ARTICLE 22
ACCOUNTING
SUMMARY OF ARTICLE

§ 2201. Accountability of legal life tenant or fiduciary, committee or conservator of legal life tenant

Every right granted by this article to or against a testamentary trustee and the fiduciary, committee of a testamentary trustee or conservator shall apply to a similar proceeding by or against a legal life tenant and by or against the fiduciary, committee or conservator of a legal life tenant.

History: Add, L 1966, ch 953, eff Sept 1, 1967 from Sur. Ct. Act § 261-a; amd, L 1981, ch 115, § 129, eff May 18, 1981.

§ 2202. Recording or filing instruments settling accounts in part or in whole

There may be recorded or filed in the court any instrument settling an account in whole or in part executed by one or more fiduciaries and one or more legatees, devisees, distributees, beneficiaries, creditors or infants who have attained majority or in the case of an infant, incompetent or conservatee whose legacy, distributive share, beneficial interest or claim has been paid, by the guardian, committee or conservator of his property or the person receiving payment. Every such instrument to be recorded shall be acknowledged and if recorded, the record thereof, or a certified copy of the record or instrument shall be presumptive evidence of the contents of such instrument and its due execution.

History: Add, L 1966, ch 953, eff Sept 1, 1967 from Sur. Ct. Act § 251; amd, L 1968, ch 222, eff Sept 1, 1968; L 1980, ch 503, eff June 24, 1980; L 1981, ch 115, § 130, eff May 18, 1981.

§ 2203. Decree on filing instruments approving accounts

1. A fiduciary may present to the court a petition showing the names and post-office addresses of all persons interested, that all taxes have been paid or that no taxes were due and that the petitioner has fully accounted and made full disclosure in writing of his administration of the estate to all persons who would be required to be served with process in a proceeding under section twenty-two hundred ten of this article and praying for a decree releasing and discharging the petitioner.

2. The petition shall also show

(a) in the case of a fiduciary other than a testamentary trustee, guardian or lifetime trustee either that his letters have been revoked or that he has been removed or that the time for creditors to present claims has expired and that all known debts of the decedent and administration expenses have been paid,

(b) in the case of a trustee whether or not the trust has been fully executed,

(c) in the case of a guardian either that the infant has reached his majority or has died.

3. The petitioner shall also file with the petition acknowledged instruments executed by all the persons who would be required to be served with process in a proceeding under section twenty-two hundred ten of this article or in the case of an infant, incompetent or conservatee whose legacy, distributive share or claim has been paid, by the guardian, committee or conservator of his property or person receiving payment, approving the account of the petitioner and releasing and discharging the petitioner.

4. The court may thereupon make a decree releasing and discharging the petitioner and the sureties on his bond, if any, from any further liability to all persons interested.

History: Add, L 1966, ch 953, eff Sept 1, 1967 from Sur. Ct. Act § 251-a; amd, L 1967, ch 685, eff Sept 1, 1967; L 1968, ch 742, Sept 1, 1968; L 1978, ch 86, § 1, eff April 25, 1978; L 1980, ch 503, § 30, eff June 24, 1980; L 1981, ch 115, § 131, eff May 18, 1981.

§ 2204. Judicial settlement where recovery has been had in negligence action

1. Where a judgment or compromise of a cause of action has been obtained and the proceeds are ready to be paid over and where the recovery is not an asset of the decedent's estate but goes by special provision of law to designated persons or classes of persons, the fiduciary may at any time file a petition for the judicial settlement of his account relating to the proceeds and upon the return of process or upon the waiver of all persons interested, if adult and competent, the court may take and settle his account and direct payment to the parties entitled according to their respective rights and interests and upon filing receipts for the payments the party paying the money and the fiduciary shall be discharged from all further liability as to such cause of action and the proceeds.

2. Where such recovery has been had and the amount thereof paid to the fiduciary, he may in like manner have a judicial settlement of his account relating to such proceeds at any time and a decree made discharging him from all further liability concerning it.

History: Add, L 1966, ch 953, eff Sept 1, 1967 from Sur. Ct. Act § 252.

§ 2205. Compulsory account and related relief on a court's own initiative or on petition; who may petition

1. In the manner provided in this section and in section 2206, the court may at any time, upon it appearing that it is for the best interests of the estate, make an order (a) requiring a fiduciary to file an intermediate or final account within such time and in such manner as directed by it, (b) suspending a fiduciary who being duly cited to account neglects to appear on the return of process without showing a satisfactory excuse therefore, or who fails to file an account within such time and in such manner as directed by the court, (c) appointing an eligible person to succeed a fiduciary whose letters have been suspended, (d) fixing a trial date for a hearing on the removal of a fiduciary whose letters have been suspended, (e) fixing a trial date to take and state an account on behalf of a fiduciary who fails to file such account or procure its settlement, and (f) granting such other and further relief as the court may direct.

2. The court may make an order as provided in subdivision one of this section either on its own initiative or on the petition of:

(a) a creditor, or

(b) a person interested, or

(c) a public administrator or county treasurer, or

(d) any person in behalf of an infant or child born after the making of the will when interested in the estate, or

(e) the fiduciary of a deceased person interested, or

(f) a surety on the bond of the fiduciary required to account, or

(g) a successor fiduciary or remaining fiduciary where letters of the predecessor or co-fiduciary have been revoked or the predecessor or co-fiduciary has been removed, or

(h) a co-fiduciary after he or she has filed his or her account and a petition for its judicial settlement, or

(i) the attorney-general of the state where any part of the estate may escheat to the state of New York.

History: Add, L 1966, ch 953, eff Sept 1, 1967 from Sur. Ct. Act §§ 253, 256, 257-a, 258,

2597; amd, L 1980, ch 503, eff June 24, 198; L 2002, ch 457, § 3, eff Nov 1, 2002.

§ 2206. Compulsory account and related relief; proceedings thereupon

1. A petition to compel an account made pursuant to 2205 may request multiple relief (a) pursuant to 711 and 719 to suspend and/or remove a fiduciary who fails to appear on the return date of process or fails to file an account within such time and in such manner as directed by the court; (b) to appoint, immediately, an eligible person to succeed a fiduciary whose letters have been suspended or revoked; and (c) to take and state an account on behalf of a fiduciary who fails to account and procure its settlement.

2. On the presentation of a petition made pursuant to 2205 or when so directed by the court, process, including a summary statement of any proposed stated account, shall issue to the fiduciary accordingly and on the return thereof if the fiduciary fails to appear or to file an account or to show good cause to the contrary or to present a petition as prescribed in 2208 the court may by order direct the fiduciary to account within the time and in the manner directed by the court, to cause process to issue requiring all persons necessary to be served under 2210 to show cause why the account should not be judicially settled, cause such process to be served upon such persons and that the fiduciary attend before the court from time to time for the purpose of the settlement of the account. In addition, the order may (a) immediately suspend the letters of a fiduciary who fails to appear on the return date of process or who fails to file an account within such time and in such manner as directed by the court, (b) immediately appoint an eligible person to succeed a fiduciary whose letters are suspended, (c) schedule a hearing for the modification or revocation of the letters of a fiduciary whose letters are suspended, and (d) schedule a hearing to take and state an account on behalf of a fiduciary who fails to file an account and procure its settlement. Such order shall also direct the issuance of supplemental process to such persons entitled to notice on an application to suspend, modify or revoke a fiduciary's letters, to appoint a successor fiduciary or to settle a fiduciary's account.

3. The pendency of a proceeding against a fiduciary to compel an accounting does not preclude the fiduciary from presenting a petition as prescribed in 2208. If such petition is presented on or before the return of process as prescribed herein, process issued thereon need not be directed to the petitioner who compelled the accounting, and the two proceedings must be consolidated.

4. After hearing the proofs of the parties the court may take and state the account and make such order or decree as justice shall require, notwithstanding the failure or refusal of the fiduciary to file such account and procure its settlement.

History: Add, L 1966, ch 953, eff Sept 1, 1967 from Sur. Ct. Act § 260; amd, L 1967, ch 685, § 126; L 1971, ch 805, eff Sept 1, 1971; L 2002, ch 457, § 4, eff Nov 1, 2002.

§ 2207. Accounting by fiduciary of deceased fiduciary, committee of incompetent fiduciary, or conservator of conservatee fiduciary

1. Where a fiduciary dies the court has the same jurisdiction upon the petition of any person required to be served upon a voluntary judicial settlement of the account of the deceased fiduciary to compel the fiduciary of the deceased fiduciary to account which it would have against the deceased fiduciary.

2. A fiduciary of a deceased fiduciary may voluntarily account for the acts and doings of the deceased fiduciary and for the property of the estate which had come into the possession

of the latter, whether or not such property has come into the hands of the fiduciary of the deceased fiduciary, provided however, that the fiduciary of the deceased fiduciary shall not be accountable for such property except to the extent that he shall have assets of the estate of the deceased fiduciary.

3. On the death of a fiduciary while an accounting by or against him as such is pending before the court, the court may continue the proceeding where his fiduciary or successor has voluntarily made himself a party thereto or has been brought in by process, and proceed with the accounting and determine all questions and grant any relief which the court would have power to determine or grant in case such fiduciary had not died or in case the fiduciary of the deceased fiduciary had voluntarily petitioned for an accounting as provided in this section.

4. On a petition filed by a fiduciary of a deceased fiduciary there shall be brought in the persons who would be necessary parties to a proceeding commenced by the deceased fiduciary for a judicial settlement of his accounts and also if a successor of the deceased fiduciary has been appointed, such successor or his fiduciary.

5. If upon the accounting the court finds that there can be a distribution in whole or in part to the parties entitled thereto it may make a decree accordingly and may also therein direct payment and delivery of the balance of the estate by the fiduciary of the deceased fiduciary upon such terms and security as it deems proper. For the purpose of payment and distribution the fiduciary of the deceased fiduciary shall have all the powers and duties of the deceased fiduciary.

6. Upon the settlement of the account the court may allow to the fiduciary of the deceased fiduciary reasonable compensation for any service rendered by him to the estate accounted for. The compensation so allowed plus any commissions retained by the deceased fiduciary or payable to his estate shall in no event exceed a full commission under 2307, 2308 or 2309, whichever section is applicable to the type of the deceased fiduciary.

7. The court may grant to the fiduciary of a deceased fiduciary all of the rights and powers of the deceased fiduciary, subject to all of the duties and liabilities of such deceased fiduciary.

8. Every right granted by this section to or against the fiduciary of a deceased fiduciary shall apply to a similar proceeding by or against the committee of an incompetent fiduciary or the conservator of a conservatee fiduciary.

History: Add, L 1966, ch 953, eff Sept 1, 1967 from Sur. Ct. Act § 257; amd, L 1967, ch 685, § 127, eff Sept 1, 1967; L 1981, ch 115, §§ 132, 133, eff May 18, 1981.

§ 2208. Voluntary account; who may petition

In any of the following cases a fiduciary may present to the court his account and a petition praying that his account be judicially settled and that all necessary and proper parties be required to show cause why such settlement should not be had:

1. By a fiduciary other than a guardian or trustee,

(a) Where the time for presentation of claims as fixed by a published notice has expired or 7 months have expired since letters were issued to the original fiduciary.

(b) Where his letters have been revoked.

(c) Where the court at any time within 6 months after the issuance of letters to the original fiduciary entertains an application by the fiduciary for the judicial settlement of his account and it appears from the petition or account that a disposition of the decedent's real property will be necessary for any of the purposes specified in 1902.

(d) Where his account has not been judicially settled within 1 year preceding the application therefor and the application is entertained.

2. By a guardian,

(a) Where a petition for a compulsory judicial settlement of his account may be presented by any other person.

(b) Where he has expended all of the estate of the infant and the court deems it proper that he should be discharged.

3. By a trustee,

(a) Where one or more distinct and separate trusts created by the will or lifetime trust instrument have been or are ready to be executed.

(b) Where his account has not been judicially settled within 1 year preceding the application therefor and the court entertains the application.

History: Add, L 1966, ch 953, eff Sept 1, 1967 from Sur. Ct. Act § 261; amd, L 1980, ch 503, § 32, eff June 24, 1980.

§ 2209. Affidavit to account

To each account filed in the court, as prescribed in this article, must be appended the affidavit of the accounting party to the effect that the account contains according to the best of his knowledge and belief a true statement of all his receipts and disbursements on account of the estate and of all money or other property belonging to the estate which have come into his hands or been received by any other person by his order or authority for his use and that he does not know of any error or omission in the account to the prejudice of any creditor of, or person interested in, the estate.

History: Add, L 1966, ch 953, eff Sept 1, 1967 from Sur. Ct. Act § 264; amd, L 1967, ch 685, § 128, eff Sept 1, 1967.

§ 2210. Voluntary account; process

Upon a voluntary judicial settlement of the account of a fiduciary process must issue to:

1. All unpaid creditors or persons claiming to be creditors of the decedent.

2. The surety on his bond, if any.

3. All cofiduciaries who do not join in the petition.

4. The successor, if one has been appointed, in a case where the petitioner has been removed or his letters have been revoked, and if no successor has been appointed, all persons interested who are required to receive process under this section.

5. The attorney general where he is required to be given notice of an accounting proceeding pursuant to clause (D) of subparagraph one of paragraph (e) of section 8-1.4 of the estates, powers and trusts law, or where the decedent, infant or beneficiary died intestate as to any part of the estate leaving one or more unknown distributees or one or more distributees whose whereabouts are unknown.

6. The distributees where the decedent, infant or beneficiary died intestate as to any property, except those who by acknowledged release appear to have been paid.

7. All devisees, all trustees of any trust created by the will or the lifetime trust instrument and all legatees except those who by acknowledged release appear to be paid and if any such be an infant, incompetent or conservatee whose legacy or claim has been paid, such release shall be executed by the guardian, committee of his property* and if payment has been made to an infant, incompetent or conservatee under the provisions of 2220, or EPTL 7-4.8** or 11-1.1, such release shall be executed by the person to whom payment was made.

8. In the case of a guardian process shall also issue to the infant.

9. In the case of a trustee process shall also issue to all persons who are entitled absolutely or contingently by the terms of the will, lifetime trust instrument or by operation of law to share in the estate.

10. Where an accounting fiduciary accounts to himself in a separate capacity as the fiduciary of a deceased beneficiary of the estate, or as trustee or as guardian of an infant beneficiary, or as the committee of an incompetent, or as the conservator of a conservatee it shall not be sufficient to issue process to or obtain the appearance of the accounting party in such separate capacity only, but in addition process shall issue to all persons interested in the estate of the deceased beneficiary, the infant, the incompetent, the conservatee or the trust of which the accounting party is trustee. The provisions of this subdivision shall not apply where the accounting fiduciary has in said separate capacity one or more co-fiduciaries who are not his co-fiduciaries in his accounting capacity.

11. Where any person to whom process is required to issue has died process shall issue to his fiduciary and if none has been appointed to all persons interested in the estate of the deceased as distributees, nominated fiduciaries or named as legatees or devisees under any will of the deceased filed in the court.

12. In any case the court may, for good cause shown, dispense with the service of process on any person provided the value of his interest in the estate does not exceed $500. Where service of process upon such person has been dispensed with the decree setting*** the account shall not be conclusive against him unless he shall before the entry of the decree appear in the proceeding, waive the issuance or service of the process or be served therewith.

13. Notwithstanding any other provision of this section to the contrary, whenever the accounting party is the public administrator, county treasurer or county officer succeeding to the duties of county treasurer, where the beneficiaries are unknown, and there are no known claimants as beneficiary, and where it appears that the value of the interests of all beneficiaries in the estate does not exceed two thousand five hundred dollars, the court may dispense with service of process on beneficiaries. In such case the attorney general must be cited and may make any objection to the account that could be made by any

---

* **Ed. Note:** It appears an error has been made, omitting a reference to conservators.

** Renumbered to § 7-4.8 by L 1981 ch 43, eff March 30, 1981.

*** So in original. Should probably be "settling".

beneficiary. The decree to be entered shall be binding upon any person who shall ultimately be determined to be entitled to share in the estate.

14. The provisions of section three hundred fifteen shall apply to a proceeding under this section.

History: Add, L 1966, ch 953, eff Sept 1, 1967 from Sur. Ct. Act § 262; amd, L 1967, ch 685, § 129, eff Sept 1, 1967; subd 13, add L 1968, ch 259, eff May 14, 1968; amd L 1968, ch 673, §§ 1, 2, eff Sept 1, 1968; L 1969, ch 551, eff Sept 1, 1969; L 1970, ch 396, § 8, eff Sept 1, 1970; L 1971, ch 805, eff Sept 1, 1971; L 1973, ch 455, eff June 5, 1973; L 1980, ch 503, § 33, eff June 24, 1980; L 1981, ch 115, §§ 134, 135, eff May 18, 1981; L 1982, ch 897, § 1, eff July 29, 1982.

§ 2211. Voluntary account; proceedings thereupon

1. On the return of process issued as prescribed in the preceding section the court must take the account, hear the proofs of the parties respecting it and make such order or decree as justice shall require.

2. The fiduciary may be examined under oath by any party to the proceeding either before or after filing objections, if any, to the account, as to any matter relating to his or her administration of the estate. The party conducting such examination shall be entitled to all rights granted under article thirty-one of the civil practice law and rules with respect to document discovery, regardless of whether such examination takes place before or after such party files objections.

History: Add, L 1966, ch 953, eff Sept 1, 1967 from Sur. Ct. Act § 263; amd, L 1967, ch 685, § 130, eff Sept 1, 1967; L 2007, ch 470, § 1, eff Jan 1, 2008.

§ 2212. Accounting for profit and loss

No profit shall be made by a fiduciary by the increase nor shall he sustain any loss by the decrease or loss without his fault of any part of the estate, but he shall be charged with the increase and credited for the decrease or loss on the settlement of his accounts.

History: Add, L 1966, ch 953, eff Sept 1, 1967 from Sur. Ct. Act § 265.

§ 2213. Accounting for claim for funeral expenses

1. If upon any accounting it shall appear that a fiduciary has failed to pay a claim for funeral expenses, the amount of which has been fixed by the court as provided in 2101 and 2102 or upon the accounting, he shall not be credited with the payment of any debt or claim against the decedent until the claim for funeral expenses has been paid, but such claim shall not be paid before the expenses of administration are paid.

2. In any accounting the claim for funeral expenses shall be separate and apart from the claim for expenses of administration.

History: Add, L 1966, ch 953, eff Sept 1, 1967 from Sur. Ct. Act § 216 in part.

§ 2214. Property of estate to be delivered on order

1. The court has jurisdiction to compel a fiduciary or the fiduciary or successor of any deceased fiduciary at any time to deliver any of the property of the estate which has come into his possession or is under his control and if it be delivered over after a decree must allow such credit upon the decree as justice shall require.

2. The court has jurisdiction when a fiduciary has died, absconded, become incompetent, has been removed or his letters have been revoked to direct him or any person, firm or corporation having possession or control of any property belonging to the estate to deliver it to the court or a successor appointed by the court or as directed by the decree made pursuant to 2207 or CPLR 2510.

> **History:** Add, L 1966, ch 953, eff Sept 1, 1967 from Sur. Ct. Act § 266; amd, L 1967, ch 685, eff Sept 1, 1967; L 1968, ch 259, § 36, eff May 14, 1968; L 1980, ch 503, § 34, eff June 24, 1980.

§ 2215. Decree for payment and distribution

1. Where an account is judicially settled as prescribed in this article and any part of the estate remains and is ready to be distributed the decree must direct the payment and distribution therefrom of the shares of the persons entitled thereto, except that no decree of distribution shall be made in an accounting proceeding in which there has been a disposition of real property pursuant to article 19 commenced within 6 months from the grant of letters until time for the presentation of claims as fixed by a published notice has expired or 7 months have expired since letters were first issued and if there be creditors who were not served with process upon the petition for accounting, until supplemental process shall have issued to them.

2. The court may award to a surviving spouse or child the same relief as to set-off of exempt property which may be awarded in such person's favor on a petition presented as prescribed in 2102.

3. If any creditor or person interested has received estate assets in excess of the amount determined on the settlement of the account to be due him the court is authorized to direct in the decree repayment by him of the excess to the fiduciary of the estate or otherwise as justice shall require and the exercise of such power by the court heretofore is confirmed.

> **History:** Add, L 1966, ch 953, eff Sept 1, 1967 from Sur. Ct. Act § 267; amd, L 1967, ch 685, § 132, eff Sept 1, 1967.

§ 2216. Distribution in kind

At any time during the administration of an estate or upon an accounting the court may direct the conveyance of any unsold realty or the delivery of any unsold chattel or the assignment of any uncollected demand or any other personal property to a party or parties entitled to payment or distribution, in lieu of the money value of the property at the fair market value at the date of distribution.

> **History:** Add, L 1966, ch 953, eff Sept 1, 1967 from Sur. Ct. Act § 268; amd, L 1967, ch 685, § 133, eff Sept 1, 1967.

§ 2217. When money or property may be retained

1. In any of the following cases the decree must direct that a sum sufficient to satisfy a debt or claim or the proportion to which it is entitled, together with the probable amount of the

interest and costs, or that any personal property the right to which is in controversy, be retained in the hands of the accounting party or be deposited in a bank or trust company, subject to the order of the court, or be paid into the court for the purpose of being applied to the payment of the debt or claim or to the satisfaction of any judgment recovered and that so much thereof as is not needed for such purposes be afterwards distributed:

(a) Where an admitted debt of the decedent, ascertainable in amount, is not yet due and the creditor will not presently accept payment with a rebate of interest, or

(b) Where a claim for a debt, ascertainable in amount, but not yet due has been disputed or rejected, or

(c) Where an action is pending between the fiduciary and a person claiming to be a creditor of the decedent, or

(d) Where on the judicial settlement of the account of a trustee a controversy respecting the right of a party to share in the estate or other personal property held by the trustee has not been determined.

2. Upon the determination of the debt or claim or the right to the personal property any party may present a petition to the court praying for directions as to the disposition of the moneys or property retained.

History: Add, L 1966, ch 953, eff Sept 1, 1967 from Sur. Ct. Act § 269; amd, L 1967, ch 685, § 134, eff Sept 1, 1967.

§ 2218. Deposit in court for benefit of legatee, distributee or beneficiary

1. (a) Where it shall appear that an alien legatee, distributee or beneficiary is domiciled or resident within a country to which checks or warrants drawn against funds of the United States may not be transmitted by reason of any executive order, regulation or similar determination of the United States government or any department or agency thereof, the court shall direct that the money or property to which such alien would otherwise be entitled shall be paid into court for the benefit of said alien or the person or persons who thereafter may appear to be entitled thereto. The money or property so paid into court shall be paid out only upon order of the surrogate or pursuant to the order or judgment of a court of competent jurisdiction.

(b) Any assignment of a fund which is required to be deposited pursuant to the provisions of paragraph one (a) of this section shall not be effective to confer upon the assignee any greater right to the delivery of the fund than the assignor would otherwise enjoy.

2. Where it shall appear that a beneficiary would not have the benefit or use or control of the money or other property due him or where other special circumstances make it desirable that such payment should be withheld the decree may direct that such money or property be paid into court for the benefit of the beneficiary or the person or persons who may thereafter appear entitled thereto. The money or property so paid into court shall be paid out only upon order of the court or pursuant to the order or judgment of a court of competent jurisdiction.

2-a. Where it appears to the court that the laws of a foreign country or sovereignty effectively deny a New York state resident beneficiary legatee or distributee of the benefit, use or control of money or other property, a decree issued in a matter concerning the right of a resident of such foreign country or sovereignty to the benefit, use or control of money or other property with a situs in New York state may direct that such money or property be paid into the court for the benefit of the beneficiary or the person or persons who may thereafter appear entitled thereto. The money or property so paid into the court shall be paid out only upon order of the court or pursuant to the order or judgment of a court of competent jurisdiction.

3. In any such proceeding where it is uncertain that an alien beneficiary or fiduciary not residing within the United States, the District of Columbia, the Commonwealth of Puerto Rico or a territory or possession of the United States would have the benefit or use or control of the money or property due him the burden of proving that the alien beneficiary will receive the benefit or use or control of the money or property due him shall be upon him or the person claiming from, through or under him.

4. Notwithstanding* any laws of inheritance or descent and distribution of any state or territory of the United States, and notwithstanding similar laws of foreign countries or sovereignties, such states or territories of the United States or foreign countries or sovereignties may not claim for themselves, as heirs or distributees or by any other theory of inheritance, any funds whose situs is in this state and which have been deposited pursuant to the laws of the state of New York for the benefit of any distributee, heir, legatee or owner of said funds, whether known or unknown, or for any person whose whereabouts are unknown.

History: Add, L 1966, ch 953, eff Sept 1, 1967 from Sur. Ct. Act § 269-a; amd, L 1968, ch 998, eff June 22, 1968; L 1977, ch 496, eff Aug 1, 1977; L 1992, ch 457, § 1, eff July 17, 1992.

§ 2219. Adjustment of advancements

Where there is a surplus of personal property to be distributed and the advancement as provided in EPTL 2-1.5 consisted of personal property or where a deficiency in the adjustment of an advancement of real property is chargeable on personal property, the decree for distribution in the court must adjust all the advances which have not been previously adjusted by a court of competent jurisdiction and if any person to be affected by the decree is not a party to the proceeding the court must cause him to be brought in by supplemental process.

History: Add, L 1966, ch 953, eff Sept 1, 1967 from Sur. Ct. Act § 270 and CPLR § 1206(1); amd, L 1968, ch 259, § 37, eff May 14, 1968.

---

* So in original. Should be "Notwithstanding".

§ 2220. Payment of share of infant, incompetent or conservatee or person under disability

1. Where an infant, incompetent, conservatee, or person under disability is entitled to money or property as beneficiary of an estate or to the proceeds of any action brought as prescribed in EPTL 5-4.1 or to the proceeds of a settlement of a cause of action for personal injuries, the decree or order shall direct that it be paid or delivered to the guardian, committee or conservator of the property of such person upon the filing of sufficient security, except as provided in EPTL 7-4.9 or 11-1.1, unless the money or property payable or deliverable to the infant, incompetent, or conservatee, or person under disability does not exceed in value $10,000, in which case the decree or order may order it to be paid or delivered to a parent of such person or to some competent adult with whom such person resides or who has some interest in such person's welfare, for the use and benefit of such person.

2. If the sum payable to a patient in an institution in the state department of mental hygiene is not in excess of the amount which the director of the institution is authorized to receive pursuant to section 29.23 of the mental hygiene law, the decree or order may order it to be paid to such director for use as provided in that section.

3. If there be no guardian, committee or conservator of the property the decree or order may provide that the sum payable to the infant, incompetent or person under substantial impairment within the meaning of the conservatorship provisions of article seventy-seven of the mental hygiene law not disposed of as above be paid into the court or the court may order that money constituting any part of the property be deposited in one or more specified insured banks or trust companies or be invested in one or more specified accounts in insured savings and loan associations subject to withdrawal only upon order of the court, except that no court order shall be required to pay over to the infant who has attained the age of eighteen years all moneys so held unless the depository is in receipt of an order from a court of competent jurisdiction directing it to withhold such payment beyond the infant's eighteenth birthday.

4. If money or property is payable or deliverable under subdivision one of this section to a person under disability as defined in article seventy-seven of the mental hygiene law, the court may pursuant to such article appoint a conservator provided that: the person under the disability resides within the county in which the proceeding is pending; no guardian, committee or conservator has been appointed by the supreme court or county court; and the money or property is to be paid or delivered to the conservator.

5. If any proceeds payable to an infant, incompetent or person under disability pursuant to this section are proposed to be paid by way of a structured settlement, which shall include any settlement whose terms contain provisions for the payment of funds on an installment basis, the court may approve such settlement, provided that, with respect to future installment payments, the court may order that each party liable for such payments shall fund such payments, in an amount necessary to assure the future payments, in the form of an annuity contract executed by a qualified insurer and approved by the superintendent of financial services pursuant to articles fifty-A and fifty-B of the civil practice law and rules.

History: Add, L 1966, ch 953, eff Sept 1, 1967 from Sur. Ct. Act § 271; amd, L 1967, ch 685, § 135; L 1968, ch 259, eff May 14, 1968; L 1973, ch 195, § 23, eff April 23, 1973; L 1973, ch 455, eff June 5, 1973; L 1975, ch 228, eff Sept 1, 1975; L 1981, ch 115, eff May 18, 1981; L 1981, ch 362, §§ 1–3, eff Sept 1, 1981; L 1982, ch 358, eff June 21, 1982; L 1988, ch 635, eff Oct 1, 1988; L 1990, ch 199, eff June 2, 1990; L 1992, ch 595, § 23, eff Sept 1, 1992; L 2011, ch 62, § 104 (Part A), eff Oct 3, 2011.

§ 2221. Payment of legacy or distributive share to foreign fiduciary

1. Where a beneficiary of an estate is entitled to money or property within the jurisdiction of the court and such beneficiary is a non-domiciliary infant, incompetent, conservatee or decedent, payment or delivery thereof may be directed by the court to the fiduciary, committee or conservator, by whatever title such foreign fiduciary may be designated, of the property or estate of the non-domiciliary infant, incompetent, conservatee or decedent, upon proof satisfactory to the court that the foreign fiduciary is entitled to receive such money or property in accordance with the terms and conditions of EPTL 13-3.4 and that the fiduciary, committee or conservator has filed at the domicile security sufficient to cover such payment or delivery or that no security is required at the domicile of the beneficiary. In the case of a deceased beneficiary there shall be submitted proof that he has no known creditors within this state.

2. The court may direct such payment or delivery in a decree judicially settling the account of a fiduciary or in an order entered upon the application of the fiduciary holding such money or property for distribution or of the foreign fiduciary, committee or conservator.

History: Add, L 1966, ch 953, eff Sept 1, 1967 from Sur. Ct. Act § 271-a; amd, L 1967, ch 685, eff Sept 1, 1967; L 1981, ch 115, §§ 139, 140, eff May 18, 1981.

§ 2222. Legacy or distributive share payable to unknown person to be paid to comptroller

1. Where the person entitled to a legacy or distributive share is unknown the decree must direct the fiduciary to pay the amount thereof to the comptroller of the state for the benefit of the person or persons who may thereafter appear to be entitled thereto.

The decree must also direct that such payment be accompanied by a copy of the decree, certified by the clerk of the court to be a true copy of the original on file in his office. The fee for such certification shall be deemed a necessary and proper disbursement, to be charged against and deducted from said legacy or distributive share prior to payment of same to the comptroller, said disbursement to be paid or credited to the person making the same, as the surrogate in said decree may direct.

2. The court or the supreme court upon the petition of a person claiming to be so entitled and upon at least 14 days' notice, accompanied with a copy of the petition, to the attorney general, the state comptroller and the public administrator of the county or if there be none, the county treasurer, may by a reference or by directing the trial of an issue by a jury or otherwise, ascertain the rights of the persons interested and grant an order directing the payment of any money which appears to be due to the claimant, but without interest and after deducting all expenses incurred by the state with respect thereto.

3. The comptroller upon the production of a certified copy of the order must draw his warrant upon the abandoned property fund for the amount therein directed to be paid payable to the person entitled thereto.

4. At any time prior to the granting of an order therein notice of the claim, accompanied with a copy of the petition, shall be given by the petitioner to such persons and in such manner as directed by the court.

History: Add, L 1966, ch 953, eff Sept 1, 1967 from Sur. Ct. Act § 272; amd, L 1967, ch 685, § 137, eff Sept 1, 1967; L 1972, ch 125, § 1, eff July 1, 1972; L 1973, ch 218, § 1, eff April 25, 1973.

§ 2222-a. Notice of legacy or distributive share payable to incarcerated individual or prisoner

Where the legatee, distributee or beneficiary is an incarcerated individual serving a sentence of imprisonment with the state department of corrections and community supervision or a prisoner confined at a local correctional facility, the court shall give prompt written notice to the office of victim services, and at the same time direct that no payment be made to such incarcerated individual or prisoner for a period of thirty days following the date of entry of the order containing such direction.

> **History:** Add, L 2001, ch 62, § 9, eff June 25, 2001, and, notwithstanding the expiration of any other statute of limitations, shall apply to: (i) all judgments originally entered prior to such effective date, regardless whether such judgment is subsequently amended or satisfied on or after such effective date; and (ii) all judgments, obligations or agreements to pay profits from a crime or funds of a convicted person entered, incurred or entered into on or after the effective date of this act; amd, L 2010, ch 56, § 45 (Part A-1), eff June 22, 2010; L 2011, ch 62, § 167 (Part C, Subpart B), eff March 31, 2011; L 2021, ch 322 § 244, eff Aug 2, 2021.

§ 2223. Funds paid into court

1. Where it appears that the whereabouts of any legatee, distributee, creditor or other person entitled to payment from the estate is unknown the decree must direct the fiduciary to pay into court the legacy, distributive share or money due such person which is not paid to the person entitled thereto within such time as directed by the court, which shall, however, be not later than 6 months from the time when the decree is made or when the legacy, distributive share or money is payable by the terms of the decree.

2. If at the expiration of 6 months after the making of the decree it is shown to the court that payment of the legacy, distributive share or money cannot be made to the person entitled thereto, an order may be made directing the payment thereof into court.

3. The money so paid into court can be paid out only by the order of the court or a court of competent jurisdiction.

4. Except in the counties wholly within the city of New York, if the amount payable does not exceed $50 a county treasurer may pay it without a court order to the person entitled thereto.

5. The state comptroller may institute any necessary proceeding before the court to compel the deposit of such moneys in court which have not been paid over or deposited after the expiration of 6 months or the expiration of such shorter period as directed by the court.

6. Where a sum of money in excess of $250 has been paid into court and subsequently paid to the state comptroller as abandoned property pursuant to paragraph (a) of subdivision 1 of section 600 of the abandoned property law an order for the payment of such money from the abandoned property fund shall be made by the court only upon notice to the state comptroller, to all persons who have made claim thereto and to such other persons as directed by the court.

> **History:** Add, L 1966, ch 953, eff Sept 1, 1967 from Sur. Ct. Act § 273; amd, L 1967, ch 685, § 138, eff Sept 1, 1967.

§ 2224. Id.; where beneficiary's name or whereabouts is unknown

1. Where it appears to the satisfaction of the court that the name or whereabouts of any person interested in the estate as a beneficiary or assignee cannot be ascertained after the exercise of due diligence and that the value of such person's interest in the estate does not

exceed the sum of $1,000, the court may direct by order or decree the fiduciary to pay the amount of such person's interest into the court for the benefit of the person or persons who may thereafter appear to be entitled thereto.

2. Upon making the payment as provided above the fiduciary shall be discharged from all futher* liability as to the amount paid into court. The order or decree may be granted on the petition of a fiduciary.

3. Notice of the application therefor shall be given to the persons and in the manner directed by the court or the court may dispense therewith.

4. The money so paid into court as above provided may be paid out only by the order of the court or pursuant to an order or judgment of a court of competent jurisdiction.

5. Except in the counties wholly within the city of New York, if the amount payable does not exceed $50 a county treasurer may pay it without a court order to the person entitled thereto.

> **History:** Add, L 1966, ch 953, eff Sept 1, 1967 from Sur. Ct. Act § 273-a; amd, L 1967, ch 685, eff Sept 1, 1967; L 1979, ch 83, § 1, eff Sept 1, 1979.

§ 2225. Determination of distributees, devisees, legatees, beneficiaries and distributive and beneficial shares

In any proceeding where the court is required to determine the distributees entitled to share in the estate under EPTL 4-1.1, or where a devisee, legatee or a beneficiary of a will or trust subject to the jurisdiction of the court is entitled to money or property upon the occurrence of a specified event, the petition may request the court as incidental thereto to adjudge that (a) a person who might otherwise be a distributee, devisee, legatee or beneficiary is dead or (b) that no distributees, devisees, legatees or beneficiaries other than those stated in the record exists. Citation shall issue to the person named and to unknown distributees or to unknown devisees, legatees or beneficiaries, if any. For the purposes of this section, a "specified event" shall be the time specified in the will or lifetime trust for the determination of the identity of the devisee, legatee, beneficiary or members of a class thereof entitled to share in the estate or trust property.

(a) If it is established to the satisfaction of the court that a person who would be a distributee, or a devisee, legatee or beneficiary upon the occurrence of a specified event, has not been heard from for a period of at least three years since the death of the decedent, or since the occurrence of such event, as the case may be, that a diligent search has been made to discover evidence that such person is still living, and that no such evidence has been found, the court may make a determination that such person is presumed dead and that he or she predeceased the decedent without issue or that such devisee, legatee or beneficiary is presumed to have died prior to the occurrence of such event and that such person died prior thereto without issue other than those issues stated in the record.

(b) If it appears to the satisfaction of the court that diligent and exhaustive efforts have been made from all available sources to ascertain the existence of distributees, or members of a class of devisees, legatees or beneficiaries, that at least three years have elapsed since the death of the decedent, or since the occurrence of the specified event upon which such

---

* So in original. Should be "further".

class is finally determined, as the case may be, that the parties before the court know of no distributees of the decedent, or of such legatees, devisees or beneficiaries, other than those stated in the record, and that no claim to a share in the estate or trust has been made by any person whose relationship or existence has not been established in the record, the court may make a determination that no distributee of the decedent or class of distributees exists, or that no such devisee, legatee or beneficiary, or members of a class of legatees, devisees or beneficiaries exists, other than those whose status is established in the record before the court.

(c) Upon making the findings under subdivision (a) or (b) of this section, the court may direct distribution of the assets to those distributees or to those devisees, legatees and beneficiaries whose relationship or present existence has been established in the record before the court.

History: Add, L 1975, ch 156, eff Sept 1, 1975; amd, L 1985, ch 106, § 1, eff May 21, 1985; L 1996, ch 89, § 1, eff May 21, 1996, applying to the estate of any person dying before or after such effective date and to any trust whenever created.

§ 2226. Rights of alleged decedent upon return

If letters shall issue upon the estate of an alleged decedent and if thereafter the person alleged to be dead shall return he or she shall on demand receive the property then in the hands of the fiduciary after reserve for any unpaid administration charges and shall have only the further rights to compel an accounting on the part of his or her fiduciary and to enforce the decree made thereon. His or her fiduciary shall not be liable for moneys or assets disbursed or delivered by him or her in good faith and the person alleged to be dead may not, upon his or her return, review any matter or recover any property embraced in any account of his or her fiduciary which may have been finally settled by decree entered prior to the date when his or her fiduciary shall have had actual notice that he or she is still living.

History: add, L 1966, ch 953, eff Sept 1. 1967 from Sur. Ct. Act §§ 119, 144, 162 in part; amd L 1967, ch 685, eff Sept 1, 1967; renumbered § 2226, L 1975, ch 156, § 1; amd L 1993, ch 514, § 54, eff Jan 1, 1994.

§ 2227. Summary statement

Each decree whereby an account is judicially settled must contain in the body thereof a summary statement of the account as settled or must refer to such summary, which must be recorded.

History: add, L 1966, ch 953, eff Sept 1, 1967 from Sur. Ct. Act § 274; renumbered § 2227, L 1975, ch 156, § 1, eff Sept 1, 1975.

ARTICLE 23
COSTS, ALLOWANCES AND COMMISSIONS
SUMMARY OF ARTICLE

§ 2301. Costs, general

1. Costs and allowances in the court shall be awarded solely in accordance with this article and shall include all disbursements of the party awarded costs which might be taxed in the supreme court.

2. Any award for costs or an allowance is in all instances discretionary with the court. The amount allowed must be fixed by the court and inserted in the decree or order.

3. All costs taxed and any allowance granted to reimburse a party in part or in whole for counsel fees or other expenses necessarily paid or incurred shall be awarded to the party but the whole or any part thereof may be made payable to an attorney rendering services to the party in the proceeding or on the appeal, except as otherwise provided in subdivision 8 of the succeeding section.

4. Except where special provision is otherwise made by law costs or an allowance may be made payable by any party personally or out of the assets of the estate or out of the share or interest of any person or from both in such proportion as directed by the court and justice requires.

5. In any proceeding the court may direct that the grant of costs or an allowance be reserved for supplemental decree to be entered after the time to appeal has expired or if an appeal be taken, after final determination of the appeal.

History: Add, L 1966, ch 953, eff Sept 1, 1967 from Sur. Ct. Act §§ 275, 276, 278 in part; amd, L 1968, ch 259, § 39, eff May 14, 1968.

§ 2302. Award of costs and allowances

1. Upon a motion the court may award costs to any party in such amount as it determines not exceeding $20 to each party, except in counties within the City of New York, where such amount shall not exceed $40.

2. Upon rendering a decree or in granting or denying an application to vacate a decree the court may award as costs such sum as it deems reasonable to the petitioner and to any other party who has succeeded in whole or in part in a contest or whose attorney, in the absence of a contest, has rendered services of substantial benefit to him, her or it, or to the estate, not exceeding

    (a) in counties within the City of New York:

      (i) $100 where there has not been a contest, or

      (ii) $300 where there has been a contest and $300 for each day, less one, necessarily occupied in the trial or hearing and in addition $100 for each day necessarily occupied in preparing therefore and $100 additional if a motion for a new trial is granted.

    (b) in all other counties:

      (i) $50 where there has not been a contest, or

      (ii) $150 where there has been a contest and $150 for each day, less one, necessarily occupied in the trial or hearing and in addition $50 for each day necessarily occupied in preparing therefore and $50 additional if a motion for a new trial is granted.

3. In a contested probate proceeding:

    (a) Costs payable out of the estate or otherwise may be awarded (1) to an unsuccessful contestant only if he, she or it be a guardian ad litem or guardian, committee or conservator of a person under disability; (2) to an unsuccessful proponent named as executor in the will when propounded by him, her or it in good faith as the last will of the decedent; and (3) to a person named as executor in a prior will on file in the court that is not admitted to probate when such person participates in the proceeding in good faith. Such nominated executor, guardian ad litem, guardian, committee or conservator, whether successful or not may be awarded costs and an allowance in such sum as the court deems reasonable for his, her or its counsel fees and other expenses incurred in the contest or attempt to sustain the will. The court may direct that such costs and allowances in whole or in part be payable by an unsuccessful contestant except that an award of the successful proponent's counsel's fees may only be allowed where the court finds that the contest was brought in bad faith or was frivolous.

    (b) Either before or after the decree granting probate the court may order that a copy of the minutes of the trial be furnished to a contestant for the purposes of appeal and charge the expense thereof initially to the estate if satisfied that the contest is in good faith. If the contestant be unsuccessful upon the appeal and he, she or it is not the guardian of an infant, the committee of an incompetent, the conservator of a conservatee or a guardian ad litem he, she or it shall refund to the estate any amount so paid by the estate for the minutes.

4. In a proceeding for probate of a will when the public administrator or county treasurer has been directed to probate a will or continue the proceedings for the probate thereof, the court may award to either of them such sum as it deems reasonable for his, her or its counsel fees and other expenses necessarily incurred therein.

5. After appeal, pursuant to the direction of the appellate court the court may award a fiduciary such sum as it deems reasonable for counsel fees and other expenses necessarily incurred on the appeal.

6. In a proceeding to construe a will or after appeal in such a proceeding, pursuant to the direction of the appellate court the court may award to a fiduciary or any party to the proceeding such sum as it deems reasonable for his, her or its counsel fees and other expenses necessarily incurred in the proceeding or on the appeal.

7. Upon a final or intermediate judicial settlement a fiduciary may be awarded for his, her or its expenses and counsel fees such sum as the court deems reasonable not exceeding:

(a) within the counties of the City of New York: $100 for each day necessarily occupied in preparing the account and in drawing, entering and executing the decree. Any sum so awarded may be in addition to any costs, allowances or commissions otherwise authorized and awarded by the court.

(b) In all other counties: $ 50 for each day necessarily occupied in preparing the account and in drawing, entering and executing the decree. Any sum so awarded may be in addition to any costs, allowances or commissions otherwise authorized and awarded by the court.

8. In a proceeding for disposition of real property a fiduciary may be awarded out of the proceeds of sale his, her or its commissions and such sum as the court deems reasonable for counsel fees and expenses necessarily incurred in the proceeding.

> **History:** Add, L 1966, ch 953, eff Sept 1, 1967 from Sur. Ct. Act §§ 277, 278, 279, 281 in part; amd, L 1968, ch 259, eff May 14, 1968; L 1969, ch 772, § 11, eff Sept 1, 1969; L 1972, ch 733, § 1, eff July 1, 1972; L 1980, ch 20, eff Sept 1, 1980; L 1981, ch 115, eff May 18, 1981; L 1993, ch 514, eff Jan 1, 1994; L 1999, ch 460, § 2, eff Sept 7, 1999, applying to the estates of decedents dying on or after such effective date.

§ 2303. Security for costs

1. In any proceeding in which an issue is raised by answer or objection by or on behalf of a non-domiciliary against the proponent of a will or a fiduciary or where the probate of a will has been tried before a jury which has disagreed, the court may require the person or persons raising such issue to give security for costs upon motion made by the proponent or fiduciary.

2. Security for costs may be required from any non-domiciliary who is the petitioner in any proceeding, provided the court finds that security is necessary for the protection of the estate.

3. If any party fails to comply with an order requiring him to give security for costs the court, upon the application of any interested party who might resort to the security if furnished, may make an order or decree dismissing the objections, answer or petition of the party in default.

> **History:** Add, L 1966, ch 953, eff Sept 1, 1967 Ct. Act § 282.

§ 2304. Costs of appeal

1. The appellate court may award costs of the appeal as follows:

(a) Upon an appeal in a proceeding to construe a will, to any party to the appeal.

(b) Upon an appeal in any other proceeding, to any party who

(i) has succeeded therein in whole or in part, or

(ii) has participated therein as a fiduciary, guardian ad litem, guardian, committee or conservator of a person under disability, or

(iii) is named as an executor in a paper propounded by him in good faith as the will of the decedent.

2. The court may direct that the costs shall abide the event of a new trial or of the subsequent proceedings in the surrogate's court.

3. Costs may be made payable out of the estate, or if awarded to a successful party, personally by the unsuccessful party, as directed by the appellate court or if such direction be not given, as directed by the court.

4. Costs of an appeal awarded in the court shall be pursuant to CPLR 8203 and 8204.

> **History:** Add, L 1966, ch 953, eff Sept 1, 1967 from Sur. Ct. Act § 283; amd, L 1981, ch 115, § 142, eff May 18, 1981.

§ 2305. Fees of appraisers

An appraiser is entitled in addition to his actual expenses, to a sum to be fixed by the court for his services in making the appraisal. He shall file with the court an affidavit showing the nature and extent of his services, and expenses if any, and the sums payable therefor shall be taxed by the court and paid by the fiduciary.

> **History:** Add, L 1966, ch 953, eff Sept 1, 1967 from Sur. Ct. Act § 284.

§ 2306. Annual statements to be furnished to beneficiaries

Any trustee, donee of a power during minority or donee of a power in trust who is not required to furnish annual statements under either 2308 or 2309 because he or she has not retained annual commissions shall nevertheless be required to furnish the annual statements referred to in those sections to any beneficiary receiving income or any person interested in the principal of the trust who shall request such statements, or in the case of a power during minority or of a power in trust, to the beneficiary of the power in trust, or to a person to whom a payment not exceeding $10,000 could be made under subdivision 1 of section 2220 of this chapter.

> **History:** Add, L 1966, ch 953, eff Sept 1, 1967 from Sur. Ct. Act § 254; L 2019, ch 601, § 1, eff Jan 1, 2020.

§ 2307. Commissions of fiduciaries other than trustees

1. Except as otherwise provided in paragraph (f) of this subdivision on the settlement of the account of any fiduciary other than a trustee, a donee of a power during minority or a donee of a power in trust, the court must allow to him or her the reasonable and necessary expenses actually paid by him or her and if he or she be an attorney of this state and shall have rendered legal services in connection with his or her official duties, such compensation for his or her legal services as appear to the court to be just and reasonable and in addition thereto it must allow to the fiduciary for his or her services as fiduciary, and if there be more than one, apportion among them according to the services rendered by them respectively the following commissions:

(a) For receiving and paying out all sums of money not exceeding $100,000 at the rate of 5 percent.

(b) For receiving and paying out any additional sums not exceeding $200,000 at the rate of 4 percent.

(c) For receiving and paying out any additional sums not exceeding $700,000 at the rate of 3 percent.

(d) For receiving and paying out any additional sums not exceeding $4,000,000 at the rate of 2½ percent.

(e) For receiving and paying out all sums above $5,000,000 at the rate of 2 percent.

(f) If the will makes provisions for specific rates or amounts of commissions for a corporate executor, or, if a corporate executor has agreed to accept specific rates or amounts of commissions, or, if the will provides that a corporate executor shall receive commissions as provided or stipulated in the corporate executor's published schedule of fees in effect at such time or times such commissions become payable, including a stipulated minimum commission and asset base for calculating such commissions, a corporate executor shall be entitled to be compensated in accordance with such provisions, agreement or schedule, as the case may be, even though such provisions, agreement or schedule are not executed in accordance with the provisions required for wills and are not attested as required for the recording of deeds in this state.

Such commission shall be computed separately for receiving and for paying out sums of money, at one-half the statutory rates for receiving and at one-half the statutory rates for paying out sums of money.

2. The value of any property, to be determined in such manner as directed by the court and the increment thereof, received, distributed or delivered, shall be considered as money in computing commissions. But this shall not apply in case of: (a) a specific legacy or devise; or (b) the recovery of awards from the September eleventh victim compensation fund of two thousand one established pursuant to title IV of the federal air transportation safety and system stabilization act, public law 107-42, as amended, which awards shall be valued at zero for purposes of this section. Whenever any portion of the dividends, interest or rent payable to a fiduciary other than a trustee is required by any law of the United States or other governmental unit to be withheld by the person paying it for income tax purposes, the amount so withheld shall be deemed to have been received and paid out.

3. In addition to the compensation hereinbefore provided the court may allow to the guardian of the person a sum of money to be fixed by it and paid by the guardian of the property out of the funds in his hands as compensation for services of the guardian of the person up to the time of the allowance.

4. If a guardian is required to receive income and pay it over and files an annual account as required by 1719 of all his receipts and disbursements, he shall be allowed and may retain the same commission on the amount of income so accounted for as he would be allowed upon principal on a judicial settlement. If the guardian fails to file an annual account as required by 1719 the guardian, notwithstanding his failure to retain in full each year the commissions on income herein prescribed, may be allowed upon the judicial settlement of his account any commissions due and theretofore uncollected by him provided that on such settlement there

is then on hand income sufficient for that purpose derived from the estate during the respective years for which further commissions are claimed. If the income on hand for any given year is insufficient to pay the uncollected commissions on the income of that year the deficiency shall not be supplied from income on hand in respect of any other year.

5. Subject to 2313 regarding multiple commissions of executors or trustees under wills of persons dying, or lifetime trusts established, after August 31, 1993, if the gross value of the principal of the estate accounted for amounts to $300,000 or more each fiduciary is entitled to the full compensation on principal and income allowed herein to a sole fiduciary unless there be more than 3, in which case the compensation to which 3 would be entitled must be apportioned among them according to the services rendered by them respectively unless the fiduciaries shall have agreed in writing among themselves to a different apportionment which, however, shall not provide for more than one full commission for any one of them. If the gross value of the principal of the estate accounted for is:

(a) less than $100,000 and there is more than 1 fiduciary the full compensation for receiving and paying out principal and income allowed herein to a sole fiduciary must be apportioned among them according to the services rendered by them respectively, or

(b) $100,000 or more but less than $300,000 each fiduciary is entitled to the full compensation for receiving and paying out principal and income allowed herein to a sole fiduciary unless there are more than 2 fiduciaries in which case the full compensation for receiving and paying out principal and income allowed herein to 2 fiduciaries must be apportioned among them according to the services rendered by them respectively,

unless the fiduciaries shall have agreed in writing between or among themselves to a different apportionment which, however, shall not provide for more than one full commission for any one of them. Where the will provides a specific compensation to a fiduciary other than a trustee he is not entitled to any allowance for his services unless by an instrument filed with the court within 4 months from the date of his letters he renounces the specific compensation. Where successive or different letters are issued to the same person on the estate of the same decedent, including a case where letters of administration are issued to a person who has previously been appointed a temporary administrator, he is entitled to a total compensation equal to the compensation allowed for the full administration of the estate by a fiduciary acting in a single capacity only. Such total compensation shall be payable in such proportions and upon such accounting as shall be fixed by the court settling the account of the person holding successive or different letters but no paying out commissions shall be allowed except upon such sums as shall actually have been paid out at the time of the respective decrees for debts, expenses of administration or to beneficiaries.

6. Where a fiduciary is for any reason entitled or required to collect the rents of and manage real property he shall be allowed and may retain for such services 5 per cent of the gross rents collected therefrom in addition to the commissions herein provided, but there shall be only one such additional commission regardless of the number of fiduciaries. In the event there are 2 or more fiduciaries the additional commission herein provided for must be apportioned among them according to the services rendered by them respectively unless they shall have agreed in writing among themselves to a different apportionment.

7. A fiduciary other than a trustee who has been acting prior to July 1, 1956 shall be entitled to have commissions on principal and income theretofore received by him computed, allowed

and paid under the methods and at the rates set forth herein, except as follows:

(a) If prior to July 1, 1956 a fiduciary other than a trustee has been allowed or has retained commissions for receiving and paying out any item of principal or income he shall be entitled to no further commissions on the item.

(b) If prior to July 1, 1956 a fiduciary other than a trustee has been allowed or has retained any commissions on any item of principal or income received but not paid out by him he shall be entitled to no further commissions for receiving the item.

History: Add, L 1966, ch 953, eff Sept 1, 1967 from Sur. Ct. Act § 285; amd, L 1967, ch 685, § 141, eff Sept 1, 1967; L 1969, ch 1050, § 1, eff Sept 1, 1969; L 1976, ch 303, § 1, eff June 8, 1976; L 1981, ch 803, §§ 2, 3, eff July 27, 1981; L 1993, ch 514, § 56, eff Jan 1, 1994; L 1994, ch 474, § 1, eff July 20, 1994; L 2002, ch 73, § 6, eff May 21, 2002; L 2019, ch 601, § 1, eff Jan 1, 2020.

§ 2307-a. Commissions of attorney-executor

1. Disclosure. When an attorney prepares a will to be proved in the courts of this state and such attorney, a then affiliated attorney, or an employee of such attorney or a then affiliated attorney is therein an executor-designee, the testator shall be informed prior to the execution of the will that:

(a) subject to limited statutory exceptions, any person, including the testator's spouse, child, friend or associate, or an attorney, is eligible to serve as an executor;

(b) absent an agreement to the contrary, any person, including an attorney, who serves as an executor is entitled to receive an executor's statutory commissions;

(c) absent execution of a disclosure acknowledgment, the attorney who prepared the will, a then affiliated attorney, or an employee of such attorney or a then affiliated attorney, who serves as an executor shall be entitled to one-half the commissions he or she would otherwise be entitled to receive; and

(d) if such attorney or an affiliated attorney renders legal services in connection with the executor's official duties, such attorney or a then affiliated attorney is entitled to receive just and reasonable compensation for such legal services, in addition to the executor's statutory commissions.

2. Testator's written acknowledgment of disclosure. An acknowledgment by the testator of the disclosure required by subdivision one of this section must be set forth in a writing executed by the testator in the presence of at least one witness other than the executor-designee. Such writing, which must be separate from the will, but which may be annexed to the will, and which may be executed prior to, concurrently with or subsequently to a will in which an attorney, a then affiliated attorney, or an employee of such attorney or a then affiliated attorney is an executor-designee and must be filed in the proceeding for the issuance of letters testamentary to the executor-designee.

3. Models of acknowledgment of disclosure. The following are models of the testator's written acknowledgment of disclosure:

(a) When set forth in a writing executed prior to or concurrently with a will:

Prior to signing my will, I was informed that:

(i) subject to limited statutory exceptions, any person, including my spouse, my child, a friend or associate, or an attorney, is eligible to serve as my executor;

(ii) absent an agreement to the contrary, any person, including an attorney, who serves as an executor for me is entitled to receive statutory commissions for executorial services rendered to my estate;

(iii) absent execution of this disclosure acknowledgment, the attorney who prepared the will, a then affiliated attorney, or an employee of such attorney or a then affiliated attorney, who serves as an executor shall be entitled to one-half the commissions he or she would otherwise be entitled to receive; and

(iv) if such attorney serves as my executor, and he or she or another attorney affiliated with such attorney renders legal services in connection with the executor's official duties, he or she is entitled to receive just and reasonable compensation for those legal services, in addition to the commissions to which an executor is entitled.

_____   _____

(Witness)   (Testator)

Dated: _____   Dated: _____

(b) When set forth in a writing executed subsequently to the will:

I,   , have designated {my attorney},   , {an attorney affiliated with my attorney} {an employee of my attorney or an affiliated attorney,} {a} {an} {executor} {alternate executor} {co-executor} (delete what is inapplicable) in my will dated _____.

Prior to signing my will, I was informed that:

(i) subject to limited statutory exceptions, any person, including my spouse, my child, a friend or associate, or an attorney, is eligible to serve as my executor;

(ii) absent an agreement to the contrary, any person, including an attorney, who serves as an executor for me is entitled to receive statutory commissions for executorial services rendered to my estate;

(iii) absent execution of this disclosure acknowledgment, the attorney who prepared my will, a then affiliated attorney, or an employee of such attorney or a then affiliated attorney, who serves as an executor shall be entitled to one-half the commissions he or she would otherwise be entitled to receive; and

(iv) if such attorney serves as my executor, and he or she or another attorney affiliated with such attorney renders legal services in connection with the executor's official duties, he or she is entitled to receive just and reasonable compensation for those legal services, in addition to the commissions to which an executor is entitled.

_____   _____

(Witness)   (Testator)

Dated: _____   Dated: _____

4. Compliance. (a) The testator's written acknowledgment of disclosure that conforms or substantially conforms to either model in subdivision 3 of this section shall be deemed compliance with subdivision 2 of this section.

(b) An attorney's compliance with subdivision 2 of this section creates neither the presumption nor the inference:

    (i) that the testator's designation of such attorney, a then affiliated attorney, or an employee of such attorney or a then affiliated attorney, as executor, is proper;

    (ii) that such attorney has complied with the disciplinary rules of the code of professional responsibility.

5. Effect of absence of acknowledgment. Absent compliance with the requirements of subdivision 2 of this section, the commissions of an attorney, or an employee of the attorney who prepared the will or a then affiliated attorney, who serves as an executor shall be one-half the statutory commissions to which such person as executor would otherwise be entitled pursuant to sections 2307 and 2313 of this article.

6. Rents. Notwithstanding the provisions of subdivision 5 of this section, the additional commissions to which an attorney, or an employee of the attorney who prepared the will or a then affiliated attorney, who serves as an executor may be entitled pursuant to subdivision 6 of section 2307 shall not be diminished.

7. Time of determination of compliance. A determination of compliance with the requirements of subdivisions 1 and 2 of this section shall be made in a proceeding for the issuance of letters testamentary to an executor-designee to whom subdivision 1 of this section applies.

8. Definitions. For purposes of this section, the words or phrases hereafter shall be construed as follows:

    (a) Affiliated attorney. An attorney who, by reason of partnership, share holding, association or other relationship, express or implied, could participate directly or indirectly, with the attorney who prepared the will in fees for legal services rendered.

    (b) Executor-designee. A person named in a will or codicil, separately or jointly with one or more persons, as a primary, successor, ancillary, or preliminary executor.

    (c) Employee. A person who was employed by the attorney who prepared the will or an affiliated attorney when the will was executed.

9. Application. (a) This section shall apply to wills executed on or after January 1, 1996 and, irrespective of the date of any will, to estates of decedents dying after December 31, 1996.

(b) With respect to wills executed prior to January 1, 1996:

    (i) subdivisions 1 and 2 of this section shall not apply if the testator has acknowledged the disclosure required by subdivision 1 of this section in a writing that conforms or substantially conforms to the model in paragraph (b) of subdivision 3 of this section; and

    (ii) the court in its discretion may waive application of subdivisions 1 and 2 of this section for good cause shown; good cause shall include, but not be limited to:

        (A) a good-faith effort after the enactment of this statute either to make to the testator the disclosure required by subdivision 1 of this section or obtain from the testator a written acknowledgment substantially conforming to that set forth in paragraph (b) of subdivision 3 of this section, or

(B) otherwise establishing to the satisfaction of the court reasonable grounds to excuse the absence of a written acknowledgement substantially conforming to that set forth in paragraph (b) of subdivision 3 of this section; and

(iii) section 4519 of the civil practice law and rules shall not apply.

History: Add, L 1995, ch 421, § 1, eff Aug 2, 1995; amd, L 2004, ch 709, § 1, eff Nov 16, 2004; L 2007, ch 488, § 1, eff Aug 31, 2007.

§ 2308. Commissions of trustees, donees of power during minority and donees of powers in trust under wills of persons dying, or under lifetime trusts created, on or before August 31, 1956

1. On the settlement of the account of any trustee or donee of power in trust under the will of a person dying on or before August 31, 1956, or under a lifetime trust established on or before August 31, 1956, the court must allow him or her his or her reasonable and necessary expenses actually paid by him or her and if he or she be an attorney of this state and shall have rendered legal services in connection with his or her official duties, such compensation for his or her legal services as shall appear to the court to be just and reasonable and in addition thereto it must allow to the trustee or to the donee of the power in trust for his or her services as trustee or donee of the power in trust the following commissions from trust principal or property subject to the power in trust:

(a) For receiving principal or property subject to the power in trust

(1) all sums of money constituting principal or property subject to the power in trust not exceeding $2,000 at the rate of 3 per cent;

(2) all additional sums of principal or property subject to the power in trust not exceeding $10,000 at the rate of 1 1/2 per cent;

(3) all sums of principal or property subject to the power in trust above $12,000 at the rate of 1 1/4 per cent; and

(b) For paying out principal or property subject to the power in trust at the rate of 1 per cent.

(c) Notwithstanding the provisions of section 8 of chapter 237 of the laws of 1978, commissions provided by paragraph (a) of this subdivision for receiving principal or property subject to the power in trust shall not be allowed to a trustee or donee of a power in trust who qualifies to act as such on or after June 5, 1978, and shall not be allowed on additions of property received on or after June 5, 1978; such commissions on any increments in property that are payable by reason of any sale, exchange or liquidation of such property shall be allowed on the lesser of (1) the amount of such increments on the date of sale, exchange or liquidation of such property and (2) the amount of such increments on June 5, 1978; and such commissions on any increments in property that are payable by reason of any distribution of such property shall be allowed on the lesser of (1) the amount of such increments on the date of distribution of such property and (2) the amount of such increments on the effective date of this paragraph.

2. In addition to the commission allowed by subdivision one a trustee or a donee of a power

in trust shall be entitled to annual commissions at the following rates:

(a) $10.50 per $1,000 or major fraction thereof on the first $400,000 of principal or property subject to the power in trust;

(b) $4.50 per $1,000 or major fraction thereof on the next $600,000 of principal or property subject to the power in trust; and

(c) $3.00 per $1,000 or major fraction thereof on all additional principal or property subject to the power in trust.

Such annual commissions shall be computed either on the value of the principal of the trust or of the property subject to the power in trust at the end of the period for which the commissions are payable or, at the option of the trustee or of the donee of the power in trust, on the value of the principal of the trust or of the property subject to the power in trust at the beginning of such period, provided that the option elected by the trustee or of the donee of the power in trust for the first period for which such commissions are payable shall be used during the continuance of the trust or of the power in trust and shall be binding on any successor or substitute trustee or trustees or successor or substitute donees of the power in trust. In the case of a trust or power in trust which prior to January 1, 1994 computed annual commissions on the basis of a 12 month period (other than a calendar year), the trustee's or donee's prior election of such 12 month period shall be binding unless, prior to January 1, 1995, the trustee or donee makes a new election to compute annual commissions on the basis of a calendar year either on the value of the principal of the trust or of the property subject to the power in trust at the end of, or at the option of the trustee or donee of the power in trust at the beginning of, the calendar year for which the commissions were payable, which new election shall be used during the remaining continuance of the trust or of the power in trust and shall be binding on any successor or substitute trustee or trustees or donee or donees of the power in trust. The computation shall be made on the basis of a 12 month period but the amount so computed payable to a trustee or donee of a power in trust shall be proportionately reduced or increased for any payments made in partial distribution of the trust or of the property subject to the power in trust or receipt of any additional property into the trust or by the donee of a power in trust within such period and shall be proportionately reduced in any period for which such commissions are payable to the trustee or donee of the power in trust if the period is less than 12 months. For the purpose of computing the annual commissions the value of any principal asset when received by the trust or by the donee of a power in trust shall be the presumptive value of the asset at the beginning and end of the period for which such commissions are payable. In computing the value of the principal of the trust or of the property subject to the power in trust the trustee or the donee of the power in trust may use the presumptive value in respect of any principal asset or may use the actual value of the asset. On the settlement of the account of the trustee or of the donee of a power in trust any person interested may dispute the amount of any commission claimed or retained. The burden of proving that the actual value of any principal asset differs from its presumptive value is upon the trustee, the donee of the power in trust or other person claiming the difference.

3. Unless the will otherwise explicitly provides, the annual commissions allowed by subdivision two of this section shall be payable one-third from the income of the trust or of the property subject to the power in trust and two-thirds from the principal of the trust or from the property subject to the power in trust. However, in the case of a trust whose definition of

income is governed by 11-2.4 of the estates, powers and trusts law, such annual commissions shall be payable from the corpus of any such trust after allowance for the unitrust amount and shall not be payable out of such unitrust amount.

4. The commissions allowed by subdivision 2 may be retained by a trustee or donee of a power in trust provided he or she furnishes annually as of a date not more than 30 days prior to the end of the trust year selected by the trustee or the calendar year, to each beneficiary currently receiving income, and to any other beneficiary interested in the income and to any person interested in the principal of the trust who shall make a demand therefor or to the beneficiary of the power in trust who shall make a demand therefor, a statement showing the principal assets or the property subject to the power in trust on hand on that date, and at least annually or more frequently if the trustee or donee of a power in trust so elects, a statement showing all his or her receipts of income and principal or property subject to the power in trust during the period with respect to which the statement is rendered including the amount of any commissions retained and the basis upon which the commissions were computed. A trustee or donee of a power in trust shall not be deemed to have waived any commissions by reason of his or her failure to retain them at the time when he or she becomes entitled thereto; provided however that commissions from income for any given trust or calendar year shall be allowed and retained only from income derived from the trust or from the property subject to the power in trust during that year and shall not be supplied from income on hand in respect of any other trust or calendar year. If a beneficiary receiving income does not desire to be furnished with any such statement his or her advice to the trustee or to the donee of the power in trust to that effect in writing shall thereafter excuse the trustee or donee of the power in trust from furnishing such statement to the beneficiary unless and until the beneficiary requests such annual statements from the trustee or donee of the power in trust.

5. (a) During the continuance of a trust created solely for public, religious, charitable, scientific, literary, educational or fraternal uses and during the period of continuance of such a trust after the termination of a life use or uses the trustee shall be entitled to and may retain commissions from income in an amount annually equal to 6 per cent of income collected in each year.

(b) In the case of a trust created solely for public, religious, charitable, scientific, literary, educational or fraternal uses the trustee shall not be entitled to any commission from principal.

(c) In the case of such a trust which continues after the termination of a life use or uses the trustee for the period of the measuring life or lives shall be entitled to commissions from income and principal at the rates and according to the terms otherwise provided in this section, except that he or she shall not be entitled to any commissions for paying out any amount of principal.

6. (a) If the gross value of the principal of the trust or of the property subject to the power in trust accounted for amounts to $400,000 or more and there is more than 1 trustee or donee of the power in trust, each trustee or donee of the power in trust is entitled to the full compensation for receiving and paying out principal or property subject to the power in trust allowed herein to a sole trustee or donee of the power in trust unless there are more than 3, in which case the compensation to which 3 would be entitled must be apportioned among the trustees or donees of the power in trust according to the services rendered by them respectively, unless the trustees or donees of the power in trust shall have agreed in

writing among themselves to a different apportionment which, however, shall not provide for more than one full commission for any one of them. If the gross value of the principal of the trust or of the property subject to the power in trust accounted for is:

(i) less than $100,000 and there is more than 1 trustee or donee of the power in trust the full compensation for receiving and paying out principal or property subject to the power in trust allowed herein to a sole trustee or donee of the power in trust must be apportioned among them according to the services rendered by them respectively, or

(ii) $100,000 or more but less than $400,000, each trustee or donee of the power in trust is entitled to the full compensation for receiving and paying out principal or property subject to the power in trust allowed pursuant to this subdivision to a sole trustee or donee of the power in trust unless there are more than 2 trustees or donees of the power in trust in which case the full compensation for paying out principal or property subject to the power in trust allowed pursuant to this subdivision to 2 trustees or donees of the power in trust must be apportioned among them according to the services rendered by them respectively,

unless the trustees or donees of the power in trust shall have agreed in writing between or among themselves to a different apportionment which, however, shall not provide for more than one full commission for any one of them.

(b) If the value of the principal of the trust or of the property subject to the power in trust for the purpose of computing the annual commissions allowed by subdivision 2 amounts to $400,000 or more and there is more than one trustee or donee of the power in trust, each trustee or donee of the power in trust is entitled to the full annual commission allowed herein to a sole trustee or donee of the power in trust unless there are more than 3, in which case the annual commissions to which 3 would be entitled must be apportioned among the trustees or donees of the power in trust according to the services rendered by them respectively, unless the trustees or donees of the power in trust shall have agreed in writing among themselves to a different apportionment which, however, shall not provide for more than one full annual commission for any one of them. If the value of the principal or of the property subject to the power in trust for the purpose of computing the annual commission allowed by subdivision 2 amounts to:

(i) less than $100,000 and there is more than 1 trustee or donee of the power in trust, the annual commissions from income and the annual commission allowed herein to a sole trustee or donee of the power in trust must be apportioned among the trustees or donee of the power in trust according to the services rendered by them respectively, or

(ii) $100,000 or more but less than $400,000, each trustee or donee of the power in trust is entitled to the full annual commission allowed pursuant to this subdivision to a sole trustee or donee of the power in trust unless there are more than 2 trustees or donees of the power in trust in which case the full annual commissions allowed pursuant to this subdivision to 2 trustees or donees of the power in trust must be apportioned among them according to the services rendered by them respectively,

unless the trustees or donees of the power in trust shall have agreed in writing between or among themselves to a different apportionment which, however, shall not provide for more than one full annual commission for any one of them. However, if from a trust or from property subject to a power in trust having a value of $400,000 or more, or if from a trust or from property subject to a power in trust having a value of $100,000 or more but less than $400,000, as the case may be, at the beginning of a trust year or of the calendar year in the case of a power in trust, any payments in partial distribution of the trust or of the property subject to the power in trust shall be made during the trust or calendar year so as to reduce the trust or of the property subject to the power in trust to a value of less than $400,000 or $100,000, as the case may be, at the end of the trust or calendar year, then the annual commission allowed herein shall, on a proportionate basis, be those allowed to a trustee of a trust or to donees of a power in trust over property having a value of $400,000 or more, of a trust or to donees of a power in trust over property having a value of $100,000 or more but less than $400,000, as the case may be, for the period from the beginning of the trust or calendar year to the date of the distribution and shall, on a proportionate basis, be those allowed to trustees of a trust or to donees of a power in trust over property having a value of either $100,000 or more but less than $400,000 or less than $100,000, as the case may be, for the remainder of the trust or calendar year and the part of such commissions payable from principal and computed from the beginning of the trust or calendar year to the date of distribution shall be charged ratably to the property remaining in the trust and to the property distributed from the trust on the basis of their respective values. Further, if during a trust year or a calendar year in the case of power in trust additional property shall be received into a trust which had a value of less than $100,000 or by a donee of a power in trust the property subject to which had a value of less than $100,000, or into a trust which had a value of $100,000 or more but less than $400,000 or by a donee of a power in trust the property subject to which had a value of $100,000 or more but less than $400,000, as the case may be, at the beginning of the trust or calendar year so that because of the additional property the trust or the property subject to the power in trust shall have a value of $100,000 or more or of $400,000 or more, as the case may be, at the end of the trust or calendar year, then the annual commission allowed herein to the trustee or to the donee of the power in trust shall, on a proportionate basis, be those allowed to trustees of a trust or to donees of a power in trust over property having a value of less than $100,000, or to trustees of a trust or to donees of the power in trust having a value of $100,000 or more but less than $400,000, as the case may be, for the period from the beginning of the trust or calendar year to the date of the receipt of the additional property and shall, on a proportionate basis, be those allowed to trustees of a trust or to donees of a power in trust over property having a value of $100,000 or more but less than $400,000, or to trustees of a trust or to donees of a power in trust over property having $400,000 or more, as the case may be, for the remainder of the trust or calendar year.

(c) Notwithstanding any provisions of paragraphs (a) and (b) of this subdivision to the contrary, if during the continuance of a trust created solely for public, religious, charitable, scientific, literary, educational or fraternal uses or during the continuance of such a trust after the termination of a life use or uses, the annual income of the trust amounts to $4,000 or more and there is more than 1 trustee, each trustee is entitled to the full commission allowed under subdivision 5 to a sole trustee unless there are more than 2, in which case the commissions to which 2 trustees would be entitled must be apportioned among the trustees according to the services rendered by them respectively, unless they shall have agreed in writing among themselves to a different apportionment which, however, shall not provide for more than one full commission to any one of them; provided however, if during the continuance of a trust created solely for public, religious, charitable, scientific, literary, educational or fraternal uses created prior to April 1, 1948, the annual income of the trust amounts to $4,000 or more and there is more than 1 trustee each trustee is entitled to the full commission allowed under subdivision 5 to a sole trustee unless there are more than 3, in which case the commission to which 3 trustees would be entitled must be apportioned among the trustees according to the services rendered by them respectively, unless they shall have agreed in writing among themselves to a different apportionment which, however, shall not provide for more than one full commission to any one of them. If the annual income of the trust amounts to less than $4,000 and there is more than 1 trustee the commissions to which a sole trustee would be entitled under subdivision 5 must be apportioned among the trustees according to the services rendered by them respectively unless they shall have agreed in writing among themselves to a different apportionment.

7. Where a trustee or donee of a power in trust is for any reason entitled or required to collect the rents of and manage real property the net amount of rents collected and not the gross amount shall be used in making computation of commissions allowed by subdivision 5 hereof and in addition to the commissions herein provided he or she shall be allowed and may retain for such services 6 per cent of the gross rents collected, but there shall be only 1 such additional commission regardless of the number of trustees or donees of the power in trust. If there are 2 or more trustees or donees of the power in trust the additional commission herein provided must be apportioned among them according to the services rendered by them respectively unless they shall have agreed in writing among themselves to a different apportionment.

8. A trustee who prior to September 1, 1966 shall have received the maximum amount of commissions on principal permitted by subdivision 8 of section 285-a of the surrogate's court act as that subdivision existed prior to that date, shall not be entitled to annual principal commissions for the period from the date when he or she shall receive such maximum and September 1, 1966, but shall be entitled to receive commissions from and after September 1, 1966 at the rates and in the manner provided in this section. A trustee who has become entitled to annual principal commissions pursuant to section 285-a of the surrogate's court act as it existed prior to September 1, 1966, but has not received them, may receive an amount of commissions not in excess of the amount he or she would have been entitled to if he or she had taken such commissions, and be entitled to receive in addition commissions from and after September 1, 1966 at the rates and in the manner provided in that section.

9. A trustee who has been acting prior to July 1, 1956 shall be entitled to have commissions on principal and income theretofore received by him or her computed, allowed and paid under the methods and at the rates set forth herein, except as follows:

(a) If prior to July 1, 1956 a trustee has been allowed or has retained commissions for receiving and paying out or for distributing any item of principal he or she shall be entitled to no further commissions on the item.

(b) If prior to July 1, 1956 a trustee has been allowed or retained commissions on any item of principal received but not paid out or distributed by him or her he or she shall be entitled to no further commissions for receiving the item.

(c) Any trustee who became entitled to an annual principal commission under subdivision 1 (b) of section 285-a of the surrogate's court act as it existed prior to April 1, 1948 and who has not retained such commission may retain an amount equal to one-half of such annual principal commission. A trustee who because of the provisions of subdivision 2 of section 285-a of the surrogate's court act as it existed prior to April 1,

1948 either was not entitled to retain an annual principal commission under subdivision 1 (b) thereof or was required to credit such annual principal commission against his or her commission for receiving principal, may retain an amount equal to 1/2 of such annual principal commission. If a trustee has been allowed by decree or has retained any such annual principal commission one-half the amount thereof shall be deducted from the amount of commissions to which the trustee would otherwise be entitled under the provisions of subdivision 1.

(d) The annual principal commissions allowed by subdivision 3 of this section as it existed on September 1, 1967 shall not be allowed or retained in respect of any trust year ending prior to April 1, 1948, but for any trust year ending on or after April 1, 1948 and prior to July 1, 1956, the annual principal commission which may be allowed or retained shall be computed at the rates in effect on the date such trust year ended.

(e) If prior to July 1, 1956 a trustee has been allowed or has retained commissions on any item of income received and paid out by him or her prior to September 1, 1943 or on any item of income collected by him or her subsequent to September 1, 1943 he or she shall be entitled to no further commission on the item.

10. The value of any property to be determined in such manner as directed by the court and the increment thereof received, distributed or delivered shall be considered as money in making computation of commissions. Whenever any portion of the dividends, interests or rents payable to a trustee or donee of a power in trust is required by any law of the United States or other governmental unit to be withheld by the person paying it for income tax purposes, the amount so withheld shall be deemed to have been collected.

11. Where the will provides a specific compensation to a trustee or donee of a power in trust he or she is not entitled to any other allowances for his or her services.

12. If a trustee of a trust or donee of a power in trust is authorized or required by the terms of the will to accumulate income for any purpose permitted by law, any income so accumulated which is not added to principal of the trust or to the principal of the property subject to the power in trust shall be deemed a separate trust or separate fund subject to the power in trust for purposes of this subdivision and the trustee or donee of the power in trust shall be entitled to commissions in respect thereof at the rates and according to the terms and provisions of subdivisions 1 and 2 of this section as though, for purposes of computing commissions of the trustee, income so accumulated was principal.

13. For the purposes of this section, the term "trustee" shall mean any trustee who is not a corporate trustee and the term "donee of a power in trust" shall mean any such donee including a donee of a power during minority who is not a corporate fiduciary of a donee of a power during minority with the rights and duties of a guardian under section 1714 of this chapter provided, however, that as used in subdivision 6 of this section, the term trustee shall include a corporate trustee.

History: Add, L 1966, ch 953, eff Sept 1, 1967 from Sur. Ct. Act § 285-a; amd, L 1967, ch 685, eff Sept 1, 1967; L 1969, ch 1050, eff Sept 1, 1969; L 1978, ch 237, eff June 5, 1978; L 1980, ch 503, § 35, eff June 24, 1980; L 1984, ch 936, eff Aug 6, 1984; L 1991, ch 245, §§ 1, 2, eff July 1, 1991; L 1993, ch 654, § 1, eff Aug 4, 1993; L 2001, ch 243, § 6, eff Jan 1, 2002; L 2001, ch 376, § 1, eff Nov 1, 2001; L 2019, ch 601, § 3, eff Jan 1, 2020.

§ 2309. Commissions of trustees, of donees of powers during minority and of donees of powers in trust under wills of persons dying, or lifetime trusts established, after August 31, 1956

1. On the settlement of the account of any trustee or donee of a power in trust under the will of a person dying after August 31, 1956, or under a lifetime trust established after August 31, 1956, the court must allow to him or her his or her reasonable and necessary expenses actually paid by him or her and if he or she be an attorney of this state and shall have rendered legal services in connection with his or her official duties, such compensation for his or her legal services as shall appear to the court to be just and reasonable and in addition thereto it must allow to the trustee or donee of a power in trust for his or her services as trustee or donee of a power in trust a commission from principal or from the property subject to the power in trust, for paying out all sums of money constituting principal or property subject to the power in trust at the rate of 1 per cent.

2. In addition to the commission allowed by subdivision 1 hereof a trustee or donee of a power in trust shall be entitled to annual commissions at the following rates:

(a) $10.50 per $1,000 or major fraction thereof on the first $400,000 of principal or property subject to the power in trust.

(b) $4.50 per $1,000 or major fraction thereof on the next $600,000 of principal or property subject to the power in trust.

(c) $3.00 per $1,000 or major fraction thereof on all additional principal or property subject to the power in trust.

Such annual commissions shall be computed either on the value of the principal of the trust or of the property subject to the power in trust at the end of the period for which the commissions are payable or, at the option of the trustee or donee of the power in trust, on the value of the principal of the trust or of the property subject to the power in trust at the beginning of such period, provided that the option elected by the trustee or donee of the power in trust for the first period for which such commissions are payable shall be used during the continuance of the trust or of the power in trust and shall be binding on any successor or substitute trustee or trustees, donee or donees. In the case of a trust which prior to January 1, 1994 computed annual commissions on the basis of a 12 month period (other than a calendar year), the trustee's prior election of such 12 month period shall be binding unless, prior to January 1, 1995, the trustee makes a new election to compute annual commissions on the basis of a calendar year either on the value of the principal of the trust at the end of, or at the option of the trustee at the beginning of, the calendar year for which the commissions were payable, which new election shall be used during the remaining continuance of the trust and shall be binding on any successor or substitute trustee or trustees. The computation shall be made on the basis of a 12-month period but the amount so computed payable to a trustee shall be proportionately reduced or increased for any payments made in partial distribution of the trust or the receipt of any additional property into the trust within such period and shall be proportionately reduced in any period for which such commissions are payable to the trustee if the period is less than 12 months. For the purpose of computing the annual commissions the value of any principal asset when received by the trust or donee of a power in trust shall be the presumptive value of the asset at the beginning and end of the period for which such commissions are payable. In computing the value of the principal of the trust or of the property subject to the power in trust the trustee or donee of the power in trust may use the presumptive value in respect of any principal asset or may use the actual value of the asset. On the settlement of the account of the trustee or donee of a power in trust any person interested may dispute the amount of any commission claimed or retained. The burden of proving that the actual value of any principal asset or asset subject to the power in trust differs from its presumptive value is upon the trustee or donee of a power in trust or other person claiming the difference.

3. Unless the will or lifetime trust instrument otherwise explicitly provides the annual commissions allowed by subdivision 2 shall be payable one-third from the income of the trust or property subject to the power in trust and two-thirds from the principal of the trust or property subject to the power in trust. However, in the case of a trust whose definition of income is governed by section 11-2.4 of the estates, powers and trusts law or a charitable remainder annuity trust or a charitable remainder unitrust, as defined in section six hundred sixty-four of the Internal Revenue Code of nineteen hundred eighty-six, as amended, such annual commissions shall be payable from the corpus of any such trust after allowance for the annuity or unitrust amounts and shall not be payable out of such annuity or unitrust amounts.

4. The commissions allowed by subdivision 2 may be retained by a trustee provided he or she furnishes annually as of a date no more than 30 days prior to the end of the trust year selected by the trustee, to each beneficiary currently receiving income, and to any other beneficiary interested in the income and to any person interested in the principal of the trust who shall make a demand therefor and by a donee of a power in trust if he or she furnishes annually as of a date no more than 30 days prior to the end of the calendar year to the beneficiary of the power in trust, a statement showing the principal assets on hand on that date, and at least annually or more frequently if the trustee or donee of the power in trust so elects, a statement showing all his or her receipts of income and principal or property subject to the power in trust during the period with respect to which the statement is rendered including the amount of any commissions retained and the basis upon which the commissions were computed. A trustee or donee of a power in trust shall not be deemed to have waived any commissions by reason of his or her failure to retain them at the time when he or she becomes entitled thereto; provided however that in the case of a trust commissions payable from income for any given trust year shall be allowed and retained only from income derived from the trust during that year and shall not be supplied from income on hand in respect of any other trust year and in the case of property subject to a power in trust commissions payable from income for any given calendar year shall be allowed and retained only from income derived from the property during that year and shall not be supplied from income on hand in respect of any other calendar year. If a beneficiary receiving income does not desire to be furnished with any such statements his or her advice to the trustee or to the donee of the power in trust to that effect in writing shall thereafter excuse the trustee or donee of the power in trust from furnishing such statement to the beneficiary unless and until the beneficiary requests such annual statements from the trustee or donee of the power in trust.

5. (a) During the continuance of a trust created solely for public, religious, charitable, scientific, literary, educational or fraternal uses and during the period of continuance of such a trust after the termination of a life use or uses the trustee shall be entitled to and may retain commissions from income in an amount annually equal to 6 per cent of income collected in each year.

(b) In the case of a trust created solely for public, religious, charitable, scientific, literary, educational or fraternal uses the trustee shall not be entitled to any commission from principal.

(c) In the case of such a trust which continues after the termination of the measuring life use or uses the trustee for the period of the measuring life use or uses shall be entitled to commissions from income and principal at the rates and according to the terms specified in subdivision 2 and except in respect of principal paid out to a charity or for charitable uses shall be entitled to a commission for distributing all sums of principal at the rate specified in subdivision 1.

6. (a) Subject to section 2313 regarding multiple commissions of executors, trustees, or donees of a power in trust created under wills of persons dying, or lifetime trusts established, after August 31, 1993, if the gross value of the principal of the trust or of the property subject to the power in trust accounted for amounts to $400,000 or more and there is more than 1 trustee or donee each trustee or donee is entitled to the full compensation for paying out principal allowed herein to a sole trustee or donee unless there are more than 3, in which case the compensation to which 3 would be entitled must be apportioned among the trustees or donees of the power in trust according to the services rendered by them respectively unless they shall have agreed in writing among themselves to a different apportionment which, however, shall not provide for more than one full commission for any one of them. If the gross value of the principal of the trust or of the property subject to the power in trust accounted for is:

(i) less than $100,000 and there is more than 1 trustee or donee of the power in trust, the full compensation for paying out principal allowed herein to a sole trustee or donee of the power in trust must be apportioned among them according to the services rendered by them respectively, or

(ii) $100,000 or more but less than $400,000, each trustee or donee of the power in trust is entitled to the full compensation for paying out principal allowed herein to a sole trustee or donee of the power in trust unless there are more than 2 trustees or donees of the power in trust in which case the full compensation for paying out principal allowed herein to 2 trustees or donees of a power of trust must be apportioned among them according to the services rendered by them respectively,

unless the trustees or donees of the power in trust shall have agreed in writing between or among themselves to a different apportionment which, however, shall not provide for more than one full commission for any one of them.

(b) Subject to section 2313 regarding multiple commissions of executors, trustees, or donees of a power in trust created under wills of persons dying, or lifetime trusts established, after August 31, 1993, if the value of the principal of the trust or of the property subject to the power in trust for the purpose of computing the annual commissions allowed by subdivision 2 amounts to $400,000 or more and there is more than one trustee or donee of a power in trust each trustee or donee of a power in trust is entitled to the full annual commission allowed herein to a sole trustee or donee of a power in trust unless there are more than 3, in which case the annual commissions to which 3 would be entitled must be apportioned among the trustees or donees of the power in trust according to the services rendered by them respectively unless the trustees or donees of the power in trust shall have agreed in writing among themselves to a different apportionment which, however, shall not provide for more than one full annual commission for any one

SCPA

of them. If the value of the principal of the trust or of the property subject to the power in trust for the purpose of computing the annual commission allowed by subdivision 2 amounts to:

    (i) less than $100,000 and there is more than 1 trustee or donee of the power in trust, the annual commission allowed herein to a sole trustee or donee of a power in trust must be apportioned among the trustees or donees of the power in trust according to the services rendered by them respectively, or

    (ii) $100,000 or more but less than $400,000, each trustee or donee of the power in trust is entitled to the full annual commission allowed herein to a sole trustee or donee of a power in trust unless there are more than 2 trustees or donees of the power in trust in which case the full annual commissions allowed herein to 2 trustees or donees of a power in trust must be apportioned among them according to the services rendered by them respectively,

unless the trustees or donees of the power in trust shall have agreed in writing between or among themselves to a different apportionment which, however, shall not provide for more than one full annual commission for any one of them. However, if from a trust or from property subject to a power in trust having a value of $400,000 or more, or if from a trust or from property subject to a power in trust having a value of $100,000, or more but less than $400,000, as the case may be, at the beginning of a trust year or of the calendar year any payments in partial distribution of the trust or of the property subject to the power in trust shall be made during the trust or calendar year so as to reduce the trust or the property subject to the power in trust to a value of less than $400,000 or $100,000, as the case may be, at the end of the trust or calendar year, then the annual commissions allowed herein shall, on a proportionate basis, be those allowed to trustees of a trust or to donees of a power in trust over property having a value of $400,000 or more, or of a trust or to donees of a power in trust over property having a value of $100,000 or more but less than $400,000, as the case may be, for the period from the beginning of the trust or calendar year to the date of the distribution and shall, on a proportionate basis, be those allowed to trustees of a trust or to donees of a power in trust over property having a value of either $100,000 or more but less than $400,000 or less than $100,000, as the case may be, for the remainder of the trust or calendar year and the part of such commissions payable from principal and computed from the beginning of the trust or calendar year to the date of distribution shall be charged ratably to the property remaining in the trust or still subject to the power in trust after such distribution and to the property distributed from the trust or to the beneficiary of the power in trust on the basis of their respective values. Further, if during a trust or calendar year additional property shall be received into a trust which had a value of less than $100,000 or by a donee of a power in trust the property subject to which had a value of less than $100,000, or into a trust which had a value of $100,000 or more but less than $400,000 or by a donee of a power in trust the property subject to which had a value of $100,000 or more but less than $400,000, as the case may be, at the beginning of the trust year or calendar year, so that because of the additional property the trust or the property subject to the power in trust has a value of $100,000 or more but less than $400,000, or of $400,000 or more, as the case may be, at the end of the trust or calendar year, then the annual commissions allowed herein to the trustee or to the donee of the power in trust shall, on a proportionate basis, be those allowed to trustees of a trust or to donees of a power in trust over property having a value of less than $100,000, or to trustees of a trust or to donees of a power in trust over property having a value of $100,000 or more but less than $400,000, as the case may be, for the period from the beginning of the trust or calendar year to the date of the receipt of the additional property and shall, on a proportionate basis, be those allowed to trustees of a trust or to donees of a power in trust over property having a value of $100,000 or more but less than $400,000, or to trustees of a trust or to donees of a power in trust over property having $400,000 or more, as the case may be, for the remainder of the trust or calendar year.

(c) Notwithstanding any provision of paragraphs (a) and (b) of this subdivision to the contrary, if during the continuance of a trust not measured at any time directly or indirectly by a life or lives or during the continuance of a trust after the termination of the measuring life or lives, the annual income of the trust amounts to $4,000 or more and there is more than 1 trustee, each trustee is entitled to the full commissions allowed under subdivision 5 to a sole trustee unless there are more than 2, in which case the commissions to which 2 trustees would be entitled must be apportioned among the trustees according to the services rendered by them respectively unless they shall have agreed in writing among themselves to a different apportionment which, however, shall not provide for more than one full commission to any one of them. If the annual income of the trust amounts to less than $4,000 and there is more than 1 trustee the commissions to which a sole trustee would be entitled under subdivision 5 must be apportioned among the trustees according to the services rendered by them respectively unless they shall have agreed in writing among themselves to a different apportionment.

7. Where a trustee or donee of a power in trust is for any reason entitled or required to collect the rents of and manage real property the net amount of rents collected and not the gross amount shall be used in making computation of commissions allowed by subdivision 5 and in addition to the commissions herein provided he or she shall be allowed and may retain for such services 6 percent of the gross rents collected, but there shall be only one such additional commission regardless of the number of trustees or donees of the power in trust. If there are 2 or more trustees or donees of the power in trust the additional commission herein provided for must be apportioned among them according to the services rendered by them respectively unless they shall have agreed in writing among themselves to a different apportionment.

8. If a trustee or donee of a power in trust is either authorized or required by the terms of the will to accumulate income for any purpose permitted by law he or she shall be entitled to commissions from the income so accumulated, including income derived from the investment of such accumulated income, at the rate of 2 percent of the first $2,500 of such income distributed during the administration of the trust and 1 percent of all such income distributed in excess of $2,500 and he or she may retain such commissions at the time or times such income is distributed.

9. The value of any property to be determined in such manner as directed by the court and the increment thereof received, distributed or delivered, shall be considered as money in making computation of commissions. Whenever any portion of the dividends, interests or rents payable to a trustee or to a donee of a power in trust is required by any law of the United States or other governmental unit to be withheld by the person paying it for income tax purposes, the amount so withheld shall be deemed to have been collected.

10. Where the will provides a specific compensation for a trustee or for a donee of a power in trust he or she is not entitled to any other allowances for his or her services.

11. For the purposes of this section, the term "trustee" shall mean any trustee who is not a corporate trustee and the term "donee of a power in trust" shall mean any such donee including a donee of a power during minority who is not a corporate fiduciary provided, however, that as used in subdivision 6 of this section, the term trustee shall include a corporate trustee and further provided that the term "property subject to the power in trust" shall include property subject to a power during minority.

History: Add, L 1966, ch 953, eff Sept 1, 1967 from Sur. Ct. Act § 285-b; amd, L 1969, ch 1050, eff Sept 1, 1969; L 1976, ch 303, eff June 8, 1976; L 1977, ch 180, eff May 24, 1977; L 1980, ch 503, § 36, eff June 24, 1980; L 1984, ch 936, eff Aug 4, 1984; L 1991, ch 245, §§ 3, 4, eff July 1, 1991; L 1993, ch 514, § 57, eff Jan 1, 1994; L 1993, ch 640, eff Aug 4, 1993; L 1993, ch 654, § 2, eff Aug 4, 1993; L 2001, ch 243, § 7, eff Jan 1, 2002; L 2019, ch 601, § 4, eff Jan 1, 2020.

§ 2310. Payment on account of commissions

1. At any time during the administration of an estate and irrespective of the pendency of a particular proceeding a fiduciary may present to the court from which his letters issued a petition praying that he be permitted to receive a sum on account of the commissions to which he would be entitled if he were then filing his account and it were judicially settled, which must show the facts upon which the application is founded.

2. If the application be entertained process shall issue to all persons whose rights or interests would be affected by the payment applied for, citing them to show cause why the relief requested be not granted.

3. Upon the return of process the court may award a sum on account of commissions or make such other order or decree, if any, as justice shall require. The payment on account shall not exceed the receiving commissions due the fiduciary, except that the court may award a greater sum where all persons whose rights or interests are affected by the payment are persons under no legal disability and by acknowledged instrument consent thereto.

4. The total expenses of the application shall be borne by the person or persons to whom an award of commissions may be made, or if the application be denied, by the petitioner personally.

5. The order or decree authorizing the payment on account shall require the fiduciary to file a bond in the amount of the payment securing its return if and to the extent the payment is disallowed, except that no such bond shall be required where the fiduciary has already filed a bond pursuant to law or is a corporate fiduciary or where all persons whose rights or interests would be affected by the payment are persons under no legal disability and by acknowledged instrument consent to waive a bond or where the will specifically dispenses with such a bond.

History: Add, L 1966, ch 953, eff Sept 1, 1967 from Sur. Ct. Act § 285-c; amd, L 1967, ch 685, § 143, eff Sept 1, 1967; L 1984, ch 636, § 1, eff July 27, 1984.

§ 2311. Ex parte application for advance payment of commissions

1. At any time during the administration of an estate and irrespective of the pendency of a particular proceeding a fiduciary may present to the court from which his letters issued a petition praying that he be permitted to receive a sum on account of the commissions to which he would be entitled if he were then filing his account and it were judicially settled, which must show that unless he is allowed such sum on account of commissions he or the estate will be deprived of substantial advantages under the income tax laws of the United States or the

state of New York or that he will suffer inconvenience or hardship or that all persons whose rights or interests would be affected by the payment applied for are persons under no legal disability and have by acknowledged instrument consented thereto. No notice of the application shall be required by the court.

2. If the application be entertained the court may award a sum on account of commissions or make such other order or decree, if any, as justice shall require.

3. In all cases where a payment on account of commissions is directed by the court the payment on account shall not exceed the receiving commissions due the fiduciary, except that the court may award a greater sum where all persons whose rights or interests are affected by the payment are persons under no legal disability and by acknowledged instrument consent thereto.

4. The total expenses of the application shall be borne by the fiduciary, by the estate, or shall be apportioned between them in such ratio as the court may determine according to the benefit derived from the payments.

5. The order or decree authorizing the payment on account shall require the fiduciary to file a bond in the amount of the payment securing its return if and to the extent that the payment is disallowed, except that no such bond shall be required where the fiduciary has already filed a bond pursuant to law or is a corporate fiduciary or where all persons whose rights or interests would be affected by the payment are persons under no legal disability and by acknowledged instrument consent to waive a bond or where the will specifically dispenses with such a bond.

History: Add, L 1966, ch 953, eff Sept 1, 1967 from Sur. Ct. Act § 285-d; amd, L 1967, ch 685, § 144, eff Sept 1, 1967; L 1968, ch 259, § 41, eff May 14, 1968; L 1984, ch 636, § 2, eff July 27, 1984.

§ 2312. Commissions of corporate trustees, including when acting as donees of powers during minority or donees of power in trust

1. If the will or lifetime trust instrument makes provisions for specific rates or amounts of commissions (other than a general reference to commissions allowed by law or words of like import) for a corporate trustee, or, if a corporate trustee has agreed to accept specific rates or amounts of commissions, a corporate trustee, whether as trustee or as donee of a power in trust, including for purposes of this section as donee of a power during minority, created under the provisions of the will or lifetime trust instrument, shall be entitled to be compensated in accordance with such provisions or agreement, as the case may be.

2. For trusts having a principal value of more than four hundred thousand dollars and as donee of a power in trust where the property subject to the power, including for purposes of this section the property subject to a power during minority, has a principal value of more than four hundred thousand dollars and subject to the provisions of subdivision 4 of this section, if the will or lifetime trust instrument does not make provisions for specific rates or amounts of commissions, or, contains only a general reference to commissions allowed by law or words of like import, a corporate trustee shall be entitled to such commissions as may be reasonable, and the court, upon application of a person interested in the trust or in the fund held by the corporate trustee as donee of a power in trust, may review the reasonableness of the commission of such corporate trustee.

3. Subject to the provisions of paragraph (a) of subdivision 4 of this section and regardless

of the principal value of the trust: (a) during the continuance of a trust created solely for public, religious, charitable, scientific, literary, educational or fraternal uses and during the period of continuance of such a trust after the termination of a life use or uses a corporate trustee shall be entitled to and may retain commissions from income in accordance with the provisions of subdivision 1 or 2 hereof, as the case may be.

(b) In the case of a trust created solely for public, religious, charitable, scientific, literary, educational or fraternal uses a corporate trustee shall not be entitled to any commission from principal.

(c) In the case of such a trust which continues after the termination of the measuring life use or uses a corporate trustee for the period of the measuring life use or uses shall be entitled to commissions from income and principal according to the provisions of subdivision 1 or 2 hereof, as the case may be, and except in respect of principal paid out to a charity or for charitable uses shall be entitled to a commission for distributing all sums of principal in accordance with the provisions of subdivision 1 or 2 hereof, as the case may be.

4. Notwithstanding anything contained in this chapter, the estates, powers and trusts law or any other provision of law to the contrary,

(a) Except as otherwise provided by paragraph (b) of this subdivision and subdivision three of this section, a corporate trustee of any trust created under will or lifetime trust instrument, or as donee of a power in trust created under will or lifetime instrument, whether in existence on or after the effective date of this section, shall be entitled to receive at least the compensation provided for an individual trustee under subdivisions 1, 2, 5 (but only as trustee), 6, 7 and 12 of section 2308 and subdivisions 1, 2, 5 (but only as trustee), 6, 7 and 8 of section 2309, as the case may be, in effect after the effective date of this section, at the time and in the manner provided by such sections, unless the will or lifetime trust instrument or an agreement between the trustee and the testator or grantor or by the trustee shall provide otherwise.

(b) A corporate trustee shall, in addition to the compensation permitted by the provisions of paragraph (a) of this subdivision, be entitled to annual commissions at the rate of not more than $12.35 per thousand or major fraction thereof, in lieu of the annual commissions provided under paragraph (a) of this subdivision, on trusts having a principal value of not more than four hundred thousand dollars and shall be entitled to annual commissions at the same rate as donee of a power in trust where the property subject to the power has a principal value of not more than four hundred thousand dollars, and such annual commissions shall be deemed reasonable compensation, unless the will or lifetime trust instrument or an agreement between the corporate trustee and the testator or grantor or by the corporate trustee shall provide otherwise. A corporate trustee shall be entitled to receive such commissions from time to time during the trust or calendar year and shall otherwise be governed by the provisions of sections 2308 and 2309, as the case may be, in effect from time to time.

5. Unless the will or lifetime trust instrument expressly provides otherwise, the commissions allowable by subdivision 1, 2 or 4 hereof, as the case may be, shall be payable one-third from the income of the trust or from the income of the property subject to the power in trust and two-thirds from the principal of the trust or from the property subject to the power in trust. However, in the case of a trust whose definition of income is governed by section 11-2.4

of the estates, powers and trusts law or a charitable remainder annuity trust or a charitable remainder unitrust, as defined in section six hundred sixty-four of the Internal Revenue Code of nineteen hundred eighty-six, as amended, such commissions shall be payable from the principal of any such trust after allowance for the annuity or unitrust amounts and shall not be payable out of such annuity or unitrust amounts.

6. The commissions allowed by subdivision 1, 2 or 4 thereof, as the case may be, may be retained, at any time or from time to time during the year in which such commissions are earned, by a corporate trustee, provided it furnishes annually as of a date no more than 30 days prior to the end of the year selected by the corporate trustee, to each beneficiary currently receiving income, and to any other beneficiary interested in the income and to any person interested in the principal of the trust who shall make a demand therefor, and, when acting as donee of a power in trust, to the beneficiary of the power in trust, a statement showing the principal assets or assets subject to the power in trust on hand on that date, and at least annually or more frequently if the trustee so elects, a statement showing all his or her receipts of income and principal or of property subject to the power in trust during the period with respect to which the statement is rendered including the amount of any commissions retained and the basis upon which the commissions were computed. A corporate trustee shall not be deemed to have waived any commissions by reason of its failure to retain them at the time when it becomes entitled thereto; provided however that commissions payable from income for any such year shall be allowed and retained only from income derived from the trust during such year and shall not be supplied from income on hand in respect of any other year. If a beneficiary receiving income or a beneficiary of a power in trust of which the corporate trustee is donee does not desire to be furnished with any such statements his or her advice to the trustee to that effect in writing shall thereafter excuse the corporate trustee from furnishing such statements to the beneficiary unless and until the beneficiary requests such annual statements from the trustee. Upon enactment of, and subject to subdivision 1 of this section, a corporate trustee shall continue to receive commissions in the manner provided for a trustee or when acting as donee of a power in trust in the manner provided for a donee of a power in trust under sections 2308 and 2309, as the case may be, in effect immediately before the effective date of this section until the end of the then current trust or calendar year, and thereafter, a corporate trustee may receive commissions in accordance with the provisions of subdivision 2 or 4 of this section. A corporate trustee shall not change from the commissions provided for by subdivision 2 or 4 of this section, as the case may be, during a trust's calendar or fiscal year or the calendar year in the case of a power in trust but a corporate trustee may change from the commissions provided for by subdivision 2 to the commissions provided for by subdivision 4 of this section, or vice versa, only at the beginning of a calendar or fiscal year of a trust or a calendar year in the case of a power in trust, as the case may be.

7. On the settlement of the account of any trustee or donee of a power in trust under a will or lifetime trust instrument, in addition to the commissions provided for by this section, the court must allow to the corporate trustee including a corporate trustee acting as donee of a power in trust the corporate trustee's reasonable and necessary expenses actually paid by the trustee.

8. The value of any property to be determined in such manner as directed by the court and the increment thereof received, distributed or delivered, shall be considered as money in making computation of commissions. Whenever any portion of the dividends, interests, rents or other income payable to a trustee or donee of a power in trust is required by any law of

the United States or other governmental unit to be withheld by the person paying it for income tax purposes, the amount so withheld shall be deemed to have been collected.

9. A trustee who prior to September 1, 1966 shall have received the maximum amount of commissions on principal permitted by subdivision 8 of section 285-a of the surrogate's court act as that subdivision existed prior to that date, shall not be entitled to annual principal commissions for the period from the date when he or she shall have received such maximum to September 1, 1966, but shall be entitled to receive commissions from and after September 1, 1966 at the rates and in the manner provided in section 2308 as in effect immediately before enactment of this section. A trustee who is entitled to annual principal commissions pursuant to section 285-a of the surrogate's court act as it existed prior to September 1, 1966, but has not received them, may receive an amount of commissions not in excess of the amount he or she would have been entitled to if he or she had taken such commissions, and be entitled to receive in addition commissions from and after September 1, 1966 at the rates and in the manner provided in section 285-a of this act.

10. A trustee who has been acting prior to July 1, 1956 shall be entitled to have commissions on principal and income theretofore received by him or her computed, allowed and paid under the methods and at the rates set forth herein, except as follows:

(a) If prior to July 1, 1956 a trustee has been allowed or has retained commissions for receiving and paying out or for distributing any item of principal he or she shall be entitled to no further commissions on the item.

(b) If prior to July 1, 1956 a trustee has been allowed or retained commissions on any item of principal received but not paid out or distributed by him or her he or she shall be entitled to no further commissions for receiving the item.

(c) Any trustee who became entitled to an annual principal commission under subdivision 1 (b) of section 285-a of the surrogate's court act as it existed prior to April 1, 1948 and who has not retained such commission may retain an amount equal to one-half of such annual principal commission. A trustee who because of the provisions of subdivision 2 of section 285-a of the surrogate's court act as it existed prior to April 1, 1948 either was not entitled to retain an annual principal commission under subdivision 1 (b) thereof or was required to credit such annual principal commission against his or her commission for receiving principal, may retain an amount equal to one-half of such annual principal commission. If a trustee has been allowed by decree or has retained any such annual principal commission one-half the amount thereof shall be deducted from the amount of commissions to which the trustee would otherwise be entitled under the provisions of subdivision 1 of surrogate's court procedure act section 2308.

(d) The annual principal commissions allowed by subdivision 3 of surrogate's court procedure act section 2308 as it existed on September 1, 1967 shall not be allowed by decree or retained in respect of any trust year ending prior to April 1, 1948, but for any trust year ending on or after April 1, 1948 and prior to July 1, 1956, the annual principal commission which may be allowed by decree or retained shall be computed at the rates in effect on the date such trust year ended.

(e) If prior to July 1, 1956 a trustee has been allowed by decree or has retained commissions on any item of income received and paid out by him or her prior to September 1, 1943 or on any item of income received by him or her subsequent to

September 1, 1943 he or she shall be entitled to no further commission on the item.

(f) For purposes of this section, the term "donee of a power in trust" shall mean any such donee including a donee of a power during minority who is a corporate fiduciary and the term "property subject to the power in trust" shall include property subject to a power during minority.

History: Add, L 1984, ch 936, § 8, eff Aug 6, 1984; amd, L 1987, ch 511, §§ 1–7, eff July 30, 1987; L 1988, ch 120, eff June 13, 1988; L 1991, ch 245, § 5, eff July 1, 1991; L 1993, ch 640, eff Aug 4, 1993; L 2001, ch 243, § 8, eff Jan 1, 2002; L 2019, ch 601, § 5, eff Jan 1, 2020.

§ 2313. Multiple commissions of executors or trustees, donees of powers during minority, or donees of power in trust under wills of persons dying, or lifetime trusts established, after August 31, 1993

With respect to wills of persons dying, or lifetime trusts established, after August 31, 1993, if there are more than two executors or trustees, donees of a power during minority, or donees of a power in trust, no more than two commissions shall be allowed unless the decedent or creator has specifically provided otherwise in a signed writing, and the compensation thus allowable must be apportioned among the fiduciaries or donees of the power in trust according to the services rendered by them respectively unless they shall have agreed in writing among themselves to a different apportionment which, however, shall not provide for more than one full commission for any one of them.

History: Add, L 1993, ch 514, eff Jan 1, 1994; amd, L 1995, ch 471, § 1, eff Aug 2, 1995; L 2019, ch 601, § 6, eff Jan 1, 2020.

SCPA

ARTICLE 24
COURT FEES

SUMMARY OF ARTICLE

§ 2401. Fees in the surrogate's court; general provisions

1. In the surrogate's court fees for service, filing and other matters shall be as provided in this article to the exclusion of other statutory provisions unless expressly stated to the contrary.

2. The clerk of each surrogate's court shall charge and receive for the services and matters herein set forth the fees indicated in this article which shall be payable in advance.

3. All fees shall be the property of the county unless otherwise provided by law.

4. Unless specifically indicated no fee is chargeable for motions made in a pending proceeding or for ex parte applications.

5. The fees in the surrogate's court of each county of the state shall be the amount specified in the rate column for the service or matter indicated.

6. Notwithstanding any other provision of law to the contrary, no filing fees payable pursuant to the provisions of this section and section twenty-four hundred two of this article shall be required in any matter relating to the estates or affairs of persons missing or deceased as a result of the terrorist attacks of September eleventh, two thousand one.

> **History:** Add, L 1966, ch 953, eff Sept 1, 1967 from Sur. Ct. Act §§ 29, 29-a to 29-d, 29-g, 29-i to 29-m; amd, L 2007, ch 21, § 3, eff April 17, 2007, applying to all matters filed on or after Sept 11, 2001 relating to the estates or affairs of persons missing or deceased as a result of the terrorist attacks of Sept 11, 2001.

§ 2402. Fees. Amount of

1. Probate. Upon filing a petition to commence a proceeding for probate of a will the fee shall be as shown by the following schedule computed initially upon the gross estate passing by will as stated in the petition; provided however that in a proceeding for ancillary probate of a will the fee shall be computed only upon the property within the state passing under such will and provided that in all cases if the value of the estate so passing as subsequently shown by a tax return filed under article twenty-six of the tax law, by a proceeding under such article, by any proceeding in surrogate's court involving such estate, or by such papers or documents in connection with such estate as court rules may require to be filed with the court, exceeds the value originally stated and upon which the fee was paid, then an additional probate fee shall be immediately payable. Such additional fee shall be the difference between the fee based on the value subsequently shown and the fee which was initially paid. In the event that the value of the estate so passing as subsequently shown is less than the value originally stated and upon which the fee was paid, then a refund shall be made which shall be the difference between the fee initially paid and the fee based on the actual value subsequently shown.

The fee paid in a probate or ancillary probate proceeding includes all charges except if probate be contested, fees as required for filing objections, demand for jury trial or for filing note of issue shall be payable.

2. Administration. Upon filing a petition to commence a proceeding for administration in intestacy the fee shall be as shown by the following schedule based initially upon the gross estate passing by intestacy as stated in the petition; provided however that if the value of the estate so passing as subsequently shown by a tax return filed under article twenty-six of the tax law, by a proceeding under such article, by any proceeding in surrogate's court involving such estate, or by such papers or documents in connection with such estate as court rules may require to be filed with the court, exceeds the value originally stated and upon which the fee was paid, then an additional fee shall be immediately payable. Such additional fee shall be the difference between the fee based on the value subsequently shown and the fee which was initially paid. In the event that the value of the estate so passing as subsequently shown is less than the value originally stated and upon which the fee was paid, then a refund shall be made which shall be the difference between the fee initially paid and the fee based on the actual value subsequently shown.

3. Accounting. (a) Upon filing a petition to commence a proceeding for an accounting the fee shall be as shown by the following schedule based on the gross value of assets accounted for including principal and income. Where more than one account is filed under a single petition the fee shall be based separately on the gross value of each separate fund or trust accounted for.

(b) Notwithstanding the provisions of paragraph (a) of this subdivision, upon filing a petition to commence an accounting proceeding for a lifetime trust or upon filing a petition for an accounting in a conservatorship proceeding, the fee shall be the same as that which is payable in the supreme court pursuant to section eight thousand eighteen of the civil practice law and rules.

4. Instruments settling accounts. For filing an instrument which releases and discharges a fiduciary but does not contain any statement of account, no fee shall be charged. For recording any such instrument, the fee shall be six dollars per page or part thereof. Upon filing or recording an instrument pursuant to section 2202, the fee shall be as shown by the following schedule based on the gross value of assets accounted for including principal and income, and such fee shall include the filing or recording of such instrument. If separate instruments executed by several beneficiaries release and discharge the same fiduciary or fiduciaries and settle in whole or in the part one and the same account, only a single fee shall be charged for the filing or recording of all such instruments.

5. Decree approving accounts. Upon filing a petition pursuant to section 2203, the fee shall be as shown by the following schedule based on the gross value of assets accounted for including principal and income. In the event no values are shown in the petition and related instruments the fee shall be as shown by the following schedule based on the estate of the decedent as shown in the estate tax return filed under article 26 of the tax law or a proceeding under such article.

6. Other proceedings. In proceedings not otherwise provided in this act the fee shall be according to the following schedule based on the value of the subject matter.

7. The fee schedule for subdivision 1 through 7 inclusive is as follows:

Value of Estate or Subject Matter	Fee Rate
Less than $10,000	$ 45.00
10,000 but under 20,000	75.00
20,000 but under 50,000	215.00
50,000 but under 100,000	280.00
100,000 but under 250,000	420.00
250,000 but under 500,000	625.00
500,000 and over	1,250.00

8. (a) For filing a petition to commence the following proceedings, the fee shall be as indicated:

SCPA		Fee Rate
607	To punish respondent for contempt	$ 30.00
711	Suspend, modify, revoke letters or remove a fiduciary other than a custodian or guardian	75.00
711	Suspend, modify, revoke letters or remove a custodian or guardian	30.00
715	Application of fiduciary to resign	30.00
717	Suspend powers-fiduciary in war	30.00
1401	Compel production of will	20.00
1420	Construction of will	75.00
1421	Determination of right of election	75.00
1502	Appointment of trustee	45.00
1508	Release against state	50.00
1703	Appointment of guardian	20.00
2003	Open safe deposit box	20.00
2102	Proceedings against a fiduciary	20.00
2103	Proceedings by fiduciary to discover property	75.00
2107	Advice and directions	75.00
2108	Continue business	45.00
2114	Review corporate trustee compensation	10.00
2205	Petition to compel fiduciary to account	30.00
EPTL		Fee Rate
7-4.6	Appointment of successor custodian	20.00

(b) For filing a petition to commence a proceeding for the appointment of a trustee of a lifetime trust or for the appointment of a conservator, the fee shall be the same as that which is payable in the supreme court pursuant to section eight thousand eighteen of the civil practice law and rules.

9. For filing:

	Fee Rate
(i) a demand for trial by jury in any proceeding, SCPA 502	$ 150.00

(ii) objections to the probate of a will

SCPA 1410	150.00
(iii) a note of issue in any proceeding	45.00
(iv) objection or answer in any action or proceeding	
other than probate	75.00
(v) a will for safekeeping pursuant to section 2507	45.00
of this act except that the court in any county may	
reduce or dispense with such fee	
(vi) a bond, including any additional bond:	
less than $10,000	20.00
$10,000 and over	30.00

10. For furnishing a transcript of a decree $20.00

11. For a certificate of letters evidencing that the appointment of a fiduciary is still in full force and effect $6.00

12. (a) For making and certifying or comparing and certifying a copy of a will or any paper on file or recorded in his office: . . . . $6.00 pg.

(b) Authenticating the same, additional: $20.00

13. For searching and certifying to any record for which search is made:

$30.00 for under 25 years
$90.00 for over 25 years

14. (a) For producing papers, documents, books of record on file in his office under a subpoena duces tecum, for use within the county where the office of the court is situated:
$30.00

(b) For use in any other county, such fee to be paid for each day or part thereof that the messenger is detailed from the office and to be in addition to mileage fee and the necessary expenses of the messenger. The clerk of the court shall not be required to make any collection or return of the money so paid for expenses: $.30

15. For recording:

(a) any instrument, decree or other paper which is required by law to be recorded:

$8.00 per pg.
or part $16.00 minimum

(b) for filing an authenticated copy of a foreign will:

$8.00 per pg.
$64.00 minimum

(c) for taxing bill of costs:

$15.00

16. No fee shall be charged:

(a) for filing objections of a guardian ad litem, or of a respondent in a proceeding brought pursuant to section three hundred eighty-four-b of the social services law

(b) for filing the annual account of a guardian

(c) for any certificate or certified copy of a paper required to be filed with the United States Veterans Administration

(d) for filing a petition in a proceeding for filing an additional bond, to reduce the penalty of a bond or substitute a new bond or discharge any bond when no accounting is required

(e) in respect to the proceedings for the appointment of a fiduciary when the appointment is made solely for the purpose of collecting bounty, arrears of pay, prize money, pension dues or other dues or gratuities due from the federal or state government for services of an infant or of a decedent formerly or now in the military or naval services of the United States or to collect the proceeds of a war risk insurance policy.

(f) to or received from the state of New York or any public agency of the state or any civil subdivision or agency thereof or with respect to a social services official when taking any proceeding with respect to the estate of a person who was a recipient of benefits from social services.

(g) or received for the filing of a petition for an order granting funds for the maintenance or other proper needs of any infant nor for any certificate or any certified copy of the order on such an application.

17. The fee charged herein for the filing of a petition shall include the recording of any decree made in that proceeding which is required by law to be recorded and shall include the recording of any letters required by law to be recorded.

> **History:** Add, L 1966, ch 953, eff Sept 1, 1967 from Sur. Ct. Act §§ 29, 29-a to 29-d, 29-g, 29-i to 29-m; amd, L 1967, ch 685, eff Sept 1, 1967; L 1968, ch 151, eff July 1, 1968; L 1968, ch 165, eff July 1, 1968; L 1968, ch 259, eff May 14, 1968; L 1969, ch 626, eff Sept 1, 1969; L 1971, ch 805, eff Sept 1, 1971; L 1972, ch 438, eff May 22, 1972; L 1972, ch 733, eff July 1, 1972; L 1973, ch 732, eff Sept 1, 1973; L 1974, ch 904, eff Sept 1, 1974; L 1977, ch 33, eff April 1, 1977; L 1979, ch 20, eff Sept 1, 1979; L 1980, ch 39, eff April 1, 1980; L 1982, ch 839, eff Sept 1, 1982; L 1984, ch 77, § 1, applicable to all estates for which letters have been issued, whether prior to, on, or after April 17, 1984; L 1987, ch 511, eff July 30, 1987; L 1987, ch 825, eff Nov 5, 1987; L 1990, ch 190, §§ 125–127, 263, eff May 25, 1990; L 1990, ch 190, § 263; L 1991, ch 62, eff April 22, 1991; L 1997, ch 389, § 33 (Part A), eff Feb 1, 2000, applying to estates of decedents dying on or after that date; L 2003, ch 62, § 30 (Part J), eff July 14, 2003.

§ 2403. Fees of court reporter in surrogate's court

Except where otherwise agreed or when special provision is otherwise made by statute a court reporter is entitled for a copy fully written out from his stenographic notes of the testimony required to be made in any proceeding for the record of the court to 20 cents for each folio and the court may order that the fees therefor be paid out of the estate to which the proceeding relates.

> **History:** Add, L 1966, ch 953, eff Sept 1, 1967 from Sur. Ct. Act § 30.

§ 2404. Expenses

Where upon the application of any party the surrogate or any of the personnel of the court goes to a place other than the court in order to take testimony or to produce records or for any purpose required by law, the person so going shall be paid by such party his actual and necessary expenses.

History: Add, L 1966, ch 953, eff Sept 1, 1967 from Sur. Ct. Act § 31.

ARTICLE 25
RECORDS AND RECORDING
SUMMARY OF ARTICLE

SCPA

§ 2501. Records to be kept by court; general requirements

1. The clerk of the court shall keep a record of and be responsible for the proper indexing, filing or recording, as the case may be, collating, arranging, restoring and preserving of all records, documents, books, maps, instruments and other matter specified in this article or by other requirement of law heretofore or hereafter deposited, filed or recorded, of all matters specified by this article or by other requirement of law.

2. He shall upon payment of the fees required by law exemplify or certify all records and papers filed or recorded and shall search and certify as to records or papers in custody of the court or that they cannot be found.

3. Records shall be kept by means of record books, cards, files or any other system, process, form or combination thereof, as may be prescribed by CPLR 9703 or directed by the court together with such appropriate index or reference system, and such topic, item or other subdivision or arrangement as deemed appropriate or convenient. When the clerk is directed to keep a record book it may be kept by one or more of the methods prescribed as may be currently utilized by the court for the purpose.

4. The expense of keeping the records required by law to be kept shall be a charge upon the county, state or other governmental unit or agency providing funds for administration of the court as may be provided by law.

5. When filing is required the paper filed shall be entered in the proper minute book, and date of filing with fee, if any, noted on the paper.

6. When recording of a paper is required an accurate copy thereof shall be made of the complete content of the paper by entry at length in a record book in plain and legible handwriting or by printing or typewriting or photographic or microphotographic or other process or any combination thereof or by making a record in any other form or process which provides or will produce an accurate copy of the paper.

7. Records and papers which are sealed and withheld from public inspection as required by law or directed by the court shall thereafter be opened only to the extent as may be authorized by the court.

8. All books and records other than those sealed are open to inspection of any person at reasonable times.

9. Records and papers relating to a proceeding and entered in the minute book shall be preserved as permanent records of the court, except as disposition is authorized by section 89 of the judiciary law.

History: Add, L 1966, ch 953, eff Sept 1, 1967 from Sur. Ct. Act § 16 in part; amd, L 1968, ch 259, § 43, eff May 14, 1968.

§ 2502. Books to be kept by clerk

The clerk shall keep and maintain:

1. A record book properly indexed in which shall be entered a description of every proceeding with proper entries under each denoting the papers filed, orders and decrees made and the steps taken therein, with the dates of filing and recording the several papers in the proceeding.

2. Such other record books, properly indexed, as may be necessary or convenient to record at length any documents required by law to be recorded.

3. A court and trust fund register in which shall be entered a reference to any proceeding in which a decree or order directs a deposit of money, the date thereof, the amount thereof, the amount so deposited, any receipt therefor and the name of the person to and for whom the deposit is made.

4. A record book, properly indexed, with proper entries denoting the name and file number of the estate and the date of filing any informal account or any release pursuant to 2202.

5. Such other books as the chief administrator of the courts in each department or the court in each county may direct to be kept.

History: Add, L 1966, ch 953, eff Sept 1, 1967 from Sur. Ct. Act §§ 16, 33 in part; amd, L 1990, ch 623, § 5, eff July 18, 1990.

§ 2504. Wills to be retained after probate; exceptions

1. A written will which has been admitted to probate must remain in the court, except where the will is on file in a court or public office of another state or country under the laws of which it cannot be removed.

2. When it appears that the laws of another jurisdiction require the production of an original will before the provisions thereof become effective in such jurisdiction the court may cause any original will on file in its office to be sent to any court which, or to any officer of such jurisdiction who, under the laws thereof, is empowered to receive the will for probate, or may deliver the will to any person interested in the probate thereof in such jurisdiction or to his fiduciary in such manner and upon such terms as it deems proper for the preservation of the will and the protection of other parties interested in the estate.

3. In the case of a joint will which has been admitted to probate in this state the court of such county may under such terms as it deems proper transmit the original joint will to the surrogate's court of any other county in this state for probate as the will of any other signer thereof. It shall be the duty of the court of such other county to keep a true copy thereof in its office and thereafter to return the original will to the surrogate's court of the county of original probate.

History: Add, L 1966, ch 953, eff Sept 1, 1967 from Sur. Ct. Act § 150.

§ 2505. Transmission of wills of non-domiciliaries and domiciliaries of another county before probate

Whenever it appears that an instrument purporting to be a will is on file or is in safekeeping and no proceeding for the probate thereof is pending and that the maker of such instrument at the time of his death was domiciled elsewhere, either within or without the state, the court, upon such notice as it may think proper, may cause the instrument to be sent to any court or officer of this state or other jurisdiction of decedent's domicile entitled under the laws thereof to receive it or to any person in this or any other jurisdiction interested in the probate of the instrument. The instrument may also be sent to any court or officer in this state or other jurisdiction in which the maker left real or personal property. Delivery is to be made in such manner and upon such terms as the court deems proper for the preservation of the instrument and for the protection of parties interested in the estate of the maker thereof.

> **History:** Add, L 1966, ch 953, eff Sept 1, 1967 from Sur. Ct. Act § 150-a; amd, L 1993, ch 514, § 59, eff Jan 1, 1994.

§ 2506. Recording wills proved within the state

1. A certified copy of a will of real property admitted to probate in any court of competent jurisdiction of the state must be recorded in the office of the county clerk or register as the case requires of any county in which real property of the testator is situated, upon the request of any person interested.

2. The fiduciary under a will of real property must cause a certified copy thereof to be recorded in each county where real property of the testator is situate, other than the county of the testator's domicile, within 20 days after letters are issued to him.

3. An exemplification of the record of such a will from any court where recorded either before or after this chapter takes effect may be in like manner recorded in the office of the clerk or register of any county.

> **History:** Add, L 1966, ch 953, eff Sept 1, 1967 from Sur. Ct. Act § 152 and Dec. Est. Law §§ 42, 43; amd, L 1967, ch 685, § 146, eff Sept 1, 1967.

§ 2507. Reception of wills for safekeeping

1. The court of any county upon being paid the fees allowed therefor by law shall receive and deposit in the court any will of a domiciliary of the county which any person shall deliver to it for that purpose and shall give a written receipt therefor to the person depositing it. An attesting witness to any will may make and sign an affidavit before any officer authorized to administer oaths setting forth such facts as he would be required to testify to in order to prove the will. The affidavit may be written upon the will or on some paper securely attached thereto and may be filed for safekeeping with the will to which it relates. There may also be filed with the will affidavits of certified medical examiners, under the provisions of the mental hygiene law, certifying that the maker of the will was of sound mind at the time of its execution, together with any facts supporting such opinion.

2. The will shall be enclosed in a sealed wrapper so that the contents thereof cannot be read and shall have endorsed thereon the name of the testator, his domicile, and the day, month and year when delivered and shall not on any pretext whatever be opened, read or examined until delivered to a person entitled to it as hereinafter directed.

3. The will shall be delivered only

(a) to the testator in person or

(b) upon his written order duly proved by the oath of the testator which shall be duly acknowledged or

(c) after his death to the persons named in the endorsement on the wrapper of the will, if such endorsement be made thereon or

(d) if there be no such endorsement or if it has been deposited with any other officer than a surrogate, then to the surrogate's court of the county.

4. If the will shall have been deposited with a surrogate's court or shall have been delivered to it as above prescribed the court after the death of the testator shall publicly open and examine the will and make known the contents thereof and shall file it in the court, there to remain until it shall have been duly proved, if capable of proof, and then to be delivered to the person entitled to the custody thereof or until required by the authority of some competent court to produce the same in such court.

> **History:** Add, L 1966, ch 953, eff Sept 1, 1967 from Dec. Est. Law §§ 30, 31, 32, 33; amd,
> L 1968, ch 259, § 44, eff May 14, 1968; L 1981, ch 177, § 1, eff Sept 1, 1981.

§ 2508. Filing of will of decedent

The court of any county may receive and file the will of any decedent domiciled in that county at the date of death which any person shall deliver, without payment of fee. A record of the receipt and filing thereof shall be made by the clerk and the will shall remain on file subject to the further order of the court.

> **History:** Add, L 1968, ch 608, eff Sept 1, 1968.

§ 2509. Firearms inventory

Whenever, by regulation, rule or statute, a fiduciary or attorney of record must file a list of assets constituting a decedent's estate, such list must include a particularized description of every firearm, shotgun and rifle, as such terms are defined in section 265.00 of the penal law, that are part of such estate. Such list must be filed with the surrogate's court in the county in which the estate proceeding, if any, is pending and a copy must be filed with the division of criminal justice services.

> **History:** Add, L 2013, ch 1, § 53, eff March 16, 2013.

ARTICLE 26
THE SURROGATE'S COURT AND ITS OFFICERS
SUMMARY OF ARTICLE

§ 2601. When court open; terms and sessions

1. The court is always open for the transaction of any business within its powers and jurisdiction.

2. The judge of a surrogate's court may appoint and may alter the times and places of transacting any business which may come before it and designate terms and sessions for trials, hearings, chamber business and other business of the court.

3. The court, in a county where the judge of the county court is also a judge of the surrogate's court, may be held at the time and place at which the county court is held and the jury in attendance may constitute the jury for the trial of any issue arising in the surrogate's court.

> **History:** Add, L 1966, ch 953, eff Sept 1, 1967 from Sur. Ct. Act §§ 34, 35; amd, L 1967, ch 685, § 147, eff Sept 1, 1967.

§ 2602. Terms of courts and powers of judges in counties having more than one judge of the surrogate's court

1. In any county having more than 1 judge of the surrogate's court

(a) all of the powers conferred by law upon a judge of the surrogate's court may be exercised by either of such judges;

(b) the disability of a judge or his illness or absence from the county after his decision upon any matter in an action or proceeding before him shall not affect the validity of such decision and the other judge may give effect thereto and make and sign an appropriate order or decree based thereon having the same force and effect as if made by the judge making the decision.

2. In any such county the judges must

S-253

(a) appoint and may alter the times of holding terms and sessions of that court for the trial of proceedings in which there is a right to trial by jury;

(b) appoint and may alter the times of holding terms and sessions of that court for the disposition of all other business;

(c) prescribe the duration of such terms and assign the judge to preside and attend at the terms and sessions so appointed.

3. In the county of New York the appointment of such terms must be published in two newspapers published in the city of New York during or before the first week in January in each year.

History: Add, L 1966, ch 953, eff Sept 1, 1967 from Sur. Ct. Act § 36; amd, L 1969, ch 772, § 12, eff Sept 1, 1969.

§ 2603. Surrogate and acting surrogate

1. The judge of the surrogate's court may be designated as the surrogate. He may sign any paper wherever he may be at any time.

2. Where the county judge is also a judge of the surrogate's court he shall be designated as such without any addition referring to his office as county judge.

3. Where a judicial officer other than the judge of the surrogate's court acts as a judge of the surrogate's court in a case prescribed by law, he may be designated as "surrogate", notwithstanding his official title.

4. No person other than the one who holds such office on the effective date of this act may serve in the office of judge of the surrogate's court unless he or she has been admitted to practice law in the state of New York for at least 10 years as of the date he or she commences the duties of office.

History: Add, L 1966, ch 953, eff Sept 1, 1967 from Sur. Ct. Act § 2, part 34; amd, L 1967, ch 685, eff Sept 1, 1967; L 1993, ch 511, § 4, eff July 26, 1993.

§ 2604. Disqualification of judge

1. In addition to his general disqualifications as a judicial officer, a judge of the surrogate's court is also disqualified

(a) from acting upon an application for the probate of a will where he is an attesting witness or is necessarily examined or to be examined as a witness,

(b) where he files a certificate that his relations to the parties or subject matter is such that it is improper for him to act.

2. An objection to the power of a judge of the surrogate's court to act based upon a disqualification is waived by an adult party unless it is taken at or before the joinder of issue by that party or, where an issue is not framed, at or before the submission of the matter to the court.

History: Add, L 1966, ch 953, eff Sept 1, 1967 from Sur. Ct. Act §§ 6, 7.

§ 2605. Chief clerk, deputy chief clerk and other personnel of the courts unless otherwise provided for a particular county

1. Chief clerk. By written order filed and recorded in his office, which he may in like

manner revoke at pleasure, a surrogate shall appoint a chief clerk of the surrogate's court, who shall be and shall perform all duties of the clerk of the surrogate's court.

2. Deputy chief clerk. In any county containing a city of the second class and in any county having a population over 500,000 the surrogate shall, and in any other county the surrogate may, in like manner appoint a deputy chief clerk of the surrogate's court. In counties under 500,000 the surrogate may designate one of the clerks of the court to act as deputy chief clerk of the court in addition to other duties.

3. Temporary chief clerk of the court. Should the chief clerk or deputy chief clerk be absent or unable to act or if the office be vacant the surrogate may designate any law assistant or other clerk to serve temporarily as chief clerk or deputy chief clerk of the court.

4. Oath and bond. Each chief clerk and deputy chief clerk shall, before entering upon the performance of his duties, take the constitutional oath of office and shall file it with the county clerk of the county together with a bond in the sum of $50,000 approved by the surrogate conditioned for the faithful performance of his duties.

5. Other personnel. Within the appropriation therefor made by the county board of supervisors each surrogate may likewise appoint and remove such law assistants, clerks, court reporters and such attendants, messengers and other court officers and employees as necessary, including temporary court attendants and other personnel.

Court attendants and officers whose duty shall be to attend terms and sessions of court as required and perform such services as the surrogate directs shall possess all the powers of an officer designated by the sheriff to attend upon the court.

History: Add, L 1966, ch 953, eff Sept 1, 1967 from Sur. Ct. Act § 21, parts of §§ 22, 23; amd, L 1967, ch 685, § 149, eff Sept 1, 1967; L 1993, ch 514, § 60, eff Jan 1, 1994.

§ 2606. Chief clerk and deputy chief clerk of the surrogate's court and other personnel in Bronx, Kings, New York, Queens and Richmond counties

1. The judge of the surrogate's court in the counties of Bronx, Kings, New York, Queens and Richmond counties may severally appoint and remove a chief clerk of the court, a deputy chief clerk and such law assistants, clerks, court reporters and other officers and employees as necessary.

2. The chief clerk shall also be and shall perform all duties of the clerk of the surrogate's court.

3. Each chief clerk and deputy chief clerk of the court shall, before entering upon the performance of his duties, take the constitutional oath of office and file the same with the county clerk, together with a bond in the sum of $50,000 approved by the surrogate conditioned on the faithful performance of the duties of his office.

4. Should the chief clerk or deputy chief clerk be absent or unable to act or if the office be vacant the surrogate may designate any law assistant or other clerk to serve temporarily as chief clerk or deputy chief clerk of the court.

5. Each surrogate may appoint and remove such attendants, messengers and court officers to attend terms and sessions of court and perform such duties as required. Such officers shall have all the powers of officers designated by sheriffs to attend upon courts of record.

6. The compensation of all court personnel in the surrogate's court of each county,

notwithstanding any other provisions of law, shall be fixed by the respective surrogates upon approval of the state administrator and shall be a city charge provided that the final determination of the estimate of annual financial needs of the court shall be made as provided by article 7-a of the judiciary law and section 29 of article 6 of the Constitution. The proper appropriating body shall annually appropriate the necessary funds for such compensation and other expenses of the court.

History: Add, L 1966, ch 953, eff Sept 1, 1967 from Sur. Ct. Act §§ 22, 23 in part; amd, L 1974, ch 615, eff Sept 1, 1974; L 1993, ch 514, § 61, eff Jan 1, 1994.

§ 2607. Court reporters

1. Each surrogate may appoint and at pleasure remove one or more court reporters for the court, whose compensation shall be determined and paid in the same manner as salaries of clerks in the court.

2. The court reporter appointed to serve in the surrogate's court may with approval of the surrogate be designated to perform duties in another court and the court reporter of another court with approval of the judge thereof may be designated to serve in the surrogate's court. The provisions of the judiciary law apply to court reporters in the court.

3. Whenever the service of a court reporter is required and no regular court reporter is available, or he is sick, absent or unable to act, or whenever a trial or hearing requires additional reportorial services, a surrogate may appoint one or more temporary court reporters to serve in an action or proceeding to be paid a reasonable compensation certified by the surrogate which shall be a charge upon the city or county and paid as other expense of the court.

History: Add, L 1966, ch 953, eff Sept 1, 1967 from Sur. Ct. Act §§ 25, 26, 28; amd, L 1968, ch 259, § 45, eff May 14, 1968.

§ 2608. Expenses of surrogate or clerk

Where, upon the application of any party, the judge or clerk of the surrogate's court goes to a place other than the court in order to take testimony, he shall be paid by such party his actual and necessary expenses.

History: Add, L 1966, ch 953, eff Sept 1, 1967 from Sur. Ct. Act § 31.

§ 2609. Powers of chief clerk and other officers of the surrogate's court

1. The chief clerk and deputy chief clerk of the surrogate's court may exercise, concurrently with the surrogate, the following powers:

   (a) To certify and sign, issue or seal in the name of the clerk

   (i) any papers or records of the court,

   (ii) any process to which a party is entitled as of course,

   (iii) any letters or other mandate of the court.

   (b) To adjourn to a definite time, not exceeding 30 days, any matter, when the surrogate is absent from his office or unable by reason of other engagements to attend thereto.

   (c) In any proceeding of which the court has jurisdiction, to administer oaths, take acknowledgments of deeds and all other written instruments and certify the same at any place within or without the state.

(d) With the approval of the surrogate or surrogates of the county to authorize or deputize one or more of the other clerks of the court, to sign his name and exercise such of the other powers conferred upon him by this section as he shall designate. The surrogate may prohibit the chief clerk or deputy chief clerk from exercising any powers specified in this subdivision but the prohibition does not affect the validity of any act of the clerk done in disregard of the prohibition.

2. In addition to the powers above enumerated, to take proof of a will, unless objections to probate of such will have been filed and are pending at such time.

3. The surrogate or surrogates in their discretion respectively may

(a) Designate the chief clerk, one of the other clerks, a law assistant or any assistant, to take and report the testimony in any proceeding, but without authority to pass upon the issue therein. The person so designated shall have the power to administer oaths to the persons testifying in such proceeding. Whenever the person so designated goes to a place other than the surrogate's office his actual and necessary expenses shall be paid by the party seeking the testimony and the chief clerk of the court shall not be required to make any collection or return of the money so paid.

(b) Authorize and deputize in writing the chief clerk, one or more other clerks, law assistants or other assistants to sign the name of the respective surrogate to decrees in uncontested proceedings for administration, for the probate of a will or for the appointment of a general guardian of the person or property of an infant, upon a written decision duly filed by the surrogate and authorize and deputize any such officer or employee to sign in his name orders on applications to open safe deposit boxes. Any decree or order signed by such officer or employee pursuant to the designation shall be valid and binding as if signed by the surrogate.

4. Where service upon a respondent is made by personal delivery of process to the chief clerk of the court designated pursuant to 307 the chief clerk shall mail such process to respondent at the address indicated by him in such designation or if not so designated, at the address last indicated by him on the records of the court.

5. Whenever the testimony is taken by commission or by any disclosure device or an attesting witness is examined under 1404, the court may direct that the commission issue to the chief clerk, deputy chief clerk or a law assistant and that the disclosure be held under the supervision of one of such persons.

6. The signature of the chief clerk upon a certificate of letters of any kind or a certificate of comparison or of a search may be a facsimile, imprinted, stamped, photographed or engraved thereon.

History: Add, L 1966, ch 953, eff Sept 1, 1967 from Sur. Ct. Act § 32; amd, L 1967, ch 685, eff Sept 1, 1967; L 1970, ch 597, eff May 8, 1970; L 1990, ch 190, § 128, eff May 25, 1990; L 1993, ch 514, § 62, eff Jan 1, 1994.

§ 2610. Commissioner of records of surrogate's court, New York county; appointment; salary; duties

1. The surrogates of New York county shall appoint a commissioner of records. The commissioner shall appoint, subject to the prior approval of the surrogates, subordinates to assist him in the performance of his duties. The salary of the commissioner and his

subordinates shall be fixed by the surrogates and shall be paid out of appropriations therefor made by the city of New York.

2. The commissioner shall examine into the arrangement and condition of the records, wills, documents, books and papers deposited or filed in the office of the surrogate's court of the county of New York and into the condition and sufficiency of the indices thereof. He shall collate and arrange the same in such manner as may be necessary for their restoration and preservation and shall take such steps as may be necessary to provide convenient references thereto and for the examination and use as the public interest and convenience may require. He shall cause copies thereof to be made whenever by reason of age, use, exposure, or any casualty such copies shall in his judgment be necessary and after the copy has been compared with the original it shall be certified by the commissioner and shall thereafter be admitted in evidence and shall be considered for all other purposes with the same effect as the original. The original shall be placed in a suitable enclosure by the commissioner and shall be preserved, properly endorsed and indexed for such examination as may be directed by an order of the court in any action or proceeding in which the accuracy of the copy may be questioned. His duties shall be performed under such conditions and regulations as may be approved by the surrogates and in a manner which shall permit the examination and use of the records, wills, documents, books, papers and indices as the public interest and convenience may require.

3. The office of commissioner of records of the surrogate's court of New York county shall terminate upon the completion of the duties in this section prescribed.

History: Add, L 1966, ch 953, eff Sept 1, 1967 from Sur. Ct. Act § 21-c.

§ 2611. Other court matters

1. Each surrogate may establish and organize within the court such departments and divisions as deemed necessary and advisable to effectively perform the various phases of work of the court including accounting, administration, adoption, guardianship, law, probate, special proceedings and such other departments and divisions as serve the needs of the court.

2. Each surrogate may assign, reassign and change at pleasure the personnel of the court to one or more departments or divisions of the court and specify the duties and responsibilities of all court personnel.

3. The court may have such auxiliary services as will serve its purpose and are within its authorized appropriation or otherwise made available to it and may utilize the auxiliary services and agencies available to any court of record.

History: Add, L 1966, ch 953, eff Sept 1, 1967.

ARTICLE 27
APPEALS

SUMMARY OF ARTICLE

§ 2701. Appeal; general applicability of CPLR
§ 2702. Proceedings upon remittitur

§ 2701. Appeal; general applicability of CPLR

1. Except as otherwise provided in this act either expressly or by necessary implication all of those provisions of the CPLR which govern appeals generally, CPLR article 55, and appeals to the appellate division from judgments and orders of the supreme court, CPLR article 57, and such other CPLR provisions as are relevant in conjunction with such appeals shall be applicable to appeals from decrees and orders of this court. For such purpose the following terms as used in the CPLR shall have the meanings ascribed:

(a) "Action" shall mean "proceeding";

(b) "Judgment" shall mean "decree";

(c) "Plaintiff" shall mean "petitioner" or "applicant"; and

(d) "Defendant" shall mean "respondent".

2. In the event a verdict was not returned an appeal may be taken from an order denying a motion for the direction of judgment.

History: Add, L 1966, ch 953, eff Sept 1, 1967.

§ 2702. Proceedings upon remittitur

Remittitur from the appellate court to this court shall also be as provided in the CPLR, except that any decree or order to be entered in this court upon the remittitur shall be as directed by the court.

History: Add, L 1966, ch 953, eff Sept 1, 1967 from Sur. Ct. Act § 310.

ARTICLE 28
REPEAL; SAVINGS CLAUSE; EFFECTIVE DATE
SUMMARY OF ARTICLE

§ 2801.   **Repeal of surrogate's court act**

§ 2802.   **Pending and subsequent actions and proceedings**

§ 2803.   **Reference to surrogate's court act**

§ 2804.   **Effect of unconstitutionality in part**

§ 2805.   **Effective date**

§ 2801. Repeal of surrogate's court act

Chapter 928 of the laws of 1920, entitled "An act in relation to surrogates and the practice and procedure in surrogate's courts" and all acts amendatory thereof and supplemental thereto, constituting the surrogate's court act, as heretofore in effect, are hereby repealed.

History: Add, L 1966, ch 953, eff Sept 1, 1967 from Sur. Ct. Act § 318.

§ 2802. Pending and subsequent actions and proceedings

This act shall apply to all actions and proceedings hereafter commenced. It shall also apply to all further proceedings in pending actions and proceedings except to the extent that the court determines that the application in a particular pending action or proceeding would not be feasible or would work injustice, in which event the former procedure applies. Proceedings pursuant to law in an action or proceeding taken prior to the time this act takes effect shall not be rendered ineffectual or impaired by this act.

History: Add, L 1966, ch 953, eff Sept 1, 1967.

§ 2803. Reference to surrogate's court act

This act shall succeed the surrogate's court act and shall be deemed substituted therefor throughout the statutes and rules of the state. Reference in any statute or rule to a particular provision of the surrogate's court act or to any part thereof shall, insofar as practicable, be deemed to refer to:

1. Such provision of this act or part thereof as replaces the prior provision or part thereof or

2. Such practice as replaces that of the prior provision or part thereof, whether the practice is supplied by statute other than this act or by authority other than statute, if the prior provision or part thereof is not superseded by a specific provision of this act.

History: Add, L 1966, ch 953, eff Sept 1, 1967.

§ 2804. Effect of unconstitutionality in part

If any clause, sentence, paragraph, subdivision, section or part of this chapter shall be adjudged by any court of competent jurisdiction to be invalid, such judgment, decree or order shall not affect, impair or invalidate the remainder thereof but shall be confined in its operation to the clause, sentence, paragraph, subdivision, section or part thereof directly involved in the controversy in which such judgment, decree or order shall have been rendered.

History: Add, L 1966, ch 953, eff Sept 1, 1967.

§ 2805. Effective date

This act shall take effect September first, nineteen hundred sixty-seven.

History: Add, L 1966, ch 953, eff Sept 1, 1967 from Sur. Ct. Act § 319.

Tables   DISTRIBUTION AND DERIVATION TABLES

SURROGATE'S COURT PROCEDURE ACT
(L. 1966, Ch. 953, effective September 1, 1967 and as amended by L. 1967, Ch. 685, 739 and 780)

An act in relation to Surrogate's Court practice and procedure governing generally the procedure in the Surrogate's Courts of the State of New York and before the judges thereof constituting Chapter 59-A of the consolidated laws.

TABLE 1

NOTE.—Distribution Table 1 and Distribution Table 2 in connection with this act which was enacted by Chapter 953 of the Laws of 1966 have been changed to read as follows:

Distribution of Surrogate's Court Act

Surrogate's Court Act	Surrogate's Court Procedure Act
1	101
2	2603
3	omitted
4	omitted
6	2604
7	2604
16	2501, 2502, 2503
17	omitted
18	omitted
19	723 in part
20	201, 209(1)(2)(7)(8)(9)(11)
21	2605
21–a	omitted
21–b	omitted
21–c	2610
21–d	omitted
22	2605, 2606
23	2605, 2606
24	omitted
25	2607
26	2607
27	omitted
28	2607

Surrogate's Court Act	Surrogate's Court Procedure Act
29	2401, 2402
29–a	2401, 2402
29–b	2401, 2402
29–c	2401, 2402
29–d	2401, 2402
29–g	2401, 2402
29–i	2401, 2402
29–j	2401, 2402
29–k	2401, 2402
29–l	2401, 2402
29–m	2401, 2402
30	2403
31	507, 2404, 2608
32	2609
33	2502 in part
34	2601, 2603 in part
35	2601
36	2602
39	omitted
40	201, 209(3)(4)(5), 501
41	203 in part
42	203 in part
43	204
44	205
45	206
46	207
47	208
48	203, 301
49	302
50	303
51	304
52	103(40), 305
53	306
54	306, 311(2)
54–a	omitted
55	307
56	307
56–a	307, 308(3)

SCPA

Surrogate's Court Act	Surrogate's Court Procedure Act
57	307
58	307, 309(2)(e)
58–a	307
59	103(25)(32), 308(1)(a)(b), 308(3)(4)
60	103(24), 311(11)
61	314 in part
—	315
62	omitted
63	103(25), 401
64	103(24)(25), 402 and 403 in part
65	501
66	506
67	502
68	502
69	omitted (referred to CPLR by 102)
70	504
71	505
72	omitted
73	507
74	506, 507
75	omitted
76	509
77	omitted
78	601
79	602
80	omitted
81	603
82	604
83	605
84	606, 607
85	720
86	721
87	referred to CPLR by Art. 27
88	701
89	702

Surrogate's Court Act	Surrogate's Court Procedure Act
90	703
91	704
92	705
93	706
94	707
95	707, 708
96	709
97	710
98	708
99	711, 719 in part
100	712
101	713, 720 in part
101–a	714
102	715
103	716
103–a	717
103–b	718
104	719
105	802
106	803
106–a	804
107	CPLR 2508
108	CPLR 2508
109	CPLR 2510
110	referred to CPLR 2510 by 811
111	801(1)(f)
112	808
113	809
114	809
115	809
115–a	809
116	omitted
117	810
117–a	2002
117–b	2003
117–c	2004
117–d	2005
117–e	2006

SCPA

Surrogate's Court Act	Surrogate's Court Procedure Act
117–f	2007
117–g	2008
117–h	2001
118	1001
119	1002, 1003, 1004, 2225 in part
120	1003, 1004
121	801(1)(a), 801(g)(2), 805
121–a	1005
122	702, 801(1)(a)
123	1219
124	1201–1218
125	1201–1218
125–a	1201–1218
125–b	1201–1218
125–c	103(33)(34), 1201–1218
126	103(44), 805 in part, 901, 902, 1118
127	903, 905
128	omitted
129	906, 908
130	904
131	904, 907
132	omitted
133	103(3), 1418
134	1419
135	801(1)(a), 805 in part
136	103(2)(4), 801(1)(a), 1007
136–a	1101
136–b	1102
136–c	1102
136–d	1104
136–e	1105
136–f	1106
136–g	1105, 1107

Surrogate's Court Act	Surrogate's Court Procedure Act
136–h	1103 in part
136–i	1103
136–j	omitted
136–k	1109
136–l	1110
136–m	1111
136–n	1112
136–o	1113
136–p	omitted
136–q	1114
136–r	1115
136–s	1117
135–t	1118
136–u	1119
136–v	1120
136–w	1121
136–x	1121
136–y	1122
136–z	1123, 1124 in part
136–aa	103(33)(34), 1123, 1125
136–bb	1124
136–cc	1125
136–dd	1123
137	omitted
137–a	1301
137–b	1302
137–c	1303
137–d	1304
137–e	1105 in part, 1305
137–f	1306
137–g	1307
137–h	1308
137–i	1309
137–j	omitted
138	1401
139	1402
140	1403
141	1404

Surrogate's Court Act	Surrogate's Court Procedure Act
142	1405
142–a	1406
143	1407
144	1408, 2225 in part
145	209(4), 1420
145–a	1421
146	1402, 1409
147	1410
148	1411
149	503
150	2504
150–a	2505
151	1422 in part
152	2506
153	1423, 1424 in part
153–a	1412
154	1413
155	1414
156	1415
157	1416
158	103(6)(7)(8), 1417
159	replaced by 1602; cf. 103(5)(6)(7)
160	1607
161	1604, 1607, 1608
162	1609, 1611, 2225 in part
163	801(1)(d), 1608
164	1610
165	1610
166	1610, 1613
167	1503, 1504
168	1502
169	801(1)(c), 806
169–a	801(1)(e),807
170	1505
171	1501
172	omitted except in 103(7)(23)
173	201, 1701

Surrogate's Court Act	Surrogate's Court Procedure Act
174	201, 1702
175	1703
176	1704
177	1705
178	CPLR 1210(b)
179	1707
180	801(1)(b), 801(2), 1708
181	702
182	708, 801(1)(c)
183	1709
184	103(7), 1716
185	801(1)(d), 1717
186	1718
187	1710, 1711
188	801(1)(e), 1711
189	1712
190	1719
191	1720
192	1721
193	1722
194	1713
194–a	103(17), 1714
194–b	1715
199	2101, 2102
200	EPTL 5-3.1
201	2101, 2102
202	EPTL 13-1.1
203	EPTL 13-1.2
204	EPTL 11-2.1(c)(2)
205	2103
206	2104
206–a	2105
207	1801
208	1802
208–a	1803
208–b	1804
209	1805
210	1806

SCPA

Surrogate's Court Act	Surrogate's Court Procedure Act
211	1807
211–a	1808
211–b	1809
211–c	1810
212	1811
212–a	1812
213	1813
215	2107
215–a	103(21), 2108
216	1811, 2101, 2102, 2103, 2213
217	2101, 2102
217–a	103(2)
218	EPTL 11-1.5
219	2101, 2102
220	2101, 2102
221	2101, 2102
222	EPTL 11-1.1
223	EPTL 11-1.2
224	EPTL 11.1-3
225	repealed
226	repealed
227	1921
228	2101, 2102
229	2109, CPLR 2609 made applicable
230	722
231	EPTL 11-1.5
231–a	2110
231–b	2111
231–c	2112
232	1905
233	1901, 1903
234	1902
235	1905
236	1904
237	1906
238	1907, 1908, 1909
239	1910

Surrogate's Court Act	Surrogate's Court Procedure Act
240	1911
241	1912
242	1907, 1911, 1914
243	1915
244	1916
245	1903
245–a	1913
246	1917
247	omitted
248	1918
249	1919
250	1920
250–a	1507
250–b	1508
250–c	See note at end of Article 15. Referred to EPTL and then omitted.
251	2202
251–a	2203
252	2204
253	2205
254	2206
256	2205
257	2207
257–a	2205
258	2205
259	2205
260	2206
261	2208
261–a	2201
262	2210
263	2211
264	2209
265	2212
266	2214
267	2215
268	2216
269	2217
269–a	2218
270	2219

SCPA

Surrogate's Court Act	Surrogate's Court Procedure Act
271	2220
271–a	2221
272	2222
273	2223
273–a	2224
274	2226
275	2301
276	2301
277	2302
278	2301, 2302
279	2302
279–a	omitted
280	405
281	2302
282	2303
283	2304
284	2305
285	2307
285–a	2308
285–b	2309
285–c	2310
285–d	2311
285–e	omitted
286	EPTL 11-1.1(b)(14)
287	omitted
288	beginning Article 27 referred to CPLR
289	beginning Article 27 referred to CPLR
290	beginning Article 27 referred to CPLR
291	beginning Article 27 referred to CPLR
292	beginning Article 27 referred to CPLR
293	beginning Article 27 referred to CPLR
294	beginning Article 27 referred to CPLR
295	beginning Article 27 referred to CPLR
296	beginning Article 27 referred to CPLR
297	beginning Article 27 referred to CPLR
298	beginning Article 27 referred to CPLR
299	beginning Article 27 referred to CPLR
300	beginning Article 27 referred to CPLR
301	beginning Article 27 referred to CPLR

Surrogate's Court Act	Surrogate's Court Procedure Act
302	beginning Article 27 referred to CPLR
303	beginning Article 27 referred to CPLR
304	beginning Article 27 referred to CPLR
305	beginning Article 27 referred to CPLR
306	beginning Article 27 referred to CPLR
307	beginning Article 27 referred to CPLR
308	beginning Article 27 referred to CPLR
309	beginning Article 27 referred to CPLR
310	2702
311	2113
312	2113
313	omitted
314	103(1)(7)(11)(12)(22)(23)(27)(28)(32)(37)(41)(42)(45)(46)(47)
315	104
316	102, 501
317	omitted
318	2801

SCPA

TABLE 2
SCPA COMPARED WITH FORMER PROVISIONS
Derivation of Surrogate's Court Procedure Act Sections

SCPA		SCA	OTHER LAWS
101		1	CPLR 101
102		316	
103 (1)	New	Derived 314 (14)	
103 (2)	New	Derived 136, 217-a	
103 (3)	New	Derived 133	
103 (4)	New	Derived 136	
103 (5)	New	Derived 159	
103 (6)	New	Derived 159	

SCPA		SCA	OTHER LAWS
103 (7)	New	Derived 159, 172, 184, 314 (13)	
103 (8)	New		
103 (9)	New		
103 (10)	New		Const., Art. 6
103 (11)	New	Derived 314 (3)	Debtor & Cred. 270
103 (12)	New		
103 (13)	New		
103 (14)	New		
103 (15)	New		
103 (16)	New		
103 (17)	New		Derived Art. 5, RPL
103 (18)	New		
103 (19)	New		
103 (20)	New		
103 (21)	New	Derived 215-a	
103 (22)		Derived 314 (3)	
103 (23)	New	Derived 172, 314 (13)	
103 (24)	New	Derived 60, 64	
103 (25)	New	Derived 59, 63, 64	
103 (26)	New		Derived Dom. Rel. 2
103 (27)	New	Derived 314 (1)	
103 (28)		Derived 314 (8)	
103 (29)	New		
103 (30)	New		
103 (31)	New		
103 (32)		Derived 59, 314 (7)	
103 (33)	New	Derived 125-c, 136-aa	
103 (34)	New	Derived 125-c, 136-aa	
103 (35)	New		
103 (36)		Derived 314 (10)	
103 (37)	New		
103 (38)	New		
103 (39)	New		
103 (40)	New	Derived 52	
103 (41)		Derived 314 (12)	Derived Gen. Const. 39
103 (42)		Derived 314 (15)	

SCPA		SCA	OTHER LAWS
103 (43)			Derived Banking Law
103 (44)	New	Derived 126	
103 (45)		Derived 314 (6)	
103 (46)		Derived 314 (9)	
103 (47)		Derived 314 (4)	
104		315	
105			R.C.P. 2, Jud. Law 7-a
201		Derived 20, 40, 173, 174	Const. Art. VI § 12
202	New		
203		Parts 41, 42 Part Derived 48	Derived CPLR 304
204		43	
205		44	
206		45 in part	
207		46 in part	
208		47 in part	
209 (1)		20 (6-a)	
209 (2)		20 (13)	
209 (3)		40 (9)	
209 (4)		20, 40, 145	Tax Law
209 (5)		40 (10)	
209 (6)	New		
209 (7)	New		
209 (8)		20 (11)	
209 (9)	New		
210			CPLR 301, 302
211	New		
212	New		Const. Art. VI § 1 (c)
301		Derived 48	Derived CPLR 203
302		Derived 49	Derived CPLR 402, 3013, 3014
303		Derived 50	CPLR 3020
304		Derived 51	
305		Derived 52	Jud. Law. § 757 Const. Art. VI § 1 (c)

SCPA	SCA	OTHER LAWS
306	53, 54 in part	CPLR 1024
307	55, 56, 56-a, 57, 58, 58-a	CPLR 307-312, 1025
308 (1) (a)	Derived 59 (2), (3)	
308 (1) (b)	New	
308 (2)	Derived 50 (4)	
308 (3)	Derived 56-a	
308 (4)	Derived 59 (5)	
309		CPLR 313
309 (2) (e)	Derived 58	
310	New	
311 (1)	Derived 60	
311 (2)	54 (3)	
312	New	
313	New	
314	61 in part	CPLR 306, 4532
315	New	
401	Derived 63	Derived CPLR 321, 322
402	Derived proposed 62-b and 64 in part	
403	Derived proposed 62-d & e and 64 in part	
404	Derived proposed 62-c & f	
405	Derived proposed 62-g & 62-b and 280	
406	Derived proposed 62-h	
407	Derived proposed 62-i & k	
408	Derived proposed 62-j	
501	Derived 40 (9), 65, 316	CPLR 325 (d), 4011, 602, 603
502	Derived 67, 68	
503	149 in part	
504	70	
505	Derived 71, 119	Derived CPLR 4211
506	66, 74 in part	CPLR 4201, 4320, 4403

SCPA		SCA	OTHER LAWS
507		Derived 31, 73, 74 in part	
508	New		
509		76	
601		78	
602		79	
603		81	
604		82	CPLR 5020, 5021
605		83	
606		84 in part	
607	New	84 in part	
701		88	
702		89, 122 & 181 in part	
703		90	
704		91	
705		92	
706		93	
707		94, 95	
708		95, 98, 182	
709		Derived 96	
710		Derived 97	
711		99 (1)–(7), (9)	
712		100	
713		101	
714		101-a	
715		102	
716		103	
717		103-a	
718		103-b	
719		99, 104	
720		85, 101	
721		86	
722		230	
723		19 in part	
801		121, 122, 135, 136, 163, 169, 169-a, 180, 182, 185, 188	
802		105	
803		106	
804		106-a	

SCPA	SCA	OTHER LAWS
805	121, 126 and 135 in part	
806	169 in part	
807	169-a	
808	112	
809	Derived 113, 114, 115, 115-a	
810	117	
811	New	
901	Derived 126	
902	Derived 126	
903	127, 129 in part	
904	130, 131	
905	127 in part	
906	129 in part	
907	131	
908	129 in part	
909	New	
910	New	
911	New	
1001	118	Bank, Law 100-a (2) (a)
1002	New Derived 119	
1003	New Derived 119, 120	
1004	New Derived 119, 120	
1005	New Derived 121-a	
1006	New	
1007	136	
1101	136-a	
1102	136-b, 136-c	
1103	136-h in part, 136-i	
1104	136-d	
1105	136-e	
1106	136-f, 136-g in part	
1107	136-g	
1108	136-h	
1109	136-k	
1110	136-l	
1111	136-m	
1112	136-n	
1113	136-o	

SCPA		SCA	OTHER LAWS
1114		136-q	
1115		136-r, 137-e	
1116	New		
1117		136-s	
1118		125 (o) (11), 136-t	
1119		136-u	
1120		136-v	
1121		136-x	
1122		136-y	
1123		136-z, 136-aa, 136-dd in part	
1124		136-s in part, 136-bb	
1125		136-cc	
1126	New		
1127	New		
1201–1218		124, 125, 125-a, b, c	
1219		123	
1301		137-a	
1302		137-b	
1303		137-c	
1304		137-d	
1305		137-e	
1306		137-f	
1307		137-g	
1308		137-h	
1309		137-i	
1310		DEL 103-a	
1311		DEL 103-b	
1401		138	
1402		139 & 146 in part	
1403		140	
1404		141	
1405		142	
1406		142-a	
1407		143	
1408		144	
1409		146	
1410		147	
1411		148	
1412		153-a	

SCPA

SCPA	SCA	OTHER LAWS
1413	154	
1414	155	
1415	156	
1416	157	
1417	158	
1418	133	
1419	134	
1420	145	
1421	145-a	
1422	151 in part	
1423	153 in part	
1424	153 in part	
1501	171	
1502	168	PPL 20, RPL 111 in part
1503	167 in part	
1504	107 in part	
1505	170	
1506	New	
1507	250-a	
1508	250-b	
1601	New	
1602	New	Replacing 159
1603	New	
1604	101 in part	
1605	New	
1606	New	
1607	160, 161 in part	
1608	164 in part, 163	
1609	162 (1)	
1610	164, 165, 166	
1611	162 (2) (3)	
1612	New	
1613	Derived 166	
1614	New	
1615	New	
1616	New	
1701	173	
1702	174	
1703	175	

SCPA	SCA	OTHER LAWS
1704	176	
1705	177	
1706		CPLR 1210 (b)
1707	179	
1708	180 in part	
1709	Derived 183	
1710	187 in part	
1711	187 in part, 188 in part	
1712	189	
1713	194	
1714	Derived 194-a	
1715	194-b in part	
1716	184 in part	
1717	185 in part	
1718	186 in part	
1719	190 in part	
1720	191	
1721	192	
1722	193	
1723	New	
1801	207	
1802	208	
1803	208-a	
1804	208-b	
1805	209	
1806	210	
1807	211	
1808	211-a	
1809	211-b	
1810	211-c	
1811	212, 216 in part	
1812	212-a	
1813	213	
1901	Derived 233 in part	
1902	934	
1903	233, 245 in part	
1904	236	
1905	Derived 235, 232	
1906	237	
1907	Derived 238, 242	

SCPA

SCPA	SCA	OTHER LAWS
1908	Derived 238	
1909	238 in part	
1910	239	
1911	Derived 241	
1912	Derived 241	
1913	245-a	
1914	Derived 242	
1915	243	
1916	244	
1917	246	
1918	248	
1919	249	
1920	250	
1921	227	
1922 New		
2001	Derived 117-h	
2002	Derived 117-a	
2003	Derived 117-b	
2004	Derived 117-c	
2005	117-d	
2006	117-e	
2007	117-f	
2008	117-g	
2101	199, 201, 216, 217, 219, 220, 221, 228 in part	
2102	199, 201, 216, 217, 219, 220, 221, 228 in part	
2103	205	
2104	206	
2105	206-a	
2106		DEL 19
2107	215	
2108	215-a	
2109	229 omitted	CPLR 2609
2110	231-a	
2111	231-b	
2112	231-c	
2113	311, 312	
2201	261-a	
2202	251	

SCPA	SCA	OTHER LAWS
2203	251-a	
2204	252	
2205	253, 256, 257-a, 258, 259	
2206	260	
2207	257	
2208	261	
2209	264	
2210	262	
2211	263	
2212	265	
2213	216 in part	
2214	266	
2215	267	
2216	268	
2217	269	
2218	269-a	
2219	270	CPLR 1206 (1)
2220	271	
2221	271-a	
2222	272	
2223	273	
2224	273-a	
2225	119, 144, 162 in part	
2226	274	
2301	275, 276, 278 in part	
2302	277, 278, 279, 281 in part	
2303	282	
2304	283	
2305	284	
2306	254	
2307	285	
2308	285-a	
2309	285-b	
2310	285-c	
2311	285-d	
2401	29, 29-a to 29-d, 29-g, 29-i to 29-m	
2402	29, 29-a to 29-d, 29-g, 29-i to 29-m	
2403	30	

SCPA

SCPA	SCA	OTHER LAWS
2404	31	
2501	16 in part	
2502	16, 33 in part	
2503	16 in part	
2504	150	
2505	150-a	
2506	152	DEL 42, 43
2507		DEL 30, 31, 32, 33
2601	34, 35	
2602	36	
2603	2, part 34	
2604	6, 7	
2605	21, parts 22, 23	
2606	22, 23 in part	
2607	25, 26, 28	
2608	31	
2609	32	
2610	21-c	
2611	New	
2701	New	
2702	310	
2801	Derived 318	
2802	New	
2803	New	
2804	New	
2805	Derived 319	

ESTATES, POWERS AND TRUSTS LAW

Table of Contents

EPTL

ARTICLE 1
GENERAL PROVISIONS
SUMMARY OF ARTICLE

PART 1 Short Title; How Cited; References; Severability; Application

§ 1-1.1. Short title; how cited

This chapter shall be known as the Estates, Powers and Trusts Law and may be cited as EPTL. A section of this law may be cited by article, part and section number, to wit, EPTL 1-1.1, which refers to article 1, part 1, section 1, without being preceded by the word article, part or section or the symbol §.

History: Add, L 1966, ch 952, eff Sept 1, 1967.

§ 1-1.2. References

Unless otherwise stated, all references in this chapter to article, part or section number refer to the articles, parts or section numbers of this chapter, and all references in any section of this chapter to a lettered or numbered paragraph or subparagraph refer to the paragraph or subparagraph so lettered or numbered in such section.

History: Add, L 1966, ch 952, eff Sept 1, 1967.

§ 1-1.3. Rules governing use of certain words

In this chapter, unless the context otherwise requires:

(a) Words in the singular number include the plural, and in the plural include the singular.

(b) Words of the masculine gender include the feminine and the neuter, and when the sense so indicates words of the neuter gender may refer to any gender.

(c) The word "writing" includes typewritten or printed matter.

History: Add, L 1966, ch 952, eff Sept 1, 1967.

§ 1-1.4. Severability

If any provision of this chapter or application thereof to any person or circumstances is held invalid, such invalidity shall not affect other provisions or applications of this chapter which can be given effect without regard to the invalid provision or application, and to this end the provisions of this chapter are declared to be severable.

History: Add, L 1966, ch 952, eff Sept 1, 1967, with substance deriving from Pers P Law § 270–a.

§ 1-1.5. Application

Unless otherwise stated therein, the provisions of this chapter apply to the estates, and to instruments making dispositions or appointments thereof, of persons living on its effective date or born subsequent thereto, without regard to the date of execution of any such instrument; except that the provisions of this chapter shall not impair or defeat any rights which have accrued under dispositions or appointments in effect prior to its effective date.

History: Add, L 1966, ch 952, eff Sept 1, 1967.

PART 2   Definitions

In this chapter, unless the context otherwise requires or a different meaning is expressly provided, the words and phrases set forth in this part shall be given their indicated meaning:

§ 1-2.1. Codicil

A codicil is a supplement to a will, either adding to, taking from or altering its provisions or confirming it in whole or in part by republication, but not totally revoking such will.

History: Add, L 1966, ch 952, eff Sept 1, 1967.

§ 1-2.2. Creator

A creator is a person who makes a disposition of property.

History: Add, L 1966, ch 952, eff Sept 1, 1967.

§ 1-2.3. Demonstrative disposition

A demonstrative disposition is a testamentary disposition of property to be taken out of specified or identified property.

History: Add, L 1966, ch 952, eff Sept 1, 1967.

§ 1-2.4. Disposition

A disposition is a transfer of property by a person during his lifetime or by will.

History: Add, L 1966, ch 952, eff Sept 1, 1967.

§ 1-2.5. Distributee

A distributee is a person entitled to take or share in the property of a decedent under the statutes governing descent and distribution.

History: Add, L 1966, ch 952, eff Sept 1, 1967, with substance deriving from Dec Est Law §§ 81, 134.

§ 1-2.6. Estate

Depending upon the context, "estate" may mean:

(a) The interest which a person has in property.

(b) The aggregate of property which a person owns.

History: Add, L 1966, ch 952, eff Sept 1, 1967.

§ 1-2.7. Fiduciary

A fiduciary is a person who meets the description, in this part, of a "personal representative" or who is designated by the creator or by the court to act as an assignee for the benefit of creditors, or a committee, conservator, curator, custodian, guardian, trustee or donee of a power during minority.

History: Add, L 1966, ch 952, eff Sept 1, 1967.

§ 1-2.8. General disposition

A general disposition is a testamentary disposition of property not amounting to a demonstrative, residuary or specific disposition.

History: Add, L 1966, ch 952, eff Sept 1, 1967.

§ 1-2.9. Incompetent

An incompetent is a person judicially declared to be incapable of managing his affairs.

History: Add, L 1966, ch 952, eff Sept 1, 1967.

§ 1-2.9-a. Infant or minor

As used in this chapter, the term "infant" or "minor" means a person who has not attained the age of eighteen years, provided, however, that such definition shall not be applicable to any provision relating to the New York Uniform Transfers to Minors Act, nor to section 13-3.4.

History: Add, L 1974, ch 903, eff Sept 1, 1974; amd L 1999, ch 231, eff July 13, 1999.

§ 1-2.10. Issue

(a) Unless a contrary intention is indicated:

(1) Issue are the descendants in any degree from a common ancestor.

(2) The terms "issue" and "descendants", in subparagraph (1), include adopted children.

History: Add, L 1966, ch 952, eff Sept 1, 1967; amd, L 1968, ch 257, eff Sept 1, 1967.

§ 1-2.11. Per capita

EPTL

A disposition or distribution of property is per capita when it is made to persons, each of whom is to take in his own right an equal portion of such property.

History: Add, L 1966, ch 952, eff Sept 1, 1967, with substance deriving from Decedent Est. Law § 47-a and § 83(9).

§ 1-2.12. Person

The term "person" includes a natural person, an association, board, any corporation, whether municipal, stock or non-stock, court, governmental agency, authority or subdivision, partnership or other firm and the state.

History: L 1966, ch 952, eff Sept 1, 1967.

§ 1-2.13. Personal representative

A personal representative is a person who has received letters to administer the estate of a decedent. The term does not include an assignee for the benefit of creditors, or a committee, conservator, curator, custodian, guardian, trustee or donee of a power during minority.

History: Add, L 1966, ch 952, eff Sept 1, 1967; amd, L 1967, ch 686, eff Sept 1, 1967.

§ 1-2.14. Per stirpes

A per stirpes disposition or distribution of property is made to persons who take as issue of a deceased ancestor in the following manner:

The property so passing is divided into as many equal shares as there are (i) surviving issue in the generation nearest to the deceased ancestor which contains one or more surviving issue and (ii) deceased issue in the same generation who left surviving issue, if any. Each surviving member in such nearest generation is allocated one share. The share of a deceased issue in such nearest generation who left surviving issue shall be distributed in the same manner to such issue.

History: Add, L 1966, ch 952, eff Sept 1, 1967, with substance deriving from Decedent Est. Law § 47-a, and § 83(10); amd, L 1967, ch 686, eff Sept 1, 1967; L 1992, ch 59, eff Sept 1, 1992.

§ 1-2.15. Property

Property is anything that may be the subject of ownership, and is real or personal property.

History: Add, L 1966, ch 952, eff Sept 1, 1967.

§ 1-2.16. Representation

By representation means a disposition or distribution of property made in the following manner to persons who take as issue of a deceased ancestor:

The property so passing is divided into as many equal shares as there are (i) surviving issue in the generation nearest to the deceased ancestor which contains one or more surviving issue and (ii) deceased issue in the same generation who left surviving issue, if any. Each surviving member in such nearest generation is allocated one share. The remaining shares, if any, are combined and then divided in the same manner among the surviving issue of the deceased issue as if the surviving issue who are allocated a share had predeceased the decedent, without issue.

History: Add, L 1992, ch 595, effective Sept 1, 1992; amd, L 1993, ch 515, eff Jan 1, 1993.

§ 1-2.17. Specific disposition

A specific disposition is a disposition of a specified or identified item of the testator's property.

History: Formerly § 1-2.16, add, L 1966, ch 952, eff Sept 1, 1967; renumbered § 1–2.17, L 1992, ch 595, eff Sept 1, 1992.

§ 1-2.18. Testamentary beneficiary

A testamentary beneficiary is a person in whose favor a disposition of property is made by will.

History: Formerly § 1-2.17, add, L 1966, ch 952, eff Sept 1, 1967; renumbered § 1-2.18, L 1992, ch 595, eff Sept 1, 1992.

§ 1-2.19. Will

(a) A will is an oral declaration or written instrument, made as prescribed by 3-2.1 or 3-2.2 to take effect upon death, whereby a person disposes of property or directs how it shall not be disposed of, disposes of his body or any part thereof, exercises a power, appoints a fiduciary or makes any other provision for the administration of his estate, and which is revocable during his lifetime.

(b) Unless the context otherwise requires, the term "will" includes a "codicil".

History: Formerly § 1-2.18, add, L 1966, ch 952, eff Sept 1, 1967, with substance deriving from Dec Est Law § 2; renumbered § 1-2.19, L 1992, ch 595, eff Sept 1, 1992.

§ 1-2.20. Lifetime trust

The term "lifetime trust" shall mean an express trust and all amendments thereto created other than by will and shall not include; a trust for the benefit of creditors, a resulting or constructive trust, a business trust where certificates of beneficial interest are issued to the beneficiary, an investment trust, voting trust, a security instrument such as a deed of trust and a mortgage, a trust created by the judgment or decree of a court, a liquidation or reorganization trust, a trust for the sole purpose of paying dividends, interest, interest coupons, salaries, wages, pensions or profits, instruments wherein persons are mere nominees for others, or a trust created in deposits in any banking institution or savings and loan institution.

History: Add, L 1997, ch 139, § 1, eff June 25, 1997, and applicable to lifetime trusts created on and after June 25, 1997.

ARTICLE 2
RULES GOVERNING DISPOSITIONS SUBJECT TO THIS LAW
SUMMARY OF ARTICLE

PART 1   Substantive Rules Governing Dispositions

§ 2-1.1. Heirs at law and next of kin defined

Whenever used in a statute or instrument, unless a contrary intention is expressed therein, the term "heirs", "heirs at law", "next of kin" or any term of like import means the distributees, as defined in 1-2.5.

> **History:** Add, L 1966, ch 952, eff Sept 1, 1967, with substance deriving from Decedent Est. Law § 47-c.

§ 2-1.2. Issue to take per capita, per stirpes or by representation

(a) Instruments executed prior to September first, nineteen hundred ninety-two. Whenever a disposition of property is made to "issue", such issue, if in equal degree of consanguinity to their common ancestor, take per capita, but if in unequal degree, per stirpes, unless a contrary intention is expressed.

(b) Instruments executed on or after September first, nineteen hundred ninety-two. Whenever a disposition of property is made to "issue", such issue take by representation as defined in 1-2.16, unless a contrary intention is expressed.

History: Add, L 1966, ch 952, eff Sept 1, 1967, with substance deriving from Decedent Est. Law § 47-a; amd, L 1992, ch 595, eff Sept 1, 1992.

§ 2-1.3. Adopted children and posthumous children as members of a class

(a)* Unless the creator expresses a contrary intention, a disposition of property to persons described in any instrument as the issue, children, descendants, heirs, heirs at law, next of kin, distributees (or by any term of like import) of the creator or of another, includes:

(1) Adopted children and their issue in their adoptive relationship. The rights of adopted children and their issue to receive a disposition under wills and lifetime instruments as a member of such class of persons based upon their birth relationship shall be governed by the provisions of subdivision two of section one hundred seventeen of the domestic relations law.

(2) Children conceived before, but born alive after such disposition becomes effective.

(3) Nonmarital children. For the purposes of this paragraph, a nonmarital child is the child of a mother and is the child of a father if the child is entitled to inherit from such father under section 4-1.2 of this chapter. The provisions of this paragraph shall apply to the wills of persons dying on and after September first, nineteen hundred ninety-one, to lifetime instruments theretofore executed which on said date are subject to the grantor's power to revoke or amend, and to all lifetime instruments executed on or after such date.

History: Add, L 1966, ch 952, eff Sept 1, 1967, with substance deriving from Decedent Est. Law § 49; amd, L 1967, ch 686, eff Sept 1, 1967; L 1986, ch 408, eff Sept 1, 1986; L 1990, ch 248, eff Sept 1, 1990; L 2008, ch 305, eff July 21, 2008.

§ 2-1.4. Words of inheritance unnecessary

The word "heirs" or words of inheritance of like import are not necessary to create or dispose of a fee.

History: Add, L 1966, ch 952, eff Sept 1, 1967, with substance deriving from RPL § 240(1).

§ 2-1.5. Advancements and their adjustment

(a) An advancement is an irrevocable gift intended by the donor as an anticipatory distribution in complete or partial satisfaction of the interest of the donee in the donor's estate, either as distributee in intestacy or as beneficiary under an existing will of the donor.

(b) No advancement shall affect the distribution of the estate of the donor unless proved by a writing contemporaneous therewith signed by the donor evidencing his intention that the gift be treated as an advancement, or by the donee acknowledging that such was the intention.

(c) When so proved, the advancement is part of the estate of the donor for the purpose of distribution. If such advancement is equal to or greater than the interest of the donee, whether in intestacy or under the will, such donee or his successor in interest may not share in the distribution of the estate; but if less than such intestate share or testamentary interest, the donee or his successor in interest may take his intestate share or testamentary interest reduced by the amount of the advancement.

---

* **Ed. Note**: There is no paragraph (b).

(d) Unless otherwise provided in a writing contemporaneous with the advancement and signed by the donor:

(1) An advancement, made as provided in this section, may be adjusted out of the property of the donor in such manner as may be equitable.

(2) The advancement shall have the value at which it is appraised for estate tax purposes, or, if not included in the gross taxable estate of the donor, the value at which it would have been appraised if included therein.

(e) Nothing in this section shall increase or decrease the elective share of a surviving spouse under either 5-1.1 or 5-1.1-A except to the extent authorized by paragraph (b) of those sections.

History: Add, L 1966, ch 952, eff Sept 1, 1967, with substance deriving from Decedent Est. Law §§ 85, 86; amd, L 1967, ch 686, eff Sept 1, 1967; L 1992, ch 595, eff Sept 1, 1992.

§ 2-1.6. Disposition of property where a person dies within one hundred twenty hours of another person or any other event

(a) Except as provided in paragraph (b) of this section:

(1) Where, under articles 4 and 5 of this chapter, the title to property or the devolution of property depends upon an individual's survivorship of the death of another individual, an individual who is not established by clear and convincing evidence to have survived the other individual by one hundred twenty hours is deemed to have predeceased the other individual.

(2) For purposes of a provision of a governing instrument that relates to an individual surviving an event, including the death of another individual, an individual who is not established by clear and convincing evidence to have survived the event by one hundred twenty hours is deemed to have predeceased the event.

(3) Where a disposition of property under a governing instrument (i) depends upon the time of death of two or more beneficiaries designated to take alternatively by reason of surviving an event, including the death of another individual, and (ii) it is not established by clear and convincing evidence that such beneficiaries have survived the event by one hundred twenty hours, the property thus disposed of shall be divided into as many equal portions as there are alternative beneficiaries and such portions shall be distributed respectively to those who would have taken the whole property in the event that the designated beneficiary through whom they take had survived.

(4) Where it is not established by clear and convincing evidence that one of two co-owners with right of survivorship survived the other co-owner by one hundred twenty hours, one-half of the property passes as if one had survived by one hundred twenty hours and one-half as if the other had survived by one hundred twenty hours. Where there are more than two co-owners and it is not established by clear and convincing evidence that at least one of them survived the others by one hundred twenty hours, the property passes in the proportion that one bears to the whole number of co-owners.

(b) The survival requirements of paragraph (a) of this section shall not apply if:

(1) The governing instrument contains language dealing explicitly with simultaneous

deaths or deaths in a common disaster and that language is operable under the facts of the case.

(2) The governing instrument expressly indicates that an individual is not required to survive an event, including the death of another individual, by any specified period or expressly requires the individual to survive the event for a specified period. However, survival of the event or the specified period must be established by clear and convincing evidence.

(3) The imposition of a one hundred twenty-hour requirement of survival would cause a nonvested property interest or a power of appointment to be invalid under section 9-1.1 of this chapter. However, survival must be established by clear and convincing evidence.

(4) The application of a one hundred twenty-hour requirement of survival to multiple governing instruments would result in an unintended failure or duplication of a disposition. However, survival must be established by clear and convincing evidence.

(5) Its application would result in a taking of the intestate estate by the state.

(6) The surviving spouse exercised the right of election under section 5-1.1-A of this chapter, but died less than one hundred twenty hours after the death of the deceased spouse.

(c) For purposes of this section, "governing instrument" means a deed, will, trust, insurance or annuity policy, bank account in trust form, security registration in beneficiary form (TOD), pension, profit-sharing, retirement, or similar benefit plan, instrument creating or exercising a power of appointment or a power of attorney, or a dispositive, appointive, or nominative instrument of any similar type.

> **History:** Add, L 2009, ch 92, § 1, eff July 21, 2009, provided that: "(1) any action or proceeding commenced prior to the effective date of this act shall not be impaired by this act. If a right is acquired, extinguished, or barred upon the expiration of a prescribed period of time that has commenced pursuant to the provisions of any statute prior to the effective date of this act, such provisions shall remain in force with respect to such right; and (2) any rule of construction or presumption provided by this act shall apply to governing instruments executed, including bank accounts opened, before the effective date of this act unless there is a clear indication of a contrary intent."

§ 2-1.7. Presumption of death from absence; effect of exposure to specific peril

(a) A person who is absent for a continuous period of three years, during which, after diligent search, he or she has not been seen or heard of or from, and whose absence is not satisfactorily explained shall be presumed, in any action or proceeding involving any property of such person, contractual or property rights contingent upon his or her death or the administration of his or her estate, to have died three years after the date such unexplained absence commenced, or on such earlier date as clear and convincing evidence establishes is the most probable date of death.

(b) The fact that such person was exposed to a specific peril of death may be a sufficient basis for determining at any time after such exposure that he or she died less than three years after the date his or her absence commenced.

(c) The three-year period provided herein shall not apply in any case in which a different period has been prescribed by statute.

> **History:** Add, L 1966, ch 952, eff Sept 1, 1967, with substance deriving from Decedent

Est. Law § 80-a; amd, L 1993, ch 514, eff Jan 1, 1994; L 2000, ch 413, eff Aug 30, 2000.

§ 2-1.8. Apportionment of federal and state estate or other death taxes; fiduciary to collect taxes from property taxed and transferees thereof

(a) Whenever it appears in any appropriate action or proceeding that a fiduciary has paid or may be required to pay an estate or other death tax, under the law of this state or of any other jurisdiction, with respect to any property required to be included in the gross tax estate of a decedent under the provisions of any such law (hereinafter called "the tax"), the amount of the tax, except in a case where a testator otherwise directs in his will, and except where by any instrument other than a will (hereinafter called a "non-testamentary instrument") direction is given for apportionment within the fund of taxes assessed upon the specific fund dealt with in such non-testamentary instrument, shall be equitably apportioned among the persons interested in the gross tax estate, whether residents or non-residents of this state, to whom such property is disposed of or to whom any benefit therein accrues (hereinafter called "the persons benefited") in accordance with the rules of apportionment herein set forth, and the persons benefited shall contribute the amounts apportioned against them.

(b) Unless otherwise provided, when a disposition is made by which any person is given an interest in income or an estate for years or for life or other temporary interest in any property or fund, the tax apportionable against such temporary interest and the remainder limited thereon is chargeable against and payable out of the principal of such property or fund without apportionment between such temporary interest and remainder. The provisions of this paragraph apply although the holder of the temporary interest has rights in the principal, but do not apply to a common law annuity.

(c) Unless otherwise provided in the will or non-testamentary instrument, and subject to paragraph (d-1) of this section:

(1) The tax shall be apportioned among the persons benefited in the proportion that the value of the property or interest received by each such person benefited bears to the total value of the property and interest received by all persons benefited, the values as finally determined in the respective tax proceedings being the values to be used as the basis for apportionment of the respective taxes.

(2) Any exemption or deduction allowed under the law imposing the tax by reason of the relationship of any person to the decedent, the fact that the property consists of life insurance proceeds or the charitable purposes of the gift shall inure to the benefit of the person bearing such relationship or receiving such insurance proceeds or charitable gift, as the case may be.

(3) Any deduction for property previously taxed and any credit for gift taxes paid by the decedent shall inure to the benefit of all persons benefited and the tax to be apportioned shall be the tax after allowance of such deduction or credit.

(4) Any interest resulting from the late payment of the tax shall be apportioned in the same manner as the tax and shall be charged wholly to principal.

(5) Any discount allowed for prepayment of the tax shall be credited wholly to the principal of the funds contributing the moneys used for prepayment in proportion to the contribution made.

(d) Subject to subparagraphs (1), (2) and (3) of this paragraph, any direction as to apportionment or non-apportionment of the tax, whether contained in a will or a non-testamentary instrument, relates only to the property passing thereunder, unless such will or instrument provides otherwise.

(1) Any such direction in a will which is later in date than a prior non-testamentary instrument and which contains a contrary direction shall govern provided that the later will specifically refers to the direction in such prior instrument.

(2) Any such direction in a non-testamentary instrument which is later in date than a prior will or non-testamentary instrument and which contains a contrary direction shall govern provided that the later instrument specifically refers to the direction in such prior will or instrument.

(3) Any such direction provided in a non-testamentary instrument only relates to the payment of the tax from the property passing thereunder and such direction shall not serve to exonerate such non-testamentary property from the payment of its proportionate share of the tax, even if otherwise directed in that non-testamentary instrument.

(d-1) (1) (A) If any part of the gross tax estate consists of property the value of which is includible in the gross tax estate by reason of § 2044 of the Internal Revenue Code of 1986 as from time to time amended, the decedent's estate shall be entitled to recover from the person receiving the property the amount by which the total tax under article twenty-six of the tax law which has been paid exceeds the total tax under such article which would have been payable if the value of such property had not been included in the gross tax estate.

(B) Clause (A) of this subparagraph shall not apply if the decedent specifically directs otherwise by will.

(2) For the purposes of this paragraph, if there is more than one person receiving the property, the right of recovery shall be against each such person.

(3) In the case of penalties and interest attributable to additional taxes described in subparagraph (1) of this paragraph, rules similar to subparagraphs (1) and (2) of this paragraph shall apply.

(e) In all cases in which any property required to be included in the gross tax estate does not come into the possession of the fiduciary, he is authorized to, and shall recover from the persons benefited or from any person in possession of such property the ratable amounts of the tax and any interest payable by the persons benefited. The surrogate may direct the payment thereof to the fiduciary and may charge such payments against the interests of the persons benefited in any assets in the possession of the fiduciary or any other person. If the fiduciary cannot recover the amount of the tax and interest apportioned against a person benefited, such amount may be charged in such manner as the surrogate determines.

(f) No fiduciary is required to pay over or distribute to any person other than the fiduciary charged with the duty to collect and pay the tax any fund or property with respect to which the tax is or may be imposed until the amount of the tax apportioned or which may be apportioned against such fund or property and any interest due from the persons entitled thereto is paid or, where the tax has not been determined or apportionment made, unless and until adequate security for such payment is furnished to the fiduciary making such payment or distribution.

(g) The surrogate shall make such preliminary, intermediate or final decrees or orders in the proceeding, as he shall deem advisable, tentatively or finally apportioning the tax and any interest, directing the fiduciary to collect the apportioned amounts from the property or interests in his possession of any persons against whom such apportionment has been made and directing all other persons against whom the tax and any interest are apportioned or from whom any part of the tax and any interest may be recovered to make payment of such apportioned amounts to such fiduciary; and if it is ascertained in such proceeding that the property in the possession of the fiduciary, otherwise payable to a person liable for any part of the tax and interest, is insufficient to discharge the liability of such person, the surrogate may direct that the balance of the apportioned amount due shall be paid to the fiduciary by such other person. If, in the course of the proceeding, it is ascertained that more than the ratable amount of the tax and interest due from any person has been paid by him or in his behalf the surrogate may direct an appropriate reimbursement of the overpayment.

(h) If the surrogate apportions any part of the tax against any person interested in non-testamentary property or apportions the tax among the respective interests created by any non-testamentary instrument, he may, in his discretion, assess against such property or interests, an equitable share of the expense in connection with the determination of the tax and the apportionment thereof. Whenever an attorney renders services to the estate or to its personal representative resulting in the exclusion from the gross taxable estate of any non-testamentary property or interests created by any non-testamentary instrument, the surrogate may, in his discretion, assess against such property or interests an equitable share of the compensation for such legal services rendered to the estate or to its personal representative in proportion to the benefit received by such property or interests from such services, unless the decedent's will or the non-testamentary instrument contains a direction that no portion of the tax shall be apportioned against such non-testamentary property or against interests created by any non-testamentary instrument. The surrogate may retain jurisdiction of any proceeding until the purposes of this section have been accomplished.

> **History:** Add, L 1966, ch 952, eff Sept 1, 1967 from Decedent Est. Law § 124; amd, L
> 1967, ch 686, eff Sept 1, 1967; L 1986, ch 480, eff Sept 21, 1986; L 1989, ch 631, eff July
> 21, 1989; L 1999, ch 380, eff Feb 1, 2000.

§ 2-1.9. Distributions in kind by executors and trustees

(a) (1) As used in this section, the terms "pecuniary disposition" and "transfer in trust of a pecuniary amount" mean, respectively, a disposition by will or a transfer under a trust agreement of a specific amount of money, which amount is either expressly stated in the instrument or determinable by means of a formula which is stated in the instrument.

(2) Whether a testamentary disposition or transfer in trust is pecuniary or fractional in character depends upon the intention of the creator.

(b) Unless the instrument expressly provides otherwise:

(1) Where a will or a trust agreement authorizes the executor or trustee (hereinafter called the "fiduciary") to satisfy wholly or partly in kind a pecuniary disposition or transfer in trust of a pecuniary amount, the assets selected by the fiduciary for that purpose shall be valued at their respective values on the dates of their distribution.

(2) Where a will or a trust agreement authorizes the fiduciary to satisfy wholly or partly in kind a pecuniary disposition or transfer in trust of a pecuniary amount and the

EPTL

instrument requires the fiduciary to value the assets selected by the fiduciary for such distribution as of a date other than the dates of their distribution, the assets selected by the fiduciary for that purpose, together with any cash distributed, shall have an aggregate value on the dates of their distribution amounting to no less than, and to the extent practicable no more than, the amount of such testamentary disposition or transfer in trust as stated in, or determined by the formula stated in, the instrument.

(c) This section applies to wills of decedents dying before, on or after its effective date and to trust agreements executed before, on or after such date, provided, however, that it shall not be applied so as to require repayment to the fiduciary of any distributions actually made prior to such date.

> **History:** Add, L 1966, ch 952, eff Sept 1, 1967, with substance deriving from PPL § 17-f; amd, L 1967, ch 686, eff Sept 1, 1967.

§ 2-1.10. Provisions relating to infants and minors

(a) Unless the creator expressly provides to the contrary, in any instrument executed prior to September first, nineteen hundred seventy-four, the words "minor", "minority", "infant", "infancy", "majority", "adult" and words of like import shall mean or refer to a person or a class of persons under the age of twenty-one years or who shall have reached such age, according to the context, and, unless otherwise expressly provided in any instrument executed on or after September first, nineteen hundred seventy-four shall mean or refer to a person or a class of persons under the age of eighteen years or who shall have reached such age, according to the context, except that any designation of a testamentary guardian of a "minor" or an "infant" shall refer to a guardianship of a person who has not reached the age of eighteen years, regardless of the date of the instrument containing the designation.

(b) This act shall not apply to distributions made subsequent to September first, nineteen hundred seventy-four and prior to the effective date of this act.

> **History:** Add, L 1975, ch 262, § 1, eff June 24, 1975.

§ 2-1.11. Renunciation of property interests

(a) A renunciation made in compliance with the provisions of this section shall not necessarily constitute a qualified disclaimer within the meaning of section 2518 of the Internal Revenue Code of 1986, as amended, or for the purposes of the taxes imposed by article twenty-six of the tax law.

(b) For purposes of this section:

(1) The term "disposition" shall include a disposition created under a will or trust agreement including, without limitation, the granting of a power of appointment, a disposition created by the exercise or nonexercise of a power of appointment, a distributive share under 4-1.1, a transfer created by a trust account as defined in 7-5.1, a transfer created by a life insurance or annuity contract, a transfer resulting from the creation of a joint tenancy or tenancy by the entirety, succession to an interest occurring by operation of law on the death of a joint tenant or tenant by the entirety, a transfer under an employee benefit plan (including, without limitation, any pension, retirement, death benefit, stock bonus or profit-sharing plan, system or trust), a transfer of a security to a beneficiary pursuant to part 4 of article 13 of this chapter, any other disposition or transfer created by any testamentary or nontestamentary instrument, or by operation of law, and any of the foregoing created or increased by reason of a renunciation made by another person.

(2) The effective date of the disposition for purposes of this section shall be:

A. If the disposition is created by will, the exercise or nonexercise of a testamentary power of appointment, a distribution pursuant to 4-1.1, the deposit of money in a trust account as defined in 7-5.1, the registration of a security in beneficiary form pursuant to part 4 of article 13 of this chapter, a life insurance or annuity contract, the death of a joint tenant or tenant by the entirety, or an employee benefit plan, the date of death of the deceased testator, holder of the power of appointment, intestate, creator of the trust account, registered owner of the security, insured, annuitant, other joint tenant or tenant by the entirety, or employee, as the case may be;

B. If the disposition is created by trust agreement, the exercise of a presently exercisable power of appointment, the creation of a joint tenancy or tenancy by the entirety, or the renunciation of a disposition created by another, the date as of which the transfer in trust is irrevocable and is a completed gift for federal gift tax purposes (regardless of whether a gift tax is imposed on the completed gift), the date of the exercise of the power of appointment, the creation of a joint tenancy or tenancy by the entirety, or renunciation, as the case may be; and

C. If the disposition is created by any other testamentary or nontestamentary instrument, or by operation of law, the date of the event by which the beneficiary is finally ascertained.

Notwithstanding the foregoing, the effective date of a disposition which is of a future estate shall be the date on which it becomes an estate in possession.

(c) (1) Any beneficiary of a disposition may renounce all or part of such beneficiary's interest; provided, however, that a surviving joint tenant or tenant by the entirety may renounce the interest to which such tenant succeeds, by operation of law upon the death of another joint tenant or tenant by the entirety, to the extent such interest could be the subject of a qualified disclaimer under section 2518 of the United States Internal Revenue Code of 1986, as amended.

(2) Such renunciation shall be in writing, signed and acknowledged by the person renouncing, and shall be filed in the office of the clerk of the court having jurisdiction over the will or trust agreement governing the property of which the disposition would otherwise be made or the court which issued letters of administration, or if there is no probate or administration, then in a surrogate's court provided by law as the place of probate or administration of the decedent's estate, within nine months after the effective date of the disposition. Such renunciation shall be accompanied by an affidavit of the renouncing party that such party has not received and is not to receive any consideration in money or money's worth for such renunciation from a person or persons whose interest is to be accelerated, unless payment of such consideration has been authorized by the court. Notice of such renunciation, which shall include a copy of the renunciation, shall be served personally or in such manner as the court may direct upon the fiduciary directed by the will or trust agreement to make the disposition or upon the administrator or such other person who was directed to make the disposition or upon any other person having custody or possession of or legal title to the property, an interest in which is being renounced, and by mail or in such manner as the court may direct upon all persons whose interest may be created or increased by reason of such renunciation. The time to file and serve such renunciation may be extended, in the discretion of the court, on a petition showing

reasonable cause and on notice to such persons and in such manner as the court may direct. The time limited in this section for filing and serving such renunciation is exclusive, and shall not be suspended or otherwise affected by any other provision of law; such renunciation shall be effective as of the date of such filing, notwithstanding that notice thereof may thereafter be required by the court.

(d) A renunciation may be made by:

(1) The guardian of the property of an infant, when so authorized by the court having jurisdiction of the estate of the infant.

(2) The committee of an incompetent when so authorized by the court that appointed the committee.

(3) The conservator of a conservatee, when so authorized by the court that appointed the conservator.

(4) A guardian appointed under article eighty-one of the mental hygiene law, when so authorized by the court that appointed the guardian.

(5) The personal representative of a decedent, provided, however, that the personal representative may seek authorization from the court having jurisdiction of the estate of the decedent.

(6) An attorney-in-fact, when so authorized under a duly executed power of attorney, provided, however, that any renunciation by an attorney-in-fact of a person under disability shall not be effective unless it is further authorized by the court with which the renunciation must be filed under subparagraph two of paragraph (c) of this section, and provided, further, that a renunciation by an attorney-in-fact of a person not under disability may be made without court authorization, unless the property which would have passed under said renunciation is, by reason of said renunciation, disposed of in favor of such attorney-in-fact or the spouse or issue of such attorney-in-fact, in which case such renunciation shall not be effective unless either (A) the instrument appointing such attorney-in-fact expressly authorizes a renunciation in favor of such attorney-in-fact or the spouse or issue of such attorney-in-fact, or (B) such renunciation has been authorized by the court with which the renunciation must be filed under subparagraph two of paragraph (c) of this section.

(e) Unless the creator of the disposition has otherwise provided, the filing of a renunciation, as provided in this section, has the same effect with respect to the renounced interest as though the renouncing person had predeceased the creator or the decedent or, if the renounced interest is a future estate, as though the renouncing person had died at the time of filing or just prior to its becoming an estate in possession, whichever is earlier in time, and shall have the effect of accelerating the possession and enjoyment of subsequent interests, but shall have no effect upon the vesting of a future estate which by the terms of the disposition is limited upon a preceding estate other than the renounced interest. If, pursuant to the preceding sentence, there would occur a per stirpes disposition of the renounced interest or a disposition or distribution of the renounced interest by representation, then solely for purposes of applying 1-2.14 or 1-2.16, as the case may be, the renouncing person shall be treated as having died on the same date as, but immediately after, the creator or decedent or, if the renounced interest is a future estate, as having died on the same date as, but immediately after, its becoming an estate in possession or, if the time of filing is earlier in time, on the same date as, but immediately after, such filing. Such renunciation is retroactive to the creation of the disposition. A person who has a present and a future interest in property and renounces the present interest in whole or in part shall be deemed to have renounced the future interest to the same extent.

(f) A beneficiary may accept one disposition and renounce another, may renounce a disposition in whole or in part, or with reference to specific amounts, parts, fractional shares or assets thereof. Notwithstanding the provisions of paragraph (e) of this section, a renunciation by a surviving spouse of a decedent of a disposition created by said decedent shall not be deemed to be a renunciation by such spouse of all or any part of any other disposition to or in favor of such spouse, regardless of whether the property which would have passed under said renounced disposition is by reason of said renunciation disposed of to or in favor of such spouse. Unless a renouncing person has provided otherwise in his renunciation, the effect of a renunciation of a fractional part of a disposition is to renounce such fraction of all property to which the renouncing person is entitled under the disposition.

(g) A renunciation may not be made under this section with respect to any property which a renouncing person has accepted, except that an acceptance does not preclude a person from renouncing all or part of any property to which such person becomes entitled when another person renounces after such acceptance. For purposes of this paragraph, a person accepts an interest in property if such person voluntarily transfers or encumbers, or contracts to transfer or encumber all or part of such interest, or accepts delivery or payment of, or exercises control as beneficial owner over all or part thereof, or executes a written waiver of the right to renounce, or otherwise indicates acceptance of all or part of such interest. A written waiver of the right to renounce shall be binding on the person waiving and all parties claiming by, through or under such person.

(h) A renunciation filed under this section is irrevocable.

(i) This section shall not abridge the right of any beneficiary or any other person to assign, convey, release or renounce any property or interest therein arising under any other section of this chapter or other statute or under common law.

(j) Except as specifically provided in the trust instrument, the will, any other instrument creating the disposition, or in this section, this section shall apply to each disposition the effective date of which (as defined in this section) is on or after the effective date of this section, except that with respect to the renunciation of a future interest this section shall apply as well to dispositions created or increased prior to the effective date of this section.

> **History:** Add, L 1977, ch 861, effective Aug 11, 1977; amd, L 1978, ch 60, eff April 11, 1978; L 1978, ch 67, eff July 1, 1978; L 1980, ch 417, eff June 23, 1980; L 1980, ch 570, eff June 26, 1980; L 1992, ch 595, eff Sept 1, 1992; L 1993, ch 515, eff Jan 1, 1994; L 2003, ch 589, eff Sept 1, 2003; L 2005, ch 325, eff Jan 1, 2006; L 2010, ch 27, eff Jan 1, 2011; L 2011, ch 285, eff Aug 3, 2011, and applying to estates of decedents dying on or after such date; L 2014, ch 315, eff Aug 11, 2014.

§ 2-1.12. Credit shelter formula bequests

If:

(a) the decedent dies after January thirty-first, two thousand; and

(b) by reason of the death of the decedent property passes or is acquired from the decedent under a will executed or a trust created prior to February first, two thousand which contains a formula providing, in sum or substance, for a bequest of the maximum amount of property that can be sheltered from federal estate tax by reason of available credits against such tax; and

(c) such formula was not amended at any time after January thirty-first, two thousand and before the death of the decedent,

then, unless the instrument containing such formula specifically provides that there are non-tax reasons for taking the federal credit for state death taxes into account, such formula shall be deemed not to include a reference to the federal credit for state death taxes.

History: Add, L 2000, ch 513, § 1, eff Oct 4, 2000, applying to estates of decedents dying after Jan 31, 2000, whether such death occurs before or after such effective date.

§ 2-1.13. Certain formula clauses to be construed to refer to the federal estate and generation-skipping transfer tax laws applicable to estates of decedents dying after December thirty-first, two thousand nine and before January first, two thousand eleven

(a) (1) If by reason of the death of a decedent property passes or is acquired under a beneficiary designation, a will or trust of a decedent who dies after December thirty-first, two thousand nine and before January first, two thousand eleven, that contains a bequest or other disposition based upon the amount of property that can be sheltered from federal estate tax by referring to the "unified credit", "estate tax exemption", "applicable exclusion amount", "applicable exemption amount", "applicable credit amount", "marital deduction", "maximum marital deduction", "unlimited marital deduction", "charitable deduction", "maximum charitable deduction" or similar words or phrases relating to the federal estate tax, or that measures a share of an estate or trust based on the amount that can pass free of federal estate taxes, or that is otherwise based on a similar provision of federal estate tax then such beneficiary designation, will or trust shall be deemed to refer to the federal estate tax law as applied with respect to decedents dying in two thousand ten, regardless of whether an election is made not to have the federal estate tax apply to a particular estate.

(2) If by reason of the death of a decedent property passes or is acquired under a beneficiary designation, a will or trust of a decedent who dies after December thirty-first, two thousand nine and before January first, two thousand eleven, that contains a bequest or other disposition based upon the amount of property that can be sheltered from federal generation-skipping transfer tax by referring to the "generation-skipping transfer tax exemption", "GST exemption", "generation-skipping transfer tax", "GST tax" or similar words or phrases that measures a share of an estate or trust based on the amount that can pass free of federal generation-skipping transfer taxes, or that is otherwise based on a similar provision of federal generation-skipping transfer tax law, then such beneficiary designation, will or trust shall be deemed to refer to the federal generation-skipping transfer tax law in effect in two thousand ten, regardless of whether an election is made not to have the federal estate tax apply to a particular estate.

(3) This paragraph shall not apply to a beneficiary designation, will or trust that manifests an intent that a contrary rule shall apply.

(b) The executor, trustee or other interested person under a beneficiary designation, will or trust referred to in paragraph (a) of this section may bring a proceeding to determine whether the beneficiary designation, will or trust manifests a contrary intention within the meaning of subparagraph three of paragraph (a) of this section. In any such proceeding, extrinsic evidence may be admitted to establish the decedent's intent.

(c) Any proceeding described in paragraph (b) of this section must be commenced by the date which is (1) twenty-four months following the date of death of the decedent, testator or grantor or (2) six months following the day on which the chapter of the laws of two thousand eleven which amended this paragraph became a law, whichever date is later, and not at any time thereafter. Notwithstanding the foregoing, the time to commence such a proceeding may be extended, in the discretion of the court, on a petition showing reasonable cause and on notice to such persons and in such manner as the court may direct.

> **History:** Add, L 2010, ch 349, § 1, eff Aug 13, 2010, deemed effective on and after Jan 1, 2010, and the provisions of this act shall apply to wills and trusts of decedents who die after Dec 31, 2009 and before Jan 1, 2011, or such earlier date that a federal estate tax or generation-skipping transfer tax becomes applicable; amd L 2011, ch 529, eff Sept 23, 2011, deemed eff on and after Jan 1, 2010, and applying to wills and trusts of decedents who die after Dec 31, 2009 and before Jan 1, 2011.

§ 2-1.14. Right to recover state estate and gift taxes where decedent retained interest

(a) (1) If any part of the gross tax estate on which tax has been paid consists of the value of property included in the gross estate by reason of section two thousand thirty-six of the internal revenue code (relating to transfers with retained life estate), the decedent's estate shall be entitled to recover from the person receiving the property the amount which bears the same ratio to the total tax under this chapter which has been paid as

  (A) the value of such property bears to

  (B) the taxable estate.

  (2) Paragraph one shall not apply if the decedent otherwise directs in a provision of his will (or a revocable trust) specifically referring to this section.

(b) For purposes of this section, if there is more than one person receiving the property, the right of recovery shall be against each such person.

(c) In the case of penalties and interest attributable to the additional taxes described in subsection (a) of this section, rules similar to the rules of subsections (a) and (b) of this section shall apply.

(d) No person shall be entitled to recover any amount by reason of this section from a trust to which section six hundred sixty-four of the internal revenue code applies (determined without regard to this section).

> **History:** Formerly § 2-1.13, add, L 1990, ch 190, eff May 25, 1990, however, that this new section shall apply only with respect to property transferred after the effective date of this act if an amount is included in the gross estate of a decedent under section 2036 of the internal revenue code other than solely by reason of subsection (c) of such section of the internal revenue code; renumbered L 2010, ch 349, § 1, eff Aug 13, 2010, deemed effective on and after Jan 1, 2010, and the provisions of this act shall apply to wills and trusts of decedents who die after Dec 31, 2009 and before Jan 1, 2011, or such earlier date that a federal estate tax or generation-skipping transfer tax becomes applicable; amd, L 1992, ch 826, eff Aug 7, 1992 (**repeal note**: Subsection (b) of section 2-1.13 of the estates, powers and trusts law, repealed by section thirty-one of this act, allowed a person to recover allocable gift tax from the original transferee of property which was treated as transferred by such person under section 2036(c) of the internal revenue code. This change is made to conform this section of the estates, powers and trusts law to section 2207B of the internal revenue code which is such section's equivalent to federal law, in which subsection (b) was repealed).

EPTL

§ 2-1.15. Consequences of partly ineffective dispositions of trust principal to two or more beneficiaries

Whenever the remainder of a lifetime or testamentary trust passes, whether outright or in further trust, to two or more designated beneficiaries, and such remainder is ineffective in part and no effective alternative disposition has been made in the governing instrument, such ineffective part shall pass to the other designated beneficiary or, if there are two or more other designated beneficiaries, to such beneficiaries in the proportions that their respective interests in such principal bear to the aggregate of the interests of such designated beneficiaries in such principal.

History: Formerly 2-1.14, add, L 1996, ch 297, § 1, eff July 10, 1996, applying to all trusts created on and after such effective date; renumbered as 2-1.15 by L 2010, ch 349, § 1, eff Aug 13, 2010, deemed eff on and after Jan 1, 2010, and the provisions of this act shall apply to wills and trusts of decedents who die after Dec 31, 2009 and before Jan 1, 2011, or such earlier date that a federal estate tax or generation-skipping transfer tax becomes applicable.

ARTICLE 3
SUBSTANTIVE LAW OF WILLS
SUMMARY OF ARTICLE

EPTL

E-23

Part 5. Rules Governing Wills Having Relation to Another Jurisdiction

§ 3-5.1.   **Formal validity, intrinsic validity, effect, interpretation, revocation or alteration of testamentary dispositions of, and exercise of testamentary powers of appointment over property by wills having relation to another jurisdiction**

PART 1   Who May Make and Receive Testamentary Dispositions of Property; What Property May Be Disposed of by Will

§ 3-1.1. Who may make wills of, and exercise testamentary powers of appointment over property

Every person eighteen years of age or over, of sound mind and memory, may by will dispose of real and personal property and exercise a power to appoint such property.

History: Add, L 1966, ch 952, eff Sept 1, 1967, with substance deriving from Decedent Est. Law § 15.

§ 3-1.2. What property may be disposed of by will

Every estate in property may be devised or bequeathed.

History: Add, L 1966, ch 952, eff Sept 1, 1967, with substance deriving from Decedent Est. Law § 11.

§ 3-1.3. Who may receive testamentary dispositions of property; testamentary dispositions to unincorporated associations

(a) A testamentary disposition of property may be made to any person having capacity to acquire and hold such property.

(b) When a will disposes of property to an association which lacks capacity to receive such property by will because it is unincorporated and the association may become incorporated under the law of this state or of the jurisdiction in which it has its principal office, such disposition is valid despite the lack of capacity of the beneficiary if within three years after probate of the will such beneficiary becomes incorporated with capacity to take such disposition, subject to the following:

(1) This section does not limit the power of the court to give effect to the intention of the testator and to preserve dispositions for the use and benefit of unincorporated associations.

(2) In the case of a testamentary disposition of property to an unincorporated association in such manner that the estate may lawfully vest in such association, as provided in paragraph (b), at a future time, the estate shall be treated as immediately vested either in the trustee in whom any estate preceding such disposition is vested or, if there is no such precedent trust, in the personal representative of the decedent's estate as trustee, subject to any intermediate estate created by the will. The trust herein created is subject to the direction and control of the surrogate's court as if it had been created by express provision in the will. If the association is incorporated and empowered to receive the disposition, the trustee shall transfer the property disposed of to the corporation so formed, but if the association is not incorporated, the trustee shall transfer the property to such persons as are entitled thereto.

(3) If a testamentary disposition to an association is made in such manner as to take effect upon the incorporation of such association, as provided in paragraph (b), and no

disposition is made of the rents, profits or other income accruing prior to such incorporation, the will shall be construed as directing the trustee described in subparagraph (2) to receive the rents, profits or other income and to hold them for the benefit of the corporation when formed or, if such corporation is not formed within the time prescribed by paragraph (b), for the benefit of the persons entitled to the property upon the failure of such disposition.

(4) Notwithstanding any other law of this state governing (A) the purposes for which trusts may be created, (B) the rule against perpetuities or (C) the accumulation of income, a trust as provided in subparagraph (2) is valid.

(5) During the continuance of any trust authorized by subparagraph (2), the unincorporated association to which the disposition is made may enforce such trust, and any such association has capacity as such, despite the fact that it is not incorporated, to exercise such right and to take such proceedings as may be appropriate for the exercise or waiver of such right or, in the manner permitted by law for renunciation by a testamentary beneficiary, to renounce the disposition. In the event of any such renunciation, the trust provided for in subparagraph (2) shall terminate and the property, including accumulations, shall vest in the persons otherwise entitled thereto as if no such disposition had been made.

(6) This section does not limit the effectiveness of 8-1.1 with respect to a disposition to which that section applies.

> **History:** Add, L 1966, ch 952, eff Sept 1, 1967, with substance deriving from Decedent Est. Law § 12 and § 47-e; amd, L 1967, ch 686, eff Sept 1, 1967.

PART 2　Execution of Wills

§ 3-2.1. Execution and attestation of wills; formal requirements

(a) Except for nuncupative and holographic wills authorized by 3-2.2, every will must be in writing, and executed and attested in the following manner:

(1) It shall be signed at the end thereof by the testator or, in the name of the testator, by another person in his presence and by his direction, subject to the following:

(A) The presence of any matter following the testator's signature, appearing on the will at the time of its execution, shall not invalidate such matter preceding the signature as appeared on the will at the time of its execution, except that such matter preceding the signature shall not be given effect, in the discretion of the surrogate, if it is so incomplete as not to be readily comprehensible without the aid of matter which follows the signature, or if to give effect to such matter preceding the signature would subvert the testator's general plan for the disposition and administration of his estate.

(B) No effect shall be given to any matter, other than the attestation clause, which follows the signature of the testator, or to any matter preceding such signature which was added subsequently to the execution of the will.

(C) Any person who signs the testator's name to the will, as provided in subparagraph (1), shall sign his own name and affix his residence address to the will but shall not be counted as one of the necessary attesting witnesses to the will. A will lacking the signature of the person signing the testator's name shall not be given effect; provided, however, the failure of the person signing the testator's name to affix his address shall not affect the validity of the will.

EPTL

(2) The signature of the testator shall be affixed to the will in the presence of each of the attesting witnesses, or shall be acknowledged by the testator to each of them to have been affixed by him or by his direction. The testator may either sign in the presence of, or acknowledge his signature to each attesting witness separately.

(3) The testator shall, at some time during the ceremony or ceremonies of execution and attestation, declare to each of the attesting witnesses that the instrument to which his signature has been affixed is his will.

(4) There shall be at least two attesting witnesses, who shall, within one thirty day period, both attest the testator's signature, as affixed or acknowledged in their presence, and at the request of the testator, sign their names and affix their residence addresses at the end of the will. There shall be a rebuttable presumption that the thirty day requirement of the preceding sentence has been fulfilled. The failure of a witness to affix his address shall not affect the validity of the will.

(b) The procedure for the execution and attestation of wills need not be followed in the precise order set forth in paragraph (a) so long as all the requisite formalities are observed during a period of time in which, satisfactorily to the surrogate, the ceremony or ceremonies of execution and attestation continue.

History: Add, L 1966, ch 952, eff Sept 1, 1967, with substance deriving from Decedent Est. Law § 21 and § 22; amd, L 1967, ch 686, eff Sept 1, 1967; L 1973, ch 618, eff Sept 1, 1973; L 1974, ch 181, eff Sept 1, 1974.

§ 3-2.2. Nuncupative and holographic wills

(a) For the purposes of this section, and as used elsewhere in this chapter:

(1) A will is nuncupative when it is unwritten, and the making thereof by the testator and its provisions are clearly established by at least two witnesses.

(2) A will is holographic when it is written entirely in the handwriting of the testator, and is not executed and attested in accordance with the formalities prescribed by 3-2.1.

(b) A nuncupative or holographic will is valid only if made by:

(1) A member of the armed forces of the United States while in actual military or naval service during a war, declared or undeclared, or other armed conflict in which members of the armed forces are engaged.

(2) A person who serves with or accompanies an armed force engaged in actual military or naval service during such war or other armed conflict.

(3) A mariner while at sea.

(c) A will authorized by this section becomes invalid:

(1) If made by a member of the armed forces, upon the expiration of one year following his discharge from the armed forces.

(2) If made by a person who serves with or accompanies an armed force engaged in actual military or naval service, upon the expiration of one year from the time he has ceased serving with or accompanying such armed force.

(3) If made by a mariner while at sea, upon the expiration of three years from the time

such will was made.

(d) If any person described in paragraph (c) lacks testamentary capacity at the expiration of the time limited therein for the validity of his will, such will shall continue to be valid until the expiration of one year from the time such person regains testamentary capacity.

(e) Nuncupative and holographic wills, as herein authorized, are subject to the provisions of this chapter to the extent that such provisions can be applied to such wills consistently with their character, or to the extent that any such provision expressly provides that it is applicable to such wills.

> **History:** Add, L 1966, ch 952, eff Sept 1, 1967, with substance deriving from Decedent Est. Law § 16; amd, L 1967, ch 686, eff Sept 1, 1967.

PART 3   Rules Governing Testamentary Dispositions

§ 3-3.1. What a testamentary disposition includes

Unless the will provides otherwise, a disposition by the testator of all his property passes all of the property he was entitled to dispose of at the time of his death.

> **History:** Add, L 1966, ch 952, eff Sept 1, 1967, with substance deriving from Decedent Est. Law § 14; amd, L 1967, ch 686, eff Sept 1, 1967.

§ 3-3.2. Competence of attesting witness who is beneficiary; application to nuncupative will

(a) An attesting witness to a will to whom a beneficial disposition or appointment of property is made is a competent witness and compellable to testify respecting the execution of such will as if no such disposition or appointment had been made, subject to the following:

(1) Any such disposition or appointment made to an attesting witness is void unless there are, at the time of execution and attestation, at least two other attesting witnesses to the will who receive no beneficial disposition or appointment thereunder.

(2) Subject to subparagraph (1), any such disposition or appointment to an attesting witness is effective unless the will cannot be proved without the testimony of such witness, in which case the disposition or appointment is void.

(3) Any attesting witness whose disposition is void hereunder, who would be a distributee if the will were not established, is entitled to receive so much of his intestate share as does not exceed the value of the disposition made to him in the will, such share to be recovered as follows:

(A) In case the void disposition becomes part of the residuary disposition, from the residuary disposition only.

(B) In case the void disposition passes in intestacy, ratibly* from the distributees who succeed to such interest. For this purpose, the void disposition shall be distributed under 4-1.1 as though the attesting witness were not a distributee.

(b) The provisions of this section apply to witnesses to a nuncupative will authorized by 3-2.2.

---

* So in original. Should probably be "ratably".

History: Add, L 1966, ch 952, eff Sept 1, 1967 from Decedent Est. Law § 27; amd, L 1967, ch 686, § 16, eff Sept 1, 1967.

§ 3-3.3. Disposition to issue or brothers or sisters of testator not to lapse; application to class dispositions

(a) Unless the will whenever executed provides otherwise:

(1) Instruments executed prior to September first, nineteen hundred ninety-two. Whenever a testamentary disposition including a disposition of a future estate other than a future estate subject to a condition precedent of surviving the testator is made to a beneficiary who is one of the testator's issue or a brother or sister, and such beneficiary dies during the lifetime of the testator leaving issue surviving such testator, such disposition does not lapse but vests in such surviving issue, by representation.[*]

(2) Instruments executed on or after September first, nineteen hundred ninety-two. Whenever a testamentary disposition including a disposition of a future estate other than a future estate subject to a condition precedent of surviving the testator is made to a beneficiary who is one of the testator's issue or a brother or sister, and such beneficiary dies during the lifetime of the testator leaving issue surviving such testator, such disposition does not lapse but vests in such surviving issue, by representation.

(3) The provisions of subparagraphs (1) and (2) of this paragraph apply to a disposition made in the form of a class gift other than a disposition to "issue," "descendents,"[**] or a class described by language of similar import, as if the disposition were made to the beneficiaries by their individual names, except that no benefit shall be conferred hereunder upon the surviving issue of an ancestor who died before the execution of the will in which the disposition to the class was made.

(b) As used in this section, the terms "issue", "surviving issue" and "issue surviving" include adopted children and their issue to the extent they would be included in a disposition to "issue" under 2-1.3 and subdivision two of section one hundred seventeen of the domestic relations law, and nonmarital children; for this purpose, a nonmarital child is the child of his mother and is the child of his father if he is entitled to inherit from his father under 4-1.2.

History: Add, L 1966, ch 952, eff Sept 1, 1967, with substance deriving from Decedent Est. Law § 29; amd, L 1967, ch 686, eff Sept 1, 1967; L 1981, ch 67, eff April 8, 1981; L 1986, ch 408, eff Sept 1, 1986; L 1992, ch 595, eff Sept 1, 1992; L 2013, ch 348, § 1, eff Sept 27, 2013, provided, however, that it shall apply only to the estates of decedents who shall have died on or after such effective date.

§ 3-3.4. Consequences of partly ineffective testamentary dispositions of property to two or more residuary beneficiaries

Whenever a testamentary disposition of property to two or more residuary beneficiaries is ineffective in part, as of the date of the testator's death, and the provisions of 3-3.3 do not apply to such ineffective part of the residuary disposition nor has an alternative disposition

---

[*] **Ed. Note:** So in original. L 2013, ch 348, § 1, eff Sept 27, 2013, amended the paragraph to change, *inter alia*, "per stirpes" to "by representation". Query whether it was error for the Legislature to change the vesting of dispositions in instruments executed prior to 9/1/92 from per stirpes to by representation.

[**] So in original. Should be "descendants".

thereof been made in the will, such ineffective part shall pass to and vest in the remaining residuary beneficiary or, if there are two or more remaining residuary beneficiaries, in such beneficiaries, ratably, in the proportions that their respective interests in the residuary estate bear to the aggregate of the interests of all remaining beneficiaries in such residuary estate.

History: Add, L 1967, ch 472, § 1, eff Sept 1, 1967.

§ 3-3.5. Conditions qualifying dispositions; conditions against contest; limitations thereon

(a) A condition qualifying a disposition of property is operative despite the failure of the testator to provide for an alternative gift to take effect upon the breach or non-occurrence of such condition.

(b) A condition, designed to prevent a disposition from taking effect in case the will is contested by the beneficiary, is operative despite the presence or absence of probable cause for such contest, subject to the following:

(1) Such a condition is not breached by a contest to establish that the will is a forgery or that it was revoked by a later will, provided that such contest is based on probable cause.

(2) An infant or incompetent may affirmatively oppose the probate of a will without forfeiting any benefit thereunder.

(3) The following conduct, singly or in the aggregate, shall not result in the forfeiture of any benefit under the will:

(A) The assertion of an objection to the jurisdiction of the court in which the will was offered for probate.

(B) The disclosure to any of the parties or to the court of any information relating to any document offered for probate as a last will, or relevant to the probate proceeding.

(C) A refusal or failure to join in a petition for the probate of a document as a last will, or to execute a consent to, or waiver of notice of a probate proceeding.

(D) The preliminary examination, under SCPA 1404, of a proponent's witnesses, the person who prepared the will, the nominated executors and the proponents in a probate proceeding and, upon application to the court based upon special circumstances, any person whose examination the court determines may provide information with respect to the validity of the will that is of substantial importance or relevance to a decision to file objections to the will.

(E) The institution of, or the joining or acquiescence in a proceeding for the construction of a will or any provision thereof.

History: Formerly 3-3.4, add, L 1966, ch 952, eff Sept 1, 1967 with substance deriving from Decedent Est. Law § 126; renumbered 3-3.5, L 1967, ch 472; L 1967, ch 686, eff Sept 1, 1967; L 1992, ch 127, eff Jan 1, 1993; L 1993, ch 514, eff Jan 1, 1994; L 2011, ch 286, eff Aug 3, 2011, and applying only to estates of decedents who shall have died on and after such effective date.

§ 3-3.6. Encumbrances on property of decedent or on proceeds of insurance policy on life of decedent not chargeable against assets of decedent's estate

(a) Where any property, subject, at the time of decedent's death, to any lien, security interest or other charge, including a lien for unpaid purchase money, is specifically disposed of by will or passes to a distributee, or where the proceeds of any policy of insurance on the life of the decedent are payable to a named beneficiary and such policy is subject to any lien, security interest or other charge, the personal representative is not responsible for the satisfaction of such encumbrance out of the property of the decedent's estate, except as provided in SCPA 1811, unless, in the case of a will, the testator has expressly or by necessary implication indicated otherwise. A general provision in the will for the payment of debts is not such an indication.

(b) Any such encumbrance is chargeable against the property of the decedent or the proceeds of a policy of insurance on the life of the decedent, subject thereto. Nothing in this section imposes upon a testamentary beneficiary, distributee or named insurance beneficiary any personal liability for the payment of the debt secured by such encumbrance.

(c) Where any lien, security interest or other charge encumbers:

(1) Property passing to two or more persons, the interest of each such person shall, only as between such persons, bear its proportionate share of the total encumbrance.

(2) Two or more properties, each such property shall, only as between the recipients thereof, bear its proportionate share of the total encumbrance.

History: Formerly § 3-3.5, add, L 1966, ch 952, eff Sept 1, 1967, with substance deriving from Decedent Est. Law § 20 and § 38; renumbered § 3-3.6, L 1967, ch 472, § 2, eff Sept 1, 1967; L 1967, ch 686, § 21, eff Sept 1, 1967.

§ 3-3.7. Testamentary disposition to trustee under, or in accordance with terms of existing inter vivos trust

(a) A testator may by will dispose of or appoint all or any part of such testator's estate to a trustee of a trust, the terms of which are evidenced by a written instrument executed by the testator, the testator and some other person, or some other person, including a trust established for the receipt of the proceeds of an annuity or pure endowment contract, or of a thrift, savings, pension, retirement, death benefit, stock bonus, or profit-sharing plan or system or a funded or unfunded life, group life, industrial life or accident and health insurance trust (although the person establishing such trust has reserved any or all rights of ownership of the insurance contracts), regardless of whether any assets have been transferred to the trust prior to the death of the testator; provided that the trust instrument is identified in the will and is executed by the person establishing the trust prior to or contemporaneously with the execution of the will and, unless such person is the sole trustee, by at least one trustee thereof prior to the death of the testator, in the manner required by the laws of this state for the recording of a conveyance of real property or, in lieu thereof, in the presence of two witnesses who shall affix their signatures to the trust instrument.

(b) The testamentary disposition or appointment is valid, even though:

(1) The trust instrument is amendable or revocable, or both, provided, however, that the disposition or appointment shall be given effect in accordance with the terms of the trust instrument, including an amendment thereto, as they appear in writing on the date of the testator's death and, where the testator so directs, including amendments to the trust instrument after his or her death, if the instrument evidencing such amendment is executed and acknowledged in the manner provided for in paragraph (b) of 7-1.17.

(2) The right is reserved in such trust instrument (A) to exercise any power over any

property transferred to or held in the trust or (B) to direct during the lifetime of the person establishing the trust or any other person, the persons and organizations to whom or in whose behalf the income shall be paid or the principal distributed.

(3) The trust instrument or any amendment thereto was not executed and attested in accordance with the formalities prescribed by 3-2.1.

(c) The property so disposed of or appointed by will becomes a part of the trust to which it is given, and title thereto vests in the trustee to be administered and disposed of in accordance with the terms of the trust instrument.

(d) Any disposition or appointment to the trustee made by a testator who died prior to the effective date of this section, which would be invalid under the applicable law of this state pre-existing the effective date of this section, shall be construed to create a testamentary trust under and in accordance with the terms of the trust instrument which the testator originally intended should embrace the property disposed of or appointed, as such terms appear in such trust instrument at the date of the testator's death.

(e) A revocation or termination of the trust before the death of the testator shall cause the disposition or appointment to fail, unless the testator has made an alternative disposition.

History: Formerly § 3-3.6, add, L 1966, ch 952, eff Sept 1, 1967, with substance deriving from Decedent Est. Law § 47-g; renumbered § 3-3.7, L 1967, ch 472, § 2, eff Sept 1, 1967; L 1967, ch 686, § 22; L 1997, ch 139, § 5, eff June 25, 1997, and applying to all lifetime trusts created on and after that date; L 2019, ch 352, eff Oct 4, 2019, and shall apply to all testamentary dispositions to a trustee occurring on or after such effective date.

§ 3-3.8. Validity of a purchase of real property notwithstanding its disposition by will

The title of a purchaser of real property, in good faith and for valuable consideration, from a distributee of a person who died owning such property shall not be affected by a testamentary disposition of such property by the decedent, unless within two years after the testator's death the will disposing of the property is admitted to probate. If, however, at the time of the testator's death, the devisee is either an infant, incompetent, imprisoned for a term less than life, without the state or if the will was concealed by one or more of the distributees of the decedent, the two year period prescribed herein does not commence until the expiration of one year from the time of the removal of such disability or the delivery of the will to the devisee or to the surrogate having jurisdiction to admit the will to probate.

History: Formerly § 3-3.7, add, L 1966, ch 952, with substance deriving from Decedent Est. Law § 46; renumbered § 3-3.8, L 1967, ch 472, § 2; L 1967, ch 686, § 23, eff Sept 1, 1967.

§ 3-3.9. Testamentary direction to purchase annuities

If a testator directs in his will the purchase of an annuity, the beneficiaries to whom the income thereof is to be paid may not elect to take the capital sum directed to be used for the purchase of such annuity in lieu thereof, unless the will expressly confers such right or except as the will expressly provides for the purchase of an assignable annuity. But nothing contained herein shall impair the right of election by a surviving spouse under 5-1.1 or 5-1.1-A.

History: Formerly § 3-3.8, add, L 1966, ch 952, with substance deriving from Decedent Est. Law § 47-b; renumbered § 3-3.9, L 1967, ch 472, § 2; L 1992, ch 595, § 7, eff Sept 1, 1992.

EPTL

PART 4 Revocation of Wills and Related Subjects

§ 3-4.1. Revocation of wills; effect on codicils

(a) Except as otherwise provided in this chapter, a revocation or alteration, if intended by the testator, may be effected in the following manner only:

(1) A will or any part thereof may be revoked or altered by:

(A) Another will.

(B) A writing of the testator clearly indicating an intention to effect such revocation or alteration, executed with the formalities prescribed by this article for the execution and attestation of a will.

(2) A will may be revoked by:

(A) An act of burning, tearing, cutting, cancellation, obliteration, or other mutilation or destruction performed by:

(i) The testator.

(ii) Another person, in the presence and by the direction of the testator; in which case, the fact that the will was so revoked in the presence and by the direction of the testator shall be proved by at least two witnesses, neither of whom shall be the person who performed the act of revocation.

(b) In addition to the methods set forth in paragraph (a), a will may be revoked or altered by a nuncupative or holographic declaration of revocation or alteration made in the circumstances prescribed by 3-2.2 by any person therein authorized to make a nuncupative or holographic will. Any such nuncupative declaration of revocation or alteration must be clearly established by at least two witnesses; any such holographic declaration, by an instrument written entirely in the handwriting of the testator, although not executed and attested in accordance with the formalities prescribed by this article for the execution and attestation of a will.

(c) The revocation of a will, as provided in this section, revokes all codicils thereto.

History: Add, L 1966, ch 952, eff Sept 1, 1967, with substance deriving from Decedent Est. Law § 34.

§ 3-4.2. Agreement to convey property previously disposed of by will not a revocation

An agreement made by a testator to convey any property does not revoke a prior testamentary disposition of such property; but such property passes under the will to the beneficiaries, subject to whatever rights were created by such agreement.

History: Add, L 1966, ch 952, eff Sept 1, 1967, with substance deriving from Dec Est Law § 37.

§ 3-4.3. Revocatory effect of a conveyance, settlement or other act affecting property previously disposed of by will

A conveyance, settlement or other act of a testator by which an estate in his property, previously disposed of by will, is altered but not wholly divested does not revoke such disposition, but the estate in the property that remains in the testator passes to the beneficiaries pursuant to the disposition. However, any such conveyance, settlement or other act of the testator which is wholly inconsistent with such previous testamentary disposition revokes it.

History: Add, L 1966, ch 952, eff Sept 1, 1967, with substance deriving from Decedent
Est. Law § 39 and § 40.

§ 3-4.4. Conveyance of property of an incompetent or conservatee, previously disposed of specifically by will, not revocation or ademption

In the case of a sale or other transfer by a committee or conservator, during the lifetime of its incompetent or conservatee, of any property which such incompetent or conservatee had previously disposed of specifically by will when he was competent or able to manage his own affairs, and no order had been entered setting aside the adjudication of incompetency at the time of such incompetent's death, or the conservatorship continued through the date of the conservatee's death, the beneficiary of such specific disposition becomes entitled to receive any remaining money or other property into which the proceeds from such sale or transfer may be traced.

History: Add, L 1966, ch 952, eff Sept 1, 1967, with substance transferred from Decedent
Est. Law § 36; amd, L 1981, ch 115, § 41, eff May 18, 1981.

§ 3-4.5. Insurance proceeds from specific disposition not subject to ademption

Where insurance proceeds from property which was the subject of a specific disposition are paid after the testator's death, such proceeds, to the extent received by the personal representative, are payable by him to the beneficiary of such disposition; and such proceeds retain the character of a specific disposition for all other purposes, including 12-1.2 and 13-1.3.

History: Add, L 1966, ch 952, with substance deriving from Decedent Est. Law § 20; amd,
L 1967, ch 686, § 24, eff Sept 1, 1967.

§ 3-4.6. Revocation or alteration of later will not to revive prior will or any provisions thereof

(a) If after executing a will the testator executes a later will which revokes or alters the prior one, a revocation of the later will does not, of itself, revive the prior will or any provision thereof.

(b) A revival of a prior will or of one or more of its provisions may be effected by:

(1) The execution of a codicil which in terms incorporates by reference such prior will or one or more of its provisions.

(2) A writing declaring the revival of such prior will or of one or more of its provisions, which is executed and attested in accordance with the formalities prescribed by this article for the execution and attestation of a will.

(3) A republication of such prior will, whether to the original witnesses or to new witnesses, which shall require a re-execution and re-attestation of the prior will in accordance with the formalities prescribed by 3-2.1.

History: Add, L 1966, ch 952, eff Sept 1, 1967 from Decedent Est. Law § 41; amd, L 1967,
ch 686, §§ 25, 26, eff Sept 1, 1967.

PART 5   Rules Governing Wills Having Relation to Another Jurisdiction

§ 3-5.1. Formal validity, intrinsic validity, effect, interpretation, revocation or alteration of testamentary dispositions of, and exercise of testamentary powers of appointment over property by wills having relation to another jurisdiction

(a) As used in this section:

(1) "Real property" means land or any estate in land, including leaseholds, fixtures and mortgages or other liens thereon.

(2) "Personal property" means any property other than real property, including tangible and intangible things.

(3) "Formal validity" relates to the formalities prescribed by the law of a jurisdiction for the execution and attestation of a will.

(4) "Intrinsic validity" relates to the rules of substantive law by which a jurisdiction determines the legality of a testamentary disposition, including the general capacity of the testator.

(5) "Effect" relates to the legal consequences attributed under the law of a jurisdiction to a valid testamentary disposition.

(6) "Interpretation" relates to the procedure of applying the law of a jurisdiction to determine the meaning of language employed by the testator where his intention is not otherwise ascertainable.

(7) "Local law" means the law which the courts of a jurisdiction apply in adjudicating legal questions that have no relation to another jurisdiction.

(b) Subject to the other provisions of this section:

(1) The formal validity, intrinsic validity, effect, interpretation, revocation or alteration of a testamentary disposition of real property, and the manner in which such property descends when not disposed of by will, are determined by the law of the jurisdiction in which the land is situated.

(2) The intrinsic validity, effect, revocation or alteration of a testamentary disposition of personal property, and the manner in which such property devolves when not disposed of by will, are determined by the law of the jurisdiction in which the decedent was domiciled at death.

(c) A will disposing of personal property, wherever situated, or real property situated in this state, made within or without this state by a domiciliary or non-domiciliary thereof, is formally valid and admissible to probate in this state, if it is in writing and signed by the testator, and otherwise executed and attested in accordance with the local law of:

(1) This state;

(2) The jurisdiction in which the will was executed, at the time of execution; or

(3) The jurisdiction in which the testator was domiciled, either at the time of execution or of death.

(d) A testamentary disposition of personal property intrinsically valid under the law of the jurisdiction in which the testator was domiciled at the time the will was executed shall not be affected by a subsequent change in the domicile of the testator to a jurisdiction by the law of which the disposition is intrinsically invalid.

(e) Interpretation of a testamentary disposition of personal property shall be made in accordance with the local law of the jurisdiction in which the testator was domiciled at the time the will was executed.

(f) Whether a testamentary disposition of personal property is effectively revoked or altered by the provisions of a subsequent testamentary instrument or by a physical act to or upon the will by which the testamentary disposition was made is determined by the law of the jurisdiction in which the testator was domiciled at the time the subsequent instrument was executed or the physical act performed.

(g) Subject to paragraphs (d), (e) and (f), the intrinsic validity, effect, revocation or alteration of a testamentary disposition by which a power of appointment over personal property is exercised, and the question of whether such power has been exercised at all, are determined by:

(1) In the case of a presently exercisable general power of appointment, the law of the jurisdiction in which the donee of such power was domiciled at the time of death.

(2) In the case of a general power of appointment exercisable by will alone or a special power of appointment:

(A) If such power was created by will, the law of the jurisdiction in which the donor of the power was domiciled at the time of death.

(B) If such power was created by inter vivos disposition, the law of the jurisdiction which the donor of the power intended to govern such disposition.

(C) If the donor is himself the donee of a general power of appointment exercisable by will alone, the law of the jurisdiction in which the donor of the power was domiciled at the time of death.

(3) The formal validity of a will by which any power of appointment over personal property is exercised is determined in accordance with paragraph (c) on the basis that the testator referred to therein is the donee of such power.

(h) Whenever a testator, not domiciled in this state at the time of death, provides in his will that he elects to have the disposition of his property situated in this state governed by the laws of this state, the intrinsic validity, including the testator's general capacity, effect, interpretation, revocation or alteration of any such disposition is determined by the local law of this state. The formal validity of the will, in such case, is determined in accordance with paragraph (c).

(i) Notwithstanding the definition of "real property" in subparagraph (a) (1), whether an estate in, leasehold of, fixture, mortgage or other lien on land is real property governed by subparagraph (b) (1) or personal property governed by subparagraph (b) (2) is determined by the local law of the jurisdiction in which the land is situated.

History: Add, L 1966, ch 952, eff Sept 1, 1967, with substance deriving from Decedent Est. Law § 22-a and § 23, § 24 and § 47.

EPTL

ARTICLE 4
DESCENT AND DISTRIBUTION OF AN INTESTATE ESTATE

SUMMARY OF ARTICLE

PART 1   Rules Governing Intestate Succession

§ 4-1.1. Descent and distribution of a decedent's estate

The property of a decedent not disposed of by will shall be distributed as provided in this section. In computing said distribution, debts, administration expenses and reasonable funeral expenses shall be deducted but all estate taxes shall be disregarded, except that nothing contained herein relieves a distributee from contributing to all such taxes the amounts apportioned against him or her under 2-1.8. Distribution shall then be as follows:

(a) If a decedent is survived by:

(1) A spouse and issue, fifty thousand dollars and one-half of the residue to the spouse, and the balance thereof to the issue by representation.

(2) A spouse and no issue, the whole to the spouse.

(3) Issue and no spouse, the whole to the issue, by representation.

(4) One or both parents, and no spouse and no issue, the whole to the surviving parent or parents.

(5) Issue of parents, and no spouse, issue or parent, the whole to the issue of the parents, by representation.

(6) One or more grandparents or the issue of grandparents (as hereinafter defined), and no spouse, issue, parent or issue of parents, one-half to the surviving grandparent or grandparents of one parental side, or if neither of them survives the decedent, to their issue, by representation, and the other one-half to the surviving grandparent or grandparents of the other parental side, or if neither of them survives the decedent, to their issue, by representation; provided that if the decedent was not survived by a grandparent or grandparents on one side or by the issue of such grandparents, the whole to the surviving grandparent or grandparents on the other side, or if neither of them survives the decedent, to their issue, by representation, in the same manner as the one-half. For the purposes of this subparagraph, issue of grandparents shall not include issue more remote than grandchildren of such grandparents.

(7) Great-grandchildren of grandparents, and no spouse, issue, parent, issue of parents, grandparent, children of grandparents or grandchildren of grandparents, one-half to the great-grandchildren of the grandparents of one parental side, per capita,

and the other one-half to the great-grandchildren of the grandparents of the other parental side, per capita; provided that if the decedent was not survived by great-grandchildren of grandparents on one side, the whole to the great-grandchildren of grandparents on the other side, in the same manner as the one-half.

(b) For all purposes of this section, decedent's relatives of the half blood shall be treated as if they were relatives of the whole blood.

(c) Distributees of the decedent, conceived before his or her death but born alive thereafter, take as if they were born in his or her lifetime.

(d) The right of an adopted child to take a distributive share and the right of succession to the estate of an adopted child continue as provided in the domestic relations law.

(e) A distributive share passing to a surviving spouse under this section is in lieu of any right of dower to which such spouse may be entitled.

History: Add, L 1966, ch 952, eff Sept 1, 1967, with substance deriving from Decedent Est. Law § 83; amd, L 1967, ch 686, eff Sept 1, 1967; L 1969, ch 596, eff Sept 1, 1969; L 1971, ch 68, eff March 30, 1971; L 1974, ch 903, eff Sept 1, 1974; L 1978, ch 423, eff June 19, 1978; L 1992, ch 595, § 8, eff Sept 1, 1992; L 2019, ch 420, § 1, eff Oct 29, 2019.

§ 4-1.2. Inheritance by non-marital children

(a) For the purposes of this article:

(1) A non-marital child is the legitimate child of his mother so that he and his issue inherit from his mother and from his maternal kindred.

(2) A non-marital child is the legitimate child of his father or non-gestating intended parent so that he and his issue inherit from such parent and such parent's kindred if:

(A) a court of competent jurisdiction has, during the lifetime of the father, made an order of filiation or parentage declaring parentage or the parentage of the child has been established through the execution of an acknowledgment of parentage pursuant to section four thousand one hundred thirty-five-b of the public health law, which has been filed with the registrar of the district in which the birth certificate has been filed or;

(B) the father of the child has signed an instrument acknowledging parentage, provided that

(i) such instrument is acknowledged or executed or proved in the form required to entitle a deed to be recorded in the presence of one or more witnesses and acknowledged by such witness or witnesses, in either case, before a notary public or other officer authorized to take proof of deeds and

(ii) such instrument is filed within sixty days from the making thereof with the putative father registry established by the state department of social services pursuant to section three hundred seventy-two-c of the social services law, as added by chapter six hundred sixty-five of the laws of nineteen hundred seventy-six and

(iii) the department of social services shall, within seven days of the filing of the instrument, send written notice by registered mail to the mother and other legal guardian of such child, notifying them that an acknowledgment of parentage instrument acknowledged or executed by such parent has been duly filed or;

(C) parentage has been established by clear and convincing evidence, which may include, but is not limited to: (i) evidence derived from a genetic marker test, or (ii) evidence that the parent openly and notoriously acknowledged the child as his or her own, however nothing in this section regarding genetic marker tests shall be construed to expand or limit the current application of subdivision four of section forty-two hundred ten of the public health law.

(3) The existence of an agreement obligating the father to support the non-marital child does not qualify such child or his issue to inherit from the father in the absence of an order of filiation made or acknowledgement of parentage as prescribed by subparagraph (2).

(4) A motion for relief from an order of filiation may be made only by the father and a motion for relief from an acknowledgement of parentage may be made by a parent or other legal guardian of such child, or the child, provided however, such motion must be made within one year from the entry of such order or from the date of written notice as provided for in subparagraph (2).

(b) If a non-marital child dies, his or her surviving spouse, issue, mother, maternal kindred, father and paternal kindred inherit and are entitled to letters of administration as if the decedent was a marital child, provided that the father and paternal kindred may inherit or obtain such letters only if the parentage of the non-marital child has been established pursuant to any of the provisions of subparagraph (2) of paragraph (a).

History: Add, L 1966, ch 952, eff Sept 1, 1967, with substance deriving from Decedent Est. Law § 83-a; amd, L 1967, ch 686, eff Sept 1, 1967; L 1979, ch 139, § 1, eff May 29, 1979; L 1981, ch 67, § 2, eff April 8, 1981; L 1981, ch 75, §§ 1, 2; L 1987, ch 434, § 2, eff July 27, 1987; L 1992, ch 595, § 9, eff Sept 1, 1992; L 1994, ch 170, § 351, eff June 15, 1994, "provided that nothing contained herein shall be deemed to affect the application, qualification, expiration or repeal of any provision of law amended by sections three hundred fifty through three hundred seventy-nine of this act and such provisions shall be applied or qualified or shall expire or be deemed repealed in the same manner, to the same extent and on the same date as the case may be as otherwise provided by law"; L 2010, ch 64, §§ 1–3, eff April 28, 2010, applying to the estates of decedents dying on or after such date; L 2020, ch 56, Pt L, § 17, eff Feb 15, 2021.

2020 Amendment

2020 N.Y. Laws 56, Pt. L, § 17, effective February 15, 2021, amended the section to conform with new provisions relating to surrogacy by clarifying the rights of inheritance after the death of an intended (formerly genetic) parent.

§ 4-1.3. Inheritance by children conceived after the death of an intended parent

(a) When used in this article, unless the context or subject matter manifestly requires a different interpretation:

(1) "Genetic material" shall mean sperm or ova provided by a genetic parent.

(2) "Child" shall mean a child conceived through assisted reproduction.

(3) "Intended parent" shall have the same meaning as defined in section 581-102 of the family court act.

(b) For purposes of this article, a genetic child is the child of his or her intended parent or parents and, notwithstanding paragraph (c) of section 4-1.1 of this part, is a distributee of his or her intended parent or parents and, notwithstanding subparagraph (2) of paragraph (a) of section 2-1.3 of this chapter, is included in any disposition of property to persons described in any instrument of which an intended parent of the genetic child was the creator as the issue, children, descendants, heirs, heirs at law, next of kin, distributees (or by any term of like import) of the creator if it is established that:

(1) the intended parent in a written instrument executed pursuant to the provisions of this section not more than seven years before the death of the intended parent expressly consented that if assisted reproduction were to occur after the death of the intended parent, the deceased individual would be a parent of the child; and

(2) the child was in utero no later than twenty-four months after the intended parent's death or born no later than thirty-three months after the intended parent's death.

(c) If the child was conceived using the genetic material of the intended parent, it must further be established that:

(1) the intended parent in a written instrument executed pursuant to the provisions of this section not more than seven years before the death of the intended parent authorized a person to make decisions about the use of the intended parent's genetic material after the death of the intended parent;

(2) the person authorized in the written instrument to make decisions about the use of the intended parent's genetic material gave written notice, by certified mail, return receipt requested, or by personal delivery, that the intended parent's genetic material was available for the purpose of conceiving a child of the intended parent, and such written notice was given;

(A) within seven months from the date of the issuance of letters testamentary or of administration on the estate of the intended parent, as the case may be, to the person to whom such letters have issued, or, if no letters have been issued within four months of the death of the intended parent, and

(B) within seven months of the death of the intended parent to a distributee of the intended parent; and

(3) the person authorized in the written instrument to make decisions about the use of the intended parent's genetic material recorded the written instrument within seven months of the intended parent's death in the office of the surrogate granting letters on the intended parent's estate, or, if no such letters have been granted, in the office of the surrogate having jurisdiction to grant them.

(d) The written instrument referred to in subparagraph (1) of paragraph (b) of this section and subparagraph (1) of paragraph (c) of this section:

(1) must be signed by the intended parent in the presence of two witnesses who also sign the instrument referred to in subparagraph (1) of paragraph (c) of this section, both of whom are at least eighteen years of age and neither of whom is a person authorized under the instrument to make decisions about the use of the intended parent's genetic material;

(2) may be revoked only by a written instrument signed by the intended parent and executed in the same manner as the instrument it revokes;

(3) may not be altered or revoked by a provision in the will of the intended parent;

(4) an instrument referred to in subparagraph (1) of paragraph (c) of this section may authorize an alternate to make decisions about the use of the intended parent's genetic material if the first person so designated dies before the intended parent or is unable to exercise the authority granted;

(5) an instrument referred to in subparagraph (1) of paragraph (b) of this section may be substantially in the following form and must be signed and dated by the intended parent and properly witnessed:

I, _____
                   (Your name and address)

consent to the use of assisted reproduction to conceive a child or children of mine after my death. I understand that, unless I revoke this consent and authorization in a written document signed by me in the presence of two witnesses who also sign the document, this consent and authorization will remain in effect for seven years from this day and that I cannot revoke or modify this consent and designation by any provision in my will.

Signed this _____ day of _____, _____

_____
                 (Your signature)

Statement of witnesses:

I declare that the person who signed this document is personally known to me and appears to be of sound mind and acting willingly and free from duress. He or she signed this document in my presence. I am not the person authorized in this document to control the use of the genetic material of the person who signed this document.

Witness:
Address:
Date:
Witness:
Address:
Date:

(6) may be substantially in the following form and must be signed and dated by the intended parent and properly witnessed:

I, _____
                   (Your name and address)

consent to the use of my (sperm or ova) (referred to below as my "genetic material") to conceive a child or children of mine after my death, and I authorize

_____
          (Name and address of person)

to decide whether and how my genetic material is to be used to conceive a child or children of mine after my death.

In the event that the person authorized above dies before me or is unable to exercise the authority granted I designate

_____
(Name and address of person)

to decide whether and how my genetic material is to be used to conceive a child or children of mine after my death.

I understand that, unless I revoke this consent and authorization in a written document signed by me in the presence of two witnesses who also sign the document, this consent and authorization will remain in effect for seven years from this day and that I cannot revoke or modify this consent and designation by any provision in my will.

Signed this _____ day of _____, _____

_____
(Your signature)

Statement of witnesses:

I declare that the person who signed this document is personally known to me and appears to be of sound mind and acting willingly and free from duress. He or she signed this document in my presence. I am not the person authorized in this document to control the use of the genetic material of the person who signed this document.

Witness:
Address:
Date:
Witness:
Address:
Date:

(e) Any authority granted in a written instrument authorized by this section to a person who is the spouse of the intended parent at the time of execution of the written instrument is revoked by a final decree or judgment of divorce or annulment, or a final decree, judgment or order declaring the nullity of the marriage between the intended parent and the spouse or dissolving such marriage on the ground of absence, recognized as valid under the law of this state, or a final decree or judgment of separation, recognized as valid under the law of this state, which was rendered against the spouse.

(f) Process shall not issue to a child who is a distributee of an intended parent under sections one thousand three and one thousand four hundred three of the surrogate's court procedure act unless the child is in being at the time process issues.

(g) Except as provided in paragraph (b) of this section with regard to any disposition of property in any instrument of which the intended parent of a child is the creator, for purposes of section 2-1.3 of this chapter a child who is entitled to inherit from an intended parent under this section is a child of the intended parent for purposes of a disposition of property to persons described in any instrument as the issue, children, descendants, heirs, heirs at law, next of kin, distributees (or by any term of like import) of the creator or of another. This paragraph shall apply to the wills of persons dying on or after September first, two thousand fourteen, to lifetime instruments theretofore executed which on said date are subject to the grantor's power to revoke or amend, and to all lifetime instruments executed on or after such date.

(h) For purposes of section 3-3.3 of this chapter the terms "issue", "surviving issue" and "issue surviving" include a child if he or she is entitled to inherit from his or her intended parent under this section.

(i) Where the validity of a disposition under the rule against perpetuities depends on the ability of a person to have a child at some future time, the possibility that such person may have a child conceived using assisted reproduction shall be disregarded. This provision shall not apply for any purpose other than that of determining the validity of a disposition under the rule against perpetuities where such validity depends on the ability of a person to have a child at some future time. A determination of validity or invalidity of a disposition under the rule against perpetuities by the application of this provision shall not be affected by the later birth of a child conceived using assisted reproduction disregarded under this provision.

(j) The use of a genetic material after the death of the person providing such material is subject exclusively to the provisions of this section and to any valid and binding contractual agreement between such person and the facility providing storage of the genetic material and may not be the subject of a disposition in an instrument created by the person providing such material or by any other person.

> **History:** Add L 2014, ch 439, § 1, eff Nov 21, 2014, except that the provisions of paragraph (f) of the new statute will apply to wills of persons dying on or after September 1, 2014, to lifetime instruments executed prior to September 1, 2014 which on that date are subject to the grantor's power to revoke or amend, and to all lifetime instruments executed on or after that date; amd L 2020, c 56, Pt L, § 29, eff Feb 15, 2021.

EPTL

2020 Amendment

2020 N.Y. Laws 56, Pt. L, § 29, effective February 15, 2021, amended the heading and the section to conform with new provisions relating to surrogacy by clarifying the legitimacy of children born by artificial insemination. This includes a new definition of "intended parent" and provisions, and a new form of consent for the use of assisted reproduction to conceive a child after death.

§ 4-1.4. Disqualification of parent to take intestate share

(a) No distributive share in the estate of a deceased child shall be allowed to a parent if the parent, while such child is under the age of twenty-one years:

(1) has failed or refused to provide for the child or has abandoned such child, whether or not such child dies before having attained the age of twenty-one years, unless the parental relationship and duties are subsequently resumed and continue until the death of the child; or

(2) has been the subject of a proceeding pursuant to section three hundred eighty-four-b of the social services law which:

(A) resulted in an order terminating parental rights, or

(B) resulted in an order suspending judgment, in which event the surrogate's court shall make a determination disqualifying the parent on the grounds adjudicated by the family court, if the surrogate's court finds, by a preponderance of the evidence, that the parent, during the period of suspension, failed to comply with the family court order to restore the parent-child relationship.

(b) Subject to the provisions of subdivision eight of section two hundred thirteen of the civil practice law and rules, the provisions of subparagraph one of paragraph (a) of this section shall not apply to a biological parent who places the child for adoption based upon:

(1) a fraudulent promise, not kept, to arrange for and complete the adoption of such child, or

(2) other fraud or deceit by the person or agency where, before the death of the child, the person or agency fails to arrange for the adoptive placement or petition for the adoption of the child, and fails to comply timely with conditions imposed by the court for the adoption to proceed.

(c) In the event that a parent or spouse is disqualified from taking a distributive share in the estate of a decedent under this section or 5-1.2, the estate of such decedent shall be distributed in accordance with 4-1.1 as though such spouse or parent had predeceased the decedent.

History: Former statute added from Decedent Est. Law § 87; Repealed and replaced L 2006, ch 285, § 1, eff Jan 1, 2007.

§ 4-1.5. Other disqualifications

No estate property, whether passing by intestacy or otherwise, which has its situs in this state, shall pass to any other state or territory of the United States, or to any foreign country or sovereignty in the event of the absence of an individual heir, distributee, legatee or owner of said property, but shall pass as abandoned property to the state of New York, and shall be held as such property pursuant to the abandoned property law.

History: Add, L 1977, ch 496, § 1, eff Aug 1, 1977.

§ 4-1.6. Disqualification of joint tenant in certain instances

Notwithstanding any other provision of law to the contrary, a joint tenant convicted of murder in the second degree as defined in section 125.25 of the penal law or murder in the first degree as defined in section 125.27 of the penal law of another joint tenant shall not be entitled to the distribution of any monies in a joint bank account created or contributed to by the deceased joint tenant, except for those monies contributed by the convicted joint tenant.

Upon the conviction of such joint tenant of first or second degree murder and upon application by the prosecuting attorney, the court, as part of its sentence, shall issue an order directing the amount of any joint bank account to be distributed pursuant to the provisions of this section from the convicted joint tenant and to the deceased joint tenant's estate. The court and the prosecuting attorney shall each have the power to subpoena records of a banking institution to determine the amount of money in such bank account and by whom deposits were made. The court shall also have the power to freeze such account upon application by the prosecuting attorney during the pendency of a trial for first or second degree murder. If, upon receipt of such court orders described in this section, the banking institution holding monies in such joint account complies with the terms of the order, such banking institution shall be held free from all liability for the distribution of such funds as were in such joint account. In the absence of actual or constructive notice of such order, the banking institution holding monies in such account shall be held harmless for distributing the money according to its ordinary course of business.

For purposes of this section, the term banking institution shall have the same meaning as provided for in paragraph (b) of subdivision three of section nine-f of the banking law.

History: Add, L 1994, ch 481, § 1, eff July 20, 1994.

ARTICLE 5
FAMILY RIGHTS

SUMMARY OF ARTICLE

PART 1　Rights of Surviving Spouse

§ 5-1.1. Right of election by surviving spouse [*Decedents dying before 9/1/92*]

(a) Election by surviving spouse against will executed after August thirty-first, nineteen hundred thirty and prior to September first, nineteen hundred sixty-six.

(1) Where a testator executes a will after August thirty-first, nineteen hundred thirty but prior to September first, nineteen hundred sixty-six, and is survived by a spouse, a personal right of election is given to the surviving spouse to take a share of the decedent's estate, subject to the following:

(A) For the purposes of this section, the elective share of the surviving spouse is one-third of the net estate if the decedent is survived by one or more issue and, in all other cases, one-half of such net estate. In computing the net estate, debts, administration and reasonable funeral expenses shall be deducted but all estate taxes shall be disregarded, except that nothing contained herein relieves the surviving spouse from contributing to all such taxes the amounts apportioned against him under 2-1.8.

E-45

(B) Where the elective share is over twenty-five hundred dollars and the testator has made a testamentary disposition in trust of an amount equal to or greater than the elective share, with income therefrom payable to the surviving spouse for life, the surviving spouse has the limited right to elect to take the sum of twenty-five hundred dollars absolutely, which shall be deducted from the principal of such trust and the terms of the will remain otherwise effective.

(C) Where the elective share of the surviving spouse does not exceed twenty-five hundred dollars, the surviving spouse has the right to elect to take his elective share absolutely, which shall be in lieu of any provision for his benefit in the will.

(D) Where the will contains an absolute disposition to the surviving spouse of or in excess of the sum of twenty-five hundred dollars and also a disposition in trust with income payable to such spouse for life of an amount equal to or greater than the difference between the absolute disposition and his elective share, the surviving spouse has no right of election.

(E) Where the will contains an absolute disposition to the surviving spouse of an amount less than the sum of twenty-five hundred dollars and also a disposition in trust with income payable to such spouse for life of an amount equal to or greater than the difference between the absolute disposition and his elective share, the surviving spouse has the limited right to elect to take the sum of twenty-five hundred dollars, inclusive of the amount of such absolute disposition, and the difference between such disposition and the sum of twenty-five hundred dollars shall be deducted from the principal of such trust and the terms of the will remain otherwise effective.

(F) Where the aggregate of the provisions in the will for the surviving spouse, including the principal of a trust, an absolute disposition or any other kind of testamentary disposition is less than the elective share, the surviving spouse has the limited right to elect to take the difference between such aggregate and the amount of the elective share, and the terms of the will remain otherwise effective. In every estate, the surviving spouse has the limited right to withdraw the sum of twenty-five hundred dollars if the elective share is equal to or greater than that amount. Such sum, however, is inclusive of any absolute disposition, whether general or specific. Where a trust is created for the life of the surviving spouse, such sum of twenty-five hundred dollars or any lesser amount necessary to make up that sum is payable from the principal of such trust.

(G) The provisions of this paragraph with respect to trusts with income payable for the life of the surviving spouse likewise apply to a legal life estate, to an annuity for life or to any other disposition in the will by which income is payable for the life of the surviving spouse. In computing the value of the dispositions in the will, the capital value of the fund or other property producing the income shall be taken and not the value of the life estate.

(H) The grant of authority in a will to a fiduciary or his successor (i) to act without bond, (ii) to name his successor to act without bond, (iii) to sell assets of the estate upon terms fixed by him, (iv) to invest the funds of the estate in other than legal investments, (v) to retain in the assets of the estate investments or property owned by the testator in his lifetime, (vi) to make distribution in kind, (vii) to make a binding and conclusive valuation of assets for the purpose of their distribution, (viii) to allocate assets either outright or in trust for the life of a surviving spouse or (ix) to conduct the affairs of the estate with partial or total exoneration from the legal responsibility of a fiduciary, shall not, either singly or in the aggregate, give the surviving spouse an absolute right to take his elective share; but the surrogate's court having jurisdiction of the estate, notwithstanding the terms of the will, may, in its discretion, in an appropriate proceeding by the surviving spouse or upon an accounting, direct and enforce for the protection of the surviving spouse an equitable distribution, allocation or valuation of the assets, enforce the liability of a fiduciary under the law and make such other directions, consistent with the provisions and purposes of this paragraph, as it may consider necessary for the protection of the surviving spouse.

(b) Inter vivos dispositions treated as testamentary substitutes for the purpose of election by surviving spouse.

(1) Where a person dies after August thirty-first, nineteen hundred sixty-six and is survived by a spouse who exercises a right of election under paragraph (c), the following transactions effected by such decedent at any time after the date of the marriage and after August thirty-first, nineteen hundred sixty-six, whether benefiting the surviving spouse or any other person, shall be treated as testamentary substitutes and the capital value thereof, as of the decedent's death, included in the net estate subject to the surviving spouse's elective right:

(A) Gifts causa mortis.

(B) Money deposited, after August thirty-first, nineteen hundred sixty-six, together with all dividends credited thereon, in a savings account in the name of the decedent in trust for another person, with a banking organization, savings and loan association, foreign banking corporation or organization or bank or savings and loan association organized under the laws of the United States, and remaining on deposit at the date of the decedent's death.

(C) Money deposited, after August thirty-first, nineteen hundred sixty-six, together with all dividends credited thereon, in the name of the decedent and another person and payable on death, pursuant to the terms of the deposit or by operation of law, to the survivor, with a banking organization, savings and loan association, foreign banking corporation or organization or bank or savings and loan association organized under the laws of the United States, and remaining on deposit at the date of the decedent's death.

(D) Any disposition of property made by the decedent after August thirty-first, nineteen hundred sixty-six whereby property is held, at the date of his death, by the decedent and another person as joint tenants with a right of survivorship or as tenants by the entirety.

(E) Any disposition of property made by the decedent after August thirty-first, nineteen hundred sixty-six, in trust or otherwise, to the extent that the decedent at the date of his death retained, either alone or in conjunction with another person, by the express provisions of the disposing instrument, a power to revoke such disposition or a power to consume, invade or dispose of the principal thereof. The provisions of this paragraph shall not affect the right of any income beneficiary to the income undistributed or accrued at the date of death.

(2) Nothing in this paragraph shall affect, impair or defeat the right of any person

entitled to receive (A) payment in money, securities or other property under a thrift, savings, pension, retirement, death benefit, stock bonus or profit-sharing plan, system or trust, (B) money payable by an insurance company or a savings bank authorized to conduct the business of life insurance under an annuity or pure endowment contract, a policy of life, group life, industrial life or accident and health insurance or a contract by such insurer relating to the payment of proceeds or avails thereof or (C) payment of any United States savings bond payable to a designated person, and such transactions are not testamentary substitutes within the meaning of this paragraph.

(3) Transactions described in subparagraphs (C) or (D) shall be treated as testamentary substitutes in the proportion that the funds on deposit were the property of the decedent immediately before the deposit or the consideration for the property held as joint tenants or as tenants by the entirety was furnished by the decedent. The surviving spouse shall have the burden of establishing the proportion of the decedent's contribution. Where the other party to a transaction described in subparagraphs (C) or (D) is a surviving spouse, such spouse shall have the burden of establishing the proportion of his contribution, if any. For the purpose of this subparagraph, the surrogate's court may accept such evidence as is relevant and competent, whether or not the person offering such evidence would otherwise be competent to testify.

(4) The provisions of this paragraph shall not prevent a corporation or other person from paying or transferring any funds or property to a person otherwise entitled thereto, unless there has been served personally upon such corporation or other person a certified copy of an order enjoining such payment or transfer made by the surrogate's court having jurisdiction of the decedent's estate or by another court of competent jurisdiction. Such order may be made, on notice to such persons and in such manner as the court may direct, upon application of the surviving spouse or any other interested party and on proof that the surviving spouse has exercised his right of election under paragraph (c). Service of a certified copy of such order on the corporation or other person holding such fund or property shall be a defense to it, during the effective period of the order, in any action or proceeding brought against it which involves such fund or property.

(5) This paragraph shall not impair or defeat the rights of creditors of the decedent with respect to any matter as to which any such creditor has rights.

(6) In case of a conflict between this paragraph and any other provision of law affecting the transactions described in subparagraph (1), this paragraph controls.

(c) Election by surviving spouse against wills executed and testamentary provisions made after August thirty-first, nineteen hundred sixty-six; election where decedent dies intestate as to all or any part of his estate.

(1) Where, after August thirty-first, nineteen hundred sixty-six, a testator executes a will disposing of his entire estate, and is survived by a spouse, a personal right of election is given to the surviving spouse to take a share of the decedent's estate, subject to the following:

(A) For the purposes of this paragraph, the decedent's estate includes the capital value, as of the decedent's death, of any property described in subparagraph (b) (1).

(B) The elective share, as used in this paragraph, is one-third of the net estate if the decedent is survived by one or more issue and, in all other cases, one-half of such net estate. In computing the net estate, debts, administration and reasonable funeral expenses shall be deducted but all estate taxes shall be disregarded, except that nothing contained herein relieves the surviving spouse from contributing to all such taxes the amounts apportioned against him under 2-1.8.

(C) The term "testamentary provision", as used in this paragraph, includes, in addition to dispositions made by the decedent's will, any transaction described as a testamentary substitute in subparagraph (b) (1).

(D) Where the elective share is over ten thousand dollars and the decedent has by testamentary provision created a trust in an amount equal to or greater than the elective share, with income therefrom payable to the surviving spouse for life, the surviving spouse has the limited right to elect to take the sum of ten thousand dollars absolutely, which shall be deducted from the principal of such trust and the terms of the instrument making the testamentary provision remain otherwise effective.

(E) Where the elective share of the surviving spouse does not exceed ten thousand dollars, the surviving spouse has the right to take the elective share absolutely, in lieu of any testamentary provision for his benefit.

(F) Where an absolute testamentary provision is made for the surviving spouse of or in excess of ten thousand dollars, and also a provision in trust with income payable to such spouse for life of an amount equal to or greater than the difference between such absolute testamentary provision and his elective share, the surviving spouse has no right of election.

(G) Where an absolute testamentary provision is made for the surviving spouse in an amount less than ten thousand dollars, and also a testamentary provision in trust with income payable to such spouse for life of an amount equal to or greater than the difference between such absolute testamentary provision and his elective share, the surviving spouse has the limited right to take the sum of ten thousand dollars, inclusive of the amount of such absolute testamentary provision, and the difference between such absolute testamentary provision and the sum of ten thousand dollars shall be deducted from the principal of the trust and the terms of the instrument making the testamentary provision remain otherwise effective.

(H) Where the aggregate of the testamentary provisions for the surviving spouse, including the principal of a trust, an absolute testamentary provision or any other kind of testamentary provision, is less than the elective share, the surviving spouse has the limited right to elect to take the difference between such aggregate and the amount of the elective share, and the terms of the instrument making such testamentary provisions remain otherwise effective. In every estate, the surviving spouse has the limited right to withdraw the sum of ten thousand dollars if the elective share is equal to or greater than that amount. Such sum, however, is inclusive of any absolute testamentary provision. Where a trust is created with income payable to the surviving spouse for life, such sum of ten thousand dollars or any lesser amount necessary to make up that sum is payable from the principal of such trust.

(I) The provisions of this paragraph with respect to trusts for the life of the surviving spouse also apply to a legal life estate, to an annuity for the life of the surviving spouse, to an annuity trust and a unitrust as provided in subparagraph (K) of paragraph one of this subdivision or to any other testamentary provision by which income is payable for the life of the surviving spouse. In computing the value of the testamentary provisions the capital value of the fund or other property producing the income shall be taken and not the value of the life estate.

(J) The surviving spouse is entitled to take the capital value (in no case to exceed such spouse's elective share) of the fund or other property producing the income whenever any instrument making a testamentary provision of income for his life authorizes:

(i) The reduction of any trust, legal life estate or annuity by invasion of the principal for another person.

(ii) The termination of any trust, legal life estate or annuity prior to the death of the surviving spouse by payment of the principal thereof to another person.

(iii) The fiduciary to pay or apply to the use of the surviving spouse less than substantially all of the net income from any trust, legal life estate or annuity.

If an instrument making any such testamentary provision contains grants of authority to a fiduciary other than the foregoing, the surrogate's court having jurisdiction of the decedent's estate may, in its discretion, in an appropriate proceeding by the surviving spouse or upon an accounting, direct and enforce for the protection of the surviving spouse an equitable distribution, allocation or valuation of the assets, enjoin any fiduciary, whether appointed by will or otherwise, from exercising any power, statutory or otherwise, which would be prejudicial to the interests of the surviving spouse, enforce the liability of a fiduciary under the law and make such other directions, consistent with the provisions and purposes of this paragraph, as it may consider necessary for the protection of the surviving spouse.

(K) If any testamentary provision for the surviving spouse provides that such spouse shall receive, for life and not less often than annually, from a charitable remainder annuity trust, as defined in paragraph one of subdivision (d) of section six hundred sixty-four of the United States Internal Revenue Code, a sum certain (which is not less than five percent of the initial net fair market value of all property placed in such trust) or from a charitable remainder unitrust, as defined in paragraph two of subdivision (d) of section six hundred sixty-four of such code, a fixed percentage (which is not less than five percent) of the net fair market value of its assets, valued annually, such testamentary provisions shall satisfy the provisions of this paragraph with respect to trusts with income payable to the surviving spouse for life.

(2) Where, after August thirty-first, nineteen hundred sixty-six, a person dies intestate as to all or any part of his estate, and, in the case of part intestacy, executes a will after such date, and is survived by a spouse, a personal right of election is given to the surviving spouse to take a share of the testamentary provisions made by the decedent, as such provisions are defined in subparagraph (1) (C), subject to the following:

(A) The share of the testamentary provisions to which the surviving spouse is entitled hereunder is his elective share, as defined in subparagraphs (1) (A) and (B), reduced by the capital value of all property passing to such spouse (i) in intestacy under 4-1.1, (ii) by testamentary substitute as described in subparagraph (b) (1) and (iii) by disposition under the decedent's last will.

(B) The satisfaction of such elective share shall not reduce the intestate share of any other distributee of the decedent.

(C) Whenever a testamentary provision for the surviving spouse takes the form of income payable for his life:

(i) The surviving spouse has the limited right to elect to take, absolutely, the sum of ten thousand dollars or the share to which he is entitled hereunder, whichever is less. Such sum, however, is inclusive of any absolute testamentary provision, as described in subparagraph (1) (C), and any amount to which the surviving spouse is entitled in intestacy under 4-1.1, and is payable from the principal of any trust, legal life estate or annuity created by such testamentary provision, the terms of which remain otherwise effective.

(ii) The provisions of subparagraph (1) (J) apply.

(d) General provisions governing right of election.

(1) Where an election has been made under this section, the will or other instrument making a testamentary provision, as the case may be, is valid as to the residue after the share to which the surviving spouse is entitled has been deducted, and the terms of such will or instrument remain otherwise effective so far as possible.

(2) Whenever a will creates a trust, legal life estate or annuity for the benefit of the surviving spouse for life, and such will commands, directs, authorizes or permits the fiduciary to allocate, apportion or charge receipts or expenses to principal or income in such manner as will or might deprive the spouse of income as defined in section 11-2.1 of this act or in any other law applicable to such trust, legal life estate or annuity, and where such trust, legal life estate or annuity, but for such will provision would satisfy the elective share of the spouse in whole or in part, such command, direction, authorization or permission shall not of itself give the surviving spouse an absolute right to take his elective share. The surrogate's court having jurisdiction of the decedent's estate may, in any appropriate proceeding, direct and enforce for the protection of the surviving spouse an allocation, apportionment or charge of all receipts and expenses in accordance with applicable legal or equitable principles so as to assure such surviving spouse of all or substantially all of the income of such trust, legal life estate or annuity consistent with the purposes and provisions of this section. The court may enjoin any fiduciary from exercising any power, authority or permission or doing any act which would be prejudicial to the rights and interests of such surviving spouse under this section. The court may enforce the liability of a fiduciary under the law and make such directions, consistent with the purposes and provisions of this section, as it may consider necessary for the protection of the surviving spouse.

(3) Except as otherwise expressly provided in the will or other instrument making a testamentary provision, ratable contribution to the share to which the surviving spouse is entitled shall be made by the beneficiaries (including the recipients of any such testamentary provision), other than the surviving spouse, under:

(A) In the case of an election under paragraph (a), the decedent's will.

(B) In the case of an election under paragraph (c), the decedent's will and other instruments making testamentary provisions.

(4) The right of election is personal to the surviving spouse, except that an election may be made by:

(A) The guardian of the property of an infant spouse, when so authorized by the surrogate having jurisdiction of the decedent's estate.

(B) The committee of an incompetent spouse, when so authorized by the supreme court.

(C) The conservator of conservatee spouse, when so authorized by the supreme court.

(5) Any question arising as to the right of election shall be determined by the surrogate's court having jurisdiction of the decedent's estate in a proceeding brought for that purpose on notice to all interested persons in such manner as the court may direct, or in a proceeding for the judicial settlement of the accounts of the personal representative.

(6) Upon application by a surviving spouse who has made an election under this section, the surrogate may make an order cancelling such election, provided that no adverse rights have intervened and no prejudice is shown to creditors of such spouse or other persons interested in the estate. Such application shall be made on notice to such persons and in such manner as the court may direct. A certified copy of such order shall be indexed and recorded in the same manner as a notice of pendency of an action in the office of the clerk of the county in which any real property of the decedent is situated.

(7) The right of election granted by this section is not available to the spouse of a decedent who was not domiciled in this state at the time of death, unless such decedent elects, under paragraph (h) of 3-5.1, to have the disposition of his property situated in this state governed by the laws of this state.

(8) The decedent's estate shall include all property of the decedent, wherever situated.

(9) An election made by the surviving spouse under this section is in lieu of any right of dower to which such spouse may be entitled.

(e) Procedure for exercise of right of election.

(1) An election under this section must be made within six months from the date of issuance of letters testamentary or of administration, as the case may be. Written notice of such election shall be served upon any personal representative in the manner herein provided, or upon a person named as executor in a will on file in the surrogate's court in a case where such will has not yet been admitted to probate, and the original thereof shall be filed and recorded, with proof of service, in the surrogate's court in which such letters were issued within six months from the date of the issuance of letters. Such notice may be served by mailing a copy thereof, addressed to any personal representative, or to the nominated executor, as the case may be, at the place of residence stated in the designation required by SCPA 708 or in such other manner as the surrogate may direct.

(2) The time to make such election may be extended before its expiration by an order of the surrogate's court from which such letters issued for a further period not exceeding six months upon any one application. If a spouse defaults in filing such election within six months from the date of issuance of such letters, the surrogate's court may relieve the spouse from such default and authorize the making of an election within the period fixed

by the order, provided that no decree settling the account of the personal representative has been made and that twelve months have not elapsed since the issuance of letters. An application for relief from a default and for an extension of time to elect shall be made upon a petition showing reasonable cause and on notice to such persons and in such manner as the surrogate may direct. A certified copy of such order shall be indexed and recorded in the same manner as a notice of pendency of an action in the office of the clerk of each county in which real property of the decedent is situated.

(3) The time limited in this paragraph for making an election is exclusive and shall not be suspended or otherwise affected by any provision of law, except that the surrogate may, in his discretion, permit an election to be made in behalf of an infant or incompetent spouse at any time up to, but not later than, the entry of the decree of the first judicial account of the permanent representative of the estate, made more than seven months after the issuance of letters.

(f) Waiver or release of right of election.

(1) A spouse, during the lifetime of the other, may waive or release a right of election, granted by this section, against a particular or any last will or a testamentary substitute, as described in subparagraph (b) (1), made by the other spouse. A waiver or release of all rights in the estate of the other spouse is a waiver or release of a right of election against any such last will or testamentary provision.

(2) To be effective under this section, a waiver or release must be in writing and subscribed by the maker thereof, and acknowledged or proved in the manner required by the laws of this state for the recording of a conveyance of real property.

(3) Such a waiver or release is effective, in accordance with its terms, whether:

(A) Executed before or after the marriage of the spouses.

(B) Executed before, on or after September first, nineteen hundred sixty-six.

(C) Unilateral in form, executed only by the maker thereof, or bilateral in form, executed by both spouses.

(D) Executed with or without consideration.

(E) Absolute or conditional.

History: Add, L 1966, ch 952, eff Sept 1, 1967, with substance deriving from Decedent Est. Law § 18, § 18-a, and 18-b; amd, L 1967, ch 686, eff Sept 1, 1967; L 1968, ch 168, eff April 9, 1968; L 1968, ch 257, eff May 14, 1968; L 1968, ch 853, eff July 1, 1968; L 1969, ch 773, § 1, eff Sept 1, 1969; L 1971, ch 798, eff Sept 1, 1971; L 1972, ch 327, eff Sept 1, 1972; L 1975, ch 87, eff May 13, 1975; L 1981, ch 115, § 42, eff May 18, 1981; L 1986, ch 246, § 1, eff Sept 29, 1986, applying to the estates, and to instruments making dispositions or appointments thereof, of persons living on its effective date or born subsequent thereto, without regard to the date of execution of any such instrument; except that this act shall not impair or defeat any rights which have accrued under dispositions or appointments in effect prior to its effective date.

§ 5-1.1-A. Right of election by surviving spouse [*Decedents dying on or after 9/1/92*]

(a) Where a decedent dies on or after September first, nineteen hundred ninety-two and is survived by a spouse, a personal right of election is given to the surviving spouse to take a share of the decedent's estate, subject to the following:

(1) For the purpose of this section, the decedent's estate includes the capital value, as of the decedent's death, of any property described in subparagraph (b) (1).

(2) The elective share, as used in this paragraph, is the pecuniary amount equal to the greater of (i) fifty thousand dollars or, if the capital value of the net estate is less than fifty thousand dollars, such capital value, or (ii) one third of the net estate. In computing the net estate, debts, administration expenses and reasonable funeral expenses shall be deducted, but all estate taxes shall be disregarded, except that nothing contained herein relieves the surviving spouse from contributing to all such taxes the amounts apportioned against him or her under 2-1.8.

(3) The term "testamentary provision", as used in this paragraph, includes, in addition to dispositions made by the decedent's will, distributions of property pursuant to 4-1.1 and any transaction described as a testamentary substitute in subparagraph (b) (1).

(4) The share of the testamentary provisions to which the surviving spouse is entitled hereunder (the "net elective share") is his or her elective share, as defined in subparagraphs (1) and (2), reduced by the capital value of any interest which passes absolutely from the decedent to such spouse, or which would have passed absolutely from the decedent to such spouse but was renounced by the spouse, (i) by intestacy, (ii) by testamentary substitute as described in subparagraph (b) (1), or (iii) by disposition under the decedent's last will.

(A) Unless the decedent has provided otherwise, if a spouse elects under this section, such election shall have the same effect with respect to any interest which passes or would have passed to the spouse, other than absolutely, as though the spouse died on the same date but immediately before the death of the decedent.

(B) For the purposes of this subparagraph (4), (i) an interest in property shall be deemed to pass other than absolutely from the decedent to the spouse if the interest so passing consists of less than the decedent's entire interest in that property or consists of any interest in a trust or trust equivalent created by the decedent; and (ii) an interest in property shall be deemed to pass absolutely from the decedent to the spouse if it is not deemed to pass other than absolutely.

(5) Where a decedent dies before September first, nineteen hundred ninety-four, paragraphs (c)(1)(D) through (c)(1)(K) of section 5-1.1 shall apply except that the words "fifty thousand dollars" shall be substituted for the words "ten thousand dollars" wherever they appear in such paragraphs.

(b) Inter vivos dispositions treated as testamentary substitutes for the purpose of election by surviving spouse.

(1) Where a person dies after August thirty-first, nineteen hundred ninety-two and is survived by a spouse who exercises a right of election under paragraph (a), the transactions affected by and property interests of the decedent described in clauses (A) through (H), whether benefiting the surviving spouse or any other person, shall be treated as testamentary substitutes and the capital value thereof, as of the decedent's death, shall be included in the net estate subject to the surviving spouse's elective right except to the extent that the surviving spouse has executed a waiver of release pursuant to paragraph (e) with respect thereto. Notwithstanding the foregoing, a transaction, other than a transaction described in clause (G), that is irrevocable or is revocable only with the consent of a person having a substantial adverse interest (including any such transactions with respect to which

the decedent retained a special power of appointment as defined in 10-3.2), will constitute a testamentary substitute only if it is effected after the date of the marriage.

(A) Gifts causa mortis.

(B) The aggregate transfers of property (including the transfer, release or relinquishment of any property interest which, but for such transfer, release or relinquishment, would come within the scope of clause (F)), other than gifts causa mortis and transfers coming within the scope of clauses (G) and (H), to or for the benefit of any person, made after August thirty-first, nineteen hundred ninety-two, and within one year of the death of the decedent, to the extent that the decedent did not receive adequate and full consideration in money or money's worth for such transfers; provided, however, that any portion of any such transfer that was excludible from taxable gifts pursuant to subsections (b) and (e) of section two thousand five hundred three of the United States Internal Revenue Code, including any amounts excluded as a result of the election by the surviving spouse to treat any such transfer as having been made one half by him or her, shall not be treated as a testamentary substitute.

(C) Money deposited, together with all dividends or interest credited thereon, in a savings account in the name of the decedent in trust for another person, with a banking organization, savings and loan association, foreign banking corporation or organization or bank or savings and loan association organized under the laws of the United States, and remaining on deposit at the date of the decedent's death.

(D) Money deposited after August thirty-first, nineteen hundred sixty-six, together with all dividends or interest credited thereon, in the name of the decedent and another person and payable on death, pursuant to the terms of the deposit or by operation of law, to the survivor, with a banking organization, savings and loan association, foreign banking corporation or organization or bank or savings and loan association organized under the laws of the United States, and remaining on deposit at the date of the decedent's death.

(E) Any disposition of property made by the decedent whereby property, at the date of his or her death, is held (i) by the decedent and another person as joint tenants with a right of survivorship or as tenants by the entirety where the disposition was made after August thirty-first, nineteen hundred sixty-six, or (ii) by the decedent and is payable on his or her death to a person other than the decedent or his or her estate.

(F) Any disposition of property or contractual arrangement made by the decedent, in trust or otherwise, to the extent that the decedent (i) after August thirty-first, nineteen hundred ninety-two, retained for his or her life or for any period not ascertainable without reference to his or her death or for any period which does not in fact end before his or her death the possession or enjoyment of, or the right to income from, the property except to the extent that such disposition or contractual arrangement was for an adequate consideration in money or money's worth; or (ii) at the date of his or her death retained either alone or in conjunction with any other person who does not have a substantial adverse interest, by the express provisions of the disposing instrument, a power to revoke such disposition or a power to consume, invade or dispose of the principal thereof. The provisions of this subparagraph shall not affect the right of any income beneficiary to the income undistributed or accrued at the date of death nor shall

EPTL

they impair or defeat any right which has vested on or before August thirty-first, nineteen hundred ninety-two.

(G) Any money, securities or other property payable under a thrift, savings, retirement, pension, deferred compensation, death benefit, stock bonus or profit-sharing plan, account, arrangement, system or trust, except that with respect to a plan to which subsection (a) (11) of section four hundred one of the United States Internal Revenue Code applies or a defined contribution plan to which such subsection does not apply pursuant to paragraph (B) (iii) thereof, only to the extent of fifty percent of the capital value thereof. Notwithstanding the foregoing, a transaction described herein shall not constitute a testamentary substitute if the decedent designated the beneficiary or beneficiaries of the plan benefits on or before September first, nineteen hundred ninety-two and did not change such beneficiary designation thereafter.

(H) Any interest in property to the extent the passing of the principal thereof to or for the benefit of any person was subject to a presently exercisable general power of appointment, as defined in section two thousand forty-one of the United States Internal Revenue Code, held by the decedent immediately before his or her death or which the decedent, within one year of his or her death, released (except to the extent such release results from a lapse of the power which is not treated as a release pursuant to section two thousand forty-one of the United States Internal Revenue Code) or exercised in favor of any person other than himself or herself or his or her estate.

(I) A transfer of a security to a beneficiary pursuant to part 4 of article 13 of this chapter.

(2) Transactions described in clause (D) or (E) (i) shall be treated as testamentary substitutes in the proportion that the funds on deposit were the property of the decedent immediately before the deposit or the consideration for the property described in clause (E) (i) was furnished by the decedent. The surviving spouse shall have the burden of establishing the proportion of the decedent's contribution; provided, however, that where the surviving spouse is the other party to the transaction, it will be conclusively presumed that the proportion of the decedent's contribution is one-half. For the purpose of this subparagraph, the court may accept such evidence as is relevant and competent, whether or not the person offering such evidence would otherwise be competent to testify.

(3) The property referred to in clause (E) shall include United States savings bonds and other United States obligations.

(4) The provisions of this paragraph shall not prevent a corporation or other person from paying or transferring any funds or property to a person otherwise entitled thereto, unless there has been served personally upon such corporation or other person a certified copy of an order enjoining such payment or transfer made by the surrogate's court having jurisdiction of the decedent's estate or by another court of competent jurisdiction. A corporation or other person paying or transferring any funds or property described in clause (G) of subparagraph one of this paragraph to a person otherwise entitled thereto, shall be held harmless and free from any liability for making such payment or transfer, in any action or proceeding which involves such funds or property. Such order may be made, on notice to such persons and in such manner as the court may direct, upon application of the surviving spouse or any other interested party and on proof that the surviving spouse has exercised his or her right of election under paragraph (a). Service of a certified copy

of such order on the corporation or other person holding such fund or property shall be a defense, during the effective period of the order, in any action or proceeding which involves such fund or property.

(5) This paragraph shall not impair or defeat the rights of creditors of the decedent with respect to any matter as to which any such creditor has rights.

(6) In case of a conflict between this paragraph and any other provision of law affecting the transactions described in subparagraph (1) of this paragraph, this paragraph controls.

(7) If any part of this section is preempted by federal law with respect to a payment or an item of property included in the net estate, a person who, not for value, received that payment or item of property is obligated to return to the surviving spouse that payment or item of property or is personally liable to the surviving spouse for the amount of that payment or the value of that item of property, to the extent required under this section.

(c) General provisions governing right of election.

(1) Where an election has been made under this section, the will or other instrument making a testamentary provision, as the case may be, is valid as to the residue after the share to which the surviving spouse is entitled has been deducted, and the terms of such will or instrument remain otherwise effective so far as possible, subject, however, to the provisions of clause (a)(4)(A).

(2) Except as otherwise expressly provided in the will or other instrument making a testamentary provision, ratable contribution to the share to which the surviving spouse is entitled shall be made by the beneficiaries and distributees (including the recipients of any such testamentary provision), other than the surviving spouse, under the decedent's will, by intestacy and other instruments making testamentary provisions, which contribution may be made in cash or in the specific property received from the decedent by the person required to make such contribution or partly in cash and partly in such property as such person in his or her discretion shall determine.

(3) The right of election is personal to the surviving spouse, except that an election may be made by:

(A) The guardian of the property of an infant spouse, when so authorized by the court having jurisdiction of the decedent's estate.

(B) The committee of an incompetent spouse, when so authorized by the court that appointed the committee.

(C) The conservator of a conservatee spouse, when so authorized by the court that appointed the conservator.

(D) The guardian ad litem for the surviving spouse when so authorized by the court that appointed such guardian.

(E) A guardian authorized under Article 81 of the mental hygiene law, when so authorized by the court that appointed the guardian.

(4) Any question arising as to the right of election shall be determined by the court having jurisdiction of the decedent's estate in a proceeding brought for that purpose on notice to all interested persons in such manner as the court may direct, or in a proceeding

for the judicial settlement of the accounts of the personal representative.

(5) Upon application by a surviving spouse who has made an election under this section, the court may make an order cancelling such election, provided that no adverse rights have intervened and no prejudice is shown to creditors of such spouse or other persons interested in the estate. Such application shall be made on notice to such persons and in such manner as the court may direct. A certified copy of such order shall be indexed and recorded in the same manner as a notice of pendency of an action in the office of the clerk of the county in which any real property of the decedent is situated.

(6) The right of election granted by this section is not available to the spouse of a decedent who was not domiciled in this state at the time of death, unless such decedent has elected, under paragraph (h) of 3-5.1, to have the disposition of his or her property situated in this state governed by the laws of this state.

(7) The decedent's estate shall include all property of the decedent wherever situated.

(8) An election made by the surviving spouse under this section is in lieu of any right of dower to which such spouse may be entitled.

(9) The references in this paragraph to sections of the United States Internal Revenue Code are to the Internal Revenue Code of 1986, as amended. Such references, however, shall be deemed to constitute references to any corresponding provisions of any subsequent federal tax code.

(d) Procedure for exercise of right of election.

(1) An election under this section must be made within six months from the date of issuance of letters testamentary or of administration, as the case may be, but in no event later than two years after the date of decedent's death, except as otherwise provided in subparagraph 2 of this paragraph. Written notice of such election shall be served upon any personal representative in the manner herein provided, or upon a person named as executor in a will on file in the surrogate's court in a case where such will has not yet been admitted to probate, and the original thereof shall be filed and recorded, with proof of service, in the surrogate's court in which such letters were issued within six months from the date of the issuance of letters but in no event later than two years from the date of decedent's death, except as otherwise provided in subparagraph 2 of this paragraph. Such notice may be served by mailing a copy thereof, addressed to any personal representative, or to the nominated executor, as the case may be, at the place of residence stated in the designation required by section 708 of the surrogate's court procedure act, to the domicile address of such nominated executor, or in such other manner as the surrogate may direct.

(2) The time to make such election may be extended before expiration by an order of the surrogate's court from which such letters issued for a further period not exceeding six months upon any one application. If the spouse defaults in filing such election within the time provided in subparagraph (1) of this paragraph, the surrogate's court may relieve the spouse from such default and authorize the making of an election within the period fixed by the order, provided that no decree settling the account of the personal representative has been made and that twelve months have not elapsed since the issuance of the letters, and two years have not elapsed since the decedent's date of death, in the case of initial application; except that the court may, in its discretion for good cause shown, extend the time to make such election beyond such period of two years. An application for relief from

the default and for an extension of time to elect shall be made upon a petition showing reasonable cause and on notice to such persons and in such manner as the surrogate may direct. A certified copy of such order shall be indexed and recorded in the same manner as a notice of pendency of an action in the office of the clerk of each county in which real property of the decedent is situated.

(3) The time limited in this paragraph for making an election is exclusive and shall not be suspended or otherwise affected by any provision of law, except that the surrogate may, in his or her discretion, permit an election to be made in behalf of an infant or incompetent spouse at any time up to, but no later than, the entry of the decree of the first judicial account of the representative of the estate, made more than seven months after the issuance of letters.

(e) Waiver or release of right of election.

(1) A spouse, during the lifetime of the other, may waive or release a right of election, granted by this section, against a particular or any last will or a testamentary substitute, as described in subparagraph (b) (1) made by the other spouse. A waiver or release of all rights in the estate of the other spouse is a waiver or release of a right of election against any such last will or testamentary provision.

(2) To be effective under this section, a waiver or release must be in writing and subscribed by the maker thereof, and acknowledged or proved in the manner required by the laws of this state for the recording of a conveyance of real property.

(3) Such a waiver or release is effective, in accordance with its terms, whether:

(A) Executed before or after the marriage of the spouses.

(B) Executed before, on or after September first, nineteen hundred sixty-six.

(C) Unilateral in form, executed only by the maker thereof, or bilateral in form, executed by both spouses.

(D) Executed with or without consideration.

(E) Absolute or conditional.

(4) If there is in effect at the time of the decedent's death a waiver, or a consent to the decedent's waiver, executed by the surviving spouse with respect to any survivor benefit, or right to such benefit, under subsection (a) (11) of section four hundred one or section four hundred seventeen of the United States Internal Revenue Code, then such waiver shall be deemed to be a waiver within the meaning of this paragraph (e) against the testamentary substitute constituting such benefit.

History: Add, L 1992, ch 595, § 10, eff Sept 1, 1992, applying only to the estate of a decedent who dies on or after September 1, 1992; amd, L 1993, ch 515, § 3, eff Jan 1, 1994; L 2005, ch 325, § 6, eff Jan 1, 2006; L 2010, ch 545, § 1, eff Jan 1, 2011; L 2018, ch 228, § 1, eff Aug 24, 2018.

§ 5-1.2. Disqualification as surviving spouse

(a)* A husband or wife is a surviving spouse within the meaning, and for the purposes of

---

* **Ed. Note**: There is no paragraph (b).

4-1.1, 5-1.1, 5-1.1-A, 5-1.3, 5-3.1 and 5-4.4, unless it is established satisfactorily to the court having jurisdiction of the action or proceeding that:

(1) A final decree or judgment of divorce, of annulment or declaring the nullity of a marriage or dissolving such marriage on the ground of absence, recognized as valid under the law of this state, was in effect when the deceased spouse died.

(2) The marriage was void as incestuous under section five of the domestic relations law, bigamous under section six thereof, or a prohibited remarriage under section eight thereof.

(3) The spouse had procured outside of this state a final decree or judgment of divorce from the deceased spouse, of annulment or declaring the nullity of the marriage with the deceased spouse or dissolving such marriage on the ground of absence, not recognized as valid under the law of this state.

(4) A final decree or judgment of separation, recognized as valid under the law of this state, was rendered against the spouse, and such decree or judgment was in effect when the deceased spouse died.

(5) The spouse abandoned the deceased spouse, and such abandonment continued until the time of death.

(6) A spouse who, having the duty to support the other spouse, failed or refused to provide for such spouse though he or she had the means or ability to do so, unless such marital duty was resumed and continued until the death of the spouse having the need of support.

History: Add, L 1966, ch 952, eff Sept 1, 1967, with substance deriving from Decedent Est. Law § 50 and § 87; amd, L 1981, ch 300, § 2, eff Sept 1, 1981; L 1993, ch 515, § 4, eff Jan 1, 1994.

§ 5-1.3. Revocatory effect of marriage after execution of will

(a) If the testator leaves a will executed prior to September first, nineteen hundred thirty and marries at any time after such will was executed, the spouse who survives such testator is entitled to succeed to the same portion of the testator's estate as would have passed to such spouse had the testator died intestate, unless provision was made for the surviving spouse by ante nuptial agreement in writing. No evidence shall be admissible to impair or defeat the rights of a surviving spouse hereunder except to establish the existence of such ante nuptial agreement.

(b) A surviving spouse may recover the portion of the testator's estate to which he is entitled under this section from the beneficiaries, ratably, out of the portions of the estate passing to such persons under the will. In abating the interests of the beneficiaries the character of the testamentary plan adopted by the testator shall be preserved to the maximum extent possible.

(c) A surviving spouse may waive his right under this section to an intestate share of the testator's estate, and may accept in lieu thereof any benefits he may have received, in whatever status, under the will.

History: Add, L 1966, ch 952, eff Sept 1, 1967, with substance deriving from Decedent Est. Law § 35.

§ 5-1.4. Revocatory effect of divorce, annulment or declaration of nullity, or dissolution of marriage on disposition, appointment, provision, or nomination regarding a former spouse

(a) Except as provided by the express terms of a governing instrument, a divorce (including a judicial separation as defined in subparagraph (f)(2)) or annulment of a marriage revokes any revocable (1) disposition or appointment of property made by a divorced individual to, or for the benefit of, the former spouse, including, but not limited to, a disposition or appointment by will, by security registration in beneficiary form (TOD), by beneficiary designation in a life insurance policy or (to the extent permitted by law) in a pension or retirement benefits plan, or by revocable trust, including a bank account in trust form, (2) provision conferring a power of appointment or power of disposition on the former spouse, and (3) nomination of the former spouse to serve in any fiduciary or representative capacity, including as a personal representative, executor, trustee, conservator, guardian, agent, or attorney-in-fact.

(b) (1) Provisions of a governing instrument are given effect as if the former spouse had predeceased the divorced individual as of the time of the revocation.

(2) A disposition, appointment, provision, or nomination revoked solely by this section shall be revived by the divorced individual's remarriage to the former spouse.

(c) Except as provided by the express terms of a governing instrument, a divorce (including a judicial separation as defined in subparagraph (f)(2)) or annulment of a marriage severs the interests of the divorced individual and the former spouse in property held by them at the time of the divorce or annulment as joint tenants with the right of survivorship, transforming their interests into interests as tenants in common.

(d) (1) A payor or other third party is not liable for having made a payment or transferred an item of property or any other benefit to a beneficiary (including a former spouse) designated in a governing instrument affected by a divorce, annulment, or remarriage, or for having taken any other action in good faith reliance on the validity of the governing instrument, before the payor or other third party received written notice of the divorce, annulment, or remarriage.

(2) Written notice of a divorce, annulment, or remarriage under subparagraph (1) must be mailed to the payor's or other third party's main office or home by registered or certified mail, return receipt requested, or served upon the payor or other third party in the same manner as a summons in a civil action and may be filed with the secretary of state if real property or a cooperative apartment is affected. Upon receipt of written notice of the divorce, annulment, or remarriage, a payor or other third party may pay any amount owed or transfer or deposit any item of property held by it or with the court having jurisdiction of the probate proceedings relating to the decedent's estate or, if no proceedings have been commenced, to or with the court having jurisdiction over the divorce, the real property or cooperative apartment, securities, bank accounts or other assets affected by the divorce or annulment under this section. The court shall hold the funds or item of property and, upon its determination under this section, shall order disbursement or transfer in accordance with the determination. Payments, transfers, or deposits made to or with the court discharge the payor or other third party from all claims for the value of amounts paid to or items of property transferred to or deposited with the court.

EPTL

(e) A person who purchases property from a former spouse or any other person for value and without notice, or who receives from a former spouse or any other person, a payment or other item of property in partial or full satisfaction of a legally enforceable obligation, is neither obligated under this section to return the payment, item of property or benefit, nor is liable under this section for the amount of the payment or the value of the item of property or benefit. But a former spouse or other person who, not for value, received a payment, item of property or any other benefit to which that person is not entitled under this section is obligated to return the payment, item of property or benefit, with interest thereon, to the person who is entitled to it under this section.

(f) For purposes of this section, the following terms shall have the following meaning and effect:

(1) "Disposition or appointment of property" includes a transfer of an item of property or any other benefit to a beneficiary designated in a governing instrument.

(2) "Divorce or annulment" means a final decree or judgment of divorce or annulment, or a final decree, judgment or order declaring the nullity of a marriage or dissolving such marriage on the ground of absence, recognized as valid under the law of this state, or a "judicial separation," which means a final decree or judgment of separation, recognized as valid under the law of this state, which was rendered against the spouse.

(3) "Divorced individual" includes an individual whose marriage has been annulled or subjected to a judicial separation.

(4) "Former spouse" means a person whose marriage to the divorced individual has been the subject of a divorce, annulment, or judicial separation.

(5) "Governing instrument" includes, but is not limited to, a will, testamentary instrument, trust agreement (including, but not limited to a totten trust account under 7-5.1(d)), insurance policy, thrift, savings, retirement, pension, deferred compensation, death benefit, stock bonus or profit-sharing plan, account, arrangement, system or trust, agreement with a bank, brokerage firm or investment company, registration of securities in beneficiary form pursuant to part 4 of article 13 of this chapter, a court order, or a contract relating to the division of property made between the divorced individuals before or after the marriage, divorce, or annulment.

(6) "Revocable," with respect to a disposition, appointment, provision, or nomination, means one under which the divorced individual, at the time of the divorce or annulment, was empowered, by law or under governing instrument, either alone or in conjunction with any other person who does not have a substantial adverse interest, to cancel the designation in favor of the former spouse, whether or not the divorced individual was then empowered to designate himself or herself in place of the former spouse and whether or not the divorced individual then had the capacity to exercise the power.

History: Former section repealed and new section added L 2008, ch 173, § 1, eff July 7, 2008. "This section shall apply only where the marriage of a person executing a disposition, appointment, provision or nomination in a governing instrument, as defined in EPTL 5-1.4(f)(5), such section as added by section one of this act, to or for the benefit of a former spouse ends in a divorce or annulment, as defined in EPTL 5-1.4(f)(2), on or after such effective date or, where such a marriage ends prior to such effective date, only where such a disposition, appointment, provision or nomination takes effect only at the death of the person who executes it and such person dies on or after the effective date of this act."

PART 3   Rights of Family Unit

§ 5-3.1. Exemption for benefit of family

(a) If a person dies, leaving a surviving spouse or children under the age of twenty-one years, the following items of property are not assets of the estate but vest in, and shall be set off to such surviving spouse, unless disqualified, under 5-1.2, from taking an elective or distributive share of the decedent's estate. In case there is no surviving spouse or such spouse, if surviving, is disqualified, such items of property vest in, and shall be set off to the decedent's children under the age of twenty-one years:

(1) All housekeeping utensils, musical instruments, sewing machine, jewelry unless disposed of in the will, clothing of the decedent, household furniture and appliances, electronic and photographic devices, and fuel for personal use, not exceeding in aggregate value twenty thousand dollars. This subparagraph shall not include items used exclusively for business purposes.

(2) The family bible or other religious books, family pictures, books, computer tapes, discs and software, DVDs, CDs, audio tapes, record albums, and other electronic storage devices, including but not limited to videotapes, used by such family, not exceeding in value two thousand five hundred dollars.

(3) Domestic and farm animals with their necessary food for sixty days, farm machinery, one tractor and one lawn tractor, not exceeding in aggregate value twenty thousand dollars.

(4) The surviving spouse or decedent's children may acquire items referred to in subparagraphs (1), (2) and (3) of this paragraph, in excess of the values set forth in such subparagraphs by payment to the estate of the amount by which the value of the items acquired exceeds the amounts set forth in such subparagraphs. If any item so acquired by the spouse or children of the decedent was a specific legacy in decedent's will, the payment to the estate for such item shall vest in the specific legatee.

(5) One motor vehicle not exceeding in value twenty-five thousand dollars. In the alternative, if the decedent shall have been the owner of one or more motor vehicles each of which exceed twenty-five thousand dollars in value, the surviving spouse or decedent's children may acquire one such motor vehicle from the estate, regardless of the fact that the decedent may also have been the owner of another motor vehicle of lesser value than twenty-five thousand dollars, by payment to the estate of the amount by which the value of the motor vehicle exceeds twenty-five thousand dollars; in lieu of receiving such motor vehicle, the surviving spouse or children may elect to receive in cash an amount equal to the value of the motor vehicle, not to exceed twenty-five thousand dollars. If any motor vehicle so acquired by the spouse or children of the decedent was a specific legacy in decedent's will, the payment to the estate of the amount by which the value of the motor vehicle exceeds twenty-five thousand dollars shall vest in the specific legatee.

(6) Money including but not limited to cash, checking, savings and money market accounts, certificates of deposit or equivalents thereof, and marketable securities, not exceeding in value twenty-five thousand dollars, reduced by the excess value, if any, of acquired items referred to in subparagraphs (1), (2), (3) and (5) of this paragraph. However, where assets are insufficient to pay the reasonable funeral expenses of the decedent, the personal representative must first apply such money to defray any deficiency in such expenses.

(7) Any set off to a child under the age of twenty-one years not exceeding ten thousand dollars shall be covered by the provisions of section twenty-two hundred twenty of the surrogate's court procedure act as if the child were a beneficiary of the estate. Any excess amounts shall be governed by the guardianship statute, if applicable.

(8) The court shall have the authority to issue such documentation as necessary to effectuate the transfer of any items under this section.

(b) No allowance shall be made in money or other property if the items of property described in subparagraph (1), (2), (3) or (5) of paragraph (a) are not in existence when the decedent dies.

(c) The items of property, set off as provided in paragraph (a), shall, at least to the extent thereof, be deemed reasonably required for the support of the surviving spouse or children under the age of twenty-one years of the decedent during the settlement of the estate.

(d) As used in this section, the term "value" shall refer to the fair market value of each item, reduced by all outstanding security interests or other encumbrances affecting the decedent's ownership of said item.

History: Add, L 1966, ch 952, eff Sept 1, 1967, with substance deriving from Sur Ct Act § 200; amd, L 1967, ch 686, eff Sept 1, 1967; L 1971, ch 149, eff Sept 1, 1971; L 1974, ch 903, eff Sept 1, 1974; L 1980, ch 82, eff April 28, 1980; L 1983, ch 103, eff May 17, 1983; L 1992, ch 595, § 11, eff Sept 1, 1992; L 2010, ch 437, § 1, eff Jan 1, 2011; L 2012, ch 123, §§ 1, 2, eff July 18, 2012, and deemed to have been in full force and effect on and after Jan 1, 2011.

§ 5-3.2. Revocatory effect of birth of child after execution of will

(a) Whenever a testator has a child born after the execution of a last will, and dies leaving the after-born child unprovided for by any settlement, and neither provided for nor in any way mentioned in the will, every such child shall succeed to a portion of the testator's estate as herein provided:

(1) If the testator has one or more children living when he executes his last will, and:

(A) No provision is made therein for any such child, an after-born child is not entitled to share in the testator's estate.

(B) Provision is made therein for one or more of such children, an after-born child is entitled to share in the testator's estate, as follows:

(i) The portion of the testator's estate in which the after-born child may share is limited to the disposition made to children under the will.

(ii) The after-born child shall receive such share of the testator's estate, as limited in subclause (i), as he would have received had the testator included all after-born children with the children upon whom benefits were conferred under the will, and given an equal share of the estate to each such child.

(iii) If it appears from the will that the intention of the testator was to make a limited provision which specifically applied only to the testator's children living at the time the will was executed, the after-born child succeeds to the portion of such testator's estate as would have passed to such child had the testator died intestate.

(iv) To the extent that it is feasible, the interest of the after-born child in the testator's estate shall be of the same character, whether an equitable or legal life estate or in fee, as the interest which the testator conferred upon his children under the will.

(2) If the testator has no child living when he executes his last will, the after-born child succeeds to the portion of such testator's estate as would have passed to such child had the testator died intestate.

(b) The term "after-born child" shall mean a child of the testator born during the testator's lifetime or in gestation at the time of the testator's death and born thereafter. For purposes of this section, a non-marital child, born after the execution of a last will shall be considered an after-born child of his or her father where paternity is established pursuant to section 4-1.2 of this chapter.

(c) The after-born child may recover the share of the testator's estate to which such child is entitled, either from the other children under subparagraph (a) (1) (B) or the testamentary beneficiaries under subparagraph (a) (2), ratably, out of the portions of such estate passing to such persons under the will. In abating the interests of such beneficiaries, the character of the testamentary plan adopted by the testator shall be preserved to the maximum extent possible.

> **History:** Add, L 1966, ch 952, eff Sept 1, 1967 from Decedent Est. Law § 26; amd, L 1967, ch 686, § 44, eff Sept 1, 1967; L 1992, ch 611, § 1, eff July 24, 1992; L 2006, ch 249, §§ 1, 2, eff July 26, 2006, for decedents dying on or after July 26, 2006; L 2007, ch 423, § 1, eff Aug 1, 2007.

§ 5-3.3. [Repealed]

§ 5-3.4. Action in supreme court by child born after execution of will, by surviving spouse upon revocation of will by marriage or by subscribing witness with interest under will

In the event that the administration of a decedent's estate in the surrogate's court has been completed and the estate distributed, an action may be maintained in the supreme court by an after-born child under 5-3.2, a surviving spouse under 5-1.3 or an attesting witness under 3-3.2 to enforce rights under such sections against testamentary beneficiaries or distributees, as the case may be.

> **History:** Formerly § 5-3.3, add, L 1966, ch 952, with substance deriving from Decedent Est. Law § 28; renumbered § 5-3.4, L 1967, ch 683, § 2, eff Sept 1, 1967.

PART 4   Rights of Members of Family Resulting From Wrongful Act, Neglect or Default Causing Death of Decedent

§ 5-4.1. Action by personal representative for wrongful act, neglect or default causing death of decedent

1. The personal representative, duly appointed in this state or any other jurisdiction, of a decedent who is survived by distributees may maintain an action to recover damages for a wrongful act, neglect or default which caused the decedent's death against a person who would have been liable to the decedent by reason of such wrongful conduct if death had not ensued. Such an action must be commenced within two years after the decedent's death; provided, however, that an action on behalf of a decedent whose death was caused by the terrorist attacks on September eleventh, two thousand one, other than a decedent identified by the attorney general of the United States as a participant or conspirator in such attacks, must be commenced within two years and six months after the decedent's death. When the

distributees do not participate in the administration of the decedent's estate under a will appointing an executor who refuses to bring such action, the distributees are entitled to have an administrator appointed to prosecute the action for their benefit.

2. Whenever it is shown that a criminal action has been commenced against the same defendant with respect to the event or occurrence from which a claim under this section arises, the personal representative of the decedent shall have at least one year from the termination of the criminal action as defined in section 1.20 of the criminal procedure law in which to maintain an action, notwithstanding that the time in which to commence such action has already expired or has less than a year remaining.

History: Add, L 1966, ch 952, eff Sept 1, 1967, with substance deriving from Decedent Est. Law § 130; amd, L 1983, ch 95, § 2, eff May 17, 1983 and applicable to all pending civil and criminal actions; L 2003, ch 114, § 1, eff July 1, 2003.

§ 5-4.2. Trial and burden of proof of contributory negligence

On the trial of an action accruing before September first, nineteen hundred seventy-five to recover damages for causing death the contributory negligence of the decedent shall be a defense, to be pleaded and proved by the defendant.

History: Add, L 1966, ch 952, with substance deriving from Decedent Est. Law § 131; amd, L 1975, ch 69, eff Sept 1, 1975.

§ 5-4.3. Amount of recovery

(a) The damages awarded to the plaintiff may be such sum as the jury or, where issues of fact are tried without a jury, the court or referee deems to be fair and just compensation for the pecuniary injuries resulting from the decedent's death to the persons for whose benefit the action is brought. In every such action, in addition to any other lawful element of recoverable damages, the reasonable expenses of medical aid, nursing and attention incident to the injury causing death and the reasonable funeral expenses of the decedent paid by the distributees, or for the payment of which any distributee is responsible, shall also be proper elements of damage. Interest upon the principal sum recovered by the plaintiff from the date of the decedent's death shall be added to and be a part of the total sum awarded.

(b) Where the death of the decedent occurs on or after September first, nineteen hundred eighty-two, in addition to damages and expenses recoverable under paragraph (a) above, punitive damages may be awarded if such damages would have been recoverable had the decedent survived.

(c) (i) In any action in which the wrongful conduct is medical malpractice or dental malpractice, evidence shall be admissible to establish the federal, state and local personal income taxes which the decedent would have been obligated by law to pay.

(ii) In any such action tried by a jury, the court shall instruct the jury to consider the amount of federal, state and local personal income taxes which the jury finds, with reasonable certainty, that the decedent would have been obligated by law to pay in determining the sum that would otherwise be available for the support of persons for whom the action is brought.

(iii) In any such action tried without a jury, the court shall consider the amount of federal, state and local personal income taxes which the court finds, with reasonable certainty, that the decedent would have been obligated by law to pay in determining the sum that would otherwise be available for the support of persons for whom the action is brought.

> **History:** Add, L 1966, ch 952, eff Sept 1, 1967, with substance deriving from Decedent Est. Law § 132; amd, L 1982, ch 100, § 1, eff Sept 1, 1982; L 1986, ch 266, § 6, eff July 8, 1986, applicable to actions commenced on or after such date.

§ 5-4.4. Distribution of damages recovered

(a) The damages, as prescribed by 5-4.3, whether recovered in an action or by settlement without an action, are exclusively for the benefit of the decedent's distributees and, when collected, shall be distributed to the persons entitled thereto under 4-1.1 and 5-4.5, except that where the decedent is survived by a parent or parents and a spouse and no issue, the parent or parents will be deemed to be distributees for purposes of this section. The damages shall be distributed subject to the following:

(1) Such damages shall be distributed by the personal representative to the persons entitled thereto in proportion to the pecuniary injuries suffered by them, such proportions to be determined after a hearing, on application of the personal representative or any distributee, at such time and on notice to all interested persons in such manner as the court may direct. If no action is brought, such determination shall be made by the surrogate of the county in which letters were issued to the plaintiff; if an action is brought, by the court having jurisdiction of the action or by the surrogate of the county in which letters were issued.

(2) The court which determines the proportions of the pecuniary injuries suffered by the distributees, as provided in subparagraph (1), shall also decide any question concerning the disqualification of a parent, under 4-1.4, or a surviving spouse, under 5-1.2, to share in the damages recovered.

(b) The reasonable expenses of the action or settlement and, if included in the damages recovered, the reasonable expenses of medical aid, nursing and attention incident to the injury causing death and the reasonable funeral expenses of the decedent may be fixed by the court which determines the proportions of the pecuniary injuries suffered by the distributees, as provided in subparagraph (1), upon notice given in such manner and to such persons as the court may direct, and such expenses may be deducted from the damages recovered. The commissions of the personal representative upon the residue may be fixed by the surrogate, upon notice given in such manner and to such persons as the surrogate may direct or upon the judicial settlement of the account of the personal representative, and such commissions may be deducted from the damages recovered.

(c) In the event that an action is brought, as authorized in this part, and there is no recovery or settlement, the reasonable expenses of such unsuccessful action, excluding counsel fees, shall be payable out of the assets of the decedent's estate.

> **History:** Add, L 1966, ch 952, eff Sept 1, 1967, with substance deriving from Decedent Est. Law § 133; amd, L 1967, ch 686, § 45, eff Sept 1, 1967; L 1975, ch 357, § 1, eff July 1, 1975, but not affecting causes of action accruing prior to its effective date; L 1992, ch 595, § 12, eff Sept 1, 1992.

§ 5-4.5. Non-marital children

For the purposes of this part, a non-marital child is the distributee of his father and paternal kindred and the father and paternal kindred of a non-marital child are that child's distributees to the extent permitted by 4-1.2.

EPTL

History: Add, L 1975, ch 357, § 2, eff July 1, 1975, but not affecting causes of action accruing prior to its effective date; amd, L 1981, ch 67, eff April 8, 1981; L 1992, ch 595, § 13, eff Sept 1, 1992.

§ 5-4.6. Application to compromise action

(a) Within sixty days of the application of an administrator appointed under 5-4.1 or a personal representative to the court in which an action for wrongful act, neglect or default causing the death of a decedent is pending, the court shall, after inquiry into the merits of the action and the amount of damages proposed as a compromise either disapprove the application or approve in writing a compromise for such amount as it shall determine to be adequate including approval of attorneys fees and other payable expenses as set forth below, and shall order the defendant to pay all sums payable under the order of compromise, within the time frames set forth in section five thousand three-a of the civil practice law and rules, to the attorney for the administrator or personal representative for placement in an interest bearing escrow account for the benefit of the distributees. The order shall also provide for the following:

(1) Upon collection of the settlement funds and creation of an interest bearing escrow account, the attorney for the administrator or personal representative shall pay from the account all due and payable expenses, excluding attorneys fees, approved by the court, such as medical bills, funeral costs and other liens on the estate.

(2) All attorneys fees approved by the court for the prosecution of the action for wrongful act, neglect or default, inclusive of all disbursements, shall be immediately payable from the escrow account upon submission to the trial court proof of filing of a petition for allocation and distribution in the surrogate's court on behalf of the decedent's estate.

(3) The attorney for the administrator or personal representative in the action for wrongful act, neglect or default who receives payment under this section shall continue to serve as attorney for the estate until the entry of a final decree in the surrogate's court.

(b) If any of the distributees is an infant, incompetent, person who is incarcerated or person under disability, the court shall determine whether a guardian ad litem is required before any payments are made, in which case the court will seek an immediate appointment of a guardian ad litem by the surrogate's court or, if the surrogate's court defers, the court shall make such appointment. Any guardian appointed for this purpose shall continue to serve as the guardian ad litem for the person requiring same for all other purposes.

(c) The filing fee in the surrogate's court shall be computed based on the amount of the gross estate prior to any payments made under this paragraph.

(d) The written approval by such court of the compromise is conclusive evidence of the adequacy of the compromise in any proceeding in the surrogate's court for the final settlement of the account of such administrator or personal representative.

(e) Nothing in this section shall be deemed to preclude the attorney for the administrator or personal representative from petitioning the surrogate's court for approval of a compromise and for allocation and distribution thereof.

(f) No letters of administration shall be issued which will in any way serve to abrogate the rights or obligations of an administrator or personal representative or an attorney representing an administrator or personal representative under this section.

History: Formerly § 5-4.5, add, L 1966, ch 952, § 1, from Decedent Est. Law § 135, renumbered § 5-4.6; amd, L 1975, ch 357, eff July 1, 1975; L 1992, ch 595, eff Sept 1, 1992; L 2005, ch 719, § 1, eff Oct 11, 2005.

EPTL

ARTICLE 6
CLASSIFICATIONS, CREATION, DEFINITION OF, AND RULES GOVERNING ESTATES IN PROPERTY
SUMMARY OF ARTICLE

EPTL

PART 1   Estates Classified as to Duration

§ 6-1.1. Estates classified

(a) Estates in property as to duration are classified as follows:

(1) Fee simple absolute.

(2) Fee on condition.

(3) Fee on limitation.

(4) Estates for life.

(5) Estates for years.

(6) Estates from period to period.

(7) Estates at will.

(8) Estates by sufferance.

History: Add, L 1966, ch 952, eff Sept 1, 1967, with substance deriving from RPL § 30.

§ 6-1.2. Estates tail abolished; future estates limited thereon

Estates tail have been abolished, and every estate which would be a fee tail, according to the law of this state as it existed before the twelfth day of July, seventeen hundred eighty-two, shall be a fee simple; and if no valid future estate is limited thereon, a fee simple absolute. Where a future estate in fee is limited on any estate which would be a fee tail, according to the law of this state as it existed previous to such date, such future estate is valid and vests in possession on the death of the first taker without issue living at the time of his death.

History: Add, L 1966, ch 952, eff Sept 1, 1967, with substance deriving from RPL § 32.

§ 6-1.3. When estate for life of third person is real property; when personal property

A disposition of real property for the life of a third person, whether limited to heirs or otherwise, is real property only during the life of the grantee or devisee; after his death it is personal property.

History: Add, L 1966, ch 952, eff Sept 1, 1967, with substance deriving from RPL § 34;
    amd, L 1967, ch 686, § 46, eff Sept 1, 1967.

PART 2   Estates Classified as to Number of Persons

§ 6-2.1. Estates in severalty, joint tenancy, tenancy by the entirety and in common

Estates as to the number of persons owning an interest therein are classified as follows:

(1) In severalty.

(2) Joint tenancy.

(3) Tenancy in common.

(4) Only as to real property and, on and after January first, nineteen hundred ninety-six, as to the shares of stock of a cooperative apartment corporation allocated to an apartment or unit together with the appurtenant proprietary lease, tenancy by the entirety.

> **History:** Add, L 1966, ch 952, eff Sept 1, 1967, with substance deriving from RPL § 65; amd, L 1995, ch 480, § 1, eff Jan 1, 1996.

§ 6-2.2. When estate is in common, in joint tenancy or by the entirety

(a) A disposition of property to two or more persons creates in them a tenancy in common, unless expressly declared to be a joint tenancy.

(b) A disposition of real property to a husband and wife creates in them a tenancy by the entirety, unless expressly declared to be a joint tenancy or a tenancy in common.

(c) A disposition on or after January first, nineteen hundred ninety-six of the shares of stock of a cooperative apartment corporation allocated to an apartment or unit together with the appurtenant proprietary lease to a husband and wife creates in them a tenancy by the entirety, unless expressly declared to be a joint tenancy or a tenancy in the common*.

(d) A disposition of real property, or a disposition on or after January first, nineteen hundred ninety-six of the shares of stock of a cooperative apartment corporation allocated to an apartment or unit together with the appurtenant proprietary lease, to persons who are not legally married to one another but who are described in the disposition as husband and wife, spouses, husbands, or wives creates in them a joint tenancy, unless expressly declared to be a tenancy in common.

(e) A disposition of property to two or more persons as executors, trustees or guardians creates in them a joint tenancy.

(f) Property passing in intestacy to two or more persons is taken by them as tenants in common.

> **History:** Add, L 1966, ch 952, eff Sept 1, 1967, with substance deriving from Decedent Est. Law § 84 and RPL § 66; amd, L 1975, ch 263, eff Sept 1, 1975; L 1995, ch 480, § 2, eff Jan 1, 1996; L 2019, ch 420, § 2, eff Oct 29, 2019.

PART 3   Estates Classified as to Time of Enjoyment and Creation

§ 6-3.1. Estates in possession and future estates

Estates in property, as to the time of their enjoyment, are classified as estates in possession and future estates.

---

* So in original. Should probably be "tenancy in common".

History: Add, L 1966, ch 952, eff Sept 1, 1967, with substance deriving from RPL § 35.

§ 6-3.2. Kinds of future estates

(a) Future estates are divided into:

(1) Estates left in the creator, consisting of:

(A) Reversions.

(B) Possibilities of reverter.

(C) Rights of reacquisition.

(2) Estates in favor of a person other than the creator, namely remainders, that are:

(A) Indefeasibly vested.

(B) Vested subject to open.

(C) Vested subject to complete defeasance.

(D) Subject to a condition precedent.

History: Add, L 1966, ch 952, eff Sept 1, 1967, with substance deriving from RPL § 36.

§ 6-3.3. Concerning the creation of certain future estates

(a) Subject to the provisions of article 9:

(1) An estate may be created to commence at a future time.

(2) An estate for life may be created in a term of years and a future estate limited thereon.

(3) A future estate may be limited after a term of years, provided that, if such future estate is subject to a condition precedent, the condition must occur within the period prescribed by article 9.

(4) A fee or a lesser estate may be limited on a fee, subject to a condition precedent which must occur within the period prescribed by article 9.

History: Add, L 1966, ch 952, eff Sept 1, 1967, with substance deriving from RPL § 50.

§ 6-3.4. When future estates are created

A future estate is created when the disposition creating it becomes legally effective.

History: Add, L 1966, ch 952, eff Sept 1, 1967, with substance deriving from RPL § 64.

PART 4   Estates Defined

§ 6-4.1. Definition of an estate in possession

An estate in possession is an estate which entitles the owner to the immediate possession of property.

History: Add, L 1966, ch 952, eff Sept 1, 1967, with substance deriving from RPL § 35.

§ 6-4.2. Definition of a future estate

A future estate is an estate limited to commence in possession at a future time, either without the intervention of a precedent estate or on the determination, by lapse of time or otherwise, of a precedent estate created at the same time.

History: Add, L 1966, ch 952, eff Sept 1, 1967, with substance deriving from RPL § 37; amd, L 1967, ch 686, § 47, eff Sept 1, 1967.

§ 6-4.3. Definition of a remainder

A remainder is a future estate, as defined in 6-4.2, created in favor of a person other than the creator.

History: Add, L 1966, ch 952, eff Sept 1, 1967, with substance deriving from RPL § 38.

§ 6-4.4. Definition of a reversion

A reversion is the future estate, other than a possibility of reverter and a right of reacquisition, left in the creator or in his successors in interest upon the simultaneous creation of one or more lesser estates than the creator originally owned.

History: Add, L 1966, ch 952, eff Sept 1, 1967, with substance deriving from RPL § 39.

§ 6-4.5. Definition of a possibility of reverter

A possibility of reverter is the future estate left in the creator or in his successors in interest upon the simultaneous creation of an estate that will terminate automatically within a period of time defined by the occurrence of a specified event.

History: Add, L 1966, ch 952, eff Sept 1, 1967, with substance deriving from former RPL § 59-a.

§ 6-4.6. Definition of a right of reacquisition

A right of reacquisition is the future estate left in the creator or in his successors in interest upon the simultaneous creation of an estate on a condition subsequent.

History: Add, L 1966, ch 952, eff Sept 1, 1967, with substance deriving from former RPL § 59-b.

§ 6-4.7. Definition of a future estate indefeasibly vested

A future estate indefeasibly vested is an estate created in favor of one or more ascertained persons in being which is certain when created to become an estate in possession whenever and however the preceding estates end and which can in no way be defeated or abridged.

History: Add, L 1966, ch 952, eff Sept 1, 1967, with substance deriving from RPL § 40.

§ 6-4.8. Definition of a future estate vested subject to open

A future estate vested subject to open is an estate created in favor of a class of persons, one or more of whom are ascertained and in being, which is certain when created to become an estate in possession whenever and however the preceding estates end, and is subject to diminution by reason of another person becoming entitled to share therein.

History: Add, L 1966, ch 952, eff Sept 1, 1967, with substance deriving from RPL § 40-a.

§ 6-4.9. Definition of a future estate vested subject to complete defeasance

A future estate vested subject to complete defeasance is an estate created in favor of one or more ascertained persons in being, which would become an estate in possession upon the expiration of the preceding estates, but may end or may be terminated as provided by the creator at, before or after the expiration of such preceding estates.

History: Add, L 1966, ch 952, eff Sept 1, 1967, with substance deriving from RPL § 40-b.

§ 6-4.10. Definition of a future estate subject to a condition precedent

A future estate subject to a condition precedent is an estate created in favor of one or more unborn or unascertained persons or in favor of one or more presently ascertainable persons upon the occurrence of an uncertain event.

History: Add, L 1966, ch 952, eff Sept 1, 1967, with substance deriving from RPL § 40-c.

PART 5   Rules Governing Future Estates

§ 6-5.1. Characteristics of future estates

Future estates are descendible, devisable and alienable, in the same manner as estates in possession.

History: Add, L 1966, ch 952, eff Sept 1, 1967, with substance deriving from RPL § 59.

§ 6-5.2. Power of appointment not to prevent vesting

The existence of an unexecuted power of appointment does not prevent the vesting of a future estate, limited in default of the execution of the power.

History: Add, L 1966, ch 952, eff Sept 1, 1967, with substance deriving from RPL § 41.

§ 6-5.3. Future estates in the alternative

Two or more future estates may be created to take effect in the alternative, so that if the first in order fails to vest, the next in succession is substituted for it and takes effect accordingly.

History: Add, L 1966, ch 952, eff Sept 1, 1967, with substance deriving from RPL § 51.

§ 6-5.4. Implication of cross remainders between tenants in common

When a limitation, if contained in a will, would create a tenancy in common, with implied cross remainders, a like limitation, if contained in a deed, has the same effect.

History: Add, L 1966, ch 952, eff Sept 1, 1967, with substance deriving from RPL § 66-a.

§ 6-5.5. Future estate valid though contingency improbable

A future estate, otherwise valid, shall not be void on the ground of the improbability of the contingency on which it is limited to take effect.

History: Add, L 1966, ch 952, eff Sept 1, 1967, with substance deriving from RPL § 52.

§ 6-5.6. Meaning of heirs, distributees and issue in certain remainders

When a remainder is limited to take effect on the death of any person without heirs, heirs of the body, distributees or issue, the word "heirs", "heirs of the body", "distributees" or "issue" mean such persons living at the death of the person named as ancestor.

History: Add, L 1966, ch 952, eff Sept 1, 1967, with substance deriving from RPL § 48.

§ 6-5.7. Posthumous children

(a) Where a future estate is limited to children, distributees, heirs or issue, posthumous children are entitled to take in the same manner as if living at the death of their ancestors.

(b) A future estate conditioned upon the death of a person without children, distributees, heirs or issue is defeated by the birth of a child conceived before but born alive after the death of such person.

History: Add, L 1966, ch 952, eff Sept 1, 1967, with substance deriving from RPL § 56.

§ 6-5.8. Heirs or distributees of life tenant take as purchasers

When a remainder is limited to the heirs, heirs of the body or distributees of a person to whom a life estate in the same property is given, the persons who, on the termination of the life estate, are the heirs, heirs of the body or distributees of the life tenant take as purchasers.

History: Add, L 1966, ch 952, eff Sept 1, 1967, with substance deriving from RPL § 54.

§ 6-5.9. Heirs or distributees of creator take as purchasers

Where a remainder is limited to the heirs or distributees of the creator of an estate in property, such heirs or distributees take as purchasers.

History: Add, L 1966, ch 952, eff Sept 1, 1967.

§ 6-5.10. When future estates are defeated

A future estate cannot be defeated or barred by any disposition or other act of the owner of the precedent estate, nor by the destruction of such precedent estate by disseizen, forfeiture, surrender, merger or otherwise; but a future estate may be defeated in any manner which the creator has provided.

History: Add, L 1966, ch 952, eff Sept 1, 1967, with substance deriving from RPL § 57.

§ 6-5.11. Non-destructibility of remainders subject to a condition precedent

A remainder is not defeated by the determination of a precedent estate before the occurrence of the condition precedent on which the remainder was limited to take effect. If such condition precedent subsequently occurs, the remainder takes effect in the same manner and to the same extent as if the precedent estate had continued.

History: Add, L 1966, ch 952, with substance deriving from RPL § 58; amd, L 1968, ch 257, § 4, eff May 14, 1968.

§ 6-5.12. Future rents and profits subject to rules governing future estates

A disposition of the rents, profits or other income from property accruing at any time subsequent to the execution of the instrument creating such disposition is subject to the rules governing future estates in property.

History: Add, L 1966, ch 952, eff Sept 1, 1967, with substance deriving from RPL § 60.

PART 6   Disposition of Community Property Rights at Death

§ 6-6.1. Application

This part applies to the disposition at death by a married person of all or the proportionate part of any personal property wherever situated which was acquired as or became, and remained, community property under the laws of another jurisdiction, and any personal property wherever situated and real property situated in this state which was acquired with the rents, issues or income of, the proceeds from, or in exchange for, property acquired as or which became, and remained, community property under the laws of another jurisdiction, or property traceable to that community property.

History: Add, L 1981, ch 187, § 1, eff Sept 1, 1981.

§ 6-6.2. Rebuttable presumptions

In determining whether this part applies to specific property acquired during a marriage by a spouse of that marriage the following rebuttable presumptions apply:

(a) Property acquired while domiciled in a jurisdiction under whose laws property could then be acquired as community property is presumed to have been acquired as or have become, and remained, property to which this part applies; and

(b) Property acquired while domiciled in a jurisdiction under whose laws property could not then be acquired as community property, title to which was taken in a form which created rights of survivorship, is presumed not to be property to which this part applies.

History: Add, L 1981, ch 187, § 1, eff Sept 1, 1981.

§ 6-6.3. Disposition upon death

Upon the death of a married person, one-half of the property to which this part applies is the property of the surviving spouse and is not subject to testamentary disposition by the decedent nor to the laws of descent and distribution. One-half of that property is the property of the decedent and is subject to testamentary disposition by the decedent or the law of descent and distribution. With respect to property to which this part applies, the one-half of the property which is the property of the decedent is not subject to the surviving spouse's right to elect against the will.

History: Add, L 1981, ch 187, § 1, eff Sept 1, 1981.

§ 6-6.4. Perfection of title

(a) If the title to any property to which this part applies was held by the decedent at the time of death, title of the surviving spouse may be perfected by an order of the surrogate's court having jurisdiction over the decedent's estate or by execution of an instrument by the personal representative or the testamentary beneficiaries or distributees of the decedent with the approval of the court, upon due notice to all persons who would be required to be served with process in a proceeding under section twenty-two hundred ten of the surrogate's court procedure act. Neither the personal representative nor the court has a duty to discover or attempt to discover whether property held by the decedent is property to which this part applies, unless a written demand is made by the surviving spouse or the spouse's successor in interest.

(b) If the title to any property to which this part applies is held by the surviving spouse at the time of the decedent's death, the personal representative or a testamentary beneficiary or distributee of the decedent may institute an action to perfect title to the property. The personal representative has no fiduciary duty to discover or attempt to discover whether any property held by the surviving spouse is property to which this part applies, unless a written demand is made by a testamentary beneficiary, distributee or creditor of the decedent.

History: Add, L 1981, ch 187, § 1, eff Sept 1, 1981; amd, L 1982, ch 847, § 1, eff July 27, 1982.

§ 6-6.5. Purchaser for value or lender

(a) If a surviving spouse has apparent title to property to which this part applies, a purchaser for value or a lender taking a security interest in the property takes his interest in the property free of any rights of the personal representative or a testamentary beneficiary or distributee of the decedent.

(b) If a personal representative or a testamentary beneficiary or distributee of the decedent has apparent title to property to which this part applies, a purchaser for value or a lender taking a security interest in the property takes his interest in the property free of any rights of the surviving spouse.

(c) A purchaser for value or a lender need not inquire whether a vendor or borrower acted properly.

(d) The proceeds of a sale or creation of a security interest shall be treated in the same manner as the property transferred to the purchaser for value or a lender.

History: Add, L 1981, ch 187, § 1, eff Sept 1, 1981.

§ 6-6.6. Effect and construction of part

This part does not effect rights of creditors nor prevent married persons from severing or altering their interests in property nor authorize testamentary dispositions of property otherwise limited or prohibited by law, and shall be so applied and construed as to effectuate its general purpose to make uniform the law with respect to the subject of this part among those states which enact similar legislation.

History: Add, L 1981, ch 187, § 1, eff Sept 1, 1981.

§ 6-6.7. Short title

This part may be cited as "The New York uniform disposition of community property rights at death act".

History: Add, L 1981, ch 187, § 1, eff Sept 1, 1981.

EPTL

ARTICLE 7
TRUSTS
SUMMARY OF ARTICLE

EPTL

E-81

PART 1   Rules Governing Trusts

§ 7-1.1. When trust interests not to merge

A trust is not merged or invalid because a person, including but not limited to the creator of the trust, is or may become the sole trustee and the sole holder of the present beneficial interest therein, provided that one or more other persons hold a beneficial interest therein, whether such interest be vested or contingent, present or future, and whether created by express provision of the instrument or as a result of reversion to the creator's estate.

> **History:** Add, L 1966, ch 952, eff Sept 1, 1967, with substance deriving from RPL § 92; amd, L 1997, ch 139, § 2, eff June 25, 1997, deleting the original text of the statute and replacing it, abrogating the doctrine of merger.

§ 7-1.2. Trustee of passive trust not to take

Every disposition of property shall be made directly to the person in whom the right to possession and income is intended to be vested and not to another in trust for such person, and if made to any person in trust for another, no estate, legal or equitable, vests in the trustee. But neither this section nor 7-1.1 shall apply to trusts arising or resulting by implicaiton[*] of law.

> **History:** Add, L 1966, ch 952, eff Sept 1, 1967, with substance deriving from RPL § 93; amd, L 1967, ch 686, § 50, eff Sept 1, 1967.

§ 7-1.3. Purchase-money resulting trust abolished

(a)[**] A disposition of property to one person for a valuable consideration paid, in whole or in part, by another is presumed fraudulent as against the creditors of the payor at the time of such disposition and, unless the presumption is rebutted, a trust results in favor of such creditors to the extent necessary to satisfy their claims; but title to the property vests in the transferee and no trust results to the payor unless the transferee either:

(1) Takes such property, in his own name, as an absolute transfer without the consent or knowledge of the payor; or

(2) In violation of some trust, purchases the property so transferred with money or property belonging to another.

> **History:** Add, L 1966, ch 952, eff Sept 1, 1967, with substance deriving from RPL § 94.

§ 7-1.4. Purposes for which trust may be created

An express trust may be created for any lawful purpose.

> **History:** Add, L 1966, ch 952, eff Sept 1, 1967, with substance deriving from RPL § 96.

§ 7-1.5. When trust interest inalienable; exception

(a) The interest of the beneficiary of any trust may be assigned or otherwise transferred, except that:

(1) The right of a beneficiary of an express trust to receive the income from property and

---

[*] So in original. Should be "implication".

[**] **Ed. Note**: There is no paragraph (b).

apply it to the use of or pay it to any person may not be transferred by assignment or otherwise unless a power to transfer such right, or any part thereof, is conferred upon such beneficiary by the instrument creating or declaring the trust.

(2) The proceeds of a life insurance policy which, under a trust or other agreement, are upon the death of the insured left with the insurance company may not be (A) transferred, (B) subject to commutation or encumbrance or (C) subject to legal process except in an action for necessaries, if provisions to such effect were incorporated in such trust or other agreement.

(b) Notwithstanding subparagraph (a) (1):

(1) he beneficiary of an express trust to receive income from property and apply it to the use of or pay it to any person may, unless otherwise provided in the instrument creating or declaring such trust, transfer any amount in excess of ten thousand dollars of the annual income to which the beneficiary is entitled from such trust to the spouse, issue, ancestors, brothers, sisters, uncles, aunts, nephews or nieces of the beneficiary, or to a trustee, committee, conservator, curator, custodian, guardian of the property of a minor, or the donee of a power during minority for the benefit only of any such person bearing such relationship to the beneficiary, provided that such transfer is evidenced by a written instrument signed and acknowledged by the beneficiary and delivered to the trustee of the trust, together with an affidavit by the beneficiary that such transfer and any like transfer concurrently in effect are for all or part of the excess over ten thousand dollars of the annual income from such trust to which such beneficiary is entitled, and that he has not received and is not to receive any consideration in money or money's worth for the transfer.

(2) Any such transfer shall be effective in any year only as to income from such trust in excess of ten thousand dollars, and for this purpose all previous like transfers applicable to a given year shall be taken into account. In the event that two or more transfers are made in or for any year in a total amount exceeding the income from such trust properly transferable hereunder, transferees shall be preferred in the order in which the instruments of transfer were delivered to the trustee.

(3) A trustee shall be exonerated and fully discharged for any payment made to a transferee in reliance on the affidavit of a beneficiary described in subparagraph (1).

(4) The provisions of this paragraph do not apply to subparagraph (a) (2):

(c) A transferee of income may, if he has not received or is not to receive any consideration in money or money's worth therefor, make a further transfer of such income only to one or more of the permissible transferees referred to in subparagraph (b) (1), other than a prior transferor; provided, however, that upon the death of a transferee any income not so transferred by him shall be an asset of his estate, subject to his testamentary disposition or passing to his distributees under the statutes of descent and distribution.

(d) The beneficiary of an express trust to receive the income from property and apply it to the use of or pay it to any person is not precluded by anything contained in this section from transferring or assigning any part or all of such income to or for the benefit of persons whom the beneficiary is legally obligated to support.

History: Add, L 1966, ch 952, eff Sept 1, 1967, with substance deriving from PPL § 15 and RPL § 103; amd, L 1967, ch 686, § 51, eff Sept 1, 1967; L 1968, ch 757, eff June 16, 1968; L 1973, ch 908, § 1, eff Sept 1, 1973.

§ 7-1.6. Application of principal to income beneficiary

(a) Notwithstanding any contrary provision of law, the court having jurisdiction of an express trust, heretofore created or declared, to receive the income from property and apply it to the use of or pay it to any person, unless otherwise provided in the disposing instrument, may in its discretion make an allowance from principal to any income beneficiary whose support or education is not sufficiently provided for, to the extent that such beneficiary is indefeasibly entitled to the principal of the trust or any part thereof or, in case the income beneficiary is not entitled to the principal of the trust or any part thereof, to the extent that all persons beneficially interested in the trust are adult and competent and consent thereto in writing; provided that the court, after a hearing on notice to all those beneficially interested in the trust in such manner as the court may direct, is satisfied that the original purpose of the creator of the trust cannot be carried out and that such allowance effectuates the intention of the creator.

(b) Notwithstanding any contrary provision of law, the court having jurisdiction of an express trust, hereafter created or declared, to receive income from property and apply it to the use of or pay it to any person, unless otherwise provided in the disposing instrument, may in its discretion make an allowance from principal to any income beneficiary whose support or education is not sufficiently provided for, whether or not such person is entitled to the principal of the trust or any part thereof; provided that the court, after a hearing on notice to all those beneficially interested in the trust in such manner as the court may direct, is satisfied that the original purpose of the creator of the trust cannot be carried out and that such allowance effectuates the intention of the creator.

(c) In the event that an income beneficiary to whom an allowance is made, as provided in this section, is or becomes entitled to a share of the principal of the trust, such allowance, without interest thereon, shall be a charge upon such share.

(d) If the application or the possibility of the application of this section to any trust would reduce or eliminate a charitable deduction otherwise available to any person or entity under the income tax, gift tax or estate tax provisions of the internal revenue code, the provisions of this section shall not apply to such trust.

(e) A supplemental needs trust which conforms to the provisions of 7-1.12 of this article shall be construed in accordance with the provisions of that section.

> **History:** Add, L 1966, ch 952, eff Sept 1, 1967, with substance deriving from PPL § 15-a and RPL § 103-a; amd, L 1967, ch 686, § 52, eff Sept 1, 1967; L 1969, ch 556, § 1; L 1978, ch 83, § 1, eff April 18, 1978; L 1993, ch 433, § 4, eff July 26, 1993, and providing, "Nothing in this act shall affect the establishment, interpretation or construction of trust instruments which do not conform with the provisions of this act, nor shall this act impair the state's authority to be paid from or seek reimbursement from any trust which does not conform with the provisions of this act or to deem the principal or income of such trust an available resource under any program of government benefits or assistance."

§ 7-1.7. Interest remaining in creator of trust

Every legal estate and interest not embraced in an express trust and not otherwise disposed of remains in the creator.

History: Add, L 1966, ch 952, eff Sept 1, 1967, with substance deriving from RPL § 102.

§ 7-1.8. Duration of trust for benefit of creditors

(a) Where an estate in real property has heretofore vested or shall hereafter vest in an assignee or other trustee for the benefit of creditors, it shall cease at the expiration of ten years from the time the trust was created, except where a different limitation is contained in the instrument creating the trust or is otherwise prescribed by law. Such estate shall thereupon revert to the assignor.

(b) This section does not apply to a trust of personal property or to a trust of real property created in connection with the salvaging of mortgage participation certificates. Nor does this section affect any rights to the proceeds of a sale of real property made by the assignee or other trustee for the benefit of creditors.

History: Add, L 1966, ch 952, eff Sept 1, 1967, with substance deriving from RPL § 110.

§ 7-1.9. Revocation of trusts

(a) Upon the written consent, acknowledged or proved in the manner required by the laws of this state for the recording of a conveyance of real property, of all the persons beneficially interested in a trust of property, heretofore or hereafter created, the creater* of such trust may revoke or amend the whole or any part thereof by an instrument in writing acknowledged or proved in like manner, and thereupon the estate of the trustees ceases with respect to any part of such trust property, the disposition of which has been revoked. If the conveyance or other instrument creating a trust of property was recorded in the office of the clerk or register of any county of this state, the instrument revoking or amending such trust, together with the consents thereto, shall be recorded in the same office of every county in which the conveyance or other instrument creating such trust was recorded.

(b) For the purposes of this section, a disposition, contained in a trust created on or after September first, nineteen hundred fifty-one, in favor of a class of persons described only as the heirs, next of kin or distributees (or by any term of like import) of the creator of the trust does not create a beneficial interest in such persons.

(c) A testamentary or lifetime trust wholly benefitting one or more charitable beneficiaries may be terminated as provided for by subparagraph two of paragraph (c) of section 8-1.1 of this chapter.

History: Add, L 1966, ch 952, eff Sept 1, 1967, with substance deriving from PPL § 23 and RPL § 118; amd, L 1967, ch 686, § 53; L 1968, ch 257, § 5, eff May 14, 1968; L 1985, ch 492, § 1, eff July 24, 1985.

§ 7-1.10. Provision by non-domiciliary creator as to law to govern trust

(a)* Whenever a person, not domiciled in this state, creates a trust which provides that it shall be governed by the laws of this state, such provision shall be given effect in determining the validity, effect and interpretation of the disposition in such trust of:

---

* So in original. Should be "creator".

* **Ed. Note**: There is no paragraph (b).

(1) Any trust property situated in this state at the time the trust is created.

(2) Personal property, wherever situated, if the trustee of the trust is a person residing, incorporated or authorized to do business in this state or a national bank having an office in this state.

History: Add, L 1966, ch 952, eff Sept 1, 1967, with substance deriving from PPL § 12-a; amd, L 1967, ch 686, § 54, eff Sept 1, 1967.

§ 7-1.11. Application of principal to creator of trust as reimbursement for taxes

(a) Notwithstanding any contrary provision of law, the trustee of an express trust, unless otherwise provided in the disposing instrument, may, from time to time, pay from principal to the creator of such trust an amount equal to any income taxes on any portion of the trust principal with which he is charged.

(b) The provisions of this section do not apply to any trust by which a future estate is indefeasibly vested in the United States or a political subdivision for exclusively public purposes; a corporation organized exclusively for religious, charitable, scientific, literary or educational purposes, including the encouragement of art and the prevention of cruelty to children or animals, no part of the net earnings of which inures to the benefit of any private shareholder or individual, and no substantial part of the activities of which is carrying on propaganda or otherwise attempting to influence legislation; a trustee, or a fraternal society, order or association operating under the lodge system, provided the principal or income of such trust is to be used by such trustee or by such fraternal society, order or association exclusively for religious, charitable, scientific, literary or educational purposes, or for the prevention of cruelty to children or animals, and no substantial part of the activities of such trustee or of such fraternal society, order or association is carrying on propaganda or otherwise attempting to influence legislation; or any veteran's organization incorporated by Act of Congress, or of its department or local chapters or posts, no part of the net earnings of which inures to the benefit of any private shareholder or individual.

History: Add, L 1969, ch 556, § 2, eff May 21, 1969.

§ 7-1.12. Supplemental needs trusts established for persons with severe and chronic or persistent disabilities

(a) Definitions: When used in this section, unless otherwise expressly stated or unless the context otherwise requires:

(1) "Developmental disability" means developmental disability as defined in subdivision twenty-two of section 1.03 of the mental hygiene law.

(2) "Government benefits or assistance" means any program of benefits or assistance which is intended to provide or pay for support, maintenance or health care and which is established or administered, in whole or in part, by any federal, state, county, city or other governmental entity.

(3) "Mental illness" means mental illness as defined in subdivision twenty of section 1.03 of the mental hygiene law.

(4) "Person with a severe and chronic or persistent disability" means a person

(i) with mental illness, developmental disability, or other physical or mental impairment;

(ii) whose disability is expected to, or does, give rise to a long-term need for specialized health, mental health, developmental disabilities, social or other related services; and

(iii) who may need to rely on government benefits or assistance.

(5) "Supplemental needs trust" means a discretionary trust established for the benefit of a person with a severe and chronic or persistent disability (the "beneficiary") which conforms to all of the following criteria:

(i) The trust document clearly evidences the creator's intent to supplement, not supplant, impair or diminish, government benefits or assistance for which the beneficiary may otherwise be eligible or which the beneficiary may be receiving, except as provided in clause (ii) of this subparagraph;

(ii) The trust document prohibits the trustee from expending or distributing trust assets in any way which may supplant, impair or diminish government benefits or assistance for which the beneficiary may otherwise be eligible or which the beneficiary may be receiving; provided, however, that the trustee may be authorized to make such distributions to third parties to meet the beneficiary's needs for food, clothing, shelter or health care but only if the trustee determines (A) that the beneficiary's basic needs will be better met if such distribution is made, and (B) that it is in the beneficiary's best interests to suffer the consequent effect, if any, on the beneficiary's eligibility for or receipt of government benefits or assistance;

(iii) The beneficiary does not have the power to assign, encumber, direct, distribute or authorize distributions from the trust;

(iv) If an inter vivos trust, the creator of the trust is a person or entity other than the beneficiary or the beneficiary's spouse; and

(v) Notwithstanding subparagraph (iv) of this paragraph, the beneficiary of a supplemental needs trust may be the creator of the trust if such trust meets the requirements of subparagraph two of paragraph (b) of subdivision two of section three hundred sixty-six of the social services law and of the regulations implementing such clauses. Provided, however, that if the trust is funded with the proceeds of retroactive payments made as a result of a court action and due the beneficiary under the federal supplemental security income program, as established under title XVI of the federal social security act, the creation of a supplemental needs trust by the beneficiary under this subparagraph shall not impair nor limit any right under applicable law of a representative payee to receive reimbursement out of such proceeds for expenses incurred on behalf of the beneficiary pending the determination of the beneficiary's eligibility for such federal supplemental security income program, nor any right under applicable law of any state or local governmental entity which provided the beneficiary with interim assistance pending the determination of the beneficiary's eligibility for such federal supplemental security income program to be repaid out of such proceeds for the amount of such interim assistance.

(6) A "beneficiary" means a person with a severe and chronic or persistent disability who is a beneficiary of a supplemental needs trust.

(b) A supplemental needs trust shall be construed in accordance with the following:

(1) It shall be presumed that the creator of the trust intended that neither principal nor income be used to pay for any expense which would otherwise be paid by government benefits or assistance for which the beneficiary might otherwise be eligible or which the beneficiary might be receiving, notwithstanding any authority the trustee may have to make distributions for food, clothing, shelter or health care as provided in clause (ii) of subparagraph five of paragraph (a) of this section;

(2) Section 7-1.6 of this article shall not be applicable to the extent that the application or possible application of that section would reduce or eliminate the beneficiary's entitlement to government benefits or assistance;

(3) Neither principal nor income held in trust shall be deemed an available resource to the beneficiary under any program of government benefits or assistance; however, actual distributions from the trust may be considered to be income or resources of the beneficiary to the extent provided by the terms of any such program;

(4) The trustee of the trust shall not be deemed to be holding assets for the benefit of the beneficiary for purposes of section 43.03 of the mental hygiene law or section one hundred four of the social services law; and

(5) If the trust provides the trustee with the authority to make distributions for food, clothing, shelter or health care as provided in clause (ii) of subparagraph five of paragraph (a) of this section, and if the mere existence of that authority would, under the terms of any program of government benefits or assistance, result in the beneficiary's loss of government benefits or assistance, regardless of whether such authority were actually exercised, then:

    (i) if the trust instrument expressly provides, such provision shall be null and void and the trustee's authority to make such distributions shall cease and shall be limited as otherwise provided; or

    (ii) the trust shall no longer be treated as a supplemental needs trust under this section and the trust shall be construed, and the trust assets considered, without regard to the provisions of this section.

(c) (1) Paragraph (b) of this section shall not apply to the extent that the trust is funded, directly or indirectly, by the beneficiary, except as provided in clause (v) of subparagraph five of paragraph (a) of this section, by someone with a legal obligation of support to the beneficiary, or by someone with another financial obligation to the beneficiary to the extent of such obligation, at the time the beneficiary is receiving or applying to receive:

    (i) Government benefits or assistance for which an income and resource calculation is made; or

    (ii) Services, care or assistance for which payment or reimbursement is or may be sought under section 43.03 of the mental hygiene law or section one hundred four of the social services law.

(2) To the extent that said paragraph (b) does not apply, the trust shall not be treated as a supplemental needs trust under this section, and the trust shall be construed, and the trust assets considered, without regard to the provisions of this section.

(d) The provisions of paragraph (b) of this section shall not apply to bar claims by

EPTL

government against persons with an interest in or under the trust other than the beneficiary.

(e) (1) The following language may be used as part of a trust instrument, but is not required, to qualify a trust as a supplemental needs trust:

1. The property shall be held, IN TRUST, for the benefit of _____ (hereinafter the "beneficiary") and shall be held, managed, invested and reinvested by the trustee, who shall collect the income therefrom and, after deducting all charges and expenses properly attributable thereto, shall, at any time and from time to time, apply for the benefit of the beneficiary, so much (even to the extent of the whole) of the net income and/or principal of this trust as the trustee shall deem advisable, in his or her sole and absolute discretion, subject to the limitations set forth below. The trustee shall add to the principal of such trust the balance of net income not so paid or applied.

2. It is the grantor's intent to create a supplemental needs trust which conforms to the provisions of section 7-1.12 of the New York estates, powers and trusts law. The grantor intends that the trust assets be used to supplement, not supplant, impair or diminish, any benefits or assistance of any federal, state, county, city, or other governmental entity for which the beneficiary may otherwise be eligible or which the beneficiary may be receiving. Consistent with that intent, it is the grantor's desire that, before expending any amounts from the net income and/or principal of this trust, the trustee consider the availability of all benefits from government or private assistance programs for which the beneficiary may be eligible and that, where appropriate and to the extent possible, the trustee endeavor to maximize the collection of such benefits and to facilitate the distribution of such benefits for the benefit of the beneficiary.

3. None of the income or principal of this trust shall be applied in such a manner as to supplant, impair or diminish benefits or assistance of any federal, state, county, city, or other governmental entity for which the beneficiary may otherwise be eligible or which the beneficiary may be receiving.

4. The beneficiary does not have the power to assign, encumber, direct, distribute or authorize distributions from this trust.

(2) (i) If the creator elects, the following additional language may be used:

5. Notwithstanding the provisions of paragraphs two and three above, the trustee may make distributions to meet the beneficiary's need for food, clothing, shelter or health care even if such distributions may result in an impairment or diminution of the beneficiary's receipt or eligibility for government benefits or assistance but only if the trustee determines that (i) the beneficiary's needs will be better met if such distribution is made, and (ii) it is in the beneficiary's best interests to suffer the consequent effect, if any, on the beneficiary's eligibility for or receipt of government benefits or assistance.

(ii) If the trustee is provided with the authority to make the distributions as described in subparagraph (2) (i), the creator may elect to add the following clause:

; provided, however, that if the mere existence of the trustee's authority to make distributions pursuant to this paragraph shall result in the beneficiary's loss of government benefits or assistance, regardless of whether such authority is actually exercised, this paragraph shall be null and void and the trustee's authority to make such distributions shall cease and shall be limited as provided in paragraphs two and three above, without exception.

(f) Nothing in this section shall affect the establishment, interpretation or construction of trust instruments which do not conform with the provisions of this section, nor shall this section impair the state's authority to be paid from or seek reimbursement from any trust which does not conform with the provisions of this section or to deem the principal or income of such trust an available resource under any program of government benefits or assistance.

History: Add, L 1993, ch 433, § 5, eff July 26, 1993, however, "nothing in this act shall affect the establishment, interpretation or construction of trust instruments which do not conform with the provisions of this act, nor shall this act impair the state's authority to be paid from or seek reimbursement from any trust which does not conform with the provisions of this act or to deem the principal or income of such trust an available resource under any program of government benefits or assistance", and "sections four and five of this act [amending EPTL 7-1.6 and enacting EPTL 7-1.12] shall not be effective to the extent that application of their provisions would adversely affect federal financial participation in the state's cost of the government benefits or assistance received by the beneficiary of a supplemental needs trust as defined therein."; amd, L 1994, ch 170, § 453, eff June 9, 1994, deemed eff April 1, 1994, "provided that nothing contained in [the] sections . . . shall be deemed to affect the application, qualification, expiration or repeal of any provision of law amended by any such sections and such provisions shall be applied or qualified or shall expire or be deemed repealed in the same manner, to the same extent and on the same date as the case may be as otherwise provided by law . . . ."

§ 7-1.13. Division of trusts and establishment of separate trusts

(a) Notwithstanding any contrary provision of law, unless expressly prohibited by the terms of the disposing instrument:

(1) the trustee of an express trust (which term as defined in paragraph (g) of this section may mean the executor or administrator) is authorized without prior court approval or the consent of the persons interested to establish two or more separate trusts in order to segregate for any of the following purposes:

(A) property held in trust in which a spouse or surviving spouse has a qualifying income interest with respect to which an election has been or will be made in whole or in part under section 2056(b)(7), 2056A or 2523(f) of the United States Internal Revenue Code of 1986 from property with respect to which no election has been or will be made;

(B) property held in trust with respect to which a marital deduction under section 2056 or 2523 of the United States Internal Revenue Code would be available, by election or otherwise, from property held in trust for persons other than the spouse or surviving spouse, so that one or more of such separate trusts qualify for the deduction under said sections;

(C) property held in trust with respect to which a charitable deduction under section 2055 or 2522 of the United States Internal Revenue Code would be available from property held in trust for persons not described in said sections, so that one or more of such separate trusts qualify for the deduction under said sections;

(D) property held in trust which is or would be excepted, excluded or exempt from or under Chapter 13 (tax on generation-skipping transfers) of the United States Internal

Revenue Code from such property which is not so excepted, excluded or exempt, so that one or more of such separate trusts will have an inclusion ratio of zero, or so that one or more of such separate trusts qualify for the grandchild exception under section 1433(b)-(d) of the Tax Reform Act of 1986, as amended;

(E) property held in trust for one (of two or more beneficiaries) from property held in trust for such other beneficiaries, so that one or more of such separate trusts shall be a qualified subchapter S trust under section 1361(d) of the United States Internal Revenue Code;

(F) property transferred in trust by a creator (including but not limited to a transfer treated as made by a spouse by reason of section 2513 of the United States Internal Revenue Code) from property transferred in trust by one or more different creators; and

(G) property transferred in trust by a creator (including but not limited to a transfer treated as made by a spouse by reason of section 2513 of the United States Internal Revenue Code) pursuant to a disposing instrument from property transferred by the same creator pursuant to another disposing instrument;

(2) the trustee of an express trust may divide such trust into two or more separate trusts, with the consent of all persons interested in the trust but without prior court approval, for any reason which is not directly contrary to the primary purpose of the trust; and

(3) the court having jurisdiction of an express trust, upon the petition of the trustee or of any person interested in the trust and upon notice to all such persons, may direct the establishment of two or more separate trusts for any reason not directly contrary to the primary purpose of the trust.

(b) Unless the court otherwise directs, the trusts established under this section shall be deemed to have been established as of the effective date of the disposing instrument; provided that the establishment of separate trusts under subparagraph two of paragraph (a) of this section may become effective upon the date or dates provided in the instrument filed under paragraph (e) of this section.

(c) Except as implicit in the establishment of separate trusts authorized by this section, the terms of the disposing instrument, subject to modifications approved by the court, shall govern each separate trust established hereunder, except that separate trusts for one or more members of a class of beneficiaries may be established under subparagraph two of paragraph (a) of this section without modification by the court if the property held in trust is distributed to such separate trusts for one or more members of such class on the basis of share per stirpes, per capita, or by representation, whichever is consistent with the terms of the disposing instrument.

(d) Unless the court otherwise directs, and except in the case of the establishment of separate trusts under clauses (F) and (G) of subparagraph one of paragraph (a) of this section where the original assets remain or can be traced, the property distributed to the separate trust shall be fairly representative of appreciation or depreciation and shall be based upon the fair market value of the assets on the date or dates of the distributions of such assets to the separate trusts.

(e) Separate trusts shall be established under subparagraphs one and two of paragraph (a) of this section by an instrument or instruments in writing, signed and acknowledged by the trustee and if under subparagraph two of paragraph (a) of this section shall also be signed and acknowledged by all the persons interested in the trust (or the guardian of the property, committee, conservator, adult guardian, or personal representative of such persons each of whom is hereby empowered to consent thereto without prior court approval). Such instruments shall be filed in the office of the clerk of the court having jurisdiction over the trust; and a copy thereof shall be served on all persons interested in the trusts (or the guardian of the property, committee, conservator, adult guardian, or personal representative of such persons), by registered or certified mail, return receipt requested, or by personal delivery or upon application of the trustee in any other manner directed by the court.

(f) The term "disposing instrument" shall mean the will, trust agreement, instrument exercising a power of appointment or other instrument creating such a trust or transferring property to such trust; provided that in the case of an instrument exercising a limited or testamentary power of appointment, the term "disposing instrument" may also refer to the instrument creating such power (if applicable under the circumstances).

(g) In any case where the United States Internal Revenue Code requires that an election or other action be made or taken by the executor or if no trustee of a trust under a will has qualified, the term "trustee" as used in this section shall mean the executor or administrator of an estate. In any such case, the trustee shall comply with any action taken by the executor or administrator under this section.

(h) For the purposes of this section, the phrase "all persons interested in the trust" shall mean all the persons upon whom service of process would be required in a proceeding for the judicial settlement of the account of the trustee, taking into account section three hundred fifteen of the surrogate's court procedure act.

(i) References to sections of the United States Internal Revenue Code shall refer to the United States Internal Revenue Code of 1986 as amended from time to time, or to corresponding provisions of subsequent internal revenue laws, and shall also refer to corresponding provisions of state law.

(j) Unless otherwise provided for in the disposing instrument, the commissions allowed to a trustee as determined under article twenty-three of the surrogate's court procedure act, as amended from time to time, shall not be increased by reason of the establishment of separate trusts pursuant to subparagraph one of paragraph (a) of this section unless the court otherwise permits an increase, provided, however, that such trustee shall be entitled to charge the trust for any additional reasonable and necessary expenses incurred in the administration of such separate trusts.

(k) For purposes of subparagraphs (a)(2) and (3) of this section, a division of a trust into two or more separate trusts to permit one or more such trusts to be governed by article 11-A and another one or more such trusts to be governed by 11-2.4 shall be deemed to be for a reason which is not directly contrary to the primary purpose of the trust unless such division is expressly prohibited by the terms of the disposing instrument.

> **History:** Add, L 1995, ch 523, § 1, eff Aug 2, 1995, and applicable to trusts whenever created; amd, L 2001, ch 243, § 9, eff Jan 1, 2002.

§ 7-1.14. Who may make a lifetime trust

Any person, as defined in 1-2.12, may by lifetime trust dispose of real and personal property. A natural person who creates a lifetime trust shall be eighteen years of age or older.

History: Add, L 1997, ch 139, § 3, eff June 25, 1997, and applicable to lifetime trusts created on and after June 25, 1997.

§ 7-1.15. What property may be disposed of by lifetime trust

Every estate in property may be disposed of by lifetime trust.

History: Add, L 1997, ch 139, § 3, eff June 25, 1997, and applicable to lifetime trusts created on and after June 25, 1997.

§ 7-1.16. Revocation of lifetime trust by will

A lifetime trust shall be irrevocable unless it expressly provides that it is revocable. In addition to the method set forth in 7-1.17, a revocable lifetime trust can be revoked or amended by an express direction in the creator's will which specifically refers to such lifetime trust or a particular provision thereof.

History: Add, L 1997, ch 139, § 3, eff June 25, 1997, and applicable to lifetime trusts created on and after June 25, 1997.

§ 7-1.17. Execution, amendment and revocation of lifetime trusts

(a) Every lifetime trust shall be in writing and shall be executed and acknowledged by the person establishing such trust and, unless such person is the sole trustee, by at least one trustee thereof, in the manner required by the laws of this state for the recording of a conveyance of real property or, in lieu thereof, executed in the presence of two witnesses who shall affix their signatures to the trust instrument.

(b) Any amendment or revocation authorized by the trust shall be in writing and executed by the person authorized to amend or revoke the trust, and except as otherwise provided in the governing instrument, shall be acknowledged or witnessed in the manner required by paragraph (a) of this section, and shall take effect as of the date of such execution. Written notice of such amendment or revocation shall be delivered to at least one other trustee within a reasonable time if the person executing such amendment or revocation is not the sole trustee, but failure to give such notice shall not affect the validity of the amendment or revocation or the date upon which same shall take effect. No trustee shall be liable for any act reasonably taken in reliance on an existing trust instrument prior to actual receipt of notice of amendment or revocation thereof.

History: Add, L 1997, ch 139, § 3, eff Dec 25, 1997, and applicable to lifetime trusts created on and after Dec 25, 1997; amd, L 2010, ch 451, § 1, eff Aug 30, 2010, and applying to all lifetime trusts created on or after Dec 25, 1997.

§ 7-1.18. Funding of lifetime trust

A lifetime trust shall be valid as to any assets therein to the extent the assets have been transferred to the trust. For purposes of this section, (a) transfer is not accomplished by recital of assignment, holding or receipt in the trust instrument, and (b) in the case of a trust of which the creator is the sole trustee, transfer shall mean in the case of assets capable of registration such as real estate, stocks, bonds, bank and brokerage accounts and the like, the recording of the deed or the completion of registration of the asset in the name of the trust or trustee, and in the case of other assets a written assignment describing the asset with particularity.

History: Add, L 1997, ch 139, § 3, eff Dec 25, 1997, and applicable to lifetime trusts created on and after Dec 25, 1997.

§ 7-1.19. Application for termination of uneconomical trust

(a) Notwithstanding sections 7-1.5 and 7-2.4 of this article or any other contrary provision of law:

(1) Any trustee or beneficiary of a lifetime or testamentary express trust (other than a wholly charitable trust) may, by application to the surrogate's court having jurisdiction over the trust, seek a termination of such trust when the expense of administering the trust is uneconomical.

(2) If, upon such application, the court finds that continuation of the trust is economically impracticable, that the express terms of the disposing instrument do not prohibit its early termination, and that such termination would not defeat the specified purpose of the trust and would be in the best interests of the beneficiaries, the court may make an order or decree terminating the trust and directing the distribution of the trust assets to and among those beneficiaries who at the time are entitled (or entitled in the discretion of the trustee) to the income and/or principal of the trust and those beneficiaries who would be entitled (or entitled in the discretion of the trustee) to the income and/or principal of the trust if it were to terminate immediately before such order or decree. The distribution of the trust assets shall be made in such manner, proportions and shares as in the judgment of the court will effectuate the intention of the creator.

(b) Notice of the application shall be given to such persons and at such time and in such manner as the court, in its discretion, may direct.

(c) If the application or the possibility of the application of this section to any trust would reduce or eliminate a charitable deduction otherwise available to any person under the income tax, gift tax, estate tax or generation-skipping transfer tax provisions of the United States Internal Revenue Code, or the laws of any state of the United States or of the District of Columbia, this section shall not apply to such trust.

(d) This section shall not apply to a supplemental needs trust which conforms to the provisions of section 7-1.12 of this part.

History: Add, L 2004, ch 359, § 1, eff Aug 10, 2004, applying to proceedings to terminate a trust whenever created.

PART 2   Rules Governing Trustees

§ 7-2.1. Extent of trustee's estate

(a) Except as otherwise provided in this article, an express trust vests in the trustee the legal estate, subject only to the execution of the trust, and the beneficiary does not take any legal estate in the property but may enforce the trust.

(b) This section does not prevent the creator of a trust from providing to whom the property shall belong in the event of the failure or termination of the trust or from disposing of the property subject to the execution of the trust. Such a transferee shall have a legal estate in the property as against all persons except the trustee and those lawfully claiming under him.

(c) A trust as described in sections 9-1.5, 9-1.6 and 9-1.7 of the estates, powers and trusts law, including a business trust as defined in subdivision two of section two of the general associations law, may acquire property in the name of the trust as such name is designated in the instrument creating said trust. Any property, so acquired can be conveyed, encumbered or otherwise disposed of only in such name by a conveyance, encumbrance or other instrument executed by:

EPTL

(1) the person or persons authorized by the instrument creating said trust; or

(2) the person or persons authorized by a resolution duly adopted by the trustees; or

(3) a majority of the trustees unless the instrument creating said trust otherwise provides.

Any instrument of conveyance, encumbrance or disposition delivered prior to the effective date of this section to or by a trust to which this section applies, in its trust name is hereby validated provided that no action or proceeding to cancel or disaffirm it shall be instituted within one year from the effective date hereof, but nothing herein contained shall affect any such pending action or proceeding.

> **History:** Add, L 1966, ch 952, eff Sept 1, 1967, with substance deriving from RPL §§ 100 and 101; amd, L 1973, ch 1031, § 1, eff June 23, 1973.

§ 7-2.2. When estate of trustee ceases

When the purpose for which an express trust is created ceases, the estate of the trustee also ceases.

> **History:** Add, L 1966, ch 952, eff Sept 1, 1967, with substance deriving from RPL § 109.

§ 7-2.3. Trust estate not to descend on death of trustee; appointment, duties and rights of successor trustee

(a) On the death of the sole surviving trustee of an express trust, the trust estate does not vest in his personal representative or pass to his distributees or devisees, but, in the absence of a contrary direction by the creator, if the trust has not been executed, the trust estate vests in the supreme court or the surrogate's court, as the case may be, and the trust shall be executed by a person appointed by the court.

(b) Upon such notice to the beneficiaries of the trust as the court may direct of an application for the appointment of a successor trustee, unless the creator has directed otherwise, the court may appoint a successor trustee, even though the trust has terminated, whenever in the opinion of the court such appointment is necessary for the effective administration and distribution of the trust estate, subject to the following:

(1) A successor trustee shall give security in such amount as the court may direct.

(2) A successor trustee shall be subject to the same duties, as to accounting and trust administration, as are imposed by law on trustees and, in addition to the reasonable expenses incurred in the course of trust administration, shall be entitled to such commissions as may be fixed by any court having jurisdiction to pass upon such trustee's final account, which shall in no case exceed the commissions allowable by law to trustees.

> **History:** Add, L 1966, ch 952, eff Sept 1, 1967, with substance deriving from PPL § 20 and RPL § 111; amd, L 1967, ch 686, § 55, eff Sept 1, 1967.

§ 7-2.4. Act of trustee in contravention of trust

If the trust is expressed in the instrument creating the estate of the trustee, every sale, conveyance or other act of the trustee in contravention of the trust, except as authorized by this article and by any other provision of law, is void.

> **History:** Add, L 1966, ch 952, eff Sept 1, 1967, with substance deriving from RPL § 105.

§ 7-2.5. Suspension of powers of trustee in war service

(a) Whenever a trustee of an express trust is engaged in war service, as defined in this section, such trustee or any other person interested in the trust estate may present a petition to the supreme court or the surrogate's court, as the case may be, to suspend the powers of such trustee while he is so engaged and until the further order of the court, and if the suspension of such trustee will leave no person acting as trustee or leave a beneficiary of such trust as the only acting trustee thereof, the petition must pray for the appointment of a successor trustee, unless a successor has been named in the trust instrument and is not engaged in war service or is not for any other reason unable or unwilling to act as such trustee.

(b) For the purposes of this section, a trustee is engaged in war service in any of the following cases:

(1) If he is a member of the armed forces of the United States or of any of its allies, or if he has been accepted for such service and is awaiting induction.

(2) If he is engaged in any work abroad in connection with a governmental agency of the United States or with the American Red Cross Society or any other body with similar objectives.

(3) If he is interned in any enemy country or is in a foreign country or a possession or dependency of the United States and is unable to return to this state.

(4) If he is a member of the Merchant Marine or similar service.

(c) Where the application is made by a trustee engaged in war service, notice shall be given to such persons and in such manner as the court may direct. Where the application is made by any other person interested in the trust estate and the trustee is in the armed forces of the United States, notice shall be given to such trustee in such manner as the court may direct. In every other case, where the application is made by a person other than the trustee, notice thereof shall be given to such persons and in such manner as the court may direct.

(d) Upon the filing of the petition and proof of service of notice prescribed in paragraph (c), the court may, notwithstanding any other provision of law, suspend the trustee engaged in war service from the exercise of all of his powers and duties while engaged in such service and until the further order of the court. The order may further provide that the remaining trustee or, if there is none, the successor named in the trust instrument or appointed by the court may exercise all of the powers and be subject to all of the duties of the original trustee.

(e) The successor trustee shall be limited to commissions as computed under SCPA 2308 or 2309, whichever is applicable, upon income received and disbursed and upon principal disbursed. Commissions may also be allowed under 2308 or 2309 upon rents if he is authorized or required to collect the rents of and manage real property. In case of the resignation or removal of the suspended trustee, or in the event of such trustee's death, the foregoing basis for computing the commissions shall not apply and his commissions shall be computed in the same manner as those of any other trustee.

(f) When the suspended trustee ceases to be engaged in war service he may, upon application to the court and upon such notice as the court may direct, be reinstated as trustee if any of the duties of such office remain unexecuted. If the suspended trustee is reinstated the court shall thereupon remove his successor and make such other order as justice requires, but such removal shall not bar the successor from subsequently qualifying as a trustee if for any reason it thereafter becomes necessary to appoint a trustee.

> **History:** Add, L 1966, ch 952, eff Sept 1, 1967, with substance deriving from PPL § 20-a
> and RPL § 111-a; amd, L 1967, ch 686, § 56, eff Sept 1, 1967.

§ 7-2.6. Resignation, suspension or removal of trustee

(a)* Subject to the relevant provisions of the civil practice law and rules, the supreme court has power:

(1) On the application of a trustee, to accept his resignation and to discharge him on such terms as it deems proper.

(2) On the application of any person interested in the trust estate, to suspend or remove a trustee who has violated or threatens to violate his trust, who is insolvent or whose insolvency is imminent or apprehended or who for any reason is a person unsuitable to execute the trust.

(3) In case of the resignation or removal of a trustee, to appoint a successor trustee and, if there is no acting trustee, to cause the trust to be executed by a receiver or other officer under its direction. This section does not apply to a trust arising or resulting by implication of law, nor where other provision is made by law for the resignation, suspension or removal of a trustee or the appointment of a successor trustee.

> **History:** Add, L 1966, ch 952, eff Sept 1, 1967, with substance deriving from RPL § 112
> amd, L 1967, ch 686, § 58, eff Sept 1, 1967.

§ 7-2.7. Accounting by trustee in supreme court

(a) Any proceeding for an accounting or other relief brought by a trustee or by a substituted or successor trustee may be commenced by such notice to the beneficiaries of the trust as the supreme court may direct.

(b) In case of the resignation, suspension or removal, pursuant to this article, of any trustee of a trust which includes real property and mortgage participation certificates held by more than one person and secured by a mortgage on real property or any estate therein, payment of which certificates is not guaranteed by the trustee or by any title or mortgage guaranty or investment company, the court in its discretion may dispense with a formal accounting by such trustee; but the trustee shall file with the court a statement of the condition of the trust and of the security underlying such certificates as of the date of his resignation, suspension or removal and shall assign, transfer or convey all of the assets of the trust to the successor trustee or to the receiver or other officer appointed by the court, as the case may be.

> **History:** Add, L 1966, ch 952, eff Sept 1, 1967, with substance deriving from RPL § 112-a;
> amd, L 1967, ch 686, § 59, eff Sept 1, 1967.

§ 7-2.8. Commissions of trustee to sell real property for benefit of creditors

A trustee of a trust to sell real property for the benefit of creditors is entitled to the same commissions as an assignee for the benefit of creditors.

> **History:** Add, L 1966, ch 952, eff Sept 1, 1967, with substance deriving from PPL § 22
> and RPL § 117.

---

* **Ed. Note**: There is no paragraph (b).

PART 3   Rights of Purchasers, Creditors and Other Persons

§ 7-3.1. Disposition in trust for creator void as against creditors

(a) A disposition in trust for the use of the creator is void as against the existing or subsequent creditors of the creator.

(b) (1) For purposes of paragraph (a) of this section, all trusts, custodial accounts, annuities, insurance contracts, monies, assets or interests established as part of, and all payments from, either an individual retirement account plan which is qualified under section 408 or section 408A of the United States Internal Revenue Code of 1986, as amended, or a Keogh (HR-10), retirement or other plan established by a corporation, which is qualified under section 401 of the United States Internal Revenue Code of 1986, as amended, shall not be considered a disposition in trust for the use of the creator, even though the creator is (i) in the case of an individual retirement account plan, an individual who is the settlor of and depositor to such account plan, or (ii) a self-employed individual, or (iii) a partner of the entity sponsoring the Keogh (HR-10) plan, or (iv) a shareholder of the corporation sponsoring the retirement or other plan.

(2) All trusts, custodial accounts, annuities, insurance contracts, monies, assets, or interests described in subparagraph one of this paragraph shall be conclusively presumed to be spendthrift trusts under this section and the common law of the state of New York for all purposes, including, but not limited to, all cases arising under or related to a case arising under sections one hundred one to thirteen hundred thirty of title eleven of the United States Bankruptcy Code, as amended.

(3) This section shall not impair any rights an individual has under a qualified domestic relations order as that term is defined in section 414(p) of the United States Internal Revenue Code of 1986, as amended.

(4) Additions to an asset described in subparagraph one of this paragraph shall not be exempt from application to the satisfaction of a money judgment if (i) made after the date that is ninety days before the interposition of the claim on which such judgment was entered, or (ii) deemed to be voidable transactions under article ten of the debtor and creditor law.

(c) A provision in any trust, other than a testamentary trust or a trust which meets the requirements of subparagraph two of paragraph (b) of subdivision two of section three hundred sixty-six of the social services law and of the regulations implementing such clauses, which provides directly or indirectly for the suspension, termination or diversion of the principal, income or beneficial interest of either the creator or the creator's spouse in the event that the creator or creator's spouse should apply for medical assistance or require medical, hospital or nursing care or long term custodial, nursing or medical care shall be void as against the public policy of the state of New York, without regard to the irrevocability of the trust or the purpose for which the trust was created.

(d) A disposition in trust shall not be considered to be for the use of the creator under paragraph (a) of this section by reason of the trustee's authority to pay trust principal to the creator pursuant to section 7-1.11 of this article. Nor shall a disposition in trust be considered to be for the use of the creator under paragraph (a) of this section where the trustee is authorized under the trust instrument or any other provision of law to pay or reimburse the creator for any tax on trust income or trust principal that is payable by the creator under the law imposing such tax or to pay any such tax directly to the taxing authorities. No creditor of a trust creator shall be entitled to reach any trust property based on the discretionary powers described in this paragraph.

History: Add, L 1966, ch 952, eff Sept 1, 1967, with substance deriving from PPL § 36; amd, L 1987, ch 108, § 2, eff June 8, 1987; L 1989, ch 280, § 3, eff July 7, 1989; L 1992, ch 41, eff April 2, 1992, only as to inter vivos trusts created on or after April 2, 1992; L 1994, ch 170, § 454, eff June 9, 1994, deemed eff April 1, 1994, "provided that nothing contained in [the] sections . . . shall be deemed to affect the application, qualification, expiration or repeal of any provision of law amended by any such sections and such provisions shall be applied or qualified or shall expire or be deemed repealed in the same manner, to the same extent and on the same date as the case may be as otherwise provided by law . . . ."; L 1995, ch 93, eff Sept 1, 1995; L 1998, ch 206, § 2, eff July 7, 1998, deemed eff on and after Jan 1, 1998; L 2005, ch 76, § 1, eff May 31, 2005, and applying to all instruments created before, on or after such effective date; L 2019, ch 580, § 5, eff April 4, 2020.

§ 7-3.2. Bona fide purchasers and creditors protected

An express trust not declared in the disposition to the trustee or an implied or resulting trust does not defeat the title of a purchaser from the trustee for value and without notice of the trust, or the rights of a creditor who extended credit to the trustee in reliance upon his apparent ownership of the trust property.

History: Add, L 1966, ch 952, eff Sept 1, 1967, with substance deriving from RPL §§ 95, 104.

§ 7-3.3. Person paying money to the trustee protected

A person who in good faith transfers money or property to a trustee is not responsible for the proper application of such money or property; and any right or title derived by him from the trustee in consideration of such transfer is not affected by the trustee's misapplication of such money or property.

History: Add, L 1966, ch 952, eff Sept 1, 1967, with substance deriving from RPL § 108.

§ 7-3.4. Excess income from trust property subject to creditors' claims

Where a trust is created to receive the income from property and no valid direction for accumulation is given, the income in excess of the sum necessary for the education and support of the beneficiary is subject to the claims of his creditors in the same manner as other property which cannot be reached by execution.

History: Add, L 1966, ch 952, eff Sept 1, 1967, with substance deriving from RPL § 98.

§ 7-3.5. Rights of creditors to obtain information concerning beneficiaries

(a) Any person who has furnished necessaries to a beneficiary of any trust may apply to the court having jurisdiction of the trust for an order directing the trustee thereof to furnish to the applicant the true and full name and residence address of any such beneficiary. As used in this section, the term "necessaries" means goods furnished and services performed suitable to the condition in life of the person to whom they are furnished or for whose benefit they are performed, and which meet his actual needs at the time such necessaries are provided.

(b) The application shall be made by a verified petition which states (1) the name and address of petitioner, (2) the nature and extent of the necessaries provided, (3) the person by whom and the circumstances under which they were provided, (4) the amount of the indebtedness claimed to exist, (5) the name of the person to whom or for whose benefit such necessaries were provided, (6) a description of the trust of which the person to whom such necessaries were provided is a beneficiary and (7) the name of the trustee administering such trust.

(c) Such petition shall also show the efforts made by the petitioner to locate the beneficiary and that more than ten days have elapsed since petitioner requested in writing that the trustee furnish the address of any such beneficiary. The petition may contain such other information as is relevant to the inquiry.

(d) The proceeding may be initiated by citation or order to show cause served on the trustee personally or in such manner and at such time as the court may direct. A copy of the petition shall be served with the process.

(e) Upon the return of the process the court, if satisfied that the allegations of the petition are true and that the petitioner is entitled to the relief sought, may make an order directing the trustee to furnish to petitioner the true and full name and residence address of any beneficiary to whom necessaries were provided. The order may fix the time within which such name and address shall be furnished. Failure to comply with an order so made shall be punishable as a contempt of court.

History: Add, L 1966, ch 952, eff Sept 1, 1967, with substance deriving from PPL § 15-b.

PART 4   Gifts to Minors[*]
PART 5   Bank Accounts in Trust Form

§ 7-5.1. Definitions

(a) A "beneficiary" is a person who is described by a depositor as a person for whom a trust account is established or maintained.

(b) A "depositor" is a person in whose name a trust account subject to this part is established or maintained.

(c) A "financial institution" is a bank, trust company, national banking association, savings bank, industrial bank, private banker, foreign banking corporation, federal savings and loan association, a savings institution chartered and supervised as a savings and loan or similar institution under federal law or the laws of a state, a federal credit union, or a credit union chartered and supervised under the laws of a state.

(d) A "trust account" includes a savings, share, certificate or deposit account in a financial institution established by a depositor describing himself as trustee for another, other than a depositor describing himself as acting under a will, trust instrument or other instrument, court order or decree.

History: Add, L 1975, ch 499, § 1, eff Sept 1, 1975.

§ 7-5.2. Terms of a trust account

The funds in a trust account, which shall include any dividends or interest thereon, shall be trust funds subject to the following terms:

(1) The trust can be revoked, terminated or modified by the depositor during his lifetime

---

[*]   Repealed. See EPTL 7-6.22 for treatment of accounts established under Part 4.

only by means of, and to the extent of, withdrawals from or charges against the trust account made or authorized by the depositor or by a writing which specifically names the beneficiary and the financial institution. The writing shall be acknowledged or proved in the manner required to entitle conveyances of real property to be recorded, and shall be filed with the financial institution wherein the account is maintained.

(2) A trust can be revoked, terminated or modified by the depositor's will only by means of, and to the extent of, an express direction concerning such trust account, which must be described in the will as being in trust for a named beneficiary in a named financial institution. Where the depositor has more than one trust account for a particular beneficiary in a particular financial institution, such a direction will affect all such accounts, unless the direction is limited to one or more accounts specifically identified by account number in addition to the foregoing requirements. A testamentary revocation, termination or modification under this paragraph can be effected by express words of revocation, termination or modification, or by a specific bequest of the trust account, or any part of it, to someone other than the beneficiary. A bequest of part of a trust account shall operate as a pro tanto revocation to the extent of the bequest.

(3) If the depositor survives the beneficiary, the trust shall terminate and title to the funds shall continue in the depositor free and clear of the trust.

(4) If the beneficiary survives the depositor, and the depositor's will contains no provision revoking, terminating or modifying the trust account under paragraph (2), the trust shall terminate and title to the funds shall vest in the beneficiary free and clear of the trust.

(5) If the beneficiary survives the depositor and the depositor's will contains language sufficient under paragraph two of this section, to revoke, terminate or modify the trust, in whole or in part, that part of the trust which is affected shall terminate and title to the funds shall be subject to disposition by the depositor's will, free and clear of the trust.

History: Add, L 1975, ch 499, § 1, eff Sept 1, 1975; amd, L 1985, ch 89, § 1, eff Sept 1, 1985.

§ 7-5.3. Payment to beneficiary

(a) If the beneficiary survives the depositor under the circumstances provided in paragraph four of section 7-5.2, the funds shall be paid to the beneficiary upon his order, if, at the time of his demand for payment of all or part of the funds, he is eighteen or more years of age.

(b) If the beneficiary survives the depositor under the circumstances provided in paragraph four of section 7-5.2, and if the beneficiary is under eighteen years of age at the time demand for payment of any part or all of the funds is made, the funds may be paid to the order of the parent or parents of the beneficiary to be held for the use and benefit of such infant beneficiary or to the order of the duly appointed guardian of the property of the beneficiary, if the funds are equal to or are less than ten thousand dollars; but if the funds are more than ten thousand dollars, the funds may be paid only to the order of the duly appointed guardian of the property of the beneficiary.

History: Add, L 1975, ch 499, § 1, eff Sept 1, 1975; amd, L 1976, ch 127, eff April 13, 1976; L 1982, ch 358, eff June 21, 1982; L 1995, ch 169, § 1, eff July 19, 1995.

§ 7-5.4. Effect of payment

A financial institution which, upon the death of a depositor and prior to service upon it of a restraining order, injunction or other appropriate process from a court of competent jurisdiction prohibiting payment, makes payment to a beneficiary or if the beneficiary is under eighteen years of age, to the guardian of the property or to the parent or parents of the infant beneficiary pursuant to section 7-5.3, shall, to the extent of such payment, be released from liability to any person claiming a right to the funds and the receipt or acquittance of the person to whom payment is made shall be a valid and sufficient release and discharge of the financial institution.

> **History:** Add, L 1975, ch 499, eff Sept 1, 1975; amd, L 1976, ch 126, § 1, eff April 13, 1976.

§ 7-5.5. Rights not affected

This part does not affect:

(1) The rights of creditors of the depositor or his estate,

(2) The rights of fiduciaries of the estate of the depositor, or

(3) The rights of the surviving spouse of the depositor.

> **History:** Add, L 1975, ch 499, § 1, eff Sept 1, 1975.

§ 7-5.6. Joint depositors

If a trust account is established in the names of more than one depositor, in form to be paid or delivered to any, or the survivor of them, in trust for another, such account shall be subject to the terms of this part, except that the title to the funds on deposit, as between the depositors, shall be governed by article XIII-E of the banking law.

> **History:** Add, L 1975, ch 499, eff Sept 1, 1975; amd, L 1994, ch 300, § 9, eff July 20, 1994, and applying to taxable periods ending on or after Aug 9, 1989.

§ 7-5.7. Multiple beneficiaries

(a) Whenever any proceeds of a trust account would pass pursuant to section 7-5.2 to two or more beneficiaries, such proceeds shall pass to such beneficiaries in equal proportions, unless the terms of the trust provide otherwise.

(b) Whenever any proceeds of a trust account would pass pursuant to section 7-5.2 to two or more beneficiaries, and one or more of the beneficiaries predeceases the depositor, such proceeds shall pass to the surviving beneficiary or beneficiaries in equal proportions, unless the terms of the trust provide otherwise.

> **History:** Add, L 1998, ch 518, § 1, eff July 29, 1998. Former § 7-5.7 was renumbered § 7-5.8.

§ 7-5.8. Application

This part shall apply to all funds in trust accounts, as defined in paragraph (d) of section 7-5.1, which are in existence on its effective date, except that its provisions shall not impair or defeat any rights which have accrued prior to such date.

> **History:** Formerly § 7-5.7, add, L 1975, ch 499, § 1; renumbered § 7-5.8, L 1998, ch 518, § 1, eff July 29, 1998.

PART 6   Uniform Transfers to Minors Act

§ 7-6.1. Definitions

In this part:

(a) "Adult" means an individual who has attained the age of twenty-one years.

(b) "Benefit plan" means an employer's plan for the benefit of an employee or partner or an individual retirement account.

(c) "Broker" means a person lawfully engaged in the business of effecting transactions in securities or commodities for the person's own account or for the account of others.

(d) "Court" means the supreme court or the surrogate's court having jurisdiction over the minor.

(e) "Custodial property" means (i) any interest in property transferred to a custodian under this part and (ii) the income from and proceeds of that interest in property.

(f) "Custodian" means a person so designated under 7-6.9 or a successor or substitute custodian designated under 7-6.18.

(g) "Financial institution" means a bank, trust company, savings institution, or credit union, chartered and supervised under state or federal law.

(h) "Guardian" means a person appointed or qualified by a court to act as general, limited, or temporary guardian of a minor's property or a person legally authorized to perform substantially the same functions.

(i) "Legal representative" means an individual's personal representative or guardian.

(j) "Member of the minor's family" means any of the minor's parents, stepparents, spouse, grandparents, brothers, sisters, uncles, and aunts, whether of the whole blood or half blood or by or through legal adoption.

(k) "Minor" means an individual who has not attained the age of twenty-one years.

(l) "Person" means an individual, corporation, organization, or other legal entity.

(m) "Personal representative" means a person who has received letters to administer the estate of a decedent or a person legally authorized to perform substantially the same functions.

(n) "State" includes any state of the United States, the District of Columbia, the Commonwealth of Puerto Rico, and any territory or possession subject to the legislative authority of the United States.

(o) "Transfer" means a transaction that creates custodial property under 7-6.9.

(p) "Transferor" means a person who makes a transfer under this part.

(q) "Trust company" means a financial institution, corporation, or other legal entity, authorized to exercise general trust powers in this state.

History: Add, L 1996, ch 304, § 2, eff July 10, 1996, applying to transfers made on or after Jan 1, 1997, and replacing the Uniform Gifts to Minors Act, EPTL 7-4.1 and 7-4.12. See EPTL 7-6.23 for applicability of this Part.

§ 7-6.2. Scope and jurisdiction

(a) This part applies to a transfer that refers to this part in the designation under paragraph (a) of 7-6.9 by which the transfer is made if at the time of the transfer, the transferor, the minor, or the custodian is a resident of this state or the custodial property is located in this state. The custodianship so created remains subject to this part despite a subsequent change in residence of a transferor, the minor, or the custodian, or the removal of custodial property from this state.

(b) A person designated as custodian under this part is subject to personal jurisdiction in this state with respect to any matter relating to the custodianship.

(c) A transfer that purports to be made and which is valid under the Uniform Transfers to Minors Act, the Uniform Gifts to Minors Act, or a substantially similar act, of another state is governed by the law of the designated state and may be executed and is enforceable in this state if at the time of the transfer, the transferor, the minor, or the custodian is a resident of the designated state or the custodial property is located in the designated state.

> **History:** Add, L 1996, ch 304, § 2, eff July 10, 1996, applying to transfers made on or after Jan 1, 1997, and replacing the Uniform Gifts to Minors Act, EPTL 7-4.1 and 7-4.12. See EPTL 7-6.23 for applicability of this Part.

§ 7-6.3. Nomination of custodian

(a) A person having the right to designate the recipient of property transferable upon the occurrence of a future event may revocably nominate a custodian to receive the property for a minor beneficiary upon the occurrence of the event by naming the custodian followed in substance by the words "as custodian for _____ (name of minor) under the New York Uniform Transfers to Minors Act." The nomination may name one or more persons as substitute custodians to whom the property must be transferred, in the order named, if the first nominated custodian dies before the transfer or is unable, declines, or is ineligible to serve. The nomination may be made in a will, a trust, a deed, an instrument exercising a power of appointment, or in a writing designating a beneficiary of contractual rights which is registered with or delivered to the payor, issuer, or other obligor of the contractual rights.

(b) A custodian nominated under this section must be a person to whom a transfer of property of that kind may be made under paragraph (a) of 7-6.9.

(c) The nomination of a custodian under this section does not create custodial property until the nominating instrument becomes irrevocable or a transfer to the nominated custodian is completed under 7-6.9. Unless the nomination of a custodian has been revoked, upon the occurrence of the future event the custodianship becomes effective and the custodian shall enforce a transfer of the custodial property pursuant to 7-6.9.

> **History:** Add, L 1996, ch 304, § 2, eff July 10, 1996, applying to transfers made on or after Jan 1, 1997, and replacing the Uniform Gifts to Minors Act, EPTL 7-4.1 and 7-4.12. See EPTL 7-6.23 for applicability of this Part.

§ 7-6.4. Transfer by gift or exercise of power of appointment

A person may make a transfer by irrevocable gift to, or the irrevocable exercise of a power of appointment in favor of, a custodian for the benefit of a minor pursuant to 7-6.9.

> **History:** Add, L 1996, ch 304, § 2, eff July 10, 1996, applying to transfers made on or after Jan 1, 1997, and replacing the Uniform Gifts to Minors Act, EPTL 7-4.1 and 7-4.12. See EPTL 7-6.23 for applicability of this Part.

§ 7-6.5. Transfer authorized by will or trust

(a) A personal representative or trustee may make an irrevocable transfer pursuant to 7-6.9 to a custodian for the benefit of a minor as authorized in the governing will or trust.

EPTL

(b) If the testator or settler has nominated a custodian under 7-6.3 to receive the custodial property, the transfer must be made to that person.

(c) If the testator or settler has not nominated a custodian under 7-6.3, or all persons so nominated as custodian die before the transfer or are unable, decline, or are ineligible to serve, the personal representative or the trustee, as the case may be, shall designate the custodian from among those eligible to serve as custodian for property of that kind under paragraph (a) of 7-6.9.

> **History:** Add, L 1996, ch 304, § 2, eff July 10, 1996, applying to transfers made on or after Jan 1, 1997, and replacing the Uniform Gifts to Minors Act, EPTL 7-4.1 and 7-4.12. See EPTL 7-6.23 for applicability of this Part.

§ 7-6.6. Other transfer by fiduciary

(a) Subject to paragraph (c), a personal representative or trustee may make an irrevocable transfer to another adult or trust company as custodian for the benefit of a minor pursuant to 7-6.9, in the absence of a will or under a will or trust that does not contain an authorization to do so.

(b) Subject to paragraph (c), a guardian may make an irrevocable transfer to another adult or trust company as custodian for the benefit of the minor pursuant to 7-6.9.

(c) A transfer under paragraph (a) or (b) may be made only if (i) the personal representative, trustee, or guardian considers the transfer to be in the best interest of the minor, (ii) the transfer is not prohibited by or inconsistent with provisions of the applicable will, trust agreement, or other governing instrument, and (iii) if the personal representative is acting in the absence of a will, the transfer is authorized by the court if it exceeds fifty thousand dollars in value.

> **History:** Add, L 1996, ch 304, § 2, eff July 10, 1996, applying to transfers made on or after Jan 1, 1997, and replacing the Uniform Gifts to Minors Act, EPTL 7-4.1 and 7-4.12. See EPTL 7-6.23 for applicability of this Part.

§ 7-6.7. Transfer by obligor

(a) Subject to paragraphs (b) and (c), a person not subject to 7-6.5 or 7-6.6 who holds property of or owes a liquidated debt to a minor not having a guardian may make an irrevocable transfer to a custodian for the benefit of the minor pursuant to 7-6.9.

(b) If a person having the right to do so under 7-6.3 has nominated a custodian under that section to receive the custodial property, the transfer must be made to that person.

(c) If no custodian has been nominated under 7-6.3, or all persons so nominated as custodian die before the transfer or are unable, decline, or are ineligible to serve, a transfer under this section may be made to an adult member of the minor's family, unless the property exceeds fifty thousand dollars in value, or to a trust company.

> **History:** Add, L 1996, ch 304, § 2, eff July 10, 1996, applying to transfers made on or after Jan 1, 1997, and replacing the Uniform Gifts to Minors Act, EPTL 7-4.1 and 7-4.12. See EPTL 7-6.23 for applicability of this Part.

§ 7-6.8. Receipt for custodial property

A written acknowledgement of delivery by a custodian constitutes a sufficient receipt and discharge for custodial property transferred to a custodian pursuant to this part.

> **History:** Add, L 1996, ch 304, § 2, eff July 10, 1996, applying to transfers made on or after

Jan 1, 1997, and replacing the Uniform Gifts to Minors Act, EPTL 7-4.1 and 7-4.12. See EPTL 7-6.23 for applicability of this Part.

§ 7-6.9. Manner of creating custodial property and effecting transfer; designation of initial custodian; control

(a) Custodial property is created and a transfer is made whenever:

(1) an uncertificated security or certificated security in registered form is either:

(i) registered in the name of the transferor, an adult other than the transferor, or a trust company, followed in substance by the words: "as custodian for _____ (name of minor) under the New York Uniform Transfers to Minors Act"; or

(ii) delivered, if in certificated form, or any document necessary for the transfer of an uncertificated security is delivered, together with any necessary endorsement, to an adult other than the transferor or to a trust company, as custodian, accompanied by an instrument in substantially the form set forth in paragraph (b);

(2) money is paid or delivered, or a security held in the name of a broker, financial institution, or its nominee is transferred, to a broker or financial institution for credit to an account in the name of the transferor, an adult other than the transferor, or a trust company, followed in substance by the words: "as custodian for _____ (name of minor) under the New York Uniform Transfers to Minors Act";

(3) the ownership of a life or endowment insurance policy or annuity contract is either:

(i) registered with the issuer in the name of the transferor, an adult other than the transferor, or a trust company, followed in substance by the words: "as custodian for _____ (name of minor) under the New York Uniform Transfers to Minors Act"; or

(ii) assigned in a writing delivered to an adult other than the transferor, or to a trust company whose name in the assignment is followed in substance by the words: "as custodian for _____ (name of minor) under the New York Uniform Transfers to Minors Act";

(4) an irrevocable exercise of a power of appointment or an irrevocable present right to future payment under a contract is the subject of a written notification delivered to the payor, issuer, or other obligor that the right is transferred to the transferor, an adult other than the transferor, or a trust company, whose name in the notification is followed in substance by the words: "as custodian for _____ (name of minor) under the New York Uniform Transfers to Minors Act";

(5) an interest in real property is recorded in the name of the transferor, an adult other than the transferor, or a trust company, followed in substance by the words: "as custodian for _____ (name of minor) under the New York Uniform Transfers to Minors Act";

(6) a certificate of title issued by a department or agency of a state or of the United States which evidences title to tangible personal property is either:

(i) issued in the name of the transferor, an adult other than the transferor, or a trust company, followed in substance by the words: "as custodian for _____ (name of minor) under the New York Uniform Transfers to Minors Act"; or

(ii) delivered to an adult other than the transferor or to a trust company, endorsed to that person followed in substance by the words: "as custodian for _____ (name of minor) under the New York Uniform Transfers to Minors Act"; or

(7) an interest in any property not described in subparagraphs (1) through (6) is transferred to an adult other than the transferor or to a trust company by a written instrument in substantially the form set forth in paragraph (b).

(b) An instrument in the following form satisfies the requirements of clause (ii) of subparagraph (1) and subparagraph (7) of paragraph (a):

"TRANSFER UNDER THE NEW YORK UNIFORM TRANSFERS TO MINORS ACT

I, _____ (name of transferor or name and representative capacity if a fiduciary) hereby transfer to _____ (name of custodian), as custodian for _____ (name of minor) under the New York Uniform Transfers to Minors Act, the following: (insert a description of the custodial property sufficient to identify it).

Dated: _____

_____

(Signature)

_____ (name of custodian) acknowledges receipt of the property described above as custodian for the minor named above under the New York Uniform Transfers to Minors Act.

Dated: _____

_____

(Signature of Custodian)

(c) A transferor shall place the custodian in control of the custodial property as soon as practicable.

History: Add, L 1996, ch 304, § 2, eff July 10, 1996, applying to transfers made on or after Jan 1, 1997, and replacing the Uniform Gifts to Minors Act, EPTL 7-4.1 and 7-4.12. See EPTL 7-6.23 for applicability of this Part.

§ 7-6.10. Single custodianship

A transfer may be made only for one minor, and only one person may be the custodian. All custodial property held under this part by the same custodian for the benefit of the same minor constitutes a single custodianship.

History: Add, L 1996, ch 304, § 2, eff July 10, 1996, applying to transfers made on or after Jan 1, 1997, and replacing the Uniform Gifts to Minors Act, EPTL 7-4.1 and 7-4.12. See EPTL 7-6.23 for applicability of this Part.

§ 7-6.11. Validity and effect of transfer

(a) The validity of a transfer made in a manner prescribed in this part is not affected by:

(1) The failure of the transferor to comply with paragraph (c) of 7-6.9 concerning possession and control;

(2) designation of an ineligible custodian, except designation of the transferor in the

case of property for which the transferor is ineligible to serve as custodian under paragraph (a) of 7-6.9; or

(3) death or incapacity of a person nominated under 7-6.3 or designated under 7-6.9 as custodian or the disclaimer of the office by that person.

(b) A transfer made pursuant to 7-6.9 is irrevocable, and the custodial property is indefeasibly vested in the minor, but the custodian has all the rights, powers, duties, and authority provided in this part, and neither the minor nor the minor's legal representative has any right, power, duty, or authority with respect to the custodial property except as provided in this part.

(c) By making a transfer, the transferor incorporates in the disposition all the provisions of this part and grants to the custodian, and to any third person dealing with a person designated as custodian, the respective powers, rights, and immunities provided in this part.

> **History:** Add, L 1996, ch 304, § 2, eff July 10, 1996, applying to transfers made on or after Jan 1, 1997, and replacing the Uniform Gifts to Minors Act, EPTL 7-4.1 and 7-4.12. See EPTL 7-6.23 for applicability of this Part.

§ 7-6.12. Care of custodial property

(a) A custodian shall:

(1) take control of custodial property;

(2) register or record title to custodial property if appropriate; and

(3) collect, hold, manage, invest, and reinvest custodial property.

(b) In dealing with custodial property, a custodian shall observe the standard of care that would be observed by a prudent person dealing with property of another and is not limited by any other statute restricting investments by fiduciaries and is specifically authorized to delegate investment and management functions in the manner of a trustee as provided in section 11-2.3. If a custodian has a special skill or expertise or is named custodian on the basis of representations of a special skill or expertise, the custodian shall use that skill or expertise. However, a custodian, in the custodian's discretion and without liability to the minor or the minor's estate, may retain any custodial property received from a transferor.

(c) A custodian may invest in or pay premiums on life insurance or endowment policies on (1) the life of the minor only if the minor or the minor's estate is the sole beneficiary, or (2) the life of another person in whom the minor has an insurable interest only to the extent that the minor, the minor's estate, or the custodian in the capacity of custodian, is the irrevocable beneficiary.

(d) A custodian at all times shall keep custodial property separate and distinct from all other property in a manner sufficient to identify it clearly as custodial property of the minor. Custodial property consisting of certificated securities may be held on deposit at a stock brokerage firm or a financial institution registered in a street name or nominee name. Custodial property consisting of an undivided interest is so identified if the minor's interest is held as a tenant in common and is fixed. Custodial property subject to recordation is so identified if it is recorded, and custodial property subject to registration is so identified if it is either registered, or held in an account designated, in the name of the custodian, followed in substance by the words: "as a custodian for _____ (name of minor) under the

New York Uniform Transfers to Minors Act."

(e) A custodian shall keep records of all transactions with respect to custodial property, including information necessary for the preparation of the minor's tax returns, and shall make them available for inspection at reasonable intervals by a parent or legal representative of the minor or by the minor if the minor has attained the age of fourteen years.

> **History:** Add, L 1996, ch 304, § 2, eff July 10, 1996, applying to transfers made on or after Jan 1, 1997, and replacing the Uniform Gifts to Minors Act, EPTL 7-4.1 and 7-4.12. See EPTL 7-6.23 for applicability of this Part.

§ 7-6.13. Powers of custodian

(a) A custodian, acting in a custodial capacity, has all the rights, powers, and authority over custodial property that unmarried adult owners have over their own property, but a custodian may exercise those rights, powers, and authority in that capacity only.

(b) This section does not relieve a custodian from liability for breach of 7-6.12.

> **History:** Add, L 1996, ch 304, § 2, eff July 10, 1996, applying to transfers made on or after Jan 1, 1997, and replacing the Uniform Gifts to Minors Act, EPTL 7-4.1 and 7-4.12. See EPTL 7-6.23 for applicability of this Part.

§ 7-6.14. Use of custodial property

(a) A custodian may deliver or pay to the minor or expend for the minor's benefit so much of the custodial property as the custodian considers advisable for the use and benefit of the minor, without court order and without regard to (1) the duty or ability of the custodian personally or of any other person to support the minor, or (2) any other income or property of the minor which may be applicable or available for the support of the minor.

(b) On petition of an interested person or the minor if the minor has attained the age of fourteen years, the court may order the custodian to deliver or pay to the minor or expend for the minor's benefit so much of the custodial property as the court considers advisable for the use and benefit of the minor.

(c) A delivery, payment, or expenditure under this section is in addition to, not in substitution for, and does not affect any obligation of a person to support the minor.

> **History:** Add, L 1996, ch 304, § 2, eff July 10, 1996, applying to transfers made on or after Jan 1, 1997, and replacing the Uniform Gifts to Minors Act, EPTL 7-4.1 and 7-4.12. See EPTL 7-6.23 for applicability of this Part.

§ 7-6.15. Custodian's expenses, compensation, and bond

(a) A custodian is entitled to reimbursement from custodial property for reasonable expenses incurred in the performance of the custodian's duties.

(b) Except for one who is a transferor under 7-6.4, a custodian has an election during each calendar year to charge reasonable compensation for services performed during that year. A custodian's election to charge reasonable compensation for a calendar year must be exercised during the calendar year.

(c) Except as provided in paragraph (f) of 7-6.18, a custodian shall not be required to give a bond.

> **History:** Add, L 1996, ch 304, § 2, eff July 10, 1996, applying to transfers made on or after

Jan 1, 1997, and replacing the Uniform Gifts to Minors Act, EPTL 7-4.1 and 7-4.12. See EPTL 7-6.23 for applicability of this Part.

§ 7-6.16. Exemption of third person from liability

A third person in good faith and without court order may act on the instructions of or otherwise deal with any person purporting to make a transfer or purporting to act in the capacity of a custodian and, in the absence of knowledge, is not responsible for determining:

(a) the validity of the purported custodian's designation;

(b) the propriety of, or the authority under this part for, any act of the purported custodian;

(c) the validity or propriety under this part of any instrument or instructions executed or given either by the person purporting to make a transfer or by the purported custodian; or

(d) the propriety of the application of any property of the minor delivered to the purported custodian.

History: Add, L 1996, ch 304, § 2, eff July 10, 1996, applying to transfers made on or after Jan 1, 1997, and replacing the Uniform Gifts to Minors Act, EPTL 7-4.1 and 7-4.12. See EPTL 7-6.23 for applicability of this Part.

§ 7-6.17. Liability to third persons

(a) A claim based on (1) a contract entered into by a custodian acting in a custodial capacity, (2) an obligation arising from the ownership or control of custodial property, or (3) a tort committed during the custodianship, may be asserted against the custodial property by proceeding against the custodian in the custodial capacity, whether or not the custodian or the minor is personally liable therefor.

(b) A custodian is not personally liable:

(1) on a contract properly entered into in the custodial capacity unless the custodian fails to reveal that capacity and to identify the custodianship in the contract; or

(2) for an obligation arising from control of custodial property or for a tort committed during the custodianship unless the custodian is personally at fault.

(c) A minor is not personally liable for an obligation arising from ownership of custodial property or for a tort committed during the custodianship unless the minor is personally at fault.

History: Add, L 1996, ch 304, § 2, eff July 10, 1996, applying to transfers made on or after Jan 1, 1997, and replacing the Uniform Gifts to Minors Act, EPTL 7-4.1 and 7-4.12. See EPTL 7-6.23 for applicability of this Part.

§ 7-6.18. Renunciation, resignation, death, or removal of custodian; designation of successor custodian

(a) A person nominated under 7-6.3 or designated under 7-6.9 as custodian may decline to serve by delivering a valid disclaimer to the person who made the nomination or to the transferor or the transferor's legal representative. If the event giving rise to a transfer has not occurred and no substitute custodian able, willing, and eligible to serve was nominated under 7-6.3, the person who made the nomination may nominate a substitute custodian under 7-6.3; otherwise the transferor or the transferor's legal representative shall designate a substitute custodian at the time of the transfer, in either case from among the persons eligible to serve as custodian for that kind of property under paragraph (a) of 7-6.9. The custodian so designated has the rights of a successor custodian.

(b) A custodian at any time may designate a trust company or an adult other than a transferor under 7-6.4 as successor custodian by executing and dating an instrument of designation before a subscribing witness other than the successor. If the instrument of designation does not contain or is not accompanied by the resignation of the custodian, the designation of the successor does not take effect until the custodian resigns, dies, become[*] incapacitated, or is removed. The transferor may designate one or more persons as successor custodian to serve in the designated order of priority, in case the custodian originally designated or a prior successor custodian is unable, declines, or is ineligible to serve or resigns, dies, becomes incapacitated, or is removed.

The designation either (1) shall be made in the same transaction and by the same document by which the transfer is made, or (2) shall be made by executing and dating a separate instrument of designation before a subscribing witness other than a successor as a part of the same transaction and contemporaneously with the execution of the document by which the transfer is made. The designation is made by setting forth the successor custodian's name, followed in substance by the words: "is designated successor custodian." A successor custodian designated by the transferor may be a trust company or an adult other than the transferor. A successor custodian effectively designated by the transferor has priority over a successor custodian designated by a custodian.

(c) A custodian may resign at any time by delivering written notice to the minor if the minor has attained the age of fourteen years and to the successor custodian and by delivering the custodial property to the successor custodian.

(d) If the transferor has not effectively designated one or more successor custodians and a custodian is ineligible, dies, or becomes incapacitated without having effectively designated a successor and the minor has attained the age of fourteen years, the minor may designate as successor custodian, in the manner prescribed in paragraph (b), an adult member of the minor's family, a guardian of the minor, or a trust company. If the minor has not attained the age of fourteen years or fails to act within sixty days after the ineligibility, death, or incapacity, the guardian of the minor becomes successor custodian. If the minor has no guardian or the guardian declines to act, the transferor, the legal representative of the transferor or of the custodian, an adult member of the minor's family, or any other interested person may petition the court to designate a successor custodian.

(e) A custodian who declines to serve under paragraph (a) or resigns under paragraph (c), or the legal representative of a deceased or incapacitated custodian, as soon as practicable, shall put the custodial property and records in the possession and control of the successor custodian. The successor custodian by action may enforce the obligation to deliver custodial property and records and becomes responsible for each item as received.

(f) A transferor, the legal representative of a transferor, an adult member of the minor's family, a guardian of the minor, or the minor if the minor has attained the age of fourteen years may petition the court to remove the custodian for cause and to designate a successor

---

[*] So in original. Should probably be "becomes".

custodian other than a transferor under 7-6.4 or to require the custodian to give appropriate bond.

History: Add, L 1996, ch 304, § 2, eff July 10, 1996, applying to transfers made on or after Jan 1, 1997, and replacing the Uniform Gifts to Minors Act, EPTL 7-4.1 and 7-4.12. See EPTL 7-6.23 for applicability of this Part.

§ 7-6.19. Accounting by and determination of liability of custodian

(a) A minor who has attained the age of fourteen years, the minor's guardian or legal representative, an adult member of the minor's family, a transferor, or a transferor's legal representative may petition the court (1) for an accounting by the custodian or the custodian's legal representative; or (2) for a determination of responsibility, as between the custodial property and the custodian personally, for claims against the custodial property unless the responsibility has been adjudicated in an action under 7-6.17 to which the minor or the minor's legal representative was a party.

(b) A successor custodian may petition the court for an accounting by the predecessor custodian.

(c) The court, in a proceeding under this part or in any other proceeding, may require or permit the custodian or the custodian's legal representative to account.

(d) If a custodian is removed under paragraph (f) of 7-6.18, the court shall require an accounting and order delivery of the custodial property and records to the successor custodian and the execution of all instruments required for transfer of the custodial property.

History: Add, L 1996, ch 304, § 2, eff July 10, 1996, applying to transfers made on or after Jan 1, 1997, and replacing the Uniform Gifts to Minors Act, EPTL 7-4.1 and 7-4.12. See EPTL 7-6.23 for applicability of this Part.

§ 7-6.20. Termination of custodianship

The custodian shall transfer in an appropriate manner the custodial property to the minor or to the minor's estate upon the earlier of:

(a) the minor's attainment of twenty-one years of age with respect to custodial property transferred under 7-6.4 or 7-6.5;

(b) the minor's attainment of age eighteen or other statutory age of majority of New York with respect to custodial property transferred under 7-6.6 or 7-6.7; or

(c) the minor's death.

History: Add, L 1996, ch 304, § 2, eff July 10, 1996, applying to transfers made on or after Jan 1, 1997, and replacing the Uniform Gifts to Minors Act, EPTL 7-4.1 and 7-4.12. See EPTL 7-6.23 for applicability of this Part.

§ 7-6.21. Age eighteen election

Notwithstanding the foregoing sections of this part, if with respect to any gift made pursuant to 7-6.9, the designations of the custodian contains, in substance, the phrase, "until age eighteen", then all records of the custodian with respect to such gift shall contain such phrase, and the gift shall be administered under this part as if the word "eighteen" were substituted for the word "twenty-one" wherever such word appears in paragraphs (a) and (k) of section 7-6.1 and in section 7-6.20.

History: Add, L 1996, ch 304, § 2, eff July 10, 1996, applying to transfers made on or after

Jan 1, 1997, and replacing the Uniform Gifts to Minors Act, EPTL 7-4.1 and 7-4.12. See EPTL 7-6.23 for applicability of this Part.

§ 7-6.22. Effect on existing custodianships

(a) Any transfer of custodial property made before January first, nineteen hundred ninety-seven is validated notwithstanding that there was no specific authority in part 4 of this article for the coverage of custodial property of that kind or for a transfer from that source at the time the transfer was made.

(b) All accounts established under part 4 of this article and in existence on January first, nineteen hundred ninety-seven shall be governed by the provisions of this part except insofar as such application impairs constitutionally vested rights. Notwithstanding the provisions of this paragraph, the age of termination in effect prior to January first, nineteen hundred ninety-seven shall remain in effect with respect to such accounts, including any additions made after December thirty-first, nineteen hundred ninety-six.

(c) To the extent that this part, by virtue of paragraph (b) of this section, does not apply to transfers made in a manner prescribed in part 4 of this article or to the powers, duties, and immunities conferred by transfers in that manner upon custodians and persons dealing with custodians, the repeal of part 4 of this article shall not affect those transfers or those powers, duties, and immunities.

History: Add, L 1997, ch 535, § 2, eff Sept 3, 1997.

§ 7-6.23. Applicability

This part applies to a transfer within the scope of 7-6.2 made on or after January first, nineteen hundred ninety-seven if:

(a) the transfer purports to have been made under the New York Uniform Gifts to Minor* Act; or

(b) the instrument by which the transfer purports to have been made uses in substance the designation "as custodian under the Uniform Gifts to Minors Act" or "as custodian under the Uniform Transfers to Minors Act" of any other state, and the application of this part is necessary to validate the transfer.

History: Formerly § 7-6.22, add, L 1996, ch 304, § 2, eff July 10, 1996, applying to transfers made on or after Jan 1, 1997, and replacing the Uniform Gifts to Minors Act, EPTL 7-4.1 and 7-4.12; renumbered § 7–6.23, L 1997, ch 535, § 2, eff Sept 3, 1997.

§ 7-6.24. Uniformity of application and construction

This part shall be applied and construed to effectuate its general purpose to make uniform the law with respect to the subject of this part among states enacting it.

History: Formerly § 7–6.23, add, L 1996, ch 304, § 2, applying to transfers made on or after Jan 1, 1997, and replacing the Uniform Gifts to Minors Act, EPTL 7-4.1 and 7-4.12. See EPTL 7-6.23 for applicability of this Part; renumbered § 7-6.24, L 1997, ch 535, § 2, eff Sept 3, 1997.

§ 7-6.25. Short title

This part may be cited as "The New York Uniform Transfers to Minors Act."

History: Formerly § 7–6.24, add, L 1996, ch 304, § 2, applying to transfers made on or

---

*, So in original. Should be "Minors".

after Jan 1, 1997, and replacing the Uniform Gifts to Minors Act, EPTL 7-4.1 and 7-4.12. See EPTL 7-6.23 for applicability of this Part; renumbered § 7–6.25, L 1997, ch 535, § 2, eff Sept 3, 1997.

§ 7-6.26. Severability

If any provisions of this part or its application to any person or circumstances is held invalid, the invalidity does not affect other provisions or applications of this part which can be given effect without the invalid provision or application, and to this end provisions of this part are severable.

> **History:** Formerly § 7–6.25, add, L 1996, ch 304, § 2, applying to transfers made on or after Jan 1, 1997, and replacing the Uniform Gifts to Minors Act, EPTL 7-4.1 and 7-4.12. See EPTL 7-6.23 for applicability of this Part; renumbered § 7–6.26, L 1997, ch 535, § 2, eff Sept 3, 1997.

PART 7   Child Performer Trust Account

§ 7-7.1. Child performer trust account

1. Scope. This section applies to contracts pursuant to which a child performer:

(a) is employed or agrees to render artistic or creative services for a fee, either directly or through a third-party individual or personal services corporation (loan-out company), or through an agency or service that provides artistic or creative services (casting agency); and

(b) agrees to purchase, or otherwise secure, sell, lease, or otherwise dispose of literary, musical, or dramatic properties, or use of a person's likeness, voice recording, performance, or story of or incidents in his or her life, either tangible or intangible, or any other rights therein for use in motion pictures, television, the production of sound recordings in any format now known or hereafter devised, the legitimate or living stage, or otherwise in the entertainment field.

2. Establishment of child performer trust account.

(a) Employer. Within thirty days following the final day of employment, except when the performance contract is a period longer than thirty days, a child performer's employer is required to transfer fifteen percent of gross earnings to the custodian of the child performer's child performer trust account. When the employment is longer than thirty days, the employer shall make the required transfer every payroll period. Transfers must conform with part six of this article. The use of an instrument to make the transfer which substantially conforms with section 7-6.9 is sufficient. If the child performer's employer has not been notified within fifteen days of the commencement of employment of the existence of a child performer trust account, or no such account has been established, then the child performer's employer shall transfer such monies together with the child performer's name and last known address to the state comptroller for placement into the child performer's holding fund established in section ninety-nine-k of the state finance law and such monies shall be administered by the state comptroller. Once transfers have been made to the child performer's trust account or the child performer's holding fund, as required by this subdivision, the child performer's employer has no further duty under this section.

(b) Custodian and guardian. Within fifteen days of the commencement of employment the child performer's guardian or custodian must establish a child performer trust account in accordance with part six of this article, unless an account has previously been established. Once the child performer trust account has been established the child performer's guardian or custodian shall notify the child performer's employer of the existence of the account and any additional information required to make transfers. The custodian of the account shall promptly notify the child performer's employer of any change in facts which affect the employer's obligation to set aside funds under this section. Upon request of the parent, legal guardian or the child performer's guardian ad litem, the custodian may require the child performer's employer to transfer more than fifteen percent of the gross earnings to the child performer trust account. The child performer's parent or legal guardian may serve as custodian. Once the child performer trust account balance reaches two hundred fifty thousand dollars or more a trust company shall be appointed as custodian of the account.

(c) Termination of child performer trust account. The child performer may terminate the child performer trust account upon reaching the age of eighteen.

3. Standard for child performer trust accounts. Custodian management of funds which are required to be placed into a child performer trust account shall be subject to part six of this article, in all respects except as provided in this section.

History: Add, L 2003, ch 630, § 4, eff March 28, 2004.

PART 8 Honorary Trusts for Pets

§ 7-8.1. Trusts for pets

(a) A trust for the care of a designated domestic or pet animal is valid. The intended use of the principal or income may be enforced by an individual designated for that purpose in the trust instrument or, if none, by an individual appointed by a court upon application to it by an individual, or by a trustee. Such trust shall terminate when the living animal beneficiary or beneficiaries of such trust are no longer alive.

(b) Except as expressly provided otherwise in the trust instrument, no portion of the principal or income may be converted to the use of the trustee or to any use other than for the benefit of all covered animals.

(c) Upon termination, the trustee shall transfer the unexpended trust property as directed in the trust instrument or, if there are no such directions in the trust instrument, the property shall pass to the estate of the grantor.

(d) A court may reduce the amount of the property transferred if it determines that amount substantially exceeds the amount required for the intended use. The amount of the reduction, if any, passes as unexpended trust property pursuant to paragraph (c) of this section.

(e) If no trustee is designated or no designated trustee is willing or able to serve, a court shall appoint a trustee and may make such other orders and determinations as are advisable to carry out the intent of the transferor and the purpose of this section.

History: Formerly § 7–6.1, add, L 1996, ch 159, § 1; renumbered § 7-8.1, L 2003, ch 630, § 3, eff March 28, 2004; L 2010, ch 70, § 1, eff May 5, 2010.

ARTICLE 8
CHARITABLE TRUSTS

SUMMARY OF ARTICLE

PART 1　Rules Governing Charitable Trusts

§ 8-1.1. Disposition of property for charitable purposes

(a) No disposition of property for religious, charitable, educational or benevolent purposes, otherwise valid under the laws of this state, is invalid by reason of the indefiniteness or uncertainty of the persons designated as beneficiaries. If a trustee is named in the disposing instrument, legal title to the property transferred for such a purpose vests in such trustee; if no person is named as trustee, title vests in the court having jurisdiction over the trust.

(b) No disposition of property made in a will, executed and attested as prescribed by law, is invalid by reason of the incorporation by reference in the will of any existing written resolution, declaration or deed of trust, identified in such will and made or adopted by any corporation authorized by law to execute or accept trusts, to assist, encourage and promote the well-being and well-doing of mankind in general or the inhabitants of any community in particular; provided that a copy of such resolution, declaration or deed of trust, certified, under its corporate seal, by the secretary or assistant secretary or the cashier or assistant cashier of such corporation, is filed for record in the office of the secretary of state and in the office of the clerk or register of the county of the corporation's principal place of business, in which the conveyances of real property are required by law to be filed for record, the secretary of state and the officer in charge of such record office being hereby authorized and directed to receive and record such resolution, declaration or deed of trust upon payment of the fees provided by law. Any such testamentary disposition to a corporation for the religious, charitable, educational or benevolent purposes set forth in such resolution, declaration or deed of trust is effective although the terms, conditions and purposes of such disposition are established only through such reference in the will.

(c) (1) The supreme court and, where the disposition is made by will, the surrogate's court in which such will is probated have jurisdiction over dispositions referred to and authorized by paragraphs (a) and (b), and whenever it appears to such court that circumstances have so changed since the execution of an instrument making a disposition for religious, charitable, educational or benevolent purposes as to render impracticable or impossible a literal compliance with the terms of such disposition, the court may, on application of the trustee or of the person having custody of the property subject to the disposition and on such notice as the court may direct, make an order or decree directing that such disposition be administered and applied in such manner as in the judgment of the court will most effectively accomplish its general purposes, free from any specific restriction, limitation or direction contained therein; provided, however, that any such order or decree is effective only with the consent of the creator of the disposition if he is living.

(2) (i) The attorney general or any trustee or beneficiary of a testamentary or lifetime trust wholly benefitting one or more charitable beneficiaries may petition a court of competent jurisdiction, on notice to the attorney general and all parties interested in the trust, seeking a termination of such trust when the trust is comprised of assets, the market value of which is one hundred thousand dollars or less and the expense of administering the trust is uneconomic when considered relative to income. When the court finds upon such application that continuation of the trust is economically impracticable or is not in the best interests of the beneficiaries, the court shall make an order or decree terminating the trust and directing the distribution of the trust assets to accomplish its charitable purposes, provided, however, that if the trust is one for the benefit of a particular charitable beneficiary or beneficiaries named therein, the court shall direct the distribution of the trust assets to such named charitable beneficiary or beneficiaries, and provided further that no such proceeding may be instituted without the consent of the creator of the disposition if he is living.

(ii) For purposes of this paragraph, the term "charitable beneficiary" shall mean the beneficiary of a disposition for a religious, charitable, educational or benevolent purpose.

(d) The power of the supreme court or the surrogate's court, as provided in paragraph (c), to prevent the failure of, and to give effect to dispositions for religious, charitable, educational or benevolent purposes is not defeated by the circumstance that the beneficiary of any such disposition does not exist or, if in existence, lacks capacity to take such disposition at the time it would otherwise become effective, whether or not the disposition creates an express trust to effectuate its purposes.

(e) Any accumulation of income from property subject to a disposition in trust for a religious, charitable, educational or benevolent purpose, or otherwise acquired by such trust, shall in all respects, including its reasonableness, amount and duration, be within the jurisdiction of the supreme court or the surrogate's court, as the case may be. In exercising such jurisdiction, (1) any accumulation of income which might otherwise be applied for the purposes of the trust may be prohibited or limited, despite a valid direction therefor in the trust instrument or authority therefor under 8-1.7 and (2) such an accumulation may be authorized by order of the court despite the absence of a direction therefor in the trust instrument. This paragraph shall not restrict in any manner the ability to release or modify restrictions relating to institutional funds under section 555 of the not-for-profit corporation law.

(f) The attorney general shall represent the beneficiaries of such dispositions for religious, charitable, educational or benevolent purposes and it shall be his duty to enforce the rights of such beneficiaries by appropriate proceedings in the courts.

(g) The supreme court or the surrogate's court, as the case may be, may authorize the trustee or any person holding title thereto to sell, mortgage or lease any real property which is the subject of a disposition for a religious, charitable, educational or benevolent purpose, whenever it appears to the satisfaction of the court that such real property, or any part thereof, has become or is likely to become unproductive, has depreciated or is likely to depreciate in value, that it is advisable to raise money to improve or erect buildings upon property so held or that it is expedient for any other reason that such real property be sold, mortgaged or leased. This paragraph shall not restrict in any manner the powers or rights any trustee may have by law or by the terms of any disposition of such real property. The provisions of this paragraph shall not apply to any corporation which is subject to sections 509 through 511 of the not-for-profit corporation law.

(h) The supreme court or the surrogate's court shall not make an order or decree under paragraph (g) unless it appears that eight days written notice, stating the time and place of the application for such order or decree, has been served upon the attorney general, who shall represent the state, the beneficiaries of any trust and the persons who might benefit from the religious, charitable, educational or benevolent purpose for which the real property, which is the subject of the application, is held. A like eight days notice of such application shall be given to any adult within the state who has a vested or contingent future estate in such real property and to any minor, incompetent, conservatee or absentee who is interested in such property, in such manner as the court may direct. Before making a final order or decree, the court shall appoint a guardian ad litem for any minor who is not represented by a guardian or parent, for any incompetent who is not represented by a committee, and for any absentee.

(i) A sale, mortgage or lease made, as required by law, in accordance with an order or decree of a court under this section is effective against the state as representative of the beneficiaries of such trust and persons who might benefit from the purposes for which such real property is held, and against persons with a vested or contingent future interest in such property and minors, incompetents, conservatees, absentees and persons not in being who have an interest in such property, as well as all other persons who, having been made parties to such proceeding, consent to such order or decree. The purchaser, mortgagee or lessee, or any person claiming under them, shall not be responsible for the disposition of the proceeds of any such sale, mortgage or lease.

(j) Whenever a voluntary association or committee has received, by public subscription, a fund for a charitable or benevolent purpose from more than one thousand contributors, a portion of which remains unexpended after the expiration of five years from the time of its receipt, and it appears that a literal compliance with the terms of the subscription is impracticable, the supreme court may make an order directing that such unexpended balance be transferred for administration and application to such domestic corporation as in the judgment of the court will most effectively accomplish the general purpose for which such fund was collected, free from any restriction, limitation or direction upon which the subscription was made; and on the transfer of such fund to the corporation designated in the order, such voluntary association, its officers and trustees, or such committee and its officers shall be fully exonerated and discharged from all liability to account for such fund. This paragraph shall not restrict in any manner the ability to release or modify restrictions relating to institutional funds under section 555 of the not-for-profit corporation law.

(k) An order shall be made under paragraph (j) on the application of the association or the treasurer of the committee, having custody of the unexpended balance, on twenty days personal notice to the attorney general and notice by publication once a week for four consecutive weeks in a newspaper of general circulation published in the county in which the treasurer of such association or committee resides. If such treasurer resides outside of the state, such notice shall be published in the county in which at least ten per cent of the contributors of such fund resided at the time of its receipt or in such other manner as the court may direct to the contributors as a class, to ten specified members of such class and to the trustees of such association or the surviving members of such committee.

(l) Where public subscriptions for charitable or benevolent purposes were made or begun prior to the year nineteen hundred twenty and the total number of subscribers exceeded five hundred but were less than one thousand, any unexpended balance of a fund obtained for such purpose which, at the time this section takes effect, is in the custody of a surviving member of a committee may be transferred for administration, on the application of such surviving member, in accordance with the procedure and with the effect set forth in paragraphs (j) and (k).

History: Add, L 1966, ch 952, eff Sept 1, 1967, with substance deriving from PPL § 12 and RPL § 113; amd, L 1967, ch 686, §§ 80, 81, eff Sept 1, 1967; L 1971, ch 1058 § 43, eff Sept 1, 1971; L 1981, ch 115, §§ 44, 45, eff May 18, 1981; L 1985, ch 492, § 2, eff July 24, 1985; L 2010, ch 490, §§ 9, 10, eff Sept 17, 2010.

§ 8-1.2. Certain charitable trusts authorized

(a) Property may be disposed of to any incorporated educational or literary institution in this state, to be held in trust for any one or more of the following purposes:

(1) To establish and maintain an observatory;

(2) To found and maintain professorships and scholarships;

(3) To provide and keep in repair a place for the burial of the dead.

(4) For any other specific purpose comprehended in the general objects authorized by its charter.

(b) The trust may be made subject to such conditions as may be prescribed by the creator and agreed to by the trustee, and all property which is hereafter disposed of to any incorporated educational or literary institution in trust for any of the foregoing purposes, may be held by such institution under such trust, subject to such conditions as may be prescribed.

(c) Property may be disposed of to any incorporated city or village of this state to be held in trust for any educational purpose, the diffusion of knowledge, or for the relief of distress, or for parks, gardens, other ornamental grounds or grounds for military parades, exercise, health and recreation, within or near such incorporated city or village, upon such conditions as may be prescribed by the creator and agreed to by such corporation; and all property so transferred to such corporation may be held by it, under such trust, subject to such conditions as may be prescribed.

(d) Property may be disposed of to commissioners of common schools of any town and to trustees of any school district, in trust for the benefit of such common schools or the schools of such district.

(e) The trusts authorized by this section may continue for such time as may be necessary to accomplish the purposes for which they are created.

History: Add, L 1966, ch 952, eff Sept 1, 1967, with substance deriving from PPL § 13 and RPL § 114; amd, L 1967, ch 686, § 82, eff Sept 1, 1967.

§ 8-1.3. Certain charitable trusts regulated

(a) Any person desiring in his lifetime to promote the public welfare by founding, endowing and maintaining, within this state, a public library, museum or other educational institution, a chapel, crematory or a board of trade or chamber of commerce may, by a disposition for such purpose, transfer property to a trustee named in such disposition or to his successor.

(b) The creator of such disposition may describe:

(1) The nature, object and purpose of the institution to be founded, endowed and maintained or of the corporation to be benefited thereby.

(2) In case of the founding of an institution, the name by which it shall be known.

(3) The powers and duties of the trustee and, if accounting is required, the manner in which and to whom he shall account; but the powers conferred shall not be exclusive of other powers which may be necessary to enable such trustee to execute fully the object of such disposition.

(4) Such rules for the management of the property as the creator may prescribe; but, unless otherwise provided, such rules shall be advisory only and shall not preclude the trustee from making such changes as new circumstances may from time to time require.

(5) The manner and by whom the successor to the trustee named in the disposition is to be appointed.

(6) The place where, and the time when, the buildings necessary and proper for the institution shall be erected, and the character and extent of such buildings. The creator may provide for all matters necessary and proper to carry out the purposes of the institution, and may provide for such lectures, exhibitions, instruction or amusement in connection therewith as he may consider desirable.

(c) The trustee named in the disposition or his successor may sue and defend, in the name of an institution established by such disposition, with respect to all matters affecting such institution.

(d) The creator of the disposition may provide for the right, during his lifetime, to personally perform the duties and exercise the powers which the disposition imposes and confers upon the trustee, and may further provide that his surviving spouse may, during her lifetime, perform such duties and exercise such powers. In all cases in which such duties and powers are performed and exercised by the creator or his spouse, during his or her lifetime, upon his death or the death of his spouse such duties and powers devolve upon and shall be performed and exercised by the trustee or his successor.

(e) The creator may reserve the right to alter, amend or modify his disposition with respect to any of the matters described in subparagraphs (1) to (6). He may also reserve the right, during his lifetime, to exercise complete control over the property subject to his disposition, without obligation to account therefor in any manner whatever, and may further provide that his surviving spouse shall, during her lifetime, have like control over such property, without obligation to account therefor in any manner whatever.

EPTL

(f) A disposition described in this section may be executed, acknowledged and recorded in the manner provided by the law of this state for the execution, acknowledgment and recording of conveyances of real property.

(g) No action or proceeding shall be maintained by any person to affect, impair, or defeat a disposition described in this section or to affect the title to property subject to such disposition or the right to the possession of such property or the income therefrom, unless such action or proceeding is commenced within two years from the time such disposition is recorded. Nor shall any defense be made to any action or proceeding maintained by a trustee or his successor which involves the legality of such disposition or affects the title to property subject thereto or the right to the possession of such property or the income therefrom, unless such defense is made in an action or proceeding commenced within two years from the time such disposition is recorded.

> **History:** Add, L 1966, ch 952, eff Sept 1, 1967, with substance deriving from PPL § 14 and RPL § 115; L 1967, ch 686, § 83, eff Sept 1, 1967.

§ 8-1.4. Supervision of trustees for charitable purposes

(a) For the purposes of this section, "trustee" means (1) any individual, group of individuals, executor, trustee, corporation or other legal entity holding and administering property for charitable purposes, whether pursuant to any will, trust, other instrument or agreement, court appointment, or otherwise pursuant to law, over which the attorney general has enforcement or supervisory powers, (2) any non-profit corporation organized under the laws of this state for charitable purposes and (3) any non-profit foreign corporation organized for charitable purposes, doing business or holding property in this state. Neither a foreign corporation nor a trustee acting under the will of, or an agreement executed by, a non-resident of this state shall become subject to the provisions of this section merely by reason of maintaining a bank, custody, investment or similar account in this state.

(b) The registration and reporting provisions of this section do not apply to (1) the United States, any state, territory or possession of the United States, the District of Columbia, the Commonwealth of Puerto Rico or to any of their agencies or governmental subdivisions, (2) any trustee which is required by any other provision of law to render a full, complete and itemized annual financial report to the congress of the United States or to the legislature of this state, provided that such report contains the information required of trustees pursuant to this article, (3) corporations organized under the religious corporations law and other religious agencies and organizations, and charities, agencies and organizations operated, supervised or controlled by or in connection with a religious organization, (4) educational institutions incorporated under the education law or by special act, (5) any hospital, (6) fraternal, patriotic, veterans, volunteer firefighters, volunteer ambulance workers, social, student or alumni organizations and historical societies chartered by the New York state board of regents, (7) a trust for which there is a corporate trustee acting as sole trustee or co-trustee under the terms of a will of a decedent who died domiciled in a state other than New York or a trust instrument executed by a non-resident of the state of New York, (8) any trust in which and so long as the charitable interest is deferred or contingent, (9) any person who, in his or her capacity as an officer, director or trustee of any corporation or organization mentioned in this paragraph, holds property for the religious, educational or charitable purposes of such corporation or organization so long as such corporation or organization is registered with the attorney general pursuant to this section, (10) any cemetery corporation subject to the provisions of article fifteen of the not-for-profit corporation law, (11) the state parent teachers association and any parent teachers association affiliated with an educational institution that is subject to the jurisdiction of the state education department, (12) any corporation organized under article forty-three of the insurance law. The provisions of this subdivision shall apply only to the registration and reporting requirements of this section and shall not limit, impair, change or alter any other provision of this article, the not-for-profit corporation law or any other provision of law.

(c) The attorney general shall establish and maintain a register of all trustees containing such information as the attorney general deems appropriate, and to that end may conduct such investigations as he or she deems necessary and shall obtain from public records, court officers, taxing authorities, trustees and other sources without the payment of any fee or charge, whatever information, copies of instruments, reports and records are needed for the establishment and maintenance of the register.

(d) Every trustee shall file with the attorney general, within six months after any property held by him or her or any income therefrom is required to be applied to charitable purposes, a copy of the instrument providing for his or her title, powers and duties; provided, however, that any trustee currently registered with the department of law pursuant to article 7-A of the executive law shall be deemed to have complied with this paragraph. If any property held by a trustee or any income therefrom is required to be applied to charitable purposes at the time this section becomes effective, the filing shall be made within six months thereafter.

(e) (1) Whenever any trustee or other person, holding property or any income therefrom, which may be required at any time to be devoted to charitable purposes, shall file in any court in this state (A) any petition for instructions relating to the administration or use of such property or income, (B) any petition for the construction of the instrument under which such property or income is held, (C) any petition respecting the disposition or distribution of such property or income or (D) any accounting, due notice of the action or proceeding shall be served by the petitioner upon the attorney general together with a copy of any petition, accounting, will or trust instrument.

(2) Whenever any instrument of a testamentary nature which provides for a disposition for charitable purposes is the subject of (A) an application for denial of probate, (B) objections to probate or (C) an application for approval of a compromise agreement in respect of probate, due notice of the action or proceeding shall be served by the petitioner upon the attorney general together with a copy of the instrument and of any such application, objections or agreement.

(f) (1) Every trustee shall, in addition to filing copies of any instrument required under paragraph (d) of this section, file with the attorney general and all identified current charitable beneficiaries written annual financial reports, under penalties for perjury, on forms prescribed by the attorney general, setting forth information as to the nature of the assets held for charitable purposes and the administration thereof by the trustee, and shall, file with the attorney general and all identified current charitable beneficiaries a notice of the termination of the interest of any party in a trust that would cause all or part of the trust assets to be applied to charitable purposes or to have the income therefrom so applied, in accordance with rules and regulations of the attorney general.

(2) Trustees required to report to the attorney general under article 7-A of the executive law shall comply with this paragraph by filing with the attorney general in addition to any other reports required herein, copies of the financial reports required by section 172-b of

the executive law unless such reports have been filed previously.

(g) Unless the filing of reports is suspended as herein provided, the first report of any trustee shall be filed no later than six months after the end of the fiscal year of the trustee during which he or she becomes subject to this section.

(h) The attorney general shall make rules and regulations necessary for the administration of this section, including rules and regulations as to the time for filing reports, the contents thereof, and any manner of executing and filing them, including but not limited to allowing or requiring any submission to the attorney general to be effected by electronic means and electronic signatures. He or she may classify trusts, estates, corporations and other trustees as to purpose, nature of assets, duration, amount of assets, amounts to be devoted to charitable purposes, or otherwise, and may establish different rules for different classes as to time and nature of the reports required, to the ends that he or she shall receive current financial reports as to all such trusts, estates, corporations or other trustees which will enable him or her to ascertain whether they are being properly administered. The attorney general may suspend the filing of financial reports as to a particular trustee for a reasonable, specifically designated time upon written application of the trustee, signed under penalties for perjury, and filed with the attorney general and after the attorney general has filed in the register of trustees a written statement that the interests of the beneficiaries will not be prejudiced thereby and that periodic reports during the term of such suspension are not required for proper supervision by his or her office. The filing of the financial reports required by this section, or the exemption from such filing or the suspension therefrom, shall not have the effect of absolving trustees from any responsibility for accounting for property or income held by them for charitable purposes. A copy of an account or other financial report filed by a trustee in any court in this state, if the account or other financial report substantially complies with the rules and regulations of the attorney general, may be filed as a financial report under this section.

(i) The attorney general may investigate transactions and relationships of trustees for the purpose of determining whether or not property held for charitable purposes has been and is being properly administered. The attorney general, his or her assistants, deputies or such other officers as may be designated by him or her, are empowered to subpoena any trustee, agent, fiduciary, beneficiary, institution, association or corporation or other witness, examine any such witness under oath and, for this purpose, administer the necessary oaths, and require the production of any books or papers which they deem relevant to the inquiry.

(j) No person shall be excused from attending such inquiry pursuant to the mandate of a subpoena, or from producing a paper or book, or from being examined or required to answer a question on the ground of failure of tender or payment of a witness fee or mileage, unless at the time of such appearance or production, as the case may be, such witness makes a demand for such payment as a condition precedent to the offering of the testimony or production required by the subpoena and such payment is not thereupon made. The provisions for payment of a witness fee or mileage do not apply to any trustee or other person holding funds for charitable purposes, or to any person in the employ of any such person, whose conduct or practices are being investigated.

(k) If a person subpoenaed to attend such inquiry fails to obey the mandate of a subpoena without reasonable cause, or if a person in attendance upon such inquiry shall without reasonable cause refuse to be sworn or to be examined or to answer a question or to produce a paper or book when ordered so to do by the officer conducting such inquiry, he or she shall be subject to proceedings under subdivision (b) of section 2308 of the civil practice law and rules.

(l) The register, copies of the instruments and the reports filed with the attorney general shall be open to public inspection, subject to reasonable rules and regulations adopted by the attorney general, which may include such limitations as to type of information subject to inspection or purpose of inspection as the attorney general shall deem to be in the public interest. The attorney general shall withhold from public inspection copies of any report filed with any other governmental agency of this state or of the United States and required by law to be kept confidential by such agency, and shall, upon request of the trustee, withhold from public inspection that portion of any instrument filed which does not relate to charitable purposes and which is not otherwise of public record.

(m) The attorney general may institute appropriate proceedings to secure compliance with this section and to secure the proper administration of any trust, corporation or other relationship to which this section applies. The powers and duties of the attorney general provided in this section are in addition to all other powers and duties he or she may have. No court shall modify or terminate the powers and responsibilities of any trust, corporation or other trustee unless the attorney general is a party to the proceeding, but nothing in this section shall otherwise impair or restrict the jurisdiction of any court with respect to the matters covered by it. The failure of any trustee to register or to file reports as required by this section may be ground for judicial removal of any person responsible for such failure.

(n) This section shall apply regardless of any contrary provisions of any instrument and shall be liberally construed so as to effectuate its general purpose of protecting the public interest in charitable uses, purposes and dispositions.

(o) Every officer, agency, board or commission of this state or political subdivisions of this state or agencies thereof receiving applications for exemption from taxation of any trustee subject to this section shall annually file with the attorney general a list of all applications received during the year and shall notify the attorney general of any suspension or revocation of a tax exempt status previously granted.

(p) The attorney general shall collect from each trustee at the time of filing of the periodic reports required by this section a fee for the filing of such reports as follows:

(1) Twenty-five dollars, if the net worth of the property held by such trustee for charitable purposes is less than fifty thousand dollars,

(2) Fifty dollars if such net worth is fifty thousand dollars or more but less than two hundred and fifty thousand dollars,

(3) One hundred dollars if such net worth is two hundred and fifty thousand dollars or more but less than one million dollars,

(4) Two hundred fifty dollars if such net worth is one million dollars or more but less than ten million dollars,

(5) Seven hundred and fifty dollars if such net worth is ten million dollars or more but less than fifty million dollars, and

(6) One thousand five hundred dollars if such net worth is fifty million dollars or more.

(q) Any trustee shall be exempt from the annual reporting requirements of this section by filing each year with the attorney general a verified statement executed by such trustee attesting that during the annual reporting period (1) the gross receipts received by said trustee during such annual reporting period were less than twenty-five thousand dollars and that (2) the total assets held by such trustee at no time during such annual reporting period exceeded twenty-five thousand dollars. For the purposes of this paragraph, gross receipts mean the total received during the financial reporting period of (A) gifts, grants, and contributions; (B) gross income and revenue from all sources; and (C) gross amounts from sales of assets, other than inventory; and total assets mean the total principal and the accumulated income, if any, held by such trustee for purposes of charitable distribution on any day during such annual reporting period.

(r) A trustee who fails to comply with paragraph (d), (f) or (g) of this section shall, after notice of said failure served upon him or her by the attorney general by certified mail, return receipt requested, be liable to the state of New York for a fine of ten dollars a day not to exceed one thousand dollars for each failure to comply after the expiration of the thirty day period following the receipt of the notice from the attorney general, except that the time to comply may be extended by the attorney general. Where the attorney general, after such thirty day period has expired, finds that the failure to comply with paragraph (d), (f) or (g) of this section is due to excusable ignorance or inadvertence or other reasonable cause, the attorney general shall waive the fine imposed by this paragraph.

(s) A trustee shall not be qualified to make application for funds or grants or to receive such funds from any department or agency of the state without certifying compliance with paragraphs (d), (f) and (g) of this section and all applicable registration and reporting requirements of article seven-A of the executive law.

> **History:** Add, L 1967, ch 686, eff Sept 1, 1967, with substance deriving from PPL § 12-b and RPL § 113-a; amd, L 1968, ch 263, deemed eff Sept 1, 1976; L 1969, ch 504, eff May 10, 1969; L 1978, ch 555, eff July 24, 1978; L 1978, ch 610, eff July 24, 1978; L 1982, ch 504, eff July 13, 1982; L 1983, ch 209, eff June 2, 1983; L 1987, ch 571, July 30, 1987, applicable to fiscal years beginning on or after Jan 1, 1988; L 1988, ch 24, eff Jan 1, 1989; L 1989, ch 61, § 34, eff April 19, 1989; L 1995, ch 83, eff April 1, 1995; L 1997, ch 329, eff Aug 5, 1997; L 1999, ch 424, eff Aug 31, 1999; L 2002, ch 43, § 17, eff Aug 1, 2002; L 2013, ch 549, § 129, eff July 1, 2014.

§ 8-1.5. Trusts for cemetery purposes

Dispositions of property in trust for the purpose of the perpetual care, maintenance, improvement or embellishment of cemeteries or private burial lots in cemeteries, and the roadways, lawns, hedges, walks, fences, monuments, structures and tombs in such cemeteries or on such private burial lots are permitted and shall be deemed to be for charitable and benevolent purposes. Such dispositions are not invalid by reason of any indefiniteness or uncertainty of the persons designated as beneficiaries, nor shall they be invalid as violating any existing rule against perpetuities. Nothing herein contained shall affect any existing authority of the courts to determine the reasonableness of the amount of such disposition. Any cemetery association may act as trustee of and execute any such trust with respect to lots, roadways, lawns, hedges, walks, fences, monuments, structures and tombs both within its own cemetery limits and outside of any cemetery under its control but within the county where such cemetery is located, whether or not such power is included among its corporate powers.

> **History:** Formerly § 8-1.4, add, L 1966, ch 952, eff Sept 1, 1967, with substance deriving

from PPL § 13-a and RPL § 114-a; renumbered § 8-1.5, L 1967, ch 686, § 88, eff Sept 1, 1967.

§ 8-1.6. Deposit of money in trust by owner of lots in private unincorporated cemetery

The owner of lots in any private unincorporated cemetery may deposit in trust for the care of such lots a sum not exceeding four hundred dollars for each lot so owned with any bank or banking institution located in a city, town or village conveniently near such private unincorporated cemetery, provided such bank or banking institution is willing to accept such money in trust and agrees to apply the proceeds of the interest thereon to the care and upkeep of such lots. Such banks or banking institutions are hereby authorized to accept such money for the purpose described herein and to apply the proceeds of the interest thereon to the care and upkeep of any such lots. The provisions of this section do not apply to savings banks.

> **History:** Formerly § 8-1.5, add, L 1966, ch 952, eff Sept 1, 1967, with substance deriving from PPL § 13-b; renumbered § 8-1.6 and amd, L 1967, ch 686, §§ 88, 89, eff Sept 1, 1967.

§ 8-1.7. Authority of trustee to accumulate income

(a) Where property has been transferred in trust for any religious, charitable, educational or benevolent purpose, or acquired by the trustee of a trust for such purpose, the trustee is authorized in his discretion, notwithstanding the absence of any direction therefor in the disposition creating the trust, to accumulate the income therefrom to the extent necessary to carry out the purposes of the trust. The authority herein granted is subject:

(1) To any express or implied prohibition by the terms of the disposition creating the trust, by any statute in force at the time of the accumulation or by the charter of a corporate trustee or other document or regulation controlling the trustee in the administration of the trust.

(2) To the supervision of the supreme court or the surrogate's court, as provided in 8-1.1, and to any contrary direction by order of the court in an action or proceeding thereunder.

(b) This section shall not restrict in any manner the appropriation for expenditure or accumulation of endowment funds as set forth in section 553 of the not-for-profit corporation law.

> **History:** Formerly § 8-1.6, add, L 1966, ch 952, eff Sept 1, 1967, with substance deriving from PPL § 16-a and RPL § 61-a; renumbered § 8-1.7, L 1967, ch 686, § 88, eff Sept 1, 1967; amd, L 2010, ch 490, § 11, eff Sept 17, 2010.

§ 8-1.8. Private foundations: administration of certain trusts as defined in the United States internal revenue code of 1954

(a) For purposes of this section, a "trust" means a private foundation as defined in section 509 of the United States Internal Revenue Code of 1986 ("code") including a private foundation charitable trust as defined in section 4947(a)(1) of the code, or a split-interest trust as defined in section 4947(a)(2) of the code, whether heretofore or hereafter created which is administered by a trustee described in subparagraph (a)(1) of section 8-1.4. The administration of a trust, as herein defined, is subject to the following provisions:

(1) The trust shall distribute for each taxable year such amounts at such time and in such manner as sufficient for such trust to avoid liability for any tax imposed on undistributed income under section 4942 of the code.

(2) The trust shall not engage in any act of self-dealing which would result in the taxation of any amount involved with respect to any such act of self-dealing under section 4941 of the code.

(3) The trust shall not retain any excess business holdings which would result in the taxation of any such excess business holdings under section 4943 of the code unless the trust is exempt from section 4943 of the code pursuant to section 4947(b)(3)(A) or (B) of the code.

(4) The trust shall not make any investments in such a manner as to jeopardize the carrying out of any such trust's exempt purposes which would result in the taxation of any such investments under section 4944 of the code unless the trust is exempt from section 4944 of the code pursuant to section 4947(b)(3)(A) or (B) of the code.

(5) The trust shall not make any taxable expenditures which would result in the liability of the trust for any tax imposed on any such taxable expenditures under section 4945 of the code.

Except as provided in paragraph (b), this paragraph applies notwithstanding any provision of the governing instrument of a trust.

(b) Paragraph (a) shall not apply with respect to assets transferred in trust prior to the effective date of this section to the extent that it conflicts with any mandatory direction in the governing instrument of the trust unless such conflicting direction is removed as impracticable under this article or in any other manner provided by law. The absence of a specific provision in the governing instrument of the trust for the current use of the principal of the fund, or the presence in such an instrument of a provision, as to the principal of a fund, limited to the principal's being held, invested and reinvested, is not such a conflicting mandatory direction.

(b-1) A trust, as defined in paragraph (a) of this section, required by section 6104(d) of the code to make available for public inspection its annual return shall publish notice of the availability of such return for inspection. Such notice shall be published, not later than the day prescribed for filing such annual return (determined with regard to any extension of time for filing), in a newspaper designated by the clerk of the county in which the principal office of the trust is located, having general circulation in that county. When such county is located within a city with a population of one million or more, such designation shall be as though the notice were a notice or advertisement of judicial proceedings. The notice shall state that the annual return of the trust is available at its principal office for inspection during regular business hours by any citizen who requests it within one hundred eighty days after the date of such publication, and shall state the address and the telephone number of the trust's principal office and the name of its principal manager. A copy or notice published in a newspaper other than the newspaper or newspapers designated by the county clerk shall not be deemed to be one of the publications required by this paragraph.

(c) All references in this section to sections of the code shall be to such sections as amended from time to time, or to corresponding provisions of subsequent internal revenue laws.

(d) Nothing in this act shall impair the rights and powers of the courts or the attorney-general of this state.

History: Add, L 1971, ch 331, eff June 1, 1971; amd, L 2000, ch 242, eff Jan 1, 2000; L 2003, ch 639, § 1, eff Oct 7, 2003, and applying "to a 'trust' as defined in paragraph (a) of section 8-1.8 of the estates, powers and trusts law, as amended by section one of this act, whether such a trust is created before, on or after the effective date of this act"; L 2005, ch 767, eff June 1, 2006; L 2006, ch 44, § 13, eff June 1, 2006.

§ 8-1.9 Trust governance

(a) For purposes of this section:

(1) A "trust" means a trust created solely for charitable purposes, or a trust that continues solely for such purposes after all non-charitable interests have terminated.

(2) "Charitable purpose" means any religious, charitable, educational or benevolent purpose.

(3) "Key person" means any person other than a trustee, whether or not an employee, who (i) has responsibilities, or exercises powers of influence over the trust as a whole similar to the responsibilities, powers, or influence of trustees and officers; (ii) manages the trust, or a segment of the trust that represents a substantial portion of the activities, assets, income or expenses of the trust; or (iii) alone or with others controls or determines a substantial portion of the trust's capital expenditures or operating budget.

(4) An "affiliate" of a trust means any entity controlled by, or in control of, such trust.

(5) "Relative" of an individual means (i) his or her spouse or domestic partner as defined in section twenty-nine hundred ninety-four-a of the public health law; (ii) his or her ancestors, brothers and sisters (whether whole or half blood), children (whether natural or adopted), grandchildren, great-grandchildren; or (iii) the spouse or domestic partner of his or her brothers, sisters, children, grandchildren, and great-grandchildren.

(6) "Related party" means (i) any trustee or key person of the trust or any affiliate of the trust; (ii) any relative of any individual described in clause (i) of this subparagraph; or (iii) an entity in which any individual described in clauses (i) and (ii) of this subparagraph has a thirty-five percent or greater ownership or beneficial interest or, in the case of a partnership or professional corporation, a direct ownership interest in excess of five percent.

(7) "Independent trustee" means a trustee who: (i) is not, and has not been within the last three years, an employee of the trust or an affiliate of the trust, and does not have a relative who is, or has been within the last three years, a key person of the trust or an affiliate of the trust; (ii) has not received, and does not have a relative who has received, in any of the last three fiscal years, more than ten thousand dollars in direct compensation from the trust or an affiliate of the trust; (iii) is not a current employee of or does not have a substantial financial interest in, and does not have a relative who is a current officer of or have a substantial financial interest in, any entity that has provided payments, property or services to, or received payments, property or services from, the trust or an affiliate of the trust if the amount paid by the trust to the entity or received by the trust from the entity for such property or services, in any of the last three fiscal years, exceeded the lesser of ten thousand dollars or two percent of such entity's consolidated gross revenue if the entity's consolidated gross revenue was less than five hundred thousand dollars; twenty-five thousand dollars if the entity's consolidated gross revenue was five hundred thousand dollars or more but less than ten million dollars; one hundred thousand dollars if the entity's consolidated gross revenue was ten million dollars or more; or (iv) is not and does not have a relative who is a current owner, whether wholly or partially, director, officer or

employee of the trust's outside auditor or who has worked on the trust's audit at any time during the past three years. For purposes of this subparagraph, the terms: "compensation" does not include reimbursement for expenses or the payment of trustee commissions or reasonable compensation as permitted by law and the governing instrument; and "payment" does not include charitable contributions, dues or fees paid to the trust for services which the trust performs as part of its nonprofit purposes, or payments made by the trust at fixed or non-negotiable rates or amounts for services received, provided that such services by and to the trust are available to individual members of the public on the same terms, and such services provided to the trust are not available from another source.

(8) "Related party transaction" means any transaction, agreement or any other arrangement in which a related party has a financial interest and in which the trust or any affiliate of the trust is a participant, except that a transaction shall not be a related party transaction if: (i) the transaction or the related party's financial interest in the transaction is de minimis, (ii) the transaction would not customarily be reviewed by the board, or boards of similar organizations, in the ordinary course of business and is available to others on the same or similar terms, or (iii) the transaction constitutes a benefit provided to a related party solely as a member of a class of the beneficiaries that the trust intends to benefit as part of the accomplishment of its mission which benefit is available to all similarly situated members of the same class on the same terms.

(9) "Independent auditor" means any certified public accountant performing the audit of the financial statements of a trust required by subdivision one of section one hundred seventy-two-b of the executive law.

(b) (1) The trustees or a designated audit committee consisting of one or more independent trustees of any trust required to file an independent certified public accountant's audit report with the attorney general pursuant to subdivision one of section one hundred seventy-two-b of the executive law shall oversee the accounting and financial reporting processes of the trust and the audit of the trust's financial statements. The trustees or designated audit committee shall annually retain or renew the retention of an independent auditor to conduct the audit and, upon completion thereof, review the results of the audit and any related management letter with the independent auditor.

(2) The trustees or a designated audit committee consisting of one or more independent trustees of any trust required to file an independent certified public accountant's audit report with the attorney general pursuant to subdivision one of section one hundred seventy-two-b of the executive law and that in the prior fiscal year had or in the current fiscal year reasonably expects to have annual revenue in excess of one million dollars shall, in addition to those duties set forth in subparagraph one of this paragraph:

(A) review with the independent auditor the scope and planning of the audit prior to the audit's commencement;

(B) upon completion of the audit, review and discuss with the independent auditor: (i) any material risks and weaknesses in internal controls identified by the auditor; (ii) any restrictions on the scope of the auditor's activities or access to requested information; (iii) any significant disagreements between the auditor and management; and (iv) the adequacy of the trust's accounting and financial reporting processes;

(C) annually consider the performance and independence of the independent auditor;

and

(D) if the duties required by this section are performed by an audit committee, report on the committee's activities to the trustees.

(3) [Repealed]

(4) If a trust is under the control of another trust or a corporation, the trustees or designated audit committee of the controlling trust, or the board or designated audit committee of the board of the controlling corporation, may perform the duties required by this paragraph.

(5) Only independent trustees may participate in deliberations or voting relating to matters set forth in this section, provided that nothing in this paragraph shall prohibit the board or designated audit committee from requesting that a person with an interest in the matter present information as background or answer questions at a committee or board meeting prior to the commencement of deliberations or voting relating thereto.

(c) (1) Notwithstanding any provision of the trust instrument to the contrary, no trust shall enter into any related party transaction unless the transaction is determined by the trustees, or an authorized committee thereof, to be fair, reasonable and in the trust's best interest at the time of such determination. Any trustee, officer or key employee who has an interest in a related party transaction shall disclose in good faith to the trustees, or an authorized committee thereof, the material facts concerning such interest.

(2) With respect to any related party transaction in which a related party has a substantial financial interest, the trustees, or an authorized committee thereof, shall:

(A) Prior to entering into the transaction, consider alternative transactions to the extent available;

(B) Approve the transaction by not less than a majority vote of the trustees or committee members present at the meeting; and

(C) Contemporaneously document in writing the basis for the trustees' or authorized committee's approval, including consideration of any alternative transactions.

(3) The trust instrument, by-laws or any policy adopted by the trustees may contain additional restrictions on related party transactions and additional procedures necessary for the review and approval of such transactions, or provide that any transaction in violation of such restrictions shall be void or voidable.

(4) The attorney general may bring an action to enjoin, void or rescind any related party transaction or proposed related party transaction that violates any provision of this article or was otherwise not reasonable or in the best interests of the trust at the time the transaction was approved, or to seek restitution, and the removal of trustees or officers, or seek to require any person or entity to:

(A) Account for any profits made from such transaction, and pay them to the trust;

(B) Pay the trust the value of the use of any of its property or other assets used in such transaction;

(C) Return or replace any property or other assets lost to the trust as a result of such transaction, together with any income or appreciation lost to the trust by reason of such transaction, or account for any proceeds of sale of such property, and pay the proceeds to the trust together with interest at the legal rate; and

(D) Pay, in the case of willful and intentional conduct, an amount up to double the amount of any benefit improperly obtained.

(5) The powers of the attorney general provided in this section are in addition to all other powers the attorney general may have under this chapter or any other law.

(6) No related party may participate in deliberations or voting relating to a related party transaction in which he or she has an interest; provided that nothing in this section shall prohibit the trustees or designated audit committee from requesting that a related party present information or answer questions concerning a related party transaction at a trustees or committee meeting prior to the commencement of deliberations or voting relating to the related party transaction.

(7) In an action by any person or entity other than the attorney general, it shall be a defense to a claim of violation of any provisions of this paragraph that a transaction was fair, reasonable and in the trust's best interest at the time the trust approved the transaction.

(8) In an action by the attorney general with respect to a related party transaction not approved in accordance with subparagraph one or two of this paragraph at the time it was entered into, whichever is applicable, it shall be a defense to a claim of violation of any provisions of this paragraph that (i) the transaction was fair, reasonable and in the trust's best interest at the time the trust approved the transaction and (ii) prior to receipt of any request for information by the attorney general regarding the transaction, the trustees have: (A) ratified the transaction by finding in good faith that it was fair, reasonable and in the trust's best interest at the time the trustee approved the transaction; and, with respect to any related party transaction involving a charitable corporation and in which a related party has a substantial financial interest, considered alternative transactions to the extent available, approving the transaction by not less than a majority vote of the trustees or committee members present at the meeting; (B) documented in writing the nature of the violation and the basis for the trustees' or committee's ratification of the transaction; and (C) put into place procedures to ensure that the trustee complies with subparagraphs one and two of this paragraph as to related party transactions in the future.

(d) (1) Except as provided in subparagraph four of this paragraph, every trust shall adopt, and oversee the implementation of, and compliance with, a conflict of interest policy to ensure that its trustees, officers and key persons act in the best interest of the trust and its beneficiaries and comply with applicable legal requirements, including but not limited to the requirements set forth in this paragraph.

(2) The conflict of interest policy shall include, at a minimum, the following provisions:

(A) a definition of the circumstances that constitute a conflict of interest;

(B) procedures for disclosing a conflict of interest or possible conflict of interest to the trustees or to a committee of the trustees, and procedures for the trustees or committee to determine whether a conflict exists;

(C) a requirement that the person with the conflict of interest not be present at or participate in any deliberation or vote on the matter giving rise to such conflict, provided that nothing in this section shall prohibit the trustees or a committee from requesting that the person with the conflict of interest present information as background or answer questions at a trustees or committee meeting prior to the commencement of deliberations or voting relating thereto;

(D) a prohibition against any attempt by the person with the conflict to influence the deliberation or voting on the matter giving rise to such conflict;

(E) a requirement that the existence and resolution of the conflict be documented in the trust's records, including in the minutes of any meeting at which the conflict was discussed or voted upon; and

(F) procedures for disclosing, addressing, and documenting related party transactions in accordance with this paragraph.

(3) The conflict of interest policy shall require that prior to a trustee's initial appointment, and annually thereafter, such trustee shall complete, sign and file with the records of the trust a written statement identifying any entity of which he or she is an officer, director, trustee, member, owner (either as a sole proprietor or a partner), or employee and with which the trust has a relationship, and any transaction in which the trust is a participant and in which the trustee might have a conflicting interest. The policy shall require that each trustee annually resubmit such written statement. The trustees shall provide a copy of all completed statements to the chair of the audit committee, if there is an audit committee.

(4) A trust that has adopted and possesses a conflict of interest policy pursuant to federal, state or local laws that is substantially consistent with the provisions of subparagraph two of this paragraph shall be deemed in compliance with provisions of this paragraph.

(5) Nothing in this paragraph shall be interpreted to require a trust to adopt any specific conflict of interest policy not otherwise required by this paragraph or any other law or rule, or to supersede or limit any requirement or duty governing conflicts of interest required by any other law or rule.

(e) (1) Except as provided in subparagraph three of this paragraph, the trustees of every trust that has twenty or more employees and in the prior fiscal year had annual revenue in excess of one million dollars shall adopt, and oversee the implementation of, and compliance with, a whistleblower policy to protect from retaliation persons who report suspected improper conduct. Such policy shall provide that no officer, trustee, employee or volunteer of a trust who in good faith reports any action or suspected action taken by or within the trust that is illegal, fraudulent or in violation of any adopted policy of the trust shall suffer intimidation, harassment, discrimination or other retaliation or, in the case of employees, adverse employment consequence.

(2) The whistleblower policy shall include the following provisions:

(A) Procedures for the reporting of violations or suspected violations of laws or trust policies, including procedures for preserving the confidentiality of reported information;

(B) A requirement that a trustee, officer or employee of the trust be designated to administer, the whistleblower policy and to report to the trustees or an authorized committee thereof, except that trustees who are employees may not participate in any board or committee deliberations or voting relating to administration of the whistle-blower policy;

(C) A requirement that the person who is the subject of a whistleblower complaint not be present at or participate in board or committee deliberation or vote on the matter relating to such complaint, provided that nothing in this subparagraph shall prohibit the board or committee from requesting that the person who is subject to the complaint present information as background or answer questions at a committee or board meeting prior to the commencement of deliberations or voting relating thereto; and

(D) A requirement that a copy of the policy be distributed to all trustees, officers, employees and volunteers, with instructions on how to comply with the procedures set forth in the policy. For purposes of this subdivision, posting the policy on the corporation's website or at the corporation's offices in a conspicuous location accessible to employees and volunteers are among the methods a corporation may use to satisfy the distribution requirement.

(3) A trust that has adopted and possesses a whistleblower policy pursuant to federal, state or local laws that is substantially consistent with the provisions of subparagraph two of this paragraph shall be deemed in compliance with the provisions of this paragraph.

(4) Nothing in this paragraph shall be interpreted to relieve any trust from any additional requirements in relation to internal compliance, retaliation, or document retention required by any other law or rule.

History: Add, L 2013, ch 549, § 130, eff July 1, 2014; amd, L 2015, ch 555, §§ 12–16, eff Dec 11, 2015; L 2016, ch 466, §§ 13-19, eff May 27, 2017.

ARTICLE 9
PERPETUITIES AND ACCUMULATIONS
SUMMARY OF ARTICLE

PART 1   Perpetuities

§ 9-1.1. Rule against perpetuities

(a) (1) The absolute power of alienation is suspended when there are no persons in being by whom an absolute fee or estate in possession can be conveyed or transferred.

(2) Every present or future estate shall be void in its creation which shall suspend the absolute power of alienation by any limitation or condition for a longer period than lives in being at the creation of the estate and a term of not more than twenty-one years. Lives in being shall include a child conceived before the creation of the estate but born thereafter. In no case shall the lives measuring the permissible period be so designated or so numerous as to make proof of their end unreasonably difficult.

(b) No estate in property shall be valid unless it must vest, if at all, not later than twenty-one years after one or more lives in being at the creation of the estate and any period of gestation involved. In no case shall lives measuring the permissible period of vesting be so designated or so numerous as to make proof of their end unreasonably difficult.

> **History:** Add, L 1966, ch 952, eff Sept 1, 1967; amd, L 1967, ch 686, §§ 90, 91, eff Sept 1, 1967.

§ 9-1.2. Reduction of age contingency

Where an estate would, except for this section, be invalid because made to depend, for its vesting or its duration, upon any person attaining or failing to attain an age in excess of twenty-one years, the age contingency shall be reduced to twenty-one years as to any or all persons subject to such contingency.

> **History:** Add, L 1966, ch 952, eff Sept 1, 1967, with substance deriving from PPL § 11-a and RPL § 42-b.

§ 9-1.3. Rules of construction

(a) Unless a contrary intention appears, the rules of construction provided in this section

E-135

govern with respect to any matter affecting the rule against perpetuities.

(b) It shall be presumed that the creator intended the estate to be valid.

(c) Where an estate would, except for this paragraph, be invalid because of the possibility that the person to whom it is given or limited may be a person not in being at the time of the creation of the estate, and such person is referred to in the instrument creating such estate as the spouse of another without other identification, it shall be presumed that such reference is to a person in being on the effective date of the instrument.

(d) Where the duration or vesting of an estate is contingent upon the probate of a will, the appointment of a fiduciary, the location of a distributee, the payment of debts, the sale of assets, the settlement of an estate, the determination of questions relating to an estate or transfer tax or the occurrence of any specified contingency, it shall be presumed that the creator of such estate intended such contingency to occur, if at all, within twenty-one years from the effective date of the instrument creating such estate.

(e) (1) Where the validity of a disposition depends upon the ability of a person to have a child at some future time, it shall be presumed, subject to subparagraph (2), that a male can have a child at fourteen years of age or over, but not under that age, and that a female can have a child at twelve years of age or over, but not under that age or over the age of fifty-five years.

(2) In the case of a living person, evidence may be given to establish whether he or she is able to have a child at the time in question.

(3) Where the validity of a disposition depends upon the ability of a person to have a child at some future time, the possibility that such person may have a child by adoption shall be disregarded.

(4) The provisions of subparagraphs (1), (2) and (3) shall not apply for any purpose other than that of determining the validity of a disposition under the rule against perpetuities where such validity depends on the ability of a person to have a child at some future time. A determination of validity or invalidity of a disposition under the rule against perpetuities by the application of subparagraph (1) or (2) or (3) shall not be affected by the later occurrence of facts in contradiction to the facts presumed or determined or the possibility of adoption disregarded under subparagraphs (1) or (2) or (3).

History: Add, L 1966, ch 952, eff Sept 1, 1967, with substance deriving from PPL § 11-b and RPL § 42-c; amd, L 1972, ch 583, § 1, eff Sept 1, 1972, applicable only to dispositions which become effective on and after such date.

§ 9-1.4. Acquisition of real property by foreign trust

Where real property situated in this state is acquired by a trust validly created under the law of another jurisdiction, whether there is a violation of the rule against perpetuities and whether a direction for the accumulation of rents and profits is valid are determined by the law of this state in effect at the time of the acquisition of such property.

History: Add, L 1966, ch 952, eff Sept 1, 1967, with substance deriving from RPL § 42-d.

§ 9-1.5. Trust with transferable certificates

A trust with transferable certificates, heretofore or hereafter created, is not invalid as violating the rule against perpetuities; but such trust may continue for such time as may be necessary to accomplish the purposes for which it is created if the instrument creating such trust provides that it may be terminated at any time by action of the trustees or by affirmative vote of the beneficiaries having a specified percentage of interest therein. This section applies to an investment trust, which is an unincorporated trust or association managed by trustees not holding any property for sale to customers in the ordinary course of its trade or business, the beneficial ownership of which is evidenced by transferable shares or by transferable certificates of beneficial interest offered for sale to the public.

History: Add, L 1966, ch 952, eff Sept 1, 1967, with substance deriving from RPL § 42-e.

§ 9-1.6. Trust for employees

A trust created by an employer, as part of a stock bonus, pension, disability or death benefit or profit-sharing plan, for the exclusive benefit of some or all of his employees, to which contributions are made by such employer or employees, or both, for the purpose of distributing to such employees the income or principal, or both, of the fund so held in trust, is not invalid as violating the rule against perpetuities; but such trust may continue for such time as may be necessary to accomplish the purposes for which it is created.

History: Add, L 1966, ch 952, eff Sept 1, 1967, with substance deriving from PPL § 13-c and RPL § 42-a.

§ 9-1.7. Trust for self-employed individuals and others

No trust created under a retirement plan, which is exempt from federal income taxation under the laws of the United States, is invalid as violating the rule against perpetuities or the rules governing the accumulation of income. Such a trust may continue for such time as may be necessary to accomplish the purposes for which it is created; may permit the accumulation of income until such time as the income is distributed to the beneficiaries under the terms of the trust; and may, according to its terms, be made irrevocable and the interest of its beneficiaries nontransferable by assignment or otherwise. A trust so made irrevocable is not subject to revocation upon the written consent of its beneficiaries as provided in 7-1.9.

History: Add, L 1966, ch 952, eff Sept 1, 1967, with substance deriving from PPL § 13-d.

§ 9-1.8. Trust created by national securities exchange to assist customers of members, member firms or member corporations

(a) A trust created by a national securities exchange for the purpose of enabling the trustees, in their discretion, to provide direct or indirect assistance to customers of a member, member firm or member corporation of such exchange, threatened with loss of their money or securities because such member, member firm or member corporation, in the opinion of the trustees, is insolvent or may be unable without assistance to meet its obligations to such customers, is not invalid as violating the rule against perpetuities or the rules governing the accumulation of income. Such a trust may continue and may accumulate the income from the property held therein for such time as may be necessary to accomplish the purposes for which it is created.

(b) As used in this section, the term "national securities exchange" means any exchange registered as a national securities exchange under the federal securities exchange act of nineteen hundred thirty-four, as the same may be amended from time to time.

History: Add, L 1966, ch 952, eff Sept 1, 1967, with substance deriving from PPL § 13-e.

PART 2   Accumulations

§ 9-2.1. Rules governing accumulations

(a) All directions for the accumulation of income are void unless authorized by statute.

(b) A direction for the accumulation of income is valid if such accumulation is to begin and terminate within the time allowed by the rule against perpetuities. An accumulation directed to continue for a period extending beyond the expiration of such time terminates upon such expiration.

(c) Where property is disposed of in trust for any religious, charitable, educational or benevolent purpose and no valid future estate, except for a similar purpose, is created by such disposition, a direction for the accumulation by the trustee of income received for such purpose is valid without regard to the time at which the accumulation is to begin or to terminate, but the accumulation is subject to the supervision and control of the supreme court or the surrogate's court as provided in 8-1.1.

(d) The income from a trust created by an employer, as part of a stock bonus, a pension, disability or death benefit or profit-sharing plan, for the exclusive benefit of some or all of his employees, to which contributions are made by such employer or employees or both, for the purpose of distributing to such employees the income or principal, or both, of the trust, may be accumulated until the funds are sufficient, in the opinion of the employer, to accomplish the purposes of such plan.

> **History:** Add, L 1966, ch 952, eff Sept 1, 1967, with substance deriving from PPL § 16 and RPL § 61; amd, L 1967, ch 686, § 92, eff Sept 1, 1967.

§ 9-2.2. Anticipation of directed accumulation

(a) When a valid accumulation is directed for the benefit of a person without other sufficient means to support or educate himself, the supreme court or, if such accumulation was directed by will, the surrogate's court of the county in which such will is admitted to probate, on the application of such person, his guardian, committee, or conservator may direct that a suitable sum from the income accumulated or to be accumulated be applied for the support or education of such person.

(b) When the proceeds of a life insurance policy issued or delivered in this state are being retained under an agreement by the insurer to credit interest thereon for the benefit of a person without other sufficient means to support or educate himself, the supreme court, on the application of such person, his guardian, committee, or conservator may direct that a suitable sum from the interest credited or agreed to be credited be applied for the support or education of such person.

> **History:** Add, L 1966, ch 952, with substance deriving from PPL § 17 and RPL § 62; amd, L 1981, ch 115, § 46, eff May 18, 1981.

§ 9-2.3. Undistributed income

When income is not disposed of and no valid direction is given for its accumulation it passes to the persons presumptively entitled to the next eventual estate.

> **History:** Add, L 1966, ch 952, eff Sept 1, 1967 with substance deriving from RPL § 63; amd, L 1967, ch 686, § 93, eff Sept 1, 1967.

ARTICLE 10
POWERS

SUMMARY OF ARTICLE

EPTL

PART 1   Common Law of Powers Established with Exceptions

§ 10-1.1. Common law of powers retained, except as modified by this article

The common law of powers as embodied in this article and as to matters not included herein, as heretofore established, is retained as the law of this state except as modified by the provisions of this article.

History: Add, L 1966, ch 952, eff Sept 1, 1967, with substance deriving from RPL § 130.

PART 2   Definitions

§ 10-2.1. Power

A power is an authority to do any act in relation to property, including the creation or revocation of an estate therein or a charge thereon, which the donor of the power might himself do, except that the term, as used in this article, does not apply to a power of attorney to convey property in the name of the owner, regulated by other statutes.

History: Add, L 1966, ch 952, eff Sept 1, 1967, with substance deriving from RPL § 131.

§ 10-2.2. Other words defined

(a) Donor. A donor is the person who creates or reserves a power.

(b) Donee. A donee is the person to whom a power is given or in whose favor a power is reserved.

(c) Appointee. An appointee is the person in whose favor a power of appointment is exercisable.

(d) Appointive property. Appointive property is property which is the subject of a power of appointment.

History: Add, L 1966, ch 952, eff Sept 1, 1967.

PART 3   Varieties of Powers

§ 10-3.1. Powers of appointment and other powers

(a) This article applies to powers of appointment. A power of appointment, as the term is used in this article, is an authority created or reserved by a person having property subject to his disposition, enabling the donee to designate, within such limits as may be prescribed by the donor, the appointees of the property or the shares or the manner in which such property shall be received.

(b) This article applies, generally, to powers which are not powers of appointment, such as a power to revoke a disposition previously made, a power during minority to manage property vested in an infant, a power to disburse the principal of a trust, a power to sell in a mortgage and a power in a life tenant to make leases. This enumeration is not exclusive but illustrative.

History: Add, L 1966, ch 952, eff Sept 1, 1967, with substance deriving from RPL § 132.

§ 10-3.2. Classification of powers of appointment as to kind; general and special; exclusive and non-exclusive

(a) A power of appointment is:

(1) general or special.

(2) exclusive or non-exclusive.

(b) A power of appointment is general to the extent that it is exercisable wholly in favor of the donee, his estate, his creditors or the creditors of his estate.

(c) All other powers of appointment are special.

(d) A special power of appointment is exclusive if it may be exercised in favor of one or more of the appointees to the exclusion of the others.

(e) A special power of appointment is non-exclusive if it must be exercised in favor of all the appointees.

History: Add, L 1966, ch 952, eff Sept 1, 1967, with substance deriving from RPL § 133.

§ 10-3.3. Classification of powers of appointment as to time of exercise; presently exercisable, testamentary and postponed

(a) A power of appointment, as to the time of its exercise, is either presently exercisable, testamentary or postponed.

(b) A power of appointment is presently exercisable if it may be exercised by the donee, during his lifetime or by his written will, at any time after its creation, and does not include

EPTL

a postponed power as described in paragraph (d).

(c) A power of appointment is testamentary if it is exercisable only by a written will of the donee.

(d) A power of appointment is postponed if it is exercisable by the donee only after the expiration of a stated time or after the occurrence or non-occurrence of a specified event.

History: Add, L 1966, ch 952, eff Sept 1, 1967, with substance deriving from RPL § 134; amd, L 1967, ch 686, § 95, eff Sept 1, 1967.

§ 10-3.4. Classification of powers of appointment as to duty to exercise; imperative and discretionary

(a) A power of appointment is either imperative or discretionary.

(b) A power of appointment is imperative if the instrument creating it imposes on the donee a duty to exercise it, and it may be imperative even though it is exclusive.

(c) A power of appointment is discretionary if the donee is authorized to exercise or not to exercise it.

History: Add, L 1966, ch 952, eff Sept 1, 1967, with substance deriving from RPL § 135.

PART 4   Creation of a Power of Appointment

§ 10-4.1. Rules for creation of a power of appointment

(a)* The donor of a power of appointment:

(1) Must be a person capable of transferring the appointive property.

(2) Must have created or reserved the power by a written instrument executed by him in the manner required by law.

(3) Must manifest his intention to confer the power on a person capable of holding the appointive property.

(4) Cannot nullify or alter the rights of creditors of the donee, as defined in this article, by any language in the instrument creating or reserving the power purporting to give the interest of such donee a spendthrift character.

History: Add, L 1966, ch 952, eff Sept 1, 1967, with substance deriving from RPL § 136.

PART 5   Extent of Donee's Authority to Appoint or Contract to Appoint an Estate in Appointive Property

§ 10-5.1. Scope of the authority of the donee

The scope of the donee's authority as to appointees and as to the time and manner of the appointment is unlimited except as the donor manifests a contrary intention.

History: Add, L 1966, ch 952, eff Sept 1, 1967 with substance deriving from RPL § 137; amd, L 1967, ch 686, eff Sept 1, 1967; L 1968, ch 257, § 6, eff May 14, 1968.

§ 10-5.2. Contract to appoint; power presently exercisable

---

* **Ed. Note:** There is no paragraph (b).

The donee of a power of appointment which is presently exercisable, or of a postponed power which has become exercisable, can contract to make an appointment to the extent that the contract or the promised appointment does not confer a benefit upon a person who is not a permissible appointee under the power.

History: Add, L 1966, ch 952, eff Sept 1, 1967, with substance deriving from RPL § 145.

§ 10-5.3. Contract to appoint; power not presently exercisable

(a) The donee of a power of appointment which is not presently exercisable, or of a postponed power which has not become exercisable, cannot contract to make an appointment; except that this prohibition shall not apply if the donor and donee are the same person. Such a prohibited contract, if made, cannot be the basis of an action for specific performance or damages, but the promisee can obtain restitution of the value given by him for the promise unless the donee has exercised the power pursuant to the contract.

(b) The provisions of this section shall not abridge the ability of the donee of a power of appointment which is not presently exercisable to release his power pursuant to 10-9.2 or to make the power, after release, an imperative power, except that where the donor designated persons or a class to take in default of the donee's exercise of the power, a release with respect to appointive property must serve to benefit all those so designated as provided by the donor.

History: Add, L 1966, ch 952, eff Sept 1, 1967, with substance deriving from RPL § 146; amd, L 1967, ch 686, § 97, eff Sept 1, 1967; L 1977, ch 341, § 1, eff June 28, 1977.

§ 10-5.4. Priority

The interest of the donee of a power of appointment, and of any appointee thereunder, has priority with respect to real property subject thereto, as against creditors, purchasers or incumbrancers, in good faith and without notice, of or from a person having an estate in such property, only from the time at which the instrument creating the power is duly recorded. As against all other persons, such interest has priority from the time at which the instrument creating the power takes effect.

History: Add, L 1966, ch 952, eff Sept 1, 1967, with substance deriving from RPL § 142.

PART 6   Rules Governing Exercise of a Power of Appointment

§ 10-6.1. Exercise of a power of appointment; manifestation of intention of donee

(a) Subject to paragraph (b), an effective exercise of a power of appointment does not require an express reference to such power. A power is effectively exercised if the donee manifests his intention to exercise it. Such a manifestation exists when the donee:

(1) Declares in substance that he is exercising all the powers he has;

(2) Sufficiently identifying the appointive property or any part thereof, executes an instrument purporting to dispose of such property or part;

(3) Makes a disposition which, when read with reference to the property he owned and the circumstances existing at the time of its making, manifests his understanding that he was disposing of the appointive property; or

(4) Leaves a will disposing of all of his property or all of his property of the kind covered by the power, unless the intention that the will is not to operate as an execution

of the power appears expressly or by necessary implication.

(b) If the donor has expressly directed that no instrument shall be effective to exercise the power unless it contains a specific reference to the power, an instrument not containing such reference does not validly exercise the power.

History: Add, L 1966, ch 952, eff Sept 1, 1967, with substance deriving from RPL § 147 and PPL § 18; amd Revisers' Notes, L 1968, ch 257, eff May 14, 1968 to add PPL § 18 as a source of the section.

§ 10-6.2. Exercise of a power of appointment; conformity to directions of donor

(a)* Subject to the power of a court of competent jurisdiction to remedy a defective execution of an imperative power of appointment, the directions of the donor as to the manner, time and conditions of the exercise of a power must be observed, except that:

(1) Where the donor has authorized it to be exercised by an instrument legally insufficient to dispose of the appointive property, the manner of exercise is to be determined by the provisions of this article.

(2) Where the donor has directed any formality to be observed in its exercise, in addition to those which would be legally sufficient to dispose of the appointive property, such additional formality is not necessary to a valid exercise of such power.

(3) Where the donor has made the power exercisable only by deed, it is also exercisable by a written will unless exercise by will is expressly excluded.

(4) Where the donor of a general power of appointment has not expressly imposed a requirement of good faith or of reasonableness with respect to the donee's exercise of such power, neither such requirement shall be implied.

History: Add, L 1966, ch 952, eff Sept 1, 1967, with substance deriving from RPL § 148.

§ 10-6.3. Exercise of a power of appointment; type of instrument

A power of appointment can be exercised only by a written instrument which would be sufficient to dispose of the estate intended to be appointed if the donee were the actual owner.

History: Add, L 1966, ch 952, eff Sept 1, 1967, with substance deriving from RPL § 149; amd, L 1967, ch 686, § 98, eff Sept 1, 1967.

§ 10-6.4. Exercise of a power of appointment; required consents

(a) When the consent of the donor or of a third person to the exercise of a power of appointment is required, such consent shall be expressed in a written instrument, subscribed by the person whose consent is required; and to entitle the instrument of exercise to be recorded, the signatures of the donee and of the person consenting must be acknowledged or proved in the manner required by the laws of this state for the recording of a deed of real property.

(b) Unless the donor expressly provides otherwise:

(1) When the consents of two or more persons are required for the exercise of a power of appointment, all must consent.

---

* **Ed. Note**: There is no paragraph (b).

(2) If before the exercise of the power:

(A) One or more of such persons die, the consent of the survivor is sufficient.

(B) One or more of such persons become incompetent, the consent of the competent person is sufficient.

History: Add, L 1966, ch 952, eff Sept 1, 1967, with substance deriving from RPL § 150; amd, L 1967, ch 686, § 99, eff Sept 1, 1967.

§ 10-6.5. Exercise of exclusive and non-exclusive power of appointment

(a)* Unless the donor expressly provides otherwise:

(1) The donee of an exclusive power may appoint all or any part of the appointive property to one or more of the appointees to the exclusion of the others.

(2) The donee of a non-exclusive power must appoint in favor of all of the appointees equally.

History: Add, L 1966, ch 952, eff Sept 1, 1967, with substance deriving from RPL § 151.

§ 10-6.6. Exercise of a power of appointment; effect when more extensive or less extensive than authorized; trustee's authority to invade principal in trust

(a) An exercise of a power of appointment is not void because its exercise is:

(1) More extensive than was authorized but is valid to the extent authorized by the instrument creating the power.

(2) Less extensive than authorized by the instrument creating the power, unless the donor has manifested a contrary intention.

(b) An authorized trustee with unlimited discretion to invade trust principal may appoint part or all of such principal to a trustee of an appointed trust for, and only for the benefit of, one, more than one or all of the current beneficiaries of the invaded trust (to the exclusion of any one or more of such current beneficiaries). The successor and remainder beneficiaries of such appointed trust may be one, more than one or all of the successor and remainder beneficiaries of such invaded trust (to the exclusion of any one, more than one or all of such successor and remainder beneficiaries).

(1) An authorized trustee exercising the power under this paragraph may grant a discretionary power of appointment as defined in paragraph (c) of section 10-3.4 of this article (including a presently exercisable power of appointment) in the appointed trust to one or more of the current beneficiaries of the invaded trust, provided that the beneficiary granted a power to appoint could receive the principal outright under the terms of the invaded trust.

(2) If the authorized trustee grants a power of appointment under subparagraph (1) of this paragraph, except as otherwise provided in subparagraph (3) of this paragraph, the granted power may only exclude as permissible appointees one or more of the beneficiary, the creator, or the creator's spouse, or any of the estates, creditors, or creditors of the estates

---

* **Ed. Note**: There is no paragraph (b).

of the beneficiary, the creator or the creator's spouse.

(3) If the authorized trustee exercises the power under this paragraph, the appointed trust may grant any power of appointment included in the invaded trust provided such power has the same class of permissible appointees as the power of appointment in the invaded trust and is exercisable in the same fashion as the power of appointment in the invaded trust.

(4) If the beneficiary or beneficiaries of the invaded trust are described by a class, the beneficiary or beneficiaries of the appointed trust may include present or future members of such class.

(c) An authorized trustee with the power to invade trust principal but without unlimited discretion may appoint part or all of the principal of the trust to a trustee of an appointed trust, provided that the current beneficiaries of the appointed trust shall be the same as the current beneficiaries of the invaded trust and the successor and remainder beneficiaries of the appointed trust shall be the same as the successor and remainder beneficiaries of the invaded trust.

(1) If the authorized trustee exercises the power under this paragraph, the appointed trust shall include the same language authorizing the trustee to distribute the income or invade the principal of the appointed trust as in the invaded trust.

(2) If the authorized trustee exercises the power under this paragraph to extend the term of the appointed trust beyond the term of the invaded trust, for any period after the invaded trust would have otherwise terminated under the provisions of the invaded trust, the appointed trust, in addition to the language required to be included in the appointed trust pursuant to subparagraph (1) of this paragraph, may also include language providing the trustees with unlimited discretion to invade the principal of the appointed trust during such extended term.

(3) If the beneficiary or beneficiaries of the invaded trust are described by a class, the beneficiary or beneficiaries of the appointed trust shall include present or future members of such class.

(4) If the authorized trustee exercises the power under this paragraph and if the invaded trust grants a power of appointment to a beneficiary of the trust, the appointed trust shall grant such power of appointment in the appointed trust and the class of permissible appointees shall be the same as in the invaded trust.

(d) An exercise of the power to invade trust principal under paragraphs (b) and (c) of this section shall be considered the exercise of a special power of appointment as defined in section 10-3.2 of this article.

(e) The appointed trust to which an authorized trustee appoints the assets of the invaded trust may have a term that is longer than the term set forth in the invaded trust, including, but not limited to, a term measured by the lifetime of a current beneficiary.

(f) If an authorized trustee has unlimited discretion to invade the principal of a trust and the same trustee or another trustee has the power to invade principal under the trust instrument which power is not subject to unlimited discretion, such authorized trustee having unlimited discretion may exercise the power of appointment under paragraph (b) of this section.

(g) An authorized trustee may exercise the power to appoint in favor of an appointed trust under paragraphs (b) and (c) of this section whether or not there is a current need to invade principal under the terms of the invaded trust.

(h) An authorized trustee exercising the power under this section has a fiduciary duty to exercise the power in the best interests of one or more proper objects of the exercise of the power and as a prudent person would exercise the power under the prevailing circumstances. The authorized trustee may not exercise the power under this section if there is substantial evidence of a contrary intent of the creator and it cannot be established that the creator would be likely to have changed such intention under the circumstances existing at the time of the exercise of the power. The provisions of the invaded trust alone are not to be viewed as substantial evidence of a contrary intent of the creator unless the invaded trust expressly prohibits the exercise of the power in the manner intended by the authorized trustee.

(i) Unless the authorized trustee provides otherwise:

(1) The appointment of all of the assets comprising the principal of the invaded trust to an appointed trust shall include subsequently discovered assets of the invaded trust and undistributed principal of the invaded trust acquired after the appointment to the appointed trust; and

(2) The appointment of part but not all of the assets comprising the principal of the invaded trust to an appointed trust shall not include subsequently discovered assets belonging to the invaded trust and principal paid to or acquired by the invaded trust after the appointment to the appointed trust; such assets shall remain the assets of the invaded trust.

(j) The exercise of the power to appoint to an appointed trust under paragraph (b) or (c) of this section shall be evidenced by an instrument in writing, signed, dated and acknowledged by the authorized trustee. The exercise of the power shall be effective thirty days after the date of service of the instrument as specified in subparagraph (2) of this paragraph, unless the persons entitled to notice consent in writing to a sooner effective date. The exercise of the power is irrevocable on such effective date, either thirty days following service of the notice or the effective date as set forth in the written consent.

(1) An authorized trustee may exercise the power authorized by paragraphs (b) and (c) of this section without the consent of the creator, or of the persons interested in the invaded trust, and without court approval, provided that the authorized trustee may seek court approval for the exercise with notice to all persons interested in the invaded trust.

(2) A copy of the instrument exercising the power and a copy of each of the invaded trust and the appointed trust shall be delivered (A) to the creator, if living, of the invaded trust, (B) to any person having the right, pursuant to the terms of the invaded trust, to remove or replace the authorized trustee exercising the power under paragraph (b) or (c) of this section, and (C) to any persons interested in the invaded trust and the appointed trust (or, in the case of any persons interested in the trust, to any guardian of the property, conservator or personal representative of any such person or the parent or person with whom any such minor person resides), by registered or certified mail, return receipt requested, or by personal delivery or in any other manner directed by the court having jurisdiction over the invaded trust.

(3) The instrument exercising the power shall state whether the appointment is of all the

assets comprising the principal of the invaded trust or a part but not all the assets comprising the principal of the invaded trust and if a part, the approximate percentage of the value of the principal of the invaded trust that is the subject of the appointment.

(4) A person interested in the invaded trust may object to the trustee's exercise of the power under this section by serving a written notice of objection upon the trustee prior to the effective date of the exercise of the power. The failure to object shall not constitute a consent.

(5) The receipt of a copy of the instrument exercising the power shall not affect the right of any person interested in the invaded trust to compel the authorized trustee who exercised the power under paragraph (b) or (c) of this section to account for such exercise and shall not foreclose any such interested person from objecting to an account or compelling a trustee to account. Whether the exercise of a power under paragraph (b) or (c) of this section begins the running of the statute of limitations on an action to compel a trustee to account shall be based on all the facts and circumstances of the situation.

(6) A copy of the instrument exercising the power shall be kept with the records of the invaded trust and, within twenty days of the effective date, the original shall be filed in the court having jurisdiction over the invaded trust. Where a trustee of an inter vivos trust exercises the power and the trust has not been the subject of a proceeding in the surrogate's court, no filing is required. The instrument shall state that in certain circumstances the appointment will begin the running of the statute of limitations that will preclude persons interested in the invaded trust from compelling an accounting by the trustees after the expiration of a given time.

(7) Prior to the effective date as provided herein, a trustee may revoke the exercise of the power to invade to a new trust. Where a trustee has served notice of the exercise of the power pursuant to subparagraph (2) of this paragraph, the trustee shall serve notice of the revocation of the exercise of the power to persons interested in the invaded trust and the appointed trust by registered or certified mail, return receipt requested, or by personal delivery or in any other manner directed by the court having jurisdiction over the invaded trust. Where the notice of the exercise of the power was filed with the court, the trustee shall file the notice of revocation of the exercise of the power with such court.

(k) This section shall not be construed to abridge the right of any trustee to appoint property in further trust that arises under the terms of the governing instrument of a trust or under any other provision of law or under common law, or as directed by any court having jurisdiction over the trust.

(l) Nothing in this section is intended to create or imply a duty to exercise a power to invade principal, and no inference of impropriety shall be made as a result of an authorized trustee not exercising the power conferred under paragraph (b) or (c) of this section.

(m) A power authorized by paragraph (b) or (c) of this section may be exercised, subject to the provisions of paragraph (h) of this section, unless expressly prohibited by the terms of the governing instrument, but a general prohibition of the amendment or revocation of the invaded trust or a provision that constitutes a spendthrift clause shall not preclude the exercise of a power under paragraph (b) or (c) of this section.

(n) An authorized trustee may not exercise a power authorized by paragraph (b) or (c) of this section to effect any of the following:

(1) To reduce, limit or modify any beneficiary's current right to a mandatory distribution of income or principal, a mandatory annuity or unitrust interest, a right to withdraw a percentage of the value of the trust or a right to withdraw a specified dollar amount, provided that such mandatory right has come into effect with respect to the beneficiary. Notwithstanding the foregoing, but subject to the other limitations in this section, an authorized trustee may exercise a power authorized by paragraph (b) or (c) of this section to appoint to an appointed trust that is a supplemental needs trust that conforms to the provisions of section 7-1.12 of this chapter;

(2) To decrease or indemnify against a trustee's liability or exonerate a trustee from liability for failure to exercise reasonable care, diligence and prudence;

(3) To eliminate a provision granting another person the right to remove or replace the authorized trustee exercising the power under paragraph (b) or (c) of this section unless a court having jurisdiction over the trust specifies otherwise;

(4) To make a binding and conclusive fixation of the value of any asset for purposes of distribution, allocation or otherwise; or

(5) To jeopardize (A) the deduction or exclusion originally claimed with respect to any contribution to the invaded trust that qualified for the annual exclusion under section 2503(b) of the internal revenue code, the marital deduction under section 2056(a) or 2523(a) of the internal revenue code, or the charitable deduction under section 170(a), 642(c), 2055(a) or 2522(a) of the internal revenue code, (B) the qualification of a transfer as a direct skip under section 2642(c) of the internal revenue code, or (C) any other specific tax benefit for which a contribution originally qualified for income, gift, estate, or generation-skipping transfer tax purposes under the internal revenue code.

(o) An authorized trustee shall consider the tax implications of the exercise of the power under paragraph (b) or (c) of this section.

(p) An authorized trustee may not exercise a power described in paragraph (b) or (c) of this section in violation of the limitations under sections 9-1.1, 10-8.1 and 10-8.2 of this chapter, and any such exercise shall void the entire exercise of such power.

(q) (1) Unless a court otherwise directs, an authorized trustee may not exercise a power authorized by paragraph (b) or (c) of this section to change the provisions regarding the determination of the compensation of any trustee; the commissions or other compensation payable to the trustees of the invaded trust may continue to be paid to the trustees of the appointed trust during the term of the appointed trust and shall be determined in the same manner as in the invaded trust.

(2) No trustee shall receive any paying commission or other compensation for appointing of property from the invaded trust to an appointed trust pursuant to paragraph (b) or (c) of this section.

(r) Unless the invaded trust expressly provides otherwise, this section applies to:

(1) Any trust governed by the laws of this state, including a trust whose governing law has been changed to the laws of this state; and

(2) Any trust that has a trustee who is an individual domiciled in this state or a trustee which is an entity having an office in this state, provided that a majority of the trustees

select this state as the location for the primary administration of the trust by an instrument in writing, signed and acknowledged by a majority of the trustees. The instrument exercising this selection shall be kept with the records of the invaded trust.

(s) For purposes of this section:

(1) The term "appointed trust" means an irrevocable trust which receives principal from an invaded trust under paragraph (b) or (c) of this section including a new trust created by the creator of the invaded trust or by the trustees, in that capacity, of the invaded trust. For purposes of creating the new trust, the requirement of section 7-1.17 of this chapter that the instrument be executed and acknowledged by the person establishing such trust shall be deemed satisfied by the execution and acknowledgment of the trustee of the appointed trust.

(2) The term "authorized trustee" means, as to an invaded trust, any trustee or trustees with authority to pay trust principal to or for one or more current beneficiaries other than (i) the creator, or (ii) a beneficiary to whom income or principal must be paid currently or in the future, or who is or will become eligible to receive a distribution of income or principal in the discretion of the trustee (other than by the exercise of a power of appointment held in a non-fiduciary capacity).

(3) References to sections of the "internal revenue code" refer to the United States internal revenue code of 1986, as amended from time to time, or to corresponding provisions of subsequent internal revenue laws, and also refer to corresponding provisions of state law.

(4) The term "current beneficiary or beneficiaries" means the person or persons (or as to a class, any person or persons who are or will become members of such class) to whom the trustees may distribute principal at the time of the exercise of the power, provided however that the interest of a beneficiary to whom income, but not principal, may be distributed in the discretion of the trustee of the invaded trust may be continued in the appointed trust.

(5) The term "invade" shall mean the power to pay directly to the beneficiary of a trust or make application for the benefit of the beneficiary.

(6) The term "invaded trust" means any existing irrevocable inter vivos or testamentary trust whose principal is appointed under paragraph (b) or (c) of this section.

(7) The term "person or persons interested in the invaded trust" shall mean any person or persons upon whom service of process would be required in a proceeding for the judicial settlement of the account of the trustee, taking into account section three hundred fifteen of the surrogate's court procedure act.

(8) The term "principal" shall include the income of the trust at the time of the exercise of the power that is not currently required to be distributed, including accrued and accumulated income.

(9) The term "unlimited discretion" means the unlimited right to distribute principal that is not modified in any manner. A power to pay principal that includes words such as best interests, welfare, comfort, or happiness shall not be considered a limitation or modification of the right to distribute principal.

(10) The creator shall not be considered to be a beneficiary of an invaded or appointed trust by reason of the trustee's authority to pay trust principal to the creator pursuant to section 7-1.11 of this chapter or by reason of the trustee's authority under the trust instrument or any other provision of law to pay or reimburse the creator for any tax on trust income or trust principal that is payable by the creator under the law imposing such tax or to pay any such tax directly to the taxing authorities.

(t) Cross-reference. For the exercise of the power under paragraph (b) or (c) of this section where there are multiple trustees, see sections 10-6.7 and 10-10.7 of this article.

> **History:** Add, L 1966, ch 952, eff Sept 1, 1967, with substance deriving from RPL § 152; amd, L 1992, ch 591, §§ 1, 2, eff July 24, 1992, and applying to trusts whenever created; L 1995, ch 479, § 1, eff Aug 2, 1995, and applying to trusts whenever created; L 2001, ch 204, § 1, eff Aug 20, 2001, and applying to trusts whenever created; L 2011, ch 451, §§ 1, 2, eff Aug 17, 2011; L 2013, ch 432, eff Oct 23, 2013, clarifying that 2011 amendment applies to trusts whether created prior to, on, or after the effective date of that 2011 amendment; L 2013, ch 482, §§ 1–5, eff Nov 13, 2013; L 2014, ch 130, § 1, eff July 22, 2014, and deemed to have been in full force and effect on and after Nov 13, 2013; L 2015, ch 441, § 1, eff Nov 20, 2015.

§ 10-6.7. Exercise by all donees; exceptions

Whenever a power of appointment, other than a power in a trustee to invade trust principal under section 10-6.6 of this article or under the terms of the dispositive instrument, is created in two or more donees, all must unite in its exercise, unless the instrument creating such power provides otherwise. But, if before its execution, one or more of such donees dies or becomes incompetent, such power may be exercised by the survivor or the competent donee, unless such exercise is explicitly barred by the terms of the instrument creating such power.

> **History:** Add, L 1966, ch 952, eff Sept 1, 1967, with substance deriving from RPL § 166 amd, L 1967, ch 686, § 100, eff Sept 1, 1967; L 2013, ch 482, § 6, eff Nov 13, 2013.

§ 10-6.8. Imperative power of appointment; effectuation

(a) The exercise of an imperative power of appointment devolves upon the supreme court or, in the case of a will, the surrogate's court in the following cases:

(1) Failure to designate the donee.

(2) Death of the designated donee without exercising the power.

(3) Incompetence of the sole donee.

(4) Defective exercise of the power, either wholly or in part, by the donee.

(b) Where an imperative power of appointment:

(1) Is exclusive, and the donee dies without exercising the power, it must be exercised for the benefit of all of the appointees equally.

(2) Has been exercised defectively by the donee, it may be properly exercised in favor of persons intended to be benefited by the donee.

(3) Has been exercised defectively by the donee, a purchaser for a valuable consideration claiming under such defective exercise is entitled to the same relief as a similar purchaser claiming under a defective disposition from an actual owner.

(4) Is non-exclusive, and the right of the appointee is assignable, creditors or assignees

of such appointee can compel the exercise of such power for their benefit.

(5) Is non-exclusive, the committee of an appointee or his assignee for the benefit of creditors can compel the exercise of such power.

History: Add, L 1966, ch 952, eff Sept 1, 1967, with substance deriving from RPL § 153.

§ 10-6.9. Exercise of a power of appointment in further trust

If the donee of a power of appointment exercises the power in favor of the trustee of a trust under a will or deed other than that under which the power was created, and if said exercise is otherwise valid, the appointive property shall be paid over to and administered by the trustee of, and under the terms of, the trust under such will or deed and jurisdiction over said appointive property shall thereafter be in the court having jurisdiction of the trust under such will or deed.

History: Add, L 1975, ch 114, § 1, eff May 27, 1975.

PART 7 Rights of Creditors in Appointive Property

§ 10-7.1. Creditors of the donee; special power

Property covered by a special power of appointment (or a general power of appointment that is exercisable solely for the support, maintenance, health and education of the donee within the meaning of sections 2041 and 2514 of the Internal Revenue Code) is not subject to the payment of the claims of creditors of the donee, his estate or the expenses of administering his estate.

History: Add, L 1966, ch 952, eff Sept 1, 1967, with substance deriving from RPL § 138; amd, L 2005, ch 700, § 1, eff Oct 4, 2005, applying to trusts created before or after the effective date of this act.

§ 10-7.2. Creditors of the donee; general power presently exercisable

Property covered by a general power of appointment (other than one exercisable solely for the support, maintenance, health and education of the donee within the meaning of sections 2041 and 2514 of the Internal Revenue Code) which is presently exercisable, or of a postponed power which has become exercisable, is subject to the payment of the claims of creditors of the donee, his estate and the expenses of administering his estate. It is immaterial whether the power was created in the donee by himself or by some other person, or whether the donee has or has not purported to exercise the power.

History: Add, L 1966, ch 952, with substance deriving from RPL § 139; amd, L 2005, ch 700, § 2, eff Oct 4, 2005, applying to trusts created before or after the effective date of this act.

§ 10-7.3. Creditors of the donee; power subject to a condition

A general power of appointment may be created subject to a condition precedent or subsequent, and until the condition is fulfilled, it is not subject to the provisions of 10-7.2.

History: Add, L 1966, ch 952, eff Sept 1, 1967, with substance deriving from RPL § 140.

§ 10-7.4. Creditors of the donee; general power not presently exercisable

(a)* Property covered by a general power of appointment which, when created, is not

---

* **Ed. Note**: There is no paragraph (b).

presently exercisable is subject to the payment of the claims of creditors of the donee, his estate and the expenses of administering his estate, only:

(1) If the power was created by the donee in favor of himself; or

(2) If a postponed power becomes exercisable in accordance with the terms of the creating instrument, except in the case of a testamentary general power.

History: Add, L 1966, ch 952, eff Sept 1, 1967, with substance deriving from RPL § 141.

PART 8   Rule Against Perpetuities and Accumulations as Affected by Powers of Appointment

§ 10-8.1. Rule against perpetuities; time at which permissible period begins

(a) Where an estate is created by an instrument exercising a power of appointment, the permissible period of the rule against perpetuities begins:

(1) In the case of an instrument exercising a general power which is presently exercisable, on the effective date of the instrument of exercise.

(2) In all other cases, at the time of the creation of the power.

(b) Where the creator of a trust reserves to himself an unqualified power to revoke, the permissible period of the rule against perpetuities begins when the power to revoke terminates by reason of the death of the creator, by a release of such power or otherwise.

History: Add, L 1966, ch 952, eff Sept 1, 1967, with substance deriving from RPL §§ 154, 155.

§ 10-8.2. Rule against perpetuities; law which determines permissible period

In all cases covered by 10-8.1, the permissible period of the rule against perpetuities is determined by the law in effect when the power is exercised or the unqualified power to revoke is terminated, and not by the law in effect when the power was created.

History: Add, L 1966, ch 952, eff Sept 1, 1967, with substance deriving from RPL § 156.

§ 10-8.3. Rules against perpetuities; facts to be considered

When the permissible period of the rule against perpetuities must be computed from the time of the creation of the power of appointment, facts and circumstances existing on the effective date of the instrument exercising the power shall be taken into account in determining the validity of interests created by the instrument exercising the power.

History: Add, L 1966, ch 952, eff Sept 1, 1967, with substance deriving from RPL § 157.

§ 10-8.4. Rule against accumulations; law determining validity in exercise of a power of appointment

When a direction for the accumulation of income is contained in an instrument exercising a power, heretofore or hereafter created, the validity of such direction is determined by the law in effect when the power is exercised, and not by the law in effect when the power was created.

History: Add, L 1966, ch 952, eff Sept 1, 1967, with substance deriving from RPL § 158.

EPTL

PART 9 Revocation and Release of a Power of Appointment

§ 10-9.1. Revocability of a power of appointment

(a) A power of appointment is irrevocable unless the donor reserves the right to revoke it.

(b) An exercise of power of appointment is irrevocable whenever:

(1) The donor of a special power manifests his intention that its exercise be irrevocable, or

(2) The donee does not manifest in the instrument exercising the power his intention to reserve a power of revocation.

(c) If the donee in exercising a power reserves a power to revoke the appointment, but does not expressly reserve a power to reappoint, upon the exercise of the power of revocation, the donee can reappoint.

(d) An instrument exercising a power of appointment is affected by fraud in the same manner as a deed or will, executed by an owner or by a trustee of property.

History: Add, L 1966, ch 952, eff Sept 1, 1967, with substance deriving from RPL § 144.

§ 10-9.2. Release of a power of appointment

(a) Any power of appointment, whether exercisable only by deed, only by will, or by either deed or will, and whether general or special, exclusive or nonexclusive other than a power which is imperative, is releasable, either with or without consideration, by written instrument signed by the donee of such power and delivered as hereinafter provided.

(b) A releasable power of appointment may be released with respect to all or any part of the appointive property and may also be released in such manner as to reduce or limit the appointees, or classes of appointees, in whose favor such power is exercisable. No release of any power of appointment shall cause the power to become imperative when such power was not imperative prior to such release, unless the instrument of release expressly so provides.

(c) Such release may be delivered to any of the following:

(1) Any person specified for such purpose in the instrument creating the power.

(2) Any trustee of the property subject to such power.

(3) Any person, other than the donee, who might be adversely affected by an exercise of the power.

(4) The county clerk of the county in which the donee resides or has a place of business or in which the instrument creating the power is filed, to be duly filed by such clerk upon the payment to him of the fees due for such filing or, if the power was created by will, to the clerk of the surrogate's court having jurisdiction of the estate of the donor.

(d) This section applies to releases delivered on or after July first, nineteen hundred forty-two.

History: Add, L 1966, ch 952, eff Sept 1, 1967, with substance deriving from RPL § 143; amd, L 1967, ch 686, § 101, eff Sept 1, 1967.

PART 10   Provisions Affecting Powers Other Than Power of Appointment

§ 10-10.1. Power to distribute principal or allocate income; restriction on exercise

A power held by a person as trustee of an express trust to make a discretionary distribution of either principal or income to such person as a beneficiary, or to make discretionary allocations in such person's favor of receipts or expenses as between principal and income, cannot be exercised by such person unless (1) such person is the grantor of the trust and the trust is revocable by such person during such person's lifetime, or (2) the power is a power to provide for such person's health, education, maintenance or support within the meaning of sections 2041 and 2514 of the Internal Revenue Code, or (3) the trust instrument, by express reference to this section, provides otherwise. If the power is conferred on two or more trustees, it may be exercised by the trustee or trustees who are not so disqualified. If there is no trustee qualified to exercise the power, its exercise devolves on the supreme court or the surrogate's court, except that if the power is created by will, its exercise devolves on the surrogate's court having jurisdiction of the estate of the donor of the power.

> **History:** Add, L 1966, ch 952, eff Sept 1, 1967, with substance deriving from RPL § 159; amd, L 1967, ch 686, eff Sept 1, 1967; L 1997, ch 139, eff June 25, 1997, and applying to all lifetime trusts created on and after that date; L 2003, ch 633, § 1, eff Sept 30, 2003; L 2004, ch 82, § 1, eff May 18, 2004.

§ 10-10.2. Power to lease in tenant for life; scope

A power may be conferred upon a tenant for life to make leases of real property for a term of not more than twenty-one years to commence in possession during his lifetime. If the power authorizes, or the life tenant makes, a lease for a term in excess of twenty-one years, such power or lease is valid for twenty-one years, but is void as to the excess.

> **History:** Add, L 1966, ch 952, eff Sept 1, 1967, with substance deriving from RPL § 160; amd, L 1967, ch 686, § 103, eff Sept 1, 1967.

§ 10-10.3. Power to lease in tenant for life; transfer and extinguishment

The power of a tenant for life to make leases is not assignable as a separate interest, but is annexed to his estate and passes by a disposition of such estate unless expressly excepted. If so excepted, it is extinguished. Such a power may be released by the tenant to a person entitled to a future estate in the property, and shall thereupon be extinguished.

> **History:** Add, L 1966, ch 952, eff Sept 1, 1967, with substance deriving from RPL § 161.

§ 10-10.4. Power to lease in tenant for life; effect of mortgage

(a)* The power of a tenant for life to make leases is neither extinguished nor suspended when such tenant executes a mortgage. The power is bound by the mortgage in the same manner as the real property embraced therein, and the lien of the mortgagee on such power:

(1) Entitles the mortgagee to an exercise of the power so far as the satisfaction of the debt requires; and

(2) Causes any subsequent interest, created by the tenant for life by an exercise of such power, to become subject to the mortgage as if in terms embraced therein.

> **History:** Add, L 1966, ch 952, eff Sept 1, 1967, with substance deriving from RPL § 162.

---

* **Ed. Note:** There is no paragraph (b).

§ 10-10.5. Power to sell in a mortgage

Where a power to sell real property is given to a mortgagee or to the transferee in any other conveyance intended to secure the payment of money, the power is deemed a part of the security, and passes to and may be exercised by any person, who by assignment or otherwise, becomes entitled to the money so secured to be paid.

History: Add, L 1966, ch 952, eff Sept 1, 1967, with substance deriving from RPL § 164.

§ 10-10.6. Effect of reserved unqualified power to revoke

Where a creator reserves an unqualified power of revocation, he remains the absolute owner of the property disposed of so far as the rights of his creditors or purchasers are concerned.

History: Add, L 1966, ch 952, eff Sept 1, 1967, with substance deriving from RPL § 163.

§ 10-10.7. Exercise of powers by multiple fiduciaries; joint and several powers

Unless contrary to the express provisions of an instrument affecting the disposition of property, a joint power other than a power of appointment but including a power in a trustee to invade trust principal under section 10-6.6 of this article or under the terms of the dispositive instrument, conferred upon three or more fiduciaries, as that term is defined in 11-1.1, by the terms of such instrument, or by statute, or arising by operation of law, may be exercised by a majority of such fiduciaries, or by a majority of survivor fiduciaries, or by the survivor fiduciary. Such a power conferred upon or surviving to two such fiduciaries may be exercised jointly by both such fiduciaries or by the survivor fiduciary, unless contrary to the express terms of the instrument creating the power. A fiduciary who fails to act through absence or disability, or a dissenting fiduciary who joins in carrying out the decision of a majority of the fiduciaries if his or her dissent is expressed promptly in writing to his or her co-fiduciaries, shall not be liable for the consequences of any majority decision, provided that liability for failure to join in administering the estate or trust or to prevent a breach of the trust may not thus be avoided. A power vested in one or more persons under a trust of real property created in connection with the salvaging of mortgage participation certificates may be executed by one or more of such persons as provided in such trust. This section shall not affect the right of any one of two or more personal representatives of a decedent to exercise a several power.

History: Add, L 1966, ch 952, eff Sept 1, 1967, with substance deriving from RPL § 166; amd, L 1967, ch 686, eff Sept 1, 1967; L 1973, ch 904, § 1, eff June 22, 1973; L 2013, ch 482, § 7, eff Nov 13, 2013.

§ 10-10.8. Irrevocability of powers other than powers of appointment

A power, other than a power of appointment, is irrevocable unless an authority to revoke it is granted or reserved in the instrument creating the power.

History: Add, L 1966, ch 952, eff Sept 1, 1967, with substance deriving from RPL § 165.

ARTICLE 11
FIDUCIARIES: POWERS, DUTIES AND LIMITATIONS; ACTIONS BY OR AGAINST IN REPRESENTATIVE OR INDIVIDUAL CAPACITIES
SUMMARY OF ARTICLE

EPTL

granted; execution on judgment recovered by predecessor representative

§ 11-4.7.   Liability of the personal representative for claims arising out of the administration of the estate

PART 1   Fiduciaries: Powers, Duties and Limitations

§ 11-1.1. Fiduciaries' powers

(a) As used in this section, unless the context or subject matter otherwise requires, (1) the term "estate" means the estate of a decedent; (2) the term "trust" means any express trust of property, created by a will, deed or other instrument, whereby there is imposed upon a trustee the duty to administer property for the benefit of a named or otherwise described income or principal beneficiary, or both. A trust shall not include trusts for the benefit of creditors, resulting or constructive trusts, business trusts where certificates of beneficial interest are issued to the beneficiary, investment trusts, voting trusts, security instruments such as deeds of trust and mortgages, trusts created by the judgment or decree of a court, liquidation or reorganization trusts, trusts for the sole purpose of paying dividends, interest, interest coupons, salaries, wages, pensions or profits, instruments wherein persons are mere nominees for others, or trusts created in deposits in any banking institution or savings and loan institution; (3) the term "fiduciary" means administrators, executors, preliminary executors, administrators d.b.n., administrators c.t.a.d.b.n., administrators c.t.a., ancillary executors, ancillary administrators, ancillary administrators c.t.a. and trustees of express trusts, including a corporate as well as a natural person acting as fiduciary, and a successor or substitute fiduciary, whether designated in a trust instrument or otherwise.

(b) In the absence of contrary or limiting provisions in the court order or decree appointing a fiduciary, or in a subsequent order or decree, or in the will, deed or other instrument, every fiduciary is authorized:

(1) To accept additions to any estate or trust from sources other than the estate of the decedent or the settlor of a trust.

(2) To acquire the remaining undivided interest in the property of an estate or trust in which the fiduciary, in his fiduciary capacity, holds an undivided interest.

(3) To invest and reinvest property of the estate or trust under the provisions of the will, deed or other instrument or as otherwise provided by law.

(4) To effect and keep in force fire, rent, title, liability, casualty or other insurance to protect the property of the estate or trust and to protect the fiduciary.

(5) With respect to any property or any estate therein owned by an estate or trust, except where such property or any estate therein is specifically disposed of:

(A) To take possession of, collect the rents from and manage the same.

(B) To sell the same at public or private sale, and on such terms as in the opinion of the fiduciary will be most advantageous to those interested therein.

(C) With respect to fiduciaries other than a trustee, to lease the same for a term not exceeding three years and, in the case of a trustee, to lease the same for a term not exceeding ten years although such term extends beyond the duration of the trust and, in either of such cases, including the right to explore for and remove mineral or other natural resources, and in connection with mineral leases to enter into pooling and unitization agreements.

(D) To mortgage the same.

(E) Any power to take possession of, collect the rent from, manage, sell, lease or mortgage, granted by this subparagraph (5), which is prohibited by the terms of the will, deed or other instrument or by the provisions of this subparagraph (5), nonetheless exists, upon the approval of the surrogate, where such power is necessary for the purposes set forth in SCPA 1902.

(F) A fiduciary acting under a will may exercise all of the powers granted by this subparagraph (5) notwithstanding the effect upon such will of the birth of a child after its execution or of any election by a surviving spouse.

(6) To make ordinary repairs to the property of the estate or trust.

(7) To grant options for the sale of property for a period not exceeding six months.

(8) With respect to any mortgage held by the estate or trust (A) to continue the same upon and after maturity, with or without renewal or extension, upon such terms as the fiduciary deems advisable; (B) to foreclose, as an incident to collection of any bond or note, any mortgage securing such bond or note, and to purchase the mortgaged property or acquire the property by deed from the mortgagor in lieu of foreclosure.

(9) To employ any bank or trust company incorporated in this state, any national bank located in this state or any private banker duly authorized by the superintendent of financial services of this state to engage in business here (who, as private banker, maintains a permanent capital of not less than one million dollars) as custodian of any stock or other securities held as a fiduciary, and the cost thereof, except in the case of a corporate fiduciary, shall be a charge upon the estate or trust. The records of such bank, trust company or private banker shall at all times show the ownership of such stock or other securities. Such stock or other securities shall at all times be kept separate from the assets of such bank, trust company or private banker and may be kept by such bank, trust company or private banker

(A) in a manner such that all certificates representing the securities from time to time constituting the assets of a particular estate, trust or other fiduciary account are held separate from those of all other estates, trusts or accounts; or

(B) in a manner such that, without certification as to ownership attached, certificates representing securities of the same class of the same issuer and from time to time constituting assets of particular estates, trusts or other fiduciary accounts are held in bulk, including, to the extent feasible, the merging of certificates of small denomination into one or more certificates of large denomination, provided that a bank, trust company or private banker, when operating under the method of safekeeping security certificates described in this subparagraph (B), shall be subject to such rules and regulations as, in the case of state chartered institutions, the state superintendent of financial services and, in the case of national banking associations, the comptroller of the currency may from time to time issue. Such bank, trust company or private banker shall, on demand by the fiduciary, certify in writing the securities held by it for such estate, trust or fiduciary account.

(10) To cause any stock or other securities (hereinafter referred to as "securities") held by any bank or trust company, when acting as fiduciary, whether alone or jointly with an individual, with the consent of the individual fiduciary, if any (who is hereby authorized to give such consent), to be registered and held in the name of a nominee of such bank or trust company without disclosure of the fiduciary relationship; and, in the case of an individual acting as fiduciary, to direct any bank or trust company incorporated under the laws of this state, any national bank located in this state or any private banker duly authorized by the superintendent of financial services of this state to engage in business here (who, as private banker, maintains a permanent capital of not less than one million dollars) to register and hold any securities deposited with such bank, trust company or private banker (hereinafter referred to as "bank") in the name of a nominee of such bank. The bank shall not redeliver such securities to the individual fiduciary, who authorized their registration in the name of a nominee of the bank, without first registering the securities in the name of the individual fiduciary, as such. But, any sale of such securities by the bank at the direction of the individual fiduciary shall not be treated as a redelivery. The bank may make any disposition of such securities which is authorized or directed by an order or decree of the court having jurisdiction of the estate or trust. Any such bank shall be absolutely liable for any loss occasioned by the acts of its nominee with respect to the securities so registered. The records of the bank shall at all times show the ownership of any such securities and of those held in bearer form. Such securities and those held in bearer form shall at all times be kept separate from the assets of the bank and may be kept by such bank

    (A) in a manner such that all certificates representing the securities from time to time constituting the assets of a particular estate, trust or other fiduciary account are held separate from those of all other estates, trusts or accounts; or

    (B) in a manner such that, without certification as to ownership attached, certificates representing securities of the same class of the same issuer and from time to time constituting assets of particular estates, trusts or other fiduciary accounts are held in bulk, including, to the extent feasible, the merging of certificates of small denomination into one or more certificates of large denomination, provided that a bank, when operating under the method of safekeeping security certificates described in this subparagraph (B), shall be subject to such rules and regulations as, in the case of state chartered institutions, the state superintendent of financial services and, in the case of national banking associations, the comptroller of the currency may from time to time issue. Such bank or trust company shall, on demand by any party to an accounting by such bank or trust company as fiduciary or on demand by the attorney for such party, certify in writing the securities held by such bank or trust company as such fiduciary.

(11) In the case of the survivor of two or more fiduciaries, to continue to administer the property of the estate or trust without the appointment of a successor to the fiduciary who has ceased to act and to exercise or perform all of the powers given to the original fiduciaries unless contrary to the express provision of the will, deed or other instrument.

(12) A successor or substitute fiduciary, to succeed to all of the powers, duties and discretion of the original fiduciary, with respect to the estate or trust, as were given to the original fiduciary, unless the exercise of such powers, duties or discretion of the original fiduciary are expressly prohibited by the will, deed or other instrument to any successor or substituted fiduciary.

(13) To contest, compromise or otherwise settle any claim in favor of the estate, trust or fiduciary or in favor of third persons and against the estate, trust or fiduciary.

(14) To vote in person or by proxy, discretionary or otherwise, shares of stock or other securities held by him as fiduciary.

(15) To pay calls, assessments and any other sums chargeable or accruing against or on account of shares of stock, bonds, debentures or other corporate securities held by a fiduciary, whenever such payments may be legally enforceable against the fiduciary or any property of the estate or trust or the fiduciary deems payment expedient and for the best interests of the estate or trust.

(16) To sell or exercise stock subscription or conversion rights, participate in foreclosures, reorganizations, consolidations, mergers or liquidations, and to consent to corporate sales, leases and encumbrances. In the exercise of such powers the fiduciary is authorized to deposit stocks, bonds or other securities with any protective or other similar committee under such terms and conditions respecting the deposit thereof as the fiduciary may approve.

(17) To execute and deliver agreements, assignments, bills of sale, contracts, deeds, notes, receipts and any other instrument necessary or appropriate for the administration of the estate or trust.

(18) In the case of a trustee, to hold the property of two or more trusts or parts of such trusts created by the same instrument as an undivided whole without separation as between such trusts or parts, provided that such separate trusts or parts shall have undivided interests and provided further that no such holding shall defer the vesting of any estate in possession or otherwise.

(19) When a legacy, a distributive share, the proceeds of any action brought as prescribed by 5-4.1, or the proceeds of a settlement of an action brought in behalf of an infant for personal injuries are payable to an infant, incompetent, conservatee or person under disability and the sum does not exceed ten thousand dollars, to make payment thereof to the father or mother or to some competent adult person with whom the infant, incompetent, conservatee or person under disability resides or who has some interest in his welfare for the use and benefit of such infant, incompetent, conservatee or person under disability. If the sum payable to a patient in an institution in the state department of mental hygiene is not in excess of the amount which the director of the institution is authorized to receive under section 29.23 of the mental hygiene law, to make payment of such sum to such director for use as provided in that section.

(20) To make distribution in cash, in kind valued at the fair market value of the property at the date of distribution, or partly in each, without being required to make pro rata distributions of specific property.

(21) To join with the surviving spouse or the executor of his will or the administrator of his estate in the execution and filing of a joint income tax return for any period prior to the death of a decedent for which he has not filed a return or a gift tax return on gifts made by the decedent's surviving spouse, and to consent to treat such gifts as being made one-half by the decedent, for any period prior to a decedent's death, and to pay such taxes thereon as are chargeable to the decedent.

(22) In addition to those expenses specifically provided for in this paragraph, to pay all other reasonable and proper expenses of administration from the property of the estate or trust, including the reasonable expense of obtaining and continuing his bond and any reasonable counsel fees he may necessarily incur.

(c) The court having jurisdiction of the estate or trust may authorize the fiduciary to exercise any other power which in the judgment of the court is necessary for the proper administration of the estate or trust.

(d) The powers set forth in this section shall apply to all estates and trusts now in existence or which may hereafter come into existence and are in addition to the powers granted by law or by the will, deed or other instrument.

> **History:** Add, L 1966, ch 952, eff Sept 1, 1967, with substance deriving from Dec Est Law § 127 and Sur Ct Act §§ 93, 222, 286; amd, L 1967, ch 686, § 107, eff Sept 1, 1967; L 1968, ch 257, §§ 7–9, eff May 14, 1968; L 1970, ch 501, § 1, eff May 8, 1970; L 1973, ch 192, eff April 25, 1973; L 1973, ch 904, §§ 2, 3, eff June 22, 1973; L 1975, ch 158, § 1, eff Sept 1, 1975; L 1984, ch 733, eff Aug 3, 1984; L 1987, ch 519, § 1, eff July 30, 1987; L 1992, ch 595, § 15, eff Sept 1, 1992; L 2011, ch 62, § 104 (Part A), eff Oct 3, 2011.

§ 11-1.2. Tax elections by personal representatives

(a) If the personal representative or other person acting in a fiduciary capacity with respect to a decedent's estate, hereinafter called the "fiduciary", claims as income tax reductions administration expenses chargeable to principal that may be claimed by such fiduciary as either estate tax deductions or as income tax deductions with the result that the income taxes paid by or chargeable to income or to any income beneficiary are reduced and with the further result that United States or New York estate taxes chargeable to principal are increased, then, unless otherwise provided or authorized by the decedent's will, each person, including the estate or any trust, who has received the use of such income tax deductions shall reimburse to the principal chargeable with such increased estate taxes an amount determined by multiplying such increase in estate taxes by a fraction having a numerator equal to the income tax deduction made available to him as the result of the aforesaid election and a denominator equal to the total amount of the income tax deductions made available thereby.

(b) Unless otherwise expressly provided by a will under which a disposition is made to or for the benefit of the surviving spouse of a decedent which qualifies for an estate tax marital deduction under any tax law of the state of New York or of the United States and the amount or size of such disposition is defined by the will in terms of the maximum marital deduction allowable under such tax law:

(1) No adjustment shall be required to be made between such disposition and the other interests in the decedent's estate by reason of (A) any increase in the amount or size of such disposition resulting from any election by the fiduciary, under such tax laws, to treat estate administration expenses as income tax deductions over the amount or size of such disposition had the contrary election been made or (B) any increase or decrease in the amount or size of such disposition resulting from an election by the fiduciary, under such tax laws, of an estate tax valuation date other than the date of the decedent's death as compared with the amount or size of such disposition had the contrary election been made.

(2) Such definition shall not be construed as a direction by the decedent to the fiduciary to exercise any election respecting the deduction of estate administration expenses or the determination of the estate tax valuation date, which the fiduciary may have under such tax

laws, only in such manner as will result in a larger allowable estate tax marital deduction than if the contrary election had been made.

> **History:** Add, L 1967, ch 686, eff Sept 1, 1967, with substance deriving from PPL § 17-e; amd, L 1968, ch 257, § 10, eff May 14, 1968; L 1969, ch 74, § 1, eff March 25, 1969.

§ 11-1.3. Power and duty of executor before probate

An executor named in a will has no power to dispose of any part of the estate of the testator before letters testamentary or preliminary letters testamentary are granted, except to pay reasonable funeral expenses, nor to interfere with such estate in any manner other than to take such action as is necessary to preserve it.

> **History:** Formerly § 11-1.2, add, L 1966, ch 952, eff Sept 1, 1967, with substance deriving from Sur Ct Act § 223; renumbered § 11-1.3 and amd, L 1967, ch 686, §§ 109, 110, eff Sept 1, 196.

§ 11-1.4. Validity of execution of power to sell, mortgage or lease real property by less than all qualifying executors

Any deed, mortgage or lease duly executed by one or more, but not all, of the executors or trustees who qualified conveys the full title and interest of the testator, and is as effective as if all the executors or trustees who qualified had joined in the execution thereof, when ten years have elapsed since the recording of such deed, mortgage or lease in the county where the property affected is situated; saving, however, the rights of every grantee, mortgagee or lessee, in good faith and for a valuable consideration, deriving title under an instrument executed by all the executors or trustees who qualified to the same property or any part thereof, whose deed, mortgage or lease is duly recorded before such period of ten years has elapsed.

> **History:** Formerly § 11-1.3, add, L 1966, ch 952, with substance deriving from Sur Ct Act § 224; renumbered § 11-1.4, L 1967, ch 686, § 109; L 1981, ch 111, § 2, eff Sept 1, 1981.

§ 11-1.5. Payment of testamentary dispositions or distributive shares

(a) Subject to his or her duty to retain sufficient assets to pay administration and reasonable funeral expenses, debts of the decedent and all taxes for which the estate is liable, a personal representative may, but, except as directed by will or court decree or order, shall not be required to, pay any testamentary disposition or distributive share before the completion of the publication of notice to creditors or, if no such notice is published, before the expiration of seven months from the time letters testamentary or of administration are granted, or, if notice of the availability of genetic material of the decedent has been given under section 4-1.3, before the birth of a genetic child who is entitled to inherit from the decedent under section 4-1.3.

(b) Whenever a disposition is directed by will to be paid in advance of such publication of notice or the expiration of such seven month period, or the birth of a genetic child entitled to inherit from the decedent under section 4-1.3, the personal representative may require a bond, conditioned as follows:

(1) That if debts of the decedent appear, and the assets of the estate are insufficient to pay them or to pay other testamentary dispositions entitled, under section 13-1.3, to payment equally with or prior to that of the disposition paid in advance, the beneficiary to whom advance payment was made will refund it, or the value thereof, together with interest thereon and any costs incurred by reason of such payment, or such ratable portion

thereof, as is necessary to pay such debts or to satisfy the rights, if any, of other beneficiaries under the will.

(2) That if the will, under which the disposition was paid, is denied probate, on appeal or otherwise, such beneficiary will refund the entire advance payment, together with interest and costs as described in subparagraph (1), to the personal representative entitled thereto.

(c) If, after the expiration of seven months from the time letters are granted or the birth of a genetic child entitled to inherit from the decedent under section 4-1.3, as the case may be, the personal representative refuses upon demand to pay a disposition or distributive share, the person entitled thereto may maintain an appropriate action or proceeding against such representative. But, for the purpose of computing the time limited for its commencement, the cause of action does not accrue until the personal representative's account is judicially settled.

History: Formerly § 11-1.4, add, L 1966, ch 952, eff Sept 1, 1967, with substance deriving from Decedent Est. Law § 146 and Sur Ct Act § 218; renumbered § 11-1.5, L 1967, ch 686, § 109, eff Sept 1, 1967; amd, L 1985, ch 634, § 1, eff July 28, 1985, applying to the estate of any person dying on or after such date; L 2014, ch 404, § 1, eff Dec 20, 2014, applying to the estates of decedents who shall have died on or after such date; amd, L 2014, ch 439, § 2, eff Nov 21, 2014.

§ 11-1.6. Property held as fiduciary to be kept separate

(a) Every fiduciary shall keep property received as fiduciary separate from his individual property. He shall not invest or deposit such property with any corporation or other person doing business under the banking law, or with any other person or institution, in his own name, but all transactions by him affecting such property shall be in his name as fiduciary; provided, however, that any bank or trust company, when acting as fiduciary, whether alone or jointly with an individual, may with the consent of the individual fiduciary, if any (who is hereby authorized to give such consent), register and hold stock or other securities (referred to in this section as "securities") in the name of the nominee of such bank or trust company; and provided, further, that any individual acting as fiduciary is authorized to direct any bank or trust company incorporated under the laws of this state, any national bank located in this state or any private banker duly authorized by the superintendent of financial services of this state to engage in business here (who, as private banker, maintains a permanent capital of not less than one million dollars) to register and hold any securities in the name of a nominee of such bank, trust company or private banker (referred to in this section as "bank"). Such bank shall not redeliver such securities to the individual fiduciary, who authorized their registration in the name of a nominee of the bank, without first registering the securities in the name of the individual fiduciary, as such. But, any sale of such securities by the bank at the direction of the individual fiduciary shall not be treated as a redelivery. The bank may make any disposition of such securities which is authorized or directed by an order or decree of the court having jurisdiction of the estate or trust.

(b) Any bank shall be absolutely liable for any loss occasioned by the acts of its nominee with respect to the securities so registered.

(c) The records of such bank shall at all times show the ownership of any such securities and of those held in bearer form. Such securities and those held in bearer form shall at all times be kept separate from the assets of the bank and may be kept by such bank

(A) in a manner such that all certificates representing the securities from time to time constituting the assets of a particular estate, trust or other fiduciary account are held separate from those of all other estates, trusts or other fiduciary accounts; or

(B) in a manner such that, without certification as to ownership attached, certificates representing securities of the same class of the same issuer and from time to time constituting assets of particular estates, trusts or other fiduciary accounts are held in bulk, including, to the extent feasible, the merging of certificates of small denomination into one or more certificates of large denomination, provided that a bank, when operating under the method of safekeeping security certificates described in this subparagraph (B), shall be subject to such rules and regulations as, in the case of state chartered institutions, the state superintendent of financial services and, in the case of national banking associations, the comptroller of the currency may from time to time issue. Such banks shall, on demand by the fiduciary, certify in writing the securities held for such fiduciary.

(d) Any person violating any of the provisions of this section shall be guilty of a misdemeanor.

(e) This section shall apply to all estates and trusts now in existence or which may hereafter come into existence.

> **History:** Formerly § 11-1.5, add, L 1966, ch 952, with substance deriving from PPL § 25 and Sur Ct Act § 231; renumbered § 11–1.6, L 1967, ch 686, § 109, eff Sept 1, 1967; L 1970, ch 501, § 2, eff May 8, 1970; L 1973, ch 470, § 1, eff June 5, 1973; L 2011, ch 62, § 104 (Part A), eff Oct 3, 2011.

§ 11-1.7. Limitations on powers and immunities of executors and testamentary trustees

(a) The attempted grant to an executor, testamentary trustee, or inter vivos trustee, or his or her successor, of any of the following enumerated powers or immunities is contrary to public policy:

(1) The exoneration of such fiduciary from liability for failure to exercise reasonable care, diligence and prudence.

(2) The power to make a binding and conclusive fixation of the value of any asset for purposes of distribution, allocation or otherwise.

(b) The attempted grant in any will or trust of any power or immunity in contravention of the terms of this section shall be void but shall not be deemed to render such will or trust invalid as a whole, and the remaining terms of the instrument shall, so far as possible, remain effective.

(c) Any person interested in an estate or trust may contest the validity of any purported grant of any power or immunity within the purview of this section without diminishing or affecting adversely his or her interest in the estate or trust any provision in any will or trust to the contrary notwithstanding.

> **History:** Formerly § 11-1.6, add, L 1966, ch 952, eff Sept 1, 1967, with substance deriving from Decedent Est. Law § 125; renumbered § 11-1.7 and amd, L 1967, ch 686, §§ 109, 113, eff Sept 1, 1967; L 2018, ch 245, eff Aug 24, 2018.

§ 11-1.8. Power of fiduciary or custodian for fiduciary to deposit United States government and agency securities with a federal reserve bank

(a) Notwithstanding any other provision of law, any bank or trust company, when acting as fiduciary and any bank, trust company or private banker, when holding securities as custodian for a fiduciary pursuant to § 11-1.1(b)(9), is authorized to deposit, or arrange through a subcustodian or otherwise for the deposit, with the federal reserve bank in its district of any securities the principal and interest of which the United States or any department, agency or instrumentality thereof has agreed to pay, or has guaranteed payment, to be credited to one or more accounts on the books of said federal reserve bank in the name of such bank, trust company or private banker, to be designated fiduciary or safekeeping accounts, to which account other similar securities may be credited. A bank, trust company or private banker so depositing securities with a federal reserve bank shall be subject to such rules and regulations with respect to the making and maintenance of such deposit as, in the case of state chartered institutions, the state superintendent of financial services, and, in the case of national banking associations, the comptroller of the currency, may from time to time issue. The records of such bank, trust company or private banker shall at all times show the ownership of the securities held in such account. Ownership of, and other interests in, the securities credited to such account may be transferred by entries on the books of said federal reserve bank without physical delivery of any securities. A bank, trust company or private banker acting as custodian for a fiduciary shall, on demand by the fiduciary, certify in writing to the fiduciary the securities so deposited by such bank, trust company or private banker with such federal reserve bank for the account of such fiduciary. A fiduciary shall, on demand by any party to its accounting or on demand by the attorney for such party, certify in writing to such party the securities deposited by such fiduciary with such federal reserve bank for its account as such fiduciary.

(b) This section shall apply to all fiduciaries, and custodians for fiduciaries, acting on the effective date of this section or who thereafter may act regardless of the date of the instrument or court order by which they are appointed.

History: Add, L 1971, ch 252, eff May 11, 1971; amd, L 1980, ch 498, § 1, eff June 24, 1980; L 2011, ch 62, § 104 (Part A), eff Oct 3, 2012.

§ 11-1.9. Power of fiduciary or custodian to deposit securities in a central depository

(a) Notwithstanding any other provision of law, any fiduciary (as defined in section 1-2.7) holding securities in its fiduciary capacity, any bank, trust company or private banker holding securities as a custodian or managing agent, and any bank, trust company or private banker holding securities as custodian for a fiduciary pursuant to section 11-1.1(b)(9), is authorized to deposit or arrange through a subcustodian or otherwise for the deposit of such securities in a clearing corporation (as defined in article eight of the Uniform Commercial Code). When such securities are so deposited, certificates representing securities of the same class of the same issuer may be merged and held in bulk in the name of the nominee of such clearing corporation with any other such securities deposited in such clearing corporation by any person regardless of the ownership of such securities, and certificates of small denomination may be merged into one or more certificates of larger denomination. The records of such fiduciary and the records of such bank, trust company or private banker acting as custodian, as managing agent or as custodian for a fiduciary shall at all times show the name of the party for whose account the securities are so deposited. Ownership of, and other interests in, such securities may be transferred by bookkeeping entry on the books of such clearing corporation without physical delivery of certificates representing such securities. A bank, trust company or private banker so depositing securities pursuant to this section shall be subject to such rules and regulations as, in the case of state chartered institutions, the state superintendent of financial services and, in the case of national banking associations, the comptroller of the currency may from time to time issue. A bank, trust company or private banker acting as custodian for a fiduciary shall, on demand by the fiduciary, certify in writing to the fiduciary the securities so deposited by such bank, trust company or private banker in such clearing corporation for the account of such fiduciary. A fiduciary shall, on demand by any party to a judicial proceeding for the settlement of such fiduciary's account or on demand by the attorney for such party, certify in writing to such party the securities deposited by such fiduciary in such clearing corporation for its account as such fiduciary.

(b) This section shall apply to any fiduciary holding securities in its fiduciary capacity, and to any bank, trust company or private banker holding securities as a custodian, managing agent or custodian for a fiduciary, acting on the effective date of this section or who thereafter may act regardless of the date of the agreement, instrument or court order by which it is appointed and regardless of whether or not such fiduciary, custodian, managing agent or custodian for a fiduciary owns capital stock of such clearing corporation.

History: Add, L 1972, ch 433, § 1, eff May 22, 1972; amd, L 1980, ch 498, § 2, eff June 24, 1980; L 2011, ch 62, § 104 (Part A), eff Oct 3, 2011.

§ 11-1.10. Power of fiduciary to employ a broker-dealer as custodian

Notwithstanding any other provision of law any fiduciary (as defined in section 1-2.7 or 11-1.1(a)(3)) is authorized: (1) to employ any broker-dealer which is registered with the Securities and Exchange Commission and the department of law of the state of New York (referred to in this section as "broker") as a custodian for a fiduciary of any stock or other securities (referred to in this section as "securities"); (2) to register such securities in the name of such broker. Such broker shall have the same power and shall be subject to the same restrictions with respect to the treatment of such securities as any bank or trust company acting as a custodian for a fiduciary and such securities shall be subject to the same treatment as securities held by such a custodian for a fiduciary as provided in sections 11-1.1(b)(9)(10), 11-1.6, 11-1.8, and 11-1.9 of this part. Any such securities held by a broker in which the broker does not have a lien for indebtedness due to it from the estate or trust may not be pledged, lent, hypothecated or disposed of except upon the specific instruction of the fiduciary.

History: Add, L 1984, ch 911, § 1, eff Aug 6, 1984.

§ 11-1.11 Limited power of fiduciary to amend trust for certain tax purposes

(a) Unless expressly prohibited by the terms of the instrument creating an express trust, the terms of the trust instrument shall be deemed to include the following provision granting the trustee, which term as defined in paragraph (h) of this section may mean the executor or administrator, a limited power to amend:

"The trustees shall have the limited power to amend the administrative and other provisions of the trust which have no significant dispositive effects within the meaning of paragraph (i) of this section on an interest described in such paragraph, by an acknowledged instrument in writing, in order to:

(i) achieve a qualified reformation of a reformable interest into a qualified interest for purposes of the charitable deduction as permitted by section 2055(e)(3) or 2522(c)(4) of the United States Internal Revenue Code ("Code") and the regulations thereto, or achieve a reformation of a charitable remainder trust permitted by section 664 of the Code and the regulations thereto;

(ii) meet the requirements of a qualified domestic trust for a surviving spouse who is not a citizen of the United States under sections 2056(d) and 2056A(a) of the Code and the regulations thereto; and

(iii) meet the requirements of a personal residence trust under section 2702(a)(3) or to meet the definition of a qualified interest under section 2702(b) of the Code, and the regulations thereto."

(b) (1) No trustee may exercise any power created under paragraph (a) of this section with respect to any trust that is exempt from tax imposed by the provisions of chapter 13 of the Code or has an inclusion ratio, as defined in section 2642(a) of the Code, of zero if the exercise of such power would cause such trust to lose in whole or in part its exemption from the tax imposed by the provisions of chapter 13 of the Code or cause such trust to have an inclusion ratio, as defined in section 2642(a) of the Code, of more than zero.

(2) If the creator of an express trust or a beneficiary (whether current, future or contingent) of income or principal of an express trust is serving as a trustee of the express trust, the creator or such beneficiary cannot participate in the exercise of the power to amend such express trust pursuant to this section. If two or more trustees are serving, the power to amend such express trust may be exercised by the trustees who are not so disqualified.

(c) Such amendment shall be embodied in one or more writings signed and acknowledged in the manner required by the laws of this state for the recording of a conveyance of real property by the trustee and filed in the office of the clerk of the court having jurisdiction over the instrument. At least thirty (30) days prior to such filing, notice of such amendment, together with a copy of the amendment, shall be sent by registered or certified mail, return receipt requested, or by personal delivery to all persons interested in the trust, or to the guardian of the property, committee, conservator, adult guardian, or personal representative of any such persons under a disability, or to the parent or person with whom a minor resides. Such notice shall include the following statement: "If you wish to object to the proposed amendment, you should notify the trustee (executor or administrator) of your objections in a writing signed and acknowledged by you before a notary in the manner required by the laws of the state of New York for the recording of a conveyance of real property. Such written objection must be personally delivered or mailed to the trustee (executor or administrator) by registered or certified mail, return receipt requested, within thirty (30) days of the date when the notice was personally delivered or mailed to you. If no such objection to the proposed amendment is made by any person interested in the trust, such amendment will become effective upon its filing in the court having jurisdiction over the trust." Proof by affidavit of such mailing or delivery of the notice or by signed acknowledgement of receipt by the person noticed, shall be filed in the office of the clerk of the court where such amendment is filed prior to or simultaneously with the filing of such amendment. If it appears by affidavit that the name or address of any person interested in the trust is unknown, mailing to such person of the notice shall not be required.

(d) Such amendment shall be effective upon filing as required by paragraph (c) of this section, provided that no written objection to such amendment, signed and acknowledged in the manner required by the laws of the state for the recording of a conveyance of real property by any person interested in the trust, has been received prior to such filing by the trustee, by personal delivery or by registered or certified mail, return receipt requested. If no such written objection has been received by the trustee prior to such filing, no judicial proceeding or consent of any person interested in the trust shall be required.

(e) Unless otherwise provided in the amendment, the amendment shall be deemed to have been effective in the case of a will as of the date of death of the decedent, and in the case of any other instrument on the date it became irrevocable.

(f) The limited power to amend granted by this section shall be exercised only if acted upon by all of the trustees, except as otherwise provided by subparagraph (b)(2) of this section.

(g) For the purposes of this section, the phrase "all persons interested in the trust" shall mean all the persons upon whom service of process would be required in a proceeding for the judicial settlement of the account of the trustee, taking into account section three hundred fifteen of the surrogate's court procedure act.

(h) In any case where the Code requires that an election or other action be made or taken by the executor or if no trustee of a trust under a will has qualified, the term "trustee" as used in this section shall mean the executor or administrator of an estate. In any such case, the trustee shall comply with any action taken by the executor or administrator under this section.

(i) An amendment pursuant to paragraph (a) of this section shall be conclusively deemed to have "no significant dispositive effect" if the difference between the actuarial value determined as of the effective date of the amendment

  (i) of the interest reformed pursuant to subparagraph (a)(i) or (a)(ii) qualifying for the marital or charitable deduction which is involved in a reformation pursuant to subparagraph (a)(i) or (a)(ii); or

  (ii) of the interest retained by the transferor or any applicable family member reformed pursuant to subparagraph (a)(iii) in order to qualify as a "personal residence trust" or a "qualified interest" under section 2702 of the Code;

and the actuarial value of the respective interest prior to such amendment does not exceed five percent of the actuarial value of such pre-amendment interest.

(j) The term "trust" shall include an arrangement treated as a "trust" for the purposes of the Code.

(k) The fact that a testamentary trust cannot be revoked, altered or amended by reason of the testator's death, or that the will or trust instrument states that the trust is irrevocable and/or cannot be altered or amended, shall not be deemed to constitute an express prohibition within the meaning of the phrase "unless expressly prohibited by the terms of the instrument creating an express trust."

(l) References to sections of the United States Internal Revenue Code or Code shall refer to the United States Internal Revenue Code of 1986 as amended from time to time, or to corresponding provisions of subsequent internal revenue laws, and regulations thereto; and shall also refer to corresponding provisions of state law.

History: Add, L 2000, ch 267, § 1, eff Aug 16, 2000, applying to all express trusts whenever created.

PART 2   Investments by Fiduciaries: Powers and Duties Relating Thereto

§ 11-2.1. Principal and income

(a) Duty of trustee as to receipts and expenditures.

(1) A trust shall be administered with due regard to the respective interests of income beneficiaries and remaindermen. A trust is so administered with respect to the allocation of receipts and expenditures if a receipt is credited or an expense is charged to income or to principal or partly to each (A) in accordance with the terms of the trust instrument, notwithstanding any contrary provisions in this section; (B) in the absence of any contrary terms of the trust instrument, in accordance with the provisions of this section; or (C) if neither of the preceding rules of administration is applicable, in accordance with what is reasonable and equitable in view of the interests of those entitled to income as well as those entitled to principal and in view of the manner in which men of ordinary prudence, discretion and judgment would act in the management of their own affairs.

(2) If the trust instrument gives the trustee discretion in crediting a receipt or charging an expenditure to income or principal or partly to each, no inference that the trustee has or has not improperly exercised such discretion arises from the fact that the trustee has made an allocation contrary to the provisions of this section.

(b) What is income and what is principal; definitions.

(1) Income is the return in money or property derived from the use of principal, including return received as:

(A) Rent from property, including sums received for the cancellation or renewal of a lease.

(B) Interest on money lent, including sums received as consideration for the privilege of prepayment of principal except as provided in paragraph (f) on bond premium and discount.

(C) Income earned during the administration of a decedent's estate, as provided in paragraph (d).

(D) Corporate distributions, as provided in paragraph (e).

(E) Accrued income on bonds or other obligations issued at a discount, as provided in paragraph (f).

(F) Receipts from principal used in business, as provided in paragraph (g).

(G) Receipts from disposition of natural resources, as provided in paragraphs (h) and (i).

(H) Receipts from other principal subject to depletion, as provided in paragraph (j).

(I) Receipts from disposition of underproductive property, as provided in paragraph (k).

(2) Principal is property, disposed of in trust, the income from which is payable to or to be accumulated for an income beneficiary and the title to which is ultimately to vest in the person entitled to the future estate. Principal includes:

(A) Consideration received by the trustee on the sale or other transfer of principal, on repayment of a loan or as a refund, replacement or change in the form of principal.

(B) Proceeds of property taken on eminent domain proceedings.

(C) Proceeds of insurance upon property forming part of the principal except proceeds of insurance upon a separate interest of an income beneficiary.

(D) Stock dividends, receipts on liquidation of a corporation and other corporate distributions, as provided in paragraph (e).

(E) Receipts with respect to bonds and other obligations, as provided in paragraph (f).

(F) Royalties and other receipts from disposition of natural resources, as provided in paragraphs (h) and (i).

(G) Receipts from other principal subject to depletion, as provided in paragraph (j).

(H) Any profit resulting from any change in the form of principal, except as provided in paragraph (k) on underproductive property.

(I) Receipts from disposition of underproductive property, as provided in paragraph (k).

(3) After determining income and principal in accordance with the terms of the trust instrument or of this section the trustee shall charge to income or principal expenses and other charges as provided in paragraph (l).

(c) When right to income arises; apportionment of income or other receipt.

(1) An income beneficiary is entitled to income from the date specified in the trust instrument or, if none is specified, from the date an asset becomes subject to the trust. In the case of an asset which becomes subject to a trust by reason of a will, it becomes subject to the trust as of the date of the death of the testator even though there is an intervening period of administration of the testator's estate.

(2) In the case of a decedent's estate, a testamentary trust or an asset received under a will by a trustee: (A) receipts due but not paid at the date of death of the testator are principal; (B) receipts in the form of periodic payments (other than corporate distributions to stockholders and savings bank and savings and loan association dividends), such as rent, interest or annuities payable from any source, not due at the date of death of the testator, shall be treated as accruing from day to day. That portion of such a receipt accruing before the date of death is principal and the balance is income.

(3) In all other cases any receipt from an income producing asset is income even though the receipt was earned or accrued in whole or in part before the date when the asset became subject to the trust.

(4) On termination of an income interest, the income beneficiary whose interest is terminated or his estate is entitled to: (A) income undistributed on the date of termination; (B) income due but not paid to the trustee on the date of termination; (C) income in the form of periodic payments (other than corporate distributions to stockholders and savings bank and savings and loan association dividends) such as rent, interest or annuities, not due on the date of termination, accrued from day to day.

(d) Income earned during administration of a decedent's estate.

(1) Unless the will provides otherwise and subject to subparagraph (2) hereof, all expenses incurred in connection with the settlement of a decedent's estate, including but not limited to debts, funeral expenses, estate taxes, interest and penalties concerning taxes, family allowances, fees of attorneys and commissions of personal representatives (other than commissions on estate income) and court fees, costs and other charges shall be charged against the principal of the estate.

(2) Unless the will provides otherwise, income from the assets of a decedent's estate after the death of the testator and before distribution, including income from property used to discharge liabilities, shall be determined in accordance with the rules applicable to a trustee under this section and distributed as follows: (A) to specific beneficiaries the net income from the property disposed of to them respectively; (B) to all other beneficiaries, except beneficiaries of pecuniary dispositions not in trust, the balance of the net income in proportion to their respective interests in the undistributed assets of the estate computed at times of distribution on the basis of inventory value; provided, however, (i) that the amount of income earned during the further administration of the estate from and after the date of payment of any estate or inheritance tax shall be distributed to such beneficiaries in proportion to their respective interests in the undistributed assets of the estate after the making of such payment on the basis of the fair market value of such assets immediately after the making of such payment, and (ii) any amount allowed as a tax deduction to the estate for income payable to a charitable organization shall be paid, without diminution for taxes, to the charitable organization entitled to receive such income. This subparagraph does not apply to any sums made payable in policies of insurance of any description or under any contract for an annuity, including a variable annuity.

(3) (A) The residuary beneficiaries are entitled to the rent from the decedent's real property, not specifically disposed of, from the date of death, in proportion to their respective interests under the will, unless the fiduciary, pursuant to a power to distribute in kind, allocates all or part of such property in whole or partial satisfaction of a pecuniary disposition in trust, in which event the rent from the property so allocated shall be distributed, as of the date of death, to the trustee of such disposition.

(B) This subparagraph applies to wills of decedents dying before, on or after its effective date, provided, however, that it shall not be so applied as to require residuary beneficiaries to repay to the estate any distributions of income from real property, not specifically disposed of, which were actually made to such beneficiaries prior to such effective date.

(4) Income and rent received by a trustee under subparagraphs (2) or (3) shall be treated as income of the trust.

(e) Distributions of corporations or associations.

(1) Notwithstanding the provisions of this paragraph, a will, deed or other instrument which creates or declares a trust may provide with respect to all matters covered by this section, and direct the manner of ascertaining income and principal and the apportionment thereof or grant discretion to the trustee or another person to do so, and such provision or direction, where otherwise not contrary to law, controls.

(2) A distribution by a corporation or association made to a trustee in the shares of the distributing corporation or association held in such trust, whether in the form of a stock

split or a stock dividend, at the rate of six per cent or less of the shares of such corporation or association upon which the distribution is made, is income. Any such distribution at a greater rate is principal.

(3) For the purpose of determining whether a will, deed or other instrument which creates or declares a trust has directed that a distribution of shares described in subparagraph (2) is income in a manner other than that provided in subparagraph (2), the following rules apply unless different rules are provided in the will, deed or other instrument:

(A) A distribution in the shares of the distributing corporation or association means a distribution in such shares, whether in the form of a stock split or a stock dividend, at the rate of six per cent or less of the shares of such corporation or association upon which the distribution is made.

(B) A distribution in the shares of the distributing corporation or association, whether in the form of a stock split or a stock dividend, at the rate of six per cent or less of the shares of such corporation or association upon which the distribution is made, is ordinary and regular and shall be deemed to be in lieu of a cash dividend.

(C) If the will, deed or other instrument which creates or declares a trust grants to the trustee or another person discretion to allocate to income or principal or between income and principal any distribution in the shares of the distributing corporation or association, such discretion may be exercised with respect to any such distribution in the shares of the distributing corporation or association, whether in the form of a stock split or a stock dividend, and no inference of imprudence or partiality shall arise from the fact that the trustee or other person has made an allocation contrary to a provision of subparagraph (2) or of this subparagraph.

(4) (A) A right issued by the distributing corporation or association to subscribe to shares or other securities, whether in the stock or other securities of the distributing corporation or association or of a corporation or association other than the distributing corporation or association, accruing to shareholders on account of their stock ownership, and the proceeds of any sale of such rights, are principal.

(B) A distribution by a corporation or association made to a trustee in the shares of the distributing corporation, but of a different type than the shares held in such trust, or a distribution of shares, securities or obligations of a corporation or association other than those of the distributing corporation or association (or the proceeds of such a distribution) shall be principal.

(5) When a corporation or association calls in shares of stock or when a corporation or association succeeds another by merger, consolidation, reorganization or other method of acquiring its assets, shares of stock issued for the shares so called in or shares of stock in the succeeding corporation or association are principal.

(6) When a corporation or association is being wholly or partially liquidated, shares of stock and cash or other assets distributed to shareholders are principal, except that if the corporation or association indicates that some part of such distribution is a settlement of preferred or guaranteed dividends, that part of the distribution settling dividends accruing since the trustee became a shareholder is income. For the purposes of this paragraph, a corporation or association is in liquidation if the corporation or association indicates that

the distribution is in total or partial liquidation, or if the corporation or association is making a distribution of assets other than cash pursuant to a court decree or final administrative order by a government agency ordering the distribution of the particular assets, unless the distributing corporation or association indicates that a distribution pursuant to such court or administrative order is wholly or partly in lieu of an ordinary cash dividend, in which case the distribution is to that extent income.

(7) Distributions made from ordinary income by a regulated investment company or by a trust qualifying and electing under federal law to be taxed as a real estate investment trust are income. All other distributions made by such company or trust, including distributions from capital gains, depreciation or depletion, whether in the form of cash or an option to take new shares or cash or an option to purchase additional shares, are principal.

(8) If the distributing corporation or association gives a shareholder an option to receive a distribution, whether in the form of cash or its own shares or cash or an option to purchase new shares, the distribution chosen is income.

(9) Except as provided in subparagraphs (2), (4), (5), (6) and (7), all distributions of corporations or associations are income including:

(A) Cash dividends.

(B) Share distributions, as provided in subparagraphs (2) and (3).

(C) Preferred or guaranteed dividends, as provided in subparagraph (6).

(D) Ordinary income from a regulated investment trust or a trust qualifying and electing under federal law to be taxed as a real estate investment trust, as provided in subparagraph (7).

(E) An option, as provided in subparagraph (8).

(10) The trustee or other person may rely upon any statement of the distributing corporation or association as to any fact, relevant under any provision of this paragraph, concerning the source or character of distributions.

(11) Where the shares of stock of a corporation or association of this state or of any other jurisdiction constitute part of an estate, trust or other fund, and the allocation of any other distribution thereof to principal or income, or between successive interests, depends on the date of accrual thereof, the date of accrual of any distribution on such shares shall be the date specified by the corporation or association declaring such distribution as that on which the shareholders of record entitled to such distribution are to be determined, or, if there be no such date specified by the corporation or association, the date of declaration of the distribution. For the purposes of this paragraph, the "date of accrual" of a distribution means that date, on and after which the distribution shall be treated in the same manner as if it had been declared and paid or distributed on such date.

(12) If a trustee or other person has heretofore received or shall hereafter receive any shares of stock distributed by any corporation or association and is uncertain as to whether any or all of them are allocable to income, the trustee or other person shall have with respect to all such shares and the proceeds thereof the same duties and powers (including powers of sale, investment and reinvestment) as though all such shares constituted part of the principal of the trust fund. The trustee or other person shall be under no obligation to

retain any of such shares in kind even though it may subsequently be determined that some or all of them were allocable to income. If and when it is determined that any or all of such shares were allocable to income, the shares allocable to income shall be distributed in kind to income, except that, if prior to such determination, the trustee or other person had sold any of the new shares comprising the distribution or any of the original shares upon which the distribution was received, income shall be entitled to receive its ratable portion of the shares remaining, if any, on hand and an amount of cash equal to its ratable portion of the proceeds received by the trustee or other person upon the sale of such shares. This subparagraph does not apply in any case in which a trustee or other person has heretofore, in good faith, made any different allocation of the shares or the proceeds of any sale thereof, or both, as between income and principal and has made distribution in accordance with such different allocation to income or to principal, or to both.

(13) Subparagraphs (1) to (6) inclusive and (8) to (11) inclusive apply to any trust, whether created or declared before, on or after the effective date hereof, except that subparagraphs (1) through (11) do not apply to any distribution described in this paragraph which accrued prior to such effective date, and subparagraph (7) applies to trusts created on and after its effective date and to the wills of persons dying on and after its effective date.

(f) Bond premium and discount.

(1) Bonds or other obligations for the payment of money are principal at their inventory value, except as provided in subparagraph (2) for discount bonds. No provision shall be made for amortization of bond premiums or for accumulation of discount, except that in the case of testamentary trusts created by the wills of persons dying, and inter vivos trusts created by instruments executed, prior to September first, nineteen hundred forty-two, premiums may, in the discretion of the trustee, be amortized if the bonds and other obligations for the payment of money were acquired prior to June first, nineteen hundred sixty-five.

The proceeds of a sale, redemption or other disposition of bonds or other obligations are principal.

(2) The increment in value of a bond or other obligation for the payment of money bearing no stated interest but payable or redeemable at maturity or at a future time at an amount in excess of the amount in consideration of which it was issued is income. If the income accrues pursuant to a fixed schedule of appreciation such income is distributable to the beneficiary at the time the increment occurs and the trustee may transfer the amount thereof from principal to income on each such date. Whenever unrealized increment is distributed as income but out of principal the principal shall be reimbursed from the income when realized.

(g) Business operations.

If a trustee uses any part of the principal in the continuance of a business of which the person who created or declared the trust was a sole proprietor or a partner, the net profits of the business, computed in accordance with generally accepted accounting principles for a comparable business, are income. If a loss results in any fiscal or calendar year, the loss falls on principal and shall not be carried into any other fiscal or calendar year for purposes of calculating net income.

EPTL

(h) Disposition of natural resources.

(1) If any part of the principal consists of a right to receive royalties, overriding or limited royalties, working interests, production payments, net profit interests or other interests in minerals or other natural resources in, on or under land, the receipts from taking the natural resources from the land shall be allocated as follows: (A) if received as rent on a lease or extension payments on a lease the receipts are income; (B) if received from a production payment, the receipts are income to the extent of any factor for interest or its equivalent provided in the governing instrument. There shall be allocated to principal the fraction of the balance of the receipts which the unrecovered cost of the production payment bears to the balance owed on the production payment, exclusive of any factor for interest or its equivalent. The receipts not allocated to principal are income; (C) if received as a royalty, overriding or limited royalty, or as a bonus, or from a working interest or from any other interest in minerals or other natural resources, receipts not provided for in the preceding subparagraphs shall be apportioned on a yearly basis in accordance with this paragraph whether or not any natural resource was being taken from the land at the time the trust was established. There shall be added to principal as an allowance for depletion such portion of the gross receipts as shall be allowed as a deduction for depletion in computing taxable income for Federal income tax purposes. The balance of the gross receipts, after payment therefrom of all expenses, direct and indirect, is income.

(2) If a trustee, on the effective date of this section, held an item of depletable property of a type specified in this paragraph, he shall allocate receipts from the property in the manner used before the effective date of this section but as to all depletable property thereafter acquired by an existing or new trust, the method of allocation provided herein shall be used.

(i) Sale of timber.

If any part of the principal consists of land from which merchantable timber may be removed, the receipts from taking the timber from the land shall be allocated in accordance with subparagraph (1)(C) of paragraph (a).

(j) Other property subject to depletion.

Except as provided in paragraphs (h) and (i), if any part of the principal consists of property subject to depletion, including leaseholds, patents, copyrights, royalty rights and rights to receive payments on a contract for deferred compensation, the receipts from such property shall be allocated in accordance with subparagraph (1)(C) of paragraph (a).

(k) Underproductive property.

(1) Except as otherwise provided in this paragraph (k), a portion of the net proceeds of a sale by a fiduciary as defined in subparagraph three of paragraph (A) of section 11-1.1 of any principal property of an estate or trust, other than securities listed on a national securities exchange or traded in over the counter, held for more than a year which has not produced over the period held an average net income of one per cent per annum of its inventory value (including as income the value of any beneficial use of the property by any income beneficiary), shall be allocated to income as delayed income, as provided in this paragraph (k). The net proceeds of such sale shall be the gross proceeds received, including the value of any property other than cash received, less the expenses of sale, including tax, if any, incurred on the gain realized, and less any carrying charges and

expenses paid from the estate or trust while such property was held by the fiduciary and was underproductive.

(2) The sum allocated to income as delayed income is the difference between the net proceeds of sale and the amount which, had such amount been invested at simple interest at five per cent per annum while the property was underproductive, would have produced the amount of the net proceeds. Such sum, plus any carrying charges and expenses charged against income while such property was held by such fiduciary and the property was underproductive, less any income actually received from the property during such period and less the value of any beneficial use of the property by any income beneficiary, is income and the balance is principal.

(3) The amount allocated to income as delayed income under this paragraph (k) shall be allocated and paid to the beneficiaries (or their respective estates), if any, who were entitled under the governing instrument to receive income from the estate or trust from time to time during the period the property was held by the fiduciary and was underproductive.

(4) If, or to the extent to which, any principal property subject to this paragraph (k) is sold or disposed of by conversion, and the proceeds of sale or conversion consist of property which cannot be readily apportioned, including, without limitation, land or mortgages (for example, real property acquired by or in lieu of foreclosure), the income beneficiary shall be entitled to the net income from any form of property or obligation received pursuant to such sale or conversion, while the received property or obligation is held, and when such property or obligation is later sold or otherwise disposed of by conversion into easily apportionable property, no allocation to income as provided in this paragraph (k) shall be made.

(5) This paragraph (k) shall not apply if the terms of the governing instrument direct otherwise. A provision in a will or trust instrument authorizing the fiduciary (A) to retain or to invest in property that is unproductive or underproductive of income (described in the instrument by the words "unproductive" or "underproductive" or words of similar import), or to retain or to invest in property expressly without regard to whether it is productive of income, (B) to transfer any portion of receipts from income to principal on account of depreciation, depletion or amortization, or (C) to accumulate income and add it to principal, shall be deemed to be a direction that this paragraph (k) shall not apply.

(l) Charges against income and principal.

(1) The following charges shall be made against income: (A) ordinary expenses incurred in connection with the administration, management and preservation of the trust property, including regularly recurring taxes assessed against any portion of the principal, water rates, insurance and bond premiums, interest paid by the trustee and ordinary repairs; (B) any tax levied upon receipts defined as income under this section or the trust instrument and payable by the trustee.

(2) If the court shall find that any judicial proceeding primarily concerns income and that it is equitable to charge the expense of such proceeding, or a part thereof, to income, the court may direct that all or a specified part of the expense of such proceeding, including attorneys' fees, shall be charged to income.

(3) If charges against income are of unusual amount, the trustee may by means of reserves or other reasonable means charge them over a reasonable period of time and

withhold from distribution sufficient sums to regularize distributions.

(4) The following charges shall be made against principal: (A) charges not provided for in subparagraphs (1) and (2), including court costs and attorneys' fees, the cost of investing and reinvesting principal, payments on principal of an indebtedness (including a mortgage amortized by periodic payments of principal), expenses of preparation of property for sale, and, unless the court directs otherwise, expenses incurred in maintaining or defending any action to protect or construe the trust or the property or assure the title of any trust property; (B) repairs or expenses incurred in making a capital improvement to principal, including special assessments; (C) any tax levied upon profits, gain or other receipts allocated to principal notwithstanding denomination of the tax as an income tax by the taxing authority.

(5) Regularly recurring charges payable from income shall be apportioned to the same extent and in the same manner that income is apportioned under paragraph (c) hereof.

(6) Notwithstanding the provisions of subparagraphs one and four of this paragraph, fees paid at least annually to banks, trust companies and registered investment advisers for investment advisory and custodial services shall be charged one-third against income and two-thirds against principal.

(m) Application of section.

Except as specifically provided in the trust instrument, the will or in this section, this section shall apply to any receipt or expense received or incurred after its effective date by any trust or decedent's estate whether established before, on or after the effective date of this section and whether the asset involved was acquired by the trustee before, on or after its effective date, provided that this section shall not apply to any receipt or expense received or incurred by any trust or decedent's estate after the effective date of article 11-A.

(n) Uniformity of interpretation.

This section shall be so construed as to effectuate its general purpose to make uniform the law of those states which enact it.

(o) Definitions.

As used in this section:

(1) "Income beneficiary" means any person to whom income is presently payable or for whom it is accumulated for distribution as income.

(2) "Remainderman" means any person entitled to principal, including income which has been accumulated and added to principal.

(3) "Trustee" means an original trustee and any successor or substituted trustee.

(4) "Inventory value" means the cost of property purchased by the trustee and the market value of other property at the time it was made subject to the trust.

History: Add, L 1966, ch 952, eff Sept 1, 1967, with substance deriving from PPL §§ 27-a–27-q; amd, L 1967, ch 527, eff Sept 1, 1967; L 1967, ch 686, eff Sept 1, 1967; L 1971, ch 670, eff June 22, 1971; L 1981, ch 402, eff July 3, 1981, applying "to instruments executed before, on or after its effective date, except that it shall not apply in any case in which a trustee or other person prior to said effective date, in good faith, charged said fees in a manner inconsistent with this act nor shall it prevent such a trustee or other person after said effective date from continuing to charge said fees in the same manner as they had been charged, in good faith, prior to said effective date"; L 1982, ch 898, § 1, eff July 29, 1982; L 1987, ch 495, § 1, eff July 30, 1987, applying to proceeds received during any period as to which the fiduciary's account has not been settled prior to July 30, 1987, whether such proceeds were received prior to or after July 30, 1987 by any trust or decedent's estate established before, on or after July 30, 1987; L 1987, ch 573, §§ 1, 2, eff July 30, 1987, applying to distributions made on or after the effective date; L 1994, ch 257, § 1, eff July 6, 1994; L 2001, ch 243, § 5, eff Jan 1, 2002.

§ 11-2.2. Power to invest

(a) Investment of trust funds

(1) A fiduciary holding funds for investment may invest the same in such securities as would be acquired by prudent men of discretion and intelligence in such matters who are seeking a reasonable income and preservation of their capital, provided, however, that nothing in this subparagraph shall limit the effect of any will, agreement, court order or other instrument creating or defining the investment powers of a fiduciary, or shall restrict the authority of a court of proper jurisdiction to instruct the fiduciary in the interpretation or administration of the express terms of any will, agreement or other instrument or in the administration of the property under the fiduciary's care. This paragraph shall apply to any investment, made on or after May first, nineteen hundred seventy, of funds held for investment by a fiduciary, and to all estates and trusts now in existence or which may hereafter come into existence.

A bank, trust company or paid professional investment advisor (whether or not registered under any federal securities or investment law) which serves as a fiduciary, and any other fiduciary representing that it has special investment skills shall exercise such diligence in investing the funds for which the fiduciary is responsible, as would customarily be exercised by prudent men of discretion and intelligence having special investment skills. This paragraph shall apply to any investment, made on or after January first, nineteen hundred eighty-six, of the funds held for investment by such a fiduciary and to all estates and trusts now in existence or which may hereafter come into existence.

This subparagraph shall not apply to any investment, made on or after January first, nineteen hundred ninety-five, of funds held for investment by a fiduciary, and to all estates and trusts in existence or which may come into existence on or after January first, nineteen hundred ninety-five.

(2) A trustee or other person holding trust funds may require such personal bonds or guaranties of payment of principal or interest or both, or such other bonds or guaranties, to accompany investments as may seem prudent, and may from time to time adjust, reduce, modify, postpone or compound the same, or any terms and conditions thereof, including the rate of interest, or any installments thereof, and may at any time release the same, and all premiums paid on such guaranties or fees for servicing mortgages may be charged to or paid out of income, provided that such charge or payment is not more than at the rate of one-half of one per centum per annum on the par value of such investments. But no trustee shall purchase securities hereunder from himself.

(3) Whenever a trustee or other person holding trust funds has heretofore lawfully invested or shall hereafter lawfully invest any trust funds in a share or part of a bond and mortgage or any part interest therein or shall hold any such share, part or part interest by

apportionment, transfer, representation or otherwise, if the property subject to such mortgage is purchased pursuant to foreclosure sale or acquired by voluntary conveyance by or in behalf of such trustee or other person holding trust funds and another person, including another such trustee, owning another such share, part or part interest in such bond and mortgage, such trustee or other person holding trust funds or a person purchasing or acquiring title in behalf of such trustee may convey the undivided interest in such real property so purchased or acquired to a corporation, formed for the purpose of acquiring such property, in exchange for a proportionate part of the capital stock and the bonds, if any, of such corporation; provided that the other person, by or in whose behalf such property has been purchased or acquired, shall exchange his undivided interest in such property for a proportionate part of the capital stock and the bonds, if any, of such corporation, issued in exchange for such real property.

(4) The corporation formed, as provided in subparagraph (3), for the acquisition of such real property shall be a business corporation, and shall have all the powers of such a corporation, and its stockholders shall have the same power to vote to authorize or confirm any sale, mortgage, lease, option or other disposition of any or all of its property that is ordinarily possessed by shareholders of a business corporation; provided, however, that the certificate of incorporation shall prohibit it from investing in any stocks, bonds or other securities, which are not under the laws of this state a proper subject for the investment of trust funds, and shall provide that upon the sale of the real property acquired by the corporation such corporation shall be dissolved. Such dissolution shall be effectuated by proceedings under article 10 of the business corporation law to be taken promptly after such sale; provided, however, that if any such corporation shall sell real property held by it for a consideration consisting in whole or in part of evidences of indebtedness secured by mortgage upon such real property or shall reacquire such property upon foreclosure of such mortgage, in either of such events, such dissolution proceedings shall not be required to be taken until final liquidation in cash by the corporation of its entire interest in or lien upon such real property.

(5) Nothing contained in this section, however, shall affect any lawful investments in shares, parts or part interests in bonds and mortgages heretofore made by any trustee or other person holding trust funds for investment, nor affect any action heretofore taken in accordance with law with respect to such bonds and mortgages or shares, parts or part interests in such bonds and mortgages. Such trustee or other person holding trust funds for investment shall have all the powers heretofore possessed under this section or any other provision of law with respect to part interests in bonds and mortgages for the protection and preservation of the trust property. It is the intention of this section to prohibit any future investments in part interests in bonds, or notes, and mortgages for any estate or fund, for which such trustee or other person may hold funds for investment.

(6) A fiduciary holding funds for investment who is directed or authorized by an instrument creating the fiduciary relationship to retain the stock of a bank or trust company that is a member of a bank holding company currently fully registered under an act of Congress entitled "Bank Holding Company Act of 1956", as the same may be amended from time to time, shall be considered as being directed or authorized to retain the stock of such bank holding company. Notwithstanding any contrary provision in this section, this subdivision shall apply to any fiduciary relationship now in existence or which may

hereafter come into existence and to all investments now held or which may hereafter be acquired in such relationship.

(7) No fiduciary holding funds for investment shall be liable for any loss incurred with respect to any investment not eligible by law for the investment of trust funds, if such ineligible investment was received by such fiduciary pursuant to a decree of court or the terms of the will, deed, or other instrument creating the fiduciary relationship, or if such ineligible investment was eligible when received or when the investment was made by the fiduciary; provided such fiduciary exercises due care and prudence in the disposition or retention of any such ineligible investment.

(8) Investment by a fiduciary in a limited partnership or investment trust, as defined in 9-1.5 of this chapter, shall not be deemed to be an improper delegation of investment authority.

(9) As used in this paragraph, the phrase "person holding trust funds" and the terms "fiduciary" and "trustee" include a personal representative, trustee, guardian, a donee of a power during minority, committee of the property of an incompetent person, and conservator of the property of a conservatee.

(b) Rights of fiduciaries to invest in securities of investment companies.

(1) A fiduciary holding funds for investment may invest the same in securities of any management type investment company or trust registered pursuant to the federal investment company act of nineteen hundred forty, as amended, in any case in which a court order, the will, agreement or other instrument creating or defining the investment powers of the fiduciary authorizes the investment of such funds in either of the following: (A) Such investments as the fiduciary may, in his discretion, select. (B) Generally in investments other than those in which fiduciaries are by law authorized to invest trust funds, notwithstanding that the fiduciary or an affiliate of the fiduciary acts as investment advisor, custodian, transfer agent, registrar, sponsor, distributor, manager or provides other services to the investment company or trust. Unless the will, lifetime trust or order appointing the fiduciary provides otherwise, the fiduciary shall elect annually either (i) to receive or have its affiliate receive compensation for providing such services to such investment company or trust for the portion of the trust invested in such investment company or trust or (ii) to take annual corporate trustees' commissions with respect to such portion.

This subparagraph shall not apply to any investment, made on or after January first, nineteen hundred ninety-five, of funds held for investment by a fiduciary, and to all estates and trusts in existence or which may come into existence on or after January first, nineteen hundred ninety-five.

(1-a) In any case in which a court order, will, agreement or other instrument creating or defining the investment powers of the fiduciary directs, requires or authorizes that the funds held for investment be invested in United States government obligations, the fiduciary may invest such funds in securities of, or other interests in, any open-end or closed-end management type investment company or investment trust registered pursuant to the federal investment company act of nineteen hundred forty, as amended, provided that the portfolio of such investment company or investment trust is limited to United States government obligations or to repurchase agreements fully collateralized by such obligations and provided further that such investment company or investment trust shall take delivery of such collateral, either directly or through an authorized custodian.

(2) As used in this paragraph, the term "fiduciary" includes a personal representative, trustee, guardian, committee of the property of an incompetent and conservator of the property of a conservatee.

History: Add, L 1966, ch 952, eff Sept 1, 1967, with substance deriving from PPL §§ 21, 26; amd, L 1967, ch 686, eff Sept 1, 1967; L 1968, ch 113, § 2, eff Apr 2, 1968; L 1968, ch 257, § 11, eff May 14, 1968; L 1968, ch 515, eff June 5, 1968; L 1968, ch 567, eff June 5, 1968; L 1970, ch 321, eff May 1, 1970; L 1972, ch 379, § 1, eff May 22, 1972; L 1972, ch 382, § 1, eff May 22, 1972, applying to existing and future fiduciary relationships and to all present and future investments; L 1981, ch 115, §§ 47, 48, eff May 18, 1981; L 1984, ch 936, eff Jan 1, 1985; L 1986, ch 104, § 1, eff May 23, 1986; L 1987, ch 511, § 9, eff July 30, 1987, deemed eff Jan 1, 1986; L 1988, ch 118, § 1, eff June 13, 1988; L 1991, ch 217, § 1, eff July 1, 1991, but not having effect on any investment prior to such date; L 1992, ch 483, § 1, eff July 17, 1992; L 1994, ch 609, §§ 2, 3, eff Jan 1, 1995.

§ 11-2.3. Prudent investor act

(a) Prudent investor rule.

A trustee has a duty to invest and manage property held in a fiduciary capacity in accordance with the prudent investor standard defined by this section, except as otherwise provided by the express terms and provisions of a governing instrument within the limitations set forth by section 11-1.7 of this chapter. This section shall apply to any investment made or held on or after January first, nineteen hundred ninety-five by a trustee.

(b) Prudent investor standard.

(1) The prudent investor rule requires a standard of conduct, not outcome or performance. Compliance with the prudent investor rule is determined in light of facts and circumstances prevailing at the time of the decision or action of a trustee. A trustee is not liable to a beneficiary to the extent that the trustee acted in substantial compliance with the prudent investor standard or in reasonable reliance on the express terms and provisions of the governing instrument.

(2) A trustee shall exercise reasonable care, skill and caution to make and implement investment and management decisions as a prudent investor would for the entire portfolio, taking into account the purposes and terms and provisions of the governing instrument.

(3) The prudent investor standard requires a trustee:

(A) to pursue an overall investment strategy to enable the trustee to make appropriate present and future distributions to or for the benefit of the beneficiaries under the governing instrument, in accordance with risk and return objectives reasonably suited to the entire portfolio;

(B) to consider, to the extent relevant to the decision or action, the size of the portfolio, the nature and estimated duration of the fiduciary relationship, the liquidity and distribution requirements of the governing instrument, general economic conditions, the possible effect of inflation or deflation, the expected tax consequences of investment decisions or strategies and of distributions of income and principal, the role that each investment or course of action plays within the overall portfolio, the expected total return of the portfolio (including both income and appreciation of capital), and the needs of beneficiaries (to the extent reasonably known to the trustee) for present and future distributions authorized or required by the governing instrument;

(C) to diversify assets unless the trustee reasonably determines that it is in the interests of the beneficiaries not to diversify, taking into account the purposes and terms and provisions of the governing instrument; and

(D) within a reasonable time after the creation of the fiduciary relationship, to determine whether to retain or dispose of initial assets.

(4) The prudent investor standard authorizes a trustee:

(A) to invest in any type of investment consistent with the requirements of this paragraph, since no particular investment is inherently prudent or imprudent for purposes of the prudent investor standard;

(B) to consider related trusts, the income and resources of beneficiaries to the extent reasonably known to the trustee, and also an asset's special relationship or value to some or all of the beneficiaries if consistent with the trustee's duty of impartiality;

(C) to delegate investment and management functions if consistent with the duty to exercise skill, including special investment skills; and

(D) to incur costs only to the extent they are appropriate and reasonable in relation to the purposes of the governing instrument, the assets held by the trustee and the skills of the trustee.

(5) Trustee's power to adjust.

(A) Where the rules in article 11-A apply to a trust and the terms of the trust describe the amount that may or must be distributed to a beneficiary by referring to the trust's income, the prudent investor standard also authorizes the trustee to adjust between principal and income to the extent the trustee considers advisable to enable the trustee to make appropriate present and future distributions in accordance with clause (b)(3)(A) if the trustee determines, in light of its investment decisions, the consideration factors incorporated in clause (b)(5)(B), and the accounting income expected to be produced by applying the rules in article 11-A, that such an adjustment would be fair and reasonable to all of the beneficiaries.

(B) In deciding whether and to what extent to exercise the power conferred by clause (b)(5)(A), a trustee may consider, in addition to the factors stated in clauses (b)(3)(B) and (b)(4)(B), the following factors to the extent relevant:

(i) the intent of the settlor, as expressed in the governing instrument; the assets held in the trust; the extent to which they consist of financial assets, interests in closely held enterprises, tangible and intangible personal property, or real property; the extent to which an asset is used by a beneficiary; and whether an asset was purchased by the trustee or received from the settlor;

(ii) the net amount allocated to income under article 11-A and the increase or decrease in the value of the principal assets, which the trustee may estimate as to assets for which market values are not readily available; and

(iii) whether and to what extent the terms of the trust give the trustee the power to invade principal or accumulate income or prohibit the trustee from invading principal or accumulating income, and the extent to which the trustee has exercised a power from time to time to invade principal or accumulate income.

(C) A trustee may not make an adjustment:

(i) with respect to a charitable remainder unitrust described in section 664 of the United States internal revenue code of 1986;

(ii) that changes the amount payable to a beneficiary as a fixed annuity or a fixed fraction of the value of the trust's assets;

(iii) from any amount that is permanently set aside for charitable purposes under a will or the terms of a trust unless the income therefrom is also permanently devoted to charitable purposes;

(iv) if possessing or exercising the power to make an adjustment causes an individual to be treated as the owner of all or part of the trust for income tax purposes, and the individual would not be treated as the owner if the trustee did not possess the power to make an adjustment;

(v) if possessing or exercising the power to make an adjustment causes all or part of the trust assets to be included for estate tax purposes in the estate of an individual who has the power to remove a trustee or appoint a trustee, or both, and the assets would not be included in the estate of the individual if the trustee did not possess the power to make an adjustment;

(vi) if the trustee is a current beneficiary or a presumptive remainderman of the trust;

(vii) if the trustee is not a current beneficiary or a presumptive remainderman, but the adjustment would benefit the trustee directly or indirectly (which, however, shall not include the possible effect on a trustee's commission); or

(viii) if the trust is an irrevocable lifetime trust which provides income to be paid for life to the grantor, and possessing or exercising the power to make an adjustment would cause any public benefit program to consider the adjusted principal or income to be an available resource or available income and the principal or income or both would in each case not be considered as an available resource or income if the trustee did not possess the power to make an adjustment;

(D) An adjustment otherwise prohibited by items (b)(5)(C)(i) through (viii) may be made if the terms of the trust, by express reference to this section, provide otherwise. If item (b)(5)(C) (iv), (v), (vi) or (vii) applies to a trustee and there is more than one trustee, the trustee or trustees to whom the provision does not apply may make the adjustment unless the exercise of the power by the remaining trustee or trustees is prohibited by the terms of the trust. If there is no trustee qualified to make the adjustment, it may be made if so directed by the court upon application of the trustee or of an interested party.

(E) A trustee may release the entire power conferred by clause (b)(5)(A) or may release only the power to adjust from income to principal or the power to adjust from principal to income if the trustee is uncertain about whether possessing or exercising the power will cause a result described in items (b)(5)(C)(i) through (vi) or (b)(5)(C)(viii) or if the trustee determines that possessing or exercising the power will or may deprive the trust of a tax benefit or impose a tax burden not described in clause (b)(5)(C). The release may be permanent or for a specified period, including a period measured by the life of an individual.

(F) Terms of a trust that limit the power of a trustee to make an adjustment between principal and income are not contrary to this section unless it is clear from the terms of the trust that the terms are intended to deny the trustee the power of adjustment conferred by clause (b)(5)(A).

(G) Any exercise of the power to adjust under this subparagraph, whether from income to principal or from principal to income, shall constitute a re-characterization of the transferred amount from income to principal or from principal to income, as the case may be, for purposes of calculating commissions under article twenty-three of the surrogate's court procedure act and, for such purposes, such re-characterization shall be deemed to take effect on the date that such transfer from income to principal or from principal to income, as the case may be, is made on a trust's records.

(6) Special investment skills.

For a bank, trust company or paid professional investment advisor (whether or not registered under any federal securities or investment law) which serves as a trustee, and any other trustee representing that such trustee has special investment skills, the exercise of skill contemplated by the prudent investor standard shall require the trustee to exercise such diligence in investing and managing assets as would customarily be exercised by prudent investors of discretion and intelligence having special investment skills.

(c) Delegation of investment or management functions.

(1) Delegation of an investment or management function requires a trustee to exercise care, skill and caution in:

(A) selecting a delegee suitable to exercise the delegated function, taking into account the nature and value of the assets subject to such delegation and the expertise of the delegee;

(B) establishing the scope and terms of the delegation consistent with the purposes of the governing instrument;

(C) periodically reviewing the delegee's exercise of the delegated function and compliance with the scope and terms of the delegation; and

(D) controlling the overall cost by reason of the delegation.

(2) The delegee has a duty to the trustee and to the trust to comply with the scope and terms of the delegation and to exercise the delegated function with reasonable care, skill and caution. An attempted exoneration of the delegee from liability for failure to meet such duty is contrary to public policy and void.

(3) By accepting the delegation of a trustee's function from the trustee of a trust that is subject to the law of New York, the delegee submits to the jurisdiction of the courts of New York even if a delegation agreement provides otherwise, and the delegee may be made a

party to any proceeding in such courts that places in issue the decisions or actions of the delegee.

(d) Investment in securities of related investment companies

A trustee holding funds for investment may invest the same in securities of any management type investment company or trust registered pursuant to the federal investment company act of nineteen hundred forty, as amended, notwithstanding that the trustee or an affiliate of the trustee acts as investment advisor, custodian, transfer agent, registrar, sponsor, distributor, manager or provides other services to the investment company or trust. Unless the will, lifetime trust or order appointing the trustee provides otherwise, the trustee shall elect annually either (i) to receive or have its affiliate receive compensation for providing such services to such investment company or trust for the portion of the trust invested in such investment company or trust or (ii) to take annual corporate trustees' commissions with respect to such portion.

(e) As used in this section:

(1) the term "trustee" includes a personal representative, trustee, guardian, donee of a power during minority, guardian under article eighty-one of the mental hygiene law, committee of the property of an incompetent person, and conservator of the property of a conservatee, but does not include an institutional fund as defined in section 551 of the not-for-profit corporation law;

(2) the term "trust" includes any fiduciary entity with property owned by a trustee as defined in this section;

(3) the term "governing instrument" includes a court order; and

(4) the term "portfolio" includes all property of every kind and character held by a trustee as defined in this section.

History: Add, L 1994, ch 609, § 1, eff Jan 1, 1995; amd, L 2001, ch 243, § 1, eff Jan 1, 2002; L 2008, ch 408, § 1, eff Aug 5, 2008; L 2010, ch 490, § 12, eff Sept 17, 2010; L 2017, ch 278, § 1, eff Jan 1, 2018.

§ 11-2.3-A. Judicial control with respect to fiduciary's power to adjust

(a) Judicial control of adjustment power.

A court shall not change a fiduciary's decision to exercise or not to exercise an adjustment power conferred by subparagraph 11-2.3(b)(5) unless it determines that the decision was an abuse of the fiduciary's discretion. A court shall not determine that a fiduciary abused his, her or its discretion merely because the court would have exercised the discretion in a different manner or would not have exercised the discretion.

(b) Applicable decisions.

The decisions to which paragraph (a) applies include:

(1) A determination under subparagraph 11-2.3(b)(5) of whether and to what extent an amount should be transferred from principal to income or from income to principal.

(2) A determination of the factors that are relevant to the trust and its beneficiaries, the extent to which they are relevant, and the weight, if any, to be given to the relevant factors, in deciding whether and to what extent to exercise the power conferred by

subparagraph 11-2.3(b)(5).

(c) Authorization for court to remedy abuse of discretion.

If a court determines that a fiduciary has abused his, her or its discretion, the court may restore the income and remainder beneficiaries to the positions they would have occupied if the fiduciary had not abused his, her or its discretion, according to the following rules:

(1) To the extent that the abuse of discretion has resulted in no distribution to a beneficiary or a distribution that is too small, the court shall require the fiduciary to distribute from the trust to the beneficiary an amount that the court determines will restore the beneficiary, in whole or in part, to his or her appropriate position.

(2) To the extent that the abuse of discretion has resulted in a distribution to a beneficiary that is too large, the court shall restore the beneficiaries, the trust, or both, in whole or in part, to their appropriate positions by requiring the fiduciary to withhold an amount from one or more future distributions to the beneficiary who received the distribution that was too large or requiring that beneficiary to return some or all of the distribution to the trust.

(3) To the extent that the court is unable, after applying subparagraphs (1) and (2), to restore the beneficiaries, the trust, or both, to the positions they would have occupied if the fiduciary had not abused his, her or its discretion, and if the court finds that the fiduciary was dishonest or arbitrary and capricious in the exercise of his, her or its discretion, the court may require the fiduciary to pay an appropriate amount from his, her or its own funds to one or more of the beneficiaries or the trust or both.

(d) Petition by fiduciary.

Upon a petition by a fiduciary who is authorized to exercise an adjustment power conferred by subparagraph 11-2.3 (b)(5), the court having jurisdiction over the trust or estate may determine whether a proposed exercise or nonexercise by the fiduciary of the adjustment power will result in an abuse of the fiduciary's discretion. If the petition describes the proposed exercise or nonexercise of the power and contains sufficient information to inform the beneficiaries of the reasons for the proposal, the facts upon which the fiduciary relies, and an explanation of how the income and remainder beneficiaries will be affected by the proposed exercise or nonexercise of the power, a beneficiary who challenges the proposed exercise or nonexercise has the burden of establishing that it will result in an abuse of discretion.

History: Add, L 2001, ch 243, § 2, eff Jan 1, 2002.

§ 11-2.4. Optional unitrust provision

(a) Unless the terms of the trust provide otherwise, the net income of any trust to which this section applies shall mean the unitrust amount as determined hereunder.

(b) Unitrust amount.

(1) For the first year of the trust as a unitrust, including a short year if applicable, the "unitrust amount" for the year shall mean an amount equal to four percent of the net fair market values of the assets held in the trust at the beginning of the first business day of the current valuation year.

(2) For the second year of a trust as a unitrust, including a first short year if applicable,

the "unitrust amount" for the year shall mean an amount equal to four percent multiplied by a fraction, the numerator of which shall be the sum of (A) the net fair market values of the assets held in the trust at the beginning of the first business day of the current valuation year and (B) the net fair market values of the assets held in the trust at the beginning of the first business day of the prior valuation year, and the denominator of which shall be two.

(3) Commencing with the third year of a trust as a unitrust, including a first short year if applicable, the "unitrust amount" for a current valuation year of the trust shall mean an amount equal to four percent multiplied by a fraction, the numerator of which shall be the sum of (A) the net fair market values of the assets held in the trust at the beginning of the first business day of the current valuation year and (B) the net fair market values of the assets held in the trust at the beginning of the first business day of each prior valuation year, and the denominator of which shall be three.

(4) The unitrust amount for the current valuation year as computed in accordance with subparagraph (b)(1), (2) or (3), as adjusted in accordance with this subparagraph, shall be proportionately reduced for any corpus distributions to beneficiaries mandated by the terms of the trust, in whole or in part (other than distributions of the unitrust amount), and shall be proportionately increased for the receipt, other than a receipt that represents a return on investment, of any additional corpus into the trust within a current valuation year.

(5) For purposes of clause (b)(2)(B), the net fair market values of the assets held in the trust at the beginning of the first business day of a prior valuation year shall be adjusted to reflect any distributions to beneficiaries mandated by the terms of the trust, in whole or in part (other than distributions of the unitrust amount), or receipts (other than receipts that represent a return on investment) of any additional principal into the trust, which have occurred after the first day of such prior valuation year and by the close of the first day of the current valuation year, as if the distribution or receipt had occurred on the first day of such prior valuation year.

(6) In the case of a short year, the trustee shall prorate the unitrust amount on a daily basis. The trustee shall prorate any adjustment under subparagraph (b)(4) on a daily basis.

(7) In the case where the unitrust amount has been incorrectly determined either in a current valuation year or in a prior valuation year, then within a reasonable time (not to exceed eighteen months) after the error was made, the trustee shall make any non-material adjustments and pay to the underpaid beneficiary (in case of non-material underpayment) or shall recover from the overpaid beneficiary (in case of non-material overpayment) an amount equal to the difference between the unitrust amount properly payable and any amount actually paid for any completed valuation year of the trust and shall properly adjust the unitrust amount for the current valuation year if affected non-materially by prior incorrect determination of a unitrust amount. A material correction shall require approval of the surrogate if applied for by the trustee or an interested party.

(c) Other definitions and special rules. For purposes of this section:

(1) A "current beneficiary" is a person to whom the income (within the meaning of this section or otherwise) of the trust is payable, or in the discretion of the trustee may be paid, in whole or in part, during the current valuation year.

(2) The term "current valuation year" shall mean the year of the trust for which the unitrust amount is being determined.

(3) The term "prior valuation year" shall mean each of the two years of the trust immediately preceding the current valuation year.

(4) The term "year" means a calendar year. A "short year" constitutes a portion of a calendar year that begins when the interest of the current beneficiary or class of current beneficiaries begins or ends when the interest of the current beneficiary or class of current beneficiaries ends.

(5) "Net fair market value" shall mean the fair market value of each asset comprising the trust reduced by the fair market value of any outstanding interest-bearing obligations of the trust, whether allocable to a specific asset or otherwise. Fair market value of an asset may be determined by any appropriate technique adopted and consistently applied by the trustee, and such techniques may include, but are not limited to, use of the asset's value at the close of business on the previous business day, and notwithstanding that such day may be in a prior year or be a day on which the trust was not subject to this section.

(6) In determining the sum of the net fair market values of the assets held in the trust for purposes of subparagraphs (b)(1), (2) and (3), and in determining whether an adjustment is required in accordance with subparagraph (b)(4) or (5), there shall not be taken into account the value:

(A) of any residential property or any tangible personal property that, as of the beginning of the first business day of the current valuation year, one or more current beneficiaries of the trust have or had the right to occupy, or have or had the right to possess or control (other than in his or her capacity as a trustee of the trust), and instead the right of occupancy or the right to possession or control shall be deemed to be the unitrust amount with respect to such residential property or such tangible personal property; provided, however, that the unitrust amount shall be adjusted in accordance with subparagraphs (b)(4) and (5) for partial distributions from or receipt into the trust of such residential property or tangible personal property during the current valuation year.

(B) of any asset specifically given to a beneficiary and the return on investment on such property, which return on investment shall be distributable to such beneficiary.

(C) of any assets while held in a testator's estate.

(D) of (i) amounts paid or distributed to the trust by a decedent's estate, another trust or another payor, as income pursuant to article 11-A attributable to an asset or amount due to the trust for a period prior to its payment or distribution to the trust, unless and except to the extent that the unitrust trustee, having the power to accumulate income, shall have determined to accumulate and add such income to principal, and such unaccumulated net income shall be distributable to the beneficiaries of the trust; or (ii) any amount paid or distributed by such decedent's estate, other trust or other payor, directly to beneficiaries of the trust in satisfaction of their ultimate entitlement to such income.

(7) In determining the net fair market value of each asset held in the trust pursuant to subparagraphs (b)(1), (2) and (3), the trustee shall, not less often than annually, determine

the fair market value of each asset of the trust that consists primarily of real property or other property that is not traded on a regular basis in an active market, and all such determinations shall, if made reasonably and in good faith, be conclusive on all persons interested in the trust. Such determination shall be conclusively presumed to have been made reasonably and in good faith unless proven otherwise in a proceeding commenced by or on behalf of a person interested in the trust within three years after the close of the year in which the determination is made.

(8) The term "trustee" does not include a personal representative.

(9) The term "trust" does not include an estate.

(d) Commencement of current beneficiary's interest.

(1) The interest of a current beneficiary or class of current beneficiaries in the unitrust amount begins on the date on which this section becomes applicable to the trust pursuant to clause (e)(4)(A), or if later the date assets first become subject to the trust. An asset becomes subject to a trust:

(A) on the date it is transferred to the trust in the case of an asset that is transferred to a trust during the transferor's life;

(B) on the date it is transferred to the trust in the case of an asset that is transferred to a testamentary trust created under a will;

(C) on the date of an individual's death in the case of an asset that is transferred to a trust by a third party by reason of the individual's death;

(D) on the date of an individual's death in the case of a trust that owns life insurance on the individual's life; or

(E) on the date a revocable trust becomes irrevocable in the case of assets then held in the trust.

(2) A trust which continues in existence for the benefit of one or more new current beneficiaries or class of current beneficiaries upon the termination of the interests of all prior current beneficiaries or classes of prior current beneficiaries, shall be deemed to be a new trust, and, for purposes of clauses (e)(1)(B) and (e)(4)(A) and subparagraph (d)(1), assets shall be deemed to first become subject to the trust on the date of the termination of such interests.

(e) Trusts to which section applies.

(1) This section shall apply to any trust if:

(A) the governing instrument provides that this section shall apply to such trust, or

(B) (i) with respect to a trust in existence prior to January first, two thousand two, on or before December thirty-first, two thousand five, the trustee, with the consent by or on behalf of all persons interested in the trust or in his, her or its discretion, elects to have this section apply to such trust, or

(ii) with respect to a trust not in existence prior to January first, two thousand two, on or before the last day of the second full year of the trust beginning after assets first become subject to the trust, the trustee, with the consent by or on behalf of all persons interested in the trust or in his, her or its discretion, elects to have this section apply to such trust.

(iii) An election in accordance with this subparagraph shall be made by an instrument, executed and acknowledged, and delivered to the creator of the trust, if he or she is then living, to all persons interested in the trust or to their representatives and to the court, if any, having jurisdiction over the trust.

(2) (A) The court having jurisdiction of a trust to which this section otherwise would apply by reason of subparagraph (e)(1) or clause (e)(2)(B), upon the petition of the trustee or any beneficiary of the trust and upon notice to all persons interested in the trust, may direct that article 11-A shall apply to the trust and that this section shall not apply to the trust; and

(B) At any time, the court having jurisdiction of a trust to which this section otherwise would not apply, upon the petition of the trustee or any beneficiary of the trust and upon notice to all persons interested in the trust, may direct that this section shall apply to the trust and that article 11-A shall not apply to the trust.

(3) For the purposes of this section, the phrase "all persons interested in the trust" shall mean all the persons upon whom service of process would be required in a proceeding for the judicial settlement of the account of the trustee, taking into account section three hundred fifteen of the surrogate's court procedure act. Where a person interested in the trust has the same interest as a person under a disability, it shall not be necessary to obtain the consent of or notify the person under a disability.

(4) (A) This section shall apply to a trust with respect to which there is:

(i) a direction in the governing instrument in accordance with clause (e)(1)(A), as of the date provided for in such governing instrument, or if there is no provision then as of the day on which assets first become subject to the trust;

(ii) an election in accordance with clause (e)(1)(B), as of the date specified in the election, which may be any day within the year in which the election is made or the first day of the year commencing after the election is made; or a

(iii) court decision rendered in accordance with clause (e)(2)(B) as of the date specified by the court in its decision;

Provided, however, that if later than any date set by this clause, this section shall not apply to the trust until January first, two thousand two.

(B) If this section applied to a trust with respect to which a court decision is rendered in accordance with clause (e)(2)(A), this section shall cease to apply to such trust and article 11-A shall apply to the trust as of the first day of the year beginning after the decision of the court becomes final, unless the court in its decision provides otherwise.

(5) In the determination of whether article 11-A or this section should apply to a trust:

(A) All of the factors relevant to the trust and its beneficiaries, including the following factors to the extent they are relevant, shall be considered:

(i) the nature, purpose, and expected duration of the trust;

(ii) the intent of the creator of the trust;

(iii) the identity and circumstances of the beneficiaries;

(iv) the needs for liquidity, regularity of payment, and preservation and appreciation of capital;

(v) the assets held in the trust; the extent to which they consist of financial assets, interests in closely held enterprises, tangible and intangible personal property, or real property; the extent to which an asset is used by a beneficiary; and whether an asset was purchased by the trustee or received from the creator of the trust.

(B) In any proceeding brought pursuant to subparagraph (e)(2), there shall be a rebuttable presumption that this section should apply to the trust.

(f) Trusts to which this section shall not apply. This section shall not apply to a trust if:

(1) the governing instrument provides in substance that this section shall not apply;

(2) the trust is a pooled income fund described in section 642(c)(5) of the United States internal revenue code of 1986;

(3) the trust is a charitable remainder annuity trust or a charitable remainder unitrust described in section 664 of the United States internal revenue code of 1986; or

(4) the trust is an irrevocable lifetime trust which provides for income to be paid for the life of a grantor, and possessing or exercising the power to make this section apply would cause any public benefit program to consider additional amounts of principal or income to be an available resource or available income, and the principal or income or both would in each case not be considered an available resource or income, if there was no power to make this section apply, if, based upon the facts and circumstances surrounding the formation of such trust, it can reasonably be concluded that the primary purpose for the establishment of the trust was to ensure that the trust principal would not be treated as an available resource for the purposes of a governmental assistance program.

History: Add, L 2001, ch 243, § 4, eff Jan 1, 2002; L 2008, ch 408, §§ 2-8, eff Aug 5, 2008.

PART 3   Actions by or Against Personal Representatives

§ 11-3.1. Actions

Any action, other than an action for injury to person or property, may be maintained by and against a personal representative in all cases and in such manner as such action might have been maintained by or against his decedent.

History: Added from Add, L 1966, ch 952, eff Sept 1, 1967, with substance deriving from Decedent Est. Law §§ 116, 117.

§ 11-3.2. Action for injury to person or property survives despite death of person in whose favor or against whom cause of action existed

(a) Action against personal representative for injury to person or property.

(1) No cause of action for injury to person or property is lost because of the death of the person liable for the injury. For any injury, an action may be brought or continued against the personal representative of the decedent, but punitive damages shall not be awarded nor penalties adjudged in any such action brought to recover damages for personal injury. This section extends to a cause of action for wrongfully causing death and an action therefor

may be brought or continued against the personal representative of the person liable therefor.

(2) Where death or an injury to person or property, resulting from a wrongful act, neglect or default, occurs simultaneously with or after the death of a person who would have been liable therefor if his death had not occurred simultaneously with such death or injury or between the wrongful act, neglect or default and the resulting death or injury, an action to recover damages for such death or injury may be maintained against the personal representative of such person.

(b) Action by personal representative for injury to person or property.

No cause of action for injury to person or property is lost because of the death of the person in whose favor the cause of action existed. For any injury an action may be brought or continued by the personal representative of the decedent, but punitive damages shall not be awarded nor penalties adjudged in any such action brought to recover damages for personal injury where the death occurs on or before August thirty-first, nineteen hundred eighty-two. On the trial of any such action accruing before September first, nineteen hundred seventy-five, which is joined with an action for causing death, the contributory negligence of the decedent is a defense, to be pleaded and proved by the defendant. No cause of action for damages caused by an injury to a third person is lost because of the death of the third person.

History: Add, L 1966, ch 952, eff Sept 1, 1967, with substance deriving from Decedent Est. Law §§ 118, 119; amd, L 1967, ch 686, § 127, eff Sept 1, 1967; L 1975, ch 69, eff Sept 1, 1975; L 1982, ch 100, § 2, eff Sept 1, 1982.

§ 11-3.3. Limitations upon recovery where injury causes death

(a) Where an injury causes the death of a person the damages recoverable for such injury are limited to those accruing before death and shall not include damages for or by reason of death, except that the reasonable funeral expenses of the decedent, paid by the estate or for the payment of which the estate is responsible, shall be recoverable in such action. The damages recovered become part of the estate of the deceased.

(b) Nothing contained herein shall affect the cause of action existing in favor of the next of kin under 5-4.1, subject to the following:

(1) Such cause of action and the cause of action, under this section, in favor of the estate to recover damages may be prosecuted to judgment in a single action; a separate verdict, report or decision shall be rendered as to each cause of action.

(2) Where an action to recover damages for personal injury has been brought, and the injured person dies, as a result of the injury, before verdict, report or decision, his personal representative may enlarge the complaint in such action to include the cause of action for wrongful death under 5-4.1.

(3) Where an action to recover damages under this section and a separate action for wrongful death under 5-4.1 are pending against the same defendant, they may be consolidated on the motion of either party.

History: Add, L 1966, ch 952, eff Sept 1, 1967, with substance deriving from Decedent Est. Law § 120; amd, L 1967, ch 686, § 128, eff Sept 1, 1967.

§ 11-3.4. Action by representative of representative

Except as otherwise prescribed by law, a personal representative of a personal representative has no authority to commence or maintain any action or proceeding relating to the estate, effects or rights of the decedent of the first representative, or to take any charge or control thereof, as such representative.

> **History:** Add, L 1966, ch 952, eff Sept 1, 1967, with substance deriving from Decedent Est. Law § 121.

PART 4   Procedural Aspects of Actions by or Against Personal Representatives

§ 11-4.1. How to sue or be sued

Actions or proceedings brought by or against a personal representative must be brought by or against him in his representative capacity.

> **History:** Add, L 1966, ch 952, eff Sept 1, 1967, with substance deriving from Decedent Est. Law § 140.

§ 11-4.2. When personal and representative causes of action may be joined

Actions or proceedings brought against a personal representative personally and in his representative capacity may be joined. In such case a judgment for the plaintiff must clearly indicate whether it is awarded against the defendant personally or in his representative capacity.

> **History:** Add, L 1966, ch 952, eff Sept 1, 1967, with substance deriving from Decedent Est. Law § 141; amd, L 1967, ch 686, § 130, eff Sept 1, 1967.

§ 11-4.3. Separate dockets and executions

In a case specified in 11-4.2 or where costs to be collected out of the individual property of a personal representative are awarded in an action or proceeding by or against him in his representative capacity, so much of the judgment as awards a sum of money against him personally may be separately docketed and a separate execution may be issued thereupon, as if the judgment contained no award against him in his representative capacity.

> **History:** Add, L 1966, ch 952, eff Sept 1, 1967, with substance deriving from Decedent Est. Law § 142; amd, L 1967, ch 686, § 131, eff Sept 1, 1967.

§ 11-4.4. Commencement of action against personal representatives; rule when some of representatives not served

Where an action or proceeding is commenced against two or more personal representatives in their representative capacities, jurisdiction of all is obtained by service of process upon any one of them and any judgment recovered may be entered and execution issued thereon against all of them, in their representative capacities, as if all had been served.

> **History:** Add, L 1966, ch 952, eff Sept 1, 1967, with substance deriving from Decedent Est. Law § 143; amd, L 1967, ch 686, § 132, eff Sept 1, 1967.

§ 11-4.5. Want of assets not to be pleaded by personal representative

In an action or proceeding against a personal representative, in his representative capacity, in which the complaint demands judgment for a sum of money, the non-existence or insufficiency of assets may not be pleaded and the plaintiff's right of recovery is not affected thereby.

> **History:** Add, L 1966, ch 952, eff Sept 1, 1967, with substance deriving from Decedent Est. Law § 150; amd, L 1967, ch 686, § 133, eff Sept 1, 1967.

§ 11-4.6. Leave to issue execution against personal representative; how procured; order and contents thereof; security before order granted; execution on judgment recovered by predecessor representative

(a) Leave to issue execution against personal representative.

Except as provided in this paragraph, an execution shall not be issued upon a judgment for a sum of money against a personal representative, in his representative capacity, until an order permitting it to be issued has been made by the surrogate's court from which letters were issued. Such an order must specify the sum to be collected, and the execution must be endorsed with a direction to collect that sum. If a judgment is rendered jointly against a personal representative in his representative capacity and one or more other parties, execution may be issued thereon, without such order, against the other party if a direction is endorsed thereon not to levy against any property which the personal representative is or may be entitled to possess in his representative capacity.

(b) How leave procured; order; contents thereof.

At least six days notice of the application for an order specified in paragraph (a) must be personally served upon the personal representative, unless it appears that service cannot be so made with due diligence, in which case notice must be given to such persons and in such manner as the surrogate directs by an order to show cause why the application should not be granted. Where it appears that the assets, after payment of all sums chargeable against them for expenses and for claims entitled to priority as against the plaintiff, are not, or will not be sufficient to pay all the debts, testamentary dispositions or other claims of the class to which the plaintiff's claim belongs, the sum directed to be collected by the execution shall not exceed the plaintiff's just proportion of the assets. In that case, one or more orders may be subsequently made in like manner, and one or more executions may be subsequently issued, whenever it appears that the sum directed to be collected by the first and subsequent execution is less than the plaintiff's just proportion.

(c) Security before grant of order.

Where a judgment has been rendered against a personal representative in his representative capacity for a testamentary disposition or distributive share, the surrogate, before granting an order permitting an execution to be issued thereupon, may, and in a proper case must, require the applicant to file in his office a bond to the defendant, in such a sum and with such sureties as the surrogate directs, to the effect that if, after collection of any sum of money by virtue of the execution, the remaining assets are not sufficient to pay all sums for which the defendant is chargeable for expenses, claims entitled to priority as against the applicant, and the other testamentary dispositions or distributive shares of the class to which the applicant's claim belongs, the plaintiff will refund to the defendant the sum so collected, or such ratable part thereof as is necessary to make up the deficiency.

(d) Execution on former judgment.

An execution may be issued in the name of a personal representative, in his representative capacity, upon a judgment recovered by any person who preceded him in the administration of the same estate, in any case where it might have been issued in favor of the original plaintiff, and without a substitution.

History: Add, L 1966, ch 952, eff Sept 1, 1967, with substance deriving from Decedent Est. Law §§ 151–154; amd, L 1967, ch 686, § 134, eff Sept 1, 1967.

EPTL

§ 11-4.7. Liability of the personal representative for claims arising out of the administration of the estate

(a) Unless otherwise provided in the contract, a personal representative is not individually liable on a contract properly entered into in his fiduciary capacity in the course of administration of the estate unless he fails to reveal his representative capacity and identify the estate or trust in the contract.

(b) A personal representative is individually liable for obligations arising from ownership or control of the estate or for torts committed in the course of administration of the estate only if he failed to exercise reasonable care, diligence and prudence.

(c) Claims based on contracts entered into by a personal representative in his fiduciary capacity, on obligations arising from ownership or control of the estate or on torts committed in the course of estate administration may be asserted against the estate by proceeding against the personal representative in his fiduciary capacity, whether or not the personal representative is individually liable therefor.

(d) In any case where liability is found against the estate as the result of an action or proceeding brought under subdivision (c), issues of liability as between the estate and the personal representative shall be determined in an accounting proceeding brought pursuant to section twenty-two hundred five of the surrogate's court procedure act.

(e) (1) For the purposes of this paragraph: (i) the term "act" shall mean the federal air transportation safety and system stabilization act, public law 107-42, as amended; (ii) the term "fund" shall mean the September eleventh victim compensation fund of two thousand one established pursuant to title IV of the act; and (iii) the term "personal representative" shall have the same meaning as that term has pursuant to section 104.4 of title twenty-eight of the code of federal regulations.

(2) Notwithstanding any other provision of law to the contrary, any person who serves as the personal representative of a victim of the terrorist attacks on September eleventh, two thousand one, and who files a claim with the fund, shall have no liability to any person resulting from any actions taken reasonably and in good faith under the act, including but not limited to: (i) the submission or prosecution of a claim to the fund; (ii) a decision not to submit such a claim, or to withdraw a claim previously submitted; (iii) the waiver pursuant to the act of the right to file a civil action (or to be a party to an action) in any federal or state court for damages sustained as a result of the terrorist attacks; (iv) the failure to identify or locate any person designated for receipt of notice under subdivision (b) of section 104.4 of title twenty-eight of the code of federal regulations, provided that the personal representative made a reasonable and good faith effort to identify and locate such person; or (v) the payment or distribution of any award received from the fund in accordance with any plan of distribution that has been submitted to and approved by the special master appointed under the act.

(3) Notwithstanding any other provision of law to the contrary, or any restrictions set forth in letters relating to any decedent who dies as a result of wounds or injury incurred as a result of the terrorist attacks on September eleventh, two thousand one, a duly appointed personal representative is authorized to file and prosecute a claim with the fund, and the filing of such a claim for an award from the fund, and the resulting compromise of any cause of action pursuant to the act, shall not violate any restriction on the powers

granted to the personal representative relating to the prosecution or compromise of any action, the collection of any settlement, or the enforcement of any judgment.

History: Add, L 1979, ch 264, § 1, eff Sept 1, 1979; amd, L 2002, ch 73, § 4, eff May 21, 2002.

EPTL

ARTICLE 11-A
UNIFORM PRINCIPAL AND INCOME ACT
SUMMARY OF ARTICLE

EPTL

PART 1   Definitions and Fiduciary Duties

§ 11-A-1.1. Short title

This article may be cited as the New York uniform principal and income act.

    History: Add, L 2001, ch 243, § 3, eff Jan 1, 2002.

§ 11-A-1.2. Definitions

In this article:

(1) "Accounting period" means a calendar year unless another twelve-month period is selected by a fiduciary. The term includes a portion of a calendar year or other twelve-month period that begins when an income interest begins or ends when an income interest ends.

(2) "Beneficiary" includes, in the case of a decedent's estate, a distributee and testamentary beneficiary and, in the case of a trust, an income beneficiary and a remainder beneficiary.

(3) "Fiduciary" means a personal representative or trustee. The term includes an executor, administrator, successor personal representative, and a person performing substantially the same function.

(4) "Income" means money or property that a fiduciary receives as current return from a principal asset. The term includes a portion of receipts from a sale, exchange, or liquidation of a principal asset, to the extent provided in part 4.

(5) "Income beneficiary" means a person to whom net income of a trust is or may be payable.

(6) "Income interest" means the right of an income beneficiary to receive all or part of net income, whether the terms of the trust require it to be distributed or authorize it to be distributed in the trustee's discretion.

(7) "Mandatory income interest" means the right of an income beneficiary to receive net income that the terms of the trust require the fiduciary to distribute.

(8) "Net income" means the total receipts allocated to income during an accounting period minus the disbursements made from income during the period, plus or minus transfers under this article or under subparagraph 11-2.3(b)(5) to or from income during the period.

(9) "Person" means an individual, corporation, business trust, estate, trust, partnership, limited liability company, association, joint venture, government; governmental subdivision, agency, or instrumentality; public corporation, or any other legal or commercial entity.

(10) "Principal" means property held in trust for distribution to a remainder beneficiary

when the trust terminates.

(11) "Remainder beneficiary" means a person entitled to receive principal when an income interest ends.

(12) "Terms of a trust" means the manifestation of the intent of a settlor or decedent with respect to the trust, expressed in a manner that admits of its proof in a judicial proceeding, whether by written or spoken words or by conduct.

(13) "Trustee" includes an original, additional, or successor trustee, whether or not appointed or confirmed by a court.

> **History:** Add, L 2001, ch 243, § 3, eff Jan 1, 2002.

§ 11-A-1.3. Fiduciary duties; general principles

(a) In allocating receipts and disbursements to or between principal and income, and with respect to any matter within the scope of parts 2 and 3, a fiduciary:

(1) shall administer a trust or estate in accordance with the terms of the trust or the will, even if there is a different provision in this article;

(2) may administer a trust or estate by the exercise of a discretionary power of administration given to the fiduciary by the terms of the trust or the will, even if the exercise of the power produces a result different from a result required or permitted by this article;

(3) shall administer a trust or estate in accordance with this article if the terms of the trust or the will do not contain a different provision or do not give the fiduciary a discretionary power of administration; and

(4) shall add a receipt or charge a disbursement to principal to the extent that the terms of the trust or the will and this article do not provide a rule for allocating the receipt or disbursement to or between principal and income.

(b) In exercising a discretionary power of administration regarding a matter within the scope of this article, whether granted by the terms of a trust, a will, or this article, a fiduciary shall administer a trust or estate impartially, based on what is fair and reasonable to all of the beneficiaries, except to the extent that the terms of the trust or the will clearly manifest an intention that the fiduciary shall or may favor one or more of the beneficiaries. A determination in accordance with this article is presumed to be fair and reasonable to all of the beneficiaries.

> **History:** Add, L 2001, ch 243, § 3, eff Jan 1, 2002.

PART 2   Decedent's Estate or Terminating Income Interest

§ 11-A-2.1. Determination and distribution of net income

After a decedent dies, in the case of an estate, or after an income interest in a trust ends, the following rules apply:

(1) A fiduciary of an estate or of a terminating income interest shall determine the amount of net income and net principal receipts received from property specifically given to a beneficiary under the rules in parts 3 through 5 which apply to trustees and the rules in paragraph (5). The fiduciary shall distribute the net income and net principal receipts to the beneficiary who is to receive the specific property.

(2) A fiduciary shall determine the remaining net income of a decedent's estate or a terminating income interest under the rules in parts 3 through 5 which apply to trustees and by:

(A) including in net income all income from property used to discharge liabilities;

(B) paying from income or principal, in the fiduciary's discretion, fees of attorneys, accountants, and fiduciaries; court costs and other expenses of administration; and interest on death taxes, but the fiduciary may pay those expenses from income of property passing to a trust for which the fiduciary claims an estate tax marital or charitable deduction only to the extent that the payment of those expenses from income will not cause the reduction or loss of the deduction; and

(C) paying from principal all other disbursements made or incurred in connection with the settlement of a decedent's estate or the winding up of a terminating income interest, including debts, funeral expenses, disposition of remains, family allowances, and death taxes and related penalties that are apportioned to the estate or terminating income interest by the will, the terms of the trust, or applicable law.

(3) Unless otherwise provided by the terms of the will or trust, commencing (A) seven months from either the date of death or other date a beneficiary is to receive a pecuniary amount outright if letters are not required, unless the beneficiary is a genetic child, then such date shall be the later of the aforementioned time periods in this subparagraph or the date of birth of the genetic child entitled to inherit from the child's genetic parent under section 4-1.3 of this chapter, or (B) seven months from the time letters, including preliminary or temporary letters, are granted if letters are required, unless the beneficiary is a genetic child, then such date shall be the later of the aforementioned time period in this subparagraph or the date of birth of the genetic child entitled to inherit from the child's genetic parent under section 4-1.3 of this chapter, a fiduciary shall distribute income to a beneficiary who receives a pecuniary amount outright, from net income determined under paragraph (2) or from principal to the extent that net income is insufficient, of an amount equal to the pecuniary amount multiplied by an income factor, which shall be set (or reset) on the first business day of each calendar year and fixed for that calendar year at the target Federal funds rate as announced by the Federal Reserve Board (or in the event the target Federal funds rate is a range of rates, the high of that range) less one percent, but in no event less than one-half of one percent.

(4) A fiduciary shall distribute the net income remaining after distributions required by paragraph (3) in the manner described in 11-A-2.2 to all other beneficiaries, including a beneficiary who receives a pecuniary amount in trust, even if the beneficiary holds an unqualified power to withdraw assets from the trust or other presently exercisable general power of appointment over the trust.

(5) A fiduciary may not reduce principal or income receipts from property described in paragraph (1) because of a payment described in 11-A-5.1 or 11-A-5.2 to the extent that the will, the terms of the trust, or applicable law requires the fiduciary to make the payment from assets other than the property or to the extent that the fiduciary recovers or expects to recover the payment from a third party. The net income and principal receipts from the property are determined by including all of the amounts the fiduciary receives or pays with respect to the property, whether those amounts accrued or became due before, on, or after the date of a decedent's death or an income interest's terminating event, and by making a

reasonable provision for amounts that the fiduciary believes the estate or terminating income interest may become obligated to pay after the property is distributed.

History: Add, L 2001, ch 243, § 3, eff Jan 1, 2002; amd, L 2008, ch 408, § 9, eff Aug 5, 2008; L 2014, ch 404, § 2, eff Dec 20, 2014, and applying to the estates of decedents who shall have died on or after such date; L 2015, ch 438, § 1, eff Nov 20, 2015.

§ 11-A-2.2. Distribution to residuary and remainder beneficiaries

(a) Each beneficiary described in paragraph 11-A-2.1 (4) is entitled to receive a portion of the net income equal to the beneficiary's fractional interest in undistributed principal assets, using values as of the distribution date, provided, however, that any amount allowed as a tax deduction to the estate for income payable to a charitable organization shall be paid, without diminution for taxes, to the charitable organization entitled to receive such income. If a fiduciary makes more than one distribution of assets to beneficiaries to whom this section applies, each beneficiary, including one who does not receive part of the distribution, is entitled, as of each distribution date, to the net income the fiduciary has received after the date of death or terminating event or earlier distribution date but has not distributed as of the current distribution date.

(b) In determining a beneficiary's share of net income, the following rules apply:

(1) The beneficiary is entitled to receive a portion of the net income equal to the beneficiary's fractional interest in the undistributed principal assets immediately before the distribution date, including assets that later may be sold to meet principal obligations.

(2) The beneficiary's fractional interest in the undistributed principal assets must be calculated without regard to property specifically given to a beneficiary and property required to pay pecuniary amounts not in trust.

(3) The beneficiary's fractional interest in the undistributed principal assets must be calculated on the basis of the aggregate value of those assets as of the distribution date without reducing the value by any unpaid principal obligation.

(4) The distribution date for purposes of this section may be the date as of which the fiduciary calculates the value of the assets if that date is reasonably near the date on which assets are actually distributed.

(c) If a fiduciary does not distribute all of the collected but undistributed net income to each person as of a distribution date, the fiduciary shall maintain appropriate records showing the interest of each beneficiary in that net income.

(d) A fiduciary may apply the rules in this section, to the extent that the fiduciary considers it appropriate, to net gain or loss realized after the date of death or terminating event or earlier distribution date from the disposition of a principal asset if this section applies to the income from the asset.

(e) The portion of a beneficiary determined under paragraph (a) is subject to the fiduciary's further power of adjustment under subparagraph 11-2.3(b)(5), which adjustment if made shall be made to or from the principal of such beneficiary's share. The fiduciary shall maintain appropriate records showing the principal interest of each beneficiary, as adjusted.

History: Add, L 2001, ch 243, § 3, eff Jan 1, 2002; amd, L 2008, ch 408, § 10, eff Aug 5, 2008.

EPTL

PART 3   Apportionment at Beginning and End of Income Interest

§ 11-A-3.1. When right to income begins and ends

(a) An income beneficiary is entitled to net income from the date on which the income interest begins. An income interest begins on the date specified in the terms of the trust or, if no date is specified, on the date an asset becomes subject to a trust or successive income interest.

(b) An asset becomes subject to a trust:

(1) on the date it is transferred to the trust in the case of an asset that is transferred to a trust during the transferor's life;

(2) on the date of a testator's death in the case of an asset that becomes subject to a trust by reason of a will, even if there is an intervening period of administration of the testator's estate; or

(3) on the date of an individual's death in the case of an asset that is transferred to a fiduciary by a third party because of the individual's death.

(c) An asset becomes subject to a successive income interest on the day after the preceding income interest ends, as determined under paragraph (d), even if there is an intervening period of administration to wind up the preceding income interest.

(d) An income interest ends on the day before an income beneficiary dies or another terminating event occurs, or on the last day of a period during which there is no beneficiary to whom a trustee may distribute income.

> **History:** Add, L 2001, ch 243, § 3, eff Jan 1, 2002.

§ 11-A-3.2. Apportionment of receipts and disbursements when decedent dies or income interest begins

(a) A trustee shall allocate an income receipt or disbursement other than one to which paragraph 11-A-2.1 (1) applies to principal if its due date occurs before a decedent dies in the case of an estate or before an income interest begins in the case of a trust or successive income interest.

(b) A trustee shall allocate an income receipt or disbursement to income if its due date occurs on or after the date on which a decedent dies or an income interest begins and it is a periodic due date. An income receipt or disbursement must be treated as accruing from day to day if its due date is not periodic or it has no due date. The portion of the receipt or disbursement accruing before the date on which a decedent dies or an income interest begins must be allocated to principal and the balance must be allocated to income.

(c) An item of income or an obligation is due on the date the payer is required to make a payment. If a payment date is not stated, there is no due date for the purposes of this article. Distributions to shareholders or other owners from an entity to which 11-A-4.1 applies are deemed to be due on the date fixed by the entity for determining who is entitled to receive the distribution or, if no date is fixed, on the declaration date for the distribution. A due date is periodic for receipts or disbursements that must be paid at regular intervals under a lease or an obligation to pay interest or if an entity customarily makes distributions at regular intervals.

History: Add, L 2001, ch 243, § 3, eff Jan 1, 2002.

§ 11-A-3.3. Apportionment when income interest ends

(a) In this section, "undistributed income" means net income received on or before the date on which an income interest ends. The term does not include an item of income or expense that is due or accrued or net income that has been added or is required to be added to principal under the terms of the trust.

(b) When a mandatory income interest ends, the trustee shall pay to a mandatory income beneficiary who survives that date, or the estate of a deceased mandatory income beneficiary whose death causes the interest to end, the beneficiary's share of the undistributed income that is not disposed of under the terms of the trust unless the beneficiary has an unqualified power to revoke more than five percent of the trust immediately before the income interest ends. In the latter case, the undistributed income from the portion of the trust that may be revoked must be added to principal.

(c) When a trustee's obligation to pay a fixed annuity or a fixed fraction of the value of the trust's assets ends, the trustee shall prorate the final payment if and to the extent required by applicable law to accomplish a purpose of the trust or its settlor relating to income, gift, estate, or other tax requirements.

History: Add, L 2001, ch 243, § 3, eff Jan 1, 2002; amd, L 2008, ch 408, § 11, eff Aug 5, 2008.

PART 4   Allocation of Receipts During Administration of Trust

SUBPART 1   Receipts from Entities

§ 11-A-4.1. Character of receipts

(a) In this section, "entity" means a corporation, partnership, limited liability company, regulated investment company, real estate investment trust, common trust fund, or any other organization in which a trustee has an interest other than a trust or estate to which 11-A-4.2 applies, a business or activity to which 11-A-4.3 applies, or an asset-backed security to which 11-A-4.15 applies.

(b) Except as otherwise provided in this section, a trustee shall allocate to income money received from an entity.

(c) A trustee shall allocate the following receipts from an entity to principal:

(1) property other than money; provided that if a trustee receives the option to receive a distribution in the form of money or property and elects to receive the distribution in the form of property such distribution shall be considered to be a distribution of money;

(2) money received in one distribution or a series of related distributions in exchange for part or all of a trust's interest in the entity;

(3) money received in total or partial liquidation of the entity; and

(4) money received from an entity that is a regulated investment company or a real estate investment trust if the money distributed is a capital gain dividend for federal income tax purposes.

(d) Money is received in partial liquidation:

EPTL

(1) to the extent that the entity, at or near the time of a distribution, indicates that it is a distribution in partial liquidation; or

(2) if the total amount of money and property received in a distribution or series of related distributions is greater than twenty percent of the entity's gross assets, as shown by the entity's year-end financial statements immediately preceding the initial receipt.

(e) Money is not received in partial liquidation, nor may it be taken into account under subparagraph (d)(2), to the extent that it does not exceed the amount of income tax that a trustee or beneficiary must pay on taxable income of the entity that distributes the money.

(f) A trustee may rely upon a statement made by an entity about the source or character of a distribution if the statement is made at or near the time of distribution by the entity's board of directors or other person or group of persons authorized to exercise powers to pay money or transfer property comparable to those of a corporation's board of directors.

History: Add, L 2001, ch 243, § 3, eff Jan 1, 2002.

§ 11-A-4.2. Distribution from trust or estate

A trustee shall allocate to income an amount received as a distribution of income from a trust or an estate in which the trust has an interest other than a purchased interest, and shall allocate to principal an amount received as a distribution of principal from such a trust or estate. If a trustee purchases an interest in a trust that is an investment entity, or a decedent or donor transfers an interest in such a trust to a trustee, 11-A-4.1 or 11-A-4.15 applies to a receipt from the trust.

History: Add, L 2001, ch 243, § 3, eff Jan 1, 2002.

§ 11-A-4.3. Business and other activities conducted by trustee

(a) If a trustee who conducts a business or other activity determines that it is in the best interest of all the beneficiaries to account separately for the business or activity instead of accounting for it as part of the trust's general accounting records, the trustee may maintain separate accounting records for its transactions, whether or not its assets are segregated from other trust assets.

(b) A trustee who accounts separately for a business or other activity may determine the extent to which its net cash receipts must be retained for working capital, the acquisition or replacement of fixed assets, and other reasonably foreseeable needs of the business or activity, and the extent to which the remaining net cash receipts are accounted for as principal or income in the trust's general accounting records. If a trustee sells assets of the business or other activity, other than in the ordinary course of the business or activity, the trustee shall account for the net amount received as principal in the trust's general accounting records to the extent the trustee determines that the amount received is no longer required in the conduct of the business.

(c) Activities for which a trustee may maintain separate accounting records include:

(1) retail, manufacturing, service, and other traditional business activities;

(2) farming;

(3) raising and selling livestock and other animals;

(4) management of rental properties;

(5) extraction of minerals and other natural resources;

(6) timber operations; and

(7) activities to which 11-A-4.14 applies.

> **History:** Add, L 2001, ch 243, § 3, eff Jan 1, 2002.

SUBPART 2   Receipts not Normally Apportioned

§ 11-A-4.4. Principal receipts

A trustee shall allocate to principal:

(1) to the extent not allocated to income under this article, assets received from a transferor during the transferor's lifetime, a decedent's estate, a trust with a terminating income interest, or a payer under a contract naming the trust or its trustee as beneficiary;

(2) money or other property received from the sale, exchange, liquidation, or change in form of a principal asset, including realized profit, subject to this part;

(3) amounts recovered from third parties to reimburse the trust because of disbursements described in subparagraph 11-A-5.2 (a)(7) or for other reasons to the extent not based on the loss of income;

(4) proceeds of property taken by eminent domain, but a separate award made for the loss of income with respect to an accounting period during which a current income beneficiary had a mandatory income interest is income;

(5) net income received in an accounting period during which there is no beneficiary to whom a trustee may or must distribute income; and

(6) other receipts as provided in subpart 3.

> **History:** Add, L 2001, ch 243, § 3, eff Jan 1, 2002.

§ 11-A-4.5. Rental property

To the extent that a trustee accounts for receipts from rental property pursuant to this section, the trustee shall allocate to income an amount received as rent of real or personal property, including an amount received for cancellation or renewal of a lease. An amount received as a refundable deposit, including a security deposit or a deposit that is to be applied as rent for future periods, must be added to principal and held subject to the terms of the lease and is not available for distribution to a beneficiary until the trustee's contractual obligations have been satisfied with respect to that amount.

> **History:** Add, L 2001, ch 243, § 3, eff Jan 1, 2002.

§ 11-A-4.6. Obligation to pay money

(a) An amount received as interest, whether determined at a fixed, variable, or floating rate, on an obligation to pay money to the trustee, including an amount received as consideration for prepaying principal, must be allocated to income without any provision for amortization of premium.

(b) A trustee shall allocate to principal an amount received from the sale, redemption, or other disposition of an obligation to pay money to the trustee. The increment in value of a bond or other obligation for the payment of money bearing no stated interest but payable or redeemable at maturity or at a future time at an amount in excess of the amount in consideration of which it was issued is income. If the income accrues pursuant to a fixed schedule of appreciation, such income is distributable to the beneficiary at the time the increment occurs, and the trustee may transfer the amount thereof from principal to income on each such date. Whenever unrealized increment is distributed as income but out of principal the principal shall be reimbursed from the income when realized.

(c) This section does not apply to an obligation to which 11-A-4.9, 11-A-4.10, 11-A-4.11, 11-A-4.12, 11-A-4.14, or 11-A-4.15 applies.

History: Add, L 2001, ch 243, § 3, eff Jan 1, 2002.

§ 11-A-4.7. Insurance policies and similar contracts

(a) Except as otherwise provided in paragraph (b), a trustee shall allocate to principal the proceeds of a life insurance policy or other contract in which the trust or its trustee is named as beneficiary, including a contract that insures the trust or its trustee against loss for damage to, destruction of, or loss of title to a trust asset. The trustee shall allocate dividends on an insurance policy to income if the premiums on the policy are paid from income, and to principal if the premiums are paid from principal.

(b) A trustee shall allocate to income proceeds of a contract that insures the trustee against loss of occupancy or other use by an income beneficiary, loss of income, or, subject to 11-A-4.3, loss of profits from a business.

(c) This section does not apply to a contract to which 11-A-4.9 applies.

History: Add, L 2001, ch 243, § 3, eff Jan 1, 2002.

SUBPART 3   Receipts Normally Apportioned

§ 11-A-4.8. Insubstantial allocations not required

If a trustee determines that an allocation between principal and income required by 11-A-4.9, 11-A-4.10, 11-A-4.11, 11-A-4.12, or 11-A-4.15 is insubstantial, the trustee may allocate the entire amount to principal unless one of the circumstances described in subparagraph 11-2.3 (b)(5) applies to the allocation. This power may be exercised by a cotrustee in the circumstances described in subparagraph 11-2.3 (b)(5) and may be released for the reasons and in the manner described in that section. An allocation is presumed to be insubstantial if:

(1) the amount of the allocation would increase or decrease net income in an accounting period, as determined before the allocation, by less than ten percent; or

(2) the value of the asset producing the receipt for which the allocation would be made is less than ten percent of the total value of the trust's assets at the beginning of the accounting period.

History: Add, L 2001, ch 243, § 3, eff Jan 1, 2002.

§ 11-A-4.9. Deferred compensation, annuities, and similar payments

(a) In this section, "payment" means a payment that a trustee may receive over a fixed number of years or during the life of one or more individuals because of services rendered or property transferred to the payer in exchange for future payments. The term includes a payment made in money or property from the payer's general assets or from a separate fund created by the payer, including a private or commercial annuity, an individual retirement account, and a pension, profit-sharing, stock-bonus, or stock-ownership plan.

(b) To the extent that a payment is characterized as interest or a dividend or a payment made in lieu of interest or a dividend, a trustee shall allocate it to income. The trustee shall allocate to principal the balance of the payment and any other payment received in the same accounting period that is not characterized as interest, a dividend, or an equivalent payment.

(c) If no part of a payment is characterized as interest, a dividend, or an equivalent payment, and all or part of the payment is required to be made, a trustee shall allocate to income ten percent of the part that is required to be made during the accounting period and the balance to principal. If no part of a payment is required to be made or the payment received is the entire amount to which the trustee is entitled, the trustee shall allocate the entire payment to principal. For purposes of this paragraph, a payment is not "required to be made" to the extent that it is made because the trustee exercises a right of withdrawal.

(d) If, to obtain an estate tax marital deduction for a trust, a trustee must allocate more of a payment to income than provided for by this section, the trustee shall allocate to income the additional amount necessary to obtain the marital deduction.

(e) This section does not apply to payments to which 11-A-4.10 applies.

History: Add, L 2001, ch 243, § 3, eff Jan 1, 2002.

§ 11-A-4.10. Liquidating asset

(a) In this section, "liquidating asset" means an asset whose value will diminish or terminate because the asset is expected to produce receipts for a period of limited duration. The term includes a leasehold, patent, copyright, royalty right, and right to receive payments during a period of more than one year under an arrangement that does not provide for the payment of interest on the unpaid balance. The term does not include a payment subject to 11-A-4.9, resources subject to 11-A-4.11, timber subject to 11-A-4.12, an activity subject to 11-A-4.14, an asset subject to 11-A-4.15, or any asset for which the trustee establishes a reserve for depreciation under 11-A-5.3.

(b) A trustee shall allocate to income ten percent of the receipts from a liquidating asset and the balance to principal.

History: Add, L 2001, ch 243, § 3, eff Jan 1, 2002.

§ 11-A-4.11. Minerals, water, and other natural resources

(a) To the extent that a trustee accounts for receipts from an interest in minerals or other natural resources pursuant to this section, the trustee shall allocate them as follows:

(1) If received as a bonus, delay rental or annual rent on a lease, a receipt of less than one thousand dollars must be allocated to income and a receipt of one thousand dollars or more must be allocated fifteen percent to principal and eighty-five percent to income;

(2) If received from a production payment, a receipt must be allocated to income if and to the extent that the agreement creating the production payment provides a factor for interest or its equivalent. The balance must be allocated to principal;

(3) If received as a royalty, shut-in-well payment, or take-or-pay payment, a receipt must be allocated fifteen percent to principal and eighty-five percent to income;

(4) If an amount is received from a working interest or any other interest not provided

for in subparagraph (a)(1), (2), or (3), a receipt must be allocated fifteen percent to principal and eighty-five percent to income.

(b) An amount received on account of an interest in water that is renewable must be allocated to income. If the water is not renewable, ninety percent of the amount must be allocated to principal and the balance to income.

(c) This article applies whether or not a decedent or donor was extracting minerals, water, or other natural resources before the interest became subject to the trust.

(d) If a trust exists on the effective date of this section, the trustee may allocate receipts from an interest in minerals, water, or other natural resources as provided in this section or in the manner used by the trustee before the effective date of this section. For every trust created after the effective date of this section, the trustee shall allocate receipts from an interest in minerals, water, or other natural resources as provided in this section. If and to the extent that the terms of a trust expressly provide for a different allocation of receipts or grants the trustee discretionary authority to determine the amount of the allocation, this section shall not apply to those receipts.

History: Add, L 2008, ch 408, § 12, eff Aug 5, 2008, which repealed the former section.

§ 11-A-4.12. Timber

(a) To the extent that a trustee accounts for receipts from the sale of timber and related products pursuant to this section, the trustee shall allocate the net receipts:

(1) to income to the extent that the amount of timber removed from the land does not exceed the rate of growth of the timber during the accounting periods in which a beneficiary has a mandatory income interest;

(2) to principal to the extent that the amount of timber removed from the land exceeds the rate of growth of the timber or the net receipts are from the sale of standing timber;

(3) to or between income and principal if the net receipts are from the lease of timberland or from a contract to cut timber from land owned by a trust, by determining the amount of timber removed from the land under the lease or contract and applying the rules in subparagraphs (1) and (2); or

(4) to principal to the extent that advance payments, bonuses, and other payments are not allocated pursuant to subparagraph (1), (2), or (3).

(b) In determining net receipts to be allocated pursuant to paragraph (a), a trustee shall deduct and transfer to principal a reasonable amount for depletion.

(c) This article applies whether or not a decedent or transferor was harvesting timber from the property before it became subject to the trust.

(d) If a trust owns an interest in timberland on the effective date of this article, the trustee may allocate net receipts from the sale of timber and related products as provided in this article or in the manner used by the trustee before the effective date of this article. If the trust acquires an interest in timberland after the effective date of this article, the trustee shall allocate net receipts from the sale of timber and related products as provided in this article.

History: Add, L 2001, ch 243, § 3, eff Jan 1, 2002.

§ 11-A-4.13. Property not productive of income

(a) If a gift tax or estate tax marital deduction is allowed for all or part of a trust whose assets consist substantially of property that does not provide the spouse with sufficient income from or use of the trust assets, and if the amounts that the trustee transfers from principal to income under paragraph 11-2.3 (b)(5) and distributes to the spouse from principal pursuant to the terms of the trust are insufficient to provide the spouse with the beneficial enjoyment required to obtain the marital deduction, the spouse may require the trustee to make property productive of income, convert property within a reasonable time, or exercise the power conferred by paragraph 11-2.3 (b)(5). The trustee may decide which action or combination of actions to take.

(b) In cases not governed by paragraph (a), proceeds from the sale or other disposition of an asset are principal without regard to the amount of income the asset produces during any accounting period.

History: Add, L 2001, ch 243, § 3, eff Jan 1, 2002.

§ 11-A-4.14. Derivatives and options

(a) In this section, "derivative" means a contract or financial instrument or a combination of contracts and financial instruments which gives a trust the right or obligation to participate in some or all changes in the price of a tangible or intangible asset or group of assets, or changes in a rate, an index of prices or rates, or other market indicator for an asset or a group of assets.

(b) To the extent that a trustee does not account under 11-A-4.3 for transactions in derivatives, the trustee shall allocate to principal receipts from and disbursements made in connection with those transactions.

(c) If a trustee grants an option to buy property from the trust, whether or not the trust owns the property when the option is granted, grants an option that permits another person to sell property to the trust, or acquires an option to buy property for the trust or an option to sell an asset owned by the trust, and the trustee or other owner of the asset is required to deliver the asset if the option is exercised, an amount received for granting the option must be allocated to principal. An amount paid to acquire the option must be paid from principal. A gain or loss realized upon the exercise of an option, including an option granted to a settlor of the trust for services rendered, must be allocated to principal.

History: Add, L 2001, ch 243, § 3, eff Jan 1, 2002.

§ 11-A-4.15. Asset-backed securities

(a) In this section, "asset-backed security" means an asset whose value is based upon the right it gives the owner to receive distributions from the proceeds of financial assets that provide collateral for the security. The term includes an asset that gives the owner the right to receive from the collateral financial assets only the interest or other current return or only the proceeds other than interest or current return. The term does not include an asset to which 11-A-4.1 or 11-A-4.9 applies.

(b) If a trust receives a payment from interest or other current return and from other proceeds of the collateral financial assets, the trustee shall allocate to income the portion of the payment which the payer identifies as being from interest or other current return and shall allocate the balance of the payment to principal.

EPTL

(c) If a trust receives one or more payments in exchange for the trust's entire interest in an asset-backed security in one accounting period, the trustee shall allocate the payments to principal. If a payment is one of a series of payments that will result in the liquidation of the trust's interest in the security over more than one accounting period, the trustee shall allocate ten percent of the payment to income and the balance to principal.

History: Add, L 2001, ch 243, § 3, eff Jan 1, 2002.

PART 5   Allocation of Disbursements During Administration of Trust

§ 11-A-5.1. Disbursements from income

A trustee shall make the following disbursements from income to the extent that they are not disbursements to which subparagraph 11-A-2.1 (2)(B) or (C) applies:

(1) one-third of the regular compensation of any person providing investment advisory or custodial services to the trustee;

(2) if the court shall find that any judicial proceeding primarily concerns income and that it is equitable to charge the expense of such proceeding, or a part thereof, to income, the court may direct that all or a specified part of the expense of such proceeding, including attorney's fees, shall be charged to income;

(3) all of the other ordinary expenses incurred in connection with the administration, management, or preservation of trust property and the distribution of income, including interest, ordinary repairs, regularly recurring taxes assessed against principal; and

(4) recurring premiums on insurance covering the loss of a principal asset or the loss of income from or use of the asset.

History: Add, L 2001, ch 243, § 3, eff Jan 1, 2002.

§ 11-A-5.2. Disbursements from principal

(a) A trustee shall make the following disbursements from principal:

(1) the remaining two-thirds of the disbursements described in paragraph 11-A-5.1 (1);

(2) all of the trustee's compensation calculated on principal as a fee for acceptance, distribution, or termination, and disbursements made to prepare property for sale;

(3) payments on the principal of a trust debt;

(4) except as provided in paragraph 11-A-5.1 (2), all expenses for accountings, judicial proceedings or other matters that involve both the income and remainder interests or that concern primarily principal, including a proceeding to construe the trust or to protect the trust or its property;

(5) premiums paid on a policy of insurance not described in paragraph 11-A-5.1 (4) of which the trust is the owner and beneficiary;

(6) estate, inheritance, and other transfer taxes, including penalties, apportioned to the trust; and

(7) disbursements related to environmental matters, including reclamation, assessing environmental conditions, remedying and removing environmental contamination, monitoring remedial activities and the release of substances, preventing future releases of

substances collecting amounts from persons liable or potentially liable for the costs of those activities, penalties imposed under environmental laws or regulations and other payments made to comply with those laws or regulations, statutory or common law claims by third parties, and defending claims based on environmental matters.

(b) If a principal asset is encumbered with an obligation that requires income from that asset to be paid directly to the creditor, the trustee shall transfer from principal to income an amount equal to the income paid to the creditor in reduction of the principal balance of the obligation.

History: Add, L 2001, ch 243, § 3, eff Jan 1, 2002.

§ 11-A-5.3. Transfers from income to principal for depreciation

(a) In this section, "depreciation" means a reduction in value due to wear, tear, decay, corrosion, or gradual obsolescence of a fixed asset having a useful life of more than one year.

(b) A trustee may transfer to principal a reasonable amount of the net cash receipts from a principal asset that is subject to depreciation, but may not transfer any amount for depreciation:

(1) of that portion of real property used or available for use by a beneficiary as a residence or of tangible personal property held or made available for the personal use or enjoyment of a beneficiary;

(2) during the administration of a decedent's estate; or

(3) under this section if the trustee is accounting under 11-A-4.3 for the business or activity in which the asset is used.

(c) An amount transferred to principal need not be held as a separate fund.

History: Add, L 2001, ch 243, § 3, eff Jan 1, 2002.

§ 11-A-5.4. Transfers from income to reimburse principal

(a) If a trustee makes or expects to make a principal disbursement described in this section, the trustee may transfer an appropriate amount from income to principal in one or more accounting periods to reimburse principal or to provide a reserve for future principal disbursements.

(b) Principal disbursements to which paragraph (a) applies include the following, but only to the extent that the trustee has not been and does not expect to be reimbursed by a third party:

(1) an amount chargeable to income but paid from principal because it is unusually large, including extraordinary repairs;

(2) a capital improvement to a principal asset, whether in the form of changes to an existing asset or the construction of a new asset, including special assessments;

(3) disbursements made to prepare property for rental, including tenant allowances, leasehold improvements, and broker's commissions;

(4) periodic payments on an obligation secured by a principal asset to the extent that the amount transferred from income to principal for depreciation is less than the periodic payments; and

(5) disbursements described in subparagraph 11-A-5.2 (a)(7).

(c) If the asset whose ownership gives rise to the disbursements becomes subject to a successive income interest after an income interest ends, a trustee may continue to transfer amounts from income to principal as provided in paragraph (a).

History: Add, L 2001, ch 243, § 3, eff Jan 1, 2002.

§ 11-A-5.5. Income taxes

(a) A tax required to be paid by a trustee based on receipts allocated to income must be paid from income.

(b) A tax required to be paid by a trustee based on receipts allocated to principal must be paid from principal, even if the tax is called an income tax by the taxing authority.

(c) A tax required to be paid by a trustee on the trust's share of an entity's taxable income must be paid proportionately:

(1) from income to the extent that receipts from the entity are allocated to income; and

(2) from principal to the extent that:

(A) receipts from the entity are allocated to principal; and

(B) the trust's share of the entity's taxable income exceeds the total receipts described in subparagraph (1) and clause (A).

(d) For purposes of this section, receipt allocated to principal or income must be reduced by the amount distributed to a beneficiary from principal or income for which the trust receives a deduction in calculating the tax.

History: Add, L 2001, ch 243, § 3, eff Jan 1, 2002.

§ 11-A-5.6. Adjustments between principal and income because of taxes

A fiduciary may make adjustments between principal and income to offset the shifting of economic interests or tax benefits between income beneficiaries and remainder beneficiaries which arise from:

(1) elections and decisions that the fiduciary makes from time to time regarding tax matters;

(2) an income tax or any other tax that is imposed upon the fiduciary or a beneficiary as a result of a transaction involving or a distribution from the estate or trust; or

(3) the ownership by an estate or trust of an interest in an entity whose taxable income, whether or not distributed, is includable in the taxable income of the estate, trust, or a beneficiary.

History: Add, L 2001, ch 243, § 3, eff Jan 1, 2002.

PART 6   Miscellaneous Provisions

§ 11-A-6.1. Uniformity of application and construction

In applying and construing this article, consideration must be given to the need to promote uniformity of the law with respect to its subject matter among states that enact it.

History: Add, L 2001, ch 243, § 3, eff Jan 1, 2002.

§ 11-A-6.2. Severability clause

If any provision of this article or its application to any person or circumstance is held invalid, the invalidity does not affect other provisions or applications of this article which can be given effect without the invalid provision or application, and to this end the provisions of this article are severable.

History: Add, L 2001, ch 243, § 3, eff Jan 1, 2002.

§ 11-A-6.3. Effective date

This article takes effect on January first, two thousand two.

History: Add, L 2001, ch 243, § 3, eff Jan 1, 2002.

§ 11-A-6.4. Application of article

Except as specifically provided in the trust instrument, the will, or in this article, this article shall apply to any receipt or expense received or incurred on or after its effective date by any trust or decedent's estate established before, on or after its effective date and whether the asset involved was acquired by the trustee before, on or after its effective date, except that this article shall not apply to a trust while any current beneficiary is interested in a unitrust amount pursuant to subparagraph 11-2.4(b)(1); but it does apply with respect to assets to which such a unitrust may become entitled but prior to their actual receipt into the unitrust.

History: Add, L 2001, ch 243, § 3, eff Jan 1, 2002; amd, L 2008, ch 2008, ch 408, § 13, eff Aug 5, 2008.

EPTL

ARTICLE 12
ACTIONS BY CREDITORS AND OTHER PERSONS AGAINST DISTRIBUTEES AND TESTAMENTARY BENEFICIARIES

SUMMARY OF ARTICLE

PART 1 Liability of Distributees and Testamentary Beneficiaries and Action Thereon

§ 12-1.1. Liability of distributees and testamentary beneficiaries

(a) Subject to the other provisions of this article, distributees and testamentary beneficiaries are liable, in an action, to the extent of the value of any property received by them as such, for the debts and reasonable funeral expenses of a decedent, the expenses of administering his estate and all taxes for which the estate is liable, which have not previously been recovered from the personal representative or from any other source described in paragraph (b).

(b) No liability may be imposed upon such distributees or testamentary beneficiaries, under paragraph (a), unless plaintiff establishes satisfactorily to the court that he cannot fully satisfy his claim:

(1) Because there is insufficient property of the estate available for such purpose in the hands of the personal representative;

(2) By action against persons prior in liability to the defendant, under paragraph (a) of 12-1.2, because such persons are not amenable to suit in this state, are insolvent or for any other reason cannot be made to answer for their liabilities; or

(3) By the enforcement, under 3-3.6, of any lien, security interest or other charge he holds against property of the decedent specifically disposed of by will or passing to a distributee, or against the proceeds of any policy of insurance on the life of the decedent payable to a named beneficiary.

> **History:** Add, L 1966, ch 952, eff Sept 1, 1967, with substance deriving from Decedent Est. Law §§ 170, 174, 176, 181, 182; amd, L 1967, ch 686, eff Sept 1, 1967; L 1968, ch 257, § 13, eff May 14, 1968.

§ 12-1.2. Order of liability; preferences

(a) Distributees and testamentary beneficiaries are liable, as provided in 12-1.1, in the following order:

(1) Distributees.

(2) Residuary beneficiaries.

(3) General beneficiaries. Demonstrative beneficiaries shall be treated as general beneficiaries, to the extent that the property or fund charged with a demonstrative disposition has adeemed.

(4) Specific beneficiaries. Demonstrative beneficiaries shall be treated as specific beneficiaries if the property or fund charged with any demonstrative disposition has not adeemed, to the extent of the value of such property or fund.

(5) A surviving spouse to whom a disposition has been made which qualifies for the estate tax marital deduction.

(b) The order of liability provided in paragraph (a) shall not apply to the liability for an estate or other death tax, under the law of this state or of any other jurisdiction, with respect to any property required to be included in the gross tax estate of a decedent under the provisions of any such law. The apportionment of such estate or other death tax, and the liability, under 12-1.1, of distributees and testamentary beneficiaries consequent to such apportionment are governed by the provisions of 2-1.8.

(c) The express or implied intention of the testator to prefer certain beneficiaries shall be effective to vary the order of liability prescribed by paragraph (a).

(d) If, in an action under this article, it is established to the satisfaction of the court that:

(1) The defendant is liable for the payment of two or more claims, preference in the payment of such claims must be given in the order prescribed by law for payment of the debts of the decedent and the obligations of his estate.

(2) An unsatisfied claim exists which is legally preferred to that of the plaintiff, the existence of such unsatisfied claim is a defense to the action if the aggregate value of the decedent's property passing to defendant and other persons in his order of liability does not exceed the amount of such unsatisfied claim; if in excess of the amount of such unsatisfied claim, the plaintiff may recover such ratable share of the excess as the amount of his claim bears to the claims of all persons in the same order of preference as his.

History: Add, L 1966, ch 952, eff Sept 1, 1967, with substance deriving from Decedent Est. Law §§ 175, 181, 182, 188, 189, 192; amd, L 1967, ch 686, eff Sept 1, 1967; L 1973, ch 663, eff Sept 1, 1973.

§ 12-1.3. Extent of liability; judgment debtor's right to indemnity and contribution

(a) Although subject, under paragraph (a) of 12-1.1, to a judgment in the full amount of the value of any property received by him, which may exceed his ratable obligation as described herein, the maximum liability to which a distributee or testamentary beneficiary is subject under this article is his ratable obligation, in the proportion that the value of the decedent's property passing to him bears to the value of all such property passing to distributees or beneficiaries, as the case may be, within the same order of liability as his under paragraph (a) of 12-1.2.

(b) Any person against whom a judgment is obtained under this article, upon payment thereof, is entitled:

(1) To be indemnified by any person prior to liability to him under paragraph (a) of 12-1.2, who remains liable under this article but against whom recovery was not available for a reason set forth in subparagraph (b)(2) of 12-1.1.

(2) To contribution, for any sum paid in excess of his ratable obligation as described in paragraph (a), from any person within the same order of liability as his under paragraph (a) of 12-1.2, but only to the extent that such person's ratable obligation is unpaid.

> **History:** Add, L 1966, ch 952, eff Sept 1, 1967, with substance deriving from Decedent Est. Law §§ 172, 173, 180, 185; amd, L 1967, ch 686, eff Sept 1, 1967.

PART 2   Rules Governing Action to Enforce Liability

§ 12-2.1. Action not impaired by failure of creditor or other person to present claim to representative as prescribed by law

The failure of the plaintiff to present his claim to the personal representative as prescribed by law shall not impair his right to maintain an action against distributees or testamentary beneficiaries under this article; but nothing contained herein shall extend the time limited for the commencement of an action to enforce plaintiff's claim.

> **History:** Add, L 1966, ch 952, eff Sept 1, 1967, with substance deriving from Decedent Est. Law § 170.

§ 12-2.2. Action may be joint or several; right to implead

An action may be brought against one or more of the persons subject to liability under this article. A person against whom an action.is brought may implead, pursuant to the provisions of CPLR article 10 governing impleader, any person who may be liable to him for indemnity or contribution under paragraph (b) of 12-1.3.

> **History:** Add, L 1966, ch 952, eff Sept 1, 1967, with substance deriving from Decedent Est. Law §§ 171, 179.

§ 12-2.3. Effect of application to surrogate to sell real property

If, during the pendency of an action to enforce a liability created by this article against a distributee or devisee of real property, a proceeding is pending or is subsequently commenced for the judicial settlement of the account of the personal representative, the action insofar as it affects any real property of the decedent shall be stayed until the accounting proceeding is concluded without an application for an order, under SCPA article 19, to dispose of real property of the decedent for the payment of debts, funeral or administration expenses having been made or, if made, without such an order having been granted. If such an order is granted, the action shall be dismissed as to the real property ordered to be disposed of and the plaintiff remitted to the enforcement of his rights against the proceeds of the real property held by the personal representative. Nothing contained herein precludes a person from asserting any right he may have under this article with respect to any other property of the decedent.

> **History:** Add, L 1966, ch 952, eff Sept 1, 1967, with substance deriving from Decedent Est. Law § 178; amd, L 1967, ch 686, § 141, eff Sept 1, 1967.

§ 12-2.4. Effect of judgment

A judgment recovered in an action brought under this article is preferred, as a lien on any property of the decedent passing to a defendant against whom the judgment was recovered, to a judgment obtained against such defendant on his personal obligation.

History: Add, L 1966, ch 952, eff Sept 1, 1967, with substance deriving from Decedent Est. Law § 185.

§ 12-2.5. Title of bona fide purchaser from distributee or testamentary beneficiary protected

The entry and filing of a judgment recovered against a distributee or testamentary beneficiary in an action brought under this article does not affect the rights of a prior purchaser, in good faith and for valuable consideration, from such distributee or beneficiary of any property of the decedent which would otherwise be subject to such judgment, unless, in the case of real property, a notice of pendency had been filed prior to such purchase. When the subsequent purchaser is protected, the judgment is enforceable against the judgment debtor to the extent of the net proceeds received by him upon the disposition of the property.

History: Add, L 1966, ch 952, eff Sept 1, 1967, with substance deriving from Decedent Est. Law §§ 186, 187.

ARTICLE 13
OTHER PROVISIONS AFFECTING ESTATES

SUMMARY OF ARTICLE

PART 1   Assets of Decedent's Estate

§ 13-1.1. Certain assets considered personal property

(a)* For purposes of the administration of an estate, the following assets of the decedent are personal property and together with every other species of personal property pass to the personal representative:

(1) Estates for years in real property, estates from year to year and estates which were held by the decedent for the life of another person.

(2) An estate for years in real property given to an executor for the payment of debts.

(3) Trade fixtures which may be removed without impairing the support of the structure to which they are annexed. All other fixtures annexed to land or structures do not pass to the personal representative, but descend to the distributees or pass to the devisees.

(4) Crops growing on the land of the decedent at the time of his death.

(5) Every kind of produce raised annually by labor or cultivation, except growing grass and fruit ungathered.

(6) Rent reserved to the decedent which had accrued at the time of his death.

(7) Debts secured by mortgages and moneys unpaid on contracts for the sale of lands.

History: Add, L 1966, ch 952, eff Sept 1, 1967, with substance deriving from SCA § 202; amd, L 1967, ch 686, Sept 1, 1967.

§ 13-1.2. Assets; debt due from executor to testator; effect of discharge by will

The designation by will of a person as executor does not operate as a discharge or testamentary disposition of any just claim which the testator had against him, but such claim must be included as an asset of the estate. The executor is liable for the value of the claim when it becomes due, and he must apply and distribute the same in the course of administering the estate. The discharge or disposition of such a claim or of a claim against any other person by will shall be treated as a specific disposition for purposes of 13-1.3. Nothing contained herein precludes an executor from raising any defense to a claim by the estate against him which would be available to any other person against whom the estate has a claim.

History: Add, L 1966, ch 952, eff Sept 1, 1967, with substance deriving from SCA § 203; amd, L 1967, ch 686, § 145, eff Sept 1, 1967; L 1986, ch 257, eff May 14, 1968 (Revisers' Note amended).

§ 13-1.3. Assets chargeable with payment of estate obligations; order in which assets appropriated; abatement

(a) All of the property of a decedent, and any income therefrom in the course of estate

---

* **Ed. Note**: There is no paragraph (b).

administration, is chargeable with the payment of:

(1) Administration and reasonable funeral expenses, debts of the decedent and any taxes for which the estate is liable.

(2) Unless such property is specifically disposed of, any general dispositions.

(b) In applying such property to the payment of any item specified in paragraph (a), no distinction shall be made between real and personal property.

(c) Whenever such property is insufficient to satisfy both the estate obligations described in subparagraph (a)(1) and all dispositions under the will, interests in the decedent's estate abate, for the purpose of paying such estate obligations, in the following order:

(1) Distributive shares in property not disposed of by will.

(2) Residuary dispositions.

(3) General dispositions. Demonstrative dispositions shall be treated as general dispositions to the extent that the property or fund charged with a demonstrative disposition has adeemed.

(4) Specific dispositions, and any income derived therefrom, ratably, in accordance with the value of the respective interests of the beneficiaries of such dispositions. For the purposes of this section, a demonstrative disposition shall be treated as a specific disposition if the property or fund charged with any demonstrative disposition has not adeemed, to the extent of the value of such property or fund.

(5) Any disposition to a surviving spouse which qualifies for the estate tax marital deduction.

(d) The order of abatement provided in paragraph (c) shall not apply to the payment of an estate or other death tax, under the law of this state or of any other jurisdiction, with respect to any property required to be included in the gross tax estate of a decedent under the provisions of any such law. The apportionment of such estate or other death tax, and the abatement of interests in the decedent's estate consequent to such apportionment, are governed by the provisions of 2-1.8.

(e) Whenever the provisions of this section are inconsistent with the express or implied intention of the testator to distinguish real property from personal property or to prefer certain beneficiaries under his will to others, the property of the estate shall be applied and the interests of beneficiaries under the will shall abate in such manner as is necessary to give effect to the intention of the testator.

(f) In the event that any property of the estate is applied to the payment of estate obligations in contravention of the order of abatement prescribed by this section, beneficiaries whose rights have been so impaired are entitled to be indemnified by other beneficiaries or distributees, as the case may be, so as to accomplish an abatement in accordance with the provisions of this section, and the amount of such indemnity shall constitute a charge on the interests of the beneficiaries or distributees liable therefor. Nothing in this paragraph shall relieve the personal representative of his liability to beneficiaries whose rights have been so impaired.

History: Add, L 1966, ch 952, eff Sept 1, 1967, with substance deriving from Decedent

Est. Law § 47-d; amd, L 1967, ch 686, eff Sept 1, 1967; L 1973, ch 663, eff Sept 1, 1973.

§ 13-1.4. Action in supreme court to compromise controversies between claimants to estate assets

An action may be maintained in the supreme court to compromise controversies between claimants to the property of an estate in accordance with and subject to the provisions of SCPA 2106.

> **History:** Add, L 1966, ch 952, eff Sept 1, 1967, with substance deriving from Decedent Est. Law § 19.

PART 2 Statute of Frauds Requirements

§ 13-2.1. Agreements involving a contract to establish a trust, to make a testamentary provision of any kind, and by a personal representative to answer for the debt or default of a decedent, required to be in writing

(a) Every agreement, promise or undertaking is unenforceable unless it or some note or memorandum thereof is in writing and subscribed by the party to be charged therewith, or by his lawful agent, if such agreement, promise or undertaking:

(1) Is a contract to establish a trust.

(2) Is a contract to make a testamentary provision of any kind.

(3) Is a promise by a personal representative to answer for the debt or default of his decedent.

(b) A contract to make a joint will, or not to revoke a joint will, if executed after the effective date of this paragraph can be established only by an express statement in the will that the instrument is a joint will and that the provisions thereof are intended to constitute a contract between the parties.

> **History:** Add, L 1966, ch 952, eff Sept 1, 1967, with substance deriving from Decedent Est. Law § 113 and GOL §§ 5-701(7), (8); amd, L 1983, ch 292, § 1, eff Sept 1, 1983.

§ 13-2.2. Transfers and mortgages of interest in decedent's estates required to be in writing and recorded

(a) Every conveyance, assignment or other transfer of, and every mortgage, security interest in or other charge upon the interest, situated in this state, of a person in the estate of a decedent, which is situated in this state, shall be in writing and acknowledged or proved in the manner prescribed by the laws of this state for the recording of a conveyance of real property. Any such instrument may be recorded as hereinafter provided, and if not so recorded, it is void against any subsequent purchaser or mortgagee of such interest, in good faith and for valuable consideration, whose conveyance or mortgage is first duly recorded. If such interest is entirely in the personal property of a decedent, the conveyance or mortgage may be recorded in the office of the surrogate granting letters on such decedent's estate or, if no such letters have been granted, in the office of the surrogate having jurisdiction to grant them. If a security interest, subject to article 9 of the uniform commercial code, is created by a transaction described in this paragraph, a financing statement shall be filed as required by section 9-501 of such code. If such interest is in both the personal and the real property of a decedent, the conveyance or mortgage may be recorded in the office of such surrogate and in the office of the recording official of the county in which the real property is situated and, if a security interest in personal property is created, a financing statement shall be filed in accordance with section 9-401* of the uniform commercial code. Such a conveyance or mortgage, when so recorded, shall be indexed under the name of the decedent in a book to be kept for that purpose by each recording officer.

(b) Such filing or recording shall not be notice of such conveyance, assignment or other transfer of, or mortgage, security interest or other charge upon the interest, situated in this state, of any person in the estate of a decedent so as to charge a personal representative of the estate with liability for payment to a beneficiary of the estate, unless and until he has received actual notice of any such transfer, mortgage or other charge.

(c) In case of a conflict between this section and article 9 of the uniform commercial code, this section controls.

> **History:** Add, L 1966, ch 952, eff Sept 1, 1967, with substance deriving from PPL § 32;
> amd, L 1967, ch 686, eff Sept 1, 1967; L 2001, ch 84, § 41, eff July 1, 2001.

§ 13-2.3. Powers of attorney in relation to decedents' estates required to be in writing and recorded

(a) Every power of attorney relating to an interest in a decedent's estate and every conveyance or assignment of an interest in an estate, or similar instrument, which contains an express or implied authorization or delegation of power to act thereunder shall be in writing and acknowledged or proved in the manner prescribed by the laws of this state for the recording of a conveyance of real property and, subject to the rules or order of the surrogate hereinafter provided, shall be recorded in the office of the surrogate granting letters on such decedent's estate or, if no such letters have been granted, in the office of the surrogate having jurisdiction to grant them. Such recording confers on the surrogate jurisdiction over the grantor of such power of attorney, the attorney in fact therein named and any other person acting thereunder. No attorney in fact named in any power of attorney or in such other instrument nor any person acting thereunder shall perform any act under such instrument unless it has been duly recorded.

(b) The surrogate may:

(1) Prescribe by rules of court or by order, consistent with the provisions of this section, the form, content, manner of execution and the conditions attached to the recording of every such instrument.

(2) Inquire into and determine the validity of every such instrument and require proof of the amount of compensation or expenses charged or to be charged by the attorney in fact and every person acting thereunder.

(3) In a proceeding authorized by SCPA 2112 or in any appropriate proceeding, fix and determine the validity and reasonableness of such compensation and expenses, whether or not the same have been previously fixed by agreement and whether or not fixed in the instrument so recorded, or otherwise.

(4) Prescribe regulations and exact a bond or undertaking to assure the payment of funds to the principal.

(c) Notwithstanding any provision contained therein, no power of attorney or other

---

* So in original. Should probably be 9-501.

EPTL

instrument which designates an agent to act for the principal shall be irrevocable, nor shall any agreement for the compensation of, or the payment of expenses by the attorney in fact or other person acting under the instrument create a power coupled with an interest in the subject matter of the agency or render the instrument irrevocable.

(d) Nothing contained herein shall authorize the practice of law by an attorney in fact or other person acting under an instrument described in this section, who is not an attorney duly licensed to practice law in the state of New York.

(e) Notwithstanding the provisions of any other statute or rule, no instrument containing a delegation of powers, assignment of interest, fee arrangement, or any instrument of like import created for the purpose of participating on behalf of an individual in any application seeking the recovery of property pursuant to section fourteen hundred sixteen of the abandoned property law or section thirteen hundred ten of the surrogate's court procedure act, nor any power of attorney, shall be accepted for filing or recording by the surrogate's court of a particular county unless the amount at issue is in excess of one thousand dollars or a fiduciary, as that term is defined by subdivision twenty-one of section one hundred three of the surrogate's court procedure act, has been appointed, or a proceeding for the appointment of a fiduciary is pending in such court. The provisions of paragraph (b) of this section shall apply to all instruments eligible for filing and recording hereunder.

> **History:** Add, L 1966, ch 952, eff Sept 1, 1967, with substance deriving from PPL § 32-a; amd, L 1968, ch 257, eff May 14, 1968; L 2014, ch 391, § 1, eff Sept 23, 2014.

PART 3   Miscellaneous Provisions

§ 13-3.1. Rights of payees in non-transferable United States savings bonds

Where any United States savings bond is payable to a designated person, whether as owner, co-owner or beneficiary, and such bond is not transferable, the right of such person to receive payment of the bond according to its terms, and the ownership of the money so received, shall not be impaired or defeated by any statute or rule of law governing the transfer of property by will, gift or intestacy, except as provided in section 5-1.1-A; provided further that nothing herein shall limit article 10 of the debtor and creditor law or 2-1.8.

> **History:** Add, L 1966, ch 952, eff Sept 1, 1967, with substance deriving from PPL § 24; amd, L 1992, ch 595, § 16, eff Sept 1, 1992.

§ 13-3.2. Rights of beneficiaries of pension, retirement, death benefit, stock bonus and profit-sharing plans, systems or trusts and of beneficiaries of annuities and supplemental insurance contracts

(a) If a person is entitled to receive (1) payment in money, securities or other property under a pension, retirement, death benefit, stock bonus or profit-sharing plan, system or trust or (2) money payable by an insurance company or a savings bank authorized to conduct the business of life insurance under an annuity or pure endowment contract or a policy of life, group life, industrial life or accident and health insurance, or if a contract made by such an insurer relating to the payment of proceeds or avails of such insurance designates a payee or beneficiary to receive such payment upon the death of the person making the designation or another, the rights of persons so entitled or designated and the ownership of money, securities or other property thereby received shall not be impaired or defeated by any statute or rule of law governing the transfer of property by will, gift or intestacy.

(b) This section does not limit article 10 of the debtor and creditor law, articles 10-C and

26 of the tax law, or 2-1.8, 5-1.1-A or 13-3.6.

(c) Paragraph (a) applies although a designation is revocable or subject to change by the person who makes it, and although the money, securities or other property receivable thereunder are not yet payable at the time the designation is made or are subject to withdrawal, collection or assignment by the person making the designation.

(d) A person entitled to receive payment includes:

(1) An employee or participant in a pension, retirement, death benefit, stock bonus or profit-sharing plan, system or trust.

(2) The owner or person purchasing an annuity, the person insured or the person effecting insurance, the person effecting a contract relating to payment of the proceeds or avails of a policy of insurance or an annuity or pure endowment contract.

(3) Any person entitled to receive payment by reason of a payee or beneficiary designation described in this section.

(e) A designation of a beneficiary or payee to receive payment upon death of the person making the designation or another must be made in writing and signed by the person making the designation and be:

(1) Agreed to by the employer or made in accordance with the rules prescribed for the pension, retirement, death benefit, stock bonus or profit-sharing plan, system or trust.

(2) Agreed to by the insurance company or the savings bank authorized to conduct the business of life insurance, as the case may be.

(f) This section applies to designations heretofore or hereafter made by persons who die on or after the date this section takes effect. This section does not invalidate any contract or designation which is valid without regard to this section.

> **History:** Added from Add, L 1966, ch 952, eff Sept 1, 1967, with substance deriving from PPL § 24-a; amd, L 1992, ch 595, § 17, eff Sept 1, 1992.

§ 13-3.3. Designation of trustee to receive proceeds of thrift, savings, pension, retirement, death benefit, stock bonus and profit-sharing plans, systems or trusts, of life, group life, industrial life or accident and health insurance policies and of annuity, endowment and supplemental insurance contracts, and taxation thereof

(a) The proceeds of thrift, savings, pension, retirement, death benefit, stock bonus and profit-sharing plans, systems or trusts, of life, group life, industrial life or accident and health insurance policies and of annuity, endowment and supplemental insurance contracts (hereinafter referred to as "proceeds") may be made payable to a trustee designated as beneficiary in the manner prescribed by this section and named as:

(1) Trustee under a trust agreement or declaration of trust in existence at the date of such designation, and identified in such designation, and such proceeds shall be paid to such trustee and be held and disposed of in accordance with the terms of such trust agreement or declaration of trust, including any amendments thereto, as they appear in writing on the date of the death of the insured, employee or participant. It shall not be necessary to the validity of any such trust agreement or declaration of trust that it have a trust corpus other than the right of the trustee as beneficiary to receive such proceeds.

(2) Trustee of a trust to be established by will, and upon qualification and issuance of letters of trusteeship such proceeds shall be payable to the trustee to be held and disposed of in accordance with the terms of such will as a testamentary trust. A designation which in substance names as such beneficiary the trustee under the will of the insured, employee or participant, shall be taken to refer to the will of such person actually admitted to probate, whether executed before or after the making of such designation.

(b) If no qualified trustee claims such proceeds from the insurer or other payor within eighteen months after the death of the insured, employee or participant, or if satisfactory evidence is furnished to the insurer or other payor within such period showing that there is or will be no trustee to receive such proceeds, such proceeds shall be paid by the insurer or other payor to the personal representative or assigns of the insured, employee or participant, unless otherwise provided by agreement with the insurer or other payor during the lifetime of the insured, employee or participant.

(c) Except to the extent otherwise provided by the trust agreement, declaration of trust or will, proceeds received by the trustee shall not be subject to the debts of the insured, employee or participant, to any greater extent than if such proceeds were payable to the beneficiaries named in the trust, and for all purposes including transfer or estate tax purposes they shall not be deemed payable to or for the benefit of the estate of the insured, employee or participant.

(d) Proceeds so held in trust may be commingled with any other assets which may properly become part of such trust.

(e) Nothing in this section shall effect the validity of any designation heretofore made of the trustee of any trust established under a trust agreement or declaration of trust or by will.

(f) This section shall be construed as declaring the law as it existed prior to its enactment and not as modifying it.

> **History:** Added from Decedent Est. Law § 47-f; repealed and replaced, L 1976, ch 626, eff July 21, 1976, broadening the scope of the trustee's authority to receive funds for the beneficiary.

§ 13-3.4. Payment or delivery of property to foreign fiduciaries

(a) Whenever any foreign fiduciary, by whatever title he is designated, of the property or estate of a non-domiciliary infant, incompetent or decedent is authorized, by the laws of the foreign jurisdiction where the infant or incompetent is domiciled or the decedent was domiciled, to receive any personal property in the possession or control of any person or fiduciary in this state, such person or fiduciary may pay or deliver the property to such foreign fiduciary without an order of the court, and the receipt and acquittance from such foreign fiduciary is a sufficient release and discharge of the person or fiduciary paying or delivering such property. For purposes of this section the status of a person as an "infant" or "incompetent" shall be determined by the law of his domicile.

(b) No person or fiduciary shall be released and discharged, as provided in paragraph (a), who:

(1) Has received written notice of the appointment, in this state, of a principal or ancillary representative of the property or estate, or of the existence of creditors, in this state, of such infant, incompetent or decedent.

(2) In the case of a testamentary disposition or a distributive share of a decedent's estate,

has reason to believe that such foreign fiduciary or the persons whom he represents would not have the benefit, use or control of such disposition or distributive share.

History: Add, L 1966, ch 952, eff Sept 1, 1967, with substance deriving from PPL § 425; amd, L 1974, ch 903, § 5, eff Sept 1, 1974, but shall not be construed to alter, change, affect, impair or defeat any rights, obligations or interests heretofore accrued, incurred or conferred prior to the effective date of the act.

§ 13-3.5. Action or proceeding by foreign personal or other legal representative

(a)* A personal or other legal representative of a non-domiciliary decedent, duly appointed or authorized by the law of any other state, territory or other jurisdiction of the United States where the decedent was domiciled, may sue in any court of this state in his capacity as personal or other legal representative in the same manner and under the same restrictions as a person residing outside of the state may sue, subject to the following:

(1) Within ten days after commencing such action or proceeding, the personal or other legal representative shall file in the office of the clerk of the court in which such action or proceeding is brought a copy of the letters issued to such representative, duly authenticated as prescribed by CPLR 4542. When the suit is brought by a foreign legal representative who is not a personal representative he shall file an affidavit setting forth the facts authorizing him to act for the decedent, and such other proof required by the court in which the action or proceeding is brought. The court may at any time, in its discretion, require the filing of authenticated copies of other papers or a bond or additional bond in an amount fixed by the court to protect the rights of interested residents of this state.

(2) Within ten days after commencing such action or proceeding, the personal or other legal representative shall file an affidavit stating that:

(A) Such decedent is not indebted to any resident of this state.

(B) More than six months have elapsed since the decedent's death and no petition for ancillary administration of the estate of such decedent has been filed in any court of this state. If made upon information and belief, such affidavit shall state the sources of affiant's information and the grounds for his belief.

(C) If it appears that the decedent is indebted to a resident of this state or that a petition for ancillary administration has been filed in this state, notice to the creditor or petitioner must be given in such manner as the court may direct.

(3) Failure to comply with the requirements of subparagraphs (1) and (2) shall stay the action or proceeding and the defendant's time to answer or move shall be extended for twenty days after plaintiff has served defendant with notice of compliance with such requirements.

(4) If ancillary letters testamentary or of administration are issued in this state after such action or proceeding is commenced, upon motion of the ancillary representative the court in which such action or proceeding is pending shall substitute the ancillary representative for the personal representative or other legal representative and shall hear and determine such action or proceeding as if the same were originally instituted by the ancillary

---

* **Ed. Note:** There is no paragraph (b).

representative, and the benefits of the judgment shall inure to the ancillary representative and be administered by him.

History: Add, L 1966, ch 952, eff Sept 1, 1967, with substance deriving from Decedent Est. Law § 160.

§ 13-3.6. Disaffirmance of fraudulent acts by personal representative and others

A fiduciary may, for the benefit of creditors or others interested in property held in trust, treat as void any act done, or disposition or agreement made in fraud of the rights of any creditor, including himself, interested in such property, and a person who fraudulently receives, takes or in any manner interferes with the property of a deceased or insolvent person is liable to such fiduciary or a receiver for such property or the value thereof, and for all damages caused by such act to the trust estate. A creditor of a deceased insolvent debtor, having a claim against the estate of such debtor exceeding in amount the sum of one hundred dollars may, without obtaining a judgment on such claim, in like manner, for the benefit of himself and other creditors interested in such property, treat as void any act done or disposition or agreement made in fraud of creditors or maintain an action to set aside such act, disposition or agreement. Such claim, if disputed, may be established in such action. The judgment in such action may provide for the sale of the property involved, when a disposition thereof is set aside, and for the payment of the proceeds thereof into the appropriate surrogate's court to be administered according to law.

History: Add, L 1966, ch 952, eff Sept 1, 1967, with substance deriving from PPL § 19; amd, L 1967, ch 686, § 150, eff Sept 1, 1967.

PART 4   Transfer-On-Death Security Registration

§ 13-4.1. Definitions

As used in this part unless the context otherwise requires:

(a) "Beneficiary form" means a registration of a security which indicates the present owner of the security and the intention of the owner regarding the person who will become the owner of the security upon the death of the owner.

(b) "Devisee" means any person to whom real property is transferred by will.

(c) "Distributee" means any person entitled to take or share in the property of a decedent under the statutes governing descent and distribution.

(d) "Legatee" means any person designated to receive a transfer by will of personal property.

(e) "Person" means an individual, a corporation, an organization or other legal entity.

(f) "Personal representative" includes executor, administrator, successor personal representative, preliminary executor, temporary administrator and persons who perform substantially the same function under the law governing their status.

(g) "Property" includes both real and personal property or any interest therein and means anything that may be the subject of ownership.

(h) "Register" including its derivatives, means to issue a certificate showing the ownership of a certificated security or, in the case of an uncertificated security, to initiate or transfer an account showing ownership of securities.

(i) "Registering entity" means a person who originates or transfers a security title by registration, and includes a broker or banking institution, as defined in paragraph (b) of subdivision three of section nine-f of the banking law maintaining security accounts for customers and a transfer agent or other person acting for or as an issuer of securities.

(j) "Security" means a share, participation or other interest in property, in a business or in an obligation of an enterprise or other issuer, and includes a certificated security, an uncertificated security and a security account.

(k) "Security account" means (i) a reinvestment account associated with a security, a securities account with a broker or banking institution, as defined in paragraph (b) of subdivision three of section nine-f of the banking law, a cash balance in a brokerage account or securities account, cash, interest, earnings, or dividends earned or declared on a security in an account, a reinvestment account or a brokerage account, whether or not credited to the account before the owner's death, or (ii) a cash balance or other property held for or due to the owner of a security as a replacement for or product of an account security, whether or not credited to the account before the owner's death.

(l) "State" includes any state of the United States, the District of Columbia, the Commonwealth of Puerto Rico, and any territory or possession subject to the legislative authority of the United States.

> **History:** Add, L 2005, ch 325, § 2, eff Jan 1, 2006; amd, L 2008 ch 420, § 1, eff Aug 5, 2008 and deemed eff on and after Jan 1, 2006.

§ 13-4.2. Registration in beneficiary form; sole or joint tenancy ownership

Only individuals whose registration of a security shows sole ownership by one individual or multiple ownership by two or more with right of survivorship, rather than as tenants in common, may obtain registration in beneficiary form. Multiple owners of a security registered in beneficiary form hold as joint tenants with right of survivorship, as tenants by the entireties or as owners of community property held in survivorship form, and not as tenants in common.

> **History:** Add, L 2005, ch 325, § 2, eff Jan 1, 2006.

§ 13-4.3. Applicable law

A security may be registered in beneficiary form if the form is authorized by this or a similar law of the state of organization of the issue or registering entity, the location of the registering entity's principal office, the office of its transfer agent or its office making the registration, or by this or a similar statute of the law of the state listed as the owner's address at the time of registration. A registration governed by the law of a jurisdiction in which this or a similar law is not in force or was not in force when a registration in beneficiary form was made is nevertheless presumed to be valid and authorized as a matter of contract law.

> **History:** Add, L 2005, ch 325, § 2, eff Jan 1, 2006.

§ 13-4.4. Origination of registration in beneficiary form

A security, whether evidenced by certificate or account, is registered in beneficiary form when the registration includes a designation of a beneficiary to take the ownership at the death of the owner or the deaths of all multiple owners.

> **History:** Add, L 2005, ch 325, § 2, eff Jan 1, 2006.

§ 13-4.5. Form of registration in beneficiary form

Registration in beneficiary form may be shown by the words "transfer on death" or the abbreviation "TOD", or by the words "pay on death" or the abbreviation "POD", after the name of the registered owner and before the name of the beneficiary.

History: Add, L 2005, ch 325, § 2, eff Jan 1, 2006.

§ 13-4.6. Effect of registration in beneficiary form

(a) The designation of a TOD beneficiary on a registration in beneficiary form has no effect on ownership until the owner's death. A registration of a security in beneficiary form may be canceled or changed at any time by the sole owner or all then surviving owners without the consent of the beneficiary.

(b) A registration in beneficiary form can be revoked or amended by an express direction in the owner's will which specifically refers to such registration.

History: Add, L 2005, ch 325, § 2, eff Jan 1, 2006.

§ 13-4.7. Ownership on death of owner

On death of a sole owner or the last to die of all multiple owners, ownership of securities registered in beneficiary form passes to the beneficiary or beneficiaries who survive all owners. On proof of death of all owners and compliance with any applicable requirements of the registering entity, a security registered in beneficiary form may be reregistered in the name of the beneficiary or beneficiaries who survived the death of all owners. Until division of the security after the death of all owners, multiple beneficiaries surviving the death of all owners hold their interests as tenants in common. If no beneficiary survives the death of all owners, the security belongs to the estate of the deceased sole owner or the estate of the last to die of all multiple owners.

History: Add, L 2005, ch 325, § 2, eff Jan 1, 2006.

§ 13-4.8. Protection of registering entity

(a) A registering entity is not required to offer or to accept a request for security registration in beneficiary form. If a registration in beneficiary form is offered by a registering entity, the owner requesting registration in beneficiary form assents to the protections given to the registering entity by this part.

(b) By accepting a request for registration of a security in beneficiary form, the registering entity agrees that the registration will be implemented on death of the deceased owner as provided in this part.

(c) A registering entity is discharged from all claims to a security by the estate, creditors, distributees, legatees or devisees of a deceased owner if it registers a transfer of the security in accordance with section 13-4.7 and does so in good faith reliance (i) on the registration, (ii) on this part, and (iii) on information provided to it by affidavit of the personal representative of the deceased owner, or by the surviving beneficiary or by the surviving beneficiary's representatives, or other information available to the registering entity. The protections of this part do not extend to a reregistration or payment made after a registering entity has received written notice from any claimant to any interest in the security objecting to implementation of a registration in beneficiary form. No other notice or other information available to the registering entity affects its right to protection under this part.

(d) The protection provided by this part to the registering entity of a security does not affect the rights of beneficiaries in disputes between themselves and other claimants to ownership of the security transferred or its value or proceeds.

EPTL

History: Add, L 2005, ch 325, § 2, eff Jan 1, 2006.

§ 13-4.9. Nontestamentary transfer on death

(a) A transfer on death resulting from a registration in beneficiary form is effective by reason of the contract regarding the registration between the owner and the registering entity and this part and is not testamentary.

(b) This part does not limit the rights of creditors of security owners against beneficiaries and other transferees under other laws of this state.

History: Add, L 2005, ch 325, § 2, eff Jan 1, 2006.

§ 13-4.10. Terms, conditions, and forms

(a) A registering entity offering to accept registrations in beneficiary form may establish the terms and conditions under which it will receive requests (i) for registrations in beneficiary form, and (ii) for implementation of registration in beneficiary form, including requests for cancellation of previously registered TOD beneficiary designations and requests for reregistration to effect a change of beneficiary. The terms and conditions so established may provide for proving death, avoiding or resolving any problems concerning fractional shares, designating primary and contingent beneficiaries, and substituting a named beneficiary's descendants to take in the place of the named beneficiary in the event of the beneficiary's death. Substitution may be indicated by appending to the name of the primary beneficiary in letters LDPS, standing for "lineal descendants per stirpes", or in letters LDPR, standing for "lineal descendants by representation". This designation substitutes a deceased beneficiary's descendants who survive the owner for a beneficiary who fails to so survive, the descendants to be identified and to share in accordance with the law of the beneficiary's domicile at the owner's death governing inheritance by descendants of an intestate. Other forms of identifying beneficiaries who are to take on one or more contingencies, and rules for providing proofs and assurances needed to satisfy reasonable concerns by registering entities regarding conditions and identities relevant to accurate implementation of registrations in beneficiary form, may be contained in a registering entity's terms and conditions.

(b) The following are illustrations of registrations in beneficiary form which a registering entity may authorize:

(1) Sole owner-sole beneficiary: John S Brown TOD (or POD) John S Brown Jr.

(2) Multiple owners-sole beneficiary: John S Brown Mary B Brown JT TEN TOD John S Brown Jr.

(3) Multiple owners-primary and secondary (substituted) beneficiaries: John S Brown Mary B Brown JT TEN TOD John S Brown Jr SUB BENE Peter Q Brown or John S Brown Mary B Brown JT TEN TOD John S Brown Jr LDPS.

History: Add, L 2005, ch 325, § 2, eff Jan 1, 2006.

§ 13-4.11. Rules of construction

(a) This part shall be liberally construed and applied to promote its underlying purposes and policy and to make uniform the laws with respect to the subject of this part among states enacting it.

(b) Unless displaced by the particular provisions of this part, the principles of law and equity supplement its provisions.

      History: Add, L 2005, ch 325, § 2, eff Jan 1, 2006.

§ 13-4.12. Application

    This part applies to registrations of securities in beneficiary form made before, on or after January first, two thousand six, by decedents dying on or after January first, two thousand six.

      History: Add, L 2005, ch 325, § 2; amd, L 2006, ch 11, § 1, eff March 21, 2006, deemed eff on and after Jan 1, 2006.

ARTICLE 13-A   ADMINISTRATION OF DIGITAL ASSETS

SUMMARY OF ARTICLE

PART 1   Definitions

§ 13-A-1. Definitions

In this article the following terms shall have the following meanings:

(a) "Account" means an arrangement under a terms-of-service agreement in which a custodian carries, maintains, processes, receives, or stores a digital asset of the user or provides goods or services to the user.

(b) "Agent" means a person granted authority to act as attorney-in-fact for the principal under a power of attorney and includes the original agent or any co-agent or successor agent.

(c) "Carries" means engages in the transmission of an electronic communication.

(d) "Catalogue of electronic communications" means information that identifies each person with which a user has had an electronic communication, the time and date of the communication, and the electronic address of the person.

(e) "Content of an electronic communication" means information concerning the substance or meaning of the communication which:

(1) has been sent or received by a user;

(2) is in electronic storage by a custodian providing an electronic-communication service to the public or is carried or maintained by a custodian providing a remote-computing service to the public; and

(3) is not readily accessible to the public.

(f) "Court" means the court in this state having jurisdiction in matters relating to the content of this article.

(g) "Custodian" means a person that carries, maintains, processes, receives, or stores a digital asset of a user.

(h) "Designated recipient" means a person chosen by a user using an online tool to administer digital assets of the user.

(i) "Digital asset" means an electronic record in which an individual has a right or interest. The term does not include an underlying asset or liability unless the asset or liability is itself an electronic record.

(j) "Electronic" means relating to technology having electrical, digital, magnetic, wireless, optical, electromagnetic, or similar capabilities.

(k) "Electronic communication" has the meaning set forth in 18 U.S.C. section 2510(12), as amended.

(l) "Electronic-communication service" means a custodian that provides to a user the ability to send or receive an electronic communication.

(m) "Fiduciary" includes an executor, preliminary executor, administrator, temporary administrator, voluntary administrator, personal representative, guardian, agent, or trustee. This term includes the successor to any fiduciary.

(n) "Guardian" means a person who has been appointed as a guardian by a court of this state pursuant to the surrogate's court procedure act or the mental hygiene law.

(o) "Information" means data, metadata, Internet protocol address, user login information, text, images, videos, sounds, codes, computer programs, software, databases, or similar intelligence of any nature.

(p) "Online tool" means an electronic service provided by a custodian that allows the user, in an agreement distinct from the terms-of-service agreement between the custodian and user, to provide directions for disclosure or nondisclosure of digital assets to a third person.

(q) "Person" means a natural person, corporation, business trust, estate, trust, partnership, limited liability company, association, joint venture, business or nonprofit entity, public corporation, government or governmental subdivision, agency, or instrumentality, or other legal or commercial entity, board and the state.

(r) "Power of attorney" means a record that grants an agent authority to act in the place of a principal.

(s) "Principal" means an individual who grants authority to an agent in a power of attorney.

(t) "Protective order" means an order appointing a guardian or another order related to management of a ward's property.

(u) "Record" means information that is inscribed on a tangible medium or that is stored in an electronic or other medium and is retrievable in perceivable form.

(v) "Remote-computing service" means a custodian that provides to a user computer-processing services or the storage of digital assets by means of an electronic communications system, as defined in 18 U.S.C. section 2510(14), as amended.

(w) "Terms-of-service agreement" means an agreement that controls the relationship between a user and a custodian.

(x) "Trustee" includes an original additional and successor trustee, and a co-trustee.

(y) "User" means a person that has an account with a custodian.

(z) "Ward" means an individual for whom a guardian has been appointed by a court of this state pursuant to the surrogate's court procedure act or the mental hygiene law. The term includes an individual for whom an application of guardianship is pending.

> **History:** Add, L 2016, ch 354, § 1, eff Sept 29, 2016.

PART 2   Applicability; Procedure for Disclosure; User Directions

§ 13-A-2.1. Applicability

(a) This article applies to:

(1) a fiduciary acting under a will, trust or power of attorney executed before, on, or after the effective date of this article;

(2) an executor, administrator or personal representative acting for a decedent who died before, on, or after the effective date of this article;

(3) a guardianship proceeding commenced before, on, or after the effective date of this article; and

(4) a trustee acting under a trust created before, on, or after the effective date of this article.

(b) This article applies to a custodian if the user resides in this state or resided in this state at the time of the user's death.

(c) This article does not apply to a digital asset of an employer used by an employee in the ordinary course of the employer's business.

> **History:** Add, L 2016, ch 354, § 1, eff Sept 29, 2016.

§ 13-A-2.2. User direction for disclosure of digital assets

(a) A user may use an online tool to direct the custodian to disclose to a designated recipient or not to disclose some or all of the user's digital assets, including the content of electronic communications. If the online tool allows the user to modify or delete a direction at all times, a direction regarding disclosure using an online tool overrides a contrary direction by the user in a will, trust, power of attorney, or other record.

(b) If a user has not used an online tool to give direction under paragraph (a) or if the custodian has not provided an online tool, the user may allow or prohibit in a will, trust, power of attorney, or other record, disclosure to a fiduciary of some or all of the user's digital assets, including the content of electronic communications sent or received by the user.

(c) A user's direction under paragraph (a) or (b) overrides a contrary provision in a terms-of-service agreement that does not require the user to act affirmatively and distinctly from the user's assent to the terms of service.

History: Add, L 2016, ch 354, § 1, eff Sept 29, 2016.

§ 13-A-2.3. Terms-of-service agreement

(a) This article does not change or impair a right of a custodian or a user under a terms-of-service agreement to access and use digital assets of the user.

(b) This article does not give a fiduciary or a designated recipient any new or expanded rights other than those held by the user for whom, or for whose estate, the fiduciary or designated recipient acts or represents.

(c) A fiduciary's or designated recipient's access to digital assets may be modified or eliminated by a user, by federal law, or by a terms-of-service agreement if the user has not provided direction under section 13-A- 2.2.

History: Add, L 2016, ch 354, § 1, eff Sept 29, 2016.

§ 13-A-2.4. Procedure for disclosing digital assets

(a) When disclosing digital assets of a user under this article, the custodian may at its sole discretion:

(1) grant a fiduciary or designated recipient full access to the user's account;

(2) grant a fiduciary or designated recipient partial access to the user's account sufficient to perform the tasks with which the fiduciary or designated recipient is charged; or

(3) provide a fiduciary or designated recipient a copy in a record of any digital asset that, on the date the custodian received the request for disclosure, the user could have accessed if the user were alive and had full capacity and access to the account.

(b) A custodian may assess a reasonable administrative charge for the cost of disclosing digital assets under this article.

(c) A custodian need not disclose under this article a digital asset deleted by a user.

(d) If a user directs or a fiduciary requests a custodian to disclose under this article some, but not all, of the user's digital assets, the custodian need not disclose the assets if segregation of the assets would impose an undue burden on the custodian. If the custodian believes the direction or request imposes an undue burden, the custodian or fiduciary may seek an order from the court to disclose:

(1) a subset limited by date of the user's digital assets;

(2) all of the user's digital assets to the fiduciary or designated recipient;

(3) none of the user's digital assets; or

(4) all of the user's digital assets to the court for review in camera.

History: Add, L 2016, ch 354, § 1, eff Sept 29, 2016.

PART 3   Disclosure of Digital Assets to Fiduciary

§ 13-A-3.1. Disclosure of content of electronic communications of deceased user

If a deceased user consented or a court directs disclosure of the contents of electronic communications of the user, the custodian shall disclose to the executor, administrator or personal representative of the estate of the user the content of an electronic communication sent or received by the user if the executor, administrator or representative gives the custodian:

(a) a written request for disclosure in physical or electronic form;

(b) a copy of the death certificate of the user;

(c) a certified copy of the letter of appointment of the executor, administrator, or personal representative or a small-estate affidavit or court order;

(d) unless the user provided direction using an online tool, a copy of the user's will, trust, or other record evidencing the user's consent to disclosure of the content of electronic communications; and

(e) if requested by the custodian:

(1) a number, username, address, or other unique subscriber or account identifier assigned by the custodian to identify the user's account;

(2) evidence linking the account to the user; or

(3) a finding by the court that:

(A) the user had a specific account with the custodian, identifiable by the information specified in subparagraph (1);

(B) disclosure of the content of electronic communications of the user would not violate 18 U.S.C. section 2701 et seq., as amended, 47 U.S.C. section 222, as amended, or other applicable law;

(C) unless the user provided direction using an online tool, the user consented to disclosure of the content of electronic communications; or

(D) disclosure of the content of electronic communications of the user is reasonably necessary for administration of the estate.

History: Add, L 2016, ch 354, § 1, eff Sept 29, 2016.

§ 13-A-3.2. Disclosure of other digital assets of deceased user

Unless the user prohibited disclosure of digital assets or the court directs otherwise, a custodian shall disclose to the executor, administrator or personal representative of the estate of a deceased user a catalogue of electronic communications sent or received by the user and digital assets, other than the content of electronic communications, of the user, if the executor, administrator or personal representative gives the custodian:

(a) a written request for disclosure in physical or electronic form;

(b) a copy of the death certificate of the user;

(c) a certified copy of the letter of appointment of the executor, administrator, or personal representative or a small-estate affidavit or court order; and

(d) if requested by the custodian:

(1) a number, username, address, or other unique subscriber or account identifier assigned by the custodian to identify the user's account;

(2) evidence linking the account to the user;

(3) an affidavit stating that disclosure of the user's digital assets is reasonably necessary for administration of the estate; or

(4) a finding by the court that:

(A) the user had a specific account with the custodian, identifiable by the information specified in subparagraph (1); or

(B) disclosure of the user's digital assets is reasonably necessary for administration of the estate.

History: Add, L 2016, ch 354, § 1, eff Sept 29, 2016.

§ 13-A-3.3. Disclosure of content of electronic communications of principal

To the extent a power of attorney expressly grants an agent authority over the content of electronic communications sent or received by the principal and unless directed otherwise by the principal or the court, a custodian shall disclose to the agent the content if the agent gives the custodian:

(a) a written request for disclosure in physical or electronic form;

(b) a copy of the power of attorney expressly granting the agent authority over the content of electronic communications of the principal;

(c) an affidavit in which the affiant attests that the copy is an accurate copy of the original power of attorney and that, to the best of the affiant's knowledge, the power remains in effect; and

(d) if requested by the custodian:

(1) a number, username, address, or other unique subscriber or account identifier assigned by the custodian to identify the principal's account; or

(2) evidence linking the account to the principal.

History: Add, L 2016, ch 354, § 1, eff Sept 29, 2016.

§ 13-A-3.4. Disclosure of other digital assets of principal

Unless otherwise ordered by the court, directed by the principal, or provided by a power of attorney, a custodian shall disclose to an agent with specific authority over digital assets or general authority to act on behalf of a principal a catalogue of electronic communications sent or received by the principal and digital assets, other than the content of electronic communications, of the principal if the agent gives the custodian:

(a) a written request for disclosure in physical or electronic form;

(b) a copy of the power of attorney that gives the agent specific authority over digital assets or general authority to act on behalf of the principal;

(c) an affidavit in which the affiant attests that the copy is an accurate copy of the original power of attorney and that, to the best of the affiant's knowledge, the power remains in effect; and

(d) if requested by the custodian:

(1) a number, username, address, or other unique subscriber or account identifier assigned by the custodian to identify the principal's account; or

(2) evidence linking the account to the principal.

History: Add, L 2016, ch 354, § 1, eff Sept 29, 2016.

§ 13-A-3.5. Disclosure of digital assets held in trust when trustee is original user

Unless otherwise ordered by the court or provided in a trust, a custodian shall disclose to a trustee that is an original user of an account any digital asset of the account held in trust, including a catalogue of electronic communications of the trustee and the content of electronic communications.

History: Add, L 2016, ch 354, § 1, eff Sept 29, 2016.

§ 13-A-3.6. Disclosure of contents of electronic communications held in trust when trustee not original user

Unless otherwise ordered by the court, directed by the user, or provided in a trust, a custodian shall disclose to a trustee that is not an original user of an account the content of an electronic communication sent or received by an original or successor user and carried, maintained, processed, received, or stored by the custodian in the account of the trust if the trustee gives the custodian:

(a) a written request for disclosure in physical or electronic form;

(b) a copy of the trust instrument that includes consent to disclosure of the content of electronic communications to the trustee;

(c) a certification by the trustee, under penalty of perjury, that the trust exists and the trustee is a currently acting trustee of the trust; and

(d) if requested by the custodian:

(1) a number, username, address, or other unique subscriber or account identifier assigned by the custodian to identify the trust's account; or

(2) evidence linking the account to the trust.

History: Add, L 2016, ch 354, § 1, eff Sept 29, 2016.

§ 13-A-3.7. Disclosure of other digital assets held in trust when trustee not original user

Unless otherwise ordered by the court, directed by the user, or provided in a trust, a custodian shall disclose, to a trustee that is not an original user of an account, a catalogue of electronic communications sent or received by an original or successor user and stored, carried, or maintained by the custodian in an account of the trust and any digital assets, other than the content of electronic communications, in which the trust has a right or interest if the trustee gives the custodian:

(a) a written request for disclosure in physical or electronic form;

(b) a copy of the trust instrument;

(c) a certification by the trustee, under penalty of perjury, that the trust exists and the trustee is a currently acting trustee of the trust; and

(d) if requested by the custodian:

(1) a number, username, address, or other unique subscriber or account identifier assigned by the custodian to identify the trust's account; or

(2) evidence linking the account to the trust.

History: Add, L 2016, ch 354, § 1, eff Sept 29, 2016.

§ 13-A-3.8. Disclosure of digital assets to guardian of ward

(a) After an opportunity for a hearing concerning the appointment or authority of a guardian, the court may grant a guardian access to the digital assets of a ward.

(b) Unless otherwise ordered by the court or directed by the user, a custodian shall disclose to a guardian the catalogue of electronic communications sent or received by a ward and any digital assets, other than the content of electronic communications, in which the ward has a right or interest if the ward gives the custodian:

(1) a written request for disclosure in physical or electronic form;

(2) a certified copy of the court order that gives the guardian authority over the digital assets of the ward; and

(3) if requested by the custodian:

(A) a number, username, address, or other unique subscriber or account identifier assigned by the custodian to identify the account of the ward; or

(B) evidence linking the account to the ward.

(c) A guardian with general authority to manage the assets of a ward may request a custodian of the digital assets of the ward to suspend or terminate an account of the ward for good cause. A request made under this section must be accompanied by a certified copy of the court order giving the guardian authority over the ward's property.

History: Add, L 2016, ch 354, § 1, eff Sept 29, 2016.

PART 4   Fiduciary Duty and Authority, Compliance and Immunity

§ 13-A-4.1. Fiduciary duty and authority

(a) The legal duties imposed on a fiduciary charged with managing tangible property apply to the management of digital assets, including:

(1) the duty of care;

(2) the duty of loyalty; and

(3) the duty of confidentiality.

(b) A fiduciary's or designated recipient's authority with respect to a digital asset of a user:

(1) except as otherwise provided in section 13-A-2.2, is subject to the applicable terms of service;

(2) is subject to other applicable law, including copyright law;

(3) in the case of a fiduciary, is limited by the scope of the fiduciary's duties; and

(4) may not be used to impersonate the user.

(c) A fiduciary with authority over the property of a decedent, ward, principal, or settlor has the right to access any digital asset in which the decedent, ward, principal, or settlor had a right or interest and hat is not held by a custodian or subject to a terms-of-service agreement.

(d) A fiduciary acting within the scope of the fiduciary's duties is an authorized user of the property of the decedent, ward, principal, or settlor for the purpose of applicable computer-fraud and unauthorized-computer- access laws, including this state's law on unauthorized computer access.

(e) A fiduciary with authority over the tangible, personal property of a decedent, ward, principal, or settlor;

(1) has the right to access the property and any digital asset stored in it; and

(2) is an authorized user for the purpose of computer-fraud and unauthorized-computer-access laws, including this state's law on unauthorized computer access.

(f) A custodian may disclose information in an account to a fiduciary of the user when the information is required to terminate an account used to access digital assets licensed to the user.

(g) A fiduciary of a user may request a custodian to terminate the user's account. A request for termination must be in writing, in either physical or electronic form, and accompanied by:

(1) if the user is deceased, a copy of the death certificate of the user;

(2) a certified copy of the letter of appointment of the executor, administrator, or personal representative or a small-estate affidavit or court order, power of attorney, or trust giving the fiduciary authority over the account; and

(3) if requested by the custodian:

(A) a number, username, address, or other unique subscriber or account identifier assigned by the custodian to identify the user's account;

(B) evidence linking the account to the user; or

(C) a finding by the court that the user had a specific account with the custodian, identifiable by the information specified in item (A).

History: Add, L 2016, ch 354, § 1, eff Sept 29, 2016.

§ 13-A-4.2. Custodian compliance and immunity

(a) Not later than sixty days after receipt of the information required under sections 13-A-3.1 through 13- A-4.1, a custodian shall comply with a request under this article from a fiduciary or designated recipient to disclose digital assets or terminate an account. If the custodian fails to comply, the fiduciary or designated recipient may apply to the court for an order directing compliance.

(b) An order under paragraph (a) directing compliance must contain a finding that compliance is not in violation of 18 U.S.C. section 2702, as amended.

(c) A custodian may notify the user that a request for disclosure or to terminate an account was made under this article.

(d) A custodian may deny a request under this article from a fiduciary or designated recipient for disclosure of digital assets or to terminate an account if the custodian is aware of any lawful access to the account following the receipt of the fiduciary's request.

(e) This article does not limit a custodian's ability to obtain or require a fiduciary or designated recipient requesting disclosure or termination under this article to obtain a court order which:

(1) specifies that an account belongs to the ward or principal;

(2) specifies that there is sufficient consent from the ward or principal to support the requested disclosure; and

(3) contains a finding required by law other than this article.

(f) A custodian and its officers, employees, and agents are immune from liability for an act or omission done in good faith in compliance with this article.

History: Add, L 2016, ch 354, § 1, eff Sept 29, 2016.

PART 5   Miscellaneous Provisions

§ 13-A-5.1. Relation to electronic signature in global and national commerce act

This article modifies, limits, or supersedes the Electronic Signatures in Global and National Commerce Act, 15 U.S.C. section 7001 et seq., but does not modify, limit, or supersede section 101(c) of such act, 15 U.S.C. section 7001(c), or authorize electronic delivery of any of the notices described in section 103(b) of such act, 15 U.S.C. section 7003(b).

History: Add, L 2016, ch 354, § 1, eff Sept 29, 2016.

§ 13-A-5.2. Severability

If any provision of this article or its application to any person or circumstance is held invalid, the invalidity does not affect other provisions or applications of this article which can be given effect without the invalid provision or application, and to this end the provisions of this article are severable.

History: Add, L 2016, ch 354, § 1, eff Sept 29, 2016.

ARTICLE 14
REPEALER; DERIVATION AND DISTRIBUTION TABLES; EFFECTIVE DATE*

SUMMARY OF ARTICLE

PART 1   Laws Repealed by This Chapter

§ 14-1.1. Schedule of laws repealed; effect of repeal

(a) The following are the laws repealed in their entirety, except as specifically noted:

Decedent Estate Law	All
General Obligations Law	Article 5, section 5-701, subdivisions 4, 7 and 8
Personal Property Law	Article 2—All Article 2-A—All Article 3—sections 32, 32-a and 36 Article 8-A—All Article 10-A—All
Real Property Law	Article 3—All Article 4—All, except sections 119, 120, 120-a, 121, 122, 122-a, 123 Article 5—All

(b) Notwithstanding the repeal of the laws prescribed by paragraph (a):

(1) Whenever any repealed statute, that has, in substance, been carried over into this chapter, contained a provision which made such statute, or a provision thereof, inapplicable to the estates of persons dying, or to instruments executed, prior to its effective date, such applicability provision is incorporated into this chapter and made part of the specified section thereof to which it relates, as if expressly included therein, to wit:

(A) Decedent Estate Law

(i) Section 26—as set forth in Laws of 1955, c. 225, § 2. . . . 11-1.1 (b)(5)(F)

---

* Amd, L 1992 ch 595, eff Sept 1, 1992

EPTL

(ii) Section 28—as set forth in Laws of 1931, c. 562, § 10. . . 5-3.4

(iii) Section 35—as set forth in Laws of 1931, c. 562, § 10. . . 5-1.3

(iv) Section 36—to the extent that it was made applicable only to wills of persons adjudicated incompetent on or after March 1, 1965. . . 3-4.4

(v) Section 46—as set forth in Laws of 1931, c. 562, § 10. . . 3-3.8

(vi) Section 47-a—to the extent that it was made applicable only to wills of persons dying after April 30, 1921. . . 2-1.2

(vii) Section 47-b—to the extent that it was made applicable only to wills of persons dying after May 12, 1936. . . 3-3.9

(viii) Section 47-c—to the extent that it has been judicially construed to apply only to wills and inter vivos instruments executed after March 28, 1938. . . 2-1.1

(ix) Section 47-d—to the extent that it was made applicable only to wills executed after August 31, 1947. . . 13-1.3(a)(2)

(x) Subdivision 7 of section 47-e. . . 3-1.3(b)

(xi) Section 47-g—to the extent that it was made applicable only to wills of persons living on or born subsequent to June 1, 1966. . . 3-3.7

(xii) Section 49—to the extent that it was made applicable only to wills of persons dying, or inter vivos instruments executed, on or after March 1, 1964, and to inter vivos instruments executed prior to such date which are, on such date, subject to the creator's power to revoke or amend. . . 2-1.3

(xiii) Section 83—as set forth in the Laws of 1959, c. 689 and the Laws of 1963, c. 712, § 2. . . 4-1.1

(xiv) Section 83-a—to the extent that it was made applicable to the estates of persons dying on or after March 1, 1964. . . 4-1.2

(xv) Subdivision 6 of section 89. . . 2-1.6

(xvi) Subdivision 8 of section 124. . . 2-1.8

(xvii) Section 125—to the extent that it was made applicable only to wills of persons dying after May 2, 1936; and as affected by the Laws of 1966, c. 16, § 2, which removed the limitation that the testator could not authorize a fiduciary to name a successor to serve without a bond, and made such change effective on March 8, 1966 and applicable to letters issued after such date to executors and testamentary trustees qualifying under wills of decedents dying after May second, nineteen hundred thirty-six. . . 11-1.7

(B) Personal Property Law

(i) Section 11—as set forth in Laws of 1960, c. 448, § 4. . . 9-1.1

(ii) Section 11-a—as set forth in Laws of 1960, c. 452, § 5. . . 9-1.2

(iii) Section 11-b—as set forth in Laws of 1960, c. 452, § 5. . . 9-1.3

(iv) Section 12—as set forth in Laws of 1953, c. 715, § 3 and Laws of 1961, c. 866, § 7. . . 8-1.1

(v) Section 13-e—as set forth in Laws of 1965, c. 401, § 2. . . 9-1.8

(vi) Subdivision 2 of section 15. . . 7-1.5

(vii) Section 16—as set forth in Laws of 1961, c. 866, § 7. . . 9-2.1

(viii) Section 16-a—as set forth in Laws of 1961, c. 866, § 7. . . 8-1.7

(ix) Section 17—as set forth in Laws of 1959, c. 453, § 4. . . 9-2.2

(x) Section 21—as set forth in Laws of 1965, c. 824. . . 11-2.2(a)(7)

(C) Real Property Law

(i) Section 42—as set forth in Laws of 1958, c. 153, § 2, as amended by Laws of 1959, c. 456, § 3 and Laws of 1960, c. 448, § 4. . . 9-1.1(a)

(ii) Section 42-b—as set forth in Laws of 1960, c. 452, § 5. . . 9-1.2

(iii) Section 42-c—as set forth in Laws of 1960, c. 452, § 5. . . 9-1.3

(iv) Section 59—as set forth in Laws of 1962, c. 146, § 3. . . 6-5.1

(v) Section 61—as set forth in Laws of 1959, c. 454, § 4 and Laws of 1961, c. 866, § 7. . . 9-2.1

(vi) Section 61-a—as set forth in Laws of 1959, c. 454, § 4 and Laws of 1961, c. 866, § 7. . . 8-1.7

(vii) Section 62—as set forth in Laws of 1959, c. 454, § 4. . . 9-2.2

(viii) Section 110—as set forth in Laws of 1953, c. 131, § 2. . . 7-1.8

(ix) Section 113—as set forth in Laws of 1953, c. 715, § 3 and Laws of 1961, c. 866, § 7. . . 8-1.1

(2) Any repealed statute shall continue to apply to any instrument to which it would have applied had it not been repealed, whenever, under 1-1.5, such instrument is not subject to the provisions of this chapter either because its creator was not living on the effective date of this chapter or because rights accrued under such instrument which cannot be impaired or defeated by this chapter.

(3) A reference in any statute of this state to any repealed law or a provision thereof shall be treated as a reference to the corresponding statute or a provision thereof, if any, of this chapter.

History: Add, L 1966, ch 952, eff Sept 1, 1967; amd, L 1967, ch 686, § 151, eff Sept 1, 1967; L 1968, ch 257, eff May 14, 1968; L 1970, ch 382, eff May 1, 1970.

PART 2   Derivation and Distribution Tables

§ 14-2.1.   Derivation of the estates, powers and trusts law from other laws

EPTL	DEL	GENOB	PPL	RPL	SCA

EPTL	DEL	GENOB	PPL	RPL	SCA
1-1.1					
1-1.2					
1-1.3					
1-1.4			270-a		
1-1.5					
1-2.1					
1-2.2					
1-2.3					
1-2.4					
1-2.5	81, 134				
1-2.6					
1-2.7					
1-2.8					
1-2.9					
1-2.10					
1-2.11	47-a, 83(9)				
1-2.12					
1-2.13					
1-2.14	47-a, 83(10)				
1-2.15					
1-2.16					
1-2.17					
11-2.19	2				
2-1.1	47-c				
2-1.2	47-a				
2-1.3	49				
2-1.4			240(1)		
2-1.5	85, 86	2-1.6	89		
2-1.7	80-a				
2-1.8	124				
2-1.9			17-f		
3-1.1	15				
3-1.2	11				
3-1.3	12, 47-e				
3-2.1	21, 22				
3-2.2	16				
3-3.1	14				
3-3.2	27				

EPTL	DEL	GENOB	PPL	RPL	SCA
3-3.3	29				
3-3.4					
3-3.5	126				
3-3.6	20, 38				
3-3.7	47-g				
3-3.8	46				
3-3.9	47-b				
3-4.1	34				
3-4.2	37				
3-4.3	39, 40				
3-4.4	36				
3-4.5	20				
3-4.6	41				
3-5.1	22-a, 23, 24, 47				
4-1.1	83				
4-1.2	83-a				
4-1.3	87-a				
4-1.4	87				
5-1.1	18, 18-a; b				
5-1.2	50, 87				
5-1.3	35				
5-1.4					
5-3.1					200
5-3.2	26				
5-3.3	17				
5-3.4	28				
5-4.1	130				
5-4.2	131				
5-4.3	132				
5-4.4	133				
5-4.5	135				
6-1.1				30	
6-1.2				32	
6-1.3				34	
6-2.1				65	
6-2.2	84			66	
6-3.1				35	
6-3.2				36	

EPTL

EPTL	DEL	GENOB	PPL	RPL	SCA
6-3.3				50	
6-3.4				64	
6-4.1				35	
6-4.2				37	
6-4.3				38	
6-4.4				39	
6-4.5				59-a	
6-4.6				50-b	
6-4.7				40	
6-4.8				40-a	
6-4.9				40-b	
6-4.10				40-c	
6-5.1				59	
6-5.2				41	
6-5.3				51	
6-5.4				66-a	
6-5.5				52	
6-5.6				48	
6-5.7				56	
6-5.8				54	
6-5.9					
6-5.10				57	
6-5.11				58	
6-5.12				60	
7-1.1				92	
7-1.2				93	
7-1.3				94	
7-1.4				96	
7-1.5			15	103	
7-1.6			15-a	103-a	
7-1.7				102	
7-1.8				110	
7-1.9			23	118	
7-1.10			12-a		
7-2.1				100, 101	
7-2.2				109	
7-2.3			20	111	
7-2.4				105	
7-2.5			20-a	111-a	
7-2.6				112	

EPTL	DEL	GENOB	PPL	RPL	SCA
7-2.7				112-a	
7-2.8			22	117	
7-3.1			36		
7-3.2				95, 104	
7-3.3				108	
7-3.4				98	
7-3.5			15-b		
7-4.1			265		
7-4.2			265-a		
7-4.3			266		
7-4.4			266-a		
7-4.5			266-b		
7-4.6			267		
7-4.7			268		
7-4.8			269		
7-4.9			270		
7-4.10					
8-1.1			12	113	
8-1.2			13	114	
8-1.3			14	115	
8-1.4			12-b	113-a	
8-1.5			13-a	114-a	
8-1.6			13-b		
8-1.7			16-a	61-a	
9-1.1			11	42, 43	
9-1.2			11-a	42-b	
9-1.3			11-b	42-c	
9-1.4				42-d	
9-1.5				42-e	
9-1.6			13-c	42-a	
9-1.7			13-d		
9-1.8			13-e		
9-2.1			16	61	
9-2.2			17	62	
9-2.3				63	
10-1.1				130	
10-2.1				131	
10-2.2					
10-3.1				132	
10-3.2				133	

EPTL	DEL	GENOB	PPL	RPL	SCA
10-3.3				134	
10-3.4				135	
10-4.1				136	
10-5.1				137	
10-5.2				145	
10-5.3				146	
10-5.4				142	
10-6.1				147	
10-6.2				148	
10-6.3				149	
10-6.4				150	
10-6.5				151	
10-6.6				152	
10-6.7				166 (former)	
10-6.8				153	
10-7.1				138	
10-7.2				139	
10-7.3				140	
10-7.4				141	
10-8.1				154, 155	
10-8.2				156	
10-8.3				157	
10-8.4				158	
10-9.1				144	
10-9.2				143	
10-10.1				159	
10-10.2				160	
10-10.3				161	
10-10.4				162	
10-10.5				164	
10-10.6				163	
10-10.7	127(2)(p)			166	
10-10.8				165	
11-1.1	127				93, 222, 286

EPTL	DEL	GENOB	PPL	RPL	SCA
11-1.2			17-e		
11-1.3					223
11-1.4					224
11-1.5	146				218
11-1.6			25		231
11-1.7	125				
11-2.1			27-a-q		
11-2.2			21, 26		
11-3.1	116, 117				
11-3.2	118, 119				
11-3.3	120				
11-3.4	121				
11-4.1	140				
11-4.2	141				
11-4.3	142				
11-4.4	143				
11-4.5	150				
11-4.6	151–154				
12-1.1	170, 174, 176, 181, 182				
12-1.2	175, 181, 182, 188, 189, 192				
12-1.3	172, 173, 180, 185				
12-2.1	170				
12-2.2	171, 179				
12-2.3	178				
12-2.4	185				
12-2.5	186, 187				
13-1.1					202
13-1.2					203

EPTL

EPTL	DEL	GENOB	PPL	RPL	SCA
13-1.3	47-d				
13-1.4	19				
13-2.1	113	5-701(7)(8)			
13-2.2			32		
13-2.3			32-a		
13-3.1			24		
13-3.2			24-a		
13-3.3	47-f				
13-3.4			425		
13-3.5	160				
13-3.6			19		

History: Add, L 1966, ch 952, eff Sept 1, 1967; amd, L 1967, ch 686, § 151, eff Sept 1, 1967; L 1968, ch 257, eff May 14, 1968; L 1970, ch 382, eff May 1, 1970.

§ 14-2.2. Distribution from other laws to the estates, powers and trusts law

DEL	EPTL	SCPA
2	*11-2.19(b)*	
11	3-1.2	
12	3-1.3(a)	
14	3-3.1	
15	3-1.1	
16	3-2.2	
17	5-3.3	
18	5-1.1(a)	
18-a	5-1.1(b)	
18-b	5-1.1(c)	
19	13-1.4	
20	3-3.6, 3-4.5	
21	3-2.1	
22	3-2.1	
22-a	3-5.1(c)	
23	3-5.1(c)	
24	3-5.1(d)	
25	omitted	
26	5-3.2	
27	3-3.2	
28	5-3.4	
29	3-3.3	
30		2507
31		2507

DEL	EPTL	SCPA
32		2507
33		2507
34	3-4.1	
35	5-1.3	
36	3-4.4	
37	3-4.2	
38	3-3.6	
39	3-4.3	
40	3-4.3	
41	3-4.6	
42		2506
43		2506
44	omitted	see 1615
45		1614
46	3-3.8	
47	3-5.1(b)(h)	
47-a	1-2.11, 1-2.14, 2-1.2	
47-b	3-3.9	
47-c	2-1.1	
47-d	13-1.3(a)(2)	
47-e	3-1.3(b)	
47-f	13-3.3	
47-g	3-3.7	
48	omitted	
49	2-1.3	
50	5-1.2	
80	omitted	
80-a	2-1.7	
81	1-2.5	
82	4-1.1(g)	
83	4-1.1	
83-a	4-1.2	
84	5-2.2(d)	
85	2-1.5	
86	2-1.5	
87	4-1.4; 5-1.2	
87-a	4-1.3	
88	omitted	
89	2-1.6	

EPTL

DEL	EPTL	SCPA
103-a		103-a
103-b		1311
112	omitted	
113	13-2.1(a)(3)	
114	omitted	
115	omitted	
116	11-3.1	
117	11-3.1	
118	11-3.2(a)	
119	11-3.2(b)	
120	11-3.3	
121	11-3.4	
124	2-1.8	
125	11-1.7	
126	3-3.5(b)(c)	
127	11-1.1	
127(2)(p)	10-10.7	
130	5-4.1	
131	5-4.2	
132	5-4.3	
133	5-4.4	
134	1-2.5	
135	5-4.5	
140	11-4.1	
141	11-4.2	
142	11-4.3	
143	11-4.4	
144	omitted	
145	omitted	
146	11-1.5	
147	omitted	
148	omitted	
149	omitted	
150	11-4.5	
151	11-4.6(a)	
152	11-4.6(b)	
153	11-4.6(c)	
154	11-4.6(d)	
155	omitted	
156	omitted	

DEL	EPTL	SCPA
157	omitted	
158	omitted	
159	omitted	
160	13-3.5	
170	12-1.1(a); 12-2.1	
171	12-2.2	
172	12-1.3(a)	
173	12-1.3(b)	
174	12-1.1(b)	
175	12-1.1(b)(2); 12-1.2(b)	
176	12-1.1(a)	
177	omitted	
178	12-2.3	
179	12-2.2	
180	12-1.3(a)	
181	12-1.1(b)(1); 12-1.2(a)	
182	12-1.1(b)(1); 12-1.2(a)	
183	omitted	
184	omitted	
185	12-1.3(a); 12-2.4	
186	12-2.5	
187	12-2.5	
188	12-1.2(c)(1)	
189	12-1.2(c)(2)	
190	omitted	
191	omitted	
192	12-1.2(b)	
193	omitted	
194	omitted	
200	omitted	
201	omitted	
202	omitted	
203	omitted	
204	omitted	
205	omitted	
210	omitted	
GENOB	EPTL	
5-701(7)	13-2.1(a)(2)	
5-701(8)	13-2.1(a)(1)	
PPL	EPTL	

EPTL

DEL	EPTL	SCPA
11	9-1.1	
11–a	9-1.2	
11–b	9-1.3(a)(b)(c)(d)	
11–c	9-1.5	
12	8-1.1	
12-a	7-1.10	
12-b	8-1.4	
13	8-1.2	
13-a	8-1.5	
13-b	8-1.6	
13-c	9-1.6	
13-d	9-1.7	
13-e	9-1.8	
14	8-1.3	
15	7-1.5	
15-a	7-1.6	
15-b	7-3.5	
16	9-2.1	
16-a	8-1.7	
17	9-2.2	
17-e	11-1.2	
17-f	2-1.9	
18	10-7.1(a)(4)	
19	13-3.6	
20	7-2.3	
20-a	7-2.5	
21	11-2.2	
22	7-2.8	
23	7-1.9	
24	13-3.1	
24-a	13-3.2	
25	11-1.6	
26	11-2.2	
27-a-q	11-2.1	
32	13-2.2	
32-a	13-2.3	
36	7-3.1	
265	7-4.1	
265-a	7-4.2	
266	7-4.3	

DEL	EPTL	SCPA
266-a	7-4.4	
266-b	7-4.5	
267	7-4.6	
268	7-4.7	
269	7-4.8	
270	7-4.9	
270-a	1-1.4	
425	13-3.4	
RPL	EPTL	
30	6-1.1	
31	omitted	
32	6-1.2	
33	omitted	
34	6-1.3	
35	6-3.1; 6-4.1	
36	6-3.2	
37	6-4.2	
38	6-4.3	
39	6-4.4	
40	6-4.7	
40-a	6-4.8	
40-b	6-4.9	
40-c	6-4.10	
41	6-5.2	
42	9-1.1(a)	
42-a	9-1.6	
42-b	9-1.2	
42-c	9-1.3(a)(b)(c)(d)	
42-d	9-1.4	
42-e	9-1.5	
43	9-1.1(b)	
48	6-5.6	
RPL	EPTL	
49	omitted	
50	6-3.3	
51	6-5.3	
52	6-5.5	
53	omitted	
54	6-5.8	
55	omitted	

EPTL

DEL	EPTL	SCPA
56	6-5.7	
57	6-5.10	
58	6-5.11	
59	6-5.1	
59-a	6-4.5	
59-b	6-4.6	
60	6-5.12	
61	9-2.1	
61-a	8-1.7	
62	9-2.2	
63	9-2.3	
64	6-3.4	
65	6-2.1	
66	6-2.2	
66-a	6-5.4	
90	omitted	
91	omitted	
92	7-1.1	
93	7-1.2	
94	7-1.3	
95	7-3.2	
96	7-1.4	
98	7-3.4	
100	7-2.1	
101	7-2.1	
102	7-1.7	
103	7-1.5	
103-a	7-1.6	
104	7-3.2	
105	7-2.4	
108	7-3.3	
109	7-2.2	
110	7-1.8	
111	7-2.3	
111-a	7-2.5	
112	7-2.6	
112-a	7-2.7	
113	8-1.1	
113-a	8-1.4	
114	8-1.2	

DEL	EPTL	SCPA
114-a	8-1.5	
115	8-1.3	
117	7-2.8	
118	7-1.9	
130	10-1.1	
131	10-2.1	
132	10-3.1	
133	10-3.2	
134	10-3.3	
135	10-3.4	
136	10-4.1	
137	10-5.1	
138	10-7.1	
139	10-7.2	
140	10-7.3	
141	10-7.4	
142	10-5.4	
143	10-9.2	
144	10-9.1	
145	10-5.2	
146	10-5.3	
147	10-6.1	
148	10-6.2	
149	10-6.3	
150	10-6.4	
151	10-6.5	
152	10-6.6	
153	10-6.8	
154	10-8.1(a)	
155	10-8.1(b)	
156	10-8.2	
157	10-8.3	
158	10-8.4	
159	10-10.1	
160	10-10.2	
161	10-10.3	
162	10-10.4	
163	10-10.6	
164	10-10.5	
165	10-10.8	

DEL	EPTL	SCPA
166	10-10.7	
240	2-1.4	
SCA	EPTL	
93	11-1.1(b)(11	
200	5-3.1	
202	13-1.1	
203	13-1.2	
218	11-1.5	
222	11-1.1(b)(23)	
223	11-1.3	
224	11-1.4	
231	11-1.6	
286	11-1.1(b)(23)	
250-c	omitted	

History: Add, L 1966, ch 952, eff Sept 1, 1967; amd, L 1967, ch 472; L 1967, ch 683, eff Sept 1, 1967; L 1967, ch 686; L 1968, ch 257, § 18; L 1973, ch 904; L 1992, ch 595, § 21, eff Sept 1, 1992.

PART 3   Effective Date

§ 14-3.1. When act becomes effective

This act shall take effect September first, nineteen hundred sixty-seven.

History: Add, L 1966, ch 952, eff Sept 1, 1967; amd, L 1967, ch 686, § 151, eff Sept 1, 1967.

UNIFORM RULES FOR SURROGATE'S COURT

Pursuant to an administrative order of the chief administrative judge of the Courts, the following Uniform Rules for Surrogate's Court were adopted, effective January 6, 1986, as part 207 of the Uniform Rules for the Trial Courts of the Unified Court System.

Also effective January 6, 1986, the following provisions of Title 22 of the Official Compilation of Codes, Rules and Regulations of the State of New York (22 NYCRR), constituting rules for the several trial courts in the State of New York, were repealed:

1810 **Rules (Surrogate's Court; Bronx County)**

1820 **Rules (Surrogate's Court; New York County)**

1830 **Uniform Rules for Surrogate's Courts in Second Judicial Department**

1940 **Uniform Rules for Surrogate's Courts in the Third Judicial Department**

1950 **Rules (Surrogate's Court; Albany County)**

1960 **Rules (Surrogate's Court; Broome County)**

1980 **Rules (Surrogate's Court; Chenango County)**

1990 **Rules (Surrogate's Court; Clinton County)**

2000 **Rules (Surrogate's Court; Columbia County)**

2050 **Rules (Surrogate's Court; Fulton County)**

2090 **Rules (Surrogate's Court; Clinton County)**

2110 **Rules (Surrogate's Court; Rensselaer County)**

2120 **Rules (Surrogate's Court; St. Lawrence County)**

2130 **Rules (Surrogate's Court; Saratoga County)**

2190 **Rules (Surrogate's Court; Tompkins County)**

2200 **Rules (Surrogate's Court; Ulster County)**

2230 **Uniform Calendar and Practice Rules for Surrogate's Courts in the Fourth Department**

2240 **Calendar and Practice Rules (Surrogate's Court; Allegany County)**

UNIFORM RULES FOR SURROGATE'S COURT

TABLE OF CONTENTS

Part 207 UNIFORM RULES FOR SURROGATE'S COURT

Official Rules

Part 207   UNIFORM RULES FOR SURROGATE'S COURT

§ 207.1   Application of part; waiver; special rules; definitions.

(a) Application. This part shall be applicable to proceedings in all Surrogates' Courts in New York State.

(b) Waiver. For good cause shown, and in the interests of justice, the court in a proceeding may waive compliance with any of these rules other than section 207.2, unless prohibited from doing so by statute or by a rule of the Chief Judge.

(c) Additional rules. Local court rules, and all court forms not inconsistent with law or with these rules, shall comply with Part 9 of the Rules of the Chief Judge (22 NYCRR Part 9).

(d) Application of SCPA, EPTL and CPLR. The provisions of this part shall be construed consistently with the Surrogate's Court Procedure Act (SCPA) and the Estates Powers and

Trusts Law (EPTL). Matters not covered by these provisions, the SCPA and the EPTL shall be governed by the Civil Practice Law and Rules (CPLR).

(e) Definitions.

(1) "Chief Administrator of the Courts" in this Part also includes a designee of the Chief Administrator.

(2) Unless the context requires otherwise, all references to "clerk" shall mean the Chief Clerk of each Surrogate's Court or the designee of the Chief Clerk.

(3) Unless otherwise defined in this Part, or the context otherwise requires, all terms used in this Part shall have the same meaning as they have in the CPLR, EPTL and the SCPA.

(effective April 1, 1998)

§ 207.2　　Terms of court.

In each Surrogate's Court there shall be held such terms as the Chief Administrator shall designate.

(effective January 6, 1986)

§ 207.3　　*Reserved*

§ 207.4　　Papers filed in court; clerk's file number; official forms.

(a) Unless otherwise specified by the court, attorneys, as well as parties appearing without attorneys, shall prepare and submit all papers, pleadings, orders and decrees to be acted upon by the Surrogate. The party causing the first paper to be filed shall communicate the clerk's file number forthwith to all other parties to the proceeding; service of the citation bearing the file number shall be sufficient. Thereafter such number shall appear on the outside cover and first page to the right of the caption of every paper tendered for filing in the proceeding. The caption also shall contain the title of the proceeding, an indication of the county of venue and a brief description of the nature of the paper. All papers shall comply and (other than wills, codicils, exhibits and forms of other governmental agencies) shall be on standard eight and one-half inch by 11-inch paper. The text of all papers must be legible and, other than prompts and instructions, must be in a standard typeface of 10 to 12-point characters and have margins that shall be no less than one-half inch. Papers also shall contain the name of the attorney or party submitting them and, whenever possible, the names, addresses and information regarding parties to the proceeding shall be printed in bold typeface.

(b) The forms set forth in Chapter VII of subtitle D of this title (22 NYCRR), designated "Surrogate Court Forms", and including forms for the Surrogates Court, shall be the official forms of the court and shall be accepted for filing pursuant to SCPA 106. Forms produced on computers or word processors shall be accepted for filing, provided (1) the text used shall be the same as that contained in the official forms and (2) the attorney or party preparing such form shall certify at the end thereof that the form is the same as the official form and that the substantive text has not been altered. Persons submitting such forms may leave out instructions (contained in brackets) and optional words or phrases that have not been selected or are irrelevant. Submitting a form to be an official form, but upon which the text has been intentionally altered to change the substance or meaning thereof, may be regarded as an attempt to mislead the court.

(c) Examples of the official forms shall be available at the clerks office of any Surrogate's Court.

(effective April 1, 1998)

§ 207.4-a Electronic filing in Surrogate's Court; consensual program

(a) Application. On consent, documents may be filed or served electronically in Surrogate's Court proceedings and counties as specified by order of the Chief Administrator of the Courts. This section shall apply only to those proceedings and counties.

(b) Definitions. The following definitions shall be used for the purposes of these rules:

(1) "New York State Courts Electronic Filing System" ("NYSCEF") shall mean the system, located at the Internet site at www.nycourts.gov/efile, established by the Chief Administrator to permit the electronic transmission of documents to courts and parties in authorized cases.

(2) "Consent" shall mean the voluntary agreement by an attorney or party to an estate proceeding to participate in that proceeding through NYSCEF pursuant to these rules.

(3) "Document" shall mean any submission to the court for filing.

(4) "Electronic filing" ("e-filing") shall mean the electronic transmission of documents through NYSCEF to the Surrogate's Court.

(5) "Electronic service" ("e-service") shall mean the electronic transmission of documents to a party or that party's attorney or representative in accordance with these rules. E-service shall not include service of process to gain jurisdiction. E-service shall be complete upon transmission of documents to NYSCEF.

(6) "E-filer" shall mean an attorney admitted to practice in New York State, or admitted pro hac vice, or an authorized agent thereof, or an unrepresented party, any of whom is registered as an e-filer with NYSCEF as set forth below.

(7) "Hard copy" shall mean a document in paper form.

(8) "Party" shall mean an individual or entity who has an interest in the proceeding and without whom the case may not proceed.

(9) "Authorized agent" shall mean a person or filing service company designated by an attorney to file and serve documents on the attorney's behalf in an estate proceeding, pursuant to a form promulgated by the Chief Administrator and filed as provided therein.

(10) "Working copy" shall mean a hard copy that is an exact copy of a document that has been electronically filed in accordance with this section.

(11) "Unrepresented litigant" shall mean a party to an action who is not represented by counsel.

(12) "Expedited processing" shall mean the expedited registration of a person as an authorized e-filing user.

(c) Intent.

(1) Except as otherwise provided in section 207.4-aa of these rules, e-filing is voluntary

and nothing herein shall preclude a party from filing and serving documents in hard copy. Except as provided in subdivision (e)(9), a party who initiates a proceeding by e-filing and any other party who chooses to participate as an e-filer must thereafter file, serve, and accept service of all documents electronically unless notice is given to the court and all other parties that the party no longer wishes to participate electronically. Notwithstanding any other provision of this rule, no party shall be compelled, directly or indirectly, to participate in e-filing pursuant to this section. An unrepresented litigant may consent to participate in e-filing hereunder provided the clerk shall first have explained his or her options for e-filing in plain language, including the option for expedited processing, and inquired whether he or she wishes to participate. Where an unrepresented litigant opts to consent hereunder, it shall be documented in the case file in a manner prescribed by the Chief Administrator. Provided, however, that where an unrepresented litigant chooses to participate in e-filing in accordance with these rules, he or she may at any time opt out of such participation by presenting the clerk of the court with a form so declaring.

(2) The court may terminate, modify, or suspend the use of e-filing in a proceeding at any time and may in its discretion excuse an e-filer from compliance with any provision of these rules.

(3) A party or that party's attorney or representative who participates as an e-filer consents to be bound by the provisions of these rules, and participates at the discretion of the Court.

(d) E-filers.

(1) In order to file documents electronically pursuant to these rules, an e-filer shall register with the Office of Court Administration of the New York State Unified Court System by filing with that Office a registration form promulgated by the Chief Administrator. Upon completion of registration, a user ID and password will be issued to the e-filer by NYSCEF. If, during the course of the proceeding, a pro se party who registered as an e-filer retains an attorney, the attorney shall register, if not already registered as an e-filer, and inform the Chief Clerk of his or her appearance on behalf of the pro se party.

(2) Registration as an e-filer shall not constitute consent to participate in any particular estate proceeding; consent to do so must be provided pursuant to subdivision (b)(2).

(3) Upon learning of the compromise of the confidentiality of either the user ID or the password, the e-filer shall immediately notify NYSCEF, which shall arrange for the issuance of a new user ID or password as appropriate.

(e) Electronic Filing of Documents.

(1) An eligible proceeding may be commenced by filing the initial documents electronically, or may become an e-filed proceeding after commencement upon the filing of documents electronically pursuant to these rules. A party commencing a proceeding electronically, or the party first filing electronically, shall serve all other parties with a Notice regarding the use of e-filing and the procedure for participating therein in a form approved by the Chief Administrator, which may be obtained through NYSCEF. Such Notice shall be served, in person or by regular mail, prior to the return date of the citation. Proof of service of such Notice shall be promptly filed with the court.

Official Rules

(2) Whenever documents are e-filed that require payment of a court filing fee, the e-filer shall pay such fee through NYSCEF, or by mail, or in person.

(3) Documents may be transmitted at any time to NYSCEF and will be deemed filed when transmission to NYSCEF is complete and payment of any court filing fee due is received by the court. A document due to be filed by a particular date shall be considered to have been timely filed if filed through NYSCEF no later than midnight of that date.

(4) Upon completion of transmission of an e-filed document, an electronic confirmation that includes the date and time of receipt shall be issued through NYSCEF to the e-filer.

(5) Receipt of documents submitted through NYSCEF and issuance of a confirmation shall not be proof of the completeness or technical or legal sufficiency of the documents. If the court identifies any defects as to form, or omissions, in any e-filed documents, the court may direct that the e-filer resubmit them in proper and complete form or amend or supplement them as appropriate.

(6) If an e-filer submits a petition for probate for which the court does not already have in its possession the original purported last will and testament and any codicils thereto being offered for probate, the e-filer shall file directly with the court the paper original purported last will and testament and any codicils thereto and a hard copy of the death certificate, attorney certified if required by the court, within two business days of the date of e-filing. Except as otherwise directed by the court, process shall not issue nor shall a fiduciary be appointed before the original purported last will and testament, any codicils thereto and the appropriate death certificate are filed with the court.

(7) If an e-filer submits a petition for administration the e-filer shall file a hard copy of the death certificate, attorney certified if required by the court, directly with the court within two business days of the date of e-filing. Except as otherwise directed by the court, process will not issue nor shall a fiduciary be appointed before the appropriate death certificate is filed with the court.

(8) Whenever a document is e-filed pursuant to this section, the official record of that document shall be the electronic record maintained by the court.

(9) Documents that cannot be e-filed because of size, content, format, or any other reasons satisfactory to the court shall be filed in hard copy directly with the court together with, when required, an affidavit of service upon all parties to the proceeding.

(10) When filing a document in hard copy pursuant to these rules, the filer shall firmly affix thereto a notice of hard copy filing indicating the basis for filing in that form.

(11) The court may require that working copies of documents be filed with the court. When filing a working copy, the filer shall firmly affix thereto a notice identifying the document as a working copy and indicating that the document has been e-filed.

(f) Signatures.

(1) Every document which is e-filed shall be signed as required by Part 130 of the Rules of the Chief Administrator in accordance with this section. The document shall provide the signatory's name, address, e-mail address of record and telephone number.

(2) A document shall be considered to have been signed by, and shall be binding upon,

a person identified therein as a signatory, if it is e-filer bearing the actual signature of such person, or, where the person identified as the signatory is the e-filer and the document is being e-filed under the e-filer's user ID and password, an "/s/" is used in the space where the signature would otherwise appear. An attorney or party who e-files a document that bears an actual signature, or causes such a document to be e-filed, represents that he or she possesses the executed hard copy of such document and that he or she shall make it available at the request of the court or any party.

(g) Service of Parties.

(1) An attorney or party seeking to obtain jurisdiction over a party to a proceeding shall serve that party by any of the methods permitted by the SCPA.

(2) In all other instances where service of documents is required, e-service may be made upon any party who is an e-filer in the proceeding. Upon e-filing of any such document, NYSCEF shall transmit notification of filing of the document to all e-mail service addresses of record. Such notification shall provide the date and time of filing and the names of those appearing on the list of e-mail service addresses of record who are receiving notification. The party receiving the notification shall be responsible for accessing NYSCEF to obtain a copy of the document filed. Proof of transmission to the party or the failure thereof shall be recorded by NYSCEF and displayed in the e-filing case record.

(h) Documents Filed by the Court. Decrees, judgments, orders, and decisions in proceedings governed by these rules shall be electronically filed by the court with the appropriate signature affixed and such e-filing shall constitute filing of the decree, judgment, order, or decision. At the time of the filing of the decree, judgment, order, or decision, NYSCEF shall transmit by e-mail to the e-mail service addresses of record a notification that the decree, judgment, order, or decision has been filed and is accessible through NYSCEF. Such notice shall not constitute service of notice of filing by any party.

(i) Technical Failures.

(1) The Chief Clerk shall deem NYSCEF to be subject to a technical failure on a given date if NYSCEF is unable to accept filings or provide access to filed documents continuously or intermittently over the course of any period of time greater than one hour after 12:00 noon of that day. The court shall provide notice of all such technical failures on the NYSCEF site. When e-filing is hindered by a technical failure, a party may file with the court in hard copy. With the exception of deadlines that by law cannot be extended, the time for filing of any paper that is delayed due to the technical failure as defined herein shall be extended for one day for each day in which such technical failure occurs, unless otherwise ordered by the court.

(2) If the e-filing or e-service does not occur or is prevented because of any of the following, the court may upon satisfactory proof enter an order permitting the document to be filed nunc pro tunc to the date it was first attempted to be sent electronically or extending the date for filing or service of the paper: an error in the transmission of the document to NYSCEF or served party which was unknown to the sending party; the party was erroneously excluded from the service list; or other technical problems experienced by the e-filer, including problems with the filer's equipment or Internet connection.

(effective October 21, 2015)

§ 207.4-aa Electronic filing in Surrogate's Court; mandatory program

(a) Application. There is hereby established a program in which all documents filed and served in Surrogate's Court proceedings and counties specified by order of the Chief Administrator of the Courts shall be filed and served electronically. Except to the extent that this section shall otherwise require, the provisions of section 207.4-a of these rules shall govern this program.

(b) Commencement of Proceedings Under this Section.

(1) Mandatory commencement in general. Except as otherwise provided in this section, every proceeding specified in subdivision (a) of this section shall be commenced by electronically filing the initiating documents with the clerk of the court through the NYSCEF site.

(2) Emergency exception. Notwithstanding paragraph (1) of this subdivision, a proceeding required to be commenced electronically may be commenced by the filing of initiating documents in hard copy provided that such documents are accompanied by the affirmation or affidavit of the filing attorney or party stating that: (i) the statute of limitations will expire on the day the documents are being filed or on the following business day; and (ii) the attorney, party, or filing agent therefor is unable to electronically file such documents because of technical problems with his or her computer equipment or Internet connection. In the event a filer shall file initiating documents in hard copy pursuant to this paragraph, each such document shall include the notice required by paragraph (10) of subdivision (e) of section 207.4-a of these rules, and the filer shall file those documents with the NYSCEF site within three business days thereafter, unless the clerk of court elects to e-file the documents on behalf of the filer. For purposes of this section, such a proceeding shall be deemed to have been commenced electronically.

(3) Service of process. Service of process upon a party in a proceeding that must be commenced electronically in accordance with this section shall be made as provided in Article 3 of the Surrogate's Court Procedure Act, or by electronic means if the party served agrees to accept such service. Such service shall be accompanied by a notice, in a form approved by the Chief Administrator, advising the recipient that the proceeding is subject to electronic filing pursuant to this section. A party served by electronic means shall, within 24 hours of service, provide the serving party or attorney with an electronic confirmation that the service has been effected.

(c) Filing and Service of Documents After Commencement in Proceedings Under this Section.

(1) All documents to be filed and served electronically. Except as otherwise provided in this section, filing and service of all documents in a proceeding that has been commenced electronically in accordance with this section shall be by electronic means.

(2) Emergency exception. Notwithstanding paragraph (1) of this subdivision, where documents are required to be filed and served electronically in accordance with such paragraph (1), such documents may nonetheless be filed and served in hard copy provided that they are accompanied by the affirmation or affidavit of the filing attorney or party stating that: (i) a deadline for their filing and service fixed by statute, rule, or order of the court will expire on the day the documents are being filed or served or on the following business day; and (ii) the attorney, party, or filing agent therefor is unable to file and serve

such documents electronically because of technical problems with his or her computer equipment or Internet connection. In the event a filer shall file and serve documents in hard copy pursuant to this paragraph, each such document shall include the notice required by paragraph (10) of subdivision (e) of section 207.4-a, and the filer shall file those documents with the NYSCEF site within three business days thereafter, unless the clerk of court elects to e-file the documents on behalf of the filer.

(d) Clerk of Court Not to Accept Hard Copies of Documents for Filing Where Electronic Filing Is Required. The clerk of the court shall refuse to accept for filing hard copies of documents sought to be filed in proceedings where such documents are required to be filed electronically.

(e) Exemption From the Requirement of Electronic Filing.

(1) Exemption of unrepresented litigants. Notwithstanding the foregoing, an unrepresented litigant or a proposed intervenor or other non-party seeking relief from the court who is unrepresented is exempt from having to file and serve documents electronically in accordance with this section. No such party shall be compelled, directly or indirectly, to participate in e-filing. As to each unrepresented litigant, the clerk shall explain his or her options for e-filing in plain language, including the option for expedited processing, and shall inquire whether he or she wishes to participate, provided however the unrepresented litigant may participate in the e-filing program only upon his or her request, which shall be documented in the case file, after he or she has been presented with sufficient information in plain language concerning the program. Where an unrepresented litigant chooses to participate in e-filing in accordance with these rules, he or she may at any time opt out of such participation by presenting the clerk of the court with a form so declaring.

(2) Exemption of represented parties. Notwithstanding the foregoing, an attorney shall be exempt from having to file and serve documents electronically in accordance with this section upon filing with the clerk of the court in which the proceeding is or will be pending a form, to be prescribed by the Chief Administrator, on which the attorney certifies in good faith that he or she:

(i) lacks the required computer hardware and/or connection to the Internet and/or scanner or other device by which documents may be converted to an electronic format; or

(ii) lacks the requisite knowledge in the operation of such computers and/or scanners necessary to comply with this section (for purposes of this paragraph, the knowledge of any employee of an attorney, or any employee of the attorney's law firm, office or business who is subject to such attorney's direction, shall be imputed to the attorney.

(3) Exemption of counsel upon a showing of good cause. Nothing in this section shall prevent a judge from exempting an attorney from having to file and serve documents electronically in accordance with this section upon a showing of good cause therefor.

(4) Procedures applicable to exempt attorneys. Where an attorney or party in a proceeding that is subject to this section is exempt from having to file and serve documents electronically in accordance with this section, he or she shall serve and file documents in hard copy, provided that each such document shall include the notice required by paragraph (10) of subdivision (e) of section 207.4-a of these rules. Notwithstanding the foregoing, all other attorneys and parties in such proceeding shall continue to be required

to file and serve documents electronically, except that, whenever they serve documents upon a person or party who is exempt from having to file and serve documents electronically in accordance with this section, they shall serve such documents in hard copy and shall file electronically proof of such service.

(effective October 21, 2015)

§ 207.5   Submission of papers to Surrogate.

All papers for signature or consideration of the Surrogate shall be presented in the first instance to the clerk of the court in the appropriate courtroom or clerk's office, except that where the clerk is unavailable or the Surrogate so directs, papers may be filed with the Surrogate and a copy filed with the clerk at the first available opportunity. Where appropriate, orders to show cause may be submitted directly to the Law Department or the Surrogate. The papers shall be clearly addressed to the Surrogate for whom they are intended, and prominently show the nature of the papers, the title and clerk's file number of the proceeding in which they are filed, and the name of the attorney or party submitting them.

(effective January 6, 1986)

§ 207.6   Transfer of actions from other courts.

(a) An application under SCPA 501 for the consent of the court to the transfer to the Surrogate's Court of an action pending in the Supreme Court or for the transfer by the Surrogate's Court to itself of any action pending in any other court or for the consolidation of such action with a proceeding pending in the Surrogate's Court shall show whether there is pending a proceeding in the Surrogate's Court and the nature of the proceeding and shall be supported by an affidavit which shall state:

    (1) the court in which such action is then pending;

    (2) the parties to the action;

    (3) the nature of the action;

    (4) whether the action is on the trial calendar;

    (5) an estimate of the time when the action will be reached for trial in the court in which the same is pending, with the facts upon which such estimate is based;

    (6) the reasons why a transfer of the action to this court is desirable;

    (7) whether a jury trial has been demanded or whether the same has been waived.

(b) There must be annexed to the moving papers a copy of the pleadings in the action sought to be transferred. Upon compliance with the foregoing requirements, an order will be issued by the court directing the adverse parties to show cause why the application should not be granted.

(effective January 6, 1986)

§ 207.7   Service and filing of papers; motions.

(a) Whenever service of a paper or notice is required, copies thereof shall be served upon all parties who have appeared and upon such other persons as the Surrogate may direct. Except as further provided in section 207.9 of this Part, a party has appeared within the meaning of these rules so as to entitle the party to be served with notices or papers (i) if the party has filed a written notice of appearance with a demand for service of all papers at a specified address; or (ii) if the party has filed a pleading upon which is endorsed the name and address of the attorney appearing for the party or the name and address of the party appearing *pro se.*

(b) Proof of service of the paper or notice upon all parties shall be filed with the original paper or notice.

(c) In all proceedings the proof of service of process, notices of motion and orders to show cause shall be filed on or before the second day preceding the return date unless the court otherwise permits. In computing such period of two days, Saturdays, Sundays and legal holidays shall not be taken into account. This provision shall not apply to an order to show cause returnable in such limited time as to make compliance with its provisions impracticable.

(d) All contested motions and proceedings shall be made returnable on any day the court is in session unless otherwise provided in the local rules of the court or by order of the Surrogate.

(e) Unless the court otherwise permits, the moving party shall serve copies of all affidavits and briefs upon all other parties at the time of service of the notice of motion. The answering party shall serve copies of all affidavits and briefs as required by CPLR 2214. Affidavits shall be for a statement of the relevant facts, and briefs shall be for a statement of the relevant law. Unless otherwise directed by the court, answering and reply affidavits and briefs and all papers required to be furnished to the court by CPLR 2214(c) must be filed no later than the time of argument or submission of the motion.

(f) The Surrogate may determine that any or all motions in that court be orally argued and may direct that moving and responding papers be filed with the court prior to the time of argument.

(g) (1) Unless oral argument has been requested by a party and permitted by the court, or directed by the court, motion papers received by the clerk of the court on or before the return date shall be deemed submitted as of the return date. (2) Attendance by counsel at the calendar call shall not be required unless (i) a party intends to make an application to the court that is not on the consent of all parties, (ii) attendance of counsel or oral argument is directed by the court, or (iii) oral argument is requested by a party. (3) Attendance by counsel for a party not requesting oral argument is not required where the hearing of oral argument is based solely upon the request of another party. (4) A party requesting oral argument shall set forth such request in its notice of motion or on the first page of the answering papers, as the case may be. A party requesting oral argument on a motion brought on by order to show cause shall do so as soon as possible prior to the time the motion is to be heard.

(effective January 6, 1986)

§ 207.8   Removal of papers.

No record or document filed in the court shall be removed therefrom by any person except on written consent of the Surrogate or the clerk. Suitable facilities shall be designated by the Surrogate for the examination or transcription of records and documents by parties or attorneys.

(effective January 6, 1986)

Official Rules

§ 207.9   Appearances.

(a) A person not named in a citation, but who claims to be interested in the proceeding and wishes to intervene therein, shall file a notice of appearance and a petition or affidavit alleging interest.

(b) Unless otherwise directed by the Surrogate, attorneys appearing on behalf of nondomiciliaries or parties not personally served within the state must furnish acknowledged evidence of authority pursuant to SCPA 401.

(c) When directed by the Surrogate, in addition to filing an appearance as required by SCPA 404, a guardian ad litem shall serve a notice of appearance upon all parties.

(effective January 6, 1986)

§ 207.10   Demand for pleadings.

Unless otherwise ordered by the Surrogate, where a party is entitled under SCPA 302(3) to a copy of a pleading on demand, it shall be served within five days of the demand.

(effective January 6, 1986)

§ 207.11   Guardians.

(a) Where application is made to appoint a guardian of two or more infants, a separate petition and proposed order must be presented with respect to each infant.

(b) The order appointing a guardian of the property of an infant shall recite the substance of, or contain a reference to, the requirements of SCPA 1719 regarding guardian's annual accounts.

(c) As soon as a ward reaches 18 years of age, the guardian shall forthwith account to the ward and proceed to obtain a discharge upon receipt and release, by a proceeding for judicial settlement of accounts, or by such other method as directed by the court.

(effective April 1, 1998)

§ 207.12   Appointment of guardian *ad litem* on nomination.

(a) In addition to the requirements of SCPA 403, all applications for the appointment of guardians *ad litem* upon the petitions of infants over 14 years of age must contain the following information:

(1) the petition of the infant must state whether the infant has been influenced by the proponent or the accounting party or the attorneys for the fiduciaries or anyone connected with them or either of them in the selection of the person the infant nominates as the infant's guardian *ad litem*, and whether the person nominated by the infant has suggested his or her employment either in person or through others.

(2) the affidavit of the attorney nominated as guardian *ad litem* must state whether the proponent in a probate proceeding or the petitioner in any other proceeding or the accounting party or the attorney for any of the foregoing persons, or anyone connected with such attorney, has suggested or accelerated the nomination of the attorney as guardian *ad litem* and, if so, must state the facts.

(b) The papers submitted on an application must satisfy the court that the attorney who is nominated for appointment as guardian *ad litem* will have no divided loyalty in the performance of his or her duties which might result in failure to protect adequately the infant's rights in the estate.

(effective January 6, 1986)

§ 207.13   Qualification of guardians ad litem; filing report.

(a) Each guardian ad litem shall qualify within ten days of notification of appointment or may be deemed unable to act. He or she shall review the courts guidelines for guardians ad litem, if available, and carefully examine all matters affecting the guardian's client and all processes and papers to ensure that they are regular and have been duly served. No decree shall be made in the proceeding until the guardian shall report these findings. The report shall be made in writing or, with the consent of the Surrogate, orally in open court, except as otherwise provided in SCPA 1754(4), within ten court days of the guardian's appointment or from the date to which the proceeding was finally adjourned, unless extended by the court.

(b) A guardian ad litem in a proceeding in which a decree has been entered directing payment of money or delivery of property to or for the benefit of the guardian's ward must file a supplemental report within 60 days after a decree settling the account, showing whether the decree has been complied with insofar as it affects the ward. In all such cases the fiduciary shall immediately notify the guardian in writing of the date and details of payment or delivery.

(c) The guardian's allowance may be authorized in the initial decree, but, except as provided in SCPA 2111, no allowance shall be paid until an appropriate report is made.

(effective April 1, 1998)

§ 207.14   Infants' funds.

(a) No allowances will be made to a guardian or otherwise for the support or maintenance of an infant unless an annual account for the preceding year has been filed or good cause is shown in the petition why it has not been filed. The petition must comply with CPLR 1211.

(b) Where an order is granted authorizing the periodic withdrawal of funds belonging to or held in trust for an infant, it shall specify the number and amounts of such withdrawals and the duration of time in which the funds may be used for the purposes stated.

(c) All guardians, persons acting jointly with a guardian, and depositories designated by the court shall produce for examination, whenever so requested by the court, all securities, evidences of deposit or investment or other records, and shall also furnish an accurate record of receipts and deposits of principal and income and of withdrawals and expenditures.

(effective January 6, 1986)

§ 207.15   Birth and death certificates.

(a) A birth certificate shall be filed upon an application for letters of guardianship or an order of adoption.

(b) A death certificate shall be filed upon an application for letters testamentary, letters of administration or voluntary administration. Alternate evidence of death may be accepted in the discretion of the court.

(c) Birth and death certificates may be required to be filed in any other proceeding in the discretion of the court.

(effective April 1, 1998)

§ 207.16　Petitions for probate and administration; proof of distributions; family tree.

(a) All petitions for probate or administration shall (1) contain the information required by SCPA 304, (2) contain an estimate of the gross estate of the decedent passing by will or intestacy, separately showing the values of personal and real property, gross rents for a period of 18 months and information about any cause of action for personal injury or wrongful death, and (2) indicate whether any distributee is a non-marital child or the issue of a non-marital person under EPTL 4-1.2(a)(1) or (a)(2).

(b) Whenever in a petition for probate or administration a party upon whom the service of process is required is a distributee whose relationship to the decedent is derived through another person who is deceased, the petition must either (1) show the relationship of the distributee to decedent and the name and relationship to decedent of each person through whom such distributee claims to be related to decedent or, (2) have annexed a family tree, table or diagram showing the name, relationship and date of death of each person through whom such distributee claims to be related to the decedent, which table or diagram shall be supported by an affidavit of a person having knowledge of the contents thereof.

(c) If the petitioner alleges that the decedent was survived by no distributees or only one distributee, or where the relationship of distributees to the decedent is grandparents, aunts, uncles, first cousins or first cousins once removed, proof must be submitted to establish (1) how each such distributee is related to the decedent and (2) that no other persons of the same or a nearer degree of relationship survived the decedent. Unless otherwise allowed by the court, the proof submitted pursuant to this subdivision must be by an affidavit or testimony of a disinterested person. Unless otherwise allowed by the court, if only one distributee survived the decedent, proof may not be given by the spouse or children of the distributee. The proof shall include as an exhibit a family tree table or diagram, except no such table or diagram shall be required if the distributee is the spouse or only child of the decedent.

(d) If the petitioner alleges that any of the distributees of the decedent or others required to be cited are unknown or that the names and addresses of some persons who are or may be distributees are unknown, petitioner must submit an affidavit showing that he or she has used due diligence in endeavoring to ascertain the identity, names and addresses of all such persons. Compliance with this due diligence requirement is not intended to burden the estate with costly or overly time-consuming searches. Absent special circumstances, the affidavit will be deemed to satisfy the requirement of due diligence if it indicates the results obtained from the following:

(1) examination of decedent's personal effects, including address books;

(2) inquiry of decedent's relatives, neighbors, friends, former business associates and employers, the post office and financial institutions;

(3) correspondence to the last known address of any missing distributees;

(4) correspondence or telephone calls to, or internet search for, persons of same or similar name in the area where the person being sought lived;

(5) examination of the records of the motor vehicle bureau and board of elections of the state or county of the last-known address of the person whose whereabouts is unknown.

In probate proceedings, the court may accept, in lieu of the above, an affidavit by decedent setting forth the efforts that he or she made to ascertain relatives.

(e) If a person requesting letters to administer an estate as sole executor or administrator is also an attorney admitted in this state, he or she shall file with the petition requesting letters a statement disclosing: (1) that the fiduciary is an attorney; (2) whether the fiduciary or the law firm with which he or she is affiliated will act as counsel; and (3) if applicable, that the fiduciary was the draftsperson of a will offered for probate with respect to that estate.

(effective October 3, 2000)

§ 207.17   *Reserved*

§ 207.18   Use of virtual representation.

(a) In any accounting proceeding where representation is to be utilized pursuant to subdivision 5 of SCPA 315, an affidavit of the petitioner or petitioner's attorney, and of the representor, must be submitted setting forth the following information:

(1) In the affidavit of the petitioner or petitioner's attorney:

(i) the name, address and the interest in the estate of the representor;

(ii) the name, address and the interest in the estate of the representees; and

(iii) the statutory basis for the use of virtual representation; and

(2) In the affidavit of the representor:

(i) that the representor has fully reviewed the proceedings;

(ii) the steps taken by the representor to adequately represent the interest of the representees in order to make a considered judgment whether to appear, default, acquiesce or contest the proceedings; and

(iii) that the representor has no conflict of interest in adequately representing the representees.

(b) If the court in any other proceeding, or in an accounting proceeding in circumstances other than set forth in subdivision (a), questions adequacy of representation by the representor, it may direct the filing of the affidavits set forth in subdivision (a) of this section.

(effective January 6, 1986)

§ 207.19   Probate; filing of will; depositions; proof by affidavit.

(a) With every petition for probate of a will there must be filed the original will and a copy thereof except in the case of lost or destroyed wills or where the Surrogate dispenses therewith or fixes a later time within which such will must be filed. With such copy there must also be filed an affidavit showing that it is a true copy of the original. If the copy be a reproduction by photographic or similar process, the affidavit shall be by one person; otherwise it shall be by the two persons who have compared the copy with the original. In a proceeding for probate of a will alleged to be lost or destroyed the Surrogate may make such order in respect of the filing of the text thereof as he or she may deem proper.

(b) (1) Unless service is by publication, a copy of the will shall be attached to all citations served and the affidavits of service of citation shall recite the service of a copy of the will.

(2) All waivers and consents filed with the court shall recite in the body of the waiver that a copy of the will was received.

(c) The clerk may require at least two days' notice before taking a deposition or testimony of any attesting witness. When any party is to be represented by a guardian ad litem, proponents should give notice of the time and place of taking a deposition of an attesting witness to such guardian ad litem.

(d) In a probate proceeding where the will purports to exercise a power of appointment, a copy of the instrument creating the power of appointment must be furnished, and the petition for probate shall list those named in said instrument who are adversely affected by the probate of such will. Jurisdiction shall be acquired over such persons in the same manner as over distributees.

(effective April 1, 1998)

§ 207.20   Inventory of assets

(a)

The fiduciary or the attorney of record shall furnish the court with an Inventory of Assets form which identifies the following:

(1) those assets that either were owned by the decedent individually, including those in which the decedent had a partial interest, or were payable or transferrable to the decedent's estate, by indicating the total value thereof by letter only for one of the following categories: A-under $10,000; B-$10,000 to under $20,000; C-$20,000 to under $50,000; D-$50,000 to under $100,000; E-$100,000 to under $250,000; F-$250,000 to under $500,000; G-$500,000 or over; and

(2) those assets held in trust; those assets over which the decedent had the power to designate a beneficiary; jointly owned property; and all other non-probate property of the decedent by checking yes or no.

(b) The Inventory of Assets form shall be filed with the court within nine months of the date letters issued to the fiduciary or as the court otherwise directs.

(c) In the event the Inventory of Assets is not filed, the court may refuse to issue certificates, may revoke the letters and may refuse to issue new ones until such list has been filed and the fees paid as provided in SCPA 2402. Failure to file such list of assets may also constitute grounds for disallowance of commissions or legal fees.

(d) If any additional filing fees are due, they shall be paid to the court at the time of the submission of the inventory.

(effective March 1, 2016207/64)

§ 207.21   Notification to foreign consuls.

Where it appears that an intestate who died, or any party interested in the estate of the intestate, is the subject of a foreign power whose consul is entitled by treaty to administration or intervention, notice of the application for the appointment of an administrator shall be given such consul.

(effective January 6, 1986)

§ 207.22   Witnesses out of county.

(a) When, in an uncontested probate proceeding, a witness to a will is outside the jurisdiction of the court, and SCPA 1406 is not utilized, the court may order that the witness be examined in the Surrogate's Court of another county or in an appropriate court of another state or county or before a commissioner designated by the court pursuant to SCPA 508, specifying the nature and manner of the examination, and shall send such other court or commissioner a copy of such order together with the original will or court-certified reproduction thereof. If the original will is sent, a court-certified copy thereof shall be retained in the office of the court wherein the proceeding is pending.

(b) When the testimony of the witness is obtained, it shall be annexed to the will or to the copy to which it relates, and together they shall be returned to and filed in the court wherein the proceeding is pending, as provided in SCPA 507.

(effective January 6, 1986)

§ 207.23   Bills of particulars in contested probate proceedings.

(a) In any probate proceeding in which objection to probate is made upon the grounds that the execution of the propounded instrument was procured by fraud or undue influence and the proponent demands or moves for a bill of particulars, the proponent shall be entitled as of course to the following information:

(1) the specific act or acts or course of conduct alleged to have constituted and effected such undue influence, the person or persons charged therewith and the time or times and place or places where it is alleged to have taken place;

(2) the particular false statements, suppressions of fact, misrepresentations, or other fraudulent acts alleged to have been practiced upon the decedent, the place or places where these events are claimed to have occurred and the persons who perpetrated them;

(3) whether such acts were accompanied by an act of physical violence or mistreatment of the decedent or threats, and if so, the nature thereof.

(b) If it is claimed by the contestant that the instrument offered for probate is not the last will of the deceased, the proponent shall be entitled to a bill of particulars as of course which shall state:

(1) whether it is claimed that there is an alleged testamentary instrument of later date than the instrument offered for probate;

(2) whether it is claimed that the instrument offered for probate was revoked, and if so, the method by which the alleged revocation was accomplished;

(3) whether it is merely claimed that the instrument offered for probate was not executed in accordance with the prescribed statutory formalities.

(c) In the demand or notice of motion it shall not be necessary for the proponent to set forth at length the foregoing items; he or she may, in lieu thereof, refer to the items specified in this rule. As to any other desired particulars, the proponent shall set them forth at length in the demand or notice of motion.

(d) Nothing contained in the foregoing shall be deemed to limit the court in denying, in a proper case, any one or more of the foregoing particulars, or in a proper case, in granting other, further or different particulars.

Official Rules

(effective January 6, 1986)

§ 207.24　　Discontinuance of proceedings.

In any discontinued action or proceeding, the attorney for the plaintiff or petitioner shall file a stipulation or statement of discontinuance with the clerk of the court within 20 days of such discontinuance. If the action or proceeding has been noticed for judicial activity within 20 days of such discontinuance, the stipulation or statement shall be filed before the date scheduled for such activity.

(effective April 1, 1998)

§ 207.25　　Kinship matters.

(a) Accounting proceedings. In all kinship matters, whether the hearing be held by the court or referred to a referee, proof must be completed by the party who seeks to establish kinship in an accounting proceeding within one year from the date fixed for a hearing by the court or the date of referral, or the party's objections shall be dismissed and the monies deposited pursuant to CPLR 2601 for the benefit of unknown distributees.

(b) Administration or withdrawal proceedings. In all kinship matters, whether the hearing be held by the court or referred to a referee, proof must be completed by the party who seeks to establish kinship in an administration proceeding or withdrawal proceeding within six months from the date fixed for a hearing by the court or the date of referral or the petition shall be dismissed, without prejudice.

(effective January 6, 1986)

§ 207.26　　Contested probate; notice of objections filed.

(a) Objections to probate of a will shall be filed and served with proof of service in conformity with SCPA 1410.

(b) Within thirty days of the filing of objections, the proponent shall present a citation in accordance with section 1411 of the SCPA. If the proponent fails to timely present such citation or, having presented it, fails to have it issued by the court, the objectant or any other person interested may present such citation to be served pursuant thereto.

(c) Since the requirements of SCPA 1411 are jurisdictional, all further pretrial procedures or proceedings shall be stayed until there is compliance with this rule.

(effective March 09, 2012)

§ 207.27　　Examinations before trial in contested probate proceedings.

In any contested probate proceeding in which objections to probate are made and the proponent or the objectant seeks an examination before trial, the items upon which the examination will be held shall be determined by the application of article 31 of CPLR. Except upon the showing of special circumstances, the examination will be confined to a three-year period prior to the date of the propounded instrument and two years thereafter, or to the date of decedent's death, whichever is the shorter period.

(effective January 6, 1986)

§ 207.28　　Examination of attesting witnesses, accountants and adverse parties or witnesses.

(a) All examinations of attesting witnesses, accountants and adverse parties or witnesses should be conducted on reasonable notice to all attorneys, guardians *ad litem* and parties entitled under SCPA 302(3). Unless the court otherwise directs, all examinations pursuant to SCPA 1404, 2102, 2103, 2104 and 2211 shall be held at the courthouse.

(b) Unless the court permits, such examinations shall not be conducted until jurisdiction has been obtained over all necessary parties to the proceeding and, where necessary, guardians *ad litem* have been appointed and qualified.

(effective June 22, 1992)

§ 207.29   Note of issue; pretrial conference.

(a) The court may establish such calenders of cases as it deems necessary or desirable for proper case management and may schedule calls of such calenders at such times and in such manner as it deems appropriate.

(b) The court may direct that a trial or hearing date shall not be fixed until after a party shall file in duplicate a note of issue with a certificate of readiness in a form prescribed by the court together with an affidavit of service of said note of issue and certificate of readiness upon all parties who have appeared. The note of issue filed shall contain a statement of the estimated trial time each party will require.

(c) A pretrial conference may be directed by the court, either before or after a trial date is fixed, at which the parties shall attend. At such conference, a schedule of dates for the completion of examinations, disclosure matters, bills of particulars and other pretrial matters may be directed. The court may direct parties to submit for inspection documents and exhibits, may require counsel to stipulate as to facts and issues, and may direct severance or consolidation of issues.

(effective April 1, 1988)

§ 207.30   Statement of issues.

(a) At least ten days prior to the trial of the issues joined in any proceeding, except where an order framing issues has theretofore been made, the petitioner shall file with the court a statement, in writing, of the nature of such issues, the party who holds the affirmative as to each issue, and the objections, if any, which the petitioner concedes to be well taken or which may have been withdrawn.

(b) In accounting proceedings, an additional notation shall be included in the statement as to any modifications of the account to which the parties consent.

(effective January 6, 1986)

§ 207.31   Jury trials; order framing issues.

(a) No matter shall be assigned a date for trial by jury until an order framing issues and directing a trial by jury has been made pursuant to SCPA 502.

(b) Whenever a jury trial has been demanded, any party on five days' notice of settlement to the attorneys for all other parties who have appeared may present a proposed order framing the issues and directing such trial by jury. Such order shall state plainly and concisely the controverted questions of fact to be determined by the jury.

(c) In such order, the court may fix a date for trial or on which the matter will be placed

Official Rules

on the calendar for assignment of trial date. Such order must be served on all parties who have appeared at least 15 days before date of trial or date of calendar call and proof of service filed at least ten days before such date of trial or calendar call.

(effective January 6, 1986)

§ 207.32   Identification of trial counsel.

(a) Where the attorney of record for any party arranges for another attorney to conduct the trial, the trial counsel must be identified in writing to the court and all parties within ten days after the filing of the notice of trial. The notice must be signed by both the attorney of record and the trial counsel.

(b) After trial counsel is designated as provided above, no substitution shall be permitted unless the substitute counsel is available to try the case on the day scheduled for trial. Written notice of such substitution shall be given promptly to the court and all parties.

(effective January 6, 1986)

§ 207.33   Engagement of counsel.

No adjournment shall be granted on the ground of engagement of counsel except in accordance with Part 125 of the Rules of the Chief Administrator.

(effective January 6, 1986)

§ 207.34   Exhibits.

(a) A party intending to offer an exhibit that can be readily duplicated or reproduced shall prepare extra copies for use at the trial. A party offering in evidence any paper in his or her possession shall submit a copy to opposing counsel for inspection.

(b) If a filed document is to form part of the evidence to be submitted at trial, such document or a certified copy shall be obtained or ordered from the clerk's office or other repository sufficiently in advance of trial to permit its production without delaying the trial.

(c) Whenever practicable, to avoid unnecessary delay during the trial, counsel shall hand exhibits for marking to the court reporter or other designated person prior to the opening statements or during a recess.

(effective April 1, 1988)

§ 207.35   Absence of attorney during trial.

All trial counsel shall remain in attendance at all stages of the trial until the jury retires to deliberate unless excused by the Surrogate. Any counsel not present during the jury deliberation, further requests to charge, or report of the jury verdict shall be deemed to stipulate that the court may proceed in his or her absence and to waive any irregularity in proceedings taken in his or her absence. The court may permit trial counsel to leave provided that counsel remain in telephone contact with the court.

(effective January 6, 1986)

§ 207.36   Failure to file timely objections.

Whenever the time to file objections in a proceeding has expired, objections shall not be accepted for filing unless accompanied by a stipulation of all parties to extend the time or unless ordered by the court.

(effective April 1, 1988)

§ 207.37   Submission of orders, judgments and decrees for signature.

(a) Proposed orders or judgments, with proof of service on all parties where the order is directed to be settled or submitted on notice, must be submitted for signature, unless otherwise directed by the court, within 60 days after the signing and filing of the decision directing that the order be settled or submitted.

(b) Failure to submit the order or judgment timely shall be deemed an abandonment of the motion or proceeding unless for good cause shown.

(c) (1) When settlement of an order or judgment is directed by the court, a copy of the proposed order or judgment with notice of settlement, returnable at the office of the clerk of the part in which the order or judgment was granted, or before the judge if the court has so directed or if the clerk is unavailable, shall be served on all parties either:

   (i) by personal service not less than five days before the day of settlement; or

   (ii) by mail not less than ten days before the date of settlement.

   (iii) by overnight delivery not less than six days before the date of settlement.

(2) Proposed counter-orders or judgments shall be made returnable on the same date and at the same place, and shall be served on all parties by personal service, not less than two days, or by mail, not less than seven days, before the date of settlement.

(effective January 30, 2013)

§ 207.38   Compromises.

(a) Upon any application for leave to compromise a claim for wrongful death or personal injuries, or both, the petition and the supporting affidavits shall set forth the time, place and manner in which the decedent sustained the injuries, and a complete statement of all such facts as would justify the granting of the application. If the cause of action did not arise under the laws of the State of New York, the laws of the jurisdiction under which said cause of action arose must be established to the satisfaction of the court.

(b) The petition also shall show the following:

   (1) the age, residence, occupation and earnings of the decedent at time of death;

   (2) the names, addresses, dates of birth and ages of all the persons entitled to take or share in the proceeds of the settlement or judgment, as provided by EPTL 5-4.4, or by the applicable law of the jurisdiction under which the claim arose, and a statement whether or not there are any children born out of wedlock;

   (3) a complete statement of the nature and extent of the disability, other than infancy, of any person set forth in paragraph (2) of this subdivision;

   (4) the gross amount of the proceeds of settlement, the amount to be paid as attorneys' fees, and the net amount to be received by petitioner as a result of the settlement;

   (5) any obligations incurred for funeral expenses, or for hospital, medical or nursing services, the name and address of each such creditor, the respective amounts of the obligations so incurred, whether such obligations have been paid in full and/or the amount

of the unpaid balance due on each of said claims as evidenced by proper bills filed with the clerk;

(6) whether any hospital notice of lien has been filed under section 189 of the Lien Law, and if so, the particulars relating thereto;

(7) on the basis of the applicable law, a tabulation showing the proposed distribution, including the names of the persons entitled to share in the proceeds and the percentage or fraction representing their respective shares, including a reference to the mortality table, if any, employed in the proceeding which resulted in the settlement or judgment, and the mortality table employed in the proposed distribution of the proceeds; and

(8) the cost of any annuities in compromises based upon structured settlements in wrongful death actions.

(c) Where the petition also makes application for the compromise of a claim for personal injuries sustained by the decedent, the petition shall set forth the amount allocated to each cause of action, the basis for such allocation, the effect of such allocation on decedent's estate tax liability, and proof of the citation of the New York State Department of Taxation and Finance, or their waiver thereof.

(d) A supporting affidavit by the attorney for petitioner must be filed with each petition for leave to compromise showing:

(1) whether the attorney has become concerned in the application or its subject matter at the instance of the party with whom the compromise is proposed or at the instance of any representative of such party;

(2) whether the attorney's fee is to be paid by the administrator, and whether any payment has been or is to be made to the attorney by any other person or corporation interested in the subject matter of the compromise;

(3) if the attorney's compensation is to be paid by any other person, the name of such person;

(4) the services rendered by the attorney in detail; and

(5) the amount to be paid as compensation to the attorney, including an itemization of disbursements on the case, and whether the compensation was fixed by prior agreement or based on reasonable value, and if by agreement, the person with whom such agreement was made and the terms thereof.

(e) In an application for the compromise of a claim solely for personal injuries, the petition shall contain all the facts in relation to such claim and comply with as much of the provisions of this rule as are applicable, and in addition, the petition shall recite the date letters were issued, whether more than seven months have elapsed from such date, the names and post-office addresses of all creditors, or those claiming to be creditors, and the distributees of the decedent, specifying such as are infants or alleged incompetents.

(f) Whenever papers are filed for the compromise of a cause of action in which the original action alleged conscious pain and suffering and wrongful death, and the action is subsequently settled for wrongful death only, the waivers and consents of any adult distributees who will not share in the recovery must recite that they are aware that, by consenting that the entire settlement be considered as a settlement of the cause of action for wrongful death, they are waiving the right to receive any distributive share out of the settlement.

(effective April 1, 1988)

§ 207.39   Costs and allowances.

(a) On the settlement of a decree, any party who shall deem himself entitled to costs may present a bill of costs, provided that at least two days' notice of the taxation thereof has been served on all attorneys appearing in the proceeding. Each bill of costs must show the items of costs to which the party deems himself entitled and must contain an itemized list of any disbursements claims, duly verified both as to amount and necessity. The disbursements for referee's and stenographer's fees may be evidenced by affidavit or by such other proof as may be satisfactory to the court.

(b) An application for an allowance may also be made on two days' notice to all attorneys appearing in the proceeding. Such application shall be accompanied by an affidavit setting forth the number of days necessarily occupied in the hearing or trial; the time occupied on each day in the rendition of the services; and a detailed statement of the nature and extent of the services rendered, including services necessarily rendered or to be rendered in the drawing, entering or executing of the decree.

(effective January 6, 1986)

§ 207.40   Accountings.

(a) Whenever a petition for a voluntary accounting is presented, the account to which it relates must be filed therewith, if not previously filed, and a citation to settle such account must thereupon be procured and served on the parties required to be cited.

(b) Unless otherwise directed by the court, upon an accounting by an executor, trustee, or administrator c.t.a., a copy of the will or trust instrument must be filed with the petition and account.

(c) Insofar as may be practical, all accounts shall conform with and contain such schedules and information as may be called for in such forms as may from time to time be provided by the Chief Administrator of the Courts or, in the absence thereof, by the court. In the account of a trustee of a common trust fund for a period that begins at the close of the prior intermediate account:

(1) the statements of increases and decreases shall also show gains and losses realized on disposition of assets based upon the fair market values at the beginning of the account of assets held at the beginning of the account and the inventory values of all other assets; and

(2) the statement of assets on hand at the close of the account shall also show the increase or decrease in the fair market values of the assets at the close of the account in relation to the fair market values at the beginning of the account of those assets which were held at the beginning of the account and in relation to the inventory values of the remainder of said assets.

(d) The schedule showing the computation of commissions shall also state in explicit terms whether any personal property listed as an asset of the estate was at the date of deceased's death pledged as collateral to any unpaid obligation of the decedent and, if so, shall set forth:

Official Rules

(1) a description of the property so pledged and the value thereof as listed in the account;

(2) the amount due at the date of death on the obligation for which it was pledged;

(3) the equity in such property at the date of death; and

(4) whether the accounting party has included in the claim for commissions any commission upon the value of the property so pledged and, if so, a statement of the capital value upon which such commissions are claimed with respect to such property.

(e) Unless service is by publication or unless otherwise directed by the court, a copy of the summary statement of account shall be attached to all citations served, and the affidavits of service of citation shall recite the service of a copy of the summary statement of account. Counsel for the accounting party or the account party, if not represented by counsel, shall furnish a copy of the full account to all persons cited in the accounting proceeding who request the full account. Failure to furnish such a copy may constitute grounds for disallowance of commissions or legal fees.

(f) Unless otherwise directed by the court, all waivers of citation and consents in accounting proceedings filed with the court shall recite in the body of the waiver that a copy of the summary statement of account was received and shall state that the person waiving understands that he or she may request a copy of the full account from the petitioner or petitioners attorney.

(g) The cost of producing and delivering a full accounting to persons interested in the estate shall be deemed a property disbursement and allowed as an expense of administration.

(effective April 1, 1998)

§ 207.41   Contested accountings.

On any accounting by an executor, administrator, temporary administrator, guardian or trustee, any creditor or any other party interested may file objections thereto in writing within such time as shall be allowed by the Surrogate. Such objections must be served upon the accounting party or the accounting party's attorney before the filing thereof in the court. A guardian ad litem appointed in an accounting proceeding shall file a report or objections within 20 days after the appointment unless for cause shown the time to file such report or objections is extended by the Surrogate.

(effective April 1, 1998)

§ 207.42   Report of estates not fully distributed.

(a) Whenever the estate of a decedent has not been fully distributed or a final accounting filed with petition for settlement within two years from the date when the first permanent letters of administration or letters testamentary were issued where the gross taxable estate of such decedent does not require the filing of a federal estate tax return, and within three years if a federal estate tax return is required, the executor or administrator shall, at or before the end of the first complete month following the expiration of such time, file with the clerk of the court a statement in substantially the following form:

SURROGATE'S COURT   Report pursuant to 22 NYCRR 207.42

. . . . COUNTY

Estate of . . . ., Deceased

File No. . . . .

Date of issuance of first permanent letters . . . .
Approximate amount of gross estate . . . .
Approximate amount that has been distributed to beneficiaries . . . .
Approximate amount remaining in fiduciary's hands at present . . . .
This estate has not yet been fully distributed for the following reason: (state briefly)

. . . .
. . . .
. . . .
. . . .

Date of this report . . . .

Fiduciary

Address: . . . .
Phone: . . . .
. . . .

Attorney for above Fiduciary

Address: . . . .
Phone: . . . .

(b) The court shall thereupon take such steps as it deems appropriate to expedite the completion of the administration of the estate and the distribution of all assets.

(c) Failure to file such statement will be considered by the court on any application for commissions or legal fees and may constitute a ground for disallowance of commissions or fees.

(d) The periods set forth in subdivision (a) hereinabove stated are not intended to set a standard time for completion of estate administration but rather to fix a period after which inquiry may be made by the court.

(e) This section shall not limit the power of the court to direct an accounting at any time on its own initiative or on petition pursuant to SCPA 2205.

(effective January 6, 1986)

§ 207.43   Filing estate tax return.

(a) For all persons who die on or after May 26, 1990, for whom an estate tax return is required to be filed pursuant to section 971 of the Tax Law, if a petition for probate or administration was filed with the Surrogate's Court, the person required to file the tax return shall file a copy of the tax return with such Surrogate's Court pursuant to section 972(c) of the Tax Law, within ten days of filing the original tax return with the Commissioner of Taxation and Finance; provided, however, this section shall not apply where the decedent died on or after February 1, 2000 and the Surrogate's Court in which the petition for probate or administration was filed has not adopted a rule pursuant to section 972(c) of the Tax Law requiring the filing of a copy of the tax return with such Court.

(b) Failure to file a copy of the estate tax return when required pursuant to this section together with any filing fee required pursuant to law shall authorize the court to compel an accounting pursuant to SCPA 2205 and may constitute grounds for revocation of letters, imposition of a surcharge or disallowance of commissions or legal fees.

(effective February 1, 2000)

§ 207.44 Payment of estate tax.

(a) No decree of final settlement of an executor's or administrator's account or of the discharge of an executor or administrator shall be signed unless the petition is accompanied or preceded by a copy of the letter from the Estate and Gift Tax Section of the New York Department of Taxation and Finance captioned "New York Estate Tax Discharge from Liability" showing that no final estate tax is due or that the final estate tax plus interest and penalties, if any, have been paid.

(b) Nothing herein shall preclude the discharge of an executor or an administrator who has complied with the requirements of section 1804(3) of the Surrogate's Court Procedure Act where a tax has been fixed but not paid because of insufficient funds in the estate, or the representative seeks a discharge before the estate has been administered, or where no return has been filed, or for other sufficient cause.

(effective February 8, 1994)

§ 207.45 Attorneys' fees; fixation of compensation.

(a) In any proceeding in which the relief requested includes the determination of compensation of an attorney or the allowance of expenses of counsel, there shall be filed with the petition an affidavit of services which shall state when and by whom the attorney was retained; the terms of the retainer; the amount of compensation requested; whether the client has been consulted as to the fee requested; whether the client consents to the same or, if not, the extent of disagreement or nature of any controversy concerning the same; the period during which services were rendered; the services rendered, in detail; the time spent; and the method or basis by which the requested compensation was determined. The affidavit also shall state whether the fee includes all services rendered and to be rendered up to and including settlement of the decree and distribution, if any, thereunder and whether the attorney waives a formal hearing as to compensation.

(b) Except when the SCPA otherwise provides or when compelling reasons exist for so doing, the court shall not fix attorneys' compensation or make allowances to parties for counsel expenses unless a proceeding is instituted under SCPA 2110 or unless, in an accounting, the petition and citation state that an application will be made for the determination of compensation, the allowance of counsel expenses and the amount thereof.

(c) Reports, affidavits and statements relating to fixation of fees and allowances shall be served upon the petitioner and upon all attorneys, guardians ad litem and parties appearing in person (other than those who have theretofore filed waivers). Proof of such service shall be filed with the court.

(d) In any proceeding for the determination of kinship in which an attorney appears for any party not a resident of the United States, the attorney shall institute a proceeding pursuant to SCPA 2110 for the fixation of his or her compensation and shall comply with the provisions set forth in subdivisions (a) through (c) of this section.

(effective April 1, 1998)

§ 207.46 Small estate proceedings.

In all proceedings for the settlement of small estates without court administration (SCPA Article 13), if additional certificates of voluntary administration are requested, other than updated or replacement certificates for the same asset or assets as the original certificate, such request shall be accompanied by an affidavit from either the voluntary administrator or the attorney of record setting forth the reasons additional certificates are required.

(effective April 1, 1998)

§ 207.47   Recording assignments of interest in estates.

(a) No assignment of any right, share or interest in an estate of a decedent shall be filed or recorded unless accompanied by an affidavit in a form satisfactory to the court, which shall state whether any power of attorney or separate agreement exists which relates to such assignment or which fixes presently or prospectively the amount payable by or to the assignor.

(b) A copy of such separate agreement shall be annexed to the affidavit, if such separate agreement be in writing, and a statement of the substance thereof shall be incorporated in the affidavit if such separate agreement be oral. No assignment accompanied by a power of attorney shall be recorded unless such power of attorney be recorded.

(effective January 6, 1986)

§ 207.48   Filing and recording of powers of attorney.

(a) No power of attorney affecting any interest in a decedent's estate shall be filed or recorded pursuant to EPTL 13-2.3 unless (1) the instrument is satisfactory to the court as to form, content and manner of execution and (2) the person offering the instrument for filing or recording shall furnish an affidavit of the attorney-in-fact, stating: the circumstances under which the power of attorney was procured; the post office address of the grantor; the amount of his or her interest and relationship, if any, to the decedent; the financial arrangement and exact terms of compensation of the attorney-in-fact or of any other person concerned with the matter; disbursements to be charged to the grantor; a copy of any agreement concerning compensation; and the name of any attorney representing the attorney-in-fact.

(b) An attorney-in-fact in a proceeding for the determination of kinship shall not accept any payment for acting pursuant to a power of attorney unless there has been filed with the court all the terms of the agreed-upon compensation or the same has been fixed by the court in a proceeding pursuant to SCPA 2112.

(effective April 1, 1998)

§ 207.49   Applications for appointment of successor custodians under EPTL 7-4.7.

(a) A petition for the appointment of a successor custodian under EPTL 7-4.7 shall show:

(1) the relationship between the petitioner and the minor;

(2) the age of the minor;

(3) the facts concerning the original gift;

(4) whether the donor was the original custodian and, if not, whether he or she joins in the application;

(5) the adult members of the minor's family;

(6) whether there is a general or testamentary guardian of the minor and, if so, whether

he or she joins in the application;

(7) what was the relationship between the custodian and the petitioner if the donor was the custodian and is now deceased;

(8) if the donor custodian and petitioner were husband and wife, whether they were living together and whether the infant resided with them;

(9) with whom the minor is now living;

(10) the monies and securities to be delivered to the successor custodian and the value of such securities.

(b) if the donor was a relative of the minor and has died leaving a will, a copy of the will should be submitted;

(c) Additional facts and affidavits shall be submitted as will permit the court to determine from the papers, in the absence of a contest, that the best interests of the minor will be served by the appointment of the petitioner as successor custodian, rather than by the appointment of some other eligible person.

(d) Unless otherwise ordered by the court, and unless such person or persons have joined in the application, notice of the application shall be served upon (i) such persons as are required to be served in a proceeding for the appointment of a guardian, (ii) the donor, if he or she is alive, and the guardian, if there is one of the minor.

(effective January 6, 1986)

§ 207.50   Reserved

§ 207.51   Appearance of a guardian, committee or conservator; affidavit required of attorney.

If the affidavit required by SCPA 402 shows that the guardian, committee or conservator is entitled to share in the distribution of the estate or fund in which the infant, incompetent or conservatee is interested or that the guardian, committee or conservator is in any way interested in the estate or fund, such affidavit must state fully the nature of his or her interest. Whenever a guardian, committee or conservator appears by an attorney, the latter shall accompany his or her notice of appearance with an affidavit showing the circumstances which led to his or her employment and whether his or her employment was suggested or accelerated either directly or indirectly by the proponent or accounting party or by the attorney for either of them or by any other person whose interest in the proceeding is adverse to that of the infant, incompetent or conservatee, and showing further that the attorney is free of any restraint, whether professional, personal or otherwise, in his or her complete independence of action on behalf of his or her client or ward.

(effective January 6, 1986)

§ 207.52   Accounting of an attorney-fiduciary.

(a) Within 12 months from the issuance of letters, or 24 months if the estate must file a federal estate tax return, if a sole executor or administrator administering an estate is also an attorney admitted in this state, and he or she or the law firm with which the attorney is affiliated is acting as counsel for the estate, the attorney-fiduciary shall file an affidavit setting forth (1) the total commissions paid or to be paid to him or her and (2) the total attorney's fees paid or to be paid (by court order, if required) to him or her or to the law firm with which he or she is affiliated, for services rendered to the estate.

(b) The court may extend the time for filing the affidavit upon good cause shown to the court in writing.

(c) The court in its discretion may require additional information or documentation from the attorney-fiduciary, including an affidavit of legal services, a cash flow statement and a full accounting pursuant to SCPA 2205.

(d) In the event the affidavit is not so filed, the court may suspend the letters until the affidavit has been filed. Failure to file the affidavit may constitute grounds for disallowance of commissions or legal fees.

(e) Except as otherwise provided by SCPA 2111(1) and (2), or SCPA 2310 or 2311, an attorney-fiduciary as defined in subdivision (a) (or the law firm with which he or she is affiliated) shall not take advances for legal services rendered to the estate, or commissions on account of compensation, until 30 days after filing the affidavit required by subdivision (a).

(f) The provisions of this section also shall apply to each co-fiduciary administering an estate who is an attorney admitted in this state if (1) he or she or the law firm with which the attorney is affiliated is acting as counsel for the estate, and (2) there is no other co-fiduciary who is not an attorney.

(effective April 1, 1998)

§ 207.53   Reserved

§ 207.54   Adoption rules; application.

(a) Sections 207.54 through 207.58 of this Part shall be applicable to all agency and private-placement adoption proceedings in Surrogate's Court.

(b) In any agency adoption, a petition may be filed to adopt a child who is the subject of a termination of parental rights proceeding and whose custody and guardianship has not yet been committed to an authorized agency, provided that:

(1) the adoption petition is filed in the same court where the termination of parental rights proceeding is pending; and

(2) the adoption petition, supporting documents and the fact of their filing shall not be provided to the judge before whom the petition for termination of parental rights is pending until such time as a fact-finding is concluded under that petition.

(effective September 30, 1991)

§ 207.55   Papers required in an adoption proceeding.

(a) All papers submitted in an adoption proceeding shall comply with section 207.4 of this Part.

(b) In addition to those papers required by the Domestic Relations Law, the following papers, unless otherwise dispensed with by the court, shall be submitted and filed prior to the placement of any adoption proceeding on the calendar:

(1) a certified copy of the birth certificate of the adoptive child;

Official Rules

(2) an affidavit or affidavits by an attorney admitted to practice in the State of New York, or, in the discretion of the court, by a person other than an attorney who is known to the court, identifying each of the parties;

(3) a certified marriage certificate, where the adoptive parents are husband and wife or where an individual adoptive parent is the spouse of the natural parent;

(4) a certified copy of a decree or judgment, where an adoptive parent's marriage has been terminated by decree or judgment;

(5) a certified death certificate, where an adoptive or natural parent's marriage has been terminated by death or where it is alleged that consent or notice is not required because of death;

(6) a proposed order of adoption;

(7) a copy of the attorney's affidavit of financial disclosure filed with the Office of Court Administration pursuant to Section 603.23, 691.23, 806.14 or 1022.33 and either an attorney's affirmation that the affidavit has been personally delivered or mailed in accordance with such rules or the dated receipt from the Office of Court Administration; and

(8) an affidavit of financial disclosure from the adoptive parent or parents, and from any person whose consent to the adoption is required by law, setting forth the following information:

(i) name, address and telephone number of the affiant;

(ii) status of the affiant in the proceeding and relationship, if any, to the adoptive child;

(iii) docket number of adoption proceeding;

(iv) the date and terms of every agreement, written or otherwise between the affiant and any attorney pertaining to any fees, compensation or other remuneration paid or to be paid by or on behalf of the adoptive parents or the natural parents, directly or indirectly, including but not limited to retainer fees on account of or incidental to the placement or adoption of the child or assistance in arrangements for such placement or adoption;

(v) the date and amount of any fees, compensation or other remuneration paid, and the total amount of fees, compensation or other remuneration to be paid to such attorney by the affiant, directly or indirectly, on account of or incidental to the placement or adoption of the child or assistance in arrangements for such placement or adoption;

(vi) the name and address of any other person, agency, association, corporation, institution, society or organization who received or will receive any fees, compensation or other remuneration from the affiant, directly or indirectly, on account of or incidental to the birth or care of the adoptive child, the pregnancy or care of the adoptive child's mother or the placement or adoption of the child and on account of or incidental to assistance in arrangements for such placement or proposed adoption; the amount of each such fee, compensation or other remuneration; and the reason for or services rendered, if any, in connection with each such fee, compensation or other remuneration;

and

(vii) the name and address of any person, agency, association, corporation, society or organization who has or will pay the affiant any fee, compensation or other remuneration, directly or indirectly, on account of or incidental to the birth or care of the adoptive child, the pregnancy or care of the adoptive child's mother, or the placement or adoption of the child and on account of or incidental to assistance in arrangements for such placement or adoption; the amount of each such fee, compensation or other remuneration; and the reason for or services rendered, if any, in connection with each such fee, compensation or other remuneration.

(9) in the case of an adoption from an authorized agency in accordance with Title 2 of Article 7 of the Domestic Relations Law, a copy of the criminal history summary report made by the New York State Office of Children and Family Services to the authorized agency pursuant to section 378-a of the Social Services Law regarding the criminal record or records of the prospective adoptive parent or parents and any adult over the age of 18 currently residing in the home.

(c) Prior to the signing of an order of adoption, the court may in its discretion require the filing of a supplemental affidavit by the adoptive parent or parents, or any person whose consent to the adoption is required, the authorized agency and the attorney for any of the aforementioned, setting forth any additional information pertaining to allegations in the petition or in any affidavit filed in the proceeding.

(effective October 8, 2003)

§ 207.56   Investigation by disinterested person; adoption.

(a) The probation service or an authorized agency or disinterested person is authorized to and, at the request of the court, shall interview such persons and obtain such data as will aid the court in determining the truth and accuracy of an adoption petition under article 7 of the Domestic Relations Law, including the allegations set forth in the schedule annexed to the petition pursuant to section 112(3) of that law and such other facts as are necessary to a determination of the petition;

(b) The adoptive parent or parents and other persons concerned with the proceeding shall be notified of the date, time and place of any interview by a disinterested person or authorized agency designated by the court in accordance with sections 112 and 116 of the Domestic Relations Law.

(c) The written report of the investigation conducted pursuant to subdivision (a) of this section shall be submitted to the court within 30 days from the date on which it was ordered, or earlier as the court may direct, unless, for good cause, the court shall grant an extension for a reasonable period of time not to exceed an additional 30 days.

(effective January 6, 1986)

§ 207.57   Special applications.

All applications, including applications to dispense with statutorily required personal appearances, period of residence of a child, or period of waiting after filing of the adoption petition, shall be made in writing and shall be accompanied by affidavits setting forth the reasons for the application and all facts relevant thereto.

(effective January 6, 1986)

Official Rules

§ 207.58   Petition for guardianship by adoptive parent.

(a) When a petition for temporary guardianship has been filed by an adoptive parent or parents pursuant to section 115-c of the Domestic Relations Law, the clerk of the court in which the petition has been filed shall distribute a written notice to the adoptive parents and lawyers who have appeared, and to the Commissioner of Social Services or the Director of the Probation Service, as appropriate, indicating that:

(1) a petition for adoption must be filed in the court in which the application for temporary guardianship has been brought within 45 days from the date of the signing of the consent to the adoption;

(2) any order or decree of temporary guardianship will expire no later than nine months following its issuance or upon the entry of a final order of adoption whichever is sooner, unless, upon application to the court, it is extended for good cause;

(3) any order or decree of temporary guardianship will terminate upon withdrawal or denial of a petition to adopt the child, unless the court orders a continuation of such order or decree;

(b) In addition to and without regard to the date set for the hearing of the petition, the clerk of the court shall calendar the case for the 45th day from the date of the signing of the consent to the adoption. If no petition for adoption has been filed by the 45th day, the court shall schedule a hearing and shall order the appropriate agency to conduct an investigation forthwith, if one had not been ordered previously.

(effective March 20, 1989)

§ 207.59   Proceedings involving custody of a Native American child.

In any proceeding in which the custody of a child is to be determined, the petition shall set forth whether the child is a Native American child subject to the Indian Child Welfare Act of 1978 (25 U.S.C. §§ 1901–1963), and the Court shall proceed further, as appropriate, in accordance with the provisions of that act.

(effective March 18, 1992)

§ 207.60   *Reserved*

§ 207.61   Proceedings for certification as a qualified adoptive parent or parents.

(a) Where the petition in a proceeding for certification as a qualified adoptive parent or parents alleges that petitioner or petitioners will cause a preplacement investigation to be undertaken, the petition shall include the name and address of the disinterested person by whom such investigation will be conducted.

(b) The report of the disinterested person conducting the preplacement investigation shall be filed by such person directly with the court, with a copy of such report delivered simultaneously to the applicant or applicants.

(c) The court shall order a report (1) from the statewide central register of child abuse and maltreatment setting forth whether the child or the petitioner is, or petitioners are, the subject of or another person named in an indicated report, as such terms are defined in section 412 of the Social Services Law, filed with such register; and (2) from the New York State Division of Criminal Justice Services setting forth any existing criminal record of such petitioner or petitioners in accordance with section 115-d(3-a) of the Domestic Relations Law; provided, however, that where the petitioner(s) have been fingerprinted pursuant to Social Services Law 378-a, the authorized agency in possession of current criminal history summary report from the New York State Office of Children and Family Services may be requested to provide such report to the court in lieu of a report from the New York State Division of Criminal Justice Services.

(effective January 31, 2001)

§ 207.62   Calendaring of proceedings for adoption from an authorized agency.

Proceedings for adoption from an authorized agency shall be calendared as follows:

(a) Within 60 days of the filing of the petition and documents specified in section 112-a of the Domestic Relations Law, the court shall schedule a review of said petition and documents to take place to determine if there is adequate basis for approving the adoption.

(b) If such basis is found, the court shall schedule the appearance of the adoptive parent(s) and child before the court, for approval of the adoption, within 30 days of the date of the review.

(c) If, upon the court's review, the court finds that there is not an adequate basis for approval of the adoption, the court shall direct such further hearings, submissions or appearances as may be required, and the proceeding shall be adjourned as required for such purposes.

(effective September 22, 1993)

§ 207.63   Annual report of public administrator.

(a) Each Surrogate shall request from the public administrator a year-end annual report which, with the participation of the counsel to the public administrator, addresses the following areas: office procedures and record keeping; case management of estates; cash management of estate accounts and financial assets; property management; sale of real and personal property; selection and compensation of outside vendors; and statistical summaries of number of estates under administration, gross value of estates under administration, statutory commissions earned by the public administrator or counsel to the public adminis-trator, legal fees earned by each counsel to the public administrator, and expenditures by the public administrator on vendors, lessors and other service providers other than counsel.

(b) Each Surrogate shall transmit to the Chief Administrator of the Courts the annual report of the public administrator and counsel to the public administrator, together with whatever written commentary thereon the Surrogate deems appropriate and necessary in view of his or her oversight role in connection with the operations and performance of the office of the public administrator and counsel to the public administrator.

(effective May 1, 2006)

§ 207.64   Omission or redaction of confidential personal information; public access to certain filings

(a) Omission or Redaction of Confidential Personal Information.

(1) Except as otherwise provided by rule or law or court order, and whether or not a sealing order is or has been sought, the parties shall omit or redact confidential personal

information in papers submitted to the court for filing. For purposes of this rule, confidential personal information ("CPI") means:

(i) the taxpayer identification number of an individual or an entity, including a social security number, an employer identification number, and an individual taxpayer identification number, except the last four digits thereof; and

(ii) other than in a proceeding under Article 13 of the SCPA, a financial account number, including a credit and/or debit card number, a bank account number, an investment account number, and/or an insurance account number, except the last four digits or letters thereof.

(2) The court sua sponte or on motion by any person may order a party to remove CPI from papers or to resubmit a paper with such information redacted; order the clerk to seal the papers or a portion thereof containing CPI in accordance with the requirement of 22 NYCRR §216.1 that any sealing be no broader than necessary to protect the CPI; for good cause permit the inclusion of CPI in papers; order a party to file an unredacted copy under seal for in camera review; or determine that information in a particular action is not confidential. The court shall consider the pro se status of any party in granting relief pursuant to this provision.

(3) Where a person submitting a paper to a court for filing believes in good faith that the inclusion of the full CPI described in Paragraph (1) of this subdivision is material and necessary to the adjudication of the proceeding before the court, he or she may apply to the court for leave to serve and file, together with a paper in which such information has been set forth in abbreviated form, a confidential affidavit or affirmation setting forth the same information in unabbreviated form, appropriately referenced to the page or pages of the paper at which the abbreviated form appears.

(4) When served with objections or a request for an inquiry or examination under SCPA 2211 or 1404 that specifies a request for particular unredacted documents previously filed in the proceeding with respect to which the objection or request for inquiry or examination relates, the party who originally served and filed the redacted document shall serve (but not file) an unredacted version upon all parties interested in the proceeding or such portion of it to which the objection or request for inquiry or examination relates.(b) Public Access to Certain Filings

The officers, clerks and employees of the court shall not permit a copy of any of the following documents to be viewed or taken by any other person than a party to the proceeding, or the attorney or counsel to a party to the proceeding, the Public Administrator or counsel thereto, counsel for any Federal, State or local governmental agency, or court personnel, or by order of the court or written permission of the Surrogate or Chief Clerk of the court. The standard for the grant of such permission in a contested matter shall be the same as required under 22 NYCRR 216.1 and applicable law:

(1) All papers and documents in proceedings instituted pursuant to Articles 17 or 17-A of the SCPA;

(2) Death certificates;

(3) Tax returns;

(4) Firearms Inventory; and

(5) Documents containing information protected from disclosure under other provisions of Federal or State law such as HIPAA for medical information, job protected services reports, material obtained from a state mental hygiene facility under MHL 33.13, and records involving alcohol or other substance abuse under 42 CFR 2.64. These examples are not intended to be exclusive.

This rule shall not preclude disclosure or copying of any index of filings maintained by the court. Any determination by the court regarding access to any filings may be the subject of an appropriate motion for clarification or reconsideration.

(*Effective March 1, 2016*)

RULES OF THE CHIEF JUDGE

Part 36 APPOINTMENT OF GUARDIANS, GUARDIANS AD LITEM, COURT EVALUATORS, ATTORNEYS FOR INCAPACITATED PERSONS, RECEIVERS, PERSONS DESIGNATED TO PERFORM SERVICES FOR A RECEIVER, AND REFEREES

TABLE OF CONTENTS
Part 36

§ 36.0   Preamble.

Public trust in the judicial process demands that appointments by judges be fair, impartial and beyond reproach. Accordingly, these rules are intended to ensure that appointees are selected on the basis of merit, without favoritism, nepotism, politics or other factors unrelated to the qualifications of the appointee or the requirements of the case.

The rules cannot be written in a way that foresees every situation in which they should be applied. Therefore, the appointment of trained and competent persons, and the avoidance of factors unrelated to the merit of the appointments or the value of the work performed, are fundamental objectives that should guide all appointments made and orders issued pursuant to this Part.

(*effective October 18, 2018*)

§ 36.1   Application.

(a) Except as set forth in subdivision (b) of this section, this Part shall apply to the following appointments made by any judge or justice of the Unified Court System:

(1) guardians;

(2) guardians ad litem, including guardians ad litem appointed to investigate and report to the court on particular issues, and their counsel and assistants;

(3) attorneys for the child who are not paid from public funds, in those judicial departments where their appointments are authorized;

(4) court evaluators;

(5) attorneys for alleged incapacitated persons;

(6) court examiners;

(7) supplemental needs trustees;

(8) receivers;

(9) referees (other than special masters and those serving otherwise in a quasi-judicial capacity); and

(10) the following persons performing services for guardians or receivers:

(i) counsel;

(ii) accountants;

(iii) auctioneers;

(iv) appraisers;

(v) property managers;

(vi) real estate brokers; and

(11) a public administrator within the City of New York and for the counties of Westchester, Onondaga, Erie, Monroe, Suffolk and Nassau and counsel to the public administrator, except that only sections 36.2(c) and 36.4(f)(e) of this Part shall apply, and that section 36.2(c) shall not apply to incumbents in these positions until one year after the effective date of this paragraph.

(b) Except for sections 36.2(c)(6) and 36.2(c)(7) of this Part, this Part shall not apply to:

(1) appointments of attorneys for the child pursuant to section 243 of the Family Court Act, guardians ad litem pursuant to section 403-a of the Surrogate's Court Procedure Act, or the Mental Hygiene Legal Service;

(2) the appointment of, or the appointment of any persons or entities performing services for, any of the following:

(i) a guardian who is a relative of the subject of the guardianship proceeding; a person or entity nominated as guardian by the subject of the proceeding; a person or entity proposed as guardian by a party to the proceeding; or a person or entity having a legally recognized duty or interest with respect to the subject of the proceeding;

(ii) a guardian ad litem nominated by an infant of 14 years of age or over;

(iii) a nonprofit institution performing property management or personal needs services, or acting as court evaluator, attorney for an alleged incapacitated person, or guardian ad litem;

(iv) a bank or trust company as a depository for funds or as a supplemental needs trustee;

(v) except as set forth in section 36.1(a)(11), a public official vested with the powers of an administrator;

(vi) a person or institution whose appointment is required by law; or

(vii) a physician whose appointment as a guardian ad litem is necessary where emergency medical or surgical procedures are required; or

(3) an appointment other than above without compensation, except that the appointee must file a notice of appointment pursuant to section 36.4(a) of this Part.

(*effective February 9, 2021*)

§ 36.2   Appointments.

(a) Appointments by the judge. All appointments of the persons set forth in section 36.1 of this Part, including those persons set forth in section 36.1(a)(10) of this Part who perform services for guardians or receivers, shall be made by the judge authorized by law to make the appointment. In making appointments of persons to perform services for guardians or receivers, the appointing judge may consider the recommendation of the guardian or receiver.

(b) Use of lists.

(1) All appointments pursuant to this Part shall be made by the appointing judge from the appropriate list of applicants established by the Chief Administrator of the Courts pursuant to section 36.3 of this Part.

(2) An appointing judge may appoint a person not on the appropriate list of applicants upon a finding of good cause, which shall be set forth in writing and shall be filed with the fiduciary clerk at the time of the making of the appointment. The appointing judge shall send a copy of such writing to the Chief Administrator. A judge may not appoint a person that has been removed from a list pursuant to section 36.3(e) of this Part.

(3) Appointments made from outside the lists shall remain subject to all of the requirements and limitations set forth in this Part, except that the appointing judge may waive any education and training requirements where completion of these requirements would be impractical.

(c) Disqualifications from appointment.

(1) No person shall be appointed who is a judge or housing judge of the Unified Court System of the State of New York, or who is a relative of, or related by marriage to, a judge or housing judge of the Unified Court System within the fourth degree of relationship.

(2) No person serving as a judicial hearing officer pursuant to Part 122 of the Rules of the Chief Administrator shall be appointed in actions or proceedings in a court in a county where he or she serves on a judicial hearing officer panel for such court.

(3) No person shall be appointed who is a full-time or part-time employee of the Unified Court System. No person who is the spouse, sibling, parent or child of an employee who holds a position at salary grade JG24 or above, or its equivalent, shall be appointed by a court within the judicial district where the employee is employed or, with respect to an employee with statewide responsibilities, by any court in the State.

(4) (i) No person who is a chair or executive director, or their equivalent, of a state or county political party (including any person or persons who, in counties of any size or population, possess or perform any of the titles, powers or duties set forth in Public Officers Law § 73[1][k]), or the spouse, sibling, parent or child of that official, shall be appointed while that official serves in that position and for a period of two years after that official no longer holds that position. This prohibition shall apply to the members, associates, counsel and employees of any law firms or entities while the official is associated with that firm or entity.

(ii) No person who has served as a campaign chair, coordinator, manager, treasurer or finance chair for a candidate for judicial office, or the spouse, sibling, parent or child of that person, or anyone associated with the law firm of that person, shall be appointed by the judge for whom that service was performed for a period of two years following the judicial election.

(5) No former judge or housing judge of the Unified Court System, or the spouse, sibling, parent or child of such judge, shall be appointed, within two years from the date the judge left judicial office, by a court within the jurisdiction where the judge served. Jurisdiction is defined as follows:

(i) the jurisdiction of a judge of the Court of Appeals shall be statewide;

(ii) the jurisdiction of a justice of an Appellate Division shall be the judicial department within which the justice served;

(iii) the jurisdiction of a justice of the Supreme Court and a judge of the Court of Claims shall be the principal judicial district within which the justice or judge served; and

(iv) with respect to all other judges, the jurisdiction shall be the principal county within which the judge served.

(6) No attorney who has been disbarred or suspended from the practice of law shall be appointed during the period of disbarment or suspension.

(7) No person convicted of a felony, or for five years following the date of sentencing after conviction of a misdemeanor (unless otherwise waived by the Chief Administrator upon application), shall be appointed unless that person receives a certificate of relief from disabilities.

(8) No receiver or guardian shall be appointed as his or her own counsel, and no person associated with a law firm of that receiver or guardian shall be appointed as counsel to that receiver or guardian, unless there is a compelling reason to do so.

(9) No attorney for an alleged incapacitated person shall be appointed as guardian to that person, or as counsel to the guardian of that person.

(10) No person serving as a court evaluator shall be appointed as guardian for the incapacitated person except under extenuating circumstances that are set forth in writing and filed with the fiduciary clerk at the time of the appointment.

(d) Limitations based upon compensation.

(1) No person shall be eligible to receive more than one appointment within a calendar year for which the compensation anticipated to be awarded to the appointee in any calendar year exceeds the sum of $15,000.

(2) If a person has been awarded more than an aggregate of $100,000 in compensation by all courts during any calendar year, the person shall not be eligible for compensated appointments by any court during the next calendar year.

(3) For purposes of this Part, the term compensation shall mean awards by a court of fees, commissions, allowances or other compensation, excluding costs and disbursements.

(4) These limitations shall not apply where the appointment is necessary to maintain continuity of representation of or service to the same person or entity in further or subsequent proceedings.

(*effective October 18, 2018*)

§ 36.3   **Procedure for appointment.**

(a) Application for appointment. The Chief Administrator shall provide for the application by persons seeking appointments pursuant to this Part on such forms as shall be promulgated by the Chief Administrator. The forms shall contain such information as is necessary to establish that the applicant meets the qualifications for the appointments covered by this Part and to apprise the appointing judge of the applicant's background.

(b) Qualifications for appointment. The Chief Administrator shall establish requirements of education and training for placement on the list of available applicants. These requirements shall consist, as appropriate, of substantive issues pertaining to each category of appointment—including applicable law, procedures, and ethics—as well as explications of the rules and procedures implementing the process established by this Part. Education and training courses and programs shall meet the requirements of these rules only if certified by the Chief Administrator. Attorney participants in these education and training courses and programs may be eligible for continuing legal education credit in accordance with the requirements of the Continuing Legal Education Board.

(c) Establishment of lists. The Chief Administrator shall establish separate lists of qualified applicants for each category of appointment, and shall make available such information as will enable the appointing judge to be apprised of the background of each applicant. The Chief Administrator may establish more than one list for the same appointment category where appropriate to apprise the appointing judge of applicants who have substantial experience in that category. Pursuant to section 81.32(b) of the Mental Hygiene Law, the Presiding Justice of the appropriate Appellate Division shall designate the qualified applicants on the lists of court examiners established by the Chief Administrator.

(d) Registration. The Chief Administrator shall establish a procedure requiring that each person on a list reregister every two years in order to remain on the list.

(e) Removal from lists. The Chief Administrator may remove any person from any list for unsatisfactory performance or any conduct incompatible with appointment from that list, or if disqualified from appointment pursuant to this Part. A person may not be removed except upon receipt of a written statement of reasons for the removal and an opportunity to provide an explanation and to submit facts in opposition to the removal.

(f) Notwithstanding section 36.3(e), pending a final determination on the issue of removal, the Chief Administrator may temporarily suspend any person from any list upon a showing of good cause that the person's conduct places clients or wards at significant risk of financial or other harm, or presents an immediate threat to the public.

(*effective October 18, 2018*)

§ 36.4   Procedure after appointment.

(a) Upon appointment of a fiduciary pursuant to this Part, the Court shall forward a copy of the appointment order to the designated fiduciary clerk within two (2) business days.

(b) Notice of appointment and certification of compliance.

(1) Every person appointed pursuant to this Part shall file with the fiduciary clerk of the court from which the appointment is made, within 30 days of the making of the appointment:

(i) a notice of appointment; and

(ii) a certification of compliance with this Part, on such form as promulgated by the Chief Administrator. Copies of this form shall be made available at the office of the fiduciary clerk and shall be transmitted by that clerk to the appointee immediately after the making of the appointment by the appointing judge. An appointee who accepts an appointment without compensation need not complete the certification of compliance portion of the form.

(2) The notice of appointment shall contain the date of the appointment and the nature of the appointment.

(3) The certification of compliance shall include:

(i) a statement that the appointment is in compliance with section 36.2(c) and (d) of this Part; and

(ii) a list of all appointments received, or for which compensation has been awarded, during the current calendar year and the year immediately preceding the current calendar year, which shall contain:

(a) the name of the judge who made each appointment;

(b) the compensation awarded; and

(c) where compensation remains to be awarded

(i) the compensation anticipated to be awarded; and

(ii) separate identification of those appointments for which compensation of $15,000 or more is anticipated to be awarded during any calendar year. The list shall include the appointment for which the filing is made.

(4) A person who is required to complete the certification of compliance, but who is unable to certify that the appointment is in compliance with this Part, shall immediately so inform the appointing judge.

(c) Approval of compensation.

(1) Upon the approval of compensation of more than $500, the court shall file with the fiduciary clerk (i) on such form as is promulgated by the Chief Administrator, a statement of approval of compensation, which shall contain a confirmation to be signed by the fiduciary clerk that the appointee has filed the notice of appointment and certification of compliance; and (ii) a copy of the proposed order approving compensation.

(2) The court shall not sign an order awarding compensation exceeding $500 until such time as the fiduciary clerk has confirmed that the appointee has properly filed the notice of appointment and certification of compliance. No compensation shall be awarded to an appointee who has not properly filed the notice of appointment and certification of compliance.

(3) Each approval of compensation of $5,000 or more to appointees pursuant to this section shall be accompanied by a statement, in writing, of the reasons therefor by the judge. The judge shall file a copy of the order approving compensation and the statement with the fiduciary clerk at the time of the signing of the order.

(4) Compensation to appointees shall not exceed the fair value of services rendered.

Appointees who serve as counsel to a guardian or receiver shall not be compensated as counsel for services that should have been performed by the guardian or receiver.

(5) Unless otherwise directed by the court, a fiduciary appointee may utilize supporting attorneys and staff in their firm without additional Court approval. Support attorneys and staff may perform tasks only under the fiduciary appointee's direct supervision; all appearances and reports must be made by the fiduciary appointee; and all compensation earned by support attorneys or personnel shall be charged to the appointee for purposes of compensation limits pursuant to this Part.

(d) Reporting of compensation received by law firms. A law firm whose members, associates and employees have had a total of $50,000 or more in compensation approved in a single calendar year for appointments made pursuant to this Part shall report such amounts on a form promulgated by the Chief Administrator.

(e) Reporting of compensation received by a referee to sell real property.

(1) A referee to sell real property shall make a letter application to the court to authorize payment over $1,100 for a "good cause" adjournment or if there is a rebid or resale.

(2) Upon approval of compensation exceeding $1,100 to a referee to sell real property, the Court shall file a copy of its compensation order with the appropriate fiduciary clerk, who shall generate the required Unified Court System forms and monitor compliance and filing with the Part 36 processing unit. Payment of such compensation may not be made until the plaintiffs in the matter have received a copy of the court's compensation order.

(3) Exception. The procedure set forth in section 36.4(b)(1) shall not apply to the appointment of a referee to sell real property and a referee to compute whose compensation for such appointments is not anticipated to exceed $1,100.

(f) Approval and reporting of compensation received by counsel to the public administrator.

(1) A judge shall not approve compensation to counsel to the public administrator in excess of the fee schedule promulgated by the administrative board of the public administrator under SCPA 1128 unless accompanied by the judge's statement, in writing, of the reasons therefor, and by the appointee's affidavit of legal services under SCPA 1108 setting forth in detail the services rendered, the time spent, and the method or basis by which the requested compensation was determined.

(2) Any approval of compensation in excess of the fee schedule promulgated by the administrative board of the public administrator shall be reported to the Office of Court Administration on a form promulgated by the Chief Administrator and shall be accompanied by a copy of the order approving compensation, the judge's written statement, and the counsel's affidavit of legal services, which records shall be published as determined by the Chief Administrator.

(3) Each approval of compensation of $5,000 or more to counsel shall be reported to the Office of Court Administration on a form promulgated by the Chief Administrator and shall be published as determined by the Chief Administrator.

(*effective March 26, 2019*)

§ 36.5   Publication of appointments.

(a) All forms filed pursuant to section 36.4 of this Part shall be public records.

(b) The Chief Administrator shall arrange for the periodic publication of the names of all persons appointed by each appointing judge, and the compensation approved for each appointee.

(*effective October 18, 2018*)

ESTATE TAX RULES

TABLE OF CONTENTS
Title 20

Part 360

Part 360

TITLE 20   DEPARTMENT OF TAXATION AND FINANCE

CHAPTER II   INCOME TAXES AND ESTATE TAXES

SUBCHAPTER G   ESTATE TAX

§ 360.1   Payment, delivery and transfer of cash, deposits and open-market securities whose value is not more than $ 30,000

(a) (1) Any trust company, corporation, bank or other institution, or person having in possession or under control cash or deposits not exceeding $ 30,000, which belong to or stand in the name of a decedent dying after June 30, 1978, or which belong to or stand in the names of such a decedent and one or more other persons jointly, may pay the same to or upon the order of the decedent's executor or administrator, a surviving joint depositor or any other person to whom payment is authorized by law, without the consent of the State Tax Commission, without notice to the commission, and without retaining any portion of such cash or deposits for the payment of estate tax. In the case of a decedent dying before July 1, 1978, payment may be made under the preceding sentence, but only if the cash and deposits do not exceed $ 2,000. Payment of cash or deposits in an amount not exceeding $ 30,000 ($ 2,000 in the case of decedents dying before July 1, 1978) should not be withheld on account of absence of waivers issued by the State Tax Commission.

(2) Any trust company, corporation, bank or other institution, or person having in possession or under control cash or deposits in excess of $ 30,000, which belong to or stand in the name of a decedent dying after June 30, 1978, or which belong to or stand in

the names of such a decedent and one or more other persons jointly, may pay not more than $ 30,000 thereof in the aggregate to or upon the order of decedent's executor or administrator, a surviving joint depositor or any other person to whom payment is authorized by law, without the consent of the State Tax Commission, without notice to the commission, and without retaining any portion of such withdrawal for the payment of estate tax. Before any payment is made, in the case of such a decedent dying after June 30, 1978, which, together with all other payments made previously or at the same time, would amount to over $ 30,000, a waiver must be obtained for the total amount on deposit in possession of or under control of the payor as of the date of the decedent's death. In the case of a decedent dying before July 1, 1978, payment may be made and waivers are required under the preceding sentences of this paragraph, but the amount of $ 2,000 shall be substituted for $ 30,000 wherever appearing in such sentences.

(b) Any person or corporation having possession or control of stock or other securities which belong to or stand in the name of a decedent dying after June 30, 1978, or which belong to or stand in the names of such a decedent and one or more other persons jointly, if such stock or other securities are customarily bought and sold in open markets, and if the market value thereof is not more than $ 30,000, may transfer or deliver the same to or upon the order of decedent's executor or administrator, a surviving joint stockholder, or any other person to whom delivery or transfer is authorized by law, without the consent of the State Tax Commission, without notice to the commission, and without retaining any portion of such stock or securities for the payment of estate tax. In the case of a decedent dying before July 1, 1978, transfer or delivery may be effected under the preceding sentence, but only if such securities have a market value of not more than $ 2,000. Transfer of securities having a market value of not more than $ 30,000 ($ 2,000 in the case of a decedent dying before July 1, 1978) should not be withheld on account of absence of waivers issued by the State Tax Commission.

(c) A corporation or its transfer agent or registrar may make such a transfer of stock or other securities issued by itself, the market value of which does not exceed $ 30,000 in the case of a decedent dying after June 30, 1978 ($ 2,000 in the case of a decedent dying before July 1, 1978), regardless of the total value of all stock or other securities issued by such corporation in the name of the decedent or in the names of the decedent and others jointly, and regardless of whether any other transfer of such stock or securities has previously been made.

(d) The State Tax Commission may defer the issuance of waivers consenting to the delivery or transfer to the executors, administrators or legal representatives of a decedent or to the survivors when held in the joint names of a decedent and one or more persons, or upon their order or request, of securities, deposits or other assets belonging to or standing in the name of said decedent or belonging to or standing in the joint names of such a decedent and one or more persons, in such amounts or portions as in the judgment of the State Tax Commission may be required to secure the payment of estate tax and interest which may thereafter be assessed on account of the delivery or transfer of such securities, deposits or other assets.

(e) Notwithstanding any other provision of this Part, in the case of a decedent dying after September 30, 1983, any cash or deposits or any stock or other security customarily bought and sold in open markets which:

(1) belongs to or stands in the name of such decedent and such decedent's surviving spouse as tenants by the entirety or as joint tenants with right of survivorship (but only if the decedent and the decedent's spouse are the only joint tenants);

(2) belongs to or stands in the name of such decedent in trust for the surviving spouse where such surviving spouse is the sole beneficiary; or

(3) belongs to or stands in the name of such decedent in an individual retirement account, an individual retirement annuity account, a Keogh account or any other account specified by the commissioner where the surviving spouse is the sole beneficiary may be transferred or delivered to such surviving spouse without notice to, or the written consent or waiver of, the Department of Taxation and Finance and without retaining any portion thereof for the payment of estate tax regardless of the value of such cash, deposit, stock or other security.

(f) Nothing in this Part shall be construed as requiring the consent of the department, notice to the department or retention of assets for the payment of estate tax for the transfer of cash, deposits, stock or other securities described in this section that, with respect to any one trust company, corporation, bank, other institution or person, do not, in the aggregate, exceed the applicable amount described in this section.

(*effective February 17, 1999*)

§ 360.2   Delivery of contents of safe deposit boxes of deceased residents

(a) In all cases, a representative of the estate shall complete an application for the release of a safe deposit box, on a form provided by the department, and mail or deliver the completed form to the department.

(b) When there is a will-search order.

(1) When a will-search order has been made pursuant to section 2003 of the Surrogate's Court Procedure Act, the department shall, after receiving a properly completed application form, advise the representative of the estate as to when the safe deposit box can be opened in the presence of a representative of the department.

(2) At the box opening, a representative of the department shall make a complete inventory of the contents of the box. The bank or safe deposit company having possession or control of such safe deposit box shall deliver the following contents thereof to the person or persons entitled to receive them without written consent or waiver of the department and without retaining any portion thereof for the payment of estate tax or interest:

(i) a will, deed to a burial plot or insurance policy to be delivered as provided in the will-search order;

(ii) papers, other than securities, which have no apparent monetary value; and

(iii) United States bonds or other securities registered in the name of any person other than the decedent, whose value is readily ascertainable from published quotations and provided that the value of all such bonds and other securities is not more than $ 30,000.

(3) If the box also contains items not distributable in accordance with such paragraph (2) of this subdivision, then, the box shall be resealed and cannot be reopened, or the remaining contents distributed, until the department has issued a waiver to the representative of the estate.

(c) When a will-search order has not been made.

Official Rules

(1) If the department, after receiving a properly completed application form, determines that a representative of the department must attend the box opening, then the provisions of subdivision (b) of this section shall apply except that for purposes of paragraph (b)(3) of this section the representative of the department may determine that no additional taxes administered by the department are likely to be due. Where the representative makes this determination, a waiver can be immediately issued releasing the contents of the box to the representative of the estate.

(2) If the department, after receiving a properly completed application form, determines that a representative of the department is not required to attend the box opening, then the department shall issue a waiver releasing the contents of the box to the representative of the estate. The representative of the state shall make, sign and send a complete inventory of the contents of the box to the department within five business days after the date that the box was opened. The signature of the representative of the estate on the inventory form shall be acknowledged by a notary public.

(d) Copying of papers regarding burial. Notwithstanding any of the provisions of this section or section 2003 of the Surrogate's Court Procedure Act, a safe deposit company, trust company, bank, corporation, firm or other person, having in its possession, or under its control, one or more safe deposit boxes, shall permit an individual or individuals, each of whom being a joint lessee with the decedent of said safe deposit box or boxes, or a deputy authorized by the decedent to have access to said safe deposit box or boxes, to examine and make copies of, in the presence of an officer of the company, bank, corporation or firm, any paper or papers found in said safe deposit box or boxes bearing upon the desire of the deceased as to the disposal of the deceased's remains, or a deed to a cemetery plot, or proof of membership in a burial society. For purposes of the preceding sentence, the term deputy shall mean the person who had access to the decedent's safe deposit box or boxes and to the contents thereof on the last day of decedent's life. After copies have been made of the paper or papers described in this subdivision, the original paper or papers shall be resealed in the safe deposit box of boxes. The contents of the box or boxes shall be distributed in accordance with subdivisions (a) and (b) or (a) and (c) of this section.

(*effective May 24, 1989*)

§ 360.3   Delivery of contents of safe deposit boxes of nonresidents

Any safe deposit company, trust company, corporation, bank or other institution may deliver the contents of a safe deposit box to the representatives of the estate of a deceased person in whose name the box was registered, and who was, at the time of death, a nonresident of this State, without obtaining the consent of the State Tax Commission, provided notice of the intended delivery is mailed or delivered to said commission at Albany, New York.

§ 360.4   Transfer of partnership assets after the death of a partner

After the death of a member of a partnership, any person or corporation having possession or control of securities, deposits or other assets belonging to or standing in the name of the partnership may transfer, pay or deliver the same to or upon the order of the surviving partner or partners, or such other person as may be entitled to receive the same on behalf of such partnership, without written consent or waiver of the State Tax Commission and without retaining any portion thereof for the payment of estate tax or interest.

§ 360.5   Payment of death benefits under employees' pension or profit-sharing plans

(a) (1) An amount payable pursuant to the terms of an employees' pension or profit-sharing plan or trust, upon the death of an employee or former employee covered thereby who dies after June 30, 1978, may be paid to any person entitled thereto without written consent or waiver of the State Tax Commission and without retaining any portion thereof for the payment of estate tax or interest, provided the total amount so payable pursuant to such plan or trust and all other employees' pension or profit-sharing plans or trusts established by the same employer or an affiliated corporation is not in excess of $ 50,000, and provided further that, if the total amount so payable exceeds $ 30,000, written notice of such payment, in duplicate and in the form set forth in subdivision (c) of this section, has been mailed to the State Tax Commission.

(2) An amount payable pursuant to the terms of an employees' pension or profit-sharing plan or trust, upon the death of an employee or former employee covered thereby who dies before July 1, 1978, may be paid to any person entitled thereto without written consent or waiver of the State Tax Commission and without retaining any portion thereof for the payment of estate tax or interest, provided the total amount so payable pursuant to such plan or trust and all other employees' pension or profit-sharing plans or trusts established by the same employer or an affiliated corporation is not in excess of $ 20,000, and provided further that, if the total amount so payable exceeds $ 2,000, written notice of such payment, in duplicate and in the form set forth in subdivision (c) of this section, has been mailed to the State Tax Commission.

(3) Notwithstanding the provisions of paragraph (1) of this subdivision, an amount payable pursuant to the terms of an employees' pension or profit-sharing plan or trust upon the death of an employee or former employee covered thereby who dies after September 30, 1983, may be paid to such employee's or former employee's surviving spouse, if such spouse is the person entitled thereto, without the written consent or waiver of the State Tax Commission and without retaining any portion thereof for the payment of estate tax or interest or giving written notice thereof to the State Tax Commission.

(b) Where the total amount payable to any person pursuant to the terms of any such plan or trust is dependent upon the duration of his life or any life or lives in being, the total amount payable to such person, for the purposes of this section, shall be deemed to mean the value of his right to receive payments pursuant to such plan or trust. In any such case, the notice to the State Tax Commission must contain all information necessary to compute the value of such person's interest.

(c) The following is the form of notice to be mailed to the Estate and Gift Tax Section, Audit Division, pursuant to this section:

NOTICE OF PAYMENT OF DEATH BENEFIT UNDER
EMPLOYEES' PENSION OR PROFIT-SHARING PLAN

_____ To: Estate and Gift Tax Section Audit Division State Campus Albany, N.Y. 12227

Notice is hereby given that the undersigned is about to make payment, pursuant to the terms of an employees' pension or profit-sharing plan, by reason of the death of the decedent named hereunder, to the persons named in the following schedule, and that the total amount to be

Official Rules

paid to each of them (including the value of all future payments) is as set forth in said schedule.

Name of decedent . . . .

Date of death . . . .

Residence address . . . .

Name	Residence address	Relationship to de-cedent	Total amount payable

Dated: _____   . . . .

(Name of corporation or person mak-ing payment)

By: . . . .

(Name of corporation or person mak-ing payment)   (Address)

Note: The above notice, in duplicate, must be mailed to Estate and Gift Tax Section, Audit Division, State Campus, Albany, N.Y. 12227, before payment is made. If any annuity or similar benefit is to be paid, there must be attached to this form a statement showing the age of the beneficiary, and all other facts necessary to compute the value of his interest.

(*effective August 25, 1983*)

§ 360.6   Payment of life insurance proceeds

(a) (1) Section 249-cc of the Tax Law imposes upon insurance companies, as to proceeds of certain life insurance policies paid by them upon the life of a resident decedent, the same liability for the estate taxes imposed by article 10-C and article 26 of the Tax Law as is imposed on all other persons or corporations having assets of a decedent in their possession. Under said section, where the amount of life insurance proceeds payable by a life insurance company to any beneficiary on the life of a resident decedent is more than $ 50,000 in the case of a decedent dying after August 31, 1977 (or $ 20,000 in the case of a decedent dying before September 1, 1977), such company must give written notice to the State Tax Commission at least 10 days prior to the payment of such proceeds, and must retain a sufficient portion of such proceeds to pay estate taxes, unless the State Tax Commission consents in writing to such payment. However, where the amount of such proceeds payable in the case of a decedent dying after August 31, 1977 is $ 50,000 or less, but more than $ 30,000 in the case of a decedent dying after June 30, 1978 ($ 2,000 in the case of a decedent dying after August 31, 1977 but before July 1, 1978), such company may make payment to the beneficiary as soon as it shall have mailed to the State Tax Commission a notice thereof. In the case of a decedent dying before September 1, 1977 where the amount of such proceeds payable is $ 20,000 or less, but more than $ 2,000, such company may make payment to the beneficiary as soon as it shall have mailed to the State Tax Commission a notice thereof.

Where the amount of such proceeds is $ 30,000 or less, in the case of a decedent dying after June 30, 1978 ($ 2,000 or less in the case of a decedent dying before July 1, 1978), no notice need be given to the State Tax Commission.

(2) Notwithstanding the provisions of paragraph (1) of this subdivision, an insurance company may pay the proceeds of life insurance policies upon the life of a decedent dying after September 30, 1983 to such decedent's surviving spouse, as beneficiary, without the written consent or waiver of the State Tax Commission and without giving written notice to the State Tax Commission or retaining any portion of the proceeds for the payment of estate tax or interest.

(b) The statute applies to the proceeds of all life insurance policies issued by any one company on the life of a decedent whether paid to a named beneficiary or to an executor or administrator. In determining the amount of such proceeds, the net amount payable under the policy shall be used; that is, the amount payable under the policy, inclusive of dividends, additional insurance, or refunds of premiums, less any outstanding indebtedness. Where a policy is payable in installments the commuted value of the installments, that is, the amount payable if the policy had been issued on a lump sum basis, shall be used. Where a company has issued more than one policy aggregating more than $ 50,000, in the case of a decedent dying after June 30, 1978 ($ 20,000 in the case of a decedent dying before July 1, 1978), waivers must be obtained.

(c) Waivers of the State Tax Commission may be secured by insurance companies, representatives of estates or beneficiaries.

(1) Applications for waivers shall, wherever possible, set forth the following information: name and address of the decedent-insured; name and address of the beneficiary; policy number; the amount of proceeds payable under each policy; name and address of the legal representative of the insured's estate; and the county in which the estate is being administered. A copy of the decedent's death certificate must be submitted with the first request for waivers. Upon issuance of a waiver by the State Tax Commission, the proceeds may be paid forthwith to the beneficiary without the giving of notice or the withholding of tax.

(2) Waivers may be secured from the New York State Department of Taxation and Finance, Audit Division-Estate Tax Section, State Campus, Albany, N.Y. 12227.

(*effective August 25, 1983*)

§ 360.7   Annuity and other payments under certain trusts, plans and accounts

(a) (1) Payments received by any beneficiary (other than the executor) under an employees' trust or a retirement annuity contract purchased by an employer, or an individual retirement account or annuity or a retirement bond, which qualify for exclusion from the Federal gross estate of a decedent under section 2039 (c) and (e) of the Internal Revenue Code of 1954, as contained in section 2 of chapter 1013 of the Laws of 1962, as last amended by chapter 916 of the Laws of 1982, are similarly excludible from a decedent's New York gross estate under section 954 of the Tax Law. Accordingly, payments pursuant to such a plan, where no contributions were made by the decedent, may be made without notice to the State Tax Commission and without obtaining a waiver if such payments do not exceed $ 100,000. However, payments pursuant to such a plan, where no contributions were made by the decedent, which exceed $ 100,000 in the aggregate may not be made unless written notice of such payment is mailed to the State Tax Commission at least 10 days prior to such payment and a sufficient portion of such payment is retained for payment of the estate tax unless a waiver is first obtained from the State Tax Commission.

(2) Notwithstanding the provisions of paragraph (1) of this subdivision, payments pursuant to such a plan, where no contributions were made by the decedent, which exceed $ 100,000 in the aggregate if made to the surviving spouse of a decedent dying after September 30, 1983 may be made without the written consent or waiver of the State Tax Commission and without giving written notice to the State Tax Commission or retaining any portion of the proceeds for the payment of estate tax. For other exemptions to waivers for payments to a surviving spouse, see sections 360.5(a)(3) and 360.6(a)(2) of this Part.

(b) To the extent that payments pursuant to such a plan are attributable to contributions made by the decedent, the provisions of section 360.5 of this Part shall be applicable. Section statutory authority: Tax Law, § 954.

(*effective August 25, 1983*)

§ 360.8 Payment or certification of checks drawn before decedent's death

(a) Any check drawn by a decedent before his death, which a bank may be authorized to pay or certify within 10 days after his death pursuant to section 4-405(2) of the Uniform Commercial Code, may be paid or certified without estate tax waiver, without notice to the State Tax Commission and without retaining any part of the deposit on account of estate tax.

(b) Checks drawn on or prior to the date of death by any person other than the decedent, such as an agent or attorney in fact, upon an account in the decedent's name, or, in the case of an account in the joint names of the decedent and another person, checks drawn on or prior to the date of death by the surviving joint depositor, may also be paid or certified within 10 days after the date of death without estate tax waiver, without notice to the State Tax Commission and without retaining any part of the deposit on account of estate tax.

(c) However, if the total of all checks paid or certified in the period of 10 days after death exceeds $ 30,000, in the case of the account in the name of a decedent dying after June 30, 1978, or in the case of an account in the joint name of such a decedent and another person, the bank shall notify the State Tax Commission within 45 days after the date of death. However, in the case of a decedent dying before July 1, 1978, such notification was required if the total exceeded $ 2,000. Such notice to the State Tax Commission shall be in substantially the form shown in subdivision (d) of this section.

(d) Waivers shall be required for the balance remaining in such accounts only if such balance, plus other deposits and assets at the same bank belonging to or standing in the name of said decedent dying after June 30, 1978, or in the joint names of such a decedent and one or more other persons, 10 days after the date of death, are in excess of $ 30,000. In the case of a decedent dying before July 1, 1978, waivers are required if such balance plus such other deposits are in excess of $ 2,000. The form of notice to be mailed by the bank to the State Tax Commission is as follows:

NOTICE OF PAYMENTS OR CERTIFICATIONS

_____ To: State Tax Commission Audit Division—Estate Tax
Section State Campus Albany, N.Y. 12227

Name of decedent . . . .

Date of death . . . .

Residence address . . . .

Notice is hereby given that the undersigned has paid or certified checks for a total amount in excess of $ 30,000 drawn on the account or accounts of the decedent named: Balance on the date of death . . . .

Total amount of checks paid or certified within

10 days after death . . . .

        Balance . . . .

                            . . . .
                                 (Paying or Certifying Bank)

                            . . . .
                                          (Address)

                      By: . . . .
                                          (Officer)

Note: The above notice, in duplicate, must be mailed within 45 days after date of decedent's death.

(_effective August 25, 1983_)

Part 361   LIEN OF TAX

§ 361.1   Releases of liens

Under articles 10, 10-C and 26 of the Tax Law, the State Tax Commission is authorized to issue releases of liens imposed by said articles on real property of decedents. Such releases will be issued, upon application therefor, in accordance with the following rules:

(a) Where an order has been entered exempting an estate from the taxes imposed by article 10, 10-C or 26, a release will be issued for any real property disclosed in the proceeding.

(b) Where an order has been entered assessing a tax under article 10, 10-C or 26, a release will be issued for any real property set forth in the return of the estate, provided the tax which is a lien on such real property, together with interest thereon, is paid.

(c) Where a proceeding to assess a tax under article 10, 10-C or 26 is pending at the time of the application, and an adequate estimated payment on account of the tax has been made, a release will be issued.

(d) Where no order fixing the tax or exempting the estate has been entered, no proceeding is pending and no estimated tax paid under article 10, 10-C or 26, the following procedure should be followed:

(1) Where the application is made by the executor, administrator, trustee, or

beneficiary of an estate, the application must be accompanied by an affidavit setting forth the date of decedent's death, all the decedent's property subject to tax, the allowable deductions, the persons interested in the estate and the amount of the distributive share of each beneficiary. If it appears from such affidavit that no tax is due, a release will be promptly issued but if it appears therefrom that a tax is due, it must be paid before a release will be issued.

(2) Where the application is made by any other person, it must be accompanied by an affidavit setting forth the relationship, directly or indirectly, of the applicant to the decedent and to any person interested in the estate, and the reason the applicant seeks the release. Such affidavit shall also set forth the date of the decedent's death, all of decedent's property subject to tax, the allowable deductions, the persons interested in the estate and the amount of the distributive share of each beneficiary. In the event that any of the facts set forth in the preceding sentence are not known and cannot reasonably be ascertained, the affidavit should state the reason why such information cannot be set forth. The affidavit should also outline the proceedings, if any, in the Surrogate's Court in regard to the decedent's estate, the assessed value of the real property for which a release is sought, (i) at the time of decedent's death, and (ii) as shown on the last preceding assessment roll, and the names of owners of such real property after the decedent's death, so far as they appear upon the public records. A release will be issued dependent upon the facts in each case upon such conditions as will not jeopardize the revenues of the State.

(e) Each application for a release must be accompanied by the statutory fee of $ 2 with respect to article 10, and $ 10 with respect to articles 10-C and 26, made payable to the State Tax Commission, and:

(1) where acceptable to the clerk of the county in which the real property is situated, the section, block, and lot numbers, and/or the book of deeds or liber number (including the page number), tax map number (where applicable), and the complete address of the property; or

(2) in those counties where the information in paragraph (1) of this subdivision is not acceptable, the legal description (metes and bounds) of the real property, in duplicate. The application must be made to the State Tax Commission, and filed with the New York State Department of Taxation and Finance, Audit Division-Estate Tax Section, State Campus, Albany, N.Y. 12227.

(*effective August 25, 1983*)

Part 362   MISCELLANEOUS

§ 362.1   Fees for searches and certificates concerning estate and transfer tax proceedings

Effective April 8, 1963, the following fees will be charged:

(a) A fee of $ 2 for a search of the estate and transfer tax records of the State Tax Commission and a certificate of the facts disclosed thereby, with reference to the estate of any decedent; and an additional fee of $ 1 for advice by telephone or telegraph as to the facts disclosed by such a search.

(b) A fee of $ 2.50 for a certificate of payment of estate tax in the form required by the

Internal Revenue Service (currently form TT 66C) for allowance of credit against the Federal estate tax.

(*effective April 4, 1963*)

Part 363   AUDIT PROCEDURES

§ 363.1   Audit of estate tax returns

In any case in which a Federal estate tax return has been filed for an estate, the legal representative of such estate, or any person having actual or constructive possession of any property includible in the New York gross estate, shall submit to the office of the Tax Commission any information, records, documents and statements, or copies thereof, within 20 days after request therefor is made. The State Tax Commission may audit the Federal estate tax return of any estate at any time before or after an order has been entered fixing tax, provided that a final Federal determination has not been made. The State Tax Commission shall notify the executor upon commencement of audit pursuant to this regulation.

(*effective May 17, 1967*)

RULES FOR TRUSTS AND ESTATES WITH A CHARITABLE INTEREST

§ 92.1   To whom this part applies

This part applies to trusts and estates with a charitable interest as defined in section 90.3 of this Chapter. The following sections of this Part contain the registration and reporting requirements applicable to trusts and estates with a charitable interest.

(a) Registration Types. Trusts and estates with a charitable interest are required to register pursuant to EPTL section 8-1.4, but are not required to register pursuant to Article 7-A. (*as of 10/04/06*)

§ 92.2   Estates

(a) Registration. Estates with a charitable interest as defined in subparagraph (a)(1) of section 90.3 of this Chapter are required to register pursuant to EPTL section 8-1.4. Estates in which the only charitable interest is a specific gift (either a specific amount of money or specific property) to one or more named charities exempt from federal taxation pursuant to Internal Revenue Code section 501(c)(3) are not required to register pursuant to the EPTL.

(1) What Registration Documents to Submit. To register with the Attorney General, an estate with a charitable interest shall submit all of the following documents:

(i) a copy of the notice of probate; and

(ii) a copy of the last will and testament and any codicils.

(2) What Registration Fees to Submit. Estates with a charitable interest are not required to pay a registration fee pursuant to the EPTL. However, an EPTL filing fee is required when the estate submits a final report pursuant to paragraph (c) of this section 92.2.

(3) When to Register. Estates with a charitable interest shall register within six months after the earlier of the date letters testamentary or preliminary letters testamentary are issued. Nothing in this Chapter shall be interpreted to waive any requirement to submit any estate-related documents to the Attorney General in a timely manner pursuant to any other provision of the laws of the State of New York, such as the requirement to submit the notice of probate pursuant to section 1409 of the Surrogate's Court Procedure Act.

(4) Where to Register. Estates with a charitable interest shall submit their registration documents to the New York City office of the Attorney General's Charities Bureau, the Albany office of the Attorney General's Charities Bureau or the applicable Attorney General's Regional Office, in accordance with instructions issued by the Attorney General,

or such other place as the Attorney General may designate.

(b) Periodic Reports. Estates with a charitable interest are not required to file periodic reports, but shall comply with any request made by the Attorney General for additional information or documentation pursuant to section 92.5 of this Part.

(c) Final Reports. Estates with a charitable interest are required to file a final report with the Attorney General.

(1) What Final Report Documents to Submit. A judicial or informal final accounting containing sufficient information for the purposes of the Attorney General's review shall constitute a complete final report for an estate with a charitable interest.

(2) What Final Report Fees to Submit. With the submission of a final report, estates with a charitable interest shall pay a filing fee based on the total value of all assets distributed or proposed to be distributed to charitable beneficiaries, including distributions resulting from specific and residuary gifts paid from principal or income, according to the following schedule:

(i) Twenty-five dollars, if the total value of all such charitable assets is less than fifty thousand dollars;

(ii) Fifty dollars, if the total value of all such charitable assets is fifty thousand dollars or more but less than two hundred fifty thousand dollars;

(iii) One hundred dollars, if the total value of such charitable assets is two hundred fifty thousand dollars or more but less than one million dollars;

(iv) Two hundred fifty dollars, if the total value of such charitable assets is one million dollars or more but less than ten million dollars;

(v) Seven hundred fifty dollars, if the total value of such charitable assets is ten million dollars or more but less than fifty million dollars; or

(vi) One thousand five hundred dollars, if the total value of such charitable assets is fifty million dollars or more. The EPTL filing fee is due at the time the final report is submitted to the Attorney General and is required for all estates with a charitable interest that are required to register with the Attorney General.

(3) Where to File Final Report. An estate with a charitable interest shall submit its final report to the New York City office of the Attorney General's Charities Bureau, the Albany office of the Attorney General's Charities Bureau or the applicable Attorney General's Regional Office, in accordance with instructions issued by the Attorney General, or such other place as the Attorney General may designate.
(*as of 10/04/06*)

§ 92.3   Charitable remainder trusts

(a) Registration with Notice of Termination. Charitable remainder trusts as defined in subparagraph (b)(1) of section 90.3 of this Part are required to register pursuant to EPTL section 8-1.4. Pursuant to EPTL section 8-1.4(f)(1), such registration shall contain a notice of the termination of the interest of any party in a trust that would cause all or part of the trust assets or income to be applied to charitable purposes. Charitable remainder trusts are not required to submit to the Attorney General a separate notice of termination.

(1) What Registration with Notice of Termination Documents to Submit. To register, a charitable remainder trust shall submit all of the following registration with notice of termination documents to the Attorney General and mail a copy to each identified current charitable beneficiary:

(i) CHAR001-RT (Registration Statement for Charitable Remainder Trusts with Notice of Termination of Intervening Trust Interest) or a successor form issued by the Attorney General, which shall include:

(a) identifying information, including the identity of the terminating interest (and, if applicable, the date of death of the individual whose interest terminated) and the identity of each charitable beneficiary,

(b) contact information for each trustee and attorney for the trust, and

(c) a statement that the trust has complied with the requirement to mail a copy of the notice of termination to each identified current charitable beneficiary; and

(ii) a copy of the trust instrument and any amendments.

(2) What Registration and Notice of Termination Fees to Submit. Charitable remainder trusts are not required to pay a registration or notice of termination fee pursuant to the EPTL. However, an EPTL filing fee is required when the trust submits a final report pursuant to paragraph (c) of this section 92.3.

(3) When to Submit and Mail Registration with Notice of Termination. Charitable remainder trusts shall submit their registration with notice of termination to the Attorney General and mail a copy of such registration with notice of termination to each identified current charitable beneficiary within six months after the date when, pursuant to the terms of the applicable trust instrument, all or part of the trust assets or income is required to be applied to charitable purposes.

(4) Where to Submit and Mail Registration with Notice of Termination. Charitable remainder trusts shall submit their registration with notice of termination to the New York City office of the Attorney General's Charities Bureau, the Albany office of the Attorney General's Charities Bureau or the applicable Attorney General's Regional Office, in accordance with instructions issued by the Attorney General, or such other place as the Attorney General may designate. Charitable remainder trusts shall also mail a copy of such registration with notice of termination to each identified current charitable beneficiary at the last known address of such beneficiary or such other address for such beneficiary as may be determined from a diligent search.

(b) Periodic Reports. Charitable remainder trusts are not required to file periodic reports, but shall comply with any request made by the Attorney General for additional information or documentation pursuant to section 92.5 of this Part.

(c) Final Reports. Charitable remainder trusts are required to file a final report with the Attorney General.

(1) What Final Report Documents to Submit. A judicial or informal final accounting containing sufficient information for the purposes of the Attorney General's review shall constitute a complete final report for a charitable remainder trust.

(2) What Final Report Fees to Submit. With the submission of a final report, charitable remainder trusts shall pay a filing fee based on the total value of all assets distributed or proposed to be distributed to charitable beneficiaries, including distributions resulting from specific and residuary gifts paid from principal or income, according to the following schedule:

(i) Twenty-five dollars, if the total value of all such charitable assets is less than fifty thousand dollars;

(ii) Fifty dollars, if the total value of all such charitable assets is fifty thousand dollars or more but less than two hundred fifty thousand dollars;

(iii) One hundred dollars, if the total value of such charitable assets is two hundred fifty thousand dollars or more but less than one million dollars;

(iv) Two hundred fifty dollars, if the total value of such charitable assets is one million dollars or more but less than ten million dollars;

(v) Seven hundred fifty dollars, if the total value of such charitable assets is ten million dollars or more but less than fifty million dollars; or

(vi) One thousand five hundred dollars, if the total value of such charitable assets is fifty million dollars or more. The EPTL filing fee is due at the time the final report is submitted to the Attorney General and is required for all charitable remainder trusts that are required to register with the Attorney General.

(3) What Final Report Fees to Submit. Charitable lead trusts shall pay a final EPTL annual filing fee of twenty-five dollars, if the total amount distributed to charity by the trust during the fiscal year is twenty-five thousand dollars or more.

(4) When to File Final Report. A charitable lead trust shall file its final report within six months after the end of its fiscal year during which the lead charitable interest terminated. The extension request provisions for charitable organizations contained in subparagraph (f)(3) of section 91.5 of this Chapter apply to final reports of charitable lead trusts.

(5) Where to File Final Report. A charitable lead trust shall submit its final report to the New York City office of the Attorney General's Charities Bureau or such other place as the Attorney General may designate.
(*as of 10/04/06*)

§ 92.4   **Charitable lead trusts**

(a) Registration. Charitable lead trusts as defined in subparagraph (b)(2) of section 90.3 of this Chapter are required to register pursuant to EPTL section 8-1.4.

(1) What Registration Documents to Submit. To register with the Attorney General, a charitable lead trust shall submit all of the following documents:

(i) CHAR001-LT (Registration Statement for Charitable Lead Trusts) or a successor form issued by the Attorney General, which shall include:

(a) identifying information, including the identity of each charitable beneficiary, and

(b) contact information for each trustee and attorney for the trust; and

(ii) a copy of the trust instrument and any amendments.

(2) What Registration Fees to Submit. Charitable lead trusts are not required to pay a registration fee pursuant to the EPTL. However, an EPTL filing fee is required when the charitable lead trust submits each periodic report and its final report pursuant to paragraphs (b) and (c) of this section 92.4.

(3) When to Register. Charitable lead trusts shall register within six months after the trust is funded.

(4) Where to Register. Charitable lead trusts shall submit their registration documents to the New York City office of the Attorney General's Charities Bureau or such other place as the Attorney General may designate.

(b) Periodic Reports. Charitable lead trusts are required to file annual reports with the Attorney General.

(1) What Annual Report Documents to Submit. The following documents constitute a complete annual filing for a charitable lead trust:

(i) CHAR004 (Annual Filing for Charitable Lead Trust) or a successor form issued by the Attorney General, which shall include:

(a) identifying information, including the identity of each charitable beneficiary and the fiscal year end of the annual report,

(b) contact information for each trustee and attorney for the trust and each financial institution where trust assets are held, and

(c) principal, income and total financial information for the trust, including charges; administration expenses, distributions to beneficiaries and other credits; liabilities; and fund balances; and

(ii) a copy of the trust's IRS Form 5227 (Split-Interest Trust Information Return) or a successor form.

(2) What Annual Report Fees to Submit. Charitable lead trusts shall pay an annual EPTL filing fee according to the following schedule:

(i) Twenty-five dollars, if the total amount distributed to charity by the trust during the fiscal year is less than fifty thousand dollars;

(ii) Fifty dollars, if the total amount distributed to charity by the trust during the fiscal year is fifty thousand dollars or more but less than two hundred fifty thousand dollars;

(iii) One hundred dollars, if the total amount distributed to charity by the trust during the fiscal year is two hundred fifty thousand dollars or more but less than one million dollars;

(iv) Two hundred fifty dollars, if the total amount distributed to charity by the trust during the fiscal year is one million dollars or more but less than ten million dollars;

(v) Seven hundred fifty dollars, if the total amount distributed to charity by the trust during the fiscal year is ten million dollars or more but less than fifty million dollars; or

(vi) One thousand five hundred dollars, if the total amount distributed to charity by the trust during the fiscal year is fifty million dollars or more.

(3) When to File Annual Reports. A charitable lead trust shall file an annual report within six months after the end of its fiscal year. The extension request provisions for charitable organizations contained in subparagraph (f)(3) of section 91.5 of this Chapter apply to annual reports of charitable lead trusts.

(4) Where to File Annual Reports. A charitable lead trust shall submit its annual reports to the New York City office of the Attorney General's Charities Bureau or such other place as the Attorney General may designate.

(c) Final Reports. Charitable lead trusts are required to file a final report with the Attorney General.

(1) What Final Report Documents to Submit. The following documents shall constitute a complete final annual report for a charitable lead trust:

(i) CHAR004 (Annual Filing for Charitable Lead Trust) or a successor form issued by the Attorney General, which shall include:

(a) identifying information, including the identity of each charitable beneficiary and the end date of the annual report,

(b) contact information for each trustee and attorney for the trust and each financial institution where trust assets are held, and

(c) principal, income and total financial information for the trust, including charges; administration expenses, distributions to beneficiaries and other credits; liabilities; and fund balances; and

(ii) a copy of the trust's IRS Form 5227 (Split-Interest Trust Information Return) or a successor form for the year during which the charitable lead interest terminates.

(3) Where to File Final Report. A charitable remainder trust shall submit its final report to the New York City office of the Attorney General's Charities Bureau, the Albany office of the Attorney General's Charities Bureau or the applicable Attorney General's Regional Office, in accordance with instructions issued by the Attorney General, or such other place as the Attorney General may designate.
(*as of 10/04/06*)

§ 92.5 Attorney General authority to require additional information or documentation

In addition to any documents the Attorney General requires of a trust or estate with a charitable interest as part of its registration, periodic report, final report or notice of termination, the Attorney General may require a trust or estate with a charitable interest to submit any information or documentation relevant to the Attorney General's review of such entity, including without limitation a periodic accounting, a detailed securities schedule, IRS Form 706 (United States Estate (and Generation-Skipping Transfer) Tax Return), IRS Form 1041 (U.S. Income Tax Return for Estates and Trusts) and New York State Department of Taxation and Finance ET-90 (New York State Estate Tax Return) or successor forms.
(*as of 10/04/06*)

§ 92.6   Certification requirement

For each registration, periodic report, final report or notice of termination required to be submitted by a trust or estate with a charitable interest pursuant to this Part, a trustee, executor or other authorized individual shall certify under penalties for perjury that, to the best of his or her knowledge and belief, such submission is true, correct and complete in accordance with the laws of the State of New York applicable to such submission.
(*as of 10/04/06*)

OFFICIAL FORMS PRESCRIBED by SURROGATE'S COURT PROCEDURE ACT[1]

Table Of Contents

---

[1] The Official Forms were originally enacted by the Chief Administrative Judge of the Courts effective May 28, 1987 by the authority given under SCPA 106 and have been periodically amended. **Ed. Note.**—These forms are for illustration only. The attorney should go to the Surrogate's Court of the county in which the action is to be commenced to obtain the necessary official forms.

SF-1

ADM/DBN–6	Affidavit of Mailing Notice of Application for Letters of Administration d.b.n. (SCPA 1005)
ADM/DBN–7	Notice to the Consul General
ADM/DBN–8	Affidavit of Service of Citation (Adult)
CPSA–1	Parentage Petition – Surrogacy Agreement
CPSA–2	Order of Parentage – Surrogacy Agreement
CPSA–3	Parentage Petition – Assisted Reproduction
CPSA–4	Order of Parentage – Assisted Reproduction
CPSA–5	Parentage Citation
CSMD–1	Petition for Appointment/Confirmation of Standby Guardian [SCPA 1757]
CSMD–2	Waiver of Process, Renunciation and Consent to Appointment of a Standby Guardian [SCPA 1757]
CSMD–3	Notice of Petition [SCPA § 1753(2)]
CSMD–4	17-A Guardianship Citation [SCPA 1757]
CSMD–5	Affidavit of Proposed Guardian [SCPA 1757]
CSMD–6	Consent, Oath and Designation [SCPA 1757]
CTA–1	Petition for Letters of Administration c.t.a. After Probate (SCPA 1418 and 1419)
CTA–2	Citation
CTA–3	Renunciation of Letters of Administration c.t.a., Waiver of Process and Consent To Dispense with Bond
FT–1	Family Tree
G–1	Guardianship Citation
G–2A	Petition for Appointment of Guardian of Person Only
G–2B	Petition for Appointment of Guardian (Person and Property/Property Only)
G–3	Affidavit of Proposed Guardian
G–4	Affidavit of Parent
G–5	Waiver, Renunciation, and Consent
G–6A	Decree Appointing Guardian (Joint Control)
G–6B	Decree Appointing Guardian
G–7A	Annual Account of Guardian (Non-Bonded)
G–7B	Annual Account of Guardian (Bonded)
G–8	Petition for Withdrawal of Infant's Property for Support and Education
G–9	Order Permitting Withdrawal of Infant's Property for Support and Education
G–10A	Petition to Close Guardianship Account (Former Infant)

G–10B	Petition to Close Guardianship Account (Guardian)
G–11	Release Settling Accounts
G–12A	Decree Closing Guardianship Account (Infant)
G–12B	Decree Closing Guardianship Account
GMD–1	Petition for Appointment of Guardian of Person/Property/Person and Property/Limited Guardian of Property
GMD–1A	Affidavit of Proposed Guardian of Person/Property/Person and Property/Limited Guardian of Property
GMD–2A	Affidavit (Certification) of Examining Physician or Licensed Psychologist
GMD–2B	Affirmation (Certification) of Examining Physician
GMD–3	Waiver of Process, Renunciation and Consent to Appointment of Guardian
GMD–4	Consent, Oath and Designation
GMD–5	Decree Appointing Guardian
GMD–6	Decree Appointing Limited Guardian of Property
GMD–7	17-A Guardianship Citation
GMD–8	Notice of Petition [SCPA § 1753(2)]
I–1	Inventory of Assets
I–2	Firearms Inventory
JA–1	Petition for Judicial Settlement of Account
JA–2	Receipt and Release
JA–3	Waiver of Citation and Consent in Accounting
JA–4	Trust Accounting with Instructions
JA–5	Decree of Judicial Settlement for Executor with Trust or Trustee
JA–6	Citation
JA–7	Non-Trust Accounting with Instructions
JA–8	Non-Trust Decree of Judicial Settlement
JA–9	Compulsory Accounting Citation
JA–10	Petition for Compulsory Accounting and Related Relief
P–1	Petition for Probate
P–2	Application for Preliminary Letters Testamentary
P–3	Affidavit of Attesting Witness
P–4	Waiver of Process; Consent to Probate
P–5	Citation
P–6	Notice of Probate
P–7	Affidavit of Service of Citation
P–8	Application and Order for Dispensing with Testimony of Attesting Witness

SLT–5	Citation—Successor Letters Testamentary
WD–1	Wrongful Death Citation
WD–2	Wrongful Death Petition
WD–3	Account
WD–4	Attorney's Affidavit
WD–5	Waiver and Consent for Insurance Company
WD–6	Waiver and Consent for Individual
WD–7	Decree
CERT	Attorney's Certification Pursuant to 22 NYCRR 207.4(a) & (b)
OCFS 3909	Request for Information Guardianship Form
REP	Report of Estate Not Fully Distributed
SD BOX–1	Petition to Search Safe Deposit Box
SD BOX–2	Order to Examine Safe Deposit Box
UCS 876	Report of Compensation Received by Law Firms for Appointments Pursuant to Part 36 of the Rules of the Chief Judge
UCS 880	Order Appointing Attorney for the Child
UCS 881	Affirmation of Services for Privately Paid Law Attorney for the Child
UCS 882	Order Approving Attorney for the Child Compensation
SUR CT-CHK	Surrogate's Court Checklists

FORM A-1   Petition for Letters of Administration

	For Office Use Only
Filling Fee Paid	$_____
_____	Certs $_____
$_____	Bond, Fee:_____
Receipt No:_____	No:_____

DO NOT LEAVE ANY ITEMS BLANK

SURROGATE'S COURT OF THE STATE OF NEW YORK

COUNTY OF_____

--- X

ADMINISTRATION PROCEEDING,

Estate of

a/k/a

                  Deceased

PETITION FOR LETTERS OF:

☐ Administration

☐ Limited Administration

☐ Administration with Limitations

☐ Temporary Administration

File No. _____

--- X

TO THE SURROGATE'S COURT, COUNTY OF_____

It is respectfully alleged:

1. The name, domicile and interest in this proceeding of the petitioner, who is of full age, is as follows:

Name: _____

Domicile: _____
           (Street Address)   (City/Town/Village)

_____
          (County)   (State)   (Zip)   (Telephone Number)

Mailing address is: _____
                                   (if different from domicile)

Citizenship (check one):   ☐ U.S.A.   ☐ Other (specify)_____

Interest of Petitioner (check one):

  [ ] Distributee of decedent (state relationship)_____

  [ ] Other (specify) _____

Is proposed Administrator an attorney?   ☐ Yes   ☐ No

  [If yes, submit statement pursuant to 22 NYCRR 207.16(e); see also 207.52 (Accounting of attorney-fiduciary).]

The proposed Administrator   ☐ is   ☐ is not a convicted felon nor is he/she otherwise
ineligible, pursuant to SCPA 707 to receive letters.

If the proposed Administrator is a convicted felon, submit a copy of the Certificate of Relief from Civil Disabilities.

2. The name, domicile, date and place of death, and national citizenship of the above-named decedent are as follows:
[The Death Certificate must be filed with this proceeding. If the decedent's domicile is different from that shown on the death certificate, check box [ ] and attach an affidavit explaining the reason for this inconsistency.]

Name: _____

Domicile: _____
           (Street Number)   (City, Village/Town)

_____
          (State)   (Zip Code)

Township of: _____   County of: _____

Date of Death: _____   Place of Death: _____

Citizenship: (check one): ☐   U.S.A.   ☐   Other (specify)_____

[Note: For Items 3a through c: Do not include any assets that are jointly held, held in trust for another, or have a named beneficiary.]

3.(a) The estimated gross value of the decedent's personal property passing by intestacy is less than

$_____

(b) The estimated gross value of the decedent's real property, in this state, which is [ ] improved, [ ] unimproved, passing by intestacy is less than

$_____

A brief description of each parcel is as follows:

_____

(c) The estimated gross rent for a period of eighteen (18) months is the sum of $ _____

(d) In addition to the value of the personal property stated in paragraph (3) the following right of action existed on behalf of the decedent and survived his/her death, or is granted to the administrator of the decedent by special provision of law,and it is impractical to give a bond sufficient to cover the probable amount to be recovered the rein: **[Write"NONE or state briefly the cause of action and the person against whom it exists, including names and carrier].**

_____

_____
_____

(e) If decedent is survived by a spouse and a parent, or parents but no issue and there is a claim for wrongful death, check here ☐ and furnish names(s) and address(es) of parent(s) in Paragraph 7. See EPTL5-4.4.

4. A diligent search and inquiry, including a search of any safe deposit box,has been made for a will of the decedent and none has been found. Petitioner(s)(has)(have) been unable to obtain any information concerning any will of the decedent and therefore allege(s),upon information and belief,that the decedent died without leaving any last will.

5. A search of the records of this Court shows that no application has ever been made for letters of administration upon the estate of the decedent or for the probate of a will of the decedent, and your petitioner is informed and verily believes that no such application ever has been made to the Surrogate's Court of any other county of this state.

6. The decedent left surviving the following who would inherit his/her estate pursuant to EPTL4-1.1 and 4-1.2:

a.   ☐ Spouse(husband/wife).

b.   ☐ Child or children or descendants of predeceased child or children. **[Must include marital, nonmarital and adopted].**

c.   ☐ Any issue of the decedent adopted by persons related to the decedent (DRLSection117).

d.   ☐ Mother/Father.

e.   ☐ Sisters or brothers, either of whole or half blood, and issue of predeceased sisters or brothers.

f.   ☐ Grandmother/Grandfather.

g.   ☐ Aunts or uncles, and children of predeceased aunts and uncles (first cousins).

h.   ☐ First cousins once removed (children of first cousins).

[Information is required only as to those classes of surviving relatives who would take the property of decedent pursuant to EPTL4-1.1.State "number" of survivors in each class. Insert "No" in all prior classes. Insert "X" in all subsequent classes].

7. The decedent left surviving the following distributees, or other necessary parties, whose names, degrees of relationship, domiciles, post office address and citizenship are as follows:

[Note: Show clearly how each person is related to decedent. If relationship is through an ancestor who is deceased, give name, date of death, and relationship of the ancestor to the decedent. Use rider sheet if space in paragraph (7) is not sufficient. See Uniform Rules 207.16(b).

If any person listed in paragraph (7) is a non-marital person, or descended from an on marital person, attach a copy of the order affiliation or Schedule A. If any person listed in paragraph (7) was adopted by any persons related by blood or marriage to decedent or descended from such persons, attach Schedule B].

7a. The following are of full age and under no disability [If non-marital or adopted-out person, so indicate by attaching Schedule A and/or B]

Name	Relationship	Domicile and Mailing Address	Citizenship Mailing Address

7b. The following are infants and/or persons under disability: [Attach applicable Schedule A, B, C, and/or D]

Name	Relationship	Domicile and Mailing Address	Citizenship Mailing Address

8 There are no outstanding debts or funeral expenses, except: [Write "NONE" or state same]

9. There are no other persons interested in this proceeding other than those here in before mentioned.

WHEREFORE, your petitioner respectfully prays that: [Check and complete all relief requested]

☐ a. process issue to all necessary parties to show cause why letters should not be issued as requested;

☐ b. an order be granted dispensing with service of process upon those persons named in Paragraph(7) who have a right to letters prior or equal to that of the person nominated, and who are non-domiciliaries or whose names or whereabouts are unknown and cannot be ascertained;

☐ c. a decree award Letters of:

     ☐ Administration to _____

     ☐ Limited Administration to _____

     ☐ Administration with Limitation to_____

     ☐ Temporary Administration to _____

or to such other person or persons having a prior right as may be entitled thereto, and;

☐ d. That the authority of the representative under the forgoing Letters be limited with respect to the prosecution or enforcement of a cause of action on behalf of the estate, as follows: the administrator(s) may not enforce a judgment or receive any funds without further order of the Surrogate.

☐ e. That the authority of the representative under the foregoing Letters be limited as follows:

_____

_____

_____

_____

_____

_____

☐ f. [State any other relief requested.] _____

_____

Dated: _____

1. _____   2. _____

     (Signature of Petitioner)   (Signature of Petitioner)

_____   _____

     (Print Name)   (Print Name)

Official Forms

STATE OF NEW YORK)
) ss:
COUNTY OF)

COMBINED VERIFICATION, OATH AND DESIGNATION

[For use when petitioner is to be appointed administrator]

I, the undersigned the petitioner named in the foregoing petition, being duly sworn, say:

1. VERIFICATION: I have read the foregoing petition subscribed by me and know the contents thereof, and the same is true of my own knowledge, except as to the matters there in stated to be alleged upon information and belief, and as to those matters I believe it to be true.

2. OATH OF ADMINISTRATOR as indicated above: I am over eighteen (18) years of age and a citizen of the United States; and I will well, faithfully and honestly discharge the duties of Administrator of the goods, chattels and credits of said decedent according to law. I am not ineligible, pursuant to SCPA 707, to receive letters and will duly account for all moneys and other property that will come into my hands.

3. DESIGNATION OF CLERK FOR SERVICE OF PROCESS: I do hereby designate the Clerk of the Surrogate's Court of _____ County, and his/her successor in office, as a person on whom service of any process, issuing from such Surrogate's Court may be made in like manner and with like effect as if it were served personally upon me, whenever I cannot be found and served within the State of New York after due diligence used.

My domicile is: _____
　　　　　　　　　(Street/Number)　　　　　　　(City, Village/Town)　　　(State)　　　(Zip)

　　　　　　　　　　　　　　　　　　_____
　　　　　　　　　　　　　　　　　　　　　　Signature of Petitioner

On the _____ day of _____ 20 _____, before me personally came

_____

to me known to be the person described in and who executed the foregoing instrument. Such person duly swore to such instrument before me and duly acknowledged that he/she executed the same.

_____

Notary Public

Commission Expires:

(Affix Notary Stamp or Seal)

Signature of Attorney: _____

Print Name: _____

Firm Name: _____ Tel. No.: _____

Address of Attorney: _____

SURROGATE'S COURT OF THE STATE OF NEW YORK

COUNTY OF

- X

PROCEEDING FOR   SCHEDULE A

Estate of   NONMARITAL PERSONS

                           (PERSONS BORN OUT OF WEDLOCK)

a/k/a

                        Deceased.   File# _____

- X

[NOTE: Nonmarital children (or their issue) who would be distributees if they (or their ancestors) were born in wedlock will not be regarded as distributees unless satisfactory proof is submitted establishing paternity]. See EPTL 4-1.2 which sets forth methods of establishing paternity.

Name of alleged distributee: _____

Date of birth: _____   Relationship to decedent: _____

Name of father: _____

Name of mother: _____

Does the birth certificate contain the father's name?   Yes ☐   No ☐

     If yes, attach copy of birth certificate.

Has an order of filiation establishing paternity been entered?   Yes ☐   No ☐

     If yes, attach copy of order.

Did the nonmarital person live with his or her father?   Yes ☐   No ☐

     If yes, give dates and places of residence: _____

_____

_____

_____

SURROGATE'S COURT OF THE STATE OF NEW YORK COUNTY OF

-- X

PROCEEDING FOR   SCHEDULE B

Estate of   ISSUE OF THE DECEDENT

                                        WHO WERE THE SUBJECT

a/k/a   OF AN ADOPTION

                    Deceased.   File # _____

-- X

Name of child: _____

Relationship to decedent prior to adoption: _____

Date of adoption: _____

Was this a step-parent adoption?(i.e.,was the child adopted by the spouse of the decedent's former spouse?)

Yes☐   No☐

If yes,name of adoptive father or mother: _____

If not a step-parent adoption,indicate below the biological relationship of the adoptive parent to the child:

☐ grandparent(s)

☐ brother or sister

☐ aunt or uncle

☐ first cousin

☐ nephew or niece

Name of the adoptive parent: _____

SURROGATE'S COURT OF THE STATE OF NEW YORK

COUNTY OF

-- X

PROCEEDING FOR   SCHEDULE C

Estate of   INFANTS

a/k/a

                         Deceased.   File # _____

-- X

[NOTE: Please furnish all of the information requested, otherwise the petition may be rejected.]

Name: _____

Date of birth: _____

_____

Relationship to the decedent: _____

With whom does the infant reside? _____

Name of mother: _____

Is she alive? _____

Name of Father: _____

Is he alive? _____

Does infant have a court-appointed guardian?   Yes ☐   No ☐

    If yes, name and address of guardian: _____

Name: _____

Date of birth: _____

Relationship to the decedent: _____

With whom does the infant reside? _____

Name of mother: _____

Is she alive? _____

Name of Father: _____

Is he alive? _____

Does infant have a court-appointed guardian?   Yes ☐   No ☐

    If yes, name and address of guardian: _____

Official Forms

SURROGATE'S COURT OF THE STATE OF NEW YORK COUNTY OF

.... X

PROCEEDING FOR

Estate of

a/k/a

SCHEDULE D

PERSONS UNDER DISABILITY

OTHER THAN INFANTS

Deceased.   File # _____

.... X

[use additional sheets if more than one]

1. Name: _____ Relationship: _____

Residence: _____

With whom does this person reside? _____

If this person is in prison, name of prison: _____

Does this person have a court-appointed fiduciary?   Yes☐   No☐

    If yes, give name, title and address: _____

_____

    If no, describe nature of disability: _____

_____

    If no, give name and address of relative or friend interested in his or her welfare: _____

_____

2. Where abouts unknown/Unknowns [persons whose addresses or names are unknown to petitioner; if known, give name and relationship to decedent]

_____

_____

_____

_____

_____

_____

_____

_____

_____

_____

_____

FORM A-2   **Administration Citation**

ADMINISTRATION CITATION   **File No.** _____

SURROGATE'S COURT - _____ COUNTY

CITATION

THE PEOPLE OF THE STATE OF NEW YORK
By the Grace of God Free and Independent,

TO _____
   _____
   _____
   _____
   _____

A petition having been duly filed by _____, who is domiciled at

_____

YOU ARE HEREBY CITED TO SHOW CAUSE before the Surrogate's Court, _____

County, at _____, New York, on _____, 20 ____

at _____ o'clock in the _____ noon of that day, why a decree should not be made in the estate

of _____

lately domiciled at _____

in the County of _____, New York, granting Letters of Administration upon

the estate of the decedent to _____ or to such other person

as may be entitled thereto.

(State any further relief requested)

_____
_____
_____

HON. _____
                                        Surrogate

                                _____
                                        Chief Clerk

Dated, Attested and Sealed,

_____, 20____
(Seal)

Name of
Attorney for Petitioner _____   Tel. No, _____
Address of Attorney _____

Note: This citation is served upon you as required by law. You are not required to appear. If
you fail to appear it will be assumed you do not object to the relief requested. You have a right
to have an attorney-at-law appear for you.
A-2

FORM A-3   **Notice of Application for Letters of Administration**

SURROGATE'S COURT OF THE STATE OF NEW YORK
COUNTY OF _____
---X
ADMINISTRATION PROCEEDING
Estate of _____

a/k/a   _____

---X
Notice is Hereby Given That:

NOTICE OF APPLICATION FOR
LETTERS OF ADMINISTRATION
(SCPA 1005)

File No. _____

    (1) an application for Letters of Administration upon the estate of the above-named decedent, has been made by _____, petitioner,

whose post office address is: _____

    (2) each and every name of the intestate decedent known to the undersigned is as indicated in the above caption.

    (3) petitioner prays that a decree be made directing the issuance of Letters of Administration to _____

    (4) the name and post office address of each and every distributee of the above-named decedent, as set forth in the petition and known to the undersigned, are as follows:

    (a) Distributees who have been duly cited, have waived citation or have appeared in this proceeding.

Name of Distributee	Domicile and Post Office Address

(b)   Other Distributees:

Name of Distributee	Domicile and Post Office Address

[CONTINUE ON REVERSE SIDE IF MORE SPACE NEEDED]

    (5) That the undersigned does not know of any other distributees of the said decedent.

    (6) That Letters of Administration will issue on or after _____, 20_____

Dated: _____, 20_____

Signature of Petitioner or Attorney

_____
Attorney for Petitioner

_____
Print Name

_____
Address (office)

_____
Address

Tel. No. _____

FORM A-4   **Affidavit of Mailing Notice of Application for Letters of Administration**

SURROGATE'S COURT OF THE STATE OF NEW YORK
COUNTY OF_____
---X
ADMINISTRATION PROCEEDING
Estate of _____

a/k/a _____

_____ Deceased.
---X

STATE OF NEW YORK
COUNTY OF _____ ss.

AFFIDAVIT OF MAILING
NOTICE OF APPLICATION FOR
LETTERS OF ADMINISTRATION
(SCPA 1005)

File No. _____

_____ , **residing at** _____ , New York,
being duly sworn, deposes and says that deponent is over the age of eighteen years; that on
_____ 20____, deponent mailed a copy of the foregoing Notice of Application for
Letters of Administration, contained in a securely closed postpaid wrapper, directed to each of
the persons named in paragraph 4(b), respectively, as follows:

whose post office address is _____

whose post office address is _____

whose post office address is _____

whose post office address is _____

whose post office address is _____

whose post office address is _____

whose post office address is _____

whose post office address is _____

by depositing the document in a letter box or other official depository under the exclusive care
and custody of the United States Post Office, located at:

_____

Sworn to before me this _____

day of _____ ,20 ___

_____
Signature

_____
Notary Public
Commission Expires:
  (Affix Stamp or Seal)

A-4

FORM A-5   Notice to Consul General

SURROGATE'S COURT OF THE STATE OF NEW YORK
COUNTY OF _____
---X
ADMINISTRATION PROCEEDING
Estate of _____

a/k/a
_____
------------------------------- Deceased. --X
---X
TO THE CONSUL GENERAL OF_____
AT THE CITY OF NEW YORK

NOTICE TO CONSUL
        GENERAL

File No. _____

PLEASE TAKE NOTICE that a petition ☐ will be ☐ has been presented to the Surrogate's Court,
County of _____, on _____ 20 ____, with respect to the Estate of
the above-named decedent and it appears from the petition that:

a. the deceased was a subject of _____ or
b. the following distributees are nonresidents of the United States:

Names	Addresses	Citizenship
_____	_____	_____
_____	_____	_____
_____	_____	_____
_____	_____	_____

_____
Attorney for Petitioner

_____
Address

_____
Telephone No.

STATE OF NEW YORK
COUNTY OF _____ ss:

_____being duly sworn, says:

That he/she resides at _____, New York; that on the
_____, 20____,he/she served a copy of the above NOTICE on the Consul General
of _____ at _____, New York City, by mailing same to the
office of the aforesaid Consul.

_____
Signature

Sworn to before me this _____

day of _____, 20___

_____
Notary Public
Commission Expires:
(Affix Stamp and Seal)

A-5

FORM A-6   **Decree Appointing Administrator**

At a Surrogate's Court of the
State of New York held in and
for the County of_____
at _____, New York
on_____, 20 ____

PRESENT:
  Hon. _____
  Surrogate.
---X
ADMINISTRATION PROCEEDING
Estate of _____

a/k/a

_____
                              Deceased.
---X

DECREE APPOINTING
  ADMINISTRATOR

File No. _____

A petition having been filed by _____ praying that administration of the goods, chattels and credits of the above-named decedent be granted to _____, and all persons named in such petition, required to be cited, having been duly cited to show cause why such relief should not be granted or having duly waived the issuance of such citation and consented thereto; and it appearing that _____ is in all respects competent to act as administrat____ of the estate of said deceased, and a

☐ bond having been filed and approved in the amount of $_____
☐ bond having been dispensed with

and such representative(s) otherwise having qualified therefore; now, after due deliberation, with no one appearing in opposition thereto, it is

ORDERED AND DECREED that Letters of Administration issue to _____

_____

ORDERED AND DECREED that the authority of such representative (s) be restricted in accordance with, and that letters herein issued contain, the limitation, if any, which appears immediately below.

_____
                Surrogate

A-6

FORM A-7   Affidavit of Regularity

SURROGATE'S COURT OF THE STATE OF NEW YORK
COUNTY OF _____X

ADMINISTRATION PROCEEDING
Estate of _____   AFFIDAVIT OF
                                                          REGULARITY
a/k/a
_____   File No. _____
_____ Deceased.
_____X

STATE OF NEW YORK
COUNTY OF_____ ss.

_____, being duly sworn, deposes and says:

   1. **That he/she is the attorney for** _____, the
_____ herein.

2. That all the parties to this proceeding have been duly cited or have waived the issuance and service of a citation herein and consented to the entry of a decree or order in the following manner and form:

a. By service of a copy of the citation issued herein upon the following persons in the manner prescribed by SCPA 307(j), as more fully appears by the proof of service thereof, made in the manner and form by law and filed on _____, 20____

Name	Address	Date of Service

b. By service pursuant to an order made herein on _____; 20____, **under** SCPA 307(2), as more fully appears by the proof of service thereof, made in the manner prescribed by law and filed herein on _____, 20 ____

Name	Address	Date of Service

(Parties who waive or consent)
C. By duly executed waivers of the issuance and service of the citation herein and a consent to the entry of a decree or order and filed herein on _____ 20____, by:

Name	Address	Date of Waiver

3. That no notice of appearance has been filed herein, except by _____

4. That all of the persons named above are of full age and are of sound mind, excepting those hereinbefore stated to be otherwise, and comprise all the parties, as deponent verily believes, who have any interest in this proceeding.

Sworn to before me this _____

day of _____, 20____   _____
                                                                Signature

_____
Notary Public
Commission Expires:
(Affix Stamp or Seal)

N.B. -Where a person cited is an infant, incarcerated, a mentally ill person, a mentally retarded person, a developmentally disabled person, an alcohol abuser or for any cause is mentally incapable of adequately protecting his/her rights, it Must so appear in the foregoing affidavit. The age of the infant also must be stated.
A-7

FORM A-8   **Waiver of Citation, Renunciation and Consent to Appointment of Administrator (Individual)**

SURROGATE'S COURT OF THE STATE OF NEW YORK
COUNTY OF _____
--X

ADMINISTRATION PROCEEDING
Estate of _____

a/k/a _____

                      Deceased.
--X

WAIVER OF CITATION,
RENUNCIATION AND CONSENT TO
APPOINTMENT OF ADMINISTRATOR
(INDIVIDUAL)

File No. _____

The undersigned, a distributee or creditor of the above named decedent and being of full age and sound mind hereby voluntarily appears in the Surrogate's Court of _____ County, New York, and waives the issuance and service of citation in this matter, renounces all right to Letters of Administration of the above captioned estate and consents that
    ☐ Letters of Administration
    ☐ Letters of Administration with Limitations
    ☐ Limited Letters of Administration

be issued to _____
or any other person or persons entitled thereto without any notice whatsoever to the undersigned, and consents

    ☐ that a bond be dispensed with and hereby specifically release any claim I might have under any bond that may be filed

    ☐ that a bond in the amount of $_____ be posted.

Date	Signature	Street Address	Relationship
	Print Name	Town/State/Zip	

STATE OF NEW YORK
COUNTY OF_____ ss.

On _____, 20___, before me personally appeared _____
to me known and known to me to be the person described in and who executed the foregoing waiver and consent and each duly acknowledged the execution thereof.

_____
Notary Public
Commission Expires:
 (Affix Stamp or Seal)

_____
Name of Attorney

_____
Address

_____

_____
Telephone No.

A-8 (10/04)

FORM A-9   Waiver of Citation and Consent to Appointment of Administrator (Corporation)

SURROGATE'S COURT OF THE STATE OF NEW YORK
COUNTY OF _____
--X
ADMINISTRATION PROCEEDING
Estate of _____

a/k/a _____

                        Deceased.
--X

WAIVER OF CITATION AND
CONSENT TO APPOINTMENT
OF ADMINISTRATOR
(CORPORATION)

File No. _____

The undersigned corporation, a creditor of the above-named decedent, hereby voluntarily appears in the Surrogate's Court of _____ County, New York, and waives the issuance and service of a citation in this matter and consents that Letters of Administration be issued to

or any other person or persons entitled thereto without any notice whatsoever to the undersigned, without furnishing a bond or other security for the faithful performance of the duties of that office and specifically releasing any claim it might have under any bond that may be furnished.

DATE: _____, 20 ____   _____
                                           (Name of Corporation)

                           By: _____
                                           (Signature of Officer)

                                    _____
                                           (Type Name and Title)

STATE OF NEW YORK
COUNTY OF _____ ss.:

On _____, 20___ before me personally came _____

_____

to me known, who being duly sworn did say that: he resides at _____

_____, he is a _____

_____ of _____

_____, the corporation described in and which executed the foregoing waiver and consent; and that he signed the same thereto by order of the board of directors of the corporation.

_____
Notary Public
Commission Expires:
 (Affix Stamp or Seal)

_____
Name of Attorney

_____
Address

_____
Telephone Number

A-9

FORM A-10   Affidavit of Service of Citation (Adult)

STATE OF NEW YORK
SURROGATE'S COURT COUNTY OF_____
-- X
ADMINISTRATION PROCEEDING,
Estate of _____

a/k/a
_____
                        Deceased.
-- X

Note: File Proof of Service at least
3 days before return date. State
clearly date, time and place of
service and name of person served
(Uniform Rule 207.7(c))

AFFIDAVIT OF SERVICE
OF CITATION (Adult)

File No. _____

STATE OF NEW YORK   COUNTY OF_____ ss.

_____ of _____
_____, being duly sworn, says that I am over the age of eighteen years; that
I made personal service of the citation herein dated _____, 20____ on each
person named below, each of whom deponent knew to be the person mentioned and described in said
citation, by delivering to and leaving with each of them personally a true copy of said citation,
as follows:

On _____, description, viz: sex _____, color of skin _____

color of hair _____, approximate age _____, weight _____, height _____, at

_____o'clock _____m. on the _____ day of _____, 20____, at _____

On _____, description, viz: sex _____, color of skin _____

color of hair _____, approximate age _____, weight _____, height _____, at

_____o'clock _____m. on the _____ day of _____, 20____, at _____

On _____, description, viz: sex _____, color of skin _____

color of hair _____, approximate age _____, weight _____, height _____, at

_____o'clock _____m. on the _____ day of _____, 20____, at _____

That none of the aforesaid persons is in the Military Service as defined by the Act of Congress
known as the "Soldiers' and Sailors' Civil Relief Act of 1940" and in the New York "Soldiers'
and Sailors, Civil Relief Act."

_____

Sworn to before me this

day of _____, 20____

_____
Notary Public
Commission Expires:
(Affix Stamp or Seal)

A-10

FORM AA-1   Petition for Ancillary Letters of Administration

DO NOT LEAVE ANY ITEMS BLANK

SURROGATE'S COURT OF THE STATE OF NEW YORK
COUNTY OF _____
---X
ANCILLARY ADMINISTRATION PROCEEDING,
ESTATE OF _____

a/k/a _____

a domiciliary of the State of _____

                              Deceased.
---X
TO THE SURROGATE'S COURT, COUNTY OF _____

**PETITION FOR ANCILLARY
LETTERS OF ADMINISTRATION
SCPA ARTICLE 16**

[ ] Ancillary Letters of Administration
[ ] Ancillary Letters of Administration d.b.n.

File No. _____

It is respectfully alleged:
1. The name, citizenship, domicile (or, in the case of a bank or trust company, its principal office) and interest in this proceeding of the petitioner(s) are as follows:

Name: _____

Domicile or Principal Office: _____
                              (Street and Number)

_____
(City, Village or Town)   (State)   (Zip Code)

     Mailing Address:_____
              (if different from domicile)
Citizen of: _____

Name: _____

Domicile or Principal Office: _____
                              (Street and Number)

_____
     (City, Village or Town)   (State)   (Zip Code)

     Mailing Address:_____
                    (if different from domicile)
Citizen of: _____

Interest(s) of Petitioner(s): [Check one]
     [ ] Administrator   [ ] Distributee of decedent [State relationship] _____
     [ ] Creditor
     [ ] Other [Specify] _____

2. The name, domicile, date and place of death, and national citizenship of the above-named decedent are as follow:

     (a) Name: _____

     (b) Date of Death: _____

     (c) Place of death: _____

     (d) Domicile: Street _____

          City, Town, Village _____

          County _____   State _____

     (e) Citizen of: _____

3. The decedent died **INTESTATE**, leaving no will.

On the _____, letters were issued to _____
by _____ Court, State of _____, being a
competent court of the state of the domicile of decedent having jurisdiction thereof, and the amount of the security given on the original
appointment was $_____.

[If additional space is needed in Paragraphs 4, 5 and 6, attach addendum.]

4.(a) The estimated gross value of decedent's property in the State of New York, consisting of real property and personal property,
is described and valued as follows: [list items and describe briefly, giving location. If space is insufficient, attach addendum].

Personal Property	$_____
Improved real property in New York State	$_____
Unimproved real property in New York State	$_____
Estimated gross rents for a period of 18 months	$_____
Total	$_____

4.(b) No other assets exist in New York State, nor does any cause of action exist on behalf of the estate, except as follows: **[Enter
"NONE" or specify]**

_____

_____

Exemplified copies of the decree and the letters issued, if any, are submitted as part of this petition.

5. The names, addresses and interests of all persons entitled to process [(a) New York State Department of Taxation and Finance,
(b) all domiciliary creditors or domiciliaries claiming to be creditors, and (c) such other persons entitled to letters pursuant to SCPA
§1607] are as follows:

Name	Address	Nature of Interest or Amount of Claim
New York State Department of Taxation and Finance	Albany, New York	_____
_____	_____	_____
_____	_____	_____
_____	_____	_____

6. The name and address of each domiciliary distributee having an interest in the property in this state is as follows:

    (a) Each distributee who is of full age and sound mind or which is a corporation or association:

Name	Address	Interest
_____	_____	_____
_____	_____	_____

    (b) Each distributee who is an infant or otherwise under a disability: [State disability and see SCPA §304(3)]

Name	Address	Interest

Disability: _____

_____   _____   _____

Disability: _____

7. There are no persons interested in this proceeding other than those hereinbefore mentioned. No previous application for ancillary administration with or without ancillary letters has been made, except _____

WHEREFORE, petitioner(s) pray(s) (a) that process issue to all necessary parties and (b) that ancillary letters issue thereon as follows:

[ ] Ancillary Letters of Administration to: _____

_____

[ ] Ancillary Letters of Administration d.b.n. to: _____

_____

(d) [State any other relief requested]

Dated: _____

1. _____   2. _____
   (Signature of Petitioner)   (Signature of Petitioner)

_____   _____
   (Print Name)   (Print Name)

3. _____
   (Name of Corporate Petitioner)

_____
   (Signature of Officer)

_____
   (Print Name and Title of Officer)

SURROGATE'S COURT OF THE STATE OF NEW YORK
COUNTY OF _____
---X

ANCILLARY ADMINISTRATION PROCEEDING
ESTATE OF _____

a/k/a_____

a domiciliary of the State of _____

Deceased.
---X

**COMBINED VERIFICATION,
OATH AND DESIGNATION**

File No. _____

STATE OF   _____)
COUNTY OF _____) ss:

The undersigned, the petitioner named in the foregoing petition, being duly sworn, says:

1. VERIFICATION: I have read the foregoing petition subscribed by me and know the contents thereof, and the same is true of my own knowledge, except as to the matters therein stated to be alleged upon information and belief, and as to those matters I believe it to be true.

2. OATH OF ANCILLARY [ ] Administrator   [ ] Administrator d.b.n.: I am over eighteen (18) years of age and a citizen of the United States; I will well, faithfully and honestly discharge the duties of ancillary administrator/administrator d.b.n.. I am not ineligible to receive letters.

3. DESIGNATION OF CLERK FOR SERVICE OF PROCESS: I do hereby designate the Clerk of the Surrogate's Court of _____ County, and his or her successor in office as a person on whom service of any process issuing from such Surrogate's Court may be made, in like manner and with like effect as if it were served personally upon me, whenever I cannot be found within the State of New York after due diligence used.

My domicile is _____
             (Street Address)   (City/Town/Village)   (State)   (Zip Code)

_____
(Signature of Petitioner)

_____
(Print Name)

On _____, before me personally came _____
to me known to be the person described in and who executed the foregoing instrument. Such person duly swore to such instrument before me and duly acknowledged that he/she executed the same.

_____
Notary Public
Commission Expires:
(Affix Notary Stamp or Seal)

Signature of New York Attorney:_____

Print Name of New York Attorney:_____

Firm Name:_____Tel. No.:_____

Address of New York Attorney:_____

AA-1 (4/98)   -4-

Official Forms

SURROGATE'S COURT OF THE STATE OF NEW YORK
COUNTY OF _____
---X
ANCILLARY ADMINISTRATION PROCEEDING,
ESTATE OF _____   **COMBINED CORPORATE VERIFICATION,**
                                                    CONSENT AND DESIGNATION
a/k/a _____

a domiciliary of the State of _____   File No. _____

                                     Deceased.
---X
STATE OF _____)
COUNTY OF _____) ss:

The undersigned, a _____of
                                    (Title)

_____
                        (Name of Bank or Trust Company)

a corporation duly qualified to act in a fiduciary capacity without further security, being duly sworn, says:

1. VERIFICATION: I have read the foregoing petition subscribed by me and know the contents thereof, and the same is true of my own knowledge, except as to the matters therein stated to be alleged upon information and belief, and as to those matters I believe it to be true.

2. CONSENT: I consent to accept the appointment as   [ ] Ancillary Administrator   [ ] Ancillary Administrator d.b.n. of the decedent described in the foregoing petition and consent to act as such fiduciary.

3. DESIGNATION OF CLERK FOR SERVICE OF PROCESS: I do hereby designate the Clerk of the Surrogate's Court of _____ County, and his or her successor in office as a person on whom service of any process issuing from such Surrogate's Court may be made, in like manner and with like effect as if it were served personally upon me, whenever I cannot be found within the State of New York after due diligence used.

_____
        (Name of Corporate Petitioner)

_____
        (Signature of Officer)

_____
        (Print Name and Title of Officer)

On _____, before me personally came _____
to me known, who duly swore to the foregoing instrument and who did say that he/she resides at _____
and that he/she is a_____of _____the corporation/national banking association described in and which executed such instrument, and the he/she signed his/her name thereto by order of the Board of Directors of the corporation.

_____
Notary Public
Commission Expires:
(Affix Notary Stamp or Seal)

Signature of New York Attorney:_____

Print Name of New York Attorney:_____

Name of New York Attorney: _____Tel. No.:_____

Address of New York Attorney: _____

AA-1 (4/98)   -5-

FORM AA-2   Citation

ANCILLARY ADMINISTRATION CITATION   File No. _____

SURROGATE'S COURT - _____ COUNTY

CITATION

THE PEOPLE OF THE STATE OF NEW YORK,
By the Grace of God Free and Independent

TO _____

_____

_____

_____

_____

A petition having been duly filed by _____, who is domiciled at

_____

YOU ARE HEREBY CITED TO SHOW CAUSE before the Surrogate's Court, _____ County, at _____

o'clock on the _____ noon of that day, why a decree should not be made in the estate of

_____

lately domiciled at _____

granting ancillary administration and directing that

☐ Ancillary Letters of Administration issue to:_____

☐ Ancillary Letters of Administration d.b.n. issue to: _____

(State any further relief requested)

Dated, Attested and Sealed,   Hon. _____

Surrogate

_____

(Seal)   Chief Clerk

_____

Attorney for Petitioner   Telephone Number

Address of Attorney,

(Note: This citation is served upon you as required by law. You are not required to appear. If you fail to appear it will be assumed you do not object to the relief request. You have a right to have an attorney appear for you.)

AA-2 (12/97)

FORM AA-3   Notice of Application for Ancillary Letters of Administration

SURROGATE'S COURT OF THE STATE OF NEW YORK
COUNTY OF _____
---X
ANCILLARY ADMINISTRATION PROCEEDING,
ESTATE OF _____

a/k/a _____

a domiciliary of the State of _____

                                          Deceased.
---X

NOTICE OF APPLICATION FOR
ANCILLARY LETTERS OF ADMINISTRATION

File No. _____

Notice is hereby given that:

1. An application for ancillary letters of administration upon the estate of _____, deceased,
domiciled at _____
State of_____ has been offered for ancillary administration in the Surrogate's Court for the County of
_____

2. Each and every name of the intestate decedent know to the undersigned is as indicated in the above caption.

3. Petitioner prays that a decree be made directing the issuance of ☐ Ancillary Letters of Administration ☐ Ancillary Letters of
Administration d.b.n. to:

_____
_____

4. The name and post office address of each and every distributee of the above-named decedent, as set forth in Paragraph 6 of the petition
and known to the undersigned, is/are as follows:

NAME OF DISTRIBUTEE	DOMICILE AND POST OFFICE ADDRESS
_____	_____
_____	_____
_____	_____
_____	_____
_____	_____

(USE ADDITIONAL SHEETS IF NECESSARY)

Date _____

(Note; Complete Affidavit of Mailing. If serving Infant 14 years of age or older, list and mail to Infant as well as parent or guardian.)

Name of New York Attorney: _____ Tel. No.:_____

Address of New York Attorney: _____

AA-3 (12/97)

NAME OF DISTRIBUTEE   DOMICILE AND POST OFFICE ADDRESS

_____   _____
_____   _____
_____   _____
_____   _____
_____   _____
_____   _____
_____   _____

AFFIDAVIT OF MAILING NOTICE OF ANCILLARY ADMINISTRATION

STATE OF NEW YORK   )
) ss.:
COUNTY OF_____)

_____, residing at _____

being duly sworn, says that he/she is over the age of 18 years, that on the _____ day of _____, he/she

deposited in the post office or in a post office box regularly maintained by the government of the United States in the

_____ of _____, State of New York, a copy of the foregoing Notice of Application for Ancillary

Letters of Administration contained in a securely closed postpaid wrapper directed to each of the persons named in said notice at the

places set opposite their respective names.

Sworn to before me this _____   _____
day of _____   Signature
                                   _____
                                   Print Name

_____
Notary Public
Commission Expires:
(Affix Notary Stamp or Seal)

Name of New York Attorney: _____ Tel. No.:_____
Address of New York Attorney: _____

AA-3 (12/97)

FORM AP-1   **Petition for Ancillary Probate**

<table>
<tr><td colspan="2">For Office Use Only</td></tr>
<tr><td>Filing Fee Paid $</td><td></td></tr>
<tr><td></td><td>Certs $</td></tr>
<tr><td>$</td><td>Bond, Fee:</td></tr>
<tr><td>Receipt No:</td><td>No:</td></tr>
</table>

DO NOT LEAVE ANY ITEMS BLANK

SURROGATE'S COURT OF THE STATE OF NEW YORK
COUNTY OF _____

-- X

ANCILLARY PROBATE PROCEEDING, WILL OF

_____

a/k/a _____

a domiciliary of the State of _____

_____ Deceased. X

PETITION FOR ANCILLARY PROBATE
   SCPA ARTICLE 16
☐ Ancillary Letters Testamentary
☐ Ancillary Letters of Administration c. t. a.
☐ Without Ancillary Letters

File No. _____

--- X

TO THE SURROGATE'S COURT, COUNTY OF _____
   It is respectfully alleged:
   1. The name, citizenship, domicile (or, in the case of a bank or trust company, its principle office) and interest in this proceeding of the petitioner(s) are as follows:

Name: _____

Domicile or Principal Office: _____
                                               (Street and Number)

   (City, Village or Town)   (State)   (Zip Code)

           Mailing address: _____
                           (If different from domicile)
Citizen of: _____

Name: _____

Domicile or Principal Office: _____
                                               (Street and Number)

   (City, Village or Town)   (State)   (Zip Code)

           Mailing address: _____
                           (If different from domicile)
Citizen of: _____

Interest (s) of Petitioner (s): [Check one]
       ☐ Executor(s) named in decedent's will   ☐ Creditor
       ☐ Other (Specify) _____

   2. The name, domicile, date and place of death, and national citizenship of the above-named decedent are as follows:

      (a)   Name: _____

      (b)   Date of Death: _____

      (c)   Place of Death: _____

      (d)   Domicile: Street _____

           City, Town, Village _____

           County _____ State _____

      (e)   Citizen of: _____

3. Decedent left a will in writing dated_____(and

codicil dated_____), which was duly admitted to probate on _____

by the_____Court, County of_____, State of _____
being a competent court of the state of the domicile of decedent having jurisdiction thereof, and the will/codicil is not subject
to contest under the laws of that state.

On_____ , letters were issued by the court to _____

and the amount of the security given on the original appointment was $_____ Under the will/codicil a
bond ☐ is ☐ is not dispensed with.

[If additional space is needed In Paragraphs 4, 5 and 6, attach addendum.]

   4. (a) The will/codicil upon ancillary probate may operate upon property in the State of New York consisting of real
property and personal property described and valued as follows: [List items and describe briefly, giving location. If space is
insufficient, attached addendum].

Personal Property	$_____
Improved real property in New York State	$_____
Unimproved real property in New York State	$_____
Estimated gross rents for a period of 18 months	$_____
Total	$_____

   4. (b) No other testamentary assets exist in New York State, nor does any cause of action exist on behalf of the estate,
except as follows: **[Enter "NONE" or specify]**

_____
_____
_____

Exemplified copies of the will/codicil, the decree admitting the will/codicil to probate, and the letters issued, if any are submitted
as part of this petition.

   5. The names, addresses and interests of all persons entitled to process [(a) New York State Department of Taxation
and Finance, (b) all domiciliary creditors or domiciliaries claiming to be creditors, and (c) such other persons entitled to letters
pursuant to SCPA §1604] are as **follows:**

Name	Address	Nature of Interest or Amount of Claim
New York State Department of Taxation and Finance	Albany, New York	

Official Forms

6. The name and address of each domiciliary beneficiary under the will/codicil having an interest in the property in this state is as follows:

(a) Each beneficiary who is of full age and sound mind or which is a corporation or association:

Name	Address	Interest [Refer to Paragraph of Will]

(b) Each beneficiary who is an infant or otherwise under a disability: [State disability and see SCPA §304(3)]

Name	Address	Interest [Refer to Paragraph of Will]

Disability:_____

Disability:_____

7. There are no persons interested in this proceeding other than those herein before mentioned. No previous application for ancillary probate with or without ancillary letters has been made, except _____

WHEREFORE, petitioner(s) pray(s) (a) that process issue to all necessary parties (b) that the Will/Codicil be admitted to ancillary probate and (c) that ancillary letters issue thereon as follows:

☐ Ancillary Letters Testamentary to:_____

☐ Ancillary Letters of administration c.t.a. to:_____

☐ No Ancillary Letters to be issued

(d) [State any other relief requested] _____

Dated-_____

1. _____   2. _____
    (Signature of Petitioner)   (Signature of Petitioner)

    _____   _____
    (Print Name)   (Print Name)

3. _____
    (Name of Corporate Petitioner)

    _____
    (Signature of Officer)

    _____
    (Print Name and Title of Officer)

SURROGATE'S COURT OF THE STATE OF NEW YORK
COUNTY OF _____
-- X

ANCILLARY PROBATE PROCEEDING, WILL OF
_____

a/k/a_____

a domiciliary of the State of _____
_____ Deceased
-- X

STATE OF_____)
COUNTY OF_____) ss:

| COMBINED VERIFICATION |
| OATH AND DESIGNATION |

File No. _____

The undersigned, the petitioner named in the foregoing petition, being duly sworn, says:

I . VERIFICATION: I have read the forgoing petition subscribed by me and know the contents -thereof, and the same is true of my own knowledge, except as to the matters therein stated to be alleged upon information and belief, and as to those matters I believe it to be true.

2. OATH OF ANCILLARY☐ Executor☐ Administrator c.t.a. I am over eighteen (18) years of age and a citizen of the United States; I will well, faithfully and honestly discharge the duties of ancillary executor/administrator c.t.a., under the will. I am not ineligible to receive letters.

3. DESIGNATION OF CLERK FOR SERVICE OF PROCESS: I do hereby designate the clerk of the Surrogate's Court of_____ County, and his or her successor in office as a person on whom service of any process issuing from such Surrogate's Court may be made, in like manner and with like effect as if it were served personally upon me, whenever I cannot be found within the State of New York after due diligence used.

My domicile is_____
      (Street Address)   (City/Town/Village)   (State)   (Zip Code)

_____
(Signature Of Petitioner)

_____
(Print Name)

On _____ , before me personally came

to me known to be the person described in and who executed the foregoing instrument. Such person duly swore to such instrument before me and duly acknowledged that he/she executed the same.

_____
Notary Public
Commission Expires:
(Affix Notary Stamp or Seal)

Signature of New York Attorney:_____

Print Name of New York Attorney:_____

Firm Name:_____ Tel. No:_____

Address of New York Attorney:_____

AP-1 (4/98)   -4-

SURROGATE'S COURT OF THE STATE OF NEW YORK
COUNTY OF _____
--- X
ANCILLARY PROBATE PROCEEDING, WILL OF

_____

a/k/a_____

a domiciliary of the State of_____
                                    Deceased.
--- X
STATE OF_____)
COUNTY OF_____)   ss:

| COMBINED CORPORATE VERIFICATION |
| CONSENT AND DESIGNATION |

File No. _____

The undersigned, a _____ of
                                              (Title)

_____
                        (Name of Bank or Trust Company)

a corporation duly qualified to act in a fiduciary capacity without further security, being duly sworn, says:

1. VERIFICATION: I have read the forgoing petition subscribed by me and know the contents thereof, and the same is true of my own knowledge, except as to the matters therein stated to be alleged upon information and belief, and as to those matters I believe it to be true.

2. CONSENT: I consent to accept the appointment as☐ Ancillary Executor☐ Ancillary Administrator c.t.a. under the will of the decedent described in the foregoing petition and consent to act as fiduciary.

3. DESIGNATION OF CLERK FOR SERVICE OF PROCESS: I do hereby designate the clerk of the Surrogate's Court of_____ County, and his or her successor in office as a person on whom service of any process issuing from such Surrogate's Court may be made, in like manner and with like effect as if it were served personally upon me, whenever I cannot be found within the State of New York after due diligence used.

_____
(Name of Corporate Petitioner)

_____
(Signature of Officer)

_____
(Print Name and Title of Officer)

On_____ , before me personally came_____
to me known, who duly swore to the foregoing instrument and who did say that he/she resides at_____
_____ and that he/she is a _____ of _____
the corporation/national banking association described in and which executed such instrument, and that he/she singed his/her name thereto by order of the Board of Directors.

_____
Notary Public
Commission Expires:
(Affix Notary Stamp or Seal)

Signature of New York Attorney:_____

Print Name of New York Attorney:_____

Firm Name:_____Tel. No:_____

Address of New York Attorney:_____

AP-1 (4/98)   -5-

FORM AP-2 **Citation**

ANCILLARY PROBATE CITATION File No_____
SURROGATES COURT-_____COUNTY
CITATION

THE PEOPLE OF THE STATE OF NEW YORK,
By the Grace of God Free and Independent

TO _____

_____

_____

A petition having been duly filed by _____ , who is

domiciled at _____

YOU ARE HEREBY CITED TO SHOW CAUSE before the Surrogate's Court, _____ County,

at _____ , New York, on _____ ,

at____o'clock in the____noon of that day, why a decree should not be made in the estate of _____

_____

lately domiciled at _____

admitting to ancillary probate an exemplified copy of the Will dated _____ .

(A Codicil dated_____), as the Will of_____

_____ deceased,

relating to real and personal property, and directing that

☐ Ancillary Letters Testamentary issue to_____

☐ Ancillary Letters of Administration c.t.a. issue to_____

☐ No Ancillary Letters to be issued

(State any further relief requested)

HON. _____
Dated, Attested and Sealed, Surrogate

_____ _____
(Seal) Chief Clerk

_____ _____
Attorney for Petitioner Telephone Number

_____
Address of Attorney
[Note: This is served upon you as required by law. You are not required to appear. If you fail to appear it will be assumed you do not object to the relief requested. You have a right to have an attorney appear for you.]
AP-2 (12/97)

FORM AP-3   Notice of Ancillary Probate

SURROGATE'S COURT OF THE STATE OF NEW YORK
COUNTY OF_____
-- X
ANCILLARY PROBATE PROCEEDING, WILL OF   NOTICE OF ANCILLARY PROBATE
_____

a/k/a _____
                                                        File No.
a domiciliary of the State of _____   _____
                            Deceased
-- X

Notice is hereby given that:

1. An exemplified copy of the Will dated_____ (and Codicil dated_____)

of the above named decedent, domiciled at _____

State of _____ has been offered for ancillary probate in the Surrogate's Court for the County

of _____.

2. The name(s) of proponent(s) of said Will/Codicil is/are_____

_____whose

address(es) is/are_____

_____

_____

3. The name and post office address of each and every domiciliary beneficiary of the above named decedent as set forth in
Paragraph 6 of the petition is/are as follows:

NAME	MAILING ADDRESS	NATURE OF INTEREST OR STATUS

(USE ADDITIONAL SHEETS IF NECESSARY)

Date _____

(Note: Complete Affidavit of Mailing. If serving infant 14 years of age or older, list and mail to Infant as well as parent
or guardian.]

Name of New York Attorney:_____ Tel. No.: _____

Address of New York Attorney: _____

AP-3   (12/97)   -1-

NAME	MAILING ADDRESS	NATURE OF INTEREST OR STATUS

AFFIDAVIT OF MAILING NOTICE OF ANCILLARY PROBATE

STATE OF NEW YORK   )
)   ss.:
COUNTY OF_____)

_____ , residing at_____

being duly sworn, says that he/she is over the age of 18 years, that on the _____ day of_____ ,

he/she deposited in the post office or in a post office box regularly maintained by the government of the United States in the

_____ of _____ , State of New York, a copy of the foregoing Notice of

Ancillary Probate contained in a securely closed postpaid wrapper directed to each of the persons named in said notice at the

place set opposite their respective names.

Sworn to before me this _____

day of_____

_____
Notary Public
Commission Expires:
(Affix Notary Stamp or Seal)

_____
Signature
_____
Print Name

Name of New York Attorney:_____ Tel. No_____

Address of New York Attorney:_____

Official Forms

FORM ADM/DBN-1   SURROGATE'S COURT   SF-40

FORM ADM/DBN-1   Petition for Letters of Administration d.b.n. (SCPA 1007)

DO NOT LEAVE ANY ITEMS BLANK

SURROGATE'S COURT OF THE STATE OF NEW YORK

COUNTY OF _____

—————————————————————————————X

LETTERS OF ADMINISTRATION d.b.n.

ESTATE OF _____

a/k/a ————————————————————————

—————————————————————————————X

           Deceased.

PETITION FOR
LETTERS OF ADMINISTRATION d.b.n.
SCPA 1007

☐ Letters of Administration d.b.n.
☐ Letters of Administration d.b.n. with Limitations
☐ Limited Letters of Administration d.b.n.

File No. _____

TO THE SURROGATE'S COURT, COUNTY OF _____

It is respectfully alleged:

1. (a) The name, citizenship, domicile (or, in the case of a blank or trust company, its principal office) and interest in this proceeding of the petitioner(s) is/are as follows:

Name: _____

Domicile or Principal Office: _____

           (Street and Number)   (City, Village or Town)

     (County)   (State)   (Zip Code)   (Telephone Number)

Mailing Address: _____

           (If different from domicile)

Citizenship (Check one):   ☐ U.S.A.   ☐ Other (specify) _____

Name: _____

Domicile or Principal Office: _____

           (Street and Number)   (City, Village or Town)

     (County)   (State)   (Zip Code)   (Telephone Number)

Mailing Address: _____

           (If different from domicile)

Citizenship (Check one):   ☐ U.S.A.   ☐ Other (specify)

Interest(s) of Petitioner(s): [Check one]

    ☐   Distributee of decedent (state relationship) _____
    ☐   Other [Specify] _____

1 - (b) Is the proposed Administrator d.b.n. an attorney?   Yes ☐   No ☐
[NOTE: If yes, submit statement pursuant to 22 NYCRR 207.16(e); see also 207.52]

2. Letters of Administration of the above-named decedent were issued by this court on _____ , to _____ , who on _____

    ☐ died   ☐ resigned   ☐ was removed.

ADM/DBN-1 (7/98)

-1-

[Note: For paragraphs 3a through c- Do not include any assets that are jointly hold, hold in trust for another, or have a named beneficiary.]

3. (a) The estimated gross value of **unadministered** personal property passing by intestacy is less than

$ _____

(b) The estimated gross value of the decedent's unadministered real property, in this state, which is
☐ improved   ☐ unimproved, passing intestacy is less then

$ _____

A brief description of each parcel is as follows:

_____

_____

(c) The estimated gross rent for a period of eighteen (18) months is the sum of

$ _____

(d) In addition to the value of the personal property stated in paragraph (3) (a), the following right of action existed on behalf of the decedent and survived his/her death, or is granted to the administrator of the decedent by special provision of law, and it is impractical to give a bond sufficient to cover the probable amount to be recovered therein: **(Write "NONE" or state briefly the cause of action and the person against who it exists, including** names and carrier].

(e) If decedent is survived by a spouse and a parent, or parents but no issue, and there is a claim for wrongful death, check here ☐ and furnish names (s) and address (es) of parent (s) in paragraph 5.
See EPTL 5-4.4.

4.   The decedent left surviving the following who would inherit his/her estate pursuant to EPTL 4-1.1 and 4-1.2-

a. _____ ☐ Spouse (husband/wife)   ☐ Divorced **[Attach copy of Divorce Decree]**

b. _____ ☐ Child or children or descendants of predeceased child or children, **[Must include marital, non-marital, and adopted].**

c. _____ ☐ Any issue of the decedent adopted by persons related to the decedent (DRL Section 117).

d. _____ ☐ Mother/Father.

e. _____ ☐ Sisters and brothers, either of whole or half blood, and issue of predeceased sisters and brothers.

f. _____ ☐ Grandmother/Grandfather.

g. _____ ☐ Aunts or uncles, and children of predeceased aunts and uncles (first cousins).

h. _____ ☐ First cousins once removed (children of first cousins).

[Information is required only as to those classes of relatives who would take the property of decedent pursuant to EPTL 4-1.1. State "number" of survivors in each class. Insert "NO" in all prior classes. Insert "X" in all subsequent classes].

5.   The decedent left surviving the following distributees, or other necessary parties, whose names, degrees of relationship, domiciles, post office addresses and citizenship are as follows:

[Note: Show clearly how each person is related to decedent. If relationship is through an ancestor who is deceased, give name, date of death, and relationship of the ancestor to the decedent. Use rider shoot if space in Paragraph (5) is not sufficient. See Uniform Rules 207.16 (b). If any person listed in paragraph (5) is a nonmarital person, or descended from a nonmarital person, attach a copy of the order of filiation or Schedule A. If any person listed in paragraph (5) was adopted by any persons related by blood or marriage to decedent or descended from such persons, attach Schedule B.]

5a.   The following are of full age and under no disability: [If nonmarital or adopted-out person, so indicate by attaching Schedule A and/or B. If any of the distributees have died subsequent to the death of the decedent, give the name and title of the legal representative appointed for such person (s), his or her address and the court that issued such letters. If any distributee who has died, subsequent to the death of the decedent, has no legal representative, then enter the name, relationship, domicile address and citizenship of that deceased person (s) distributee (s).]

Name	Relationship	Domicile and Mailing address	Citizenship

5b.   The following are infants and/or persons under disability: [Attach applicable Schedule A, B, C and/or D]

Name	Relationship	Domicile and Mailing address	Citizenship

6. There are no persons interested in this proceeding other than those herein mentioned.

7. There are no outstanding debts or funeral expenses, except: [Write "NONE" or state same)

WHEREFORE, your petitioner (s) respectfully pray (s) that: [Check and complete all relief requested]

☐　a.　　Process issue to all necessary parties to show cause why letters should not be issued as requested;

☐　b.　　An order be granted dispensing with service of process upon those persons named in paragraph 5 who have a right to letters prior or equal to that of the person nominated, and who are non-domiciliaries or whose names or whereabouts are unknown and cannot be ascertained;

☐　c.　　A decree award Letters of Administration d.b.n. to _____

_____

or to such other person or persons having a prior right as may be entitled thereto, and;

☐　d.　　That the authority of the representative under the foregoing Letters be limited with respect to the prosecution of a cause of action on behalf of the estate, as follows: the administrator (s) may not enforce a judgment or receive any funds without further order of the Surrogate.

☐　e.　　That the authority of the representative under the foregoing Letters be limited as follows:

_____

_____

_____

☐　f.　　[State any other relief requested]._____

_____

Dated:_____

1 _____　　2. _____
　　　(Signature of Petitioner)　　　　　　　　　　(Signature of Petitioner)

_____　　　_____
　　　　(Print Name)　　　　　　　　　　　　　　　　(Print Name)

3. _____
　　(Name of Corporate Petitioner)

_____
　　　(Signature of Officer)

_____
　　(Print Name and Title of Officer)

-4-

SURROGATE'S COURT OF THE STATE OF NEW YORK
COUNTY OF _____
---X
LETTERS OF ADMINISTRATION d.b.n.
ESTATE OF
     _____

a/k/a _____

---X
                     Deceased.
                                X

**SCHEDULE A
NON MARITAL PERSONS
(PERSONS BORN OUT OF WEDLOCK)**

File No. _____

[NOTE: Non marital children (or their issue) who would be distributees if they (or their ancestors) were born in wedlock will not be regarded as distributees unless satisfactory proof is submitted establishing paternity]. See EPTL 4-1.2, which sets forth methods of establishing paternity.

Name of alleged distributee: _____

Date of birth: _____ Relationship to decedent: _____

Name of father: _____

Name of mother: _____

Does the birth certificate contain the father's name?   Yes ☐   No ☐

     If yes, attach a copy of birth certificate.

Has an order of filiation establishing paternity been entered?

Yes ☐   No ☐   If yes, attach a copy of order.

Did the nonmarital person live with his or her father?   Yes ☐   No ☐

     If yes, give dates and place of residence: _____

_____

_____

SURROGATE'S COURT OF THE STATE OF NEW YORK
COUNTY OF _____

---X
LETTERS OF ADMINISTRATION d.b.n.
ESTATE OF
_____

a/k/a   _____

                              Deceased.
---X

SCHEDULE B
**ISSUE OF THE DECEDENT
WHO WERE THE SUBJECT OF AN ADOPTION**

File No. _____

Name of child: _____

Relationship to decedent prior to adoption: _____

Date of adoption: _____

Was this a step-parent adoption? (i.e., was the child adopted by the spouse of the decedent's former spouse?)
     Yes   ☐   No   ☐

          If yes, name of adoptive father or mother: _____

If not a step-parent adoption, indicate below the biological relationship of the adoptive parent to the child:

     ☐   grandparents (s)

     ☐   brother or sister

     ☐   aunt or uncle

     ☐   first cousin

     ☐   nephew or niece

Name of the adoptive parent _____

SURROGATE'S COURT OF THE STATE OF NEW YORK
COUNTY OF _____
--X
LETTERS OF ADMINISTRATION d.b.n.   SCHEDULE C
ESTATE OF_____   INFANTS

_____   File No. _____
a/k/a

                  Deceased.
--X

Name: _____ Date of birth: _____

Relationship to the decedent: _____

With whom does the infant reside? _____

Name of mother: _____ Is she alive? _____

Name of father: _____ Is he alive? _____

Does the infant have a court-appointed guardian?   Yes ☐   No ☐

      If yes, name and address of guardian: _____

      _____

Name: _____ Date of birth: _____

Relationship to the decedent: _____

With whom does the infant reside? _____

Name of mother: _____ Is she alive? _____

Name of father: _____ Is he alive? _____

Does the infant have a court-appointed guardian?   Yes ☐   No ☐

      If yes, name and address of guardian: _____

      _____

SURROGATE'S COURT OF THE STATE OF NEW YORK
COUNTY OF _____
---X
LETTERS OF ADMINISTRATION d.b.n.
ESTATE OF

_____

a/k/a

_____

                                    Deceased
---X

SCHEDULE D
PERSONS UNDER DISABILITY
OTHER THAN INFANTS

File No. _____

[Use additional sheets if needed]

1.   Name: _____ Relationship: _____

Residence: _____

With whom does this person reside? _____

If this person is in prison, name of prison: _____

Does this person have a court-appointed fiduciary?   Yes ☐   No ☐

        If yes, give name, title and address: _____

        _____

        If no, describe nature of disability: _____

        _____

        If no, give name and address of relative or friend interested in his or her welfare: _____

        _____

2.   Whereabouts unknown/Unknowns [persons whose addresses or names are unknown to petitioner; if known, give name and relationship to decedent]:

_____

_____

_____

_____

_____

_____

_____

_____

COMBINED VERIFICATION, OATH & DESIGNATION

[For use when petitioner is to be appointed administrator d.b.n.]

STATE OF_____)
COUNTY OF_____) **ss:**

      The undersigned, the petitioner named in the foregoing petition, being duly sworn, says:

      1.   VERIFICATION: I have read the foregoing petition subscribed by me and know the contents thereof, and the same is true of my own knowledge, except as to the matters therein stated to be alleged upon information and belief, and as to those matters I believe it to be true.

      2.   OATH OF ADMINISTRATOR d.b.n. I am over eighteen (18) years of age and a citizen of the United States; I will well, faithfully and honestly discharge the duties of the administrator d.b.n. I am not ineligible to receive letters.

      3.   DESIGNATION OF CLERK FOR SERVICE OF PROCESS: I do hereby designate the Clerk of the Surrogate's Court of _____ County, and his or her successor in office, as a person on whom service of any process issuing from such Surrogate's Court may be made, in like manner and with like effect as if it were served personally upon me, whenever I cannot be found within the State of New York after due diligence used.

My domicile is _____
                 (Street Address)   (City/Town/Village)   (State)   (Zip Code)

_____

      (Signature of Petitioner)

_____

        (Print Name)

      On _____ , _____ , before me personally came

_____
to me known to be the person described in and who executed the foregoing instrument. Such person duly swore to such instrument before me and duly acknowledged that he/she executed the same.

_____
Notary Public
Commission Expires:
(Affix Notary Stamp or Seal)

Signature of Attorney: _____

Print Name: _____

Firm Name: _____ Tel. No.: _____

Address of Attorney: _____

COMBINED CORPORATE VERIFICATION, CONSENT AND DESIGNATION

[For use when a petitioner to be appointed is a bank or trust company]

STATE OF_____)
COUNTY OF_____) ss:

The undersigned, a _____ Of
                                                        (Title)

_____
                                (Name of Bank or Trust Company)

a corporation duly qualified to act in a fiduciary capacity without further security, being duly sworn, says:

    1.   VERIFICATION: I have read the foregoing petitioner subscribed by me and know the contents thereof, and the same is true of my own knowledge, except as to the matters therein stated to be alleged upon information and belief, and as to those matters I believe it to be true.

    2.   CONSENT: I consent to accept the appointment as Administrator d.b.n. of the decedent described in the foregoing petition and consent to act as such fiduciary.

    3.   DESIGNATION OF CLERK FOR SERVICE OF PROCESS: I do hereby designate the Clerk of the Surrogate's Court of _____ County, and his or her successor in office, as a person on whom service of any process issuing from such Surrogate's Court may be made, in like manner and with like effect as if it were served personally upon me, whenever I cannot be found within the State of New York after due diligence used.

_____
    (Name of Corporate Petitioner)

_____
    (Signature of Officer)

_____
    (Print Name and Title of Officer)

    On the _____ , _____ before me personally came _____
to me known, who duly sworn to the foregoing instrument and who did say that he/she resides at _____
_____ and that he/she is a _____ Of
_____ the corporation/national banking association described in and which executed such instrument, and the he/she signed his/her name thereto by order of the Board of Directors of the corporation.

_____
Notary Public
Commission Expires:
(Affix Notary Stamp or Seal)

Signature of Attorney: _____

Print Name: _____

Firm Name: _____ Tel. No.: _____

Address of Attorney: _____

FORM ADM/DBN-2   **Citation**

LETTERS OF ADMINISTRATION d.b.n. CITATION   File No. _____

SURROGATE'S COURT - _____ COUNTY

CITATION

THE PEOPLE OF THE STATE OF NEW YORK,
By the Grace of God Free and Independent

TO | _____ |

_____

_____

A petition having been duly filed by _____ , who is

domiciled at _____

YOU ARE HEREBY CITED TO SHOW CAUSE before the Surrogate's Court, _____ County,

at _____ , New York, on _____ , _____

at _____ o'clock in the_____ noon of that day, why a decree should not be made in the estate

of _____

lately domiciled at _____

granting administration d.b.n. and directing that

☐   Letters of Administration d.b.n. issue to: _____

☐   Letters of Administration d.b.n. with Limitations issue to: _____

☐   Limited Letters of Administration d.b.n. issue to _____

(State any further relief requested)

_____

_____

HON. _____

Dated, Attested and Sealed,

                                        Surrogate

_____ , _____   _____
(Seal)   Chief Clerk

_____
Attorney For Petitioner   Telephone Number

_____
Address of Attorney

[Note: This citation is served upon you as required by law. You are not required to appear. If you fail to appear it **will** be assumed you do not object to the relief requested. You have a right to have an attorney appear for you.]

ADM/DBN-2 (7/98)

FORM ADM/DBN-3 **Waiver of Citation Renunciation and Consent to Appointment of Administrator d.b.n. (Individual)**

SURROGATE'S COURT OF THE STATE OF NEW YORK
COUNTY OF _____-------------X

LETTERS OF ADMINISTRATION d.b.n.
ESTATE OF _____

a/k/a _____

_____ Deceased.-------X

WAIVER OF CITATION,
RENUNCIATION AND CONSENT
TO APPOINTMENT OF ADMINISTRATION d.b.n.
(INDIVIDUAL)

File No. _____

The undersigned, a distributee or creditor of the above-named decedent, and being of full age and sound mind, hereby voluntarily appears in the Surrogate's Court of _____ County, New York, and waives the issuance and service of citation in this matter, renounces all rights to Letters of Administration d.b.n. of the above captioned estate and consents that

☐ Letters of Administration d.b.n.

☐ Letters of Administration d.b.n. with Limitations

☐ Limited Letters of Administration d.b.n.

be issued to _____

or any other person or persons entitled thereto without any notice whatsoever to the undersigned, and consents

☐ that a bond be dispensed with and hereby specifically releases any claim the undersigned might have under any bond that may be filed.

☐ that a bond in the amount of $ _____ be posted.

Date	Signature	Street Address	Relationship
	Print Name	Town/State/Zip	

STATE OF NEW YORK
COUNTY OF _____ ss.:

On _____ , _____, before me personally came

to me known and known to be the person described in and who executed the foregoing instrument. Such person duly swore to such instrument before me and duly acknowledged that he/she executed the same.

_____
Notary Public
Commission Expires:
(Affix Notary Stamp or Seal)

Name of Attorney: _____ Tel. No.: _____

Address of Attorney: _____

ADM/DBN-3 (10/04)

FORM ADM/DBN-4   Consent to Appointment of Administrator d.b.n.
(Corporation)

SURROGATE'S COURT OF THE STATE OF NEW YORK
COUNTY OF _____
--X
LETTERS OF ADMINISTRATION d.b.n.
ESTATE OF_____

a/k/a   _____

                       Deceased.
--X

CONSENT TO APPOINTMENT OF
ADMINISTRATOR d.b.n.
(CORPORATION)

File No. _____

     The undersigned corporation voluntarily appears in the Surrogate's Court of_____ County,
New York, and consents that

☐   Letters of Administration d.b.n.

☐   Letters of Administration d.b.n. with Limitations

☐   Limited Letters of Administration d.b.n.

be issued to _____

or any other person or persons entitled thereto without any notice whatsoever to the undersigned, and consents

☐   that a bond be dispensed with and hereby specifically releases any claim the undersigned might have
under any bond that may be filed.

☐   that a bond in the amount of $ _____ be posted.

_____   _____
Date   Name of Corporation

      By: _____
               (Signature of Officer)

           _____
           (Type Name and Title)

STATE OF NEW YORK
COUNTY OF _____ ss.:

    On _____ , _____, before me personally came
_____
to me known, who being duly sworn did say that: (s)he resides at _____
_____ of _____
the corporation described in and which executed the foregoing consent; and that (s)he signed the same thereto by order of
the board of directors of the above corporation.

_____
Notary Public
Commission Expires:
(Affix Notary Stamp or Seal)

Name of Attorney: _____ Tel. No.: _____

Address of Attorney: _____

ADM/DBN-4 (10/04)

FORM ADM/DBN-5   Notice of Application for Letters of Administration d.b.n.
(SCPA 1005)

SURROGATE'S COURT OF THE STATE OF NEW YORK
COUNTY OF _____
---X

LETTERS OF ADMINISTRATION d.b.n.
ESTATE OF _____

a/k/a _____

                      Deceased.
---X

NOTICE OF APPLICATION FOR
LETTERS OF ADMINISTRATION d.b.n.
(SCPA 1005)

File No. _____

Notice is Hereby Given That:

1. An application for Letters of Administration d.b.n. upon the estate of the above-named decedent, has been made by _____ , petitioner, whose post office address is: _____

2. Each and every name of the intestate decedent known to the undersigned is as indicated in the above caption.

3. Petitioner prays that a decree be made directing the issuance of Letters of Administration d.b.n. to _____

4. The name and post office address of each and every distributee of the above-named decedent, as set forth in the petition and known to the undersigned, are as follows:

    (a). Distributees who have been duly cited, or have waived citation or have appeared in this proceeding:

        Name of Distributee   Domicile and Post Office Address

        _____   _____

        _____   _____

        _____   _____

    (b). Other Distributees:

        Name of Distributee   Domicile and Post Office Address

        _____   _____

        _____   _____

        _____   _____

                [IF MORE SPACE IS NEEDED ADD RIDER]

5. The undersigned does not know of any other distributees of the said decedent.

6. Letters of Administration d.b.n. will issue on or after _____ , _____

Dated _____ , _____

                        _____
                        Signature of Petitioner or Attorney

                        _____
                            Print Name

                        _____
                            Address

Name of Attorney: _____ Tel. No.: _____

Address of Attorney: _____

ADM/DBN-5 (7/98)

Official Forms

FORM ADM/DBN-6   **Affidavit of Mailing Notice of Application for Letters of Administration d.b.n. (SCPA 1005)**

SURROGATE'S COURT OF THE STATE OF NEW YORK
COUNTY OF _____
--X
LETTERS OF ADMINISTRATION d.b.n.
ESTATE OF _____

a/k/a   _____

                            Deceased.
--X

                                   AFFIDAVIT OF MAILING
                          NOTICE OF APPLICATION FOR
              LETTERS OF ADMINISTRATION d.b.n.
                               (SCPA 1005)

                         File No. _____

STATE OF NEW YORK
COUNTY OF _____ ss.:

_____ , residing at _____, New York, being
duly sworn, deposes and says that deponent is over the age of eighteen years; that on _____, _____
deponent mailed a copy of the foregoing Notice of Application for Letters of Administration d.b.n. , contained in a securely
closed postpaid wrapper, directed to each of the persons named in paragraph 4 (b), respectively, as follows:

whose post office address is _____

whose post office address is _____

whose post office address is _____

whose post office address is _____

whose post office address is _____

whose post office address is _____

whose post office address is _____

whose post office address is _____

by depositing the document in a letters box or other official depository under the exclusive care and custody of the United
States Post Office located at:

_____

_____

                                  _____
                                        Signature

Sworn to before me this _____

day of _____, _____

_____
Notary Public
Commission Expires:
(Affix Notary Stamp or Seal)

ADM/DBN-6 (7/98)

FORM ADM/DBN-7   **Notice to the Consul General**

SURROGATE'S COURT OF THE STATE OF NEW YORK
COUNTY OF _____
---X

LETTERS OF ADMINISTRATION d.b.n.
ESTATE OF   _____

a/k/a   _____

                              Deceased.
---X

NOTICE TO THE CONSUL
           GENERAL

File No. _____

TO THE CONSUL GENERAL OF
AT THE CITY OF NEW YORK

PLEASE TAKE NOTICE that a petition ☐ (will be) ☐ (has been). presented to the Surrogate's Court, County of
_____ on _____, _____ , with respect to the Estate of
the above-named decedent, and it appears from the petition that:

a.   the deceased was a subject of _____ or

b.   the following distributees are nonresidents of the United States:

Names	Addresses	Citizenship

Attorney for Petitioner

_____
Address

_____
Telephone Number

STATE OF NEW YORK
COUNTY OF_____ ss.:

_____, being duly sworn, says:

That he/she resides at _____, New York; that
on the _____ , _____ , he/she served a copy of the above

NOTICE on the Counsel General of _____ at _____ ,
New York City, by mailing same to the office of the aforesaid Consul.

Sworn to before me this _____

day of _____ , _____

_____
Notary Public
Commission Expires:
(Affix Notary Stamp or Seal)

ADM/DBN-7 (7/98)

FORM ADM/DBN-8   **Affidavit of Service of Citation (Adult)**

SURROGATE'S COURT OF THE STATE OF NEW YORK
COUNTY OF _____
_____X

LETTERS OF ADMINISTRATION d.b.n.
ESTATE OF _____

a/k/a _____

_____ Deceased.
_____X

Note- File Proof of Service at least
3 days before return date. State
clearly date, time and place of
service and name of person served
(Uniform Rule 207.7 (c)).

AFFIDAVIT OF SERVICE
OF CITATION (Adult)

File No. _____

STATE OF NEW YORK   COUNTY OF_____ss.:

_____ of _____

_____, being duly sworn, says that I am over the age of eighteen years; that I made personal
service of the citation herein dated_____,20_____ on each person named below,
each of whom deponent knew to be the person mentioned and described in said citation, by delivering to and leaving with
each of them personally a true copy of said citation, as follows:

On _____, description, viz: sex _____, color of skin _____

color of hair _____, approximate age _____, weight _____, height _____, at

_____ o'clock _____ m   on the _____ day of _____,20_____, at _____

On _____, description, viz: sex _____, color of skin _____

color of hair _____, approximate age _____, weight _____, height _____, at

_____ o'clock _____ m   on the _____ day of _____,20_____, at _____

On _____, description, viz: sex _____, color of skin _____

color of hair _____, approximate age _____, weight _____, height _____, at

_____ o'clock _____ m   on the _____ day of _____,20_____, at _____

That none of the aforesaid persons is in the Military Service as defined by the Act of Congress known as the "Soldiers'
and "Sailors' Civil Relief of 1940" and in the New York "Soldiers' and Sailors' Civil Relief Act."

_____

Sworn to before me this_____

day of _____,20_____

_____
Notary Public
Commission Expires:
(Affix Notary Stamp or Seal)

ADM/DBN-8 (7/98)

FORM CPSA-1   **Parentage Petition – Surrogacy Agreement**

For Office Use Only
(Filing Fee Paid $_____)
(Receipt No:_____No:_____)

SURROGATE'S COURT OF THE STATE OF NEW YORK
COUNTY OF
---x
In the Matter of a Parentage Proceeding Concerning

_____

A Child conceived as a result of a Surrogacy Agreement.
---x
TO THE SURROGATE'S COURT, COUNTY OF _____.

PARENTAGE PETITION –
SURROGACY AGREEMENT

File No. _____

It is respectfully alleged:

1. The name, relationship, domicile, interest and telephone number of the petitioner(s) are as follows:

    a. Name: _____ Interest: _____

    Domicile:_____
                  (Street Address)   (City/Town/Village)

    (County)   (State)   (Zip)   (Telephone Number)

    Mailing address: _____
                      (If different from domicile)

    b. Name: _____ Interest: _____

    Domicile:_____
                  (Street Address)   (City/Town/Village)

    (County)   (State)   (Zip)   (Telephone Number)

    Mailing address: _____
                      (If different from domicile)

2. [Check applicable box] ☐ The person acting as the surrogate gave birth to the following child: ☐ male ☐ female ☐ non-binary/other

    Name:_____
                                           (Date of Birth)
    Address:_____
              (Street Address)   (City/Town/Village)

             (County)   (State)   (Zip)
    Who was born in _____
                   (County)   (State)

    OR

    ☐ The person acting as the surrogate is now pregnant with a child who is expected to be born on or about _____ in _____
    (specify date)   (County)   (State)

Official Forms

3. a. The following is the person acting as the surrogate:

Name: _____

                                               (Date of Birth)

Address: _____

       (Street Address)   (City/Town/Village)

_____

      (County)   (State)   (Zip)

    b. [Delete if inapplicable]   The person acting as surrogate is married to _____

                                                     (specify name)

4. The person acting as the surrogate and the spouse, if any, of the person acting as surrogate, and the intended parent(s) knowingly and voluntarily executed a surrogacy agreement.   A copy of the agreement is annexed to this petition.

5. I am/We are submitting this petition to request an order declaring the following

Name: _____

                                               (Date of Birth)

Address: _____

       (Street Address)   (City/Town/Village)

_____

      (County)   (State)   (Zip)

Name: _____

                                               (Date of Birth)

Address: _____

       (Street Address)   (City/Town/Village)

_____

      (County)   (State)   (Zip)

to be the legal parent(s) of the child.

6. [Check all that apply]
    ☐ At the time that the surrogacy agreement was executed, the following intended parent(s), _____ _____, had resided in New York State for at least six months;
    ☐ At the time that the surrogacy agreement was executed, the person acting as surrogate had resided in New York State for at least six months.

7. The following attorneys, _____, representing the intended parent(s) and the following attorneys, _____, representing the person acting as surrogate (and spouse, if applicable) have certified that the surrogacy agreement complies with Part 4 of Article 5-C of the Family Court Act.   Copies of the attorneys' certifications are annexed to this Petition.

8. Annexed to this petition is/are a statement from all parties to the surrogacy agreement that they knowingly and voluntarily entered into the surrogacy agreement and that they are jointly requesting an order/judgment/decree of parentage.

9. Upon information and belief:
    a. no individual has been adjudicated as a parent of this child, either in this court, or any other court, including a Native-American court, except _____
                          (specify)

    b. no individual has signed an Acknowledgement of Parentage admitting parentage of this child except

_____
        (specify)

10. Upon information and belief, the subject child ☐ is ☐ is not a Native American child who may be subject to the *Indian Child Welfare Act of 1978* (25 U.S.C. §§ 1901-1963).

11. No prior application has been made to any Court for the relief requested herein.

WHEREFORE, your petitioner(s) respectfully requests that this court issue an order/judgment/decree and declaration of parentage, an order that the intended parent(s) is/are the legal parent(s) of the child and that the person acting as surrogate and her spouse (if applicable) is/are not a legal parent(s) and such other and further relief as may be appropriate under the circumstances.

Dated:_____

_____
(Signature of Petitioner)

_____
(Print Name)

_____
(Signature of Petitioner)

_____
(Print Name)

VERIFICATION

STATE OF NEW YORK   )
) ss.:
COUNTY OF   )

_____, being duly sworn deposes and says that I am the petitioner above named. I have read the foregoing petition and the same is true of my own knowledge except as the matters therein stated to be alleged upon information and belief and as to those matters, I believe them to be true.

Sworn to before me this

_____ day of _____ 20___

                                         _____
                                         (Signature of Petitioner)

_____   _____
Notary Public   (Print Name)
Commission Expires:
(Affix Notary Stamp or Seal)

Signature of Attorney: _____

Print Name: _____

Firm Name: _____ Tel.No.:_____

Address of Attorney:_____
                                              (e-mail address)

CPSA-1 (2/2021)   3

FORM CPSA-2   **Order of Parentage – Surrogacy Agreement**

---x

In the Matter of a Parentage Proceeding Concerning   ORDER OF PARENTAGE–
                                                                       SURROGACY AGREEMENT

_____   File No. _____

A Child conceived as a result of a Surrogacy Agreement.
---x

    Upon reading and filing the petition of _____
_____, duly verified the _____ day of _____, 20 ___, alleging that _____
_____ is/are the
intended parent(s) of [specify name of child or, if not yet born, expected name, if known, of child] _____
_____

[Applicable to a child already born]: ☐ The child, who was born on:_____
                                                   (Date of Birth)
is ☐ male ☐ female ☐ non-binary/other

                     OR

[Applicable where child has not yet been born]: ☐ The child is expected to be born on or about: _____
                                                         (specify date)

    The following person, _____, ☐ has acted ☐ is acting as a
surrogate.

    The intended parent(s) _____and the person
acting as a surrogate and the spouse, if any, of the person acting as surrogate having executed a surrogacy
agreement on _____;
             (date)

    And the following parties [specify] _____
having ☐ contested ☐ not contested the allegations of the petition; and

    The issues having duly come on to be heard before this Court,

    NOW, after examination and inquiry into the facts and circumstances of the proceeding [and after hearing
the proofs and testimony offered in relation thereto], the Court finds and determines the following to be true:

    The person acting as surrogate became pregnant in conjunction with a surrogacy agreement.

    The residency requirement was satisfied.

    A certification was submitted by the attorneys for the intended parents and the person acting as surrogate
and the spouse, if any, of the person acting as surrogate, attesting that the requirements of Part 4 of Article 5-C of
the Family Court Act regarding the surrogacy agreement have been satisfied.

    The intended parents and the person acting as surrogate, and the spouse, if any, of the person acting as
surrogate, knowingly and voluntarily entered into the surrogacy agreement.

CPSA-2 (2/2021)

[Applicable to a child already born]:

☐ IT IS, THEREFORE, ORDERED, ADJUDGED and DECLARED that [specify name(s)]:_____
_____ is/are the legal parent(s) of [child's name]
_____ and the parent(s) shall forthwith assume responsibility for the
child's maintenance and support;

OR

[Applicable where child has not yet been born]:

☐ IT IS, THEREFORE, ORDERED, ADJUDGED and DECLARED that upon the child's birth, [specify name(s)]
_____ will be
the legal parent(s) of the child who is expected to be born on [due date] _____ and upon
the birth of such child, shall immediately assume responsibility for the child's maintenance and support and further
that, within _____ days of the child's birth, the intended parent(s) shall provide to this Court notification
thereof, together with such other facts as may assist in identifying the birth record of the child whose parentage is
in issue in this proceeding;

IT IS FURTHER ORDERED, ADJUDGED AND DECLARED that [specify the person acting as surrogate]: _____
_____ is not a legal parent to the child and the spouse, if any, of the
person acting as surrogate [specify] _____ is not a parent to the child;

IT IS FURTHER ORDERED that [specify the person acting as surrogate] _____
and the spouse, if any, of the person acting as surrogate [specify] _____
shall transfer the child to the intended parent(s) if this has not already occurred;

IT IS FURTHER ORDERED THAT:

(i) Pursuant to Judiciary Law §254, the clerk of the court shall transmit to the state commissioner of health, or for
a person born in New York City, to the commissioner of health of the city of New York, on a form prescribed by
the commissioner, a written notification of such entry together with such other facts as may assist in identifying
the birth record of the person whose parentage was in issue and, if such person whose parentage has been
determined is under eighteen years of age, the clerk shall also transmit forthwith to the registry operated by the
department of social services, pursuant to Social Services Law §372-c, a notification of such determination; and

(ii) Pursuant to Public Health Law §4138 and NYC Public Health Code §207.05, upon receipt of a judgment of
parentage, the local registrar where a child is born will report the parentage of the child to the appropriate
department of health in conformity with this court order. If an original birth certificate has already been issued, the
appropriate department of health will amend the birth certificate in an expedited manner and seal the previously
issued birth certificate except that it may be rendered accessible to the child at eighteen years of age or the legal
parent or parents.

[Check box if applicable]:

☐ IT IS FURTHER ORDERED THAT [specify]:_____

_____

Dated:
                    , New York   _____
                                                                                  SURROGATE

CPSA-2 (2/2021)

FORM CPSA-3   SURROGATE'S COURT   SF-62

FORM CPSA-3   Parentage Petition – Assisted Reproduction

SURROGATE'S COURT OF THE STATE OF NEW YORK
COUNTY OF
---x
In the Matter of a Parentage Proceeding Concerning

_____

A Child conceived as a result of Assisted Reproduction.
---x

PARENTAGE PETITION –
ASSISTED REPRODUCTION

File No. _____

TO THE SURROGATE'S COURT, COUNTY OF_____,

It is respectfully alleged:

1. The name, relationship, domicile, and telephone number of the petitioner(s) are as follows:

   a. Name: _____ ☐ child ☐ parent ☐ participant ☐ person with a claim to parentage ☐ social services official or other governmental agency ☐ representative authorized by law to act for an individual who would otherwise be entitled to maintain a proceeding but who is deceased, incapacitated or a minor ☐ other individual with claim to parentage [specify]_____.

   Domicile:_____
         (Street Address)   (City/Town/Village)

   _____
      (County)   (State)   (Zip)   (Telephone Number)

   Mailing address:_____
              (If different from domicile)

   b. Name: _____ ☐ gestating intended parent ☐ non-gestating intended parent

   Domicile:_____
         (Street Address)   (City/Town/Village)

   _____
      (County)   (State)   (Zip)   (Telephone Number)

   Mailing address:_____
              (If different from domicile)

2. I am/We are submitting this petition to request an order declaring the following

   Name:_____
                            (Date of Birth)
   Address:_____
         (Street Address)   (City/Town/Village)

   _____
      (County)   (State)   (Zip)

   Name:_____
                            (Date of Birth)
   Address:_____
         (Street Address)   (City/Town/Village)

   _____
      (County)   (State)   (Zip)

   to be the legal parent(s) of the child.

CPSA-3 (2/2021)   1

3. [Check applicable boxes]
    a. ☐ The gestating intended parent became pregnant as a result of assisted reproduction and gave birth to the following child:
        ☐ male   ☐ female   ☐ non-binary/other

        Name: _____
                                                            (Date of Birth)
        Address: _____
                    (Street Address)   (City/Town/Village)

        _____
                    (County)   (State)   (Zip)
        Who was born in _____
                                (County)   (State)

    b. ☐ The gestating intended parent became pregnant as a result of assisted reproduction and is now pregnant with a child who is expected to be born on or about _____ in _____.
                                                                (specify date) (County) (State)

4. ☐ An intended parent has been a resident (s) of New York State for a period of at least six months

        OR

    ☐ The child   ☐ was born in New York State within 90 days of the filing of this petition.
                  ☐ will be born in New York State within 90 days of the filing of this petition.

5. The intended parent(s) both consented to assisted reproduction.

6. Check applicable boxes for court to consider proof of a donor's donative intent pursuant to Section 581-202 of the Family Court Act:

    ☐ **[Known donor]** The child was conceived with a gamete or embryo from a known gamete or embryo donor(s).
        ☐ A record from the donor acknowledging the donation and confirming that the donor has no parental or proprietary interest in the gametes or embryos. Said record is signed by both the donor and the gestating intended parent and is attached hereto.
    OR
        ☐ The following constitutes evidence for the court to consider that the donor has no parental or proprietary interest in the gametes or embryos [specify evidence]: _____.

    ☐ **[Anonymous donor or where gametes or embryos have previously been released to a gamete or embryo storage facility or in the presence of a healthcare practitioner]**. The child was conceived with a gamete or embryo released to a storage facility or healthcare practitioner.
        ☐ A statement or documentation from the storage facility or healthcare practitioner that the embryo or gamete was donated anonymously or previously released to the facility or practitioner is attached hereto.
    OR
        ☐ The following constitutes evidence for the court to consider that the donor intended the donation to be anonymous or previously released the embryo or gamete to a storage facility or healthcare practitioner [specify evidence]: _____.

7. [Check applicable boxes]
    Petitioner 1a: I ☐ have ☐ have not   acknowledged parentage on the Public Health Law form.
    Petitioner 1b: I ☐ have ☐ have not   acknowledged parentage on the Public Health Law form.

    ☐ No other person has acknowledged parentage on the Public Health Law form.

8. Upon information and belief, no individual has been adjudicated as a parent of this child, either in this court, or any other court, including a Native-American court, except_____.
                                                                    (specify)

9. Upon information and belief, the subject child ☐ is ☐ is not a Native American child who may be subject to the *Indian Child Welfare Act of 1978* (25 U.S.C. §§ 1901-1963).

10.   No prior application has been made to any Court for the relief requested herein.

WHEREFORE, I am requesting that this Court issue an order/judgment/decree and declaration of parentage, an order that the embryo or gamete donor is not a legal parent and such other and further relief as may be appropriate under the circumstances.

Dated: _____   _____
                                                                  (Signature of Petitioner)

                                                                  _____
                                                                  (Print Name)

                                                                  _____
                                                                  (Signature of Petitioner)

                                                                  _____
                                                                  (Print Name)

VERIFICATION

STATE OF   )
) ss.:
COUNTY OF   )

_____, being duly sworn deposes and says that I am the petitioner above named.   I have read the foregoing petition and the same is true of my own knowledge except as the matters therein stated to be alleged upon information and belief and as to those matters, I believe them to be true.

Sworn to before me this

_____ day of _____ 20___   _____
                                                                            (Signature of Petitioner)

_____   _____
Notary Public   (Print Name)
Commission Expires:
(Affix Notary Stamp or Seal).

Signature of Attorney: _____
Print Name: _____
Firm Name: _____ Tel. No.: _____
Address of Attorney: _____
                                                                                      (e-mail address)

CPSA-3 (2/2021)   3

FORM CPSA-4 **Order of Parentage – Assisted Reproduction**

--x

In the Matter of a Parentage Proceeding Concerning

_____

A Child conceived as a result of Assisted Reproduction.

--x

ORDER OF PARENTAGE–
ASSISTED REPRODUCTION

File No. _____

Upon reading and filing the petition of _____
_____, duly verified the _____ day of _____, 20 ____, alleging that _____
_____ is/are the
intended parent(s) of [specify name of child or, if not yet born, expected name, if known, of child] _____
_____

[Applicable to a child already born]: ☐ The child, who was born on: _____
(Date of Birth)

Is: ☐ male ☐ female ☐ non-binary/other

OR

[Applicable where child has not yet been born]: ☐ The child is expected to be born on or about: _____
(specify date)

The child's conception was accomplished through assisted reproduction; and

The petitioner(s) is/are [specify]:
    ☐ child
    ☐ parent
    ☐ participant
    ☐ person with a claim to parentage
    ☐ social services official or other governmental agency
    ☐ representative authorized by law to act for an individual who would otherwise be entitled to
    maintain a proceeding but who is deceased, incapacitated or a minor
    ☐ other individual with claim to parentage [specify] _____.

And all persons named in such petition required to be cited having duly been cited to show cause why such relief should not be granted or having consented thereto; and having ☐ appeared ☐ not appeared to answer the petition [specify] _____

And the following parties [specify] _____
having ☐ contested ☐ not contested the allegations of the petition; and

The issues having duly come on to be heard before this Court,

NOW, after examination and inquiry into the facts and circumstances of the proceeding, the Court finds:

    ☐ The gestating parent became pregnant as a result of assisted reproduction.
    ☐ The residency requirement was satisfied as follows:
        ☐ An intended parent has been a resident of New York for at least six months.
        ☐ The child ☐ was ☐ will be born in New York within 90 days of filing of the petition.

    ☐ The Court received a statement from both intended parents that the non-gestating intended parent consented to assisted reproduction.

CPSA-4 (2/2021)

[Applicable to a known donor]:
☐ the Court received a record from the donor, signed by both the donor and the gestating intended parent, confirming that the donor has no parental or proprietary interest in the gametes or embryos.

OR

☐ the Court found by clear and convincing evidence that the donor has no parental or proprietary interest in the gametes or embryos.

[Applicable to an anonymous donor or where gametes or embryos have previously been released to a gamete or embryo storage facility or in the presence of a healthcare practitioner]:
☐ the Court received a statement or documentation from the storage facility or healthcare practitioner that the embryo or gamete was donated anonymously or previously released to the facility or practitioner.

OR

☐ the Court found by clear and convincing evidence that the donor intended the donation to be anonymous or previously released the embryo or gamete to a storage facility or healthcare practitioner.

[Applicable to a child already born]: ☐ IT IS, THEREFORE ORDERED, ADJUDGED and DECLARED that [name(s) of parent(s)] _____
is/are the legal parent(s) of [child's name] _____,
a child born on [date of birth] _____, and the parent(s) shall forthwith assume responsibility for the child's maintenance and support;
OR

[Applicable where child has not yet been born]: ☐ IT IS, THEREFORE ORDERED, ADJUDGED and DECLARED that upon the child's birth, [name(s) of parent(s)] _____
will be the legal parent(s) of the child who is expected to be born on or about [date] _____,
and upon the birth of such child, shall immediately assume responsibility for the child's maintenance and support and further that, within _____ days of the child's birth, the intended parent(s) shall provide to this Court notification thereof, together with such other facts as may assist in identifying the birth record of the child whose parentage is in issue in this proceeding;

AND IT IS FURTHER ORDERED and ADJUDGED that the donor, whether known or unknown, is not a parent of the child;

IT IS FURTHER ORDERED THAT:

(i) Pursuant to Judiciary Law §254, the clerk of the court shall transmit to the state commissioner of health, or for a person born in New York City, to the commissioner of health of the city of New York, on a form prescribed by the commissioner, a written notification of such entry together with such other facts as may assist in identifying the birth record of the person whose parentage was in issue and, if such person whose parentage has been determined is under eighteen years of age, the clerk shall also transmit forthwith to the registry operated by the department of social services, pursuant to Social Services Law §372-c, a notification of such determination; and

(ii) Pursuant to Public Health Law §4138 and NYC Public Health Code §207.05, upon receipt of a judgment of parentage, the local registrar where a child is born will report the parentage of the child to the appropriate department of health in conformity with this court order. If an original birth certificate has already been issued, the appropriate department of health will amend the birth certificate in an expedited manner and seal the previously issued birth certificate except that it may be rendered accessible to the child at eighteen years of age or the legal parent or parents.

CPSA-4 (2/2021)

[Check box, if applicable]: ☐ IT IS FURTHER ORDERED THAT _____

_____

Dated:

          , New York

_____
SURROGATE

FORM CPSA-5　　**Parentage Citation**

PARENTAGE CITATION

File No. _____

SURROGATE'S COURT - _____ COUNTY

CITATION

THE PEOPLE OF THE STATE OF NEW YORK

By the Grace of God Free and Independent

TO: _____
_____

A petition having been duly filed by _____ , who
resides or is found at _____ .

YOU ARE HEREBY CITED TO SHOW CAUSE before the Surrogate's Court, _____ County,
at _____ , New York, on
_____ 20 _____ at _____ o'clock in the _____ noon of that day, why the declaration
of parentage, order/judgment/decree of parentage and other and further relief requested in the petition, a copy of
which is attached, should not be made.

(State any further relief requested)
_____
_____
_____

Hon. _____

Dated, Attested and Sealed　　　　　　　　　　　　　　　　Surrogate
_____ , 20 _____

_____
Chief Clerk

_____
Attorney for Petitioner　　　　　　　　Telephone Number

_____
Address of Attorney

[NOTE: This citation is served upon you as required by law. You are not required to appear. If you fail to appear it will be
assumed you do not object to the relief requested. You have a right to have an attorney appear for you.]
CPSA-5 (2/2021)

FORM CSMD-1   Petition for Appointment/Confirmation of Standby Guardian
[SCPA 1757]

SURROGATE'S COURT OF THE STATE OF NEW YORK
COUNTY OF _____
--X
In the Matter of the Application of
_____ for
Appointment/Confirmation as Standby Guardian of

Pursuant to SCPA Article 17-A
--X

Filing Fee Paid $ _____
_____ Certs $ _____
_____ Certs $ _____
$_____ Bond, Fee $ _____
Receipt No: _____ No: _____

PETITION FOR APPOINTMENT/CONFIRMATION
OF STANDBY GUARDIAN [SCPA 1757] OF
[   ] PERSON
[   ] PROPERTY
[   ] PERSON AND PROPERTY
[   ] LIMITED GUARDIAN OF THE PROPERTY

File No. _____

TO THE SURROGATE'S COURT OF THE COUNTY OF_____

It is respectfully alleged that:

1.   The name, date of birth, permanent address and telephone number of the petitioning [   ] guardian   [   ] standby
guardian [   ] alternate standby guardian [   ] second alternate standby guardian [   ] third alternate standby
guardian(s) to the [   ] intellectually disabled [   ] developmentally disabled person (hereafter known as Respondent)
is:

Name:_____ Telephone Number; _____

Permanent Address or Corporate Office: _____
                                                                        (Street and Number)

_____
            (City, Village, Town)   (State)   (Zip Code)
        Mailing Address: _____
                                                    (If different from permanent address)
Date of Birth: _____ Interest/Relationship to Respondent: _____

2(a). The name, permanent address, date of birth and marital status of the Respondent of this proceeding is as follows:

Name: _____

Permanent Address: _____
                                                    (Street and Number)

_____
            (City, Village, Town)   (State)   (Zip Code)
        Mailing Address: _____
                                                    (If different from permanent address)
Date of Birth: _____ Marital Status: _____
[Attach certified copy of birth certificate if not already filed with the court.]

2(b). [   ] The Respondent is not admitted to a group home or facility as defined in Section 1.03 and/or Article 15 of the Mental
Hygiene Law.

        [   ] The Respondent has been admitted to a group home or facility as defined in Section 1.03 and/or Article 15 of the
Mental Hygiene Law.

Name of group home or facility: _____

Address of group home or facility: _____

Name of Director of group home or facility: _____

Address of Director of group home or facility: _____

Name of the Director of the Mental Hygiene Legal Service: _____

Address of the Director of the Mental Hygiene Legal Service: _____

CSMD-1(4/2018)   -1-

Official Forms

3. The Petitioner was appointed [   ] guardian [   ] standby guardian [   ] alternate standby guardian [   ] second alternate standby guardian [   ] third alternate standby guardian in the above-titled matter by decree on _____, _____ and letters issued appointing _____ as guardian of the above-named Respondent. Within said decree the Petitioner was appointed as [   ] standby guardian [   ] alternate standby guardian [   ] second alternate standby guardian [   ] third alternate standby guardian(s) subject to confirmation.

4. The guardian(s) is/are no longer able to act due to the following:

    [   ] death **[attach a certified copy of the death certificate(s)]**
    [   ] incapacity **[attach proof of incapacity]**
    [   ] adjudication of incompetency **[attach proof]**
    [   ] renunciation **[attach proof of renunciation]**

    [Please note: Paragraph 5 to be completed only if new or different standby guardian(s) is/are to be designated in this proceeding.]

5. The names, permanent addresses, dates of birth and relationship of the guardian(s) is/are:

    (a) Name of the Standby Guardian: _____

    Permanent Address: _____
    _____
    (Street and Number)

    _____
    (City, Village, Town)   (State)   (Zip Code)

    Date of Birth: _____ Interest/Relationship to Respondent: _____

    Education: _____ Qualifications: _____

    to be appointed Standby Guardian of the   [   ] person
                                                      [   ] property
                                                      [   ] person and property
                                                      [   ] limited guardian of the property

    (b) Name of the Alternate Standby Guardian: _____

    Permanent Address: _____
    _____
    (Street and Number)

    _____
    (City, Village, Town)   (State)   (Zip Code)

    Date of Birth: _____ Interest/Relationship to Respondent: _____

    Education: _____ Qualifications: _____

    to be appointed Alternate Standby Guardian of the   [   ] person
                                                         [   ] property
                                                         [   ] person and property
                                                         [   ] limited guardian of the property

    (c) Name of the Second Alternate Standby Guardian: _____

    Permanent Address: _____
    _____
    (Street and Number)

    _____
    (City, Village, Town)   (State)   (Zip Code)

    Date of Birth: _____ Interest/Relationship to Respondent: _____

    Education: _____ Qualifications: _____

    to be appointed Second Alternate Standby Guardian of the   [   ] person
                                                                [   ] property
                                                                [   ] person and property
                                                                [   ] limited guardian of the property

(d) Name of the Third Alternate Standby Guardian: _____

Permanent Address: _____
                                        (Street and Number)

_____
         (City, Village, Town)   (State)   (Zip Code)

Date of Birth: _____ Interest/Relationship to Respondent: _____

Education: _____ Qualifications: _____

to be appointed Third Alternate Standby Guardian of the   [   ] person
                                                           [   ] property
                                                           [   ] person and property
                                                           [   ] limited guardian of the property

[Please note: Paragraph 6 and 7 to be completed if seeking confirmation of standby guardian or alternate standby guardian.]

6.   Petitioner has assumed the duties of the standby guardian in accordance with the decree dated _____, _____
     and pursuant to the provisions of SCPA 1757 and has been so acting as such standby guardian since _____, _____
     and that one hundred eighty (180) days have not elapsed since the assumption of such duties.

7.   Petitioner is requesting confirmation as standby guardian of the Respondent's   [   ] person   [   ] property
     [   ] person and property   [   ] limited guardian of the property.

8.   Petitioner [   ] has [   ] does not have knowledge that the person nominated herein to be a guardian or any individual eighteen years of age or over who resides in the home of the proposed guardian:

     a.   Is the subject of a report filed with the Statewide Central Register of Child Abuse and Maltreatment pursuant to the rules of Child Protective Services, following an investigation which determines that some credible evidence of alleged abuse or maltreatment exists, and/or

     b.   Has been the subject of or the Respondent in a Child Protective Proceeding commenced pursuant to law, which proceeding resulted in an order finding that the child is an abused or neglected child.

               [If Petitioner has such knowledge, attach an affidavit explaining in detail.]

9.   Petitioner has completed and submitted to the court the Request For Information Guardianship Form (OCFS 3909) required to be submitted to the New York State Central Register of Child Abuse and Maltreatment.

10. **[Answer if required by court.]**
     The names and addresses of persons interested (i.e.: parents, spouse, adult children and/or adult siblings) in this proceeding upon whom service of process is required or concerning whom the court is required to have information are:

     [Set forth names, addresses and relationship to the intellectually disabled or developmentally disabled person and whether any person is under a disability along with details required by SCPA 304(3).]

     _____

     _____

     _____

11. There are no other persons than those mentioned interested in this application or proceeding.

-3-

WHEREFORE, your Petitioner(s) respectfully request(s) that: **[Check and complete all relief requested]**

(a)   Petitioner be confirmed as _____ guardian, and appropriate letters be issued
to _____, as the standby guardian of the
[   ] person
[   ] property
[   ] person and property
[   ] limited guardianship of the property
of the Respondent

(b)   Appointment of _____ as Standby Guardian of the
[   ] person
[   ] property
[   ] person and property
[   ] limited guardianship of the property
of the Respondent

(c)   Appointment of _____ as Alternate Standby Guardian of the
[   ] person
[   ] property
[   ] person and property
[   ] limited guardianship of the property
of the Respondent

(d)   Appointment of _____ as Second Alternate Standby Guardian of the
[   ] person
[   ] property
[   ] person and property
[   ] limited guardianship of the property
of the Respondent

(e)   Appointment of _____, as Third Alternate Standby Guardian of the
[   ] person
[   ] property
[   ] person and property
[   ] limited guardianship of the property
of the Respondent

be granted, or to such other person or corporation as may be entitled thereto and that process issue to all interested
persons who have not waived the issuance of same requiring them to show cause why such relief should not be
granted.

(f)   A hearing [   ] be held [   ] not be held.

(g)   The appearance of the Respondent [   ] be required [   ] not be required at any hearings directed by the Court.

(h)   The guardian of the person be authorized and empowered to make all decisions with respect to the medical and dental
needs of the Respondent and to render consent to any medical procedures which are necessary to the health and
welfare of the Respondent unless the court directs otherwise. A health care decision may include a decision to withhold
or withdraw life-sustaining treatment as defined in subdivision (j) of 81.03 of the Mental Hygiene Law.

(I)   The guardian of the property be directed to continue to collect and receive all moneys and other property of the
Respondent jointly with a clerk of the Surrogate's Court, or depository subject to the provisions of SCPA 1708, and shall
deposit same in the name of the guardian, subject to order of the court with either:

**[Designate a sufficient number of banks/depositories, located in this county, so that the deposit does not
exceed the maximum amount insured by the federal deposit insurance corporation or the national credit union
share insurance fund ($250,000.00).]**

1. _____
    Name of Bank/Depository   Branch Address

2. _____
    Name of Bank/Depository   Branch Address

(j)   The bond of the guardian be dispensed with.

(k)   Additional relief requested _____

_____

Dated: _____

1. _____   2. _____
         (Signature of Petitioner)   (Name of Corporate Petitioner)

_____   _____
         (Print Name)   (Signature of Officer)

                                                     _____
                                                              (Print Name and Title of Officer)

STATE OF NEW YORK   )
COUNTY OF _____) ss.:

_____, being duly sworn deposes and says that I am the
Petitioner(s) above named. I/we have read the foregoing petition and the same is true of my own knowledge except as to
matters therein stated to be alleged upon information and belief and as to those matters I/we believe them to be true.

_____   _____
         (Signature of Petitioner)   (Name of Corporate Petitioner)

_____   _____
         (Print Name)   (Signature of Officer)

                                                     _____
                                                              (Print Name and Title of Officer)

Sworn to before me this

_____ day of _____, _____

_____
Notary Public
Commission Expires:
(Affix Notary Stamp or Seal)

Signature of Attorney: _____

Print Name: _____

Firm Name: _____   Telephone Number: _____

Address of Attorney: _____

COMBINED OATH & DESIGNATION
[For use when Petitioner is an individual]

STATE OF NEW YORK   )
COUNTY OF _____) ss.:

_____ being duly sworn, deposes and says:

1.   OATH OF GUARDIAN: I am over eighteen (18) years of age, that I will well, faithfully and honestly discharge the duties of such guardian: That I am acquainted with the estate of said (intellectually disabled) (developmentally disabled) person and that I am not ineligible to receive letters.

2.   DESIGNATION OF CLERK FOR SERVICE OF PROCESS: I hereby designate the Clerk of the Surrogate's Court of _____ County, and his/her successor in office, as a person on whom service of any process issuing from such Surrogate's Court may be made in like manner and with like effect as if it were served personally upon me, whenever I cannot be found within the State of New York after due diligence used.

My permanent address is: _____
                (Street Address)   (City, Town, Village)   (State)   (Zip Code)

_____
(Signature of Proposed Guardian)

_____
(Print Name)

On _____, _____ , before me personally came

_____
to me known to be the person(s) described in and who executed the foregoing instrument. Such person(s) duly swore to such instrument before me and duly acknowledged that he/she/they executed the same.

_____
Notary Public
Commission Expires:
(Affix Notary Stamp or Seal)

COMBINED CORPORATE CONSENT & DESIGNATION
[For use when a Petitioner to be appointed is a corporation]

STATE OF NEW YORK   )
COUNTY OF _____) ss.:

I, the undersigned, a _____ of
(Title)

_____
(Name of Corporation)
a corporation duly qualified to act in a fiduciary capacity without further security, being duly sworn, say:

1.   VERIFICATION: I have read the foregoing petition subscribed by me and know the contents thereof, and the same is true of my own knowledge, except as to the matters therein stated to be alleged upon information and belief, and as to those matters I believe it to be true.

2.   CONSENT: I consent to accept the appointment as | | Standby Guardian [   ] Alternate Standby Guardian [   ] Second Alternate Standby Guardian of the   [   ] person [   ] property [   ] person and property | | limited guardianship of the property of the Respondent described in the foregoing petition and consent to act as such fiduciary.

3.   DESIGNATION OF CLERK FOR SERVICE OF PROCESS: I hereby designate the Clerk of the Surrogate's Court of _____ County, and his/her successor in office, as a person on whom service of any process issuing from such Surrogate's Court may be made in like manner and with like effect as if it were served personally upon me, whenever I cannot be found within the state of New York after due diligence used.

_____
(Proposed Corporate Guardian)

_____
(Signature of Officer)

_____
(Print Name and Title of Officer)

On_____ , _____ , before me personally came _____ , to me known, who duly swore to the foregoing instrument and which did say that he/she resides at _____ _____ and that he/she is a _____ of _____ the corporation described in and which executed such instrument, and that he/she signed his/her name thereto by order of the Board of Directors of the corporation.

_____
Notary Public
Commission Expires:
(Affix Notary Stamp or Seal)

Official Forms

FORM CSMD-2   **Waiver of Process Renunciation and Consent to Appointment of a Standby Guardian [SCPA 1757]**

SURROGATE'S COURT OF THE STATE OF NEW YORK
COUNTY OF _____
--X
In the Matter of the Application of
_____ for
Appointment/Confirmation as Standby Guardian of

                                      WAIVER OF PROCESS
                                      RENUNCIATION AND CONSENT TO
                                      APPOINTMENT OF A STANDBY GUARDIAN

Pursuant to SCPA Article 17-A   File No. _____
--X

The undersigned _____, whose permanent address is

_____
          (Street and Number)   **(City, Village, Town)**

_____
              (State)   **(Zip Code)**

and who is a competent person over the age of eighteen (18) years and whose interest in the above-named proceeding is as follows:

[Check appropriate interest.]

      [   ] Parent of the above-named [   ] intellectually disabled   [   ] developmentally disabled person.

      [   ] Spouse of the above-named [   ] intellectually disabled   [   ] developmentally disabled person.

      [   ] An adult child of the above-named [   ] intellectually disabled   [   ] developmentally disabled person.

      [   ] An adult brother/sister of the above-named [   ] intellectually disabled   [   ] developmentally disabled person.

      Other **[Specify]** _____

hereby personally appears in this proceeding and

1. renounces my right to act as a guardian under decree dated _____, and

2. waives the issuance and service of process in this matter, and

3. consents that _____ be appointed the _____
Guardian of the

     [   ] person
     [   ] property
     [   ] person and property
     [   ] limited guardianship of the property

and that _____ be appointed the Alternate Standby
Guardian of the

     [   ] person
     [   ] property
     [   ] person and property
     [   ] limited guardianship of the property

CSMD-2 (4/2018)   -1-

and that _____ be appointed the Second Alternate
Standby Guardian of the

      [ ] person
      [ ] property
      [ ] person and property
      [ ] limited guardianship of the property

and that _____ be appointed the Third Alternate Standby
Guardian of the

      [ ] person
      [ ] property
      [ ] person and property
      [ ] limited guardianship of the property

and that such letters may be granted to said person(s) or to any other person(s) entitled thereto without notice to the
undersigned.

_____
(Signature)

Date: _____

_____
(Print Name)

STATE OF _____)
) ss:
COUNTY OF_____)

    On _____, _____, before me personally came
_____ to
me known to be the person described in and who executed the foregoing instrument. Such person duly swore to such
instrument before me and duly acknowledged that he/she executed the same.

_____
Notary Public
Commission Expires:
(Affix Notary Stamp or Seal)

FORM CSMD-3   Notice of Petition [SCPA § 1753(2)]

SURROGATE'S COURT OF THE STATE OF NEW YORK
COUNTY OF _____
--X
In the Matter of the Application of
_____ for
Appointment/Confirmation as Standby Guardian of   **NOTICE OF PETITION**
                                                                   SCPA §1753 (2)

                                                         File No. _____

Pursuant to SCPA Article 17-A
--X

Notice is hereby given that:

1. On the _____ day of _____, 20_____, _____,
                                                    (Name of Petitioner)
whose address is _____,

filed a petition with the Surrogate's Court, County of _____. Letters of guardianship will issue on or after
_____, _____, for the appointment/confirmation of

[   ] _____, _____ guardian
                        (Name)

[   ] _____, alternate standby guardian
                        (Name)

[   ] _____, second alternate standby guardian
                        (Name)

[   ] _____, third alternate standby guardian
                        (Name)

of the   [   ] person
                [   ] property
                [   ] person and property
                [   ] limited guardianship of the property.

2. The name and post office address of each person entitled to notice of the petition who has not been served or has not appeared, or waived service of process, with a statement with regard to such person's relationship, if any, to the intellectually disabled or developmentally disabled person, is as follows:

NAME	MAILING ADDRESS	RELATIONSHIP

(USE ADDITIONAL SHEETS IF NECESSARY)

Date: _____, _____

Attorney for Petitioner(s) _____ Telephone Number: _____

Address of Attorney: _____

CSMD-3 (4/2018)   -1-

AFFIDAVIT OF MAILING NOTICE OF PETITION

STATE OF NEW YORK   )
COUNTY OF   ) ss.:

_____, residing at _____
being duly sworn, deposes and says that he/she is over the age of 18 years, that on the _____ day of
_____, _____, he/she mailed, by certified mail, a copy of the foregoing Notice of Petition contained
in a securely closed, postpaid wrapper directed to each of the persons named in said notice at the places set opposite their
respective names.

_____
(Signature)

Sworn to before me this

_____
(Print Name)

_____ day of_____, _____

_____
Notary Public
Commission Expires:
(Affix Notary Stamp or Seal)

Attorney for Petitioner(s): _____ Telephone Number: _____

Address of Attorney: _____

-2-

FORM CSMD-4 **17-A Guardianship Citation [SCPA 1757]**

File No. _____

SURROGATE'S COURT- COUNTY

17-A GUARDIANSHIP CITATION [SCPA 1757]

THE PEOPLE OF THE STATE OF NEW YORK

By the Grace of God Free and Independent

TO:

A petition having been filed by _____, who is/are
domiciled at _____

YOU ARE HEREBY CITED TO SHOW CAUSE before the Surrogate's Court, _____ County,
at _____, New York , on _____, _____, at
_____ o'clock in the _____ noon of that day, why letters of _____ guardianship of the

[ ] person
[ ] property
[ ] person and property
[ ] limited guardianship of the property
of _____ should not be granted to _____ ;

why the appointment of _____ as Alternate Standby Guardian of the
[ ] person
[ ] property
[ ] person and property
[ ] limited guardianship of the property
of _____ should not be granted;

why the appointment of _____ as Second Alternate Standby Guardian of the
[ ] person
[ ] property
[ ] person and property
[ ] limited guardianship of the property
of _____ should not be granted;

why the appointment of _____ as Third Alternate Standby Guardian of the
[ ] person
[ ] property
[ ] person and property
[ ] limited guardianship of the property
of _____ should not be granted;

and why a hearing [ ] should be held   [ ] should not be held;
and why the appearance of Respondent [ ] should be [ ] should not be required at the hearing;
and why the guardian of the person should not be authorized and empowered to make all decisions with respect to the medical
and dental needs of the Respondent and to render consent to any medical procedures which are necessary to the health and
welfare of the Respondent, unless the court directs otherwise. A health care decision may include a decision to withhold or
withdraw life-sustaining treatment as defined in subdivision (j) of 81.03 of the Mental Hygiene Law.
[State further relief requested]

Dated, Attested and Sealed,

_____, _____, HON.
(Seal) Surrogate

_____
, Chief Clerk
Attorney for Petitioner(s): _____ Telephone Number: _____
Address of Attorney: _____
[Note: This citation is served upon you as required by law. You are not required to appear. However, if you fail to appear it will be assumed by
the court that you do not object to the relief requested. You have a right to have an attorney appear for you.]
CSMD-4 (4/2018)

FORM CSMD-5   **Affidavit of Proposed Guardian [SCPA 1757]**

SURROGATE'S COURT OF THE STATE OF NEW YORK
COUNTY OF _____
--X

In the Matter of the Application of

_____ for

Appointment/Confirmation as Standby Guardian of

AFFIDAVIT OF PROPOSED
GUARDIAN OF THE
| | PERSON
| | PROPERTY
| | PERSON AND PROPERTY
| | LIMITED GUARDIAN OF THE PROPERTY

Pursuant to SCPA Article 17-A

--X   File No. _____

STATE OF NEW YORK   )
COUNTY OF   ) ss.:

To the Surrogate's Court, County of _____

The undersigned _____, being duly sworn, deposes and says:

1.   I am a competent person over the age of eighteen (18) years, and I submit this affidavit in support of my petition to
      be confirmed in my appointment as guardian of _____ a
      [⸜] intellectually disabled   (Name)
      [   ] developmentally disabled person
      (hereafter known as Respondent).

2.   I have known the Respondent since _____ by reason of the
following: **[State relationship if any.]**

_____

_____

_____

_____

3.   I reside at_____, and the
other resident members of the household are: **[Include all persons residing there and their dates of birth.]**

_____   _____

_____   _____

_____   _____

4.   My educational background is as follows:

_____

5.   Not including minor traffic offenses and adjudications as a youthful offender or juvenile delinquent,

      (a) I have never been convicted of an offense against the law, except _____

_____

_____(b) I have never forfeited bail or other collateral, except_____

_____

Official Forms

(c) I do not have any criminal charges pending against me, except _____

_____

6. I have no physical or mental impairment, or medical condition, which would interfere with my ability to perform the duties of guardian of the Respondent, except

_____

_____

7. I am not addicted to narcotics or to alcohol.

8. I am willing and able to undertake and perform the duties and responsibilities of guardian of the Respondent until the court determines otherwise.

9. I believe that my appointment as guardian would be in the best interests of the Respondent for the following reasons:

_____

_____

_____

_____

_____
(Signature of Proposed Guardian)

_____
(Print Name)

Sworn to before me this

_____ day of _____, _____

_____
Notary Public
Commission Expires:
(Affix Notary Stamp or Seal)

-2-

FORM CSMD-6   **Consent, Oath and Designation [SCPA 1757]**[1]

SURROGATE'S COURT OF THE STATE OF NEW YORK
COUNTY OF _____
---X
In the Matter of the Application of

_____ for   **CONSENT, OATH AND**
Appointment/Confirmation as Standby Guardian of   **DESIGNATION**

Pursuant to SCPA Article 17-A   File No. _____
---X
STATE OF NEW YORK   )
COUNTY OF _____) ss.:

_____, being duly sworn, deposes and says: I am an adult competent person and I do hereby consent to the relief requested in the petition and my appointment as [   ] standby guardian [   ] alternate standby guardian [   ] second alternate standby guardian [   ] third alternate standby guardian
of the [   ] person
       [   ] property
       [   ] person and property
       [   ] limited guardianship of the property

of the above-named Respondent and I waive the issuance and service of process upon me herein. I will make an application for confirmation in accordance with SCPA §1757 and will be subject to a formal hearing if the Respondent is eighteen years of age or over. I agree that upon the death, incapacity, renunciation or adjudication of incompetency of the last guardian who has been designated to serve prior to me, I will immediately assume the duties of guardian
of the [   ] person
       [   ] property
       [   ] person and property
       [   ] limited guardianship of the property

and will seek to have this Court confirm my appointment within (180) days of my assumption of duties.

    1. OATH OF   [   ] STANDBY GUARDIAN [   ] ALTERNATE STANDBY GUARDIAN   [   ] SECOND ALTERNATE STANDBY GUARDIAN [   ] THIRD ALTERNATE STANDBY GUARDIAN: I am over eighteen (18) years of age and that I will well, faithfully and honestly discharge the duties of [   ] standby guardian [   ] alternate standby guardian [   ] second alternate standby guardian [   ] third alternate standby guardian
of the [   ] person
       [   ] property
       [   ] person and property
       [   ] limited guardianship of the property

of the above named Respondent, that I am acquainted with the estate of the Respondent; and that I am not ineligible to receive letters.

    2. DESIGNATION OF CLERK FOR SERVICE OF PROCESS: I do hereby designate the Clerk of the Surrogate's Court of _____ County, and his/her successor in office, as a person on whom service of any process issuing from such Surrogate's Court may be made, in like manner and with like effect as if it were served personally upon me whenever I cannot be found and served within the State of New York after due diligence used.

---

[1] In the opening paragraph, the phrase "and will seek to have this Court confirm my appointment within (60) days of my assumption of duties" should read "and will seek to have this Court confirm my appointment within (180) days of my assumption of duties", pursuant to 2009 N.Y. Laws 260, effective July 29, 2009, which amended SCPA 1757(2).

My permanent address is : _____
    (Street Address)   (City/Town/Village)   (State)   (Zip)

                        _____
                             (Signature of Proposed Guardian)

                        _____
                                      (Print Name)

    On _____, _____, before me personally came

to me known to be the person described in and who executed the foregoing instrument. Such person duly swore to such
instrument before me and duly acknowledged that he/she executed the same.

_____
Notary Public
Commission Expires:
(Affix Notary Stamp or Seal)

FORM CTA-1   Petition for Letters of Administration c.t.a. After Probate (SCPA 1418 and 1419)

<table>
<tr><td colspan="2">For Office Use Only</td></tr>
<tr><td colspan="2">Filing Fee Paid $_____</td></tr>
<tr><td>_____</td><td>Certs: _____</td></tr>
<tr><td>$_____</td><td>Bond, Fee: _____</td></tr>
<tr><td>Receipt No:_____</td><td>No:_____</td></tr>
</table>

DO NOT LEAVE ANY ITEMS BLANK

SURROGATE'S COURT OF THE STATE OF NEW YORK
COUNTY OF _____

_____X

LETTERS OF ADMINISTRATION c.t.a.,
WILL OF _____

a/k/a _____

_____ Deceased.

_____X

PETITION FOR
LETTERS OF ADMINISTRATION c.t.a
AFTER PROBATE
SCPA 1418 AND 1419

File No. _____

TO THE SURROGATE'S COURT, COUNTY OF _____ :
   It is respectfully alleged:

   1. (a)   The name, citizenship, domicile (or, in the case of a bank or trust company, its principal office) and interest in this proceeding of the petitioner(s) is/are as follows:_____

Name: _____

Domicile or Principal Office:_____
                        (Street and Number)   (City, Village or Town)

(County)   (State)   (Zip)   (Telephone Number)

Mailing Address: _____
                        (If different from domicile)

Citizenship (check one):   USA   Other (specify) _____

Name:_____

Domicile or Principal Office: _____
                        (Street and Number)   (City, Village or Town)

(County)   (State)   (Zip)   (Telephone Number)

Mailing Address: _____
                        (If different from domicile)

Citizenship (check one):   U.S.A.   Other (specify) _____

Interest (s) of Petitioner (s):   [Check one]

          Sole Beneficiary   Residuary Beneficiary
          Other [Specify] _____

   1.(b)   The proposed Administrator c.t.a.   is   is not an attorney.
             [NOTE: An Administrator c.t.a. - Attorney must comply with Uniform Court Rule 207.16 (e). (See also 207.52)]
   2.   The will of the above-named decedent was admitted to probate by the Surrogate's Court
of _____County on _____ and Letters Testamentary were issued to
_____ , who on_____,
   died   resigned   was removed.

CTA-1

-1-

Official Forms

3.   The names and addresses of all persons and parties interested in this proceeding having a right to letters of administration c.t.a. (with the will annexed) prior or equal to the petitioner under the provisions of SCPA §1418 and 1419, are as follows: [Furnish all information specified in **NOTE** below, if required]

Name_____ Domicile Address and_____Description of Legacy, Devisee
Relationship_____Mailing Address_____ or Other Interest, or Nature
of Fiduciary Status: _____
_____
_____

4.   The names and addresses of all persons and parties who are beneficiaries named in the will other than those named in paragraph 3 above are as follows: [Furnish all information specified in **NOTE** below, if required]

Name_____ Domicile Address and_____Description of Legacy, Devisee
Relationship_____Mailing Address_____ or Other Interest, or Nature
of Fiduciary Status:_____
_____
_____

5.   There are no persons other than those hereinbefore mentioned interested in this proceeding.

6.   There are no outstanding debts or funeral expenses, except: [If "**NONE**" so state] _____

7.   (a) To the best of the knowledge of the undersigned, property of the estate remains **unadministered** as follows:

Personal Property $ _____   Improved real property in New York State $ _____

Unimproved real property in New York State $ _____

Estimated gross rents for a period of 18 months $ _____

(b) No other testamentary assets exist in New York State, nor does any cause of action exist on behalf of the estate as follows: **[Enter "NONE" or specify]** _____

[NOTE: In the case of each infant, state (a) name, birth date, relationship to decedent, domicile and residence address, and the person with whom he/she resides, (b) whether or not he/she has a court-appointed guardian (if not, so state), and whether or not his/her father and/or mother is living, and (c) the name and residence address of any court-appointed guardian and the information regarding such appointment. In the case of each other person under a disability, state (a) name, relationship to decedent, and residence address, (b) facts regarding this disability including whether or not a committee, conservator, guardian, or any other fiduciary has been appointed and whether or not he/she has been committed to any institution, and (c) the names and addresses of any committee, person or institution having care and custody of him/her; conservator; guardian; and any relative or friend having an interest in his/her welfare. In the case of a person confined as a prisoner, state place of incarceration and list any person having an interest in his/her welfare.

Wherefore, petitioner (s) pray (s)   (a) that process issue to all necessary parties and
(b) that letters issue as follows:
    Letters of Administration c.t.a. to: _____
(c)   [State any other relief requested] _____
Dated: _____

1. _____   2._____
(Signature of Petitioner)   (Signature of Petitioner)

_____   _____
(Print Name)   (Print Name)
3._____
(Name of Corporate Petitioner)

_____
(Signature of Officer)

_____
(Print Name and Title of Officer)

COMBINED VERIFICATION, OATH & DESIGNATION

[For use when petitioner is to be appointed administrator c.t.a.]

STATE OF _____)

COUNTY OF _____) SS.:

The undersigned, the petitioner named in the foregoing petition, being duly sworn says:

1. VERIFICATION: I have read the foregoing petition subscribed by me and know the contents thereof, and the same is true of my own knowledge, except as to the matters therein stated to be alleged upon information and belief, and as to those matters I believe it to be true.

2. OATH OF ADMINISTRATOR c.t.a.: I am over eighteen (18) years of age and a citizen of the United States; I will well, faithfully and honestly discharge the duties of the administrator c.t.a.. I am not ineligible to receive letters.

3. DESIGNATION OF CLERK FOR SERVICE OF PROCESS: I do hereby designate the Clerk of the Surrogate's Court of _____County, and his or her successor in office, as a person on whom service of any process issuing from such Surrogate's Court may be made, in like manner and with like effect as if it were served personally upon me, whenever I cannot be found within the State of New York after due diligence used.

My domicile is _____
　　　　　　(Street Address)　　　(City/Town/Village)　　　　　　　　　　(State)

_____
(Signature of Petitioner)

_____
(Print Name)

On _____ , _____ , before me personally
　　came _____
to me known to be the person described in and who executed the foregoing instrument. Such person duly sworn to such instrument before me and duly acknowledge that he/she executed the same.

_____
Notary Public
Commission Expires:
(Affix Notary Stamp or Seal)

Signature of Attorney: _____

Print Name: _____

Firm Name: _____ Tel. No.: _____

Address of Attorney: _____

Official Forms

FORM CTA-1   SURROGATE'S COURT   **SF-88**

COMBINED CORPORATE VERIFICATION, CONSENT AND DESIGNATION

[For use when a petitioner to be appointed is a bank or trust company]

STATE OF _____)

COUNTY OF _____) ss:

The undersigned, a _____ of

_____ (Title)_____

_____

(Name of Bank or Trust Company)

a corporation duly qualified to act in a fiduciary capacity without further security, being duly sworn, say:

    1. VERIFICATION: I have read the foregoing petition subscribed by me and know the contents thereof, and the same is true of my own knowledge, except as to the matters therein stated to be alleged upon information and belief, and as to those matters I believe it to be true.

    2. CONSENT: I consent to accept the appointment as Administrator c.t.a. of the decedent described in the foregoing petition and consent to act as such fiduciary.

    3. DESIGNATION OF CLERK FOR SERVICE OF PROCESS: I do hereby designate the Clerk of the Surrogate's Court of _____ County, and his or her successor in office, as a person on whom service of any process issuing from such Surrogate's Court may be made, in like manner and with like effect as if it were served personally upon me, whenever I cannot be found within the State of New York after due diligence used.

_____

    (Name of Corporate Petitioner)

_____

    (Signature of Officer)

_____

    (Print Name and Title of Officer)

    On the _____ , _____ , before me personally came to me known, who duly swore to the foregoing instrument and who did say that he/she resides at _____

_____ and that he/she is a _____

of_____the corporation/national banking association described in and which executed such instrument, and the he/she signed his/her name thereto by order of the Board of Directors of the corporation.

Notary Public _____
Commission Expires:
(Affix Notary Stamp or Seal)

Signature of Attorney: _____

Print Name: _____

Firm Name: _____   Tel. No.: _____

Address of Attorney: _____

-4-

FORM CTA-2   **Citation**

LETTERS OF ADMINISTRATION c.t.a. CITATION   File No._____
                    SURROGATE'S COURT- _____COUNTY

CITATION
THE PEOPLE OF THE STATE OF NEW YORK,
By the Grace of God Free and Independent

TO _____

_____

_____

_____

A petition having been duly filed by_____, who is domiciled at_____
_____YOU ARE HEREBY CITED TO SHOW
CAUSE before the Surrogate's Court,_____ County, at _____, New
York, on _____at _____ o'clock in the
_____noon of that day, why a decree should not be -made in the estate of _____
lately domiciled at _____
granting administration c.t.a. and directing that Letters of Administration c.t.a. issue to _____
_____(State any
further relief requested)_____

_____

_____

_____

HON._____

Dated, Attested and Sealed,   Surrogate

_____ ,   Chief Clerk _____
(Seal)

Attorney for Petitioner   Telephone Number

Address of Attorney

[Note: This citation is served upon you as required by law. You are not required to appear. If you fail to appear
it will be assumed you do not object to the relief requested. You have a right to have an attorney appear for you.]

-5-

FORM CTA-3   **Renunciation of Letters of Administration c.t.a., Waiver of Process and Consent to Dispense with Bond**

SURROGATE'S COURT OF THE STATE OF NEW YORK
COUNTY OF _____ X

LETTERS OF ADMINISTRATION c.t.a.
WILL OF_____

a/k/a_____

_____ Deceased.
_____ X

RENUNCIATION OF LETTERS OF
ADMINISTRATION c.t.a.
WAIVER OF PROCESS AND
CONSENT TO DISPENSE WITH BOND

File No. _____

The undersigned, _____ , a person interested in this estate as

☐   a beneficiary with equal or prior right to receive letters

☐   a beneficiary of the estate

☐   a creditor

☐   other (specify) _____

hereby personally appears in this proceeding in the Surrogate's Court of _____
County and

1.   Renounces all rights to Letters of Administration c.t.a.

2.   Waives the issuance and service of citation in the above entitled proceeding.

3.   Consents that Letters of Administration c.t.a. be granted by the Court
to_____ or any other person or persons entitled there to without any notice
whatsoever to the undersigned.

4.   Consents to dispense with bond of the Administrator c.t.a. and if such consent be filed by some
but not all of the persons interested in the estate, specifically releases any claim under any bond that may be
required of such Administrator c.t.a.

Date	Signature	Street Address	Relationship

Print Name

Town/State/Zip

STATE OF NEW YORK
COUNTY OF _____   ss.: _____

On   _____ , _____ before me personally came to me
known to be the person described in and who executed the foregoing instrument. Such person duly swore to such
instrument before me and duly acknowledged that he/she executed the same.

Notary Public_____
Commission Expires:_____
(Affix Notary Stamp or Seal)

Name of Attorney _____   Tel. No.:_____

Address of Attorney: _____

CTA-3 (7/98)

-6-

FORM FT-1   **Family Tree**

<u>FAMILY TREE</u>

Cross Out Class That is Not Applicable	Children or Brothers/Sisters	Grandchildren or Nieces/Nephews	Great Grandchildren or Grandnieces/Grandnephews

_____

_____ Decedent

_____

_____ Name of Spouse

_____ Deceased_____
                  Date

_____ Divorced_____
                  Date

_____ Never Married

STATE OF NEW YORK
COUNTY OF
_____ being duly sworn, states that the charts contained on this paper are correct.

Sworn to me on _____

_____
NOTARY PUBLIC   NOTE: Complete reverse side of family tree form also

Official Forms

FORM FT-1   SURROGATE'S COURT   SF-92

Form FT-1

Grandparents	Aunts and Uncles	First Cousins #	**First Cousins Once Removed #

Grandparents   Aunts and Uncles   First Cousins #   **First Cousins Once Removed #

(___)_____   (___)_____
(___)_____   (___)_____
(___)_____   (___)_____

_____

(___)_____   (___)_____
(___)_____   (___)_____
(___)_____   (___)_____

_____

(___)_____

_____

(___)_____   (___)_____
Paternal Grandfather   (___)_____   (___)_____
(___)_____   (___)_____

_____

Paternal Grandmother   Father of Decedent

(___)_____   (___)_____
(___)_____   (___)_____
_____   (___)_____   (___)_____
(___)_____

(___)_____   (___)_____
_____   (___)_____   (___)_____
(___)_____   (___)_____
(___)_____

(___)_____   (___)_____
_____   (___)_____   (___)_____
Maternal Grandfather   (___)_____   (___)_____
(___)_____

_____

Maternal Grandmother   Mother of Decedent

STATE OF NEW YORK
COUNTY OF
_____ being duly sworn, states that the charts contained on this paper are correct.

Sworn to before me on _____

_____
NOTARY PUBLIC

**List First Cousins Once Removed by # that corresponds
with deceased first cousin.

FORM G-1   Guardianship Citation

GUARDIANSHIP CITATION   File No._____

SURROGATE'S COURT - _____ COUNTY

CITATION

THE PEOPLE OF THE STATE OF NEW YORK
By the Grace of God Free and Independent,

TO: _____
_____
_____

A petition having been filed by _____ who

permanently resides at _____

YOU ARE HEREBY CITED TO SHOW CAUSE before the Surrogate's Court, _____ County

at _____, New York, on _____, _____

at _____ ☐ a.m. ☐ p.m. , why a decree should not be made appointing _____

_____ as

☐   Guardian of the Person

☐   Guardian of the Property

☐   Guardian of the Person and Property

of _____, an infant.
(State any further relief requested)

_____

HON. _____
Surrogate

Dated, Attested and Sealed,

_____,   _____, Chief Clerk

(Seal)

Name of
Attorney or Petitioner _____ Tel. No. _____

Address of Attorney _____

Note: This citation is served upon you as required by law. You are not required to appear. If you fail to appear it will be assumed that you do not object to the relief requested. You have the right to have an attorney-at-law appear for you.

G-1 (9/00)

FORM G-2A   Petition for Appointment of Guardian of Person Only

SURROGATE'S COURT OF THE STATE OF NEW YORK
COUNTY OF _____
---X
Proceeding for the Appointment of a
Guardian for

_____

_____ an Infant.
---X

Filing Fee Paid $ _____
                    Certs $ _____
                    Certs $ _____
$ _____ Bond, $ _____
Receipt No: _____ No: _____

PETITION FOR APPOINTMENT OF
GUARDIAN OF PERSON ONLY

File No. _____

TO THE SURROGATE'S COURT, COUNTY OF _____

It is respectfully alleged:

1.   The name, permanent address, date of birth and telephone number of the petitioner, and the petitioner's relationship to the infant are as follows:
Name: _____ Telephone Number: _____

Permanent Address: _____
                                        (Street and Number)

_____   _____   _____
(City, Village, Town)   (State)   (Zip Code)

Mailing address: _____
                                        (if different from Permanent address)
Date of Birth: _____ Relationship to Infant: _____

Name: _____ Telephone Number: _____

Permanent Address: _____
                                        (Street and Number)

_____   _____   _____
(City, Village, Town)   (State)   (Zip Code)

Mailing address: _____
                                        (if different from permanent address)
Date of Birth: _____ Relationship to Infant: _____

2.   The name, permanent address, date of birth and marital status of the infant of this proceeding is as follows:

Name: _____

Permanent Address: _____
                                        (Street and Number)

_____   _____   _____
(City, Village, Town)   (State)   (Zip Code)
Mailing address: _____
                          (If different from permanent address)
Date of Birth: _____ Marital Status: _____
(Attach certified copy of birth certificate]

3.   The names and permanent addresses of the parents of the infant and, if the infant is married, the infant's spouse are:
[If both parents of the infant are deceased, give date of death and complete Number 5 and Number 6]

Name of Father: _____ Date of Birth: _____ Date of Death: _____

Permanent Address: _____.
                                        (Street and Number)

_____   _____   _____
(City, Village, Town)   (State)   (Zip Code)

Mailing Address: _____
G-2A (9/00)   (If different from permanent address)

-1-

Name of Mother:_____ Date of Birth:_____ Date of Death:_____

Permanent Address:_____
                                    (Street and Number)

_____
      (City, Village, Town)   (State)   (Zip Code)

      Mailing Address:_____
                                  (If different from permanent address)

Name of Spouse:_____ Date of Birth:_____ Date of Death:_____

Permanent Address:_____
                                    (Street and Number)

_____
      (City, Village, Town)   (State)   (Zip Code)

      Mailing Address:_____
                                  (If different from permanent address)

4.   The names and addresses if the adult persons with whom the infant resides if other than parents are:

Name:_____

Permanent Address:_____
                                    (Street and Number)

_____
      (City, Village, Town)   (State)   (Zip Code)

      Mailing Address:_____
                                  (if different from permanent address)
Relationship to infant:_____

5.   If father and mother are deceased, list the names and addresses of and addresses of the nearest distributees of full age who live within the state. **[If not applicable, so state]**

      Name   Permanent Address   Relationship

_____

_____

_____

6.   The names and permanent addresses of the infant's grandparents: **[If not applicable, so state and If deceased, add date of death].**

      Name   Permanent Address

_____ Maternal Grandmother

_____ Maternal Grandfather

_____ Paternal Grandmother

_____ Paternal Grandfather

7.   Petitioner is requesting appointment as guardian of the Infant's person only and alleges that the petitioner is capable of providing care, custody and control of the infant during minority and is motivated solely by the best interests of the child in requesting this appointment.

Official Forms

8. (a) The infant has never had, at any time, a guardian appointed for him/her, and,

   (b) Custody of the infant has never been surrendered by any person lawfully charged therewith nor has custody been the subject of any court order, except as hereinafter listed: [Attach copies of all surrenders, court orders, or divorce decrees].

   _____

   _____

9.   Petitioner ☐ has ☐ does not have knowledge that a person nominated to be a guardian, or any individual eighteen years of age or over who resides in the home of the proposed guardian:

   a.   Is the subject of a reported filed with the Statewide Central Register of Child Abuse and Maltreatment pursuant to the rules of Child Protective Services, following an investigation which determines that some credible evidence of alleged abuse or maltreatment exists, and/or

   b.   Has been the subject of, or the respondent in a Child Protective Proceeding commenced pursuant to law, which proceeding resulted in an order finding that the child is an abused or neglected child.

   [If Petitioner has such knowledge, attach an affidavit explaining in detail].

10.   Petitioner has completed and annexed the Request For Information Guardianship Form (OCFS 3909) required to be submitted to the New York State Central Register of Child Abuse and Maltreatment.

11.   The infant ☐ is ☐ is not a Native American child under the Indian Child Welfare Act of 1978 1901-1963).

12.   There are no other persons interested in this proceeding upon whom process is required to be served other than those listed above.

13.   No prior application has been made to any Court for the relief requested herein.

WHEREFORE, your petitioner respectfully prays that:

   Letters of Guardianship of the Person

   be granted to _____

   _____

   or such other person or corporation as may be entitled thereto and that process issue to all interested persons who have not waived issuance of same requiring them to show cause why such relief should not be granted.

Dated: _____

_____   _____
      (Signature of Petitioner)   (Signature of Petitioner)

_____   _____
         (Print Name)   (Print Name)

STATE OF _____)
COUNTY OF _____) ss.:

_____ , being duly sworn deposes and says that I am the petitioner above named. I have read the foregoing petition and the same is true of my own knowledge except as to matters therein stated to be alleged upon information and belief and as to those matters I believe them to be true.

Sworn to before me this
_____ day of _____ _____

_____   _____
                                                   (Signature of Petitioner)

_____   _____
Notary Public   (Print Name)
Commission Expires:
(Affix Notary Stamp or Seal)   _____
                                                   (Signature of Petitioner)

                                           _____
                                                   (Print Name)

COMBINED OATH & DESIGNATION

STATE OF _____)
COUNTY OF _____) ss.:

_____ being duly sworn, deposes and says:

1.   OATH OF GUARDIAN: I am over eighteen (18) years of age and a citizen of the United States; that I will well, faithfully and honestly discharge the duties of such guardian: That I am acquainted with estate of said infant and have read the statement contained in the foregoing petition as to the estimated value of same, and believe same to be correct, and that I am not ineligible to receive letters.

2.   DESIGNATION OF CLERK FOR SERVICE OF PROCESS: I hereby designate the Clerk of the Surrogate's Court of _____ County, and his/her successor in office, as a person on whom service of any process issuing from such Surrogate's Court may be made in like manner and with like effect as if it were served personally upon me, whenever I cannot be found within the state of New York after due diligence used.

My permanent address is _____
                         (Street Address)   (City/Town/Village)   (State)   (zip)

_____   _____
(Signature of Proposed Guardian)   (Signature of Proposed Guardian)

_____   _____
        (Print Name)   (Print Name)

On _____ , _____ , before me personally came

to me known to be the person described in and who executed the foregoing instrument. Such person duly sworn to such instrument before me and duly acknowledged that he/she executed the same.

_____
Notary Public
Commission Expires:
(Affix Notary Stamp or Seal)

Signature of Attorney: _____

Print Name: _____

Firm Name: _____ Tel. No.: _____

Address of Attorney: _____

-4-

SURROGATE'S COURT OF THE STATE OF NEW YORK
COUNTY OF _____

---X

Proceeding for the Appointment of a
Guardian for

_____

JOINDER AND STATEMENT OF
PREFERENCE OF INFANT 14 YEARS AND OVER

_____ an Infant.

---X

FILE NO. _____

I, _____ , the Infant, hereby join in the foregoing petition and request that

_____ of _____ be appointed guardian

of my   ☐ person and property
           ☐ person
           ☐ property

STATE OF _____)
COUNTY OF _____) ss.:

_____ being duly sworn says: that I am the infant in the foregoing petition
and joinder statement, that I have read the same and believe them to be true, and join in the prayer for the relief requested.

_____
(Signature of Infant)

_____
(Print Name)

Sworn to before me this
_____ day of _____ , _____

_____
Notary Public
Commission Expires:
(Affix Notary Stamps or Seal)

Note: If the petition is prepared by an attorney, the attorney's name, address and telephone number must be set forth.

Signature of Attorney: _____

Print Name: _____

Firm Name: _____ Tel. No.: _____

Address of Attorney: _____

FORM G-2B   **Petition for Appointment of Guardian (Person and Property/Property Only)**

SURROGATE'S COURT OF THE STATE OF NEW YORK
COUNTY OF _____
--X
Proceeding for the Appointment of a
Guardian for

_____

                                                    an Infant.
--X

TO THE SURROGATE'S COURT, COUNTY OF _____

Filing Fee Paid	$ _____
_____ Certs	$ _____
_____ Certs	$ _____
$ _____ Bond,	$ _____
Receipt No: _____	No: _____

PETITION FOR
APPOINTMENT OF GUARDIAN OF
☐ PERSON AND PROPERTY
☐ PROPERTY ONLY

File No._____

It is respectfully alleged:
1.   The name, permanent address, date of birth and telephone number of the petitioner, and the petitioner's relationship to the infant are as follows:

Name:_____ Telephone Number:_____

Permanent Address:_____
                                            (Street and Number)

_____
    (City, Village, Town)   (State)   (Zip Code)
    Mailing address:_____
                                    (If different from permanent address)
Date of Birth:_____   Relationship to Infant:_____

Name:_____ Telephone Number:_____

Permanent Address:_____
                                            (Street and Number)

_____
    (City, Village, Town)   (State)   (Zip Code)
    Mailing address:_____
                                    (if different from permanent address)
Date of Birth:_____   Relationship to infant:_____

2.   The name, Permanent address, date of birth and marital status of the infant of this proceeding is as follows:

Name:_____

Permanent Address:_____
                                            (Street and Number)

_____
    (City, Village, Town)   (State)   (Zip Code)
    Mailing address:_____
                                    (If different from permanent address)
Date of Birth:_____   Marital Status:_____
[Attach certified copy of birth certificate]

3.   The names and permanent addresses of the parents of the infant and, if the infant is married, the infant's spouse are:
[If deceased give date of death and complete Number 5 and Number 6]
Name of Father:_____ Date of Birth:_____ Date of Death:_____

Permanent Address:_____
                                            (Street and Number)

_____
    (City, Village, Town)   (State)   (Zip Code)

    Mailing Address:_____
                                    (If different from permanent address)

G-2-13 (9/00)

-I-

Name of Mother:_____ Date of Birth:_____ Date of Death:_____

Permanent Address:_____
                          (Street and Number)

_____
(City, Village, Town)   (State)   (Zip Code)

Mailing Address:_____
                   (If different from permanent address)

Name of Spouse:_____ Date of Birth:_____ Date of Death:_____

Permanent Address:_____
                          (Street and Number)

_____
(City, Village, Town)   (State)   (Zip Code)

Mailing Address:_____
                   (If different from permanent address)

4.   The names and addresses of the adult persons with whom the infant resides if other than parents are:

Name:_____

Permanent Address:_____
                          (Street and Number)

_____
(City, Village, Town)   (State)   (Zip Code)

Mailing Address:_____
                   (If different from permanent address)
Relationship to infant:_____

5.   If father and mother are deceased, list the names and addresses of the nearest distributees; of full age who live within the state. [if not applicable, so state]

Name	Permanent Address	Relationship

6.   The names and permanent addresses of the infant's grandparents: **[If not applicable, so state and if deceased, add date of death]**

Name	Permanent Address	
		Maternal Grandmother
		Maternal Grandfather
		Paternal Grandmother
		Paternal Grandfather

7.   **[Please check (a) and (b) for guardian of the infant's person and property or check (b) for guardianship of the infant's property only]**
(a)   ☐   Petitioner is requesting appointment as guardian of the infant's person and alleges the petitioner is capable of providing care, custody and control of the infant during minority and is motivated solely by the best interests of the child in requesting this appointment.

(b) ☐   Petitioner is requesting appointment as guardian of the infant's property, and alleges that the estimated value of all REAL and PERSONAL property to which the infant is entitled is:

                        $ _____

[Answer question 8 only if requesting guardianship of the property]
8. (a) PERSONAL PROPERTY **[State exact title of all bank accounts with account number and balance, and/or list insurance policies by company, policy number, amount insured, and name of insured and relationship to infant and/or list the name, number of shares and value of all stocks, bonds, and any other personal property. List value of infant's interest].**

_____
_____
_____
_____
_____

(b) REAL PROPERTY **[State whether real property is mortgaged or under a lien and the amount thereof. Indicate whether property is to be occupied as a residence by the infant. If not, indicate rental income or whether a sale of the property is contemplated.]**

Location of Property _____   Gross Value _____

Infant's Interest _____   Annual Income _____

Amount Mortgaged or Under a Lien _____

_____

(c)   ANNUAL INCOME OF INFANT FROM ALL SOURCES:

    (1)   Compensation or pension to be received from: _____ $ _____

    (2)   Income from Trust _____ $ _____

    (3)   Other Income _____ $ _____

(d) STATE SOURCE OF ALL PROPERTY listed above. **If any property is derived from an estate or as a result of the death of any person, name the decedent, his or her date of death and relationship to the infant, whether a fiduciary has been appointed, court name, file number, and type of letters. Provide a copy of any will or decree directing payment. List names and addresses of all banks, insurance companies and persons from whom payment is expected].**

_____
_____
_____
_____

9. (a) The infant has never had, at any time, a guardian appointed for him/her, and,

    (b)   Custody of the infant has never been surrendered by any person lawfully charged therewith nor has custody been the subject of any court order, except as hereinafter listed: **[Attach copies of all surrenders, court orders, or divorce decrees].**

_____
_____
_____

10.   That if the infant is a non-domiciliary married person and the petition relates to property only, that the property is not subject to the control or disposition of the person's spouse by the law of his or her domicile. (SCPA 1705(5))

11. Petitioner ☐ has ☐ does not have knowledge that a person nominated to be a guardian, or any individual eighteen years of age or over who resides in the home of the proposed guardian:

  a. Is the subject of a reported filed with the Statewide Central Register of Child Abuse and Maltreatment pursuant to the rules of Child Protective Services, following an Investigation which determines that some credible evidence of alleged abuse or maltreatment exists, and/or

  b. Has been the subject of, or the respondent in a Child Protective Proceeding commenced pursuant to law, which proceeding resulted in an order finding that the subject infant is an abused or neglected child.

  [If petitioner has such knowledge, attach an affidavit explaining in detail].

12. Petitioner has completed and annexed the Request For Information Guardianship Form (OCFS 3909) required to be submitted to the New York State Central Register of Child Abuse and Maltreatment.

13. The infant ☐ is ☐ is not a Native American child under the Indian Child Welfare Act of 1978. (25 U.S.C. Sections 1901-1963)

14. There are no other persons interested in this proceeding upon whom process is required to be served other than those listed above.

15. No prior application has been made to any Court for the relief requested herein.

WHEREFORE, your petitioner respectfully prays that: **[Check and complete all relief requested]**

(a) Letters of Guardianship of the

  ☐   Person and Property

  ☐   Property

  be granted to _____

  _____

  or such other person or corporation as may be entitled thereto and that process issue to all interested persons who have not waived issuance of same requiring them to show cause why such relief should not be granted,

(b) The guardian of the property be directed to collect and receive all moneys and other property of the infant jointly with a clerk of the Surrogate's Court, or Depository subject to the provisions of SCPA 1708, and shall deposit same in the name of guardian, subject to order of the court with either:

  1. _____
     Name of Bank/Depository   Branch Address

  2. _____
     Name of Bank/Depository   Branch Address

(c) The bond of the guardian be dispensed with.

Dated: _____

_____   _____
(Signature of Petitioner)   (Signature of Petitioner)

_____   _____
(Print Name)   (Print Name)

STATE OF _____)
COUNTY OF_____) ss.:

_____, being duly sworn deposes and says that I am the petitioner above named. I have read the foregoing petition and the same is true of my own knowledge except as to matters therein stated to be alleged upon information and belief and as to those matters I believe them to be true.

Sworn to before me this
_____ day of_____. _____

_____
_____
(Signature of Petitioner)

Notary Public
Commission Expires:
(Affix Notary Stamp or Seal)

_____
(Print Name)

_____
(Signature of Petitioner)

_____
(Print Name)

COMBINED OATH & DESIGNATION

STATE OF _____)
COUNTY OF _____) ss.:

_____ being duly sworn, deposes and says:

1.   OATH OF GUARDIAN: I am over eighteen (18) years of age and a citizen of the United States; that I will well, faithfully and honestly discharge the duties of such guardian: That I am acquainted with estate of said Infant and have read the statement contained in the foregoing petition as to the estimated value of same, and believe same to be correct, and that I am not ineligible to receive letters.

2.   DESIGNATION OF CLERK FOR SERVICE OR PROCESS: I hereby designate the Clerk of the Surrogate's Court of _____ County, and his/her successor in office, as a person on whom service of any process issuing from such Surrogate's Court may be made in like manner and with like effect as if it were served personally upon me, whenever I cannot be found within the state of New York after due diligence used.

My permanent address is _____
     (Street Address)   (City/Town/Village)   (State)   (Zip)

_____
(Signature of Proposed Guardian)

_____
(Signature of Proposed Guardian)

_____
(Print Name)

_____
(Print Name)

On _____, _____, before me personally came to me known to be the person described in and who executed the foregoing instrument. Such person duly sworn to such instrument before me and duly acknowledged that he/she executed the same.

_____
Notary Public
Commission Expires:
(Affix Notary Stamp or Seal)

Signature of Attorney: _____

Print Name: _____

Firm Name: _____ Tel. No.: _____

Address of Attorney: _____

-5-

FORM G-2B　　　　SURROGATE'S COURT　　　　SF-104

SURROGATE'S COURT OF THE STATE OF NEW YORK
COUNTY OF _____
---X
Proceeding for the Appointment of a
Guardian for

_____

_____ an Infant.
---X

JOINDER AND STATEMENT OF
PREFERENCE OF INFANT 14 YEARS AND OVER

FILE NO. _____

I, _____ , the infant, hereby join in the foregoing petition and request that

_____ of _____ be appointed guardian

of my　☐ person and property
　　　　☐ person
　　　　☐ property

STATE OF _____ }
COUNTY OF _____) ss.:

_____ being duly sworn says: that I am the infant in the foregoing petition
and joinder statement, that I have read the same and believe them to be true, and join in the prayer for the relief requested.

_____
(Signature of Infant)

_____
(Print Name)

Sworn to before me this
_____ day of _____, _____

_____
Notary Public
Commission Expires:
(Affix Notary Stamp or Seal)

Note:　If the petition is prepared by an attorney, the attorney's name, address and telephone number must be set forth.

Signature of Attorney: _____

Print Name: _____

Firm Name: _____ Tel. No.: _____

Address of Attorney: _____

FORM G-3   Affidavit of Proposed Guardian

SURROGATE'S COURT OF THE STATE OF NEW YORK
COUNTY OF _____
--X
Proceeding for the Appointment of a
Guardian for

_____

AFFIDAVIT OF PROPOSED
GUARDIAN OF THE PERSON

File No. _____

_____ an Infant.
--X

STATE OF _____)
COUNTY OF _____) ss.:

To the Surrogate's Court, County of _____

The undersigned _____, being duly sworn deposes and says:

1.   I am a competent person over the age of eighteen (18) years, and I submit this affidavit in support of my petition to be appointed guardian of the person of _____, an infant.

2.   I have known the infant since _____ by reason of the following: [State relationship, if any. Set forth when and by whom the custody of the infant was transferred to you]

_____
_____
_____
_____
_____

3.   I reside at _____, and the other resident members of the household are: (Include all persons residing there and their respective ages]

_____   _____
_____   _____
_____   _____

4.   Not including minor traffic offenses and adjudications as a youthful offender, wayward minor or juvenile delinquent,

      (a)   I have never been convicted of an offense against the law, except _____

      _____

      (b)   I have never forfeited bail or other collateral, except _____

      _____

      (c)   I do not have any criminal charges pending against me, except _____

      _____

5.   I have no physical or mental impairment, or medical condition, which would interfere with my ability to perform the duties of guardian of the Infant, except

_____
_____
_____

6.   I am not addicted to unlawful narcotics or to alcohol.

G-3 (9/00)

Official Forms

7.　　I am willing and able to undertake care, custody and control of the infant until the infant attains the age of eighteen (18) or until the court determines otherwise.

8.　　I believe that my appointment as guardian would be in the best interest of the infant for the following reasons:

_____

_____

_____

_____

_____

(Signature of Proposed Guardian)

_____

(Print Name)

Sworn to before me this
_____ day of _____, _____

_____

Notary Public
Commission Expires:
(Affix Notary Stamp or Seal)

-2-

FORM G-4   Affidavit of Parent

SURROGATE'S COURT OF THE STATE OF NEW YORK
COUNTY OF _____
---X
Proceeding for the Appointment of a
Guardian for   AFFIDAVIT OF PARENT

_____

_____ an Infant.   File No. _____
---X

STATE OF NEW YORK   )
COUNTY OF_____) ss.:

    The undersigned, _____ , being duly sworn, deposes and says:
1.
    I am a competent person over the age of eighteen (18) years and I am the natural/adoptive parent
_____of_____
             (Mother/Father)   (Infant)
and I reside at _____

2.   As the natural/adoptive parent of the above-named infant, I have determined that it would be in the best interests of
the child if_____ was/were appointed guardian (s) of the
           (Proposed Guardian (s))
was/were appointed guardian (s) of the infant for the following reasons:
_____
_____
_____
_____

3.   No guardian has ever been appointed for the infant herein nor has custody thereof been surrendered by me nor
otherwise judicially awarded to any other person or agency except as listed below:
_____
_____
_____

4.   I understand that I am relinquishing all rights to care, custody and control of my infant_____ ,
                               (Son/Daughter)
in favor of_____ , the proposed guardian (s) of the person of said infant.

5.   I further understand that such care, custody and control of the Infant shall remain in_____
                                (Proposed Guardian (s))
as guardian of the person _____ until the infant shall attain the age of eighteen
                 (Infant)
(18) years, and that the proposed guardian (s) is/are capable of assuming such care, custody, and control over the infant.

_____
                Signature of Parent

Sworn to before me this
_____ day of _____ , _____

_____
Notary Public
Commission Expires
(Affix Notary Stamp or Seal)

G-4 (9/00)

FORM G-5   Waiver, Renunciation, and Consent

SURROGATE'S COURT OF THE STATE OF NEW YORK
COUNTY OF _____
---X
Proceeding for the Appointment of a
Guardian for

_____

_____ an Infant.
---X

WAIVER OF PROCESS
RENUNCIATION AND CONSENT
TO LETTERS OF GUARDIANSHIP

File No. _____

The undersigned _____ whose permanent address is:

_____

      (Street and Number)   (City, Village, Town)

_____

         (State)   (Zip Code)
and who is a competent person over the age of eighteen (18) years and whose interest in the above-entitled proceeding is
as follows:

    [Check appropriate interest]

        ☐   Parent of the above-named infant
        ☐   Grandparent of the above named infant
        ☐   Other (Specify) _____

hereby personally appears in this proceeding and

    (1)   renounces all right to Letters of Guardianship of the   ☐ person and property
                ☐ person   ☐ property of infant

    (2)   waives the issuance and service of process in this matter, and

    (3)   consents that _____ be appointed the guardian of the

        a.   ☐   Person of the above-named Infant
        b.   ☐   Property of the above-named infant
        c.   ☐   Person and Property of the above-named infant

and that such letters may be granted to said person or to any other person entitled thereto without notice to the undersigned.

Date:_____   _____

                                                  (Signature)

                                      _____

                                            (Print Name)

STATE OF _____) ss.:
COUNTY OF _____)

    On _____ , _____ , before me personally came
_____ known to me to be the
individual described in and who executed the foregoing instrument, and to me such person duly acknowledged that_____
executed the same.

_____
Notary Public
Commission Expires:
(Affix Notary Stamp or Seal)

G-5 (9/00)

FORM G-6A   Decree Appointing Guardian (Joint Control)

At a Surrogate's Court of the
State of New York, held in and
for the County of_____ ,
at _____ , New York on
_____ , _____ .

PRESENT:
HON._____
      SURROGATE
---X
Proceeding for the Appointment of a   DECREE APPOINTING
Guardian for   GUARDIAN
                                             (Joint Control Decree)
_____

_____ an Infant.   File No. _____
---X

Upon reading and filing the petition, duly verified on _____ , _____
applying for the appointment of a guardian of the person and property of the above-named infant, and it appearing
that jurisdiction has been obtained over all necessary parties, and the court being satisfied that the interests of the
infant will be promoted by the appointment of guardian of the person and property of the infant and that
_____ , is in all respects competent to act as such guardian, it is hereby

ORDERED AND DECREED, that_____ of _____
be and is hereby appointed guardian of the person and property of said infant, and it is further

ORDERED AND DECREED, that a bond be dispensed with and that said guardian collect and receive all
money and property of said infant pursuant to SCPA 1708 jointly with the Clerk of the Surrogate's Court of
_____ , County and that all such money and property be deposited or invested
in the name of the guardian subject to the further order of the Court with the depository or depositories hereby
designated, namely: _____ provided however, that no deposit or investment in any one
depository shall exceed the maximum insured amount and such deposit or investment shall be withdrawn or
removed only on the order of the Court, it is

ORDERED AND DECREED, that said guardian is restrained from collecting and receiving any money or
property except under joint control as aforesaid, and the letters to be issued shall be limited to the receiving and
administration of the money or property under such joint control, and it is further

ORDERED AND DECREED, that upon taking and filing the oath and designation required by law, Letters
of Guardianship issue as aforesaid.

_____
_____ , Surrogate

G-6A (9/00)

FORM G-6B   **Decree Appointing Guardian (Bond)**

At a Surrogate's Court of the
State of New York, held in and
for the County of _____
at _____ , New York on
_____ , _____ .

PRESENT:
HON _____
.   SURROGATE
---X

Proceeding for the Appointment of a
Guardian for

_____

_____ an Infant.
---X

DECREE APPOINTING
GUARDIAN
(Bond)

File No. _____

    Upon reading and filing the petition, duly verified on _____ , _____
applying for the appointment of a guardian of the person and property of the above-named infant, and it appearing
that jurisdiction has been obtained over all necessary parties, and the court being satisfied that the interests of the
infant will be promoted by the appointment of guardian of the person and property of the infant and that
_____ , is in all respects competent to act as such guardian, it is hereby

    ORDERED AND DECREED, that _____ of _____
be and is hereby appointed guardian of the person and property of said infant, and that Letters of Guardianship
issue, upon said guardian filing the oath and designation required by law, and executing a bond, with sufficient
sureties in the sum of _____ dollars ($ _____).

_____ , Surrogate

G-6B (9/00)

FORM G-7A   Annual Account of Guardian (Non-Bonded)

SURROGATE'S COURT OF THE STATE OF NEW YORK
COUNTY OF _____
---X

Annual Account of _____   File No._____

Guardian of _____   Annual Account of Non-Bonded Guardian
                                             for the Period Ending

_____ an Infant.   _____
---X

TO THE SURROGATE'S COURT, COUNTY OF _____

I, _____ whose permanent address is
        (Name of Guardian)

_____   _____
(Street Address)   (City/Town/Village)

_____   _____   _____
(County)   (State)   (Zip)   (Telephone Number)

Mailing address is: _____
                        (if different from permanent address)

appointed Guardian of the property of the above named infant by this Court on _____ ,
respectfully submit the following account and declare the same to be a full and true statement of my account of the
property of said infant covering the period:

From: _____ To: _____
and state that I accounted for all the property of the above infant, to the dates covered by this account.

Name of Infant: _____

Present Address: _____

INSTRUCTIONS TO GUARDIAN

    File original account with the Surrogate's Court and retain a copy for your records to assist you in preparing
your next account.

    Do not send deposit books to this office. Furnish letter or certificate of deposit from bank or depository.

Official Forms

SCHEDULE A
ASSETS ON HAND AT BEGINNING OF PERIOD COVERED

List all assets in the infant's estate at beginning of period covered by this account which are the assets on hand at the close of last accounting, unless this is a **first account,** in which case state first account in this schedule and enter receipts in Schedule B.

Name of Bank or Depository	Account Number	Amount at opening date of this account
1.		
2.		
3.		
4.		

Other property held at opening date of this accounting period.

Total Schedule A _____

SCHEDULE B

LIST ALL RECEIPTS OF PRINCIPAL OR INCOME

Show receipts and source, including interest on bank accounts during the period covered by this account.

Name of Bank or Depository	Account Number	Interest Accrued (this period)
1.		
2.		
3.		
4.		

Additional property received:

Total Schedule B _____

SCHEDULE C

LIST ALL MONEYS PAID OUT

Show all disbursements during the period covered by this account.
Withdrawals with Court Order

Name of Bank or Depository	Account Number	Order Dated Amount
1.		
2.		
3.		
4.		

Other disbursements:

Total Schedule C

The guardian is not permitted to expend any funds of the Infant without first obtaining an order of the Court. Any change of guardian's address must be reported in writing to the Clark of the Court.

SCHEDULE D

ASSETS ON HAND AT END OF PERIOD COVERED

Show assets on hand at the end of the period covered by this account. Show name of bank or depository, account number and balance at close of this account.

SUBMIT PROOF OF BANK BALANCES, LETTER OR CERTIFICATE OF DEPOSIT FROM BANK OR DEPOSITORY; DO NOT SEND DEPOSIT BOOKS.

Name of Bank or Depository	Account Number	Amount on deposit at closing date of accounting period
1.		
2.		
3.		
4.		

Other property held at the closing date of the accounting period:

Total Schedule D

-3-

Official Forms

SCHEDULE E

SUMMARY OF RECEIPTS AND DISBURSEMENTS AS SHOWN BY ABOVE SCHEDULES

I charge myself with total balance as shown by
last account Schedule "A" $_____

I charge myself with receipts as shown by
Schedule "B" $_____

              Total debits (Schedule A and B above) $_____

I credit myself with disbursements as shown by
Schedule "C" $_____

I credit myself with balance on hand, to be
charged to me in my next account $_____

(This balance should be the same as total
of Schedule "D".)
Total credits (Schedule C and D above) $_____

SCHEDULE E

SET FORTH THE NAME(S) AND PRESENT ADDRESS(ES) OF BANK(S) OR DEPOSITORY(IES) IN WHICH FUNDS
ARE HELD IN JOINT CONTROL

1 _____   _____
      (Name of Bank or Depository)   (Address of Bank or Depository)

2 _____   _____
      (Name of Bank or Depository)   (Address of Bank or Depository)

3 _____   _____
      (Name of Bank or Depository)   (Address of Bank or Depository)

4 _____   _____
      (Name of Bank or Depository)   (Address of Bank or Depository)

State of _____)

County of _____) ss.:

I _____ being duly sworn do say: I am the Guardian of the property
of the within infant; that the foregoing Account is to the best of my knowledge and belief a true statement.

Sworn to before me this   _____
_____ day of _____   Signature of Guardian

_____   _____
Notary Public   Print Name
Commission Expires:
(Affix Stamp or Seal)

Signature of Attorney: _____

Print Name: _____

Firm Name: _____ Tel. No: _____

Address of Attorney: _____

-4-

FORM G-7B   **Annual Account of Guardian (Bonded)**

SURROGATE'S COURT OF THE STATE OF NEW YORK
COUNTY OF _____
---X   File No. _____
Annual Account of_____

Guardian of _____   Annual Account of Bonded Guardian for
                                                    the Period Ending
                          an Infant.   _____
---X

TO THE SURROGATE'S COURT, COUNTY OF _____

    I, _____ , whose permanent address is
              (Name of Guardian)

_____
    (Street Address)   (City/Town/Village)

_____
    (County)   (State)   (Zip)   (Telephone Number)

Mailing address is:_____,
                          (If different from permanent address)

appointed Guardian of the property of the above named infant by this Court on _____
_____ , respectfully submit the following account and declare the same to be a
full and true statement of my account of the property of said infant covering the period:

From: _____To: _____
and state that I heretofore accounted for all the property of the above infant, to the dates covered by this
account.

Name of Infant: _____

Present Address: _____

INSTRUCTIONS TO GUARDIAN

    File original account with the Surrogate's Court and retain a copy for your records to assist you
in preparing your next account.

    Do not send deposit books to this office. Furnish letter or certificate of deposit from bank or
depository.

Official Forms

SCHEDULE A

ASSETS ON HAND AT BEGINNING OF PERIOD COVERED

List all assets in the infant's estate at beginning of period covered by this account which will be assets on hand at close of the last accounting, unless this is a **first account**, in which case state first account in this schedule and enter receipts in Schedule B.

At the opening date of this accounting period, namely _____ ,
the infant's estate consisted of : (State value of all items listed)

(1)   Cash deposited in the banks named below and evidenced by bank books of which the numbers are given below. (State whether savings, special interest or checking accounts.)

_____

_____

_____

_____

_____

(2)   Securities which are listed and identified below by (a) par value, (b) name, (c) certificate number, (d) interest rate, (e) interest dates, (f) due date, (g) inventory value.

_____

_____

_____

_____

(3)   Other Personal Property listed below with full description and value. (Include here books, pictures, jewelry, furniture, etc.)

_____

_____

_____

_____

_____

G-7B (9/00)

(4)   Interests, described below, in personal property not in my possession. (Include here interests in trust funds, insurance funds or uncollected legacies or distributive shares due from other estates.)

_____
_____
_____
_____
_____
_____

(5)   Interests, described below, in real property.

_____
_____
_____
_____
_____
_____

TOTAL: $_____

SCHEDULE B

LIST ALL ADDITIONAL PRINCIPAL RECEIVED

Show date received, source and amount.

_____
_____
_____
_____
_____
_____
_____
_____
_____
_____

TOTAL: $ _____

-3-

SCHEDULE C

LIST ALL RECEIPTS OF INCOME

Show source, including interest on specified bank accounts, rents on realty, and dividends received on investments, during the period covered by this account, as well as date of payment.)

Interest credited to bank accounts: _____

Dividends received: _____

Rents on realty: _____

TOTAL $ _____

SCHEDULE D

LIST ALL LOSSES INCURRED

Show all realized decreases on principal assets whether due to sale -or liquidation, indicating the asset sold or liquidated, and the date of same.)

TOTAL: $ _____

-4-

SCHEDULE   E

LIST ALL MONEYS PAID OUT

Show all disbursements, not investments, during the period covered by this account, including date of payment, payee, and amount paid.

_____

_____

_____

_____

_____

_____

_____

_____

_____

_____

_____ TOTAL: $ _____

SCHEDULE   F

ASSETS ON HAND AT END OF PERIOD COVERED

Show assets on hand at the end of the period covered by this account and the valuation thereof.

(1)   Cash deposited in the banks named below, evidenced by bank books of which the numbers are given below. (State whether savings, special interest, or checking accounts.)

_____

_____

_____

_____

_____

(2)   Securities listed and identified below by (a) par value, (b) name, (c) certificate number, (d) interest rate, (e) interest dates, (f) due dates, (g) cost or inventory value.

_____

_____

_____

_____

_____

_____

(3)   Other personal property listed below, with full description and value. (Include books, pictures, jewelry, furniture, etc.)

_____

_____

_____

_____

_____

_____

(4)   Interests, described below, in personal property not in my possession. (Include interests in trust funds, insurance funds or uncollected legacies or distributive shares due from other estates.)

_____

_____

_____

_____

_____

_____

(5)   Interests, described below, in real property.

_____

_____

_____

_____

_____

_____

TOTAL: $ _____

SCHEDULE G

THIS IS AN INFORMATION SCHEDULE AND THE FIGURES THEREIN ARE NOT TO BE INCLUDED IN THE SUMMARY STATEMENT

Changes were made in said infant's estate during this accounting period as shown below.

(1)   I invested cash in securities and state below (a) date of purchase, (b) name of security, (c) certificate number, (d) par value, (e) cost price, (f) commission paid, (g) accrued interest, (h) from whom purchased, (i) interest rate, (j) interest dates.

_____
_____
_____
_____
_____
_____

(2)   I sold securities for cash and state below (a) date of sale, (b) name of security, (c) certificate number, (d) inventory value, (e) amount received, (f) accrued interest, (g) to whom sold, (h) commission paid, (i) profit or loss on sale.

_____
_____
_____
_____
_____
_____

(3)   Securities were redeemed as stated below by (a) date, (b) name of security, (c) certificate number, (d) inventory value, (e) amount received, (f) accrued interest, (g) gain or loss.

_____
_____
_____
_____
_____
_____

Official Forms

(4)   I exchanged securities for other securities and state below (a) name of original security, (b) certificate number, (c) cash paid in exchange, (d) name of new security, (e) certificate number, (f) cash received in exchange, (g) reason for exchange, (h) with whom exchange made.

_____
_____
_____
_____
_____
_____

(5)   Other changes not due to investment, sale, redemption or exchange of securities are stated below, with the reasons therefor.

_____
_____
_____
_____
_____
_____

SCHEDULE H

SUMMARY OF RECEIPTS AND DISBURSEMENTS AS SHOWN BY ABOVE SCHEDULES

I charge myself with total balance as shown
by last account on Schedule A $_____

I charge myself with total additional principal
received as shown on Schedule B $_____

I charge myself with total income received as
shown on Schedule C $_____

                                      TOTAL: $_____

I credit myself with total losses as shown on
Schedule D $_____

I credit myself with total monies paid out as
shown on Schedule E $_____

                                      TOTAL: $_____

Principal balance on hand (This balance
should be the same as total on Schedule F) $_____

-8-

SCHEDULE I

SET FORTH THE NAME (S) AND PRESENT ADDRESS (ES) OF THE BANK (S) OR DEPOSITORY (IES) AND THE SURETY (IES) ON THE BOND AND WHETHER THE SECURITY OF THE BOND (S) HAS BECOME IMPAIRED.

1. _____   _____
   (Name of Bank or Depository)   (Address of Bank or Depository)

2. _____   _____
   (Name of Bank or Depository)   (Address of Bank or Depository)

3. _____   _____
   (Name of Surety)   (Address of Surety)

   Impaired ☐ Yes ☐ No

4. _____   _____
   (Name of Surety)   (Address of Surety)

   Impaired ☐ Yes ☐ No

State of _____

County of _____ SS.

I _____ being duly sworn do say: I am the Guardian of the property of the within infant; that the foregoing Account is to the best of my knowledge and belief a true statement.

_____
Signature of Guardian

Sworn to before me this
_____ day of _____

_____
Notary Public   Print Name
Commission Expires:
(Affix Notary Stamp or Seal)

Signature of Attorney: _____

Print Name: _____

Firm Name: _____   Tel. No.: _____

Address of Attorney: _____

-9-

FORM G-8 **Petition for Withdrawal of Infant's Property for Support and Education**

SURROGATE'S COURT OF THE STATE OF NEW YORK
COUNTY OF _____
---X
In the Matter of the Guardianship of

_____

an Infant.
---X

PETITION FOR WITHDRAWAL
OF INFANTS PROPERTY FOR
SUPPORT AND EDUCATION

File No. _____

TO THE SURROGATE'S COURT, COUNTY OF _____

The petition of the guardian respectfully alleges:

1.   Name of guardian: _____ Phone Number: _____
     Permanent Address: _____
     Relation to infant: _____ Present Occupation: _____
     Name of infant: _____
     Permanent Address: _____
     Date of birth: _____

2.   Date Letters of Guardianship were issued: _____
     [Check one]   ☐ Person and Property   ☐ Property only

3.   The name and address of depository or depositories in which funds of the infant are deposited is or are:
     [List all, attach additional sheet If needed]

     Name: _____
     Address: _____
     Amount on deposit at date of this petition $ _____

4.   The property and income of the infant is set forth in the annexed Schedule A summarized as follows:

                    Yearly Income $_____
          Value of infants property $_____

5.   Petitioner requests authorization for withdrawal of the following amounts for the support or education of the infant:

     (a)   A lump sum of $_____

     (b)   A sum of $_____ by periodic withdrawals of $_____ each month
           for a period of _____ months beginning _____ and ending _____

     The funds are needed and are to be used for the following reasons and purposes: [Complete Schedule B]

     _____
     _____
     _____

6.   The parent or parents of the infant are: **[If deceased, state date of death]**

      Father:_____

      Permanent Address:_____

      Mother: _____

      Permanent Address: _____

      The income and resources of infant's parent or parents are as set forth in Schedule C hereto annexed.

7.   The reason the parent (s) of the infant cannot provide for the support or education of the infant is:

      _____

      _____

      The estimated yearly household expenditures of infant's parent or parents are as set forth in Schedule D hereto annexed.

8.   The funds of the infant withdrawn during the past calendar year of_____ are as follows: **[If "NONE", must so state]**

          Date of order: $_____

          Amount authorized to be withdrawn $_____

          Total withdrawn and spent $_____

          Amount unexpended, if any $_____

                  [Attach additional sheets as needed]

9.   No previous application has been made for the relief now sought.

    WHEREFORE, petitioner requests:

1.   That the court authorize the withdrawal from funds of the infant on deposit in the name of the guardian in the _____

      _____

               [Insert name and address of Depository]

    for support, maintenance and education of the infant as follows:

    (a)   A lump sum of $_____

    (b)   A sum of $_____ , by periodic withdrawals of not over $ _____ each month for one year beginning with the month of_____ and ending with the month of _____ provided that any monthly sum not withdrawn for one month may be withdrawn during any succeeding month during the year.

    (c)   That petitioner may have such other or further relief as may be proper.

Dated: _____   _____
                                            (Signature of Petitioner)

                                       _____
                                              (Print Name)

Official Forms

State of _____)

County of _____)   ss.:

I, _____, the petitioner named in the foregoing petition, being duly sworn, say:

I have read the foregoing petition subscribed by me and know the contents thereof, and the same is true of my own knowledge, except as to the matters therein stated to be alleged on information and belief and as to these matters, I believe it to be true.

_____
(Signature of Petitioner)

Sworn to before me this
_____ day of_____ : _____

_____
(Print Name)

_____
Notary Public
Commission Expires:
(Affix Notary Stamp or Seal)

NOTE: 1.   Withdrawal is subject to guardian filing any required annual account.
          2.   Court may require additional information relative to circumstances of parents or other facts justifying use of infant's funds.
          3.   Infant 14 years and over must join in and sign consent to petition, otherwise must be given notice as Court directs.
          4.   Generally periodic withdrawals will be limited to a period of 12 months or less.

CONSENT OF INFANT TO WITHDRAWAL

I, _____ , the infant named in the foregoing petition, being over the age of fourteen years, do hereby join in the petition and ask that the withdrawal be made as therein requested.

Dated: _____

_____
(Signature of Infant)

_____
(Print Name)

State of _____)

County of_____) ss.

_____ being duly sworn, says that: I have read the foregoing petition, and the same is true of my own knowledge, except as to the matters therein stated to be alleged on information and belief, as to those matters, I believe them to be true.

_____
(Signature of Infant)

Sworn to before me this
_____ day of_____ , _____

_____
(Print Name)

_____
Notary Public
Commission Expires:
(Affix Notary Stamp or Seal)

Official Forms

SCHEDULE A (PARAGRAPH 4)

(Income & Property of Infant)

Annual Income -   Interest on bank deposits $_____

Social Security benefits $_____

Veterans benefits $_____

Wages $_____

Other income $_____

Total $_____

Property: Bank Deposits   (Name Bank)

_____ $_____

_____ $_____

Other Property (Describe-State Value)

_____ $_____

_____ $_____

Total $_____

SCHEDULE B (PARAGRAPH 5)
(List items for which funds are requested and amount,
e.g. tuition-name school and attach bill;
for medical, name doctor and amount.)

Item	Amount
_____	$_____
_____	$_____
_____	$_____
_____	$_____
_____	$_____

SCHEDULE C (PARAGRAPH 6)

Income and Resources of Parents:

	Mother	Father
Earnings: Salary and Wages	$	$
Income from dividends, interest, etc.	$	$
Social Security (for Parent)	$	$
Social Security (for all infants)	$	$
Rents, Business income, etc.	$	$
Total:	$	$

Assets:

	Mother	Father
Bank accounts and securities	$	$
Real estate (Home)	$	$
Real estate (Other)	$	$
Total:	$	$

Indebtedness:

	Mother	Father
Mortgages	$	$
Other debts	$	$
Total:	$	$

Names and ages of any dependents

NAME	RELATIONSHIP	AGE

-6-

SCHEDULE D (PARAGRAPH 7)

Parent's Household

Estimated yearly household expenditures: $ _____

a. Home: Taxes, Mortgages, Insurance $ _____

Heat, Light, Water, Repairs $ _____

Rent $ _____

Other home costs $ _____

b. Family Maintenance:

Food $ _____

Clothing $ _____

Medical $ _____

Income Taxes $ _____

All Other $ _____

Total number of persons in household _____

Are infant's funds to be used toward paying any of the above expenses? If so, state which and how much:

_____ $ _____

_____ $ _____

_____ $ _____

Signature of Attorney: _____

Print Name: _____

Firm Name: _____   Tel. No.: _____

Address of Attorney: _____

FORM G-9   **Order Permitting Withdrawal of Infant's Property for Support and Education**

At a Surrogate's Court of the State
of New York, held in and for the
County of _____ at _____ ,
New York, on _____

PRESENT:
HON. _____
_____ Surrogate.
---X

In the Matter of the Guardianship of

_____

ORDER FOR WITHDRAWAL OF
INFANT'S PROPERTY FOR
SUPPORT AND EDUCATION

File No. _____

_____ an Infant.
---X

Upon reading and filing the petition dated _____ , of

_____ Guardian of _____ , Infant, it is

ORDERED that the Guardian is hereby permitted to draw the sum of _____

_____ ($_____) from funds in _____

to be applied for the purpose of _____ during the period beginning

_____ and ending _____

_____ , SURROGATE

G-9 (9/00)

Official Forms

FORM G-10A   **Petition to Close Guardianship Account (Former Infant)**

SURROGATE'S COURT OF THE STATE OF NEW YORK
COUNTY OF _____
--X

In the Matter of the Guardianship of

_____

                                    a Former Infant.
--X

PETITION TO CLOSE
GUARDIANSHIP ACCOUNT
(Former Infant)

File No _____

TO THE SURROGATE'S COURT, COUNTY OF _____

1. The name, permanent address and birth date of the petitioner (former infant) as well as the name and permanent address of the guardian of the former infant, are as follows:

Former Infant's Name: _____

Permanent Address of Former Infant: _____

Date of Birth: _____

Guardian's Name: _____

Guardian's Permanent Address: _____

2. The guardian has custody and control of the following property of the petitioner to which the petitioner is now entitled by reason of having attained the age of eighteen.

        The sum of $_____ deposited in Account No._____ in the

_____ with accrued
                        (Name and Address of Depository)
interest. **[Attach current bank statement]**

                    [Attach additional sheets as needed]

3. There are no persons interested in this proceeding other than those herein above mentioned.

WHEREFORE, petitioner requests that a Decree be entered directing the payment to petitioner (former infant) the property described in paragraph (2) above.

Dated: _____

                                    _____
                                    Signature of Petitioner (FORMER INFANT)

                                    _____
                                            Print Name

STATE OF NEW YORK
COUNTY OF _____) ss.:

I, the undersigned petitioner being duly sworn, say: That I have read the foregoing petition subscribed by me and know the contents thereof, and that the same is true of my own knowledge, except as to those matters therein stated to be alleged on information and belief and as to those matters I believe it to be true.

Sworn to before me this   Signature of Guardian
_____ day of _____

_____   _____
Notary Public   Print Name
Commission Expires:
(Affix Notary Stamp or Seal)

Signature of Attorney: _____

Print Name: _____

Firm Name: _____ Tel. No _____

Address of Attorney: _____

-2-

FORM G-10B   SURROGATE'S COURT   SF-134

FORM G-10B   Petition to Close Guardianship Account (Guardian)

SURROGATE'S COURT OF THE STATE OF NEW YORK
COUNTY OF _____

In the Matter of the Guardianship of

_____

_____ a Former Infant. ___x

PETITION TO GUARDIANSHIP
ACCOUNT (Guardian)

File No. _____

TO THE SURROGATE'S COURT OF THE COUNTY OF _____

1.   The name and permanent address of petitioner (guardian) and the name and permanent address and birth date of the former infant, are as follows:

Name of guardian: _____ Phone Number: _____

Permanent Address: _____

Relationship to former infant: _____

Name of former infant: _____

Permanent Address: _____

Date of birth: _____

2.   The guardian has custody and control of the following property to which the former infant is now entitled by reason of having attained the age of eighteen.

The sum of $ _____ deposited in Account No. _____ in the

_____ with accrued interest. [Attach current bank statement]
(Name and Address of Depository)

[Attach additional sheets as needed]

3.   I have informally accounted to the former infant whose consent to this petition is submitted herewith.

4.   There are no persons interested in this proceeding other than those herein above mentioned.

WHEREFORE, petitioner requests a decree directing and authorizing payment to the former infant of the property above-mentioned, and for such other relief as may be proper.

Dated: _____

_____
Signature of Petitioner

_____
Print Name

STATE OF _____)
COUNTY OF _____) ss.:

I, the undersigned petitioner being duly sworn, say: That I have read the foregoing petition, subscribed by me and know the contents thereof, and that the same is true of my own knowledge, except as to those matters I believe it to be true.

_____
Signature of Petitioner

Sworn to before me this _____
day of _____, _____

_____
Print Name

_____
Notary Public
Commission Expires:
(Affix Notary Stamp or Seal)

CONSENT OF FORMER INFANT

I, _____, residing at

_____

do hereby state:

I hereby join in the within petition and consent to the relief requested.

_____, as guardian, has informally accounted to me for the administration
of all property which was received by said guardian and I hereby request that said guardian be directed to turn over to me the
balance of all property mentioned in the annexed petition.

Dated: _____

                                   _____
                                          Signature of Former Infant

                                     _____
                                                Print Name

STATE OF _____)
COUNTY OF _____) ss.:

On the _____ day of _____, _____ , before me personally came

_____, to me known to be the person described in and who executed the foregoing instrument.
Such person duly swore to such instrument before me and duly acknowledged that _____ executed the same.

_____
Notary Public
Commission Expires:
(Affix Notary Stamp or Seal)

Signature of Attorney: _____

Print Name: _____

Firm Name: _____ Tel.No.: _____

Address of Attorney: _____

FORM G-11　　**Release Settling Accounts**

SURROGATE'S COURT OF THE STATE OF NEW YORK
COUNTY OF _____
--X

In the Matter of the Guardianship of

_____

　　　　　　　　　　A Former Infant.
--X

RELEASE SETTLING ACCOUNTS

File No. _____

TO THE SURROGATE'S COURT OF THE COUNTY OF_____ :

WHEREAS, _____ of
　　　　　　　　　　　　　(Name of Guardian)
_____, State of_____ ,
　　　　　　(Permanent Address)
was duly appointed guardian of the (person and) property of _____ ,
an infant, on _____ , by the Surrogate's Court of _____ ,
County, and thereupon duly qualified as guardian; and

　　WHEREAS, the former infant attained the age of eighteen on _____ , _____ , and

　　WHEREAS, the guardian has settled with the former infant all matters relating to the guardianship and to the property of the former infant, in which settlement the guardian is charged:

With amount of personal property and income thereof received	$ _____
With amount of income from infant's real estate received	$ _____
Total	$ _____

And is credited:

With amount expended in care of infant	$ _____
With amount applied to support, maintenance and education of infant	$ _____
Total	$ _____

Leaving a Balance of	$ _____

NOW, THEREFORE, in consideration of the payment and delivery to me,

_____ of _____,
(Name of Former Infant)   (Permanent Address)

$_____ in cash and property, the receipt of which is hereby acknowledged, being the balance in the hands of the guardian and also in consideration of a mutual agreement to waive a judicial accounting, I do for myself, my executors and administrators, release and forever discharge _____
(Name of Guardian)

and _____
          (Name of Depositories)

☐ Clerk of the Court, ☐ Guardianship Clerk of the Court, from any and every claim, demand, action and cause of action, account, liability or reckoning of every name and nature for and on account of any and every matter and thing whatsoever arising from or in any manner relating to or connected with my estate and guardianship.

IN WITNESS WHEREOF, we, the guardian and former infant, have set our hands and seals this _____ day of _____, _____ .

_____   _____
Signature of Guardian   Signature of Former Infant

_____   _____
Print Name   Print Name

On this _____ day of_____ , _____ , before me personally came
_____ and _____
known to me to be the individual(s) described In and who executed the foregoing instrument. Such person (s) duly swore to such instrument before me and duly acknowledged that he/she/they executed the same.

_____
Notary Public
Commission Expires:
(Affix Notary Stamp or Seal)

Signature of Attorney: _____

Print Name: _____

Firm Name: _____ Tel. No.: _____

Address of Attorney: _____

G-11   (9/00)   -2-

FORM G-12A   **Decree Closing Guardianship Account (Infant)**

At a Surrogate's Court of the
State of New York, held in and
for the County of _____,
at _____ , New York on
_____ , _____

PRESENT:
HON. _____
     SURROGATE
--X

Proceeding for the Appointment of a
Guardian for

_____

                   an Infant.
--X

DECREE TO CLOSE
GUARDIANSHIP ACCOUNT
(Infant)

File No. _____

     Upon reading the annexed petition of _____ , a former infant,
showing that (s) he attained majority on _____ _____ , and is presently entitled to
_____ , estate, and the supported affidavit of _____ ,
dated _____ , _____ ,

     Now on the motion of _____ , attorney for petitioner
_____ , it is

     ORDERED AND DECREED, that _____ , guardian of said former infant,
_____ , is hereby authorized and directed to pay to said former infant all
monies in the guardian's possession or in any bank standing to credit as such guardian of said infant and to
transfer and deliver to said former infant all other property of every character in the guardian's possession
belonging to the former infant, and to execute and deliver any and all assignments or other instruments in writing
necessary or requisite to transfer the legal title and possession of said property to the former infant, and it is further

     ORDERED AND DECREED, that any bank or trust company or savings and loan association or person
having possession of any of said former infant's estate Is hereby directed to pay over and deliver the same as
hereinabove ordered on presentation of a certified copy of this decree, and it is further

     ORDERED AND DECREED, that upon completion of payments and transfers aforesaid, the Letters of
Guardianship heretofore issued are revoked.

_____ , Surrogate

G- 12A (9/00)

FORM G-12B   Decree Closing Guardianship Account (Guardian)

At a Surrogate's Court of the
State of New York, held in and
for the County of _____ ,
at _____ , New York on
_____ , _____ .

PRESENT:
HON. _____
_____ SURROGATE
--X

Proceeding for the Appointment of a
Guardian for

_____
_____

         an Infant.
--X

DECREE TO CLOSE
GUARDIANSHIP ACCOUNT
(Guardian)

File No. _____

  Upon reading the annexed petition of _____ , guardian of
_____ , a former infant over 18, and the consent of said former infant
acknowledged the _____ day of _____ , _____ to the relief requested by the guardian,
and the instrument releasing the guardian pursuant to SCPA 2202.

  Now on the motion of _____ , attorney for the petitioner
_____ , it is

  ORDERED AND DECREED, that the guardian of former infant, _____ ,
is hereby authorized and directed to pay to the former infant all monies in the guardian's possession or in any bank
standing to credit as such guardian of the infant and to transfer and deliver to the former infant all other property
of every character in the guardian's possession belonging to the former infant, and to execute and deliver any and
all assignments or other instruments in writing necessary or requisite to transfer the legal title and possession of
said property to the former infant, and it is further

  ORDERED AND DECREED, that any bank or trust company or savings and load association or person
having possession of any of the former infant's estate is hereby directed to pay over and deliver the same as
hereinabove ordered on presentation of a certified copy of this decree, and it is further

  ORDERED AND DECREED, that upon completion of payments and transfers aforesaid, the Letters of
Guardianship heretofore issued are revoked.

            _____
            _____ , Surrogate

G-12B (9/00)

FORM GMD-1   SURROGATE'S COURT   SF-140

FORM GMD-1   **Petition for Appointment of Guardian of Person/Property/Person and Property/Limited Guardian of Property**

SURROGATE'S COURT OF THE STATE OF NEW YORK
COUNTY OF _____
--X
Proceeding for the Appointment of a
Guardian for

Pursuant to SCPA Article 17-A
--X

Filing Fee Paid $ _____
_____ Certs $ _____
_____ Certs $ _____
$ _____ Bond, Fee $ _____
Receipt No: _____ No: _____

PETITION FOR
APPOINTMENT OF GUARDIAN OF
[   ] PERSON
[   ] PROPERTY
[   ] PERSON AND PROPERTY
[   ] LIMITED GUARDIAN OF THE PROPERTY

File No. _____

TO THE SURROGATE'S COURT OF THE COUNTY OF _____

It is respectfully alleged:

1.   The name, permanent address, date of birth and telephone number of the Petitioner(s), and the Petitioner's(s') relationship to the [   ] intellectually disabled person   [   ] developmentally disabled person (hereafter known as Respondent) is as follows:

Name: _____ Telephone Number: _____

Permanent Address or Corporate Office: _____
                                       (Street and Number)

_____   _____   _____
        (City, Village, Town)   (State)   (Zip Code)

Mailing Address: _____
                            (If different from permanent address)

Date of Birth: _____ Interest/Relationship to Respondent: _____

Name: _____ Telephone Number: _____

Permanent Address or Corporate Office: _____
                                       (Street and Number)

_____   _____   _____
        (City, Village, Town)   (State)   (Zip Code)

Mailing Address: _____
                            (If different from permanent address)

Date of Birth: _____ Interest/Relationship to Respondent: _____

2(a). The name, permanent address, date of birth and marital status of the Respondent of this proceeding is as follows:

Name: _____

Permanent Address: _____
                                 (Street and Number)

_____   _____   _____
        (City, Village, Town)   (State)   (Zip Code)

Mailing Address: _____
                            (If different from permanent address)

Date of Birth: _____ Marital Status: _____
[Attach certified copy of birth certificate.]

2(b). [✔] The Respondent is not admitted to a group home or facility as defined in Section 1.03 and/or Article 15 of the Mental Hygiene Law.

[   ] The Respondent has been admitted to a group home or facility as defined in Section 1.03 and/or Article 15 of the Mental Hygiene Law.

_____, Name of group home or facility

_____, Address of group home or facility

_____, Name of Director of group home or facility

_____, Address of Director of group home or facility

_____, Name of the Director of the Mental Hygiene Legal Service

_____, Address of the Director of the Mental Hygiene Legal Service

3.   The names and permanent addresses of the parents of the Respondent and, if the Respondent is married, the Respondent's spouse are: **[If deceased give date of death and complete Number 6]**

Name of Parent: _____ Date of Birth: _____ Date of Death: _____

Permanent Address: _____
(Street and Number)

_____ _____ _____
(City, Village, Town)   (State)   (Zip Code)
Mailing Address: _____
(If different from permanent address)

Name of Parent: _____ Date of Birth: _____ Date of Death: _____

Permanent Address: _____
(Street and Number)

_____ _____ _____
(City, Village, Town)   (State)   (Zip Code)
Mailing Address: _____
(If different from permanent address)

Name of Spouse: _____ Date of Birth: _____ Date of Death: _____

Permanent Address: _____
(Street and Number)

_____ _____ _____
(City, Village, Town)   (State)   (Zip Code)
Mailing Address: _____
(If different from permanent address)

4.   The names of the adult children and adult siblings, eighteen (18) years of age or older, of the Respondent are as follows: **[Add rider if necessary.]**

Name: _____ Relationship to Respondent: _____

Permanent Address: _____
(Street and Number)

_____ _____ _____
(City, Village, Town)   (State)   (Zip Code)
Mailing Address: _____
(If different from permanent address)

Name: _____ Relationship to Respondent: _____

Permanent Address: _____
                              (Street and Number)

_____
        (City, Village, Town)   (State)   (Zip Code)
    Mailing Address: _____
                              (If different from permanent address)

Name: _____ Relationship to Respondent: _____

Permanent Address: _____
                              (Street and Number)

_____
        (City, Village, Town)   (State)   (Zip Code)
    Mailing Address: _____
                              (If different from permanent address)

Name: _____ Relationship to Respondent: _____

Permanent Address: _____
                              (Street and Number)

_____
        (City, Village, Town)   (State)   (Zip Code)
    Mailing Address: _____
                              (If different from permanent address)

5. The name and address of the primary care physician if other than a physician having submitted a certification with the petition:

Name of primary care physician: _____

Post Office Address: _____
                              (Street and Number)

_____
        (City, Village, Town)   (State)   (Zip Code)

6. If the Respondent's parents are both deceased, list the names and addresses of the nearest distributees of full age who live within the State of New York. **[If not applicable, so state.]**

Name	Permanent Address	Relationship

7. The name and address of the person(s) with whom the Respondent resides and/or the person(s) charged with his/her care and custody, if other than the parents or spouse:

Name	Permanent Address	Relationship

8.   If Respondent's parents, spouse, adult children or adult siblings are living but not proposed to be appointed guardian, standby guardian or alternate standby guardian, explain why below.

_____

_____

_____

9.   The persons proposed to be appointed guardian(s), standby guardian or alternate standby guardian are of sound mind, adult and competent.

10. **[Please check (a) and (b) for guardian of the Respondent's person and property; check (a) for guardianship of the Respondent's person only; or (b) for the guardianship of the Respondent's property only.]**

    (a)   [ ]   Petitioner(s) (is/are) requesting appointment of a guardian(s) of the Respondent's person and allege(s) the Petitioner(s) (is/are) motivated solely by the best interest of the Respondent for the reasons set forth below:

        _____

        _____

        _____

    (b)   [ ]   Petitioner(s) (is/are) requesting appointment of a guardian(s) of the Respondent's property and allege(s) that the estimated value of all REAL and PERSONAL property to which the Respondent is entitled is:

        $_____

[Answer question 11 only if requesting guardianship of the property.]

11. (a) PERSONAL PROPERTY **[State exact title of all bank accounts with account number and balance; any insurance policies by company, policy number, amount insured, name of insured and relationship to Respondent; the name, number of shares and value of all stocks, bonds, and any other personal property including all causes of action the Respondent may have.]**

_____

_____

_____

_____

    (b) REAL PROPERTY **[State whether real property is mortgaged or under a lien and the amount thereof. Indicate whether property is to be occupied as a residence by the Respondent. If not, indicate rental income or whether a sale of the property is contemplated.]**

Location of Property_____   Gross Value $_____

Respondent's Interest_____   Annual Income $_____

[ ] Mortgaged or [ ] Under a Lien $_____   Rental Income $_____

Residence to be occupied by Respondent [ ] yes [ ] no   Sale of property contemplated [ ] yes [ ] no

Official Forms

(c) ANNUAL INCOME OF RESPONDENT FROM ALL SOURCES:

(1) Wages to be received from: _____ $ _____
(2) Pension to be received from: _____ $ _____
(3) Income from trust: _____ $ _____
(4) Governmental entitlements from: _____ $ _____
(5) Other Income: _____ $ _____

    (d) STATE SOURCE OF ALL PROPERTY listed above. **[If any property is derived from an estate or as a result of the death of any person, name the decedent; his or her date of death and relationship to the Respondent; whether a fiduciary has been appointed; court name; file number; and type of letters. Provide a copy of any will or decree directing payment. List names and addresses of all banks, insurance companies and persons from whom payment is expected.]**

_____

_____

_____

12. Respondent has been duly certified as a person incapable of managing himself/herself and/or his/ her affairs by reason of [ ] intellectual disability   [ ] developmental disability, and such condition is permanent in nature or likely to continue indefinitely, as shown by the certification of:

_____Physician   dated: _____and

_____Physician/Licensed Psychologist   dated: _____

Said certifications shall be attached hereto and made part of the petition. **[Where certifications of two licensed physicians are used, at least one certification must evidence special qualifications to make the certification as set forth in SCPA Section 1750 or Section 1750-a. At least one certification must evidence that the physician is familiar with or has professional knowledge in the care and treatment of persons with an intellectual disability or developmental disability, as appropriate.]**

13. **[If application for a limited guardian of the property]** Respondent is over the age of 18 years and is employed by

_____ , located at _____

_____
    (Street/Number)   (City, Village/Town)   (State)   (Zip Code)

and is wholly or substantially self supporting by means of his/her wages or earnings from employment.

14. The names, permanent addresses, dates of birth and relationship of the guardian(s) is/are:

(a)   Name of Guardian, if other than Petitioner: _____

Permanent Address: _____
                                 (Street and Number)

_____
    (City, Village, Town)   (State)   (Zip Code)
Date of Birth:_____ Interest/Relationship to Respondent: _____

Education: _____ Qualifications: _____

to be appointed Guardian of the [ ] person
                              [ ] property
                              [ ] person and property
                              [ ] limited guardian of the property

Name of Guardian, if other than Petitioner: _____

Permanent Address: _____
                         (Street and Number)

_____
  (City, Village, Town)   (State)   (Zip Code)
Date of Birth:_____ Interest/Relationship to Respondent: _____

Education: _____ Qualifications: _____

to be appointed Guardian of the [   ] person
                    [   ] property
                    [   ] person and property
                    [   ] limited guardian of the property

(b)   Name of the Standby Guardian: _____

Permanent Address: _____
                         (Street and Number)

_____
  (City, Village, Town)   (State)   (Zip Code)
Date of Birth:_____ Interest/Relationship to Respondent: _____

Education: _____ Qualifications: _____

to be appointed Standby Guardian of the [   ] person
                          [   ] property
                          [   ] person and property
                          [   ] limited guardian of the property

(c)   Name of the First Alternate Standby Guardian: _____

Permanent Address:_____
                         (Street and Number)

_____
  (City, Village, Town)   (State)   (Zip Code)
Date of Birth: _____ Interest/Relationship to Respondent: _____

Education: _____ Qualifications: _____

to be appointed First Alternate Standby Guardian of the [   ] person
                                [   ] property
                                [   ] person and property
                                [   ] limited guardian of the property

(d)   Name of the Second Alternate Standby Guardian: _____

Permanent Address:_____
                         (Street and Number)

_____
  (City, Village, Town)   (State)   (Zip Code)
Date of Birth: _____ Interest/Relationship to Respondent: _____

Education: _____ Qualifications: _____

to be appointed Second Alternate Standby Guardian of the [   ] person
                                  [   ] property
                                [   ] person and property
                                [   ] limited guardian of the property

Official Forms

15. **[Check appropriate box]:**

[   ] (a) Respondent is able to attend the hearing to be scheduled by the court.

[   ] (b) Respondent's presence at the hearing should be dispensed with because Respondent is medically
            incapable of being present to the extent that attendance is likely to result in physical harm to Respondent.
            [Certification of certifying physician must so attest]

[   ] (c) Respondent's presence at the hearing should be dispensed with because **[Specify other circumstances
            enabling the court to determine that Respondent's presence at the hearing would not be in his/her
            best interest, attach rider if necessary.]**_____

            _____

[   ] (d) Respondent is less than 18 years of age, and Petitioner(s) request(s) that a hearing be dispensed with.

16. Respondent never has had a guardian appointed by will or deed or an acting guardian in socage, or a guardian of the
     person appointed pursuant to Section 384 or 384-b of the Social Services Law.

17. Petitioner(s) [   ] has/have [   ] does/do not have knowledge that a person nominated to be a guardian, or any individual
     eighteen years of age or over who resides in the home of the proposed guardian:

     a.   Is the subject of a report filed with the Statewide Central Register of Child Abuse and Maltreatment pursuant to
            the rules of Child Protective Services, following an investigation which determines that some credible evidence
            of alleged abuse or maltreatment exists, and/or

     b.   Has been the subject of or the Respondent in a Child Protective Proceeding commenced pursuant to law, which
            proceeding resulted in an order finding that the Respondent is an abused or neglected individual.

            [If Petitioner has such knowledge, attach an affidavit explaining in detail.]

18. Petitioner(s) has/have completed and submitted to the court the Request For Information Guardianship Form (OCFS
     3909) required to be submitted to the New York State Central Register of Child Abuse and Maltreatment.

19. **[If the Respondent is under the age of 18 years complete the following]:**

     The Respondent [   ] is   [   ] is not a Native American child under the Indian Child Welfare Act of 1978 (25 U.S.C.
     Sections 1901 - 1963).

20. There are no other persons interested in this proceeding upon whom process is required to be served other than those
     listed above.

21. No prior application has been made to any court for the relief requested herein, except: **[Enter "NONE" or specify]**

WHEREFORE, your Petitioner(s) respectfully request(s) that: **[Check and complete all relief requested]**

(a)   Letters of Guardianship of the

    [   ] person
    [   ] property
    [   ] person and property
    [   ] limited guardianship of the property
    of the Respondent be granted to _____

(b)   Appointment of _____ as Standby Guardian of the

    [   ] person
    [   ] property
    [   ] person and property
    [   ] limited guardianship of the property
    of the Respondent

(c)   Appointment of _____ as First Alternate Standby Guardian of the

    [   ] person
    [   ] property
    [   ] person and property
    [   ] limited guardianship of the property
    of the Respondent

(d)   Appointment of _____ as Second Alternate Standby Guardian of the

    [   ] person
    [   ] property
    [   ] person and property
    [   ] limited guardianship of the property
    of the Respondent

be granted, or to such other person or corporation as may be entitled thereto and that process issue to all interested persons who have not waived the issuance of same requiring them to show cause why such relief should not be granted.

(e)   The appearance of the Respondent   [   ] should be   [   ] should not be required at any hearing.

(f)   The guardian(s) of the person be authorized and empowered to make all decisions with respect to the medical and dental needs of the Respondent and to render consent to any medical procedures which are necessary to the health and welfare of the Respondent unless the court directs otherwise. A health care decision may include a decision to withhold or withdraw life-sustaining treatment treatment as defined in Section 1750-b(1) of the Surrogate's Court Procedure Act.

(g)   The guardian(s) of the property be directed to collect and receive all moneys and other property of the Respondent jointly with a clerk of the Surrogate's Court, or depository subject to the provisions of SCPA 1708, and shall deposit same in the name of the guardian(s), subject to order of the court with either:

    1. _____

        Name of Bank/Depository   Branch Address

    2. _____

        Name of Bank/Depository   Branch Address

    [List two Banks/Depositories in _____ County.]

(h)   The bond of the guardian(s) be dispensed with.

(l)   Additional relief requested _____

_____

Dated: _____

1. _____   2. _____
    (Signature of Petitioner)   (Signature of Petitioner)

_____   _____
    (Print Name)   (Print Name)

3. _____
    (Name of Corporate Petitioner)

_____
    (Signature of Officer)

_____
    (Print Name and Title of Officer)

STATE OF NEW YORK   )
COUNTY OF _____) ss.:

_____, being duly sworn deposes and says that I am/we are the
Petitioner(s) above named. I/we have read the foregoing petition and the same is true of my own knowledge except as to
matters therein stated to be alleged upon information and belief and as to those matters I/we believe them to be true.

_____   _____
    (Signature of Petitioner)   (Signature of Petitioner)

_____   _____
    (Print Name)   (Print Name)

_____
    (Name of Corporate Petitioner)

_____
    (Signature of Officer)

_____
    (Print Name and Title of Officer)

Sworn to before me this

_____ day of _____, _____

_____
Notary Public
Commission Expires:
(Affix Notary Stamp or Seal)

Signature of Attorney: _____

Print Name: _____

Firm Name: _____   Telephone Number: _____

Address of Attorney: _____

COMBINED OATH & DESIGNATION
[For use when Petitioner is an individual]

STATE OF NEW YORK   )
COUNTY OF _____) ss.:

_____ being duly sworn, deposes and says:

1.   OATH OF GUARDIAN: I am over eighteen (18) years of age, that I will well, faithfully and honestly discharge the duties of such guardian: That I am acquainted with the estate of said (intellectually disabled) (developmentally disabled) person and have read the statement contained in the foregoing petition as to the estimated value of same, and believe same to be correct, and that I am not ineligible to receive letters.

2.   DESIGNATION OF CLERK FOR SERVICE OF PROCESS: I hereby designate the Clerk of the Surrogate's Court of _____ County, and his/her successor in office, as a person on whom service of any process issuing from such Surrogate's Court may be made in like manner and with like effect as if it were served personally upon me, whenever I cannot be found within the state of New York after due diligence used.

My permanent address is: _____
                     (Street Address)   (City, Town, Village)   (State)   (Zip Code)

My permanent address is: _____
                     (Street Address)   (City, Town, Village)   (State)   (Zip Code)

_____   _____
  (Signature of Proposed Guardian)   (Signature of Proposed Guardian)

_____   _____
  (Print Name)   (Print Name)

On _____, _____, before me personally came

_____
to me known to be the person(s) described in and who executed the foregoing instrument. Such person(s) duly swore to such instrument before me and duly acknowledged that he/she/they executed the same.

_____
Notary Public
Commission Expires:
(Affix Notary Stamp or Seal)

-10-

FORM GMD-1   SURROGATE'S COURT   **SF-150**

COMBINED CORPORATE CONSENT & DESIGNATION
[For use when a Petitioner to be appointed is a corporation]

STATE OF NEW YORK)
COUNTY OF _____) ss.:

I, the undersigned, a _____ of
(Title)

_____
(Name of Corporation)
a corporation duly qualified to act in a fiduciary capacity without further security, being duly sworn, say:

1.   VERIFICATION: I have read the foregoing petition subscribed by me and know the contents thereof, and the same is true of my own knowledge, except as to the matters therein stated to be alleged upon information and belief, and as to those matters I believe it to be true.

2.   CONSENT: I consent to accept the appointment as [ ] Guardian [ ] Standby Guardian [ ] First Alternate Standby Guardian [ ] Second Alternate Standby Guardian of the [ ] person [ ] property [ ] person and property [ ] limited guardianship of the property of the Respondent described in the foregoing petition and consent to act as such fiduciary.

3.   DESIGNATION OF CLERK FOR SERVICE OF PROCESS: I hereby designate the Clerk of the Surrogate's Court of _____ County, and his/her successor in office, as a person on whom service of any process issuing from such Surrogate's Court may be made in like manner and with like effect as if it were served personally upon me, whenever I cannot be found within the state of New York after due diligence used.

_____
(Proposed Corporate Guardian)

_____
(Signature of Officer)

_____
(Print Name and Title of Officer)

On _____, _____, before me personally came _____,
to me known, who duly swore to the foregoing instrument and which did say that he/she resides at _____
_____ and that he/she is a _____ of
_____ the corporation described in and which executed such instrument, and
that he/she signed his/her name thereto by order of the Board of Directors of the corporation.

_____
Notary Public
Commission Expires:
(Affix Notary Stamp or Seal)

**FORM GMD-1A   Affidavit of Proposed Guardian of Person/Property/Person and
Property/Limited Guardian of Property**

SURROGATE'S COURT OF THE STATE OF NEW YORK
COUNTY OF _____
---X
Proceeding for the Appointment of a
Guardian for

                                        AFFIDAVIT OF PROPOSED
                                        GUARDIAN OF THE
                                        | | PERSON
                                        | | PROPERTY
                                        | | PERSON AND PROPERTY
                                        | | LIMITED GUARDIAN OF THE PROPERTY

Pursuant to SCPA Article 17-A
---X   File No. _____
STATE OF NEW YORK   )
COUNTY OF   ) ss.:

To the Surrogate's Court, County of _____

The undersigned _____, being duly sworn, deposes and says:

1.   I am a competent person over the age of eighteen (18) years, and I submit this affidavit in support of my petition to
be appointed guardian of [   ] an intellectually disabled person [   ] a developmentally disabled person.

2.   I have known the subject Respondent since _____ by reason of the
following: **[State relationship if any.]**

_____

_____

_____

_____

3.   I reside at_____, and the
other resident members of the household are: **[Include all persons residing there and their dates of birth.]**

_____   _____

_____   _____

_____   _____

4.   My educational background is as follows:

_____

5.   Not including minor traffic offenses and adjudications as a youthful offender or juvenile delinquent,

      (a) I have never been convicted of an offense against the law, except _____

_____

      (b) I have never forfeited bail or other collateral, except _____

_____

Official Forms

(c) I do not have any criminal charges pending against me, except _____

_____

6.   I have no physical or mental impairment, or medical condition, which would interfere with my ability to perform the duties of guardian of the [   ] intellectually disabled person   [   ] developmentally disabled person, except

_____

_____

7.   I am not addicted to narcotics or to alcohol.

8.   I am willing and able to undertake care, custody and control of the Respondent until the court determines otherwise.

9.   I believe that my appointment as guardian would be in the best interests of the Respondent for the following reasons:

_____

_____

_____

_____

_____
(Signature of Proposed Guardian)

_____
(Print Name)

Sworn to before me this

_____ day of _____, _____

_____
Notary Public
Commission Expires:
(Affix Notary Stamp or Seal)

FORM GMD-2A   Affidavit (Certification) of Examining Physician or Certified Psychologist

SURROGATE'S COURT OF THE STATE OF NEW YORK
COUNTY OF _____
---X
Proceeding for the Appointment of a
Guardian for

                              AFFIDAVIT (CERTIFICATION) OF EXAMINING
                              PHYSICIAN OR LICENSED PSYCHOLOGIST

                              File No. _____

Pursuant to SCPA Article 17-A
---X
STATE OF NEW YORK   )
COUNTY OF _____   ) ss.:

    I, _____ . [   ] Physician [   ] Licensed Psychologist,
being duly sworn, deposes and says:

[PLEASE ANSWER ALL QUESTIONS]

1. My license number is : _____

2. My offices are located at: _____

_____

3. My professional knowledge and/or background in the care and treatment of persons with [   ] intellectual disabilities
[   ] developmental disabilities is as follows:

_____

_____

_____

_____

4(a). I have examined the Respondent on: **[Set forth date(s).]**

_____

(b). **[Check appropriate box(es) and explain where requested]:**

     [   ] I have performed the following tests or evaluations of the Respondent. **[Set forth in detail the names
     of tests and/or evaluations, dates performed and results.]**

     _____

     _____

     [   ] I have reviewed the following tests or evaluations performed on Respondent. **[Set forth in detail the
     names of tests and/or evaluations, dates performed, results and names of doctors who performed the
     tests and/or evaluations.]**

     _____

     _____

Official Forms

5. The mental and physical condition of the Respondent is as follows: **[Describe in detail.]**

_____

_____

_____

6. **[Check appropriate box(es)]:**

INTELLECTUALLY DISABLED

[ ]   Based upon the foregoing, it is my conclusion the Respondent is an intellectually disabled person and in my opinion incapable of managing himself/herself and/or his/her affairs by reason of an intellectual disability. The nature and degree of the intellectual disability is as follows:

_____

_____

_____

DEVELOPMENTALLY DISABLED

[ ]   Based upon the foregoing, it is my conclusion that the Respondent is developmentally disabled and in my opinion he/she has an impaired ability to understand and appreciate the nature and consequences of decisions, which results in Respondent being incapable of managing himself/herself and/or his/her affairs by reason of developmental disability, and whose disability is attributable to:

[ ] (a) Cerebral palsy, which originated before the Respondent attained the age of twenty-two.
[Describe, in detail, the nature, degree and origin of the disability.]

_____

_____

_____

[ ] (b) Epilepsy, which originated before the Respondent attained the age of twenty-two.
[Describe, in detail, the nature, degree and origin of the disability.]

_____

_____

_____

[ ] (c) Neurological impairment, which originated before the Respondent attained the age of twenty-two.
[Describe, in detail, the nature, degree and origin of the disability.]

_____

_____

_____

[   ] (d) Autism, which originated before the Respondent attained the age of twenty-two.
[Describe, in detail, the nature, degree and origin of the disability.]

_____

_____

_____

[   ] (e) Traumatic head injury.
[Describe, in detail, the nature, degree and origin of the disability.]

_____

_____

_____

[   ] (f) A condition, which originated before the Respondent attained the age of twenty-two, found
to be closely related to an intellectual disability, because such condition results in similar impairment
of general intellectual functioning or adaptive behavior to that of intellectually disabled persons.
[Describe in detail the condition, and the nature, degree and origin of the disability.]

_____

_____

_____

[   ] (g) Dyslexia resulting from a disability described in subdivision (a) through (f) or an intellectual
disability which condition originated before the Respondent attained the age of twenty-two. **[Describe
in detail the nature, degree and origin of the developmental disability or intellectual disability.]**

_____

_____

_____

7. **[Check appropriate box]:**

[   ] The condition of the Respondent is permanent in nature or likely to continue indefinitely.

[   ] The condition of the Respondent is not permanent in nature nor likely to continue indefinitely.

8. **[Check appropriate box]:**

[   ] There are no circumstances warranting Respondent's nonappearance at the hearing required by the
court.

[   ] Respondent's presence at the hearing should be dispensed with because he/she is medically incapable
of being present to the extent that attendance is likely to result in physical harm to the Respondent.
[Explain in detail.]

_____

_____

_____

[ ] Respondent's presence at the hearing should be dispensed with for the following reasons: **[Set forth facts and circumstances which would result in the court finding that the Respondent's presence at the hearing would not be in his/her best interest.]**

_____

_____

_____

9. **[Check appropriate box for an intellectually disabled person]:**

[ ] Based upon the foregoing, it is my conclusion that the Respondent **is not capable** of understanding and appreciating the nature and consequences of health care decisions, including the benefits and risks of and alternatives to any proposed health care, and of reaching an informed decision in order to promote his/her own well being. A health care decision **may include** a decision to withhold or withdraw life-sustaining treatment as defined in Section 1750-b.1 of the Surrogate's Court Procedure Act.

[ ] Based upon the foregoing, it is my conclusion that the Respondent **is capable** of understanding and appreciating the nature and consequences of health care decisions, including the benefits and risks of and alternatives to any proposed health care, and of reaching an informed decision in order to promote his/her own well being. A health care decision **may include** a decision to withhold or withdraw life-sustaining treatment as defined in Section 1750-b.1 of the Surrogate's Court Procedure Act.

10. **[Check appropriate box for a developmentally disabled person]:**

[ ] Based upon the foregoing, it is my conclusion that the Respondent has a developmental disability, as defined in Section 1750-b(1) of the Surrogate's Court Procedure Act, which includes an intellectual disability, or results in a similar impairment of general intellectual functioning or adaptive behavior so that such person is incapable of managing himself or herself, and/or his or her affairs by reason of such developmental disability, and that the Respondent **is not capable** of understanding and appreciating the nature and consequences of health care decisions, including the benefits and risks of and alternatives to any proposed health care, and of reaching an informed decision in order to promote his/her own well being. A health care decision **may include** a decision to withhold or withdraw life-sustaining treatment as defined in Section 1750-b.1 of the Surrogate's Court Procedure Act.

[ ] Based upon the foregoing, it is my conclusion that the Respondent **is capable** of understanding and appreciating the nature and consequences of health care decisions, including the benefits and risks of and alternatives to any proposed health care, and of reaching an informed decision in order to promote his/her own well being. A health care decision **may include** a decision to withhold or withdraw life-sustaining treatment as defined in Section 1750-b.1 of the Surrogate's Court Procedure Act.

_____

Signature of Physician/Licensed Psychologist

_____

Print Name

Sworn to before me this

_____ day of _____

_____

Notary Public
Commission Expires:
(Affix Notary Stamp or Seal)

-4-

FORM GMD-2B   Affirmation (Certification) of Examining Physician

SURROGATE'S COURT OF THE STATE OF NEW YORK
COUNTY OF _____
---X
Proceeding for the Appointment of a
Guardian for

**AFFIRMATION (CERTIFICATION)
OF EXAMINING PHYSICIAN**

File No. _____

Pursuant to SCPA Article 17-A
---X

STATE OF NEW YORK   )
COUNTY OF _____) ss.:

I, _____, a physician duly licensed to practice
medicine in the State of New York, under penalty of perjury affirms as follows:

[PLEASE ANSWER ALL QUESTIONS]

1.   My license number is : _____

2.   My offices are located at: _____
_____

3.   My professional knowledge and/or background in the care and treatment of persons with [   ] intellectual
disabilities [   ] developmental disabilities is as follows:

_____
_____
_____
_____

4(a).   I have examined the Respondent on: **[Set forth date(s).]**

_____

(b).   **[Check appropriate box(es) and explain where requested]:**

[   ]   I have performed the following tests or evaluations of the Respondent. **[Set forth in detail the names of
tests and/or evaluations, dates performed and results.]**

_____
_____

[   ]   I have reviewed the following tests or evaluations performed on Respondent. **[Set forth in detail the
names of tests and/or evaluations, dates performed, results and names of doctors who performed
the tests and/or evaluations.]**

_____
_____

Official Forms

5. The mental and physical condition of the Respondent is as follows: **[Describe in detail.]**

_____

_____

_____

6. **[Check appropriate box(es)]:**

INTELLECTUALLY DISABLED

[ ] Based upon the foregoing, it is my conclusion the Respondent is an intellectually disabled person and in my opinion incapable of managing himself/herself and/or his/her affairs by reason of intellectual disability. The nature and degree of the intellectual disability is as follows:

_____

_____

_____

DEVELOPMENTALLY DISABLED

[ ] Based upon the foregoing, it is my conclusion that the Respondent is developmentally disabled and in my opinion he/she has an impaired ability to understand and appreciate the nature and consequences of decisions, which results in Respondent being incapable of managing himself/herself and/or his/her affairs by reason of developmental disability, and whose disability is attributable to:

[ ] (a) Cerebral palsy, which originated before the Respondent attained the age of twenty-two. **[Describe, in detail, the nature, degree and origin of the disability.]**

_____

_____

_____

[ ] (b) Epilepsy, which originated before the Respondent attained the age of twenty-two. **[Describe, in detail, the nature, degree and origin of the disability.]**

_____

_____

_____

[ ] (c) Neurological impairment, which originated before the Respondent attained the age of twenty-two. **[Describe, in detail, the nature, degree and origin of the disability.]**

_____

_____

_____

[   ] (d) Autism, which originated before the Respondent attained the age of twenty-two.
[Describe, in detail, the nature, degree and origin of the disability.]

_____

_____

[   ] (e) Traumatic head injury.
 [Describe, in detail, the nature, degree and origin of the disability.]

_____

_____

_____

[   ] (f) A condition, which originated before the Respondent attained the age of twenty-two, found to
be closely related to an intellectual disability, because such condition results in similar impairment of
general intellectual functioning or adaptive behavior to that of intellectually disabled persons.
[Describe in detail the condition, and the nature, degree and origin of the disability.]

_____

_____

_____

[   ] (g) Dyslexia resulting from a disability described in subdivision (a) through (f) or an intellectual
disability which condition originated before the Respondent attained the age of twenty-two.
**[Describe in detail the nature, degree and origin of the developmental disability or intellectual
disability.]**

_____

_____

_____

7. **[Check appropriate box]:**

[   ] The condition of the Respondent is permanent in nature or likely to continue indefinitely.

[   ] The condition of the Respondent is not permanent in nature nor likely to continue indefinitely.

8. **[Check appropriate box]:**

[   ] There are no circumstances warranting Respondent's nonappearance at the hearing required by the court.

[   ] Respondent's presence at the hearing should be dispensed with because he/she is medically incapable of
being present to the extent that attendance is likely to result in physical harm to the Respondent.
[Explain in detail.]

_____

_____

_____

| | Respondent's presence at the hearing should be dispensed with for the following reasons: **[Set forth facts and circumstances which would result in the court finding that the Respondent's presence at the hearing would not be in his/her best interest.]**

_____

_____

_____

9. **[Check appropriate box for intellectually disabled person]:**

[ ] Based upon the foregoing, it is my conclusion that the Respondent **is not capable** of understanding and appreciating the nature and consequences of health care decisions, including the benefits and risks of and alternatives to any proposed health care, and of reaching an informed decision in order to promote his/her own well being. A health care decision **may include** a decision to withhold or withdraw life-sustaining treatment as defined in Section 1750-b.1 of the Surrogate's Court Procedure Act.

[ ] Based upon the foregoing, it is my conclusion that the Respondent **is capable** of understanding and appreciating the nature and consequences of health care decisions, including the benefits and risks of and alternatives to any proposed health care, and of reaching an informed decision in order to promote his/her own well being. A health care decision **may include** a decision to withhold or withdraw life-sustaining treatment as defined in Section 1750-b.1 of the Surrogate's Court Procedure Act.

10. **[Check appropriate box for a developmentally disabled person]:**

[ ] Based upon the foregoing, it is my conclusion that the Respondent has a developmental disability, as defined in Section 1750-b(1) of the Surrogate's Court Procedure Act, which includes an intellectual disability, or results in a similar impairment of general intellectual functioning or adaptive behavior so that such person is incapable of managing himself or herself, and/or his or her affairs by reason of such developmental disability, and that the Respondent **is not capable** of understanding and appreciating the nature and consequences of health care decisions, including the benefits and risks of and alternatives to any proposed health care, and of reaching an informed decision in order to promote his/her own well being. A health care decision **may include** a decision to withhold or withdraw life-sustaining treatment as defined in Section 1750-b.1 of the Surrogate's Court Procedure Act.

[ ] Based upon the foregoing, it is my conclusion that the Respondent **is capable** of understanding and appreciating the nature and consequences of health care decisions, including the benefits and risks of and alternatives to any proposed health care, and of reaching an informed decision in order to promote his/her own well being. A health care decision **may include** a decision to withhold or withdraw life-sustaining treatment as defined in Section 1750-b.1 of the Surrogate's Court Procedure Act.

_____

Signature of Physician

_____

Print Name

Dated: _____

-4-

FORM GMD-3   **Waiver of Process, Renunciation and Consent to Appointment of Guardian**

SURROGATE'S COURT OF THE STATE OF NEW YORK
COUNTY OF _____
---X
Proceeding for the Appointment of a
Guardian for

WAIVER OF PROCESS
RENUNCIATION AND CONSENT
TO APPOINTMENT OF A GUARDIAN

File No. _____

Pursuant to SCPA Article 17-A
---X

The undersigned _____, whose permanent address is

_____
(Street and Number)   (City, Village, Town)

_____
(State)   (Zip Code)

and who is a competent person over the age of eighteen (18) years and whose interest in the above-named proceeding is as follows:

[Check appropriate interest]

    [ ] Parent of the above-named alleged [ ] intellectually disabled person [ ] developmentally disabled person.

    [ ] Spouse of the above-named alleged [ ] intellectually disabled person [ ] developmentally disabled person.

    [ ] An adult child of the above-named alleged [ ] intellectually disabled person [ ] developmentally disabled person.

    [ ] An adult brother/sister of the above-named alleged [ ] intellectually disabled person
                                   [ ] developmentally disabled person

    | Other **[Specify]** _____

hereby personally appears in this proceeding and

1. renounces all right to apply as a guardian under Article 17-A of the SCPA

2. waives the issuance and service of process in this matter, and

3. consents that _____ be named the Guardian(s) of the

    [ ] person
    [ ] property
    [ ] person and property
    [ ] limited guardianship of the property

and that _____ be named the Standby
Guardian of the

    [ ] person
    [ ] property
    [ ] person and property
    [ ] limited guardianship of the property

GMD-3 (4/2018)   -1-

and that _____ be named the First Alternate
Standby Guardian of the

      [ ] person
      [ ] property
      [ ] person and property
      [ ] limited guardianship of the property

and that _____ be named the Second Alternate
Standby Guardian of the

      [ ] person
      [ ] property
      [ ] person and property
      [ ] limited guardianship of the property

and that such letters may be granted to said person(s) or to any other person(s) entitled thereto without notice to the undersigned.

                                                  _____

Date: _____

                                                  (Signature)

                                                _____

                                                (Print Name)

STATE OF _____) ss.:
COUNTY OF _____)

    On _____, _____, before me personally came

_____ to
me known to be the person described in and who executed the foregoing instrument. Such person duly swore to such instrument before me and duly acknowledged that he/she executed the same.

_____
Notary Public
Commission Expires:
(Affix Notary Stamp or Seal)

FORM GMD-4   Consent, Oath and Designation

SURROGATE'S COURT OF THE STATE OF NEW YORK
COUNTY OF _____
---X
Proceeding for the Appointment of a
Guardian for

CONSENT, OATH AND
DESIGNATION

File No. _____

Pursuant to SCPA Article 17-A
---X
STATE OF NEW YORK   )
COUNTY OF _____) ss.:

_____, being duly sworn, deposes and says:
I am an adult competent person and I do hereby consent to the relief requested in the petition and my appointment as
[   ] standby guardian   [   ] first alternate standby guardian   [   ] second alternate standby guardian
of the   [   ] person
         [   ] property
         [   ] person and property
         [   ] limited guardianship of the property

of the above-named Respondent and I waive the issuance and service of process upon me herein. I will make an application for confirmation in accordance with SCPA §1757 and will be subject to a formal hearing if the Respondent is eighteen years of age or over. I agree that upon the death, incapacity, renunciation or removal of the last guardian who has been designated to serve prior to me, I will immediately assume the duties of guardian
of the   [   ] person
         [   ] property
         [   ] person and property
         [   ] limited guardianship of the property

and will seek to have this Court confirm my appointment within (180) days of my assumption of duties.

     1. OATH OF   [   ] STANDBY GUARDIAN   [   ] FIRST ALTERNATE STANDBY GUARDIAN |]
SECOND ALTERNATE STANDBY GUARDIAN: I am over eighteen (18) years of age, that I will well, faithfully and honestly discharge the duties of
[   ] standby guardian   [   ] first alternate standby guardian   [   ] second alternate standby guardian
of the   [   ] person
         [   ] property
         [   ] person and property
         [   ] limited guardianship of the property

of the above named Respondent, that I am acquainted with the estate of the Respondent; and that I am not ineligible to receive letters.

     2. DESIGNATION OF CLERK FOR SERVICE OF PROCESS: I do hereby designate the Clerk of the Surrogate's Court of _____ County, and his/her successor in office, as a person on whom service of any process issuing from such Surrogate's Court may be made, in like manner and with like effect as if it were served personally upon me whenever I cannot be found and served within the State of New York after due diligence used.

My permanent address is : _____

    (Street Address)   (City/Town/Village)   (State)   (Zip)

                            _____

                            (Signature of Proposed Guardian)

                            _____

                            (Print Name)

On _____, _____, before me personally came

_____
to me known to be the person described in and who executed the foregoing instrument. Such person duly swore to such instrument before me and duly acknowledged that he/she executed the same.

_____
Notary Public
Commission Expires:
(Affix Notary Stamp or Seal)

FORM GMD-5   Decree Appointing Guardian*

At a Surrogate's Court of the State of New
York, held in and for the County of
_____ at _____,
New York on _____ 20 _____.

PRESENT:
HON: _____

  SURROGATE

In the Matter of the Guardianship of

_____,

Pursuant to SCPA Article 17-A

DECREE
APPOINTING
GUARDIAN

File No. _____

(*as of 1/1/04*)

    Upon the reading and filing of the petition of _____, duly verified
the _____ day of _____, 20 _____, applying for appointment of a guardian of the (person) (and) (property) of _____ a
(mentally retarded) (developmentally disabled) person, and the certifications
of _____ dated _____, 20 _____, and _____
dated _____, 20 _____, and the matter having come on to be
heard before this Court on _____, 20 _____, and the Court having
found that _____ is a (mentally retarded) (developmentally disabled)
person, incapable of managing (himself/herself) and/or his/her affairs by
reason of (mental retardation) (developmental disability), and that such
condition is permanent in nature or likely to continue indefinitely and the
best interests of said person would be promoted by the appointment of a
guardian of his/her (person) (and) (property) [and the proposed guardian
having filed a bond with sureties pursuant to statute, which has been
approved by the Surrogate], it is hereby

    ORDERED that _____, upon taking the official oath and filing

_____

    * Official Forms GMD-5 and GMD-6 are no longer included in the list of official forms
provided by the Office of Court Administration. Please consult your local Surrogate's Court
for their preferred forms of Decrees.

Official Forms

the designation as required by law, be and hereby is appointed guardian of the (person) (and) (property) of _____, and it is further

[If applicable] ORDERED that the filing of the bond is dispensed with the guardian is directed to collect and receive the money and property belonging to _____ jointly with _____ and it is further

ORDERED that _____ file with the Court the annual account required by law, and it is further

ORDERED that _____ (are) (is) appointed standby guardian(s) for said (mentally retarded) (developmentally disabled) person, subject to the confirmation of this Court pursuant to section 1757 of the Surrogate's Court Procedure Act, and it is further

ORDERED that _____ (are) (is) appointed alternate standby guardian(s) for said (mentally retarded) (developmentally disabled) person, subject to the confirmation of this Court pursuant to section 1757 of the Surrogate's Court Procedure Act, and it is further

ORDERED that Letters of Guardianship be issued accordingly.

_____

                                                    SURROGATE

FORM GMD-6   Decree Appointing Limited Guardian of Property[*]

At a Surrogate's Court of the State of New
York held in and for the County of
_____, at _____,
New York on _____ 20 _____.

PRESENT:
HON: _____

     SURROGATE

In the Matter of the Guardianship of _____ Pursuant to SCPA Article 17-A	DECREE APPOINTING LIMITED GUARDIAN OF PROPERTY File No. _____ *(as of 1/1/04)*

     Upon reading and filing the petition of _____ duly verified the
_____ day of _____, 20 _____, applying for the appointment of a limited guardian of the property of _____, a (mentally
retarded) (developmentally disabled) person, and the certifications of
_____, dated _____, 20 _____, and _____, 20
_____, and the matter having come on to be heard before this Court on
_____, 20 _____, and the Court having found that _____
is a (mentally retarded) (developmentally disabled) person, incapable of
handling his/her affairs by reason of (mental retardation) (developmental
disability) and that such condition is permanent in nature or likely to
continue indefinitely and that said person is at least eighteen years of age and
it wholly or substantially self supporting by means of his/her wages or
earnings from employment, and that the best interests of said person would
be promoted by the appointment of a limited guardian of his/her property
[and the proposed guardian having filed a bond with sureties pursuant to
statute, which has been approved by the Surrogate], it is hereby

     ORDERED that _____, upon taking the official oath and filing
the designation as required by law, be and hereby is appointed limited

_____

[*] Official Forms GMD-5 and GMD-6 are no longer included in the list of official forms
provided by the Office of Court Administration. Please consult your local Surrogate's Court
for their preferred forms of Decrees.

guardian of the property of _____ and that letters be issued accordingly, and it is further,

   ORDERED that these letters are limited to the receiving and administration of only such property of _____ as shall be received from other than his/her wages or earnings, and it is further

   [If applicable] ORDERED that the filing of the bond is dispensed with and the guardian is directed to collect and receive the money and property belonging to _____ jointly with _____, and it is further

   ORDERED that the guardian file with the Court the annual account required by law.

_____

                                                    SURROGATE

FORM GMD-7   **17-A Guardianship Citation**

File No. _____

SURROGATE'S COURT-   COUNTY

17-A GUARDIANSHIP CITATION

THE PEOPLE OF THE STATE OF NEW YORK
By the Grace of God Free and Independent

TO:

A petition having been filed by _____, who is/are
domiciled at _____

YOU ARE HEREBY CITED TO SHOW CAUSE before the Surrogate's Court, _____ County,
at _____, New York , on _____, _____, at
_____ o'clock in the _____noon of that day, why letters of guardianship of the

[ ] person
[ ] property
[ ] person and property
[ ] limited guardianship of the property
of _____ should not be granted to _____;

why the appointment of _____ as Standby Guardian of the
[ ] person
[ ] property
[ ] person and property
[ ] limited guardianship of the property
of _____ should not be granted;

why the appointment of _____ as First Alternate Standby Guardian of the
[ ] person
[ ] property
[ ] person and property
[ ] limited guardianship of the property
of _____ should not be granted;

why the appointment of _____ as Second Alternate Standby Guardian of the
[ ] person
[ ] property
[ ] person and property
[ ] limited guardianship of the property
of _____ should not be granted;

and why a hearing [ ] should be held [ ] should not be held;
and why the appearance of Respondent [ ] should be [ ] should not be required at the hearing;
and why the guardian(s) of the person should not be authorized and empowered to make all decisions with respect to the
medical and dental needs of the Respondent and to render consent to any medical procedures which are necessary to the
health and welfare of the Respondent, unless the court directs otherwise. A health care decision may include a decision to
withhold or withdraw life-sustaining treatment as defined in Section 1750-b(1) of the Surrogate's Court Procedure Act.
[State further relief requested]

Dated, Attested and Sealed,   HON.
          Surrogate
_____, _____
(Seal)

_____
, Chief Clerk

Attorney for Petitioner(s): _____ Telephone Number: _____
Address of Attorney: _____

[Note: This citation is served upon you as required by law. You are not required to appear. If you fail to appear it will be assumed you do not
object to the relief requested. You have a right to have an attorney appear for you.]
GMD-7 (4/2018)

FORM GMD-8   Notice of Petition

SURROGATE'S COURT OF THE STATE OF NEW YORK
COUNTY OF _____
---X
Proceeding for the Appointment of a
Guardian for

                                     NOTICE OF PETITION
                                      SCPA §1753 (2)

                        File No. _____

Pursuant to SCPA Article 17-A
---X

Notice is hereby given that:

1. On the _____ day of _____, 20____, _____,
                                          (Name of Petitioner(s))
whose address is/are_____,

filed a petition with the Surrogate's Court, County of _____, which is returnable on
_____, _____, at _____ o'clock in the _____ noon of that day for the appointment of

[   ] _____, guardian(s)
                        (Name(s))
[   ] _____, standby guardian
                        (Name)
[   ] _____, first alternate standby guardian
                        (Name)
[   ] _____, second alternate standby guardian
                        (Name)

of the [   ] person
       [   ] property
       [   ] person and property
       [   ] limited guardianship of the property.

2. The name and post office address of each person entitled to notice of the petition who has not been served or has not appeared, or waived service of process, with a statement with regard to such person's relationship, if any, to the intellectually disabled person developmentally disabled person, is as follows:

NAME	MAILING ADDRESS	RELATIONSHIP

(USE ADDITIONAL SHEETS IF NECESSARY)

Date: _____, _____

Attorney for Petitioner(s) _____ Telephone Number: _____

Address of Attorney: _____

GMD-8 (4/2018)   -1-

AFFIDAVIT OF MAILING NOTICE OF PETITION

STATE OF NEW YORK   )
COUNTY OF   ) ss.:

_____, residing at _____
being duly sworn, deposes and says that he/she is over the age of 18 years, that on the _____ day of
_____, _____, he/she mailed, by certified mail, a copy of the foregoing Notice of Petition contained
in a securely closed, postpaid wrapper directed to each of the persons named in said notice at the places set opposite their
respective names.

_____
(Signature)

Sworn to before me this

_____
(Print Name)

_____ day of_____, _____

_____
Notary Public
Commission Expires:
(Affix Notary Stamp or Seal)

Attorney for Petitioner(s): _____ Telephone Number: _____

Address of Attorney: _____

-2-

FORM I-1   Inventory of Assets

SURROGATE'S COURT OF THE STATE OF NEW YORK
COUNTY OF

--x

In the Matter of

Deceased.

--x

TO BE COMPLETED BY FIDUCIARY or ATTORNEY FOR FIDUCIARY	
Total Estate Assets (see below)*	
Filing fee SCPA 2402(7)	
Filing fee initially paid	
Balance (Refund) Due	$0.00

INVENTORY OF ASSETS (Rule §207.20)

File No: _____

The undersigned, a fiduciary or attorney for the fiduciary of the above Decedent's estate, certifies that the following constitutes the gross estate for tax purposes and identifies whether non-estate assets exist. Complete below according to the following value categories:

Category **A** - under $10,000; Category **B** - $10,000 to under $20,000; Category **C** - $20,000 to under $50,000;
Category **D** - $50,000 to under $100,000; Category **E** - $100,000 to under $250,000;
Category **F** - $250,000 to under $500,000; Category **G** - $500,000 or over.

Date of Death: _____   Date of Letters: _____   Type of Letters: _____

Name of Fiduciary(ies) and, if changed, fiduciary(ies) address: _____

ASSETS INDIVIDUALLY OWNED BY DECEDENT   **CATEGORY**
OR PAYABLE TO ESTATE

1. Real Estate
2. Stocks and Bonds
3. Insurance Payable to Estate
4. IRAs, 401 Ks Payable to Estate
5. Mortgages or Notes Held by Decedent
6. Cash
7. Miscellaneous
8. Firearms (Check appropriate box)   ○ Yes   see attached firearms inventory
                                              ○ None

  ***TOTAL ESTATE ASSETS**

NON-ESTATE ASSETS - CHECK YES OR NO TO EACH OF THE FOLLOWING:

9.   Living Trust   ○ Yes   ○ No
     If yes, set forth the Name of the Trustee(s)
10. Gifts in Excess of Federal Annual Exclusion Made   ○ Yes   ○ No
     Within 3 Years of Decedent's Death
11. Jointly Held Property (Real or Personal)   ○ Yes   ○ No
12. Insurance Payable to Beneficiary   ○ Yes   ○ No
13. IRAs, 401K's Payable to Beneficiary   ○ Yes   ○ No
14. Annuities   ○ Yes   ○ No
15. Powers of Appointment   ○ Yes   ○ No
16. Cause(s) of Action Pending   ○ Yes   ○ No
     If yes, identify Court and Index Number

Certified to be true on the _____ day of _____ , 20 _____

Signature _____   Attorney's Name _____

Print Name _____   Attorney's Address _____

I-1 3/2016   Attorney's Telephone No. _____

FORM I-2   Firearms Inventory

SURROGATE'S COURT OF THE STATE OF NEW YORK _____ **COUNTY**

In The Matter of the Estate of   **FIREARMS INVENTORY**
                                   (SCPA §2509)

_____

_____ Deceased.   **FILE NUMBER** _____

The undersigned, [ ] a fiduciary, or [ ] an attorney of record certifies that the following firearms, as defined by Section 265.00 of the Penal Law, make up part of the decedent's estate.

Name of Fiduciary or Attorney: _____
         (Address, if changed): _____

	Make:	Model:	Caliber or Gauge:	Serial #:	Valuation:
1					$
2					
3					
4					
5					
6					
7					
8					
9					
10					
11					
12					
			TOTAL: *(as indicated in section F2 of Inventory of Assets)*		

☐ *(mark box if more entries are necessary - and attach extra pages)*

        ATTORNEY   Certified to be true on _____, 20____

Name: _____   _____

Address: _____   **Signature**

_____

Telephone: _____   **Print Name**

A copy of this Inventory must also be filed with DCJS at:

    Firearms Inventories filed with the Surrogate's Court will be kept in a secure location separate from the estate file and will be made available for inspection only to persons interested in the proceeding and their counsel, unless otherwise ordered by the Court.

      Division of Criminal Justice Services
      Alfred E. Smith Building
      80 South Swan Street
      Albany, NY 12110

I-2   5/2013

FORM JA-1   **Petition for Judicial Settlement of Account**

DO NOT LEAVE ANY ITEMS BLANK

SURROGATE'S COURT OF THE STATE OF NEW YORK
COUNTY OF _____
---X

ACCOUNTING BY _____

as the _____

of the ESTATE OF _____

a/k/a _____
                                           Deceased.
---X

PETITION FOR JUDICIAL
SETTLEMENT OF ACCOUNT OF

☐ Executor
☐ Administrator
☐ Trustee
☐ Other [specify] _____

File No. _____

TO THE SURROGATE'S COURT, COUNTY OF _____

It is respectfully alleged:

1.   The name(s), and address(es) of the petitioner(s), the type and date of letters issued, and the amount and surety of petitioner's (s') bond, if any, are as follows:

Name: _____

Address: _____
             (Street Address)   (City/Town/Village)

_____
   (County)   (State)   (Zip)   (Telephone Number)

Mailing address: _____
             (if different from above)

Type of letters issued: _____   Date letters issued: _____

Amount of bond: $ _____   Name of surety: _____

Name: _____

Address: _____
             (Street Address)   (City/Town/Village)

_____
   (County)   (State)   (zip)   (Telephone Number)

Mailing address: _____
   (if different from above)

Type of letters issued: _____   Date letters issued: _____

JA-1 (4/98)

2.   The decedent's name, date of death and domicile are as follows:

Name: _____   Date of death: _____

Domicile: _____
                (Street Address)   (City/Town/Village)

_____
                (State)   (Zip Code)

Township of: _____   County of: _____

3.   The petitioner(s) present (s) and render (s) herewith, a verified account of petitioner's (s') proceedings in this estate or trust, for the period from _____ to _____, showing the gross value of assets, including principal and income, to be the sum of $ _____

4.   ☐   (a)   An order was entered in this Court on _____ ,20___

          ☐   Exempting the estate from tax

          ☐   Fixing and assessing the tax due

    [Attach a copy of the tax order and receipt]

      ☐   (b)   The following return (s) (was) (were) filed:

          ☐   ET-90 [For decedent's dying on or after May 25, 1990]. A copy was filed with the Surrogate's Court   ☐ Yes   ☐ No

          ☐   TT-385 (For decedent's dying before May 25, 1990]

          ☐   706 or 706NA

    The estate taxes with respect to this estate were paid in full. [Attach a copy of letter of discharge.]

      ☐   (c.)   No tax proceeding or return was required for this estate.

5.   The rendering of such account at this time is proper because check appropriate reason]

      ☐   seven months have elapsed since letters were issued to petitioner(s);

      ☐   letters issued to the petitioner(s) have been revoked,

      ☐   more than one year has elapsed since the preceding account of the petitioner(s) was settled;

      ☐   other reason [specify]:

6.   The names and post-office addresses of all persons and parties interested in this proceeding who are required to be cited under the provisions of Surrogate's Court Procedure Act §221 0, or otherwise, or concerning whom or which the Court is required to have information, are set forth in subdivision (a) or (b):

      (a)   All persons and parties so interested herein who are of full age and sound mind, or which are corporations or associations, are as follows:

Official Forms

Name	Nature of Interest	P.O. Address

(b)   **All persons so interested herein who are infants or incompetents** or persons believed to be mentally incapable to adequately protect their rights, or persons whose existence, identity, or whereabouts are unknown (including persons who are virtually represented under SCPA §315) are as follows:

[Furnish **all information specified in NOTE** at bottom of page]

Name	Nature of Interest	P.O. Address

[NOTE: In the case of each infant, state (a) name, birth date, age, nature of interest, domicile, residence address, and the person with whom he/she resides; (b) whether or not he/she has a guardian or testamentary guardian, and whether or not his/her father, or if he/she be dead, his/her mother is living; and (c) the name and post office address of any guardian and any living parent. In the case of each incompetent or person incapable of adequately protecting his/her rights, state (a) name, nature of interest, and post office address; (b) facts regarding his/her incompetency, including whether or not a committee has been appointed and whether or not he/she has been committed at any institution; (c) the names and post office addresses of any committee, conservator, guardian, and person or institution having care and custody of him/her, and any relative or friend having an interest in his/her welfare. In the case of unknowns, describe in identical language to be used in citation for publication. In the case of a person confined as a prisoner, state place of incarceration. With respect to virtual representation see Uniform Court Rule, §207.18.]

7.   There are no persons interested in this proceeding other than those herein about mentioned.

8.   No prior application has been made to this or any other court for the relief requested in this petition.

WHEREFORE the petitioner(s) pray (s) that the account of proceedings be judicially settled

[specify any other relief requested.]

_____
_____
_____
_____
_____

and that process be issued to all necessary parties who have not appeared to show cause why the relief requested should not be granted; and that an order be granted directing the service of process pursuant to the provisions of SCPA Article 3 upon such persons named in Paragraph (6) whose names or whereabouts are unknown and cannot be ascertained or who may be persons on whom service by personal delivery cannot be made.

Dated: _____

1. _____   2. _____
    (Signature of Petitioner)   (Signature of Petitioner)

_____   _____
    (Print Name)   (Print Name)

3. _____
    (Name of Corporate Petitioner)

_____
    (Signature of Officer)

_____
    (Print Name and Title of Officer)

Official Forms

FORM JA-1   SURROGATE'S COURT   **SF-178**

VERIFICATION

[For use when petitioner is an individual]

STATE OF NEW YORK   )

COUNTY OF _____)   ss.:

    The undersigned, the petitioner (s), named in the foregoing petition, being duly sworn, say (s): (1) (We) have read the foregoing petition subscribed by me (us) and know the contents thereof, and the same is true of (my) (our) own knowledge, except as to the matters therein stated to be alleged upon information and belief, and as to those matters (1) (we) believe it to be true.

_____   _____
(Signature of Petitioner)   (Signature of Petitioner)

_____   _____
(Print Name)   (Print Name)

Sworn to before me on
_____, 20____

_____
Notary Public
Commission Expires:
(Affix Notary Stamp or Seal)

Signature of Attorney: _____

Print Name: _____

Name of Attorney: _____   Tel. No.: _____

Address of Attorney: _____

VERIFICATION

[For use when petitioner is a bank or trust company]

STATE OF NEW YORK   )

COUNTY OF _____)   ss.:

I, the undersigned, a _____ of
                                                               (Title)

_____
                                 (Name of Bank or Trust Company)

being duly sworn, say (s),

I have read the foregoing petition subscribed by me and know the contents thereof, and the same is true of my own knowledge, except as to the matters stated to be alleged upon information and belief, and as to those matters I believe it to be true.

                      (Name of Bank or Trust)

BY _____
               (Signature of Officer)

_____
               (Print Name and Title)

Sworn to before me on
_____,20____

Notary Public
Commission Expires:
(Affix Notary Stamp or Seal)

Signature of Attorney: _____

Print Name: _____

Name of Attorney: _____   Tel. No.: _____

Address of Attorney: _____

FORM JA-2   **Receipt and Release**

SURROGATE'S COURT OF THE STATE OF NEW YORK
COUNTY OF _____
---x
ACCOUNTING BY _____   RECEIPT AND RELEASE

as the _____   File No. _____

of the ESTATE OF _____

a/k/a _____

                     Deceased.
---x

The undersigned, being of full age, sound mind and under no disability, and entitled to share in the estate of the above named decedent as a [check one] ☐ legatee under a will, ☐ distributee of an intestate share, ☐ trust beneficiary, ☐ creditor of the estate, ☐ other [specify]

(a)   Acknowledges that each fiduciary named above has fully and satisfactorily accounted for all assets of the estate;

(b)   Approves the written account verified on _____,20_____ as submitted to the undersigned;
(Delete paragraphs (a) and (b) if the undersigned is not interested in or affected by the amount of the residuary estate or trust, or if being made pursuant to a decree of the court.]

(c)   Acknowledges receipt of money paid or property transferred or delivered as follows:

         money (cash or check): $ _____

         the following property: valued at $ _____

The following payment and/or transfer is in full payment or distribution of :

☐ a legacy under Paragraph/Article _____ of the will or trust;
☐ a claim against the estate;
☐ the amount directed to be paid by a decree of this court dated:
☐ other [specify]:

(d)   Releases and discharges each fiduciary named above from all liability to the undersigned for any and all matters relating to or derived from the administration of the estate; waives the issuance and service of a citation to attend any and all proceedings for the judicial settlement of the account; and authorizes the Surrogate to make and enter a decree settling the account and fully releasing and discharging each fiduciary named above as to all matters embraced therein.

Dated: _____

_____   _____
          (Signature)   (Corporate Name)

_____   _____
         (Print Name)   (Signature of Officer)

JA-2 (12/96)

STATE OF NEW YORK   )

COUNTY OF _____)   ss.:

On _____ 20_____, before me personally appeared

[INDIVIDUAL]

☐   _____ to me known and known to me to be the person

described in and who executed the foregoing receipt and release and duly acknowledged the execution thereof.

[CORPORATION]

☐   _____ to me known, who duly swore to the foregoing instrument and who did say

that he/she resides at _____

and that he/she is a _____ of _____ the

corporation/national banking association described in and which executed such instrument; and that he/she signed his/her

name thereto by order of the Board of Directors of the corporation.

_____

Notary Public
Commission Expires:
(Affix Notary Stamp or Seal)

Name of Attorney: _____   Tel. No.: _____

Address of Attorney: _____

FORM JA-3   Waiver of Citation and Consent in Accounting

SURROGATE'S COURT OF THE STATE OF NEW YORK
COUNTY OF _____
--- X
ACCOUNTING BY _____

as the _____

of the ESTATE OF _____

a/k/a _____
                                            Deceased.
--- X

WAIVER OF CITATION AND CONSENT
IN ACCOUNTING

File No. _____

The undersigned, being of full age, and sound mind, residing at the address written below, having an interest in this proceeding, waives the issuance and service of citation in this proceeding, and consents to the submission of a decree settling the account as filed and adjusted without further notice. I acknowledge receipt of a copy of the summary statement of account.

Date	Signature	Street Address	Interest
	Print Name	City/Town/Village	State/Zip

STATE OF NEW YORK   )
COUNTY OF _____) ss.:

                On _____, 20 ____, before me personally appeared _____

[INDIVIDUAL]

_____ to me known and known to me to be the person described in and who executed the foregoing waiver and consent and duly acknowledged the execution thereof.

[CORPORATION]

_____ to me known, who duly swore to the foregoing instrument and who did say that

he/she resides at _____

and that he/she is a _____ of _____ the

corporation/national banking association described in and which executed such instrument; and that he/she signed his/her

name by order of the Board of Directors of the corporation.

_____
Notary Public
Commission Expires:
(Affix Notary Stamp or Seal)

Name of Attorney: _____ Tel. No.: _____

Address of Attorney: _____

[Note: You may request a copy of the full account from the petitioner or petitioner's attorney.)

JA-3 (12/96)

FORM JA-4   Trust Accounting with Instructions

SURROGATE'S COURT OF THE STATE OF NEW YORK
COUNTY OF_____
--- X

ACCOUNTING BY_____   ACCOUNTING BY:

as the _____   ☐ Executor with Trust
                                         ☐ Trustee
of the ESTATE OF_____   ☐ Other [Specify]_____

a/k/a_____   File No. _____
                              Deceased.
--- X

TO THE SURROGATE'S COURT OF THE COUNTY OF_____
   The undersigned does hereby render the account of proceedings as follows:

   Period of account from _____ to _____ . This is a
☐(final) ☐(intermediate) account.

    [The instructions concerning the schedules need not be stated at the head of each schedule. It will be sufficient to set forth only the schedule letter and heading. For convenience of reference, the schedule letter and page number of the schedule should be shown at the bottom of each sheet of the account.]

PRINCIPAL

Schedule A	-	Principal Received, page _____
Schedule A - 1	-	Realized Increases, page _____
Schedule B	-	Realized Decreases, page _____
Schedule C	-	Funeral and Administration Expenses and Taxes, page _____
Schedule C - 1	-	Unpaid Administration Expenses, page _____
Schedule D	-	Creditor's Claims, page _____ **[Does not apply in a trustee's account]**
Schedule E	-	Distributions of Principal, page _____
Schedule F	-	New Investments, Exchanges and Stock Distribution, page _____
Schedule G	-	Principal remaining on Hand, page _____

INCOME

Schedule A-2	-	Income Collected, page _____
Schedule C-2	-	Administration, Expenses Chargeable to Income, page _____
Schedule E-1	-	Distributions of Income, page _____
Schedule G-1	-	Income Remaining on Hand, page _____
Schedule H	-	Interested Parties, page _____
Schedule I	-	Computation of Commissions, page _____
Schedule J	-	Other Pertinent Facts and Cash Reconciliation, page _____
Schedule K	-	Estate Taxes Paid and Allocation of Estate Taxes, page _____

JA-4 (6/98)

Official Forms

SUMMARY

PRINCIPAL ACCOUNT

CHARGES:

Schedule "A" - (Principal received) $ _____

Schedule "A- 1 " - (Realized increases in principal) $ _____

  Total principal charges $ _____

CREDITS:

Schedule "B" - (Realized decreases in principal) $ _____

Schedule "C" - (Funeral and administration expenses) $ _____

Schedule "D" - (Creditor's claims actually paid) $ _____
[Does not apply In trustee's account]

Schedule "E" - (Distributions of principal) $ _____

  Total principal credits $ _____

Principal balance on hand shown by Schedule "G" $ _____

INCOME ACCOUNT

CHARGES:

Schedule "A-2" - (Income collected) $ _____

  Total income charges $ _____

CREDITS

Schedule "C-2" - (Administration expenses) $ _____

Schedule "E-1" - (Distributions of income) $ _____

  Total income credits $ _____

Balance of undistributed income remaining on hand as shown in Schedule "G-1" $ _____

<u>**COMBINED-ACCOUNTS**</u>

Principal on hand | Cash | $ _____
| Other Property | $ _____
| Total | $ _____

Income on hand: | Cash | $ _____
| Other Property | $ _____
| Total | $ _____

Total on hand as of _____,20____ | $ _____

The foregoing principal balance of $ _____ consists of $ _____ in cash and $ _____ in other property on hand as of the _____ day of 20____ It is subject to deduction of estimated principal commissions amounting to $ _____ as shown in Schedule I, and to the proper charge to principal of expenses of this accounting.

The foregoing income balance of $ _____ consists of $ _____ in cash and $ _____ in other property on hand as of the _____ day of 20____. It is subject to deduction of estimated income commissions amounting to $ _____ as shown in Schedule 1, and to the proper charge to income expenses of this accounting.

The attached schedules are part of this account.

_____
(Name of Corporate Fiduciary)

_____
(Signature of Officer)

_____
(Signature of Fiduciary)

_____
(Signature of Fiduciary)

FORM JA-4   SURROGATE'S COURT   **SF-186**

AFFIDAVIT OF ACCOUNTING PARTY

STATE OF NEW YORK   )

COUNTY OF _____)   ss.:

_____ being duly sworn, says: that the schedules of assets of the estate reported herein are true and complete and include all money and property of any kind, and all increment thereon, which have come into the hands of any of the accounting parties or have been received by any other persons for the use of any accounting party by order of authority of such accounting party, and include all indebtedness due by any accounting party to the estate whether discharged or not; that the moneys stated in the account as collected were all that could be collected; that all claims for credit for losses or decreases of value of assets are correctly reported; that the reported payments out of estate assets for funeral and administration expenses were actually made and made in the amounts scheduled; that the reported payments to creditors and beneficiaries were actually made at the dates and in the amounts scheduled; that no payments have been made by any accounting party on any fiduciary's claims against the estate except after prior approval and allowance by the Surrogate; that all receipts and disbursements are correctly and fully reported and scheduled; that the accounting parties do not know of any error in the account or in any schedule thereof or of any matter or thing relating to the estate omitted therefrom to the prejudice of rights of any creditor or of any person interested in the estate; and that the schedule of commissions has been computed in conformity with the statute regulating commissions and the Rules of the Surrogate's Court applicable thereto.

Sworn to before me on

_____, 20____

_____
Notary Public
Commission Expires:
(Affix Notary Stamp or Seal)

_____
Signature

_____
Print Name

Signature of Attorney: _____   Tel. No.: _____

Address of Attorney: _____

INSTRUCTIONS

PRINCIPAL

Schedule A

Statement of Principal Received

This schedule must contain an itemized statement of all the moneys and other personal property constituting principal for which each accounting party is charged, together with the date of receipt or acquisition of such money or property. If real property has been sold by the fiduciary, this schedule must set forth the proceeds of sale of such property, including a copy of the closing statement.

Schedule A-1

Statement of Increases on Sales, Liquidation or Distribution

This schedule must contain a full and complete statement of all realized increases derived from principal assets whether due to sale, liquidation, or distribution or any other reason. It should also show realized increases on new investments or exchanges. In each instance, the date of realization of the increase must be shown and the property from which the increase was derived must be identified.

Schedule B

Statement of Decreases Due to Sales, Liquidation, Collection, Distribution or
Uncollectibility

This schedule must contain a full and complete statement of all realized decreases on principal assets whether due to sale, liquidation, collection or distribution, or any other reason. It should show decreases on new investments or exchanges and also sales, liquidations or distributions that result in neither gain nor loss. In each instance, the date of realization of the decrease must be shown and the property from which the decrease was incurred must be identified. It should also report any asset which the fiduciary intends to abandon as worthless, together with a full statement of the reasons for abandoning it.

Schedule C

Statement of Funeral and Administration Expenses and Taxes Charged to Principal

This schedule must contain an itemized statement of all moneys chargeable and paid for funeral, administration and other necessary expenses, together with the date and the reason for each expenditure. Consolidate all similar expenditures; i.e. funeral expenses, taxes, accountant fees, legal fees, filing fees, commissions, other. Where the will directs that all inheritance and death taxes are to be paid out of the estate, credit for payment of the same should be taken in this schedule.

Schedule C-1

Statement of Unpaid Administration Expenses

This schedule must contain an itemized statement of all unpaid claims for administration and other necessary expenses, together with a statement of the basis for each such claim.

Schedule D

Statement of All Creditor's Claims

This schedule must contain an itemized statement of all creditor's claims subdivided to show:

1. Claims presented, allowed, paid and credited and appearing in the Summary Statement together with the date of payment.
2. Claims presented and allowed but not paid.
3. Claims presented but rejected, and the date of and the reason for such rejection.
4. Contingent and possible claims.
5. Personal claims requiring approval by the court pursuant to SCPA §1805.

In the event of insolvency, preference of various claims should be stated, with the order of their priority.

Schedule E

Statement of Distributions of Principal

This schedule must contain an itemized statement of all moneys paid and all property delivered from principal to the beneficiaries, legatees, trustees, surviving spouse or distributees of the deceased, the date of payment or delivery thereof, and the name of the person to whom payment or delivery was actually made.

Where estate taxes are required to be apportioned and payments have been made on account of the taxes, the amounts apportioned in Schedule K against beneficiaries of the estate shall be charged against the respective individuals share.

Schedule F

Statement of New Investments, Exchanges and Stock Distributions

This schedule must contain an itemized statement of (a) all new investments made by the fiduciary with the date of acquisition and cost of all property purchased, (b) all exchanges made by the fiduciary, specifying dates and items received and items surrendered, and (c) all stock dividends, stock splits, right and warrants received by the fiduciary, showing the securities to which each relates and their allocation as between principal and income.

Schedule G

Statement of Principal Remaining on Hand

This schedule must contain an itemized statement showing all property constituting principal remaining on hand including a statement of all uncollected receivables and property rights due to the estate. Show the date and cost of all such property that was acquired by purchase, exchange or transfers made or received, together with the date of acquisition and the cost thereof and indicate such sums in the appropriate lines of the summary schedule. Show all unrealized increases and decreases relating to assets on hand, and report the same in the appropriate places in the summary schedule.

INCOME

Schedule A-2

Statement of All Income Collected

This schedule must contain a full and complete statement of all interest, dividends, rents and other income received, and the date of each receipt. Each receipt must be separately accounted for and identified, except that where a security had been held for an entire year, the interest or ordinary dividends may be reported on a calendar year basis.

Schedule C-2

Statement of Administration Expenses Charged to Income

This schedule must contain an itemized statement of all moneys chargeable to income and paid for administration, maintenance and other expenses, together with the date and reason for each such expenditure.

Schedule E-1

Statement of Distribution of Income

This schedule must contain an itemized statement of all moneys paid and of property delivered out of income to the beneficiaries, the date of payment or delivery thereof and the name of the person to whom payment or delivery was actually made. If convenient, distributions of income to any one beneficiary may be reported by the calendar year.

Schedule G-1

Statement of Income on Hand

This schedule must contain a statement showing all undistributed income.

Schedule H

Statement of Interested Parties

This schedule must contain the names of all persons entitled as beneficiary, legatee, devisee, trustee, surviving spouse, distributee, unpaid creditor or otherwise to a share of the estate or fund, with their post office addresses and the degree of relationship, if any, of each to the deceased, and a statement showing the nature of and the value or approximate value of the interest of each such person.

This schedule also must contain a statement that the records of this court have been searched for powers of attorney and assignments and encumbrances made and executed by any of the persons interested in or entitled to a share of the estate and a list detailing each power of attorney, assignment and encumbrance, disclosed by such search, with the date of its recording and the name and address of each attorney in fact and of each assignee and of each person beneficially interested under the encumbrance to in the respective instruments, and also whether the accounting party had any knowledge of the execution of any such power of attorney or assignment not so filed and recorded.

Schedule I

Statement of Computation of Commissions

This schedule must contain a computation of the amount of commissions due upon this accounting. See Uniform Court Rule, §207.40 (d).

Schedule J

Statement of Other Pertinent Facts, and Cash Reconciliation

This schedule must contain a statement of all other pertinent facts affecting the administration of the estate and the rights of those interested therein. It must also contain a statement of any real property left by the decedent that it is not necessary to include as an estate asset to be accounted for, a brief description thereof, its gross value, and the amount of mortgages or liens thereon at the date of death of the deceased. A cash reconciliation must also be set forth in this schedule so that verification with bank statements and cash on hand may be readily made.

Schedule K

Statement of Estate Taxes Paid and Allocation Thereof

This schedule must contain a statement showing all estate taxes assessed and paid with respect to any property required to be included in the gross estate of the decedent under the provisions of the Tax Law or under the laws of the United States. This schedule must also contain a computation setting forth the proposed allocation of taxes paid and to be paid and the amounts due the estate from each person in whose behalf a tax payment has been made and also the proportionate amount of the tax paid by each of the named persons interested in this estate or charged against their respective interest, as provided in §2-1.8 of the Estates, Powers and Trusts Law.

Where an allocation of taxes is required, the method of computing the allocation of said taxes must be shown in this schedule.

Official Forms

FORM JA-5   **Decree of Judicial Settlement for Executor with Trust or Trustee**

SURROGATE'S COURT OF THE STATE OF NEW YORK
COUNTY OF _____
---X

ACCOUNTING BY_____

as the_____

of the ESTATE OF _____

a/k/a
_____
                                          Deceased.
---X

FINAL/INTERMEDIATE
DECREE OF JUDICIAL SETTLEMENT
EXECUTOR WITH TRUST OR TRUSTEE

File No. _____

      A petition praying for a decree judicially settling the final/intermediate account having been presented and filed in this court and the time to present claims against the estate having expired, and a citation having been issued directed to all persons interested in this proceeding requiring them to show cause why a decree should not be granted judicially settling the account prayed for in the petition, and the citation having been returned with proof of due service thereof on the following:

_____
_____
_____

and duly executed waivers of the service of citation or receipts and releases having been filed for the following:

_____
_____
_____

and the following parties having appeared in answer to the citation:

_____

and _____ attorneys, having appeared for the petitioner, and there being no other appearances; and the Surrogate having appointed as guardian ad litem for the following persons under a disability:

_____
_____

and each guardian ad litem having filed a report recommending that the account be judicially settled and no objection having been filed to the account;

and it appearing that all tax returns required by law have been filed and all New York State estate taxes have been fully paid, provision made therefore, or the estate is exempt from tax; and the Surrogate having examined the account and having found that each petitioner has fully accounted for all of the monies and property of the estate that have come into the petitioner's hands for the period of the account, as adjusted, it is

      ORDERED, ADJUDGED AND DECREED, that the final/intermediate account be and the same hereby is judicially settled and allowed as filed (and adjusted), and that the following is a summary thereof as settled:

_____
_____
_____
_____
_____

JA-5 (12/96)

SUMMARY

PRINCIPAL ACCOUNT

CHARGES:

Schedule "A"	(Principal received)	$ _____
Schedule "A-1"	(Realized increases in principal)	$ _____
Total Principal Charges		$ _____

CREDITS:

Schedule "B"	(Realized decreases in principal)	$ _____
Schedule "C"	(Funeral and administration expenses)	$ _____
Schedule "D"	(Creditor's claims actually paid) **[Does not apply in a trustee's account]**	$ _____
Schedule "E"	(Distributions of principal)	$ _____
Total Principal Credits		$ _____
Principal balance on hand shown by Schedule "G",		$ _____

INCOME ACCOUNT

CHARGES:

Schedule "A-2"	(Income collected)	$ _____
Total income charges		$ _____

CREDITS

Schedule "C-2",	(Administration expenses)	$ _____
Schedule "E-1"	(Distributions of Income)	$ _____
Total income credits		$ _____
Balance of undistributed income remaining on hand as shown in Schedule "G-1"		$ _____

COMBINED ACCOUNTS

Principal on hand	Cash	$ _____
	Other Property	$ _____
	Total	$ _____

-18-

Income on hand: Cash $ _____

Other Property $ _____

Total $ _____

Total on hand as of _____ ,20____ $ _____

and it is further

ORDERED, ADJUDGED AND DECREED, that petitioner(s) pay the remaining cash and transfer, assign and deliver the other remaining assets as shown in the account as follows:

To the petitioner:
as and for commissions the sum of $ _____

To the petitioner:
as and for commissions the sum of $ _____

To the attorney:
for legal services rendered for
the benefit of the estate the sum of $ _____

and for costs and disbursements
(which sums are in addition to any payments
made on account and allowed by the court) $ _____

To the guardian ad litem:
for services as guardian ad litem $ _____

and it is further

ORDERED, ADJUDGED AND DECREED, that the balance remaining on hand in the amount of $ _____ be paid as follows:

To _____ $ _____
To _____ $ _____
To _____ $ _____

ORDERED, ADJUDGED AND DECREED, that upon complying with the directions of this decree and the filing of the receipts for the payments herein directed, the petitioner (s)- hereby shall be discharged as to all matters and things contained in this accounting and decree.

Dated: _____

_____
Judge of the Surrogate's Court

FORM JA-6   Citation

ACCOUNTING CITATION   File No. _____

SURROGATE'S COURT - _____ COUNTY

CITATION

THE PEOPLE OF THE STATE OF NEW YORK,
By the Grace of God Free and Independent

TO _____
   _____
   _____
   _____

A petition and an account having been duly filed by _____ , whose address is
_____

YOU ARE HEREBY CITED TO SHOW CAUSE before the Surrogate's Court, _____ County,

at _____ , New York, on _____ , 20 ___ , at _____ o'clock in the _____

noon of that day, why the account of _____ , a summary of which has been served herewith,

as _____ , of the estate of _____ should not be judicially settled.

[State any further relief requested]

_____
_____
_____
_____

                                          HON. _____
Dated, Attested and Sealed,   Surrogate

_____ , 20 ___   _____
(Seal)   Chief Clerk

Name of Attorney: _____   Tel. No.: _____
Address of Attorney: _____

[Note: This citation is served upon you as required by law. You are not required to appear; however, if you fail to appear it will
be assumed you do not object to the relief requested. You have a right to have an attorney appear for you, and you or your
attorney may request a copy of the full account from the petitioner or petitioner's attorney.]

JA-6 (12/96)

FORM JA-7   Non-Trust Accounting with Instructions

SURROGATE'S COURT OF THE STATE OF NEW YORK
COUNTY OF _____
-- X
ACCOUNTING BY_____

as the_____

of the ESTATE OF_____

a/k/a _____

-- X

ACCOUNTING BY:

☐ Executor
☐ Administrator
☐ Other [specify]

File No._____

TO THE SURROGATE'S COURT OF THE COUNTY OF _____

The undersigned does hereby render the account of proceedings as follows:

Period of account from _____ to _____

This is a ☐ (final) ☐ (intermediate) account.

[The instructions concerning the schedules need not be stated at the head of each schedule. It will be sufficient to set forth only the schedule letter and heading. For convenience of reference, the schedule letter and page number of the schedule should be shown at the bottom of each sheet of the account.]

Schedule A	-	Principal Received, page _____
Schedule A - I	-	Realized Increases, page _____
Schedule A - 2	-	Income Collected, page _____
Schedule B	-	Realized Decreases, page _____
Schedule C	-	Funeral and Administration Expenses and Taxes, page _____
Schedule C - 1	-	Unpaid Administration Expenses, page _____
Schedule D	-	Creditors Claims, page _____
Schedule E	-	Distributions Made, page _____
Schedule F	-	New Investments, Exchanges and Stock Distribution, page _____
Schedule G	-	Personal Property Remaining on Hand, page _____
Schedule H	-	Interested Parties and Proposed Distribution, page _____
Schedule I	-	Computation of Commissions, page _____
Schedule J	-	Other Pertinent Facts and Cash Reconciliation, page _____
Schedule K	-	Estate Taxes Paid and Allocation of Estate Taxes, page _____

JA-7 (6/98)

SUMMARY

CHARGES:

Schedule "A"　　-　(Principal received)　　　　　　　$ _____

Schedule "A - 1 "　-　(Realized increases in principal)　$ _____

Schedule "A - 2"　-　(Income Collected)　　　　　　$ _____

　　Total Charges　　　　　　　　　　　　　　　　　$ _____

CREDITS:

Schedule "B"　　-　(Realized decreases in principal)　$ _____

Schedule "C"　　-　(Funeral and administration expenses　$ _____

Schedule "D"　　-　(Creditor's claims actually paid)　$ _____

Schedule "E"　　-　(Distributions of principal)　　　$ _____

　　Total Charges　　　　　　　　　　　　　　　　　$ _____

Balance on hand shown by Schedule "G"　　　　　　$ _____

　　The foregoing balance of $ _____ consists of $ _____ in cash and
$ _____ in other property on hand as of the _____ day of _____ ,
20_____　It is subject to deduction of estimated principal commissions amounting to $ _____ as
shown in Schedule I and to the proper charge to principal of expenses of this accounting.

　　The attached schedules are part of this account.

_____　　　_____
(Name of Corporate Fiduciary)　　　　　　(Signature of Fiduciary)

_____　　　_____
(Signature of Officer)　　　　　　　　　(Signature of Fiduciary)

Official Forms

AFFIDAVIT OF ACCOUNTING PARTY

STATE OF NEW YORK   )

COUNTY OF _____)   ss.:

_____ being duly sworn, says: that the schedules of assets of the estate reported herein are true and complete and include all money and property of any kind, and all increment thereon, which have come into the hands of any of the accounting parties or have been received by any other persons for the use of any accounting party by order of authority of such accounting party, and include all indebtedness due by any accounting party to the estate whether discharged or not; that the moneys stated in the account as collected were all that could be collected; that all claims for credit for losses or decreases of value of assets are correctly reported; that the reported payments out of estate assets for funeral and administration expenses were actually made and made in the amounts scheduled; that the reported payments to creditors and beneficiaries were actually made at the dates and in the amounts scheduled; that no payments have been made by any accounting party on any fiduciary's claims against the estate except after prior approval and allowance by the Surrogate; that all receipts and disbursements are correctly and fully reported and scheduled; that the accounting parties do not know of any error in the account or in any schedule thereof or of any matter or thing relating to the estate omitted therefrom to the prejudice of rights of any creditor or of any person interested in the estate; and that the schedule of commissions has been computed in conformity with the statute regulating commissions and the Rules of the Surrogate's Court applicable thereto.

Sworn to before me on

_____,20____

_____   _____
                                                                        Signature

Notary Public   _____
Commission Expires: Print Name
(Affix Notary Stamp or Seal)

Name of Attorney: _____   Tel. No.: _____

Address of Attorney: _____

INSTRUCTIONS

PRINCIPAL

Schedule A

Statement of Principal Received

     This schedule must contain an itemized statement of all the moneys and other personal property constituting principal for which each accounting party is charged, together with the. date of receipt or acquisition of such money or property. If real property has been sold by the fiduciary, this schedule must set forth the proceeds of sale of such property, including a copy of the closing statement.

Schedule A-1

Statement of Increases on Sales, Liquidation or Distribution

     This schedule must contain a full and complete statement of all realized increases derived from principal assets whether due to sale, liquidation, or distribution or any other reason. It should also show realized increases on new investments or exchanges. In each instance, the date of realization of the increase must be shown and the property from which the increase was derived must be identified.

Schedule A-2

Statement of All Income Collected

     This schedule must contain a full and complete statement of all interest, dividends, rents and other income received, and the date of each receipt. Each receipt must be separately accounted for and identified, except that where a security had been held for an entire year, the interest or ordinary dividends may be reported on a calendar year basis.

Schedule B

Statement of Decreases Due to Sales, Liquidation, Collection, Distribution or Uncollectibility

     This schedule must contain a full and complete statement of all realized decreases on principal assets whether due to sale, liquidation, collection or distribution, or any other reason. It should show decreases on new investments or exchanges and also sales, liquidations or distributions that result in neither gain nor loss. In each instance, the date of realization of the decrease must be shown and the property from which the decrease was incurred must be identified. It should also report any asset which the fiduciary intends to abandon as worthless, together with a full statement of the reasons for abandoning it.

Schedule C

Statement of Funeral and Administration Expenses and Taxes Actually Paid

     This schedule must contain an itemized statement of all moneys chargeable and paid for funeral, administration and other necessary expenses, together with the date and the reason for each expenditure. Consolidate all similar expenditures; i.e. funeral expenses, taxes, accountant fees, legal fees, filing fees, commissions, other. Where the will directs that all inheritance and death taxes are to be paid out of the estate, credit for payment of the same should be taken in this schedule.

Schedule C-1

Statement of Unpaid Administration Expenses

     This schedule must contain an itemized statement of all unpaid claims for administration and other necessary expenses, together with a statement of the basis for each such claim.

Schedule D

Statement of All Creditor's Claims

This schedule must contain an itemized statement of all creditor's claims subdivided to show:

     1. Claims presented, allowed, paid and credited and appearing in the Summary Statement together

Official Forms

with the date of payment.

2. Claims presented and allowed but not paid.
3. Claims presented but rejected, and the date of and the reason for such rejection.
4. Contingent and possible claims.
5. Personal claims requiring approval by the court pursuant to SCPA §1805.

In the event of insolvency, preference of various claims should be stated, with the order of their priority.

Schedule E

Statement of Distributions Made

This schedule must contain an itemized statement of all moneys paid and all property delivered to the beneficiaries, legatees, trustees, surviving spouse or distributees of the deceased, the date of payment or delivery thereof, and the name of the person to whom payment or delivery was actually made.

Where estate taxes are required to be apportioned and payments have been made on account of the taxes, the amounts apportioned in Schedule K against beneficiaries of the estate shall be charged against the respective individuals share.

Schedule F

Statement of New Investments, Exchanges and Stock Distributions

This schedule must contain an itemized statement of (a) all new investments made by the fiduciary with the date of acquisition and cost of all property purchases, (b) all exchanges made by the fiduciary, specifying dates and items received and items surrendered, and (c) all stock dividends, stock splits, right and warrants received by the fiduciary, showing the securities to which each relates and their allocation as between principal and income.

Schedule G

Statement of Personal Property Remaining on Hand

This schedule Must contain an itemized statement showing all property constituting principal remaining on hand including a statement of all uncollected receivables and property rights due to the estate. Show the date and cost of all such property that was acquired by purchase, exchange or transfers made or received, together with the date of acquisition and the cost thereof and indicate such sums in the appropriate lines of the summary schedule. Show all unrealized increases and decreases relating to assets on hand, and report the same in the appropriate places in the summary schedule.

Schedule H

Statement of Interested Parties

This schedule must contain the names of all persons entitled as beneficiary, legatee, devisee, trustee, surviving spouse, distributee, unpaid creditor or otherwise to a share of the estate or fund, with their post office addresses and the degree of relationship, if any, of each to the deceased, and a statement showing the nature of and the value or approximate value of the interest of each such person.

This schedule also must contain a statement that the records of this court have been searched for powers of attorney and assignments and encumbrances made and executed by any of the persons interested in or entitled to a share of the estate and a list detailing each power of attorney, assignment and encumbrance, disclosed by such search , with the date of its recording and the name and address of each attorney in fact and of each assignee and of each person beneficially interested under the encumbrance to in the respective instruments, and also whether the accounting party had any knowledge of the execution of any such power of attorney or assignment not so filed and recorded.

Schedule I

Statement of Computation of Commissions

This schedule must contain a computation of the amount of commissions due upon this accounting. See Uniform Court Rule, §207.40 (e).

Schedule J

Statement of Other Pertinent Facts, Cash Reconciliation and Proposed Distribution

This schedule must contain a statement of all other pertinent facts affecting the administration of the estate and the rights of those interested therein. It must also contain a statement of any real property left by the decedent that it is not necessary to include as an estate asset to be accounted for, a brief description thereof, its gross value, and the amount of mortgages or liens thereon at the date of death of the deceased. A cash reconciliation must also be set forth in this schedule so that verification with bank statements and cash on hand may be readily made.

Schedule K

Statement of Estate Taxes Paid and Allocation Thereof

This schedule must contain a statement showing all estate taxes assessed and paid with respect to any property required to be included in the gross estate of the decedent under the provisions of the Tax Law or under the laws of the United States. This schedule must also contain a computation setting forth the proposed allocation of taxes paid and to be paid and the amounts due the estate from each person in whose behalf a tax payment has been made and also the proportionate amount of the tax paid by each of the named persons interested in this estate or charged against their respective interest, as provided in §2-1.8 of the Estates, Powers and Trusts Law.

Where an allocation of taxes is required, the method of computing the allocation of said taxes must be shown in this schedule.

Official Forms

FORM JA-8   **Non-Trust Decree of Judicial Settlement**

SURROGATE'S COURT OF THE STATE OF NEW YORK
COUNTY OF _____
--- X
ACCOUNTING BY _____   FINAL/INTERMEDIATE
                                                  DECREE OF JUDICIAL SETTLEMENT
as the_____   FOR EXECUTOR-ADMINISTRATOR

of the ESTATE OF_____   File No. _____

a/k/a _____
                          Deceased.
--- X

     A petition praying for a decree judicially settling the final/intermediate account having been presented and filed in this court and the time to present claims against the estate having expired, and a citation having been issued directed to all persons interested in this proceeding requiring them to show cause why a decree should not be granted judicially settling the account prayed for in the petition, and the citation having been returned with proof of due service thereof on the following:

_____

_____

and duly executed waivers of the service of citation or receipts and releases having been filed for the following:

_____

_____

and the following parties having appeared in answer to the citation:

_____

_____

and _____, attorneys, having appeared for the petitioner, and there being no other appearances; and the Surrogate having appointed _____as guardian ad litem for the following persons under a disability:

_____

_____

and each guardian ad litem having filed a report recommending that the account be judicially settled and no objection having been filed to the account;

and it appearing that all tax returns required by law have been filed and all New York State estate taxes have been fully paid, provision made therefore, or the estate is exempt from tax; and the Surrogate having examined the account and having found that each petitioner has fully accounted for all of the monies and property of the estate that have come into the petitioner's hands for the period of the account, as adjusted, it is

     ORDERED, ADJUDGED AND DECREED, that the final/intermediate account be and the same hereby is judicially settled and allowed as filed (and adjusted), and that the following is a summary thereof as settled:

JA-8 (12/96)

SUMMARY

PRINCIPAL ACCOUNT

CHARGES:

Schedule "A"	-	(Principal received)	$ _____
Schedule "A - 1"	-	(Realized increases in principal)	$ _____
Schedule "A - 2"	-	(Income Collected)	$ _____
Total Charges			$ _____

CREDITS:

Schedule "B"	-	(Realized decreases in principal)	$ _____
Schedule "C"	-	(Funeral and administration expenses)	$ _____
Schedule "D"	-	(Creditor's claims actually paid)	$ _____
Schedule "E"	-	(Distributions of principal)	$ _____
Total Charges			$ _____
Balance on hand shown by Schedule G			$ _____

and it is further

    ORDERED, ADJUDGED AND DECREED, that petitioner(s) pay the remaining cash and transfer, assign and deliver the other remaining assets as shown in the account as follows:

To the petitioner: as and for commissions the sum of	$ _____
To the petitioner: as and for commissions the sum of	$ _____
To the attorney: for legal services rendered for the benefit of the estate the sum of	$ _____

and for costs and disbursements
(which sums are in addition to any payments
made on account and allowed by the court) $ _____

To the guardian ad litem:
for services as guardian ad litem $ _____

and it is further

      ORDERED, ADJUDGED AND DECREED, that the balance remaining on hand in the amount
of $ _____ be paid as follows:

To: _____ $ _____
To: _____ $ _____
To: _____ $ _____

      ORDERED, ADJUDGED AND DECREED, that upon complying with the directions of this decree and
the filing of the receipts for the payments herein directed, the petitioner (s) hereby shall be discharged as to all
matters and things contained in this accounting and decree.

Dated: _____,20____

                                   _____

                                   Judge of the Surrogate's Court

FORM JA-9   Compulsory Accounting Citation

COMPULSORY ACCOUNTING CITATION   File No. _____

SURROGATE'S COURT: _____ COUNTY

CITATION

THE PEOPLE OF THE STATE OF NEW YORK,

By the Grace of God Free and Independent

TO: _____
_____
_____

A petition having been filed by _____ ,

who is/are domiciled, or in the case of a corporation, its principal office, at _____
_____
_____

YOU ARE HEREBY CITED TO SHOW CAUSE before the Surrogate's Court, _____ County, at

_____ , New York, on _____

at _____ o'clock in the _____ noon of that day why _____ should
not file his/her account and cause same to be judicially settled, and upon failure to file his/her account, with petition for judicial settlement,
on the return date of citation, that the court issue an order requiring him/her to file an account in the estate of
_____

[For additional relief pursuant to SCPA §2205 and §2206, check appropriate box]:

☐ upon failure to appear on the return date of process without satisfactory excuse therefore, or upon failure to file an account in the
time and manner directed by the court, show cause why his/her letters should not be suspended and why the court should not appoint
_____ , an eligible person(s), as temporary fiduciary(ies) and to fix a trial date for a
hearing on the removal of _____ whose letters have been suspended and for the
appointment of _____ , as Successor Fiduciary(ies).

☐ if the fiduciary's letters are suspended or the fiduciary fails to account in the time and manner directed by the court, why the court
should not fix a date for a hearing to take and state the fiduciary's account, in accordance with the proposed accounting attached to the
petition, the summary statement of such account has been served herewith.

[State any further relief requested]

_____
_____
_____

Dated, Attested and Sealed,

HON. _____
Surrogate

_____ , _____

(Seal)

_____ , Chief Clerk

Attorney for Petitioner(s): _____ Telephone No.: _____

Address of Attorney: _____

[Note: This citation is served upon you as required by law. You are not required to appear. If you fail to appear, it will be assumed you do not
object to the relief requested. You have a right to have an attorney appear for you, and you or your attorney may request a copy of the full account
from the petitioner or petitioner's attorney.]

JA-9 (1/2004)

FORM JA-10   Petition for Compulsory Accounting and Related Relief

Filing Fee Paid $ _____
Receipt No.: _____

SURROGATE'S COURT OF THE STATE OF NEW YORK
COUNTY OF _____
---X
Petition for a Compulsory Accounting and Related Relief
in the Estate of

_____

PETITION FOR A COMPULSORY
ACCOUNTING AND RELATED RELIEF
SCPA 2205

File No. _____

                                        Deceased.
---X

To the Surrogate's Court of the County of _____

It is respectfully alleged:

1. The name, citizenship and domicile (or, in the case of a corporation, its principal office) of the petitioner(s) are as follows:

Name: _____

Domicile or Principal Office: _____
                                        (Street and Number)

_____
     (City, Village or Town)   (State)   (Zip Code)

Citizen of: _____

Name: _____

Domicile or Principal Office: _____
                                        (Street and Number)

_____
     (City, Village or Town)   (State)   (Zip Code)

Citizen of: _____

2. That the decedent died on _____

3. That letters ☐ testamentary ☐ of administration ☐ of trusteeship ☐ other (specify) _____

were granted by the Surrogate's Court of the County of _____ on _____ ,

to _____ residing at _____

_____

4. That the fiduciary has not filed an account.

5. The petitioner(s) is/are a ☐ distributee ☐ legatee ☐ creditor ☐ other (specify) _____ and the reason
why petitioner(s) wish(es) the fiduciary to account is:

_____

_____

_____

_____

[NOTE: Complete paragraph 6, If relief requested Is In addition to a compulsory accounting.]

6. The persons entitled to notice on an application to suspend, modify or revoke a fiduciary's letters, to appoint a successor fiduciary or to settle a fiduciary's account (See SCPA Section 2206(2)) are:

Name	Address	Nature of Interest

WHEREFORE your petitioner(s) pray(s) that process issue requiring _____
                                                                                (Name of Fiduciary)
to show cause why he/she should not file his/her account and cause same to be judicially settled and upon failure to file his/her account with petition for judicial settlement on the return date of citation, that the court issue an order requiring him/her to file an account.

[For additional relief pursuant to SCPA §2205 and §2206, check the appropriate box]:

☐ upon failure to appear on the return date of process without satisfactory excuse therefore, or upon failure to file an account in the time and manner directed by the court, show cause why his/her letters should not be suspended and why the court should not appoint _____, an eligible person(s), as temporary fiduciary(ies) and to fix a trial date for a hearing on the removal of _____ whose letters have been suspended and for the appointment of _____ as Successor Fiduciary(ies).

☐ if the fiduciary's letters are suspended or the fiduciary fails to account in the time and manner directed by the court, why the court should not fix a date for a hearing to take and state the fiduciary's account, in accordance with the proposed accounting attached to the petition, the summary statement of such account has been served herewith.
                                    [State any further relief requested]

_____

_____

_____

Dated: _____

1. _____   2. _____
        (Signature of Petitioner)   (Signature of Petitioner)

   _____   _____
           (Print Name)   (Print Name)

3. _____
      (Name of Corporate Petitioner)

   _____
         (Signature of Officer)

   _____
      (Print Name and Title of Officer)

Official Forms

STATE OF NEW YORK   )
COUNTY OF _____) ss.:

_____, being duly sworn deposes and says that I am/we are the petitioner(s) above named. I/we have read the foregoing petition and the same is true of my/our own knowledge except as to matters therein stated to be alleged upon information and belief and as to those matters I/we believe them to be true.

_____   _____
(Signature of Petitioner)   (Signature of Petitioner)

_____   _____
(Print Name)   (Print Name)

On _____, before me personally came

to me known to be the person(s) described in and who executed the foregoing instrument. Such person(s) duly swore to such instrument before me and duly acknowledged that he/she/they executed the same.

_____
Notary Public
Commission Expires:
(Affix Notary Stamp or Seal)

STATE OF NEW YORK   )
COUNTY OF _____) ss.:

The undersigned, a _____ of _____
                                         (Title)   (Name of Corporation)
a corporation duly qualified to act in a fiduciary capacity without further security, being duly sworn, say:

　　1. VERIFICATION: I have read the foregoing petition subscribed by me and know the contents thereof, and the same is true of my own knowledge, except as to the matters therein stated to be alleged upon information and belief, and as to those matters I believe it to be true

_____
(Name of Corporate Petitioner)

_____
(Signature of Officer)

_____
(Print Name and Title of Officer)

On _____, before me personally came _____
to me known, who duly swore to the foregoing instrument and which did say that he/she resides at _____ and
that he/she is a _____ of _____ the
corporation described in and which executed such instrument, and that he/she signed his/her name thereto by the order of the Board of Directors of the corporation.

_____
Notary Public
Commission Expires:
(Affix Notary Stamp or Seal)

Signature of Attorney: _____

Print Name: _____

Firm Name: _____ Tel. No. _____

Address of Attorney: _____

FORM P-1   Petition for Probate

Filing Fee Paid $_____
_____ Certs $_____
_____ Certs $_____
$_____ Bond, Fee: $_____
Receipt No: _____ No:_____

STATE OF NEW YORK
SURROGATE'S COURT: COUNTY OF
--X
PROBATE PROCEEDING,
WILL OF

a/k/a

                                        Deceased.
--X

PETITION FOR PROBATE AND:
[ ] **Letters Testamentary**
[ ] **Letters of Trusteeship**
[ ] **Letters of Administration c.t.a.**

File No._____

To the Surrogate's Court, County of
   It is respectfully alleged:
   1.(a)   The name, citizenship, domicile (or, in the case of a bank or trust company, its principal office) and interest in this proceeding of the petitioner are as follows:

Name:_____
Domicile or Principal Office:_____
                                                        (Street and Number)

_____
       (City, Village or Town)   (State)   (Zip Code)   (Telephone Number)
                     Mailing Address:_____
                                                        (If different from domicile)
Citizen of:_____

Name:_____
Domicile or Principal Office:_____
                                                        (Street and Number)

_____
       (City, Village or Town)   (State)   (Zip Code)   (Telephone Number)
                     Mailing Address:_____
                                                        (If different from domicile)
Citizen of:_____

Interest (s) of Petitioner (s): [Check one] [ ] Executor (s) named in decedent's Will
                                           [ ] Other (Specify) _____

   1.(b)   The proposed Executor [ ] is [ ] is not an attorney.
           [NOTE: A sole Executor-Attorney must comply with 22 NYCRR 207.16(e)]

   1.(c)   The proposed Executor [ ] is [ ] is not the attorney-draftsperson, a then-affiliated attorney or employee thereof.
           [NOTE: An attorney-draftsperson, a then-affiliated attorney or employee thereof must comply with SCPA 2307-a]

   1.(d)   The proposed Executor [ ] is [ ] is not a convicted felon nor is he/she otherwise ineligible, pursuant to SCPA 707 to
           receive letters. If the proposed Executor is a convicted felon, submit a copy of the Certificate of Relief from Civil
           Disabilities.

   2.   The name, domicile, date and place of death, and national citizenship of the above-named decedent as follows:

           (a) Name: _____
           (b) Date of death _____
           (c) Place of death _____
           (d) Domicile: Street _____
               City, Town, Village _____
               County_____ State _____
           (e) Citizen of:_____

   3.   The Last Will, herewith presented, relates to both real and personal property and consists of an instrument or instruments
dated as shown below and signed at the end thereof by the decedent and the following attesting witnesses:

_____   _____
   (Date of Will)   (Names of All Witnesses to Will)

_____   _____
   (Date of Codicil)   (Names of All Witnesses to Codicil)

_____   _____
   (Date of Codicil)   (Names of All Witnesses to Codicil)

P-1 (03/18)   -1-

4.   No other will or codicil of the decedent is on file in this Surrogate's Court, and upon information and belief, after a diligent search and inquiry, including a search of any safe deposit box, there exists no will, codicil or other testamentary instrument of the decedent later in date to any of the instruments mentioned in Paragraph 3 except as follows: **[Enter "NONE" or specify]**

5.   The decedent was survived by distributees classified as follows: [Information is required only as to those classes of surviving relatives who would take the property of decedent pursuant to EPTL 4-1.1 and 4-1.2. State the **number** of survivors in each class. Insert "**NO**" in all prior classes. Insert "**X**" in all subsequent classes].

a.   [ ]   Spouse (husband/wife).

b.   [ ]   Child or children and/or issue of predeceased child or children. **[Must include marital, nonmarital, adopted, or adopted-out of child under DRL Section 117]**

c.   [ ]   Mother/Father.

d.   [ ]   Sisters and/or brothers, either of the whole or half blood, and issue of predeceased sisters and/or brothers (nieces/nephews, etc.)

e.   [ ]   Grandparents. [Include maternal and paternal]

f.   [ ]   Aunts and/or uncles, and children of predeceased aunts and/or uncles (first cousins). [Include maternal and paternal]

g.   [ ]   First cousins once removed (children of predeceased first cousins). [Include maternal and paternal]

6.   The names, relationships, domicile and addresses of all distributees (under EPTL 4-1.1 and 4-1.2), of each person designated in the Will herewith presented as primary executor, of all persons adversely affected by the purported exercise by such Will of any power of appointment, of all persons adversely affected by any codicil and of all persons having an interest under any other will of the decedent on file in the Surrogate's Court, are hereinafter set forth in subdivisions (a) and (b).

[If the propounded will purports to revoke or modify an inter vivos trust or any other testamentary substitute, list the names, relationships, domicile and addresses of the trustee and beneficiaries affected by the will in subparagraphs (a) and (b) below. **Submit trust agreement**]

(a)   All persons and parties so interested who are of **full age and sound mind** or which are corporations or associations, are as follows:

Name and Relationship	Domicile Address and Mailing Address	Description of Legacy, Devise or Other Interest, or Nature of Fiduciary Status

(b)   All persons so interested who are **persons under disability**, are as follows:
[Furnish all information specified in NOTE following 7b]

Name and Relationship	Domicile Address and Mailing Address	Description of Legacy, Devise or Other Interest, or Nature of Fiduciary Status
_____	_____	_____
_____	_____	_____
_____	_____	_____
_____	_____	_____

7. (a)   The names and domiciliary of all substitute or successor executors and of all trustees, guardians, legatees, devisees, and other beneficiaries named in the Will and/or trustees and beneficiaries of any inter vivos trust designated in the propounded Will other than those named in Paragraph 6 herewith are as follows:

Name	Domicile Address and Mailing Address	Description of Legacy, Devise or Other Interest, or Nature of Fiduciary Status
_____	_____	_____
_____	_____	_____
_____	_____	_____
_____	_____	_____

(b)   All such legatees, devisees and other beneficiaries who are persons under disability are as follows: [Furnish all information specified in NOTE below]

Name	Domicile Address and Mailing Address	Description of Legacy, Devise or Other Interest, or Nature of Fiduciary Status
_____	_____	_____
_____	_____	_____
_____	_____	_____
_____	_____	_____

[NOTE: In the case of each infant, state (a) name, birth date, relationship to decedent, domicile and residence address, and the person with whom he/she resides, (b) whether or not he/she has a court-appointed guardian (if not, so state), and whether or not his/her father and/or mother is living, and (c) the name and residence address of any court-appointed guardian and the information regarding such appointment. In the case of each other person under a disability, state (a) name, relationship to decedent, and residence address, (b) facts regarding his disability including whether or not a committee, conservator, guardian, or any other fiduciary has been appointed and whether or not he/she has been committed to any institution, and (c) the names and addresses of any committee, person or institution having care and custody of him/her, conservator, guardian, and any relative or friend having an interest in his/her welfare. In the case of a person confined as a prisoner, state place of incarceration and list any person having an interest in his/her welfare. In the case of unknowns, describe such person in the same language as will be used in the process.]

Official Forms

FORM P-1   SURROGATE'S COURT   SF-210

8. (a) No beneficiary under the propounded will, listed in Paragraph 6 or 7 above, had a confidential relationship to the decedent, such as attorney, accountant, doctor, or clergyperson, except: **[Enter "NONE" or indicate the nature of the confidential relationship].** _____

(b) No persons, corporations or associations are interested in this proceeding other than those mentioned above.

9. (a) To the best of the knowledge of the undersigned, the approximate total value of all property constituting the decedent's gross testamentary estate is greater than $_____ but less than $_____.

Personal Property $_____ Improved real property in New York State $_____

Unimproved real property in New York State $_____

Estimated gross rents for a period of 18 months $_____

(b) No other testamentary assets exist in New York State, nor does any cause of action exist on behalf of the estate, except as follows: **[Enter "NONE" or specify]**
_____
_____

10. Upon information and belief, no other petition for the probate of any will of the decedent or for letters of administration of the decedent's estate has heretofore been filed in any court.

WHEREFORE your petitioner (s) pray (s) that process be issued to all necessary parties to show cause why the Will and the Codicil (s) set forth in Paragraph 3 and presented herewith should not be admitted to probate; (b) that an order be granted directing the service of process, pursuant to the provisions of Article 3 of the S.C.P.A., upon the persons named in Paragraph (6) hereof whose names or whereabouts are unknown and cannot be ascertained, or who may be persons on whom service by personal delivery cannot be made; and (c) that such Will and Codicil (s) be admitted to probate as a Will of real and personal property and that letters issue thereon as follows: [Check and complete all relief requested.]

[ ] Letters Testamentary to _____

_____

[ ] Letters of Trusteeship to _____ f/b/o _____

_____ f/b/o _____

_____ f/b/o _____

[ ] Letters of Administration c.t.a. to _____
and that petitioner (s) have such other relief as may be proper.

Dated:_____

1. _____   2. _____
    (Signature of Petitioner)   (Signature of Petitioner)

_____   _____
      (Print Name)   (Print Name)

3. _____
    (Name of Corporate Petitioner)

_____
    (Signature of Officer)

_____
    (Print Name and Title of Officer)

COMBINED VERIFICATION, OATH AND DESIGNATION
[For use when petitioner is an individual]

STATE OF NEW YORK   )
COUNTY OF   ) ss.:

The undersigned, the petitioner named in the foregoing petition, being duly sworn, says:

1.   VERIFICATION: I have read the foregoing petition subscribed by me and know the contents thereof, and the same is true of my own knowledge, except as to the matters therein stated to be alleged upon information and belief, and as to those matters I believe it to be true.

2.   OATH OF [ ] EXECUTOR [ ] ADMINISTRATOR c.t.a. [ ] TRUSTEE as indicated above: I am over eighteen (18) years of age, and I will well, faithfully and honestly discharge the duties of Fiduciary of the goods, chattels and credits of said decedent according to law. I am not ineligible, pursuant to SCPA 707, to receive letters and will duly account for all moneys and other property that will come into my hands.

3.   DESIGNATION OF CLERK FOR SERVICE OF PROCESS: I hereby designate the Clerk of the Surrogate's Court of _____ County, and his/her successor in office, as a person on whom service of any process, issuing from such Court may be made in like manner and with like effect as if it were served personally upon me, whenever I cannot be found and served within the State of New York after due diligence used.

My domicile is :_____
               (Street Address)   (City/Town/Village)   (State)   (Zip)

_____
(Signature of Petitioner)

_____
(Print Name)

On _____ , 20 _____ , before me personally came

_____
to me known to be the person described in and who executed the foregoing instrument. Such person duly swore to such instrument before me and duly acknowledged that he/she executed the same.

_____
Notary Public
Commission Expires:
(Affix Notary Stamp or Seal)

Signature of Attorney:_____

Print Name:_____

Firm Name:_____Tel No.:_____ e-mail:_____

Address of Attorney:_____

Official Forms

FORM P-1   SURROGATE'S COURT   **SF-212**

COMBINED CORPORATE VERIFICATION, CONSENT AND DESIGNATION
[For use when a petitioner to be appointed is a bank or trust company]

STATE OF NEW YORK   )
COUNTY OF   ) ss.:

    I, the undersigned, a _____ of
                                            (Title)

_____
                           (Name of Bank or Trust Company)

a corporation duly qualified to act in a fiduciary capacity without further security, being duly sworn says:

    1.   VERIFICATION: I have read the foregoing petition subscribed by me and know the contents thereof, and the same is true of my own knowledge, except as to the matters therein stated to be alleged upon information and belief, and as to those matters I believe it to be true.

    2.   CONSENT: I consent to accept the appointment as   [ ] Executor   [ ]   Administrator c.t.a
[ ] Trustee under the Last Will and Testament of the decedent described in the foregoing petition and consent to act as such fiduciary.

    3.   DESIGNATION OF CLERK FOR SERVICE OF PROCESS: I designate the Chief Clerk of the Surrogate's Court of _____ County, and his/her successor in office, as a person on whom service of any process issuing from such Surrogate's Court may be made, in like manner and whenever one of its proper officers cannot be found and served within the State of New York after due diligence used.

_____
    (Name of Bank or Trust Company)

BY_____
        (Signature)

_____
    (Print Name and Title)

    On _____, 20 _____ , before me personally came _____,
to me known, who duly swore to the foregoing instrument and who did say that he/she resides at _____
and that he/she is a _____ of _____
the corporation/national banking association described in and which executed such instrument, and that he/she signed his/her name thereto by order of the Board of Directors of the corporation.

_____
Notary Public
Commission Expires:
(Affix Notary Stamp or Seal)

Signature of Attorney:_____

Print Name:_____

Firm Name:_____ Tel No.:_____ e-mail: _____

Address of Attorney:_____

FORM P-2   Application for Preliminary Letters Testamentary

SURROGATE'S COURT OF THE STATE OF NEW YORK
COUNTY OF _____
-- X

PROBATE PROCEEDING,
WILL OF _____

a/k/a _____

_____ Deceased.
-- X

APPLICATION FOR
PRELIMINARY LETTERS TESTAMENTARY
(See SCPA 1412)

File # _____

1.   The proposed preliminary executor (s) is/are _____
     _____, and is/are designated as executor (s) in the Will of the above named
     decedent dated _____
     (together with Codicil (s) dated _____) and duly filed
     with the court.

2.   The person (s) who would have a right to letters testamentary pursuant to Section 1412.1 is/are: [Enter **"NONE"**
     or specify name and interest]

3.   Preliminary letters are requested for the following reasons:

4.   Probate is expected to be completed by: _____

5.   A contest ☐ is   ☐ is not expected.

6.   The testamentary assets of decedent's estate are estimated as follows: [describe and state value; annex
     schedule if space is insufficient]

     Personal Property: _____

                                        Total Personal Property: $ _____
     Real Property: _____

                                        Total Real Property: $ _____
     18 months rent, if applicable: _____

                                        Total of 18 months rent: $ _____
7.   The liabilities of this estate are: _____

P-2 (10/96)

8.   By provision in the propounded will, the applicant(s) [is/are] [are not] required to file a bond or other security
       for the performance of his/her/their duties.

       Your applicant (s) respectfully request the issuance to _____

       _____

       of preliminary letters testamentary upon qualifying.

Dated: _____   _____
                                                                            Applicant

                                                          _____
                                                                            Applicant

OATH & DESIGNATION OF PRELIMINARY EXECUTOR

STATE OF NEW YORK   )
COUNTY OF _____) ss.:

I, the undersigned, _____ being duly sworn say:

1.   OATH OF PRELIMINARY EXECUTOR: I am over eighteen (18) years of age and a citizen of the United States; I am an executor named in the Will described in the foregoing petition and will well, faithfully and honestly discharge the duties of preliminary executor and duly account for all money or property which may come into my hands. I am not ineligible to receive letters.

2.   DESIGNATION OF CLERK FOR SERVICE OF PROCESS: I hereby designate the Clerk of the Surrogate's Court of _____ County, and his/her successor in office, as a person on whom service of any process issuing from such Surrogate's Court may be made, in like manner and with like effect as if it were served personally upon me whenever I cannot be found and served within the State of New York after due diligence used.

My domicile is _____
            (Street Address)   (City/Town/Village)   (State)   (Zip)

                                     _____
                                     (Signature of Petitioner)

                                     _____
                                        (Print Name)

On _____ ,20___ , before me personally came _____

to me known to be the person described in and who executed the foregoing instrument. Such person duly swore to such instrument before me and duly acknowledged that he/she executed the same.

_____
Notary Public
Commission Expires:
(Affix Notary Stamp or Seal)

Signature of Attorney: _____

Print Name: _____

Firm Name: _____ Tel No. _____

Address of Attorney: _____

NOTE: Each Preliminary Executor must complete a combined Oath & Designation of Preliminary Executor.

Official Forms

CONSENT AND DESIGNATION OF CORPORATE PRELIMINARY EXECUTOR

STATE OF NEW YORK   )
COUNTY OF_____) ss.:

    I, the undersigned, a _____ of
                                     (Title)

_____
                       (Name of Bank or Trust Company)
a corporation duly qualified to act in a fiduciary capacity without further security, being duly sworn, says:

1.   CONSENT: I consent to accept the appointment as Preliminary Executor under the Last Will and Testament of the decedent described in this application and consent to act as such fiduciary.

2.   DESIGNATION OF CLERK FOR SERVICE OF PROCESS: I designate the Chief Clerk of the Surrogate's Court of County, and his/her successor in office, as a person on whom service of any process issuing from such Surrogate's Court may be made, in like manner and whenever one of its proper officers cannot be found and served within the State of New York after due diligence used.

_____
    (Name of Bank or Trust Company)

BY: _____
          (Signature)

_____
    (Print Name and Title)

    On _____ ,20___, before me personally came _____, to me known, who duly swore to the foregoing instrument and who did say that he/she resides at and that he/she is a _____ of _____ the corporation/national banking association described in and which executed such instrument, and that he/she signed his/her name thereto by order of the Board of Directors of the corporation.

_____
Notary Public
Commission Expires:
(Affix Notary Stamp or Seal)

Signature of Attorney: _____

Print Name: _____

Firm Name: _____ Tel No. _____

Address of Attorney: _____

FORM P-3   Affidavit of Attesting Witness

SURROGATE'S COURT STATE OF NEW YORK
COUNTY OF _____
--- X
PROBATE PROCEEDING,
WILL OF_____
a/k/a   _____
                       Deceased.
--- X

AFFIDAVIT OF ATTESTING WITNESS
(After Death)
Pursuant to SCPA 1406

File No. _____

STATE OF NEW YORK   )
COUNTY OF _____) ss.:

The undersigned witness, being duly sworn, deposes and says:

(1)   I have been shown [check one]
      ☐ the original instrument dated , _____,
      ☐ a court-certified photographic reproduction of the original instrument dated _____,
         purporting to be the last Will and Testament/Codicil of the above-named decedent.

(2)   On the date indicated in such instrument (under the supervision of an attorney), I saw the decedent subscribe the same at the place where decedent's signature appears, and I heard the decedent declare such instrument to be his/her last Will and Testament/Codicil.

(3)   I thereafter signed my name to such instrument as a witness thereto at the request of the decedent, and I saw the other witness(es) _____ sign his/her/their names (s) at the end of such instrument as a witness thereto.

(4)   At the time the decedent subscribed and executed such instrument, the decedent was to the best of my knowledge and belief upwards of 18 years of age, and in all respects appeared to be of sound and disposing mind, memory and understanding, competent to make a will, and not under any restraint.

(5)   The decedent could read, write and converse in the English language, and was not suffering from defects of sight, hearing or speech, or any other physical or mental impairment, which would affect his/her capacity to make a valid will. The purported instrument was the only copy of said Will/Codicil executed on that occasion, and was not executed in counterparts.

(6)   I am making this affidavit at the request of_____

                                         _____
                                            (Witness Signature)
                                            _____
                                              (Print Name)
                                            _____
                                             (Street Address)
                                             _____
                                              (Town/State/Zip)

Sworn to before me this _____

day of_____ , _____

_____
Notary Public
Commission Expires:
(Affix Notary Stamp or Seal)

[Note: Each witness must be shown either the Original Will or a Court-Certified Reproduction thereof. The Notary Public subscribing to this affidavit may Not be a party or witness to the Will.]
P-3 (10/96)

Official Forms

FORM P-4   Waiver of Process; Consent to Probate

SURROGATE'S COURT STATE OF NEW YORK
COUNTY OF _____
--- X
PROBATE PROCEEDING,   WAIVER OF PROCESS;
WILL OF_____   CONSENT TO PROBATE

a/k/a _____   File No. _____

                                        Deceased.
--- X

To the Surrogate's Court, County of _____

The undersigned, being of full age and sound mind, residing at the address written below and interested in this proceeding as set forth in paragraph 6a of the petition, hereby waives the issuance and service of citation, in this matter and consents that the court admit to probate the decedent's Last Will and Testament dated _____ 20____ (and codicils, if any, dated_____), a copy of each of which testamentary instrument had been received by me, and that

☐ Letters Testamentary issue to _____
                                  _____
                                  _____
                                  _____

☐ Letters of Trusteeship issue to
   of the following trusts: _____
                           _____
                           _____
                           _____

Date	Signature	Street Address	Relationship
	Print Name	Town/State/Zip	

STATE OF NEW YORK
COUNTY OF _____ ss.:

    On _____ ,20____ before me personally appeared _____
to me known and known to me to be the person described in and who executed the foregoing waiver and consent and duly acknowledged the execution thereof.

_____
Notary Public
Commission Expires:
(Affix Notary Stamp or Seal)

Signature of Attorney: _____
Print Name: _____
Firm Name: _____ Tel No. _____
Address of Attorney: _____

P-4 (10/96)

FORM P-5   Citation

PROBATE CITATION   File No. _____

SURROGATE'S COURT - _____ COUNTY
CITATION

THE PEOPLE OF THE STATE OF NEW YORK,
By the Grace of God Free and Independent

TO _____
_____
_____

A petition having been duly filed by _____, who is

domiciled at _____

YOU ARE HEREBY CITED TO SHOW CAUSE before the Surrogate's Court, _____ County,

at _____, New York, on _____ 20___ at _____ o'clock in

the _____ noon of that day, why a decree should not be made in the estate of_____

lately domiciled at _____ admitting to probate

a Will dated _____, (a Codicil dated _____)

(a Codicil dated _____) , a copy of which is attached, as the Will of_____

_____ deceased, relating to real and personal property, and directing that

☐ Letters Testamentary issue to: _____

☐ Letters of Trusteeship issue to: _____

☐ Letters of Administration c.t.a. issue to: _____

(State any further relief requested)

_____
_____
_____

HON. _____

Dated, Attested and Sealed   _____
_____ ,20 ___   Surrogate
(Seal)   _____
                                                    Chief Clerk

_____
Attorney for Petitioner   Telephone Number

_____
Address of Attorney

[NOTE: This citation is served upon you are required by law. You are not required to appear. If you fail to appear it will be assumed you do not object to the relief requested. You have a right to have an attorney appear for you.]

P-5 (10/96)

-13-

FORM P-6   Notice of Probate

SURROGATE'S COURT OF THE STATE OF NEW YORK
COUNTY OF _____
--X

PROBATE PROCEEDING,   NOTICE OF PROBATE
WILL OF _____   (SCPA 1409)

a/k/a _____
                          Deceased.   File No. _____
--X

Notice is hereby given that:

1   The Will dated _____, (and Codicil dated _____)
(and Codicil dated _____) of the above named decedent, domiciled at
_____ County of _____, New York,
has been/will be offered for probate in the Surrogate's Court for the County of _____

2.   The name (s) of proponent (s) of said Will is/are _____
       whose address(es) is/are _____
       _____
       _____

3.   The name and post office address of each person named or referred to in the petition who has not been served or
       has not appeared, or waived service of process, with a statement whether such person is named or referred to in
       the will as legatee, devisee, trustee, guardian or substitute or successor executor, trustee or guardian, and as to
       any such person who is an infant or an incompetent, the name and post office address of a person upon whom
       service of process may be made on behalf of such infant or incompetent, is as follows:

NAME	MAILING ADDRESS	NATURE OF INTEREST OR STATUS

(USE ADDITIONAL SHEETS IF NECESSARY)

Date _____, 20____

[Note: Complete Affidavit of Mailing. If serving Infant 14 years of age or older, list and mail to infant as well as parent or guardian.]

Name of Attorney: _____ Tel. No: _____
Address of Attorney: _____

P-6 (10/96)

-14-

AFFIDAVIT OF MAILING NOTICE OF PROBATE

STATE OF NEW YORK   )

) ss.:

COUNTY OF_____)

_____, residing at _____ being duly sworn,

says that he/she is over the age of 18 years, that on the day of_____, 20___ he/she deposited in the post

office box regularly maintained by the government of the United States in the _____ of_____

_____, State of New York, a copy of the foregoing Notice of Probate contained in a securely closed postpaid

wrapper directed to each of the persons named in said notice at the places set opposite their respective names.

_____
Signature

_____
Print Name

Sworn to before me this _____
day of_____, 20____

_____
Notary Public
Commission Expires:
(Affix Notary Stamp or Seal)

Name of Attorney: _____ Tel. No: _____
Address of Attorney: _____

-15-

FORM P-7   Affidavit of Service of Citation

SURROGATE'S COURT OF THE STATE OF NEW YORK
COUNTY OF _____

---X

PROBATE PROCEEDING,
WILL OF
_____

a/k/a _____

Deceased.

---X

Note: File Proof of Service at least 2 days before return date. State clearly date, time and place of service and name of person served. (Uniform Rule 207.7 (c) [22 NYCRR])

AFFIDAVIT OF SERVICE
OF CITATION

File No. _____

STATE OF NEW YORK   )
COUNTY OF _____) ss.:

_____ of _____
_____, being duly sworn, says that I am over the age of eighteen years; that I made personal service of the citation herein dated _____,20___, and a copy of the Will/Codicil on each person named below, each of whom deponent knew to be the person mentioned and described in said citation, by delivering to and leaving with each of them personally a true Copy of said citation and Will/Codicil, as follows:

_____, description: sex _____, color of skin _____, color of hair
_____, approximate age _____, weight _____, height _____, at _____ o'clock
_____.m. on the _____ day of _____,20____,
at _____

_____, description: sex _____, color of skin _____, color of hair
_____, approximate age _____, weight _____, height _____, at _____ o'clock
_____.m. on the _____ day of _____,20____,
at _____

_____, description: sex _____, color of skin _____, color of hair
_____, approximate age _____, weight _____, height _____, at _____ o'clock
_____.m. on the _____ day of _____,20____,
at _____

That none of the aforesaid persons is in the military service as defined by the Act of Congress known as the "Soldiers' and Sailors' Civil Relief Act of 1940" and in the New York "Soldiers' and Sailors' Civil Relief Act."

_____
Signature

_____
Print Name

Sworn to before me this _____
day of _____,20____

_____
Notary Public
Commission Expires:
(Affix Notary Stamp or Seal)

Name of Attorney: _____ Tel. No: _____
Address of Attorney: _____

P-7 (10/96)

FORM P-8   Application and Order for Dispensing with Testimony of Attesting Witness

SURROGATE'S COURT OF THE STATE OF NEW YORK
COUNTY OF_____
---X
PROBATE PROCEEDING,
WILL OF _____

a/k/a_____
_____ Deceased.
---X

APPLICATION TO DISPENSE WITH
TESTIMONY OF ATTESTING WITNESS
(SCPA 1405)

File No. _____

STATE OF NEW YORK   )
COUNTY OF_____) ss.:

_____, being duly sworn, deposes and says:

The testimony of _____, an attesting witness to the

Will/Codicil of the above named decedent, dated _____, _____, offered for probate, cannot be obtained

because of   ☐ death   ☐ absence   ☐ **disability**   ☐ inability to locate.

[Explain in detail and add additional affidavit if necessary] _____

_____

_____

_____

_____

        Wherefore it is respectfully requested, pursuant to SCPA 1405, that the testimony of said witness be dispensed
with.

                                    _____
                                                Signature

                                    _____
                                               Print Name

Sworn to before me this _____
day of_____,20____

_____
Notary Public
Commission Expires:
(Affix Notary Stamp or Seal)

-17-

Official Forms

SURROGATE'S COURT OF THE STATE OF NEW YORK
COUNTY OF_____

--x

PROBATE PROCEEDING,
WILL OF _____

ORDER DISPENSING
WITH TESTIMONY OF
ATTESTING WITNESS

a/k/a_____

                            Deceased:

--x

Upon reading and filing the foregoing affidavit which states why the attesting witness therein named is unable to appear in this Court, it is

ORDERED that the testimony of , as an attesting witness to the instrument offered for probate herein, is hereby dispensed with in this probate proceeding.

Dated _____,20 ____

_____

_____, Surrogate

P-8 (10/96)

FORM P-9   Affidavit Proving Handwriting

SURROGATE'S COURT OF THE STATE OF NEW YORK
COUNTY OF _____
-- X

PROBATE PROCEEDING,   AFFIDAVIT PROVING
WILL OF _____   HANDWRITING

a/k/a _____
                 Deceased.   File No. _____
-- X

STATE OF NEW YORK   )
) ss.:
COUNTY OF _____)

_____ being duly sworn, deposes and says:

1.   My address is _____

2.   I was well-acquainted with ☐ the testator ☐ an attesting witness to the testator's Will/Codicil.

3.   I am familiar with the manner and style of the testator's/witness's handwriting, having often seen him/her write his/her signature and having seen his/her signature on documents I know to have been signed by him/her,

4.   The signature subscribed at the end of the instrument in writing now produced and shown to me, purporting to be the testator's Last Will and Testament dated _____, _____, is the signature of and is the handwriting of _____

_____
              Signature

_____
              Print Name

Sworn to before me this _____
day of_____ ,20____

_____
Notary Public
Commission Expires:
(Affix Notary Stamp or Seal)

Name of Attorney _____ Tel. No.: _____
Address of Attorney: _____

P-9 (10/96)

FORM P-10   **Renunciation of Nominated Executor and/or Trustee**

SURROGATE'S COURT OF THE STATE OF NEW YORK
COUNTY OF_____
---X

PROBATE PROCEEDING, WILL OF_____ a/k/a_____ _____ Deceased.	RENUNCIATION OF NOMINATED EXECUTOR and/or TRUSTEE File No. _____

---X

    I, _____, domiciled at (or, in the case of a bank or trust company, its principal office) _____, nominated as an executor and/or trustee in the (Will) (Codicil) of_____ dated _____, late of_____ in the County of_____, New York, hereby renounce the appointment and all right and claim to letters testamentary and/or letters of trusteeship of and under the (Will) (Codicil) or to act as executor and/or trustee thereof.

    I hereby waive the issuance and service of a citation in the above entitled matter, and consent that the Will dated _____ (and Codicil dated _____) (and Codicil dated _____), a copy of which has been received by the undersigned, be forthwith admitted to probate. I hereby consent that Letter   Testamentary ☐ of Administration c.t.a. ☐ of Trusteeship issue to _____ without the necessity of furnishing a bond. If a bond is furnished, I hereby waive and release all right to make any claim on the bond in any capacity whatsoever.

_____ (Signature)	_____ (Name of Corporation)
_____ (Print Name)	_____ (Name of Officer)

Date: _____

STATE OF NEW YORK
COUNTY OF_____   ss.:

    On _____, 20___, before me personally appeared [INDIVIDUAL] ☐ :_____ to me known and known to me to be the person described in and who executed the foregoing renunciation and duly acknowledged the execution thereof. [CORPORATION]   ☐ _____to me known, who duly swore to the foregoing instrument and who did say that he/she resides at _____ and that he/she is a _____ of _____ the corporation/national banking association described in and which executed such instrument; and that he/she signed his/her name thereto by order of the Board of Directors of the corporation.

_____
Notary Public
Commission Expires:
(Affix Notary Stamp or Seal)

Name of Attorney _____ Tel. No.: _____
Address of Attorney: _____

P-10 (10/96)

FORM P-11   **Renunciation of Letters of Administration c.t.a. and Waiver of Process**

SURROGATE'S COURT OF THE STATE OF NEW YORK
COUNTY OF _____

\- X

PROBATE PROCEEDING,
Will of _____

a/k/a _____

_____ Deceased.

\- X

RENUNCIATION OF LETTERS OF
ADMINISTRATION c.t.a. AND
WAIVER OF PROCESS
(SCPA 1418)

File No. _____

The undersigned, _____ , a person interested in this estate, and in all respects eligible to receive letters, hereby personally appears in this proceeding in the Surrogate's Court of _____
County and

1. Renounces all rights to Letters of Administration c.t.a.

2. Waives the issuance and service of citation in the above entitled proceeding and consents that the will dated _____ ,20___ , a copy of which has been received by the undersigned, be admitted to probate.

3. Consents that Letters of Administration c.t.a. be granted by the Court to _____ _____ or any other person or persons entitled thereto without any notice whatsoever to the undersigned.

4. Consents to dispense with the bond of the Administrator c.t.a., and if such consent be filed by some but not all of the persons interested in the estate, specifically releases any claim by me under any bond that may be required of such Administrator c.t.a.

Date	Signature	Street Address	Relationship

| Print Name | | Town/State/Zip | |

STATE OF NEW YORK
COUNTY OF_____ss.:

On _____ ,20___ , before me personally came_____
to me known and known to me to be the person described in and who executed the foregoing waiver and consent and duly acknowledged the execution thereof.

_____
Notary Public
Commission Expires:
(Affix Notary Stamp or Seal)

Name of Attorney: _____
Address of Attorney: _____

P- 11 (10/96)

FORM P-12 **Affidavit of No Debt**

SURROGATE'S COURT OF THE STATE OF NEW YORK
COUNTY OF_____
--- X

PROBATE PROCEEDING,
WILL OF _____

a/k/a _____

_____ Deceased.
--- X

AFFIDAVIT OF NO DEBT
(For use with Letters of
Administration c.t.a.)

File No._____

STATE OF NEW YORK   )
)ss.:
COUNTY OF_____)

_____, being duly sworn, deposes and says that

he/she resides at_____, County of _____,

State of _____, that he/she is the person seeking appointment as administrator c.t.a. in the

above entitled proceeding; that the value of all personal property receivable by the fiduciary of the estate of the above-named

decedent plus estimated gross rents receivable by said fiduciary for 18 months will not exceed the sum of

$_____, that deponent has made a diligent search to ascertain whether or not there are any debts or claims

against the estate of said decedent and that there are no claims, including unpaid funeral and medical bills, except as follows:

[If "none", write "NONE"] _____

NAME	ADDRESS	NATURE OF CLAIM	AMOUNT

Sworn to before me this_____

day of_____,20_____

_____
Signature

_____
Notary Public
Commission Expires:
(Affix Notary Stamp or Seal)

_____
Print Name

Name of Attorney_____ Tel. No.:_____

Address of Attorney_____

P- 12 (10/96)

FORM P-13   **Affidavit of Comparison**

SURROGATE'S COURT OF THE STATE OF NEW YORK
COUNTY OF _____
-- X
PROBATE PROCEEDING,
WILL OF _____

a/k/a _____
                            Deceased.
-- X

(Note: Attach a copy of the Will/Codicil to this Affidavit of Comparison executed by any two persons; if a photocopy of the Will is used, only one person need make the affidavit.)

AFFIDAVIT OF COMPARISON

File No._____

STATE OF NEW YORK   )
)   ss.:
COUNTY OF _____)

    I/We _____ (and) _____ being duly

sworn, say(s), that (he/she has) (we have) carefully compared the copy of decedent's Will/Codicil propounded herein to which

this affidavit is annexed with the original Will dated the _____ day of _____, _____, (and the original

Codicil dated the _____ day of _____, _____), about to be filed for probate, and that the same is in all

respects a true and correct copy of said original Will/Codicil and of the whole thereof.

_____
Signature

_____
Print Name

_____
Signature

_____
Print Name

Sworn to before me this_____
day of_____ ,20____

_____
Notary Public
Commission Expires:
(Affix Notary Stamp or Seal)

Name of Attorney _____ Tel. No.: _____
Address of Attorney: _____

P- 13 (10/96)

FORM P-14   SURROGATE'S COURT   SF-230

FORM P-14   Petition for Successor Letters Testamentary

Filing Fee Paid $_____
_____ Certs $_____
Receipt No: _____ No:_____

DO NOT LEAVE ANY ITEMS BLANK

STATE OF NEW YORK
SURROGATE'S COURT: COUNTY OF _____
_____X
In the Matter of the Petition for Successor Letters Testamentary
in the Estate of

a/k/a

                                                 Deceased.
_____X

**PETITION FOR SUCCESSOR
LETTERS TESTAMENTARY**

File No. _____

To the Surrogate's Court, County of _____

It is respectfully alleged:

1.(a)   The name, citizenship, domicile (or, in the case of a bank or trust company, its principal office) and interest in this proceeding of the petitioner(s) are as follows:

Name:_____

Domicile or Principal Office:_____
                                        (Street and Number)

_____
        (City, Village or Town)   (State)   (Zip Code)
        Mailing Address:_____
                                        (If different from domicile)
Citizen of:_____

Name:_____

Domicile or Principal Office:_____
                                        (Street and Number)

_____
        (City, Village or Town)   (State)   (Zip Code)
        Mailing Address:_____
                                        (If different from domicile)
Citizen of:_____

Interest(s) of Petitioner(s): [Check one]   [ ] Successor Executor(s) named in decedent's Will
                                               [ ] Other (Specify) _____

1.(b)   The proposed Successor Executor [ ] is [ ] is not an attorney.
          [Note: A sole Successor Executor-Attorney must comply with 22 NYCRR §207.16(e)]

1.(c)   The proposed Successor Executor [ ] is [ ] is not the attorney-draftsperson, a then-affiliated attorney or employee thereof.
          [NOTE: An attorney-draftsperson, a then-affiliated attorney or employee thereof must comply with SCPA §2307-a]

2.   The will of the above-named decedent was admitted to probate by the Surrogate's Court of _____
County on _____ and Letters Testamentary were issued to _____
who on _____, [ ] died   [ ] other (specify) _____.
[Note: If prior fiduciary is deceased, please provide court with certified copy of death certificate.]

SLT-1 (04/2011)

-1-

3. The names and addresses of all persons and parties interested in this proceeding having a right to successor letters testamentary prior or equal to the petitioner(s) are as follows:

Name and
Relationship

Domicile Address and
Mailing Address

Nature of Fiduciary Status

4. The names and addresses of all persons and parties who are named in the will as fiduciaries or beneficiaries, other than those named in paragraph 3 above, are as follows:

Name and
Relationship

Domicile Address and
Mailing Address

Description of Legacy, Devise
or Other Interest, or Nature of
Fiduciary Status

[Note: If any such person is under a disability state name and post office address of a person upon whom service of process may be made on behalf of such person.]

5. There are no persons other than those hereinbefore mentioned interested in this proceeding.

6.(a) To the best of the knowledge of the undersigned, the property of the estate that remains **unadministered** is as follows:

Personal Property \$_____ Improved real property in New York State \$_____

Unimproved real property in New York State \$_____

Estimated gross rents for a period of 18 months \$_____

(b) No other testamentary assets exist in New York State, nor does any cause of action exist on behalf of the estate, except as follows: **[Enter "NONE" or specify]**
_____

_____

WHEREFORE, petitioner(s) pray(s):

That Successor Letters Testamentary issue to _____
in the same manner as original letters, and that he/she/they be authorized to complete the administration of the estate of
_____, deceased.

Dated:_____

1. _____   2. _____
   (Signature of Petitioner)   (Signature of Petitioner)

_____   _____
   (Print Name)   (Print Name)

3. _____
   (Name of Corporate Petitioner)

_____
   (Signature of Officer)

_____
   (Print Name and Title of Officer)

-2-

Official Forms

FORM P-14   SURROGATE'S COURT   **SF-232**

COMBINED VERIFICATION, OATH AND DESIGNATION
[For use when petitioner is an individual]

STATE OF NEW YORK   )
COUNTY OF _____) ss.:

The undersigned, the petitioner named in the foregoing petition, being duly sworn, says:

1.   VERIFICATION: I have read the foregoing petition subscribed by me and know the contents thereof, and the same is true of my own knowledge, except as to the matters therein stated to be alleged upon information and belief, and as to those matters I believe them to be true.

2.   OATH OF SUCCESSOR EXECUTOR as indicated above: I am over eighteen (18) years of age and a citizen of the United States and I will well, faithfully and honestly discharge the duties of Fiduciary of the goods, chattels and credits of said decedent according to law. I am not ineligible to receive letters and will duly account for all moneys and other property that will come into my hands.

3.   DESIGNATION OF CLERK FOR SERVICE OF PROCESS: I hereby designate the Clerk of the Surrogate's Court of _____ County, and his/her successor in office, as a person on whom service of any process issuing from such Court may be made in like manner and with like effect as if it were served personally upon me, whenever I cannot be found and served within the State of New York after due diligence is used.

My domicile is :_____
                  (Street Address)   (City/Town/Village)   (State)   (Zip)

_____
    (Signature of Petitioner)

_____
      (Print Name)

On_____ , _____, before me personally appeared
_____,
to me known to be the person described in and who executed the foregoing instrument. Such person duly swore to such instrument before me and duly acknowledged that he/she executed the same.

_____
Notary Public
Commission Expires:
(Affix Notary Stamp or Seal)

Signature of Attorney:_____

Print Name:_____

Firm Name:_____ Tel No. :_____

Address of Attorney:_____

-3-

COMBINED CORPORATE VERIFICATION, CONSENT AND DESIGNATION
[For use when a petitioner to be appointed is a bank or trust company]

STATE OF NEW YORK   )
COUNTY OF _____) ss.:

I, the undersigned, a_____ of

(Title)

_____,

(Name of Bank or Trust Company)

a corporation duly qualified to act in a fiduciary capacity without further security, being duly sworn say:

1.   VERIFICATION: I have read the foregoing petition subscribed by me and know the contents thereof, and the same is true of my own knowledge, except as to the matters therein stated to be alleged upon information and belief, and as to those matters I believe them to be true.

2.   CONSENT: I consent to accept the appointment as Successor Executor under the Last Will and Testament of the decedent described in the foregoing petition and consent to act as such fiduciary.

3.   DESIGNATION OF CLERK FOR SERVICE OF PROCESS: I designate the Chief Clerk of the Surrogate's Court of _____ County, and his/her successor in office, as a person on whom service of any process issuing from such Surrogate's Court may be made, in like manner and with like effect as if it were served personally upon me, whenever one of the fiduciary's proper officers cannot be found and served within the State of New York after due diligence is used.

_____

(Name of Bank or Trust Company)

By_____   _____

(Signature)   (Principal Office Street Address)

_____   _____

(Print Name and Title)   (City/Town/Village)   (State)   (Zip)

On _____ , _____ , before me personally appeared _____,
to me known, who duly swore to the foregoing instrument and who did say that he/she resides at _____
_____and that he/she is a _____ of
_____, the corporation/national banking association described in and which executed such instrument; and that he/she signed his/her name thereto by order of the Board of Directors of the corporation.

_____

Notary Public
Commission Expires:
(Affix Notary Stamp or Seal)

Signature of Attorney:_____

Print Name:_____

Firm Name:_____ Tel. No.:_____

Address of Attorney:_____

FORM P-15   **Renunciation of Successor Letters Testamentary and Waiver of Process (Individual)**

-4-

STATE OF NEW YORK
SURROGATE'S COURT: COUNTY OF _____

_____X

In the Matter of the Petition for Successor Letters Testamentary
in the Estate of

**RENUNCIATION OF SUCCESSOR
LETTERS TESTAMENTARY AND
WAIVER OF PROCESS (INDIVIDUAL)**

a/k/a

File No._____

_____
                              Deceased.
_____X

    The undersigned, _____, a person interested in this estate as alternate executor, hereby personally appears in this proceeding in the Surrogate's Court of _____ County and

    1. Renounces all rights to Successor Letters Testamentary.

    2. Waives the issuance and service of citation in the above-entitled proceeding.

    3. Consents that Successor Letters Testamentary be granted by the Court to _____ or any other person or persons entitled thereto without any notice whatsoever to the undersigned.

_____   _____   _____
Date   Signature   Street Address

       _____   _____
                          Print Name   City/State/Zip

STATE OF NEW YORK
COUNTY OF _____   ss.:

    On _____, _____, before me personally appeared
_____,
to me known to be the person described in and who executed the foregoing instrument. Such person duly swore to such instrument before me and duly acknowledged that he/she executed the same.

_____
Notary Public
Commission Expires:
(Affix Notary Stamp or Seal)

Name of Attorney_____   Tel. No.:_____

Address of Attorney_____

SLT-2 (04/2011)

FORM P-16   **Renunciation of Successor Letters Testamentary and Waiver of Process (Corporation)**

STATE OF NEW YORK
SURROGATE'S COURT: COUNTY OF _____
_____X
In the Matter of the Petition for Successor Letters Testamentary
in the Estate of

a/k/a

**RENUNCIATION OF SUCCESSOR
LETTERS TESTAMENTARY AND
WAIVER OF PROCESS (CORPORATION)**

File No._____

                    Deceased.
_____X

The undersigned, _____, a person
interested in this estate as alternate executor, hereby personally appears in this proceeding in the Surrogate's Court of
_____ County and

　　1. Renounces all rights to Successor Letters Testamentary.

　　2. Waives the issuance and service of citation in the above-entitled proceeding.

　　3. Consents that Successor Letters Testamentary be granted by the Court to _____
or any other person or persons entitled thereto without any notice whatsoever to the undersigned.

_____   _____
            (Signature)   (Name of Corporation)

_____   _____
            (Print Name)   (Principal Office Street Address)

                                            _____
                                            (City/Town/Village)   (State)   (Zip)

Date: _____

STATE OF NEW YORK
COUNTY OF   ss.:

　　On _____, _____, before me personally appeared
_____, to me known, who
duly swore to the foregoing instrument and who did say that he/she resides at _____ and that
he/she is a _____ of _____, the corporation/national banking
association described in and which executed such instrument; and that he/she signed his/her name thereto by order of the
Board of Directors of the corporation.

_____
Notary Public
Commission Expires:
(Affix Notary Stamp or Seal)

Name of Attorney_____ Tel. No.:_____

Address of Attorney_____

SLT-3 (04/2011)

FORM P-17   Notice of Petition for Appointment of Successor Executor

STATE OF NEW YORK
SURROGATE'S COURT: COUNTY OF _____

_____X
In the Matter of the Petition for Successor Letters Testamentary
in the Estate of

**NOTICE OF PETITION FOR
APPOINTMENT OF
SUCCESSOR EXECUTOR**

a/k/a

File No. _____

_____
                              Deceased.
_____X

Notice is hereby given that:

1.   The Will of the above-named decedent was admitted to probate by the Surrogate's Court of _____

County on _____, and Letters Testamentary were issued to _____,

who on _____, [   ] died [   ] other (specify) _____.

2.   The name (s) of the Successor Executor (s) of said Will is/are _____

_____, whose

address(es) is/are _____

_____

_____

3.   The names and address of all persons and parties who are named in the will as fiduciaries or beneficiaries who have
not appeared or have been served or waived service of process.

NAME	MAILING ADDRESS	NATURE OF INTEREST OR STATUS

[Note: If serving infant 14 years of age or older, list and mail to infant as well as parent or guardian.]

(USE ADDITIONAL SHEETS IF NECESSARY)

Date: _____, 20_____

**[Note: Notice of Petition for Appointment of Successor Executor may or may not be required in all
counties. If Notice is required, complete Affidavit of Mailing.]**

Name of Attorney: _____ Tel. No.: _____

Address of Attorney: _____

SLT-4 (04/2011)

-1-

AFFIDAVIT OF MAILING
NOTICE OF PETITION FOR APPOINTMENT OF SUCCESSOR EXECUTOR

STATE OF NEW YORK   )
) ss.:
COUNTY OF   )

_____, residing at _____, being duly

sworn, says that he/she is over the age of 18 years, that on the _____ day of _____,

20_____, he/she deposited in a post office box regularly maintained by the government of the United States in the

_____of _____, State of New York, a copy of the foregoing Notice of Petition for

Appointment of Successor Executor contained in a securely closed postpaid wrapper directed to each of the persons named

in said Notice at the places set opposite their respective names.

Sworn to before me this _____   _____
                                                                        Signature
day of _____, 20____   _____
                                                                        Print Name
_____
Notary Public
Commission Expires:
(Affix Notary Stamp or Seal)

Name of Attorney_____ Tel. No.:_____

Address of Attorney_____

FORM P-17　　　　　SURROGATE'S COURT　　　　　**SF-238**

-2-

SUCCESSOR LETTERS TESTAMENTARY　　　　　File No. _____

SURROGATE'S COURT - _____ COUNTY

CITATION

THE PEOPLE OF THE STATE OF NEW YORK,
By the Grace of God Free and Independent

TO:

A petition having been filed by _____, who is

domiciled at _____,

YOU ARE HEREBY CITED TO SHOW CAUSE before the Surrogate's Court, _____ County,

at _____, New York, on _____ 20____, at _____ o'clock in

the _____ noon of that day, why a decree should not be made in the estate of _____

lately domiciled at _____, directing that

[   ] Successor Letters Testamentary issue to _____.

HON. _____

Dated, Attested and Sealed,　　　　　　　　　　　　　　　Surrogate

_____, _____

(Seal)　　　　　　　　　　　　　　　　　　　　　　　Chief Clerk

_____

Attorney for Petitioner　　　　　　　　　　　　　Telephone Number

_____

Address of Attorney

[NOTE: This citation is served upon you as required by law. You are not required to appear. If you fail to appear it will be assumed you do not object to the relief requested. You have a right to have an attorney appear for you.]

SLT-5 (04/2011)

FORM SE-1C   **Renunciation of Voluntary Administration**

SURROGATE'S COURT OF THE STATE OF NEW YORK

COUNTY OF _____

VOLUNTARY ADMINISTRATION, Estate of   RENUNCIATION OF VOLUNTARY
ADMINISTRATION
(as of 11/2019)

_____,

                           Deceased.   File No. _____

TO THE SURROGATE'S COURT:

     The undersigned, whose domiciliary address is

_____

   (Street Address)   (City/Town/Village)   (State)   (Zip)

Mailing Address _____

                        (If different from domicile)

being of full age and [check and complete]

         [   ] a distributee of the above-named decedent and related as a

         _____

                   (state relationship)

         [   ] a fiduciary or legatee named in the decedent's will dated _____

hereby personally appears herein and renounces all right to act as voluntary administrator of the goods, chattels and credits of the decedent.

                         _____

                                  (Renouncing Party)

                         _____

                                     (Print Name)

STATE OF _____)

) ss.:

COUNTY OF_____)

     On the _____day of_____, 20__, before me personally came

_____, known to me to be the individual described in and who executed the foregoing instrument, and to me such person duly acknowledged that he/she executed the same.

                         _____

                                  Notary Public

            My commission expires: _____

Signature of Attorney: _____

Print Name of Attorney:_____

Firm Name:_____ Tel. No._____

Address of Attorney:_____

SE-1C (11/2019)

FORM SE-1D   **Report and Account in Settlement of Estate Pursuant to Article 13, SCPA**

SURROGATE'S COURT OF THE STATE OF NEW YORK

COUNTY OF _____

VOLUNTARY ADMINISTRATION, Estate of   REPORT AND ACCOUNT IN
                                                       SETTLEMENT OF ESTATE PURSUAN
_____,   TO ARTICLE 13, SCPA
                                                       (as of 11/2019)

                          Deceased.   File No. _____

        The undersigned, authorized by this court to act as the voluntary administrator of the above entitled estate, reports and accounts as follows:

1.   There has come into my possession the following personal property of the deceased, which is on hand or has been converted into cash in the amounts indicated:

                          Item   Value

_____

_____

_____

                [If more space is needed add a sheet of paper]

Total value of personal property and cash: $ _____

2.   All of this personal property and cash have been disbursed or distributed as follows:

                   Item or Cash   To Whom

_____

_____

_____

Receipts or canceled checks showing the payment of expenses of administration, disbursements, or distributions are annexed.

3.   No part of the estate of the decedent remains in my possession.

                                        _____
                                                Voluntary Administrator

                                        _____
                                         Print Name of Voluntary Administrator

STATE OF _____)
) ss.:
COUNTY OF _____)

_____, being duly sworn, deposes and says:
I have read the foregoing Report and Account and know the contents thereof; the matters and things therein stated are true of my own knowledge; the foregoing Account is in all respects just and true and contains a full, particular and true account of all money and property of the deceased coming into my possession; and the administration expenses, disbursements and distribution shown have been actually made for the purposes and reasons therein stated.

Sworn to before me on
_____, 20____   _____
                                                      (Affiant)

_____
Notary Public
My Commission expires: _____

SE-1D (11/2019)

FORM SE-3A   Affidavit in Relation to Settlement of Estate Under Article 13, SCPA

SURROGATE'S COURT OF THE STATE OF NEW YORK
COUNTY OF _____
---X
VOLUNTARY ADMINISTRATION, Estate of

**AFFIDAVIT IN RELATION TO
SETTLEMENT OF ESTATE UNDER
ARTICLE 13, SCPA**

_____,

_____ Deceased.
---X

File No. _____
(as of 11/2019)

(INSTRUCTIONS: In completing this form, answer
each question. This may be done in some instances
by crossing out words in parenthesis and in some
instances by inserting the required information.)

STATE OF _____)

COUNTY OF_____) ss.:

I, _____, being duly sworn, depose and say

(1) My permanent address is: _____
                                                     (Street Address)

                                                                                              (City/Town/Village)

_____
          (County)   (State)   (Zip)   (Telephone Number)

My mailing address is: _____
                                          (If different from permanent address)

My email address is: _____

(2) My interest is: ☐ Distributee of decedent _____
                                                                        (Relationship)

                             ☐ Other (Specify) _____

(3) The name, permanent address, date, place of death, and citizenship of the decedent, to whose estate this proceeding
relates, are as follows:

Name of Decedent (a/k/a, if applicable): _____

Permanent Address: _____
                                  (Street Address)   (City/Town/Village)   (County)   (State)

Date of Death: _____ Place of Death: _____
                                                                                      (City/Town/Village)   (State)

Citizenship of Decedent: _____

(4) Decedent died: ☐ Intestate (without a will)
                             ☐ Testate (the original will is attached)

(5) A search of the records of the Court shows that no application has been made in, the estate of the decedent for voluntary
administration, letters of administration or for probate of a will, and your affiant is informed and verily believes that no such
application ever has been made to any other Surrogate's Court in this state.

Official Forms

SE-3A   (11/2019)   -1-

(6) The names and addresses of the decedent's distributees under New York law, including non-marital children and descendants of predeceased non-marital children, and their relationship to the decedent, are as follows: (If more space is needed, add a sheet of paper)

Name	Mailing Address, (Including Zip)	Relationship Indicate if non-marital)

(7) (If decedent had a will) The name and address of all beneficiaries in the will of the decedent filed herewith are as follows: (If more space is needed, add a sheet of paper)

Name	Mailing Address, (Including Zip)	Bequest

8) The value of the entire personal property, wherever located, of the decedent, exclusive of joint bank accounts, trust accounts, U.S. savings bonds POD (payable on death), and jointly owned personal property, or property exempt under the EPTL §5-3.1, **does not exceed $50,000.00.**

9) The following, exclusive of joint bank accounts, trust accounts, U.S. savings bonds POD (payable on death), and jointly owned personal property, or property exempt under EPTL §5-3.1, is a complete list of all personal property owned by the decedent, either standing in his/her own name or owned by him/her beneficially and including items of value in any safe deposit box. (If more space is needed, add a sheet of paper)

Items of Personal Property Separately Listed	Value of Each Item

TOTAL $ _____

(10) All the **liabilities** of the decedent known to me are as follows: (If more space is needed, add a sheet of paper)

　　Name of Creditor　　　　　　　　　　　　　　　　　　　Amount Owed

_____　　_____

_____　　_____

_____　　_____

(11) I undertake to act as voluntary administrator of the decedent's estate, and to administer it pursuant to Article 13 of the Surrogate's Court Procedure Act. I agree to reduce all of the decedent's assets to possession; to liquidate such assets to the extent necessary; to open an estate bank account in a bank of deposit or savings bank in this state, in which I shall deposit all money received; to sign all checks drawn on or withdrawals from such account in the name of the estate by myself, as voluntary administrator; to pay the expenses of administration, the decedent's reasonable funeral expenses and his/her debts in the order provided by law; and to distribute the balance to the person or persons and in the amount or amounts provided by law. As voluntary administrator, I shall file in this court an account of all receipts and of disbursements made.

(12)　I understand that this proceeding will not determine the estate tax liability, if any, in the event that the decedent had any interest in real property or any joint bank accounts, trust accounts, U.S. savings bonds POD (payable on death), or jointly owned or trust property.

(13) If letters testamentary or of administration are later granted, I acknowledge that my powers as voluntary administrator shall cease, and I shall deliver to the court-appointed fiduciary a complete statement of my account and all assets and funds of the estate in my possession.

_____
　　　　　　　　　　　Signature of Affiant

_____
　　　　　　　　　　　Print Name

Sworn to before me on

_____, 20 _____

_____
Notary Public
My Commission Expires:
(Affix Notary Stamp or Seal)

Signature of Attorney: _____

Print Name: _____

Firm Name: _____Tel. No.: _____

Address of Attorney: _____

Official Forms

FORM SE-3B

SURROGATE'S COURT

SF-244

FORM SE-3B   Affidavit in Relation to Settlement of Estate Under Article 13, SCPA

SURROGATE'S COURT OF THE STATE OF NEW YORK
COUNTY OF _____
---X
VOLUNTARY ADMINISTRATION, Estate of

_____ ,
                                    Deceased.
---X

STATE OF _____)
) ss.:
COUNTY OF _____)

**AMENDED AFFIDAVIT
IN RELATION TO SETTLEMENT
OF ESTATE
UNDER ARTICLE 13, SCPA**
(as of 11/2019)

File No._____

I, _____ , being duly sworn, depose and say:
     (Name)

1.   I am the voluntary administrator of the above-named decedent and make this affidavit pursuant to Article 13 of the Surrogate's Court Procedure Act. The original and any amended affidavits were filed on the following dates: [list dates]

_____

2.   I was found qualified to act as the voluntary administrator of the above captioned estate by the
_____ County Surrogate's Court on the _____ day of _____, 20 _____.

3.   The following items of personal property, owned by the above-named decedent, were not listed in paragraph 9 of the Affidavit of Voluntary Administration originally filed nor in any amended affidavits filed with the court.

Items of Personal Property Separately Listed	Value of Each Item
_____	_____
_____	_____
_____	_____
Total $	_____

4.   For the item of personal property listed in paragraph 3, I require _____ additional certificates of voluntary administration.

The value of all of the decedent's non-exempt assets still does not exceed **$50,000.00**.

Sworn to before me on
_____, 20 _____

_____
(Affiant)

_____
(Print Name)

_____
Notary Public
My Commission Expires:
(Affix Notary Stamp or Seal)

Signature of Attorney:_____

Print Name:_____

Firm Name:_____ Tel No. : _____

Address of Attorney:_____

SE-3B (11/2019)

FORM SG-1   Petition for Standby Guardianship [SCPA 1726(3)]

For Office Use Only
. (Filing Fee Paid $)
(Receipt No: No:)

SURROGATE'S COURT OF THE STATE OF NEW YORK
COUNTY OF
---x
Proceeding for the Appointment
of a Standby Guardian for

PETITION FOR APPOINTMENT OF
A STANDBY GUARDIAN
(SCPA 1726 (3))

_____ An Infant.
---x

File No.

TO THE SURROGATE'S COURT, COUNTY OF

It is respectfully alleged:

1. The name, relationship, domicile, and telephone number of the petitioner are as follows: [Petitioner must be a parent, legal guardian or legal custodian of the infant. If legal guardian or legal custodian submit a copy of the order of appointment.]

    Name: ☐ Mother   ☐ Father   ☐ Legal Guardian   ☐ Legal Custodian

    Domicile:
                    (Street Address)   (City/Town/Village)

            (County)   (State)   (Zip)   (Telephone Number)

    Mailing address:
                                                        (If different from domicile)

2. The name, domicile, date of birth and marital status of the infant are as follows: [Birth Certificate Must be filed with this petition]

    Name:
                                                        (Date of Birth)
    Domicile:
                    (Street Address)   (City/Town/Village)

            (County)   (State)   (Zip)

    Mailing address:
                                    (If different from domicile)

    Marital Status:

3. The names and addresses of the adult persons with whom the infant resides are :   [If same as above so state]
    Name:

    Domicile:
                    (Street Address)   (City/Town/Village)

            (County)   (State)   (Zip)

    Mailing address:
                                    (If different from domicile)

SG-1 (7/2018)

1

4.   The name and domicile of the proposed standby guardian(s) are as follows:

Name:

(Relationship, if any, to infant)

Domicile:

(Street Address)   (City/Town/Village)

(County)   (State)   (Zip)

Mailing address:

(If different from domicile)

5.   The name and domicile, of the other parent of the infant and, if the infant is married, the infant's spouse, or if the other parent is deceased and there is no spouse, the grandparents residing within the county, are as follows:

Father/Mother:

Domicile:

Spouse:

(Date of Birth)

Domicile:

Maternal Grandparents:

Domicile:

Paternal Grandparents:

Domicile:

The foregoing persons are adult and competent, except: [If any of the above is an infant attach a Schedule containing the name of the infant, with whom he or she resides, whether he or she has a court-appointed guardian, and if so, provide the name and address of the guardian. If disability is other than infancy, fill out and attach Schedule A.]

6.   No other persons or agencies are interested in this proceeding other than those mentioned above, except:

7a.   No guardian or standby guardian ever has been appointed for the infant except as follows: [See SCPA Section 1704 (3)]

7b.   Custody of the infant never has been surrendered by a person lawfully charged therewith, nor has custody of the infant been the subject of any court order, except as hereinafter listed: [So specify and attach copies of all surrenders, court orders, or divorce decrees]

8. [If you seek the appointment of a Standby Guardian of the **person only**, DO NOT complete this paragraph]. The estimated value of all real and personal property owned by the infant and the infant's resources are as follows:

    a. PERSONAL PROPERTY [State exact title of all bank accounts with account number and balance. List insurance policies by Company, policy number, amount insured, name of insured and relationship to infant. List the value of infant's interest.]

    The personal property of the infant is not subject to the control of the infant's spouse under the laws of a jurisdiction other than New York. [If property is so subject, so state]

    b. REAL PROPERTY [State whether the real property is mortgaged or under a lien and the amount thereof. Indicate whether the property is to be occupied as a residence by the infant. If not, indicate rental income or whether a sale of the property is contemplated.]

    Location of Property

    Gross Value $ Less Mortgage or Lien $ = Net value $

    Infant's interest   Annual Income $

    c. ANNUAL INCOME OF INFANT FROM ALL SOURCES:

        (1) Compensation or pension to be received from : $

        (2) Income from Trusts $

        (3) Income from Real Property $

        (4) Other Income $

9. The authority of the standby guardian is to become effective upon the petitioner's [Check as many boxes as are appropriate:]

    a. ☐ incapacity   b. ☐ death

    c. ☐ administrative separation with consent   d. ☐ consent

10. Petitioner:

    ☐ suffers from a progressively chronic illness

    ☐ suffers from an irreversible fatal illness

    ☐ may become subject to an administrative separation

    [State the basis for the above statement, such as the date and source of the medical diagnosis. You need not identify the illness.]

11. If administrative separation [Check appropriate box]

  a. ☐ Petitioner has a basis to believe that she/he may be the subject of a federal immigration matter because
      [See SCPA 1726 (3)(b)(iii)(C)]

  b. ☐ Petitioner is in receipt of official communication regarding immigration enforcement.

12. The infant ☐is ☐is not a Native American Child subject to the Indian Child Welfare Act of 1978 (25 USC Section 1901-1963).

13. Petitioner☐(has)☐(does not have) knowledge that the person nominated to be Standby Guardian has ever been named as a subject of an indicated report filed pursuant to Title 6 of Article 6 of the SocialServices Law, or has been the subject of or the respondent in a child protective proceedingcommenced under Article 10 of the Family Court Act, which proceeding resulted in an order finding thatthe child is an abused or neglected child. [If the petitioner has such knowledge, attach an affidavitexplaining in detail].

14. Completed and annexed hereto is the Request for Information Guardianship Form required to be submitted to the New York Central Register of Child Abuse and Maltreatment.

15. [Check appropriate box]:

  a. ☐ The petitioner is able to attend any hearing to be scheduled by the court.

  b. ☐ The petitioner is medically unable to appear and asks that the court dispense with his/her appearance.

  c. ☐ The petitioner may not be available to attend any court scheduled hearing due to administrative separation.

16. No prior application has been made to any Court for the relief requested herein.

WHEREFORE, your petitioner respectfully prays that: [Check and complete all relief requested].

(a) Letters of Standby Guardianship of the

      ☐ Person only
      ☐ Property only
      ☐ Person and Property

    be granted to

    or such other person or corporation as may be entitled thereto upon petitioner's ☐death ☐incapacity☐ administrative separation ☐consent [Check appropriate boxes] and that process issue to all interested persons who have not waived the issuance of same requiring them to show cause why such relief should not be granted.

4

(b)   The standby guardian of the property be prohibited from collecting or receiving any money or property of the infant until he or she qualifies and complies with the provisions of SCPA 1708.

Dated: _____
                                              (Signature of Petitioner)

                                              (Print Name)

STATE OF NEW YORK   )
) ss.:
COUNTY OF   REMOVE   )

                    REMOVE   , being duly sworn deposes and says that I am the petitioner above named. I have read the foregoing petition and the same is true of my own knowledge except as the matters therein stated to be alleged upon information and belief and as to those matters I believe them to be true.

Sworn to before me this

         day of   20   _____
                                              (Signature of Petitioner)

_____   _____
Notary Public   (Print Name)
Commission Expires:
(Affix Notary Stamp or Seal)

Signature of Attorney: ADD LINE FOR SIGNATURE

Print Name:

Firm Name: Tel.No.:

Address of Attorney:

FORM SG-1   SURROGATE'S COURT   **SF-250**

File #

SURROGATE'S COURT OF THE STATE OF NEW YORK
COUNTY OF
---x
Proceeding for the Appointment   SCHEDULE A
of a Standby Guardian for   PERSONS UNDER DISABILITY
                                                            OTHER THAN INFANTS

                                    An Infant.
---x

[use additional sheets if more than one]

1.   Name: Relationship:

      Residence:

      With whom does this person reside?

      If this person is in prison, name of prison:

      Does this person have a court-appointed fiduciary?   Yes ☐   No ☐

            If yes, give name, title and address:

            If no, describe nature of disability:

            If no, give name and address of relative or friend interested in his or her welfare:

6

FORM SG-2 **Physician's Opinion of Progressively Chronic or Fatal Illness [SCPA 1726(3)]**

SURROGATE'S COURT OF THE STATE OF NEW YORK
COUNTY OF
---x
Proceeding for the Appointment
of a Standby Guardian for

PHYSICIAN'S OPINION
OF PROGRESSIVELY
CHRONIC OR FATAL ILLNESS

An Infant.
---x File No.

I,   , am a physician duly licensed to practice medicine in the State of New York.

1. My license number is:

2. My office is located at:

3. [Check appropriate box]:

☐ I am the physician who has primary responsibility for the treatment and care of the petitioner, or

☐ I am physician who is acting on behalf of   , the physician who has primary responsibility for the treatment and care of the petitioner, or

☐ I am a physician who is familiar with the petitioner's medical condition.

4. [Check appropriate box(es) and explain where requested]:

☐ [i] I have performed tests or evaluations of the petitioner. [Set forth the dates performed.]

☐ [ii] I have reviewed the tests or evaluations performed on petitioner. [Set forth the dates performed, and the names of the doctors who performed the tests and/or evaluations.]

5. [Check appropriate box]:

Based upon the foregoing tests or evaluations of the petitioner, it is my opinion, with a reasonable degree of medical certainty, that the petitioner

☐ has an irreversible fatal illness
☐ has a progressively chronic illness
☐ may become incapacitated by reason of a chronic and substantial inability, as a result of mental impairment, to understand the nature and consequences of decisions concerning the care of the petitioner's dependent infant or ward and a consequent inability by petitioner to care for said infant or ward.

6. Petitioner is ☐ medically capable, ☐ medically incapable, of appearing at the hearing. [If medically incapable of appearing, explain]

7. I am not a party to this proceeding and affirm the foregoing opinion to be true under the penalties of perjury.

Dated: _____
                                                    Signature of Physician

SG-2 (7/2018)

FORM SG-3 **Waiver of Citation, Renunciation and Consent to Appointment of Standby Guardian [SCPA 1726(3)]**

SURROGATE'S COURT OF THE STATE OF NEW YORK
COUNTY OF
---X

Proceeding for the Appointment
of a Standby Guardian for

WAIVER OF CITATION
RENUNCIATION AND CONSENT
TO APPOINTMENT OF STANDBY GUARDIAN
(SCPA 1726 (3))

An Infant. File No.

---X

I, whose domicile is:

(Street Address) (City/Town/Village)

(County) (State) (Zip)

am a competent person over the age of eighteen years. My interest in the above entitled proceeding is as follows:
[Check appropriate interest]

☐ Parent of the above named infant
☐ Grandparent of the above named infant
☐ Other (Specify)

I hereby personally appear and waive the issuance and service of a citation in this matter and

(1) Consent that be appointed the standby guardian of the

a. ☐ Person only
b. ☐ Property only
c. ☐ Person and Property

(2) Renounce all right to letters of Guardianship which may hereafter be issued by the Court upon the qualification of the Standby Guardian.

Dated:

ADD LINE FOR SIGNATURE
(Signature)

_____
(Print Name)

STATE OF NEW YORK)
COUNTY OF REMOVE) ss.:
)

On , 20 , before me personally appeared
  REMOVE to be the same
person described in and who executed the foregoing instrument. Such person duly swore such instrument and duly acknowledge that he/she executed the same.

_____
Notary Public
Commission Expires:
(Affix Notary Stamp or Seal)

_____
Name of Attorney

_____
Address

Telephone Number

SG-3 (7/2018)

8

FORM SG-4   Citation [SCPA 1726(3)]

STANDBY GUARDIANSHIP CITATION   File No.

SURROGATE'S COURT -   COUNTY

CITATION

THE PEOPLE OF THE STATE OF NEW YORK

TO

   A petition having been filed by   , who is
domiciled at

   YOU ARE HEREBY CITED TO SHOW CAUSE before the Surrogate's Court,
County, at   , New York, on   , 20
at   o'clock of that day why an order should not be granted pursuant to SCPA 1726 appointing
                                    as Standby Guardian (s) of   , an infant.

(State any further relief requested)

                    HON.
                         Surrogate

Dated, Attested and Sealed,

              , 20

                       Chief Clerk

(Seal)

Name of
Attorney for Petitioner   Tel. No.

Address of Attorney

Note: This citation is served upon you as required by law. You are not required to appear. If you fail to
appear it will be assumed that you do not object to the relief requested. You have the right to have an
attorney-at-law appear for you.

SG-4 (7/2018)

9

FORM SG-5 **Affidavit and Consent of Proposed Standby Guardian [SCPA 1726(3)]**

SURROGATE'S COURT OF THE STATE OF NEW YORK
COUNTY OF
-- X
Proceeding for the Appointment
of a Standby Guardian for

                                An Infant.
-- X

STATE OF NEW YORK   )
) ss.:
COUNTY OF   )

AFFIDAVIT AND CONSENT
OF PROPOSED STANDBY
GUARDIAN PURSUANT TO
SCPA (1726) (3)

File No.

, being duly sworn, deposes and says:

1.   I am a competent person over the age of eighteen years, and I submit this affidavit in support of the petition to have me appointed standby guardian of the ☐person only, ☐property only, or ☐person and property of the above named infant.   [Check one]

2.   I have known the subject infant since   by reason of the following [State relationship, if any]:

3.   I reside at   and the other resident members of my household are [Include all persons residing there and their respective ages]:

SG-5 (7/2018)

10

4. Except for minor traffic offenses and adjudications as a youthful offender or juvenile delinquent:

(a) Have you ever been convicted of a crime? ☐ yes ☐ no

(b) Have you ever forfeited bail or other collateral? ☐ yes ☐ no

(c) Do you have criminal charges pending against you? ☐ yes ☐ no

(d) Do you have a physical impairment or mental or medical condition that would interfere with your ability to perform the duties of guardian of the infant? ☐ yes ☐ no

(e) Have you ever used controlled substances or narcotics or been addicted to alcohol? ☐ yes ☐ no

[If you have answered "yes" to any of the questions set forth in (a) - (e), set forth details in space provided].

5. I am willing and able to undertake the care, custody and control of the infant until the infant attains the age of eighteen or until the court determines otherwise.

6. Upon the petitioner's ☐ incapacity, ☐ death, ☐ administrative separation or upon written consent, I agree to file all necessary documentation with the court within 90 days of the receipt of the determination of the incapacity, death, or 60 days of the date of the standby guardian's receipt of documentation of the petitioner's administrative separation and written consent.

_____
Signature of the Proposed Standby Guardian

Sworn to before me this
    day of _____ , 20 ___

_____
Notary Public
Commission Expires:
(Affix Notary Stamp or Seal)

11

Official Forms

FORM SG-6   Consent of Petitioner for Standby Guardian [SCPA 1726(3)]

SURROGATE'S COURT OF THE STATE OF NEW YORK
COUNTY OF
---X
Proceeding for the Appointment   CONSENT OF PETITIONER
of a Standby Guardian for   FOR STANDBY GUARDIAN
                                                            (Pursuant to SCPA 1726 (3)(e)(iv))

                              An Infant.   File No.
---X

I   , state that:

1.   I am the petitioner in the proceeding for the appointment of a Standby Guardian of my minor
      child.

2.   A decree was signed on
      appointing   standby guardian effective upon the execution
      of this consent.

3.   Notwithstanding the request in the petition that the Standby Guardian's authority be effective
      upon my ☐ incapacity ☐ death ☐ administrative separation, [Delete inapplicable provision]
      I hereby consent to commencement of the Standby Guardian's authority upon (his) (her) receipt
      of this written consent executed in accordance with the provisions of Section 1726 (3)(e)(iv) of
      the Surrogate's Court Procedure Act.

4.   I am physically unable to sign this written consent and have directed
      (Name of person other than Standby Guardian) to sign on my behalf in my presence and in the
      presence of two witnesses whose signatures are set forth below. [Delete if inapplicable]

Dated: _____
                                             Petitioner's Signature

                                    _____
                                          Signature of Person other than Petitioner

    I declare that the person whose name appears above (signed this consent in my presence) (was
physically unable to sign and asked another to sign this document, who did so in my presence).   I further
declare that I am at least eighteen years old and am not the person designated as standby guardian.

Dated: Witness:
                                    _____
                                                Signature
                                    _____
                                                Print Name
                                    _____
                                                Address
Dated: Witness:

                                    _____
                                                Signature
                                    _____
                                                Print Name
                                    _____
                                                Address

SG-6 (7/2018)

12

I _____ appointed or designated as

(Name of Standby Guardian)

such by _____ hereby acknowledge that I have

received the foregoing consent of the following date _____

_____

Signature

_____

Print Name

[Note: The Standby Guardian must file this written consent with the Court within 90 days of receipt of the written consent.   Failure to file may result in the guardian's authority being rescinded by the Court.]

Name of Attorney: _____   Tel No. _____

Address of Attorney: _____

FORM SG-7   SURROGATE'S COURT   **SF-258**

FORM SG-7   **Consent of Infant Over 14 [SCPA 1726(3)]**

SURROGATE'S COURT OF THE STATE OF NEW YORK
COUNTY OF
-- X
Proceeding for the Appointment
of a Standby Guardian for   CONSENT OF INFANT OVER 14

-- An Infant. ----- X   File No.

I, the infant herein, being over 14 years of age, join in the foregoing petition and consent that
be appointed standby guardian of my

☐   person only
☐   property only
☐   person and property

ADD LINE FOR SIGNATURE
(Signature)

_____
(Print Name)

STATE OF NEW YORK   )
)   SS.:
COUNTY OF   REMOVE   )

On   20   , before me personally came
to me known and the person described in and who executed the foregoing instrument. Such person swore
such instrument before me and duly acknowledged to me that she/he executed the same.

_____
Notary Public
Commission Expires:
(Affix Notary Stamp or Seal)

Name of Attorney: Tel No.

Address of Attorney

SG-7 (7/2018)

14

FORM SG-8   **Decree Appointing a Standby Guardian [SCPA 1726(3)]**

SURROGATE'S COURT OF THE STATE OF NEW YORK
COUNTY OF
-- X
Proceeding for the Appointment
of a Standby Guardian for

                                    An Infant.
-- X

| | DECREE APPOINTING
                                       A STANDBY GUARDIAN
                                       (SCPA 1726 (3)) |

File No.

A petition having been filed by   , praying for the appointment of a
Standby Guardian for the above named infant, and it appearing that the petitioner suffers from a progressively
chronic or irreversible fatal illness or has been administratively separated from their infant child and that the
interests of the infant will be promoted by the appointment of a Standby Guardian of the infant's person and/or
property; and that   is in all respects competent to act as such
Standby Guardian; it is hereby

ORDERED, ADJUDGED AND DECREED, that
be and is hereby appointed Standby Guardian of the person and/or property of the infant, whose authority
shall be effective upon the receipt by the standby guardian of

☐   a determination of the petitioner's incapacity
☐   a certificate of petitioner's death
☐   evidence of death that may satisfy the court
☐   documentation of petitioner's administrative separation

The authority of the Standby Guardian shall also be effective upon the petitioner's written consent
pursuant to Section 1726 (3)(e)(iv) of the Surrogate's Court Procedure Act; and it is further

ORDERED, ADJUDGED AND DECREED, that the Standby Guardian of the infant shall file a copy of a
determination of incapacity or certificate of death or other such evidence of death that may satisfy the court of
the petitioner with this court within 90 days or his or her authority may be rescinded by the court or the standby
guardian shall file a copy of documentation of the administrative separation within 60 days of the date of the
standby guardian's receipt of documentation of the petitioner's administrative separation or his or her authority
may be rescinded by the court; and it is further

ORDERED, ADJUDGED AND DECREED, that letters of Guardianship shall be issued to the Standby
Guardian upon his or her filing the Confirmation Affidavit of Standby Guardian, qualifying pursuant to SCPA
Section 708, and complying with the provisions of SCPA Section 1708, if applicable.

_____
                                                              , Surrogate

Dated: , 20

SG-8 (7/2018)

15

Official Forms

FORM SG-9   **Confirmation Affidavit of Standby Guardian [SCPA 1726(3)]**

SURROGATE'S COURT OF THE STATE OF NEW YORK
COUNTY OF
-- X

Proceeding for the Appointment   CONFIRMATION AFFIDAVIT
of a Standby Guardian for   OF STANDBY GUARDIAN

                                 An Infant.   File No.
-- X

STATE OF NEW YORK   )
) ss.:
COUNTY OF   )

The undersigned, Standby Guardian, being duly sworn says:

1.   I was appointed standby guardian of the above named infant by this Court by decree dated

2.   There has been ☐ no material change ☐ a material change in the circumstances of the infant since the filing of the petition. [If any material changes, so specify]

3.   The petitioner has ☐ died ☐ been incapacitated ☐ submitted documentation of petitioner's administrative separation ☐ made a written consent whereby I am now entitled to receive letters of Guardianship.

4.   I have never been named as a subject of an indicated report filed pursuant to Title 6 of Article 6 of the Social Services Law, or have been the subject of or the respondent in a child protective proceeding commenced under Article 10 of the Family Court Act, which proceeding resulted in an order finding that the child is an abused or neglected child, except: [Explain in detail].

5.   OATH OF GUARDIAN: I am over eighteen years of age and domiciled in the State of New York; that I will well, faithfully and honestly discharge the duties as a standby guardian. I am acquainted with the infant and have read the statement contained in the petition filed with the Court as to the value, if any, of the infants property, and believe it to be correct. I am not ineligible to receive letters.

6.   DESIGNATION OF CLERK FOR SERVICE OF PROCESS: I hereby designated the Clerk of the Surrogate's Court of   County, and his or her successor in office, as a person on whom service of any process issuing from such Surrogate's Court may be made, in like manner and with like effects as if it were served personally upon me whenever I cannot be found and served within the State of New York after due diligence is used.

My domicile is :
               (Street Number)   (City, Village/Town)   (State)   (Zip)

If I change my address I shall promptly notify the court of the new address.

                                                       _____
SG-9 (7/2018)   Signature of Proposed Guardian

STATE OF NEW YORK)
) ss.:
COUNTY OF REMOVE)

On _____ , 20 _____ , before me personally appeared _____
to me known and known to me to be the person described in and who
executed the foregoing instrument, and duly acknowledged to me that REMOVE he executed the same.

Sworn to before me on this
REMOVE day of REMOVE , 20

REMOVE
_____
Notary Public   Name of Attorney
Commission Expires:
(Affix Notary Stamp or Seal)

                                                 Address

                                                 Telephone Number

18

FORM SG-10   SURROGATE'S COURT   **SF-262**

FORM SG-10   **Designation of Standby Guardian [SCPA 1726(3)]**

For Office Use Only
(Filing Fee Paid $)
(Receipt No: No:)

SURROGATE'S COURT OF THE STATE OF NEW YORK
COUNTY OF
---x
Proceeding for the Appointment   DESIGNATION OF
of a Standby Guardian for   STANDBY GUARDIAN
                                                    (SCPA 1726 (3))

                              An Infant.   File No.
---x
TO THE SURROGATE'S COURT, COUNTY OF

       I   , hereby designate
           (Name of Parent)   (Name of Designee)
                                          and

           (Address)   (Telephone No.)

as standby guardian of the ☐person, ☐property or ☐person and property of my child(ren), namely

                 (Name of child(ren))
The appointment of   , as standby guardian of the
                 (Name of Designee/Standby Guardian)
person and/or property of my children would be in their best interests because

The standby guardian's authority shall take effect: (1) if my doctor concludes in writing that I am mentally
incapacitated, and thus unable to care for my child(ren); (2) if my doctor concludes in writing that I am
physically debilitated, and thus unable to care for my child(ren) and I consent in writing, before two witnesses,
to the standby guardian's authority taking effect; (3) If I become subject to an administrative separation such
that care and supervision of the child will be interrupted or cannot be provided; or (4) upon my death.

In the event the person I designate above is unable or unwilling to act as guardian for my child(ren), I hereby
designate

           (Name)   (Address)
                 as standby guardian of my child(ren).
       (Telephone No.)

SG-10 (7/2018)

1

I also understand that my standby guardian's authority will cease sixty days after commencing unless by such date he or she petitions the court for appointment as guardian.

I understand that I retain full parental, guardianship, custodial or caretaker rights even after the commencement of the standby guardian's authority, and may revoke the standby guardianship at any time.

Dated: _____
     mm/dd/yyyy

_____
(Signature of Petitioner)

_____
(Print Name)

I declare that the person whose name appears above signed this document in my presence, or was physically unable to sign and asked another to sign this document, who did so in my presence. I further declare that I am at least eighteen years old and am not the person designated as standby guardian.

Date: _____
     mm/dd/yyyy

_____
Witness's Signature

Address:

Date: _____
     mm/dd/yyyy

_____
Witness's Signature

Address:

FORM SLT-1   **Petition for Successor Letters Testamentary**

Filing Fee Paid	$
_____ Certs	$
Receipt No: _____	No: _____

DO NOT LEAVE ANY ITEMS BLANK

STATE OF NEW YORK
SURROGATE'S COURT: COUNTY OF _____
_____X
In the Matter of the Petition for Successor Letters Testamentary
in the Estate of

**PETITION FOR SUCCESSOR
LETTERS TESTAMENTARY**

File No. _____

a/k/a

Deceased.

_____X

To the Surrogate's Court, County of _____

It is respectfully alleged:

1.(a)   The name, citizenship, domicile (or, in the case of a bank or trust company, its principal office) and interest in this proceeding of the petitioner(s) are as follows:

Name:_____

Domicile or Principal Office:_____
(Street and Number)

_____
(City, Village or Town)   (State)   (Zip Code)
      Mailing Address:_____
(If different from domicile)

Citizen of:_____

Name:_____

Domicile or Principal Office:_____
(Street and Number)

_____
(City, Village or Town)   (State)   (Zip Code)
      Mailing Address:_____
(If different from domicile)

Citizen of:_____

Interest(s) of Petitioner(s): [Check one]   [ ] Successor Executor(s) named in decedent's Will
                                             [ ] Other (Specify) _____

1.(b)   The proposed Successor Executor [ ] is [ ] is not an attorney.
        [Note: A sole Successor Executor-Attorney must comply with 22 NYCRR §207.16(e)]

1.(c)   The proposed Successor Executor [ ] is [ ] is not the attorney-draftsperson, a then-affiliated attorney or employee thereof.
        [NOTE: An attorney-draftsperson, a then-affiliated attorney or employee thereof must comply with SCPA §2307-a]

2.   The will of the above-named decedent was admitted to probate by the Surrogate's Court of _____

County on _____ and Letters Testamentary were issued to _____

who on _____, [ ] died   [ ] other (specify) _____.

[Note: If prior fiduciary is deceased, please provide court with certified copy of death certificate.]

SLT-1 (04/2011)

3.   The names and addresses of all persons and parties interested in this proceeding having a right to successor letters testamentary prior or equal to the petitioner(s) are as follows:

Name and   Domicile Address and   Nature of Fiduciary Status
Relationship   Mailing Address

4. The names and addresses of all persons and parties who are named in the will as fiduciaries or beneficiaries, other than those named in paragraph 3 above, are as follows:

Name and   Domicile Address and   Description of Legacy, Devise
Relationship   Mailing Address   or Other Interest, or Nature of
                                                                                 Fiduciary Status

[Note: If any such person is under a disability state name and post office address of a person upon whom service of process may be made on behalf of such person.]

5. There are no persons other than those hereinbefore mentioned interested in this proceeding.

6.(a) To the best of the knowledge of the undersigned, the property of the estate that remains **unadministered** is as follows:

Personal Property $_____ Improved real property in New York State $_____

Unimproved real property in New York State $_____

Estimated gross rents for a period of 18 months $_____

(b) No other testamentary assets exist in New York State, nor does any cause of action exist on behalf of the estate, except as follows: **[Enter "NONE" or specify]**

_____

_____

WHEREFORE, petitioner(s) pray(s):

That Successor Letters Testamentary issue to _____
in the same manner as original letters, and that he/she/they be authorized to complete the administration of the estate of
_____, deceased.

Dated:_____

1. _____   2. _____
    (Signature of Petitioner)   (Signature of Petitioner)

_____   _____
       (Print Name)   (Print Name)

3. _____
    (Name of Corporate Petitioner)

_____
       (Signature of Officer)

_____
  (Print Name and Title of Officer)

Official Forms

COMBINED VERIFICATION, OATH AND DESIGNATION
[For use when petitioner is an individual]

STATE OF NEW YORK)
COUNTY OF) ss.:

The undersigned, the petitioner named in the foregoing petition, being duly sworn, says:

1. VERIFICATION: I have read the foregoing petition subscribed by me and know the contents thereof, and the same is true of my own knowledge, except as to the matters therein stated to be alleged upon information and belief, and as to those matters I believe them to be true.

2. OATH OF SUCCESSOR EXECUTOR as indicated above: I am over eighteen (18) years of age and a citizen of the United States and I will well, faithfully and honestly discharge the duties of Fiduciary of the goods, chattels and credits of said decedent according to law. I am not ineligible to receive letters and will duly account for all moneys and other property that will come into my hands.

3. DESIGNATION OF CLERK FOR SERVICE OF PROCESS: I hereby designate the Clerk of the Surrogate's Court of _____ County, and his/her successor in office, as a person on whom service of any process issuing from such Court may be made in like manner and with like effect as if it were served personally upon me, whenever I cannot be found and served within the State of New York after due diligence is used.

My domicile is :_____
                        (Street Address)   (City/Town/Village)   (State)   (Zip)

_____
        (Signature of Petitioner)

_____
        (Print Name)

On_____ , _____, before me personally appeared

_____
to me known to be the person described in and who executed the foregoing instrument. Such person duly swore to such instrument before me and duly acknowledged that he/she executed the same.

_____
Notary Public
Commission Expires:
(Affix Notary Stamp or Seal)

Signature of Attorney:_____

Print Name:_____

Firm Name:_____ Tel No. :_____

Address of Attorney:_____

-3-

COMBINED CORPORATE VERIFICATION, CONSENT AND DESIGNATION
[For use when a petitioner to be appointed is a bank or trust company]

STATE OF NEW YORK   )
COUNTY OF _____) ss.:

I, the undersigned, a_____ of
(Title)

_____,
(Name of Bank or Trust Company)

a corporation duly qualified to act in a fiduciary capacity without further security, being duly sworn say:

1.   VERIFICATION: I have read the foregoing petition subscribed by me and know the contents thereof, and the same is true of my own knowledge, except as to the matters therein stated to be alleged upon information and belief, and as to those matters I believe them to be true.

2.   CONSENT: I consent to accept the appointment as Successor Executor under the Last Will and Testament of the decedent described in the foregoing petition and consent to act as such fiduciary.

3.   DESIGNATION OF CLERK FOR SERVICE OF PROCESS: I designate the Chief Clerk of the Surrogate's Court of _____ County, and his/her successor in office, as a person on whom service of any process issuing from such Surrogate's Court may be made, in like manner and with like effect as if it were served personally upon me, whenever one of the fiduciary's proper officers cannot be found and served within the State of New York after due diligence is used.

_____
(Name of Bank or Trust Company)

By_____   _____
(Signature)   (Principal Office Street Address)

_____   _____
(Print Name and Title)   (City/Town/Village)   (State)   (Zip)

On _____ ,_____ , before me personally appeared _____, to me known, who duly swore to the foregoing instrument and who did say that he/she resides at _____ _____and that he/she is a _____ of _____, the corporation/national banking association described in and which executed such instrument; and that he/she signed his/her name thereto by order of the Board of Directors of the corporation.

_____
Notary Public
Commission Expires:
(Affix Notary Stamp or Seal)

Signature of Attorney:_____

Print Name:_____

Firm Name:_____ Tel. No.:_____

Address of Attorney:_____

FORM SLT-2   **Renunciation of Successor Letters Testamentary and Waiver of Process (Individual)**

-4-

STATE OF NEW YORK
SURROGATE'S COURT: COUNTY OF _____
_____X
In the Matter of the Petition for Successor Letters Testamentary
in the Estate of

a/k/a

RENUNCIATION OF SUCCESSOR LETTERS TESTAMENTARY AND WAIVER OF PROCESS (INDIVIDUAL)

File No._____

Deceased.
_____X

The undersigned, _____, a person interested in this estate as alternate executor, hereby personally appears in this proceeding in the Surrogate's Court of _____ County and

1. Renounces all rights to Successor Letters Testamentary.

2. Waives the issuance and service of citation in the above-entitled proceeding.

3. Consents that Successor Letters Testamentary be granted by the Court to _____
or any other person or persons entitled thereto without any notice whatsoever to the undersigned

Date _____   _____   _____
                        Signature   Street Address

               _____   _____
                        Print Name   City/State/Zip

STATE OF NEW YORK
COUNTY OF _____   ss.:

On _____, _____, before me personally appeared
_____
to me known to be the person described in and who executed the foregoing instrument. Such person duly swore to such instrument before me and duly acknowledged that he/she executed the same.

_____
Notary Public
Commission Expires:
(Affix Notary Stamp or Seal)

Name of Attorney_____ Tel. No.:_____

Address of Attorney_____

SLT-2 (04/2011)

FORM SLT-3   Renunciation of Successor Letters Testamentary and Waiver of Process (Corporation)

STATE OF NEW YORK
SURROGATE'S COURT: COUNTY OF _____
_____X
In the Matter of the Petition for Successor Letters Testamentary
in the Estate of

**RENUNCIATION OF SUCCESSOR
LETTERS TESTAMENTARY AND
WAIVER OF PROCESS (CORPORATION)**

a/k/a

File No._____

_____
                    Deceased.
_____X

The undersigned, _____, a person
interested in this estate as alternate executor, hereby personally appears in this proceeding in the Surrogate's Court of
_____ County and

    1. Renounces all rights to Successor Letters Testamentary.

    2. Waives the issuance and service of citation in the above-entitled proceeding.

    3. Consents that Successor Letters Testamentary be granted by the Court to _____
or any other person or persons entitled thereto without any notice whatsoever to the undersigned.

_____   _____
        (Signature)   (Name of Corporation)

_____   _____
        (Print Name)   (Principal Office Street Address)

                         _____
                       (City/Town/Village)   (State)   (Zip)

Date: _____

STATE OF NEW YORK
COUNTY OF _____   ss.:

    On _____, _____, before me personally appeared

_____, to me known, who
duly swore to the foregoing instrument and who did say that he/she resides at _____ and that
he/she is a_____ of_____, the corporation/national banking
association described in and which executed such instrument; and that he/she signed his/her name thereto by order of the
Board of Directors of the corporation.

_____
Notary Public
Commission Expires:
(Affix Notary Stamp or Seal)

Name of Attorney_____ Tel. No.:_____

Address of Attorney_____

SLT-3 (04/2011)

FORM SLT-4   SURROGATE'S COURT   **SF-270**

FORM SLT-4   **Notice of Petition for Appointment of Successor Executor**

STATE OF NEW YORK
SURROGATE'S COURT: COUNTY OF _____
_____X
In the Matter of the Petition for Successor Letters Testamentary
in the Estate of

                                                          NOTICE OF PETITION FOR
                                                          APPOINTMENT OF
                                                          SUCCESSOR EXECUTOR
a/k/a
                                                          File No. _____

                            Deceased.
_____X

Notice is hereby given that:

1.   The Will of the above-named decedent was admitted to probate by the Surrogate's Court of _____

County on _____, and Letters Testamentary were issued to _____,

who on _____, [   ] died [   ] other (specify)_____.

2.   The name (s) of the Successor Executor (s) of said Will is/are _____

_____, whose

address(es) is/are _____

_____

_____

3.   The names and address of all persons and parties who are named in the will as fiduciaries or beneficiaries who have not appeared or have been served or waived service of process.

          NAME   **MAILING ADDRESS**   **NATURE OF INTEREST**
                                                                          OR STATUS

[Note: If serving infant 14 years of age or older, list and mail to infant as well as parent or guardian.]

(USE ADDITIONAL SHEETS IF NECESSARY)

Date: _____, 20_____

[Note: Notice of Petition for Appointment of Successor Executor may or may not be required in all counties. If Notice is required, complete Affidavit of Mailing.]

Name of Attorney:_____ Tel. No.:_____

Address of Attorney:_____

SLT-4 (04/2011)

AFFIDAVIT OF MAILING
NOTICE OF PETITION FOR APPOINTMENT OF SUCCESSOR EXECUTOR

STATE OF NEW YORK   )
) ss.:
COUNTY OF   )

_____, residing at _____, being duly

sworn, says that he/she is over the age of 18 years, that on the _____ day of _____,

20_____, he/she deposited in a post office box regularly maintained by the government of the United States in the

_____of _____, State of New York, a copy of the foregoing Notice of Petition for

Appointment of Successor Executor contained in a securely closed postpaid wrapper directed to each of the persons named

in said Notice at the places set opposite their respective names.

Sworn to before me this _____   _____
                                                                        Signature

day of _____, 20____   _____
                                                                        Print Name

_____
Notary Public
Commission Expires:
(Affix Notary Stamp or Seal)

Name of Attorney_____ Tel. No.:_____

Address of Attorney_____

Official Forms

FORM SLT-5   Citation—Successor Letters Testamentary

-2-

SUCCESSOR LETTERS TESTAMENTARY   File No. _____

SURROGATE'S COURT - _____ COUNTY

CITATION

THE PEOPLE OF THE STATE OF NEW YORK,
By the Grace of God Free and Independent

TO:

A petition having been filed by _____, who is

domiciled at _____,

YOU ARE HEREBY CITED TO SHOW CAUSE before the Surrogate's Court, _____ County,

at _____, New York, on _____ 20_____, at _____ o'clock in

the _____ noon of that day, why a decree should not be made in the estate of _____

lately domiciled at _____, directing that

[   ] Successor Letters Testamentary issue to _____.

Dated, Attested and Sealed,

HON. _____
                                        Surrogate

_____, _____

(Seal)   _____
                                        Chief Clerk

_____   _____
Attorney for Petitioner   Telephone Number

_____
Address of Attorney

[NOTE: This citation is served upon you as required by law. You are not required to appear. If you fail to appear it will be assumed you do not object to the relief requested. You have a right to have an attorney appear for you.]

SLT-5 (04/2011)

FORM WD-1   Wrongful Death Citation

Official Form WD-1   File # _____
(4/98)

CITATION
THE PEOPLE OF THE STATE OF NEW YORK
BY THE GRACE OF GOD, FREE AND INDEPENDENT,

TO: _____
_____, an infant over the age of 14 years, of _____, New York
                            [List other parties]
_____
_____
_____
_____
_____

being persons interested as creditors, legatees, devisees, beneficiaries, distributees or otherwise of the
estate of _____, deceased, who at the time of death resided at
_____.

    A petition having been duly filed by _____, who is domiciled at
_____.

    YOU ARE HEREBY CITED TO SHOW CAUSE before the Surrogate's Court, _____ County
at _____, New York on _____, at _____ a.m.

    WHY the account of the proceedings of _____ as Administrat_____
of the estate of _____, deceased, a copy of which is attached, should not be
judicially settled, and

    WHY the administrat_____ should not be empowered to compromise and settle a certain claim
for wrongful death against _____ for the sum of $_____
and to discontinue any claim for conscious pain and suffering, and

    WHY the provisions in the limited Letters of Administration issued to the petitioner on _____,
restraining the compromise or collecting upon the aforesaid claim and cause of action, should not be
modified to permit said compromise, and

    WHY the filing of a bond should not be dispensed with, and

    WHY the defendant, _____, or defendant's insurance company,
should not pay to _____, Esqs., out of the proceeds of the settlement for the
claim for wrongful death, the sum of $_____ as and for attorneys' fees, together with
disbursements in the sum of $_____, and

    WHY the entire recovery of $_____ should not be allocated to the cause of
action for decedent's wrongful death, and

    WHY the balance of the settlement, to wit the sum of $_____, should not be distributed
to those distributees having sustained a pecuniary loss as follows:

Official Forms

_____ % of the balance to _____ widow/widower of decedent;
_____ % of the balance to _____, child of decedent; _____% of the
balance to _____, child of decedent,

and

WHY the claim of _____ should not be rejected, as a nondistributee, and

WHY the claim of _____ in the amount of $ _____ should not be rejected, and

WHY upon payments as hereinbefore mentioned the said administrat_____ should not be permitted to execute and deliver general releases and all other necessary papers to the defendant, _____, or defendant's insurance company, releasing them from all claims against them arising out of the aforesaid action for wrongful death, together with any other papers necessary to effectuate the said compromise.

DATED, ATTESTED AND SEALED

HON. _____
                                    County Surrogate

(L.S.)

_____
_____, Chief Clerk

ATTORNEY

Name of Attorney: _____
Address of Attorney: _____.

Telephone Number of Attorney: _____

NOTE: This citation is served upon you as required by law. You are not obliged to appear in person. You have a right to have an attorney appear for you. If you fail to appear it will be assumed that you do not object to the relief requested.

FORM WD-2   Wrongful Death Petition

Form WD-2
(Wrongful Death Petition)

SURROGATE'S COURT OF THE STATE OF NEW YORK
COUNTY OF _____
---X
In the Matter of the Application of

_____,

as Administrat____ of the Goods, Chattels
and Credits which were of

_____, Deceased,

For leave to compromise a certain cause
of action for wrongful death of the
decedent and to render and have judicially
settled an account of the proceedings as
such Administrat____
---X

PETITION
File No._____

(as of 4/98)

TO THE SURROGATE'S COURT:

It is respectfully alleged:

1. Petitioner_____ is the _____ of the above-named decedent

and presently resides at _____.

2. The decedent died a resident of _____, County of _____, New York

on _____, and had resided there with _____.

3. On _____, Letters of Guardianship of the person and property of

_____, infant son/daughter of the decedent (copy attached), were issued to your

petitioner by the Surrogate's Court, _____County.

4. On _____Limited Letters of Administration of the Goods, Chattels and Credits

which were of _____, deceased, were issued to petitioner by the Surrogate's

Court of _____County, which letters were of limited authority and restrained your petitioner from

compromising or collecting upon said claim for wrongful death until further order of this court. To date, said

letters have not been revoked and are presently in full force and effect. No bond was required of your

administrat____ to cover any probable amount to be realized from said action.

Form WD-2 Page 2

5. The decedent at the time of death was employed as a _____ by _____

_____ at _____, earning approximately $_____ per week.

6. The decedent at the time of death was _____ years of age, having been born on _____.

7. The injuries that resulted in the decedent's death were sustained on [give date, time] _____

_____ at [location] _____.

[Describe fatal incident]

_____

_____

_____

_____

_____

_____

_____

8. The decedent was taken to _____ Hospital where he/she died on _____ at

or about _____ a.m./p.m. of that day without having regained consciousness. [Describe circumstances, e.g.,

length of hospitalization, etc. resulting in death _____

_____

_____

_____

_____

_____

Decedent did not regain consciousness, and all of the proceeds of the settlement of the action are to be allocated

for wrongful death and not for conscious pain and suffering.

Form WD-2 Page 3

9. A combined action for decedent's wrongful death and conscious pain and suffering was commenced against the defendant _____.
[Include references to court where action commenced, pleadings, etc.] Thereafter, negotiations were entered into with the representative of _____ Insurance Company, and a final offer has been made to settle this claim for the sum of $_____ out of maximum insurance coverage of $_____.

10. An investigation of the personal resources of the defendant _____
has been undertaken and it has been discovered that [provide details as to assets] _____
_____
_____
_____

11. Petitioner believes that it is in the best interests of the distributees and the estate of the decedent and those interested therein to accept the settlement so offered and that this is the largest amount that can be obtained without further litigation.

12. The grounds of petitioner's belief are [indicate reasons why acceptance of the settlement is advisable] _____
_____
_____
_____

13. The decedent at the time of death was married and left the following survivors:

Name	Relationship	Date of Birth	Present Age

Form WD-2 Page 4

14. On _____, Petitioner retained _____ Esq. of

_____ as his/her attorney (a copy of the retainer agreement and affidavit of

legal services are attached). In view of the results achieved, petitioner would request the court to approve a fee

as follows: That the attorney's disbursements in the sum of $_____ first be deducted from the gross

settlement of _____; that of the balance of $_____ a fee of $_____ or

_____ % be allowed, which together would amount to total compensation of $_____.

     15. Petitioner has been advised that the proceeds of an action for wrongful death are allocated according

to the pecuniary loss sustained by the widow/widower and infants. Petitioner has further been advised that the

share of the petitioner and the children are computed in accordance with the years of dependency each of the

survivors could look forward to but for the decedent's death. At the time of death, decedent was _____ years of

age, having been born on_____ and having died on and had a life expectancy of _____ years,

based on the table of vital statistics, United States Health Department - copy attached. As petitioner as

husband/wife and widower/widow was born on _____ and had a life expectancy of _____ years,

the life expectancy of the decedent must be used. Therefore, the years of dependency are as follows:

Name	Age on Date of Death	Anticipated Years of Dependency	Percentage Net Amount of Settlement

Form WD-2 Page 5

NOTE: WHERE RECOVERY OR PART THEREOF IS ALLOCATED TO CONSCIOUS PAIN AND SUFFERING, THE PROCEEDS PASS THROUGH THE DECEDENT'S ESTATE EITHER IN ACCORDANCE WITH THE PROVISIONS OF HIS/HER WILL, OR IN THE EVENT OF INTESTACY, IN ACCORDANCE WITH EPTL 4-1.1.

16. All of the above persons are of sound mind and full age (except for the infant _____)

and are citizens of the United States.

17. Petitioner as administrat_____ hereby waives any claim for statutory commissions and waives the

filing of a surety bond.

18. Decedent's funeral bill in the sum of $_____ has been paid by _____.

Annexed hereto is the paid bill. No reimbursement is sought. There are no medical bills or hospital bills

outstanding, and there are no assignments, compensation claims or liens filed with petitioner as administrat____

except for the following:

a) The Commissioner of Social Services has submitted a claim of $_____ for public

assistance rendered to decedent and his/her family for the years_____. This claim is rejected

since the Department would have a lien only against a recovery for conscious pain and suffering, which would

be an estate asset, and here there is to be no recovery for conscious pain and suffering.

b) _____ has submitted a claim for _____

based on an _____

_____.

This claim is also rejected for the same reasons as the rejection of the claim of the Department of Social

Services. (List other creditors, if any) _____

_____

_____

_____

Official Forms

c) Decedent's father/mother _____, seeks a share of the recovery by

claiming the suffering of a pecuniary loss by virtue of decedent's death. This claim is rejected on the grounds

that in spite of any possible demonstrated pecuniary injury, decedent's father/mother is nevertheless a

nondistributee and thus ineligible to share in the recovery.

19. [If applicable] During the years through _____, the decedent was the recipient of public

assistance in the form of Aid to Dependent Children.

20. No previous application has been made for the relief sought herein.

21. Petitioner desires leave of this court to compromise and settle with_____

Insurance Company the claim against_____

for the wrongful death of the decedent, to discontinue the action for conscious pain and suffering and to fix

reasonable attorney's fees and to pay the distributees their share of the settlement pursuant to the provisions of

law (and to settle the account of the Administrat____).

22. The only persons interested in this proceeding entitled to notice thereof are the following:

Name	Relationship	Address
_____	Husband-Administrator	_____
_____	Wife-Administratrix	_____
_____	Daughter	_____
_____	Son	_____
_____	Father	_____
_____	Mother	_____
_____	Alleged Creditor	_____
NYS Tax Comm.	Possible Creditor	_____
Dept. Social Services	Possible Creditor	_____

Form WD-2 Page 7

_____ Defendant   _____

Insurance Co.   Defendant's Ins. Co.   _____

None of the above are under a disability except_____,

an infant under the age of fourteen years.

23. Petitioner has not become interested in the within matter at the instance of the defendant or anyone

acting on defendant's behalf, directly or indirectly.

WHEREFORE, your Petitioner prays that a Citation herein be directed to the following:

<u>NAME</u>   <u>ADDRESS</u>

_____   _____

_____   _____

_____   _____

_____   _____

[List names of distributees and, if applicable, Department of Social Services, New York State Tax Commission,

Defendant, and Defendant's Insurance Company.]requiring them to show cause as follows: (include as

applicable) _____

_____

_____

WHY the administrat___ should not be authorized and empowered to compromise and settle a certain

claim for the wrongful death of the decedent, against_____

for the sum of $_____to discontinue the action for conscious pain and suffering, and

WHY the entire recovery of $_____ should not be allocated to the cause of action for

decedent's wrongful death, and

WHY the provisions in the Letters of Administration heretofore issued to your petitioner on

_____ restraining the administrat_____ from compromising or collecting upon the aforesaid claim should not be modified to permit said compromise, and

    WHY the filing of a bond should not be dispensed with, and

    WHY the account of_____ as Administrat_____ in this proceeding, should

not be judicially settled, and

    WHY defendant _____or defendant's insurance company should

not pay to the firm of _____ Esqs. out of the proceeds of the settlement for the claim of

wrongful death, the sum of $_____ as and for attorney's fees, together with disbursements of $_____

_____, and

    WHY, the balance of the settlement, to wit the sum of $_____ should not be distributed to

those distributees having sustained a pecuniary loss as follows: _____% of the balance to _____

_____, widow/widower of the decedent; _____% of the balance to _____,

child of decedent; _____% of the balance to _____, child of decedent, and

    WHY the claim of the Department of Social Services should not be rejected as a nondistributee, and

    WHY the claim of _____ should not be rejected as a nondistributee, and

    WHY the claim of _____ in the amount of $_____ should not be rejected,

and

    WHY upon payments as hereinbefore mentioned by the said defendant _____ or

defendant's insurance company, the _____ Insurance Company, the petitioner, as administrat_____

of the goods, chattels and credits that were of _____, deceased, should not execute

and deliver to the said defendant, _____, or defendant's Insurance Company a full, final

and complete release in the claim against them arising out of the aforesaid cause of action together with any other papers necessary to effectuate said compromise.

Dated: _____

_____
              Petitioner

STATE OF NEW YORK)
) ss.:
COUNTY OF _____)

_____ being duly sworn, deposes and says, that he/she is the petitioner in

the within action, that he/she has read the foregoing petition and knows the contents thereof that the same is true

of his/her own knowledge, except as to those matters therein stated to be alleged upon information and belief,

and as to those matters he/she believes them to be true.

_____

Sworn to before me this
____ day of _____,_____.

_____
      Notary Public
(affix stamp or seal)

Signature of Attorney:_____

Print Name:_____

Firm Name:_____ Tel. No.:_____

Address of Attorney:_____

Official Forms

FORM WD-3   **Account**

Form WD-3
 (4/98)

SURROGATE'S COURT OF THE STATE OF NEW YORK
COUNTY OF _____

In the Matter of the Application of
as Administrat_____ of the Goods, Chattels and
Credits which were of   **ACCOUNT**

_____
                          Deceased.   File # _____

For leave to compromise a certain cause of action for
wrongful death of the decedent and to render and have
judicially settled an account of the proceedings as such
Administrat_____.

TO THE SURROGATE'S COURT:

    1. I _____ do render the following account of my
proceedings as administrat_____ of the goods, chattels and credits which were of _____,
deceased, consisting of a claim against _____, who is insured by
_____ Insurance Company, for wrongful death arising on or about _____,
as the result of an automobile accident involving the decedent and _____

    2. Letters of Administration of the goods, chattels and credits of the decedent were issued to me on
_____, said letters being limited to the prosecution only, and not for the collection of
any proceeds of, any action or claim for wrongful death. Simultaneously herewith, leave is being asked to
compromise the claim for wrongful death of the decedent for the sum of $_____.

    3. There is submitted with this account my petition as administrat_____ ; and affidavit by
_____, Esq., attorney for the petitioner herein; a copy of the paid
funeral bill; and waivers of the necessary parties.

    4. In view of the facts and circumstances, it is my opinion that a satisfactory result has been
achieved through the efforts of my attorneys, and they are requesting disbursements in the sum of
$_____ and that they receive thereafter a fee of _____ % of the net proceeds.

    5. The funeral bill in the sum of $_____ has been paid through no-fault insurance.

    6. There are no outstanding hospital bills or doctors' bills.

    7. The only property coming into my hands is by reason of the compromise of the claim against the
Insurance Company in the sum of $_____ .

    8. The decedent left surviving no other next of kin except _____,
his/her widow/widower, and _____
_____
his/her children. All of the above persons are entitled to share in the proceeds of the compromise.

(NOTE: WHERE THERE ARE NO DISTRIBUTEES UNDER A DISABILITY, THE RENDERING OF AN ACCOUNT IS USUALLY NOT REQUIRED.)

(NOTE: REIMBURSEMENT OF FUNDS PAID FOR FUNERAL AND OTHER ADMINISTRATIVE EXPENSES, UNDER MOST CIRCUMSTANCES, ARE ALLOWABLE, AS ARE STATUTORY COMMISSIONS TO THE ADMINISTRAT(OR)(RIX). IF REIMBURSEMENT OR COMMISSIONS ARE NOT SOUGHT, THE PETITION SHOULD CONTAIN A WAIVER THEREOF).

9. There are no other claims or creditors of the estate that have been presented to or have come into my hands or knowledge except for the following:

a) The Commissioner of Social Services has submitted a claim of $_____ for public assistance rendered to decedent and his/her family for the years ___ _____. This claim was rejected.

b) _____ has submitted a claim for $_____ _____ based on _____ This claim was rejected.

c) Decedent's father/mother, _____ has sought a share of the recovery based on an alleged pecuniary loss. This claim was rejected.

10. The following are the only persons interested in this proceeding:

[List names of distributees, etc.]

NAME	RELATIONSHIP	DATE OF BIRTH
_____	_____	_____
_____	_____	_____
_____	_____	_____
County Department of Social Services	Possible Creditor	
New York State Tax Commission	Possible Creditor	
_____	Attorneys	
_____	Defendant	_____
Insurance Company	Defendant's Insurance Company	

11. I charge myself as follows with the amount to be received on compromise of the claim for wrongful death against _____ Insurance Company: $_____

-2-

12. I credit myself as follows:

a) With the amount to be paid to _____,
   Esqs., attorneys, including disbursements: $_____

b) With the amount to be paid to _____,
   widow/widower and distributee: (_____ %) $_____

c) With the amount to be paid to the guardian of the person
   and property of _____,
   infant, jointly with the Trust Officer of _____
   Bank (_____ %): $_____

d) with the amount to be paid to _____,
   son/daughter (_____ %): $_____

                        Total: $_____

Leaving no balance.

Dated: _____

                                    _____

STATE OF NEW YORK
COUNTY OF _____ **ss.:**

_____ being duly sworn, deposes and says:
That I am the administrat_____ /accountant in the above estate, having been duly appointed by a decree of this Court.

The foregoing account of proceedings contains to the best of my knowledge and belief a true and complete statement of my receipts and disbursements in the estate of _____
of all monies and other property belonging to the estate or fund which have come into my hands or which have been received by any person or persons by my order or authority for use since my appointment, and a full and true statement of account of the manner in which I have disposed of same and all property remaining in my hands at the present time, and a full and true account of the nature of each and every transaction may by me since my appointment.

I do not know of any error or omission in said account to the prejudice of any person interested in said estate or fund.

                                    _____
                                    _____

Sworn to before me this _____
day of _____.

_____
Notary Public

FORM WD-4   **Attorney's Affidavit**

[describe defendant's defense]

_____
_____
_____
_____

8. After intensive negotiations with _____ Insurance Company, it finally has made an offer in the sum of $_____ out of a total of $_____ coverage for the wrongful death of decedent.

9. All of the proceeds of the settlement of the claim are to be allocated to the action for wrongful death, the decedent never having regained consciousness following the occurrence complained of.

10. That _____ was, in addition thereto, appointed Guardian of the person and property of the infant, _____, by the Surrogate's Court, _____ County, on _____, under File No. _____.

11. In light of the fact that the owner of the vehicle involved in the accident alleges that the accident was the fault of the decedent and *[provide other details]*

_____
_____
_____ your deponent submits that the settlement is fair and reasonable and should be accepted for the best interests of the estate.

12. Your deponent will prepare all papers necessary to accomplish said settlement and obtain approval of the Surrogate's Court and do whatever is necessary on behalf of the estate and the next of kin.

13. The following expenses have been incurred *[list all expenses]*:

Police reports	$_____
Hospital records	$_____
Surrogate's Court fees	$_____
Motor Vehicle Bureau	$_____
TOTAL	$_____

14. Your deponent has not become concerned in this action at the request of the defendants or their attorneys or representatives, and no compensation has been or will be received by deponent from defendants or their attorneys or representatives. Any compensation to be received by way of fees herein is to be paid out of the proceeds of the proposed settlement and not otherwise. Your deponent has a written retainer with the administrat____ herein providing for a fee of _____ % of the net recovery, which your deponent submits is fair and reasonable in light of all of the facts and circumstances.

Official Forms

15. On _____, your deponent caused a check of the records of this court to be made for liens, assignments and encumbrances and found none, and your deponent has been advised by petitioner that petitioner does not know of any filed or recorded, and your deponent has inquired of the petitioner and is satisfied that the only claims that have been filed with the administrat____ are those shown in the petition. Your deponent waives notice and the requirement that any security be filed and consents to the entry of a decree without any further notice.

16. No previous application for the relief requested herein has been made to any court or judge.

17. Your deponent requests that a fair and reasonable sum for services rendered and to be rendered be allowed in te sum of S_____, together with disbursements in the sum of S_____.

WHEREFORE, deponent respectfully prays that the relief requested herein be granted.

_____

Sworn to before me this _____
day of _____, 20____.

_____
Notary Public

FORM WD-5   **Waiver and Consent for Insurance Company**

Form WD-5 (Waiver and Consent for Insurance Company)

NOTE: If the action was settled with the assistance of the Supreme Court, or if the amount of the settlement has been otherwise approved, this form will not be required.

SURROGATE'S COURT OF THE STATE OF NEW YORK
COUNTY OF _____

In the Matter of the Application of
_____ as   **WAIVER AND CONSENT**
Administrat_____ of the Goods,   **FOR INSURANCE COMPANY**
Chattels and Credits which were of
_____, deceased,
for leave to compromise a certain cause of action   FILE # _____
for wrongful death of the decedent and to render and
have judicially settled an account of the proceedings
as such Administrat _____ .

TO THE SURROGATE'S COURT:

    The _____ Insurance Company, with offices at
_____
as the insurer of _____ and pursuant to its obligations
to its insured under said liability insurance policy, does hereby appear and waive issuance and
service of a citation in the above entitled proceeding. It further consents to pay the sum of
$_____ in full settlement of the claim for wrongful death of _____
_____ .deceased. It further consents that the filing of a bond or other
security be dispensed with and waive any further notice.

DATED: _____

                              _____ Insurance Company

                    BY: _____

STATE OF NEW YORK   )
COUNTY OF _____   )ss:.

    On the _____ day of _____, 20____, before me personally
came and appeared _____, known to me to be a Corporate
Officer of the _____ Insurance Company, to wit, _____,
who had the authority and who did execute the foregoing Waiver and Consent on behalf of the
_____ Insurance Company and acknowledged that _____
executed the same.

                    _____
                    Notary Public
                    Commission Expires:
                    (Affix Stamp)

Official Forms

FORM WD-6   Waiver and Consent for Individual

Form WD-6 (Waiver and Consent for Individual)

SURROGATE'S COURT OF THE STATE OF NEW YORK
COUNTY OF _____

In the Matter of the Application of

_____ as   **WAIVER AND CONSENT**

Administrat_____ of the Goods,
Chattels and Credits which were of
_____, deceased,
for leave to compromise a certain cause of action   FILE # _____
for wrongful death of the decedent and to render and   (as of 9/87)
have judicially settled an account of the proceedings
as such Administrat_____.

TO THE SURROGATE'S COURT:

The undersigned, _____ being over the age of 21 years,
having been born on _____ and residing at _____
being a person interested as *(state relationship)* _____ of decedent, hereby appears and
waives the issuance and service of a citation in the above proceeding and consents to the following relief:
*(The adult distributee, or other adult interested party, must specifically consent to each and every item of relief
requested by the petitioner) NOTE: If the adult distributee is entitled to share in the proceeds of the settlement,
but is voluntarily relinquishing that right, this must be clearly stated as well.*

THAT the account of the proceedings of _____, as administrat_____ of the
estate of _____, deceased, a copy of which is attached, should be judicially
settled, and

THAT the administrat_____ should be empowered to compromise and settle a certain claim for the
wrongful death against _____ for the sum of $ _____ and to
discontinue any claim for conscious pain and suffering, and

THAT the provisions of the limited Letters of administration issued to the petitioner on
restraining the compromise or collecting upon the aforesaid claim and cause of action should be modified to
permit said compromise, and

THAT the filing of a bond should be dispensed with, and

THAT the defendant, _____, or defendant's insurance company should
pay to _____, Esqs., out of the proceeds of the settlement for the claim for
wrongful death, the sum of $ _____ As and for attorneys' fees together with disbursements in the sum
of $ _____ , and

THAT the entire recovery of $ _____ should be allocated to the cause of action for
decedent's wrongful death, and

THAT the balance of the settlement, to wit the sum of $ _____ , should be distributed to
those distributees having sustained a pecuniary loss as follows: _____ % of the balance to _____
_____ widow/widower of decedent; _____ % of the balance to _____,

child of decedent; _____% of the balance to _____ , child of decedent, and

THAT the claim of _____should be rejected, as a non distributee, and

THAT the claim of _____ in the amount of $ _____ should be rejected, and

THAT upon payments as hereinbefore mentioned, the said administrat_____ should be permitted to execute and deliver general releases and all other necessary papers to the defendant or defendant's insurance company, releasing them from all claims against them arising out of the aforesaid action for wrongful death, together with any other papers necessary to effectuate the said compromise, and

THAT the entire settlement be considered as a settlement for a cause of action for wrongful death and a waiver of my right to receive any distributee share of the settlement.

DATED: _____

_____

STATE OF NEW YORK   )
COUNTY OF _____)ss:

On the _____ day of _____ , 20 ____ , before me personally came _____ known to me to be the person who is described in the foregoing Waiver and Consent, and acknowledged to me that he/she executed same.

_____
Notary Public
Commission Expires:
(Affix Stamp)

2

FORM WD-7   **Decree**

Form WD-7 (as of 4/98)

At a Surrogate's Court held in and for the
County of _____, at the
Courthouse in_____,
New York, on the _____ day of
_____, 20____.

PRESENT:

    HON. _____
_____ County Surrogate

In the Matter of the Application of	
_____ as	**DECREE**
Administrat_____ of the Goods,	
Chattels and Credits which were of	
Administrat_____, deceased,	
for leave to compromise and settle the claim and	
cause of action arising out of the death of the	FILE # _____
decedent and to judicially settle his/her account	
relating to the proceeds thereof.	

    Upon the Petition of _____, as Administrat_____
of the Estate of _____, deceased, duly verified the _____ day
of _____, 20____, in which application was made for an Order permitting the
said _____, as Administrat_____ to compromise and settle
for the sum of $_____ the cause of action against _____
for the wrongful death of the decedent, _____.

    And to discontinue the action for conscious pain and suffering and to discharge and
release said defendant and insurance company from all suits and claims upon the payment of the
said $_____ in settlement of the cause of action herein,

    And that the entire recovery of said action should be allocated to the cause of action for
decedent's wrongful death, to modify the Letters of Administration to permit said compromise,
dispense with the filing of a bond, judicially settle the account, pay to _____,
Esqs., their fee for services rendered, reject the claim of the Department of Social Services, and
reject the claims of _____ and _____.

    And more than seven months having elapsed since the granting of Letters of
Administration to _____, and the Surrogate having
issued a Citation to all persons interested in the estate of said deceased to attend such judicial
settlement on the _____ day of _____, 20____, at _____ a.m., at the Surrogate's
Court, _____ County,

And the said Citation having been duly returned with proof of due service thereof, or the due appearance and waiver of notice, by the following named person or corporations, to wit: *[List names of distributees, and, if applicable, _____ County Department of Social Services, New York State Tax Commission, Defendant, and Defendant's Insurance Company]*

And the said _____, petitioner herein, having appeared by _____ his/her attorney,

And the said _____ having appeared by _____, his/her attorneys, and having filed objections to said account,

And said _____ County Department of Social Services having appeared by _____ _____, its attorney, and having filed objections to said account,

And said New York State Tax Commission having appeared by _____, its attorney, and having filed objections to said account,

And the Court having appointed _____, as Guardian Ad Litem for _____,

And _____ having filed objections on behalf of his/her ward, _____,

And _____ having filed a report as such guardian,

And a hearing having been held, and the Court having rendered a decision dated _____ _____, granting the petition to compromise the cause of action for wrongful death and to judicially settle the account,

And the Court having examined the said account and having found the state and condition of said account to be as set forth in the following statement recorded with the Court:

SUMMARY STATEMENT OF THE SETTLEMENT PROCEEDS

The Administrat_____ is charged with $_____ the proceeds of the action of wrongful death to be distributed:

TOTAL CHARGES $_____

The Administrat_____ is credited with $_____ the following amounts

TOTAL CREDITS $_____

BALANCE OF THE SETTLEMENT PROCEEDS
TO BE DISTRIBUTED $_____

And it appearing the said Administrat_____ has fully accounted for all monies and properties of the estate in said summary statement, and the Administrat_____ having waived any claim to statutory commissions, it is hereby

ORDERED, ADJUDGED AND DECREED that the petitioner's application for leave to compromise and settle the cause of action for wrongful death and to allocate the entire amount of the proceeds to the cause of action for wrongful death and to grant leave to discontinue the cause of action for conscious pain and suffering is granted; and it is further

ORDERED, ADJUDGED AND DECREED that the petitioner as Administrat_____ of the decedent's estate is authorized to settle and discontinue the claims and causes of action for conscious pain and suffering and wrongful death against the defendant, _____, and petitioner is authorized to deliver general releases and discontinues and any other papers or documents that may be required to effectuate a settlement and discontinuances or withdrawals of the said claims and causes of actions for conscious pain and suffering and wrongful death; and it is further

ORDERED, ADJUDGED AND DECREED that the entire settlement sum of $_____ is allocated to the cause of action for wrongful death, and the personal injury action is discontinued with prejudice and without interest, costs or disbursements; and it is further

ORDERED, ADJUDGED AND DECREED that the entire settlement sum of $_____ be paid by the defendant, or defendant's insurance company as follows:

To _____ as fee for services as
    Guardian Ad Litem $_____
To _____ as fee for services as
    attorney for the Administrat_____ herein $_____
To _____ in reimbursement of
    disbursements as attorney for the Administrat_____
    herein $_____
To _____ as and for his/her share
    as surviving spouse and beneficiary of said decedent
    pursuant to EPTL section 5-4.4, equal to _____ % $_____
To _____, child and next of kin by
    payment to _____,
    Guardian of the property of_____,
    jointly with the Trust Officer of the _____
    Bank, as and for his/her share as next of kin of said
    decedent pursuant to EPTL section 5-4.4, equal to _____ % $_____
and it is further

ORDERED, ADJUDGED AND DECREED that the claims of the Department of Social Services, the New York State Tax Commission, and _____ hereby are disallowed and objections filed by these parties are dismissed; and it is further

ORDERED, ADJUDGED AND DECREED that upon the defendant; or the defendant's insurance company, making payments as aforesaid, _____, as Administrat_____ of the estate of _____, deceased, be and hereby is discharged from any and all further liability as to all matters and things embraced in the aforesaid account and determined by this decree; and it is further

ORDERED, ADJUDGED AND DECREED that the giving of a bond or other security in connections therewith be dispensed with, and that the restrictions on the Letters of Administration be modified to allow the above settlement; and it is further

ORDERED, ADJUDGED AND DECREED that the account of _____ as Administrat_____ is hereby judicially settled.

ENTER: _____

DATED: _____   _____
                                                        Surrogate

NOTICE OF ENTRY

_____, Chief Clerk
_____ County Surrogate's Court

FORM CERT   **Attorney's Certification Pursuant to 22 NYCRR 207.4(a) & (b)**

SURROGATE'S COURT OF THE STATE OF NEW YORK
COUNTY OF

_____

a/k/a

ATTORNEY'S CERTIFICATION
(22 NYCRR 207.4 (a) & (b))

File No. _____

Deceased.

_____

    The undersigned attorney hereby certifies pursuant to Sections 207.4 (a) and (b) of the Uniform Rules for Surrogate's Court, that the typeface utilized complies with subsection (a) of the aforesaid rule and the text used in the foregoing forms is the same contained in the official forms and that the substantive text has not been altered.

Signature of Attorney : _____

Print Name : _____

Firm Name : _____   Tel. No. : _____

Address of Attorney: _____

FORM OCFS 3909   **Request for Information Guardianship Form**

OCFS-3909 (Rev. 10/2016) FRONT

NEW YORK STATE
OFFICE OF CHILDREN AND FAMILY SERVICES
REQUEST FOR INFORMATION GUARDIANSHIP FORM
(FOR COURT USE ONLY)

| SCR USE ONLY: |
| Request I.D. # |
| Date of request: |
| / / |

Section 1706 of the Surrogate's Court Procedure Act and Section 81.19(g) of the Mental Hygiene Law require that an inquiry be made of the New York Statewide Central Register of Child Abuse and Maltreatment as to whether the proposed guardian or any other individual eighteen years of age or over who resides in the home of the proposed guardian is a subject of an indicated child abuse or maltreatment report.

| RESOURCE ID # | COURT LIAISON | AREA CODE/PHONE # ( ) |
| DOCKET FILE # | COURT NAME AND ADDRESS | ZIP CODE |

INFORMATION CONCERNING PROPOSED GUARDIAN(S) AND MEMBERS OF THE HOUSEHOLD - Please Print Clearly.
Complete each column for every household member regardless of age. The proposed guardian(s) are listed first with maiden name or alias listed directly below each individual. If there is no maiden name or alias for that individual please write **"NONE"** in the row underneath that individual's name. For all other household members, indicate his/her relationship to the guardian in the second column using the relationship to guardian code on the reverse of this form. List the maiden name or alias for that household member in the row below their name indicating maiden or alias or **"NONE"** if applicable.

RELATIONSHIP TO GUARDIAN CODES: (see page 2 for codes)	LAST NAME (Please print clearly)	FIRST NAME (Please print clearly)	MI	SEX	DATE OF BIRTH (mm/dd/yyyy)
(G) Guardian				☐ M ☐ F	/ /
(M) Maiden/alias				☐ M ☐ F	/ /
				☐ M ☐ F	/ /
				☐ M ☐ F	/ /
				☐ M ☐ F	/ /
				☐ M ☐ F	/ /
				☐ M ☐ F	/ /
				☐ M ☐ F	/ /
				☐ M ☐ F	/ /
				☐ M ☐ F	/ /

Please provide your CURRENT ADDRESS and any PREVIOUS ADDRESSES at which you have resided over the last 28 years, including CITY, STATE, and ZIP CODE for each individual being cleared.
Include month/year in the FROM and TO columns. Attach additional pages if necessary.

CURRENT ADDRESS: STREET	CITY	STATE	ZIP	FROM (mo/yr) /	TO (mo/yr) /
PREVIOUS ADDRESS: STREET	CITY	STATE	ZIP	FROM (mo/yr) /	TO (mo/yr) /
PREVIOUS ADDRESS: STREET	CITY	STATE	ZIP	FROM (mo/yr) /	TO (mo/yr) /
PREVIOUS ADDRESS: STREET	CITY	STATE	ZIP	FROM (mo/yr) /	TO (mo/yr) /
PREVIOUS ADDRESS: STREET	CITY	STATE	ZIP	FROM (mo/yr) /	TO (mo/yr) /
PREVIOUS ADDRESS: STREET	CITY	STATE	ZIP	FROM (mo/yr) /	TO (mo/yr) /

ADDRESS HISTORY FOR OTHER PERSON(S) 18 YEARS OLD OR OLDER, RESIDING WITH PROPOSED GUARDIAN.
Include month/year in the FROM and TO columns. Attach additional pages if necessary

LAST NAME & MAIDEN/ALIAS		FIRST NAME				MI
CURRENT STREET ADDRESS	CITY	STATE	ZIP	FROM (mo/yr) /	TO (mo/yr) /	
PREVIOUS STREET ADDRESS	CITY	STATE	ZIP	FROM (mo/yr) /	TO (mo/yr) /	
PREVIOUS STREET ADDRESS	CITY	STATE	ZIP	FROM (mo/yr) /	TO (mo/yr) /	
PREVIOUS STREET ADDRESS	CITY	STATE	ZIP	FROM (mo/yr) /	TO (mo/yr) /	
PREVIOUS STREET ADDRESS	CITY	STATE	ZIP	FROM (mo/yr) /	TO (mo/yr) /	
PREVIOUS STREET ADDRESS	CITY	STATE	ZIP	FROM (mo/yr) /	TO (mo/yr) /	

* ADDITIONAL SPACE PROVIDED ON REVERSE SIDE OF FORM

Official Forms

OCFS-3909 (Rev. 10/2016) REVERSE

RESOURCE ID #	Record Resource ID # as appropriate. If you need assistance, email: mailto:ocfs.sm.conn_app@ocfs.ny.gov
DOCKET/FILE #:	Record your Court Docket File # as appropriate.
COURT LIAISON:	Record Name of Court Liaison.
Relationship to Guardian Codes: (list the code and/or the relationships as appropriate)	G – Guardian(s) (at least one person must be designated) M – Maiden name/alias (must be completed for every guardian) E – 18-year-old or older (residing in a proposed guardian's household) F – Family member (under 18 years of age) O – Other household member (under 18 years of age)

Mail your completed **OCFS-3909, Request for Information Guardianship Form** to the: **New York Statewide Central Register of Child Abuse and Maltreatment, Attn: Service Center Unit P.O. Box 4480, Albany, N.Y. 12204-0480**	For questions regarding how to fill out the **OCFS-3909, Request for Information Guardianship Form** call: **(518-474-1567)**

To order a supply of the form, OCFS-3909, *Request for Information Guardianship:* Please access and completely fill out form OCFS-4627, *Request for Forms and Publications* from the Internet: http://ocfs.ny.gov/main/documents/defaultkeyword1.asp

Mail your completed OCFS-4627, *Request for Forms and Publications* to the: **Office of Children and Family Services, Mailroom, 52 Washington Street, Rensselaer, NY 12144.** If you have difficulty accessing the form from the web-site, you can call the **Forms Request Line** at: 518-473-0971 and leave a detailed message to receive one.

ADDITIONAL ADDRESSES

LAST NAME		FIRST NAME					M.I.
PREVIOUS STREET ADDRESS	CITY		STATE	ZIP	FROM (mo/yr) /	TO (mo/yr) /	
LAST NAME		FIRST NAME					M.I.
PREVIOUS STREET ADDRESS	CITY		STATE	ZIP	FROM (mo/yr) /	TO (mo/yr) /	
LAST NAME		FIRST NAME					M.I.
PREVIOUS STREET ADDRESS	CITY		STATE	ZIP	FROM (mo/yr) /	TO (mo/yr) /	
LAST NAME		FIRST NAME					M.I.
PREVIOUS STREET ADDRESS	CITY		STATE	ZIP	FROM (mo/yr) /	TO (mo/yr) /	
LAST NAME		FIRST NAME					M.I.
PREVIOUS STREET ADDRESS	CITY		STATE	ZIP	FROM (mo/yr) /	TO (mo/yr) /	
LAST NAME		FIRST NAME					M.I.
PREVIOUS STREET ADDRESS	CITY		STATE	ZIP	FROM (mo/yr) /	TO (mo/yr) /	
LAST NAME		FIRST NAME					M.I.
PREVIOUS STREET ADDRESS	CITY		STATE	ZIP	FROM (mo/yr) /	TO (mo/yr) /	
LAST NAME		FIRST NAME					M.I.
PREVIOUS STREET ADDRESS	CITY		STATE	ZIP	FROM (mo/yr) /	TO (mo/yr) /	
LAST NAME		FIRST NAME					M.I.
PREVIOUS STREET ADDRESS	CITY		STATE	ZIP	FROM (mo/yr) /	TO (mo/yr) /	
LAST NAME		FIRST NAME					M.I.
PREVIOUS STREET ADDRESS	CITY		STATE	ZIP	FROM (mo/yr) /	TO (mo/yr) /	

OCFS-3909 (Rev. 10/2016) REVERSE

LAST NAME			FIRST NAME					M.I.
PREVIOUS STREET ADDRESS		CITY		STATE	ZIP	FROM (mo/yr) /	TO (mo/yr) /	
LAST NAME			FIRST NAME					M.I.
PREVIOUS STREET ADDRESS		CITY		STATE	ZIP	FROM (mo/yr) /	TO (mo/yr) /	
LAST NAME			FIRST NAME					M.I.
PREVIOUS STREET ADDRESS		CITY		STATE	ZIP	FROM (mo/yr) /	TO (mo/yr) /	
LAST NAME			FIRST NAME					M.I.
PREVIOUS STREET ADDRESS		CITY		STATE	ZIP	FROM (mo/yr) /	TO (mo/yr) /	
LAST NAME			FIRST NAME					M.I.
PREVIOUS STREET ADDRESS		CITY		STATE	ZIP	FROM (mo/yr) /	TO (mo/yr) /	
LAST NAME			FIRST NAME					M.I.
PREVIOUS STREET ADDRESS		CITY		STATE	ZIP	FROM (mo/yr) /	TO (mo/yr) /	
LAST NAME			FIRST NAME					M.I.
PREVIOUS STREET ADDRESS		CITY		STATE	ZIP	FROM (mo/yr) /	TO (mo/yr) /	
LAST NAME			FIRST NAME					M.I.
PREVIOUS STREET ADDRESS		CITY		STATE	ZIP	FROM (mo/yr) /	TO (mo/yr) /	
LAST NAME			FIRST NAME					M.I.
PREVIOUS STREET ADDRESS		CITY		STATE	ZIP	FROM (mo/yr) /	TO (mo/yr) /	
LAST NAME			FIRST NAME					M.I.
PREVIOUS STREET ADDRESS		CITY		STATE	ZIP	FROM (mo/yr) /	TO (mo/yr) /	
LAST NAME			FIRST NAME					M.I.
PREVIOUS STREET ADDRESS		CITY		STATE	ZIP	FROM (mo/yr) /	TO (mo/yr) /	
LAST NAME			FIRST NAME					M.I.
PREVIOUS STREET ADDRESS		CITY		STATE	ZIP	FROM (mo/yr) /	TO (mo/yr) /	
LAST NAME			FIRST NAME					M.I.
PREVIOUS STREET ADDRESS		CITY		STATE	ZIP	FROM (mo/yr) /	TO (mo/yr) /	
LAST NAME			FIRST NAME					M.I.
PREVIOUS STREET ADDRESS		CITY		STATE	ZIP	FROM (mo/yr) /	TO (mo/yr) /	

FORM REP   SURROGATE'S COURT   SF-300

FORM REP   Report of Estate Not Fully Distributed

(Rev. 6/98)

REPORT OF ESTATE NOT FULLY DISTRIBUTED (22 NYCRR 207.42)

SURROGATE'S COURT
_____ COUNTY

Estate of _____, Deceased

File No. _____

Date of issuance of first permanent letters _____

Approximate amount of gross estate $ _____

Approximate amount that has been distributed to beneficiaries
$ _____

Approximate amount remaining in fiduciary's hands at present
$ _____

This estate has not yet been fully distributed for the following reason: [state briefly and state date by which distribution may be expected]

_____
_____
_____

Date of this report _____

                                    _____
                                              Fiduciary

                        Address: _____
                                 _____

                        Phone: _____

                                    _____
                                    Attorney for above Fiduciary

                        Address: _____
                                 _____

                        Phone: _____

Uniform Rule §207.42 Report of estates not fully distributed

(a) Whenever the estate of a decedent has not been fully distributed or a final accounting filed with petition for settlement within two years from the date when the first permanent letters of administration or letters testamentary were issued where the gross taxable estate of such decedent does not require the filing of a federal estate tax return, and within three years if a federal estate tax return is required, the executor or administrator shall, at or before the end of the first complete month following the expiration of such time, file with the clerk of the court a statement in substantially the following form: (see other side of this sheet for form)

(b) The court shall thereupon take steps as it deems appropriate to expedite the completion of the administration of the estate and the distribution of all assets.

(c) Failure to file such statement will be considered by the court on any application for commissions or legal fees and may constitute a ground for disallowance of commissions or fees.

(d) The periods set forth in subdivision (a) hereinabove stated are not intended to set a standard time for completion of estate administration but rather to fix a period after which inquiry may be made by the court.

(e) This section shall not limit the power of the court to direct an accounting at any time on its own initiative or on petition pursuant to SCPA 2205.

SCPA, see McKinney's Book 58A

NOTE: IF YOU HAVE NOT TAKEN THE NECESSARY STEPS TO CLOSE OUT THE ESTATE IN OUR OFFICE, (Judicial Settlement - Affidavit & Final Order. filed all necessary releases and affirmation by attorney or proceedings under SCPA § 2202 and § 2203), THE ESTATE IS **NOT** CONSIDERED CLOSED BY THE SURROGATE'S OFFICE.

THEREFORE, EVEN THOUGH THE ESTATE ASSETS MAY HAVE BEEN DISTRIBUTED, THE PROPER STEPS TO CLOSE OUT THE ESTATE MUST BE TAKEN. IT IS **NOT** SUFFICIENT TO FILE THE ATTACHED FORM AND INDICATE THAT THERE ARE NO FUNDS REMAINING IN THE FIDUCIARY'S HANDS.

FORM SD BOX-1   **Petition to Search Safe Deposit Box**

Fee Pd _____
Receipt No. _____

STATE OF NEW YORK
SURROGATE'S COURT: COUNTY OF _____

IN THE MATTER OF THE APPLICATION TO SEARCH A
SAFE DEPOSIT BOX FOR THE WILL OR OTHER PAPERS
OF

_____ ,

         Deceased.

PETITION TO SEARCH
SAFE DEPOSIT BOX

FILE # _____

To the Surrogate's Court of _____ County, it is respectfully alleged:

(1) The name and domicile of the petitioner is as follows:

Name: _____

Domicile or if a financial institution, Principal Office:

_____
 (Street address) *(City, Town or Village)* *(County)* *(State)* *(Zip)* *(Telephone Number)*

Mailing address, if different from domicile, is: _____

(2) The petitioner is [*indicate*] [ ] the nearest surviving distributee of the decedent [ ] the executor named in the
decedent's will [ ] has an interest in the decedent's estate as follows:

(3) The name, date, place of death, and domicile of the decedent are as follows:

Name: _____ Date of death: _____

Place of death: _____

Domicile: _____
   (Street address) *(City, Town or Village)* *(P.O. if different)* *(State)* *(Zip)*

(4) The decedent has a safe deposit box in the vault of _____ , a banking corporation doing
business in _____ County, New York. Petitioner is informed and believes that the decedent left a will
or other papers in the safe deposit box.

  Wherefore petitioner prays that an Order be made pursuant to SCPA § 2003 permitting the petitioner, in the presence
of an officer of the banking corporation, to examine the safe deposit box for the purposes of ascertaining if the decedent's
will is contained therein, and to obtain a deed to a burial plot and any insurance policies made payable to a named beneficiary,
and further directing the petitioner to make an inventory of the contents of the safe deposit box.

Dated: _____ , 20___

            _____
              Signature of Petitioner

STATE OF NEW YORK   )

COUNTY _____)

_____ , being duly sworn, says:

    I have read the foregoing petition subscribed by me and know the contents thereof, and the same is true of my own

knowledge except as to matters stated to be alleged upon information and belief and as to those matters I believe it to be true.

_____
Signature of Petitioner

Sworn to before me this

_____ day of _____, 20____

_____
Notary Public
My Commission Expires:
(Affix Notary Stamp or Seal)

Signature of Attorney: _____ _____

Print Name:_____Tel No.:_____

Firm Name:_____

Official Forms

FORM SD BOX-2   **Order to Examine Safe Deposit Box**

At a Surrogate's Court of the
State of New York Held in and
for the County of _____,
at _____ New York
on _____, 20 _____

PRESENT, _____, SURROGATE

IN THE MATTER OF

The Application of _____ for an

(Petitioner)

Order Directing _____

(Name of Bank)

to **Permit Petitioner to Examine the Contents of a Safe Deposit Box** in the said

bank, standing in the name of _____

(Deceased)

**Order to Examine
Safe Deposit Box**

Upon reading and filing the petition of _____ ,
duly verified the ___ day of _____, _____, showing among other things that _____ ,
in his lifetime rented of the _____ ,
a safe deposit box, and that there was deposited in said safe deposit box certain papers belonging to said _____
_____, and among others a paper purporting to be the Last Will and Testament of the said _____
_____

It is Ordered, that the _____
permit the said _____ to examine said papers in
the presence of an officer of said _____ ,
and if a paper purporting to be the Will of said _____
is found, to deliver said Will **PERSONALLY OR BY REGISTERED MAIL to the Chief Clerk of the
Surrogate's Court,** County of _____, _____
and if a deed to a burial plot is found among such papers to deliver said deed to _____
_____ ; and if a policy of insurance in the name of the decedent and payable to a named
beneficiary is found among said papers to deliver said policy of insurance to the beneficiary named therein.

DATED: _____   _____

, Surrogate

<u>**Note to Bank Official**</u>: The term Will means any instrument of a Testamentary Character. Wills are NOT to be sent to the court by ordinary mail.

FORM UCS 876 **Report of Compensation Received by Law Firms for Appointments Pursuant to Part 36 of the Rules of the Chief Judge**

UCS - 876 - Rev. 10/18

REPORT OF COMPENSATION RECEIVED BY LAW FIRMS FOR APPOINTMENTS PURSUANT TO PART 36 OF THE RULES OF THE CHIEF JUDGE (§ 36.4(d))

(Complete if total compensation from appointment of law firm's members, associates and employees pursuant to Part 36 of the Rules of the Chief Judge exceeds $50,000 in a single calendar year (January 1 to December 31). File by March 31ˢᵗ following the calendar year reported.)

1. Calendar Year Reported:

Year ☐ ☐ ☐ ☐

2. Law Firm Tax ID Number

TID# ☐☐ – ☐☐☐☐☐☐☐

3. Name of Law Firm:

4. Address/Phone/FAX/ E-mail:

Street   City/Town/Village   State   Zip

Phone   Fax   E-Mail

5. List the names and Fiduciary Identification Numbers of the members, associates and employees of the law firm for whom compensation from appointments has been approved during the calendar year reported, and enter for each the total compensation approved during that year. For a member, associate or employee with no Fiduciary Identification Number (FID#), enter "Non-List" and his/her Social Security Number in space provided for FID#. (Attach additional sheets as needed.)

CLICK BOX   TO ADD ADDITIONAL ITEMS

NAME	FIDUCIARY IDENTIFICATION NUMBER	TOTAL APPROVED COMPENSATION IN CALENDAR YEAR REPORTED
		$
		$
		$
		$
		$
		$
		$

6. Total of all compensation entered in item 5: $

Date:_____   Signature: _____

Print Name: _____

Title: _____
(e.g., managing attorney, member)

Mail to: OCA, Appointment Processing Unit, 25 Beaver Street, Room 840, New York NY 10004

Official Forms

FORM UCS 880   **Order Appointing Attorney for the Child**

Court: _____

County: _____

---X

<table>
<tr><td>Title of Action/Proceeding</td><td><u>ORDER APPOINTING</u>
<u>ATTORNEY FOR THE CHILD</u></td></tr>
</table>

_____

_____   INDEX NO. _____ / _____

_____   No.   Yr.

---X

Name of Judge: _____:

Upon all of the prior proceedings in this action/proceeding, it is

1. ORDERED that the following is appointed Attorney for the Child:

   Name: _____

   Address: _____

   _____

   _____

   Phone/FAX: _____ / _____

   Email: _____

for the following child(ren) of the parties *(provide name(s) and date(s) of birth of child(ren)):*

_____

_____

_____

_____ ;

2. ORDERED that upon receipt of this order and UCS 872 (Notice of Appointment and Certification of Compliance), the Attorney for the Child shall complete, execute and return UCS 872 to the Fiduciary Clerk;

3. ORDERED that within 10 days of service of a copy of this order of appointment the parties shall pay to the Attorney for the Child a retainer of $_____ *(enter "None" if a retainer is not authorized)*;

4. ORDERED that no less often than every 60 days from the date of this order of appointment the Attorney for the Child shall send to counsel for the parties bills for compensation and the reimbursement of disbursements;

5. ORDERED that the Attorney for the Child shall bill at a rate of compensation of $_____ per hour;

6. ORDERED that subject to reallocation at trial the retainer and all subsequent compensation, including reimbursement for disbursements, shall be paid to the Attorney for the Child by the parties according to the following percentages:

Plaintiff _____% Defendant _____%;

7. ORDERED that once the retainer is expended, or where no retainer is authorized, the parties shall pay all bills sent by the Attorney for the Child within 20 days of the date of the bill;

8. ORDERED that all compensation and reimbursement for disbursements billed by the Attorney for the Child during the pendency of this action/proceeding shall be approved by the Court in the final order of compensation, which shall be settled by the Attorney for the Child, on five days notice, at the conclusion of the Attorney for the Child's service in the action/proceeding, or as otherwise directed by the Court;

9. ORDERED that the final order of compensation shall be supported by the Attorney for the Child's affirmation of services on a form approved by the Chief Administrator of the

Courts;

10. ORDERED that within 10 days of service of a copy of the final order of compensation the Attorney for the Child shall return to a party any amount paid by that party in excess of his/her share of compensation and reimbursement for disbursements, as approved by the Court in the final order of compensation;

11. ORDERED that

a.   counsel for the parties shall immediately contact the Attorney for the Child to schedule the interview(s) of the child(ren) with the Attorney for the Child outside the presence of the parties and their counsel;

b.   the parties shall make themselves, the child(ren), and anyone living in either party's household, available for interviews with the Attorney for the Child (counsel for the parties may be present at any interview between the Attorney for the Child and counsel's client, or the party may, upon written consent of his/her counsel, waive counsel's presence);

c.   each party, on written consent of his/her counsel, may schedule interviews with the Attorney for the Child, with or without his/her counsel present, to discuss all issues relevant to custody and visitation (the sequence and frequency of such interviews shall be at the sole discretion of the Attorney for the Child);

d.   the parties and counsel shall cooperate with the Attorney for the Child in providing any documents, papers or information requested, including executing releases permitting the Attorney for the Child to speak with, or receive information from, any mental health professionals, social service workers or agencies, physicians, schools, or other persons or entities having material and necessary information regarding the parties or the child(ren);

e.   the parties shall provide reasonable, private and unhampered access by the children to the Attorney for the Child, including contact in person or by phone, FAX, email or regular mail;

12. ORDERED that the Attorney for the Child shall make such applications to the

court as

deemed appropriate, including requests for the appointment of forensic experts to conduct evaluations, the cost of which shall be borne by the parties in the same percentages as have been established for the payment of the Attorney for the Child's compensation;

      13. ORDERED that counsel for the parties shall immediately send the Attorney for the Child

copies of all papers in the action/proceeding, including pleadings, motions and prior orders, and

      14. ORDERED that the parties, counsel and the Attorney for the Child shall appear for

conference in this Part at_____ am/pm on _____, 20 ____ .

DATED:

                 _____

                         Judge

Attorney for Plaintiff/Petitioner: **Attorney for Defendant/Respondent:**

*Name:*_____   *Name:*_____

*Address:*_____   *Address:*_____

_____   _____

*Phone/FAX:*_____/_____   *Phone/FAX:*_____/_____

*Email:*_____   *Email:*_____

Official Forms

FORM UCS 881   **Affirmation of Services for Privately Paid Attorney for the Child**

Court: _____

County: _____
---X

Title of Action

_____

_____

_____

---X

**AFFIRMATION OF SERVICES
FOR
PRIVATELY PAID
ATTORNEY FOR THE CHILD**

COMPENSATION FOR PERIOD:
___/___/___ to ___/___/___
Mo Day Yr   Mo Day Yr

INDEX NO. _____ ___/_____
No.   Yr.

State of New York   )
) ss:
County of _____)

_____affirms under penalties of perjury:
Name of Appointee

1. By order of this Court (Hon._____), dated _____, 20 ,

I was appointed Attorney for the following child(ren) of the parties :[1]

Name(s) of child(ren):_____

_____ *(11)*

2. During my period of service, this action/proceeding was *(Choose one by marking "X" in box):*

☐ contested **OR** ☐ not contested *(12)*

_____

[1]Text boxes are key-numbered *(##)* to items on UCS 875 (Statement of Approval of Compensation).

3. The nature of the services provided is evidenced by my time records, attached as Exhibit A, which itemize and total my charges, plus disbursements, and separately itemize and total all payments received from each party;

4. Compensation, excluding disbursements, is requested for:

    a. the hours spent during the current period (see Exhibit A):

    > _____ *(14)*
    > *Number of Hours*

    b. at the hourly rate of:
        (Attach, as Exhibit B, a copy of the order of appointment fixing hourly rate.)

    $_____ per hour

    c. for total compensation[2] of:

    > _____ *(15)*
    > *Total Compensation*

5. I request reimbursement for disbursements in the amount of: $_____ .

WHEREFORE, I respectfully request that the Court grant fair and reasonable compensation, plus reimbursement for disbursements, for a total award of: $_____ .

DATED: _____

Signature: _____

Print Name: _____

Address: _____

_____

_____

Phone/FAX: _____ / _____

Email: _____

---

[2]Compensation, *excluding disbursements*, is the amount to be entered in item 15 of UCS 875 (Statement of Approval of Compensation).

Official Forms

FORM UCS 882   SURROGATE'S COURT   **SF-312**

FORM UCS 882   **Order Approving Attorney for the Child Compensation**

Court: _____
County: _____
---X

<table>
<tr><td>Title of Action/Proceeding</td><td><u>ORDER APPROVING
ATTORNEY FOR THE CHILD
COMPENSATION</u></td></tr>
</table>

_____

_____   INDEX NO. _____ / _____

_____   No.   Yr.

---X

Name of Judge: _____:

Upon the order of this Court, dated _____, 20 , appointing as Attorney for the Child:

Name: _____

Address: _____

_____

_____

Phone/FAX: _____ / _____

Email: _____,

and upon his/her affirmation of services, dated _____, 20 , it is

ORDERED that the Attorney for the Child's compensation is approved in the amount of $_____, plus disbursements in the amount of $_____, for a total of $_____;

ORDERED that the parties shall be liable for the approved compensation and reimbursement for disbursements in the following percentages:

Plaintiff/Petitioner _____%: for a total of $_____,

Defendant/Respondent _____%: for a total of $_____;

ORDERED that the foregoing percentages are *(Mark "X" in box (a)* <u>OR</u> *(b))*

    a. ☐ as established by the order of appointment;

    b. ☐ as otherwise determined by the Court;

ORDERED that *(Enter "None" if no credit is given.)*

    a. Plaintiff/Petitioner is credited $ _____ for payments made;

    b. Defendant/Respondent is credited $ _____ for payments made;

ORDERED that within 10 days of service of a copy of this order *(Mark "X" in appropriate box(es), and enter dollar amount for item(s) marked.)*

    a. ☐ Plaintiff/Petitioner shall pay Attorney for the Child　　$_____

    _____

    b. ☐ Defendant/Respondent shall pay Attorney for the Child　　$____

    _____

    _____

    c. ☐ Attorney for the Child shall pay Plaintiff/Petitioner　　$_____

    _____

    d. ☐ Attorney for the Child shall pay Defendant/Respondent $_____

    _____

DATED:

                     _____

                            Judge

<u>Attorney for Plaintiff/Petitioner:</u>　　　　　<u>Attorney for Defendant/Respondent::</u>

*Name:*_____　　*Name:*_____

*Address:*_____　　*Address:*_____

_____　　_____

_____　　_____

*Phone/FAX:*_____/_____   *Phone/FAX:*_____/_____

*Email:*_____   *Email:*_____

SUR CT-CHK   Surrogate's Court Checklists

Surrogate's Court Checklists:

These checklists formulated by the Fourth Judicial District are supplied for your use in completing petitions of common proceedings filed in Surrogate's Court and for which there are official forms. A checklist works through each paragraph of any particular petition. It is anticipated that the 4JD Checklist Committee will annually update these forms so please contact the court for information as to which checklists may have been changed, corrected or added by the committee within the past year. **Your office should not submit checklists to Surrogate's Court when filing a proceeding.**

Probate Proceeding Checklist	(P-CHKLST release 2/22/07)	7 pages
Ancillary Probate Proceeding Checklist	(ANCP-CHK release 8/9/04)	4 pages
Administration c.t.a. (after probate) Proceeding Checklist	(Acta-CHKLST release 8/9/04)	4 pages
Administration Proceeding Checklist	(A-CHKLST release 2/22/07)	6 pages
Ancillary Administration Proceeding Checklist	(ANCA-CHK release 8/9/04)	4 pages
Administration d.b.n. Proceeding Checklist	(Adbn-CHKLST release 2/22/07)	5 pages
Voluntary Administration Checklist	(V-CHKLST release 2/22/07)	4 pages
Guardianship Proceeding Checklist Person Only	(G-CHKLST [person only] release 8/9/04)	4 pages
Guardianship Proceeding Checklist Person and/or Property	(G-CHKLST [person & prop] release 8/9/04)	5 pages
17-A Guardianship Proceeding Checklist of Mentally Retarded/Developmentally Disabled Person	(G17A-CHK release 2/22/07)	5 pages
17-A Guardianship Proceeding Checklist Standby Appointment/Confirmation	(G17A-CONF-STNDBY-CHK release 2/22/07)	4 pages
Standby Guardianship Proceeding Checklist	(STBY-GRDNSHP-CHKLST release 8/9/04)	7 pages
Wrongful Death Compromise Settlement Proceeding Checklist	(WDCS-CHK release 8/9/04)	5 pages
Informal Accounting with/without Decree Proceeding Checklist	(INF-ACTG-CHK release 8/9/04)	4 pages
Judicial Settlement of Account Proceeding Checklist	(JUD-ACTG-CHK release 8/9/04)	7 pages
Compulsory Accounting and Related Relief Proceeding Checklist	(COMP-ACTG-CHK release 8/9/04)	2 pages
Private Placement Adoption Proceeding Checklist	(PRIV-ADPTN-CHK release 2/22/07)	6 pages
Agency Adoption Proceeding Checklist	(AGNCY-ADPTN-CHK release 2/22/07)	5 pages

CHCKLST-INST.FRM

Probate Proceeding Checklist

(see Surrogate's Court Form P-1, rev. 2/08)

This Checklist is provided for your convenience while completing the petition and the checklist should not be returned to the Court.

If the will was previously admitted to probate the petitioner should submit Administration c.t.a. form CTA-1.

Check All Forms To Make Sure Venue Is Correct - Appropriate County Is Listed
Fill In All Areas On All Pages of Petition - Also Mark When Not Applicable Where Necessary

PET ¶ #	DESCRIPTION	YES	NO
	Is the captioned name the same as the signature on the Will and ¶2 of petition?		
	If A/K/A's, are they listed in the caption and also under ¶2 of petition?		
	Has the type of Letters been checked?		
1.(a)	**Is the name of each fiduciary the same as in Will?**		
	If <u>NO</u>, does petitioner explain why?		
	Is the petitioner ...　the nominated executor		
	alternate executor		
	or person eligible under SCPA §1402 or 1418 (admin. c.t.a.)		
	NOTE: A Non-domiciliary alien is ineligible to be sole fiduciary (SCPA §707)		
1.(b)	**If an attorney and sole executor: has a statement been filed pursuant to Court Rules §207.16(e)?**		
1.(c)	**Has SCPA §2307-a been complied with?**		
2.(a)	**Is the name of the decedent the same as the signature on Will?**		
	Are all A/K/A's listed?		
2.(b)	**Does date of death agree with death certificate?**		
	Certified death certificate must be filed with petition		
2.(c)	**Is the place of death the same as that listed on death certificate?**		
2.(d)	**Is the address on petition and death certificate the same? this county?**		
	If <u>NOT</u>, has an explanatory affidavit with proofs of domicile been filed? (SCPA §206 & 208)		
	If decedent was a non-domiciliary of the State, has information been furnished pursuant to SCPA §1605 showing ...		

PET ¶ #	DESCRIPTION	YES	NO
2.(d) cont.	(1) no original probate or administration proceeding has been or will be filed in any other jurisdiction		
	(2) statement that testator left probatable assets in this jurisdiction		
	(3) statement listing the distributees in the domiciliary jurisdiction or that they are the same as under New York State Law		
2.(e)	**Is the citizenship of decedent listed?**		
	NOTE: Does all information provided under ¶2 agree with death certificate; if not, has an explanatory affidavit been provided? Check that marital status is correct; submit divorce decree if requested by the court.		
3.	*Make sure that original will and codicil are filed with affidavit(s) of attesting witnesses or necessary documents requesting that the affidavits be dispensed with are filed. (With one surviving witness submit form P-8; if all witnesses are deceased submit forms P-8 and P-9 for one witness and P-9 for decedent.)*		
	Are dates listed correctly for Will and Codicils?		
	Are all witnesses listed correctly?		
	If necessary - did witnesses see original will or a court-certified copy? see SCPA §1406(2)		
	Is affidavit of comparison with copy of will (& codicils) submitted?		
	NOTE: Witnesses may not notarize each other's signatures on witness depositions.		
4.	**Answer "NONE" or specify?**		
5.	*NOTE: Distributee: Any person entitled to take/share in property under EPTL §4-1.1 and 4-1.2.*		
	Has the number of survivors been listed?		
	Has "NO" been inserted in all prior classes?		
	Has an "X" been inserted in all subsequent classes?		
	NOTE: If alleged that the decedent was survived by no distributee or only one distributee or where the relationship of distributees to the decedent is grandparents, aunts, uncles, first cousins or first cousins once removed, has an Affidavit of Heirship been submitted - see Court Rules §207.16(c).		
6.(a)	**Are all distributees (who are of full age and sound mind) listed with the required information? (Court needs Form P-4 [Acknowledged Waiver of Process/Consent to Probate] see SCPA §401(4), or proposed citation for each person listed under 6(a). Provide copy of death certificate or date of death for any deceased distributee.) NOTE: Administrator c.t.a. see SCPA §1418 - use waiver P-11.**		

Official Forms

PET ¶ #	DESCRIPTION	YES	NO
6.(a) cont.	Is each person designated as primary executor listed?		
	Are all persons adversely affected by the purported exercise by such Will of any power of appointment listed?		
	Are all persons adversely affected by any codicil listed?		
	Are all persons listed under any other Will of the decedent on file in the Surrogate's Court listed?		
	If there is an inter vivos trust or other testamentary substitute, are trustees and beneficiaries affected by the will listed?		
	Has a copy of the Trust been submitted?		
6.(b)	Same as 6.(a) above but are persons under disability		
	NOTE: IF THERE ARE PERSONS UNDER DISABILITY LISTED UNDER 6(b) A GUARDIAN AD LITEM WILL HAVE TO BE APPOINTED AND A CITATION ISSUED. (see SCPA §306 & 307)		
	NOTE: THE FOLLOWING INFORMATION HAS TO BE PROVIDED UNDER 6(b) AND 7(b) IF THERE ARE PERSONS UNDER DISABILITY.		
	INFANTS:		
	Name, birth date, relationship to decedent, domicile/residence address, person with whom he/she resides		
	Is there a court-appointed guardian? If so, submit name and residence address and information regarding appointment (submit proof of appointment).		
	Are parents living?		
	ALL OTHER PERSONS UNDER DISABILITY:		
	Name, relationship to decedent, residence address		
	Facts regarding disability: has a committee, conservator, guardian, or any other fiduciary been appointed (submit proof of appointment)		
	Has the person under disability been committed to any institution?		
	Are the names and addresses of any committee, person or institution having care and custody of him/her, conservator, guardian and any relative or friend having an interest in his/her welfare listed?		
	If a person is confined as a prisoner: place of incarceration listed and name and address of any person(s) having an interest in his/her welfare		
	Unknowns: described in the same language as will be used in the citation		

PET ¶ #	DESCRIPTION	YES	NO
6.(b) cont.	*NOTE: IF THERE ARE UNKNOWNS, the following proof has to be submitted:* *affidavit showing that diligent efforts have been made to locate unknown* *distributees or distributees whose whereabouts are unknown [Court Rules* *§207.16(d)]* *"DILIGENT SEARCH" requires extensive research, e.g.:* *cemetery and marriage records; telephone books; conversation with other distributees,* *neighbors, etc.; records of varied Surrogate's Court; military records; Bureau of* *Immigration & Naturalization; Social Security Administration; Bureau of Vital Statistics;* *Department of Motor Vehicles; Bureau of the Census; City directories; Internet*		
7.(a)	Court needs Form P-6 [Notice of Probate/Affidavit of Mailing] for all persons listed under 7(a) & 7(b) - see SCPA §1409.		
	Are the names and domiciliary addresses of all substitute or successor executors, trustees, guardians listed? If predeceased - provide death certificate or date of death.		
	Are all legatees (any person designated to receive a transfer by will of personal property) who is of full age and sound mind listed?		
	Are all devisees (any person to whom real property is transferred by will) who is of full age and sound mind listed?		
	Are all other beneficiaries, who are of full age and sound mind, named in the will listed?		
	Are charities receiving a residuary share? If so the State Attorney General must receive a notice of probate.		
	Are any trustees and beneficiaries of any inter vivos trust designated in the purported will other than those named in paragraph 6 listed?		
7.(b)	Same as 7.(a) above but are persons under a disability (see ¶6b). see SCPA §1409(2) and SCPA §307(3) and (4).		
8.	Has "NONE" been entered or is there an indication of the confidential relationship? (May require a PUTNAM hearing.)		
9.(a)	Has value of estate been listed? (do not include joint assets, insurance left to a beneficiary, non-probate assets)		
9.(b)	Has "NONE" been entered or has cause of action been specified?		
10.	Under WHEREFORE Clause: has type of letters and all relief requested been checked and completed?		

PET ¶ #	DESCRIPTION	YES	NO
10. cont.	Is petition dated, signed, verified, properly notarized (including proper jurat and expiration date of notary's commission)?		
	Is oath and designation signed?		
	does it set forth proposed fiduciary's physical address?		
	Is proposed fiduciary a Bank? use combined corporate verification, consent and designation [use page 6 of the petition]		
	Is attorney's name, address and phone number listed?		
	Is Part 130 Certification completed by attorney or self-represented party?		
	if NOT, has a separate certification as to Part 130 signing requirements been included?		
If forms are computer generated, has a certification pursuant to Court Rules §207.4 been attached?			

PARTIAL FEE SCHEDULE	SCPA/EPTL§ or Rule #
Have the proper fees been included with petition?	2402
Fees per schedule; $6.00 for each Certificate of Appointment.	
Filing fee is based upon the values of the estate owned individually by the decedent or payable to the Estate - see SCPA §2402(8)	
0 but under 10,000 $ 45.00 10,000 but under 20,000 75.00 20,000 but under 50,000 215.00 50,000 but under 100,000 280.00 100,000 but under 250,000 420.00 250,000 but under 500,000 625.00 500,000 and over 1,250.00	
If Letters of Trusteeship are requested include an additional $45.00 for this appointment (after checking with individual court of filing as to fee policies).	

COMMENTS AND COURT NOTES		Form Number	SCPA/EPTL§ or Rule #
When Permitted	Whenever decedent dies with a Will.		1402
Forms Always Required	•Petition for Probate	P-1	1402
	•Original Will of decedent and Codicil(s), if any		
	•Affidavit of Comparison (unless waived by court)	P-13	
	•Certified Death Certificate		207.15(b)
	•Affidavit of Attesting Witnesses	P-3	1406
	•Self-addressed stamped envelope (if court requires)		
Forms or Documents Sometimes Required	•Application to Dispense with Testimony of Attesting Witness	P-8	1405
	•Waiver of Process; Consent to Probate	P-4	
	•Notice of Appearance		
	•Authorization to Appear on Behalf of Party		
	•Attorney/Fiduciary Statement		207.16(e) & 2307-a
	•Family Tree Chart (if required by court)	FT-1	207.16(c)
	•Affidavit Proving Handwriting of Decedent/Witness	P-9	
	•Renunciation of Nominated Executor and/or Trustee	P-10	
	•Renunciation of Letters of Admin. c.t.a./Waiver of Process	P-11	
	•Affidavit of No Debt (Admin. c.t.a.)	P-12	
	•Citation on Probate	P-5	1403
	•Affidavit for Supplemental Citation		
	•Order for Mailing and/or Publication		
	•Notice to Consul General		
	•Notice of Probate & Affidavit of Service	P-6	
	•Affidavit of Due Diligence		
	•Application for Preliminary Letters Testamentary & Oath & Designation of Preliminary Executor	P-2	1412
	•Sole Heir Affidavit		207.16(c)
	•Affidavit of Service (Personal/Mail/Publication)		314
	•Affidavit as to Military Service		
	•Bond		801-805
	•Death Certificate of deceased spouse, distributee, beneficiary or named executor		207.15(c)
	•Notice of Election by Surviving Spouse		5-1.1
	•Waiver or Release of the Right of Election		5-1.1
	•Obituary Notice (if court requires)		

Official Forms

COMMENTS AND COURT NOTES (continued)

All Waivers and Proofs of Service must show that each interested party actually received a copy of the Will.

Proofs of Service of Citation must be filed with the Court at least two (2) working days before the return date.

Guardian Ad Litem will be appointed on or before the return day of process for all unknowns and persons under disability (SCPA §403).

Petition & Notice of Probate must include names of all persons designated in Will as legatee, devisee, fiduciary or alternate fiduciary not otherwise listed as an interested party.

Letters will not be delivered until Notice of Probate and Mailing Affidavit are filed.

Review carefully instructions to paragraphs 6 and 7 of the Petition and be sure interested parties are listed in the correct places.

NYS Department of Taxation & Finance may be a necessary party for estates of non-domiciliary decedents. Review SCPA §1403(1)(g).

Documents signed by Power of Attorney (Provide certified copy of POA and comply with Section 13-2.3 EPTL and 207.48 Uniform Rules).

Check to be certain all documents are properly acknowledged.

THIS MATERIAL IS PROVIDED FOR INFORMATIONAL/TRAINING PURPOSES ONLY. – It is intended for use in conjunction with review of the applicable statutes and rules of the Surrogate's Court and the Surrogate's Court Operations Manual.

Ancillary Probate Proceeding Checklist
(see Surrogate's Court Form AP-1, 12/97, rev. 4/98)

This Checklist is provided for your convenience while completing the petition and the checklist should not be returned to the Court.

> **NOTE: An ancillary probate may be used when a non-domiciliary leaves real and/or personal property which needs to be administered under New York State law and there has been probate in the foreign (domiciliary) jurisdiction.**

Fill In All Areas On All Pages of Petition - Also Mark When Not Applicable Where Necessary
Check All Forms To Make Sure Venue Is Correct - Appropriate County Is Listed

CHECK: IS THE ATTORNEY OF RECORD LICENSED TO PRACTICE IN THE STATE OF NEW YORK?

PET ¶ #	DESCRIPTION	YES	NO
	Is the captioned name the same as the signature on the Will and ¶2 of the petition?		
	If A/K/A's are they listed in the caption and also under ¶2 of the petition?		
	Has the type of Letters been checked?		
1.	**Is the petitioner the person expressly appointed in the Will as executor with respect to property located in this State or his/her designee?** (see SCPA §1604)		
	If Not: **Is petitioner the fiduciary appointed to act in the domiciliary jurisdiction or his/her designee?**		
	If Not: **Is petitioner the person acting in the domiciliary jurisdiction to administer and distribute the testator's estate?**		
	If Not: **Is petitioner a person entitled to letters of administration c.t.a. or his/her designee?** (see SCPA §1418)		
	If Not: **Is petitioner a creditor, public administrator (County Treasurer) or person interested or to whom letters may issue?** (see SCPA §1609.1)		
	NOTE: Non-domiciliary alien executor, though ineligible to act in this jurisdiction (unless said executor has a co-executor who is a citizen), has a right to designate an ancillary fiduciary. (see SCPA §707 and §1608)		
2.	**Verify information set forth in Authenticated documents from foreign state.**		
	NOTE: Exemplified/Authenticated Record should include copies of Will, Decree or Order Admitting Will to probate in the foreign (domiciliary) jurisdiction, and Letters issued thereon in the foreign jurisdiction (if the issuance of Ancillary Letters are being requested). (see SCPA §1614 and CPLR §4540) If no letters were issued in foreign jurisdiction then explanatory affidavit may be required.		
	NOTE: Exemplifications and/or authenticated documents must be <u>unaltered</u> - i.e. should <u>not be</u> unstapled to photocopy and <u>should not be attached to petition.</u>		

Official Forms

PET ¶ #	DESCRIPTION	YES	NO
2 cont.	*NOTE: Documents filed in a foreign language shall be accompanied by an English translation and an affidavit by the translator stating his/her qualifications and that the translation is accurate. [see CPLR §2101(b)].*		
3.	**Verify again that all information set forth is as indicated in the Exemplified and/or Authenticated documents from foreign state.**		
	NOTE: If petition indicates that time has not yet passed for Will to be subject to contest under the laws of the foreign state, do not admit to ancillary probate, hold in abeyance until such time as verification from foreign Court is filed indicating that time has passed and it is not being contested.		
	NOTE: Bond of Ancillary Fiduciary may be required. [see SCPA §801(c)(ii)]		
4a.	**Is all the New York State property listed with complete address, description and value?**		
	Verify jurisdiction at this time with property situate in your County, real or personal. (see SCPA §206)		
	All items must be completed. If non-applicable, please indicate.		
	NOTE: Filing fee on Ancillary Probate is based on the value of New York Property only. (see SCPA §2402)		
4b.	**If cause of action is listed <u>complete details must be included</u>; if none, so state.**		
5.	**Issue citation for service on Interested parties listed here as set forth in form (unless waivers and consents to ancillary probate have been submitted).**		
	<u>**Always cite**</u> **the New York State Department of Taxation and Finance** (see SCPA §1609.3) <u>**UNLESS**</u> **a Notice of Appearance and Consent by Tax Commissioner has been filed with Stipulation Reserving Domicile.**		
	If Letters Are Requested Cite: 1) Domiciliary (New York State) Creditors or those claiming to be creditors; 2) Those entitled to letters or entitled to designate an appointee. (see instructions on item 1 of this checklist for those entitled to letters - SCPA §1604)		
6.	**Only beneficiaries who reside in New York State (domiciliary beneficiaries) and who are named in the Will/Codicil being offered for Ancillary Probate need be listed here.**		
	<u>**If Letters are Requested:**</u> **Notice of Ancillary Probate with proof of mailing to all listed if they have not been served with process, waiver, or otherwise appeared in the proceeding. Both (a) and (b) must be completed. If none applicable, so indicate.**		

PET ¶ #	DESCRIPTION	YES	NO
7.	This must be completed. Either "except" crossed out or "none" indicated.		
	Under WHEREFORE Clause: has all relief requested been checked and completed?		
	Is petition dated, signed, verified, properly notarized (including proper jurat and expiration date of notary's commission)?		
	Is Combined Verification, Oath and Designation signed?		
	Does it set forth proposed fiduciary's physical address?		
	Is proposed fiduciary a bank? (If yes, submit a combined Corporate Verification, Consent and Designation)		
	NOTE: Certification must be provided from a financial institution that they are qualified to act as a fiduciary in the State of New York.		
	Is attorney's name, address and phone number listed?		
	Is Part 130 Certification completed by attorney or self-represented party?		
	If NOT, has a separate certification as to Part 130 signing requirements been included?		
If forms are computer generated, has a certification pursuant to Court Rules §207.4 been attached?			

	PARTIAL FEE SCHEDULE	SCPA/EPTL§ or Rule #
Filing Fee	**Have the proper fees been included with petition?**	2402
	Fees per schedule; $6.00 for each Certificate of Appointment.	
	Filing fee is based upon the values of the <u>New York State Property only</u> owned individually by the decedent or payable to the Estate - see SCPA §2402(8)	

0 but under 10,000	$ 45.00
10,000 but under 20,000	75.00
20,000 but under 50,000	215.00
50,000 but under 100,000	280.00
100,000 but under 250,000	420.00
250,000 but under 500,000	625.00
500,000 and over	1,250.00

Official Forms

COMMENTS AND COURT NOTES		Form Number	SCPA/EPTL§ or Rule #
When Permitted	Whenever a non-domiciliary decedent leaves real and/or personal property which needs to be administered under NYS law and there has been probate in the foreign jurisdiction.		1602
Forms Always Required	•Petition for Ancillary Probate •Exemplified/Authenticated Record of Foreign Proceeding (Will, Order Appointing, Letters of Appointment) •Citation (or waiver and consent from tax department)	AP-1 AP-2	1609 1614 CPLR 4540 1609
Forms or Documents Sometimes Required	•Certified Death Certificate •Notice of Ancillary Probate with Affidavit of Mailing •Renunciation of Nominated Executor •Self-addressed stamped envelope •Bond	 AP-3 P-10 	 1608(5) 801(c)(ii)

Proofs of Service of Citation must be filed with the Court at least two (2) working days before the return date.

Letters will not be delivered until Notice of Ancillary Probate and Affidavit of Mailing are filed if applicable.

Documents signed by Power of Attorney (Provide certified copy of POA and comply with Section 13-2.3 EPTL and 207.48 Uniform Rules).

Check to be certain all documents are properly acknowledged.

THIS MATERIAL IS PROVIDED FOR INFORMATIONAL/TRAINING PURPOSES ONLY. – It is intended for use in conjunction with review of the applicable statutes and rules of the Surrogate's Court and the Surrogate's Court Operations Manual.

Administration c.t.a. (after Probate)
Proceeding Checklist
(see Surrogate's Court Form CTA-1, rev. 7/98)

This Checklist is provided for your convenience while completing the petition and the checklist should not be returned to the Court

> **NOTE: If, subsequent to the admission of a will to probate, the executor or administrator c.t.a. dies, resigns or for any reason is removed from office, and there is no executor or administrator c.t.a. qualified to act, a proceeding for the appointment of an administrator c.t.a. or administrator c.t.a., d.b.n. may be commenced in order to complete the administration of the estate. (SCPA §1418 and 1419).**

NOTE: According to the Opinion of the State Comptroller 89-49, dated 11/27/1989, the fee to be charged on an administration c.t.a. proceeding is $45.00.

Check that the office of the executor or administrator c.t.a. is vacant [SCPA §1418(1)]:
1. death certificate
2. proof of revocation
3. resignation (NOTE: an accounting may be required before fiduciary is discharged - SCPA §716)

> **NOTE: The Court may refuse to issue Letters of Administration c.t.a. if distribution is possible pursuant to SCPA §2207.**

Fill In All Areas On All Pages of Petition - Also Mark When Not Applicable Where Necessary
Check All Forms To Make Sure Venue Is Correct - Appropriate County Is Listed

PET ¶ #	DESCRIPTION	YES	NO
	Secure the estate file folder		
	Is the captioned name exactly the same as it appears on the original proceeding?		
	Make sure that the file number is on the petition and all other supporting documents and should be the same file number as the original proceeding		
1a.	**Is the petitioner eligible to act and qualify pursuant to SCPA §1418?**		
	(a) sole beneficiary or if he/she is dead, to his/her fiduciary (b) to one or more residuary beneficiaries or, if any are dead, to his/her fiduciary (c) if there is no one eligible under (a) or (b) who will accept, the Court may issue letters to one or more persons interested in the estate or, if any be dead, to his/her fiduciary *NOTE: [see SCPA §1418(2)-(8) for additional classes] Check citizenship		
	Has the interest of the petitioner been checked and specified?		

Official Forms

PET ¶ #	DESCRIPTION	YES	NO
1b.	Is the proposed administrator an attorney?		
	If so, has a statement been provided pursuant to 22NYCRR 207.16(e)?		
	NOTE: Latter will need an accounting (see 22NYCRR 207.52)		
2.	**Check that the date of admission of Will to probate is correct and that the name of the original fiduciary is listed along with date of death or removal.**		
3.	*NOTE: Verify that all persons and parties interested in this proceeding having a right to letters of administration c.t.a. prior or equal to the petitioner under the provisions of SCPA §1418 and 1419 are listed.*		
	Check that the names, relationships, domiciles and interest of all parties are listed in the petition.		
	NOTE: If there are any deceased interested parties, provide a copy of the death certificate or provide the date of death.		
4.	**Check that all names, relationships, domiciles and interest of all persons and parties are listed who are beneficiaries named in the will other than those named in paragraph 3.**		
	NOTE: Form CTA-3 has to be submitted from all adult competent persons listed under 3 & 4 having a right to letters equal or prior to petitioner or a citation will be issued. ALL INTERESTED PARTIES MUST CONSENT THAT BOND BE DISPENSED WITH OR FILING OF A BOND WILL BE REQUIRED.		
	NOTE: If any interested parties have died subsequent to the death of the decedent, a statement should be included as to whether a legal representative has been appointed, and if so, their name and title, his/her address and the court which issued letters must be listed. If there has been no appointment the distributees of such post-deceased distributee must be listed giving names, relationship, domiciles and citizenship.		
	NOTE: FOR INFANTS (Attach copy of birth certificate if required by court)		
	NOTE: IF THERE IS A COURT-APPOINTED GUARDIAN (FIDUCIARY) SUBMIT PROOF OF APPOINTMENT.		
	NOTE: IF THERE ARE UNKNOWNS, the following proof has to be submitted: affidavit showing that diligent efforts have been made to locate unknown distributees or distributees whose whereabouts are unknown [Court Rules §207.16(d)]		
	"DILIGENT SEARCH" requires extensive research, e.g.: cemetery and marriage records; telephone books; conversation with other distributees, neighbors, etc.; records of varied Surrogate's Court; military records; Bureau of Immigration & Naturalization; Social Security Administration; Bureau of Vital Statistics; Department of Motor Vehicles; Bureau of the Census; City directories; Internet		

PET ¶ #	DESCRIPTION	YES	NO
5.	Verify that there are no other persons interested in this proceeding other than those already mentioned.		
6.	Make sure outstanding debts or funeral expenses are listed. If NONE, so state.		
7a.& 7b.	Check value of unadministered property		
	Check estimated gross rents of real property (if any) for period of eighteen (18) months		
	Check that any pending or contemplated causes of action on behalf of the decedent are listed and complete information is given		
	NOTE: If inconsistent with amount shown in original proceeding, an explanatory affidavit may be required.)		
	Under WHEREFORE Clause: has all relief requested been checked and completed?		
	Is petition dated, signed, verified, properly notarized (including proper jurat and expiration date of notary's commission)?		
	Is Combined Verification, Oath and Designation signed?		
	does it set forth proposed fiduciary's physical address?		
	Is proposed fiduciary a Bank? use combined corporate verification, consent and designation [use page 4 of the petition]		
	Is attorney's name, address and phone number listed?		
	Is Part 130 Certification completed by attorney or self-represented party?		
	if <u>NOT</u>, has a separate certification as to Part 130 signing requirements been included?		
If forms are computer generated, has a certification pursuant to Court Rules §207.4 been attached?			

Official Forms for this type of proceeding are:

    ✍   CTA-1 (7/98) Petition for Letters of Administration c.t.a. after Probate

    ✍   CTA-2 (7/98) Citation (make sure that the full relief requested is included in citation)

    ✍   CTA-3 (7/98) Renunciation of Letters of Administration c.t.a., Waiver of Process and Consent to Dispense with Bond (to be submitted by an adult competent party having a prior or equal right to that of petitioner) **NOTE:** The Court may fix a bond in an amount which will adequately protect creditors and interested persons who have not consented to dispense with a bond

Official Forms

COMMENTS AND COURT NOTES

The Court may fix a bond in an amount which will adequately protect creditors and interested persons who have not consented to dispense with a bond.

Proofs of Service of Citation must be filed with the Court at least two (2) working days before the return date.

Guardian Ad Litem will be appointed on or before the return day of process for all unknowns and persons under disability (SCPA §403).

Review carefully instructions to paragraphs 3 and 4 of the Petition and be sure interested parties are listed in the correct places.

Documents signed by Power of Attorney (Provide certified copy of POA and comply with Section 13-2.3 EPTL and 207.48 Uniform Rules).

Check to be certain all documents are properly acknowledged.

THIS MATERIAL IS PROVIDED FOR INFORMATIONAL/TRAINING PURPOSES ONLY. – It is intended for use in conjunction with review of the applicable statutes and rules of the Surrogate's Court and the Surrogate's Court Operations Manual.

Administration Proceeding Checklist
(see Surrogate's Court Form A-1, rev. 12/98)

> *This Checklist is provided for your convenience while completing the petition and the checklist should not be returned to the Court.*

Check All Forms To Make Sure Venue Is Correct - Appropriate County Is Listed
Fill In All Areas On All Pages of Petition - Also Mark When Not Applicable Where Necessary

PET ¶ #	DESCRIPTION	YES	NO
	Is the captioned name exactly the same as it appears on the Death Certificate?		
	If A/K/A's, are they listed in the caption and also under ¶2 of petition?		
	Has the type of Letters been checked?		
1.	**Is the petitioner eligible to act and qualify pursuant to SCPA §1001?**		
	(a) surviving adult spouse of decedent		
	(b) adult child		
	(c) adult grandchild		
	(d) parent		
	(e) brother or sister		
	(f) any other person who is a distributee and who is eligible to qualify		
	(g) others as set forth in SCPA §1001(3) to (9)		
	Check citizenship		
	NOTE: A Non-domiciliary alien is ineligible to act as a sole fiduciary [see SCPA §707]		
	Has the interest of the petitioner been checked and specified?		
	Is the proposed administrator an attorney?		
	If so, has a statement been provided pursuant to 22NYCRR 207.16(e)?		
	NOTE: Latter will need an accounting [see 22NYCRR 207.52]		
2.	**Does the information under ¶2 of the Petition agree with the death certificate?**		
	(certified copy of death certificate must be filed with petition)		
	(a) if address on petition does not agree with death certificate, has an explanatory affidavit been filed [see SCPA §206-208]		
	(b) if decedent was a non-domiciliary of the State, has an explanatory affidavit and a request for non-domiciliary treatment been filed setting forth the following:		
	(1) statement that no original probate or administration proceeding has been or will be filed in any jurisdiction		
	(2) statement that the decedent left estate assets in this jurisdiction		

PET ¶#	DESCRIPTION	YES	NO
2. cont.	(3) statement listing the distributees in the domiciliary jurisdiction or that they are the same as under New York State Law		
3.	**Has everything been answered?**		
	(a) & (b) is all property in decedent's name alone? do not include: jointly held property with right of survivorship; property held in trust for another; assets that have a named beneficiary		
	(c) estimated rent for 18 months has to be included; this amount needs to be considered in determining whether a bond is required and if so, the amount of the bond		
	(d) if there is a pending or contemplated cause of action on behalf of the decedent, has all information requested in petition been provided?		
	(e) has it been checked, if so, is information provided under ¶7 of Petition?		
4.	**This paragraph states that a diligent search has been made to find a will.**		
5.	**Were the court's records searched for a will for safekeeping or an estate/file previously opened? [See SCPA §2507 and §2508]**		
6.	*NOTE: <u>Distributee:</u> Any person entitled to take or share in property under EPTL §4-1.1 and 4-1.2. (SUBMIT A FAMILY TREE IF REQUIRED BY THE COURT.)*		
	Has the number of survivors been listed?		
	Has "<u>NO</u>" been inserted in all prior classes?		
	Has an " <u>X</u> " been inserted in all subsequent classes?		
	NOTE: If alleged that the decedent was survived by no distributee or only one distributee or where the relationship of distributees to the decedent is grandparents, aunts, uncles, first cousins or first cousins once removed, has an Affidavit of Heirship been submitted - see Court Rules 207.16(c). NOTE: If there are any deceased distributees, provide a copy of the death certificate or provide the date of death.		
7a.	**Are all distributees or other necessary parties who are of full age and under no disability listed with required information? [see Court Rules §207.16(b)]**		
	<u>Renunciation and Waiver:</u> Renunciation of letters of administration and waiver of process may be submitted from any adult, competent person who has a prior or equal right to letters of administration and must consent to the granting of all relief in the "wherefore clause" of the petition. Waivers must be signed and acknowledged. If letters of administration are to be granted to a designee, the name of such designee must be inserted. (Form A-8 to be used by individuals and Form A-9 from a Corporation [example: funeral director and creditors]).		

PET ¶ #	DESCRIPTION	YES	NO
7a. cont.	If non-marital or adopted-out person, has Schedule A and/or B been attached to Petition?		
	Notice of Application for Letters of Administration: This notice (Form A-3) must be given to all those listed in the petition who have a right to letters inferior to that of the nominated administrator, or persons who share in the decedent's estate as distributees, but are not eligible to receive letters. If any of these have waived, notice to them is not required. An original affidavit of mailing must accompany the filed notice.		
NOTE: *ALL INTERESTED PARTIES MUST CONSENT THAT BOND BE DISPENSED WITH OR FILING OF BOND WILL BE REQUIRED.*			
7b.	Same as 7a above but are persons under disability		
	Are infants and persons under disability listed with required information?		
	Are Schedules A, B, C and/or D attached?		
	NOTE: FOR INFANTS (Attach copy of birth certificate if required by court)		
	NOTE: IF THERE IS A COURT-APPOINTED GUARDIAN (FIDUCIARY) SUBMIT PROOF OF APPOINTMENT.		
	NOTE: IF THERE ARE UNKNOWNS, the following proof has to be submitted: affidavit showing that diligent efforts have been made to locate unknown distributees or distributee whose whereabouts are unknown [see Court Rules §207.16(d)]		
	"DILIGENT SEARCH" requires extensive research, e.g.: cemetery and marriage records; telephone books, conversation with other distributees, neighbors, etc.; records of varied Surrogate's Courts; military records; Bureau of Immigration & Naturalization; Social Security Administration; Bureau of Vital Statistics; Department of Motor Vehicles; Bureau of the Census; City directories, Internet		
	NOTE: PURSUANT TO SCPA §1003(4) Jurisdiction over unknown distributees or distributees whose whereabouts are not known need not be secured prior to the issuance of letters, but is required by publication of citation in the accounting proceeding. The Decree granting Administration must so state.		
8.	Make sure outstanding debts or funeral expenses are listed (attach copy of funeral bill if paid). If no outstanding expenses, so state. If outstanding expenses, use Form A-9.		
9.	Under WHEREFORE Clause: has all relief requested been checked and completed?		
	Is petition dated, signed, verified, properly notarized (including proper jurat and expiration date of notary's commission)?		

Official Forms

PET ¶#	DESCRIPTION	YES	NO
9. cont.	**Is Combined Verification, Oath and Designation signed?**		
	does it set forth proposed fiduciary's physical address?		
	Is proposed fiduciary a bank? (submit a Consent and Designation)		
	Is attorney's name, address and phone number listed?		
	Is Part 130 Certification completed by attorney or self-represented party?		
	if NOT, has a separate certification as to Part 130 signing requirements been included?		
If forms are computer generated, has a certification pursuant to Court Rules §207.4 been attached?			

PARTIAL FEE SCHEDULE	SCPA/EPTL§ or Rule #
Have the proper fees been included with petition?	2402
Fees per schedule; $6.00 for each Certificate of Appointment.	
Filing fee is based upon the values of the estate owned individually by the decedent or payable to the Estate - see SCPA §2402(8)	
0 but under 10,000 $ 45.00 10,000 but under 20,000 75.00 20,000 but under 50,000 215.00 50,000 but under 100,000 280.00 100,000 but under 250,000 420.00 250,000 but under 500,000 625.00 500,000 and over 1,250.00	

	COMMENTS AND COURT NOTES	Form Number	SCPA/EPTL§ or Rule #
When Permitted	Whenever decedent dies without a Will, OR Will filed with Court is not offered for Probate.		1001-1004
Forms Always Required	•Petition for Administration •Oath and Designation •Death Certificate •Copy of paid funeral bill or Waiver from funeral director •Self-addressed stamped envelope (if court requires)	A-1 A-1 A-9	1402 207.15(b)

COMMENTS AND COURT NOTES (continued)		Form Number	SCPA/EPTL§ or Rule #
Forms or Documents Sometimes Required	•Administration Citation	A-2	1003
	•Waiver, Renunciation & Consent:		1003(3)
	Individual	A-8	
	Corporation	A-9	
	•Notice of Application for Letters Administration	A-3	1005
	•Affidavit of Mailing Notice of Application	A-4	
	•Notice to Consul General	A-5	207.21
	•Affidavit of Regularity	A-7	
	•Attorney/Fiduciary Affidavit		207.16(e)
	•Affidavit of Due Diligence for Publication		207.16(c)
	•Affidavit of Service	A-10	307
	•Bond		801-805
	•Family Tree Chart	FT-1	207.16(d)
	•Affidavit of Sole Heirship		207.16(c)
	•Death Certificate of deceased spouse, distributee		207.15(c)
	•Obituary Notice (if court requires)		

If the assets exceed $30,000 and one or more distributees refuse to consent that the Administrator serve without bond (or are unable to consent by reason of their being under disability) it may be necessary to obtain a fiduciary bond. See SCPA Article 8.

Proofs of Service of Citation must be filed with the Court at least two (2) working days before the return date.

Guardian Ad Litem will be appointed on or before the return day of process for all unknowns and persons under disability (SCPA §403).

Letters will not be delivered until Notice of Application *(if required)* and Mailing Affidavit are filed.

Review carefully instructions to paragraphs 6 and 7 of the Petition and be sure interested parties are listed in the correct places.

Documents signed by Power of Attorney (Provide certified copy of POA and comply with Section 13-2.3 EPTL and 207.48 Uniform Rules).

Check to be certain all documents are properly acknowledged.

THIS MATERIAL IS PROVIDED FOR INFORMATIONAL/TRAINING PURPOSES ONLY. – It is intended for use in conjunction with review of the applicable statutes and rules of the Surrogate's Court and the Surrogate's Court Operations Manual.

Official Forms

Ancillary Administration Proceeding Checklist

(see Surrogate's Court Form AA-1, 12/97, rev. 4/98)

This Checklist is provided for your convenience while completing the petition and the checklist should not be returned to the Court.

> **NOTE: An ancillary administration may be used when a non-domiciliary dies without a will and leaves real and/or personal property located in New York State or a cause of action exists which needs to be administered and there has been an administration in the foreign (domiciliary) jurisdiction.**

**Fill In All Areas On All Pages of Petition - Also Mark When Not Applicable Where Necessary
Check All Forms To Make Sure Venue Is Correct - Appropriate County Is Listed**

CHECK: IS THE ATTORNEY OF RECORD LICENSED TO PRACTICE IN THE STATE OF NEW YORK?

PET ¶#	DESCRIPTION	YES	NO
	Is the captioned name the same as that on the foreign documents and ¶2 of the petition?		
	If A/K/A's are they listed in the caption and also under ¶2 of the petition?		
	Has the type of Letters been checked?		
1.	**Is the petitioner the person appointed administrator in the foreign/domiciliary jurisdiction or the person acting in that jurisdiction? [see SCPA §1607(2)]**		
	If Not: **Is petitioner a person entitled to original letters of administration?**		
	If Not: **Is petitioner the designee of person(s) in either the two classes listed above? [see SCPA §1607(3)]**		
	If Not: **Is petitioner a creditor, public administrator (County Treasurer) or person interested or to whom letters may issue? [see SCPA §1609(1)]**		
	NOTE: Non-domiciliary alien administrator, though ineligible to act in this jurisdiction (unless said administrator has a co-administrator who is a citizen), has a right to designate an ancillary fiduciary. (see SCPA §707 and §1608)		
2.	**Verify information set forth in Authenticated documents from foreign state.**		
	NOTE: Exemplified/Authenticated Record should include copies of the foreign administration proceeding, Decree or Order and Letters issued thereon in the foreign jurisdiction. (see SCPA §1614 and CPLR §4540 and §4542)		
	NOTE: Exemplifications and/or authenticated documents must be <u>unaltered</u> - i.e. should <u>not be</u> unstapled to photocopy and <u>should not be</u> attached to petition.		
	NOTE: Documents filed in a foreign language shall be accompanied by an English translation and an affidavit by the translator stating his/her qualifications and that the translation is accurate. [see CPLR §2101(b)].		

PET ¶#	DESCRIPTION	YES	NO
3.	Verify again that all information set forth is as indicated in the Authenticated documents from foreign state.		
	NOTE: Bond of Ancillary Fiduciary may be required. [see SCPA §801(c)(ii)]		
4a.	Is all the New York State property listed with complete address, description and value?		
	Verify jurisdiction at this time with property situate in your County, real or personal. (see SCPA §206)		
	All items must be completed. If non-applicable, please indicate.		
	NOTE: Filing fee on Ancillary Administration is based on the value of New York Property only. (see SCPA §2402)		
4b.	If cause of action is listed <u>complete details must be included</u>; if none, so state.		
5.	Issue citation for service on Interested parties listed here as set forth in form (unless waivers and consents have been submitted).		
	<u>Always cite</u> the New York State Department of Taxation and Finance (see SCPA §1609.3) <u>UNLESS</u> a Notice of Appearance and Consent by Tax Commissioner has been filed with Stipulation Reserving Domicile.		
	If Letters Are Requested Cite: 1) Domiciliary (New York State) creditors or those claiming to be creditors; 2) Those entitled to letters or entitled to designate an appointee. (see instructions on item 1 of this checklist for those entitled to letters - SCPA §1607)		
6.	Only domiciliary distributees who reside in New York State need to be listed.		
	Notice of Application for Letters of Ancillary Administration with proof of mailing to all domiciliary distributees who have not waived or otherwise appeared in the proceeding must be submitted. Both 6(a) and 6(b) must be completed. If none applicable, so indicate.		
7.	This must be completed. Either "except" crossed out or "none" indicated.		
	Under WHEREFORE Clause: has all relief requested been checked and completed?		
	Is petition dated, signed, verified, properly notarized (including proper jurat and expiration date of notary's commission)?		
	Is Combined Verification, Oath and Designation signed?		
	Does it set forth proposed fiduciary's physical address?		
	Is proposed fiduciary a bank? (If yes, submit a combined Corporate Verification, Consent and Designation)		

Official Forms

PET ¶ #	DESCRIPTION	YES	NO
	NOTE: Certification must be provided from a financial institution that they are qualified to act as a fiduciary in the State of New York.		
	Is attorney's name, address and phone number listed?		
	Is Part 130 Certification completed by attorney or self-represented party?		
	If <u>NOT</u>, has a separate certification as to Part 130 signing requirements been included?		
If forms are computer generated, has a certification pursuant to Court Rules §207.4 been attached?			

	PARTIAL FEE SCHEDULE	SCPA/EPTL§ or Rule #
Filing Fee	**Have the proper fees been included with petition?**	2402
	Fees per schedule; $6.00 for each Certificate of Appointment.	
	Filing fee is based upon the values of the <u>New York State Property only</u> owned individually by the decedent or payable to the Estate - see SCPA §2402(8)	
	0 but under 10,000 $ 45.00 10,000 but under 20,000 75.00 20,000 but under 50,000 215.00 50,000 but under 100,000 280.00 100,000 but under 250,000 420.00 250,000 but under 500,000 625.00 500,000 and over 1,250.00	

COMMENTS AND COURT NOTES		Form Number	SCPA/EPTL§ or Rule #
When Permitted	Whenever a non-domiciliary decedent leaves real and/or personal property or a cause of action which needs to be administered under NYS law and there has been an administration in the foreign jurisdiction.		1607
Forms Always Required	•Petition for Ancillary Administration •Exemplified/Authenticated Record of Foreign Proceeding, Decree or Order Appointing, Letters of Appointment •Citation (or waiver and consent from Tax Department)	AA-1 AA-2	1609 1614 CPLR 4540 1609
Forms or Documents Sometimes Required	•Certified Death Certificate •Notice of Ancillary Administration with Affidavit of Mailing •Self-addressed stamped envelope •Bond	AA-3	1608(5) 801(c)(ii)

Proofs of Service of Citation must be filed with the Court at least two (2) working days before the return date.

Letters will not be delivered until Notice of Ancillary Administration and Affidavit of Mailing are filed if applicable.

Documents signed by Power of Attorney (Provide certified copy of POA and comply with Section 13-2.3 EPTL and 207.48 Uniform Rules).

Check to be certain all documents are properly acknowledged.

THIS MATERIAL IS PROVIDED FOR INFORMATIONAL/TRAINING PURPOSES ONLY. – It is intended for use in conjunction with review of the applicable statutes and rules of the Surrogate's Court and the Surrogate's Court Operations Manual.

Official Forms

Administration d.b.n. Proceeding Checklist

(see Surrogate's Court Form ADM/DBN-1, rev. 7/98)

This Checklist is provided for your convenience while completing the petition and the checklist should not be returned

> **NOTE:** An Administrator De Bonis Non (d.b.n.) may be appointed to complete the administration of an estate if the administrator dies, resigns, or for any other reason is removed from office. The procedure for the appointment of an administrator d.b.n. shall be the same as an application for letters of administration (SCPA §1007).

NOTE: According to the Opinion of the State Comptroller 89-49, dated 11/27/1989, the fee to be charged on an administration d.b.n. proceeding is $45.00.

Check that the office of the administrator is vacant [SCPA §1007(1)]:
1. death certificate
2. proof of revocation
3. resignation (NOTE: the Court may require an accounting before permitting a fiduciary to resign)

> **NOTE:** The Court may refuse to issue Letters of Administration d.b.n. if distribution is possible pursuant to SCPA §2207.

Fill In All Areas On All Pages of Petition - Also Mark When Not Applicable Where Necessary
Check All Forms To Make Sure Venue Is Correct - Appropriate County Is Listed

PET ¶ #	DESCRIPTION	YES	NO
	Secure the estate file folder		
	Is the captioned name exactly the same as it appears on the original proceeding?		
	Make sure that the file number is on the petition and all other supporting documents and should be the same file number as the original proceeding		
1a.	Is the petitioner eligible to act and qualify pursuant to SCPA §1001?		

	(a) surviving adult spouse of decedent
	    (b) adult child
	    (c) adult grandchild
	    (d) parent
	    (e) brother or sister
	    (f) any other person who is a distributee and who is eligible to qualify
	    (g) others as set forth in SCPA §1001(2) to (9)		

	Check citizenship		
	Has the interest of the petitioner been checked and specified?		

PET ¶ #	DESCRIPTION	YES	NO
1b.	Is the proposed administrator an attorney?		
	If so, has a statement been provided pursuant to 22NYCRR 207.16(e)?		
	NOTE: Latter will need an accounting (see 22NYCRR 207.52)		
2.	**Check date original letters were issued; insert name of original administrator and date of death, resignation or removal**		
3.a-3.e	**Check value of unadministered property**		
	Check estimated gross rents of real property (if any) for period of eighteen (18) months		
	Check that any pending or contemplated causes of action on behalf of the decedent are listed and complete information is given		
	NOTE: If inconsistent with amount shown in original administration proceeding, an explanatory affidavit may be required.)		
4.	*NOTE: Distributee - Any person entitled to take/share in property under EPTL §4-1.1 and 4-1.2.* *(SUBMIT A FAMILY TREE IF REQUIRED BY THE COURT)*		
	Has the number of survivors been listed?		
	Has "NO" been inserted in all prior classes?		
	Has an " X " been inserted in all subsequent classes?		
	NOTE: If alleged that the decedent was survived by no distributee or only one distributee or where the relationship of distributees to the decedent is grandparents, aunts, uncles, first cousins or first cousins once removed, has an Affidavit of Heirship been submitted - see Court Rules §207.16(c). *NOTE: If there are any deceased distributes, provide a copy of the death certificate or provide the date of death.*		
5a.	**Check that the names, relationship, domicile, mailing address and citizenship of all distributees are listed in the petition**		
	NOTE: Form ADM/DBN-3 has to be submitted from all adult competent persons listed under 5a having a right to letters equal or prior to petitioner or a citation will be issued. Use ADM/DBN-4 form for all companies listed. All persons with an inferior right to letters should receive a notice of application (forms ADM/DBN-5 & 6). ALL INTERESTED PARTIES MUST CONSENT THAT BOND BE DISPENSED WITH OR FILING OF BOND WILL BE REQUIRED.		
	NOTE: If any have died subsequent to the death of the decedent, a statement should be included as to whether a legal representative has been appointed, and if so, name and title of such representative, his/her address and the court which issued letters. If no legal representative has been appointed, the distributees of such post-deceased distributee must be listed giving names, relationship, domiciles, mailing addresses and citizenship.		

Official Forms

PET ¶ #	DESCRIPTION	YES	NO
5b.	Same as 5a. above but are persons under disability		
	Are infants and persons under disability listed with required information?		
	Are Schedules A, B, C and/or D attached?		
	NOTE: FOR INFANTS (Attach copy of birth certificate if required by court)		
	NOTE: IF THERE IS A COURT-APPOINTED GUARDIAN (FIDUCIARY) SUBMIT PROOF OF APPOINTMENT.		
	NOTE: IF THERE ARE UNKNOWNS, the following proof has to be submitted: affidavit showing that diligent efforts have been made to locate unknown distributees or distributees whose whereabouts are unknown [Court Rules §207.16(d)] "DILIGENT SEARCH" requires extensive research, e.g.: *cemetery and marriage records; telephone books; conversation with other distributees, neighbors, etc.; records of varied Surrogate's Court; military records; Bureau of Immigration & Naturalization; Social Security Administration; Bureau of Vital Statistics; Department of Motor Vehicles; Bureau of the Census; City directories; Internet*		
	NOTE: PURSUANT TO SCPA §1003(4) Jurisdiction over unknown distributees or distributees whose whereabouts are not known need not be secured prior to the issuance of letters, but is required by publication of citation in the accounting proceeding. The Decree granting Administration must so state.		
6.	Verify that there are no other persons interested in this proceeding other than those already mentioned.		
7.	Make sure outstanding debts or funeral expenses are listed. If none, so state.		
	Under WHEREFORE Clause: has all relief requested been checked and completed?		
	Is petition dated, signed, verified, properly notarized (including proper jurat and expiration date of notary's commission)?		
	Is Combined Verification, Oath and Designation signed?		
	does it set forth proposed fiduciary's physical address?		
	Is proposed fiduciary a bank? (submit a Consent and Designation)		
	Is attorney's name, address and phone number listed?		
	Is Part 130 Certification completed by attorney or self-represented party?		
	if <u>NOT</u>, has a separate certification as to Part 130 signing requirements been included?		
If forms are computer generated, has a certification pursuant to Court Rules §207.4 been attached?			

Official Forms for this type of proceeding are:

- ✍ ADM/DBN-1 Petition for Letters of Administration d.b.n. (7/98)
- ✍ ADM/DBN-2 Citation (make sure full relief requested is included in citation) (7/98)
- ✍ ADM/DBN-3 Waiver of Citation, Renunciation and Consent to Appointment of Administrator d.b.n. (Individual) (10/04)
- ✍ ADM/DBN-4 Consent to Appointment of Administrator d.b.n. (Corporation) (10/04)
- ✍ ADM/DBN-5 Notice of Application for Letters of Administration d.b.n. (7/98)
- ✍ ADM/DBN-6 Affidavit of Mailing Notice of Application for Letters of Administration d.b.n. (7/98)
- ✍ ADM/DBN-7 Notice to the Consul General (7/98)
- ✍ ADM/DBN-8 Affidavit of Service of Citation (Adult) (7/98)

COMMENTS AND COURT NOTES

If the assets exceed $30,000 and one or more distributees refuse to consent that the Administrator serve without bond (or are unable to consent by reason of their being under disability) it may be necessary to obtain a fiduciary bond. See SCPA Article 8.

Proofs of Service of Citation must be filed with the Court at least two (2) working days before the return date.

Guardian Ad Litem will be appointed on or before the return day of process for all unknowns and persons under disability (SCPA §403).

Letters will not be delivered until Notice of Application *(if required)* and Mailing Affidavit are filed.

Review carefully instructions to paragraphs 5a and 5b of the Petition and be sure interested parties are listed in the correct places.

Documents signed by Power of Attorney (Provide certified copy of POA and comply with Section 13-2.3 EPTL and 207.48 Uniform Rules).

Check to be certain all documents are properly acknowledged.

THIS MATERIAL IS PROVIDED FOR INFORMATIONAL/TRAINING PURPOSES ONLY. – It is intended for use in conjunction with review of the applicable statutes and rules of the Surrogate's Court and the Surrogate's Court Operations Manual.

Official Forms

Voluntary Administration Checklist
(see Surrogate's Court Form SE-3A rev. 11/2019)

> *This Checklist is provided for your convenience while completing the petition and the checklist should not be returned to the Court.*

Check Form To Make Sure Venue Is Correct - Appropriate County Is Listed.
Fill In All areas On All Pages Of Affidavit - Also Mark When Not Applicable, Where Necessary.

PET ¶ #	Description	YES	NO
	Is the captioned name exactly the same as it appears on the Death Certificate?		
	If A/K/A's, are they listed in the caption and also under ¶3 of affidavit?		
1.	**Is the petitioner eligible to act and qualify pursuant to SCPA §1303(a) or 1303(b)?** (a) named executor, if there is a will (b) surviving adult spouse of decedent (c) adult child (d) adult grandchild (e) parent (f) brother or sister (g) niece or nephew or aunt or uncle (h) others as set forth in SCPA §1303(a) or SCPA §1303(b)		
2.	**Has the interest of the affiant been checked and specified?**		
3.	**Enter decedent's name, including a/k/a's, domicile, date of death, place of death and citizenship. Does the information agree with the death certificate?**		
	NOTE: A certified copy of the death certificate must be filed with affidavit. [see SCPA §1304(3)]		
4.	**Check appropriate box. If decedent died with a will, the original will must be submitted with Affidavit. [SCPA §1303(b)].**		
5.	**Check records of Surrogate's Court to make sure no previous application has been made in this estate for a voluntary administration or for letters of administration or for the probate of a will.**		
6.	*NOTE: Distributee: Any person entitled to take or share in property under EPTL §4-1.1 and 4-1.2. (SUBMIT A FAMILY TREE IF REQUIRED BY THE COURT.)*		
	Check that name, complete mailing address and relationship of each distributee is listed.		
	NOTE: If alleged that the decedent was survived by no distributee or only one distributee or where the relationship of distributees to the decedent is grandparents, aunts, uncles, first cousins or first cousins once removed, the Court may require an Affidavit of Heirship as set forth in Uniform Rules 207.16 (c).		
	NOTE: If there are any deceased distributees, provide a copy of the death certificate or provide the date of death.		

PET ¶ #	Description	YES	NO
7.	Must be listed: name, bequest and full mailing address of each individual named in the will.		
	NOTE: Postcard Notices (may be in letter form) are to be mailed to each distributee and beneficiary listed in affidavit under ¶6 and ¶7, excluding affiant. [see SCPA §1304(4)]		
8.	Check to be certain that value of personal property does not exceed $50,000.		
9.	Must be listed: all assets of the decedent including bank accounts, stocks, insurance policies not payable to a named beneficiary and the value of each item. JOINT ASSETS AND SET-OFF PROPERTY ARE EXCLUDED. [see EPTL §5-3.1] Give specifics for each asset, i.e. name of bank, account number, etc. A certificate will be issued for each asset listed.		
10.	Must be listed: names of all creditors, including unpaid funeral expenses, and the amount owed to each creditor.		
11.	Court should advise the voluntary administrator of his or her duties and that they are required to account for the disposition of all assets.		
12.	This paragraph states that this proceeding will not determine the estate tax liability.		
13.	This paragraph states that if an administration or probate proceeding is commenced, voluntary administrator must file an account with the Court appointed fiduciary. [see SCPA §1307(2)]		
	Is affidavit signed and properly notarized (including proper jurat and expiration date of notary's commission)? Affiant is represented by an attorney. Is the attorney's name, address and phone number listed and has the Part 130 Certification been completed?		

If forms are computer generated, has a certification pursuant to Court Rules §207.4 been attached?

Official Forms

FEE SCHEDULE	SCPA/EPTL § or Rule #
Have the proper fees been included with affidavit? $1.00 for filing affidavit	1304(4)

	COMMENTS AND COURT NOTES	Form Number	SCPA/EPTL § or Rule #
When permitted	May be used when a fiduciary is needed to transfer estate assets (personal property only) and the value of the assets does not exceed $50,000. Amounts exclusive of property set off under EPTL §5-3.1.		1301
Documents Always Required	• Affidavit in Relation to Settlement of Estate under Article 13 • Certified Death Certificate • Original Will (if one exists) • Report and Account in Settlement of Estate	SE-3A SE-1D	1304(3) 1304(3) 1303(b) 1307(2)
Documents Sometimes Required	• Renunciation of Voluntary Administration • Copy of funeral bill • Obituary Notice • Affidavit of Disinterested Party/Sole Heirship Affidavit • Family Tree Chart • Amended Affidavit • Death Certificate of deceased spouse, distributee	SE-1C FT-1 SE-3B	1303 207.16(c) 207.16(c) 207.46

COMMENTS AND COURT NOTES (continued)

Only one certificate of appointment will be issued for each asset or item listed in paragraph 9 of the Affidavit (SE-3A). If additional certificates are needed after Affidavit is filed, use Amended Affidavit (Form SE-3B).

A voluntary administrator MAY NOT be used to pass title to real property held in the decedent's name. **[However, pursuant to Real Property Law §321(5)(a) a voluntary administrator may sign a discharge of mortgage.]**

A bank account must be opened for any money received by the voluntary administration, see SCPA §1307(1).

Review carefully instructions to ¶6 and ¶7 of the Affidavit and be sure interested parties are listed in the correct places.

Documents signed by Power of Attorney (Provide certified copy of POA and comply with Section 13-2.3 EPTL and 207.48 Uniform Rules).

Check to be certain all documents are properly notarized.

Estates, Powers and Trusts Law Section 5-3.1 - Exemption for Benefit of Family

If a person dies leaving a surviving spouse the following items of personal property vest in such surviving spouse, and if there is no surviving spouse, such items of property vest in the decedent's children under the age of 21 years, if any:

(1) Household items (furniture, clothing, etc....) not exceeding a total value of $20,000.

(2) Family Bible, pictures, videotapes, discs, computer tapes, software, books not exceeding a total value of $2,500.

(3) Domestic animals with their necessary food for 60 days, farm machinery, one tractor and one lawn tractor, not exceeding in aggregate value $20,000.

(4) One motor vehicle not exceeding in value $25,000.

(5) Money not exceeding in value $25,000, including but not limited to cash, checking, savings, and money market accounts, certificates of deposit or equivalents there-of, and marketable securities, except that where assets are insufficient to pay the reasonable funeral expense of the decedent, the personal representative must apply such money or other personal property to defray any deficiency in such expenses.

(This is not a complete reprint of the law regarding family exemptions. Please see EPTL §5-3.1 for the full text of the law.)

THIS MATERIAL IS PROVIDED FOR INFORMATION/TRAINING PURPOSES ONLY. -It is intended for use in conjunction with review of the applicable statutes and rules of the Surrogate's Court and the Surrogate's Court Operations Manual.

Official Forms

Guardianship Proceeding Checklist
Person Only
(see Surrogate's Court Form G-2A, rev. 12/6/00)

This Checklist is provided for your convenience while completing the petition and the checklist should not be returned to the Court.

**Fill in All Areas On All Pages - Also Mark When Not Applicable When Necessary
Check All Forms To Make Sure Venue Is Correct - Appropriate County Is Listed**

PET ¶ #	DESCRIPTION	YES	NO
	Does the Court have jurisdiction over the subject infant [see SCPA §1702]?		
	NOTE: The infant must be domiciled in the county, have sojourned in the county immediately preceding the application for guardianship, or if a non-domiciliary of the state, must have property situate in the county.		
	Is the captioned name the same as the birth certificate and ¶2 of petition?		
1.	**Is the petitioner a proper party?** [see SCPA §1703]		
	Is the petitioner ... the infant, if over fourteen (14) years of age		
	a parent		
	a person with whom the infant resides		
	the public administrator or chief fiscal officer (where no one else is available to act as guardian of the property; would not act as guardian of the person)		
	any other person representing the interest of the infant		
	Has all required information been provided? [name, telephone #, permanent address (mailing address), date of birth and relationship]		
	Are all A/K/A's listed?		
2.	**Is the name of the infant in ¶2 the same as that listed on the birth certificate?**		
	Has all requested information been provided? [name, permanent address (mailing address), date of birth and marital status]		
	Birth Certificate from official registrar (not hospital) to be filed with petition [see NYCRR §207.15(a)]		
	Are all A/K/A's listed?		
3.	**Check that names and addresses of <u>both</u> natural parents are listed.** If infant is married-provide requested information [see SCPA §1704(2)]		
	If one or both are deceased their names must still be shown and date of death noted. (Court may require copy of death certificate)		
3. cont.	If the name of the father is not shown on petition or birth certificate, determine if a proceeding has been brought to establish paternity. (Court may require copy of filiation order) *[see page 4 - Comments & Court Notes]*		

PET ¶ #	DESCRIPTION	YES	NO
	NOTE: If it is claimed that the identity of the father is unknown, the Court may require an affidavit showing diligent efforts to identify him.		
	NOTE: If the natural mother was married at the time of infant's birth, there is a rebuttable presumption that her husband is the father of the infant and is a necessary party unless a filiation order has established otherwise. [see DRL §24(1)]		
4.	List names/addresses of adults with whom infant resides if other than parent or name of agency having custody of infant.		
5.	If both parents are deceased, check that names and addresses of adult domiciliary distributees are listed. [see SCPA §1704(2)]		
6.	Have the names and permanent addresses of the infant's grandparents been provided? [see SCPA §1705]		
	If not applicable, so state.		
	If deceased, add date of death.		
7.	This paragraph is a sworn statement by petitioner.		
8a.	Verify that the infant has never had a guardian appointed.		
8b.	Verify that custody of the infant has never been surrendered by any person and that no court order has ever awarded custody of the infant. If exceptions list information on petition and see note below.		
	NOTE: Check that applicable copies of surrenders, court orders or divorce decrees have been attached.		
9.	Verify whether petitioner indicated knowledge that a person nominated to be a guardian, or any individual eighteen years of age or over who resides in the home of the proposed guardian:		
	a. Is the subject of a report filed with the Statewide Central Register of Child Abuse and Maltreatment pursuant to the rules of Child Protective Services, following an investigation which determines that some credible evidence of alleged abuse or maltreatment exists and/or		
	b. Has been the subject of, or the respondent in, a Child Protective Proceeding commenced pursuant to law, which proceeding resulted in an order finding that the child is an abused or neglected child.		
	NOTE: If knowledge of a report is indicated, verify that an affidavit explaining circumstances in detail is included.		
10.	Check that Request for Information Guardianship form [OCFS 3909] has been submitted with petition and includes all persons over age of 18 in the household.		
	NOTE: Some Courts may require submission of form DCJS-6, Fingerprint Card, for each proposed guardian in order to conduct a criminal record search.		

Official Forms

PET ¶ #	DESCRIPTION	YES	NO
11.	Verify that the petitioner has indicated whether the child is or is not a Native American Child under the Indian Child Welfare Act of 1978 (25 U.S.C. sections 1901-1963).		
12.	This paragraph is a sworn statement that there are no other persons interested in this proceeding other than those already mentioned.		
13.	This paragraph is a sworn statement that no prior application has been made in any court for the relief requested in the petition.		
	Under WHEREFORE Clause: has all relief requested been checked and completed?		
	Is petition dated, signed, verified, properly notarized (including proper jurat and expiration date of notary's commission)?		
	Is oath and designation signed by proposed fiduciary?		
	Does it set forth proposed fiduciary's physical(street) address?		
	Is attorney's name, address and phone number listed? (Or if self-represented, add none.)		
	Has Part 130 Certification been completed?		
	If NOT, has a separate attorney certification as to Part 130 signing requirements been included?		
	Has Joinder and Statement of Preference of Infant Over 14 been included? [see SCPA §1706(1)]		
	Is the joinder dated, signed, verified, properly notarized (including proper jurat and expiration date of notary's commission)?		
If forms are computer generated, has a certification pursuant to Court Rules §207.4 been attached?			

FEE SCHEDULE	SCPA/EPTL§ or Rule #
Have the proper fees been included with petition?	2402
$20.00 for filing petition $6.00 for each Certificate of Appointment.	

	COMMENTS AND COURT NOTES	Form Number	SCPA/EPTL§ or Rule #
When Permitted	Whenever the interests of an infant will be promoted by the appointment of a guardian of the person		1701

COMMENTS AND COURT NOTES		Form Number	SCPA/EPTL § or Rule #
Forms Always Required	•Petition for Guardianship	G-2A	1704
	•Birth Certificate		207.15(a)
	•Affidavit of Proposed Guardian of the Person	G-3	
	•Request for Information Guardianship Form	OCFS-3909	1706(2)
Forms or Documents Sometimes Required	•Guardianship Citation	G-1	1705
	•Affidavit of Parent	G-4	
	•Waiver, Renunciation and Consent	G-5	1705
	•Affidavit of Service		
	•Affidavit of Due Diligence		
	•Affidavit of Service (Personal/Mail/Publication)		
	•Death Certificate of deceased spouse, distributee or parent		
	•Copies of Divorce Decrees, Surrenders, Court Orders		
	•Orders of Filiation		
	•Fingerprint Card	DCJS-6	

Proofs of Service of Citation must be filed with the Court at least two (2) working days before the return date.

Some courts may conduct additional inquiries of Putative Father Registry. (Court submits inquiry form to Registry - NYS OCFS Form LDSS-2725,); some courts may also check if natural father has acknowledged being father in any other manner (possible sources of information may be Family Court, Department of Social Services, hospital of birth, local registrar and/or Department of Health).

Guardian Ad Litem will be appointed on or before the return day of process for all unknowns and persons under disability (SCPA §403).

Documents signed by Power of Attorney (Provide certified copy of POA and comply with Section 13-2.3 EPTL and 207.48 Uniform Rules).

Check to be certain all documents are properly acknowledged.

THIS MATERIAL IS PROVIDED FOR INFORMATIONAL/TRAINING PURPOSES ONLY. – It is intended for use in conjunction with review of the applicable statutes and rules of the Surrogate's Court and the Surrogate's Court Operations Manual.

Official Forms

Guardianship Proceeding Checklist
Person and/or Property
(see Surrogate's Court Form G-2-B, rev. 12/6/00)

This Checklist is provided for your convenience while completing the petition and the checklist should not be returned to the Court.

Fill in All Areas On All Pages - Also Mark When Not Applicable When Necessary
Check All Forms To Make Sure Venue Is Correct - Appropriate County Is Listed

PET ¶ #	DESCRIPTION	YES	NO
	Does the Court have jurisdiction over the subject infant [see SCPA §1702]?		
	NOTE: The infant must be domiciled in the county, have sojourned in the county immediately preceding the application for guardianship, or if a non-domiciliary of the state, must have property situate in the county.		
	Is the captioned name the same as the birth certificate and ¶2 of petition?		
1.	**Is the petitioner a proper party?** [see SCPA §1703]		
	Is the petitioner ... **the infant, if over fourteen (14) years of age**		
	a parent		
	a person with whom the infant resides		
	the public administrator or chief fiscal officer (where no one else is available to act as guardian of the property; would not act as guardian of the person)		
	any other person representing the interest of the infant		
	Has all requested information been provided [name, permanent address, date of birth, telephone # and relationship]?		
	Are all A/K/A's listed?		
2.	**Is the name of the infant in ¶2 the same as that listed on the birth certificate?**		
	Birth Certificate from official registrar (not hospital) to be filed with petition [see NYCRR §207.15(a)]		
	Has all requested information been provided [name, permanent address, date of birth, marital status]		
	Are all A/K/A's listed?		
3.	**Check that names and addresses of <u>both</u> natural parents are listed. If infant is married, has the information been provided regarding the spouse?** [see SCPA §1704(2)]		
	If one or both parents are deceased their names must still be shown and date of death noted. (Court may require copy of death certificate)		

PET ¶ #	DESCRIPTION	YES	NO
5.	**Complete ¶5 only if new or different standby guardian(s) is/are to be designated in this proceeding.**		
	If applicable enter required information in (a) through (d).		
6.	**Complete ¶6 only if seeking confirmation of standby guardian or alternate standby guardian.**		
	If applicable enter required information.		
7.	**Complete ¶7 only if seeking confirmation of standby guardian or alternate standby guardian.**		
	If applicable check appropriate box.		
8.	**Check appropriate box.** [see SCPA §1704(6) and §1761].		
	NOTE: If knowledge of a report is indicated, verify that an affidavit explaining circumstances in detail is included.		
9.	**Confirm that Request for Information Guardianship form has been submitted.**		
	NOTE: Some Courts may require submission of form DCJS-6, Fingerprint Card, for each proposed guardian in order to conduct a criminal record search.		
10.	**List names and addresses of all interested parties.** [see SCPA §1753 and 304(3)]		
11.	**This paragraph states that there are no other persons interested in this proceeding other than those already mentioned.**		
	If new or different standby guardian(s) is/are to be designated furnish any necessary waivers/renunciations/consents. (Form GMD-3)		
	NOTE: SCPA §1753(1) requires that process shall issue to: *1. Parent or Parents (if other than petitioner)* *2. Adult children, adult siblings (if petitioner is other than a parent)* *3. Spouse (if respondent is married);* *4. Person having care and custody or with whom respondent resides (if other than parent or spouse);* *5. The respondent (if fourteen (14) years of age or older).*		
	NOTE: SCPA §1753(2) requires that a Notice of Petition be served by certified mail to: *1. Adult siblings (if petitioner is a parent)* *2. Mental Hygiene Legal Services* *3. Director of any State Facility where respondent resides* *4. Adult children (if petitioner is a parent)* *5. Any other person Court deems proper* *6. Any person designated in writing by respondent*		
	NOTE: No process or notice is necessary to any person above who has been declared by the court as incompetent or who has, as appears to the Court's satisfaction, abandoned the respondent or to a spouse who is divorced from the respondent. [see SCPA §1754(2)]		

PET ¶ #	DESCRIPTION	YES	NO
	Under WHEREFORE Clause: has all relief requested for sections (a) through (k) been checked and completed?		
	Is petition dated, signed, verified, properly notarized (including proper jurat and expiration date of notary's commission)?		
	Is attorney's name, address and phone number listed?		
	Is oath and designation signed?		
	does it set forth proposed guardian's physical address?		
	Is proposed guardian a Bank?		
	has corporate consent and designation been submitted? [see SCPA §708(4)]		
	Has Part 130 Certification been completed?		
	if **NOT**, has a separate attorney certification as to Part 130 signing requirements been included?		

If forms are computer generated, has a certification pursuant to Court Rules §207.4 been attached?

FEE SCHEDULE	SCPA/EPTL§ or Rule #
Have the proper fees been included with petition? $20.00 for filing petition $6.00 for each Certificate of Appointment.	2402

	COMMENTS AND COURT NOTES	Form Number	SCPA/EPTL§ or Rule #
When Permitted	Whenever the interests of a respondent will be promoted by the confirmation or designation of a standby guardian of the person or of the property or of both person and property.		1750, 1750-a 1750-b

COMMENTS AND COURT NOTES	Form Number	SCPA/EPTL§ or Rule #
Forms Always Required •Petition for Appointment/Confirmation of Standby Guardian	CSMD-1	1757
•Affidavit of Proposed Guardian	CSMD-5	
•Birth Certificate (if not already filed with court)		207.15(a)
•Request for Information Guardianship Form	OCFS-3909	1706(2)
•Affidavit (Certification) of Examining Physician or Licensed Psychologist (if not already filed or required by court)	GMD-2A	1750,1750-a, 1750-b
•Affirmation (Certification) of Examining Physician (if not already filed or required by court)	GMD-2B	1750,1750-a 1750-b
•Citation	CSMD-4	1757
•Notice of Petition	CSMD-3	1753(2)
Forms or Documents Sometimes Required •Waiver, Renunciation and Consent	CSMD-2	1753(1)
•Consent, Oath and Designation of Guardian/Standby Guardian	CSMD-6	
•Guardian's Annual Account	G-7	1719, 1761
•Affidavit of Due Diligence		
•Affidavit of Service (Personal/Mail/Publication)		
•Bond		801, 1708, 1761
•Death Certificate of deceased spouse, distributee or parent		207.15(b)
•Birth Certificate of spouse or distributees who are under the age of 18		207.15(a)
•Copies of Divorce Decrees, Surrenders, Court Orders		
•Orders of Filiation	DCJS-6	
•Fingerprint Card		

Proofs of Service of Citation must be filed with the Court at least two (2) working days before the return date in compliance with Uniform Rule 207.7(e).

Guardian Ad Litem will be appointed when respondent is not a resident of a state facility. Guardian ad litem will be appointed on or before the return day of process for all unknowns and persons under disability (SCPA §403).

Documents signed by Power of Attorney (Provide certified copy of POA and comply with Section 13-2.3 EPTL and 207.48 Uniform Rules).

Check to be certain all documents are properly acknowledged.

THIS MATERIAL IS PROVIDED FOR INFORMATIONAL/TRAINING PURPOSES ONLY. – It is intended for use in conjunction with review of the applicable statutes and rules of the Surrogate's Court and the Surrogate's Court Operations Manual.

Official Forms

17-A Guardianship Proceeding Checklist
of Intellectually Disabled/Developmentally Disabled Person
(Person and/or Property)
(see Surrogate's Court Form GMD-1, rev. 7/2016)

This Checklist is provided for your convenience while completing the petition and the checklist need not be returned to the Court.

Check All Forms To Make Sure Venue Is Correct - Appropriate County Is Listed
Fill in All Areas On All Pages of Petition - Also Mark When Not Applicable
Where Necessary

PET ¶ #	DESCRIPTION	YES	NO
	Does the Court have jurisdiction over the subject ID/DDP, hereinafter referred to as <u>respondent</u> [see SCPA §1702]?		
	NOTE: The respondent must be domiciled in the county, have sojourned in the county immediately preceding the application for guardianship, or if a non-domiciliary of the state, must have property situate in the county. The domicile of the respondent's parent(s) or spouse if respondent is married, or custodial parent in the case of an infant respondent is the domicile of the respondent.		
	Is the captioned name the same as the birth certificate and ¶2 of petition? [see 22NYCRR §207.15(a) and SCPA §1752(1)]		
1.	**Is the petitioner a proper party?** [see SCPA §1751]		
	Is the petitioner ... both parents or the survivor, or one parent;		
	any person eighteen (18) years of age or older, including a corporation authorized to serve as a guardian, interested in the welfare of the respondent;		
	the respondent when such person is eighteen (18) years of age or older.		
	Complete all required information.		
	Are all A/K/A's listed?		
2a.	**Is the name and date of birth of the respondent in ¶2 the same as that listed on the Birth Certificate?** [see SCPA §1752(1)]		
	Attach Birth Certificate from official registrar (not hospital) to be filed with petition [see NYCRR §207.15(a)]		
	Complete all required information.		
2b.	**Check whether respondent is admitted to a group home or facility.** [see MHL §1.03 and/or Article 15]		
	If admitted, complete required information.		
3.	**List the names and post office addresses of the parents and spouse of the respondent.** [see SCPA §1752(3)]		

PET ¶ #	DESCRIPTION	YES	NO
3. cont.	If any relatives are deceased their names must still be shown and date of death noted. (Court may require copy of death certificate)		
	If the name of the father is not shown on petition or birth certificate, determine if a proceeding has been brought to establish paternity. (Court may require copy of filiation order) *[see page 5 - Comments & Court Notes]*		
	NOTE: If it is claimed that the identity of the father is unknown, the Court may require an affidavit showing diligent efforts to identify him.		
	NOTE: If the natural mother was married at the time of respondent's birth, there is a rebuttable presumption that her husband is the father of the respondent and is a necessary party unless a filiation order has established otherwise. [see DRL §24(1)]		
4.	List names and addresses of adult children, adult siblings, and their relationship to respondent. [see SCPA §1752(3)]		
5.	If the respondent has a primary care physician other than the physician submitting the certification, complete required information.		
6.	If the father and mother are deceased, list the names and addresses of New York State distributees (those persons entitled to take a share of the respondent's property). [see EPTL §4-1.1]		
7.	If respondent resides with person(s) other than parents or spouse, list names, addresses and relationship to respondent of person(s) charged with their care and custody.		
8.	Give detailed information why those relatives listed in this paragraph are not petitioning to be appointed.		
9.	This paragraph states that proposed guardian(s), standby or alternate standby guardian(s) are of sound mind, adult and competent.		
10a.	Choose the box that reflects the relief requested and indicate reasons.		
10b.	Choose the box that reflects the relief requested and indicate value.		
11a.	Describe and state the value of personal property as directed in this paragraph. [see SCPA §1752(6)]		
11b.	Describe and state the value of real property as directed in this paragraph. [see SCPA §1752(6)]		
11c.	Describe and state the value of annual income as directed in this paragraph. [see SCPA §1752(6)]		
11d.	State the source of all property as directed in this paragraph.		
	NOTE: Court only requires information as to respondent's property. All information in paragraph 11 will be used to compare and verify the guardian's report on the first annual account.		

PET ¶ #	DESCRIPTION	YES	NO
12.	Confirm that the licensed doctors' certifications (Form GMD-2A and 2B) are attached to petition and that their names and the dates of the certifications are completed on the petition. Check certifications/affidavits to be certain all required information is contained therein. [see SCPA §1750, 1750-a, 1750-b]		
13.	For a limited guardianship, insert applicable employment information. [see SCPA §1756]		
14a. to 14d.	List names and addresses of the proposed guardians (other than petitioner), all standby guardians or alternate guardians are listed and confirm that the boxes checked reflect the relief requested.		
	Confirm that proper consents/oaths/designations or consents/designations are completed by any proposed alternate/standby guardians. (GMD-4)		
15.	Check appropriate box. If request is made to dispense with respondent's presence, confirm that physician's certification so attests or that other circumstances are stated. [see SCPA §1754]		
16.	Confirm that the respondent has never had a guardian appointed by will or deed or any acting guardian in socage, or a guardian appointed pursuant to Social Services Law §384 or §284-b. [see SCPA §1704(3) and SCPA §1761]		
17.	Check appropriate box. [see SCPA §1704(6) and §1761].		
	NOTE: If knowledge of a report is indicated, verify that an affidavit explaining circumstances in detail is included.		
18.	Confirm that Request for Information Guardianship form has been submitted.		
	NOTE: Some Courts may require electronic fingerprinting for each proposed guardian in order to conduct a criminal record search.		
19.	Check appropriate box.		
20.	This paragraph states that there are no other persons interested in this proceeding other than those already mentioned.		
	Confirm that any necessary waivers/renunciations/consents have been filed. (Form GMD-3)		

	NOTE: SCPA §1753(1) requires that process shall issue to:
	    1. Parent or Parents (if other than petitioner)
	    2. Adult children, adult siblings (if petitioner is other than a parent)
	    3. Spouse (if respondent is married);
	    4. Person having care and custody or with whom respondent resides (if other than parent or spouse);
	    5. The respondent (if fourteen (14) years of age or older).		

	NOTE: No process or notice is necessary to any person above who has been declared by the court as incompetent or who has, as appears to the Court's satisfaction, abandoned the respondent or to a spouse who is divorced from the respondent. [see SCPA §1754(2)]		

PET ¶ #	DESCRIPTION	YES	NO

20. cont.	*NOTE: SCPA §1753(2) requires that a Notice of Petition (GMD-8) be served by certified mail to:*
	   1. Adult siblings (if petitioner is a parent)
	   2. Mental Hygiene Legal Services
	   3. Director of any State Facility where respondent resides
	   4. Adult children (if petitioner is a parent)
	   5. Any other person Court deems proper
	   6. Any person designated in writing by respondent		

21.	State whether any prior application for guardianship of the subject respondent has been made in any court.		
	Under WHEREFORE Clause: has all relief requested for sections (a) through (i) been checked and completed?		
	Is petition dated, signed, verified, properly notarized (including proper jurat and expiration date of notary's commission)?		
	Is attorney's name, address and phone number listed?		
	Is oath and designation signed?		
	does it set forth proposed guardian's physical address?		
	Is proposed guardian a Bank?		
	has corporate consent and designation been submitted? [see SCPA §708(4)]		
	Is Part 130 Certification completed by attorney or self-represented party?		
	if NOT, has a separate certification as to Part 130 signing requirements been included?		
If forms are computer generated, has a certification pursuant to Court Rules §207.4 been attached?			

FEE SCHEDULE	SCPA/EPTL§ or Rule #

Have the proper fees been included with petition?
   $20.00 for filing petition
   $6.00 for each Certificate of Appointment.
	2402

	COMMENTS AND COURT NOTES	Form Number	SCPA/EPTL§ or Rule #
When Permitted	Whenever the interests of a respondent will be promoted by the appointment of a guardian of the person or of the property or of both person and property.		1750, 1750-a 1750-b

Official Forms

COMMENTS AND COURT NOTES		Form Number	SCPA/EPTL§ or Rule #
Forms Always Required	•Petition for Appointment of Guardian	GMD-1	1751, 1752
	•Affidavit of Proposed Guardian	GMD-1A	
	•Birth Certificate		207.15(a)
	•Request for Information Guardianship Form	OCFS-3909	1706(2)
	•Affidavit (Certification) of Examining Physician or Licensed Psychologist	GMD-2A	1750,1750-a, 1750-b
	•Affirmation (Certification) of Examining Physician	GMD-2B	1750,1750-a 1750-b
	•Citation	GMD-7	1753(1)
	•Notice of Petition	GMD-8	1753(2)
Forms or Documents Sometimes Required	•Waiver, Renunciation and Consent	GMD-3	1753(1)
	•Consent, Oath and Designation of Guardian/Standby Guardian	GMD-4	
	•Decree Appointing Limited Guardian of Property	GMD-6	1756
	•Affidavit of Due Diligence		
	•Affidavit of Service (Personal/Mail/Publication)		
	•Bond		801, 1708, 1761
	•Death Certificate of deceased spouse, distributee or parent		
	•Birth Certificate of spouse or distributees who are under the age of 18		207.15(b) 207.15(a)
	•Copies of Divorce Decrees, Surrenders, Court Orders		
	•Orders of Filiation		

Proofs of Service of Citation must be filed with the Court at least two (2) working days before the return date in compliance with Uniform Rule 207.7(c).

Some courts may conduct additional inquiries of Putative Father Registry. (Court submits inquiry form to Registry - NYS OCFS Form LDSS-2725,); some courts may also check if natural father has acknowledged being father in any other manner (possible sources of information may be Family Court, Department of Social Services, hospital of birth, local registrar and/or Department of Health).

Guardian Ad Litem will be appointed when respondent is not a resident of a state facility. Guardian ad litem will be appointed on or before the return day of process for all unknowns and persons under disability (SCPA §403).

Documents signed by Power of Attorney (Provide certified copy of POA and comply with Section 13-2.3 EPTL and 207.48 Uniform Rules).

Check to be certain all documents are properly acknowledged.

THIS MATERIAL IS PROVIDED FOR INFORMATIONAL/TRAINING PURPOSES ONLY. – It is intended for use in conjunction with review of the applicable statutes and rules of the Surrogate's Court and the Surrogate's Court Operations Manual.

17-A Guardianship Proceeding Checklist
Appointment/Confirmation of Standby Guardian [SCPA 1757]
(Person and/or Property)
(see Surrogate's Court Form CSMD-1, rev. 9/2006)

> *This Checklist is provided for your convenience while completing the petition and the checklist need not be returned to the Court.*

> *If you are using Surrogate's Court form CSMD-1 to confirm a Standby Guardian appointment, the CSMD-1 must be filed as soon as possible. Confirmation must be finalized within 180 days of assumption of duties.*

Check All Forms To Make Sure Venue Is Correct - Appropriate County Is Listed
Fill in All Areas On All Pages of Petition - Also Mark When Not Applicable Where Necessary

PET ¶#	DESCRIPTION	YES	NO
	Does the Court have jurisdiction over the subject MR/DDP, hereinafter referred to as <u>respondent</u> [see SCPA §1702]?		
	NOTE: The respondent must be domiciled in the county, have sojourned in the county immediately preceding the application for guardianship, or if a non-domiciliary of the state, must have property situate in the county. The domicile of the respondent's parent(s) or spouse if respondent is married, or custodial parent in the case of an infant respondent is the domicile of the respondent.		
	Is the captioned name the same as the birth certificate and ¶2(a) of petition? [see 22NYCRR 207.15(a) and SCPA §1752(1)]		
1.	**Is the petitioner a proper party?** [see SCPA §1757]		
	Is the petitioner ... **the guardian,** **standby guardian,** **alternate standby guardian,** **second alternate standby guardian,** **third alternate standby guardian,** **mentally retarded/respondent,** **developmentally disabled/respondent**		
	Complete all required information.		
	Are all A/K/A's listed?		
2a.	**Is the name and date of birth of the respondent in ¶2 the same as that listed on the Birth Certificate?** [see SCPA §1752(1)]		
	Attach Birth Certificate from official registrar (not hospital) to be filed with petition [see NYCRR §207.15(a)] - if not already on file with the court		
	Complete all required information.		

Official Forms

PET ¶ #	DESCRIPTION	YES	NO
2b.	**Check whether respondent is admitted to a group home or facility.** [see MHL §1.03 and/or Article 15] **If admitted, complete required information.**		
3.	**Indicate previous types of appointments and date of decree and to whom original letters were issued.**		
4.	**Choose the box that reflects the relief requested and attach required proof.**		
5.	**Complete ¶5 only if new or different standby guardian(s) is/are to be designated in this proceeding.** If applicable, enter required information in (a) through (d).		
6.	**Complete ¶6 only if seeking confirmation of standby guardian or alternate standby guardian.** If applicable, enter required information.		
7.	**Complete ¶7 only if seeking confirmation of standby guardian or alternate standby guardian.** If applicable, check appropriate box.		
8.	**Check appropriate box.** [see SCPA §1704(6) and §1761]. *NOTE: If knowledge of a report is indicated, verify that an affidavit explaining circumstances in detail is included.*		
9.	**Confirm that a Request for Information Guardianship form [OCFS 3909] has been submitted.** *NOTE: Some Courts may require electronic fingerprinting for each proposed guardian in order to conduct a criminal record search.*		
10.	**List names and addresses of all interested parties.** [see SCPA §1753 and 304(3)]		
11.	**This paragraph states that there are no other persons interested in this proceeding other than those already mentioned.** **If new or different standby guardian(s) is/are to be designated, furnish any necessary waivers/renunciations/consents. (Form CSMD-2)**		

	NOTE: SCPA §1753(1) requires that process shall issue to:
	    1. Parent or Parents (if other than petitioner)
	    2. Adult children, adult siblings (if petitioner is other than a parent)
	    3. Spouse (if respondent is married);
	    4. Person having care and custody or with whom respondent resides (if other than parent or spouse);
	    5. The respondent (if fourteen (14) years of age or older).		

PET ¶ #	DESCRIPTION	YES	NO
11. cont.	*NOTE: No process or notice is necessary to any person above who has been declared by the court as incompetent or who has, as appears to the Court's satisfaction, abandoned the respondent or to a spouse who is divorced from the respondent. [see SCPA §1754(2)]*		
	NOTE: SCPA §1753(2) requires that a Notice of Petition (CSMD-3) be served by certified mail to: *1. Adult siblings (if petitioner is a parent)* *2. Mental Hygiene Legal Services* *3. Director of any State Facility where respondent resides* *4. Adult children (if petitioner is a parent)* *5. Any other person Court deems proper* *6. Any person designated in writing by respondent*		
	Under WHEREFORE Clause: has all relief requested for sections (a) through (k) been checked and completed?		
	Is petition dated, signed, verified, and properly notarized (including proper jurat and expiration date of notary's commission)?		
	Is attorney's name, address and phone number listed?		
	Is oath and designation signed?		
	does it set forth proposed guardian's physical address?		
	Is proposed guardian a Bank?		
	has corporate consent and designation been submitted? [see SCPA §708(4)]		
	Is Part 130 Certification completed by attorney or self-represented party?		
	if **NOT**, has a separate certification as to Part 130 signing requirements been included?		
If forms are computer generated, has a certification pursuant to Court Rules §207.4 been attached?			

FEE SCHEDULE	SCPA/EPTL§ or Rule #
Have the proper fees been included with petition? $20.00 for filing petition $6.00 for each Certificate of Appointment.	2402

Official Forms

COMMENTS AND COURT NOTES		Form Number	SCPA/EPTL§ or Rule #
When Permitted	Whenever the interests of a respondent will be promoted by the confirmation or designation of a standby guardian of the person or of the property or of both person and property.		1750, 1750-a 1750-b
Forms Always Required	•Petition for Appointment/Confirmation of Standby Guardian	CSMD-1	1757
	•Affidavit of Proposed Guardian	CSMD-5	
	•Birth Certificate (if not already filed with court)		207.15(a)
	•Request for Information Guardianship Form	OCFS-3909	1706(2)
	•Affidavit (Certification) of Examining Physician or Licensed Psychologist (if not already filed or required by court)	GMD-2A	1750,1750-a, 1750-b
	•Affirmation (Certification) of Examining Physician (if not already filed or required by court)	GMD-2B	1750,1750-a 1750-b
	•Citation	CSMD-4	1757
	•Notice of Petition	CSMD-3	1753(2)
Forms or Documents Sometimes Required	•Waiver, Renunciation and Consent	CSMD-2	1753(1)
	•Consent, Oath and Designation of Guardian/Standby Guardian	CSMD-6	
	•Guardian's Annual Account	G-7	1719, 1761
	•Affidavit of Due Diligence		
	•Affidavit of Service (Personal/Mail/Publication)		
	•Bond		801, 1708, 1761
	•Death Certificate of deceased spouse, distributee or parent		207.15(b)
	•Birth Certificate of spouse or distributees who are under the age of 18		207.15(a)
	•Copies of Divorce Decrees, Surrenders, Court Orders		
	•Orders of Filiation		

Proofs of Service of Citation must be filed with the Court at least two (2) working days before the return date in compliance with Uniform Rule 207.7(c).

Guardian Ad Litem will be appointed when respondent is not a resident of a state facility. Guardian ad litem will be appointed on or before the return day of process for all unknowns and persons under disability (SCPA §403).

Documents signed by Power of Attorney (Provide certified copy of POA and comply with Section 13-2.3 EPTL and 207.48 Uniform Rules).

Check to be certain all documents are properly acknowledged.

THIS MATERIAL IS PROVIDED FOR INFORMATIONAL/TRAINING PURPOSES ONLY. – It is intended for use in conjunction with review of the applicable statutes and rules of the Surrogate's Court and the Surrogate's Court Operations Manual.

Standby Guardianship Proceeding Checklist
Person and/or Property
(see Surrogate's Court Form SG-1, rev. 4/98)

This Checklist is provided for your convenience while completing the petition and the checklist should not be returned to the Court.

A separate petition and supporting papers <u>must</u> be submitted for each infant child of the petitioner.

CAREFULLY follow instructions when checking off boxes or crossing out words that are inapplicable to the facts of your case as these forms must conform to a number of different fact situations.

ALL QUESTIONS MUST BE ANSWERED.

Check All Forms To Make Sure Venue Is Correct - Appropriate County Is Listed

PET ¶ #	DESCRIPTION	YES	NO
	Does the Court have jurisdiction over the subject infant?		
	NOTE: The infant must be domiciled in the county, have sojourned in the county immediately preceding the application for standby guardianship, or if a non-domiciliary of the state, must have property situate in the county.		
	Is the captioned name the same as the birth certificate and ¶2 of petition?		
1.	**Is the petitioner a proper party? [see SCPA §1726(3)(a)]**		
	Is the petitioner ... a parent		
	a legal guardian of the infant		
	Does the petition set forth the following:		
	Name, relationship of the petitioner to the infant and date of birth		
	Mailing address, residence and telephone number of petitioner		
2.	**Is the name of the infant in ¶2 the same as that listed on the birth certificate?**		
	Birth Certificate from official registrar (not hospital) to be filed with petition [see NYCRR §207.15(a)]		
	Does the petition set forth the following:		
	Name, marital status and date of birth of infant		
	Mailing address and residence		
3.	**Are the names, mailing addresses, residences and dates of birth of the adult persons with whom the infant resides listed?**		
4.	**Is the name, mailing address, residence, and date of birth of the proposed standby guardian listed?**		

Official Forms

PET ¶ #	DESCRIPTION	YES	NO
	NOTE: Include relationship of proposed standby guardian to infant if required.		
5.	**Has the name and address, of the other parent been provided?**		
	If deceased, his/her name must still be shown and death noted. (Court may require copy of death certificate)		
	If the name of the father is not shown on petition or birth certificate, determine if a proceeding has been brought to establish paternity. (Court may require copy of filiation order) *[see page 7 - Comments & Court Notes]*		
	NOTE: If it is claimed that the identity of the father is unknown, the Court may require an affidavit showing diligent efforts to identify him.		
	NOTE: If the natural mother was married at the time of infant's birth, there is a rebuttable presumption that her husband is the father of the infant and is a necessary party unless a filiation order has established otherwise. [see DRL §24(1)]		
	If the infant is married, is the infant's spouse, date of birth and address listed?		
	If one parent is deceased, and there is no spouse of the infant, is the name of the grandparents (if residing within the county) listed with address?		
	NOTE: If any of the above is an infant attach a schedule providing the name of the infant, with whom he/she resides with, whether he/she has a court-appointed guardian, if so, provide the name and address of the guardian. If the disability is other than infant, fill out and attach Schedule A.		
6.	**Are there any other persons or agencies interested in this proceeding other than those mentioned above?**		
7a.	**Has any guardian or standby guardian ever been appointed for the infant? See SCPA §1704(3)**		
7b.	**Has information regarding custody of the infant been provided?**		
	NOTE: Include all specifics regarding any court ordered custody or surrender and attach copies of all surrenders, court orders or divorce decrees.		
8.	*NOTE: COMPLETE THIS PARAGRAPH IF YOU ARE SEEKING THE APPOINTMENT OF A STANDBY GUARDIAN OF THE __PROPERTY__.* **Has all the infant's financial information been included in 8a, 8b, and 8c?** *NOTE: This information will be used to compare and verify the guardian's report on the first annual inventory and account.*		
9.	**Has the appropriate box been checked as to when the authority of the standby guardian is to become effective?**		
10.	**Has the information regarding the petitioner's illness (i.e., date and source of medical diagnosis) been sufficiently provided?**		

PET ¶ #	DESCRIPTION	YES	NO
11.	**Has the information as to whether the infant is or is not a Native American Child been provided?** [The Indian Child Welfare Act of 1978 (25 USC §1901-1963]		
12.	**Verify whether petitioner indicated knowledge that the person nominated to be Standby Guardian has ever been the subject of or another person pursuant to Title 6 of Article 6 of the Social Services Law, or has been subject of or a respondent in a child protective proceeding commenced under Article 10 of the Family Court Act, which resulted in a court order finding that the child is an abused or neglected child.** [If petitioner has such knowledge, an affidavit needs to be attached explaining in detail]		
13.	**Check that Request for Information Guardianship form has been submitted with petition and includes all persons over the age of 18 in the household.**		
	NOTE: Some Courts may require submission of form DCJS-6, Fingerprint Card, for each proposed guardian in order to conduct a criminal record search.		
14.	**Has the appropriate box been checked as to whether or not the petitioner is able to attend any hearing scheduled by the Court?**		
15.	**Has any prior application been made to any Court for the relief requested herein?**		
	Under WHEREFORE Clause: has all relief requested been checked and completed?		
	a.) Has the type of Letters been checked?		
	Has all other information been deleted, if not applicable?		
	Is petition dated, signed, verified, properly notarized (including proper jurat and expiration date of notary's commission)?		
	Is attorney's name, address and phone number listed? (Or if self-represented, add none.)		
	Has Part 130 Certification been completed?		
	If <u>NOT</u>, has a separate attorney certification as to Part 130 signing requirements been included?		
If forms are computer generated, has a certification pursuant to Court Rules §207.4 been attached?			

Official Forms

FEE SCHEDULE	SCPA/EPTL§ or Rule #
	2402
Have the proper fees been included with petition?	
$20.00 for filing petition	
$6.00 for each Certificate of Appointment	

COMMENTS AND COURT NOTES	Form Number	SCPA/EPTL§ or Rule #
When Permitted — When the parent or legal guardian of an infant(s) has a progressively chronic or fatal illness		1726
Always Required		
•Petition for Guardianship	SG-1	1726
•Birth Certificate		207.15(a)
•Request for Information Guardianship Form	OCFS-3909	1706(2)
•Physician's Opinion	SG-2	1726(6)(a)
•Affidavit and Consent of Proposed Standby Guardian	SG-5	1726(3)
•Decree Appointing a Standby Guardian	SG-8	1726(3)
Forms or Documents Sometimes Required		
•Waiver, Renunciation and Consent	SG-3	1705
•Guardianship Citation	SG-4	1705
•Consent of Petitioner for Standby Guardian	SG-6	1726(3)(e)(iii)
•Consent of Infant Over 14	SG-7	1706(1)
•Confirmation Affidavit of Standby Guardian	SG-9	
•Affidavit of Service		
•Affidavit of Due Diligence		
•Affidavit of Service (Personal/Mail/Publication)		
•Bond		801(1)(b)
•Death Certificate of deceased spouse or parent		
•Copies of Divorce Decrees, Surrenders, Court Orders		
•Orders of Filiation		
•Fingerprint Card	DCJS-6	
•Document by parent appointing/designating standby grdn.		1726(4)(b)(iii)

COMMENTS AND COURT NOTES	Form Number	SCPA/EPTL§ or Rule #
Proofs of Service of Citation must be filed with the Court at least two (2) working days before the return date. Some courts may conduct additional inquiries of Putative Father Registry. (Court submits inquiry form to Registry - NYS OCFS Form LDSS-2725,); some courts may also check if natural father has acknowledged being father in any other manner (possible sources of information may be Family Court, Department of Social Services, hospital of birth, local registrar and/or Department of Health). Guardian Ad Litem will be appointed on or before the return day of process for all unknowns and persons under disability (SCPA §403). Documents signed by Power of Attorney (Provide certified copy of POA and comply with Section 13-2.3 EPTL and 207.48 Uniform Rules). Check to be certain all documents are properly acknowledged.		

THIS MATERIAL IS PROVIDED FOR INFORMATIONAL/TRAINING PURPOSES ONLY. – It is intended for use in conjunction with review of the applicable statutes and rules of the Surrogate's Court and the Surrogate's Court Operations Manual.

Official Forms

BACKGROUND INFORMATION
STANDBY GUARDIANSHIPS
(pertains only to infants; does not include 17A's)
SCPA §1726

STANDBY GUARDIAN: Definition - for purposes of this proceeding a person judicially appointed pursuant to SCPA §1726(3) as standby guardian of an infant whose authority becomes effective upon the happening of an event specified in the order of appointment

BACKGROUND:

In 1992 the legislature enacted SCPA §1726 to allow a parent to nominate a standby guardian who could step into office upon the incapacity or death of the parent.

In 1994 the legislature amended the statute to make it equally applicable to legal guardians, as well as parents.

A standby guardian can be appointed by means of two methods:
1. Petition and Decree, pursuant to SCPA §1726(3)
2. Designation subject to later confirmation, pursuant to SCPA §1726(4)

APPOINTMENT BY PETITION & DECREE:

All the information required for the appointment of a guardian under SCPA §1704 is required, plus the parent must show that she has either "a progressively chronic illness" or an "irreversibly fatal disease". SCPA §1726(3)(b)(ii)

The petition **must** also specify whether the standby guardian takes office when the parent becomes incapacitated, when she dies, or when she consents to the guardian's assumption of office. SCPA §1726(3)(b)(i)

When the guardian takes office, the parent retains joint authority with the guardian. SCPA §1726(7)

NOMINATION OF STANDBY GUARDIAN:

Statute permits nomination by a written document rather than a court proceeding SCPA §1726(4)

This paper **must** be signed by the parent or legal guardian before two disinterested adult witnesses - SCPA §1726(4)

The appointment/designation may be filed with Surrogate's Court for safekeeping accompanied with any applicable fee and would be released only to the parent, the standby, or other persons directed by the court - SCPA §1726(8)(b)

The filing of the appointment/designation of a standby guardian in the court does not enhance its validity in any way - SCPA §1726(8)

THE STANDBY GUARDIAN CAN BEGIN TO SERVE WHEN:
- The attending doctor produces a determination of incapacity (definition found at SCPA §1726(1)(d))
- A determination of debilitation with the parent's consent (definition found at SCPA §1726(1)(c))

NOTE: these statements must be in writing, and must describe the parent's physical condition and prognosis.
- The standby guardian can petition for appointment on notice to the parent - SCPA §1726(5)

The standby guardian may act as guardian immediately upon the occurrence of one of these events, but if he/she fails to file a petition within sixty (60) days, his/her authority will cease.

- May also commence to serve if the parent consents - SCPA§ 1726(3)(e)(iii)

The parent has to sign the consent in the presence of two disinterested witnesses. The standby guardian has to file the written consent in the court within ninety (90) days.

TERMINATION OR REVOCATION:
If the parent recovers, the court may terminate the guardianship - SCPA §1726(3)(d)(iii)
A parent may revoke her designation, either by informing the standby guardian or, if the petition has been filed, by filing a written revocation in the court - SCPA §1726(4)(f); (3)(f)(g)
The court may rescind its decree appointing the standby guardian before he/she begins to serve if it finds that the appointment no longer serves the child's best interests - SCPA §1726 (3)(d)(iii)

Wrongful Death Compromise Settlement
Proceeding Checklist
(see Surrogate's Court Form WD-2, rev. 4/98)
(see 22 NYCRR Uniform Rule §207.38)

This Checklist is provided for your convenience while completing the petition and the checklist should not be returned to the Court.

Fill in All Areas On All Pages - Also Mark When Not Applicable When Necessary
Strike Any Paragraphs/Sections Which Do Not Apply
Check All Forms To Make Sure Venue Is Correct - Appropriate County Is Listed

PET ¶#	DESCRIPTION	YES	NO
	Does this Surrogate's Court have jurisdiction over the proceeding?		
	NOTE: If an action has been commenced in Supreme Court - proof of disposition of the matter must be provided: withdrawal, discontinuance, Supreme Court order transferring action/part of action, etc.		
	Does the caption mirror the estate file name and appointee.		
1.	**Is the petitioner a proper party?** [see EPTL §5-4.6(a)]		
	Is the petitioner ... **the appointed fiduciary**		
	a personal representative		
2.	**Is the decedent's residence and persons resided with listed?**		
3.	**Is the date letters of guardianship were issued for any infant children listed?**		
	Are the names of the infant children listed as well as the name of the Court where the guardianship issued?		
	Is a copy of the letters of guardianship attached?		
	NOTE: A guardian must be appointed for any child receiving funds in excess of $10,000.[see SCPA §2220(1)]		
4.	**Is the date Limited Letters were issued, the decedent's name and mention of bond status listed?**		
5.	**Is the occupation of the decedent listed?**		
	Are the place of employment and address of employment listed?		
	Are the weekly earnings of the decedent listed?		
6.	**Are the age of the decedent and date of birth listed?**		
7.	**Are the date and time of the injuries which caused the decedent's death listed?**		
	Is the location of the place of injury listed?		
	NOTE: If the cause of action did not arise under New York law, the laws of the jurisdiction under which the cause of action arose must be established to the satisfaction of the Court.		
	Has the fatal incident been described?		
8.	**Is the name of the hospital listed?**		

PET ¶ #	DESCRIPTION	YES	NO
	Is the date, time of death and hospital stay detailed?		
	Are all the proceeds of the action to be allocated to wrongful death?		
	Is there an allocation for "conscious pain and suffering"?		
	NOTE: If any of the compromise settlement is to be attributed to "conscious pain and suffering" the court will require a full description of the injury/incident to include but not limited to: police reports, hospital records, affidavits, pleadings, discovery/investigation documents, etc.		
9.	Are all defendants, court location, title, and type of any other action commenced listed?		
	Is the name of the insurance company listed?		
	Is the amount of the settlement listed?		
	Is the maximum insurance policy coverage listed?		
10.	Has a complete listing of the assets of the defendant(s) been provided?		
11.	This paragraph states that the settlement being compromised is the largest obtainable amount.		
12.	Are the petitioner's reasons for acceptance of the settlement listed?		
13.	Are the names of all survivors listed?		
	Are the relationships of all survivors indicated?		
	Are the dates of birth of all survivors listed?		
	Are the present ages of all survivors indicated?		
14.	Is the date the petitioner retained counsel indicated?		
	Is a copy of the retainer agreement attached?		
	Affidavit of services must be attached (unless attorney's fees were previously approved by another court transferring action).		
	Are the proper amounts listed for: Attorney's disbursements?		
	Attorney's fees?		
	Additional disbursements?		
15.	Are the following statistics indicated?		
	Decedent's age and date of birth		
	Decedent's date of death and life expectancy		
	Petitioner's date of birth and life expectancy		

Official Forms

PET ¶ #	DESCRIPTION	YES	NO
15. cont.	All distributee's names, age as of decedent's date of death, anticipated years of dependency and percent of net amount of settlement (Kaiser formula may apply)		
	If a structured settlement, set forth cost of any annuity		
	If parents are sole distributees and distribution is unequal, give reasons		
	NOTE: Where recovery or part thereof is allocated to conscious pain and suffering, the proceeds pass through the decedent's estate either in accordance with the provisions of the will, or in the event of intestacy, in accordance with EPTL §4-1.1.		
16.	Are all infant distributees listed?		
17.	This paragraph states that petitioner waives statutory commissions and filing of a surety bond.		
18.	Is cost of decedent's funeral bill listed?		
	Is copy of paid bill attached?		
	Are any hospital/medical bills listed as outstanding?		
18a.	Are the facts of any social services claim detailed?		
18b.	Are the facts of any creditor's claims detailed?		
18c.	If a pecuniary loss by a parent is being sought, has that been indicated?		
19.	Is information as to decedent receiving public assistance in form of Aid to Dependent Children provided?		
20.	Has any previous application been made for same type of relief?		
21.	Has the name of the insurance company and the claim holder been listed?		
	Has a request been made by the fiduciary to close the estate?		
22.	Are the names, relationships, and addresses of all interested parties listed?		
	NOTE: Interested parties may include but are not limited to - Husband, Wife, Administrator or Administratrix, Executor or Executrix, Daughter, Son, Father, Mother, Alleged Creditor, Department of Social Services, New York State Tax Commission, Insurance Company, Additional Defendants.		
	Are all persons under disability and/or infants under the age of fourteen indicated? A complete statement of the nature and extent of the disability other than infancy of distributees must be attached.		
	NOTE: A guardian ad litem may be appointed for any person listed in the petition as a person under disability. If the person under disability appears by a guardian of the property, committee, conservator or guardian of the property pursuant to Article 81 of the Mental Hygiene Law whom the Court finds has no adverse interest, no guardian ad litem is necessary.		
23.	Are all persons/agencies required to be cited indicated with name and address?		

PET ¶ #	DESCRIPTION	YES	NO
23. cont.	Under WHEREFORE Clause: has all relief requested been checked and completed?		
	Has any relief not applicable been struck out?		
	Is petition dated, signed, verified, properly notarized (including proper jurat and expiration date of notary's commission)?		
	Is attorney's name, address and phone number listed?		
	Has Part 130 Certification been completed?		
	if <u>NOT</u>, has a separate attorney certification as to Part 130 signing requirements been included?		
If forms are computer generated, has a certification pursuant to Court Rules §207.4 been attached?			

FEE SCHEDULE	SCPA/EPTL§ or Rule #
Has the proper fee been included with the petition? Filing fee is according to the following schedule based upon the gross value of the compromise settlement - see SCPA §2402(6) 0 but under 10,000 $ 45.00 10,000 but under 20,000 75.00 20,000 but under 50,000 215.00 50,000 but under 100,000 280.00 100,000 but under 250,000 420.00 250,000 but under 500,000 625.00 500,000 and over 1,250.00	2402

Official Forms

COMMENTS AND COURT NOTES	Form Number	SCPA/EPTL§ or Rule #
When Permitted	Whenever the interests of an estate require the approval of an offer of settlement in a wrongful death proceeding and/or personal injury proceeding.		5-4.6 5-4.1 5-4.3
Forms Always Required	•Wrongful Death Petition •Attorney's Affidavit •Waiver and Consent/Citation for Tax Department •Proposed Decree	WD-2 WD-4 WD-7	
Forms or Documents Sometimes Required	•Wrongful Death Citation •Account •Waiver and Consent for Insurance Company •Waiver and Consent for Individual •Copy of Supreme Court Order (in transferred actions) •Affidavit of Service (Personal/Mail/Publication) •Bond •Copy of Kaiser Formula •Tax Discharge of Liability Letter	WD-1 WD-3 WD-5 WD-6	5-4.4

Make sure all waivers and consents from distributees/beneficiaries are on the official form including all necessary wherefore clauses from petition.

Proposed Citation must include all relief requested in petition wherefore clauses.

Proofs of Service of Citation must be filed with the Court at least two (2) working days before the return date.

Guardian Ad Litem will be appointed for interested parties under a disability. Guardian ad litem will be appointed on or before the return day of process for all unknowns and persons under disability (SCPA §403).

Documents signed by Power of Attorney (Provide certified copy of POA and comply with Section 13-2.3 EPTL and 207.48 Uniform Rules).

Check to be certain all documents are properly acknowledged.

THIS MATERIAL IS PROVIDED FOR INFORMATIONAL/TRAINING PURPOSES ONLY. – It is intended for use in conjunction with review of the applicable statutes and rules of the Surrogate's Court and the Surrogate's Court Operations Manual.

Informal Accounting with/without Decree
Proceeding Checklist
(see Surrogate's Court Form JA-2, rev. 12/96)

This Checklist is provided for your convenience while completing the petition and the checklist should not be returned to the Court.

Fill in All Areas On All Pages - Also Mark When Not Applicable When Necessary
Strike Any Paragraphs/Sections Which Do Not Apply
Check All Forms To Make Sure Venue Is Correct - Appropriate County Is Listed

PET ¶ #	DESCRIPTION	YES	NO
	CHECK WITH THE COURT YOU ARE FILING WITH AS TO SPECIFIC CLOSING REQUIREMENTS.		
	Has more than seven months passed since letters of appointment were issued?		
	NOTE: If an action for this estate was ever commenced in Supreme Court - proof of disposition of the matter must be provided: withdrawal, discontinuance, Supreme Court order, etc.		
	Have any claims been filed with the Surrogate's Court?		
	NOTE: If claims are on file, the court will not accept any type of informal accounting until the creditor issue has been resolved through: the filing of general releases or satisfactions; a hearing was held previously to determine the validity of the claim(s) which were deemed invalid; the claim(s) have been withdrawn.		
	Are all residuary beneficiaries of sound mind and body and of legal age?		
	Are any residuary beneficiaries under a disability?		
	NOTE: If any residuary beneficiaries are under a disability you must do a formal accounting and a guardian ad litem must be appointed.		
	Has a guardian been appointed for any minor child receiving more than $10,000?		
	NOTE: A guardian must be appointed for any child receiving funds in excess of $10,000. Proof of payment to a minor receiving funds of $10,000 or less may be substantiated by having a parent sign a receipt and release.		
	Does the inventory of assets reflect that no tax return filing was required?		
	Has a tax return been filed with the Court?		
	Has a tax discharge of liability letter been filed with the Court?		
	Have receipts/releases been filed for all specific bequests and/or legacies?		
	If certain bequests or legacies have not been satisfied, has an affidavit with sufficient details as to the circumstances been filed?		
	Have receipts/releases been filed from all residuary beneficiaries?		
	Are you requesting that the informal documents settling an account be recorded?		
	Has the appropriate $5 per page recording fee been enclosed? [see SCPA §2402(4)]		

Official Forms

PET ¶ #	DESCRIPTION	YES	NO

	NOTE: For the purposes of an informal accounting the term Receipt/Release may include but is not limited to the following types of documents:
	    •*Waiver-Receipt and Release* •*Receipt and Release (form JA-2)*
	    •*Release and Discharge* •*Attorney/Fiduciary Affidavit of Informal Settlement*
	    •*Agreement and Assignment* •*Release Settling Account*
	    •*Indemnity Agreement* •*Executor's Release*
	    •*Receipt and Discharge* •*Release-Receipt and Waiver*
	    •*Release* •*Receipt*
	    •*Receipt and Waiver* •*Release of Fiduciary*
	    •*Trustee Release* •*Satisfaction*
	    •*Partial Receipt and Release* •*Agreement Settling Account*
	    •*Receipt-Release and Discharge* •*Release of Distributive Share*
	    •*Release of Residuary Share* •*Receipt-Release and Agreement*
	    •*Voluntary Release and Discharge* •*Receipt-Release and Refunding Agreement*
	                         •*Voluntary Receipt and Discharge*		

	Has the appropriate fee been enclosed for any account form submitted to the Court?		
	NOTE: Under SCPA §2402(4) the Surrogate's Court is obliged to collect a filing fee on any document recorded or filed which contains an informal statement of account. This fee includes the filing and recording of such instruments. An informal statement of account and/or attorney's affidavit of services may be required by some courts which may also waive the statutory filing fee.		
	NOTE: Under SCPA §2402(5) the Surrogate's Court is obliged to collect a filing fee for any proceeding requesting a Decree Settling Accounts. The fee is based on the informal statement of account filed. If no statement of account is filed the fee will be based on the tax return or inventory amount.		
	Are you requesting a decree settling the informal account? (see SCPA §2203)		
	If requesting a decree - has the necessary petition been filed?		
	Are the names and post office addresses of all interested parties listed?		
	Is there a statement that all taxes have been paid or that no taxes were due?		
	Is there a statement that the petitioner has fully accounted and made full disclosure in writing of the administration of the estate to all interested parties?		
	Is there a statement that the petitioner is seeking a decree releasing and discharging the fiduciary?		
	Is there a statement that the fiduciary's letters have not been revoked and the fiduciary has not been removed?		
	Is there a statement that the time to present claims has expired and that all known debts and administrative expenses have been paid?		
	If this is a trusteeship accounting - is there a statement whether or not the trust has been fully executed?		
	If this is a guardianship accounting is there a statement whether the infant has reached majority or has died?		

PET ¶ #	DESCRIPTION	YES	NO
	Have acknowledged instruments accompanying the petition been executed by all interested parties or their guardian, committee, conservator or designated payee and do they contain a statement approving the account and releasing and discharging the petitioner?		
	Is petition dated, signed, verified, properly notarized (including proper jurat and expiration date of notary's commission)?		
	Is the attorney's signature, name, address and phone number listed?		
	Is there a Part 130 Certification?		
Has the proposed decree settling informal account been submitted to the Court?			
	Does the proposed decree contain language releasing and discharging the fiduciary, or the sureties of the bond, from any further liability?		
If forms are computer generated, has a certification pursuant to Court Rules §207.4 been attached?			

FEE SCHEDULE	SCPA/EPTL§ or Rule #
Have the proper fees been included with the proceeding?	2402
Filing fee is according to the following schedule based upon:	
the subject matter of an informal statement of account that has been filed	2402(4)
or the value of the estate's tax return/inventory when a petition for Decree on Filing Instruments Approving Accounts has been submitted	2402(5)
0 but under 10,000 $ 45.00	
10,000 but under 20,000 75.00	
20,000 but under 50,000 215.00	
50,000 but under 100,000 280.00	
100,000 but under 250,000 420.00	
250,000 but under 500,000 625.00	
500,000 and over 1,250.00	
Recording fee for instruments releasing and discharging a fiduciary but which do not contain any statement of account is	
$6.00 per page	2402(4)

Official Forms

	COMMENTS AND COURT NOTES	Form Number	SCPA/EPTL§ or Rule #
When Permitted	Whenever distribution can be made by agreement of all parties concerned by the filing of receipts and releases concerning the accounting.		
Forms Always Required	•Receipts and Releases (or similar documents)	JA-2	
Forms or Documents Sometimes Required	•Petition •Varied Titled Receipts and Releases (see note above) •Proposed Decree Approving Informal Accounting •Final Report •Tax Discharge of Liability Letter •Tax Department Waiver •Statement of Account •Attorneys Affidavit of Services •Waiver/Consent from State Attorney General •Waiver and Consent for Individual •Copy of Supreme Court Order		2203(2) 207.42

Documents signed by Power of Attorney (Provide certified copy of POA and comply with Section 13-2.3 EPTL and 207.48 Uniform Rules).

Check to be certain all documents are properly acknowledged.

THIS MATERIAL IS PROVIDED FOR INFORMATIONAL/TRAINING PURPOSES ONLY. – It is intended for use in conjunction with review of the applicable statutes and rules of the Surrogate's Court and the Surrogate's Court Operations Manual.

Judicial Settlement of Account
Proceeding Checklist
(see Surrogate's Court Form JA-1, rev. 12/96)

This Checklist is provided for your convenience while completing the petition and the checklist should not be returned to the Court.

Fill in All Areas On All Pages - Also Mark When Not Applicable When Necessary
Strike Any Paragraphs/Sections Which Do Not Apply
Check All Forms To Make Sure Venue Is Correct - Appropriate County Is Listed

PET ¶ #	DESCRIPTION	YES	NO
	Does this Surrogate's Court have jurisdiction over the proceeding?		
	NOTE: If an action has been commenced in Supreme Court - proof of disposition of the matter must be provided: withdrawal, discontinuance, Supreme Court order transferring action/part of action, etc.		
	Does the caption mirror the estate file name and appointee?		
	Is the correct type of account checked? [and has the correct account form been used?]		
1.	**Is the petitioner a proper party? [see SCPA §2208]**		
	Is the petitioner ... the appointed fiduciary		
	the appointed guardian		
	the appointed trustee		
	a fiduciary of a deceased fiduciary [see SCPA §2207]		
	Is the petitioner's name, residence and mailing address listed?		
	Is the type of letters and date of issuance listed?		
	Is the amount of bond and name of surety listed, if applicable?		
	Are additional petitioner's information listed, if applicable?		
2.	**Is the decedent's name, date of death and domicile listed?**		
3.	**Are the dates which cover the account and gross sum of account listed?**		
4a.	**Has all tax information been listed?**		
4b.	**Has a tax return been filed?**		
4b.	**Was there no tax proceeding requirement for this estate?**		
	NOTE: Some courts may require a notice of appearance/waiver/consent form from the tax department (as an interested party) if a tax discharge letter is not on file.		
5.	**Has seven months passed since letters were issued?**		
	Were letters issued to the petitioner(s) revoked?		
	Has more than one year passed since a preceding account was filed?		

Official Forms

PET ¶ #	DESCRIPTION	YES	NO
6a.	Are the names and mailing addresses of all interested parties listed?		
6b.	Are the names of any interested persons under a disability listed?		
	NOTE: Interested parties may include but are not limited to the following: unpaid creditors or persons claiming to be creditors, surety of the bond, co-fiduciaries not joining in petition, successor fiduciary of petitioner removed or suspended, state attorney general [see EPTL §8-1.4], distributees, beneficiaries, legatees, devisees, trustees, trust beneficiaries, guardians, infants over the age of fourteen, fiduciaries of deceased beneficiaries or all distributees of deceased beneficiaries if fiduciary has not been appointed, guardian ad litems, chief fiscal officers/county treasurers.		
	NOTE: A guardian ad litem may be appointed for any person listed in the petition as a person under disability. If the person under disability appears by a guardian of the property, committee, conservator or guardian of the property pursuant to Article 81 of the Mental Hygiene Law whom the Court finds has no adverse interest, no guardian ad litem is necessary.		
7.	This paragraph states that there are no additional interested parties.		
8.	This paragraph states that there are no prior applications made in any court for the relief requested in this petition.		
	Under WHEREFORE Clause: has all relief requested been checked and completed?		
	Has any relief not applicable been struck out?		
	Is petition dated, signed, verified, properly notarized (including proper jurat and expiration date of notary's commission)?		
	Is attorney's name, address and phone number listed?		
	Has Part 130 Certification been completed?		
	if NOT, has a separate attorney certification as to Part 130 signing requirements been included?		
If forms are computer generated, has a certification pursuant to Court Rules §207.4 been attached?			

ACCOUNT FORMS - SCHEDULE REQUIREMENTS		
USE THE CORRECT ACCOUNT FORM [JA-4 or JA-7] AND MATCHING SUMMARY STATEMENT - Certain Accounts may not use all of the following schedules.		
List proper title of matter, correct accounting type, dates for period of account; page number where each schedule starts must be listed		
A PRINCIPAL RECEIVED		
Itemized statement of all moneys and personal property constituting principal assets with their date of receipt or acquisition		

	Proceeds of sale of real property including a copy of the closing statement		
	Do not include total amount of principal assets exchanged which would incorrectly inflate gross account total (such as stocks sold to buy other stocks, bank accounts transferred to other banks or alternate types of accounts, etc. - these are reported under Schedule B (if no loss/gain) or Schedule F		
A-1	**REALIZED INCREASES**		
	Actual increases due to sales, liquidation or distribution of principal assets		
	Realized increases on new investments or exchanges		
	Detail date increase was realized and identify property from which increase was derived		
A-2	**INCOME COLLECTED**		
	Report all Interest		
	Report all Dividends		
	Report all Rents		
	Report any other income		
	Each receipt must be separately accounted for and identified except where a security has been held for an entire year, then interest or ordinary dividends may be reported on a calendar year basis		
B	**REALIZED DECREASES**		
	Full and complete statement of all realized decreases on principal assets whether due to sale, liquidation, collection or distribution, or any other reason		
	Show decreases on new investments or exchanges and also sales, liquidations or distributions that result in neither gain nor loss		
	Show date of realization of each decrease and identify property from which decrease was incurred		
	Report any asset which the fiduciary intends to abandon as worthless accompanied by a full statement of the reasons for abandoning it		
C	**FUNERAL AND ADMINISTRATION EXPENSES AND TAXES: FUNERAL AND ADMINISTRATION EXPENSES AND TAXES CHARGED TO PRINCIPAL**		
	Itemized statement of all moneys chargeable (to principal) and paid for funeral, administration and other necessary expenses, together with date and reason for each expenditure		
	Consolidate similar expenditures (funeral expenses, taxes, accountant fees, legal fees, filing fees, commissions, other)		
	Where will directs all inheritance and death taxes are to be paid out of the estate, credit for payment of the same should be taken in this schedule		

Official Forms

C-1	**UNPAID ADMINISTRATION EXPENSES**		
	Itemized statement of all unpaid claims for administration and other necessary expenses		
	Include a statement as to the basis of each claim		
C-2	**ADMINISTRATION EXPENSES CHARGEABLE TO INCOME**		
	Itemized statement of all moneys chargeable to income and paid for administration, maintenance and other expenses, together with date and reason for each such expenditure		
D	**CREDITOR'S CLAIMS** - *does not apply in trustee's account*		
	List claims presented, allowed, paid and credited and appearing in the summary statement together with the date of payment		
	List claims presented and allowed but not paid		
	List claims presented but rejected and the date of and reason for such rejection		
	List contingent and possible claims		
	List personal claims requiring approval by the court pursuant to SCPA §1805		
	If estate is insolvent - preference of claims should be stated with the order of their priority		
E	**DISTRIBUTIONS OF PRINCIPAL; DISTRIBUTIONS MADE**		
	Itemized statement of all moneys paid and all property delivered (from principal) to beneficiaries, legatees, trustees, surviving spouse or distributees of the deceased, date of payment or delivery and name of the person to whom payment or delivery was actually made		
	If estate taxes were required to be apportioned and payments have been made on account of the taxes, the amounts apportioned in Schedule K against beneficiaries of the estate shall be charged against the respective individuals share		
E-1	**DISTRIBUTIONS OF INCOME**		
	Itemized statement of all moneys paid and of property delivered out of income to the beneficiaries, the date of payment or delivery and the name of the person to whom payment or delivery was made		
	Distributions of income to any one beneficiary may be reported by the calendar year		
F	**NEW INVESTMENTS, EXCHANGES AND STOCK DISTRIBUTIONS**		
	Itemized statement of all new investments with date of acquisition and cost of all property purchased		
	Itemized statement of all exchanges made, specifying dates and items received and items surrendered		

	Itemized statement of all stock dividends, stock splits, rights and warrants received, showing securities to which each relates and their allocation as between principal and income		
G	**PRINCIPAL REMAINING ON HAND; PERSONAL PROPERTY REMAINING ON HAND**		
	Itemized statement showing all property constituting principal remaining on hand		
	Statement of all uncollected receivables and property rights due the estate		
	Show date and cost of all such property acquired by purchase, exchange or transfers made or received, together with date of acquisition and cost - indicate such sums in appropriate lines of the summary schedule		
	Show all unrealized increases and decreases relating to assets on hand and report the same in the appropriate places in the summary schedule		
G-1	**INCOME REMAINING ON HAND**		
	Statement showing all undistributed income		
H	**INTERESTED PARTIES AND PROPOSED DISTRIBUTION**		
	List names of all persons/parties entitled as beneficiary, legatee, devisee, trustee, surviving spouse, distributee, unpaid creditor or otherwise to a share of the estate or fund with their post office addresses and the degree of relationship if any of each to the deceased and a statement showing the nature of the value or approximate value of the interest of each person/party		
	Enclose statement that court records have been searched for powers of attorney and assignments and encumbrances made and executed by any of the persons interested in or entitled to a share of the estate		
	Enclose a list detailing each power of attorney, assignment and incumbrance, disclosed by such search, with the date of its recording and the name and address of each attorney in fact of each assignee and of each person beneficially interested under the encumbrance referred to in the respective instruments		
	Enclose statement as to whether accounting party has any knowledge of the execution of any such power of attorney or assignment not so filed and recorded		
I	**COMPUTATION OF COMMISSIONS**		
	Compute the amount of commissions due upon this account pursuant to SCPA §2307		
	Specifically bequeathed property or very specific legacies can not be included in commission computations		

J	OTHER PERTINENT FACTS AND CASH RECONCILIATION		
	State all other pertinent facts affecting the administration of the estate and the rights of those interested therein		
	Include statement of any real property left by the decedent that it is not necessary to include as an estate asset to be accounted for, a brief description thereof, its gross value, and the amount of mortgages or liens thereon at the date of death of the deceased		
	Include a cash reconciliation in this schedule so that verification with bank statements and cash on hand may be readily made		
K	ESTATE TAXES PAID AND ALLOCATION OF ESTATE TAXES		
	State all estate taxes assessed and paid with respect to any property required to be included in the gross estate under the provisions of the Tax Law or under the laws of the United States		
	Include a computation setting forth the proposed allocation of taxes paid and to be paid and the amounts due the estate from each person in whose behalf a tax payment has been made, and also the proportionate amount of the tax paid by each of the named persons interested in this estate or charged against their respective interest, as provided in EPTL §2-1.8		
	Where an allocation of taxes is required, the method of computing the allocation of said taxes must be shown in this schedule		

FEE SCHEDULE	SCPA/EPTL§ or Rule #
Has the proper fee been included with the petition? Filing fee is according to the following schedule based upon the gross value of the principal (and income) - see SCPA §2402(5) 0 but under 10,000 $ 45.00 10,000 but under 20,000 75.00 20,000 but under 50,000 215.00 50,000 but under 100,000 280.00 100,000 but under 250,000 420.00 250,000 but under 500,000 625.00 500,000 and over 1,250.00	2402

COMMENTS AND COURT NOTES		Form Number	SCPA/EPTL§ or Rule #
When Permitted	Whenever the interests of an estate require judicial approval of an account of the estate proceeding.		2208

COMMENTS AND COURT NOTES		Form Number	SCPA/EPTL§ or Rule #
Forms Always Required	•Petition for Judicial Settlement of Account •Trust Accounting or •Non-trust Accounting •Proposed Decree		
Forms or Documents Sometimes Required	•Copies of Will, Codicils, Trust Agreements •Receipt and Release •Waiver of Citation and Consent in Accounting •Citation •Waiver and Consent from State Attorney General •Waiver and Consent from State Tax Department •Copy of Supreme Court Orders •Affidavit of Service (Personal/Mail/Publication) •Tax Discharge of Liability Letter		

Account forms must include a summary statement and an affidavit of the accounting party.

Waivers and consents must recite fact that party received a summary statement of the account. Any party is entitled to request a complete copy of the account from the petitioner.

Make sure all waivers and consents from interested parties are on the official form including all necessary wherefore clauses from petition.

Proposed Citation must include all relief requested in petition wherefore clauses.

Proofs of Service of Citation must be filed with the Court at least two (2) working days before the return date.

Guardian Ad Litem will be appointed for interested parties under a disability. Guardian ad litem will be appointed on or before the return day of process for all unknowns and persons under disability (SCPA §403).

Documents signed by Power of Attorney - provide certified copy of POA and comply with Section 13-2.3 EPTL and 207.48 Uniform Rules.

Check to be certain all documents are properly acknowledged.

THIS MATERIAL IS PROVIDED FOR INFORMATIONAL/TRAINING PURPOSES ONLY. – It is intended for use in conjunction with review of the applicable statutes and rules of the Surrogate's Court and the Surrogate's Court Operations Manual.

Official Forms

Compulsory Accounting and Related Relief
Proceeding Checklist
(see Surrogate's Court Form JA-10, rev. 1/2004)

This Checklist is provided for your convenience while completing the petition and the checklist should not be returned to the Court.

Fill in All Areas On All Pages - Also Mark When Not Applicable When Necessary
Strike Any Paragraphs/Sections Which Do Not Apply
Check All Forms To Make Sure Venue Is Correct - Appropriate County Is Listed

PET ¶ #	DESCRIPTION	YES	NO
	Does the caption mirror the estate file name and appointee?		
1.	Is the petitioner a proper party? [see SCPA §2205(2)]		
	Is the petitioner ... a creditor		
	a person interested [see SCPA 103(39)]		
	a public administrator or county treasurer		
	a person on behalf of an infant or child born after the making of the will		
	a fiduciary of a deceased person interested		
	a surety on the bond of the fiduciary		
	a successor fiduciary or a remaining fiduciary		
	a co-fiduciary after the filing of an account and petition for judicial settlement		
	the attorney general of the state where any part of the estate may escheat to the state of New York		
	Is the petitioner's name, address and citizenship listed?		
2.	Is the decedent's date of death listed?		
3.	Is the type of letters, county and date of issuance listed?		
	Is fiduciary's name and address listed?		
4.	Check that fiduciary has not filed an account.		
5.	Is the interest of the petitioner and reasons for requesting a compulsory accounting described?		
6.	If additional relief other than a compulsory accounting is requested, are the names, addresses and nature of interest of all parties listed? [see SCPA §2206(2)]		
	Under WHEREFORE Clause: has all relief requested been checked and completed?		
	Has any relief not applicable been struck out?		

PET ¶#	DESCRIPTION	YES	NO
	Is petition dated, signed, verified, properly notarized (including proper jurat and expiration date of notary's commission)?		
	Is attorney's name, address and phone number listed?		
	Has Part 130 Certification been completed?		
	if **NOT**, has a separate attorney certification as to Part 130 signing requirements been included?		
If forms are computer generated, has a certification pursuant to Court Rules §207.4 been attached?			

FEE SCHEDULE	SCPA/EPTL§ or Rule #
Has the proper fee been included with the petition?	2402
Filing fee is according to SCPA §2402(8)(a) $30.00	

	COMMENTS AND COURT NOTES	Form Number	SCPA/EPTL§ or Rule #
When Permitted	On Court's own motion or by petition of proper party.		2205
Forms Always Required	•Petition for a Compulsory Accounting and Related Relief •Compulsory Accounting Citation	JA-10 JA-9	
Forms or Documents Sometimes Required	•Order Directing Compulsory Accounting •Affidavit of Service of Citation •Copy of Supreme Court Order (proof of disposition of the matter must be provided: withdrawal, discontinuance, order transferring action/part of action, etc.)		

Proposed Citation must include all relief requested in petition wherefore clauses.

Proofs of Service of Citation must be filed with the Court at least two (2) working days before the return date.

Documents signed by Power of Attorney - provide certified copy of POA and comply with Section 13-2.3 EPTL and 207.48 Uniform Rules.

Check to be certain all documents are properly acknowledged.

THIS MATERIAL IS PROVIDED FOR INFORMATIONAL/TRAINING PURPOSES ONLY. – It is intended for use in conjunction with review of the applicable statutes and rules of the Surrogate's Court and the Surrogate's Court Operations Manual.

Official Forms

Private Placement Adoption Proceeding Checklist

(see Surrogate's Court Form 1-C, rev. 9/06)
[references DRL §§111, 111-a, 112, 115, and SCPA §1725(1)]

This Checklist is provided for your convenience while completing the petition and the checklist should not be returned to the Court.

> **NOTE:** If adoptive child has resided with adoptive step-parent and birth parent <u>less</u> than one year, a petition for certification (Form 22) must be filed. [See D.R.L. §115-d(8)]

Fill In All Areas On All Pages - Also Mark When Not Applicable When Necessary
Check All Forms To Make Sure Venue Is Correct - Appropriate County Is Listed

> **NOTE:** Check SCPA §1725 to see if you need to do a Temporary Guardianship (Form 21-A) by adoptive parents, prior to the adoption.

PET ¶ #	DESCRIPTION	YES	NO
	BE SURE THE SURNAME OF THE CHILD IS NOT LISTED IN ANY DOCUMENT HEADING.		
1	**Is the name of the first petitioning adoptive parent filled in?** See Domestic Relations Law.		
1(a)	**Is the residency of the adoptive parent, including county listed?**		
	NOTE: The proposed adoptive parent(s) must reside in the county, or if the proposed adoptive parent(s) do not reside in New York State, the child must reside in the county.		
1(b)	**Is the age and date of birth listed?**		
	NOTE: At least one of the petitioners must be over eighteen (18) years of age.		
1(c)	**Is the marital status and living arrangements filled in?**		
1(d)	**Is the adoptive parent's religious faith filled in?** See Social Services Law §373.3.		
1(e)	**Is the occupation and earnings of the adoptive parent filled in?**		
	NOTE: If any monies are received from the Commissioner of Social Services on behalf of the adoptive child that amount must be included.		
2	**Follow above instructions in #1 for second adoptive parent.**		
2(a)	**Follow above instructions in #1(a).**		
2(b)	**Follow above instructions in #1(b).**		
2(c)	**Follow above instructions in #1(c).**		
2(d)	**Follow above instructions in #1(d).**		
2(e)	**Follow above instructions in #1(e).**		

PET ¶ #	DESCRIPTION	YES	NO
3	Is the full name, date and place of birth of the adoptive child noted?		
	NOTE: A certified copy of the child's birth certificate from the official registrar must be attached to the petition.		
4	Is the child's religious faith, if any, noted? See Social Services Law §373.3		
5(a)	Is the name and address of the birth or legal parents of the adoptive child listed?		
5(b)	Is the age and date of birth of the birth or legal parents of the adoptive child listed?		
5(c)	Is the heritage (specific nationality, ethnic background, race) of the adoptive child listed?		
5(d)	Is the religious faith, if any, of the birth or legal parents of the adoptive child listed? See Social Services Law §373.3.		
5(e)	Is the education (specific number of years of school, or degrees completed at time of birth of adoptive child) of the birth or legal parents of the adoptive child listed?		
5(f)	Is the height, weight, hair color, eye color, skin of the birth or legal parents listed?		
5(g)	Is Form 1-D, which provides health and medical history at time of birth of adoptive child, including conditions or diseases believed to be hereditary and any drugs or medications taken during pregnancy by the child's mother annexed to the petition?		
	NOTE: Some courts may require additional separate forms as to medical history of the birth mother and birth father.		
5(h)	Are the talents, hobbies and special interests of the birth or legal parents of the adoptive child listed?		
6	Is the manner in which the adoptive parent(s) obtained the adoptive child noted? See Domestic Relations Law §115(1)(a).		
7	Has the time span the adoptive child has resided with the adoptive parents been indicated?		
8	Has the names and dates of birth of other persons living in the household been indicated?		
9	If the adoptive child's name is to be changed, is the proposed name listed and spelled correctly?		
10	Is it stated whether the adoptive child has or has not been previously adopted?		

Official Forms

PET ¶ #	DESCRIPTION	YES	NO
11	Are the name(s) and address(es) of any person(s) having lawful custody of the adoptive child, if known, listed?		
12 (a-d)	Does the petition set forth that all necessary consents are attached or have sufficient facts been detailed for the Court to dispense with the consent(s). See Domestic Relations Law §109(6), §111, §111-a, §115, §115-b. Use appropriate consent form(s): 2D, 2F, 2Fa, 2G or 2Ga.		
	NOTE: Some courts may dispense with consent(s) only after a citation has been issued and properly served.		
	NOTE: If the adoptee is over eighteen (18) years of age, the consent of the natural parent(s) is not required.		
13 (a-b)	Has the name(s) of the consenting birth or legal parent(s) been listed with the date of the consent(s); if extra-judicial, has the correct 45th date been noted? See D.R.L. §115-b(3).		
14	This paragraph states that on information and belief that the named court in an extra-judicial consent has not received any written notice of revocation and that more than 45 days have elapsed.		
15	If there has been a guardian (general or testamentary) named for the adoptive child, has the nature, date and place of appointment been listed?		
16	Have the names of any further interested persons entitled to notice been listed along with their relationship? See D.R.L. §111(3) and §111-a.		
17	Check appropriate boxes and submit form 1-E if required.		
18	Make sure that Form 1-D has been attached with child's medical information along with any other medical forms required by court.		
19	If child was brought from another state has proper documentation been attached from the Interstate Compact? See S.S.L. §374-a and §382.		
20(a)	Is it indicated whether there is any knowledge of child abuse or maltreatment involving the child or the adoptive parent? See S.S.L. §412.		
	NOTE: Form DSS-4156 must be submitted.		
20(b)	Is it indicated whether any adult residing in the adoptive parent(s) household has a criminal record?		
	NOTE: Fingerprint cards (Form DCJS-6 rev. 1/89) must be submitted.		
21	Is it indicated whether there are any prior or pending proceedings affecting this adoptive child? If so, has sufficient information been provided?		
22	Is it indicated whether the adoptive child is an Indian (Native American) child? See 25 U.S.C. §§1901-1963.		

PET ¶ #	DESCRIPTION	YES	NO
23	Have any additional allegations been indicated?		
	Check that the "Wherefore" clause lists all relief requested including the correct listing and spelling of a change in the adoptive child's name.		
	Is petition dated, signed, verified, properly notarized (including proper jurat and expiration date of notary's commission)?		
	Is attorney's name, address and phone number listed?		
	Has Part 130 Certification been completed?		
	if <u>NOT</u>, has a separate attorney certification as to Part 130 signing requirements been included?		
If forms are computer generated, has a certification pursuant to Court Rules §207.4 been attached?			

	ADDITIONAL ADOPTION DOCUMENT REQUIREMENTS		
	Certified Birth Certificate of Adoptive Child (from official registrar)		
	Certified copy of marriage record of the adoptive parents.		
	Confidential Affidavit with certified copies of divorce decrees.		
	Photocopies of adoptive parent's birth certificates.		
	Doctor's certificate of health for adoptive parents and adoptee (examinations must be done within six months of filing petition).		
	Report of Adoption (Form VS-43 10/71). [If adoptee was born in another state the report of adoption form should be obtained from that state's vital statistics bureau.]		
1-C	Petition for Adoption		
1-Ca	Affidavit of Change in Circumstances (required if there has been a change in circumstances since certification).		
1-D	Child's Medical History (with additional birth parent health information required by Court).		
1-E	Affirmation Regarding Venue		
1-F	Determination of Family Court Judge Regarding Venue		
1-G	Order Regarding Venue		
2-B	Agreement of Adoption.		
2-D	Consent of Child Over 14		

Official Forms

2-E	Affidavit & Consent of Person having Lawful Custody of adoptee other than birth or legal parent.		
	Affidavit of Paternity (if applicable).		
2-F	Judicial Consent (consent taken before judge of birth or legal parent relinquishing parental rights)		
	Additional Adoption Documentation Requirements (continued)		
2-Fa	Judicial Consent (consent taken before judge of birth or legal parent consenting to step-parent adopting child)		
2-G	Extrajudicial Consent (consent taken before notary of birth or legal parent relinquishing parental rights)		
2-Ga	Extrajudicial Consent (consent taken before notary of birth or legal parent consenting to step-parent adopting child)		
6-B	Order for Investigation		
7	Report of Investigation by Probation Department or Social Services		
8-B	Affidavit of Identifying Party (where affiant is not the attorney of record)		
8-C	Affidavit of Identifying Party (where affiant is the attorney of record)		
	Affirmation (by attorney of record) [with attached retainer agreement]		
9-B	Affidavit of Financial Disclosure - Parents		
	Attorney's Affidavit (Form UCS-836) [an index number from the Court is required before mailing original affidavit to Office of Court Administration with a copy to Court - OCA requires that a 3"x5" postcard be supplied with affidavit for return notice of state tracking number, the postcard must be filed with Court.]		
10-B	Supplemental Affidavit		
	Narrative Affidavit by adoptive parent(s) (if required by court)		
13-B	Order of Adoption (proposed)		
15-A	Application for Certified Copy of Adoption Order (before sealing of records)		
15-B	Order for Certified Copy of Adoption Order (before sealing of records)		
	CERTIFICATION DOCUMENTATION REQUIREMENTS		
22	Petition (Certification as a Qualified Adoptive Parent)		
	Certified Birth Certificate (from official registrar)		
	Consents to Adoption (if applicable)		
	Certified copy of Marriage Certificate		
	Affidavit of Prior Marriages (if required by court)		

	Certified copies of divorce decrees.		
	DSS-4156 Request for Information		
	Fingerprint Cards		
23	Affidavit and Report (of Disinterested Person)		
	TEMPORARY GUARDIANSHIP DOCUMENTATION REQUIREMENTS		
21-A	Petition for Temporary Guardianship		
2-F	Judicial Consent (Natural Parent) [copy to be attached to petition]		
21-E	Affidavit (Change of circumstances since certification as qualified adoptive parent)		

THIS MATERIAL IS PROVIDED FOR INFORMATIONAL/TRAINING PURPOSES ONLY. – It is intended for use in conjunction with review of the applicable statutes and rules of the Surrogate's Court and the Surrogate's Court Operations Manual.

Official Forms

Agency Adoption Proceeding Checklist
(see Surrogate's Court Form 1-A, rev. 9/06)
[references DRL §§111-a(1), 112]

> *This Checklist is provided for your convenience while completing the petition and the checklist should not be returned to the Court.*

> **NOTE: DRL §112-a and 22 NYCRR 207.62 require expeditious calendaring of agency adoption hearings. The mandated time schedules begin to run "upon the filing of the adoption." The adoption is deemed filed upon receipt by the Clerk of the following: Petition (Form 1-A), Child's Medical History (Form 1-D), Agency's Verified Schedule (Form 1-B), any required agreements and consents (Form 2-A, surrender[s]), completed DSS Request for Information Form, and Certificate of Readiness.**

Fill In All Areas On All Pages - Also Mark When Not Applicable When Necessary
Check All Forms To Make Sure Venue Is Correct - Appropriate County Is Listed

PET ¶ #	DESCRIPTION	YES	NO
	BE SURE THE SURNAME OF THE CHILD IS NOT LISTED IN ANY DOCUMENT HEADING.		
	NOTE: to determine the Court's jurisdiction - the petition must be filed in the county where termination of parental rights or judicial surrender proceedings are pending; in any other agency adoption proceeding, the petition must be filed in the county in which parental rights have been terminated or a judicial surrender was approved or in the county where the adoptive parent(s) reside or if such parents do not reside in the state in the county where the authorized agency has its principal office. [DRL §113(3)].		
1	Is the name of the first petitioning adoptive parent filled in? See Domestic Relations Law.		
1(a)	Is the residency of the adoptive parent, including county listed?		
1(b)	Is the age and date of birth listed?		
	NOTE: At least one of the petitioners must be over eighteen (18) years of age.		
1(c)	Is the marital status and living arrangements filled in?		
1(d)	Is the adoptive parent's religious faith filled in? See Social Services Law §373.3.		
1(e)	Is the occupation and earnings of the adoptive parent filled in?		
	NOTE: If any monies are received from the Commissioner of Social Services on behalf of the adoptive child that amount must be included.		
2	Follow above instructions in #1 for second adoptive parent.		
2(a)	Follow above instructions in #1(a).		
2(b)	Follow above instructions in #1(b).		
2(c)	Follow above instructions in #1(c).		

PET ¶ #	DESCRIPTION	YES	NO
2(d)	Follow above instructions in #1(d).		
2(e)	Follow above instructions in #1(e).		
3	Is the first name, date and place of birth, and religious faith of the adoptive child noted?		
	NOTE: A certified copy of the child's birth certificate from the official registrar must be attached to the petition.		
4	Is the name of the agency's official listed?		
	Is the verified schedule (form 1-B) included? See DRL §112(3)		
5(a)	Is the age and date of birth of the birth or legal parents of the adoptive child listed?		
5(b)	Is the heritage (specific nationality, ethnic background, race) of the adoptive child listed?		
5(c)	Is the religious faith, if any, of the birth or legal parents of the adoptive child listed? See Social Services Law §373.3.		
5(d)	Is the education (specific number of years of school, or degrees completed at time of birth of adoptive child) of the birth or legal parents of the adoptive child listed?		
5(e)	Is the height, weight, hair color, eye color, skin of the birth or legal parents listed?		
5(f)	Is Form 1-D, which provides health and medical history at time of birth of adoptive child, including conditions or diseases believed to be hereditary and any drugs or medications taken during pregnancy by the child's mother annexed to the petition?		
	NOTE: Some courts may require additional separate forms as to medical history of the birth mother and birth father.		
5(g)	Are the talents, hobbies and special interests of the birth or legal parents of the adoptive child listed?		
6	Is it indicated whether the adoptive child is an Indian (Native American) child? Refer to the Indian Child Welfare Act of 1978 (25 U.S.C. §§1901-1963).		
7	Is the manner in which the adoptive parent(s) obtained the adoptive child noted?		
8	If child was brought from another state has proper documentation been attached from the Interstate Compact? See S.S.L. §374-a and §382.		
9	Has the time span the adoptive child has resided with the adoptive parents been indicated with specific dates?		

Official Forms

PET ¶ #	DESCRIPTION	YES	NO
10	Has the names and dates of birth of other persons living in the household been indicated?		
11	If the adoptive child's name is to be changed, is the proposed name listed and spelled correctly?		
12	Is it stated whether the adoptive child has or has not been previously adopted?		
13	Have the names of any further interested persons entitled to notice been listed along with their relationship? See D.R.L. §111(3) and §111-a.		
14(a)	Is it indicated whether there is any knowledge of child abuse or maltreatment involving the child or the adoptive parent? See S.S.L. §412.		
	NOTE: Form DSS-4156 must be submitted.		
14(b)	Is it indicated whether any adult residing in the adoptive parent(s) household has a criminal record?		
	NOTE: Fingerprint cards (Form DCJS-6 rev. 1/89) must be submitted.		
15	Is it indicated whether there are any prior or pending proceedings affecting this adoptive child? If so, has sufficient information been provided?		
16	Is there a post-adoption contact agreement? If so, has sufficient information been provided?		
17	Check appropriate box and submit form 1-E if required.		
18	Have any additional allegations been indicated?		
	Check that the "Wherefore" clause lists all relief requested including the correct listing and spelling of a change in the adoptive child's name.		
	Is petition dated, signed, verified, properly notarized (including proper jurat and expiration date of notary's commission)?		
	Is attorney's name, address and phone number listed?		
	Has Part 130 Certification been completed?		
	if **NOT**, has a separate attorney certification as to Part 130 signing requirements been included?		
If forms are computer generated, has a certification pursuant to Court Rules §207.4 been attached?			

MANDATED TIME SCHEDULE - 22 NYCRR 207.62
Within sixty (60) days of the filing of the above documents, the Court must schedule a review of the documents and determine if there is an adequate basis for approving the adoption.
If there is an adequate basis for approving the adoption, within thirty (30) days of the review, the Court shall schedule the appearance of the proposed adoptive parent(s) and the child.
If after the review, the Court finds that there is not an adequate basis for the approval of the adoption, the Court shall direct such further hearings, submissions or appearances as may be required, and the proceeding shall be adjourned as required for such purposes.

	COMMENTS AND COURT NOTES	Form Number	DRL/SSL§ or Rule #
Forms Required from Adoptive Parent(s) or Attorney	•Petition for Adoption	1-A	111-a(1), 112
	•Copy of Birth Certificate(s) of Adoptive Parent(s) if required by court		
	•Certified Copy of Marriage Record		207.55(b)
	•Certified Copy of Divorce Decree(s)		
	•Agreement of Adoption and Consent (previously executed and acknowledged by agency)	2-A	111(1)(f), 112(2)(b), 113
	•Consent of Child Over 14	2-C	111(1)(a)
	•Affidavit of Identifying Party	8-A	207.55(b)(2)
	•Affidavit of Financial Disclosure	9-A	374(6)
	•Attorney's Affirmation if required by court		
	•Affidavit of Attorney	UCS-836	
	•Supplemental Affidavit	10-A	207.55(c)
	•Confidential Affidavit if required by court		
	•Report of Adoption		
	•Narrative Affidavit from Adoptive Parent(s) - if required by court		
	•Fingerprint Card(s)		
	•Proposed Order of Adoption	13-A	111, 112(b), 113, 114

COMMENTS AND COURT NOTES	Form Number	DRL/SSL§ or Rule #
Forms Required from Adoption Agency •Certified Birth Certificate of Adoptive Child		207.55(b)(1)
•Doctor's Certificate of Health for Adoptive Parent(s) and Adoptive Child - if required by court		
•Verified Schedule	1-B	111-a, 112(3), 384
•Child's Medical History	1-D	112(3)(6), 373-a
•Affirmation Regarding Venue	1-E	
•NYS Child Abuse & Maltreatment Registry Letter		
•Original Surrender(s)		
•Affidavit by Adoptive Parent(s) as to Receipt of Medical History of Adoptive Child		
•Completed Report of Investigation		
•Affidavit from Agency (if required by court)		
•Application for Certified Copy of Order (if required by court)	15-A	
•Proof that agency is authorized to place child in NYS Pursuant to Interstate Compact Agreement		
•Copy of Social History Form - that was given to attorney prior to filing of petition (if required by court)		
•Miscellaneous Documents received at time of surrender which may include but are not limited to: Affidavit Regarding Paternity, Affidavit of Financial Disclosure (from birth parent(s) surrendering child), Background Information Form, Religious Preference Form		

If any of the documents submitted are in a foreign language, you must attach an English translation along with an Affidavit of Authority of Translator to act as same, and Certificate of Authorization by U.S. Consulate (if applicable).[see CPLR §2101(b)]

Check to be certain all documents are properly acknowledged.

THIS MATERIAL IS PROVIDED FOR INFORMATIONAL/TRAINING PURPOSES ONLY. – It is intended for use in conjunction with review of the applicable statutes and rules of the Surrogate's Court and the Surrogate's Court Operations Manual.

Voluntary Administration Checklist

(see Surrogate's Court Form SE-3A, rev. 1/2009)

This Checklist is provided for your convenience while completing the petition and the checklist should not be returned to the Court.

Check Form To Make Sure Venue Is Correct - Appropriate County Is Listed
Fill In All Areas On All Pages of Affidavit - Also Mark When Not Applicable Where Necessary

PET ¶ #	DESCRIPTION	YES	NO
	Is the captioned name exactly the same as it appears on the Last Will and Testament? (if there is no Will the name should be the same as that listed on the Death Certificate)		
	If A/K/A's, are they listed in the caption and also under ¶3 of affidavit?		
1.	**Is the petitioner eligible to act and qualify pursuant to SCPA §1303(a) or 1303(b)?** (a) named executor/executrix if there is a will (b) surviving adult spouse of decedent (c) adult child (d) adult grandchild (e) parent (f) brother or sister (g) niece or nephew or aunt or uncle (h) others as set forth in SCPA §1303(a) or SCPA §1303(b) **Complete all required information.**		
2.	**Has the interest of the affiant been checked and specified?**		
3.	**Enter decedent's name, including a/k/a's, domicile, date of death, place of death and citizenship. Does the information agree with the death certificate?** *NOTE: A certified copy of the death certificate must be filed with affidavit.[see SCPA §1304(3)]*		
4.	**Check appropriate box. If decedent died with a will, the original will must be submitted with Affidavit [SCPA §1303(b)].**		
5.	**Check records of Surrogate's Court to make sure no previous application has been made in this estate for a voluntary administration or for letters of administration or for the probate of a will.**		
6.	**Check that name, complete mailing address and relationship of each distributee is listed. If an address is unknown detail efforts made to locate the individual.** *NOTE: Distributee: Any person entitled to take or share in property under EPTL §4-1.1 and 4-1.2. (SUBMIT A FAMILY TREE IF REQUIRED BY THE COURT.) If there are any deceased distributees, provide a copy of the death certificate or provide the date of death.*		
	If there are no issue, state "no issue" otherwise list names, addresses and the name of the deceased distributee that connects them to decedent.		

Official Forms

PET ¶ #	DESCRIPTION	YES	NO
6. cont.	*NOTE: If it is alleged that the decedent was survived by no distributee or only one distributee or where the relationship of distributees to the decedent is grandparents, aunts, uncles, first cousins or first cousins once removed, the Court may require an Affidavit of Heirship as set forth in Uniform Rules 207.16(c).*		
7.	Information that must be listed: name, bequest and full mailing address of each individual named in the will.		
	NOTE: Notices will be mailed by the Court to each distributee and beneficiary listed in the affidavit under ¶6 and ¶7, excluding affiant. [see SCPA §1304(4)] Some Courts require a stamped addressed envelope to each individual listed.		
8.	Check to be certain that value of personal property does not exceed $30,000 for decedent dying on or after 1/1/09 ($20,000.00 for decedent dying prior to 1/1/09 but on or after 8/29/96; $10,000.00 for decedent dying prior to 8/29/96). [see SCPA §1301(1) and EPTL §5-3.1(a)(1-5)]		
9.	Information that must be listed: all assets of the decedent including bank accounts, stocks, insurance policies not payable to a named beneficiary and the value of each item. JOINT ASSETS AND SET-OFF PROPERTY ARE EXCLUDED. [see EPTL §5-3.1] Give specific details for each asset, i.e. name of bank, account number, etc. A certificate will be issued for each asset listed.		
10.	Must be listed: names of all creditors, including unpaid funeral expenses, and the amount owed to each creditor.		
	NOTE: Some Courts require proof of payment of the funeral bill if not listed.		
11.	Court should advise the voluntary administrator of his or her duties and that they are required to account for the distribution of all assets.		
12.	This paragraph states this proceeding will not determine the estate tax liability.		
13.	This paragraph states that if an administration or probate proceeding is commenced, voluntary administrator/trix must file account with the Court appointed fiduciary. [see SCPA §1307(2)]		
	Is affidavit signed and properly notarized (including proper jurat and expiration date of notary's commission)?		
	Is attorney or self-represented party's name, address and phone number listed?		
	Is Part 130 Certification completed by attorney or self-represented party?		
	if **NOT**, has a separate certification as to Part 130 signing requirements been included?		
If forms are computer generated, has a certification pursuant to Court Rules §207.4 been attached?			

FEE SCHEDULE	SCPA/EPTL§ or Rule #
Has the proper fee been included with affidavit?	1304(4)
$1.00 for filing affidavit	

	COMMENTS AND COURT NOTES	Form Number	SCPA/EPTL§ or Rule #
When Permitted	May be used when a fiduciary is needed to transfer estate assets (personal property only) and the value of the assets does not exceed the following: $30,000 - for decedents dying on or after 1/1/09 $20,000 - for decedents dying from 8/29/96 through 12/31/08 $10,000 - for decedents dying from 6/15/81 through 8/28/96 $5,000 - for decedents dying from 6/24/75 through 6/14/81 $3,000 - for decedents dying prior to 6/24/75 Amounts exclusive of property set off under EPTL §5-3.1.		1301
Documents Always Required	•Affidavit in Relation to Settlement of Estate under Article 13 •Certified Death Certificate •Original Will (if one exists) •Report and Account in Settlement of Estate	SE-3A SE-1D	1304(3) 1304(3) 1303(b) 1307(2)
Documents Sometimes Required	•Renunciation of Voluntary Administration •Copy of funeral bill •Obituary Notice •Affidavit of Disinterested Party/Sole Heirship Affidavit •Family Tree Chart •Amended Affidavit •Death Certificate of deceased spouse, distributee	SE-1C FT-1 SE-3B	1303 207.16(c) 207.16(c) 207.46

Official Forms

COMMENTS AND COURT NOTES (continued)

Certificates will be issued only for assets or items listed in paragraph 9 of the Affidavit (SE-3A). If additional certificates are needed for assets discovered after the Affidavit is filed, submit Amended Affidavit (Form SE-3B).

A voluntary administrator MAY NOT be used to pass title to real property held in the decedent's name. **[However, pursuant to Real Property Law §321(5)(a) a voluntary administrator may sign a discharge of mortgage.]**

A bank account must be opened for any money received by the voluntary administrator, see SCPA §1307(1).

Review carefully instructions to ¶6 and ¶7 of the Affidavit and be sure interested parties are listed in the correct places.

Documents signed by Power of Attorney (Provide certified copy of POA and comply with Section 13-2.3 EPTL and 207.48 Uniform Rules).

Check to be certain all documents are properly notarized.

Estates, Powers and Trusts Law Section 5-3.1 - Exemption for Benefit of Family

If a person dies leaving a surviving spouse the following items of personal property vest in such surviving spouse, and if there is no surviving spouse, such items of property vest in the decedent's children under the age of 21 years, if any:

(1) Household items (furniture, clothing, etc...) not exceeding a total value of $10,000.00.

(2) Family Bible, pictures, videotapes, computer tapes, discs, software, books not exceeding a total value of $1,000.00.

(3) Domestic animals with their necessary food for 60 days, farm machinery, one tractor and one lawn tractor, not exceeding in aggregate value $15,000.00.

(4) One motor vehicle not exceeding in value $15,000.00.

(5) Money or other personal property not exceeding in value $15,000.00, except that where assets are insufficient to pay the reasonable funeral expense of the decedent, the personal representative must apply such money or other personal property to defray any deficiency in such expenses.

(This is not a complete reprint of the law regarding family exemptions. Please see EPTL §5-3.1 for the full text of the law.)

OFFICIAL FORMS PRESCRIBED
by
SURROGATES' COURT PROCEDURE ACT
for use in
ADOPTIONS*

Table Of Contents

---

* By administrative order dated March 13, 1987, "Adoption Forms of the Family Court and Surrogate's Court of the State of New York" were designated as Official Forms of the Court. These forms have been periodically amended and/or repealed and replaced.

AF-1

---

* **Ed. Note**: There are currently no forms numbered 19 or 20.

21–E	Affidavit (Change of Circumstance Since Certification as Qualified Adoptive Parent)
22	Petition (Certification as a Qualified Adoptive Parent)
23	Affidavit and Report (Disinterested Person Certification Proceeding) (Private-Placement)
24	Order (Certification as a Qualified Adoptive Parent)
25	Order (Conditional Certification as a Qualified Adoptive Parent)
26	Petition for Extension of Expired Certification (Private Placement)
26–A	Affidavit and Report (Disinterested Person-Extension of Expired Certification)
27–A	Petition for Access to Sealed Adoption Records (Domestic Relations Law-Section 114)
27–B	Notice of Petition for Access to Sealed Adoption Records (Domestic Relations Law-Section 114)
27–C	Affidavit of Service of Notice of Petition for Access to Sealed Adoption Records
27–D	Waiver of Notice of Petition for Access to Sealed Adoption Records/Consent (Domestic Relations Law-Section 114)
27–E	Adoption-Order on Petition for Access to Sealed Adoption Records
28	Petition for Registration of Foreign Adoption Order (and Name Change)
28–A	Order of Foreign Adoption (and Name Change)
29–A	Petition for Adult Adoption
29–B	Consent to Adult Adoption by Adoptee
29–C	Consent to Adult Adoption by Spouse
30	Petition for Access to Sealed Birth Certificate [PHL § 4138-e]
DOH-1928	Report of Adoption
DOH-4455	Adoption Information Registry Birth Parent Registration Form
FORM 12/99	Order for Child Protective Inquiry
LDSS-2725	Request/Response for Name and/or Address of Father of Child Born Out of Wedlock
OCFS-3937	Request for Information -Private Adoption
OCFS-4156	Order of Adoption Family Court/Surrogate Court Request Form
UCS-836	Attorney's Affidavit (Agency and Private Placement Adoptions)

FORM 1-A   Petition for Adoption (Agency)

D.R.L. §§ 111-a(l), 112

Form 1-A
(Adoption
Petition-Agency)
(9/2006)

SURROGATE'S COURT OF THE STATE OF NEW YORK
COUNTY OF _____

In the Matter of the Adoption of
A Child Whose First Name is

(Docket)(File) No. _____

_____

_____

PETITION FOR
ADOPTION
(Agency)

The Petitioner(s) respectfully allege(s) to this Court that [Delete inapplicable provisions]:

1. Petitioning adoptive parent [specify name]: _____

    a. resides at [specify address, including county]: _____

    _____

    b. is of full age, having been born on [specify date of birth]: _____

    c. is ☐ unmarried

          ☐ married to [specify name]: _____ and living together;

          ☐ married to [specify name]: _____ and living separate and apart
pursuant to a decree or judgment of separation or pursuant to a separation agreement subscribed by the
parties thereto and acknowledged or proved in the form required to entitle a deed to be recorded;

          ☐ married to [specify name]: _____ and living separate and
apart for at least three years prior to commencement of the proceeding);

    d. is of the following religious faith, if any [specify]: _____

    e. is engaged in the following occupation [specify]: _____ and earns
$_____ in approximate annual income [delete if inapplicable] of which $_____ is
support and maintenance to be received from the Commissioner of Social Services on behalf of the
adoptive child.

2. Petitioning adoptive parent [specify name]: _____

    a. resides at [specify address, including county]: _____

    _____

    b. is of full age, having been born on [specify date of birth]: _____

    c. is ☐ unmarried

          ☐ married to [specify name]: _____ and living together;

          ☐ married to [specify name]: _____ and living separate and apart
pursuant to a decree or judgment of separation or pursuant to a separation agreement subscribed by the
parties thereto and acknowledged or proved in the form required to entitle a deed to be recorded;

☐ married to [specify name]: _____ and living separate and apart for at least three years prior to commencement of the proceeding);

         d. is of the following religious faith [specify]: _____

         e. is engaged in the following occupation [specify]: _____
and earns $_____ in approximate annual income [delete if applicable]: of which $_____ is support and maintenance to be received from the Commissioner of Social Services on behalf of the adoptive child.

     3. Upon information and belief, the adoptive child, whose first name is [specify]: _____ ; was born on _____, ___, at _____ and the religious faith of such child is [specify]: _____ _____

     4. Upon information and belief, there will be annexed to this petition a schedule verified by a duly constituted official of [specify agency]: _____, an authorized agency, as required by section 112(3) of the Domestic Relations Law, concerning the adoptive child who is the subject of this proceeding.

     5. The following is information, as nearly as can be ascertained, concerning the birth or legal parents of the adoptive child:

        (a)   Age and date of birth

Parent [specify name]: _____
Parent [specify name]: _____

        (b)   Heritage (specify nationality, ethnic background, race)

Parent [specify name]: _____
Parent [specify name]: _____

        (c)   Religious faith, if any

Parent [specify name]: _____
Parent [specify name]: _____

        (d)   Education [specify number of years of school or degrees completed at time of birth of adoptive child]: _____

Parent [specify name]: _____
Parent [specify name]: _____

        (e)   General physical appearance at time of birth of adoptive child [specify height, weight, color of hair, eyes, skin]:

Parent [type name]: _____
    Ht: _____ Wt: _____
    Hair Color: _____ Eye Color: _____
    Skin Color: _____

Parent [type name]: _____
    Ht: _____ Wt: _____
    Hair Color: _____ Eye Color: _____
    Skin Color: _____

FORM 1-A

SURROGATE'S COURT

AF-6

(f) Annex Form 1-D which provides health and medical history of birth parents at time of birth of adoptive child, including conditions or diseases believed to be hereditary and any drugs or medication taken during pregnancy by child's mother.

(g)   Specify any other information which may be a factor influencing the adoptive child's present or future we being, including talents, hobbies and special interests of parents: [attach separate sheet if necessary]

6. The subject child ☐ is ☐ is not a Native-American child, who is subject to the Indian Child Welfare Act of 1978 (25 U.S.C. §§ 1901-1963). If so, the following have been notified [check applicable box(es)]:
☐ parent/custodian [specify name and give notification date]: _____
☐ tribe/nation [specify name and give notification date]: _____
☐ United States Secretary of the Interior [give notification date]: _____

7. The manner in which the adoptive parent(s) obtained the adoptive child is as follows:
_____

[Delete if inapplicable]: 8. The placement is subject to the provisions of section(s) ☐ 374-a ☐ 382 of the Social Services Law and the provisions of such sections have been complied with. The original approval signed by the Administrator of the Interstate Compact on the placement of Children is attached hereto.

9. The adoptive child resided with the adoptive parent(s) from [specify date]: _____

10. Other persons living in the household are [specify names and dates of birth]: _____
_____

11.   The name by which the adoptive child is to be known is: _____

12.   Upon information and belief, the adoptive child ☐ has ☐ has not been previously adopted.

13. To the best of Petitioner(s)' information and belief, there are no persons other than those mentioned herein or in the verified schedule annexed hereto who are entitled, pursuant to Sections 111(3) and 11 -a of the Domestic Relations Law, to notice of this proceeding (except):

Name: _____   Relationship: _____
Last known address: _____

Name: _____   Relationship: _____
Last known address: _____

Name: _____   Relationship: _____
Last known address: _____

14 (a). The adoptive parent(s) ☐ (has)(have) ☐ (has)(have) no knowledge that the child or an adoptive parent is the subject of an indicated report, or is another person named in an indicated report of child abuse or maltreatment, as such terms are defined in section 412 of the Social Services Law, or has been the subject of or the respondent in a child protective proceeding which resulted in an order

finding that the child is an abused or neglected child.

(b)[Check applicable box(es)]: Upon information and belief,
☐ Neither the adoptive parent(s) nor any other adult over the age of 18 residing in the household have a criminal record.
☐ The following adoptive parent(s)[specify]: _____ have been convicted of the following offenses [specify including dates) of conviction]: _____
However, denial of Petitioner's petition will create an unreasonable risk of harm to the physical or mental health of the child and granting the petition will not place the child's safety in jeopardy and will be in the best interests of the child, pursuant to Social Services Law §378-a(2)(e)(1), for the following reason(s) [specify]: _____

☐ The following adult over the age of 18 living in the home [specify]: _____
has the following record of criminal conviction(s) [specify, including date(s)]: _____

15.   There are no prior or pending proceedings affecting the custody or status of the adoptive child, including any proceeding[s] dismissed or withdrawn, (except) [specify type of proceeding, court, disposition, if any, and date of disposition, if any]: _____

[If there is a post-adoption contact agreement, attach it and answer Question 16]:
16 ☐ On [specify date]: _____, at the time of the approval of the surrender of the child, the Family Court, [specify]: _____ County, approved the annexed post-adoption contact agreement as being in the child's best interests. The agreement was consented to in writing by the following [specify]: _____
Adoptive parent(s) [specify]: _____
Birth parent(s) [specify]: _____
Adoptive child's law guardian [specify]: _____
Sibling(s) or half-sibling(s) over the age of 14, if contact is with siblings or half-siblings [specify]: _____

17. This petition ☐ has ☐ has not been filed in the Court that exercised jurisdiction over the most recent permanency or other proceeding involving this child. [If it has not, petitioner must file affirmation, Adoption Form 1 -E].

18. [Insert any additional allegations.]

WHEREFORE, the Petitioner(s) requests an order:
approving the adoption of the adoptive child [specify first name]: _____ by the Petitioner(s), and [delete if inapplicable]: _____ the post-adoption contact agreement, and
directing that the adoptive child shall be treated in all respects as the child of the Petitioner(s), and directing that the name of the adoptive child be changed and that (s)he shall henceforth be known by the name of [specify]: _____, together with such other and further relief as may be just and proper.

Dated: _____

_____/_____
Adoptive Parent: typed or printed name/ signature

_____/_____
Adoptive Parent: typed or printed name / signature

_____/_____
Adoptive child if over 18- typed or printed name/ signature'

_____/_____
Attorney if any: typed or printed name/signature

_____
Attorney's Address and Telephone number

---

[1] If the child is over the age of 14, written consent to the adoption must also be attached.

VERIFICATION

STATE OF NEW YORK   )
                      :ss.:
COUNTY OF _____)

being duly sworn, says that (he)(she) (they)(is)(are) the Petitioner(s) in the above-named proceeding and that the foregoing petition is true to (his)(her)(their) own knowledge, except as to matters where in stated to be alleged on information and belief and as to those matters (he)(she) (they) believe(s) it to be true.

_____ / _____
Adoptive Parent: typed or printed name/ signature

_____ / _____
Adoptive Parent: typed or printed name/ signature

_____ / _____
Adoptive child if over 18: typed or printed name/ signature

Sworn to before me this
_____ day of _____, ____.

_____
(Deputy)Clerk of the Court
    Notary Public

Resworn to before me this
____day of _____, _____.

_____
Judge of the _____ Court

FORM 1-B   Verified Schedule (Agency)

D.R.L.; §§111-a, 112(3), 112-b   Adoption Form 1-B
S.S.L. §§383-c, 384   (Verified Schedule-Agency)
                                                  9/2008

FAMILY COURT OF THE STATE OF NEW YORK
COUNTY OF _____

_____

In the Matter of the Adoption of   (Docket) (File) No.
A Child Whose First Name is

_____   VERIFIED SCHEDULE
                                       (Agency)

TO THE _____ COURT:

     1. I, _____ , am a duly constituted official of
_____ , the authorized agency whose principal office is at
_____ , and who ☐ has custody of ☐ is placing
the adoptive child named in the caption of this proceeding for adoption.

     2. On information and belief, the full name, date and place of birth of the adoptive child are:
                           [Attach certified copy of birth certificate]
_____

_____ .

     3a. On information and belief, the full name and last known address of the birth mother of
the adoptive child are: _____
_____

     3b. On information and belief, the full name and last known address of the birth father of
the adoptive child are: _____
_____

     4. This agency obtained custody of the adoptive child in the following manner: _____
_____

     5. [Applicable to *Interstate Compact on Placement of Children* cases]: The administrator of
the *Interstate Compact for the Placement of Children* of the State of New York or his or her designee,
has certified that such placement complied with the provisions of the compact. A true copy of the
signed document is attached and made a part of this schedule.

     6. [Check applicable box(es)]:
        (a) The consent to this adoption by [specify]: _____ ,
birth mother of the adoptive child, ☐ is attached hereto ☐ is unnecessary for the following reasons
[specify]: _____
_____

Official Forms

Form 1-B page 2

(b) The consent to this adoption by [specify]:_____,
birth father of the adoptive child, ☐ is attached hereto ☐ is unnecessary for the following reasons
[specify]:_____

_____

7. [Extra-judicial surrenders ONLY; delete applicable box; skip paragraph if inapplicable]:
☐ [Applicable to child surrendered from foster care, pursuant to Soc. Serv. Law §383-c]:
The birth parent(s) of the adoptive child ☐ has/have ☐ has/have not requested this agency
to return the adoptive child to the birth parent(s) within 45 days of the execution and delivery of an
instrument of surrender to an authorized agency, ☐ except [specify, if applicable]:_____

_____

☐ [Applicable to child surrendered who was NOT in foster care, pursuant to Soc. Serv. Law
§384]: The birth parent(s) of the adoptive child ☐ has/have ☐ has/have not requested this agency to
return the adoptive child to the birth parent(s) within 30 days of the execution and delivery of an
instrument of surrender to an authorized agency, ☐ except [specify, if applicable]:_____

_____

8. Attached hereto and made a part hereof is a document setting forth all available
information comprising the adoptive child's medical history.

9. [Applicable if there is a Post-adoption Contact Agreement; attach true copy]:
☐ On [specify date]:_____, at the time of the approval of the surrender
of the child, the Family Court, [specify]:_____County, approved the attached Post-adoption
Contact Agreement as being in the child's best interests. The agreement was consented to in writing by
the following [specify]:_____
Adoptive parent(s)[specify]:_____
Birth parent(s) [specify]:_____
Adoptive child's law guardian [specify]:_____
Sibling(s) or half-sibling(s) over the age of 14, if contact is with siblings or half-siblings [specify]:
_____

Date:_____,____.

                              _____
                              Authorized Agency

                              By _____

                              _____
                              Title

                              _____
                              Signature of Attorney, if any

                              _____
                              Attorney's Name (Print or Type)

                              _____
                              _____

Form 1-B page 3

_____
Attorney's Address and Telephone Number

VERIFICATION

STATE OF NEW YORK　　　）
　　　　　　　　　　　　ss.:
COUNTY OF _____）

_____being duly sworn,
deposes and says:

　　　That (he) (she) is a duly constituted official of the above-named authorized agency, to wit, its

_____
_____;

　　　That (he) (she) has read the foregoing Schedule and knows the contents thereof; that the same is true to (his) (her) own knowledge except as to matters therein stated to be alleged on information and belief and that as to those matters (he) (she) believes it to be true.

_____
　　　　　　　　　　　　　　Agency Official

Sworn to before me this
　　　day of _____, ____.

_____
(Deputy) Clerk of the Court
Notary Public

FORM 1-C   Petition for Adoption (Private-Placement)

D.R.L.§§ 111, 111-a, 112, 115
S.C.P.A. § 1725(1)

Form 1-C
(Petition-Private
-Placement)
9/2008

FAMILY COURT OF THE STATE OF NEW YORK
COUNTY OF _____
....

In the Matter of Adoption of
A Child Whose First Name Is

(Docket)(File) No.

_____

_____

PETITION FOR
ADOPTION
(Private-Placement)

....

The Petitioner(s) respectfully allege(s) to this Court that :

[Delete inapplicable provisions.]:

1. Petitioning adoptive parent [specify name]: _____

    a. resides at [specify address, including county]: _____
_____

    b. is of full age, having been born on [specify date of birth]:_____
_____

    c. is (unmarried)
       (married to [specify name]:_____and living together
       (married to [specify name]:_____ and living separate
and apart pursuant to a decree or judgment of separation or pursuant to a separation agreement
subscribed by the parties thereto and acknowledged or proved in the form required to entitle a
deed to be recorded);
       (married to [specify name]: _____and living separate and
apart for at least three years prior to commencement of the proceeding);

    d. is of the following religious faith, if any: _____

    e. is engaged in the following occupation [specify]:_____and earns $_____
(of which $_____is support and maintenance to be received from the Commissioner of
Social Services on behalf of the adoptive child).

2. Petitioning adoptive parent [specify name]:_____

    a. resides at [specify address, including county]: _____
_____

Form 1-C page 2

    b. is of full age, having been born on [specify date of birth]: _____

    c. is (unmarried)

          (married to [specify name]: _____ and living together

          (married to [specify name]: _____ and living separate

and apart pursuant to a decree or judgment of separation or pursuant to a separation agreement subscribed by the parties thereto and acknowledged or proved in the form required to entitle a deed to be recorded);

          (married to [specify name]:_____ and living separate and apart for at

least three years prior to commencement of the proceeding);

    d. is of the following religious faith, if any: _____

    e. is engaged in the following occupation [specify]:_____ and earns $_____

  in approximate annual income (of which $_____ is support and maintenance to be received from the Commissioner of Social Services on behalf of the adoptive child).

   3. The full name, date and place of birth of the adoptive child is

          [attach certified copy of birth certificate]

_____

   4. Upon information and belief, the religious faith of the adoptive child, if any, is

_____.

   5. The following is information, as nearly as can be ascertained, concerning the birth or legal parents of the adoptive child:

      (a) Full name and last known address

Parent (specify full name and address, if known): _____
_____
_____

Parent (specify full name and address, if known): _____
_____
_____

      (b) Age and date of birth

Parent (specify name): _____
Parent (specify name): _____

      (c) Heritage (specify nationality, ethnic background, race)

Parent (specify name): _____
Parent (specify name): _____

(d)   Religious faith, if any

Parent (specify name): _____
Parent (specify name): _____

(e)   Education (specify number of years of school or degrees completed at time of birth of adoptive child)

Parent (specify name):_____
Parent (specify name):_____

(f)   General physical appearance at time of birth of adoptive child (height, weight, color of hair, eyes, skin)

Parent (specify name):
               Ht:_____ Wt:_____
          Hair Color: _____ Eye Color: _____
          Skin Color: _____

Parent (specify name):
               Ht:_____ Wt: _____
          Hair Color: _____ Eye Color:_____
          Skin Color: _____

(g) Annex Form 1-D which provides health and medical history at time of birth of adoptive child, including conditions or diseases believed to be hereditary and any drugs or medication taken during pregnancy by child's mother.

(h) Any other information which may be a factor influencing the adoptive child's present or future well-being, including talents, hobbies and special interests of parents: [attach separate sheet if necessary]

6. The manner in which the adoptive parent(s) obtained the adoptive child is as follows:
_____

7. The adoptive child resided with the adoptive parent(s) from [indicate date]: _____
_____ .

8. Other persons living in the household are: [Specify names and dates of birth]:_____
_____
_____ .

9.   The name by which the adoptive child is to be known is: _____

10.   Upon information and belief, the adoptive child (has) (has not) been previously adopted.

11. The full name(s) and address(es) of any person(s) having lawful custody of the adoptive child, if known (is)(are) _____
_____

12.   On information and belief, pursuant to Domestic Relations Law §111,

Form 1-C page 4

(a) the consent of the birth or legal parent of the adoptive child ☐ is attached hereto ☐ is not required because _____

(b) the consent of the birth or legal parent of the adoptive child ☐ is attached hereto ☐ is not required because _____

(c) the consent(s) of the above-named person(s) having lawful custody of the adoptive child child ☐ is attached hereto ☐ is not required because _____

(d) The consent(s) of other person(s)[specify name(s)]: child ☐ is attached hereto ☐ is not required because _____
_____

13(a)(The consent of the birth or legal parent [specify name]:_____was executed pursuant to section 115-b(3) of the Domestic Relations Law on _____, _____; the 45th day after execution of the consent is _____, _____.

(b) (The consent of the birth or legal parent [specify name]:_____ was executed pursuant to Section 115-b(3) of the Domestic Relations Law on _____, _____; the 45th day after execution of the consent is _____, _____.)

[DELETE IF INAPPLICABLE]: 14. This court is not the court named in the consent(s) of the parent(s) of the adoptive child, attached hereto, as the court in which the adoption proceeding will be commenced, but more than 45 days have elapsed since the date of execution of said consent(s) and, on information and belief, no written notice of revocation has been received by that court.)

[DELETE IF INAPPLICABLE]: 15. On information and belief, the minor child has a ☐ general ☐ testamentary guardian. [state nature, date and place of appointment]: _____
_____

16. To the best of the Petitioner(s)' information and belief, there are no persons other than those mentioned herein or in the verified scheduled annexed hereto who are entitled, pursuant to Domestic Relation Law §111(3) and 111-a, to notice of this proceeding (except)

Name _____Relationship: _____
Last known address:_____.

Name _____Relationship: _____
Last known address:_____.

Name _____ Relationship: _____
Last known address: _____ .

17. The child ☐ is ☐ is not under the jurisdiction of the Family Court. If so, this petition ☐ has ☐ has not been filed in the Court that exercised jurisdiction over the most recent permanency or other proceeding involving this child. [If it has not been so filed, petitioner must file affirmation, Adoption Form 1-E].

18. Attached hereto and made a part hereof is Form 1-D setting forth all available information comprising the adoptive child's medical history.

[DELETE IF INAPPLICABLE]: 19. The placement is subject to the provisions of Social Services Law section(s)☐374-a ☐ 382 and the provisions of such section(s) have been complied with. The original approval signed by the Administrator of the Interstate Compact on the Placement of Children is attached hereto.

20. (a) The adoptive parent(s) ☐has/have ☐ has/have no knowledge that the child or an adoptive parent is the subject of an indicated report or is another person named in an indicated report of child abuse or maltreatment, as such terms are defined in section 412 of the Social Services Law, or has been the subject of or the respondent in a child protective proceeding which resulted in an order finding that the child is an abused or neglected child.

(b) The adoptive parent(s) ☐ has/have ☐ has/have no knowledge of any criminal record concerning themselves or any other adult over the age of 18 residing in the household (except)

_____
_____

21. There are no prior or pending proceedings affecting the custody or status of the adoptive child, including any proceedings dismissed or withdrawn, (except) [specify type of proceeding, court, disposition, if any, and date of disposition, if any]:_____
_____

22. The subject child ☐ is ☐ is not a Native-American child, who is subject to the Indian Child Welfare Act of 1978 (25 U.S.C. §§ 1901-1963). If so, the following have been notified [check applicable box(es)]:
☐ parent/custodian [specify name and give notification date]: _____
☐ tribe/nation [specify name and give notification date]: _____
☐ United States Secretary of the Interior [give notification date]:_____

23. [Insert any additional allegations.]
_____
_____
_____
_____
_____
_____.

WHEREFORE, the Petitioner(s) request(s) an order approving granting temporary guardianship of the child to Petitioner(s) and the adoption of the adoptive child [specify first name]:_____by the Petitioner(s) and directing that the adoptive child shall be treated in all respects as the child of the Petitioner(s) and directing that the name of

the adoptive child be changed and that (s)he shall henceforth be known by the name of [specify]:
_____ together with such other and further relief as may be just and proper.

Dated:_____,____.

_____ / _____
Adoptive Parent: typed or printed name/ signature

_____ / _____
Adoptive Parent: typed or printed name / signature

_____ / _____
Adoptive child if over 18: typed or printed name / signature*

_____ / _____
Attorney , if any: typed or printed name/ signature

_____
Attorney's Address and Telephone Number

* Note: Consent of a child over 14 must be attached.

<u>VERIFICATION</u>

STATE OF NEW YORK   )
                                      :ss.:
COUNTY OF_____)

_____being duly sworn, says that (he)(she)
(they)(is)(are) the Petitioner(s) in the above-named proceeding and that the foregoing petition is
true to (his)(her)(their) own knowledge, except as to matters where in stated to be alleged on
information and belief and as to those matters (he)(she) (they) believe(s) it to be true.

_____/_____
Adoptive Parent: typed or printed name/ signature

_____/_____
Adoptive Parent: typed or printed name/ signature

_____/_____
Adoptive child if over 18: typed or printed name/ signature

Sworn to before me this
         day of_____,_____.

_____
(Deputy)Clerk of the Court
      Notary Public

Resworn to before me this
         day of_____,_____.

_____
Judge of the _____ Court

FORM 1-Ca   **Affidavit (Change of Circumstance Since Certification as Qualified Adoptive Parent) (Private-Placement)**

D.R.L. §115, 115-d

Form 1-Ca
(Affidavit - Change of
Circumstance)
Private-Placement
9/99

SURROGATE'S COURT OF THE STATE OF NEW YORK
COUNTY OF

_____

In the Matter of Adoption of
A Child Whose First Name Is

(Docket)(File) No.

AFFIDAVIT
(Change of
circumstance since
certification as qualified
adoptive parent)
(Private-Placement)

_____

STATE OF NEW YORK   )
                      :ss..
COUNTY OF   )

, being duly sworn depose(s) and say(s):

1. Deponent(s) (was)(were) certified as (a) qualified adoptive parent(s) by ord of the court County of   , dated   ,   ;

2. The following change(s) in circumstance relevant and material to such certification (has)(have) taken place since that date:

Date:

_____
Petitioner

_____
Print or type name

_____
Signature of Attorney, if any

_____
Attorney's Name (Print or Type)

_____
_____
Attorney's Address and Telephone Number

Sworn to before me this
   day of   ,   .

_____

Official Forms

FORM 1-D   **Child's Medical History**

D.R.L. §§112(3)(6)
S.S.L. §373-a

Form 1-D
(Child's Medical
History - Agency or
Private-Placement)
3/2017

FAMILY COURT OF THE STATE OF NEW YORK
COUNTY OF

_____

In the Matter of the Adoption of
A Child whose First Name is

(Docket)(File) No.

Child's Medical
History (Agency or
Private-Placement)

_____

1. Age and date of birth of child:

2. Has the child had any of the following illnesses or health problems: (Where indicated, specify below
or on additional sheet).

___ (AIDS Infection)
(HIV positive status)[1]
___ Allergy to foods/other
substances
___ Allergy to medications
(prescription or over-
the-counter)
___ Asthma
___ Chicken Pox
___ Circulatory system
disorders (specify):
___ Diabetes
___ Diphtheria
___ German Measles (Rubella)
___ Measles (Rubeola)
___ Hay Fever
___ Heart problems (specify):

___ Hepatitis
___ Kidney disease
___ Malaria
___ Mental/Behavioral disorders (specify):
___ Mumps
___ Parasites in stool
___ Rheumatic Fever
___ Scarlet Fever
___ Sickle Cell Anemia/Trait
___ Tuberculosis
___ Typhoid Fever
___ Urinary tract infection
___ Whooping Cough (Pertussis)
___ Other (specify):
___ Operations/Accidents/Fractures
(specify):

3. Immunizations: give dates of the following:
D.P.T/D.T. _____
Polio (oral) _____
Measles _____ Mumps _____ Rubella _____
Hemophilus Influenza B. (H.I.B.) _____
Heptavax/Hepatitis Immune Globulin _____
Influenza (Flu) _____
Pneumonia vaccine _____

_____

[1] Delete inapplicable provision.

Other (specify) _____
Tuberculosis test (most recent/result) _____

4.   List Pre-natal History:

___ First trimester bleeding   ___ Drugs (such as marijuana,
___ Toxemia (high blood pressure   heroin, methadone or
     or protein in the urine)   amphetamines) (specify):
___ Medications (other than
     vitamins or iron)   ___ Alcohol (occasional)(moderate)(heavy)[2]
                                              (specify):
___ Diabetes or thyroid
     problem (specify):

Birth:

Birth weight _____ length _____
Apgar score: 1 min. _____ 5 mins. _____
Date baby was due _____
Date baby was born _____
Complications of delivery:
___ Premature rupture of membranes
___ Caesarian: routine _____ emergency _____
___ Excessive bleeding: abruption _____ placenta previa _____

Newborn:

___ Resuscitation required
___ Yellow jaundice:
     lights _____ exchange transfusion _____
___ Infection (specify):
___ Breathing problem (specify):
___ Other (specify):

5. List congenital impairments, including physical defects, if any.

6. State present health or cause of death (give ages), if known, of:

_____

   [2]Delete inapplicable provision.

Form 1-D page 3

Birth father:
Birth mother:
Siblings: full:

           half:

7. If known, indicate whether birth mother had any of the following:

___ Tuberculosis
___ Diabetes
___ Mental or nervous
     disorder e.g.,
     schizophrenia,
     depression, manic
     depressive illness
     (specify):

___ Thyroid disease
___ Stroke
___ Sickle cell anemia
___ (Aids infection)
     (HIV positive status)*
___ High blood pressure
___ Bleeding tendency
___ Eye or ear disorder
___ Intellectual disability: mental
___ Physical disability (specify):
___ Circulatory or blood
     disorders (specify):
___ Obesity

___ Asthma
___ Gastrointestinal disease,
     (e.g., gall bladder, ulcer,
     irritable bowel disorder)
     (specify):

___ Breast cancer
___ Colon cancer
___ Cancer, other (specify):

___ Arthritis or rheumatism
___ Kidney disease
     (specify):
___ Alcoholism or other substance
     abuse (specify):
___ Developmental disorder
     (e.g., learning disability,
     (attention deficit)(specify):

___ Other (specify):

8. If known, indicate whether birth father had any of the following:

___ Tuberculosis
___ Diabetes
___ Mental or nervous
     schizophrenia,
     depression, manic
     depressive illness
     (specify):
___ Thyroid disease
___ Stroke
___ Sickle cell anemia

___ Asthma
___ Gastrointestinal disease
     (e.g., gall bladder, ulcer,
     irritable bowel disorder)
     (specify):

___ Colon cancer
___ Cancer, other
     (specify):

Form 1-D page 4

___ (AIDS infection)
(HIV positive status)*

___ Arthritis or rheumatism
___ Kidney disease
(specify):

_____
*Delete inapplicable provision.

___ High blood pressure
___ Bleeding tendency
___ Eye or ear disorders
___ Intellectual disability
___ Physical disability
(specify)
___ Circulatory or blood
disorders (specify):
___ Obesity

___ Alcoholism or other substance
abuse (specify):

___ Developmental disorder
(e.g., learning disability,
attention deficit disorder)
(specify):
___ Other (specify):

Indicate source for information about child's medical history
and the source(s) for information about medical history of birth father and birth mother and whether from
direct or indirect source:

Completed by (state official
title, if any): _____

_____
Petitioner

_____
Print or type name

_____
Signature of Attorney, if any

_____
Attorney's Name (Print or Type)

_____
_____
Attorney's Address and Telephone Number

FORM 1-E   **Affirmation Regarding Venue**

D.R.L. § 113
[This form <u>must</u> be submitted
in cases where adoption has been filed before
judge <u>other than</u> judge who heard most recent
Family Court proceeding]

Adoption Form 1-E
(Affirmation Regarding Venue)
(9/2006)

SURROGATE'S COURT OF THE STATE OF NEW YORK
COUNTY OF _____

In the Matter of the Adoption of
A Child Whose First Name Is:

_____

Docket No. _____
AFFIRMATION
REGARDING VENUE

I, [specify name]: _____ , an attorney
duly admitted to practice law in the State of New York, affirm the following: _____

1. I represent [specify]: _____ , the prospective adoptive
parents in the above-entitled proceeding regarding the adoption of [specify child's first name]:__

2. Upon information and belief, according to [specify agency having custody or
guardianship of child or other source of information): _____
the child was freed for adoption as follows [check applicable box(es)]: _____
a. The child's birth mother:
☐ surrendered her parental rights in a _____
☐ judicial surrender executed before Judge [specify]:_____ in Family Court,
[specify county]: _____ on [specify date]:_____ in Docket # [specify]:_____
☐ extra-judicial surrender approved by Judge [specify]:_____ in Family Court,
[specify county]: _____ on [specify date]:_____ in Docket # [specify]:_____
☐ had her parental rights terminated by order of Judge [specify]:_____ in Family
Court, [specify county]:_____ on [specify date]:____ in Docket # [specify]:_____
☐ is unknown.
☐ is deceased.

b. The child's birth father or any other individual entitled to consent to the adoption:
☐ surrendered his parental rights in a _____
☐ judicial surrender executed before Judge [specify]:_____ in Family Court,
[specify county]: _____ on [specify date]:_____ in Docket # [specify]:_____
☐ extra-judicial surrender approved by Judge [specify]:_____ in Family Court,
[specify county]:_____ on [specify date]:_____ in Docket # [specify]:_____
☐ had his parental rights terminated by order of Judge [specify]:_____ in Family
Court, [specify county]: _____ on [specify date]:____ in Docket # [specify]:_____

☐ is unknown.
☐ is deceased.

3. Upon information and belief, according to [specify agency having custody or guardianship of child or other source of information]: _____
the child's most recent permanency hearing was held before [specify judge or referee]
in Family Court, [specify county]: _____ , on [specify date]: _____

4. This adoption proceeding has been filed before this Court for the following reasons [check applicable box(es) and explain]: _____
☐ This Court is more familiar with the facts and circumstances regarding permanency planning for, and the needs and best interests of this child, because [specify]: _____

☐ The child's law guardian [specify]: _____ is able to continue to represent the child in this proceeding.

☐ The prospective adoptive parents reside in [specify county]: _____
and would find it inconvenient to travel to the Family Court in [specify county]: _____

☐ This Court will be able to proceed in this matter more expeditiously because [specify]:
_____

☐ Other [specify]: _____
_____

WHEREFORE, for the reasons stated above, I am requesting that this Court retain jurisdiction over this adoption proceeding.

_____
Signature of Affirmant

_____
Affirmant's Name (print or type)

_____
Affirmant's Address and Telephone Number

FORM 1-F   **Determination of Family Court Judge Regarding Venue**

D.R.L. § 113
[Applicable where adoption was filed before
a judge other than the Family Court Judge
who heard most recent Family Court proceeding.
This form should be submitted by the Family Court judge,
who heard the most recent proceeding, to the judge
before whom the adoption is pending so that the
latter judge can incorporate the determination into the
Order Regarding Venue, Adoption Form 1-G]

Adoption Form 1-F
Determination of Family Court Judge
Regarding Venue)
(9/2006)

FAMILY COURT OF THE STATE OF NEW YORK
COUNTY OF _____

In the Matter of the Adoption of
A Child Whose First Name Is:

_____

Docket No. _____

DETERMINATION OF
FAMILY COURT JUDGE
REGARDING VENUE

     I, [specify name]: _____ , _____ , a Judge of
the Family Court, _____ County, affirm the following:

     1. I am the judge who presided over the following proceeding(s) in Family Court,
     County, regarding [specify child's first name]: _____
       ☐ surrender proceeding(s) regarding the child's ☐ birth mother ☐ birth father or other
individual entitled to consent to the adoption.
       ☐ termination of parental rights proceeding(s) regarding the child's
         ☐ birth mother ☐ birth father ☐ other individual entitled to consent to the adoption.
       ☐ permanency hearing regarding the child on [specify date]: _____
       ☐ other [specify, including date]: _____

     2. This Court has notified the Petitioner and law guardian in the above Family Court
proceeding(s) and has given them the opportunity to ☐ present facts and legal argument
☐ participate in the communication with the Court in which the adoption proceeding has been
filed. Their positions regarding the venue of this adoption are as follows:
       ☐ Petitioner [specify]: _____
       ☐ Law guardian [specify]: _____

     3. After communicating with the Court in which the adoption proceeding has been filed.
and after consideration of the positions of the Petitioner and law guardian in the above Family
Court proceedings, I have determined the following:

     ☐ The adoption proceeding should be transferred to this Court forthwith, but in no event
more than 35 days from the filing of the adoption petition;
               O R

☐ The adoption petition should be heard by the Court in which it has been filed.

4. The reasons for this determination are as follows [check applicable box(es); explain]: _____

☐ Relative familiarity of each Court with the facts and circumstances regarding permanency planning for, and the needs and best interests of this child [explain]: _____

☐ Ability of the child's law guardian [specify]: _____ to continue to represent the child in the adoption proceeding, if appropriate [explain]:_____

☐ Relative convenience of each Court to the residence of the prospective adoptive parents [explain]: _____

☐ Relative ability of each Court to proceed in the adoption proceeding expeditiously [explain]:_____

☐ Other [explain]: _____

   WHEREFORE, for the reasons stated above, I am requesting that the Court in which the adoption has been filed incorporate the above determination into an Order to be issued within 30 days of the filing of the adoption petition.

                              _____
                                    Signature of Affirmant

                              _____
                                 Affirmant's Name (print or type)

                              _____
                              _____
                              Family Court Address and Telephone Number

Official Forms

FORM 1-G   Order Regarding Venue

D.R.L. § 113   Adoption Form 1-G
[This Order must be issued <u>within 30 days of filing</u>   (Order Regarding Venue)
of adoption petition in cases filed before a judge other   **(9/2006)**
than the judge who heard most recent Family Court proceeding]

At a term of the Surrogate's Court of the State of New York,
held in and for the County of _____
at _____ , New York, on _____ .

PRESENT:
Hon. _____
Judge _____

SURROGATE'S COURT OF THE STATE OF NEW YORK
COUNTY OF _____

In the Matter of the Adoption of   Docket No. _____
A Child Whose First Name Is: ORDER REGARDING
                                                     VENUE
_____

        The petition regarding the adoption of the above-named child having been filed in this
Court, and the affirmation of Petitioner's attorney regarding venue, dated [specify]: _____
having been presented to this Court, and this Court having notified the parties to this action and
given them an opportunity to present facts and legal argument regarding venue,

        And this Court having communicated with the Hon. _____ , Judge of
the _____ Court, _____ County, and the Hon. _____ , Judge of
the _____ Court, _____ County, having submitted a Determination Regarding
Venue (Form 1-F) to this Court, dated [specify]: _____ , that contains a determination
regarding the venue of this action,

        NOW, and upon all the papers and proceedings herein, it is hereby
        ORDERED that the determination of venue by the _____ Court, _____ County, and
the reasons stated therein be incorporated into this Order, and it is further

[Check applicable box]:
        ☐ ORDERED that the adoption petition regarding the above-named child be heard in this
Court forthwith;
                                            OR
        ☐ ORDERED that the adoption petition regarding the above-named child be transferred
to the Hon. _____ , Judge of the _____ Court, _____ County,
forthwith, <u>but in no event more than 35 days</u> from the date of filing of the adoption petition;

        AND IT IS FURTHER ORDERED that [specify; delete if inapplicable]: _____
_____

Adoption Form 1-G   Page 2

ENTER

_____

☐ Judge of the Family Court ☐ Surrogate

Dated: _____ , _____

PURSUANT TO SECTION 11 13 OF THE FAMILY COURT ACT,
AN APPEAL FROM THIS ORDER MUST BE TAKEN WITHIN 30
DAYS OF RECEIPT OF THE ORDER BY APPELLANT IN COURT,
35 DAYS FROM THE DATE OF MAILING OF THE ORDER TO
APPELLANT BY THE CLERK OF COURT, OR 30 DAYS AFTER
SERVICE BY A PARTY OR THE LAW GUARDIAN UPON
THE APPELLANT, WHICHEVER IS EARLIEST.

Check applicable box:
☐ Order mailed on [specify date(s) and to whom mailed]:_____
☐ Order received in court on [specify date(s) and to whom given]:_____

FORM 2-A   Agreement of Adoption and Consent (Agency)

D.R.L.§ 111(1)(f), 112(2)(b)113

Form 2-A
(Agreement of Adoption
and Consent -- Agency)
8/2002

SURROGATE'S COURT OF THE STATE OF NEW YORK
COUNTY OF
_____

In the Matter of the Adoption of   (Docket)(File) No.
A Child Whose First Name Is

AGREEMENT OF
ADOPTION AND
CONSENT (Agency)

_____
     The undersigned petitioning adoptive parent(s) hereby agree(s) to adopt the above-named
adoptive child and to treat said child in all respects as (his) (her) (their) own lawful child and to extend
and assure to said child all the rights, benefits and privileges incident to such relationship, and to incur
and fulfill all the responsibilities of (a parent) (parents) with respect to said child.

Dated:

_____/_____
Adoptive Parent: typed or printed name/ signature

_____/_____
Adoptive Parent: typed or printed name / signature

_____/_____
Adoptive child if over 14: typed or printed name/ signature

_____/_____
Attorney if any: typed or printed name/signature

_____
Attorney's Address and Telephone number

Form 2-A Page 2

The undersigned authorized agency hereby consents to the adoption of the above-named adoptive child by the petitioning adoptive parent(s).

Name of Authorized Agency: _____

By: _____

_____
Title

STATE OF NEW YORK)
                 ss:
COUNTY)

On [specify date]:   , [specify name]:
personally appeared before me. (He)(She) is personally known to me or proved (his)(her) identity to me by satisfactory evidence as the person whose name is subscribed on this agreement of adoption and consent. (He)(She) acknowledged to me that (he)(she) executed this agreement and consent.

_____
Notary Public

STATE OF NEW YORK)
                 ss:
COUNTY)

On [specify date]:   , [specify name]:
personally appeared before me. (He)(She) is personally known to me or proved (his)(her) identity to me by satisfactory evidence as the person whose name is subscribed on this agreement of adoption and consent. (He)(She) acknowledged to me that (he)(she) executed this agreement and consent.

_____
Notary Public

Form 2-A Page 3

STATE OF NEW YORK   )
) ss:
COUNTY   )

On this   day of   ,   , before me personally came   , to me known and who by me being duly sworn did depose and say:
That he/she resides at

County of   State of   :
that he/she is [specify position]:
of [specify authorized agency]:

(an authorized agency), the corporation described in and which executed the foregoing instrument, that he/she knows the seal of said corporation; that such seal affixed to said instrument is such corporate seal; that it was affixed to said instrument by order of the Board of   of such corporation in writing, and that he/she signed his/her name thereto.

_____
Notary Public

State of New York   )
) ss.:
County of   )

On this   day of   ,   ,
, proven to me by the oath of   ,
an attorney admitted to practice in the State of New York, to be the person who executed the foregoing instrument, personally came before me and acknowledged that (he)(she) executed the same.

_____
Judge of the   Court

FORM 2-B **Agreement of Adoption (Private-Placement)**

D.R.L. §§ 111(1)(f), 115(4)

Form 2-B
(Agreement of Adoption
Private-Placement)
8/2002

SURROGATE'S COURT OF THE STATE OF NEW YORK
COUNTY OF
_____

In the Matter of the Adoption of
A Child whose First Name is

(Docket)(File) No.

AGREEMENT OF
ADOPTION
(Private-Placement)

_____

    The under signed petitioning adoptive parent(s) hereby agree(s) to adopt the above-named adoptive child and to treat said child in all respects as (his)(her)(their) own lawful child and to extend and assure to said child all the rights, benefits and privileges incident to such relationship, and to incur and fulfill all the responsibilities of (a) parent(s) with respect to said child.

Dated:

_____/_____
Adoptive Parent: typed or printed name/ signature

_____/_____
Adoptive Parent: typed or printed name / signature

_____/_____
Adoptive child if over 14: typed or printed name/ signature

_____/_____
Attorney if any: typed or printed name/signature

_____
Attorney's Address and Telephone number

Form 2-B page 2

STATE OF NEW YORK　　　)
　　　　　　　　　　　　　　ss:
COUNTY　　　　　　　　　　)

On [specify date]:　　　　　　　　　　, [specify name]:
personally appeared before me. (He)(She) is personally known to me or proved (his)(her) identity to me by satisfactory evidence as the person whose name is subscribed on this agreement of adoption and consent. (He)(She) acknowledged to me that (he)(she) executed this agreement of adoption and consent.

_____
　　　　　　　　　　　Notary Public

STATE OF NEW YORK　　　)
　　　　　　　　　　　　　　ss:
COUNTY　　　　　　　　　　)

On [specify date]:　　　　　　　　, [specify name]:
personally appeared before me. (He)(She) is personally known to me or proved (his)(her) identity to me by satisfactory evidence as the person whose name is subscribed on this agreement of adoption and consent. (He)(She) acknowledged to me that (he)(she) executed this agreement of adoption and consent.

_____
　　　　　　　　　　　Notary Public

STATE OF NEW YORK　　　)
　　　　　　　　　　　　　　ss:
COUNTY　　　　　　　　　　)

On this　day of　　　　,　,　　　　　, proven to me by the oath of　　　　　　　　　,
an attorney admitted to practice in the State of New York, to be the person(s) who executed the foregoing instrument, personally came before me and acknowledged that (he)(she) executed the same.

_____
Judge of the　　　　　　　Court

FORM 2-C   Consent of Child Over 14 (Agency)

D.R.L. §111(1) (a)

Adoption Form 2-C
(Consent of Child-
Agency)
8/2002

SURROGATE'S COURT OF THE STATE OF NEW YORK
COUNTY OF
_____

In the Matter of Adoption of   (Docket)(File) No.
A Child Whose First Name Is

CONSENT OF CHILD
OVER 14

_____

    The undersigned adoptive child, who is   years old, having been born on   ,
hereby consents to (his)(her) adoption by
        (and   ), the petitioning adoptive parent(s) in the above-entitled
proceeding.

Dated:

_____
            Child
_____/_____
Adoptive Parent: typed or printed name/ signature
_____/_____
Adoptive Parent: typed or printed name / signature
_____/_____
Adoptive child if over 14: typed or printed name/ signature
_____/_____
Attorney if any: typed or printed name/signature
_____
Attorney's Address and Telephone number

STATE OF NEW YORK   )
                 :ss.:
COUNTY OF   )

    On [specify date]:   , [specify name]:
personally appeared before me. (He)(She) is personally known to me or proved (his)(her) identity to
me by satisfactory evidence as the person whose name is subscribed on this consent. (He)(She)
acknowledged to me that (he)(she) executed this consent.

_____
        Notary Public

Form 2-C page 2

STATE OF NEW YORK   )
                           :ss.:
COUNTY OF   )

    On this   day of   ,   , before me personally came
, proven to me by the oath of
an attorney admitted to practice in the State of New York to be the attorney admitted to practice in the
State of New York to be the person described in and who executed the foregoing instrument and
duly acknowledged that (he)(she) executed the same.

                                      _____
                                      Judge of the   Court

FORM 2-D   **Consent of Child Over 14 (Private-Placement)**

D.R.L. § 111(1) (a)   Form 2-D
                                                       (Consent of Child -
                                                       Private-Placement)
                                                       8/2002

SURROGATE'S COURT OF THE STATE OF NEW YORK
COUNTY OF
....

In the Matter of the Adoption of A Child   (Docket)(File) No.
Whose first Name Is

                                                       CONSENT OF CHILD
                                                            OVER 14
                                                       (Private-Placement)

....

          The undersigned adoptive child, who is   years old, having been born on   ,
hereby consents to (his) (her) adoption by   ) , the
petitioning adoptive parent(s) in the above-entitled proceeding.

Dated:

                              _____
                                                       Child

          _____/_____
                  Adoptive Parent: typed or printed name/ signature

          _____/_____
                  Adoptive Parent: typed or printed name / signature

          _____/_____
                  Adoptive child if over 14: typed or printed name/ signature

          _____/_____
                  Attorney if any: typed or printed name/signature

          _____
                  Attorney's Address and Telephone number

Form 2-D page 2

STATE OF NEW YORK   )
                          ss.:
COUNTY OF   )

        On [specify date]:   , [specify name]:
personally appeared before me. (He)(She) is personally known to me or proved (his)(her) identity to me
by satisfactory evidence as the person whose name is subscribed on this consent. (He)(She) acknowledged
to me that (he)(she) executed this consent.

_____
        Notary Public

STATE OF NEW YORK   )
                          ss.:
COUNTY OF   )

        On this   day of   ,   , before me personally came
        proven to me by the oath of   an attorney
admitted to practice in the State of New York to be the person described in and who executed the foregoing
instrument and   duly acknowledged that
executed the same.

_____
        Judge of the   Court

FORM 2-E   Affidavit and Consent of Person Having Lawful Custody (Other than Birth or Legal Parent-Private-Placement)

D.R.L. §§ 109(6), 111(1)(f),
115(6)

Form 2-E
(Affidavit and Consent
- Person Having Custody
Private-Placement)
8/2002

SURROGATE'S COURT OF THE STATE OF NEW YORK
COUNTY OF
_____

In the Matter of the Adoption of
A Child whose First Name is

(Docket)(File) No.

AFFIDAVIT AND
CONSENT
OF PERSON HAVING
LAWFUL CUSTODY
(Other than Birth
or Legal Parent-
Private-Placement)

_____

STATE OF NEW YORK   )
                        ss.:
COUNTY OF   )

    (I) (we) [specify name(s)]:
                (and   ),
being duly sworn, depose(s) and say(s):

            Deponent(s) reside(s) at

and (is)(are) the person(s) having lawful custody of the above-named adoptive child in that:

          [recite facts showing how lawful custody was obtained]

    Deponent(s) hereby consent(s) to said child's adoption by the petitioning adoptive parent(s)
(and   ).

_____

_____

FORM 2-E   SURROGATE'S COURT   **AF-40**

_____/_____
Affiant (Person Having Legal Custody) typed or printed name/ signature

_____/_____
Attorney if any: typed or printed name/signature

_____
Attorney's Address and Telephone number

STATE OF NEW YORK   )
                                               ss.:
COUNTY OF   )

        On [specify date]:   , [specify name]:
personally appeared before me. (He)(She) is personally known to me or proved (his)(her) identity to
me by satisfactory evidence as the person whose name is subscribed on this affidavit and consent.
(He)(She) acknowledged to me that (he)(she) executed this affidavit and consent.

                                 _____
                                               Notary Public

STATE OF NEW YORK   )
                                               ss.:
COUNTY OF   )

        On [specify date]:   , [specify name]:
personally appeared before me. (He)(She) is personally known to me or proved (his)(her) identity to
me by satisfactory evidence as the person whose name is subscribed on this affidavit and consent.
(He)(She) acknowledged to me that (he)(she) executed this affidavit and consent.

                                 _____
                                               Notary Public

FORM 2-F   Judicial Consent (Birth or Legal Parent-Private-Placement)

D.R.L. §§115, 115-b

Form 2-F
Judicial Consent -
Birth or Legal Parent -
Private-Placement)
8/2002

SURROGATE'S COURT OF THE STATE OF NEW YORK
COUNTY OF
_____

In the Matter of the Adoption of
A child whose First Name is

(Docket)(File) No.

JUDICIAL CONSENT
(Birth or Legal Parent
-- Private-Placement)

_____

THIS CONSENT BECOMES IRREVOCABLE UPON EXECUTION OR
ACKNOWLEDGMENT BEFORE ANY JUDGE OR SURROGATE IN
NEW YORK STATE OR A COURT OF COMPETENT JURISDICTION IN
ANOTHER STATE HAVING JURISDICTION OVER ADOPTION
PROCEEDING(S). NO ACTION OR PROCEEDING FOR THE CUSTODY
OF THE ADOPTIVE CHILD MAY BE MAINTAINED BY THE PARENT
EXECUTING OR ACKNOWLEDGING THE WITHIN CONSENT.
                      ; optional]:

    1.   I, [specify name]:   , residing at   , (birth)(legal)
parent of [specify first name]:
          , do hereby consent to the adoption of my (daughter)(son) who was born on [specify
date]:   (by [specify name(s); optional]:   , adoptive
parent(s)).

    2. I have been advised that this consent becomes irrevocable when executed or acknowledged
before a judge or surrogate, and thereafter no action or proceeding may be maintained by me for the
custody of the child. I also have been advised that before I acknowledge or execute this consent, I have
a right to be represented by a lawyer of my own choosing and, if I am financially unable to obtain
same, a lawyer will be assigned at public cost. I further have been advised that I have a right to obtain
supportive counseling.

    *3. The full name and last known address of the other (birth)(legal) parent of the adoptive child
are:

Dated: Signature:

Official Forms

Form 2-f Page 2

_____ / _____
(Birth)(Legal) parent: typed or printed name/ signature

_____ / _____
Attorney if any: typed or printed name/signature

_____
Attorney's Address and Telephone number

State of　　　　　　　　　　)
　　　　　　　　　　　　　　　ss.:
County of　　　　　　　　　　)

　　　　On [specify date]:　　　　　　　　　　, [specify name]:
personally appeared before me. (He)(She) is personally known to me or proved (his)(her) identity to
me by satisfactory evidence as the person whose name is subscribed on this judicial surrender.
(He)(She) acknowledged to me that (he)(she) executed this surrender. I have informed (him)(her) of the
consequences of the act of execution and acknowledgment pursuant to the provisions of section 115-b
of the Domestic Relations Law and have informed (him)(her) of the right to be represented by legal
counsel of (his)(her) own choosing; of the right to obtain supportive counseling and of any rights to
assigned counsel pursuant to section 262 of the Family Court Act, section 407 of the Surrogate's Court
Procedure Act, or section 35 of the Judiciary Law. I have given (him)(her) a copy of this consent upon
execution thereof.

　　　　　　　　　　_____
　　　　　　　　　　　　Judge of the Court

(Seal of Court to be
affixed together
with Court Clerk's
certification)

FORM 2-Fa   Judicial Consent (Birth or Legal Parent-Private-Placement-Step-parent)

D.R.L. §§115, 115-b(8)

Form 2-Fa
(Judicial Consent of
Birth or Legal Parent to
Adoption by Step-parent)
(12/2009)

SURROGATE'S COURT OF THE STATE OF NEW YORK
COUNTY OF

In the Matter of the Adoption of
A Child whose First Name is

(Docket)(File) No.

JUDICIAL CONSENT OF BIRTH
OR LEGAL PARENT TO
ADOPTION BY STEP-PARENT

1.   I, [specify name]:   , residing at
, □ birth □legal parent of
[specify first name of child]:   , do hereby consent to the adoption
of my □daughter   □son, who was born on specify date]:   by [specify name]:
, adoptive parent.

2. The full name and last known address of the other □birth □legal parent of the adoptive child arc [optional]:

Dated:

_____/_____
□Birth □Legal Parent: type or print name   / Signature

_____/_____
Attorney if any: type or print name   /signature

_____
Attorney's Address and Telephone number

State of   )
                            : ss.:
County of   )
    On [specify date]:   , [specify name]:
personally appeared before me. □ He □She is personally known to me or proved □his □her
identity to me by satisfactory evidence as the person whose name is subscribed on this judicial consent.
□ He □ She acknowledged to me that □ he □ she executed this judicial consent.

_____
Judge of the   Court

_____
(Seal of Court to be
affixed together
with Court Clerk's
certification)

FORM 2-G   Extrajudicial Consent (Birth or Legal Parent-Private-Placement)

D.R.L. §§ 115,115-b

Form 2-G
(Extrajudicial Consent -Birth or Legal
Parent -- Private-placement)
9/2009

COURT OF THE STATE OF NEW YORK

COUNTY OF _____

In the Matter of the Adoption of
A Child whose First Name is _____

(Docket)(File) No.
EXTRAJUDICIAL CONSENT
(Birth or Legal Parent --
Private-Placement)

THIS CONSENT MAY BE REVOKED WITHIN 45 DAYS OF THE EXECUTION OF THIS DOCUMENT. IF THE CONSENT IS NOT REVOKED WITHIN SAID 45 DAYS, NO PROCEEDING MAY BE MAINTAINED BY THE PARENT FOR THE RETURN OF THE CUSTODY OF THE CHILD. THE REVOCATION MUST BE IN WRITING AND RECEIVED BY THE COURT WHERE THE ADOPTION PROCEEDING IS TO BE COMMENCED WITHIN 45 DAYS OF THE EXECUTION OF THE CONSENT. THE NAME AND ADDRESS OF THE COURT IN WHICH THE ADOPTION PROCEEDING HAS BEEN OR IS TO BE COMMENCED IS:
[specify name and address of court]:

IF THE ADOPTIVE PARENTS CONTEST THE REVOCATION, TIMELY NOTICE OF REVOCATION WILL NOT NECESSARILY RESULT IN THE RETURN OF THE CHILD TO THE PARENT, AND THE RIGHT OF THE PARENT TO THE CUSTODY OF THE CHILD WILL NOT BE SUPERIOR TO THOSE OF THE ADOPTIVE PARENTS. A HEARING BEFORE A JUDGE WILL BE REQUIRED TO DETERMINE: (1) WHETHER THE NOTICE OF REVOCATION WAS TIMELY AND PROPERLY GIVEN; AND IF NECESSARY, (2) WHETHER THE BEST INTERESTS OF THE CHILD WILL BE SERVED: (A) BY RETURNING CUSTODY OF THE CHILD TO THE PARENT; OR (B) BY CONTINUING THE ADOPTION PROCEEDING COMMENCED BY THE ADOPTIVE PARENTS; OR (C) BY DISPOSITION OTHER THAN ADOPTION BY THE ADOPTIVE PARENTS; OR (D) BY PLACEMENT OF

Form 2g Page 2

THE CHILD WITH AN AUTHORIZED AGENCY. IF ANY SUCH
DETERMINATION IS MADE, THE COURT WILL MAKE SUCH
DISPOSITION OF THE CUSTODY OF THE CHILD AS WILL
BEST SERVE THE INTERESTS OF THE CHILD.

THE PARENT HAS THE RIGHT TO LEGAL REPRESENTATION
OF THE PARENT'S OWN CHOOSING, THE RIGHT TO
SUPPORTIVE COUNSELING AND MAY HAVE THE RIGHT TO
HAVE THE COURT APPOINT AN ATTORNEY PURSUANT TO
SECTION 262 OF THE FAMILY COURT ACT, SECTION 407 OF
THE SURROGATE'S COURT PROCEDURE ACT, OR SECTION
35 OF THE JUDICIARY LAW.

1. I, [specify name]:   , residing at
                              , am the ☐ birth ☐legal parent of [specify first name of
child]:   . I do hereby consent to the adoption of my ☐daughter ☐son, who was , born on
[specify date]:   by [specify name]:   adoptive parent(s).

2. The full name and last known address of the other ☐birth ☐legal parent of the adoptive child are
[optional]:

3. I ☐have ☐ have not been represented by counsel. If represented, state counsel's name, address and
telephone number:

4. I [print name of consenting parent]:
this ___ day of _____, ____, have received a copy of this consent.

Date:
                    _____/_____
                    ☐ birth ☐legal parent: type or print name/ signature
                    _____/_____
                    Attorney, if any: type or print name/   signature
                    _____
                    Attorney's Address and Telephone number

STATE OF NEW YORK)
                              : ss.:
COUNTY OF   )
    On [specify date]:   , [specify name]:
personally appeared before me. (He)(She) is personally known to me or proved (his)(her) identity to me by satisfactory
evidence as the person whose name is subscribed on this extrajudicial surrender. (He)(She) acknowledged to me that (he)(she)
executed this surrender.
                    _____
                              Notary Public

FORM 2-Ga   **Extrajudicial Consent (Birth or Legal Parent-Private-Placement-Step-parent)**

D.R.L. §§ 115, 115-b(8)

Form 2-Ga
(Extrajudicial Consent
Birth or Legal Parent -
Private-Placement
Step-parent)
8/2002

SURROGATE'S COURT OF THE STATE OF NEW YORK
COUNTY OF
_____

In the Matter of the Adoption of   (Docket)(File) No.
A Child whose First Name is

EXTRAJUDICIAL CONSENT
(Birth or Legal Parent -
Private-Placement -
Step-parent)

_____

1. I, _____ , residing at _____
_____ , am the (birth) (legal) parent of _____ . I do hereby consent
to the adoption of my (daughter) (son) _____
_____ , born on _____
by [specify name]: _____ , adoptive parent.

2. The name and last known address of the other (birth)(legal) parent of the adoptive child are
[delete if inapplicable]: _____

Dated: _____

_____/_____
(Birth)(Legal) Parent: typed or printed name/ signature

_____/_____
Attorney if any: typed or printed name/signature

_____
Attorney's Address and Telephone number

STATE OF NEW YORK   )
                      :ss:
COUNTY OF   )

On [specify date]: _____ , [specify name]: _____
personally appeared before me. (He)(She) is personally known to me or proved (his)(her) identity to
me by satisfactory evidence as the person whose name is subscribed on this extrajudicial surrender.
(He)(She) acknowledged to me that (he)(she) executed this surrender.

_____
Notary Public

FORM 3   **Order Directing Service of Notice**

D.R.L. §§ 111(3), 111-a(4),115(9)

Form 3
(Order Directing
Service of Notice)
12/97

At a term of the Court of the
State of New York, held in and for the
County of
at   New York,
on   ,20   .

P R E S E N T
    Hon.
      Judge

In the Matter of the Adoption of
A Child Whose First Name Is

(Docket)(File) No.

ORDER
DIRECTING
SERVICE OF
NOTICE

    A petition for the adoption of the above-named adoptive child having been filed with this Court, and

    It appearing that notice should be given to the person(s) hereinafter named, it is

    ORDERED that notice of the filing of said petition requesting an order approving and allowing the said adoption be given to

in the following manner:

Form 3 page 2

ENTER

_____

Surrogate.

Dated: , 20   .

Check applicable box:
☐Order mailed on [specify date(s) and to whom mailed]:_____
☐Order received in court on [specify date(s) and to whom given]:_____

FORM 4   **Notice of Proposed Adoption**

D.R.L. §§ 111(3), 111-a(6),115(9).

Adoption Form 4
(Notice of Proposed Adoption)
10/2004

SURROGATE'S COURT OF THE STATE OF NEW YORK
COUNTY OF

In the Matter of the Adoption of
A Child whose First Name is

☐ Docket ☐ File No.

NOTICE OF PROPOSED
ADOPTION

To:

PLEASE TAKE NOTICE that a petition requesting an order approving and allowing the adoption of an adoptive child whose first name is [specify]:   , who is alleged to be your [specify relationship]:   , and whose full name and date and place of birth is set forth in a Schedule annexed to the petition for adoption herein, together with an agreement to adopt and consents to the adoption pursuant to the Domestic Relations Law, has been filed with the [specify]:   Court of the State of New York,   County. A hearing on the petition will be held at the Court, located at [specify address]:
on [specify date]:   , at [specify time]:   o'clock in the ☐ morning ☐ afternoon of that day, at which time and place all persons having any interest therein will be heard.

[Check box if applicable pursuant to Domestic Relations Law §111-a(6)]:
☐ PLEASE TAKE FURTHER NOTICE that your failure to appear may constitute a denial of your interest in the child, which may result, without further notice to you, in the adoption or other disposition of the custody of the child.

_____
Signature of Petitioner's Attorney

_____
Attorney's Name (print or type)

_____
Attorney's Address and Telephone Number

Official Forms

FORM 5 **Order of Publication**

D.R.L.§§ 111(3), S.C.P.A. 307(2)(a)
(iv),CPLR 315

Form 5
(Order of Publication
Agency)
9/99

At a term of the Court of the
State of New York, held in and for the
County of   ,
at   New York,
on   ,   .

P R E S E N T
   Hon.
    Judge

In the Matter of the Adoption of
A Child whose First Name Is

(Docket) (File) No.

ORDER OF
PUBLICATION

Upon reading and filing the petition herein duly verified on
    applying for the adoption of the above-named person and upon the affidavit of
duly sworn to on   and it appearing to the satisfaction of the Court that the present
whereabouts of   are unknown and cannot, after due diligence, be ascertained, it
is hereby

ORDERED, that service of a copy of a notice of application for adoption be made upon
    by publication thereof in (one) (two) newspaper(s), to wit: in the
    published in the County of   , State of
    (and in the   published in the County of
State of   , (once)[1] (not less than once in each of four successive weeks)[2], the (first)
publication to be made at least   days before the return day fixed in the said notice of application
for adoption; and it is further

(ORDERED that on or before the day of first publication the petitioner deposit in a post office
or in any post office box regularly maintained by the government of the United States in the State of
New York a copy of said notice of application for adoption, contained in a securely closed, post-paid
wrapper, directed to said   at
    that being last known address of said person.)

---

[1]S.C.P.A. § 307(2)(a)(iv)

[2]CPLR 315 et seq

Form 5 page 2

(ORDERED that the mailing of said notice of application for adoption is hereby dispensed with, the Court being satisfied by said petition and affidavit that the petitioner cannot with reasonable diligence ascertain a place or places where the said   would probably receive the matter transmitted through the post office.)

PURSUANT TO SECTION 1113 OF THE FAMILY COURT ACT, AN APPEAL FROM THIS ORDER MUST BE TAKEN WITHIN 30 DAYS OF RECEIPT OF THE ORDER BY APPELLANT IN COURT, 35 DAYS FROM THE DATE OF MAILING OF THE ORDER TO APPELLANT BY THE CLERK OF COURT, OR 30 DAYS AFTER SERVICE BY A PARTY OR THE LAW GUARDIAN UPON THE APPELLANT, WHICHEVER IS EARLIEST.

ENTER

_____
(J.F.C.) (SURROGATE)

Date:

Check applicable box:
☐ Order mailed on [specify date(s) and to whom mailed]:_____
☐ Order received in court on [specify date(s) and to whom given]:_____

FORM 6   Order for Investigation

D.R.L. §§ 112(7), 113

Form 6
(Adoption--Order for
Investigation)
9/99

At a term of the Court of the
State of New York, held in and for the
County of   ,
at   New York,
on   ,

PRESENT:
   Hon.
    Judge

In the Matter of Adoption of   (Docket)(File) No.
A Child Whose First Name Is

ORDER FOR
INVESTIGATION

     UPON reading and filing the petition, agreement of adoption and consents and other papers submitted herein, it is

     ORDERED that   be and hereby is designated and appointed to investigate the truth and accuracy of the allegations of the petition; and it is further

     ORDERED that said investigator shall ascertain as fully as possible and incorporate in a report such other factors relating to the adoptive child and the adoptive parents as will give the court adequate time for determining the propriety of approving the adoption; and it is further

     ORDERED that within thirty (30) days of the date of this order, unless this Court shall grant an extension of such period for good cause shown, said investigator shall make a written report of such investigation and submit the same to this Court; (and it is further

     ORDERED

).

Form 6 Page 2

ENTER

_____
Surrogate

Date: _____ , __ .

Check applicable box:
☐ Order mailed on [specify date(s) and to whom mailed]:_____
☐ Order received in court on [specify date(s) and to whom given]:_____

FORM 7   Report of Investigation (Private-Placement)

D.R.L. § 116

Adoption Form 7
(Adoption--Report of
Investigation-
Private-Placement)
9/2008

SURROGATE'S COURT OF THE STATE OF NEW YORK
COUNTY OF _____

In the Matter of Adoption of
A Child Whose First Name Is   (Docket)(File) No.

_____

_____   REPORT OF
                                                   INVESTIGATION
_____   (Private-Placement)

TO THE _____COURT OF THE COUNTY OF _____ ;

Pursuant to the order for investigation dated the____day of _____from the Honorable
_____Judge of the_____ Court, I,_____, have
investigated the allegations set forth in the petition herein and any statements contained in the
affidavits required by the Domestic Relations Law. On the basis of such investigation, I respectfully
submit the following report:

     1. The marital status, family members and history, religious affiliation, if any, of the adoptive
parent(s) and adoptive child are:_____
_____
_____
_____
_____ ;

     2. The physical and mental health of the adoptive parent(s) and adoptive child are:
_____
_____
_____
_____
_____ ;

     3. The adoptive parent(s) have an income of and own the following property: _____
_____
_____
_____

     4. The following fees, compensation or other remuneration have been paid or agreed upon with
respect to the placement of the child for adoption:

To the birth parent: _____

To the attorney for the birth parent:_____

To agency:_____

Form 7 page 2

To attorney for agency:_____

To attorney for adoptive parent:_____

Other (specify):_____

5. The adoptive parent(s) (has)(have) not been (a) respondent(s) in any proceeding involving children alleged to be neglected, abandoned, abused, delinquent or in need of supervision except:

_____
_____
_____
_____ ;

6. The following other facts relations to the familial, social, emotional and financial circumstances or the adoptive parent(s) may be relevant to a determination of adoption: _____

_____
_____
_____

Dated:_____,___.

_____
Investigator

_____
Petitioner

_____
Print or type name

_____
Signature of Attorney, if any

_____
Attorney's Name (Print or Type)

_____
_____
Attorney's Address and Telephone Number

FORM 8-A   Affidavit Identifying Party (Agency)

22 NYCRR 205.53(b)(2)   Form 8-A
                                                        (Adoption– Affidavit
                                                        Identifying
                                                        Party-Agency)
                                                        4/2002

SURROGATE'S COURT OF THE STATE OF NEW YORK
COUNTY OF
....
In the Matter of Adoption of   (Docket)(File) No.
A Child Whose First Name Is

                                                        AFFIDAVIT
                                                        IDENTIFYING
                                                        PARTY
                                                        (Agency)

....

STATE OF NEW YORK   )
)ss.:
COUNTY OF   )

        I [specify name of affiant]:   , having been duly sworn, deposes and states
the following:

        1. [Delete if inapplicable]:   I am an attorney at law duly licensed to practice under the laws
of the State of New York and have an office at [specify address]:

        2. I know [specify name of party]:
                and I know that ☐ he   ☐ she is the same person described in and who
executed the annexed [specify]:   [delete if inapplicable]: and who is
now present before the Court.

        3. [Delete if inapplicable]: I know [specify name of additional party]:
                and I know that ☐ he   ☐ she is the same person described in and who
executed the annexed [specify]:   [delete if inapplicable]: and who is
now present before the Court.

                                    _____
                                    Affiant

Sworn to before me this
day of   ,

_____
Judge of the   Court

FORM 8-B   Affidavit Identifying Party (Private-Placement) (Where Affiant Not Attorney of Record)

22 NYCRR 205.53(b)(2)

Form 8-B
(Affidavit
Identifying Party)
9/2009

SURROGATE'S COURT OF THE STATE OF NEW YORK
COUNTY OF _____
In the Matter of Adoption of   (Docket)(File) No.
A Child Whose First Name is

                                                               AFFIDAVIT IDENTIFYING
                                                               PARTY

_____

STATE OF NEW YORK   )
)ss.:
COUNTY OF   )

     I, [specify name of affiant]: _____ , having been duly sworn, deposes and states the following:

     1. Check applicable box(es)]:
☐ I am an attorney at law duly licensed to practice under the laws of the State of New York and have an office at [specify address]:
☐ I am counsel of record for [specify]:
☐ I am not an attorney but am known to the court. [See 22 NYCRR 205.53(b)(2)].

     2. I know [specify name of party]: _____
and I know that ☐ he ☐ she is the same person described in and who executed the annexed ;specify document]:   [delete if inapplicable]: and
who is now present before the Court.

     3. [Delete if inapplicable]: I know [specify name of additional party]: _____
and I know that ☐ he ☐ she is the same person described in and who executed the annexed [specify]:   [delete if inapplicable]: and
who is now present before the Court.

                                            _____
                                            Affiant

Sworn to before me this_____
day of_____, _____.

_____
Judge of the   Court

FORM 9-A   Affidavit of Financial Disclosure-Parents (Agency)

S.S.L. § 374(6);
22 NYCRR 205.53(b)(8)

Form 9-A
(Affidavit of Financial
Disclosure - Parents
- Agency)
9/99

SURROGATE'S COURT OF THE STATE OF NEW YORK

COUNTY OF

In the Matter of the Adoption of
A Child whose First Name is

(Docket)(File) No.

AFFIDAVIT OF
FINANCIAL
DISCLOSURE -
PARENTS
(Agency)

STATE OF NEW YORK   )
                                        ss:
COUNTY   )

(and   )

being duly sworn, depose(s) and say(s):

    1. That deponent(s) reside(s) at
                                        and (is)(are)
the (petitioning adoptive parent(s) (birth or legal parent(s)) of the above-named adoptive child; and

    2. That deponent(s) (has)(have) paid or given or caused to be paid or given or undertaken to pay or give the following expenses, contributions, compensation or things of value, either directly or indirectly, to any person, agency, association, corporation, institution, society or organization, in connection with the placing out of said adoptive child with deponent(s) or with the adoption of said child by deponent(s):

        [Specify recipient, amount, form, and purpose of each payment. If none, so state.]

;

    3. That deponent(s)(has)(have) requested, received or accepted, either directly or indirectly, the following compensation or things or value from any person, agency, association, corporation, institution, society or other organization in connection with the placing out of said adoptive child with deponent(s) or with the adoption of said child by deponent(s).

Form 9-A page 2

[Specify source, amount, form
and purpose of each payment
requested or received. If none,
so state.]

_____/_____

*(Adoptive) (Birth)(Legal) Parent: typed or printed name/ signature

_____/_____

*(Adoptive)(Birth) (Legal) Parent: typed or printed name/ signature

_____/_____

*Attorney if any: typed or printed name/signature

_____

*Attorney's Address and Telephone number

Sworn to before me this
    day of   , .

_____

Judge of the   Court

_____

*Delete inapplicable provisions

FORM 9-B   **Affidavit of Financial Disclosure-Parents (Private-Placement)**

S.S.L. §374(6);
22 NYCRR 205.53(b)(8)

Form 9-B
(Affidavit of Financial
Disclosure - Parents -
Private-Placement)
9/99

SURROGATE'S COURT OF THE STATE OF NEW YORK
COUNTY OF
....

In the Matter of the Adoption of
A Child whose First Name is

(Docket)(File) No.

AFFIDAVIT OF
FINANCIAL
DISCLOSURE -
PARENTS
(Private Placement)

....

STATE OF NEW YORK)
                   ss:
COUNTY   )

                           (and   )
being duly sworn, depose(s) and say(s):

     1. That deponent(s) reside(s) at
            and (is)(are)
the (petitioning adoptive parent(s) (birth or legal parent(s)) of the above-named adoptive child;
and

     2. That deponent(s) (has)(have) paid or given or caused to be paid or given or
undertaken to pay or give the following expenses, contributions, compensation or things of
value, either directly or indirectly, to any person, agency, association, corporation, institution,
society or organization, in connection with the placing out of said adoptive child with
deponent(s) or with the adoption of said child by deponent(s):

                     [Specify recipient, amount, form,
                     and purpose of each payment. If
                     none, so state.]

                          ;

     3. That deponent(s) (has)(have) requested, received or accepted, either directly or
indirectly, the following compensation or things or value from any person, agency, association,
corporation, institution, society or other organization in connection with the placing out of said
adoptive child with deponent(s) or with the adoption of said child by deponent(s).

                     [Specify source, amount, form

Form 9-B page 2

and purpose of each payment
requested or received. If none,
so state.]

_____/_____
*(Adoptive)(Birth)(Legal) Parent: typed or printed name/ signature

_____/_____
*(Adoptive) (Birth)(Legal) Parent: typed or printed name / signature

_____/_____
*Attorney if any: typed or printed name/signature

_____
*Attorney's Address and Telephone number

Sworn to before me this
    day of   ,   .

_____
Judge of the   Court

_____
*Delete inapplicable provisions.

FORM 10-A   **Supplemental Affidavit (Agency)**

22 NYCRR 205.53(c)

Form 10-A
(Supplemental Affidavit
Agency)
9/99

SURROGATE'S COURT OF THE STATE OF NEW YORK
COUNTY OF
_____

In the Matter of the Adoption of
A Child whose First Name is

(Docket)(File) No.

SUPPLEMENTAL
AFFIDAVIT
(AGENCY)

_____

STATE OF NEW YORK   )
                    ss:
COUNTY   )

(and   )

being duly sworn, depose(s) and say(s):

That deponent(s) (is) (are) the same person(s) who on
filed in this Court a petition for adoption of the above-named adoptive
child. Deponent(s) reallege(s) and reaffirm(s) each of the matters set forth in said petition heretofore
filed and represent(s) to the Judge of this Court that there has been no change of circumstances
whatsoever since the filing of said original petition, dated: , except as follows:

Date:

_____/_____
Adoptive Parent: typed or printed name/ signature

_____/_____
Adoptive Parent: typed or printed name / signature

_____/_____
Adoptive child if over 18: typed or printed name/ signature

_____/_____
Attorney if any: typed or printed name/signature

_____
Attorney's Address and Telephone number

Sworn to before me this
     day of   ,   .

_____
Judge of the   Court

FORM 10-B   Supplemental Affidavit (Private-Placement)

22 NYCRR 205.53(c)

Form 10-B
(Supplemental Affidavit
Private-Placement)
9/99

SURROGATE'S COURT OF THE STATE OF NEW YORK
COUNTY OF
_____

In the Matter of the Adoption of   (Docket)(File) No.
A child whose First Name is

SUPPLEMENTAL
AFFIDAVIT
(Private-Placement)

_____

STATE OF NEW YORK   )
                         ss:
COUNTY   )

                              (and   )

being duly sworn, depose(s) and say(s):

    1. Deponent(s) (is) (are) the same person(s) who on
        filed in this Court a petition for adoption of the above-named adoptive
child.

    2. Deponent(s) (is) (are) over the age of twenty-one years, citizen(s) of the United States, and
(unmarried)(married and living together) (married and living apart).

    3. The post-office addresses, place(s) of residence and home telephone number(s) of
petitioner(s) (is) (are)

Petitioner (specify name):

Petitioner (specify name):

    4. Petitioner(s) hereby state(s) that there has been no change of circumstances whatsoever since
the filing of said original petition, dated   , except as follows:

Form 10-B page 2

Date:

_____/_____

Adoptive Parent: typed or printed name/ signature

_____/_____

Adoptive Parent: typed or printed name / signature

_____/_____

Adoptive child if over 18: typed or printed name/ signature

_____/_____

Attorney if any: typed or printed name/signature

_____

Attorney's Address and Telephone number

Sworn to before this
   day of   .

_____

Judge of the   Court

FORM 10-C   **Affidavit Regarding Status of Appeal (Agency)**

D.R.L. §112

Adoption Form 10-C
(Affidavit Regarding
Status of Appeal –
Agency Adoption)
(9/2005)

SURROGATE'S COURT OF THE STATE OF NEW YORK
COUNTY OF
....

In the Matter of the Adoption of   Docket No.
A Child Whose First Name Is: AFFIDAVIT REGARDING
         STATUS OF APPEAL[1]

....

STATE OF NEW YORK   )
)ss.:
COUNTY OF   )

     I , [specify name]:   ,   , an attorney
duly admitted to practice law in the State of New York, swear the following to be true under the
penalties of perjury:

     1. I represented [specify authorized agency]:   in the
following proceeding(s) that resulted in the above-named child being freed for adoption [specify
termination of parental rights and/or surrender proceeding(s)]:

     2. The parental rights of the child's birth mother were terminated as a result of [check
applicable box(es)]:
         ☐ an order of disposition in a termination of parental rights proceeding, dated [specify]:
             which was served upon the:
                 ☐ law guardian ☐ counsel for the mother ☐ mother, if self-represented; and
                 ☐ other parties [specify]:
                 [Check box if applicable]: ☐ The order was not served upon the mother, because
                               she never appeared in the proceeding.
This order has not been reversed, modified or vacated and [check applicable box(es)]:
                 ☐ a notice of appeal has not been filed and the time to file a notice ☐ has ☐has not
             lapsed.
                 ☐ a notice of appeal was filed and:
                     ☐ the appeal was dismissed as it was not perfected.
                     ☐ the appeal was not perfected and the time to perfect ☐ has ☐has not
             lapsed.
                     ☐ the appeal was perfected and has been disposed of as follows [specify]:

                 and ☐ is ☐ is not the subject of any further appeal or proceeding on

---

[1] This form must be filed for all agency adoptions involving children freed for adoption by termination of
parental rights or surrender and should be completed by the attorney representing the agency in those proceedings.

remand pending in any Court;

□ a surrender of the child, dated [specify]:
    The surrender has not been revoked or vacated and [check applicable box(es)]:
        □ it is not the subject of revocation proceedings.
        □ revocation proceedings were brought but were disposed of as follows [specify]:
        □ a notice of appeal has not been filed and the time to file a notice □ has □has not
            lapsed.
        □ a notice of appeal was filed and:
                □ the appeal was dismissed as it was not perfected.
                □ the appeal was not perfected and the time to perfect □ has □has not
                    lapsed.
                □ the appeal was perfected and has been disposed of as follows [specify]:

                and □ is   □ is not the subject of any further appeal or proceeding on
                remand pending in any Court;

3. The parental rights of the child's birth father or any other individual entitled to consent to
the adoption were terminated as a result of [check applicable box(es)]:
        □ an order of disposition in a termination of parental rights proceeding, dated [specify]:
    which was served upon the:
        □ law guardian □ counsel for the father □ father, if self-represented; and
        □ other parties [specify]:
        [Check box if applicable]: □ The order was not served upon the father because
                                he never appeared in the proceeding.
    This order has not been reversed, modified or vacated and [check applicable box(es)]:
        □ a notice of appeal has not been filed and the time to file a notice □ has □has not
            lapsed.
        □ a notice of appeal was filed and:
                □ the appeal was dismissed as it was not perfected.
                □ the appeal was not perfected and the time to perfect □ has □has not
                    lapsed.
                □ the appeal was perfected and has been disposed of as follows [specify]:

                and □ is   □ is not the subject of any further appeal or proceeding on
                remand pending in any Court;

□ a surrender of the child, dated [specify]:
    The surrender has not been revoked or vacated and [check applicable box(es)]:
        □ it is not the subject of revocation proceedings.
        □ revocation proceedings were brought but were disposed of as follows [specify]:
        □ a notice of appeal has not been filed and the time to file a notice □ has □has not
            lapsed.
        □ a notice of appeal was filed and:
                □ the appeal was dismissed as it was not perfected.
                □ the appeal was not perfected and the time to perfect □ has □has not

lapsed.

□ the appeal was perfected and has been disposed of as follows [specify]:

and □ is □ is not the subject of any further appeal or proceeding on remand pending in any Court;

_____
Signature of Attorney, if any

_____
Attorney's Name (print or type)

_____
_____
_____
Attorney's Address and Telephone Number

Sworn to before me this
     day of

_____
(Deputy) (Clerk of the Court)
(Notary Public)

FORM 11   **Order to Show Cause (Removal of Child from Adoptive Home)**

D.R.L. §116(2)

Form 11
(Order to Show Cause
Removal of Child from
Adoptive Home)
9/99

At a term of the Surrogate's Court of the
State of New York, held in and for the
County of   ,
at   , New York,
on

P R E S E N T
    Hon.
      Judge

....

In the Matter of the Adoption of
A Child Whose First Name Is

(Docket) (File) No.

ORDER TO SHOW
CAUSE (Removal of
Child from Adoptive
Home)

....

    UPON reading and filing the report dated   ,   of   , the
investigator designated by an order of this Court to examine into the allegations set forth in the
petition herein; it is

    ORDERED THAT

                ,the petitioner(s) herein show cause before this Court at
        , New York, on the   day of   , at   o'clock in
the   noon of that day or as soon thereafter as counsel can be heard why an order should
not be granted removing
the above-named adoptive child, from the home of
            (and   ), the proposed adoptive
parent(s), and why such other and further relief should not be granted as may be just and
proper; and it is further

Form 11 page 2

ORDERED that service of a copy of this order (and the report upon which it was granted) upon the persons above-named (and upon
and), personally within the State of New York on or before the day of , , be deemed sufficient service.

PURSUANT TO SECTION 1113 OF THE FAMILY COURT ACT, AN APPEAL FROM THIS ORDER MUST BE TAKEN WITHIN 30 DAYS OF RECEIPT OF THE ORDER BY APPELLANT IN COURT, 35 DAYS FROM THE DATE OF MAILING OF THE ORDER TO APPELLANT BY THE CLERK OF COURT, OR 30 DAYS AFTER SERVICE BY A PARTY OR THE LAW GUARDIAN UPONTHE APPELLANT, WHICHEVER IS EARLIEST.

Dated: , .

ENTER

_____
(J.F.C.) (SURROGATE)

Check applicable box:
☐Order mailed on [specify date(s) and to whom mailed]:
☐Order received in court on [specify date(s) and to whom given]:

FORM 12   Order Removing Child from Adoptive Home

D.R.L. §§116 (2)   Form 12
                                                   (Order Removing Child From
     Adoptive   Home)
                                                   9/99

                         At a term of the Surrogate's court of the
                         State of New York, held in and for the
                         County of   ,
                         at   New York
                         on   ,   .

PRESENT:
     Hon.
     Judge

_____

In the Matter of the Adoption of   (Docket)(File) No.
A Child Whose First Name Is
                                                   ORDER REMOVING
                                                   CHILD FROM
                                                   ADOPTIVE HOME

_____

                                        ,the adoptive child above named having been
placed for adoption on or about   ,   , with the petitioner(s)
herein, and a petition having been duly filed in this Court praying for an order of adoption
pursuant to section 116 of the Domestic Relations Law; and

            This Court having on the   day of   ,   , issued an
     order of investigation designating
to examine into the allegations set forth in the petition and to make a written report of the
investigation; and the investigator having duly made and submitted a written report
of investigation dated   ,   ; and it appearing from the report that good cause
exists for the removal of the adoptive child from the home of said petitioner(s); and

            The petitioner(s) having been ordered to show cause why the adoptive child
should not be removed from the home of said petitioner(s); and due notice of this proceeding
having been given to   (and
                                          );
and the Court having taken proof of the facts shown by the investigations and the Court being
satisfied that the welfare of the adoptive child requires that (he)(she) be removed from the
home of the petitioner(s);

Form 12 page 2

Now, therefore, it is hereby

ORDERED that   ,the adoptive child, be and
(he)(she) hereby is removed from the home of   (and   )
and is (transferred to the Family Court) (returned to) (placed with [specify]:
    );(and it is further)

(ORDERED that a copy of this order be served upon

        , an authorized agency.)

PURSUANT TO SECTION 1113 OF THE FAMILY COURT ACT,
AN APPEAL FROM THIS ORDER MUST BE TAKEN WITHIN 30
DAYS OF RECEIPT OF THE ORDER BY APPELLANT IN COURT,
35 DAYS FROM THE DATE OF MAILING OF THE ORDER TO
APPELLANT BY THE CLERK OF COURT, OR 30 DAYS AFTER
SERVICE BY A PARTY OR THE LAW GUARDIAN UPON
THE APPELLANT, WHICHEVER IS EARLIEST.

ENTER

_____
(J.F.C.) (SURROGATE.)

Dated: ,   .

Check applicable box:
□ Order mailed on [specify date(s) and to whom mailed]:_____
□ Order received in court on [specify date(s) and to whom given]:_____

FORM 13-A　　　**Order of Adoption (Agency)**

D.R.L. §§ 111, 112(b), 113, 114

Form 13-A
(Order of Adoption -
Agency)
(9/2006)

At a term of the Surrogate's Court of the
State of New York, held in and for the
County of ——————————— ,
at _____ , New York,
on _____ , _____ .

PRESENT:
　　Hon. _____
　　　　Judge _____

——————————————————

In the Matter of the Adoption of　　　　　(Docket) (File) No. _____
A Child Whose First Name Is

——————————————　　**ORDER OF**
　　　　　　　　　　　　　　　ADOPTION
——————————————　　(Agency)

　　　The Petition of _____ (and _____), verified the
day of _____ , having been duly presented to this Court, together with an agreement on
the part of the petitioning adoptive parent(s) to adopt and treat as (his)(her)(their) own lawful child the
adoptive child having the given first name of _____
and whose full name is _____ , and whose birthday is_____,____, and who
was born at_____ , as set forth in the verified schedule attached to the
petition for adoption and having been made a part thereof; together with a document setting forth all
available information comprising the adoptive child's medical history; together with the affidavit(s) of
and the consent(s) of _____

　　　[Delete if inapplicable]: AND together with the written post-adoption contact agreement,
consented to by Petitioner(s), by the child's birth parent(s)[specify]: _____,
by the child's law guardian [specify]: _____ , by the child's sibling(s) or half-
sibling(s) [specify; delete if inapplicable]: _____
and by the child, attached and incorporated into this Order;[1]

　　　AND, although (his)(her)(their) consent(s) (is)(are) not required, the Court having given notice
of the proposed adoption to [specify]: _____

_____

_____ ,

　　　AND the above-named petitioning adoptive parent(s) and the adoptive child and all other
persons whose consents are required having personally appeared before this Court for examination,
(except [specify]: _____

_____ ;

　　　[Required in cases involving Native-American children; check if applicable]:

_____

　　　[1]NOTE: If a post-adoption contact agreement is incorporated into this order, the court-ordered
agreement, but not this Order, shall be given to the birth parents.

☐ And the following having been duly notified [check applicable box(es)]:
☐ parent/custodian ☐ tribe/nation ☐ United States Secretary of the Interior;
And the tribe/nation having: ☐ appeared ☐ not appeared;

AND the agency having obtained a New York State and national criminal history of the petitioning adoptive parents and adults over 18 residing in their home and [check applicable box]:
☐ such check having revealed no disqualifying convictions, as provided in Section 378-a of the Social Services Law;
☐ such check having revealed that Petitioner [specify]: _____ was criminally convicted but the Court having determined that denial of Petitioner's petition will create an unreasonable risk of harm to the physical or mental health of the child and that granting the petition will not place the child's safety in jeopardy and will be in the best interests of the child, pursuant to Social Services Law §378-a(2)(e)(1);
☐ such check having revealed that another adult over 18 in the home [specify]: _____ was criminally convicted but the Court having determined that adoption by the Petitioner(s) will nonetheless be in the child's best interests;

AND an investigation having been ordered and made and the written report of such investigation having been filed with the Court, as required by the Domestic Relations Law;

[Check if applicable]: ☐ AND the verified report of _____ , the authorized agency, dated _____ , is hereby accepted, pursuant to section 113 of the Domestic Relations Law, as the report of investigation required by section 12 of the Domestic Relations Law;

AND the adoptive child having resided with the petitioning adoptive parent(s) since [specify date]: _____ and [check box, if applicable]: ☐ the judge having dispensed with the three month period of residency with the adoptive parent(s), pursuant to section 112 of the Domestic Relations Law because [specify]: _____

AND the court having inquired of the statewide central register of child abuse and maltreatment and having been informed that [check applicable box(es)]:
☐ Neither the adoptive parent(s) (is) (are) not the subject of, or another person named in, an indicated report filed with such register as such terms are defined in section 412 of the Social Services Law);
☐ The adoptive parent(s) (is) (are) the subject of, or another person named in, an indicated report filed with such register as such terms are defined in section 412 of the Social Services Law, as follows [specify]: _____
and the Court having given due consideration to the information contained therein;

AND this Court having determined that the best interests of the adoptive child will be promoted by the adoption and that there is no reasonable objection to the proposed change of the name of the adoptive child;

NOW, on motion of _____ , **attorney for the petitioner(s) herein, and upon all the papers and proceedings herein, it is**

ORDERED that the petition of _____ (and _____) for the adoption of [specify]: _____ , a person born on [specify date]: _____ at [specify]: _____ , is allowed and approved; and it is further

ORDERED that the adoptive child shall henceforth be regarded and treated in all respects as the lawful child of the adoptive parent(s); and it is further

ORDERED that the name of the adoptive child is changed to [specify]: _____ and that the adoptive child shall hereafter be known by that name; and it is further

ORDERED that the Clerk prepare, certify and deliver to [specify]:_____ a copy of this order; and it is further

ORDERED that the child's medical history; heritage of the parents, which shall include nationality, ethnic background and race; education, which shall be the number of years of school completed by the parents at the time of the birth of the adoptive child; general physical appearance of the parents at the time of the birth of the adoptive child, including height, weight, color of hair, eyes, skin; occupation of the parents at the time of birth of the adoptive child; health and medical history of the parents at the time of birth of the adoptive child, including all available information setting forth conditions or diseases believed to be hereditary, any drugs or medication taken during pregnancy by the mother; and other information which may be a factor influencing the child's present or future well-being; and talents, hobbies and special interests of the parents as contained in the petition, shall be furnished to the adoptive parent(s); and it is

[Check box if applicable]: ☐ ORDERED that the post-adoption contact agreement, which was approved as being in the child's best interests by the Court that approved the child's conditional surrender and which was consented to in writing by the following [specify]: _____
Adoptive parent(s)[specify]: _____
Birth parent(s) [specify]: _____
Adoptive child's law guardian [specify]:_____
Sibling(s) or half-sibling(s) over the age of 14, if contact is with siblings or half-siblings [specify]: _____
is hereby incorporated into this Order of Adoption; and a true copy of such post-adoption contact agreement and Order of Incorporation shall be given to all parties to the post-adoption contact agreement;[2] and it is further

[Check box if applicable]: ☐ ORDERED that, if required by a governmental agency, including but not limited to, the United States Social Security Administration, the United States Passport Office and the New York State Department of Motor Vehicles, in connection with an application submitted by

_____

[2] The Order of Incorporation and Post-Adoption Contact Agreement, but not this Order of Adoption, must be given to the parties to the agreement.

or on behalf of the adoptive child, the adoptive parent(s)' attorney [specify]: _____
is authorized to deliver a certified copy of this Order of Adoption to such agency directly or to the
adoptive parent, as he or she deems appropriate; and it is further

ORDERED that this order, together with all other papers pertaining to the adoption, shall be
filed and kept as provided in the Domestic Relations Law and shall not be subject to access or
inspection except as provided in this Order or such Law.

ENTER

_____
☐ Judge of the Family Court ☐ Surrogate

Dated: _____, _____ .

PURSUANT TO SECTION 1113 OF THE FAMILY COURT ACT,
AN APPEAL FROM THIS ORDER MUST BE TAKEN WITHIN 30
DAYS OF RECEIPT OF THE ORDER BY APPELLANT IN COURT,
35 DAYS FROM THE DATE OF MAILING OF THE ORDER TO
APPELLANT BY THE CLERK OF COURT, OR 30 DAYS AFTER
SERVICE BY A PARTY OR THE LAW GUARDIAN UPON
THE APPELLANT, WHICHEVER IS EARLIEST.

Check applicable box:
☐ Order mailed on [specify date(s) and to whom mailed]:_____
☐ Order received in court on [specify date(s) and to whom given]:_____

FORM 13-B   Order of Adoption (Private-Placement)

D.R.L. §§111, 112(b), 113, 114

Adoption Form 13-B
(Order of Adoption-
Private-Placement)
9/2009

At a term of the _____ Court of the
State of New York, held in and for the
County of _____ ,
at _____ New York
on _____,_____ .

PRESENT:
Hon. _____
    Judge

_____

In the Matter of the Adoption of   ☐Docket ☐File No.
A Child Whose First Name Is   _____

_____   ORDER OF
                                                    ADOPTION
_____   (Private-Placement)

The Petition of _____ (and
_____), verified the _____day of _____, ____, having been duly
presented to this Court, together with an agreement on the part of the petitioning adoptive parent(s) to
adopt and treat as ☐his ☐her ☐their own lawful child the adoptive child, whose first name is [specify]:
_____ and whose birth day is [specify]:_____, and who was born at
[specify]:_____,
as set forth in the petition for adoption herein, and the petition having a document attached thereto and
made a part thereof setting forth all available information comprising the adoptive child's medical history;
together with the affidavit(s) of [specify]:_____
and the consent(s) of [specify]:_____;

[Check applicable box(es)]: AND, although ☐his ☐her ☐their consent(s) ☐is/are
☐is/are not required, the Court having given notice of the proposed adoption to [specify]: _____

_____

AND the aforesaid petitioning adoptive parents and the adoptive child and all
other persons whose consents are required having personally appeared before this Court for examination,
except [specify]:_____;

AND an investigation having been ordered and made and the written report of such
investigation having been filed with the Court, as required by the Domestic Relations Law;

[Check box(es) if applicable]: ☐ AND the Court having ☐ shortened
☐dispensed with the three-month waiting period between its receiving the petition to adopt and this order
of adoption, pursuant to section 116 of the Domestic Relations Law, because [specify reason(s)]:

_____ ;

AND the adoptive child having resided with the petitioning adoptive parent(s) since
_____(and the judge

having dispensed with the three-month period of residency with the adoptive parent(s), pursuant to section 112 and 116 of the Domestic Relations Law because _____ ;

[Check box(es) if applicable]: ☐AND the court having inquired of the statewide central register of child abuse and maltreatment and having been informed that the ☐child ☐adoptive parent(s) ☐is/are ☐is/are not a subject of, or another person named in, an indicated report filed with the register as such terms are defined in section 412 of the Social Services Law,
☐AND there being available to this Court findings of a court inquiry made within the preceding twelve months, of the statewide central register of child abuse and maltreatment that the ☐ child ☐adoptive parent(s) ☐is/are ☐is/are not a subject of, or another person named in, an indicated report filed with such register as such terms are defined in section 412 of the Social Services Law, and the Court having given due consideration to any information contained therein;

AND this Court being satisfied that the best interests of the adoptive child will be promoted by the adoption and that there is no reasonable objection to the proposed change of the name of the adoptive child;

[Required in cases involving Native-American children; check if applicable]:
☐And the following having been duly notified [check applicable box(es)]:
☐parent/custodian
☐tribe/nation
And the tribe/nation having: ☐appeared ☐not appeared;
☐United States Secretary of the Interior;

NOW, on motion of [specify]: _____
Attorney for the petitioners herein, and upon all the papers and proceedings herein, it is

ORDERED that the petition of _____ (and _____
_____) for the adoption of _____
a person born on _____, _____, at _____ , is
allowed and approved; and it is further

ORDERED that the adoptive child shall henceforth be regarded and treated in all respects as the lawful child of the adoptive parent(s); and it is further

ORDERED that the name of the adoptive child is changed to [specify]: _____ and that the adoptive child shall hereafter be known by that name; and it is further

[Check box if applicable]: ☐ORDERED that the Clerk prepare, certify and deliver a copy of this order to [specify]: _____ ; and it is further

ORDERED that the child's medical history; heritage of the parents, which shall include nationality, ethnic background and race; education, which shall be the number of years of school completed by the parents at the time of the birth of the adoptive child; general physical appearance of the parents at the time of the birth of the adoptive child, including height, weight, color of hair, eyes, skin; occupation of the parents at the time of birth of the adoptive child; health and medical history of the parents at the time of birth of the adoptive child, including all available information setting forth conditions or diseases believed to be hereditary, any drugs or medication taken during pregnancy by the mother; and other information which may be a factor influencing the child's present or future well-being; and talents, hobbies and special interests of the parents as contained in the petition, shall be furnished to the adoptive parents; and it is

[Check box if applicable]: ☐ ORDERED that, if required by a governmental agency, including but not limited to, the United States Social Security Administration, the United States Passport Office and the New York State Department of Motor Vehicles, in connection with an application submitted by or on behalf of the adoptive child, the adoptive parent(s)' attorney [specify]: _____
is authorized to deliver a certified copy of this Order of Adoption to such agency directly or to the adoptive parent, as he or she deems appropriate; and it is further

ORDERED that this order, together with all other papers pertaining to the adoption, shall be filed and kept as provided in the Domestic Relations Law and shall not be subject to access or inspections except as provided in this Order or such Law.

ENTER:

_____
☐ Judge of the Family Court ☐ Surrogate

Dated: _____, 20 ____.

[Applicable to orders of the Family Court]:

PURSUANT TO SECTION 1113 OF THE FAMILY COURT ACT, AN APPEAL FROM AN ORDER OF THE FAMILY COURT MUST BE TAKEN WITHIN 30 DAYS OF RECEIPT OF THE ORDER BY APPELLANT IN COURT, 35 DAYS FROM THE DATE OF MAILING OF THE ORDER TO APPELLANT BY THE CLERK OF COURT, OR 30 DAYS AFTER SERVICE BY A PARTY OR THE LAW GUARDIAN UPON THE APPELLANT, WHICHEVER IS EARLIEST.

Check applicable box:
☐ Order mailed on [specify date(s) and to whom mailed]:_____
☐ Order received in court on [specify date(s) and to whom given]:_____

FORM 14   **Certificate of Adoption**

D.R.L. §114

Adoption Form 14
(Certificate of Adoption)
(9/2005)

SURROGATE'S COURT OF THE STATE OF NEW YORK
COUNTY OF

CERTIFICATE OF ADOPTION

I,   , Clerk of the
        Court of   County, do hereby certify that I have inspected the records of
this Court and find that:

       AN ORDER OF ADOPTION was signed on the   day of   ,   , by Honorable
       , Judge of the   Court of the County of   , granting the petition
of   (and   ), adoptive parent(s) of a child now known
and called by the name of [specify]:   , who was born at   , on
the   day of   ,   ;

       This certificate as to the facts recited herein shall have the same force and effect as a
certified copy of an order of adoption.

       IN TESTIMONY WHEREOF, I have hereunto set my hand
       and affixed the seal of the   Court
       of the County of   this
       day of   ,   .

_____
Clerk of the   Court
of the County of

**FORM 14-A   Order of Incorporation of Post- Adoption Contact Agreement
(Agency)**

D.R.L. §112-b   Adoption Form 14-A
                                          (Order of Incorporation of Post-adoption
                                          Contact Agreement - Agency Adoption)
                                                      (9/2005)

                              At a term of the Surrogate's Court of the
                              State of New York, held in and for the
                              County of   ,
                              at   , New York,
                              on   . .

PRESENT:
        Hon.
              Judge
....
In the Matter of the Adoption of   (Docket) (File) No.
A Child Whose First Name Is

                                          ORDER OF INCORPORATION OF
                                          POST-ADOPTION CONTACT
                                          AGREEMENT (Agency Adoption)

....

        A Petition having been presented to this Court regarding the adoption of the
above named child, and the Petition having included a surrender/consent to
adopt signed by the following birth parent(s)[specify]:
before Judge [specify]:   of [specify Court and County]:
on [specify date]:

        And the Court that approved the execution of the surrender having also approved the
attached Post-adoption Contact Agreement signed and agreed to by the following [specify]:

as being in the best interests of the child;[1]

        And this Court having issued an Order, Docket No. [specify]:
for the child to be adopted, it is hereby

        ORDERED that the terms and conditions of the attached Post-adoption Contact
Agreement are hereby incorporated into the Adoption order such that the terms and conditions
survive the adoption order and are subject to proceedings under DRL 112-b; and it is
further

_____

[1] A true copy of the approved Post-adoption Contact Agreement must be attached to this Order.

ORDERED that the [check applicable box]: □ Clerk of Court   □ Other [specify]: shall provide a copy of this incorporation order and the attached Post-adoption Contact Agreement to all those persons and their attorneys who are listed above as those who signed and agreed to the terms and conditions of the Post-adoption Contact Agreement.

And it is further ORDERED that:

ENTER

_____
□ Judge of the Family Court □ Surrogate

PURSUANT TO SECTION 1113 OF THE FAMILY COURT ACT, AN APPEAL FROM THIS ORDER MUST BE TAKEN WITHIN 30 DAYS OF RECEIPT OF THE ORDER BY APPELLANT IN COURT, 35 DAYS FROM THE DATE OF MAILING OF THE ORDER TO APPELLANT BY THE CLERK OF COURT, OR 30 DAYS AFTER SERVICE BY A PARTY OR THE LAW GUARDIAN UPON THE APPELLANT, WHICHEVER IS EARLIEST.

Dated: ,   .
Check applicable box:
□ Order mailed on [specify date(s) and to whom mailed]:_____
□ Order received in court on [specify date(s) and to whom given]:_____

FORM 15-A   **Application for Certified Copy of Adoption Order (Before sealing of records)**

D.R.L. §114

Form 15-A
(Application for
Certified Copy of
Adoption Order Before
sealing of records)
9/99

SURROGATE'S COURT OF THE STATE OF NEW YORK
COUNTY OF
_____

In the matter of the Adoption of   (Docket)(File) No .

APPLICATION FOR
CERTIFIED COPY OF
ADOPTION ORDER
(Before sealing of
records)

A Minor of the Age of   years
_____

The undersigned applicants) respectfully show(s) that:

1. The applicant(s)   (and)
reside(s) at   (and) (respectively) in the
County of   State of   .

2. On or about the   day of   ,   , an order was made by the
Honorable Judge of the   Court of   County, State
of New York, approving the adoption of the above-named child by
, and thereafter, said order was duly filed in the office of the Clerk of the
Court of the County of

3. It is necessary for the applicant (s) to obtain a certified copy of said order approving the
adoption because of the following facts and circumstances:

WHEREFORE, applicant (s) pray (s) that the Court make an order directing the Clerk of the
                        Court of the County of   to prepare,
certify and deliver to the applicant a copy of the original order of adoption granted herein, and for such
other and further relief as to the Court may be just and proper.

_____
Applicant

_____
Applicant

Form 15-A page 2

_____
Petitioner

_____
Print or type name

_____
Signature of Attorney, if any

_____
Attorney's Name (Print or Type)

_____
_____
Attorney's Address and Telephone Number

VERIFICATION

STATE OF NEW YORK   )
)ss.:
COUNTY OF   )

   being duly sworn, say(s) that (he)(she)(they)(is)(are) the applicants above named; that (he)(she)(they)(have)(has) read the foregoing application and the same is true to (his)(her) (their) knowledge except as to matters therein stated to be alleged on information and belief and as to those matters (he)(she)(they) believers) it to be true.

_____
Applicant

_____
Applicant

Subscribed and sworn to before me this
day of

_____
 (Deputy) Clerk of the Court
   Notary Public

FORM 15-B   **Order for Certified Copy of Adoption Records (Before Sealing of Records)**

D.R.L.§114

Form 15-B
(Order for Certified Copy
of Adoption Order-Before
sealing of records)
9/99

At a term of the Surrogate's Court of the
State of New York, held in and for the
County of   ,
at   , New York
on   .

PRESENT:
    Hon.
      Judge

_____

In the matter of the Adoption of

(Docket)(File) No.

ORDER FOR
CERTIFIED COPY OF
ADOPTION ORDER
A Minor of the Age of   years   (Before sealing of
records)

_____

    UPON reading and filing the application of   and
             duly verified the   day of   ,
requesting this Court to issue an order authorizing the Clerk of the   Court of the
County of   to prepare, certify and deliver to said applicant (s) a copy of the
original order of adoption granted herein; and the Court being satisfied that there is good and proper
cause for granting such request; and upon all of the proceedings had herein; it is

    ORDERED that the Clerk of the   Court of the County of
        be and (s)he hereby is authorized to prepare, certify and deliver to said applicant (s) a
copy of the original order of adoption granted herein.,

Form 15-B page 2

PURSUANT TO SECTION 1113 OF THE FAMILY COURT ACT,
AN APPEAL FROM THIS ORDER MUST BE TAKEN WITHIN 30 DAYS OF RECEIPT OF
THE ORDER BY APPELLANT IN COURT, 35 DAYS FROM THE DATE OF MAILING OF
THE ORDER TO APPELLANT BY THE CLERK OF COURT, OR 30 DAYS AFTER
SERVICE BY A PARTY OR THE LAW GUARDIAN UPON THE APPELLANT,
WHICHEVER IS EARLIEST.

ENTER

_____
(J.F.C.) (Surrogate)

Dated: ,   .

Check applicable box:
❑ Order mailed on [specify date(s) and to whom mailed]: _____
❑ Order received in court on [specify date(s) and to whom given]: _____

FORM 16-A   **Application for Certified Copy of Adoption Records (After Sealing of Records)**

D.R.L. §114

Form 16-A
(Application for Certified
Copy of Adoption Order-
After sealing of records)
(9/2006)

SURROGATE'S COURT OF THE STATE OF NEW YORK
COUNTY OF
....

In the Matter of the Adoption of   (Docket)(File) No.

APPLICATION FOR
CERTIFIED COPY
OF ADOPTION
ORDER (After sealing
of records)

A Minor of the Age of   years
....

The undersigned applicant(s) respectfully show(s) that:

1. The applicants)
(and)
reside(s) at   (and)
    (respectively) in the County of   , State of

2. On or about the day of   ,   , an order was made by the Honorable
    , a judge of the   Court
of   County, State of New York, approving the adoption of the above-
named child by   , and thereafter the order was duly filed in the office
of the Clerk of the   Court of the County of
    , and sealed.

3. It is necessary for the applicant(s) to obtain a certified copy of the order approving the
adoption because of the following facts and circumstances [Explain. Note: if the applicant is a
Native-American individual 18 years of age or older who is seeking information and/or records
regarding the birth parents' tribal affiliation, so indicate]:

    WHEREFORE, applicant(s) request(s) that the Court make an order directing the Clerk of
the   Court of the County of   to prepare, certify

and deliver to the applicant(s) a copy of the original order of adoption granted herein, and for such other and further relief as to the Court may be just and proper.

_____

Applicant

_____

Applicant

_____

Print or type name(s)

_____

Signature of Attorney, if any

_____

Attorney's Name (Print or Type)

_____

_____

Attorney's Address and Telephone Number

VERIFICATION

STATE OF NEW YORK   )
)ss.:
COUNTY OF   )

, being duly sworn, say(s) that (he)(she)(they)(is)(are) the applicants) above named; that (he)(she)(they)(have)(has) read the foregoing application and the same is true to (his)(her)(their) knowledge except as to matters therein stated to be alleged on information and belief and as to those matters (he)(she)(they) believe(s) it to be true.

_____

Applicant

_____

Applicant

Subscribed and sworn to before me this
          day of   ,   .

_____
(Deputy) Clerk of the Court
   Notary Public

FORM 16-B   **Order for Certified Copy of Adoption Records (After Sealing of Records)**

D.R.L. § 114

Form 16-B
(Order for Certified Copy of
Adoption Order - After sealing
of records)
(9/2006)

At a term of the Surrogate's Court of the State of New York,
held in and for the County of   ,
at   , New York, on   ,

PRESENT

        Hon.

                Judge

In the Matter of the Adoption of   (Docket) (File) No.

A Minor of the Age of   years

                                                ORDER ON
                                                APPLICATION FOR
                                                CERTIFIED COPY OF
                                                ADOPTION ORDER
---   (After sealing of records)

UPON reading and filing the application of
    and   duly verified the day of   ,   , requesting this Court to issue an
order authorizing the Clerk of the   Court of the County of   to prepare,
certify and deliver to the applicant(s) a copy of the original order of adoption granted herein; and the
Court being satisfied that there is good and proper cause for granting such request; and upon all of the
proceedings had herein; it is [check applicable box]:

    ☐ ORDERED that the application is GRANTED and the Clerk of the   Court of the
County of   is directed to prepare, certify and deliver to the applicant(s) a copy of the
original order of adoption granted herein.

                        OR

    ☐ ORDERED that the application is DENIED.

PURSUANT TO SECTION 1113 OF THE FAMILY COURT ACT, AN APPEAL FROM
THIS ORDER MUST BE TAKEN WITHIN 30 DAYS OF RECEIPT OF THE ORDER BY
APPELLANT IN COURT, 35 DAYS FROM THE DATE OF MAILING OF THE ORDER TO
APPELLANT BY THE CLERK OF COURT, OR 30 DAYS AFTER SERVICE BY A PARTY
OR THE LAW GUARDIAN UPON THE APPELLANT, WHICHEVER IS EARLIEST.
                                        Enter

                        _____
                        Judge of the Family Court/Surrogate
Dated:
Check applicable box:
☐ Order mailed on [specify date(s) and to whom mailed]:_____
☐ Order received in court on [specify date (s) and to whom given]:_____

FORM 17   **Petition for Enforcement of Post- Adoption Contact Agreement (After Adoption Finalization)**

Domestic Relations Law §112-b

Adoption Form 17
(Agency Adoption– Petition for
Enforcement of Post-adoption Contact
Agreement After Adoption Finalization)
(9/2005)

SURROGATE'S COURT OF THE STATE OF NEW YORK
COUNTY OF
....
In the Matter of a Post-adoption
Contact Agreement Concerning

Child's Name:
Date of Birth:

Docket No.
PETITION FOR ENFORCEMENT
OF POST-ADOPTION CONTACT
AGREEMENT (After Adoption
Finalization)

Pursuant to Section 112-b of the
Domestic Relations Law
....

**NOTICE: WILLFUL FAILURE TO OBEY THE TERMS AND CONDITIONS OF AN
ORDER OF THE FAMILY COURT MAY RESULT IN COMMITMENT TO JAIL
FOR A TERM NOT TO EXCEED SIX MONTHS.**

TO THE FAMILY COURT OF THE COUNTY OF [specify]:   :

The undersigned Petitioner respectfully alleges upon information and belief that:
   1. Petitioner, [specify]:   , is [check applicable box]:
☐ an authorized agency having its office and place of business at [specify]:
in the County of [specify]:   , State of New York;
☐ a party to a post-adoption contact agreement regarding the above-named child;
☐ the law guardian of the above-named child.

   2. On [specify date]:   , in conjunction with the surrender of the child, the Family Court,
        County, approved a Post-adoption Contact Agreement regarding the above-named child as being in
the child's best interests. This Post-adoption Contact Agreement was incorporated into the Order of
Adoption by the [specify Court and County]: ☐ Family ☐ Surrogate's Court,   County,
on [specify date]:   . True copies of the Order of Incorporation and the Post-
adoption Contact Agreement are attached to this petition.

   3. The following Respondent [specify]:   has violated the Post-adoption Contact
Agreement as follows [specify facts and circumstances, including dates]:

   4. Enforcement of the terms and conditions of the Post-adoption Contact Agreement is in the best
interests of the child because [specify]:

5. No previous application has been made for enforcement of the Post-adoption Contact Agreement to any court or judge, except [specify; delete if inapplicable]:

WHEREFORE, Petitioner requests that this Court enter an order enforcing the Post-adoption Contact Agreement.

_____
Petitioner

_____   _____
Print or type name

_____
Signature of Attorney, if any

_____
Attorney's Name (Print or Type)

_____   _____
Attorney's Address and Telephone #

<u>VERIFICATION</u>

STATE OF NEW YORK   )
)SS.:
COUNTY OF   )

_____, being duly sworn, deposes and says:

That (s)he is _____ and is acquainted with the facts and circumstances of the above-entitled proceeding; that (s)he has read the foregoing petition and knows the contents thereof; that the same is true to (his)(her) own knowledge except as to those matters therein stated to be alleged upon information and belief, and that as to those matters (s)he believes it to be true.

_____
Petitioner

Sworn to before me this
      day of   ,

_____
(Deputy) Clerk of the Court
Notary Public

FORM 18   **Order Determining Petition for Enforcement of Post-Adoption Contact Agreement (After Adoption Finalization)**

Domestic Relations Law §112-b

Adoption Form 18
(Agency Adoption– Order Determining Petition
for Enforcement of Post -adoption Contact
Agreement After Adoption Finalization)
(9/2005)

At a term of the Surrogate's Court of the
State of New York, held in and for the
County of   ,
at   New York,
on   ,   .

PRESENT:
        Hon.
            Judge
_____

In the Matter of a Post-adoption
Contact Agreement Concerning

Child's Name:
Date of Birth:

Pursuant to Section 112-b
of the Domestic Relations Law

Docket No.
ORDER DETERMINING PETITION
FOR ENFORCEMENT OF
POST-ADOPTION
CONTACT AGREEMENT (After
Adoption Finalization)

_____

NOTICE: WILLFUL FAILURE TO OBEY THE TERMS AND CONDITIONS OF THIS ORDER MAY RESULT IN COMMITMENT TO JAIL FOR A TERM NOT TO EXCEED SIX MONTHS.

The petition of [specify]:   , dated [specify]:   , having been filed requesting enforcement of a Post-adoption Contact Agreement, approved by the Family Court,   County, and incorporated into the Order of Adoption by Order of Incorporation, dated [specify]:   by the [specify]: ☐ Family ☐ Surrogate's Court,   County;

And all parties to the Post-adoption Contact Agreement, including the law guardian, having been duly served with notice of this proceeding and the following having personally appeared [specify]:

And the matter having duly come on for a hearing before this Court, and the Court, after hearing the proof and testimony offered in relation to the case, having determined that [check applicable box]:

☐ The following Respondent [specify]:   violated the Post-adoption Contact Agreement as follows [specify]:

and enforcement of the Post-adoption Contact Agreement ☐ is ☐ is not in the child's best interests for

FORM 18   SURROGATE'S COURT   **AF-92**

the following reasons [specify]:

OR

    ☐ The Post-adoption Contact Agreement has not been violated.

NOW THEREFORE, it is

    ☐ ORDERED that the petition is GRANTED and the Post-adoption Contact Agreement is enforced. as follows [specify]:

OR

    ☐ ORDERED that the petition for enforcement of the Post-adoption Contact Agreement is DISMISSED.

ENTER

_____
Judge of the Family Court

Dated:

    PURSUANT TO SECTION 1113 OF THE FAMILY COURT ACT, AN APPEAL FROM THIS ORDER MUST BE TAKEN WITHIN 30 DAYS OF RECEIPT OF THE ORDER BY APPELLANT IN COURT, 35 DAYS FROM THE DATE OF MAILING OF THE ORDER TO APPELLANT BY THE CLERK OF COURT, OR 30 DAYS AFTER SERVICE BY A PARTY OR THE LAW GUARDIAN UPON THE APPELLANT, WHICHEVER IS EARLIEST.

Check applicable box:
☐ Order mailed on [specify date(s) and to whom mailed]:_____
☐ Order received in court on [specify date(s) and to whom given]:_____

FORM 21-A   Petition for Temporary Guardianship

D.R.L.§115-c; S.C.P.A.§1725

Form 21-A
(Petition for
Temporary
Guardianship)
9/2008

FAMILY COURT OF THE STATE OF NEW YORK
COUNTY OF _____
....

In the Matter of the Temporary
Guardianship of A Child Whose
First Name is   (Docket)(File)No.
_____   _____
                                                 Petition for Temporary
                                                 Guardianship

....

The Petitioner(s) respectfully allege(s) to the Court that:

1. Physical custody of [specify child's first and last name]: _____,
a child born on _____, was transferred to [specify]:_____
and _____ for the purposes of adoption on the _____ day of
_____ , by [specify]:_____ , the child's ☐ parent(s)
☐ guardian(s), and the requirements for certification of [specify]: _____
as qualified adoptive parents herein were [check applicable box]: ☐complied with
☐ duly waived by order of the _____ , Court, County of _____
dated _____,___.

2. The residence and telephone number of Petitioner(s) are:_____
_____

3. The full name(s) and address(es) of the birth parent(s) of the child are: _____
_____
_____.

4. The anticipated name of the child subsequent to adoption will be: _____
_____
_____.

5. The anticipated residence of the child subsequent to adoption will be: _____

Form 21-A page 2

6. A consent to the adoption of the child was duly executed pursuant to section 115-b of the Domestic Relations Law on _____,____ . A copy of the consent to the adoption is annexed hereto.

7. The child will be residing with Petitioner(s), and a petition for adoption of the child by Petitioner(s) will be filed in the _____ Court of the County of _____, State of New York, within 45 days of the execution of the consent to adoption of the child.

8. No previous petition has been filed or application made to any court or judge for the relief sought herein (except)[include any proceedings dismissed or withdrawn]: _____
_____
_____
_____

WHEREFORE, Petitioner(s) request(s) an order granting temporary guardianship of the child to Petitioner(s).

_____
Petitioner(s)

_____

_____
Applicant

_____
Print or type name

_____
Signature of Attorney, if any

_____
Attorney's Name (Print or Type)

_____
_____
_____
Attorney's Address and Telephone Number

Dated: _____,____ .

Form 21-A page 3

VERIFICATION

STATE OF NEW YORK   )
)ss.:
COUNTY OF_____)

_____ , being duly sworn, says
that (he) (she) (they) (is)(are) the Petitioner(s) in the above-named proceeding and that the
foregoing petition is true to (his) (her) (their) own knowledge, except as to matters therein
stated to be alleged on information and belief, and as to those matters (he)(she)(they) believe(s)
it to be true.

                              _____
                              Petitioner(s)

Subscribed and sworn to before me
this_____day of_____,____.

_____
(Deputy) Clerk of the Court
      Notary Public

FORM 21-B   Order (Temporary Guardianship of the Person)

D.R.L.§ 115-c
S.C.P.A.§ 1725.

Form 21-B
(Temporary
Guardianship)
12/97

At a term of the Surrogate's court of the
State of New York, held in and for the
County of   ,
at   New York
on   , 19   .

PRESENT:
    Hon.
      Judge

_____

In the Matter of the Temporary
Guardianship of A Child Whose
First Name is

(Docket)(File) No.

ORDER
(Temporary
Guardianship
of the Person)

_____

Upon reading and filing the petition herein duly verified on   applying for
(temporary guardianship of   , a child placed for adoption,) (an
order approving the adoption of   , an adoptive child) and
it appearing that the child will be residing with the Petitioner(s) and that Petitioner(s) intend to
file for adoption of the child within 45 days of the execution of the consent to the adoption of
the child, and the Court having inquired of the statewide central register of child abuse and
maltreatment and having been informed that the (child)(Petitioner(s)) (is)(are)not) a subject of
or another person named in an indicated report filed with such register as such terms are
defined in section 412 of the Social Services Law, and the Court having given due
consideration to any information contained therein,

          And it appearing further it is (not) in the best interests of the child to grant said
petition

          NOW therefore, it is hereby

Form 21-b Page 2

(ORDERED that said application for temporary guardianship is granted; and it is further

ORDERED that   be appointed temporary guardians) of the person of   :and it is further .

ORDERED that this order shall expire on or the date a final order of adoption is entered, whichever is sooner.)

(ORDERED, that said application for temporary guardianship is denied;) (and it is further)

(ORDERED that the proceeding herein be continued for further investigation;) (and it is further)

(ORDERED that upon notice to   ,the Petitioner(s) shall appear on the   day of   , 19   , at   to show cause why the child should not be removed from their home;)

PURSUANT TO SECTION 1113 OF THE FAMILY COURT ACT, AN APPEAL FROM THIS ORDER MUST BE TAKEN WITHIN 30 DAYS OF RECEIPT OF THE ORDER BY APPELLANT IN COURT, 35 DAYS FROM THE DATE OF MAILING OF THE ORDER TO APPELLANT BY THE CLERK OF COURT, OR 30 DAYS AFTER SERVICE BY A PARTY OR THE LAW GUARDIAN UPON THE APPELLANT, WHICHEVER IS EARLIEST.

ENTER

_____
(J.F.C) (Surrogate)

Dated: , 19   .

Check applicable box:
☐ Order mailed on [specify date(s) and to whom mailed]:_____
☐ Order received in court on [specify date(s) and to whom given]:_____

FORM 21-C   Notice (Temporary Guardianship of the Person)

D.R.L. § 115-c
S.C.P.A. § 1725

SURROGATE'S COURT OF THE STATE OF NEW YORK
COUNTY OF

Form 21-C
(Temporary
Guardianship)
12/97

_____

In the Matter of the Temporary   (Docket) (File) No.
Guardianship of A Child Whose
First Name is   NOTICE

_____

TO:

       PLEASE TAKE NOTICE that pursuant to section 1725 of the Surrogate's Court Procedure Act and section 661 of the Family Court Act:

       1. A petition for adoption must be filed int his Court within 45 days form the date of the signing of the consent to the adoption which has been filed as part of the above-entitled proceeding.

       2. Any order or decree of temporary guardianship entered in the above-entitled proceeding will expire no later than nine (9) months following its issuance or upon the entry of a final order of adoption, whichever is sooner, unless, upon application to the court, it is extended for good cause.

       3. Any order or decree of temporary guardianship entered int he above-entitled proceeding will terminate upon withdrawal or denial of a petition to adopt the above-named child, unless the court orders a continuation of such order or decree.

Dated: , 19 .

_____
Clerk of the Court

_____
Petitioner

_____
Print or type name

_____
Signature of Attorney, if any

_____
Attorney's Name (Print or Type)

_____
_____
Attorney's Address and Telephone Number

FORM 21-D   **Notice (Denial or Withdrawal of Application) (Removal of Child)**

D.R.L.§115-C
S.C.P.A.§1725

Form 21-D
(Temporary
Guardianship)
12/97

SURROGATE'S COURT OF THE STATE OF NEW YORK
COUNTY OF
_____

In the Matter of the Temporary
Guardianship of A Child Whose
First Name is

(Docket) (File) No.

NOTICE
(Denial of Withdrawal of
Application; Removal of
Child)

_____

TO.

PLEASE TAKE NOTICE that on the   day of   19 :

(   ) the petition of   for an order of temporary
     guardianship was denied.

(   ) the petition for adoption filed by   has been
     (withdrawn) (denied).

(   ) the child,   , has been removed from the physical
     custody of

(   ) the order dated the   day of   19 , granting temporary
     guardianship of the child,   , to
     has expired without the entry of a final order of adoption.

     The law requires this notice to be sent to you. You may wish to consult a lawyer about your legal rights at this time.

Dated: ,19 .

Form 21-D page 2

_____

CLERK OF THE COURT

_____

 Petitioner

_____

Print or type name

_____

Signature of Attorney, if any

_____

Attorney's Name (Print or Type)

_____
_____

Attorney's Address and Telephone Number

FORM 21-E   **Affidavit (Change of Circumstance Since Certification as Qualified Adoptive Parent)**

D.R.L. § 115-c
S.C.P.A.§ 1725

Form 21-E
(Temporary
Guardianship)
12/97

SURROGATE'S COURT OF THE STATE OF NEW YORK
COUNTY OF _____

In the Matter of the Temporary
Guardianship of A Child Whose
First Name is

(Docket)(File) No.

AFFIDAVIT
(Change of circumstance
since certification as qualified
adoptive parent)

_____

STATE OF NEW YORK   )
                       :ss..
COUNTY OF   )

_____, being duly sworn depose(s) and say(s):

1. Deponent(s) (was)(were) certified as (a) qualified adoptive parent(s) by order of the _____ Court, County of _____, dated _____ 19____ ;

2. The following change(s) in circumstance relevant and material to such certification (has)(have) taken place since that date:

Dated:

_____
Petitioner

_____
Print or type name

_____
Signature of Attorney, if any

_____
Attorney's Name (Print or Type)

_____
Attorney's Address and Telephone Number

Sworn to before me this
    day of _____, 19 .

FORM 22   Petition (Certification as a Qualified Adoptive Parent)

D.R.L. §§ 115, 115-d

Form 22
(Certification
As Qualified
Adoptive Parent)
9/99

....

In the Matter of the Adoption of
A Child whose First Name is

by Adoptive Parent(s)

(Docket)(File) No.

PETITION
(Certification
as a Qualified
Adoptive Parent)
(Private-Placement)

....

The Petitioner(s) respectfully allege(s) to this Court that:

[Delete inapplicable provisions]:

1. (His)(Her)(Their) name(s), residential address and telephone number are:

Petitioner (specify name):

Petitioner (specify name):

2. (He)(She)(They) (is)(are) seeking certification by this court as (a) person(s) qualified to take custody of the adoptive child [specify first name]:   , (prior to) (contemporaneous with) the filing of a private-placement adoption petition.

3. (He)(She)(They) (has) (have) (not) been the subject of a pending child protective investigation or of an indicated report, as such term is defined in section 412 of the Social Services Law, filed with the statewide register of child abuse and maltreatment pursuant to Title six of Article six of the Social Services Law.

4. A pre-placement investigation will be undertaken by a disinterested person, as such term is defined in section four of 115-d of the Domestic Relations Law, and a written report of such investigation will be furnished directly to the court by such disinterested person.

5. The marital, family status and history of the Petitioner(s) (is) (are):

Petitioner (specify name):

Petitioner (specify name):

6. The physical and mental health of the Petitioner(s) (is)(are):

Petitioner (specify name):

Petitioner (specify name):

7. Attached hereto and made a part hereof is a statement of all property owned by and income of the Petitioner(s).

8. Petitioner(s) (has) (have)(not ever been) (a) respondent(s) in any proceeding in a court concerning alleged (abused) (neglected) (abandoned) children, (except as follows):

Form 22 page 2

Petitioner (specify name):

Petitioner (specify name):

(b) (Petitioner(s) (have) no prior criminal convictions or founded findings of child abuse or neglect (except as follows):[1]

Petitioner (specify name):

Petitioner (specify name):

9. Petitioner(s) (has)(have) (not) made any prior application for certification as (a) qualified adoptive parent(s); if so, the disposition and disposition date of such application was as follows:

Petitioner (specify name):

Petitioner (specify name):

);

10. Petitioner(s) (do)(does) (not) intend to cause a pre-placement investigation to be undertaken (and request(s) this court to appoint a disinterested person to conduct such pre-placement investigation;)

WHEREFORE, Petitioner (s) pray(s) for an order (conditionally)[2] certifying Petitioner(s) as (a) qualified adoptive parent(s).

/_____
Petitioner: typed or printed name   / signature

/_____
Petitioner: typed or printed name   / signature

/_____
Attorney: typed or printed name/ signature

_____
Attorney's Address and Telephone Number

---

[1]Fingerprint cards must be provided to the Court so that a criminal history report can be obtained from the N.Y.S. Division of Criminal Justice Services pursuant to Domestic Relations Law Section 115-d(3-a).

[2]Applicable only if petition seeks conditional certification pursuant to D.R.L. Section 115-d(6).

Form 22 Page 3

<u>VERIFICATION</u>

STATE OF NEW YORK   )
                             ss:
COUNTY   )

being duly sworn, says that (he)(she)(they) (is)(are) the Petitioner(s) in the above-named proceeding and that the foregoing petition is true to (his)(her)(their) own knowledge, except as to matters therein stated to be on information and belief and as to those matters (he)(she)(they) believe(s) to be true.

_____/_____
Petitioner: typed or printed name/ signature

_____/_____
Petitioner: typed or printed name/ signature

Sworn to before me this
day of   ,   .

_____
(Deputy) Clerk of the Court
     Notary Public

FORM 23   Affidavit and Report (Disinterested Person Certification Proceeding) (Private-Placement)

D.R.L §§ 115, 115-d.

Form 23
(Certification
as Qualified
Adoptive Parent)
9/99

SURROGATE'S COURT OF THE STATE OF NEW YORK
COUNTY OF

In the Matter of the Adoption of
A Child Whose First Name Is   (Docket)(File) No.

AFFIDAVIT and
REPORT (Disinterested
Person-Certification

by
  Proceeding)
Adoptive Parent   (Private-Placement)

State of New York   )
                           :ss..
County of   )

                                        being duly sworn deposes and says that:

        1. (He)(She) is a disinterested person as such person is defined in section 115-d of the
Domestic Relations Law in that:
and has no interest in the out come of the application of the part(y)(ies) herein for certification as
qualified adoptive apparent(s);

        2. The following fee(s) (have been) (will be) paid to deponent for services rendered in
connection with the pre-placement investigation performed in connection with this certification
proceeding:

                                                ;

        3. The following is deponent's report of (his)(her) investigation into the truth and accuracy
of the allegations set forth in the petition of   , as qualified
adoptive parents in the proceeding for certification and (deponent's investigation of the various factors
relevant to the suitability of the petitioners as qualified adoptive parents:

FORM 23   SURROGATE'S COURT   **AF-106**

Form 23 page 2

(a) Date, place and duration of personal interview and visit at petitioners home:

(b) Report:

(c) other facts relating to familial, social, religious, emotional and financial circumstances of petitioners relevant to certification as a qualified adoptive parent(s).

Dated:

_____
Affiant (Disinterested Person)

_____
Print or type name

Sworn to before me
this   day
of   ,

_____
Notary Public

FORM 24   Order (Certification as a Qualified Adoptive Parent)

D.R.L§§ 115, 115-d

Form 24
(Certification as
Qualified Adoptive
Parent)
(9/2006)

At a term of the Surrogate's Court of the
State of New York, held in and for the
County of_____ ,
at_____New York
on_____ ,_____ .

PRESENT:
    Hon. _____
        Judge

_____

In the Matter of the Adoption of
A Child Whose First Name is

(Docket)(File) No.

_____

ORDER
(Certification as a
Qualified Adoptive
Parent)

_____

by
Adoptive Parent

_____

NOTICE: THIS ORDER IS VALID ONLY UNTIL

The petition of_____, verified the_____day of_____,_____,
and filed in this court on the_____ day of _____,_____, applying for certification
as (a) qualified parent(s) of the above-named adoptive child and a report having been filed herein
by _____, a disinterested person as defined in section 115-d of the
Domestic Relations Law,

AND a criminal history check having been performed and such check having revealed no
criminal convictions enumerated in section 115-d(3-a) of the Domestic Relations Law (except
[specify; delete if inapplicable]: _____

AND this Court having determined that the best interests of the above-named adoptive
child [check applicable box]: ☐ will ☐will not be promoted by the adoption by the Petitioner(s),

Now therefore upon consideration of the report and all other relevant and material factors,
it is hereby

☐ ORDERED that _____are certified as (a) qualified adoptive

parent(s) of the above-named adoptive child and may accept physical custody of a child for the purposes of adoption prior to or contemporaneous with the filing of an adoption petition.

OR

☐ ORDERED that the application by for certification as (a) qualified adoptive parent(s) is hereby denied for the following reasons:_____

_____

_____.)

PURSUANT TO SECTION 1113 OF THE FAMILY COURT ACT, AN APPEAL FROM THIS ORDER MUST BE TAKEN WITHIN 30 DAYS OF RECEIPT OF THE ORDER BY APPELLANT IN COURT, 35 DAYS FORM THE DATE OF MAILING OF THE ORDER TO APPELLANT BY THE CLERK OF COURT, OR 30 DAYS AFTER SERVICE BY A PARTY OR THE LAW GUARDIAN UPON THE APPELLANT, WHICHEVER IS EARLIEST.

ENTER

_____
(Judge of the Family Court)(Surrogate).

Dated:_____,_____ .

Check applicable box:
☐ Order mailed on specify date(s) and to whom mailed]: _____
☐ Order received in court on [specify date(s) and to whom given]: _____

FORM 25   Order (Conditional Certification as a Qualified Adoptive Parent)

D.R.L.§§ 115, 115-d

Form 25
(Conditional Certification
as Qualified Adoptive Parent)
(9/2006)

At a term of the Surrogate's Court of the
State of New York, held in and for the
County of _____ ,
at _____ ,New York
on _____

P R E S E N T:
   Hon._____
      Judge
....

In the Matter of the Adoption of
A Child Whose First Name is   (Docket) (File) No.

                                                    _____
                                                    ORDER
_____   (Conditional Certification
                                                    as a Qualified Adoptive
                                                    Parent)

by
Adoptive Parent(s)
....

The petition of _____ verified the _____ day of _____ ,____,
having been filed in this court on the _____ day of _____,____, applying for certification
as (a) qualified parent(s) of the adoptive child above-named; and

The petition and criminal history check indicating no prior criminal convictions as
enumerated in Domestic Relations Law §115-d (3-a), pending child protective investigations,
or founded findings of child abuse or neglect; and

A report having been filed herein by_____, a disinterested
person as defined in section 115-d of the Domestic Relations Law; and

This Court having determined, based upon the information submitted, that adoption
of the above-named child by the Petitioner(s) is in the child's best interests; and

Pending completion of any further reports, investigations or inquiries ordered by the
Court or required by any other statute or Court rule;

Now, therefore, upon consideration of said report and all other relevant and material factors, it is hereby

ORDERED that _____ (is) (are) conditionally certified as (a) qualified adoptive parent(s) of the above-named adoptive child and may accept physical custody of such child for the purposes of adoption prior to or contemporaneous with the filing of an adoption petition.

NOTICE: THIS ORDER OF CONDITIONAL CERTIFICATION IS VALID UNTIL REPLACED BY AN ORDER OF CERTIFICATION OR BY AN ORDER DENYING CERTIFICATION, BUT IN NO EVENT BEYOND 180 DAYS OF THIS DATE.

PURSUANT TO SECTION 1113 OF THE FAMILY COURT ACT, AN APPEAL FROM THIS ORDER MUST BE TAKEN WITHIN 30 DAYS OF RECEIPT OF THE ORDER BY APPELLANT IN COURT, 35 DAYS FROM THE DATE OF MAILING OF THE ORDER TO APPELLANT BY THE CLERK OF COURT, OR 30 DAYS AFTER SERVICE BY A PARTY OR THE LAW GUARDIAN UPON THE APPELLANT, WHICHEVER IS EARLIEST.

ENTER

_____
(Judge of the Family Court.) (Surrogate)

Dated:_____,_____.

Check applicable box:
☐ Order mailed on [specify date(s) and to whom mailed]:_____
☐ Order received in court on [specify date(s) and to whom given]:_____

FORM 26   Petition for Extension of Expired Certification (Private Placement)

D.R.L. §§ 115, 115-d(9)

Form 26
(Certification Petition
for Extension of Expired
Certification - Private
Placement)
9/99

....
In the Matter of the Adoption of
A Child whose First Name is

by Adoptive Parent(s)

(Docket)(File) No.

PETITION
FOR EXTENSION
OF EXPIRED
CERTIFICATION
(Private Placement)

....

The Petitioner(s) respectfully allege(s) to this Court that:

1. (He)(She)(They) filed a petition to adopt the above-described child in this Court on   ,

2. Petitioner(s) (was)(were) certified as a qualified adoptive parent(s), by order of the Court, County of
                    , dated   ,   , which order expired on   ,   , within one year
prior to the filing of the adoption petition.

3. The following change(s) in circumstances relevant and material to such certification (has)(have)
taken place since issuance and expiration of the last certification:

4. Submitted herewith is written verification of any such change in circumstances or lack thereof by
, a disinterested person as defined in section 115-d(4) of the Domestic Relations Law.

WHEREFORE, Petitioner(s) (prays) (prays) for an order extending the termination date of the earlier
certification until eighteen months from the date of filing of the adoption petition, that is,

_____/_____
Adoptive Parent: typed or printed name/ signature

_____/_____
Adoptive Parents: typed or printed name/ signature

_____/_____
Attorney: typed or printed name/ signature

_____
Attorney's Address and Telephone Number

Form 26 page 2

<u>VERIFICATION</u>

STATE OF NEW YORK)
                                    ss:
COUNTY)

being duly sworn, says that (he)(she) (they)(is)(are) the Petitioner(s) in the above-named proceeding and that the foregoing petition is true to (his)(her)(their) own knowledge, except as to matters therein stated to be alleged on information and belief and as to those matters (he)(she) (they) believe(s) it to be true.

_____ /_____
Adoptive Parent: typed or printed name/ signature

_____ /_____
Adoptive Parent: typed or printed name/ signature

Sworn to before me this
   day of   ,

_____
(Deputy)Clerk of the Court
   Notary Public

Resworn to before me this
   day of   ,   .

_____
Judge of the   Court

FORM 26-A **Affidavit and Report (Disinterested Person-Extension of Expired Certification)**

D.R.L. §§ 115, 115-d (9)

Form 26-a
(Certification as
Qualified Adoptive
Parent)
9/99

SURROGATE'S COURT OF THE STATE OF NEW YORK
COUNTY OF

In the Matter of the Adoption of
A Child Whose First Name is

(Docket) (File) No.

AFFIDAVIT and
REPORT
(Disinterested Person-
Extension of Expired by
Certification)

Adoptive Parent(s)

　　　[Name]　　　　　　　　　　　　　　, being duly sworn, deposes and
says that:

　　　1. I am a disinterested person as defined in section 115-d (4) of the Domestic Relations Law
in that (he) (she) has no interest in the outcome of the application of the part (y) (ies) herein for
certification as (a) qualified adoptive parent (s).

　　　2. The following fee (s) (have been) (will be) paid to deponent for services rendered in
connection with the application for extension of certification:

　　　3. I have read the affidavit and report prepared by
and submitted in support of the petition for certification as (a) qualified adoptive parent (s) submitted
by petitioner (s) on　　　　　　　,　　. On information and belief, an order granting
certification as a qualified adoptive parent (s) was made by the　　　　　　　　　Court,
　　　　　　　　County, on　　　　,　, and expired on　　　,　.

　　　4. The following Change (s) in circumstances relevant and material to the extension of such
certification (has) (have) taken place since the issuance and expiration of the last certification:

　　　5. The source of my knowledge concerning the circumstances of the petitioner's (s') family
and household is: [include date, place and duration of personal interview and visit at petitioner's (s')
home.]

FORM 26-A　　　　　SURROGATE'S COURT　　　　　**AF-114**

Form 26-a page 2

Dated:

_____
Affiant (Disinterested Person)

_____
Print or type name

Sworn to before me this
　　day of　　　　　　　　　,　　.

_____
　　Notary Public

FORM 27-A   **Petition for Access to Sealed Adoption Records (Domestic Relations Law-Section 114)**

D.R.L. § 114

Adoption Form 27-A
(Adoption--Petition for Access to
Sealed Adoption Records)
(9/2006)

SURROGATE'S COURT OF THE STATE OF NEW YORK
COUNTY OF _____

In the Matter of the Adoption of   (Docket)(File) No. _____
A Child Whose First Name is

_____   PETITION FOR
                                                     ACCESS TO SEALED
                                                     ADOPTION RECORDS
_____

TO THE SURROGATE'S COURT OF THE COUNTY OF [specify]: _____
_____

The Petitioner respectfully alleges to this Court that:

1.   [Check applicable box]:
      ☐ I am the child who was adopted in the above-entitled proceeding.
      ☐ My relationship to the above-named child is as follows [specify]: _____
      _____

2.   a. I reside at [specify address and telephone number]: _____
      _____

      b. My mailing address, if different from the above, is [specify]: _____
      _____

3.   Upon information and belief, [check applicable box]:
      ☐ [Applicable where Petitioner is the adoptee]: I was born in [specify city, village or town and
State]: _____ on or about [specify date]: _____A certified copy of my birth
certificate is attached.
      ☐ [Applicable where Petitioner is not the adoptee]: [specify adoptee's name]: _____
was born in [specify city, village or town and State]: _____ on or about [specify date]: ____
      A certified copy of the birth certificate is attached.

4.   Upon information and belief, [check applicable box]:
      ☐ [Applicable where Petitioner is the adoptee]: I was adopted pursuant to court order in the
[specify county and court, if known]: _____

      ☐ [Applicable where Petitioner is not the adoptee]: [specify adoptee's name]:_____
was adopted pursuant to court order in the [specify county and court, if known]: _____

5.   A request for information ☐ has ☐ has not been made of the Adoption Information Registry.
      **[Direct inquiries to: NYS Department of Health, Adoption Information Registry, P.O.
      Box 2602, Albany, New York 12220- 2602, (518)474-9600]**

6.   The names, dates of death, permanent addresses of the adoptive parents, if living, and the
      adoptee's birth name, if known, are as follows [specify]: _____
      _____

7.   [Check applicable box(es)]:
      ☐ I am requesting access to sealed adoption records on medical grounds for the following

reasons [specify]: _____

[NOTE: If your request is based on medical grounds, you must attach a medical certification from a physician licensed to practice medicine in the State of New York addressing a serious physical or mental illness. Such certification shall identify the information required to address the illness.]

☐ I am requesting access to sealed adoption records for good cause, other than medical, for the following reasons [specify]: _____

☐ [Applicable to Native-American individuals 18 years of age and older]: I am requesting access to sealed adoption records, including information about my birth parents' tribal affiliation(s), if any, and other information necessary to protect any rights flowing from such tribal affiliations.

8. No previous application has been made for the relief requested herein except as follows: [Enter "NONE", or specify]: _____

I understand that the Court may appoint a law guardian for the purpose of reviewing the file and determining whether the information being sought is in the file and to undertake such other and further instructions that the Court may require.

WHEREFORE, for the reasons stated above, I respectfully request access to the sealed adoption records and information sought above and for such other and further relief as this Court deems just and proper.

Dated: _____, _____.

_____
Petitioner's signature

_____
Petitioner: Print or type name

_____
Attorney' signature, if any

_____
Attorney's Address and Telephone number

VERIFICATION

STATE OF NEW YORK)
                 :ss.:
COUNTY OF _____)

being duly sworn, says that (he)(she) is the Petitioner(s) in the above-named proceeding and that the foregoing petition is true to (his)(her) own knowledge, except as to matters stated to be alleged on information and belief and as to those matters (he)(she) believe(s) them to be true.

_____/_____
Petitioner: typed or printed name/   Signature

Sworn to before me this
_____ day of _____, _____.

_____
(Deputy)Clerk of the Court
Notary Public

FORM 27-B　　**Notice of Petition for Access to Sealed Adoption Records (Domestic Relations Law-Section 114)**

D.R.L. § 114

Adoption Form 27-B
(Adoption-Notice of Petition for
Access to Sealed Adoption Records)
(9/2006)

SURROGATE'S COURT OF THE STATE OF NEW YORK
COUNTY OF _____

In the Matter of the Adoption of
A Child Whose First Name is

(Docket)(File) No. _____

_____

NOTICE OF PETITION
FOR ACCESS TO SEALED
ADOPTION RECORDS

NOTICE IS HEREBY GIVEN THAT:

1.　A petition has been filed in Surrogate's Court, _____County, requesting an order permitting access to sealed adoption records regarding the above-named child. This petition will be heard in the Surrogate's Court, _____County, located at [specify address and court part]: _____
on [specify date and time]: _____

2.　The Petitioner [specify name and address, unless confidential]: _____
　　is seeking access　☐ for medical reasons.
　　　　　　　　　　　☐ for good cause other than medical reasons
　　　　　　　　　　　☐ in order to obtain information about tribal affiliation.

3.　The following are the names and post office addresses of each person named or referred to in the petition as the living adoptive parents who have not already waived notice of this proceeding or consented to the relief requested in the petition, and each additional person to whom the Court may direct service of this Notice of Petition for Access to Sealed Adoption Records:

Name	Mailing Address	Relationship

Date: _____

_____
Name of Attorney, if any

_____
Attorney's Address and Telephone number

[Note: This Notice of Petition for Access to Sealed Adoption Records is served upon you as required by law. You are **not** required to appear or to respond. However, should you fail to appear or respond on or before the date set forth in Paragraph 1, it will be assumed you do not object to the relief requested. You may have an attorney appear for you.]

Official Forms

FORM 27-C   **Affidavit of Service of Notice of Petition for Access to Sealed Adoption Records**

D.R.L. § 114
[This form must be filed at least two days
before the return date in Court. It must state
the date, time and place of service]

Adoption Form 27-C
(Adoption- Affidavit of Service
of Petition for Access to Sealed
Adoption Records)
(9/2006)

SURROGATE'S COURT OF THE STATE OF NEW YORK
COUNTY OF _____

In the Matter of the Adoption of
A Child Whose First Name is

(Docket)(File) No. _____

_____

_____

AFFIDAVIT OF SERVICE
OF PETITION FOR
ACCESS TO SEALED
ADOPTION RECORDS

STATE OF _____)

COUNTY OF _____) ss:

    I, [name]: _____ of [state residence of business address]: _____
_____ having been duly sworn, deposes and states the following under penalties of perjury:
    1. I am over the age of eighteen years.
    2. I personally served the Notice of Petition for Access to Sealed Adoption Records on
each person named below, each of whom I knew to be the person mentioned and described in the
Notice, by delivering to and leaving with each of them personally a true copy of the Notice:
Name: _____
Date and Time served: _____
Place served: _____
Physical description Of person served: Sex: _____ Skin color: _____ Hair color: _____
                 Approximate age: _____ Weight: ____ Height: _____

Name: _____
Date and Time served: _____
Place served: _____
Physical description of person served: Sex: _____ Skin color: _____ Hair color: _____
                 Approximate age: _____ Weight: ____ Height: _____

    3. None of the persons named above is in the military service as defined by the Act of
Congress known as the "Soldiers' and Sailors' Civil Relief Act of 1940" and the New York
"Soldiers' and Sailors' Civil Relief Act."
Dated: _____, _____.

_____
Affiant

_____
Print or Type Name

Sworn to before me this
___ day of _____, _____.

_____
(Deputy) Clerk of the Court
Notary Public

FORM 27-D   **Waiver of Notice of Petition for Access to Sealed Adoption Records/ Consent (Domestic Relations Law-Section 114)**

D.R.L. § 1 14

Adoption Form 27-D
(Adoption-Waiver of Notice of
Petition for Access to
Sealed Adoption Records)
(9/2006)

SURROGATE'S COURT OF THE STATE OF NEW YORK
COUNTY OF _____

In the Matter of the Adoption of
A Child Whose First Name is

_____

(Docket)(File) No. _____

WAIVER OF NOTICE OF PETITION
FOR ACCESS TO SEALED
ADOPTION RECORDS

_____

1.   I am the [check applicable box]: ☐ Adoptive Mother ☐ Adoptive Father ☐ Other
[specify]:_____ of the above-named child. I am 18 years of age or older.

2.   I am waiving the service of Notice of Petition for Access to Sealed Adoption Records in this
matter and am consenting to the release of sealed adoption records to [specify]. _____
_____

Dated: _____

_____
(Signature of Interested Party)

_____
(Print Name)

STATE OF_____)

COUNTY OF_____) ss:

On the_____ day of_____ in the year_____, before me, the
undersigned, _____
personally appeared_____, personally known to me or proved to me on
the basis of satisfactory evidence to be the individual (s) whose name (s) is/are subscribed to the within
instrument and acknowledged to me that he/she/they executed the same in his/her/their capacity (ies), and
that by his/her/their signatures (s) on the instrument, the individual (s), or the person, upon behalf of which
the individual (s) acted, executed the instrument.

_____
Notary Public
(Deputy) Clerk of Court

_____
Signature of Attorney, if any

_____
Attorney's Name (print or type)

_____
Attorney's Address and Telephone Number

FORM 27-E   Adoption-Order on Petition for Access to Sealed Adoption Records

D.R.L. § 114

Adoption Form 27-E
(Adoption-Order on Petition for
Access to Sealed Adoption Records)
(9/2006)

At a term of the Surrogate's Court of the
State of New York, held in and for the
County of ―――――――――――――――,
at ――――――――――, New York,
on ――――――――, ―――――― .

PRESENT:
   Hon. ――――――――――――――――――――
       Judge ――――――――――――――――

In the Matter of the Adoption of
A Child Whose First Name is

――――――――――――――――――――――

(Docket)(File) No. ――――――――

ORDER ON PETITION
FOR ACCESS TO SEALED
ADOPTION RECORDS

   The petition for access to sealed adoption records of the above-named child having been filed in this Court, and notice having been given to necessary parties,

   NOW, and upon all the papers and proceedings herein, it is hereby [check applicable box(es)]: ―――――――――――――――――――――――――――――――

   ☐ ORDERED that the Petition is GRANTED and that [specify]: ――――――――――
――――――― shall be given, access to sealed adoption records on the following grounds:
   ☐ To obtain medical information [specify]: ――――――――――――――――――

   ☐ Other good cause [specify]: ――――――――――――――――――――――

   ☐ [Applicable to petitions brought by Native-American adults, 18 and older]: to obtain information on tribal affiliation [specify]: ――――――――――――――――――
――――――――――――――――――――――――――――――――――――
OR
☐ ORDERED that the Petition is DENIED for the following reason(s) [specify]: ――――
――――――――――――――――――――――――――――――――――――

   AND IT IS FURTHER ORDERED that [specify; delete if inapplicable]: ――――――
――――――――――――――――――――――――――――――――――――

                            ENTER

Dated: ――――――――――
――――――――, ―――― .

――――――――――――――――――
☐ Judge of the Family Court ☐ Surrogate

Adoption Form 27-E Page 2

PURSUANT TO SECTION 11 13 OF THE FAMILY COURT ACT,
AN APPEAL FROM THIS ORDER MUST BE TAKEN WITHIN 30
DAYS OF RECEIPT OF THE ORDER BY APPELLANT IN COURT,
35 DAYS FROM THE DATE OF MAILING OF THE ORDER TO
APPELLANT BY THE CLERK OF COURT, OR 30 DAYS AFTER
SERVICE BY A PARTY OR THE LAW GUARDIAN UPON
THE APPELLANT, WHICHEVER IS EARLIEST.

Check applicable box:
☐ Order mailed on [specify date(s) and to whom mailed]:_____
☐ Order received in court on [specify date(s) and to whom given]:_____

FORM 28   Petition for Registration of Foreign Adoption Order (and Name Change)

DRL §111-c

Adoption Form 28
Petition for Registration of Foreign
Adoption Order
9/2008

FAMILY COURT OF THE STATE OF NEW YORK
COUNTY OF _____

....

In the Matter of Adoption of
A Child Whose First Name Is

Docket No._____
PETITION FOR
REGISTRATION OF A
FOREIGN ADOPTION ORDER
(AND NAME CHANGE)

_____

....

The Petitioner(s) respectfully allege(s) to this Court that :

1. (I am)(We are) the ☐adoptive parent(s)☐guardian ☐ guardian ad litem
of [child's name]:_____, who was born on [date of birth]:
_____in [country]:_____.
The child was adopted in [country]:_____ on [date]:_____
(I am) (We are) submitting this petition to register the attached Order of Adoption
and [delete if inapplicable]: to change the child's name to [specify]:_____
_____

2. The adoptive parent(s) and the child reside at:[specify address(es)]:[1]

Child	Adoptive Parents	Full Address
_____	_____	_____
_____	_____	_____

3. The child was granted an IR-3 immigrant visa by the United States Citizenship
and Immigration Services on [specify date]: _____

4. The name by which the adoptive child is to be known is [specify]:
_____

WHEREFORE, the Petitioner(s) request(s) an order registering the attached Order
of Adoption, [delete if inapplicable] changing the child's name, and such other and
further relief as the Court deems just and proper.

_____

[1] Unless the Court has ordered the address to be confidential on the ground that disclosure would pose an
unreasonable health or safety risk. If so, so indicate and simply list the STATE of residence. *See* Family Court Act
§154-b; Form 21 (available at www.nycourts.gov).

Dated:_____,_____.

_____/_____
Adoptive Parent: typed or printed name/ signature

_____/_____
Adoptive Parent: typed or printed name / signature

_____/_____
☐ Guardian ☐ Guardian ad Litem : typed or printed name / signature

_____/_____
Attorney , if any: typed or printed name/ signature

_____
Attorney's Address and Telephone Number

VERIFICATION

STATE OF NEW YORK   )
                                          :ss.:
COUNTY OF_____)

being duly sworn, says that (he)(she) (they)(is)(are) the Petitioner(s) in the above-named proceeding and that the foregoing petition is true to (his)(her)(their) own knowledge, except as to matters where in stated to be alleged on information and belief and as to those matters (he)(she) (they) believe(s) it to be true.

_____/_____
Adoptive Parent: typed or printed name/ signature

_____/_____
Adoptive Parent: typed or printed name / signature

_____/_____
☐ Guardian ☐ Guardian ad Litem : typed or printed name / signature

Sworn to before me this
       day of_____,_____.

_____
(Deputy)Clerk of the Court
Notary Public

FORM 28-A   **Order of Foreign Adoption (and Name Change)**

D.R.L. §§111-c

Adoption Form 28-A
(Order of Foreign Adoption
and Name Change)
9/2008

At a term of the Family Court of the
State of New York, held in and for the
County of _____,
at _____New York
on _____,_____ .

PRESENT:
    Hon. _____
      Judge

_____

In the Matter of the Adoption of
A Child Whose First Name Is

_____

             ☐Docket☐File No.

     ORDER OF FOREIGN
        ADOPTION
    (AND NAME CHANGE)

_____

        The Petition of _____ (and _____
_____), verified the_____day of _____,_____, together with the Order of
Adoption of [specify country]:_____ , dated [specify]:_____,
having been presented to this Court,

        This Court hereby finds and determines the following:
1. The names and states of residence of the adoptive parent(s) is/are [specify]:_____
_____.

2. The child [specify name]: _____
   was reported to have been born on [specify date]:_____in [country]:
_____

3. The child was adopted in [country]:_____on [specify date]:_____

4. The child was granted an IR-3 immigrant visa by the United States Citizenship and
Immigration Services on [specify date]: _____

       NOW, and upon all the papers and proceedings herein, it is

       ORDERED that the petition of _____ (and
_____) for the registration of the adoption of [child's name]:_____
is GRANTED; and it is further

       ORDERED that the Order of Adoption issued in [country]: _____

is registered in this State and is incorporated into and made a part of this Order and such Order of Adoption is deemed to have the same force and effect and is enforceable as if it had been issued by a court in the State of New York; and it is further

ORDERED that the adoptive child shall be regarded and treated in all respects as the lawful child of the adoptive parent(s); and it is further

ORDERED that the name of the adoptive child is changed to [specify]:_____ and that the adoptive child shall hereafter be known by that name; and it is further

[Check box if applicable]: ☐ORDERED that the Clerk prepare, certify and deliver a copy of this order to [specify]:_____ ; and it is further

[Check box if applicable]: ☐ORDERED that, if required by a governmental agency, including but not limited to, the United States Social Security Administration, the United States Passport Office and the New York State Department of Motor Vehicles, in connection with an application submitted by or on behalf of the adoptive child, the adoptive parent(s)' attorney [specify]: _____
is authorized to deliver a certified copy of this Order of Foreign Adoption to such agency directly or to the adoptive parent(s), as he or she deems appropriate; and it is further

ORDERED that this order, together with all other papers pertaining to the adoption, shall be filed and kept as provided in the Domestic Relations Law and shall not be subject to access or inspections except as provided in this Order or by such Law.

ENTER:

_____
☐Judge of the Family Court ☐Surrogate

Dated:_____ ,_____ .

[Applicable to orders of the Family Court]:

PURSUANT TO SECTION 1113 OF THE FAMILY COURT ACT,
AN APPEAL FROM AN ORDER OF THE FAMILY COURT MUST BE TAKEN
WITHIN 30 DAYS OF RECEIPT OF THE ORDER BY APPELLANT IN COURT, 35
DAYS FROM THE DATE OF MAILING OF THE ORDER TO APPELLANT BY THE
CLERK OF COURT, OR 30 DAYS AFTER SERVICE BY A PARTY OR THE LAW
GUARDIAN UPON THE APPELLANT, WHICHEVER IS EARLIEST.

Check applicable box:
☐ Order mailed on [specify date(s) and to whom mailed]:_____
☐ Order received in court on [specify date(s) and to whom given]:_____

Official Forms

FORM 29-A   **Petition for Adult Adoption**

SURROGATE'S COURT OF THE STATE OF NEW YORK
COUNTY OF _____

---X
In the Matter of the Adoption of

                                                                    PETITION FOR ADULT ADOPTION
_____ An Adult,
                                                                    File No. _____
---X

The Petitioner(s) respectfully allege(s) to this court that:

1. Petitioning adoptive parent is: _____

    (a) resides at: _____

        _____

    (b) is of full age, having been born on: _____

    (c) is (unmarried); or
        (married) to: _____ and living together; or living separate and
        apart pursuant to a decree or judgment of separation or pursuant to a separation agreement subscribed by
        the parties and acknowledged or proved in the form required to entitle a deed to be recorded; or living
        separate and apart for at least three years prior to commencement of the proceeding.

2. Petitioning adoptive parent is: _____

    (a) resides at: _____

        _____

    (b) is of full age, having been born on: _____

Note: If the petitioning adoptive parent is married, and his/her spouse is not joining in the petition, please
provide consent to the petition by such spouse. If consent cannot be obtained, please submit an affidavit
explaining why the spouse's consent should be dispensed with.

3. Petitioning adoptee: _____, who resides at

_____, was born on _____.

(A certified copy of the birth certificate is annexed).

29-A   (12/2016)

4. The following is information, as nearly as can be ascertained, concerning the legal parent(s) of the adoptee.

  (a) Full name, last known address of the adult adoptee's legal parent(s), date of birth:

Parent: _____

Parent: _____

5. The adoptee is seeking to change her/his name to _____ or is not seeking a name change.

6. Neither the adoptive parent nor the adoptee has been the subject of a proceeding for a Guardian under Article 81 of the Mental Hygiene Law or under Article 17-A of the Surrogate's Court Procedure Act.

7. If the adoptee is not a petitioner, his or her consent is attached.

WHEREFORE, the Petitioner(s) request(s) an order granting the adoption of _____ by the Petitioner(s) and directing that such adoptee _____ shall be treated in all respects as the child of the Petitioner(s) and directing that

[   ] the name of the adoptee be changed and henceforth be known by the name of

_____

together with such other and further relief as may be just and proper.

Dated: _____ , _____

_____ / _____
Adoptive Parent   (Print Name)   (Signature)

_____ / _____
Adoptive Parent   (Print Name)   (Signature)

_____ / _____
Adoptee   (Print Name)   (Signature)

_____
Signature of Attorney   Print Name

_____
Firm Name   Telephone Number

_____
Address of Attorney

Official Forms

FORM 29-A　　　　　SURROGATE'S COURT　　　　　**AF-128**

<u>VERIFICATION</u>

STATE OF NEW YORK　　　　　)
　　　　　　　　　　　　　　　:ss.
COUNTY OF _____)

_____

being duly sworn, says that (he)(she)(they)(is)(are) the Petitioner(s) in the above-named proceeding and that the foregoing petition is true to (his)(her)(their) own knowledge, except as to matters wherein stated to be alleged on information and belief and as to those matters (he)(she)(they) believe(s) it to be true.

_____
Petitioner

_____
Petitioner

_____
Petitioner

Sworn to before me on

_____,_____

_____
Notary Public
Commission Expires:
(Affix Notary Stamp or Seal)

Sworn to before me

_____,_____
Judge of the _____ Court

FORM 29–B   Consent to Adult Adoption by Adoptee

SURROGATE'S COURT OF THE STATE OF NEW YORK
COUNTY OF _____

---X

In the Matter of the Adoption of

                                    CONSENT TO ADULT ADOPTION
                                            BY ADOPTEE

_____ An Adult,

                                    File No. _____

---X

The undersigned _____ whose permanent address is:

_____   _____
          (Street and Number)   (City, Village, Town)

_____   _____
              (State)   (Zip Code)

who is a competent person over the age of eighteen (18) years and whose interest in the above-entitled
proceeding is the subject adoptee, hereby consents to being adopted by the petitioner(s) and consents to being
treated in all respects as the child of the petitioning adoptive parent(s).

Date: _____   _____
                                                     (Signature)

                                    _____
                                                     (Print Name)

STATE OF _____) ss.:
COUNTY OF _____)

        On _____, _____, before me personally came

_____ known to me to be the
individual described in and who executed the foregoing instrument, and to me such person duly acknowledged
that he/she executed the same.

_____
Notary Public
Commission Expires:
(Affix Notary Stamp or Seal)

29-B (2/2016)

FORM 29–C   Consent to Adult Adoption by Spouse

SURROGATE'S COURT OF THE STATE OF NEW YORK
COUNTY OF _____

---X

In the Matter of the Adoption of

                                                                    CONSENT TO ADULT ADOPTION
                                                                              BY SPOUSE

_____ An Adult,

                                                                    File No. _____
---X

The undersigned _____ whose permanent address is:

_____
          (Street and Number)   (City, Village, Town)

_____
                (State)   (Zip Code)

who is a competent person over the age of eighteen (18) years and whose interest in the above-entitled
proceeding is spouse of the petitioning adoptive parent, hereby consents to the adult adoption of
_____ by the petitioner(s) and consents to the adoptee being
treated in all respects as the child of the petitioning adoptive parent(s).

Date: _____   _____
                                                              (Signature)

                                                              _____
                                                              (Print Name)

STATE OF _____) ss.:
COUNTY OF _____)

          On _____, _____, before me personally came

_____ known to me to be the
individual described in and who executed the foregoing instrument, and to me such person duly acknowledged
that he/she executed the same.

_____
Notary Public
Commission Expires:
(Affix Notary Stamp or Seal)

29-C (2/2016)

FORM 30   **Petition for Access to Sealed Birth Certificate [PHL § 4138-e]**

SURROGATE'S COURT OF THE STATE OF NEW YORK
COUNTY OF _____
---X

In the Matter of the Adoption of
of a Child Whose First Name is

	PETITION FOR ACCESS TO
	SEALED BIRTH CERTIFICATE
	PHL § 4138-e

_____

---X

To the Surrogate's Court, County of _____

File No. _____

It is respectfully alleged that:

1. The name, address and interest in this proceeding of the petitioner who is of full age, is as follows:

Name: _____

Address: _____
      (Street address)   (City/ Town/Village)

_____
      (County)   (State)   (Zip)   (Telephone No.)

Mailing Address: _____
                   (If different from street address)

Email Address: _____

2. [Check applicable box, if adopted person is living]

   ☐   a.   I am the adopted person, and am 18 years old or older. Submit proof of adoption, if available.

   ☐   b.   I am the lawful representative of _____.
                                 (Name of adopted person)
        My authority being: *(Check one below)*

          ☐   SCPA Article 17-A guardian of the person

          ☐   MHL Article 81 guardian of the person

          ☐   Other *(Specify)* _____

        [Submit a copy of the certificate of appointment or other such authority to act]

3. [Check applicable box, if adopted person is deceased and attach proof of death]

   Name of adopted person: _____

   ☐ a. I am the deceased adopted person's direct line descendant (child, grandchild, great grandchild, etc.).

   State relationship _____

   [Submit a family tree affidavit or other proof of relationship to adopted person]

   ☐ b. I am the lawful representative of the deceased's adopted person's direct line descendant,

   _____ (child, grandchild, great grandchild, etc.)
   (Name of direct line descendant)

   [Submit a family tree affidavit or other proof of relationship to the adopted person]

   My authority being: (*Check one below*)

   ☐ SCPA Article 17-A guardian of the person

   ☐ MHL Article 81 guardian of the person

   ☐ Other (*Specify*) _____

   [Submit a copy of the certificate of appointment or other such authority to act]

4. Name(s) of adoptive parent(s): _____

   If known, name(s) of birth parent(s): _____

   If known, birth name of adopted person: _____

   If known, date of adoption: _____

   Date of birth of adopted person: _____

5. A request for information has been made pursuant to Public Health Law Section 4138-e for a certified copy of the original

   birth certificate of the adopted person to the following authority: (*Check all that apply*)

   ☐ The State Commissioner of Health (Bureau of Vital Records)

   ☐ The Commissioner of Health and Mental Hygiene of the City of New York (Office of Vital Records)

   ☐ The local registrar of the City of Albany for birth records prior to 1/1/1914

   ☐ The local registrar of the City of Buffalo for birth records prior to 1/1/1914

   ☐ The local registrar of the City of Yonkers for birth records prior to 1/1/1914

   It has been determined by the aforementioned Commissioner or Registrar that it is impossible to provide the requested

   copies. **[Attach a copy of the determination of the Commissioner or Registrar.]**

Wherefore, I respectfully request a court - certified copy of the birth certificate on file with the court, or any identifying information that would have appeared on such original birth certificate.

Dated: _____, 20___   _____
                                      Petitioner's Signature

                                     _____
                                      Print/Type Petitioner's Name

VERIFICATION

State of _____   )
) ss.:
County of _____   )

The undersigned, the petitioner named in the foregoing petition, being duly sworn, says I have read the foregoing petition subscribed by me and know the contents thereof, and the same is true of my own knowledge, except as to matters therein stated to be alleged upon information and belief, and as to those matters I believe it to be true.

My address is _____
                       (Street address)   (City/Town/Village)   (State)   (Zip)

                                       _____
                                      Signature of Petitioner

                                       _____
                                      Print/Type Name of Petitioner

On _____, 20___, before me personally came _____ to me known to be the person described in and who executed the foregoing instrument. Such person duly swore to such instrument before me and duly acknowledged that he/she executed same.

_____
Notary Public
Commission Expires: _____
(Affix Notary Stamp or Seal)

Signature of Attorney: _____   Tel. No.: _____

Print Name of Attorney: _____   Email: _____

Firm Name: _____

Address of Attorney: _____

Official Forms

FORM DOH-1928   SURROGATE'S COURT   AF-134

FORM DOH-1928   Report of Adoption

NEW YORK STATE DEPARTMENT OF HEALTH
Vital Records Section

Report of Adoption

SEND TO: Amendment Unit, Vital Records Section, P.O. 2602, Albany, NY 12220-2602

1. Information on Original Certificate

Infant

1. Name: First   Middle   Last   2. Sex: ☐ Male ☐ Female

3. Date of Birth: Month Day Year   4a. County (NYS) of Birth: 4b. Town of Birth: 4c. City or Village of Birth:

Mother

5a. Maiden Name: First   Middle   Last

5b. Social Security Number: 5c. Was mother's consent to the adoption required at the time of adoption or was mother's signature required on an instrument of surrender? ☐ Yes ☐ No   If NO, were parental rights terminated? ☐ Yes ☐ No

6a. Name: First   Middle   Last

Father

6b. Social Security Number: 6c. Was father's consent to the adoption required at the time of adoption or was father's signature required on an instrument of surrender? ☐ Yes ☐ No   If NO, were parental rights terminated? ☐ Yes ☐ No

2. Information on Amended Birth Record Following Adoption

Infant

7. Name by Adoption: First   Middle   Last

Adoptive Parents

Mother

8a. Maiden Name: First   Middle   Last

8b. Date of Birth: Month Day Year   8c. State of Birth: (Country if not USA)   8d. Social Security Number:

9a. Residence: State   9b. County: 9c. Town: 9d. City or Village:

9e. Within the corporate limits? ☐ Yes ☐ No   9f. Residence: Street and Number

10. Mailing Address for Notice of Birth Registration: (Include Zip Code)

Father

11a. Name: First   Middle   Last

11b. Date of Birth: Month Day Year   11c. State of Birth: (Country if not USA)   11d. Social Security Number:

3. Attorney

Attorney

12a. Name: First   Middle   Last

12b. Firm:

12c. Mailing Address: (Include Zip Code)

DOH-1928 (12/2003)

4. Certification

SEAL OF THE COURT

Print Form

Pursuant to Section 254 of the Judiciary Law, I hereby certify that the child described was adopted by the parents cited in this report on the

_____ day of _____ , _____

as set forth in the decree made in the _____

Court of _____ County, State of New York.

Signed: _____   Clerk of Court   Date

CLEAR FORM

FORM DOH-4455   **Adoption Information Registry Birth Parent Registration Form**

NEW YORK STATE DEPARTMENT OF HEALTH   **Adoption Information Registry Birth Parent Registration Form**
Vital Records Section

This form is to be completed by birth parents who consent to the adoption or who execute an instrument of surrender. It is used to register a birth parent's agreement or non-agreement to the release of the birth parent's name and address by the Adoption Registry to the adoptee (the adopted child). This identifying information will be given to the adopted child only when the child reaches at least eighteen years of age and voluntarily registers with the Adoption Registry.

FOR OFFICIAL NYS USE ONLY
Registry # _____
Date _____

This form may also be used at any time after the adoption to agree to the release of identifying information, to withdraw your agreement or to update your contact information.

Instructions for the birth parent, adoption agencies, attorneys, courts and the NYC Department of Health and Mental Hygiene are on page 2.

1. Birth Parent Information:

Check One: Birth Mother ☐   Birth Father ☐   Date of your birth: _____
                                                                        MM/DD/YYYY

Name of birth parent
First Name: _____   Middle Name: _____

Current Last Name: _____   Maiden Last Name: _____
                                                                   (If Applicable)

Contact Information:
Mailing address
Street: _____   City/Town: _____

State: _____   ZIP: _____

Email Address: _____   Phone: (____) _____ - _____

2. Adoptee Information:

Name given to child at birth
First Name: _____   Middle Name: _____

Last Name: _____   Date of Birth: _____
                                                                MM/DD/YYYY
Town, city or village
of birth of adoptee: _____ , New York State.

3. Agency Information:

Name of Adoption Agency or Attorney if private adoption: _____

Name of Court: _____

4. Birth Parent Statement:

I have read the Notice to Birth Parents on the reverse side of this form and I understand that if I agree to the release of identifying information the adoptee can be given my name and known address and that I will not be notified when the information is released. Further, I swear of affirm under penalty of perjury that all of the information provided on this application is true and accurate to the best of my knowledge and belief.

☐ Yes, I agree that my name and address can be given to the adopted child if he or she registers with the Adoption Information Registry on or after his or her eighteenth birthday.

☐ No, I do not wish my name and address to be given to the adopted child.

If you change your mind after submitting this form, please complete a new form, checking either Yes or No, have the form notarized and send it to the Adoption Registry. The form with the most recent date will be kept on file.

STATE OF _____
                                        SS:
COUNTY OF _____

Subscribed and sworn to
(affirmed) before me this _____

Day of _____ . _____

_____   _____
Signature of Applicant   Signature of Notary Public

DOH-4455 (10/2008)   Page 1 of 2

FORM DOH-4455   SURROGATE'S COURT   **AF-136**

NEW YORK STATE DEPARTMENT OF HEALTH   Adoption Information Registry Birth Parent Registration Form
Vital Records Section

This form was developed in accordance with the provisions of Public Health Law section 4138-c(10).

Notice to Birth Parents

Do not complete this form for children born or adopted outside of new York State. The completed form will be submitted to the Court by the agency or attorney handling the adoption. The Court will send it to the Adoption Registry.

This form allows you to choose whether or not you would like the Adoption Registry to provide your name and address ("identifying information") to the adopted child. If you agree to the release of this information, the contact information will be provided to the child only if he or she registers with the Adoption Registry. The child will be able to register once he or she has reached at least eighteen years of age.

Checking **Yes** in item 4 on this form is not the same as giving consent to adoption or surrender. Whether you check **Yes** or **No**, your consent to or acknowledgment of the adoption or surrender will still be legal.

If you do not check either **Yes** or **No** we will treat your answer as No unless we already have a completed form from you on file. In that case, your previous choice will be retained and only your contact information will be updated.

You will not be notified if or when the Adoption Registry gives your information to the adopted child. It will be up to the adopted child whether or not he or she will request information or contact you.

If both parents consented to the adoption or executed a surrender instrument, then each must complete one of these forms. If either parent does not agree to the release of identifying information or later changes his or her mind and revokes agreement to the release of identifying information, the Adoption Registry will not release the name and address of either parent to the adopted child.

If you change your mind in the future you can complete a new form and agree to the release of identifying information or cancel your agreement by checking either **Yes** or **No**, having the form notarized and submitting the new form to the *NYS Department of Health, Adoption Information Registry, P.O. Box 2602, Albany, NY 12220-2602.*

The adopted child will receive the most current name and address that you have on file with the Adoption Registry. To make sure the child gets your current information, it is your responsibility to notify the Adoption Registry, in writing, if you change your name, address or other information. You may use this form to notify the registry of changes in your contact information.

You can file medical information updates with the Adoption Registry. Medical information must be submitted on your medical care provider's letterhead and include: medical care provider's name, address, telephone number and signature.

Further information about the services of the Adoption Registry and forms you can download can be found at http://www.nyhealth.gov/vital_records/adoption.htm *and* http://www.nycourts.gov/forms/familycourt/adoption.shtml

Adoption Agencies & Attorneys

For a child born in New York State, this form must be completed by the birth parent at the time the birth parent is either executing or acknowledging a consent to adoption pursuant to section 115-b of the Domestic Relations Law or is executing a surrender instrument pursuant to sections 383-c or 384 of the Social Services Law.

Completed forms must be filed with the court of adoption with the consent or instrument of surrender.

Court of Adoption

For a child born in New York State, this form must be completed by each birth parent at the time such birth parent is executing or acknowledging a consent to adoption or is executing a surrender instrument for the relinquishment of the child named in this form.

Send the Report of Adoption (DOH-1928) or, for New York City, Notification of order of Adoption (VR-47) and a copy of this form to:

Adoptee born in New York City:	**Adoptee born elsewhere in New York State:**
NYC Department of Health & Mental Hygiene	NYS Department of Health
Office of Vital Records	Vital Records Birth Amendment Unit
125 Worth St., Rm. 133, CN4	P.O. Box 2602
New York, NY 10013	Albany, NY 12220-2602

NYC Department of Health & Mental Hygiene

Send copies of this form, the Notification of Order of Adoption, the original birth certificate and the amended birth certificate to:

NYS Department of Health, Adoption Information Registry, P.O. Box 2602, Albany, NY 12220-2602

FORM 12/99   **Order for Child Protective Inquiry**

At a term of the Court of the State of
New York, held in and for the County of
_____ , at _____ , New York on
_____ , _____

P R E S E N T:
   Hon. _____
        Judge
_____
A Child Whose First Name Is   File No.

                                  ORDER FOR
                        CHILD PROTECTIVE INQUIRY

_____

       UPON reading and filing of the petition for a private placement adoption, agreement
of adoption, consents and other papers submitted herein, the Court finds pursuant to Social
Services Law §422(4)(A)(e) that _____ is an adult member of the
petitioner(s) household and that a report from the New York State Office of Children & Family
Services as to whether s/he has a history of indicated child protective reports is necessary to
determine whether the best interests of the child would be served by granting the adoption
petition;

       NOW THEREFORE, it is hereby

       ORDERED that the New York State Office of Children & Family Services shall
conduct an investigation/inquiry on _____ , a person over the age of eighteen
and a member of the prospective adoptive parent(s) household and submit the report to the
_____ County Surrogate's Court located at_____ , _____ , NY
_____ within 30 days of this Order.

Date: _____

                                  _____
                                  Hon._____
                                  Surrogate

Check applicable box:
[   ] Order mailed on _____ and to whom
mailed:_____

[   ] Order received in court on_____ and to whom
given:_____

Form 12/99 Order for Investigation

FORM LDSS-2725   **Request/Response for Name and/or Address of Father of**
Child Born Out of Wedlock

LDSS-2725 (Rev. 9/2009)

	NEW YORK STATE OFFICE OF CHILDREN AND FAMILY SERVICES **REQUEST/RESPONSE FOR NAME AND/OR ADDRESS** **OF FATHER OF CHILD BORN OUT OF WEDLOCK** *(Print or Type All Information)*	FORWARD ORIGINAL TO: NYS OCFS Putative Father Registry

REQUEST

REQUEST DATE:

(Please: One form per child)

FATHER'S NAME:	FATHERS SOCIAL SECURITY # (If Known):	REQUESTING AGENCY (Name and Address):
CHILD'S NAME	CHILD'S DATE OF BIRTH	REQUIRED
MOTHER'S NAME:	MOTHER'S SOCIAL SECURITY # (If Known)	
SIGNATURE OF AGENCY OFFICIAL: REQUIRED	PRINT NAME OF AGENCY OFFICIAL:	AGENCY TEL. NO.(Include Area Code):

**The department shall, upon request, provide the names and addresses of persons listed with the
registry to any court or authorized NYS agency, and such information shall not be divulged to any
other person, except upon order of a court for good cause shown. Social Service Law 372-c Putative
Father Registry**

INSTRUCTIONS:

1. COMPLETE ALL THE BOXES ABOVE. If you complete on-line, *print and then sign* the document. If you complete
   hard copy please print neatly and sign in the Agency Official Box.

2. IF THE MOTHER DOES NOT NAME THE FATHER IN ANY AFFIDAVIT, OR IF THE FATHER'S NAME DOES NOT
   APPEAR ON THE CHILD'S BIRTH CERTIFICATE, LIST THE FATHER'S NAME AS "**UNKNOWN**".

3. **MAIL ONLY** ONE **(1) COPY TO:**

   NYS-OCFS
   NYSAS/Putative Father Registry
   52 Washington Street, Room 323 North
   Rensselaer, New York, 12144

RESPONSE   STAFF REGISTRAR – PUTATIVE FATHER REGISTRY: RESPONSE DATE:

REGISTRY INFORMATION

DOCUMENT TYPE:

☐ Acknowledgement of Paternity   ☐ Court Order   ☐ Instrument to Acknowledge Paternity   ☐ Other

PUTATIVE FATHER'S NAME:	DATE OF BIRTH:	SOCIAL SECURITY NUMBER:	DATE REGISTERED:
ADDRESS:			

DATE OF COURT ORDER:	DOCKET NUMBER:	COURT:

FORM OCFS-3937 Request for Information-Private Adoption

OCFS-3937 (Rev. 2/2009) FRONT

NEW YORK STATE
OFFICE OF CHILDREN AND FAMILY SERVICES
REQUEST FOR INFORMATION – PRIVATE ADOPTION
FOR USE BY COURTS OR DISINTERESTED PERSONS ONLY – Please Complete

	SCR USE: BATCH #

RESOURCE ID #	ADOPTION LIAISON	AREA CODE/PHONE #
DOCKET FILE #	COURT NAME AND ADDRESS	ZIP CODE

Section 422.4(A)(p) of the Social Services Law allows a disinterested person** conducting an investigation relating to a pending private placement adoption application access to child protective services information in the possession of the Statewide Central Register of Child Abuse and Maltreatment (SCR).

This court, as part of such an investigation, has decided to request such access.

**See reverse for explanation of Disinterested Person

INFORMATION TO BE FILLED OUT BY PROSPECTIVE ADOPTIVE PARENT(S)

LAST NAME	FIRST NAME		MI	SEX ☐ M ☐ F	DATE OF BIRTH
MAIDEN NAME ALIAS		FIRST NAME			
LAST NAME	FIRST NAME		MI	SEX ☐ M ☐ F	DATE OF BIRTH

CURRENT ADDRESS	CITY	STATE	ZIP	FROM	TO
PREVIOUS ADDRESS FOR THE LAST 28 YEARS	CITY	STATE	ZIP	FROM	TO
PREVIOUS ADDRESS FOR THE LAST 28 YEARS	CITY	STATE	ZIP	FROM	TO
PREVIOUS ADDRESS FOR THE LAST 28 YEARS	CITY	STATE	ZIP	FROM	TO
PREVIOUS ADDRESS FOR THE LAST 28 YEARS	CITY	STATE	ZIP	FROM	TO
PREVIOUS ADDRESS FOR THE LAST 28 YEARS	CITY	STATE	ZIP	FROM	TO

See reverse for additional space for recording separate previous addresses

MEMBERS OF PROSPECTIVE ADOPTIVE PARENT(S) HOUSEHOLD

LAST NAME AND MAIDEN/ALIAS	FIRST NAME	MI	SEX ☐ M ☐ F	DATE OF BIRTH
LAST NAME	FIRST NAME	MI	SEX ☐ M ☐ F	DATE OF BIRTH
LAST NAME	FIRST NAME	MI	SEX ☐ M ☐ F	DATE OF BIRTH
LAST NAME	FIRST NAME	MI	SEX ☐ M ☐ F	DATE OF BIRTH
LAST NAME	FIRST NAME	MI	SEX ☐ M ☐ F	DATE OF BIRTH

See reverse for additional space for recording separate previous addresses

I (we) understand that the information I (we) have provided to this court will be used to inquire of the New York State Office of Children and Family Services whether I (we) am (are) named in a pending or indicated child abuse or maltreatment report(s) on file with the SCR and to provide relevant information to the court.

I (we) affirm that all the information provided on this form is true. I (we) understand that if I (we) knowingly give false statements such action could be grounds for dismissal of my adoption petition and for opening, vacating or setting aside any order of adoption arising from such petition.

_____   _____   _____   _____
DATE   SIGNATURE OF ADOPTIVE PARENT(S)   DATE   SIGNATURE OF ADOPTIVE PARENT(S)

Official Forms

OCFS-3937 (Rev. 2/2009) REVERSE

"NOTIFICATION TO PROSPECTIVE ADOPTIVE PARENTS OF THE SECTION 422.4(A)(p) PROCEDURE"

I (we) understand that if I (we) am (are) named in a pending or indicated child abuse or maltreatment report(s) on file with the SCR then all information contained in my (our) SCR record concerning such pending or indicated reports will be provided by the court to the disinterested person conducting the court ordered private placement adoption investigation, with the exception of the name(s) or identifying description(s) of the person(s) who reported the suspected child abuse or maltreatment unless written permission for release of identity has been authorized by such reporting person(s).

I (we) further understand that the results of the inquiry will be considered by the court pursuant to Section 116 of the Domestic Relations Law as one of the factors which may bear upon the outcome of my (our) adoption application.

This form is not an application for adoption. It is to be used solely for the purposes described in Section 422.4(A)(p) of the Social Services Law. I (we) understand that the purpose of collecting the demographic data on other persons in my (our) household is to enable the New York State Office of Children and Family Services to identify with the greatest degree of certainty whether or not I (we) am (are) named in a child abuse or maltreatment report(s). The utilization of this information in a discriminatory manner is contrary to the Human Rights Law.

**A disinterested person as defined in Section 116(5) of the Domestic Relations Law includes the probation service of the Family Court, a licensed master social worker, licensed clinical social worker, or an authorized agency specifically designated by the court to conduct pre-placement investigations.

COURT INSTRUCTIONS

RESOURCE ID #:   Record your Resource ID # as appropriate. If you need assistance, email:
ocfs.sm.conn_app@ocfs.state.ny.us

DOCKET/FILE #:   Record your Court Docket File # as appropriate.

AGENCY LIAISON: Record name of Adoption Liaison or Disinterested Person**.

Adoption forms are to be sent to: **The New York Statewide Central Register
Of Child Abuse and Maltreatment
P.O. Box 4480, Attn: Service Center Unit
Albany, N.Y. 12204-0480**

ADDITIONAL ADDRESSES

LAST NAME		FIRST NAME					M.I.
PREVIOUS STREET ADDRESS	CITY		STATE	ZIP	FROM	TO	
LAST NAME		FIRST NAME					M.I.
PREVIOUS STREET ADDRESS	CITY		STATE	ZIP	FROM	TO	
LAST NAME		FIRST NAME					M.I.
PREVIOUS STREET ADDRESS	CITY		STATE	ZIP	FROM	TO	
LAST NAME		FIRST NAME					M.I.
PREVIOUS STREET ADDRESS	CITY		STATE	ZIP	FROM	TO	
LAST NAME		FIRST NAME					M.I.
PREVIOUS STREET ADDRESS	CITY		STATE	ZIP	FROM	TO	
LAST NAME		FIRST NAME					M.I.
PREVIOUS STREET ADDRESS	CITY		STATE	ZIP	FROM	TO	
LAST NAME		FIRST NAME					M.I.

TO ORDER MORE FORMS:
Please access the **Request for Forms and Publications** form, **(OCFS-4627)** from the Internet:
http://www.ocfs.state.ny.us/main/forms/management_services/

Mail your completed **Request for Forms and Publications**, **(OCFS-4627)** to the **Office of Children and Family Services, Forms Management Unit, Resource Distribution Center, 11, 4th Ave, Rensselaer, NY 12144-2629.** If you have difficulty accessing the form from the web-site, you can call **The Forms Hot Line at: 518-473-0971.**

FORM OCFS-4156   **Order of Adoption Family Court/Surrogate Court Request Form**

OCFS-4156 (Rev. 06/2007) FRONT

NEW YORK STATE
OFFICE OF CHILDREN AND FAMILY SERVICES
ORDER OF ADOPTION
FAMILY COURT/SURROGATE COURT REQUEST FORM

		SCR USE: BATCH#
RESOURCE ID #:	COURT LIAISON	AREA CODE/PHONE # ( ) -
DOCKET FILE #	COURT NAME AND ADDRESS	ZIP CODE

Section 112 of the Domestic Relations Law, as amended by Chapter 164 of the laws of 1991, requires that an inquiry be made of the New York Statewide Register of Child Abuse and Maltreatment (SCR) to determine if the adoptive parent(s) are the subject of an indicated child abuse or maltreatment report.

Date of Request: _____

TO BE FILLED OUT BY ADOPTIVE PARENT(S)

LAST NAME (father)	FIRST NAME	MI	SEX ☐ M ☐ F	DATE OF BIRTH		
ALIAS NAME(S)						
CURRENT ADDRESS: STREET	CITY	STATE	ZIP	FROM	TO	
PRIOR ADDRESS(ES) (STREET) FOR THE LAST 28 YEARS.	CITY	STATE	ZIP	FROM	TO	
	CITY	STATE	ZIP	FROM	TO	
	CITY	STATE	ZIP	FROM	TO	
	CITY	STATE	ZIP	FROM	TO	
	CITY	STATE	ZIP	FROM	TO	
	CITY	STATE	ZIP	FROM	TO	
LAST NAME (mother)	FIRST NAME	MI	SEX ☐ M ☐	DATE OF BIRTH		
ALIAS NAME(S)						
CURRENT ADDRESS: STREET	CITY	STATE	ZIP	FROM	TO	
PRIOR ADDRESS(ES) (STREET) FOR THE LAST 28 YEARS	CITY	STATE	ZIP	FROM	TO	
	CITY	STATE	ZIP	FROM	TO	
	CITY	STATE	ZIP	FROM	TO	
	CITY	STATE	ZIP	FROM	TO	
	CITY	STATE	ZIP	FROM	TO	
	CITY	STATE	ZIP	FROM	TO	

MEMBERS OF ADOPTIVE PARENT(S) HOUSEHOLD

LAST NAME & MAIDEN/ALIAS	FIRST NAME	MI	SEX ☐ M ☐	DATE OF BIRTH
LAST NAME & MAIDEN/ALIAS	FIRST NAME	MI	SEX ☐ M ☐	DATE OF BIRTH
LAST NAME & MAIDEN/ALIAS	FIRST NAME	MI	SEX ☐ M ☐	DATE OF BIRTH
LAST NAME & MAIDEN/ALIAS	FIRST NAME	MI	SEX ☐ M ☐	DATE OF BIRTH
LAST NAME & MAIDEN/ALIAS	FIRST NAME	MI	SEX ☐ M ☐	DATE OF BIRTH
LAST NAME & MAIDEN/ALIAS	FIRST NAME	MI	SEX ☐ M ☐	DATE OF BIRTH
LAST NAME & MAIDEN/ALIAS	FIRST NAME	MI	SEX ☐ M ☐	DATE OF BIRTH

Official Forms

FORM OCFS-4156   SURROGATE'S COURT   AF-142

OCFS-4156 (Rev. 02/2009) REVERSE

COURT INSTRUCTIONS

RESOURCE ID #   Record your Resource ID # as appropriate. If you need assistance, email: ocfs.sm.conn_app@ocfs.state.ny.us

DOCKET/FILE #:   Record your Court Docket File # as appropriate.

COURT LIAISON: Record name of Court Liaison.

DATE OF REQUEST: Record the Court processing date.

Order of Adoption Family Court/Surrogate Court forms are to be sent to:

> **The New York Statewide Central Register**
> **Of Child Abuse and Maltreatment**
> **P.O. Box 4480, Attn: Service Center Unit**
> **Albany, N.Y. 12204-0480**

TO ORDER MORE FORMS:
Please access the **Request for Forms and Publications** form, **(OCFS-4627)** from the Internet:
http://www.ocfs.state.ny.us/main/forms/management_services/

Mail your completed **Request for Forms and Publications**, **(OCFS-4627)** to the **Office of Children and Family Services, Forms Management Unit, Resource Distribution Center, 11, Fourth Ave, Rensselaer, NY 12144-2629.** If you have difficulty accessing the form from the web-site, you can call **The Forms Hot Line at: 518-473-0971.**

FORM UCS-836   **Attorney's Affidavit (Agency and Private Placement Adoptions)**

NEW YORK STATE UNIFIED COURT SYSTEM ATTORNEY'S AFFIDAVIT
Agency and Private Placement Adoptions

Names or other information likely to identify the birth or adoptive parents or the adoptive child
are to be omitted from the information to be supplied in the attorney's statement

Pursuant to 22 NYCRR 603.23; 691.23; 806.14; 1022.33

(a) Every attorney appearing for an adoptive parent, a natural parent, or an adoption agency in an adoption proceeding in the courts within this judicial department, shall, prior to the entry of an adoption decree, file with the Office of Court Administration of the State of New York and with the Court in which the adoption proceeding has been initiated, a signed statement under oath setting forth the following information (please type or print, use additional pages where necessary):

1. Name of Attorney: Last Name: _____ First Name _____ Initial _____

2. Association with firm: (if any) _____

3. Business Address: Street _____

   City _____ State _____ Zip _____

4. Telephone Number: _____

5. Docket Number of Adoption proceeding: _____

6. Court where adoption has been filed: (include county) _____

7. The date and terms of every **agreement**, written or otherwise, between the attorney and the adoptive parents, the birth parents, or anyone else on their behalf, pertaining to any compensation or thing of value paid or given, or to be paid or given by or on behalf of the adoptive parents or the birth parents, including but not limited to retainer fees. (Indicate whether the agreement is in writing or oral by checking the appropriate box).

   Date of Agreement: ___ mm / dd / yyyy   ☐ Written Agreement   ☐ Oral Agreement

   Terms of Agreement: _____

   _____

   _____

8. The date and amount of any **compensation** paid or thing of value given, and the amount of total compensation to be paid or thing of value to be given to the attorney by the adoptive parents, the birth parents, or by anyone else on account of or incidental to any assistance or service in connection with the proposed adoption. (If the source of compensation or thing of value is the birth parents or the adoptive parents check appropriate box only; if other, specify name).

   Date: ___ mm / dd / yyyy   Compensation paid or thing of value given: _____

   Source of compensation or thing of value given: ☐ Birth parents $ _____ ☐ Adoptive parents $ _____

   ☐ Other $ _____ (specify name) _____

   Total compensation to be paid or thing of value to be given: _____

   Source of compensation to be paid or thing of value to be given ☐ Birth parents $ _____ ☐ Adoptive parents $ _____

   ☐ Other $ _____ (specify name) _____

9. A brief statement of the nature of the services rendered: _____

   _____

Complete items 10-11 if another attorney or attorneys will share in the fees received in connection with the proposed adoption:

10. The name and address of any other attorney or attorneys, who shared in the fees received in connection with the services or to whom any compensation or thing of value was paid or is to be paid, directly or indirectly, **by the attorney**. Include the amount of such compensation or thing of value.

    Name: _____

    Address: _____

    Compensation paid or thing of value given: _____ Date paid: ___ mm / dd / yyyy

    Compensation to be paid or thing of value to be given: _____

11. The name and address of any other attorney or attorneys, if known, who received or will receive any compensation or thing of value, directly or indirectly, **from the adoptive parents, birth parents, agency or other source**, on account of or incidental to any assistance or service in connection with the proposed adoption. Include the amount of such compensation or thing of value, if known. If the source of compensation or thing of value is the birth or adoptive parents, check appropriate box only; if other, specify name.

    Name: _____

    Address: _____

    Compensation paid or thing of value given: _____ Date paid: ___ mm / dd / yyyy

    Source of compensation: ☐ Birth parents $ _____ ☐ Adoptive parents $ _____

    ☐ Other $ _____ Specify name and address: _____

    Compensation to be paid or thing of value to be given: _____

    Source of compensation: ☐ Birth parents $ _____ ☐ Adoptive parents $ _____

    ☐ Other $ _____ Specify name and address: _____

Official Forms

Complete items 12-13 if another person, agency, association, corporation, institution, society or organization will share in the fees received in connection with the proposed adoption:

12. The name and address of any other person, agency, association, corporation, institution, society or organization who received or will receive any compensation or thing of value **from the attorney**, directly or indirectly, on account of or incidental to any assistance or service in connection with the proposed adoption. The amount of such compensation or thing of value.

    Name: _____

    Address: _____

    Compensation paid or thing of value received: $ _____ Date paid: _mm / dd / yyyy_

    Compensation or thing of value to be received: _____

13. The name and address, if known, of any person, agency, association, corporation, institution, society or organization to whom compensation or thing of value has been paid or given or is to be paid or given **by any source** for the placing out of or on account of or incidental to assistance in arrangements for the placement or adoption of the adoptive child. The amount of such compensation or thing of value and the services performed or the purpose for which the payment was made. If the source of compensation or thing of value is the birth parents or the adoptive parents, check appropriate box only; if other, specify name. If additional space is needed, attach separate page.

    Name: _____

    Address: _____

    Compensation paid or thing of value given: _____ Date paid: _mm / dd / yyyy_

    Source of Compensation: ☐ Birth parents $ _____ ☐ Adoptive parents $ _____

    ☐ Other $ _____ Specify name and address: _____

    Compensation to be paid or thing of value to be given: _____

    Source of Compensation to be paid or thing of value to be given: ☐ Birth parents $ _____ ☐ Adoptive parents $ _____

    ☐ Other $ _____ Specify name and address: _____

    Service performed or purpose of payment: _____

14. **A brief statement** as to the date and manner in which the initial contact occurred between the attorney and the adoptive parents or birth parents with respect to the proposed adoption.

    Date: _mm / dd / yyyy_

    _____

    _____

    _____

    _____

I affirm that I have read this form, (including any attachments), in its entirety and that all statements I have made are true, to the best of my knowledge. False statements made in this affidavit are punishable under the penal law (§ 210.45).

Signature: _____ Date: _mm / dd / yyyy_

Department: _____ District: _____

Note:
Statements may be filed personally by the attorney or his/her representative at the main office of the Office of Court Administration in the City of New York, and upon such filing he/she shall receive a date stamped receipt containing the code number assigned to the original so filed. Statements may also be filed by ordinary mail, enclosing a self addressed stamped postcard.

Mail to: / All inquiries should be directed to:

ADOPTION AFFIDAVITS
Office of Court Administration
P.O. Box 2016
New York, N.Y. 10008

212-428-2796

For Office of Court Administration Use Only

All statements filed by attorneys shall be deemed to be confidential, and the information therein contained shall not be divulged or made available for inspection or examination to any person other than the client of the attorney in the adoption proceeding, except upon written order of the Presiding Justice of the Appellate Division.

NEW YORK STATE TAX LAW

ARTICLE 26   ESTATE TAX

PART I
COMPUTATION OF TAX

PART II
RETURNS AND PAYMENTS OF TAX

PART III
LIENS, DISCHARGES AND SURROGATE'S COURT

PART IV
PROCEDURE AND ADMINISTRATION

PART I   COMPUTATION OF TAX

§ 951. Applicable internal revenue code provisions

(a) General. For purposes of this article, any reference to the internal revenue code means the United States Internal Revenue Code of 1986, with all amendments enacted on or before January first, two thousand fourteen and, unless specifically provided otherwise in this article, any reference to December thirty-first, nineteen hundred seventy-six or January first, nineteen hundred seventy-seven contained in the provisions of such code which are applicable to the determination of the tax imposed by this article shall be read as a reference to June thirtieth, nineteen hundred seventy-eight or July first, nineteen hundred seventy-eight, respectively.

(b) [Expires and is repealed July 1, 2022] Disposition to surviving spouse who is not a United States citizen. In the case of an estate where a federal estate tax return is not required for federal estate tax purposes, a disposition to a surviving spouse that would qualify for the federal estate tax marital deduction under section 2056 of the internal revenue code if not for the limitation imposed by subsection (d)(1) of such section shall nonetheless be treated as qualifying for the federal estate tax marital deduction for purposes of computing the tax imposed by section nine hundred fifty-two of this part, without requiring that such disposition pass to the surviving spouse in a qualified domestic trust as required for federal purposes by internal revenue code section 2056(d)(2).

History: Add, L 1962, ch 1013, § 1; amd, L 1968, ch 1010, § 1; L 1971, ch 350, § 1; L 1971, ch 352, § 1; L 1977, ch 879, § 6; L 1978, ch 67, § 1, eff July 1, 1978; L 1980, ch 417, § 1; L 1982, ch 916, § 1; L 1984, ch 446, § 1; L 1985, ch 543, § 2, eff July 24, 1985; L 1990, ch 190, §§ 56, 142, eff May 25, 1990, applicable to estates of decedents dying after May 25, 1990; L 1992, ch 826, § 1, eff Aug 7, 1992, but only as to estates of decedents dying after the effective date; L 1997, ch 389, § 4 (Part A), eff Aug 7, 1997, § 5 (Part A), eff Jan 1, 2000; L 1998, ch 56, § 33 (Part A), eff April 28, 1998; L 1999, ch 407, § 1 (Part A), eff Aug 9, 1999; L 2010, ch 57, § 1 (Part T), eff Aug 11, 2010, and applying to estates of decedents dying on or after Jan 1, 2010; L 2013, ch 538, § 1, eff Dec 18, 2013, applying to the estates of decedents dying on or after Jan 1, 2010, and expiring and deemed repealed July 1, 2016; L 2014, ch 59, § 1 (Part X), eff April 1, 2014, applying to estates of decedents dying on and after that date; L 2019, ch 89, § 1, eff July 3, 2019.

§ 951-a. General provisions and definitions

When used in this article:

(a) The term "executor" means the executor or administrator of the estate of the decedent, or, if there is no executor or administrator appointed, qualified and acting, then any person or entity in actual or constructive possession of any property of the decedent.

(b) The term "person" includes an individual, a trustee, a corporation, an association, a joint-stock company, a partnership, a limited liability company and a bank.

(c) The term "tangible personal property" means corporeal personal property, including money held for numismatic purposes, and does not include deposits in banks, mortgages, debts, receivables, shares of stock, bonds, notes, credits, evidences of an interest in property, evidences of debt, or choses in action generally.

(d) The term "persons interested in the estate" shall include all persons who may be entitled to receive or who have received any property or interest which is required to be included in the gross estate of a decedent, or any benefit whatsoever with respect to any such property or interest, whether under a will, or intestacy, or by reason of any of the transfers, trusts, estates, interests, rights, powers and relinquishments of powers which are required to be included in the gross estate.

(e) The term "taxpayer" means the estate of the decedent and any other person subject to or liable for any tax imposed by this article.

(f) Tax treatment of charitable contributions for determining domicile. Notwithstanding any other provision of any other law to the contrary, the making of a financial contribution, gift, bequest, donation or any other financial instrument or pledge in any amount or the donation or loan of any object of any value, or the volunteering, giving or donation of uncompensated time, or any combination of the foregoing, considered a charitable contribution under subsection (c) of section one hundred seventy of the internal revenue code, or to a not-for-profit organization, as defined in subdivision seven of section one hundred seventy-nine-q of the state finance law, shall not be used in any manner to determine where an individual is domiciled at the time of his or her death.

History: Add, L 1990, ch 190, § 110, eff May 25, 1990, applicable to estates of decedents dying after May 25, 1990; amd, L 1994, ch 576, § 44, eff July 26, 1994; L 1997, ch 389, §§ 6, 7 (Part A), eff Feb 1, 2000; L 2016, ch 60, §§ 1, 2 (Part Y), eff April 13, 2016.

§ 952. Tax imposed

(a) A tax is hereby imposed on the transfer of the New York estate by every deceased individual who at his or her death was a resident of New York state.

(b) Computation of tax. The tax imposed by this section shall be computed on the deceased resident's New York taxable estate as follows:

If the New York taxable estate is:	The tax is:
Not over $ 500,000	3.06% of taxable estate
Over $ 500,000 but not over $ 1,000,000	$ 15,300 plus 5.0% of excess over $ 500,000
Over $ 1,000,000 but not over $ 1,500,000	$ 40,300 plus 5.5% of excess over $ 1,000,000
Over $ 1,500,000 but not over $ 2,100,000	$ 67,800 plus 6.5% of excess over $ 1,500,000
Over $ 2,100,000 but not over $ 2,600,000	$ 106,800 plus 8.0% of excess over $ 2,100,000
Over $ 2,600,000 but not over $ 3,100,000	$ 146,800 plus 8.8% of excess over $ 2,600,000
Over $ 3,100,000 but not over $ 3,600,000	$ 190,800 plus 9.6% of excess over $ 3,100,000
Over $ 3,600,000 but not over $ 4,100,000	$ 238,800 plus 10.4% of excess over $ 3,600,000

Over $ 4,100,000 but not over $ 5,100,000	$ 290,800 plus 11.2% of excess over $ 4,100,000
Over $ 5,100,000 but not over $ 6,100,000	$ 402,800 plus 12.0% of excess over $ 5,100,000
Over $ 6,100,000 but not over $ 7,100,000	$ 522,800 plus 12.8% of excess over $ 6,100,000
Over $ 7,100,000 but not over $ 8,100,000	$ 650,800 plus 13.6% of excess over $ 7,100,000
Over $ 8,100,000 but not over $ 9,100,000	$ 786,800 plus 14.4% of excess over $ 8,100,000
Over $ 9,100,000 but not over $ 10,100,000	$ 930,800 plus 15.2% of excess over $ 9,100,000
Over $ 10,100,000	$ 1,082,800 plus 16.0% of excess over $ 10,100,000

(c) Applicable credit amount.

(1) A credit of the applicable credit amount shall be allowed against the tax imposed by this section as provided in this subsection. In the case of a decedent whose New York taxable estate is less than or equal to the basic exclusion amount, the applicable credit amount shall be the amount of tax that would be due under subsection (b) of this section on such decedent's New York taxable estate. In the case of a decedent whose New York taxable estate exceeds the basic exclusion amount by an amount that is less than or equal to five percent of such amount, the applicable credit amount shall be the amount of tax that would be due under subsection (b) of this section if the amount on which the tax is to be computed were equal to the basic exclusion amount multiplied by one minus a fraction, the numerator of which is the decedent's New York taxable estate minus the basic exclusion amount, and the denominator of which is five percent of the basic exclusion amount. Provided, however, that the credit allowed by this subsection shall not exceed the tax imposed by this section, and no credit shall be allowed to the estate of any decedent whose New York taxable estate exceeds one hundred five percent of the basic exclusion amount.

(2) (A) For purposes of this section, the basic exclusion amount shall be as follows:

In the case of decedents dying on or after: The basic exclusion amount is:

April 1 2014 and before April 1, 2015	$ 2,062,500
April 1, 2015 and before April 1, 2016	3,125,000
April 1, 2016 and before April 1, 2017	4,187,500
April 1, 2017 and before January 1, 2019	5,250,000

(B) In the case of any decedent dying in a calendar year beginning on or after January first, two thousand nineteen, the basic exclusion amount shall be equal to:

(i) five million dollars, multiplied by

(ii) one plus the cost-of-living adjustment, which shall be the percentage by which the consumer price index for the preceding calendar year exceeds the consumer price index for calendar year two thousand ten.

(C) (i) For purposes of this paragraph, "consumer price index" means the most recent consumer price index for all-urban consumers published by the United States department of labor.

(ii) For purposes of clause (ii) of subparagraph (B) of this paragraph, the consumer price index for any calendar year shall be the average of the consumer price index as of the close of the twelve-month period ending on August thirty-first of such calendar year.

(iii) If any amount adjusted under this paragraph is not a multiple of ten thousand dollars, such amount shall be rounded to the nearest multiple of ten thousand dollars.

History: Add, L 1997, ch 389, § 9 (Part A), eff Feb 1, 2000; amd, L 2004, ch 60, § 3 (Part I), eff Aug 20, 2004; L 2014, ch 59, § 2 (Part X), eff April 1, 2014, applying to estates of decedents dying on and after that date; L 2015, ch 59, § 1 (Part BB), eff April 13, 2015, deemed to have been in full force and effect on and after April 1, 2014.

§ 954. Resident's New York gross estate

(a) General.—The New York gross estate of a deceased resident means his or her federal gross estate as defined in the internal revenue code (whether or not a federal estate tax return is required to be filed) modified as follows:

(1) Reduced by the value of real or tangible personal property having an actual situs outside New York state.

(2) Increased by the amount determined under section nine hundred fifty-seven of this part (relating to limited powers of appointment created prior to September first, nineteen hundred thirty).

(3) Increased by the amount of any taxable gift under section 2503 of the internal revenue code not otherwise included in the decedent's federal gross estate, made during the three year period ending on the decedent's date of death, but not including any gift made: (A) when the decedent was not a resident of New York state; or (B) before April first, two thousand fourteen; or (C) between January first, two thousand nineteen and January fifteenth, two thousand nineteen; or (D) that is real or tangible personal property having an actual situs outside New York state at the time the gift was made. Provided, however that this paragraph shall not apply to the estate of a decedent dying on or after January first, two thousand twenty-six.

(4) Increased by the value of any property not otherwise already included in the decedent's federal gross estate in which the decedent had a qualifying income interest for life if a deduction was allowed on the return of the tax imposed by this article with respect to the transfer of such property to the decedent by reason of the application of paragraph (7) of subsection (b) of section 2056 of the internal revenue code, as made applicable to the tax imposed by this article by section nine hundred ninety-nine-a of this article, whether or not a federal estate tax return was required to be filed by the estate of the transferring spouse.

(b) Valuation.—

(1) The New York gross estate shall be valued as of the time of the decedent's death, except that if a federal estate tax return is filed and the alternate valuation under section 2032 of the internal revenue code is elected for federal estate tax purposes, the New York gross estate shall be valued as of the applicable federal valuation date or dates. Any real

property qualified under section two thousand thirty-two-A of the internal revenue code shall have the same value for purposes of the New York gross estate as it has for federal estate tax purposes.

(2) If such alternate valuation could have been elected pursuant to paragraph one of this subsection, but for the absence of an estate sufficient to require the filing of a federal return, the New York gross estate may, upon the election of the executor, be valued as of the federal valuation date or dates which would have applied if a federal return had been filed. However, no election may be made under this paragraph unless such election will decrease the value of the New York gross estate and the amount of tax imposed by this article (reduced by credits allowable against such tax). Any election made under this paragraph shall be irrevocable. The election allowed by this paragraph shall be made no later than the date prescribed for the filing of the return under this article (including extensions) or any time thereafter as the commissioner may prescribe.

(c) Cross references.—

(1) For provisions of the internal revenue code defining the federal gross estate, see:

Sec. 2031. Definition of gross estate.

Sec. 2032. Alternate valuation.

Sec. 2032A. Valuation of certain farm, etc., real property.

Sec. 2033. Property in which the decedent had an interest.

Sec. 2034. Dower or curtesy interest.

Sec. 2035. Adjustments for gifts made within three years of decedent's death.

Sec. 2036. Transfers with retained life estate.

Sec. 2037. Transfers taking effect at death.

Sec. 2038. Revocable transfers.

Sec. 2039. Annuities.

Sec. 2040. Joint interests.

Sec. 2041. Powers of appointment.

Sec. 2042. Proceeds of life insurance.

Sec. 2043. Transfers for insufficient consideration.

Sec. 2044. Certain property for which marital deduction was previously allowed.

Sec. 2045. Prior interests.

Sec. 2046. Disclaimers.

(2) For provisions of the internal revenue code which, except to the extent they are inconsistent with the provisions of this article, are pertinent to the computation of taxable gifts and the tax under this article, see:

Sec. 2503. Taxable gifts.

Sec. 2511. Transfers in general.

Sec. 2512. Valuation of gifts.

Sec. 2513. Gift by husband or wife to third party.

Sec. 2514. Powers of appointment.

(3) For effect of federal estate tax determinations, see section nine hundred sixty-one of this article.

History: Add, L 1962, ch 1013, § 1; amd, L 1978, ch 67, § 4, eff July 1, 1978; L 1982, ch 916, § 3, eff Dec 19, 1982; L 1984, ch 446, § 2, eff July 19, 1984; L 1985, ch 543, § 3, eff July 24, 1985; L 1990, ch 190, § 57, eff May 25, 1990, applying to estates of decedents dying after May 25, 1990; L 1992, ch 826, § 3, eff Aug 7, 1992; L 1997, ch 389, §§ 7, 10–12 (Part A), eff Feb 1, 2000, applying to estates of decedents dying on or after Feb 1, 2000; L 1998, ch 56, § 34 (Part A), eff April 28, 1998, applying to estates of decedents dying after Dec 31, 1997; L 1998, ch 56, § 91 (Part A), eff April 28, 1998, deemed eff April 1, 1963; L 1999, ch 407, § 2 (Part A), eff Aug 9, 1999, applying to estates of decedents dying after December 31, 1997; § 3 (Part A), eff Feb 1, 2000; L 2014, ch 59, § 3 (Part X), eff April 1, 2014, applying to estates of decedents dying on and after that date; L 2015, ch 59, § 2 (Part BB), eff April 13, 2015, deemed to have been in full force and effect on and after April 1, 2014; L 2019, ch 59, § 1 (Part F), eff April 12, 2019 (applying to estates of decedents dying on or after January 16, 2019) and § 2 (Part F), eff April 12, 2019 (applying to estates of decedents dying on or after April 1, 2019).

§ 955. Resident's New York taxable estate

(a) General.—The taxable estate of a New York resident shall be his or her New York gross estate, minus the deductions allowable for determining his or her federal taxable estate under the internal revenue code (whether or not a federal estate tax return is required to be filed), except to the extent that such deductions relate to real or tangible personal property sitused outside New York state.

(b) Waiver of deductions.—If the right to any deduction otherwise allowable is waived for federal estate tax purposes, it shall be considered waived for New York estate tax purposes.

(c) Qualified terminable interest property election.—Except as otherwise provided in this subsection, the election referred to in paragraph (7) of subsection (b) of section 2056 of the internal revenue code shall not be allowed under this article unless such election was made with respect to the federal estate tax return required to be filed under the provisions of the internal revenue code. If such election was made for the purposes of the federal estate tax, then such election must also be made by the executor on the return of the tax imposed by this article. Where no federal estate tax return is required to be filed, the executor must make the election referred to in such paragraph (7) with respect to the tax imposed by this article on the return of the tax imposed by this article. Any election made under this subsection shall be irrevocable.

(d) Cross references.—For provisions of the internal revenue code specifying the deductions allowable for federal estate tax purposes, see:

Sec. 2032(b).   Alternate valuation—special rule for deductions.

Sec. 2046.   Disclaimers.

Sec. 2053.   Expenses, indebtedness, and taxes.

Sec. 2054.   Losses.

Sec. 2055.   Transfers for public, charitable, and religious uses.

Sec. 2056.   Bequests, etc., to surviving spouse.

> **History:** Add, L 2014, ch 59, § 4 (Part X), eff April 1, 2014, applying to estates of decedents dying on and after that date; L 2019, ch 59, § 3 (Part F), eff April 12, 2019, applying to estates of decedents dying on or after April 1, 2019.

§ 957. Modification for limited powers of appointment created prior to September first, nineteen hundred thirty

(a) General

In determining the New York gross estate, there shall be added to the federal gross estate of a deceased resident the value of all property (other than real and tangible personal property situated outside New York state) passing under a limited power of appointment exercised by the decedent (A) by will or (B) by a disposition which is of such nature that if it were a transfer of property owned by him, such property would be includible in his federal gross estate under section two thousand thirty-five, two thousand thirty-six, two thousand thirty-seven or two thousand thirty-eight of the internal revenue code.

(b) Definition

For purposes of this section, a limited power of appointment means a power—

(1) with respect to property which is not or was not subject to New York death tax in the estate of the grantor of such power, but would have been so taxable except for a statute providing that the tax on the transfer of such property should be imposed in the estate of the grantee of such power in the event of its exercise; and

(2) the exercise of which has not required the inclusion of the property in the decedent's federal gross estate under section two thousand forty-one of the internal revenue code (relating to general powers of appointment).

> **History:** Add, L 1962, ch 1013, § 1, eff April 1, 1963, and applicable to estates of all decedents dying on or after such date; amd, L 1964, ch 229, § 2, eff March 29, 1964; L 1965, ch 159, § 2, eff May 11, 1965; L 1997, ch 389, § 7 (Part A), eff Feb 1, 2000.

§ 958. Exemptions in other laws not applicable

No exemption provided for in any other article of this chapter or any other law of this state shall be construed as being applicable in any manner under this article.

> **History:** Formerly § 959–b, add, L 1990, ch 190, § 112, eff May 25, 1990; renumbered § 958, L 1997, ch 389, § 13 (Part A), eff Feb 1, 2000, applying to estates of decedents dying on or after Feb 1, 2000.

§ 960. Nonresident's estate tax

(a) General.—A tax is hereby imposed on the transfer, from any deceased individual who at his death was not a resident of New York state, of real and tangible personal property having an actual situs in New York state and either (i) includible in his federal gross estate or (ii) which would be includible in his New York gross estate pursuant to section nine hundred fifty-seven (relating to certain limited powers of appointment) if he were a resident of New York state.

(b) Computation of tax.—The tax imposed under subsection (a) shall be the same as the tax that would be due, if the decedent had died a resident, under subsection (a) of section nine hundred fifty-two, except that for purposes of computing the tax under subsection (b) of section nine hundred fifty-two, "New York taxable estate" shall not include the value of, or any deduction allowable under the Internal Revenue Code related to, any intangible personal property otherwise includible in the deceased individual's New York gross estate, and shall not include the amount of any gift unless such gift consists of real or tangible personal property having an actual situs in New York state or intangible personal property employed in a business, trade or profession carried on in this state.

(c) Cross references.—

(1) For valuation of property includible in the New York gross estate if the decedent had been a resident, see section nine hundred fifty-four.

(2) For provisions of the internal revenue code applicable to the federal gross estate of a decedent who was neither a resident nor a citizen of the United States, see:

Sec. 2103.   Definition of gross estate.

Sec. 2104.   Property within the United States.

Sec. 2105.   Property without the United States.

(d) Works of art on loan for exhibition.—Notwithstanding the foregoing, the tax imposed under subsection (a) of this section on the transfer, from any deceased individual who at his or her death was not a resident of the state of New York, of works of art having an actual situs in the state of New York and either (i) includible in his or her federal gross estate or (ii) which would be includible in his or her New York gross estate pursuant to section nine hundred fifty-seven (relating to certain limited powers of appointment) if he or she were a resident of the state of New York, shall not be subject to the tax imposed by this section if such works of art are loaned to a public gallery located within the state of New York solely for exhibition purposes but only if no part of the net earnings of such public gallery or museum inure to the benefit of any private stockholder or individual, and, at the time of the death of such individual such works of art are on exhibition or en route to or from exhibition in such a public gallery or museum.

History: Add, L 1962, ch 1013, § 1, eff April 1, 1963, and applicable to estates of all decedents dying on or after such date; amd, L 1963, ch 273, § 4; L 1971, ch 350, § 2, eff June 1, 1971; L 1977, ch 879, § 3; L 1978, ch 67, §§ 14, 15, eff July 1, 1978, and applicable to estates of decedents dying after June 30, 1978; L 1980, ch 190, § 1, eff June 3, 1980; L 1990, ch 190, §§ 138, 139, eff May 25, 1990, applying to estates of decedents dying after May 25, 1990; L 1994, ch 170, § 252, eff June 9, 1994, applying to estates of decedents dying after such effective date; L 1997, ch 389, §§ 14, 15 (Part A), eff Feb 1, 2000, applying to estates of decedents dying on or after Feb 1, 2000; L 2004, ch 60, § 4 (Part I), eff Aug 20, 2004, applying to estates of decedents dying on or after Jan 1, 2002; L 2014, ch 59, § 5 (Part X), eff April 1, 2014, applying to estates of decedents dying on and after that date; L 2015, ch 59,

§ 3 (Part BB), eff April 13, 2015, deemed to have been in full force and effect on and after April 1, 2014.

1992 Note

L 1992 ch 826, § 32, effective August 7, 1992 added a Note:

Notwithstanding subsection (c) of section 955 of the tax law, in computing the tax imposed under section 960 of the tax law on transfers by a decedent who was not a citizen or resident of the United States but was a resident of a foreign country with which the United States has a tax treaty with respect to estate, inheritance or gift taxes at the time of such decedent's death, a marital deduction shall be allowed for a transfer to his or her spouse even though such spouse is not a citizen of the United States at the time of such decedent's death if a marital deduction is allowed for such transfer for federal estate tax purposes. Notwithstanding subsection (c) of section 1004 of the tax law, where the donor of a gift to his or her spouse is not a citizen or resident of the United States but is a resident of a foreign country with which the United States has a tax treaty with respect to estate, inheritance or gift taxes when such gift is made, a marital deduction shall be allowed under article 26-A of the tax law for such gift even though such spouse is not a citizen of the United States at the time of such gift if a marital deduction is allowed for such gift for federal gift tax purposes. In the case of the estate of an individual dying after the effective date of this section but before December 20, 1992, the requirements of the preceding sentences that the individual not be a citizen or resident of the United States shall not apply in computing the tax imposed under section 960 of the tax law on transfers by nonresidents or under section 952 of the tax law on transfers by residents, whichever estate tax is applicable, or in computing the gift tax imposed by article 26-A of the tax law. Except to the extent inconsistent with the provisions of this section, the provisions of article 26 and 26-A of the tax law relating to the transfers or gifts covered by the provisions of this section shall apply. The provisions of this section are intended to take into account section 7815(d)(14) of the Omnibus Budget Reconciliation Act of 1989 (Public Law 101–239) which provides as follows: "(14) in the case of the estate of, or gift by an individual who was not a citizen or resident of the United States but was a resident of a foreign country with which the United States has a tax treaty with respect to estate, inheritance, or gift taxes, the amendments made by section 5033 of the 1988 act shall not apply to the extent such amendments would be inconsistent with the provisions of such treaty relating to estate, inheritance, or gift tax marital deductions. In the case of the estate of an individual dying before the date three years after the date of the enactment of this act, or a gift by an individual before the date three years after the date of the enactment of this act, the requirement of the preceding sentence that the individual not be a citizen or resident of the United States shall not apply."

§ 960-a. Reciprocity

The tax imposed by this article in respect of personal property (except tangible personal property having an actual situs in this state) shall not be payable if the transferor is a resident of a state or territory of the United States the laws of which, at the time of the transfer, contained a reciprocal provision under which nonresidents were exempted from transfer taxes or death taxes of every character in respect of personal property (except tangible personal property having an actual situs therein) provided the state or territory of residence of such nonresident allowed a similar exemption to residents of the state or territory of residence of such transferor. For the purposes of this section, the District of Columbia and the Commonwealth of Puerto Rico shall be considered territories of the United States.

History: Add, L 1973, ch 640, § 3, eff June 11, 1973.

§ 961. Effect of federal determination

(a) General

A final federal determination as to

(1) the inclusion in the federal gross estate of any item of property or interest in

property,

(2) the allowance of any item claimed as a deduction from the federal gross estate, or

(3) the value or amount of any such item, shall also determine the same issue for purposes of the tax under this article unless such final federal determination is shown by a preponderance of the evidence to be erroneous.

(b) Definition

For the purpose of this section a final federal determination means:

(1) A decision by the tax court or a judgment, decree or other order by any court of competent jurisdiction which has become final.

(2) A final disposition by the secretary of the treasury or his delegate of a claim for refund. Such disposition shall be deemed to have occurred—

(A) as to items of the claim which are allowed, upon allowance of refund or upon disallowance of the claim by reason of offsetting items; and

(B) as to items of the claim which are disallowed, or as to items applied by the secretary of the treasury or his delegate as an offset against the claim, (i) upon expiration of the time for instituting suit for refund with respect to such items, unless suit is instituted before the expiration of such time, or (ii) upon filing with the surrogate or appraiser a written statement, in such form as may be required by the tax commission, that suit for refund will not be instituted.

(3) A closing agreement made under section seven thousand one hundred twenty-one of the internal revenue code.

(4) An assessment pursuant to a waiver of restrictions on assessment, or a notification in writing issued by the secretary of the treasury or his delegate that the federal estate tax return has been accepted where such notification is issued after an audit of such return, as filed, unless the executor shall have filed with the commissioner of taxation and finance a written statement, in such form as may be required by the commissioner, that a claim for refund of federal estate taxes has been or will be filed.

(c) Items determined

If there has been a final federal determination with respect to a decedent's federal estate tax, any item entering into the computation of such tax shall be deemed to have been the subject of the final federal determination, whether or not specifically adjusted thereby.

History: Add, L 1962, ch 1013, § 1, eff April 1, 1963, and applicable to estates of all decedents dying on or after such date; amd, L 1990, ch 190, § 113, eff May 25, 1990, applicable to estates of decedents dying after May 25, 1990.

PART II   RETURNS AND PAYMENTS OF TAX

§ 971. Estate tax returns

(a) Returns by executor

(1) Residents. In the case of the estate of every individual dying on or after April first, two thousand fourteen, who at his or her death was a resident of New York state, his or her executor shall make a return with respect to the estate tax imposed by section nine

hundred fifty-two of this article if the decedent's federal gross estate, increased by the amount of any gift includible in his or her New York gross estate, exceeds the basic exclusion amount applicable to the decedent's date of death in paragraph two of subsection (c) of section nine hundred fifty-two of this article.

(2) Nonresidents. In the case of the estate of every individual dying on or after April first, two thousand fourteen, who at his or her death was not a resident of New York state, if such individual's federal gross estate includes real or tangible personal property having an actual situs in New York state, the executor shall make a return with respect to the estate tax imposed by section nine hundred sixty of this article if the decedent's federal gross estate, increased by the amount of any gift includible in his or her New York gross estate, exceeds the basic exclusion amount applicable to the decedent's date of death in paragraph two of subsection (c) of section nine hundred fifty-two of this article.

(b) Joint fiduciaries

If two or more executors are acting jointly, the return may be made by any one of them.

(c) Tax a debt Any tax under this article, and any increase, interest or penalty thereon, shall, from the time of the death of the decedent, be a debt owed by the estate of the decedent and from the time it is due and payable, be a personal debt of the person liable to pay the same, to the state of New York.

(d) Cross reference

For requirement of filing federal returns, see subsection (b) of section nine hundred seventy-seven of this article.

> **History:** Add, L 1990, ch 190, § 114, eff May 25, 1990, applicable to estates of decedents dying after May 25, 1990; amd, L 1987, ch 389, § 16 (Part A), eff Aug 7, 1997; L 1994, ch 170, § 253, eff June 9, 1994, applying to estates of decedents dying after such effective date; L 1997, ch 389, § 17 (Part A), eff Feb 1, 2000, applicable to estates of decedents dying on or after February 1, 2000.; L 2014, ch 59, § 6 (Part X), eff April 1, 2014, applying to estates of decedents dying on and after that date.

§ 971-a. Additional proceedings in estates of non-domiciliary decedents

(a) Condition to appointment of executor for nonresident

Every petition for ancillary letters testamentary or of administration and every petition for original letters testamentary or of administration in the estate of a decedent who at the time of his death was not domiciled in this state, shall set forth the commissioner of taxation and finance as a party to be cited, and upon the presentation thereof the surrogate shall issue a citation directed to the commissioner. The decree of the surrogate awarding the letters may contain any provision for the payment of the tax imposed by this article or the giving of security therefor which might be made by such surrogate if the commissioner of taxation and finance were a creditor of the decedent.

(b) Notification in case of estate of nonresident

Whenever the commissioner of taxation and finance is cited on the issuance of original letters testamentary or of administration in the estate of a decedent not domiciled in this state as provided in subsection (a) of this section, the commissioner shall notify the proper taxing authorities of the state in which such decedent was domiciled of the fact of the filing of the petition and shall furnish information submitted by the executor to the commissioner as to the decedent's property and value thereof. No executor shall be entitled to a final accounting or discharge in a surrogate's court of this state unless he shall have filed with the surrogate, in addition to the certificate or final receipt required under section nine hundred eighty-one of this article, (i) proof that all death taxes, together with interest and penalties thereon, due to the state of domicile of such decedent or to any political subdivision thereof have been paid or secured, or (ii) a consent by the proper taxing authorities of the state of domicile to such final accounting or discharge.

(c) Domiciliary state's tax authority as interested party

The official charged with administration of the death tax laws of the domiciliary state shall be deemed a party interested in the estate of a deceased individual who at his death was not a resident of New York state, to the extent that such official may petition for an accounting therein if the death taxes, interest and penalties due to such domiciliary state or a political subdivision thereof are not paid or secured. Upon such petition the surrogate may decree such accounting and may decree the remission to a fiduciary appointed by the domiciliary probate court of so much of the personal property of such estate as may be necessary to insure the payment to the state of domicile, or political subdivision thereof, of the amount of death taxes, interest and penalties due to such state or political subdivision.

(d) Requirement of reciprocity

This section shall apply to the estate of a deceased individual who at his death was not a resident of New York state only (i) if the laws of the state of his domicile contain a provision, of any nature or however expressed, whereby this state is given reasonable assurance of the collection of its death taxes, interest and penalties, from the estates of decedents dying domiciled in this state in cases where the estates of such decedents are being administered by the probate court of such other state by virtue of original letters testamentary or of administration, or (ii) if the state in which such decedent was domiciled does not grant letters testamentary or of administration in estates of nonresidents, until after letters have been issued by the state of domicile.

(e) Cooperation by commissioner of taxation and finance

The commissioner of taxation and finance shall cooperate with the taxing authorities of the state of domicile of a deceased individual who at his death was not a resident of New York state and shall furnish them with such information as may be requested with respect to any such estate. The provisions of this section shall be liberally construed to insure that the state of domicile of a decedent shall receive any death taxes together with interest and penalties thereon, due to it from such decedent's estate.

(f) Definition of state

For the purpose of this section, the term "state" means the states of the United States, the District of Columbia, any territory of the United States and the Dominion of Canada or any province thereof.

> **History**: Add, L 1990, ch 190, § 114, eff May 25, 1990, applicable to estates of decedents dying after May 25, 1990; amd, L 1992, ch 826, § 8, eff Aug 7, 1992, deemed eff May 25, 1990 ("shall take effect immediately and shall be deemed to have been in full force and effect on May 25, 1990, provided, however, that each such section of this act shall apply as if included in the provisions of chapter 190 of the laws of 1990 to which it relates.").

§ 972. Time and place for filing returns

(a) Time for filing returns

A person required to make and file a return under this article shall file returns, statements, or other documents, or copies thereof, within nine months after the date of the decedent's death.

(b) Place for filing returns

The commissioner of taxation and finance shall prescribe the place for filing any return, statement, other document, or copies thereof, required to be filed with such commissioner pursuant to this article.

(c) Simultaneous filing of returns with surrogate's court

If required by rule of any surrogate's court, a person required to make and file returns, statements, or other documents, or copies thereof, under this article shall simultaneously file a duplicate copy of such returns, statements, or other documents, or copies thereof, with the surrogate's court in the county where the petition was filed to commence either a proceeding for probate of a will or a proceeding for administration in intestacy. The office of court administration shall promptly notify the commissioner after receiving notice that any surrogate's court has adopted such a rule, so that the commissioner will be able to properly inform taxpayers of their responsibility to file such returns, statements or other documents with the surrogate's court.

> **History:** Add, L 1990, ch 190, § 114, eff May 25, 1990, applicable to estates of decedents dying after May 25, 1990; amd, L 1997, ch 389, §§ 7, 18 (Part A), eff Feb 1, 2000, applicable to estates of decedents dying on or after February 1, 2000.

§ 973. Signing of returns and other documents

(a) General

Any return, statement or other document required to be made pursuant to this article shall be signed in accordance with instructions prescribed by the commissioner of taxation and finance.

(b) Signature presumed authentic

The fact that the name of the executor or other individual is signed to a return, statement or other document, or copies thereof, shall be prima facie evidence for all purposes that the return, statement or other document, or copy was actually signed by him.

(c) Certifications

The making or filing of any return, statement or other document, or copy thereof, required to be made or filed pursuant to this article, including a copy of a federal return, shall constitute a certification by the person making or filing such return, statement or other document or copy thereof that the statements contained therein are true and that any copy filed is a true copy.

> **History:** Add, L 1990, ch 190, § 114, eff May 25, 1990, applicable to estates of decedents dying after May 25, 1990.

§ 974. Payment of tax

(a) General

The tax imposed by this article shall without assessment, or notice and demand be paid at the time prescribed in this article by the executor, subject to being by him charged against and collected from the persons interested in the estate, to the commissioner of taxation and finance.

(b) Payment

The entire tax due shall, unless otherwise provided in this article, be paid on or before the date fixed for filing the return required under this article.

(c) Cross reference

For interest on underpayment, see sections six hundred eighty-four and nine hundred ninety of this chapter.

> **History:** Add, L 1990, ch 190, § 114, eff May 25, 1990, , applicable to estates of decedents dying after May 25, 1990; amd, L 1997, ch 389, § 19 (Part A), eff Feb 1, 2000, applicable to estates of decedents dying on or after Feb 1, 2000.

§ 975. Liability for tax

(a) Duty of executor to pay tax

(1) The tax imposed by this article shall e paid by the executor, who shall thereupon charge the same against and collect it from the persons interested in the estate in accordance with the rules of apportionment of section 2-1.8 and other relevant provisions of the estates, powers and trusts law.

(2) If the tax imposed by this article, or any part thereof, is paid by, or collected out of, that part of the estate passing to or in the possession of any person other than the executor in his capacity as such, such person shall be entitled to reimbursement out of any part of the estate still undistributed or by a just and equitable contribution by the persons whose interest in the estate of the decedent would have been reduced if the tax had been paid before the distribution of the estate or whose interest is subject to equal or prior liability for the payment of taxes, debts or other charges against the estate, it being the purpose and intent of this section that so far as is practicable and unless otherwise directed by the will or non-testamentary instrument of the decedent, the tax shall be paid out of the estate before its distribution.

(b) Liability of executor

An executor who pays, in whole or in part, any debt due by the estate for which he or she acts, except for a debt owed to the United States or to New York state, or who distributes any asset of the estate, prior to the payment in full of the tax imposed by this article, shall be answerable in his or her own person and estate for the payment of such tax to the extent that the assets of the estate have been so paid out or distributed. The liability of the executor under this subsection shall continue until his or her discharge as provided in section nine hundred eighty-one of this article.

(c) Liability of life insurance beneficiaries

Unless the decedent directs otherwise in his or her will, if any part of the New York gross estate on which tax has been paid consists of proceeds of policies of insurance on the life of the decedent receivable by a beneficiary other than the executor, the executor shall be entitled to recover from such beneficiary such portion of the total tax paid as the proceeds of such policies bear to the federal taxable estate, reduced by the value of any real or tangible personal property located outside New York state, and increased by any federal estate tax deductions attributable to such property. If there is more than one such beneficiary, the executor shall be entitled to recover from such beneficiaries in the same ratio. In the case of such proceeds receivable by the surviving spouse of the decedent for which a deduction is allowed under section two thousand fifty-six of the internal revenue code (relating to marital deduction), this section shall not apply to such proceeds.

(d) Liability of recipients of property over which decedent had power of appointment

Unless the decedent directs otherwise in his or her will, if any part of the New York gross estate on which the tax has been paid consists of the value of property included in the gross estate under section two thousand forty-one of the internal revenue code, the executor shall be entitled to recover from the person receiving such property by reason of the exercise, nonexercise, or release of a power of appointment such portion of the total tax paid as the value of such property bears to the federal taxable estate, reduced by the value of any real or tangible personal property located outside New York state, and increased by any federal estate tax deductions attributable to such property. If there is more than one such person, the executor shall be entitled to recover from such persons in the same ratio. In the case of such property received by the surviving spouse of the decedent for which a deduction is allowed under section two thousand fifty-six of the internal revenue code (relating to marital deduction), this section shall not apply to such property.

(e) Liability of transferees and others

If the tax imposed by this article is not paid when due, then the spouse, transferee, trustee, surviving tenant, person in possession of the property by reason of the exercise, nonexercise, or release of a power of appointment, or beneficiary, who receives, or has on the date of the decedent's death, property included in the New York gross estate to the extent of the value, at the time of the decedent's death, of such property, shall be personally liable for such tax. Any part of such property transferred by (or transferred by a transferee of) such spouse, transferee, trustee, surviving tenant, person in possession of property by reason of the exercise, nonexercise, or release of a power of appointment, or beneficiary, to a bona fide purchaser, mortgagee, or pledgee, for an adequate and full consideration in money or money's worth shall be divested of the lien provided in section nine hundred eighty-two of this article and a like lien shall then attach to all the property of such spouse, transferee, trustee, surviving tenant, person in possession, beneficiary, or transferee of any such person, except any part transferred to a bona fide purchaser, mortgagee, or pledgee for an adequate and full consideration in money or money's worth. Provided, however, where any interest in such property was held by the decedent and the decedent's surviving spouse as tenants by the entirety, such interest in such property shall be divested of the lien provided in section nine hundred eighty-two of this article.

History: Add, L 1990, ch 190, § 114, eff May 25, 1990, applicable to estates of decedents dying after May 25, 1990; amd, L 1992, ch 826, § 9, eff Aug 7, 1992; L 1994, ch 170, § 254, eff June 9, 1994, applying to estates of decedents dying after such effective date; L 1997, ch 389, § 20 (Part A), eff Feb 1, 2000, applicable to estates of decedents dying on or after Feb 1, 2000.

§ 976. Extensions of time

(a) General

(1) The commissioner of taxation and finance may grant a reasonable extension of time for payment of tax (or any installment), or for filing any return, statement or other document required pursuant to this article, on such terms and conditions as he may require. Except in the case of executors who are outside the United States, no such extension for filing any return, statement or other document shall exceed six months. Except as

otherwise provided in this article, no such extension for payment shall exceed twelve months from the date fixed for payment.

(2) Where there is included in the value of the gross estate the value of a reversionary or remainder interest in property, the payment of the part of the tax imposed by this article attributable to such interest may, at the election of the executor, be postponed until six months after the termination of the precedent interest or interests in the property, and the amount the payment of which is so postponed shall then be payable, together with interest thereon. If the commissioner of taxation and finance finds that the payment of the tax within such six months would result in undue hardship to the estate and said commissioner has approved payment in respect of such tax over a longer period, he may extend the time for a payment for a reasonable period not in excess of three years from the expiration of such six months. The postponement of the payment of any such amount shall be under such regulations as the commissioner of taxation and finance may prescribe, and shall be upon condition that the executor, or any other person liable for the tax, shall comply with subsection (c) of this section (relating to furnishing of security).

(3) If the commissioner of taxation and finance finds that the payment on the due date of any part of the amount of the tax imposed by this article would result in undue hardship to the estate, he may extend the time for payment for such period as he may deem reasonable, but not to exceed four years from the date of death, and may require payment to be made in annual installments.

(b) Whenever the commissioner extends the time for the payment of tax under this section, that portion of the tax as to which an extension is granted shall bear interest from the date the tax is required to be paid, to the date of payment without regard to any extension of time for the payment of the tax or filing of the return, at the rate prescribed in subsection (a) of section six hundred eighty-four of this chapter.

(c) Furnishing of security

If any extension of time is granted for payment of any amount of tax, the commissioner of taxation and finance may require the taxpayer to furnish a bond issued by a surety company approved by the superintendent of financial services as to solvency and responsibility and authorized to transact business in this state or other security acceptable to such commissioner in an amount not exceeding twice the amount for which the extension of time for payment is granted, on such terms and conditions as such commissioner may require.

(d) Cross reference

For extensions of time for payment of estate tax where an estate consists largely of interest in closely held businesses, see section nine hundred ninety-seven of this article.

(e) If the decedent has a cause of action pending at the time of death, or a cause of action arises which is related to the decedent's death, and any recovery under the cause of action is to be taxable under this article, the commissioner shall waive any penalty and interest associated with such cause of action which accrues from the date that the return disclosing such cause of action is filed, provided that such penalty and interest may not be waived for periods beyond one year after the date of final judgment or settlement of the cause of action.

History: Add, L 1990, ch 190, § 114, eff May 25, 1990, applicable to estates of decedents dying after May 25, 1990; amd, L 1999, ch 232, § 1, eff July 13, 1999, applying to the estates of decedents dying on or after such effective date; L 2004, ch 60, § 2 (Part I), eff Aug 20, 2004,

Tax Law Art 26

and applying to estates of decedents dying on or after Feb. 1, 2000; L 2011, ch 62, § 104 (Part A), eff Oct 3, 2011.

§ 977. Requirements concerning returns, notices, records and statements

(a) General

The commissioner of taxation and finance may prescribe regulations as to the keeping of records, the content and form of returns, statements or other documents, and the filing of copies of federal estate tax returns and determinations. The commissioner may require any executor or other person, by regulation, instruction or notice served upon such person, to make such returns or documents, render such statements, or keep such records as the commissioner may deem sufficient to show whether or not such executor or other person is liable under this article for tax.

(b) Federal return

(1) If a federal estate tax return is required for federal estate tax purposes, a copy thereof, together with such summary and additional information as the commissioner of taxation and finance may prescribe, shall be filed with the return of tax under this article.

For the purposes of this article, the phrase "return, statement or other document" shall include a copy of the federal estate tax return, document or statement.

(2) If a federal estate tax return is not required for federal estate tax purposes, the return of tax under this article shall include such schedules and information as the commissioner of taxation and finance shall prescribe.

(c) Identifying numbers

(1) When required by the commissioner of taxation and finance:

(A) Inclusion in returns. Any person required under the authority of this article to make a return, statement, or other document, or copies thereof, shall include in such return, statement, or other document, or copies thereof, such identifying number as may be prescribed for securing proper identification of such person, or of the decedent.

(B) Furnishing number to other persons. Any person with respect to whom a return, statement, or other document, or copy thereof, is required under the authority of this article to be made by another person shall furnish to such other person such identifying number as may be prescribed for securing his proper identification.

(C) Furnishing number of another person. Any person required under the authority of this article to make a return, statement, or other document, or copy thereof, with respect to another person, shall request from such other person, and shall include in any such return, statement, or other document, or copy thereof, such identifying number as may be prescribed for securing proper identification of such other person.

(2) Limitation. For purposes of subparagraphs (B) and (C) of paragraph (1) of this subsection, a return, statement, or other document, or copies thereof, of an estate, with respect to its liability for tax, hall be considered as a return, statement, or other document, or copies thereof, with respect to each beneficiary of such estate under this article.

(3) Requirement of information. For purposes of this subsection, the commissioner of taxation and finance is authorized to require such information as may be necessary to

assign an identifying number to any person or estate.

(4) Use of social security account number. The social security account number issued to an individual may, except as otherwise specified by the commissioner of taxation and finance, be used as the identifying number for such individual for purposes of this title.

(d) Notice of qualification as executor

Every executor shall give notice of his qualifications as such to the commissioner of taxation and finance in such manner and at such time as may be required by the commissioner. The commissioner may provide such exemptions from the requirements of this section as he deems proper.

> History: Add, L 1990, ch 190, § 114, eff May 25, 1990, applicable to estates of decedents dying after May 25, 1990.

§ 978. Compromise agreements in cases of disputed domicile

(a) Determining tax under this article

Where the commissioner of taxation and finance claims that a decedent was domiciled in this state at the time of his death and the taxing authorities of another state or states make a similar claim with respect to their state or states, the commissioner of taxation and finance may enter into a written agreement with such taxing officials and with the executor that a certain sum shall be accepted in full payment of the tax imposed by this article, provided that said agreement also fixes the amount to be paid to such other state or states in full payment of the death taxes thereof. Full power and authority is hereby conferred upon the executor to enter into the agreement provided for herein. The execution of such agreement shall finally and conclusively fix and determine the amount of tax imposed by this article, except as otherwise provided in such agreement with respect to the valuation of estates devoted to farming or closely held business and except as provided in subsection (b) of this section, without regard to any other provision of the laws of this state.

(b) Payment of agreed tax

The executor shall pay to the commissioner of taxation and finance the amount of tax fixed in the agreement described in subsection (a) of this section. In the event the aggregate amount payable under such agreement to the states involved is less than the maximum credit allowable to the estate against the United States estate tax imposed with respect thereto, the executor forthwith shall also pay to the commissioner of taxation and finance so much of the difference between such aggregate amount and the amount of such credit, as the amount payable to the commissioner under the agreement bears to such aggregate amount.

(c) Definition

As used in this section the word "state" means any state, territory, or possession of the United States, the District of Columbia and the Dominion of Canada or any province thereof.

> History: Add, L 1990, ch 190, § 114, eff May 25, 1990, applicable to estates of decedents dying after May 25, 1990.

§ 979. Report of change in federal taxable estate, adjusted taxable gifts, additional estate tax imposed by section 2032A of the internal revenue code

(a) General

If the amount of the federal taxable estate reported on the federal estate tax return for an estate is changed or corrected by the United States internal revenue service or other competent authority, the executor shall report such change or correction in the federal taxable estate within ninety days after the final determination of such change or correction or as otherwise required by the commissioner of taxation and finance, and shall concede the accuracy of such determination or state wherein it is erroneous. Any executor filing an amended federal estate tax return shall also file within ninety days thereafter an amended return under this article, and shall give such further information as the commissioner may require. The commissioner may by regulation prescribe such exceptions to the requirements of this section as he or she deems appropriate.

(b) Final federal determination

The executor of every estate which is subject to the United States estate tax shall file with the commissioner of taxation and finance a copy of the final federal determination thereof forthwith after the same is made.

> History: Add, L 1990, ch 190, § 114, eff May 25, 1990, applicable to estates of decedents dying after May 25, 1990; amd, L 1997, ch 389, § 21 (Part A), eff Feb 1, 2000, applicable to estates of decedents dying on or after Fe 1, 2000.

§ 979-a. Notification by surrogate to commissioner concerning tax

A surrogate, in his discretion, may notify the commissioner of taxation and finance of any and all matters which come to the surrogate's attention as a result of any proceeding commenced in surrogate's court, or the filing therein of papers or documents, and which affect the tax imposed by this article.

> History: Add, L 1990, ch 190, § 114, eff May 25, 1990, applicable to estates of decedents dying after May 25, 1990.

§ 980. Change of election

The commissioner of taxation and finance may change, by regulation, any election expressly authorized by this article in order to conform such election to its equivalent federal election.

> History: Add, L 1990, ch 190, § 114, eff May 25, 1990, applicable to estates of decedents dying after May 25, 1990.

PART III   LIENS, DISCHARGES AND SURROGATE'S COURT

§ 981. Discharge from liability

(a) Certificate of no tax due

If a return has been filed and the commissioner of taxation and finance determines that no tax is due, he shall issue to the executor a certificate that no tax is due.

(b) Final receipt for tax due

If a return has been filed and the commissioner of taxation and finance is satisfied that the tax paid is the full amount of tax due, he shall issue to the executor a final receipt for tax due.

(c) Final receipt for agreed tax

If the commissioner of taxation and finance enters into an agreement under section nine hundred seventy-eight of this article (relating to compromise agreements in cases of disputed domicile) and if the amount due under such section is paid, he shall issue to the executor a final receipt for tax due.

(d) Discharge of executor upon accounting

If a return is required to be filed under section nine hundred seventy-one of this article, except as provided in subdivision three of section eighteen hundred four of the surrogate's court procedure act, no executor shall be entitled to a final accounting or discharge in the surrogate's court unless he has filed with the surrogate's court a certificate under subsection (a) or a final receipt under subsection (b) or (c) of this section. For additional requirement in case of the estate of a nonresident, see section nine hundred seventy-one-a of this article.

(e) Duplicate certificate or receipt

Any person interested in the estate shall, upon request, be entitled to a duplicate certificate of no tax due or duplicate final receipt for tax due or for agreed tax upon the payment of ten dollars to the commissioner of taxation and finance.

(f) Record of access to safe deposit boxes

The commissioner of taxation and finance may by regulation prescribe requirements for safe deposit companies, trust companies, banks, corporations, firms or other persons holding safe deposit boxes for rental to the public to maintain and retain records as to the persons who have had access to such safe deposit boxes.

(g) Cross reference

For criminal penalties for unlawful entry of safe deposit box, see article thirty-seven of this chapter.

> **History**: Add, L 1990, ch 190, § 114, eff May 25, 1990, applicable to estates of decedents dying after May 25, 1990; amd, L 1994, ch 170, § 255, eff June 9, 1994, applying to estates of decedents dying after such effective date; L 1997, ch 389, § 22 (Part A), eff Feb 1, 2000, applicable to estates of decedents dying on or after Feb 1, 2000.

§ 982. Lien for estate tax

(a) General

Unless the tax imposed by this article is sooner paid in full, it shall be a lien upon all property includible in the New York gross estate of the decedent for fifteen years from the date of death of the decedent, except that such part of the New York gross estate as is used for the payment of charges against the estate and expenses of its administration, allowed by any court having jurisdiction thereof, shall be divested of such lien. In the case of a decedent who at his death was not a resident of New York state, the lien shall apply to all property subject to tax under this article.

(b) Prior mortgages on real property

The lien under subsection (a) of this section shall be subject to the lien of any mortgage indebtedness on real property incurred in good faith prior to the time when the tax under this article became a lien. Such real property may be sold and conveyed free from any such tax lien in an action to foreclose such mortgage to which the people of the state of New York shall have been made a party defendant by reason of the existence of the lien for the tax. The lien may then attach to any surplus moneys which result from such sale, to be determined in the proceedings for the distribution of such surplus moneys.

(c) Discharge of lien

Subject to such rules or regulations as the commissioner may prescribe, the commissioner may issue a certificate of discharge of any or all of the property subject to the lien imposed by this section if he or she finds that the liability secured by such lien as been fully satisfied or provided for, upon application for such discharge. A certificate of discharge issued under this subsection shall be held conclusive that the lien upon the property covered by the certificate is extinguished.

(d) Recording of certificate of discharge

A certificate of discharge issued under subsection (c) of this section may be recorded in the office of the recording officer of the county where real property described therein is situated.

(e) Power of executor to sell

The executor shall have full power to sell so much of the property of the estate as will enable him to pay the tax imposed by this article in the same manner that he is permitted by law to do for payment of debts of the estate.

> **History:** Add, L 1990, ch 190, § 114, eff May 25, 1990, applicable to estates of decedents dying after May 25, 1990; amd, L 1997, ch 389, § 23 (Part A), eff Feb 1, 2000, applicable to estates of decedents dying on or after Feb 1, 2000; L 1997, ch 577, § 17, eff Sept 10, 1997, and applying to applications for discharge filed after Sept 10, 1997.

§ 983. Surrogates; assistants and clerks; district tax attorneys

(a) The commissioner of taxation and finance may, upon the recommendation of the surrogate, appoint, and may at pleasure remove, assistants and clerks in the surrogate's offices of the following counties, and shall fix their salaries within the amounts appropriated for that purpose:

(1) In New York county, a transfer and estate tax assistant; a deputy transfer and estate tax assistant; a transfer and estate tax clerk; an assistant clerk; a recording clerk; a stenographer; and shall be entitled to expend not more than seven hundred fifty dollars a year in such office for the expenses necessarily incurred in the administration of taxes under this article and articles ten and ten-C (as such article ten-C existed before its repeal) of this chapter.

(2) In Kings county, a transfer and estate tax assistant; a deputy transfer and estate tax assistant; two transfer and estate tax clerks; and shall be entitled to expend not more than five hundred dollars a year for expenses necessarily incurred in the administration of taxes under this article and articles ten and ten-C (as such article ten-C existed before its repeal) of this chapter.

(3) In Erie county, a transfer and estate tax clerk.

(4) In Westchester county, a transfer and estate tax clerk and a transfer and estate tax assistant.

(5) In Albany county, a transfer and estate tax clerk.

(6) In Queens county, two transfer and estate tax clerks and a typist.

(7) In Onondaga county, a transfer and estate tax clerk; and shall be entitled to expend not more than two hundred dollars a year for expenses necessarily incurred in the administration of taxes under this article and articles ten and ten-C (as such article ten-C existed before its repeal) of this chapter.

(8) In Monroe county, a transfer and estate tax clerk; and shall be entitled to expend not

more than three hundred dollars a year for expenses necessarily incurred in the administration of taxes under this article and articles ten and ten-C (as such article ten-C existed before its repeal) of this chapter.

(9) In Dutchess county, a transfer and estate tax clerk.

(10) In Oneida county, a transfer and estate tax clerk.

(11) In Suffolk county, two transfer and estate tax clerks.

(12) In Ulster county, a transfer and estate tax clerk.

(12-a) In Otsego county, a transfer and estate tax clerk.

(13) In Richmond county, a transfer and estate tax clerk.

(14) In Nassau county, two transfer and estate tax clerks.

(15) In Bronx county, a transfer and estate tax clerk and a transfer and estate tax assistant.

(16) In Orange county, a transfer and estate tax clerk.

(b) The positions of assistants and clerks in each surrogate's office described in subsection (a) of this section may be filled by promotion from among officers and employees of such office. Persons occupying such positions of assistants and clerks in each surrogate's office may be eligible for promotion to other positions in such office.

(c) In each county of the state having a population of over one million, and in each county of the state having a population of over three hundred thousand inhabitants, included in or adjoining a city or county containing a population of over one million inhabitants, the surrogate or surrogates shall each annually receive for compensation for services rendered in connection with the administration of transfer and estate taxes the sum of six thousand eight hundred eighty-two dollars in addition to the salary or compensation paid to such surrogate by the county, but such salary and compensation shall not together exceed the entire salary and compensation paid to a justice of the supreme court in the judicial district in which the county is included. Where a city pays the salary of a surrogate of a county wholly included within such city and such salary is equal to the entire salary and compensation paid to a justice of the supreme court in the judicial district in which the county is included, the state shall pay such city on behalf of such county the sum of six thousand eight hundred eighty-two dollars multiplied by the number of surrogates in such county. Where a county pays the salary of a surrogate and such salary is equal to the entire compensation paid to a justice of the supreme court in the judicial district in which the county is included, the state shall pay such county the sum of six thousand eight hundred eighty-two dollars multiplied by the number of surrogates in such county. The additional compensation provided for by this subsection shall be payable in the same manner as salaries and expenses under this section. The moneys provided to be paid by this subsection to a city or county in lieu of additional compensation shall be paid upon warrant of the comptroller drawn in favor of the city treasurer of the city or of the county treasurer of the county due such amount, which sum shall be paid to said city or county treasurer out of any moneys in the treasury not otherwise appropriated.

(d) (1) In each county of the state the surrogate shall receive annually for such services rendered in connection with the administration of transfer and estate taxes as are not incident to holding courts or performing duties as a judicial officer the respective sums following:

(A) In any such county having a population of less than ten thousand, five hundred seventy-three dollars;

(B) In any such county having a population of ten thousand or more but less than fifty thousand, one thousand eight hundred eighty-six dollars;

(C) In any such county having a population of fifty thousand or more but less than one hundred thousand, two thousand two hundred twenty-one dollars;

(D) In any such county having a population of one hundred thousand or more but less than two hundred thousand, three thousand two hundred thirty dollars;

(E) In any such county having a population of two hundred thousand or more but less than five hundred thousand, four thousand two hundred fifty-one dollars;

(F) In any such county having a population of five hundred thousand or more, six thousand eight hundred fifty-one dollars.

(2) No provision of this subsection shall repeal or affect the provisions of subsection (c) of this section, but the provisions of this subsection shall apply to the surrogate or surrogates mentioned in subsection (c) of this section, provided that any payment or payments made to him or them, whether under this subsection or subsection (c), or both, shall not in all exceed the sum of six thousand eight hundred eighty-two dollars annually. Such sum shall not, however, in addition to the salary or compensation paid to any surrogate by the state, together exceed the entire salary and compensation paid to a justice of the supreme court in the judicial district in which the county is included. The moneys provided to be paid for services by this subsection shall be payable in the same manner as salaries and expenses under this section. Such salaries and expenses shall be paid upon proper vouchers, out of moneys appropriated for such purpose.

(e) The commissioner of taxation and finance is authorized to designate and retain counsel to represent the department and to pay the expenses thereby incurred out of money appropriated for such purpose in the following circumstances:

(1) when the department is cited as a party under section nine hundred seventy-one-a of this article,

(2) in a special proceeding under section nine hundred ninety-eight or any appeal therefrom, of this article,

(3) to examine securities, deposits or other assets pursuant to subsection (e) of section nine hundred seventy-five of this article, and

(4) for such other duties under this chapter as the commissioner may assign.

History: Add, L 1990, ch 190, § 114, eff May 25, 1990, applicable to estates of decedents dying after May 25, 1990; amd, L 1991, ch 166, § 302, eff June 12, 1991.

PART IV   PROCEDURE AND ADMINISTRATION

§ 990. Applicability of other tax law provisions

(a) General

Except as otherwise provided in this article, all of the provisions of sections six hundred eighty-one through six hundred eighty-eight and six hundred ninety-one through six hundred ninety-seven of this chapter shall apply to the provisions of this article with the same force and effect as if the language of those sections had been incorporated in full into this article and had expressly referred to the tax under this article, except to the extent that any such provision is either inconsistent with or not relevant to this article and except as modified in subsection (b) of this section or with such other modifications as may be necessary to adapt the language of such provisions to the provisions of this article.

(b) Modifications

Sections six hundred eighty-one through six hundred eighty-eight and six hundred ninety-one through six hundred ninety-seven shall be read as modified by this subsection.

(1) The phrase "income tax" shall be read as "estate tax."

(2) The phrases "income" and "taxable income" shall be read as "federal taxable estate".

(3) The phrase "section six hundred fifty-nine" shall be read as "section nine hundred seventy-nine".

(4) The phrase "federal income tax" shall be read as "federal estate tax."

(5) The phrase "taxable year" shall be read as "tax under this article."

(6) Subsection (d) of section six hundred eighty-three shall be read as follows: The tax may be assessed at any time within six years after the return was filed if an estate omits from its federal gross estate, federal taxable estate or New York gross estate an amount properly includible therein which is in excess of twenty-five percent of the amount stated in the return of the federal gross estate, federal taxable estate or New York gross estate.

(7) References to sections six hundred eighty-nine or six hundred ninety of this chapter shall be deemed references to section nine hundred ninety-eight; references to the hearing process shall be deemed references to the procedures under section nine hundred ninety-eight; references to the division of tax appeals or the tax appeals tribunal in relation to the administration of the hearing process shall be deemed references to the surrogate's court; and references to filing a petition shall be deemed references to commencing a special proceeding under section nine hundred ninety-eight.

(8) In subsection (e) of section six hundred eighty-three of this chapter, the following sentence is added: "The running of the period of limitation for the collection of any tax imposed by this article shall be suspended for the period of any extension of time for payment granted under the provisions of subsection (a) of section nine hundred seventy-six and section nine hundred ninety-seven of this article."

(9) In subsection (a) of section six hundred eighty-four of this chapter, the phrase "to the date paid" shall be read as "to the date paid, except as otherwise provided in subsection (j) of section nine hundred ninety-seven of this article."

(10) In subsection (k) of section six hundred eighty-five of this chapter, the reference to "subsection (b) of section six hundred fifty eight" shall be read as "subsection (c) of section nine hundred seventy-seven of this article."

(11) In subsection (a) of section six hundred eighty-six of this chapter, the phrase

"person who made the overpayment" shall mean "estate, persons interested in the estate or other person making the overpayment."

(12) In subsections (f) and (i) of section six hundred eighty-seven of this chapter, the phrases "for taxable year" and "for such year" shall be read as "in respect of the tax imposed by this article" and, in subsection (i) thereof, the phrase "the fifteenth day of the fourth month following the close of his taxable year" shall be read as "such last day, determined without regard to any extension of time granted."

(13) In subsection (b) of section six hundred ninety-one of this chapter, the term "address given in the last return filed by him" shall be read as "address given in the notice of qualification filed by the executor under subsection (d) of section nine hundred seventy-seven of this article."

(14) In section six hundred ninety-two of this chapter, the term "person" shall be read as "estate or any other person."

(15) In section six hundred ninety-three of this chapter, the term "transferee" shall include

(A) any donee, heir, testamentary beneficiary or distributee, and

(B) any other person who under section nine hundred seventy-five of this article is personally liable for any part of the tax imposed by this article, and

(C) an executor to the extent of his personal liability under section nine hundred seventy-five of this article for the tax imposed by this article; and in subsection (d) of such section, the reference to subsection (e) of section six hundred ninety-seven of this chapter shall mean section nine hundred ninety-four of this article.

History: Add, L 1990, ch 190, § 114, eff May 25, 1990, applicable to estates of decedents dying after May 25, 1990; amd, L 1994, ch 170, § 256, eff June 9, 1994, applying to estates of decedents dying after such effective date; L 1997, ch 389, § 24 (Part A), eff Feb 1, 2000, applicable to estates of decedents dying on or after Feb 1, 2000.

§ 991. Interest accrual relief for additional tax attributable to newly-discovered abandoned property

Notwithstanding any other provision of law, in computing the interest due on an addition to tax owed by an estate attributable to the inclusion in the estate's federal gross estate of an asset held by the comptroller as abandoned property, the commissioner shall apply the interest rate used by the comptroller, pursuant to section fourteen hundred five of the abandoned property law, in computing the interest due on such abandoned property while in the comptroller's possession (including a zero rate if the comptroller did not pay interest on such property) if, as of the date prescribed for the filing of a return required by this article, including any extensions granted for filing, information pertaining to the asset had not yet appeared in the public records of abandoned property required to be maintained by the comptroller pursuant to section fourteen hundred one of the abandoned property law.

History: Add, L 2013, ch 197, § 1, eff July 31, 2013, applying to estates of decedents dying on or after June 1, 1944).

§ 992. Addition to tax in the case of valuation understatement

In the case of any underpayment of a tax imposed by this article which is attributable to a valuation understatement, there shall be added to the tax an amount equal to the applicable percentage of the underpayment so attributed.

(a) For purposes of this section, the applicable percentage shall be determined under the following table:

If the valuation claimed is the following percent of the correct valuation:	The applicable percentage is:
fifty percent or more but not more than sixty-six and two-thirds percent	ten
forty percent or more but less than fifty percent	twenty
less than forty percent	thirty

(b) For purposes of this section, there is a valuation understatement if the claimed value of any property is sixty-six and two-thirds percent or less of the amount determined to be the correct amount of such valuation.

(c) This section shall not apply if the underpayment is less than one thousand dollars with respect to the estate of the decedent.

(d) The commissioner may waive all or any part of the addition to tax provided by this section on showing by the executor that there was a reasonable basis for the claimed valuation and that such claim was made in good faith.

History: Add, L 1990, ch 190, § 114, eff May 25, 1990, applicable to estates of decedents dying after May 25, 1990; amd, L 1997, ch 389, § 26 (Part A), eff Feb 1, 2000, applicable to estates of decedents dying on or after Feb 1, 2000.

§ 994. Secrecy requirement and penalties for violation

(a) Secrecy requirements.

(1) Except in accordance with proper judicial order or as otherwise provided by law, it shall be unlawful for the commissioner of taxation and finance, any officer or employee of the department of taxation and finance, any person engaged or retained by such department on an independent contract basis, or any person who, pursuant to this section, is permitted to inspect any report or return or to whom a copy, an abstract or a portion of any report or return is furnished, or to whom any information contained in any report or return is furnished, to divulge or make known in any manner the value of the estate or any particulars set forth or disclosed in any report or return required under this article.

(2) The officers charged with the custody of such reports and returns shall not be required to produce any of them or evidence of anything contained in them in any action or proceeding in any court, except on behalf of the commissioner of taxation and finance in an action or proceeding under the provisions of this chapter, or in any other action or proceeding involving the collection of a tax due under this chapter to which the state or the commissioner of taxation and finance is a party or claimant, or on behalf of any party to any action or proceeding under the provisions of this article when the reports, returns or facts shown thereby are directly involved in such action or proceeding or in any proceeding under the surrogate's court procedure act to assist the surrogate to carry out his powers or duties under such act including, but not limited to the determination of the amount of court fees required to be paid under article twenty-four of such act, in any of which events the court may require the production of, and may admit in evidence, so much

of said reports, returns or of the facts shown thereby, as are pertinent to the action or proceeding and no more.

(3) Nothing herein shall be construed to prohibit the delivery to a surrogate or to any person liable for the payment of the tax imposed by this article or such liable person's duly authorized representative of a certified copy of any return, correspondence or other data filed in connection with the tax for which such person is liable or a copy of any workpaper, document or other data prepared or developed by the department during the processing, audit or investigation of that return or the collection of the tax derived therefrom or the delivery of any such copy to any person interested in the estate, any heir at law, next of kin, or beneficiary under the will, of such decedent, or a donee of property, but only if the commissioner or the surrogate, as the case may be, finds that such person, heir at law, next of kin, beneficiary, or donee has a material interest which will be affected by information contained therein. Further, nothing herein shall be construed to prohibit the publication of statistics so classified as to prevent the identification of particular reports or returns and the items thereof, or the inspection by the attorney general or other legal representatives of the state of the return of any person (or any report related to such return or any copy mentioned in the preceding sentence) who shall bring action to set aside or review the tax based thereon, or against whom an action or proceeding under this chapter has been recommended by the commissioner or the attorney general or has been instituted, or the inspection of the reports or returns required under this article by the comptroller or duly designated officer or employee of the state department of audit and control, for purposes of the audit of a refund of any tax paid by a taxpayer under this article. Further, nothing contained herein shall be construed to prevent an examination of any documents concerning an estate that are under the control of the surrogate by a title abstractor, attorney at law or title examiner or to prevent a title abstractor, attorney at law or title examiner from applying for and obtaining a discharge of lien in accordance with subsection (c) of section nine hundred eighty-two of this article or from receiving information needed in order to obtain such discharge, for the sole purpose of insuring title to real property or a chattel real and/or preparing a title abstract, title search, or title report in connection with real property or chattel real. The commissioner or the surrogate, as the case may be, may require such title abstractor, attorney at law or title examiner to certify that the sole purpose of such examination is for insuring title to real property or a chattel real and/or preparing a title abstract, title search or title report. Furthermore, nothing herein shall be construed to prohibit the delivery to a person entitled thereto under the provisions of this article of a receipt or certificate that the tax imposed under this article has been paid, in whole or in part.

(4) (A) Any officer or employee of the state who willfully violates the provisions of this subsection shall be dismissed from office and be incapable of holding any public office in this state for a period of five years thereafter.

(B) Cross-reference: For criminal penalties, see article thirty-seven of this chapter

(b) Cooperation with the United States and other states

Notwithstanding the provisions of subsection (a) of this section, the commissioner of taxation and finance may permit the secretary of the treasury of the United States or his delegates, or the proper tax officer of any state imposing an estate, inheritance or death tax on the transfer of the estate of a deceased individual or on the transfer by will or the intestate laws of such state from any person dying seized or possessed of property in such state, or the authorized representative of either such officer, to inspect any return filed under this article, or may furnish to such officer or his authorized representative an abstract of any such return or supply him with information concerning an item contained in any such return, or disclosed by an investigation of tax liability under this article, but such permission shall be granted or such information furnished to such officer or his representative only if the laws of the United States or of such other state, as the case may be, grant substantially similar privileges to the commissioner of taxation and finance or such other officer of this state charged with the administration of the tax imposed by this article and such information is to be used for tax purposes only; and provided further the commissioner of taxation and finance may furnish to the commissioner of internal revenue or his authorized representative such returns filed under this article and other tax information, as he may consider proper, for use in court actions or proceedings under the internal revenue code, whether civil or criminal, where a written request therefor has been made to the commissioner of taxation and finance by the secretary of the treasury of the United States or his delegates, provided the laws of the United States grant substantially similar powers to the secretary of the treasury of the United States or his delegates. Where the commissioner of taxation and finance has so authorized use of returns and other information in such actions or proceedings, officers and employees of the department of taxation and finance may testify in such actions or proceedings in respect to such returns or other information. Nothing herein shall be construed to prohibit the delivery of any return or the furnishing of information thereon by the commissioner of taxation and finance to the taxing authorities of another state for the purpose of complying with the provisions of section nine hundred seventy-one-a of this article relating to additional proceedings in estates of nondomiciliary decedents.

(b-1) Cooperation with investigations by certain committees of the United States Congress

(1) Notwithstanding the provisions of subsection (a) of this section, upon written request from the chairperson of the committee on ways and means of the United States House of Representatives, the chairperson of the committee on finance of the United States Senate, or the chairperson of the joint committee on taxation of the United States Congress, the commissioner shall furnish such committee with any current or prior year reports or returns specified in such request that were filed under this article by the president of the United States, vice-president of the United States, member of the United States Congress representing New York state, or any person who served in or was employed by the executive branch of the government of the United States on the executive staff of the president, in the executive office of the president, or in an acting or confirmed capacity in a position subject to confirmation by the United States senate; or, in New York state: a statewide elected official, as defined in paragraph (a) of subdivision one of section seventy-three-a of the public officers law; a state officer or employee, as defined in subparagraph (i) of paragraph (c) of subdivision one of such section seventy-three-a; a political party chairperson, as defined in paragraph (h) of subdivision one of such section seventy-three-a; a local elected official, as defined in subdivisions one and two of section eight hundred ten of the general municipal law; a person appointed, pursuant to law, to serve due to vacancy or otherwise in the position of a local elected official, as defined in subdivisions one and two of section eight hundred ten of the general municipal law; a member of the state legislature; or a judge or justice of the unified court system; or filed by a partnership, firm, association, corporation, joint-stock company, trust or similar entity directly or indirectly controlled by any individual listed in this paragraph, whether by contract, through ownership or control of a majority interest in such entity, or otherwise, or filed by a partnership, firm, association, corporation, joint-stock

company, trust or similar entity of which any individual listed in this paragraph holds ten percent or more of the voting securities of such entity; provided however that, prior to furnishing any report or return, the commissioner shall redact any copy of a federal return (or portion thereof) attached to, or any information on a federal return that is reflected on, such report or return, and any social security numbers, account numbers and residential address information.

(2) No reports or returns shall be furnished pursuant to this subsection unless the chairperson of the requesting committee certifies in writing that such reports or returns have been requested related to, and in furtherance of, a legitimate task of the Congress, that the requesting committee has made a written request to the United States secretary of the treasury for related federal reports or returns or report or return information, pursuant to 26 U.S.C. Section 6103(f), and that if such requested reports or returns are inspected by and/or submitted to another committee, to the United States House of Representatives, or to the United States Senate, then such inspection and/or submission shall occur in a manner consistent with federal law as informed by the requirements and procedures established in 26 U.S.C. Section 6103(f).

(c) Procedure and preservation of returns

(1) Reports and returns or in lieu thereof, copies or reproductions of such reports and returns, shall be preserved for eighteen years and thereafter until the commissioner of taxation and finance orders them to be destroyed.

(2) Requests for the inspection or disclosure of a report or return and such inspection or disclosure shall be made in such manner and at such time and place as shall be prescribed by the commissioner of taxation and finance.

(3) (A) A reproduction of a report or return shall, upon written request, be furnished to any person to whom disclosure or inspection of such report or return is authorized under this section. A reasonable fee may be prescribed for furnishing each page of such reproduction.

(B) Any reproduction of any report, return, document, or other matter made in accordance with this subsection shall have the same legal status as the original, and any such reproduction shall be admissible in evidence in any judicial or administrative proceeding as if it were the original, whether or not the original is in existence.

(d) Filing returns and making payment to depository banks

Notwithstanding the provisions of subsection (a) of this section, the commissioner of taxation and finance, in his discretion, may require or permit any or all of the estates, executors, beneficiaries and other persons liable for any tax imposed by this article to make payments on account of any tax, penalty or interest imposed by this article to banks, banking houses or trust companies designated by the commissioner of taxation and finance and to file returns with such banks, banking houses or trust companies as agents of the commissioner of taxation and finance, in lieu of making such payment to, or filing such returns with the commissioner of taxation and finance. However, the commissioner of taxation and finance shall designate only such banks, banking houses or trust companies as are or shall be designated by the comptroller as depositories pursuant to this article.

History: Add, L 1990, ch 190, § 114, eff May 25, 1990, applicable to estates of decedents dying after May 25, 1990; amd, L 1993, ch 286, § 1, eff July 21, 1993; L 2019, ch 91 (the "Tax

Returns Released Under Specific Terms Act"), § 10, eff July 8, 2019; L 2019, ch 92, § 9, eff July 8, 2019.

§ 997. Extensions of time for payment of estate tax where estate consists largely of interest in closely held businesses

The provisions of section 6166 of the internal revenue code shall apply to this section to the same extent as if such section of such code were contained in and made part of this section (whether or not a federal estate tax return required to be filed) except as provided herein:

(a) The phrase "adjusted gross estate" shall be read as "adjusted federal gross estate determined without reference to paragraphs (1), (2) and (3) of subsection (a) of section nine hundred fifty-four" of this article.

(b) The phrase "section 2001" shall be read as "section nine hundred fifty-two or section nine hundred sixty" of this article.

(c) The phrase "the date prescribed by section 6151(a) for payment of the tax" shall be read as "the date prescribed by this article for the payment of the tax (without regard to any extension of time)."

(d) The term "secretary" shall be read as "commissioner of taxation and finance."

(e) Election. The election under this section shall not be allowed unless a similar election was made and allowed with respect to the federal estate tax return required to be filed under the provisions of the internal revenue code. If such election was made for the purposes of the federal estate tax, the time for making the election under this article shall be the same as is required under the federal estate tax. Where no federal estate tax return is required to be filed, the election with respect to the tax imposed under this article shall be made no later than the date prescribed for the filing of the return under this article (including extensions thereof) or any time thereafter as the commissioner of taxation and finance may by regulation prescribe.

(f) The commissioner of taxation and finance may, at any time, require a bond to be filed with him, which bond has been issued by a surety company approved by the superintendent of financial services as to solvency and responsibility and authorized to transact business in this state or other security acceptable to such commissioner, in an amount not exceeding twice the amount for which the time for payment has been extended under this section, to secure the payment of the estate tax and interest, the time for payment of which has been extended under this section.

(g) If an acceleration of payment occurs with respect to the tax imposed by this article, the extension of time for payment of the tax imposed by this article shall cease to apply and any unpaid portion of the tax payable in installments shall be paid upon notice and demand from the commissioner of taxation and finance. If any such acceleration of payment is avoided by a payment within six months of the due date thereof, then the provisions of subsection (j) of this section with respect to a two percent rate of interest shall not apply to said payment and there is imposed a penalty of five percent of the amount of such payment multiplied by the number of months, or fractions thereof, after the due date of the payment and before payment is made. Such acceleration of payment shall occur if:

(1) any installment of estate tax imposed by this article is not paid on or before the

date fixed for its payment (including any extension of time for the payment of such installment), or

(2) the executor has been notified by the commissioner of taxation and finance that a bond or other security is required, but no such bond or other security has been filed within thirty days from the date of mailing of such notification, or

(3) an acceleration of payment has occurred with respect to the election by the executor to pay part or all of the federal estate tax in installments or, where no federal estate tax return is required to be filed, an acceleration of payment has occurred by virtue of the provisions of subsection (g) of section 6166 of the internal revenue code.

(h) The commissioner of taxation and finance may, for reasonable cause and if his interests would not be jeopardized thereby, extend the time for payment of any part of any installment under this subsection, including any part of a deficiency prorated to any installment under this subsection, for a reasonable period (1) not in excess of ten years from the date prescribed for the filing of the return under this article (without regard to any extension of time to file) or (2) if the date prescribed for such filing is earlier than the date which is twelve months after the due date of the last installment, such later date.

(i) If the time for payment of any amount of tax has been extended under this subsection, interest shall be paid annually together with the installment of tax on any unpaid portion of such amount (including the amount of any deficiency), at the rate prescribed in subsection (b) of section nine hundred seventy-six of this article with respect to extensions of time for payment of estate tax (other than the extensions of time provided for in this section) or as otherwise provided for in subsection (j) of this section.

(j) If the time for payment of any amount of tax has been extended under this section, the provisions of section 6166 of the internal revenue code applicable to the payment of interest are modified as follows:

(1) Interest on the two percent portion of such amount shall be paid at the rate of two percent per annum. For purposes of this section, the amount of any deficiency which is prorated to installments payable under this section, shall be treated as an amount of tax payable in installments under such section.

(2) For purposes of this paragraph, the term "two percent portion" means the lesser of fifty-four thousand dollars or the amount of the tax imposed by this article which is extended as provided in this section.

(3) If the amount of tax imposed by this article which is extended exceeds the two percent portion, any payment of a portion of such amount shall, for purposes of computing interest for periods after such payment, be treated as reducing the two percent portion by an amount which bears the same ratio to the amount of such payment as the amount of the two percent portion (determined without regard to this paragraph) bears to the amount of tax which is extended.

(4) Interest on any portion of the amount of tax which is not includible in the two percent portion of such amount shall be payable at the rate provided for in subsection (I) of this section.

(5) (A) Interest payable on any unpaid portion of the amount of tax due attributable to the first five years after the date prescribed for payment of the tax shall be paid

annually;

(B) interest payable on any unpaid portion of such amount of tax attributable to any period after the five year period referred to in subparagraph (a) of this paragraph shall be paid annually at the same time as and as part of, each installment payment of the tax;

(C) in the case of a deficiency to which subsection (e) of 6166 of the internal revenue code applies is determined after the close of the five year period referred to in subparagraph (A) of this paragraph, interest attributable to such five year period, and interest assigned under subparagraph (B) of this paragraph to any installment, the date of payment of which has arrived on or before the date of such determination, shall be paid upon notice and demand from the commissioner of taxation and finance; and

(D) if the executor has selected a period shorter than five years, such shorter period shall be substituted for five years in subparagraphs (A), (B) and (C) of this paragraph. Any period of time selected for the purposes of the tax under this article shall in no event be greater than the period of time selected for the purpose of the estate tax imposed by the internal revenue code.

(k) The lien of the tax provided for in section nine hundred eighty-two of this article shall be applicable to the same extent as if no election had been made to extend the time for payment of estate tax under this section.

History: Add, L 1990, ch 190, § 114, eff May 25, 1990, applicable to estates of decedents dying after May 25, 1990; amd, L 1992, ch 826, § 12, eff Aug 7, 1992; L 1994, ch 170, § 258, eff June 9, 1994, applying to estates of decedents dying after such effective date; L 1997, ch 389, §§ 7, 27 (Part A), eff Feb 1, 2000, ; L 1998, ch 56, §§ 41, 42 (Part A), eff April 28, 1998, applying to estates of decedents dying after Dec 31, 1998; L 2011, ch 62, § 104 (Part A), eff Oct 3, 2011; L 2014, ch 59, § 7 (Part X), eff April 1, 2014, applying to estates of decedents dying on and after that date.

§ 998. Petition to the surrogate's court and appeal

(a) General

A taxpayer shall have the right to protest a notice of deficiency or a notice of disallowance of a claim for refund issued by the commissioner of taxation and finance with respect to tax under this article as provided in this section. A proceeding under this section shall be a special proceeding under article four of the civil practice law and rules and shall be commenced by filing a notice of petition and verified petition with the surrogate's court and service of such notice of petition and verified petition on the commissioner of taxation and finance or the commissioner's attorney. In any county which has designated a transfer and estate clerk of the court, the filing of the notice of petition and verified petition with the surrogate's court shall be effected by filing such notice of petition and verified petition with such clerk. The notice of petition, together with the petition and any affidavits specified in the notice, shall be so filed and served at least forty-five days before the time at which the petition is noticed to be heard. An answer and supporting affidavits, if any, shall be served at least ten days before such time. A reply, together with supporting affidavits, if any, shall be served at least five days before such time. No petition shall be denied without opportunity for a hearing of any issues of fact raised therein.

(b) Conciliation conferences

The provisions of subdivision three-a of section one hundred seventy of this chapter regarding conciliation conferences in the bureau of conciliation and mediation services shall be applicable with respect to a notice of deficiency or disallowance of a refund of tax under this article provided, however, the references to "the division of tax appeals" shall be deemed to be references to "the surrogate's court" for purposes of the tax under this article and references to filing a petition shall be deemed to be references to the commencement of a special proceeding under this section.

(c) Jurisdiction and venue

The surrogate's court of every county having jurisdiction of the estate of a decedent under the provisions of sections two hundred five and two hundred six of the surrogate's court procedure act shall have jurisdiction of proceedings under this section. Venue of such proceedings shall be as provided in such sections.

(d) Petition for review of a deficiency

Within ninety days, or one hundred fifty days if the notice is addressed to a person outside of the United States, after the mailing of the notice of deficiency of estate tax, the taxpayer may commence a special proceeding pursuant to this section in the surrogate's court for review of the deficiency. Such petition may also assert a claim for refund of tax under this article, subject to the limitations of subsection (g) of section six hundred eighty-seven of this chapter, as made applicable to the tax imposed under this article by section nine hundred ninety.

(e) Petition for refund

(1) A taxpayer may commence a special proceeding with the surrogate's court under this section for the amounts asserted in a claim for refund if

(A) the taxpayer has filed a timely claim for refund with the commissioner of taxation and finance,

(B) the taxpayer has not previously commenced a special proceeding under subsection (d) regarding the tax imposed by this article with respect to the death of the same decedent unless the petition under this subsection relates to a separate claim for refund properly filed under subsection (f) of section six hundred eighty-seven, as made applicable to the tax imposed by this article by section nine hundred ninety, and

(C) either (i) six months have expired since the claim was filed, or (ii) the commissioner has mailed to the taxpayer, by registered or certified mail, a notice of disallowance of such claim in whole or in part.

(2) No special proceeding under this subsection shall be filed more than two years after the date of mailing of a notice of disallowance, unless prior to the expiration of such two year period it has been extended by written agreement between the taxpayer and the commissioner of taxation and finance. If a taxpayer files a written waiver of the requirement that such taxpayer be mailed a notice of disallowance, the two year period prescribed by this paragraph for filing a petition for refund shall begin on the date such waiver is filed.

(f) Assertion of deficiency after filing petition

(1) Petition for review of deficiency. If a taxpayer commences a special proceeding for

review of a deficiency, the commissioner may assert and the surrogate's court shall have power to determine a greater deficiency than asserted in the notice of deficiency and the commissioner may assert and the surrogate's court shall have power to determine any addition to tax or penalty.

(2) Petition for refund. If the taxpayer commences a special proceeding for refund, the commissioner may assert and the surrogate's court may determine:

(A) a deficiency as to any amount of deficiency asserted within the period in which an assessment would be timely, or

(B) deny so much of the amount for which refund is sought in the petition, as is offset by other issues pertaining to the taxpayer.

(3) Opportunity to respond. A taxpayer shall be given a reasonable opportunity to respond to any matters asserted by the commissioner under this subsection.

(4) Restriction on further notices of deficiency. If the taxpayer commences a special proceeding under this section, no notice of deficiency of estate tax may thereafter be issued to the taxpayer regarding the tax imposed by this article with respect to the death of the same decedent, except in case of fraud or with respect to a change or correction required to be reported under section nine hundred seventy-nine.

(g) Burden of proof

In any case before the surrogate's court under this section, the burden of proof shall be upon the petitioner, except for the following issues, as to which the burden of proof shall be upon the commissioner:

(1) whether the petitioner has been guilty of fraud with intent to evade tax;

(2) whether the petitioner is liable as the transferee of property of a taxpayer, but not to show that the taxpayer was liable for the tax;

(3) whether the petitioner is liable for any increase in a deficiency where such increase is asserted initially after a notice of deficiency was mailed and a special proceeding commenced under this section, unless such increase in deficiency is the result of a change or correction required to be reported under section nine hundred seventy-nine, and of which change or correction the commissioner of taxation and finance had no notice at the time the commissioner mailed the notice of deficiency; and

(4) whether any person is liable for a penalty under subsection (k) or (r) of section six hundred eighty-five of this chapter, as made applicable to the tax imposed by this article by section nine hundred ninety.

(h) Review under this section exclusive

The review of a deficiency or denial of a refund provided by this section shall be the exclusive remedy available for the judicial review of the liability of the taxpayer for the taxes imposed by this article.

(i) Appeal; assessment pending appeal; appeal bond

(1) The taxpayer or the commissioner of taxation and finance may appeal from a decree entered in a special proceeding pursuant to this section as provided in section two thousand

seven hundred one of the surrogate's court procedure act.

(2) Irrespective of any restrictions on the assessment and collection of deficiencies, the commissioner may assess a deficiency determined by the surrogate's court after the expiration of the period during which a notice of appeal may be filed, notwithstanding that a notice of appeal has been filed by the taxpayer with respect to such deficiency, unless the taxpayer, at or before the time his notice of appeal is filed, has paid the deficiency, has deposited with the commissioner the amount of the deficiency, or has filed with the commissioner a bond or other security acceptable to the commissioner (which may be a jeopardy bond under subsection (h) of section six hundred ninety-four, as made applicable to the tax imposed by this article by section nine hundred ninety) in the amount of the portion of the deficiency (including interest and other amounts) in respect of which the appeal is made and all costs and charges which may accrue against the taxpayer in the prosecution of the proceeding, including costs of all appeals, conditioned upon the payment of the deficiency (including interest and other amounts) as finally determined and such costs and charges. If as a result of a waiver of the restrictions on the assessment and collection of a deficiency any part of the amount determined by the commissioner is paid after the filing of the review bond or other security, such bond or other security shall, at the request of the taxpayer, be proportionately reduced.

(3) If the amount of a deficiency determined by the commissioner is disallowed in whole or in part by the court, the amount so disallowed shall be credited or refunded to the taxpayer, without the making of a claim therefor, or, if payment has not been made, shall be abated.

(j) Date of finality of decree

A decree of the surrogate's court shall become final upon the expiration of the time for filing a notice of appeal if no such notice is filed within such time, or if a notice of appeal has been duly filed, upon expiration of the time for all judicial review, or upon the entry of a decree of the surrogate's court in accordance with the mandate of the court on appeal.

> **History:** Add, L 1990, ch 190, § 114, eff May 25, 1990, applicable to estates of decedents dying after May 25, 1990.

§ 999. Deposit and disposition of revenue

All taxes, interest, penalties and fees collected or received by the tax commission under this article shall be deposited and disposed of pursuant to the provisions of section one hundred seventy-one-a of this chapter.

> **History:** Formerly § 963, add, L 1978, ch 69, § 24, eff Oct 1, 1978; renumbered § 999, L 1990, ch 190, § 115, eff May 25, 1990, applicable to estates of decedents dying after May 25, 1990.

§ 999-a. Appendix to article twenty-six

The following provisions of the United States Internal Revenue Code of 1986, with all amendments enacted on or before January first, two thousand fourteen, shall apply to the tax imposed by this article, to the extent specified in this article.

§ 2031. Definition of Gross Estate.

(a) General.—The value of the gross estate of the decedent shall be determined by including to the extent provided for in this part, the value at the time of his death of all property, real or personal, tangible or intangible, wherever situated.

(b) Valuation of unlisted stock and securities.—In the case of stock and securities of a corporation the value of which, by reason of their not being listed on an exchange and by reason of the absence of sales thereof, cannot be determined with reference to bid and asked prices or with reference to sales prices, the value thereof shall be determined by taking into consideration, in addition to all other factors, the value of stock or securities of corporations engaged in the same or a similar line of business which are listed on an exchange.

(c) Estate tax with respect to land subject to a qualified conservation easement.—

(1) In general.—If the executor makes the election described in paragraph (6), then, except as otherwise provided in this subsection, there shall be excluded from the gross estate the lesser of—

(A) the applicable percentage of the value of land subject to a qualified conservation easement, reduced by the amount of any deduction under section 2055(f) with respect to such land, or

(B) the exclusion limitation.

(2) Applicable percentage.—For purposes of paragraph (1), the term "applicable percentage" means 40 percent reduced (but not below zero) by 2 percentage points for each percentage point (or fraction thereof) by which the value of the qualified conservation easement is less than 30 percent of the value of the land (determined without regard to the value of such easement and reduced by the value of any retained development right (as defined in paragraph (5)). The values taken into account under the preceding sentence shall be such values as of the date of the contribution referred to in paragraph (8)(B).

(3) Exclusion limitation.—For purposes of paragraph (1), the exclusion limitation is the limitation determined in accordance with the following table:

In the case of estates of decedents dying during:	The exclusion limitation is:
1998	100,000
1999	200,000
2000	300,000
2001	400,000
2002 or thereafter	500,000

(4) Treatment of certain indebtedness.—

(A) In general.—The exclusion provided in paragraph (1) shall not apply to the extent that the land is debt-financed property.

(B) Definitions.—For purposes of this paragraph—

(i) Debt-financed property.—The term "debt-financed property" means any property with respect to which there is an acquisition indebtedness (as defined in clause (ii)) on the date of the decedent's death.

(ii) Acquisition indebtedness.—The term "acquisition indebtedness" means, with respect to debt-financed property, the unpaid amount of—

(I) the indebtedness incurred by the donor in acquiring such property,

(II) the indebtedness incurred before the acquisition of such property if such indebtedness would not have been incurred but for such acquisition,

(III) the indebtedness incurred after the acquisition of such property if such indebtedness would not have been incurred but for such acquisition and the incurrence of such indebtedness was reasonably foreseeable at the time of such acquisition, and

(IV) the extension, renewal, or refinancing of an acquisition indebtedness.

(5) Treatment of retained development right.—

(A) In general.—Paragraph (1) shall not apply to the value of any development right retained by the donor in the conveyance of a qualified conservation easement.

(B) Termination of retained development right.—If every person in being who has an interest (whether or not in possession) in the land executes an agreement to extinguish permanently some or all of any development rights (as defined in subparagraph (D)) retained by the donor on or before the date for filing the return of the tax imposed by section 2001, then any tax imposed by section 2001 shall be reduced accordingly. Such agreement shall be filed with the return of the tax imposed by section 2001. The agreement shall be in such form as the Secretary shall prescribe.

(C) Additional tax.—Any failure to implement the agreement described in subparagraph (B) not later than the earlier of—

(i) the date which is 2 years after the date of the decedent's death, or

(ii) the date of the sale of such land subject to the qualified conservation easement, shall result in the imposition of an additional tax in the amount of the tax which would have been due on the retained development rights subject to such agreement. Such additional tax shall be due and payable on the last day of the 6th month following such date.

(D) Development right defined.—For purposes of this paragraph, the term "development right" means any right to use the land subject to the qualified conservation easement in which such right is retained for any commercial purpose which is not subordinate to and directly supportive of the use of such land as a farm for farming purposes (within the meaning of section 2032A(e)(5)).

(6) Election.—The election under this subsection shall be made on or before the due date (including extensions) for filing the return of tax imposed by section 2001 and shall be made on such return. Such an election, once made, shall be irrevocable.

(7) Calculation of estate tax due.—An executor making the election described in paragraph (6) shall, for purposes of calculating the amount of tax imposed by section 2001, include the value of any development right (as defined in paragraph (5)) retained by the donor in the conveyance of such qualified conservation easement. The computation of tax on any retained development right prescribed in this paragraph shall be done in such manner and on such forms as the Secretary shall prescribe.

(8) Definitions.—For purposes of this subsection—

(A) Land subject to a qualified conservation easement.—The term "land subject to a qualified conservation easement" means land—

(i) which is located in the United States or any possession of the United States,

(ii) which was owned by the decedent or a member of the decedent's family at all times during the 3-year period ending on the date of the decedent's death, and

(iii) with respect to which a qualified conservation easement has been made by an individual described in subparagraph (C), as of the date of the election described in paragraph (6).

(B) Qualified conservation easement.—The term "qualified conservation easement" means a qualified conservation contribution (as defined in section 170(h)(1)) of a qualified real property interest (as defined in section 170(h)(2)(C)), except that clause (iv) of section 170(h)(4)(A) shall not apply, and the restriction on the use of such interest described in section 170(h)(2)(C) shall include a prohibition on more than a de minimis use for a commercial recreational activity.

(C) Individual described.—An individual is described in this subparagraph if such individual is—

(i) the decedent,

(ii) a member of the decedent's family,

(iii) the executor of the decedent's estate, or

(iv) the trustee of a trust the corpus of which includes the land to be subject to the qualified conservation easement.

(D) Member of family.—The term "member of the decedent's family" means any member of the family (as defined in section 2032A(e)(2)) of the decedent.

(9) Treatment of easements granted after death.—In any case in which the qualified conservation easement is granted after the date of the decedent's death and on or before the due date (including extensions) for filing the return of tax imposed by section 2001, the deduction under section 2055(f) with respect to such easement shall be allowed to the estate but only if no charitable deduction is allowed under chapter 1 to any person with respect to the grant of such easement.

(10) Application of this section to interests in partnerships, corporations, and trusts.—This section shall apply to an interest in a partnership, corporation, or trust if at least 30 percent of the entity is owned (directly or indirectly) by the decedent, as determined under the rules described in section 2057(e)(3).

(d) Cross reference.—For executor's right to be furnished on request a statement regarding any valuation made by the Secretary within the gross estate, see section 7517.

§ 2032. Alternate Valuation.

(a) General.—The value of the gross estate may be determined, if the executor so elects, by valuing all the property included in the gross estate as follows:

(1) In the case of property distributed, sold, exchanged, or otherwise disposed of, within 6 months after the decedent's death such property shall be valued as of the date of distribution, sale, exchange, or other disposition.

(2) In the case of property not distributed, sold, exchanged, or otherwise disposed of, within 6 months after the decedent's death such property shall be valued as of the date 6 months after the decedent's death.

(3) Any interest or estate which is affected by mere lapse of time shall be included at its value as of the time of death (instead of the later date) with adjustment for any difference in its value as of the later date not due to mere lapse of time.

(b) Special rules.—No deduction under this chapter of any item shall be allowed if allowance for such items is in effect given by the alternate valuation provided by this section. Wherever in any other subsection or section of this chapter reference is made to the value of property at the time of the decedent's death, such reference shall be deemed to refer to the value of such property used in determining the value of the gross estate. In case of an election made by the executor under this section, then—

(1) for purposes of the charitable deduction under section 2055 or 2106(a)(2), any bequest, legacy, devise, or transfer enumerated therein, and

(2) for the purpose of the marital deduction under section 2056, any interest in property passing to the surviving spouse, shall be valued as of the date of the decedent's death with adjustment for any difference in value (not due to mere lapse of time or the occurrence or nonoccurrence of a contingency) of the property as of the date 6 months after the decedent's death (substituting, in the case of property distributed by the executor or trustee, or sold, exchanged, or otherwise disposed of, during such 6-month period, the date thereof).

(c) Election must decrease gross estate and estate tax.—No election may be made under this section with respect to an estate unless such election will decrease—

(1) the value of the gross estate, and

(2) the sum of the tax imposed by this chapter and the tax imposed by chapter 13 with respect to property includible in the decedent's gross estate (reduced by credits allowable against such taxes).

(d) Election.—

(1) In general.—The election provided for in this section shall be made by the executor on the return of the tax imposed by this chapter. Such election, once made, shall be irrevocable.

(2) Exception.—No election may be made under this section if such return is filed more than 1 year after the time prescribed by law (including extensions) for filing such return.

§ 2032A. Valuation of Certain Farm, Etc., Real Property.

(a) Value based on use under which property qualifies.—

(1) General rule.—If—

(A) the decedent was (at the time of his death) a citizen or resident of the United States, and

(B) the executor elects the application of this section and files the agreement referred to in subsection (d)(2), then, for purposes of this chapter, the value of qualified real property shall be its value for the use under which it qualifies, under subsection (b), as qualified real property.

(2) Limitation on aggregate reduction in fair market value.—The aggregate decrease in the value of qualified real property taken into account for purposes of this chapter which results from the application of paragraph (1) with respect to any decedent shall not exceed $750,000.

(3) Inflation adjustment.—In the case of estates of decedents dying in a calendar year after 1998, the $750,000 amount contained in paragraph (2) shall be increased by an amount equal to—

(A) $750,000, multiplied by

(B) the cost-of-living adjustment determined under section 1(f)(3) for such calendar year by substituting "calendar year 1997" for "calendar year 1992" in subparagraph (B) thereof.

If any amount as adjusted under the preceding sentence is not a multiple of $10,000, such amount shall be rounded to the next lowest multiple of $10,000.

(b) Qualified real property.—

(1) In general.—For purposes of this section, the term "qualified real property" means real property located in the United States which was acquired from or passed from the decedent to a qualified heir of the decedent and which, on the date of the decedent's death, was being used for a qualified use by the decedent or a member of the decedent's family, but only if—

(A) 50 percent or more of the adjusted value of the gross estate consists of the adjusted value of real or personal property which—

(i) on the date of the decedent's death, was being used for a qualified use by the decedent or a member of the decedent's family, and

(ii) was acquired from or passed from the decedent to a qualified heir of the decedent.

(B) 25 percent or more of the adjusted value of the gross estate consists of the adjusted value of real property which meets the requirements of subparagraphs (A)(ii) and (C),

(C) during the 8-year period ending on the date of the decedent's death there have been periods aggregating 5 years or more during which—

(i) such real property was owned by the decedent or a member of the decedent's family and used for a qualified use by the decedent or a member of the decedent's family, and

(ii) there was material participation by the decedent or a member of the decedent's family in the operation of the farm or other business, and

(D) such real property is designated in the agreement referred to in subsection (d)(2).

(2) Qualified use.—For purposes of this section, the term "qualified use" means the devotion of the property to any of the following:

(A) use as a farm for farming purposes, or .

(B) use in a trade or business other than the trade or business of farming.

(3) Adjusted value.—For purposes of paragraph (1), the term "adjusted value" means—

(A) in the case of the gross estate, the value of the gross estate for purposes of this chapter (determined without regard to this section), reduced by any amounts allowable as a deduction under paragraph (4) of section 2053(a), or

(B) in the case of any real or personal property, the value of such property for purposes of this chapter (determined without regard to this section), reduced by any amounts allowable as a deduction in respect of such property under paragraph (4) of section 2053(a).

(4) Decedents who are retired or disabled.—

(A) In general.—If, on the date of the decedent's death, the requirements of paragraph (1)(C)(ii) with respect to the decedent for any property are not met, and the decedent—

(i) was receiving old-age benefits under title II of the Social Security Act for a continuous period ending on such date, or

(ii) was disabled for a continuous period ending on such date, then paragraph (1)(C)(ii) shall be applied with respect to such property by substituting "the date on which the longer of such continuous periods began" for "the date of the decedent's death" in paragraph (1)(C).

(B) Disabled defined.—For purposes of subparagraph (A), an individual shall be disabled if such individual has a mental or physical impairment which renders him unable to materially participate in the operation of the farm or other business.

(C) Coordination with recapture.—For purposes of subsection (c)(6)(B)(i), if the requirements of paragraph (1)(C)(ii) are met with respect to any decedent by reason of subparagraph (A), the period ending on the date on which the continuous period taken into account under subparagraph (A) began shall be treated as the period immediately before the decedent's death.

(5) Special rules for surviving spouses.—

(A) In general.—If property is qualified real property with respect to a decedent (hereinafter in this paragraph referred to as the "first decedent") and such property was acquired from or passed from the first decedent to the surviving spouse of the first decedent, for purposes of applying this subsection and subsection (c) in the case of the estate of such surviving spouse, active management of the farm or other business by the surviving spouse shall be treated as material participation by such surviving spouse in the operation of such farm or business.

(B) Special rule.—For the purposes of subparagraph (A), the determination of whether property is qualified real property with respect to the first decedent shall be made without regard to subparagraph (D) of paragraph (1) and without regard to whether an election under this section was made.

(C) Coordination with paragraph (4).—In any case in which to do so will enable the requirements of paragraph (1)(C)(ii) to be met with respect to the surviving spouse, this subsection and subsection (c) shall be applied by taking into account any application of paragraph (4).

(c) Tax treatment of dispositions and failures to use for qualified use.—

(1) Imposition of additional estate tax.—If, within 10 years after the decedent's death and before the death of the qualified heir—

(A) the qualified heir disposes of any interest in qualified real property (other than by a disposition to a member of his family), or

(B) the qualified heir ceases to use for the qualified use the qualified real property which was acquired (or passed) from the decedent,

then, there is hereby imposed an additional estate tax.

(2) Amount of additional tax.—

(A) In general.—The amount of the additional tax imposed by paragraph (1) with respect to any interest shall be the amount equal to the lesser of—

(i) the adjusted tax difference attributable to such interest, or

(ii) the excess of the amount realized with respect to the interest (or, in any case other than a sale or exchange at arm's length, the fair market value of the interest) over the value of the interest determined under subsection (a).

(B) Adjusted tax difference attributable to interest.—For purposes of subparagraph (A), the adjusted tax difference attributable to an interest is the amount which bears the same ratio to the adjusted tax difference with respect to the estate (determined under subparagraph (C)) as—

(i) the excess of the value of such interest for purposes of this chapter (determined without regard to subsection (a)) over the value of such interest determined under subsection (a), bears to

(ii) a similar excess determined for all qualified real property.

(C) Adjusted tax difference with respect to the estate.—For purposes of subparagraph (B), the term "adjusted tax difference with respect to the estate" means the excess of what would have been the estate tax liability but for subsection (a) over the estate tax liability. For purposes of this subparagraph, the term "estate tax liability" means the tax imposed by section 2001 reduced by the credits allowable against such tax.

(D) Partial dispositions.—For purposes of this paragraph, where the qualified heir disposes of a portion of the interest acquired by (or passing to) such heir (or a predecessor qualified heir) or there is a cessation of use of such a portion—

(i) the value determined under subsection (a) taken into account under subparagraph (A)(ii) with respect to such portion shall be its pro rata share of such value of such interest, and

(ii) the adjusted tax difference attributable to the interest taken into account with respect to the transaction involving the second or any succeeding portion shall be reduced by the amount of the tax imposed by this subsection with respect to all prior transactions involving portions of such interest.

(E) Special rule for disposition of timber.—In the case of qualified woodland to which an election under subsection (e)(13)(A) applies, if the qualified heir disposes of (or severs) any standing timber on such qualified woodland—

    (i) such disposition (or severance) shall be treated as a disposition of a portion of the interest of the qualified heir in such property, and

    (ii) the amount of the additional tax imposed by paragraph (1) with respect to such disposition shall be an amount equal to the lesser of—

        (I) the amount realized on such disposition (or, in any case other than a sale or exchange at arm's length, the fair market value of the portion of the interest disposed or severed), or

        (II) the amount of additional tax determined under this paragraph (without regard to this subparagraph) if the entire interest of the qualified heir in the qualified woodland had been disposed of, less the sum of the amount of the additional tax imposed with respect to all prior transactions involving such woodland to which this subparagraph applied.

For purposes of the preceding sentence, the disposition of a right to sever shall be treated as the disposition of the standing timber. The amount of additional tax imposed under paragraph (1) in any case in which a qualified heir disposes of his entire interest in the qualified woodland shall be reduced by any amount determined under this subparagraph with respect to such woodland.

(3) Only 1 additional tax imposed with respect to any 1 portion.—In the case of an interest acquired from (or passing from) any decedent, if subparagraph (A) or (B) of paragraph (1) applies to any portion of an interest, subparagraph (B) or (A), as the case may be, of paragraph (1) shall not apply with respect to the same portion of such interest.

(4) Due date.—The additional tax imposed by this subsection shall become due and payable on the day which is 6 months after the date of the disposition or cessation referred to in paragraph (1).

(5) Liability for tax; furnishing of bond.—The qualified heir shall be personally liable for the additional tax imposed by this subsection with respect to his interest unless the heir has furnished bond which meets the requirements of subsection (e)(11).

(6) Cessation of qualified use.—For purposes of paragraph (1)(B), real property shall cease to be used for the qualified use if—

    (A) such property ceases to be used for the qualified use set forth in subparagraph (A) or (B) of subsection (b)(2) under which the property qualified under subsection (b), or

    (B) during any period of 8 years ending after the date of the decedent's death and before the date of the death of the qualified heir, there had been periods aggregating more than 3 years during which—

        (i) in the case of periods during which the property was held by the decedent, there was no material participation by the decedent or any member of his family in the operation of the farm or other business, and

(ii) in the case of periods during which the property was held by any qualified heir, there was no material participation by such qualified heir or any member of his family in the operation of the farm or other business.

(7) Special rules.—

(A) No tax if use begins within 2 years.—If the date on which the qualified heir begins to use the qualified real property (hereinafter in this subparagraph referred to as the commencement date) is before the date 2 years after the decedent's death—

(i) no tax shall be imposed under paragraph (1) by reason of the failure by the qualified heir to so use such property before the commencement date, and

(ii) the 10-year period under paragraph (1) shall be extended by the period after the decedent's death and before the commencement date.

(B) Active management by eligible qualified heir treated as material participation.—For purposes of paragraph (6)(B)(ii), the active management of a farm or other business by—

(i) an eligible qualified heir, or

(ii) a fiduciary of an eligible qualified heir described in clause (ii) or (iii) of subparagraph (C), shall be treated as material participation by such eligible qualified heir in the operation of such farm or business. In the case of an eligible qualified heir described in clause (ii), (iii), or (iv) of subparagraph (C), the preceding sentence shall apply only during periods during which such heir meets the requirements of such clause.

(C) Eligible qualified heir.—For purposes of this paragraph, the term "eligible qualified heir" means a qualified heir who—

(i) is the surviving spouse of the decedent,

(ii) has not attained the age of 21,

(iii) is disabled (within the meaning of subsection (b)(4)(B)), or

(iv) is a student.

(D) Student.—For purposes of subparagraph (C), an individual shall be treated as a student with respect to periods during any calendar year if (and only if) such individual is a student (within the meaning of section 152(f)(2)) for such calendar year.

(E) Certain rents treated as qualified use.—For purposes of this subsection, a surviving spouse or lineal descendant of the decedent shall not be treated as failing to use qualified real property in a qualified use solely because such spouse or descendant rents such property to a member of the family of such spouse or descendant on a net cash basis. For purposes of the preceding sentence, a legally adopted child of an individual shall be treated as the child of such individual by blood.

(8) Qualified conservation contribution is not a disposition.—A qualified conservation contribution (as defined in section 170(h)) by gift or otherwise shall not be deemed a

disposition under subsection (c)(1)(A).

(d) Election; agreement.—

(1) Election.—The election under this section shall be made on the return of the tax imposed by section 2001. Such election shall be made in such manner as the Secretary shall by regulations prescribe. Such an election, once made, shall be irrevocable.

(2) Agreement.—The agreement referred to in this paragraph is a written agreement signed by each person in being who has an interest (whether or not in possession) in any property designated in such agreement consenting to the application of subsection (c) with respect to such property.

(3) Modification of election and agreement to be permitted.—The Secretary shall prescribe procedures which provide that in any case in which the executor makes an election under paragraph (1) (and submits the agreement referred to in paragraph (2)) within the time prescribed therefor, but—

(A) the notice of election, as filed, does not contain all required information, or

(B) signatures of 1 or more persons required to enter into the agreement described in paragraph (2) are not included on the agreement as filed, or the agreement does not contain all required information, the executor will have a reasonable period of time (not exceeding 90 days) after notification of such failures to provide such information or signatures.

(e) Definitions; special rules.—For purposes of this section—

(1) Qualified heir.—The term "qualified heir" means, with respect to any property, a member of the decedent's family who acquired such property (or to whom such property passed) from the decedent. If a qualified heir disposes of any interest in qualified real property to any member of his family, such member shall thereafter be treated as the qualified heir with respect to such interest.

(2) Member of family.—The term "member of the family" means, with respect to any individual, only—

(A) an ancestor of such individual,

(B) the spouse of such individual,

(C) a lineal descendant of such individual, of such individual's spouse, or of a parent of such individual, or

(D) the spouse of any lineal descendant described in subparagraph (C).

For purposes of the preceding sentence, a legally adopted child of an individual shall be treated as the child of such individual by blood.

(3) Certain real property included.—In the case of real property which meets the requirements of subparagraph (C) of subsection (b)(1), residential buildings and related improvements on such real property occupied on a regular basis by the owner or lessee of such real property or by persons employed by such owner or lessee for the purpose of operating or maintaining such real property, and roads, buildings, and other structures and

improvements functionally related to the qualified use shall be treated as real property devoted to the qualified use.

(4) Farm.—The term "farm" includes stock, dairy, poultry, fruit, furbearing animal, and truck farms, plantations, ranches, nurseries, ranges, greenhouses or other similar structures used primarily for the raising of agricultural or horticultural commodities, and orchards and woodlands.

(5) Farming purposes.—The term "farming purposes" means—

(A) cultivating the soil or raising or harvesting any agricultural or horticultural commodity (including the raising, shearing, feeding, caring for, training, and management of animals) on a farm;

(B) handling, drying, packing, grading, or storing on a farm any agricultural or horticultural commodity in its unmanufactured state, but only if the owner, tenant, or operator of the farm regularly produces more than one-half of the commodity so treated; and

(C) (i) the planting, cultivating, caring for, or cutting of trees, or

(ii) the preparation (other than milling) of trees for market.

(6) Material participation.—Material participation shall be determined in a manner similar to the manner used for purposes of paragraph (1) of section 1402(a) (relating to net earnings from self-employment).

(7) Method of valuing farms.—

(A) In general.—Except as provided in subparagraph (B), the value of a farm for farming purposes shall be determined by dividing—

(i) the excess of the average annual gross cash rental for comparable land used for farming purposes and located in the locality of such farm over the average annual State and local real estate taxes for such comparable land, by

(ii) the average annual effective interest rate for all new Federal Land Bank loans.

For purposes of the preceding sentence, each average annual computation shall be made on the basis of the 5 most recent calendar years ending before the date of the decedent's death.

(B) Value based on net share rental in certain cases.—

(i) In general.—If there is no comparable land from which the average annual gross cash rental may be determined but there is comparable land from which the average net share rental may be determined, subparagraph (A)(i) shall be applied by substituting "average annual net share rental" for "average annual gross cash rental".

(ii) Net share rental.—For purposes of this paragraph, the term "net share rental" means the excess of—

(I) the value of the produce received by the lessor of the land on which such produce is grown, over

(II) the cash operating expenses of growing such produce which, under the lease, are paid by the lessor.

(C) Exception.—The formula provided by subparagraph (A) shall not be used—

(i) where it is established that there is no comparable land from which the average annual gross cash rental may be determined, or

(ii) where the executor elects to have the value of the farm for farming purposes determined and that there is no comparable land from which the average net share rental may be determined under paragraph (8).

(8) Method of valuing closely held business interests, etc.—In any case to which paragraph (7)(A) does not apply, the following factors shall apply in determining the value of any qualified real property:

(A) The capitalization of income which the property can be expected to yield for farming or closely held business purposes over a reasonable period of time under prudent management using traditional cropping patterns for the area, taking into account soil capacity, terrain configuration, and similar factors,

(B) The capitalization of the fair rental value of the land for farmland or closely held business purposes,

(C) Assessed land values in a State which provides a differential or use value assessment law for farmland or closely held business,

(D) Comparable sales of other farm or closely held business land in the same geographical area far enough removed from a metropolitan or resort area so that nonagricultural use is not a significant factor in the sales price, and

(E) Any other factor which fairly values the farm or closely held business value of the property.

(9) Property acquired from decedent.—Property shall be considered to have been acquired from or to have passed from the decedent if—

(A) such property is so considered under section 1014(b) (relating to basis of property acquired from a decedent),

(B) such property is acquired by any person from the estate, or

(C) such property is acquired by any person from a trust (to the extent such property is includible in the gross estate of the decedent).

(10) Community property.—If the decedent and his surviving spouse at any time held qualified real property as community property, the interest of the surviving spouse in such property shall be taken into account under this section to the extent necessary to provide a result under this section with respect to such property which is consistent with the result which would have obtained under this section if such property had not been community property.

(11) Bond in lieu of personal liability.—If the qualified heir makes written application to the Secretary for determination of the maximum amount of the additional tax which may be imposed by subsection (c) with respect to the qualified heir's interest,

the Secretary (as soon as possible, and in any event within 1 year after the making of such application) shall notify the heir of such maximum amount. The qualified heir, on furnishing a bond in such amount and for such period as may be required, shall be discharged from personal liability for any additional tax imposed by subsection (c) and shall be entitled to a receipt or writing showing such discharge.

(12) Active management.—The term "active management" means the making of the management decisions of a business (other than the daily operating decisions).

(13) Special rules for woodlands.—

(A) In general.—In the case of any qualified woodland with respect to which the executor elects to have this subparagraph apply, trees growing on such woodland shall not be treated as a crop.

(B) Qualified woodland.—The term "qualified woodland" means any real property which—

(i) is used in timber operations, and

(ii) is an identifiable area of land such as an acre or other area for which records are normally maintained in conducting timber operations.

(C) Timber operations.—The term "timber operations" means—

(i) the planting, cultivating, caring for, or cutting of trees, or

(ii) the preparation (other than milling) of trees for market.

(D) Election.—An election under subparagraph (A) shall be made on the return of the tax imposed by section 2001. Such election shall be made in such manner as the Secretary shall by regulations prescribe. Such an election, once made, shall be irrevocable.

(14) Treatment of replacement property acquired in section 1031 or 1033 transactions.—

(A) In general.—In the case of any qualified replacement property, any period during which there was ownership, qualified use, or material participation with respect to the replaced property by the decedent or any member of his family shall be treated as a period during which there was such ownership, use, or material participation (as the case may be) with respect to the qualified replacement property.

(B) Limitation.—Subparagraph (A) shall not apply to the extent that the fair market value of the qualified replacement property (as of the date of its acquisition) exceeds the fair market value of the replaced property (as of the date of its disposition).

(C) Definitions.—For purposes of this paragraph—

(i) Qualified replacement property.—The term "qualified replacement property" means any real property which is—

(I) acquired in an exchange which qualifies under section 1031, or

(II) the acquisition of which results in the nonrecognition of gain under section 1033.

Such term shall only include property which is used for the same qualified use as the replaced property was being used before the exchange.

(ii) Replaced property.—The term "replaced property" means—

(I) the property transferred in the exchange which qualifies under section 1031, or

(II) the property compulsorily or involuntarily converted (within the meaning of section 1033).

(f) Statute of limitations.—If qualified real property is disposed of or ceases to be used for a qualified use, then—

(1) the statutory period for the assessment of any additional tax under subsection (c) attributable to such disposition or cessation shall not expire before the expiration of 3 years from the date the Secretary is notified (in such manner as the Secretary may by regulations prescribe) of such disposition or cessation (or if later in the case of an involuntary conversion or exchange to which subsection (h) or (i) applies, 3 years from the date the Secretary is notified of the replacement of the converted property or of an intention not to replace or of the exchange of property), and

(2) such additional tax may be assessed before the expiration of such 3-year period notwithstanding the provisions of any other law or rule of law which would otherwise prevent such assessment.

(g) Application of this section and section 6324B to interests in partnerships, corporations, and trusts.—The Secretary shall prescribe regulations setting forth the application of this section and section 6324B in the case of an interest in a partnership, corporation, or trust which, with respect to the decedent, is an interest in a closely held business (within the meaning of paragraph (1) of section 6166(b)). For purposes of the preceding sentence, an interest in a discretionary trust all the beneficiaries of which are qualified heirs shall be treated as a present interest.

(h) Special rules for involuntary conversions of qualified real property.—

(1) Treatment of converted property.—

(A) In general.—If there is an involuntary conversion of an interest in qualified real property—

(i) no tax shall be imposed by subsection (c) on such conversion if the cost of the qualified replacement property equals or exceeds the amount realized on such conversion, or

(ii) if clause (i) does not apply, the amount of the tax imposed by subsection (c) on such conversion shall be the amount determined under subparagraph (B).

(B) Amount of tax where there is not complete reinvestment.—The amount determined under this subparagraph with respect to any involuntary conversion is the amount of the tax which (but for this subsection) would have been imposed on such conversion reduced by an amount which—

(i) bears the same ratio to such tax, as

(ii) the cost of the qualified replacement property bears to the amount realized on the conversion.

(2) Treatment of replacement property.—For purposes of subsection (c)—

(A) any qualified replacement property shall be treated in the same manner as if it were a portion of the interest in qualified real property which was involuntarily converted; except that with respect to such qualified replacement property the 10-year period under paragraph (1) of subsection (c) shall be extended by any period, beyond the 2-year period referred to in section 1033(a)(2)(B)(i), during which the qualified heir was allowed to replace the qualified real property,

(B) any tax imposed by subsection (c) on the involuntary conversion shall be treated as a tax imposed on a partial disposition, and

(C) paragraph (6) of subsection (c) shall be applied—

(i) by not taking into account periods after the involuntary conversion and before the acquisition of the qualified replacement property, and

(ii) by treating material participation with respect to the converted property as material participation with respect to the qualified replacement property.

(3) Definitions and special rules.—For purposes of this subsection—

(A) Involuntary conversion.—The term "involuntary conversion" means a compulsory or involuntary conversion within the meaning of section 1033.

(B) Qualified replacement property.—The term "qualified replacement property" means—

(i) in the case of an involuntary conversion described in section 1033(a)(1), any real property into which the qualified real property is converted, or

(ii) in the case of an involuntary conversion described in section 1033(a)(2), any real property purchased by the qualified heir during the period specified in section 1033(a)(2)(B) for purposes of replacing the qualified real property.

Such term only includes property which is to be used for the qualified use set forth in subparagraph (A) or (B) of subsection (b)(2) under which the qualified real property qualified under subsection (a).

(4) Certain rules made applicable.—The rules of the last sentence of section 1033(a)(2)(A) shall apply for purposes of paragraph (3)(B)(ii).

(i) Exchanges of qualified real property.—

(1) Treatment of property exchanged.—

(A) Exchanges solely for qualified exchange property.—If an interest in qualified real property is exchanged solely for an interest in qualified exchange property in a transaction which qualifies under section 1031, no tax shall be imposed by subsection (c) by reason of such exchange.

(B) Exchanges where other property received.—If an interest in qualified real property is exchanged for an interest in qualified exchange property and other property in a transaction which qualifies under section 1031, the amount of the tax imposed by subsection (c) by reason of such exchange shall be the amount of tax which (but for this subparagraph) would have been imposed on such exchange under subsection (c)(1), reduced by an amount which—

(i) bears the same ratio to such tax, as

(ii) the fair market value of the qualified exchange property bears to the fair market value of the qualified real property exchanged.

For purposes of clause (ii) of the preceding sentence, fair market value shall be determined as of the time of the exchange.

(2) Treatment of qualified exchange property.—For purposes of subsection (c)—

(A) any interest in qualified exchange property shall be treated in the same manner as if it were a portion of the interest in qualified real property which was exchanged,

(B) any tax imposed by subsection (c) by reason of the exchange shall be treated as a tax imposed on a partial disposition, and

(C) paragraph (6) of subsection (c) shall be applied by treating material participation with respect to the exchanged property as material participation with respect to the qualified exchange property.

(3) Qualified exchange property.—For purposes of this subsection, the term "qualified exchange property" means real property which is to be used for the qualified use set forth in subparagraph (A) or (B) of subsection (b)(2) under which the real property exchanged therefor originally qualified under subsection (a).

§ 2033. Property in Which the Decedent had an Interest. The value of the gross estate shall include the value of all property to the extent of the interest therein of the decedent at the time of his death.

§ 2034. Dower or Curtesy Interests. The value of the gross estate shall include the value of all property to the extent of any interest therein of the surviving spouse, existing at the time of the decedent's death as dower or curtesy, or by virtue of a statute creating an estate in lieu of dower or curtesy.

§ 2035. Adjustments for Certain Gifts Made Within Three Years of Decedent's Death.

(a) Inclusion of certain property in gross estate.—If—

(1) the decedent made a transfer (by trust or otherwise) of an interest in any property, or relinquished a power with respect to any property, during the 3-year period ending on the date of the decedent's death, and

(2) the value of such property (or an interest therein) would have been included in the decedent's gross estate under section 2036, 2037, 2038, or 2042 if such transferred interest or relinquished power had been retained by the decedent on the date of his death, the value of the gross estate shall include the value of any property (or interest therein) which would have been so included.

(b) Inclusion of gift tax on gifts made during 3 years before decedent's death.—The amount of the gross estate (determined without regard to this subsection) shall be increased by the amount of any tax paid under chapter 12 by the decedent or his estate on any gift made by the decedent or his spouse during the 3-year period ending on the date of the decedent's death.

(c) Other rules relating to transfers within 3 years of death.—

(1) In general.—For purposes of—

(A) section 303(b) (relating to distributions in redemption of stock to pay death taxes),

(B) section 2032A (relating to special valuation of certain farms, etc., real property), and

(C) subchapter C of chapter 64 (relating to lien for taxes),

the value of the gross estate shall include the value of all property to the extent of any interest therein of which the decedent has at any time made a transfer, by trust or otherwise, during the 3-year period ending on the date of the decedent's death.

(2) Coordination with section 6166.—An estate shall be treated as meeting the 35 percent of adjusted gross estate requirement of section 6166(a)(1) only if the estate meets such requirement both with and without the application of subsection (a).

(3) Marital and small transfers.—Paragraph (1) shall not apply to any transfer (other than a transfer with respect to a life insurance policy) made during a calendar year to any donee if the decedent was not required by section 6019 (other than by reason of section 6019(2)) to file any gift tax return for such year with respect to transfers to such donee.

(d) Exception.—Subsection (a) and paragraph (1) of subsection (c) shall not apply to any bona fide sale for an adequate and full consideration in money or money's worth.

(e) Treatment of certain transfers from revocable trusts.—For purposes of this section and section 2038, any transfer from any portion of a trust during any period that such portion was treated under section 676 as owned by the decedent by reason of a power in the grantor (determined without regard to section 672(e)) shall be treated as a transfer made directly by the decedent.

§ 2036. Transfers with Retained Life Estate.

(a) General rule.—The value of the gross estate shall include the value of all property to the extent of any interest therein of which the decedent has at any time made a transfer (except in case of a bona fide sale for an adequate and full consideration in money or money's worth), by trust or otherwise, under which he has retained for his life or for any period not ascertainable without reference to his death or for any period which does not in fact end before his death—

(1) the possession or enjoyment of, or the right to the income from, the property, or

(2) the right, either alone or in conjunction with any person, to designate the persons who shall possess or enjoy the property or the income therefrom.

(b) Voting rights.—

(1) In general.—For purposes of subsection (a)(1), the retention of the right to vote (directly or indirectly) shares of stock of a controlled corporation shall be considered to be a retention of the enjoyment of transferred property.

(2) Controlled corporation.—For purposes of paragraph (1), a corporation shall be treated as a controlled corporation if, at any time after the transfer of the property and during the 3-year period ending on the date of the decedent's death, the decedent owned (with the application of section 318), or had the right (either alone or in conjunction with any person) to vote, stock possessing at least 20 percent of the total combined voting power of all classes of stock.

(3) Coordination with section 2035.—For purposes of applying section 2035 with respect to paragraph (1), the relinquishment or cessation of voting rights shall be treated as a transfer of property made by the decedent.

(c) Limitation on application of general rule.—This section shall not apply to a transfer made before March 4, 1931; nor to a transfer made after March 3, 1931, and before June 7, 1932, unless the property transferred would have been includible in the decedent's gross estate by reason of the amendatory language of the joint resolution of March 3, 1931 (46 Stat. 1516).

§ 2037. Transfers Taking Effect at Death.

(a) General rule.—The value of the gross estate shall include the value of all property to the extent of any interest therein of which the decedent has at any time after September 7, 1916, made a transfer (except in case of a bona fide sale for an adequate and full consideration in money or money's worth), by trust or otherwise, if—

(1) possession or enjoyment of the property can, through ownership of such interest, be obtained only by surviving the decedent, and

(2) the decedent has retained a reversionary interest in the property (but in the case of a transfer made before October 8, 1949, only if such reversionary interest arose by the express terms of the instrument of transfer), and the value of such reversionary interest immediately before the death of the decedent exceeds 5 percent of the value of such property.

(b) Special rules.—For purposes of this section, the term "reversionary interest" includes a possibility that property transferred by the decedent—

(1) may return to him or his estate, or

(2) may be subject to a power of disposition by him,

but such term does not include a possibility that the income alone from such property may return to him or become subject to a power of disposition by him. The value of a reversionary interest immediately before the death of the decedent shall be determined (without regard to the fact of the decedent's death) by usual methods of valuation, including the use of tables of mortality and actuarial principles, under regulations prescribed by the Secretary. In determining the value of a possibility that property may be subject to a power of disposition by the decedent, such possibility shall be valued as if it were a possibility that such property may return to the decedent or his estate. Notwithstanding the foregoing, an interest so transferred shall not be included in the decedent's gross estate under this section if possession or enjoyment of the property could have been obtained by any beneficiary during the decedent's life through the exercise of a general power of appointment (as defined in section 2041) which in fact was exercisable immediately before the decedent's death.

§ 2038. Revocable Transfers.

(a) In general.—The value of the gross estate shall include the value of all property—

(1) Transfers after June 22, 1936.—To the extent of any interest therein of which the decedent has at any time made a transfer (except in case of a bona fide sale for an adequate and full consideration in money or money's worth), by trust or otherwise, where the enjoyment thereof was subject at the date of his death to any change through the exercise of a power (in whatever capacity exercisable) by the decedent alone or by the decedent in conjunction with any other person (without regard to when or from what source the decedent acquired such power), to alter, amend, revoke, or terminate, or where any such power is relinquished during the 3-year period ending on the date of the decedent's death.

(2) Transfers on or before June 22, 1936.—To the extent of any interest therein of which the decedent has at any time made a transfer (except in case of a bona fide sale for an adequate and full consideration in money or money's worth), by trust or otherwise, where the enjoyment thereof was subject at the date of his death to any change through the exercise of a power, either by the decedent alone or in conjunction with any person, to alter, amend, or revoke, or where the decedent relinquished any such power during the 3-year period ending on the date of the decedent's death. Except in the case of transfers made after June 22, 1936, no interest of the decedent of which he has made a transfer shall be included in the gross estate under paragraph (1) unless it is includible under this paragraph.

(b) Date of existence of power.—For purposes of this section, the power to alter, amend, revoke, or terminate shall be considered to exist on the date of the decedent's death even though the exercise of the power is subject to a precedent giving of notice or even though the alteration, amendment, revocation, or termination takes effect only on the expiration of a stated period after the exercise of the power, whether or not on or before the date of the decedent's death notice has been given or the power has been exercised. In such cases proper adjustment shall be made representing the interests which would have been excluded from the power if the decedent had lived, and for such purpose, if the notice has not been given or the power has not been exercised on or before the date of his death, such notice shall be considered to have been given, or the power exercised, on the date of his death.

§ 2039. Annuities.

(a) General.—The gross estate shall include the value of an annuity or other payment receivable by any beneficiary by reason of surviving the decedent under any form of contract or agreement entered into after March 3, 1931 (other than as insurance under policies on the life of the decedent), if, under such contract or agreement, an annuity or other payment was payable to the decedent, or the decedent possessed the right to receive such annuity or payment, either alone or in conjunction with another for his life or for any period not ascertainable without reference to his death or for any period which does not in fact end before his death.

(b) Amount includible.—Subsection (a) shall apply to only such part of the value of the annuity or other payment receivable under such contract or agreement as is proportionate to that part of the purchase price therefor contributed by the decedent. For purposes of this section, any contribution by the decedent's employer or former employer to the purchase price of such contract or agreement (whether or not to an employee's trust or fund forming part of a pension, annuity, retirement, bonus or profit sharing plan) shall be considered to be contributed by the decedent if made by reason of his employment.

§ 2040. Joint Interests.

(a) General rule.—The value of the gross estate shall include the value of all property to the extent of the interest therein held as joint tenants with right of survivorship by the decedent and any other person, or as tenants by the entirety by the decedent and spouse, or deposited, with any person carrying on the banking business, in their joint names and payable to either or the survivor, except such part thereof as may be shown to have originally belonged to such other person and never to have been received or acquired by the latter from the decedent for less than an adequate and full consideration in money or money's worth: Provided, That where such property or any part thereof, or part of the consideration with which such property was acquired, is shown to have been at any time acquired by such other person from the decedent for less than an adequate and full consideration in money or money's worth, there shall be excepted only such part of the value of such property as is proportionate to the consideration furnished by such other person: Provided further, That where any property has been acquired by gift, bequest, devise, or inheritance, as a tenancy by the entirety by the decedent and spouse, then to the extent of one-half of the value thereof, or, where so acquired by the decedent and any other person as joint tenants with right of survivorship and their interests are not otherwise specified or fixed by law, then to the extent of the value of a fractional part to be determined by dividing the value of the property by the number of joint tenants with right of survivorship.

(b) Certain joint interests of husband and wife.—

(1) Interests of spouse excluded from gross estate.—Notwithstanding subsection (a), in the case of any qualified joint interest, the value included in the gross estate with respect to such interest by reason of this section is one-half of the value of such qualified joint interest.

(2) Qualified joint interest defined.—For purposes of paragraph (1), the term "qualified joint interest" means any interest in property held by the decedent and the decedent's spouse as—

(A) tenants by the entirety, or

(B) joint tenants with right of survivorship, but only if the decedent and the spouse of the decedent are the only joint tenants.

§ 2041. Powers of Appointment.

(a) In general.—The value of the gross estate shall include the value of all property—

(1) Powers of appointment created on or before October 21, 1942.—To the extent of any property with respect to which a general power of appointment created on or before October 21, 1942, is exercised by the decedent—

(A) by will, or

(B) by a disposition which is of such nature that if it were a transfer of property owned by the decedent, such property would be includible in the decedent's gross estate under sections 2035 to 2038, inclusive;

but the failure to exercise such a power or the complete release of such a power shall not be deemed an exercise thereof. If a general power of appointment created on or before October 21, 1942, has been partially released so that it is no longer a general power of appointment, the exercise of such power shall not be deemed to be the exercise of a general power of appointment if—

(i) such partial release occurred before November 1, 1951, or

(ii) the donee of such power was under a legal disability to release such power on October 21, 1942, and such partial release occurred not later than 6 months after the termination of such legal disability.

(2) Powers created after October 21, 1942.—To the extent of any property with respect to which the decedent has at the time of his death a general power of appointment created after October 21, 1942, or with respect to which the decedent has at any time exercised or released such a power of appointment by a disposition which is of such nature that if it were a transfer of property owned by the decedent, such property would be includible in the decedent's gross estate under sections 2035 to 2038, inclusive. For purposes of this paragraph (2), the power of appointment shall be considered to exist on the date of the decedent's death even though the exercise of the power is subject to a precedent giving of notice or even though the exercise of the power takes effect only on the expiration of a stated period after its exercise, whether or not on or before the date of the decedent's death notice has been given or the power has been exercised.

(3) Creation of another power in certain cases.—To the extent of any property with respect to which the decedent—

(A) by will, or

(B) by a disposition which is of such nature that if it were a transfer of property owned by the decedent such property would be includible in the decedent's gross estate under section 2035, 2036, or 2037,

exercises a power of appointment created after October 21, 1942, by creating another power of appointment which under the applicable local law can be validly exercised so as to postpone the vesting of any estate or interest in such property, or suspend the absolute ownership or power of alienation of such property, for a period ascertainable without regard to the date of the creation of the first power.

(b) Definitions.—For purposes of subsection (a)—

(1) General power of appointment.—The term "general power of appointment" means a power which is exercisable in favor of the decedent, his estate, his creditors, or the creditors of his estate; except that—

(A) A power to consume, invade, or appropriate property for the benefit of the decedent which is limited by an ascertainable standard relating to the health, education, support, or maintenance of the decedent shall not be deemed a general power of appointment.

(B) A power of appointment created on or before October 21, 1942, which is exercisable by the decedent only in conjunction with another person shall not be deemed a general power of appointment.

(C) In the case of a power of appointment created after October 21, 1942, which is exercisable by the decedent only in conjunction with another person—

(i) If the power is not exercisable by the decedent except in conjunction with the creator of the power—such power shall not be deemed a general power of appointment.

(ii) If the power is not exercisable by the decedent except in conjunction with a person having a substantial interest in the property, subject to the power, which is adverse to exercise of the power in favor of the decedent—such power shall not be deemed a general power of appointment. For the purposes of this clause a person who, after the death of the decedent, may be possessed of a power of appointment (with respect to the property subject to the decedent's power) which he may exercise in his own favor shall be deemed as having an interest in the property and such interest shall be deemed adverse to such exercise of the decedent's power.

(iii) If (after the application of clauses (i) and (ii)) the power is a general power of appointment and is exercisable in favor of such other person—such power shall be deemed a general power of appointment only in respect of a fractional part of the property subject to such power, such part to be determined by dividing the value of such property by the number of such persons (including the decedent) in favor of whom such power is exercisable.

For purposes of clauses (ii) and (iii), a power shall be deemed to be exercisable in favor of a person if it is exercisable in favor of such person, his estate, his creditors, or the creditors of his estate.

(2) Lapse of power.—The lapse of a power of appointment created after October 21, 1942, during the life of the individual possessing the power shall be considered a release of such power. The preceding sentence shall apply with respect to the lapse of powers during any calendar year only to the extent that the property, which could have been appointed by exercise of such lapsed powers, exceeded in value, at the time of such lapse, the greater of the following amounts:

(A) $5,000, or

(B) 5 percent of the aggregate value, at the time of such lapse, of the assets out of which, or the proceeds of which, the exercise of the lapsed powers could have been satisfied.

(3) Date of creation of power.—For purposes of this section, a power of appointment created by a will executed on or before October 21, 1942, shall be considered a power created on or before such date if the person executing such will dies before July 1, 1949, without having republished such will, by codicil or otherwise, after October 21, 1942.

§ 2042. Proceeds of Life Insurance.

The value of the gross estate shall include the value of all property—

(1) Receivable by the executor.—To the extent of the amount receivable by the executor as insurance under policies on the life of the decedent.

(2) Receivable by other beneficiaries.—To the extent of the amount receivable by all other beneficiaries as insurance under policies on the life of the decedent with respect to which the decedent possessed at his death any of the incidents of ownership, exercisable either alone or in conjunction with any other person. For purposes of the preceding sentence, the term "incident of ownership" includes a reversionary interest (whether

arising by the express terms of the policy or other instrument or by operation of law) only if the value of such reversionary interest exceeded 5 percent of the value of the policy immediately before the death of the decedent. As used in this paragraph, the term "reversionary interest" includes a possibility that the policy, or the proceeds of the policy, may return to the decedent or his estate, or may be subject to a power of disposition by him. The value of a reversionary interest at any time shall be determined (without regard to the fact of the decedent's death) by usual methods of valuation, including the use of tables of mortality and actuarial principles, pursuant to regulations prescribed by the Secretary. In determining the value of a possibility that the policy or proceeds thereof may be subject to a power of disposition by the decedent, such possibility shall be valued as if it were a possibility that such policy or proceeds may return to the decedent or his estate.

§ 2043. Transfers for Insufficient Consideration.

(a) In general.—If any one of the transfers, trusts, interests, rights, or powers enumerated and described in sections 2035 to 2038, inclusive, and section 2041 is made, created, exercised, or relinquished for a consideration in money or money's worth, but is not a bona fide sale for an adequate and full consideration in money or money's worth, there shall be included in the gross estate only the excess of the fair market value at the time of death of the property otherwise to be included on account of such transaction, over the value of the consideration received therefor by the decedent.

(b) Marital rights not treated as consideration.—

(1) In general.—For purposes of this chapter, a relinquishment or promised relinquishment of dower or curtesy, or of a statutory estate created in lieu of dower or curtesy, or of other marital rights in the decedent's property or estate, shall not be considered to any extent a consideration "in money or money's worth".

(2) Exception.—For purposes of section 2053 (relating to expenses, indebtedness, and taxes), a transfer of property which satisfies the requirements of paragraph (1) of section 2516 (relating to certain property settlements) shall be considered to be made for an adequate and full consideration in money or money's worth.

§ 2044. Certain Property for Which Marital Deduction Was Previously Allowed.

(a) General rule.—The value of the gross estate shall include the value of any property to which this section applies in which the decedent had a qualifying income interest for life.

(b) Property to which this section applies.—This section applies to any property if—

(1) a deduction was allowed with respect to the transfer of such property to the decedent—

(A) under section 2056 by reason of subsection (b)(7) thereof, or

(B) under section 2523 by reason of subsection (f) thereof, and

(2) section 2519 (relating to dispositions of certain life estates) did not apply with respect to a disposition by the decedent of part or all of such property.

(c) Property treated as having passed from decedent.—For purposes of this chapter and chapter 13, property includible in the gross estate of the decedent under subsection (a) shall be treated as property passing from the decedent.

§ 2045. Prior Interests.

Except as otherwise specifically provided by law, sections 2034 to 2042, inclusive, shall apply to the transfers, trusts, estates, interests, rights, powers, and relinquishment of powers, as severally enumerated and described therein, whenever made, created, arising, existing, exercised, or relinquished.

§ 2046. Disclaimers.

For provisions relating to the effect of a qualified disclaimer for purposes of this chapter, see section 2518.

§ 2053. Expenses, indebtedness, and taxes.

(a) General rule.—For purposes of the tax imposed by section 2001, the value of the taxable estate shall be determined by deducting from the value of the gross estate such amounts—

(1) for funeral expenses,

(2) for administration expenses,

(3) for claims against the estate, and

(4) for unpaid mortgages on, or any indebtedness in respect of, property where the value of the decedent's interest therein, undiminished by such mortgage or indebtedness, is included in the value of the gross estate, as are allowable by the laws of the jurisdiction, whether within or without the United States, under which the estate is being administered.

(b) Other administration expenses.—Subject to the limitations in paragraph (1) of subsection (c), there shall be deducted in determining the taxable estate amounts representing expenses incurred in administering property not subject to claims which is included in the gross estate to the same extent such amounts would be allowable as a deduction under subsection (a) if such property were subject to claims, and such amounts are paid before the expiration of the period of limitation for assessment provided in section 6501.

(c) Limitations.—

(1) Limitations applicable to subsections (a) and (b).—

(A) Consideration for claims.—The deduction allowed by this section in the case of claims against the estate, unpaid mortgages, or any indebtedness shall, when founded on a promise or agreement, be limited to the extent that they were contracted bona fide and for an adequate and full consideration in money or money's worth; except that in any case in which any such claim is founded on a promise or agreement of the decedent to make a contribution or gift to or for the use of any donee described in section 2055 for the purposes specified therein, the deduction for such claims shall not be so limited, but shall be limited to the extent that it would be allowable as a deduction under section 2055 if such promise or agreement constituted a bequest.

(B) Certain taxes.—Any income taxes on income received after the death of the decedent, or property taxes not accrued before his death, or any estate, succession, legacy, or inheritance taxes, shall not be deductible under this section.

(C) Certain claims by remaindermen.—No deduction shall be allowed under this section for a claim against the estate by a remainderman relating to any property described in section 2044.

(D) Section 6166 interest.—No deduction shall be allowed under this section for any interest payable under section 6601 on any unpaid portion of the tax imposed by section 2001 for the period during which an extension of time for payment of such tax is in effect under section 6166.

(2) Limitations applicable only to subsection (a).—In the case of the amounts described in subsection (a), there shall be disallowed the amount by which the deductions specified therein exceed the value, at the time of the decedent's death, of property subject to claims, except to the extent that such deductions represent amounts paid before the date prescribed for the filing of the estate tax return. For purposes of this section, the term "property subject to claims" means property includible in the gross estate of the decedent which, or the avails of which, would under the applicable law, bear the burden of the payment of such deductions in the final adjustment and settlement of the estate, except that the value of the property shall be reduced by the amount of the deduction under section 2054 attributable to such property.

(d) Certain foreign death taxes.—

(1) In general.—Notwithstanding the provisions of subsection (c)(1)(B), for purposes of the tax imposed by section 2001, the value of the taxable estate may be determined, if the executor so elects before the expiration of the period of limitation for assessment provided in section 6501, by deducting from the value of the gross estate the amount (as determined in accordance with regulations prescribed by the Secretary) of any estate, succession, legacy, or inheritance tax imposed by and actually paid to any foreign country, in respect of any property situated within such foreign country and included in the gross estate of a citizen or resident of the United States, upon a transfer by the decedent for public, charitable, or religious uses described in section 2055. The determination under this paragraph of the country within which property is situated shall be made in accordance with the rules applicable under subchapter B (sec. 2101 and following) in determining whether property is situated within or without the United States. Any election under this paragraph shall be exercised in accordance with regulations prescribed by the Secretary.

(2) Condition for allowance of deduction.—No deduction shall be allowed under paragraph (1) for a foreign death tax specified therein unless the decrease in the tax imposed by section 2001 which results from the deduction provided in paragraph (1) will inure solely for the benefit of the public, charitable, or religious transferees described in section 2055 or section 2106(a)(2). In any case where the tax imposed by section 2001 is equitably apportioned among all the transferees of property included in the gross estate, including those described in sections 2055 and 2106(a)(2) (taking into account any exemptions, credits, or deductions allowed by this chapter), in determining such decrease, there shall be disregarded any decrease in the Federal estate tax which any transferees other than those described in sections 2055 and 2106(a)(2) are required to pay.

(3) Effect on credit for foreign death taxes of deduction under this subsection.—

(A) Election.—An election under this subsection shall be deemed a waiver of the right to claim a credit, against the Federal estate tax, under a death tax convention with any foreign country for any tax or portion thereof in respect of which a deduction is taken under this subsection.

(B) Cross reference.—

See section 2011(d) for the effect of a deduction taken under this paragraph on the credit for foreign death taxes.

(e) Marital rights.—

For provisions treating certain relinquishments of marital rights as consideration in money or money's worth, see section 2043(b)(2).

§ 2054. Losses.

For purposes of the tax imposed by section 2001, the value of the taxable estate shall be determined by deducting from the value of the gross estate losses incurred during the settlement of estates arising from fires, storms, shipwrecks, or other casualties, or from theft, when such losses are not compensated for by insurance or otherwise.

§ 2055. Transfers for public, charitable, and religious uses.

(a) In general.—For purposes of the tax imposed by section 2001, the value of the taxable estate shall be determined by deducting from the value of the gross estate the amount of all bequests, legacies, devises, or transfers—

(1) to or for the use of the United States, any State, any political subdivision thereof, or the District of Columbia, for exclusively public purposes;

(2) to or for the use of any corporation organized and operated exclusively for religious, charitable, scientific, literary, or educational purposes, including the encouragement of art, or to foster national or international amateur sports competition (but only if no part of its activities involve the provision of athletic facilities or equipment), and the prevention of cruelty to children or animals, no part of the net earnings of which inures to the benefit of any private stockholder or individual, which is not disqualified for tax exemption under section 501(c)(3) by reason of attempting to influence legislation, and which does not participate in, or intervene in (including the publishing or distributing of statements), any political campaign on behalf of (or in opposition to) any candidate for public office;

(3) to a trustee or trustees, or a fraternal society, order, or association operating under the lodge system, but only if such contributions or gifts are to be used by such trustee or trustees, or by such fraternal society, order, or association, exclusively for religious, charitable, scientific, literary, or educational purposes, or for the prevention of cruelty to children or animals, such trust, fraternal society, order, or association would not be disqualified for tax exemption under section 501(c)(3) by reason of attempting to influence legislation, and such trustee or trustees, or such fraternal society, order, or association, does not participate in, or intervene in (including the publishing or distributing of statements), any political campaign on behalf of (or in opposition to) any candidate for public office;

(4) to or for the use of any veterans' organization incorporated by Act of Congress, or of its departments or local chapters or posts, no part of the net earnings of which inures to the benefit of any private shareholder or individual; or

(5) to an employee stock ownership plan if such transfer qualifies as a qualified gratuitous transfer of qualified employer securities within the meaning of section 664(g).

For purposes of this subsection, the complete termination before the date prescribed for the filing of the estate tax return of a power to consume, invade, or appropriate property for the benefit of an individual before such power has been exercised by reason of the death of such individual or for any other reason shall be considered and deemed to be a qualified disclaimer with the same full force and effect as though he had filed such qualified disclaimer. Rules similar to the rules of section 501(j) shall apply for purposes of paragraph (2).

(b) Powers of appointment.—Property includible in the decedent's gross estate under section 2041 (relating to powers of appointment) received by a donee described in this section shall, for purposes of this section, be considered a bequest of such decedent.

(c) Death taxes payable out of bequests.—If the tax imposed by section 2001, or any estate, succession, legacy, or inheritance taxes, are, either by the terms of the will, by the law of the jurisdiction under which the estate is administered, or by the law of the jurisdiction imposing the particular tax, payable in whole or in part out of the bequests, legacies, or devises otherwise deductible under this section, then the amount deductible under this section shall be the amount of such bequests, legacies, or devises reduced by the amount of such taxes.

(d) Limitation on deduction.—The amount of the deduction under this section for any transfer shall not exceed the value of the transferred property required to be included in the gross estate.

(e) Disallowance of deductions in certain cases.—

(1) No deduction shall be allowed under this section for a transfer to or for the use of an organization or trust described in section 508(d) or 4948(c)(4) subject to the conditions specified in such sections.

(2) Where an interest in property (other than an interest described in section 170(f)(3)(B)) passes or has passed from the decedent to a person, or for a use, described in subsection (a), and an interest (other than an interest which is extinguished upon the decedent's death) in the same property passes or has passed (for less than an adequate and full consideration in money or money's worth) from the decedent to a person, or for a use, not described in subsection (a), no deduction shall be allowed under this section for the interest which passes or has passed to the person, or for the use, described in subsection (a) unless—

(A) in the case of a remainder interest, such interest is in a trust which is a charitable remainder annuity trust or a charitable remainder unitrust (described in section 664) or a pooled income fund (described in section 642(c)(5)), or

(B) in the case of any other interest, such interest is in the form of a guaranteed annuity or is a fixed percentage distributed yearly of the fair market value of the property (to be determined yearly).

(3) Reformations to comply with paragraph (2).—

(A) In general.—A deduction shall be allowed under subsection (a) in respect of any qualified reformation.

(B) Qualified reformation.—For purposes of this paragraph, the term "qualified reformation" means a change of a governing instrument by reformation, amendment, construction, or otherwise which changes a reformable interest into a qualified interest but only if—

    (i) any difference between—

        (I) the actuarial value (determined as of the date of the decedent's death) of the qualified interest, and

        (II) the actuarial value (as so determined) of the reformable interest, does not exceed 5 percent of the actuarial value (as so determined) of the reformable interest,

    (ii) in the case of—

        (I) a charitable remainder interest, the nonremainder interest (before and after the qualified reformation) terminated at the same time, or

        (II) any other interest, the reformable interest and the qualified interest are for the same period, and

    (iii) such change is effective as of the date of the decedent's death.

A nonremainder interest (before reformation) for a term of years in excess of 20 years shall be treated as satisfying subclause (I) of clause (ii) if such interest (after reformation) is for a term of 20 years.

    (C) Reformable interest.—For purposes of this paragraph—

    (i) In general.—The term "reformable interest" means any interest for which a deduction would be allowable under subsection (a) at the time of the decedent's death but for paragraph (2).

    (ii) Beneficiary's interest must be fixed.—The term "reformable interest" does not include any interest unless, before the remainder vests in possession, all payments to persons other than an organization described in subsection (a) are expressed either in specified dollar amounts or a fixed percentage of the fair market value of the property. For purposes of determining whether all such payments are expressed as a fixed percentage of the fair market value of the property, section 664(d)(3) shall be taken into account.

    (iii) Special rule where timely commencement of reformation.—Clause (ii) shall not apply to any interest if a judicial proceeding is commenced to change such interest into a qualified interest not later than the 90th day after—

        (I) if an estate tax return is required to be filed, the last date (including extensions) for filing such return, or

        (II) if no estate tax return is required to be filed, the last date (including extensions) for filing the income tax return for the 1st taxable year for which such a return is required to be filed by the trust.

    (iv) Special rule for will executed before January 1, 1979, etc.—In the case of any interest passing under a will executed before January 1, 1979, or under a trust created before such date, clause (ii) shall not apply.

    (D) Qualified interest.—For purposes of this paragraph, the term "qualified interest" means an interest for which a deduction is allowable under subsection (a).

(E) Limitation.—The deduction referred to in subparagraph (A) shall not exceed the amount of the deduction which would have been allowable for the reformable interest but for paragraph (2).

(F) Special rule where income beneficiary dies.—If (by reason of the death of any individual, or by termination or distribution of a trust in accordance with the terms of the trust instrument) by the due date for filing the estate tax return (including any extension thereof) a reformable interest is in a wholly charitable trust or passes directly to a person or for a use described in subsection (a), a deduction shall be allowed for such reformable interest as if it had met the requirements of paragraph (2) on the date of the decedent's death. For purposes of the preceding sentence, the term "wholly charitable trust" means a charitable trust which, upon the allowance of a deduction, would be described in section 4947(a)(1).

(G) Statute of limitations.—The period for assessing any deficiency of any tax attributable to the application of this paragraph shall not expire before the date 1 year after the date on which the Secretary is notified that such reformation (or other proceeding pursuant to subparagraph (J)1 []]* has occurred.

(H) Regulations.—The Secretary shall prescribe such regulations as may be necessary to carry out the purposes of this paragraph, including regulations providing such adjustments in the application of the provisions of section 508 (relating to special rules relating to section 501(c)(3) organizations), subchapter J (relating to estates, trusts, beneficiaries, and decedents), and chapter 42 (relating to private foundations) as may be necessary by reason of the qualified reformation.

(I) Reformations permitted in case of remainder interests in residence or farm, pooled income funds, etc.—The Secretary shall prescribe regulations (consistent with the provisions of this paragraph) permitting reformations in the case of any failure—

(i) to meet the requirements of section 170(f)(3)(B) (relating to remainder interests in personal residence or farm, etc.), or

(ii) to meet the requirements of section 642(c)(5).

(J) Void or reformed trust in cases of insufficient remainder interests.—In the case of a trust that would qualify (or could be reformed to qualify pursuant to subparagraph (B)) but for failure to satisfy the requirement of paragraph (1)(D) or (2)(D) of section 664(d), such trust may be—

(i) declared null and void ab initio, or

(ii) changed by reformation, amendment, or otherwise to meet such requirement by reducing the payout rate or the duration (or both) of any noncharitable beneficiary's interest to the extent necessary to satisfy such requirement, pursuant to a proceeding that is commenced within the period required in subparagraph (C)(iii). In a case described in clause (i), no deduction shall be allowed under this title for any transfer to the trust and any transactions entered into by the trust prior to being

---

* The bracketed punctuation has been inserted by the Publisher.

declared void shall be treated as entered into by the transferor.

(4) Works of art and their copyrights treated as separate properties in certain cases.—

(A) In general.—In the case of a qualified contribution of a work of art, the work of art and the copyright on such work of art shall be treated as separate properties for purposes of paragraph (2).

(B) Work of art defined.—For purposes of this paragraph, the term "work of art" means any tangible personal property with respect to which there is a copyright under Federal law.

(C) Qualified contribution defined.—For purposes of this paragraph, the term "qualified contribution" means any transfer of property to a qualified organization if the use of the property by the organization is related to the purpose or function constituting the basis for its exemption under section 501.

(D) Qualified organization defined.—For purposes of this paragraph, the term "qualified organization" means any organization described in section 501(c)(3) other than a private foundation (as defined in section 509). For purposes of the preceding sentence, a private operating foundation (as defined in section 4942(j)(3)) shall not be treated as a private foundation.

(5) Contributions to donor advised funds.—A deduction otherwise allowed under subsection (a) for any contribution to a donor advised fund (as defined in section 4966(d)(2)) shall only be allowed if—

(A) the sponsoring organization (as defined in section 4966(d)(1)) with respect to such donor advised fund is not—

(i) described in paragraph (3) or (4) of subsection (a), or

(ii) a type III supporting organization (as defined in section 4943(f)(5)(A)) which is not a functionally integrated type III supporting organization (as defined in section 4943(f)(5)(B)), and

(B) the taxpayer obtains a contemporaneous written acknowledgment (determined under rules similar to the rules of section 170(f)(8)(C)) from the sponsoring organization (as so defined) of such donor advised fund that such organization has exclusive legal control over the assets contributed.

(f) Special rule for irrevocable transfers of easements in real property.—A deduction shall be allowed under subsection (a) in respect of any transfer of a qualified real property interest (as defined in section 170(h)(2)(C)) which meets the requirements of section 170(h) (without regard to paragraph (4)(A) thereof).

(g) Cross references.—

(1) For option as to time for valuation for purpose of deduction under this section, see section 2032.

(2) For treatment of certain organizations providing child care, see section 501(k).

(3) For exemption of gifts and bequests to or for the benefit of Library of Congress, see section 5 of the Act of March 3, 1925, as amended (2 U.S.C. 161).

(4) For treatment of gifts and bequests for the benefit of the Naval Historical Center as gifts or bequests to or for the use of the United States, see section 7222 of Title 10, United States Code.

(5) For treatment of gifts and bequests to or for the benefit of National Park Foundation as gifts or bequests to or for the use of the United States, see section 8 of the Act of December 18, 1967 (16 U.S.C. 191).

(6) For treatment of gifts, devises, or bequests accepted by the Secretary of State, the Director of the International Communication Agency, or the Director of the United States International Development Cooperation Agency as gifts, devises, or bequests to or for the use of the United States, see section 25 of the State Department Basic Authorities Act of 1956.

(7) For treatment of gifts or bequests of money accepted by the Attorney General for credit to "Commissary Funds, Federal Prisons" as gifts or bequests to or for the use of the United States, see section 4043 of Title 18, United States Code.

(8) For payment of tax on gifts and bequests of United States obligations to the United States, see section 3113(e) of Title 31, United States Code.

(9) For treatment of gifts and bequests for benefit of the Naval Academy as gifts or bequests to or for the use of the United States, see section 6973 of Title 10, United States Code.

(10) For treatment of gifts and bequests for benefit of the Naval Academy Museum as gifts or bequests to or for the use of the United States, see section 6974 of Title 10, United States Code.

(11) For exemption of gifts and bequests received by National Archives Trust Fund Board, see section 2308 of Title 44, United States Code.

(12) For treatment of gifts and bequests to or for the use of Indian tribal governments (or their subdivisions), see section 7871.

§ 2056. Bequests, etc., to surviving spouse.

(a) Allowance of marital deduction.—For purposes of the tax imposed by section 2001, the value of the taxable estate shall, except as limited by subsection (b), be determined by deducting from the value of the gross estate an amount equal to the value of any interest in property which passes or has passed from the decedent to his surviving spouse, but only to the extent that such interest is included in determining the value of the gross estate.

(b) Limitation in the case of life estate or other terminable interest.—

(1) General rule.—Where, on the lapse of time, on the occurrence of an event or contingency, or on the failure of an event or contingency to occur, an interest passing to the surviving spouse will terminate or fail, no deduction shall be allowed under this section with respect to such interest—

(A) if an interest in such property passes or has passed (for less than an adequate and full consideration in money or money's worth) from the decedent to any person other than such surviving spouse (or the estate of such spouse); and

(B) if by reason of such passing such person (or his heirs or assigns) may possess or enjoy any part of such property after such termination or failure of the interest so passing to the surviving spouse;

and no deduction shall be allowed with respect to such interest (even if such deduction is not disallowed under subparagraphs (A) and (B))—

(C) if such interest is to be acquired for the surviving spouse, pursuant to directions of the decedent, by his executor or by the trustee of a trust.

For purposes of this paragraph, an interest shall not be considered as an interest which will terminate or fail merely because it is the ownership of a bond, note, or similar contractual obligation, the discharge of which would not have the effect of an annuity for life or for a term.

(2) Interest in unidentified assets.—Where the assets (included in the decedent's gross estate) out of which, or the proceeds of which, an interest passing to the surviving spouse may be satisfied include a particular asset or assets with respect to which no deduction would be allowed if such asset or assets passed from the decedent to such spouse, then the value of such interest passing to such spouse shall, for purposes of subsection (a), be reduced by the aggregate value of such particular assets.

(3) Interest of spouse conditional on survival for limited period.—For purposes of this subsection, an interest passing to the surviving spouse shall not be considered as an interest which will terminate or fail on the death of such spouse if—

(A) such death will cause a termination or failure of such interest only if it occurs within a period not exceeding 6 months after the decedent's death, or only if it occurs as a result of a common disaster resulting in the death of the decedent and the surviving spouse, or only if it occurs in the case of either such event; and

(B) such termination or failure does not in fact occur.

(4) Valuation of interest passing to surviving spouse.—In determining for purposes of subsection (a) the value of any interest in property passing to the surviving spouse for which a deduction is allowed by this section—

(A) there shall be taken into account the effect which the tax imposed by section 2001, or any estate, succession, legacy, or inheritance tax, has on the net value to the surviving spouse of such interest; and

(B) where such interest or property is encumbered in any manner, or where the surviving spouse incurs any obligation imposed by the decedent with respect to the passing of such interest, such encumbrance or obligation shall be taken into account in the same manner as if the amount of a gift to such spouse of such interest were being determined.

(5) Life estate with power of appointment in surviving spouse.—In the case of an interest in property passing from the decedent, if his surviving spouse is entitled for life to all the income from the entire interest, or all the income from a specific portion thereof, payable annually or at more frequent intervals, with power in the surviving spouse to appoint the entire interest, or such specific portion (exercisable in favor of such surviving spouse, or of the estate of such surviving spouse, or in favor of either, whether or not in each case the power is exercisable in favor of others), and with no power in any other

person to appoint any part of the interest, or such specific portion, to any person other than the surviving spouse—

    (A) the interest or such portion thereof so passing shall, for purposes of subsection (a), be considered as passing to the surviving spouse, and

    (B) no part of the interest so passing shall, for purposes of paragraph (1)(A), be considered as passing to any person other than the surviving spouse.

This paragraph shall apply only if such power in the surviving spouse to appoint the entire interest, or such specific portion thereof, whether exercisable by will or during life, is exercisable by such spouse alone and in all events.

(6) Life insurance or annuity payments with power of appointment in surviving spouse.—In the case of an interest in property passing from the decedent consisting of proceeds under a life insurance, endowment, or annuity contract, if under the terms of the contract such proceeds are payable in installments or are held by the insurer subject to an agreement to pay interest thereon (whether the proceeds, on the termination of any interest payments, are payable in a lump sum or in annual or more frequent installments), and such installment or interest payments are payable annually or at more frequent intervals, commencing not later than 13 months after the decedent's death, and all amounts, or a specific portion of all such amounts, payable during the life of the surviving spouse are payable only to such spouse, and such spouse has the power to appoint all amounts, or such specific portion, payable under such contract (exercisable in favor of such surviving spouse, or of the estate of such surviving spouse, or in favor of either, whether or not in each case the power is exercisable in favor of others), with no power in any other person to appoint such amounts to any person other than the surviving spouse—

    (A) such amounts shall, for purposes of subsection (a), be considered as passing to the surviving spouse, and

    (B) no part of such amounts shall, for purposes of paragraph (1)(A), be considered as passing to any person other than the surviving spouse.

This paragraph shall apply only if, under the terms of the contract, such power in the surviving spouse to appoint such amounts, whether exercisable by will or during life, is exercisable by such spouse alone and in all events.

(7) Election with respect to life estate for surviving spouse.—

    (A) In general.—In the case of qualified terminable interest property—

      (i) for purposes of subsection (a), such property shall be treated as passing to the surviving spouse, and

      (ii) for purposes of paragraph (1)(A), no part of such property shall be treated as passing to any person other than the surviving spouse.

    (B) Qualified terminable interest property defined.—For purposes of this paragraph—

      (i) In general.—The term "qualified terminable interest property" means property—

        (I) which passes from the decedent,

        (II) in which the surviving spouse has a qualifying income interest for life, and

(III) to which an election under this paragraph applies.

(ii) Qualifying income interest for life.—The surviving spouse has a qualifying income interest for life if—

(I) the surviving spouse is entitled to all the income from the property, payable annually or at more frequent intervals, or has a usufruct interest for life in the property, and

(II) no person has a power to appoint any part of the property to any person other than the surviving spouse.

Subclause (II) shall not apply to a power exercisable only at or after the death of the surviving spouse. To the extent provided in regulations, an annuity shall be treated in a manner similar to an income interest in property (regardless of whether the property from which the annuity is payable can be separately identified).

(iii) Property includes interest therein.—The term "property" includes an interest in property.

(iv) Specific portion treated as separate property.—A specific portion of property shall be treated as separate property.

(v) Election.—An election under this paragraph with respect to any property shall be made by the executor on the return of tax imposed by section 2001. Such an election, once made, shall be irrevocable.

(C) Treatment of survivor annuities.—In the case of an annuity included in the gross estate of the decedent under section 2039 (or, in the case of an interest in an annuity arising under the community property laws of a State, included in the gross estate of the decedent under section 2033) where only the surviving spouse has the right to receive payments before the death of such surviving spouse—

(i) the interest of such surviving spouse shall be treated as a qualifying income interest for life, and

(ii) the executor shall be treated as having made an election under this subsection with respect to such annuity unless the executor otherwise elects on the return of tax imposed by section 2001.

An election under clause (ii), once made, shall be irrevocable.

(8) Special rule for charitable remainder trusts.—

(A) In general.—If the surviving spouse of the decedent is the only beneficiary of a qualified charitable remainder trust who is not a charitable beneficiary nor an ESOP beneficiary, paragraph (1) shall not apply to any interest in such trust which passes or has passed from the decedent to such surviving spouse.

(B) Definitions.—For purposes of subparagraph (A)—

(i) Charitable beneficiary.—The term "charitable beneficiary" means any beneficiary which is an organization described in section 170(c).

(ii) ESOP beneficiary.—The term "ESOP beneficiary" means any beneficiary which is an employee stock ownership plan (as defined in section 4975(e)(7)) that holds a remainder interest in qualified employer securities (as defined in section 664(g)(4)) to be transferred to such plan in a qualified gratuitous transfer (as defined in section 664(g)(1)).

(iii) Qualified charitable remainder trust.—The term "qualified charitable remainder trust" means a charitable remainder annuity trust or a charitable remainder unitrust (described in section 664).

(iv)

(9) Denial of double deduction.—Nothing in this section or any other provision of this chapter shall allow the value of any interest in property to be deducted under this chapter more than once with respect to the same decedent.

(10) Specific portion.—For purposes of paragraphs (5), (6), and (7)(B)(iv), the term "specific portion" only includes a portion determined on a fractional or percentage basis.

(c) Definition.—For purposes of this section, an interest in property shall be considered as passing from the decedent to any person if and only if—

(1) such interest is bequeathed or devised to such person by the decedent;

(2) such interest is inherited by such person from the decedent;

(3) such interest is the dower or curtesy interest (or statutory interest in lieu thereof) of such person as surviving spouse of the decedent;

(4) such interest has been transferred to such person by the decedent at any time;

(5) such interest was, at the time of the decedent's death, held by such person and the decedent (or by them and any other person) in joint ownership with right of survivorship;

(6) the decedent had a power (either alone or in conjunction with any person) to appoint such interest and if he appoints or has appointed such interest to such person, or if such person takes such interest in default on the release or nonexercise of such power; or

(7) such interest consists of proceeds of insurance on the life of the decedent receivable by such person.

Except as provided in paragraph (5) or (6) of subsection (b), where at the time of the decedent's death it is not possible to ascertain the particular person or persons to whom an interest in property may pass from the decedent, such interest shall, for purposes of subparagraphs (A) and (B) of subsection (b)(1), be considered as passing from the decedent to a person other than the surviving spouse.

§ 2103. Definition of Gross Estate.

For the purpose of the tax imposed by section 2101, the value of the gross estate of every decedent nonresident not a citizen of the United States shall be that part of his gross estate (determined as provided in section 2031) which at the time of his death is situated in the United States.

§ 2104. Property Within the United States.

(a) Stock in corporation.—For purposes of this subchapter shares of stock owned and held by a nonresident not a citizen of the United States shall be deemed property within the United

States only if issued by a domestic corporation.

(b) Revocable transfers and transfers within 3 years of death.—For purposes of this subchapter, any property of which the decedent has made a transfer, by trust or otherwise, within the meaning of sections 2035 to 2038, inclusive, shall be deemed to be situated in the United States, if so situated either at the time of the transfer or at the time of the decedent's death.

(c) Debt obligations.—For purposes of this subchapter, debt obligations of

(1) a United States person, or

(2) the United States, a State or any political subdivision thereof, or the District of Columbia, owned and held by a nonresident not a citizen of the United States shall be deemed property within the United States. With respect to estates of decedents dying after December 31, 1969, deposits with a domestic branch of a foreign corporation, if such branch is engaged in the commercial banking business, shall, for purposes of this subchapter, be deemed property within the United States. This subsection shall not apply to a debt obligation to which section 2105(b) applies.

§ 2105. Property Without the United States.

(a) Proceeds of life insurance.—For purposes of this subchapter, the amount receivable as insurance on the life of a nonresident not a citizen of the United States shall not be deemed property within the United States.

(b) Bank deposits and certain other debt obligations.—For purposes of this subchapter, the following shall not be deemed property within the United States—

(1) amounts described in section 871(i)(3), if any interest thereon would not be subject to tax by reason of section 871(i)(1) were such interest received by the decedent at the time of his death,

(2) deposits with a foreign branch of a domestic corporation or domestic partnership, if such branch is engaged in the commercial banking business,

(3) debt obligations, if, without regard to whether a statement meeting the requirements of section 871(h)(5) has been received, any interest thereon would be eligible for the exemption from tax under section 871(h)(1) were such interest received by the decedent at the time of his death, and

(4) obligations which would be original issue discount obligations as defined in section 871(g)(1) but for subparagraph (B)(i) thereof, if any interest thereon (were such interest received by the decedent at the time of his death) would not be effectively connected with the conduct of a trade or business within the United States.

Notwithstanding the preceding sentence, if any portion of the interest on an obligation referred to in paragraph (3) would not be eligible for the exemption referred to in paragraph (3) by reason of section 871(h)(4) if the interest were received by the decedent at the time of his death, then an appropriate portion (as determined in a manner prescribed by the Secretary) of the value (as determined for purposes of this chapter) of such debt obligation shall be deemed property within the United States.

(c) Works of art on loan for exhibition.—For purposes of this subchapter, works of art owned by a nonresident not a citizen of the United States shall not be deemed property within the United States if such works of art are—

    (1) imported into the United States solely for exhibition purposes,

    (2) loaned for such purposes, to a public gallery or museum, no part of the net earnings of which inures to the benefit of any private stockholder or individual, and

    (3) at the time of the death of the owner, on exhibition, or enroute to or from exhibition, in such a public gallery or museum.

§ 2503.

    (a) General Definition.—The term "taxable gifts" means the total amount of gifts made during the calendar year, less deductions provided in subchapter C (section 2522 and following).

    (b) Exclusions from gifts.

    (1) In general.—In the case of gifts (other than gifts of future interests in property) made to any person by the donor during the calendar year, the first $10,000 of such gifts to such person shall not, for purposes of subsection (a), be included in the total amount of gifts made during such year. Where there has been a transfer to any person of a present interest in property, the possibility that such interest may be diminished by the exercise of a power shall be disregarded in applying this subsection, if no part of such interest will at any time pass to any other person.

    (2) Inflation adjustment.—In the case of gifts made in a calendar year after 1998, the $10,000 amount contained in paragraph (1) shall be increased by an amount equal to—

    (A) $10,000, multiplied by

    (B) the cost-of-living adjustment determined under section 1(f)(3) for such calendar year by substituting "calendar year 1997" for "calendar year 1992" in subparagraph (B) thereof.

If any amount as adjusted under the preceding sentence is not a multiple of $1,000, such amount shall be rounded to the next lowest multiple of $1,000.

    (c) Transfer for the benefit of minor.—No part of a gift to an individual who has not attained the age of 21 years on the date of such transfer shall be considered a gift of a future interest in property for purposes of subsection (b) if the property and the income therefrom—

    (1) may be expended by, or for the benefit of, the donee before his attaining the age of 21 years, and

    (2) will to the extent not so expended—

    (A) pass to the donee on his attaining the age of 21 years, and

    (B) in the event the donee dies before attaining the age of 21 years, be payable to the estate of the donee or as he may appoint under a general power of appointment as defined in section 2514(c).

    (d) (d) Repealed. Pub. L. 97-34, title III, Section 311(h)(5), Aug. 13, 1981, 95 Stat. 282

    (e) Exclusion for certain transfers for educational expenses or medical expenses.

(1) In general. Any qualified transfer shall not be treated as a transfer of property by gift for purposes of this chapter.

(2) Qualified transfer. For purposes of this subsection, the term "qualified transfer" means any amount paid on behalf of an individual—

(A) as tuition to an educational organization described in section 170(b)(1)(A)(ii) for the education or training of such individual, or

(B) to any person who provides medical care (as defined in section 213(d)) with respect to such individual as payment for such medical care.

(f) Waiver of certain pension rights. If any individual waives, before the death of a participant, any survivor benefit, or right to such benefit, under section 401(a)(11) or 417, such waiver shall not be treated as a transfer of property by gift for purposes of this chapter.

(g) Treatment of certain loans of artworks.

(1) In general. For purposes of this subtitle, any loan of a qualified work of art shall not be treated as a transfer (and the value of such qualified work of art shall be determined as if such loan had not been made) if—

(A) such loan is to an organization described in section 501(c)(3) and exempt from tax under section 501(c) (other than a private foundation), and

(B) the use of such work by such organization is related to the purpose or function constituting the basis for its exemption under section 501.

(2) Definitions. For purposes of this section—

(A) Qualified work of art. The term "qualified work of art" means any archaeological, historic, or creative tangible personal property.

(B) Private foundation. The term "private foundation" has the meaning given such term by section 509, except that such term shall not include any private operating foundation (as defined in section 4942(j)(3)).

§ 2511. Transfers in general.

(a) Scope. Subject to the limitations contained in this chapter, the tax imposed by section 2501 shall apply whether the transfer is in trust or otherwise, whether the gift is direct or indirect, and whether the property is real or personal, tangible or intangible; but in the case of a nonresident not a citizen of the United States, shall apply to a transfer only if the property is situated within the United States.

(b) Intangible property. For purposes of this chapter, in the case of a nonresident not a citizen of the United States who is excepted from the application of section 2501(a)(2)—

(1) shares of stock issued by a domestic corporation, and

(2) debt obligations of—

(A) a United States person, or

(B) the United States, a State or any political subdivision thereof, or the District of Columbia, which are owned and held by such nonresident shall be deemed to be property situated within the United States.

§ 2512. Valuation of gifts.

(a) If the gift is made in property, the value thereof at the date of the gift shall be considered the amount of the gift.

(b) Where property is transferred for less than an adequate and full consideration in money or money's worth, then the amount by which the value of the property exceeded the value of the consideration shall be deemed a gift, and shall be included in computing the amount of gifts made during the calendar year.

§ 2513. Gift by husband or wife to third party.

(a) Considered as made one-half by each.

(1) In general. A gift made by one spouse to any person other than his spouse shall, for the purposes of this chapter, be considered as made one-half by him and one-half by his spouse, but only if at the time of the gift each spouse is a citizen or resident of the United States. This paragraph shall not apply with respect to a gift by a spouse of an interest in property if he creates in his spouse a general power of appointment, as defined in section 2514(c), over such interest. For purposes of this section, an individual shall be considered as the spouse of another individual only if he is married to such individual at the time of the gift and does not remarry during the remainder of the calendar year.

(2) Consent of both spouses. Paragraph (1) shall apply only if both spouses have signified (under the regulations provided for in subsection (b)) their consent to the application of paragraph (1) in the case of all such gifts made during the calendar year by either while married to the other.

(b) Manner and time of signifying consent.

(1) Manner. A consent under this section shall be signified in such manner as is provided under regulations prescribed by the Secretary.

(2) Time. Such consent may be so signified at any time after the close of the calendar year in which the gift was made, subject to the following limitations—

(A) The consent may not be signified after the 15th day of April following the close of such year, unless before such 15th day no return has been filed for such year by either spouse, in which case the consent may not be signified after a return for such year is filed by either spouse.

(B) The consent may not be signified after a notice of deficiency with respect to the tax for such year has been sent to either spouse in accordance with section 6212(a).

(c) Revocation of consent. Revocation of a consent previously signified shall be made in such manner as in[*] provided under regulations prescribed by the Secretary, but the right to revoke a consent previously signified with respect to a calendar year—

(1) shall not exist after the 15th day of April following the close of such year if the

---

[*] Should probably read "is".

consent was signified on or before such 15th day; and

(2) shall not exist if the consent was not signified until after such 15th day.

(d) Joint and several liability for tax. If the consent required by subsection (a)(2) is signified with respect to a gift made in any calendar year, the liability with respect to the entire tax imposed by this chapter of each spouse for such year shall be joint and several.

§ 2514. Powers of appointment.

(a) Powers created on or before October 21, 1942. An exercise of a general power of appointment created on or before October 21, 1942, shall be deemed a transfer of property by the individual possessing such power; but the failure to exercise such a power or the complete release of such a power shall not be deemed an exercise thereof. If a general power of appointment created on or before October 21, 1942, has been partially released so that it is no longer a general power of appointment, the subsequent exercise of such power shall not be deemed to be the exercise of a general power of appointment if—

(1) such partial release occurred before November 1, 1951, or

(2) the donee of such power was under a legal disability to release such power on October 21, 1942, and such partial release occurred not later than six months after the termination of such legal disability.

(b) Powers created after October 21, 1942. The exercise or release of a general power of appointment created after October 21, 1942, shall be deemed a transfer of property by the individual possessing such power.

(c) Definition of general power of appointment. For purposes of this section, the term "general power of appointment" means a power which is exercisable in favor of the individual possessing the power (hereafter in this subsection referred to as the "possessor"), his estate, his creditors, or the creditors of his estate; except that—

(1) A power to consume, invade, or appropriate property for the benefit of the possessor which is limited by an ascertainable standard relating to the health, education, support, or maintenance of the possessor shall not be deemed a general power of appointment.

(2) A power of appointment created on or before October 21, 1942, which is exercisable by the possessor only in conjunction with another person shall not be deemed a general power of appointment.

(3) In the case of a power of appointment created after October 21, 1942, which is exercisable by the possessor only in conjunction with another person—

(A) if the power is not exercisable by the possessor except in conjunction with the creator of the power-such power shall not be deemed a general power of appointment;

(B) if the power is not exercisable by the possessor except in conjunction with a person having a substantial interest, in the property subject to the power, which is adverse to exercise of the power in favor of the possessor-such power shall not be deemed a general power of appointment. For the purposes of this subparagraph a person who, after the death of the possessor, may be possessed of a power of appointment (with respect to the property subject to the possessor's power) which he may exercise in his own favor shall be deemed as having an interest in the property and such interest shall be deemed adverse to such exercise of the possessor's power;

(C) if (after the application of subparagraphs (A) and (B)) the power is a general power of appointment and is exercisable in favor of such other person-such power shall be deemed a general power of appointment only in respect of a fractional part of the property subject to such power, such part to be determined by dividing the value of such property by the number of such persons (including the possessor) in favor of whom such power is exercisable.

For purposes of subparagraphs (B) and (C), a power shall be deemed to be exercisable in favor of a person if it is exercisable in favor of such person, his estate, his creditors, or the creditors of his estate.

(d) Creation of another power in certain cases. If a power of appointment created after October 21, 1942, is exercised by creating another power of appointment which, under the applicable local law, can be validly exercised so as to postpone the vesting of any estate or interest in the property which was subject to the first power, or suspend the absolute ownership or power of alienation of such property, for a period ascertainable without regard to the date of the creation of the first power, such exercise of the first power shall, to the extent of the property subject to the second power, be deemed a transfer of property by the individual possessing such power.

(e) Lapse of power. The lapse of a power of appointment created after October 21, 1942, during the life of the individual possessing the power shall be considered a release of such power. The rule of the preceding sentence shall apply with respect to the lapse of powers during any calendar year only to the extent that the property which could have been appointed by exercise of such lapsed powers exceeds in value the greater of the following amounts:

(1) $5,000, or

(2) 5 percent of the aggregate value of the assets out of which, or the proceeds of which, the exercise of the lapsed powers could be satisfied.

(f) Date of creation of power. For purposes of this section a power of appointment created by a will executed on or before October 21, 1942, shall be considered a power created on or before such date if the person executing such will dies before July 1, 1949, without having republished such will, by codicil or otherwise, after October 21, 1942.

§ 2516. Certain property settlements.

Where a husband and wife enter into a written agreement relative to their marital and property rights and divorce occurs within the 3-year period beginning on the date 1 year before such agreement is entered into (whether or not such agreement is approved by the divorce decree), any transfers of property or interests in property made pursuant to such agreement—

(1) to either spouse in settlement of his or her marital or property rights, or

(2) to provide a reasonable allowance for the support of issue of the marriage during minority,

shall be deemed to be transfers made for a full and adequate consideration in money or money's worth.

§ 2518. Disclaimers.

(a) General Rule.—For purposes of this subtitle, if a person makes a qualified disclaimer with respect to any interest in property, this subtitle shall apply with respect to such interest as if the interest had never been transferred to such person.

(b) Qualified Disclaimer Defined.—For purposes of subsection (a), the term "qualified disclaimer" means an irrevocable and unqualified refusal by a person to accept an interest in property but only if—

(1) such refusal is in writing,

(2) such writing is received by the transferor of the interest, his legal representative, or the holder of the legal title to the property to which the interest relates not later than the date which is 9 months after the later of—

(A) the date on which the transfer creating the interest in such person is made, or

(B) the day on which such person attains age 21,

(3) such person has not accepted the interest or any of its benefits, and

(4) as a result of such refusal, the interest passes without any direction on the part of the person making the disclaimer and passes either—

(A) to the spouse of the decedent, or

(B) to a person other than the person making the disclaimer.

(c) Other rules. For purposes of subsection (a)—

(1) Disclaimer of undivided portion of interest. A disclaimer with respect to an undivided portion of an interest which meets the requirements of the preceding sentence shall be treated as a qualified disclaimer of such portion of the interest.

(2) Powers. A power with respect to property shall be treated as an interest in such property.

(3) Certain transfers treated as disclaimers. A written transfer of the transferor's entire interest in the property—

(A) which meets requirements similar to the requirements of paragraphs (2) and (3) of subsection (b), and

(B) which is to a person or persons who would have received the property had the transferor made a qualified disclaimer (within the meaning of subsection (b)),

shall be treated as a qualified disclaimer.

§ 2519. Dispositions of certain life estates.

(a) General rule

For purposes of this chapter and chapter 11, any disposition of all or part of a qualifying income interest for life in any property to which this section applies shall be treated as a transfer of all interests in such property other than the qualifying income interest.

(b) Property to which this subsection applies. This section applies to any property if a deduction was allowed with respect to the transfer of such property to the donor—

(1) under section 2056 by reason of subsection (b)(7) thereof, or

(2) under section 2523 by reason of subsection (f) thereof.

(c) Cross reference

For right of recovery for gift tax in the case of property treated as transferred under this section, see section 2207A(b).

§ 2522. Charitable and similar gifts.

(a) Citizens or residents. In computing taxable gifts for the calendar year, there shall be allowed as a deduction in the case of a citizen or resident the amount of all gifts made during such year to or for the use of—

(1) the United States, any State, or any political subdivision thereof, or the District of Columbia, for exclusively public purposes;

(2) a corporation, or trust, or community chest, fund, or foundation, organized and operated exclusively for religious, charitable, scientific, literary, or educational purposes, or to foster national or international amateur sports competition (but only if no part of its activities involve the provision of athletic facilities or equipment), including the encouragement of art and the prevention of cruelty to children or animals, no part of the net earnings of which inures to the benefit of any private shareholder or individual, which is not disqualified for tax exemption under section 501(c)(3) by reason of attempting to influence legislation, and which does not participate in, or intervene in (including the publishing or distributing of statements), any political campaign on behalf of (or in opposition to) any candidate for public office;

(3) a fraternal society, order, or association, operating under the lodge system, but only if such gifts are to be used exclusively for religious, charitable, scientific, literary, or educational purposes, including the encouragement of art and the prevention of cruelty to children or animals;

(4) posts or organizations of war veterans, or auxiliary units or societies of any such posts or organizations, if such posts, organizations, units, or societies are organized in the United States or any of its possessions, and if no part of their net earnings insures* to the benefit of any private shareholder or individual.

Rules similar to the rules of section 501(j) shall apply for purposes of paragraph (2).

(b) Nonresidents. In the case of a nonresident not a citizen of the United States, there shall be allowed as a deduction the amount of all gifts made during such year to or for the use of—

(1) the United States, any State, or any political subdivision thereof, or the District of Columbia, for exclusively public purposes;

(2) a domestic corporation organized and operated exclusively for religious, charitable, scientific, literary, or educational purposes, including the encouragement of art and the prevention of cruelty to children or animals, no part of the net earnings of which inures to the benefit of any private shareholder or individual, which is not disqualified for tax exemption under section 501(c)(3) by reason of attempting to influence legislation, and

---

*   Should probably read "inures".

which does not participate in, or intervene in (including the publishing or distributing of statements), any political campaign on behalf of (or in opposition to) any candidate for public office;

(3) a trust, or community chest, fund, or foundation, organized and operated exclusively for religious, charitable, scientific, literary, or educational purposes, including the encouragement of art and the prevention of cruelty to children or animals, no substantial part of the activities of which is carrying on propaganda, or otherwise attempting, to influence legislation, and which does not participate in, or intervene in (including the publishing or distributing of statements), any political campaign on behalf of (or in opposition to) any candidate for public office; but only if such gifts are to be used within the United States exclusively for such purposes;

(4) a fraternal society, order, or association, operating under the lodge system, but only if such gifts are to be used within the United States exclusively for religious, charitable, scientific, literary, or educational purposes, including the encouragement of art and the prevention of cruelty to children or animals;

(5) posts or organizations of war veterans, or auxiliary units or societies of any such posts or organizations, if such posts, organizations, units, or societies are organized in the United States or any of its possessions, and if no part of their net earnings inures to the benefit of any private shareholder or individual.

(c) Disallowance of deductions in certain cases.

(1) No deduction shall be allowed under this section for a gift to of 1 for the use of an organization or trust described in section 508(d) or 4948(c)(4) subject to the conditions specified in such sections.

(2) Where a donor transfers an interest in property (other than an interest described in section 170(f)(3)(B)) to a person, or for a use, described in subsection (a) or (b) and an interest in the same property is retained by the donor, or is transferred or has been transferred (for less than an adequate and full consideration in money or money's worth) from the donor to a person, or for a use, not described in subsection (a) or (b), no deduction shall be allowed under this section for the interest which is, or has been transferred to the person, or for the use, described in subsection (a) or (b), unless—

(A) in the case of a remainder interest, such interest is in a trust which is a charitable remainder annuity trust or a charitable remainder unitrust (described in section 664) or a pooled income fund (described in section 642(c)(5)), or

(B) in the case of any other interest, such interest is in the form of a guaranteed annuity or is a fixed percentage distributed yearly of the fair market value of the property (to be determined yearly).

(3) Rules similar to the rules of section 2055(e)(4) shall apply for purposes of paragraph (2).

(4) Reformations to comply with paragraph (2).

(A) In general—A deduction shall be allowed under subsection (a) in respect of any qualified reformation (within the meaning of section 2055(e)(3)(B)).

(B) Rules similar to section 2055(e)(3) to apply—For purposes of this paragraph, rules similar to the rules of section 2055(e)(3) shall apply.

(5) Contributions to donor advised funds. A deduction otherwise allowed under subsection (a) for any contribution to a donor advised fund (as defined in section 4966(d)(2)) shall only be allowed if—

(A) the sponsoring organization (as defined in section 4966(d)(1)) with respect to such donor advised fund is not—

(i) described in paragraph (3) or (4) of subsection (a), or

(ii) a type III supporting organization (as defined in section 4943(f)(5)(A)) which is not a functionally integrated type III supporting organization (as defined in section 4943(f)(5)(B)), and

(B) the taxpayer obtains a contemporaneous written acknowledgment (determined under rules similar to the rules of section 170(f)(8)(C)) from the sponsoring organization (as so defined) of such donor advised fund that such organization has exclusive legal control over the assets contributed.

(d) Special rule for irrevocable transfers of easements in real property. A deduction shall be allowed under subsection (a) in respect of any transfer of a qualified real property interest (as defined in section 170(h)(2)(C)) which meets the requirements of section 170(h) (without regard to paragraph (4)(A) thereof).

(e) Special rules for fractional gifts

(1) Denial of deduction in certain cases

(A) In general
No deduction shall be allowed for a contribution of an undivided portion of a taxpayer's entire interest in tangible personal property unless all interests in the property are held immediately before such contribution by—

(i) the taxpayer, or

(ii) the taxpayer and the donee.

(B) Exceptions
The Secretary may, by regulation, provide for exceptions to subparagraph (A) in cases where all persons who hold an interest in the property make proportional contributions of an undivided portion of the entire interest held by such persons.

(2) Recapture of deduction in certain cases; addition to tax

(A) In general. The Secretary shall provide for the recapture of an amount equal to any deduction allowed under this section (plus interest) with respect to any contribution of an undivided portion of a taxpayer's entire interest in tangible personal property—

(i) in any case in which the donor does not contribute all of the remaining interests in such property to the donee (or, if such donee is no longer in existence, to any person described in section 170(c)) on or before the earlier of—

(I) the date that is 10 years after the date of the initial fractional contribution, or

(II) the date of the death of the donor, and

(ii) in any case in which the donee has not, during the period beginning on the date of the initial fractional contribution and ending on the date described in clause (i)—

(I) had substantial physical possession of the property, and

(II) used the property in a use which is related to a purpose or function constituting the basis for the organizations' exemption under section 501.

(B) Addition to tax. The tax imposed under this chapter for any taxable year for which there is a recapture under subparagraph (A) shall be increased by 10 percent of the amount so recaptured.

(C) Initial fractional contribution. For purposes of this paragraph, the term "initial fractional contribution" means, with respect to any donor, the first gift of an undivided portion of the donor's entire interest in any tangible personal property for which a deduction is allowed under subsection (a) or (b).

(f) Cross references

(1) For treatment of certain organizations providing child care, see section 501(k).

(2) For exemption of certain gifts to or for the benefit of the United States and for rules of construction with respect to certain bequests, see section 2055(f).

(3) For treatment of gifts to or for the use of Indian tribal governments (or their subdivisions), see section 7871.

§ 2523. Gift to spouse[.]*

(a) Allowance of deduction. Where a donor transfers during the calendar year by gift an interest in property to a donee who at the time of the gift is the donor's spouse, there shall be allowed as a deduction in computing taxable gifts for the calendar year an amount with respect to such interest equal to its value.

(b) Life estate or other terminable interest. Where, on the lapse of time, on the occurrence of an event or contingency, or on the failure of an event or contingency to occur, such interest transferred to the spouse will terminate or fail, no deduction shall be allowed with respect to such interest—

(1) if the donor retains in himself, or transfers or has transferred (for less than an adequate and full consideration in money or money's worth) to any person other than such donee spouse (or the estate of such spouse), an interest in such property, and if by reason of such retention or transfer the donor (or his heirs or assigns) or such person (or his heirs or assigns) may possess or enjoy any part of such property after such termination or failure of the interest transferred to the donee spouse; or

(2) if the donor immediately after the transfer to the donee spouse has a power to appoint an interest in such property which he can exercise (either alone or in conjunction with any person) in such manner that the appointee may possess or enjoy any part of such property

---

* The bracketed punctuation has been inserted by the Publisher as it was inadvertently omitted by the Legislature.

after such termination or failure of the interest transferred to the donee spouse. For purposes of this paragraph, the donor shall be considered as having immediately after the transfer to the donee spouse such power to appoint even though such power cannot be exercised until after the lapse of time, upon the occurrence of an event or contingency, or on the failure of an event or contingency to occur.

An exercise or release at any time by the donor, either alone or in conjunction with any person, of a power to appoint an interest in property, even though not otherwise a transfer, shall, for purposes of paragraph (1), be considered as a transfer by him. Except as provided in subsection (e), where at the time of the transfer it is impossible to ascertain the particular person or persons who may receive from the donor an interest in property so transferred by him, such interest shall, for purposes of paragraph (1), be considered as transferred to a person other than the donee spouse.

(c) Interest in unidentified assets. Where the assets out of which, or the proceeds of which, the interest transferred to the donee spouse may be satisfied include a particular asset or assets with respect to which no deduction would be allowed if such asset or assets were transferred from the donor to such spouse, then the value of the interest transferred to such spouse shall, for purposes of subsection (a), be reduced by the aggregate value of such particular assets.

(d) Joint interests. If the interest is transferred to the donee spouse as sole joint tenant with the donor or as tenant by the entirety, the interest of the donor in the property which exists solely by reason of the possibility that the donor may survive the donee spouse, or that there may occur a severance of the tenancy, shall not be considered for purposes of subsection (b) as an interest retained by the donor in himself.

(e) Life estate with power of appointment in donee spouse. Where the donor transfers an interest in property, if by such transfer his spouse is entitled for life to all of the income from the entire interest, or all the income from a specific portion thereof, payable annually or at more frequent intervals, with power in the donee spouse to appoint the entire interest, or such specific portion (exercisable in favor of such donee spouse, or of the estate of such donee spouse, or in favor of either, whether or not in each case the power is exercisable in favor of others), and with no power in any other person to appoint any part of such interest, or such portion, to any person other than the donee spouse—

    (1) the interest, or such portion, so transferred shall, for purposes of subsection (a) be considered as transferred to the donee spouse, and

    (2) no part of the interest, or such portion, so transferred shall, for purposes of subsection (b)(1), be considered as retained in the donor or transferred to any person other than the donee spouse.

This subsection shall apply only if, by such transfer, such power in the donee spouse to appoint the interest, or such portion, whether exercisable by will or during life, is exercisable by such spouse alone and in all events. For purposes of this subsection, the term "specific portion" only includes a portion determined on a fractional or percentage basis.

(f) Election with respect to life estate for donee spouse.

    (1) In general

    In the case of qualified terminable interest property—

(A) for purposes of subsection (a), such property shall be treated as transferred to the donee spouse, and

(B) for purposes of subsection (b)(1), no part of such property shall be considered as retained in the donor or transferred to any person other than the donee spouse.

(2) Qualified terminable interest property. For purposes of this subsection, the term "qualified terminable interest property" means any property—

(A) which is transferred by the donor spouse,

(B) in which the donee spouse has a qualifying income interest for life, and

(C) to which an election under this subsection applies.

(3) Certain rules made applicable. For purposes of this subsection, rules similar to the rules of clauses (ii), (iii), and (iv) of section 2056(b)(7)(B) shall apply and the rules of section 2056(b)(10) shall apply.

(4) Election.

(A) Time and manner. An election under this subsection with respect to any property shall be made on or before the date prescribed by section 6075(b) for filing a gift tax return with respect to the transfer (determined without regard to section 6019(2)) and shall be made in such manner as the Secretary shall by regulations prescribe.

(B) Election irrevocable. An election under this subsection, once made, shall be irrevocable.

(5) Treatment of interest retained by donor spouse.

(A) In general. In the case of any qualified terminable interest property—

(i) such property shall not be includible in the gross estate of the donor spouse, and

(ii) any subsequent transfer by the donor spouse of an interest in such property shall not be treated as a transfer for purposes of this chapter.

(B) Subparagraph (A) not to apply after transfer by donee spouse. Subparagraph (A) shall not apply with respect to any property after the donee spouse is treated as having transferred such property under section 2519, or such property is includible in the donee spouse's gross estate under section 2044.

(6) Treatment of joint and survivor annuities. In the case of a joint and survivor annuity where only the donor spouse and donee spouse have the right to receive payments before the death of the last spouse to die—

(A) the donee spouse's interest shall be treated as a qualifying income interest for life,

(B) the donor spouse shall be treated as having made an election under this subsection with respect to such annuity unless the donor spouse otherwise elects on or before the date specified in paragraph (4)(A),

(C) paragraph (5) and section 2519 shall not apply to the donor spouse's interest in the annuity, and

(D) if the donee spouse dies before the donor spouse, no amount shall be includible in the gross estate of the donee spouse under section 2044 with respect to such annuity.

An election under subparagraph (B), once made, shall be irrevocable.

(g) Special rule for charitable remainder trusts.

(1) In general. If, after the transfer, the donee spouse is the only noncharitable beneficiary (other than the donor) of a qualified charitable remainder trust, subsection (b) shall not apply to the interest in such trust which is transferred to the donee spouse.

(2) Definitions. For purposes of paragraph (1), the term "noncharitable beneficiary" and "qualified charitable remainder trust" have the meanings given to such terms by section 2056(b)(8)(B).

(h) Denial of double deduction. Nothing in this section or any other provision of this chapter shall allow the value of any interest in property to be deducted under this chapter more than once with respect to the same donor.

§ 2524. Extent of deductions. The deductions provided in sections 2522 and 2523 shall be allowed only to the extent that the gifts therein specified are included in the amount of gifts against which such deductions are applied.

§ 2701. Special valuation rules in case of transfers of certain interests in corporations or partnerships.

(a) Valuation rules.

(1) In general. Solely for purposes of determining whether a transfer of an interest in a corporation or partnership to (or for the benefit of) a member of the transferor's family is a gift (and the value of such transfer), the value of any right—

(A) which is described in subparagraph (A) or (B) of subsection (b)(1), and

(B) which is with respect to any applicable retained interest that is held by the transferor or an applicable family member immediately after the transfer,

shall be determined under paragraph (3). This paragraph shall not apply to the transfer of any interest for which market quotations are readily available (as of the date of transfer) on an established securities market.

(2) Exceptions for marketable retained interests, etc. Paragraph (1) shall not apply to any right with respect to an applicable retained interest if—

(A) market quotations are readily available (as of the date of the transfer) for such interest on an established securities market,

(B) such interest is of the same class as the transferred interest, or

(C) such interest is proportionally the same as the transferred interest, without regard to nonlapsing differences in voting power (or, for a partnership, nonlapsing differences with respect to management and limitations on liability).

Subparagraph (C) shall not apply to any interest in a partnership if the transferor or an applicable family member has the right to alter the liability of the transferee of the transferred property. Except as provided by the Secretary, any difference described in subparagraph (C) which lapses by reason of any Federal or State law shall be treated as a nonlapsing difference for purposes of such subparagraph.

(3) Valuation of rights to which paragraph (1) applies.

(A) In general. The value of any right described in paragraph (1), other than a distribution right which consists of a right to receive a qualified payment, shall be treated as being zero.

(B) Valuation of certain qualified payments. If—

(i) any applicable retained interest confers a distribution right which consists of the right to a qualified payment, and

(ii) there are 1 or more liquidation, put, call, or conversion rights with respect to such interest, the value of all such rights shall be determined as if each liquidation, put, call, or conversion right were exercised in the manner resulting in the lowest value being determined for all such rights.

(C) Valuation of qualified payments where no liquidation, etc. rights. In the case of an applicable retained interest which is described in subparagraph (B)(i) but not subparagraph (B)(ii), the value of the distribution right shall be determined without regard to this section.

(4) Minimum valuation of junior equity.

(A) In general. In the case of a transfer described in paragraph (1) of a junior equity interest in a corporation or partnership, such interest shall in no event be valued at an amount less than the value which would be determined if the total value of all of the junior equity interests in the entity were equal to 10 percent of the sum of—

(i) the total value of all of the equity interests in such entity, plus

(ii) the total amount of indebtedness of such entity to the transferor (or an applicable family member).

(B) Definitions. For purposes of this paragraph—

(i) Junior equity interest. The term "junior equity interest" means common stock or, in the case of a partnership, any partnership interest under which the rights as to income and capital (or, to the extent provided in regulations, the rights as to either income or capital) are junior to the rights of all other classes of equity interests.

(ii) Equity interest. The term "equity interest" means stock or any interest as a partner, as the case may be.

(b) Applicable retained interests. For purposes of this section—

(1) In general. The term "applicable retained interest" means any interest in an entity with respect to which there is—

(A) a distribution right, but only if, immediately before the transfer described in subsection (a)(1), the transferor and applicable family members hold (after application of subsection (e)(3)) control of the entity, or

(B) a liquidation, put, call, or conversion right.

(2) Control. For purposes of paragraph (1)—

(A) Corporations. In the case of a corporation, the term "control" means the holding of at least 50 percent (by vote or value) of the stock of the corporation.

(B) Partnerships. In the case of a partnership, the term "control" means—

(i) the holding of at least 50 percent of the capital or profits interests in the partnership, or

(ii) in the case of a limited partnership, the holding of any interest as a general partner.

(C) Applicable family member. For purposes of this subsection, the term "applicable family member" includes any lineal descendant of any parent of the transferor or the transferor's spouse.

(c) Distribution and other rights; qualified payments. For purposes of this section—

(1) Distribution right.

(A) In general. The term "distribution right" means—

(i) a right to distributions from a corporation with respect to its stock, and

(ii) a right to distributions from a partnership with respect to a partner's interest in the partnership.

(B) Exceptions. The term "distribution right" does not include—

(i) a right to distributions with respect to any interest which is junior to the rights of the transferred interest,

(ii) any liquidation, put, call, or conversion right, or

(iii) any right to receive any guaranteed payment described in section 707(c) of a fixed amount.

(2) Liquidation, etc. rights.

(A) In general. The term "liquidation, put, call, or conversion right" means any liquidation, put, call, or conversion right, or any similar right, the exercise or nonexercise of which affects the value of the transferred interest.

(B) Exception for fixed rights.

(i) In general. The term "liquidation, put, call, or conversion right" does not include any right which must be exercised at a specific time and at a specific amount.

(ii) Treatment of certain rights. If a right is assumed to be exercised in a particular manner under subsection (a)(3)(B), such right shall be treated as so exercised for purposes of clause (i).

(C) Exception for certain rights to convert. The term "liquidation, put, call, or conversion right" does not include any right which—

(i) is a right to convert into a fixed number (or a fixed percentage) of shares of the same class of stock in a corporation as the transferred stock in such corporation under subsection (a)(1) (or stock which would be of the same class but for nonlapsing differences in voting power),

(ii) is nonlapsing,

(iii) is subject to proportionate adjustments for splits, combinations, reclassifications, and similar changes in the capital stock, and

(iv) is subject to adjustments similar to the adjustments under subsection (d) for accumulated but unpaid distributions.

A rule similar to the rule of the preceding sentence shall apply for partnerships.

(3) Qualified payment.

(A) In general. Except as otherwise provided in this paragraph, the term "qualified payment" means any dividend payable on a periodic basis under any cumulative preferred stock (or a comparable payment under any partnership interest) to the extent that such dividend (or comparable payment) is determined at a fixed rate.

(B) Treatment of variable rate payments. For purposes of subparagraph (A), a payment shall be treated as fixed as to rate if such payment is determined at a rate which bears a fixed relationship to a specified market interest rate.

(C) Elections.

(i) In general. Payments under any interest held by a transferor which (without regard to this subparagraph) are qualified payments shall be treated as qualified payments unless the transferor elects not to treat such payments as qualified payments. Payments described in the preceding sentence which are held by an applicable family member shall be treated as qualified payments only if such member elects to treat such payments as qualified payments.

(ii) Election to have interest treated as qualified payment. A transferor or applicable family member holding any distribution right which (without regard to this subparagraph) is not a qualified payment may elect to treat such right as a qualified payment, to be paid in the amounts and at the times specified in such election. The preceding sentence shall apply only to the extent that the amounts and times so specified are not inconsistent with the underlying legal instrument giving rise to such right.

(iii) Elections irrevocable. Any election under this subparagraph with respect to an interest shall, once made, be irrevocable.

(d) Transfer tax treatment of cumulative but unpaid distributions.

(1) In general. If a taxable event occurs with respect to any distribution right to which subsection (a)(3)(B) or (C) applied, the following shall be increased by the amount determined under paragraph (2):

(A) The taxable estate of the transferor in the case of a taxable event described in paragraph (3)(A)(i).

(B) The taxable gifts of the transferor for the calendar year in which the taxable event occurs in the case of a taxable event described in paragraph (3)(A)(ii) or (iii).

(2) Amount of increase.

(A) In general. The amount of the increase determined under this paragraph shall be the excess (if any) of—

(i) the value of the qualified payments payable during the period beginning on the date of the transfer under subsection (a)(1) and ending on the date of the taxable event determined as if—

(I) all such payments were paid on the date payment was due, and

(II) all such payments were reinvested by the transferor as of the date of payment at a yield equal to the discount rate used in determining the value of the applicable retained interest described in subsection (a)(1), over

(ii) the value of such payments paid during such period computed under clause (i) on the basis of the time when such payments were actually paid.

(B) Limitation on amount of increase.

(i) In general. The amount of the increase under subparagraph (A) shall not exceed the applicable percentage of the excess (if any) of—

(I) the value (determined as of the date of the taxable event) of all equity interests in the entity which are junior to the applicable retained interest, over

(II) the value of such interests (determined as of the date of the transfer to which subsection (a)(1) applied).

(ii) Applicable percentage. For purposes of clause (i), the applicable percentage is the percentage determined by dividing—

(I) the number of shares in the corporation held (as of the date of the taxable event) by the transferor which are applicable retained interests of the same class, by

(II) the total number of shares in such corporation (as of such date) which are of the same class as the class described in subclause (I).

A similar percentage shall be determined in the case of interests in a partnership.

(iii) Definition. For purposes of this subparagraph, the term "equity interest" has the meaning given such term by subsection (a)(4)(B).

(C) Grace period. For purposes of subparagraph (A), any payment of any distribution during the 4-year period beginning on its due date shall be treated as having been made on such due date.

(3) Taxable events. For purposes of this subsection—

(A) In general. The term "taxable event" means any of the following:

(i) The death of the transferor if the applicable retained interest conferring the distribution right is includible in the estate of the transferor.

(ii) The transfer of such applicable retained interest.

(iii) At the election of the taxpayer, the payment of any qualified payment after the period described in paragraph (2)(C), but only with respect to such payment.

(B) Exception where spouse is transferee.

(i) Deathtime transfers

Subparagraph (A)(i) shall not apply to any interest includible in the gross estate of the transferor if a deduction with respect to such interest is allowable under section 2056 or 2106(a)(3).

(ii) Lifetime transfers. A transfer to the spouse of the transferor shall not be treated as a taxable event under subparagraph (A)(ii) if such transfer does not result in a taxable gift by reason of—

(I) any deduction allowed under section 2523, or the exclusion under section 2503(b), or

(II) consideration for the transfer provided by the spouse.

(iii) Spouse succeeds to treatment of transferor. If an event is not treated as a taxable event by reason of this subparagraph, the transferee spouse or surviving spouse (as the case may be) shall be treated in the same manner as the transferor in applying this subsection with respect to the interest involved.

(4) Special rules for applicable family members.

(A) Family member treated in same manner as transferor. For purposes of this subsection, an applicable family member shall be treated in the same manner as the transferor with respect to any distribution right retained by such family member to which subsection (a)(3)(B) or (C) applied.

(B) Transfer to applicable family member. In the case of a taxable event described in paragraph (3)(A)(ii) involving the transfer of an applicable retained interest to an applicable family member (other than the spouse of the transferor), the applicable family member shall be treated in the same manner as the transferor in applying this subsection to distributions accumulating with respect to such interest after such taxable event.

(C) Transfer to transferors. In the case of a taxable event described in paragraph (3)(A)(ii) involving a transfer of an applicable retained interest from an applicable family member to a transferor, this subsection shall continue to apply to the transferor during any period the transferor holds such interest.

(5) Transfer to include termination. For purposes of this subsection, any termination of an interest shall be treated as a transfer.

(e) Other definitions and rules. For purposes of this section—

(1) Member of the family. The term "member of the family" means, with respect to any transferor—

(A) the transferor's spouse,

(B) a lineal descendant of the transferor or the transferor's spouse, and

(C) the spouse of any such descendant.

(2) Applicable family member. The term "applicable family member" means, with respect to any transferor—

(A) the transferor's spouse,

(B) an ancestor of the transferor or the transferor's spouse, and

(C) the spouse of any such ancestor.

(3) Attribution of indirect holdings and transfers. An individual shall be treated as holding any interest to the extent such interest is held indirectly by such individual through a corporation, partnership, trust, or other entity. If any individual is treated as holding any interest by reason of the preceding sentence, any transfer which results in such interest being treated as no longer held by such individual shall be treated as a transfer of such interest.

(4) Effect of adoption. A relationship by legal adoption shall be treated as a relationship by blood.

(5) Certain changes treated as transfers. Except as provided in regulations, a contribution to capital or a redemption, recapitalization, or other change in the capital structure of a corporation or partnership shall be treated as a transfer of an interest in such entity to which this section applies if the taxpayer or an applicable family member—

(A) receives an applicable retained interest in such entity pursuant to such transaction, or

(B) under regulations, otherwise holds, immediately after such transaction, an applicable retained interest in such entity.

This paragraph shall not apply to any transaction (other than a contribution to capital) if the interests in the entity held by the transferor, applicable family members, and members of the transferor's family before and after the transaction are substantially identical.

(6) Adjustments. Under regulations prescribed by the Secretary, if there is any subsequent transfer, or inclusion in the gross estate, of any applicable retained interest which was valued under the rules of subsection (a), appropriate adjustments shall be made for purposes of chapter 11, 12, or 13 to reflect the increase in the amount of any prior taxable gift made by the transferor or decedent by reason of such valuation or to reflect the application of subsection (d).

(7) Treatment as separate interests. The Secretary may by regulation provide that any applicable retained interest shall be treated as 2 or more separate interests for purposes of this section.

§ 2702. Special valuation rules in case of transfers of interests in trusts.

(a) Valuation rules.

(1) In general. Solely for purposes of determining whether a transfer of an interest in trust to (or for the benefit of) a member of the transferor's family is a gift (and the value of such transfer), the value of any interest in such trust retained by the transferor or any

applicable family member (as defined in section 2701(e)(2)) shall be determined as provided in paragraph (2).

(2) Valuation of retained interests.

(A) In general. The value of any retained interest which is not a qualified interest shall be treated as being zero.

(B) Valuation of qualified interest. The value of any retained interest which is a qualified interest shall be determined under section 7520.

(3) Exceptions.

(A) In general. This subsection shall not apply to any transfer—

(i) if such transfer is an incomplete gift,

(ii) if such transfer involves the transfer of an interest in trust all the property in which consists of a residence to be used as a personal residence by persons holding term interests in such trust, or

(iii) to the extent that regulations provide that such transfer is not inconsistent with the purposes of this section.

(B) Incomplete gift. For purposes of subparagraph (A), the term "incomplete gift" means any transfer which would not be treated as a gift whether or not consideration was received for such transfer.

(b) Qualified interest. For purposes of this section, the term "qualified interest" means—

(1) any interest which consists of the right to receive fixed amounts payable not less frequently than annually,

(2) any interest which consists of the right to receive amounts which are payable not less frequently than annually and are a fixed percentage of the fair market value of the property in the trust (determined annually), and

(3) any noncontingent remainder interest if all of the other interests in the trust consist of interests described in paragraph (1) or (2).

(c) Certain property treated as held in trust. For purposes of this section—

(1) In general. The transfer of an interest in property with respect to which there is 1 or more term interests shall be treated a transfer of an interest in a trust.

(2) Joint purchases. If 2 or more members of the same family acquire interests in any property described in paragraph (1) in the same transaction (or a series of related transactions), the person (or persons) acquiring the term interests in such property shall be treated as having acquired the entire property and then transferred to the other persons the interests acquired by such other persons in the transaction (or series of transactions). Such transfer shall be treated as made in exchange for the consideration (if any) provided by such other persons for the acquisition of their interests in such property.

(3) Term interest. The term "term interest" means—

(A) a life interest in property, or

(B) an interest in property for a term of years.

(4) Valuation rule for certain term interests. If the nonexercise of rights under a term interest in tangible property would not have a substantial effect on the valuation of the remainder interest in such property—

(A) subparagraph (A) of subsection (a)(2) shall not apply to such term interest, and

(B) the value of such term interest for purposes of applying subsection (a)(1) shall be the amount which the holder of the term interest establishes as the amount for which such interest could be sold to an unrelated third party.

(d) Treatment of transfers of interests in portion of trust. In the case of a transfer of an income or remainder interest with respect to a specified portion of the property in a trust, only such portion shall be taken into account in applying this section to such transfer.

(e) Member of the family. For purposes of this section, the term "member of the family" shall have the meaning given such term by section 2704(c)(2).

§ 2703. Certain rights and restrictions disregarded

(a) General rule. For purposes of this subtitle, the value of any property shall be determined without regard to—

(1) any option, agreement, or other right to acquire or use the property at a price less than the fair market value of the property (without regard to such option, agreement, or right), or

(2) any restriction on the right to sell or use such property.

(b) Exceptions. Subsection (a) shall not apply to any option, agreement, right, or restriction which meets each of the following requirements:

(1) It is a bona fide business arrangement.

(2) It is not a device to transfer such property to members of the decedent's family for less than full and adequate consideration in money or money's worth.

(3) Its terms are comparable to similar arrangements entered into by persons in an arms' length transaction

§ 2704. Treatment of certain lapsing rights and restrictions.

(a) Treatment of lapsed voting or liquidation rights.

(1) In general. For purposes of this subtitle, if—

(A) there is a lapse of any voting or liquidation right in a corporation or partnership, and

(B) the individual holding such right immediately before the lapse and members of such individual's family hold, both before and after the lapse, control of the entity, such lapse shall be treated as a transfer by such individual by gift, or a transfer which is includible in the gross estate of the decedent, whichever is applicable, in the amount determined under paragraph (2).

(2) Amount of transfer. For purposes of paragraph (1), the amount determined under this

paragraph is the excess (if any) of—

(A) the value of all interests in the entity held by the individual described in paragraph (1) immediately before the lapse (determined as if the voting and liquidation rights were nonlapsing), over

(B) the value of such interests immediately after the lapse.

(3) Similar rights. The Secretary may by regulations apply this subsection to rights similar to voting and liquidation rights.

(b) Certain restrictions on liquidation disregarded.

(1) In general. For purposes of this subtitle, if—

(A) there is a transfer of an interest in a corporation or partnership to (or for the benefit of) a member of the transferor's family, and

(B) the transferor and members of the transferor's family hold, immediately before the transfer, control of the entity,

any applicable restriction shall be disregarded in determining the value of the transferred interest.

(2) Applicable restriction. For purposes of this subsection, the term "applicable restriction" means any restriction—

(A) which effectively limits the ability of the corporation or partnership to liquidate, and

(B) with respect to which either of the following applies:

(i) The restriction lapses, in whole or in part, after the transfer referred to in paragraph (1).

(ii) The transferor or any member of the transferor's family, either alone or collectively, has the right after such transfer to remove, in whole or in part, the restriction.

(3) Exceptions. The term "applicable restriction" shall not include—

(A) any commercially reasonable restriction which arises as part of any financing by the corporation or partnership with a person who is not related to the transferor or transferee, or a member of the family of either, or

(B) any restriction imposed, or required to be imposed, by any Federal or State law.

(4) Other restrictions. The Secretary may by regulations provide that other restrictions shall be disregarded in determining the value of the transfer of any interest in a corporation or partnership to a member of the transferor's family if such restriction has the effect of reducing the value of the transferred interest for purposes of this subtitle but does not ultimately reduce the value of such interest to the transferee.

(c) Definitions and special rules. For purposes of this section—

(1) Control. The term "control" has the meaning given such term by section 2701(b)(2).

(2) Member of the family. The term "member of the family" means, with respect to any individual—

(A) such individual's spouse,

(B) any ancestor or lineal descendant of such individual or such individual's spouse,

(C) any brother or sister of the individual, and

(D) any spouse of any individual described in subparagraph (B) or (C).

(3) Attribution. The rule of section 2701(e)(3) shall apply for purposes of determining the interests held by any individual.

§ 7872. Treatment of loans with below-market interest rates

(a) Treatment of gift loans and demand loans.

(1) In general. For purposes of this title, in the case of any below-market loan to which this section applies and which is a gift loan or a demand loan, the forgone interest shall be treated as—

(A) transferred from the lender to the borrower, and

(B) retransferred by the borrower to the lender as interest.

(2) Time when transfers made. Except as otherwise provided in regulations prescribed by the Secretary, any forgone interest attributable to periods during any calendar year shall be treated as transferred (and retransferred) under paragraph (1) on the last day of such calendar year.

(b) Treatment of other below-market loans.

(1) In general. For purposes of this title, in the case of any below-market loan to which this section applies and to which subsection (a)(1) does not apply, the lender shall be treated as having transferred on the date the loan was made (or, if later, on the first day on which this section applies to such loan), and the borrower shall be treated as having received on such date, cash in an amount equal to the excess of—

(A) the amount loaned, over

(B) the present value of all payments which are required to be made under the terms of the loan.

(2) Obligation treated as having original issue discount. For purposes of this title—

(A) In general. Any below-market loan to which paragraph (1) applies shall be treated as having original issue discount in an amount equal to the excess described in paragraph (1).

(B) Amount in addition to other original issue discount. Any original issue discount which a loan is treated as having by reason of subparagraph (A) shall be in addition to any other original issue discount on such loan (determined without regard to subparagraph (A)).

(c) Below-market loans to which section applies.

(1) In general. Except as otherwise provided in this subsection and subsection (g), this section shall apply to—

(A) Gifts. Any below-market loan which is a gift loan.

(B) Compensation-related loans. Any below-market loan directly or indirectly between—

(i) an employer and an employee, or

(ii) an independent contractor and a person for whom such independent contractor provides services.

(C) Corporation-shareholder loans. Any below-market loan directly or indirectly between a corporation and any shareholder of such corporation.

(D) Tax avoidance loans. Any below-market loan 1 of the principal purposes of the interest arrangements of which is the avoidance of any Federal tax.

(E) Other below-market loans. To the extent provided in regulations, any below-market loan which is not described in subparagraph (A), (B), (C), or (F) if the interest arrangements of such loan have a significant effect on any Federal tax liability of the lender or the borrower.

(F) Loans to qualified continuing care facilities. Any loan to any qualified continuing care facility pursuant to a continuing care contract.

(2) $10,000 de minimis exception for gift loans between individuals.

(A) In general. In the case of any gift loan directly between individuals, this section shall not apply to any day on which the aggregate outstanding amount of loans between such individuals does not exceed $10,000.

(B) De minimis exception not to apply to loans attributable to acquisition of income-producing assets.

Subparagraph (A) shall not apply to any gift loan directly attributable to the purchase or carrying of income-producing assets.

(C) Cross reference. For limitation on amount treated as interest where loans do not exceed $100,000, see subsection (d)(1).

(3) $10,000 de minimis exception for compensation-related and corporate-shareholder loans.

(A) In general. In the case of any loan described in subparagraph (B) or (C) of paragraph (1), this section shall not apply to any day on which the aggregate outstanding amount of loans between the borrower and lender does not exceed $10,000.

(B) Exception not to apply where 1 of principal purposes is tax avoidance. Subparagraph (A) shall not apply to any loan the interest arrangements of which have as 1 of their principal purposes the avoidance of any Federal tax.

(d) Special rules for gift loans.

(1) Limitation on interest accrual for purposes of income taxes where loans do not

exceed $100,000.

(A) In general. For purposes of subtitle A, in the case of a gift loan directly between individuals, the amount treated as retransferred by the borrower to the lender as of the close of any year shall not exceed the borrower's net investment income for such year.

(B) Limitation not to apply where 1 of principal purposes is tax avoidance. Subparagraph (A) shall not apply to any loan the interest arrangements of which have as 1 of their principal purposes the avoidance of any Federal tax.

(C) Special rule where more than 1 gift loan outstanding. For purposes of subparagraph (A), in any case in which a borrower has outstanding more than 1 gift loan, the net investment income of such borrower shall be allocated among such loans in proportion to the respective amounts which would be treated as retransferred by the borrower without regard to this paragraph.

(D) Limitation not to apply where aggregate amount of loans exceed $100,000. This paragraph shall not apply to any loan made by a lender to a borrower for any day on which the aggregate outstanding amount of loans between the borrower and lender exceeds $100,000.

(E) Net investment income. For purposes of this paragraph—

(i) In general. The term "net investment income" has the meaning given such term by section 163(d)(4).

(ii) De minimis rule. If the net investment income of any borrower for any year does not exceed $1,000, the net investment income of such borrower for such year shall be treated as zero.

(iii) Additional amounts treated as interest. In determining the net investment income of a person for any year, any amount which would be included in the gross income of such person for such year by reason of section 1272 if such section applied to all deferred payment obligations shall be treated as interest received by such person for such year.

(iv) Deferred payment obligations. The term "deferred payment obligation" includes any market discount bond, short-term obligation, United States savings bond, annuity, or similar obligation.

(2) Special rule for gift tax. In the case of any gift loan which is a term loan, subsection (b)(1) (and not subsection (a)) shall apply for purposes of chapter 12.

(e) Definitions of below-market loan and forgone interest. For purposes of this section—

(1) Below-market loan. The term "below-market loan" means any loan if—

(A) in the case of a demand loan, interest is payable on the loan at a rate less than the applicable Federal rate, or

(B) in the case of a term loan, the amount loaned exceeds the present value of all payments due under the loan.

(2) Forgone interest. The term "forgone interest" means, with respect to any period during which the loan is outstanding, the excess of—

(A) the amount of interest which would have been payable on the loan for the period if interest accrued on the loan at the applicable Federal rate and were payable annually on the day referred to in subsection (a)(2), over

(B) any interest payable on the loan properly allocable to such period.

(f) Other definitions and special rules. For purposes of this section—

(1) Present value. The present value of any payment shall be determined in the manner provided by regulations prescribed by the Secretary—

(A) as of the date of the loan, and

(B) by using a discount rate equal to the applicable Federal rate.

(2) Applicable Federal rate.

(A) Term loans. In the case of any term loan, the applicable Federal rate shall be the applicable Federal rate in effect under section 1274(d) (as of the day on which the loan was made), compounded semiannually.

(B) Demand loans. In the case of a demand loan, the applicable Federal rate shall be the Federal short-term rate in effect under section 1274(d) for the period for which the amount of forgone interest is being determined, compounded semiannually.

(3) Gift loan. The term "gift loan" means any below-market loan where the forgoing of interest is in the nature of a gift.

(4) Amount loaned. The term "amount loaned" means the amount received by the borrower.

(5) Demand loan. The term "demand loan" means any loan which is payable in full at any time on the demand of the lender. Such term also includes (for purposes other than determining the applicable Federal rate under paragraph (2)) any loan if the benefits of the interest arrangements of such loan are not transferable and are conditioned on the future performance of substantial services by an individual. To the extent provided in regulations, such term also includes any loan with an indefinite maturity.

(6) Term loan. The term "term loan" means any loan which is not a demand loan.

(7) Husband and wife treated as 1 person. A husband and wife shall be treated as 1 person.

(8) Loans to which section 483, 643(i), or 1274 applies. This section shall not apply to any loan to which section 483, 643(i), or 1274 applies.

(9) No withholding. No amount shall be withheld under chapter 24 with respect to—

(A) any amount treated as transferred or retransferred under subsection (a), and

(B) any amount treated as received under subsection (b).

(10) Special rule for term loans. If this section applies to any term loan on any day, this section shall continue to apply to such loan notwithstanding paragraphs (2) and (3) of subsection (c). In the case of a gift loan, the preceding sentence shall only apply for purposes of chapter 12.

(11) Time for determining rate applicable to employee relocation loans.

(A) In general. In the case of any term loan made by an employer to an employee the proceeds of which are used by the employee to purchase a principal residence (within the meaning of section 121), the determination of the applicable Federal rate shall be made as of the date the written contract to purchase such residence was entered into.

(B) Paragraph only to apply to cases to which section 217 applies. Subparagraph (A) shall only apply to the purchase of a principal residence in connection with the commencement of work by an employee or a change in the principal place of work of an employee to which section 217 applies.

(g) Exception for certain loans to qualified continuing care facilities.

(1) In general. This section shall not apply for any calendar year to any below-market loan made by a lender to a qualified continuing care facility pursuant to a continuing care contract if the lender (or the lender's spouse) attains age 65 before the close of such year.

(2) $90,000 limit. Paragraph (1) shall apply only to the extent that the aggregate outstanding amount of any loan to which such paragraph applies (determined without regard to this paragraph), when added to the aggregate outstanding amount of all other previous loans between the lender (or the lender's spouse) and any qualified continuing care facility to which paragraph (1) applies, does not exceed $90,000.

(3) Continuing care contract. For purposes of this section, the term "continuing care contract" means a written contract between an individual and a qualified continuing care facility under which—

(A) the individual or individual's spouse may use a qualified continuing care facility for their life or lives,

(B) the individual or individual's spouse—

(i) will first—

(I) reside in a separate, independent living unit with additional facilities outside such unit for the providing of meals and other personal care, and

(II) not require long-term nursing care, and

(ii) then will be provided long-term and skilled nursing care as the health of such individual or individual's spouse requires, and

(C) no additional substantial payment is required if such individual or individual's spouse requires increased personal care services or long-term and skilled nursing care.

(4) Qualified continuing care facility.

(A) In general. For purposes of this section, the term "qualified continuing care facility" means 1 or more facilities—

(i) which are designed to provide services under continuing care contracts, and

(ii) substantially all of the residents of which are covered by continuing care contracts.

(B) Substantially all facilities must be owned or operated by borrower. A facility shall not be treated as a qualified continuing care facility unless substantially all facilities which are used to provide services which are required to be provided under a continuing care contract are owned or operated by the borrower.

(C) Nursing homes excluded. The term "qualified continuing care facility" shall not include any facility which is of a type which is traditionally considered a nursing home.

(5) Adjustment of limit for inflation.

(A) In general. In the case of any loan made during any calendar year after 1986 to which paragraph (1) applies, the dollar amount in paragraph (2) shall be increased by the inflation adjustment for such calendar year. Any increase under the preceding sentence shall be rounded to the nearest multiple of $100 (or, if such increase is a multiple of $50, such increase shall be increased to the nearest multiple of $100).

(B) Inflation adjustment. For purposes of subparagraph (A), the inflation adjustment for any calendar year is the percentage (if any) by which

(i) the CPI for the preceding calendar year exceeds

(ii) the CPI for calendar year 1985.

1. For purposes of the preceding sentence, the CPI for any calendar year is the average of the Consumer Price Index as of the close of the 12-month period ending on September 30 of such calendar year.

(6) Suspension of application. Paragraph (1) shall not apply for any calendar year to which subsection (h) applies.

(h) Exception for loans to qualified continuing care facilities.

(1) In general. This section shall not apply for any calendar year to any below-market loan owed by a facility which on the last day of such year is a qualified continuing care facility, if such loan was made pursuant to a continuing care contract and if the lender (or the lender's spouse) attains age 62 before the close of such year.

(2) Continuing care contract. For purposes of this section, the term "continuing care contract" means a written contract between an individual and a qualified continuing care facility under which—

(A) the individual or individual's spouse may use a qualified continuing care facility for their life or lives,

(B) the individual or individual's spouse will be provided with housing, as appropriate for the health of such individual or individual's spouse—

(i) in an independent living unit (which has additional available facilities outside such unit for the provision of meals and other personal care), and

(ii) in an assisted living facility or a nursing facility, as is available in the continuing care facility, and

(C) the individual or individual's spouse will be provided assisted living or nursing care as the health of such individual or individual's spouse requires, and as is available in the continuing care facility.

The Secretary shall issue guidance which limits such term to contracts which provide only facilities, care, and services described in this paragraph.

(3) Qualified continuing care facility.

(A) In general. For purposes of this section, the term "qualified continuing care facility" means 1 or more facilities—

(i) which are designed to provide services under continuing care contracts,

(ii) which include an independent living unit, plus an assisted living or nursing facility, or both, and

(iii) substantially all of the independent living unit residents of which are covered by continuing care contracts.

(B) Nursing homes excluded. The term "qualified continuing care facility" shall not include any facility which is of a type which is traditionally considered a nursing home.

(i) Regulations.

(1) In general. The Secretary shall prescribe such regulations as may be necessary or appropriate to carry out the purposes of this section, including—

(A) regulations providing that where, by reason of varying rates of interest, conditional interest payments, waivers of interest, disposition of the lender's or borrower's interest in the loan, or other circumstances, the provisions of this section do not carry out the purposes of this section, adjustments to the provisions of this section will be made to the extent necessary to carry out the purposes of this section,

(B) regulations for the purpose of assuring that the positions of the borrower and lender are consistent as to the application (or nonapplication) of this section, and

(C) regulations exempting from the application of this section any class of transactions the interest arrangements of which have no significant effect on any Federal tax liability of the lender or the borrower.

(2) Estate tax coordination. Under regulations prescribed by the Secretary, any loan which is made with donative intent and which is a term loan shall be taken into account for purposes of chapter 11 in a manner consistent with the provisions of subsection (b).

§ 6166. Extension of Time for Payment of Estate Tax Where Estate Consists Largely of Interest in Closely Held Business.

(a) 5-year deferral; 10-year installment payment.—

(1) In general.—If the value of an interest in a closely held business which is included in determining the gross estate of a decedent who was (at the date of his death) a citizen or resident of the United States exceeds 35 percent of the adjusted gross estate, the executor may elect to pay part or all of the tax imposed by section 2001 in 2 or more (but not exceeding 10) equal installments.

(2) Limitation.—The maximum amount of tax which may be paid in installments under this subsection shall be an amount which bears the same ratio to the tax imposed by section

2001 (reduced by the credits against such tax) as—

    (A) the closely held business amount, bears to

    (B) the amount of the adjusted gross estate.

  (3) Date for payment of installments.—If an election is made under paragraph (1), the first installment shall be paid on or before the date selected by the executor which is not more than 5 years after the date prescribed by section 6151(a) for payment of the tax, and each succeeding installment shall be paid on or before the date which is 1 year after the date prescribed by this paragraph for payment of the preceding installment.

(b) Definitions and special rules.—

  (1) Interest in closely held business.—For purposes of this section, the term "interest in a closely held business" means—

    (A) an interest as a proprietor in a trade or business carried on as a proprietorship;

    (B) an interest as a partner in a partnership carrying on a trade or business, if—

      (i) 20 percent or more of the total capital interest in such partnership is included in determining the gross estate of the decedent, or

      (ii) such partnership had 45 or fewer partners; or

    (C) stock in a corporation carrying on a trade or business if—

      (i) 20 percent or more in value of the voting stock of such corporation is included in determining the gross estate of the decedent, or

      (ii) such corporation had 45 or fewer shareholders.

  (2) Rules for applying paragraph (1).—For purposes of paragraph (1)—

    (A) Time for testing.—Determinations shall be made as of the time immediately before the decedent's death.

    (B) Certain interests held by husband and wife.—Stock or a partnership interest which—

      (i) is community property of a husband and wife (or the income from which is community income) under the applicable community property law of a State, or

      (ii) is held by a husband and wife as joint tenants, tenants by the entirety, or tenants in common, shall be treated as owned by one shareholder or one partner, as the case may be.

    (C) Indirect ownership.—Property owned, directly or indirectly, by or for a corporation, partnership, estate, or trust shall be considered as being owned proportionately by or for its shareholders, partners, or beneficiaries. For purposes of the preceding sentence, a person shall be treated as a beneficiary of any trust only if such person has a present interest in the trust.

    (D) Certain interests held by members of decedent's family.—All stock and all partnership interests held by the decedent or by any member of his family (within the meaning of section 267(c)(4)) shall be treated as owned by the decedent.

(3) Farmhouses and certain other structures taken into account.—For purposes of the 35-percent requirement of subsection (a)(1), an interest in a closely held business which is the business of farming includes an interest in residential buildings and related improvements on the farm which are occupied on a regular basis by the owner or lessee of the farm or by persons employed by such owner or lessee for purposes of operating or maintaining the farm.

(4) Value.—For purposes of this section, value shall be value determined for purposes of chapter 11 (relating to estate tax).

(5) Closely held business amount.—For purposes of this section, the term "closely held business amount" means the value of the interest in a closely held business which qualifies under subsection (a)(1).

(6) Adjusted gross estate.—For purposes of this section, the term, "adjusted gross estate" means the value of the gross estate reduced by the sum of the amounts allowable as a deduction under section 2053 or 2054. Such sum shall be determined on the basis of the facts and circumstances in existence on the date (including extensions) for filing the return of tax imposed by section 2001 (or, if earlier, the date on which such return is filed).

(7) Partnership interests and stock which is not readily tradable.—

(A) In general.—If the executor elects the benefits of this paragraph (at such time and in such manner as the Secretary shall by regulations prescribe), then—

(i) for purposes of paragraph (1)(B)(i) or (1)(C)(i) (whichever is appropriate) and for purposes of subsection (c), any capital interest in a partnership and any non-readily-tradable stock which (after the application of paragraph (2)) is treated as owned by the decedent shall be treated as included in determining the value of the decedent's gross estate,

(ii) the executor shall be treated as having selected under subsection (a)(3) the date prescribed by section 6151(a), and

(iii) for purposes of applying section 6601(j), the 2-percent portion (as defined in such section) shall be treated as being zero.

(B) Non-readily-tradable stock defined.—For purposes of this paragraph, the term "non-readily-tradable stock" means stock for which, at the time of the decedent's death, there was no market on a stock exchange or in an over-the-counter market.

(8) Stock in holding company treated as business company stock in certain cases.—

(A) In general.—If the executor elects the benefits of this paragraph, then—

(i) Holding company stock treated as business company stock.—For purposes of this section, the portion of the stock of any holding company which represents direct ownership (or indirect ownership through 1 or more other holding companies) by such company in a business company shall be deemed to be stock in such business company.

(ii) 5-year deferral for principal not to apply.—The executor shall be treated as having selected under subsection (a)(3) the date prescribed by section 6151(a).

(iii) 2-percent interest rate not to apply.—For purposes of applying section 6601(j), the 2-percent portion (as defined in such section) shall be treated as being zero.

(B) All stock must be non-readily-tradable stock.—

(i) In general.—No stock shall be taken into account for purposes of applying this paragraph unless it is non-readily-tradable stock (within the meaning of paragraph (7)(B)).

(ii) Special application where only holding company stock is non-readily-tradable stock.—If the requirements of clause (i) are not met, but all of the stock of each holding company taken into account is non-readily-tradable, then this paragraph shall apply, but subsection (a)(1) shall be applied by substituting "5" for "10".

(C) Application of voting stock requirement of paragraph (1)(C)(i).—For purposes of clause (i) of paragraph (1)(C), the deemed stock resulting from the application of subparagraph (A) shall be treated as voting stock to the extent that voting stock in the holding company owns directly (or through the voting stock of 1 or more other holding companies) voting stock in the business company.

(D) Definitions.—For purposes of this paragraph—

(i) Holding company.—The term "holding company" means any corporation holding stock in another corporation.

(ii) Business company.—The term "business company" means any corporation carrying on a trade or business.

(9) Deferral not available for passive assets.—

(A) In general.—For purposes of subsection (a)(1) and determining the closely held business amount (but not for purposes of subsection (g)), the value of any interest in a closely held business shall not include the value of that portion of such interest which is attributable to passive assets held by the business.

(B) Passive asset defined.—For purposes of this paragraph—

(i) In general.—The term "passive asset" means any asset other than an asset used in carrying on a trade or business.

(ii) Stock treated as passive asset.—The term "passive asset" includes any stock in another corporation unless—

(I) such stock is treated as held by the decedent by reason of an election under paragraph (8), and

(II) such stock qualified under subsection (a)(1).

(iii) Exception for active corporations.—If—

(I) a corporation owns 20 percent or more in value of the voting stock of another corporation, or such other corporation has 45 or fewer shareholders, and

(II) 80 percent or more of the value of the assets of each such corporation is attributable to assets used in carrying on a trade or business, then such corporations shall be treated as 1 corporation for purposes of clause (ii). For purposes of applying subclause (II) to the corporation holding the stock of the other corporation, such stock shall not be taken into account.

(10) Stock in qualifying lending and finance business treated as stock in an active trade or business company.—

(A) In general.—If the executor elects the benefits of this paragraph, then—

(I) Stock in qualifying lending and finance business treated as stock in an active trade or business company.—For purposes of this section, any asset used in a qualifying lending and finance business shall be treated as an asset which is used in carrying on a trade or business.

(II) 5-year deferral for principal not to apply.—The executor shall be treated as having selected under subsection (a)(3) the date prescribed by section 6151(a).

(iii) 5 equal installments allowed.—For purposes of applying subsection (a)(1), "5" shall be substituted for "10".

(B) Definitions.—For purposes of this paragraph—

(i) Qualifying lending and finance business.—The term "qualifying lending and finance business" means a lending and finance business, if—

(I) based on all the facts and circumstances immediately before the date of the decedent's death, there was substantial activity with respect to the lending and finance business, or

(II) during at least 3 of the 5 taxable years ending before the date of the decedent's death, such business had at least 1 full-time employee substantially all of whose services were the active management of such business, 10 full-time, nonowner employees substantially all of whose services were directly related to such business, and $5,000,000 in gross receipts from activities described in clause (ii).

(ii) Lending and finance business.—The term "lending and finance business" means a trade or business of—

(I) making loans,

(II) purchasing or discounting accounts receivable, notes, or installment obligations,

(III) engaging in rental and leasing of real and tangible personal property, including entering into leases and purchasing, servicing, and disposing of leases and leased assets,

(IV) rendering services or making facilities available in the ordinary course of a lending or finance business, and

(V) rendering services or making facilities available in connection with activities described in subclauses (I) through (IV) carried on by the corporation rendering services or making facilities available, or another corporation which is a member of the same affiliated group (as defined in section 1504 without regard to section 1504(b)(3)).

(iii) Limitation.—The term "qualifying lending and finance business" shall not include any interest in an entity, if the stock or debt of such entity or a controlled group (as defined in section 267(f)(1)) of which such entity was a member was readily tradable on an established securities market or secondary market (as defined by the Secretary) at any time within 3 years before the date of the decedent's death.

(c) Special rule for interest in 2 or more closely held businesses.—For purposes of this section, interest in 2 or more closely held businesses, with respect to each of which there is included in determining the value of the decedent's gross estate 20 percent or more of the total value of each such business, shall be treated as an interest in a single closely held business. For purposes of the 20-percent requirement of the preceding sentence, an interest in a closely held business which represents the surviving spouse's interest in property held by the decedent and the surviving spouse as community property or as joint tenants, tenants by the entirety, or tenants in common shall be treated as having been included in determining the value of the decedent's gross estate.

(d) Election.—Any election under subsection (a) shall be made not later than the time prescribed by section 6075(a) for filing the return of tax imposed by section 2001 (including extensions thereof), and shall be made in such manner as the Secretary shall by regulations prescribe. If an election under subsection (a) is made, the provisions of this subtitle shall apply as though the Secretary were extending the time for payment of the tax.

(e) Proration of deficiency to installments.—If an election is made under subsection (a) to pay any part of the tax imposed by section 2001 in installments and a deficiency has been assessed, the deficiency shall (subject to the limitation provided by subsection (a)(2)) be prorated to the installments payable under subsection (a). The part of the deficiency so prorated to any installment the date for payment of which has not arrived shall be collected at the same time as, and as a part of, such installment. The part of the deficiency so prorated to any installment the date for payment of which has arrived shall be paid upon notice and demand from the Secretary. This subsection shall not apply if the deficiency is due to negligence, to intentional disregard of rules and regulations, or to fraud with intent to evade tax.

(f) Time for payment of interest.—If the time for payment of any amount of tax has been extended under this section—

(1) Interest for first 5 years.—Interest payable under section 6601 of any unpaid portion of such amount attributable to the first 5 years after the date prescribed by section 6151(a) for payment of the tax shall be paid annually.

(2) Interest for periods after first 5 years.—Interest payable under section 6601 on any unpaid portion of such amount attributable to any period after the 5-year period referred to in paragraph (1) shall be paid annually at the same time as, and as a part of, each installment payment of the tax.

(3) Interest in the case of certain deficiencies.—In the case of a deficiency to which subsection (e) applies which is assessed after the close of the 5-year period referred to in paragraph (1), interest attributable to such 5-year period, and interest assigned under paragraph (2) to any installment the date for payment of which has arrived on or before

the date of the assessment of the deficiency, shall be paid upon notice and demand from the Secretary.

(4) Selection of shorter period.—If the executor has selected a period shorter than 5 years under subsection (a)(3), such shorter period shall be substituted for 5 years in paragraphs (1), (2), and (3) of this subsection.

(g) Acceleration of payment.—

(1) Disposition of interest; withdrawal of funds from business.—

(A) If—

(i) (I) any portion of an interest in a closely held business which qualifies under subsection (a)(1) is distributed, sold, exchanged, or otherwise disposed of, or

(II) money and other property attributable to such an interest is withdrawn from such trade or business, and

(ii) the aggregate of such distributions, sales, exchanges, or other dispositions and withdrawals equals or exceeds 50 percent of the value of such interest, then the extension of time for payment of tax provided in subsection (a) shall cease to apply, and the unpaid portion of the tax payable in installments shall be paid upon notice and demand from the Secretary.

(B) In the case of a distribution in redemption of stock to which section 303 (or so much of section 304 as relates to section 303) applies—

(i) the redemption of such stock, and the withdrawal of money and other property distributed in such redemption, shall not be treated as a distribution or withdrawal for purposes of subparagraph (A), and

(ii) for purposes of subparagraph (A), the value of the interest in the closely held business shall be considered to be such value reduced by the value of the stock redeemed.

This subparagraph shall apply only if, on or before the date prescribed by subsection (a)(3) for the payment of the first installment which becomes due after the date of the distribution (or, if earlier, on or before the day which is 1 year after the date of the distribution), there is paid an amount of the tax imposed by section 2001 not less than the amount of money and other property distributed.

(C) Subparagraph (A)(i) does not apply to an exchange of stock pursuant to a plan of reorganization described in subparagraph (D), (E), or (F) of section 368(a)(1) nor to an exchange to which section 355 (or so much of section 356 as relates to section 355) applies; but any stock received in such an exchange shall be treated for purposes of subparagraph (A)(i) as an interest qualifying under subsection (a)(1).

(D) Subparagraph (A)(i) does not apply to a transfer of property of the decedent to a person entitled by reason of the decedent's death to receive such property under the decedent's will, the applicable law of descent and distribution, or a trust created by the decedent. A similar rule shall apply in the case of a series of subsequent transfers of the property by reason of death so long as each transfer is to a member of the family (within the meaning of section 267(c)(4)) of the transferor in such transfer.

(E) Changes in interest in holding company.—If any stock in a holding company is treated as stock in a business company by reason of subsection (b)(8)(A)—

(i) any disposition of any interest in such stock in such holding company which was included in determining the gross estate of the decedent, or

(ii) any withdrawal of any money or other property from such holding company attributable to any interest included in determining the gross estate of the decedent, shall be treated for purposes of subparagraph (A) as a disposition of (or a withdrawal with respect to) the stock qualifying under subsection (a)(1).

(F) Changes in interest in business company.—If any stock in a holding company is treated as stock in a business company by reason of subsection (b)(8)(A)—

(i) any disposition of any interest in such stock in the business company by such holding company, or

(ii) any withdrawal of any money or other property from such business company attributable to such stock by such holding company owning such stock,

shall be treated for purposes of subparagraph (A) as a disposition of (or a withdrawal with respect to) the stock qualifying under subsection (a)(1).

(2) Undistributed income of estate.—

(A) If an election is made under this section and the estate has undistributed net income for any taxable year ending on or after the due date for the first installment, the executor shall, on or before the date prescribed by law for filing the income tax return for such taxable year (including extensions thereof), pay an amount equal to such undistributed net income in liquidation of the unpaid portion of the tax payable in installments.

(B) For purposes of subparagraph (A), the undistributed net income of the estate for any taxable year is the amount by which the distributable net income of the estate for such taxable year (as defined in section 643) exceeds the sum of—

(i) the amounts for such taxable year specified in paragraphs (1) and (2) of section 661(a) (relating to deductions for distributions, etc.);

(ii) the amount of tax imposed for the taxable year on the estate under chapter 1; and

(iii) the amount of the tax imposed by section 2001 (including interest) paid by the executor during the taxable year (other than any amount paid pursuant to this paragraph).

(C) For purposes of this paragraph, if any stock in a corporation is treated as stock in another corporation by reason of subsection (b)(8)(A), any dividends paid by such other corporation to the corporation shall be treated as paid to the estate of the decedent to the extent attributable to the stock qualifying under subsection (a)(1).

(3) Failure to make payment of principal or interest.—

(A) In general.—Except as provided in subparagraph (B), if any payment of principal or interest under this section is not paid on or before the date fixed for its payment by this section (including any extension of time), the unpaid portion of the tax payable in installments shall be paid upon notice and demand from the Secretary.

(B) Payment within 6 months.—If any payment of principal or interest under this section is not paid on or before the date determined under subparagraph (A) but is paid within 6 months of such date—

(i) the provisions of subparagraph (A) shall not apply with respect to such payment,

(ii) the provisions of section 6601(j) shall not apply with respect to the determination of interest on such payment, and

(iii) there is imposed a penalty in an amount equal to the product of—

(I) 5 percent of the amount of such payment, multiplied by

(II) the number of months (or fractions thereof) after such date and before payment is made. The penalty imposed under clause (iii) shall be treated in the same manner as a penalty imposed under subchapter B of chapter 68.

(h) Election in case of certain deficiencies.—

(1) In general.—If—

(A) a deficiency in the tax imposed by section 2001 is assessed,

(B) the estate qualifies under subsection (a)(1), and

(C) the executor has not made an election under subsection (a), the executor may elect to pay the deficiency in installments. This subsection shall not apply if the deficiency is due to negligence, to intentional disregard of rules and regulations, or to fraud with intent to evade tax.

(2) Time of election.—An election under this subsection shall be made not later than 60 days after issuance of notice and demand by the Secretary for the payment of the deficiency, and shall be made in such manner as the Secretary shall by regulations prescribe.

(3) Effect of election on payment.—If an election is made under this subsection, the deficiency shall (subject to the limitation provided by subsection (a)(2)) be prorated to the installments which would have been due if an election had been timely made under subsection (a) at the time the estate tax return was filed. The part of the deficiency so prorated to any installment the date for payment of which would have arrived shall be paid at the time of the making of the election under this subsection. The portion of the deficiency so prorated to installments the date for payment of which would not have so arrived shall be paid at the time such installments would have been due if such an election had been made.

(i) Special rule for certain direct skips.—To the extent that an interest in a closely held business is the subject of a direct skip (within the meaning of section 2612(c)) occurring at the same time as and as a result of the decedent's death, then for purposes of this section any tax imposed by section 2601 on the transfer of such interest shall be treated as if it were additional tax imposed by section 2001.

(j) Regulations.—The Secretary shall prescribe such regulations as may be necessary to the application of this section.

(k) Cross references.—

(1) Security.—For authority of the Secretary to require security in the case of an extension under this section, see section 6165.

(2) Lien.—For special lien (in lieu of bond) in the case of an extension under this section, see section 6324A.

(3) Period of limitation.—For extension of the period of limitation in the case of an extension under this section, see section 6503(d).

(4) Interest.—For provisions relating to interest on tax payable in installments under this section, see subsection (j) of section 6601.

(5) Transfers within 3 years of death.—For special rule for qualifying an estate under this section where property has been transferred within 3 years of decedent's death, see section 2035(c)(2).

History: Add, L 2014, ch 59, § 10 (Part X), eff April 1, 2014.

GENERAL OBLIGATIONS LAW

ARTICLE 5   CREATION, DEFINITION AND ENFORCEMENT OF CONTRACTUAL OBLIGATIONS

---

* L 2010 ch 340, effective Sept 12, 2010, deemed effective on and after Sept 1, 2009, provided, that any statutory short form power of attorney and any statutory gifts rider executed after Aug 31, 2009 shall remain valid as will any revocation of a prior power of attorney that was delivered to the agent before the effective date of this act, amended the heading.

§ 5-1513. Statutory short form power of attorney

§ 5-1501. Application and definitions

1. This title shall apply to all powers of attorney except powers of attorney excluded from this title by section 5-1501C of this title.

2. As used in this title the following terms shall have the following meanings:

(a) "Agent" means a person granted authority to act as attorney-in-fact for the principal under a power of attorney, and includes the original agent and any co-agent or successor agent. Unless the context indicates otherwise, an "agent" designated in a power of attorney shall mean "attorney-in-fact" for the purposes of this title. An agent acting under a power of attorney has a fiduciary relationship with the principal.

(b) "Benefits from governmental programs or civil or military service" means any benefit, program or assistance provided under a statute or governmental regulation, including social security, medicare and medicaid.

(c) "Capacity" means ability to comprehend the nature and consequences of the act of executing and granting, revoking, amending or modifying a power of attorney, any provision in a power of attorney, or the authority of any person to act as agent under a power of attorney.

(d) "Compensation" means reasonable compensation authorized to be paid to the agent from assets of the principal for services actually rendered by the agent pursuant to the authority granted in a power of attorney.

(e) "Financial institution" means a financial entity, including, but not limited to: a bank, trust company, national bank, savings bank, federal mutual savings bank, savings and loan association, federal savings and loan association, federal mutual savings and loan association, credit union, federal credit union, branch of a foreign banking corporation, public pension fund, retirement system, securities broker, securities dealer, securities firm, and insurance company.

(f) "Incapacitated" means to be without capacity.

(g) "Internal Revenue Code" means the United States Internal Revenue Code of 1986, as amended. Such references, however, shall be deemed to constitute references to any corresponding provisions of any subsequent federal tax code.

(h) "Monitor" means a person appointed in the power of attorney who has the authority to request, receive, and seek to compel the agent to provide a record of all receipts, disbursements, and transactions entered into by the agent on behalf of the principal.

(i) "Person" means an individual, whether acting for himself or herself, or as a fiduciary or as an official of any legal, governmental or commercial entity (including, but not limited to, any such entity identified in this subdivision), corporation, business trust, estate, trust, partnership, limited liability company, association, joint venture, government, governmental subdivision, government agency, government entity, government instrumentality, public corporation, or any other legal or commercial entity.

(j) "Power of attorney" means a written document, other than a document referred to in section 5-1501C of this title, by which a principal with capacity designates an agent to act on his or her behalf and includes both a statutory short form power of attorney and a non-statutory power of attorney.

(k) "Principal" means an individual who is eighteen years of age or older, acting for himself or herself and not as a fiduciary or as an official of any legal, governmental or commercial entity, who executes a power of attorney.

(l) "Record" means information that is inscribed on a tangible medium or that is stored in an electronic or other medium and is retrievable in perceivable form.

(m) "Sign" means to place any memorandum, mark or sign, written, printed, stamped, photographed, engraved or otherwise upon an instrument or writing, or to use an electronic signature as that term is defined in subdivision three of section three hundred two of the state technology law, with the intent to execute the instrument, writing or electronic record. In accordance with the requirements of section three hundred seven of the state technology law, a power of attorney or any other instrument executed by the principal or agent that is recordable under the real property law shall not be executed with an electronic signature.

(n) "Statutory short form power of attorney" means a power of attorney that meets the requirements of paragraphs (a), (b) and (c) of subdivision one of section 5-1501B of this title, and that substantially conforms to the wording of the form set forth in section 5-1513 of this title; provided however, that any section indicated as "Optional" that is not used may be omitted and replaced by the words "Intentionally Omitted". A given power of attorney substantially conforms to the form required pursuant to section 5-1513 of this title notwithstanding that the form contains (i) an insignificant mistake in wording, spelling, punctuation or formatting, or the use of bold or italic type; or (ii) uses language that is essentially the same as, but is not identical to, the statutory form, including utilizing language from a previous statute. The determination of whether there is substantial conformity with the form set forth in section 5-1513 of this title shall not depend on the presence or absence of a particular clause. Failing to include clauses that are not relevant to a given power of attorney shall not in itself cause such power of attorney to be found to not substantially conform with the requirements of such form. The use of the form set forth in section 5-1513 of this title is lawful and when used, it shall be construed as a statutory short form power of attorney. A statutory short form power of attorney may be used to grant authority provided in sections 5-1502A through 5-1502N of this title. A "statutory short form power of attorney" may contain modifications or additions as provided in section 5-1503 of this title.

(o) "Non-statutory power of attorney" means a power of attorney that is not a statutory short form power of attorney.

(p) "Third party" means a financial institution or person other than a principal or an agent.

History: Add, L 2008, ch 644, § 2, eff Sept 1, 2009, as amended by L 2009 ch 4, effective Sept 1, 2009, which repealed the former section; amd, L 2010, ch 340, § 2, eff Sept 12, 2010, deemed eff on and after Sept 1, 2009, provided, that any statutory short form power of attorney and any statutory gifts rider executed after Aug 31, 2009 shall remain valid as will any revocation of a prior power of attorney that was delivered to the agent before the effective date of this act; L 2020, ch 323, §§ 1-3, eff June 13, 2021.

§ 5-1501A. Power of attorney not affected by incapacity

1. A power of attorney is durable unless it expressly provides that it is terminated by the incapacity of the principal.

2. The subsequent incapacity of a principal shall not revoke or terminate the authority of an agent who acts under a durable power of attorney. All acts done during any period of the principal's incapacity by an agent pursuant to a durable power of attorney shall have the same effect and inure to the benefit of and bind a principal and his or her distributees, devisees, legatees and personal representatives as if such principal had capacity. If a guardian is thereafter appointed for such principal, such agent, during the continuance of the appointment, shall account to the guardian rather than to such principal.

> **History:** Add, L 2008, ch 644, § 2, eff Sept 1, 2009, as amended by L 2009 ch 4, eff Sept 1, 2009.

§ 5-1501B. Creation of a valid power of attorney; when effective

1. To be valid, except as otherwise provided in section 5-1512 of this title, a statutory short form power of attorney, or a non-statutory power of attorney, executed in this state by a principal, must:

(a) Be typed or printed using letters which are legible or of clear type no less than twelve point in size, or, if in writing, a reasonable equivalent thereof.

(b) Be signed, initialed and dated by a principal with capacity, or in the name of such principal by another person, other than a person designated as the principal's agent or successor agent, in the principal's presence and at the principal's direction, in either case with the signature of the person signing duly acknowledged in the manner prescribed for the acknowledgment of a conveyance of real property and witnessed by two persons who are not named in the instrument as agents or as permissible recipients of gifts, in the manner described in subparagraph two of paragraph (a) of section 3-2.1 of the estate, powers and trusts law in the presence of the principal. The person who takes the acknowledgement under this paragraph may also serve as one of the witnesses. When a person signs at the direction of a principal he or she shall sign by writing or printing the principal's name, and printing and signing his or her own name.

(c) Be signed and dated by any agent acting on behalf of the principal with the signature of the agent duly acknowledged in the manner prescribed for the acknowledgment of a conveyance of real property. A power of attorney executed pursuant to this section is not invalid solely because there has been a lapse of time between the date of acknowledgment of the signature of the principal and the date or dates of acknowledgment of the signature or signatures of any agent or agents or successor agent or successor agents authorized to act on behalf of the principal or because the principal became incapacitated during any such lapse of time.

(d) Substantially conform to the wording of the:

(1) "Caution to the Principal" in paragraph (a) of subdivision one of section 5-1513 of this title; and

(2) "Important Information for the Agent" in paragraph (n) of subdivision one of section 5-1513 of this title.

2. Insubstantial variation in the wording of the "Caution to the Principal" of paragraph (a) of subdivision one of section 5-1513 of this title or of the "Important Information for the

Agent" of paragraph (n) of subdivision one of section 5-1513 of this title shall not prevent a power of attorney from being deemed a statutory short form power of attorney or a non-statutory power of attorney.

3. (a) The date on which an agent's signature is acknowledged is the effective date of the power of attorney as to that agent; provided, however, that if two or more agents are designated to act together, the power of attorney takes effect when all the agents so designated have signed such power of attorney with their signatures acknowledged.

(b) If the power of attorney states that it takes effect upon the occurrence of a date or a contingency specified in the document, then the power of attorney takes effect only when the date or contingency identified in the document has occurred, and the signature of the agent acting on behalf of the principal has been acknowledged. If the document requires that a person or persons named or otherwise identified therein declare, in writing, that the identified contingency has occurred, such a declaration satisfies the requirement of this paragraph without regard to whether the specified contingency has occurred.

4. Nothing of this title shall be construed to bar the use or validity of any other or different form of power of attorney desired by a person other than a principal as the term principal is defined in section 5-1501 of this title.

History: Add, L 2008, ch 644, § 2, eff Sept 1, 2009, as amended by L 2009 ch 4, eff Sept 1, 2009; amd, L 2010, ch 340, §§ 3–5, eff Sept 12, 2010, deemed eff on and after Sept 1, 2009, provided, that any statutory short form power of attorney and any statutory gifts rider executed after Aug 31, 2009 shall remain valid as will any revocation of a prior power of attorney that was delivered to the agent before the effective date of this act; L 2020, ch 323, § 4, eff June 13, 2021; L 2021, ch 84 § 1, eff June 13, 2021.

§ 5-1501C. Powers of attorney excluded from this title

The provisions of this title shall not apply to the following powers of attorney:

1. A power of attorney given primarily for a business or commercial purpose, including without limitation:

(a) a power to the extent it is coupled with an interest in the subject of the power;

(b) a power given to or for the benefit of a creditor in connection with a loan or other credit transaction;

(c) a power given to facilitate transfer or disposition of one or more specific stocks, bonds or other assets, whether real, personal, tangible or intangible;

2. a proxy or other delegation to exercise voting rights or management rights with respect to an entity;

3. a power created on a form prescribed by a government or governmental subdivision, agency or instrumentality for a governmental purpose;

4. a power authorizing a third party to prepare, execute, deliver, submit and/or file a document or instrument with a government or governmental subdivision, agency or instrumentality or other third party;

5. a power authorizing a financial institution or employee of a financial institution to take action relating to an account in which the financial institution holds cash, securities, commodities or other financial assets on behalf of the person giving the power;

6. a power given by an individual who is or is seeking to become a director, officer, shareholder, employee, partner, limited partner, member, unit owner or manager of a corporation, partnership, limited liability company, condominium or other legal or commercial entity in his or her capacity as such;

7. a power contained in a partnership agreement, limited liability company operating agreement, declaration of trust, declaration of condominium, condominium bylaws, condominium offering plan or other agreement or instrument governing the internal affairs of an entity authorizing a director, officer, shareholder, employee, partner, limited partner, member, unit owner, manager or other person to take lawful action relating to such entity;

8. a power given to a condominium managing agent to take action in connection with the use, management and operation of a condominium unit;

9. a power given to a licensed real estate broker to take action in connection with a listing of real property, mortgage loan, lease or management agreement;

10. a power authorizing acceptance of service of process on behalf of the principal; and

11. a power created pursuant to authorization provided by a federal or state statute, other than this title, that specifically contemplates creation of the power, including without limitation a power to make health care decisions or decisions involving the disposition of remains.

Nothing in this section shall be deemed to prohibit use of a statutory short form power of attorney or a nonstatutory power of attorney in connection with any of the transactions described in this section.

History: Add, L 2010, ch 340, § 6, eff Sept 12, 2010, deemed eff on and after Sept 1, 2009, provided, that any statutory short form power of attorney and any statutory gifts rider executed after Aug 31, 2009 shall remain valid as will any revocation of a prior power of attorney that was delivered to the agent before the effective date of this act.

§ 5-1502A. Construction—real estate transactions

In a statutory short form power of attorney, the language conferring general authority with respect to "real estate transactions," must be construed to mean that the principal authorizes the agent:

1. To accept as a gift, or as security for a loan, to reject, to demand, to buy, to lease, to receive, or otherwise to acquire either ownership or possession of any estate or interest in land;

2. To sell, to exchange, to convey either with or without covenants, to quit-claim, to release, to surrender, to mortgage, to incumber, to partition or to consent to the partitioning, to create, modify or revoke a trust to grant options concerning, to lease or to sublet, or otherwise to dispose of, any estate or interest in land;

3. To release in whole or in part, to assign the whole or a part of, to satisfy in whole or in part, and to enforce by action, proceeding or otherwise, any mortgage, incumbrance, lien or other claim to land which exists, or is claimed to exist, in favor of the principal;

4. To do any act of management or of conservation with respect to any estate or interest in land owned, or claimed to be owned, by the principal, including by way of illustration, but not of restriction, power to insure against any casualty, liability or loss, to obtain or to

regain possession or to protect such estate or interest by action, proceeding or otherwise, to pay, to compromise or to contest taxes or assessments, to apply for refunds in connection therewith, to purchase supplies, to hire assistance or labor and to make repairs or alterations in the structures or lands;

5. To utilize in any way, to develop, to modify, to alter, to replace, to remove, to erect or to install structures or other improvements upon any land in which the principal has, or claims to have, any estate or interest;

6. To demand, to receive, to obtain by action, proceeding or otherwise, any money, or other thing of value to which the principal is, or may become, or may claim to be entitled as the proceeds of an interest in land or of one or more of the transactions enumerated in this section, to conserve, to invest, to disburse or to utilize anything so received for purposes enumerated in this section, and to reimburse the agent for any expenditures properly made by him in the execution of the powers conferred on him by the statutory short form power of attorney;

7. To participate in any reorganization with respect to real property and to receive and to hold any shares of stock or instrument of similar character received in accordance with such plan of reorganization, and to act with respect thereto, including by way of illustration, but not of restriction, power to sell or otherwise to dispose of such shares, or any of them, to exercise or to sell any option, conversion or similar right with respect thereto, and to vote thereon in person or by the granting of a proxy;

8. To agree and to contract, in any manner, and with any person and on any terms, which the agent may select, for the accomplishment of any of the purposes enumerated in this section, and to perform, to rescind, to reform, to release or to modify any such agreement or contract or any other similar agreement or contract made by or on behalf of the principal;

9. To execute, to acknowledge, to seal and to deliver any deed, creation, modification or revocation of a trust, mortgage, lease, notice, check or other instrument which the agent may think useful for the accomplishment of any of the purposes enumerated in this section;

10. To prosecute, to defend, to submit to alternative dispute resolution, to settle, and to propose or to accept a compromise with respect to, any claim existing in favor of, or against, the principal based on or involving any real estate transaction or to intervene in any action or proceeding relating thereto;

11. To hire, to discharge, and to compensate any attorney, accountant, expert witness or other assistant or assistants when the agent shall think such action to be desirable for the proper execution by him of any of the powers described in this section, and for the keeping of needed records thereof; and

12. In general, and in addition to all the specific acts in this section enumerated, to do any other act or acts, which the principal can do through an agent, with respect to any estate or interest in land.

All powers described in this section 5-1502A of the general obligations law shall be exercisable equally with respect to any estate or interest in land owned by the principal at the giving of the power of attorney or thereafter acquired, and whether located in the state of New York or elsewhere.

History: Add, L 1963, ch 576, § 1, eff Sept 27, 1964, with substance transferred from Gen Bus § 222; amd, L 2008, ch 644, § 3, eff Sept 1, 2009, as amended by L 2009 ch 4; L 2010, ch 340, § 7, eff Sept 12, 2010, deemed eff on and after Sept 1, 2009, provided, that any statutory short form power of attorney and any statutory gifts rider executed after Aug 31, 2009 shall remain valid as will any revocation of a prior power of attorney that was delivered to the agent before the effective date of this act; L 2020, ch 323, § 5, eff June 13, 2021.

§ 5-1502B. Construction—chattel and goods transactions

In a statutory short form power of attorney, the language conferring general authority with respect to "chattel and goods transactions," must be construed to mean that the principal authorizes the agent:

1. To accept as a gift, or as security for a loan, to reject, to demand, to buy, to receive, or otherwise to acquire either ownership or possession of, any chattel or goods or any interest in any chattel or goods;

2. To sell, to exchange, to convey either with or without covenants, to release, to surrender, to mortgage, to incumber, to pledge, to hypothecate, to pawn, to create, modify or revoke a trust to grant options concerning, to lease or to sublet to others, or otherwise to dispose of any chattel or goods or any interest in any chattel or goods;

3. To release in whole or in part, to assign the whole or a part of, to satisfy in whole or in part, and to enforce by action, proceeding or otherwise, any mortgage, incumbrance, lien or other claim, which exists, or is claimed to exist, in favor of the principal, with respect to any chattel or goods or any interest in chattel or goods;

4. To do any act of management or of conservation, with respect to any chattel or goods or to any interest in any chattel or goods owned, or claimed to be owned, by the principal, including by way of illustration, but not of restriction, power to insure against any casualty, liability or loss, to obtain or to regain possession, or to protect such chattel or goods or interest in any chattel or goods, by action, proceeding or otherwise, to pay, to compromise or to contest taxes or assessments, to apply for refunds in connection therewith, to move from place to place, to store for hire or on a gratuitous bailment, to use, to alter, and to make repairs or alterations of any such chattel or goods, or interest in any chattel or goods;

5. To demand, to receive, to obtain by action, proceeding or otherwise, any money or other thing of value to which the principal is, or may become, or may claim to be entitled as the proceeds of a chattel or goods or of any interest in any chattel or goods, or of one or more of the transactions enumerated in this section, to conserve, to invest, to disburse or to utilize anything so received for purposes enumerated in this section, and to reimburse the agent for any expenditures properly made by him in the execution of the powers conferred on him by the statutory short form power of attorney;

6. To agree and to contract, in any manner, and with any person and on any terms, which the agent may select, for the accomplishment of any of the purposes enumerated in this section, and to perform, to rescind, to reform, to release or to modify any such agreement or contract or any other similar agreement or contract made by or on behalf of the principal;

7. To execute, to acknowledge, to seal and to deliver any conveyance, mortgage, lease,

creation, revocation or modification of a trust, notice, check or other instrument which the agent may think useful for the accomplishment of any of the purposes enumerated in this section;

8. To prosecute, to defend, to submit to alternative dispute resolution, to settle, and to propose or to accept a compromise with respect to, any claim existing in favor of, or against, the principal based on or involving any chattel or goods transaction or to intervene in any action or proceeding relating thereto;

9. To hire, to discharge, and to compensate any attorney, accountant, expert witness or other assistant or assistants when the agent shall think such action to be desirable for the proper execution by him of any of the powers described in this section, and for the keeping of needed records thereof; and

10. In general, and in addition to all the specific acts in this section enumerated, to do any other act or acts, which the principal can do through an agent, with respect to any chattel or goods or interest in any chattel or goods.

All powers described in this section 5-1502B of the general obligations law shall be exercisable equally with respect to any chattel or goods or interest in any chattel or goods owned by the principal at the giving of the power of attorney or thereafter acquired, and whether located in the state of New York or elsewhere.

> **History:** Add, L 1963, ch 576, § 1, eff Sept 27, 1964, with substance transferred from Gen Bus § 223; amd, L 2008, ch 644, § 4, eff Sept 1, 2009, as amended by L 2009, ch 4; L 2010, ch 340, § 8, eff Sept 12, 2010, deemed eff on and after Sept 1, 2009, provided, that any statutory short form power of attorney and any statutory gifts rider executed after Aug 31, 2009 shall remain valid as will any revocation of a prior power of attorney that was delivered to the agent before the effective date of this act; L 2020, ch 323, § 6, eff June 13, 2021.

§ 5-1502C. Construction—bond, share and commodity transactions

In a statutory short form power of attorney, the language conferring general authority with respect to "bond, share and commodity transactions," must be construed to mean that the principal authorizes the agent:

1. To accept as a gift, or as security for a loan, to reject, to demand, to buy, to receive, or otherwise to acquire either ownership or possession of, any bond, share, instrument of similar character, commodity interest or any instrument with respect thereto, together with the interest, dividends, proceeds or other distributions connected therewith;

2. To sell (including short sales), to exchange, to transfer either with or without a guaranty, to release, to surrender, to hypothecate, to pledge, to create, modify or revoke a trust to grant options concerning, to loan, to trade in, or otherwise to dispose of any bond, share, instrument of similar character, commodity interest or any instrument with respect thereto;

3. To release in whole or in part, to assign the whole or a part of, to satisfy in whole or in part, and to enforce by action, proceeding or otherwise, any pledge, incumbrance, lien or other claim as to any bond, share, instrument of similar character, commodity interest or any interest with respect thereto, when such pledge, incumbrance, lien or other claim is owned, or claimed to be owned, by the principal;

4. To do any act of management or of conservation with respect to any bond, share, instrument of similar character, commodity interest or any instrument with respect thereto,

owned or claimed to be owned by the principal or in which the principal has or claims to have an interest, including by way of illustration, but not of restriction, power to insure against any casualty, liability or loss, to obtain or to regain possession or to protect the principal's interest therein by action, proceeding or otherwise, to pay, to compromise or to contest taxes or assessments, to apply for refunds in connection therewith, to consent to and to participate in any reorganization, recapitalization, liquidation, merger, consolidation, sale or lease, or other change in or revival of a corporation or other association, or in the financial structure of any corporation or other association, or in the priorities, voting rights or other special rights with respect thereto, to become a depositor with any protective, reorganization or similar committee of the bond, share, other instrument of similar character, commodity interest or any instrument with respect thereto, belonging to the principal, to make any payments reasonably incident to the foregoing, to exercise or to sell any option, conversion or similar right, to vote in person or by the granting of a proxy (with or without the power of substitution), either discretionary, general or otherwise, for the accomplishment of any of the purposes enumerated in this section;

5. To carry in the name of a nominee selected by the agent any evidence of the ownership of any bond, share, other instrument of similar character, commodity interest or instrument with respect thereto, belonging to the principal;

6. To employ, in any way believed to be desirable by the agent, any bond, share, other instrument of similar character, commodity interest or any instrument with respect thereto, in which the principal has or claims to have any interest, for the protection or continued operation of any speculative or margin transaction personally begun or personally guaranteed, in whole or in part, by the principal;

7. To demand, to receive, to obtain by action, proceeding or otherwise, any money or other thing of value to which the principal is, or may become, or may claim to be entitled as the proceeds of any interest in a bond, share, other instrument of similar character, commodity interest or any instrument with respect thereto, or of one or more of the transactions enumerated in this section, to conserve, to invest, to disburse or to utilize anything so received for purposes enumerated in this section, and to reimburse the agent for any expenditures properly made by him in the execution of the powers conferred on him by the statutory short form power of attorney;

8. To agree and to contract, in any manner, and with any broker or other person, and on any terms, which the agent may select, for the accomplishment of any of the purposes enumerated in this section, and to perform, to rescind, to reform, to release or to modify any such agreement or contract or any other similar agreement made by or on behalf of the principal;

9. To execute, to acknowledge, to seal and to deliver any consent, agreement, authorization, creation, modification or revocation of a trust, assignment, notice, waiver of notice, check, or other instrument which the agent may think useful for the accomplishment of any of the purposes enumerated in this section;

10. To execute, to acknowledge and to file any report or certificate required by law or governmental regulation;

11. To prosecute, to defend, to submit to alternative dispute resolution, to settle and to propose or to accept a compromise with respect to, any claim existing in favor of, or

against, the principal based on or involving any bond, share or commodity transaction or to intervene in any action or proceeding relating thereto;

12. To hire, to discharge, and to compensate any attorney, accountant, expert witness or other assistant or assistants when the agent shall think such action to be desirable for the proper execution by him of any of the powers described in this section, and for the keeping of needed records thereof; and

13. In general, and in addition to all the specific acts in this section enumerated, to do any other act or acts, which the principal can do through an agent, with respect to any interest in any bond, share or other instrument of similar character, commodity, or instrument with respect to a commodity.

All powers described in this section 5-1502C of the general obligations law shall be exercisable equally with respect to any interest in any bond, share or other instrument of similar character, commodity, or instrument with respect to a commodity owned by the principal at the giving of the power of attorney or thereafter acquired, whether located in the state of New York or elsewhere.

History: Add, L 1963, ch 576, § 1, eff Sept 27, 1964, with substance transferred from Gen Bus § 224; amd, L 2008, ch 644, § 5, as amd by L 2009, ch 4, eff Sept 1, 2009; L 2010, ch 340, § 9, eff Sept 12, 2010, deemed eff on and after Sept 1, 2009, provided, that any statutory short form power of attorney and any statutory gifts rider executed after Aug 31, 2009 shall remain valid as will any revocation of a prior power of attorney that was delivered to the agent before the effective date of this act; L 2020, ch 323, § 7, eff June 13, 2021.

§ 5-1502D. Construction—banking transactions

In a statutory short form power of attorney, the language conferring general authority with respect to "banking transactions," must be construed to mean that the principal authorizes the agent:

1. To continue, to modify, to terminate and to make deposits to and withdrawals from any deposit account, including any joint account with the agent or totten trust for the benefit of the agent, or other banking arrangement made by or on behalf of the principal prior to the creation of the agency, provided, however, that:

(a) with respect to joint accounts existing at the creation of the agency, the authority granted hereby shall not include the power to change the title of the account by the addition of a new joint tenant or the deletion of an existing joint tenant, unless the authority to make such changes is expressly stated otherwise in the "Modifications" section of a statutory short form power of attorney or in a non-statutory power of attorney signed and dated by the principal with the signature of the principal duly acknowledged in the manner prescribed for the acknowledgement of a conveyance of real property, and which is executed pursuant to the requirements of section 5-1501B of this title, and

(b) with respect to totten trust accounts existing at the creation of the agency, the authority granted hereby shall not include the power to add, delete, or otherwise change the designation of beneficiaries in effect for any such accounts, unless the authority to make such additions, deletions or changes is expressly stated otherwise in the "Modifications" section of a statutory short form power of attorney or in a non-statutory power of attorney signed and dated by the principal with the signature of the principal duly acknowledged in the manner prescribed for the acknowledgment of a conveyance of real property, and which is executed pursuant to the requirements of section 5-1501B of this title.

2. To open in the name of the principal or on behalf of the principal a deposit account of any type with any banker or in any banking institution selected by the agent, to make deposits to and withdrawals from any such deposit account, to hire such safe deposit box or vault space and to make such other contracts for the procuring of other services made available by any such banker or banking institution as the agent shall think to be desirable;

3. To make, to sign and to deliver checks or drafts for any purpose, to withdraw by check, order or otherwise any funds or property of the principal deposited with, or left in the custody of, any banker or banking institution, wherever located, either before or after the creation of the agency;

4. To prepare from time to time financial statements concerning the assets and liabilities or income and expenses of the principal, and to deliver statements so prepared to any banker, banking institution or other person, whom the agent believes to be reasonably entitled thereto;

5. To receive statements, vouchers, notices or other documents from any banker or banking institution and to act with respect thereto;

6. To have free access at any time or times to any safe deposit box or vault to which the principal might have access, if personally present;

7. To borrow money by bank overdraft, or by promissory note of the principal given for such period and at such interest rate as the agent shall select, to give such security out of the assets of the principal as the agent shall think to be desirable or necessary for any such borrowing, to pay, to renew or to extend the time of payment of any note so given or given by or on behalf of the principal, and to procure for the principal a loan from any banker or banking institution by any other procedure made available by such banker or institution;

8. To make, to assign, to indorse, to discount, to guarantee, and to negotiate, for any and all purposes, all promissory notes, bills of exchange, checks, drafts or other negotiable or non-negotiable paper of the principal, or payable to the principal or to his order, to receive the cash or other proceeds of any such transactions, to accept any bill of exchange or draft drawn by any person upon the principal, and to pay it when due;

9. To receive for the principal and to deal in and to deal with any trust receipt, warehouse receipt or other negotiable or non-negotiable instrument, in which the principal has or claims to have an interest;

10. To apply for and to receive letters of credit or travelers checks from any banker or banking institution selected by the agent, giving such indemnity or other agreements in connection therewith as the agent shall think to be desirable or necessary;

11. To consent to an extension in the time of payment with respect to any commercial paper or any banking transaction in which the principal has an interest or by which the principal is, or might be, affected in any way;

12. To pay, to compromise or to contest taxes or assessments and to apply for refunds in connection therewith;

13. To demand, to receive, to obtain by action, proceeding, or otherwise any money or other thing of value to which the principal is, or may become, or may claim to be entitled as the proceeds of any banking transaction conducted by the principal himself, or by the agent in the execution of any of the powers described in this section, or partly by the principal and partly by the agent so acting, to conserve, to invest, to disburse or to utilize anything so received for purposes enumerated in this section, and to reimburse the agent for any expenditures properly made by him in the execution of the powers conferred upon him by the statutory short form power of attorney;

14. To execute, to acknowledge, to seal and to deliver any instrument of any kind, in the name of the principal or otherwise, which the agent may think useful for the accomplishment of any of the purposes enumerated in this section;

15. To prosecute, to defend, to submit to alternative dispute resolution, to settle, and to propose or to accept a compromise with respect to, any claim existing in favor of, or against, the principal based on or involving any banking transaction or to intervene in any action or proceeding relating thereto;

16. To hire, to discharge, and to compensate any attorney, accountant, expert witness or other assistant or assistants when the agent shall think such action to be desirable for the proper execution by him of any of the powers described in this section, and for the keeping of needed records thereof; and

17. In general, and in addition to all the specific acts in this section enumerated, to do any other act or acts, which the principal can do through an agent, in connection with any banking transaction which does or might in any way affect the financial or other interests of the principal.

18. If a power of attorney requires that two or more agents act together as co-agents, one or more agents may delegate to the co-agent the authority to conduct banking transactions if the principal initialed subject (o) in the grant of authority provisions of paragraph (f) of the statutory short form set forth in section 15-1513 of this title.

All powers described in this section 5-1502D of the general obligations law shall be exercisable equally with respect to any banking transaction engaged in by the principal at the giving of the power of attorney or thereafter engaged in, and whether conducted in the state of New York or elsewhere.

History: Add, L 1963, ch 576, § 1, eff Sept 27, 1964, with substance transferred from Gen Bus § 225; amd, L 2008, ch 644, § 6, as amd by L 2009, ch 4, eff Sept 1, 2009; L 2010, ch 340, §§ 10, 11, eff Sept 12, 2010, deemed eff on and after Sept 1, 2009, provided, that any statutory short form power of attorney and any statutory gifts rider executed after Aug 31, 2009 shall remain valid as will any revocation of a prior power of attorney that was delivered to the agent before the effective date of this act; L 2020, ch 323, §§ 8, 8-a, eff June 13, 2021.

§ 5-1502E. Construction—business operating transactions

In a statutory short form power of attorney, the language conferring general authority with respect to "business operating transactions," must be construed to mean that the principal authorizes the agent:

1. To the extent that an agent is permitted by law thus to act for a principal, to discharge and to perform any duty or liability and also to exercise any right, power, privilege or option which the principal has, or claims to have, under any contract of partnership

whether the principal is a general or special partner thereunder, to enforce the terms of any such partnership agreement for the protection of the principal, by action, proceeding or otherwise, as the agent shall think to be desirable or necessary, and to defend, submit to alternative dispute resolution, settle or compromise any action or other legal proceeding to which the principal is a party because of his membership in said partnership;

2. To exercise in person or by proxy or to enforce by action, proceeding or otherwise, any right, power, privilege or option which the principal has as the holder of any bond, share, or other instrument of similar character and to defend, submit to alternative dispute resolution, settle or compromise any action or other legal proceeding to which the principal is a party because of any such bond, share, or other instrument of similar character;

3. With respect to any business enterprise which is owned solely by the principal

a. to continue, to modify, to renegotiate, to extend and to terminate any contractual arrangements made with any person, firm, association or corporation whatsoever by or on behalf of the principal with respect thereto prior to the creation of the agency;

b. to determine the policy of such enterprise as to the location of the site or sites to be utilized for its operation, as to the nature and extent of the business to be undertaken by it, as to methods of manufacturing, selling, merchandising, financing, accounting and advertising to be employed in its operation, as to the amount and types of insurance to be carried, as to the mode of securing, compensating and dealing with accountants, attorneys, servants and other agents and employees required for its operation, to agree and to contract, in any manner, and with any person and on any terms, which the agent thinks to be desirable or necessary for effectuating any or all of such decisions of the agent as to policy, and to perform, to rescind, to reform, to release or to modify any such agreement or contract or any other similar agreement or contract made by or on behalf of the principal;

c. to change the name or form of organization under which such business is operated and to enter into such partnership agreement with other persons or to organize such corporation to take over the operation of such business, or any part thereof, as the agent shall think to be desirable or necessary;

d. to demand and to receive all moneys which are, or may become, due to the principal, or which may be claimed by the principal or on his behalf, in the operation of such enterprise, and to control and to disburse such funds in the operation of such enterprise in any way which the agent shall think to be desirable or necessary, to engage in any banking transactions which the agent shall think to be desirable or necessary for effectuating the execution of any of the powers of the agent described in this subdivision;

4. To prepare, to sign, to file and to deliver all reports, compilations of information, returns or other papers with respect to any business operating transaction of the principal, which are required by any governmental agency, department or instrumentality or which the agent shall think to be desirable or necessary for any purpose, and to make any payments with respect thereto;

5. To pay, to compromise or to contest taxes or assessments and to do any act or acts which the agent shall think to be desirable or necessary to protect the principal from illegal

or unnecessary taxation, fines, penalties or assessments in connection with his business operations, including power to attempt to recover, in any manner permitted by law, sums paid before or after the creation of the agency as taxes, fines, penalties or assessments;

6. To demand, to receive, to obtain by action, proceeding or otherwise, any money, or other thing of value to which the principal is, or may become, or may claim to be entitled as the proceeds of any business operation of such principal, to conserve, to invest, to disburse or to utilize anything so received for purposes enumerated in this section, and to reimburse the agent for any expenditures properly made by him in the execution of the powers conferred upon him by the statutory short form power of attorney;

7. To execute, to acknowledge, to seal and to deliver any deed, assignment, mortgage, lease, notice, consent, agreement, authorization, check or other instrument which the agent may think useful for the accomplishment of any of the purposes enumerated in this section;

8. To prosecute, to defend, to submit to alternative dispute resolution, to settle, and to propose or to accept a compromise with respect to, any claim existing in favor of, or against, the principal based on or involving any business operating transaction or to intervene in any action or proceeding relating thereto;

9. To hire, to discharge, and to compensate any attorney, accountant, expert witness or other assistant or assistants when the agent shall think such action to be desirable for the proper execution by him of any of the powers described in this section, and for the keeping of needed records thereof; and

10. In general, and in addition to all the specific acts in this section enumerated, to do any other act or acts, which the principal can do through an agent, in connection with any business operated by the principal, which the agent shall think to be desirable or necessary for the furtherance or protection of the interests of the principal.

All powers described in this section 5-1502E of the general obligations law shall be exercisable equally with respect to any business in which the principal is interested at the creation of the agency or in which the principal shall thereafter become interested, and whether operated in the state of New York or elsewhere.

History: Add, L 1963, ch 576, § 1, eff Sept 27, 1964, with substance transferred from Gen Bus § 226; amd, L 2010, ch 340, § 12, eff Sept 12, 2010, deemed eff on and after Sept 1, 2009, provided, that any statutory short form power of attorney and any statutory gifts rider executed after Aug 31, 2009 shall remain valid as will any revocation of a prior power of attorney that was delivered to the agent before the effective date of this act.

§ 5-1502F. Construction—insurance transactions

In a statutory short form power of attorney, the language conferring general authority with respect to "insurance transactions," must be construed to mean that the principal authorizes the agent:

1. To continue, to pay the premium or assessment on, to modify, to rescind, to release or to terminate any contract of life, accident, health, disability or liability insurance or any combination of such insurance procured by or on behalf of the principal prior to the creation of the agency which insures either the principal or any other person, without regard to whether the principal is or is not a beneficiary thereunder; provided, however, with respect to life insurance contracts existing at the creation of the agency, the authority

granted hereby shall not include the power to add, delete or otherwise change the designation of beneficiaries in effect for any such contract, unless the authority to make such additions, deletions or changes is stated otherwise in the "Modifications" section of a statutory short form power of attorney or in a non-statutory power of attorney signed and dated by the principal with the signature of the principal duly acknowledged in the manner prescribed for the acknowledgment of a conveyance of real property, and which is executed pursuant to the requirements of section 5-1501B of this title;

2. To procure new, different or additional contracts of insurance protecting the principal with respect to ill-health, disability, accident or liability of any sort, to select the amount, the type of insurance contract and the mode of payment under each such policy, to pay the premium or assessment on, to modify, to rescind, to release or to terminate, any contract so procured by the agent;

3. To apply for and to receive any available loan on the security of the contract of insurance, whether for the payment of a premium or for the procuring of cash, to surrender and thereupon to receive the cash surrender value, to exercise an election as to beneficiary or mode of payment, to change the manner of paying premiums, and to change or to convert the type of insurance contract, with respect to any contract of life, accident, health, disability or liability insurance as to which the principal has, or claims to have, any one or more of the powers described in this section; provided, however, that the authority granted hereby shall not include the power to add, delete or otherwise change the designation of beneficiaries in effect for any such contract, unless the authority to make such additions, deletions or changes is expressly stated otherwise in the "Modifications" section of a statutory short form power of attorney or in a non-statutory power of attorney signed and dated by the principal with the signature of the principal duly acknowledged in the manner prescribed for the acknowledgment of a conveyance of real property, and which is executed pursuant to the requirements of section 5-1501B of this title;

4. To demand, to receive, to obtain by action, proceeding or otherwise, any money, dividend, or other thing of value to which the principal is, or may become, or may claim to be entitled as the proceeds of any contract of insurance or of one or more of the transactions enumerated in this section, to conserve, to invest, to disburse or to utilize anything so received for purposes enumerated in this section, and to reimburse the agent for any expenditures properly made by him in the execution of the powers conferred on him by the statutory short form power of attorney;

5. To apply for and to procure any available governmental aid in the guaranteeing or paying of premiums of any contract of insurance on the life of the principal;

6. To sell, to assign, to hypothecate, to borrow upon, or to pledge the interest of the principal in any contract of insurance;

7. To pay, from such proceeds or otherwise, to compromise or to contest, and to apply for refunds in connection with, any tax or assessment levied by a taxing authority with respect to any contract of insurance or the proceeds thereof or liability accruing by reason of such tax or assessment;

8. To agree and to contract, in any manner, and with any person and on any terms, which the agent may select for the accomplishment of any of the purposes enumerated in this

section, and to perform, to rescind, to reform, to release or to modify any such agreement or contract;

9. To execute, to acknowledge, to seal and to deliver any consent, demand, request, application, agreement, indemnity, authorization, assignment, pledge, notice, check, receipt, waiver or other instrument which the agent may think useful for the accomplishment of any of the purposes enumerated in this section;

10. To continue, to procure, to pay the premium or assessment on, to modify, to rescind, to release, to terminate or otherwise to deal with any contract of insurance, other than those enumerated in subdivisions one or two of this section, whether fire, marine, burglary, compensation, disability, liability, hurricane, casualty, or other type, or any combination of insurance, to do any act or acts with respect to any such contract or with respect to its proceeds or enforcement which the agent thinks to be desirable or necessary for the promotion or protection of the interests of the principal;

11. To prosecute, to defend, to submit to alternative dispute resolution, to settle, and to propose or to accept a compromise with respect to any claim existing in favor of, or against, the principal based on or involving any insurance transaction or to intervene in any action or proceeding relating thereto;

12. To hire, to discharge, and to compensate any attorney, accountant, expert witness or other assistant or assistants when the agent shall think such action to be desirable for the proper execution by him of any of the powers described in this section and for the keeping of needed records thereof; and

13. In general, and in addition to all the specific acts in this section enumerated, to do any other act or acts, which the principal can do through an agent, in connection with procuring, supervising, managing, modifying, enforcing and terminating contracts of insurance in which the principal is the insured or is otherwise in any way interested.

All powers described in this section 5-1502F of the general obligations law shall be exercisable with respect to any contract of insurance in which the principal is in any way interested, whether made in the state of New York or elsewhere.

History: Add, L 1963, ch 576, § 1, eff Sept 27, 1964, with substance transferred from Gen Bus § 227; amd, L 2008, ch 644, § 7, as amd by L 2009, ch 4, eff Sept 1, 2009; L 2010, ch 340, § 13, eff Sept 12, 2010, deemed eff on and after Sept 1, 2009, provided, that any statutory short form power of attorney and any statutory gifts rider executed after Aug 31, 2009 shall remain valid as will any revocation of a prior power of attorney that was delivered to the agent before the effective date of this act; L 2020, ch 323, § 9, eff June 13, 2021.

§ 5-1502G. Construction—estate transactions

In a statutory short form power of attorney, the language conferring general authority with respect to "estate transactions," must be construed to mean that the principal authorizes the agent:

1. To the extent that an agent is permitted by law thus to act for a principal, to apply for and to procure, in the name of the principal, letters of administration, letters testamentary, letters of trusteeship, or any other type of authority, either judicial or administrative, to act as a fiduciary of any sort;

2. To the extent that an agent is permitted by law thus to act for a principal, to represent and to act for the principal in all ways and in all matters affecting any estate of a decedent,

absentee, infant or incompetent, or any trust or other fund, out of which the principal is entitled, or claims to be entitled, to some share or payment, or with respect to which the principal is a fiduciary;

3. Subject to the provisions of paragraph (d) of section 2-1.11 of the estates, powers and trusts law, to accept, to reject, to receive, to receipt for, to sell, to assign, to release, to pledge, to exchange, or to consent to a reduction in or modification of, any share in or payment from any estate, trust or other fund;

4. To demand, to obtain by action, proceeding or otherwise any money, or other thing of value to which the principal is, or may become, or may claim to be entitled by reason of the death testate or intestate of any person or of any testamentary disposition or of any trust or by reason of the administration of the estate of a decedent or absentee or of the guardianship of an infant or incompetent or the administration of any trust or other fund, to initiate, to participate in and to oppose any proceeding, judicial or otherwise, for the ascertainment of the meaning, validity or effect of any deed, will, declaration of trust, or other transaction affecting in any way the interest of the principal, to initiate, to participate in and to oppose any proceeding, judicial or otherwise, for the removal, substitution or surcharge of a fiduciary, to conserve, to invest, to disburse or to utilize anything so received for purposes enumerated in this section, and to reimburse the agent for any expenditures properly made by him in the execution of the powers conferred on him by the statutory short form power of attorney;

5. To prepare, to sign, to file and to deliver all reports, compilations of information, returns or papers with respect to any interest had or claimed by or on behalf of the principal in any estate, trust, or other fund, to pay, to compromise or to contest, and to apply for refunds in connection with, any tax or assessment, with respect to any interest had or claimed by or on behalf of the principal in any estate, trust or other fund or by reason of the death of any person, or with respect to any property in which such interest is had or claimed;

6. To agree and to contract, in any manner, and with any person and on any terms, which the agent may select, for the accomplishment of the purposes enumerated in this section, and to perform, to rescind, to reform, to release, or to modify any such agreement or contract or any other similar agreement or contract made by or on behalf of the principal;

7. To execute, to acknowledge, to verify, to seal, to file and to deliver any consent, designation, pleading, notice, demand, election, conveyance, release, assignment, check, pledge, waiver, admission of service, notice of appearance or other instrument which the agent may think useful for the accomplishment of any of the purposes enumerated in this section;

8. To submit to alternative dispute resolution or to settle, and to propose or to accept a compromise with respect to any controversy or claim which affects the estate of a decedent, absentee, infant or incompetent, or the administration of a trust or other fund, in any one of which the principal has, or claims to have, an interest, and to do any and all acts which the agent shall think to be desirable or necessary in effectuating such compromise;

9. To hire, to discharge, and to compensate any attorney, accountant, expert witness or other assistant or assistants, when the agent shall think such action to be desirable for the

proper execution by him of any of the powers described in this section, and for the keeping of needed records thereof; and

10. In general, and in addition to all the specific acts in this section enumerated, to do any other act or acts, which the principal can do through an agent, with respect to the estate of a decedent, absentee, infant or incompetent, or the administration of a trust or other fund, in any one of which the principal has, or claims to have, an interest, or with respect to which the principal is a fiduciary.

All powers described in this section shall be exercisable equally with respect to any estate of a decedent, absentee, infant or incompetent, or the administration of any trust or other fund, in which the principal is interested at the giving of the power of attorney or may thereafter become interested, regardless of whether the estate, trust or other fund is specifically identified at the giving of the power of attorney and whether located in the state of New York or elsewhere.

> **History:** Add, L 1963, ch 576, § 1, eff Sept 27, 1964, with substance transferred from Gen Bus § 228; amd, L 2003, ch 589, § 2, eff Sept 1, 2003; L 2008, ch 644, § 8, as amd by L 2009, ch 4, eff Sept 1, 2009; L 2010, ch 27, § 2, eff Jan 1, 2011; L 2010, ch 340, § 14, eff Sept 12, 2010, deemed eff on and after Sept 1, 2009, provided, that any statutory short form power of attorney and any statutory gifts rider executed after Aug 31, 2009 shall remain valid as will any revocation of a prior power of attorney that was delivered to the agent before the effective date of this act.

§ 5-1502H. Construction—claims and litigation

In a statutory short form power of attorney, the language conferring general authority with respect to "claims and litigation," must be construed to mean that the principal authorizes the agent:

1. To assert and to prosecute before any court, administrative board, department, commissioner or other tribunal, any cause of action, claim, counterclaim, offset or defense, which the principal has, or claims to have, against any individual, partnership, association, corporation, government, or other person or instrumentality, including, by way of illustration and not of restriction, power to sue for the recovery of land or of any other thing of value, for the recovery of damages sustained by the principal in any manner, for the elimination or modification of tax liability, for an injunction, for specific performance, or for any other relief;

2. To bring an action of interpleader or other action to determine adverse claims, to intervene or to interplead in any action or proceeding, and to act in any litigation as amicus curiae;

3. In connection with any action or proceeding or controversy, at law or otherwise, to apply for and, if possible, to procure a libel, an attachment, a garnishment, an order of arrest or other preliminary, provisional or intermediate relief and to resort to and to utilize in all ways permitted by law any available procedure for the effectuation or satisfaction of the judgment, order or decree obtained;

4. In connection with any action or proceeding, at law or otherwise, to perform any act which the principal might perform, including by way of illustration and not of restriction, acceptance of tender, offer of judgment, admission of any facts, submission of any controversy on an agreed statement of facts, consent to examination before trial, and

generally to bind the principal in the conduct of any litigation or controversy as seems desirable to the agent;

5. To submit to alternative dispute resolution, to settle, and to propose or to accept a compromise with respect to, any claim existing in favor of or against the principal, or any litigation to which the principal is, or may become or be designated a party;

6. To waive the issuance and service of a summons, citation or other process upon the principal, to accept service of process, to appear for the principal, to designate persons upon whom process directed to the principal may be served, to execute and to file or deliver stipulations on the principal's behalf, to verify pleadings, to appeal to appellate tribunals, to procure and to give surety and indemnity bonds at such times and to such extent as the agent shall think to be desirable or necessary, to contract and pay for the preparation and printing of records and briefs, to receive and to execute and to file or deliver any consent, waiver, release, confession of judgment, satisfaction of judgment, notice, agreement, or other instrument which the agent shall think to be desirable or necessary in connection with the prosecution, settlement or defense of any claim by or against the principal or of any litigation to which the principal is or may become or be designated a party;

7. To appear for, to represent and to act for the principal with respect to bankruptcy or insolvency proceedings, whether voluntary or involuntary, whether of the principal or of some other person, with respect to any reorganization proceeding, or with respect to any receivership or application for the appointment of a receiver or trustee which, in any way, affects any interest of the principal in any land, chattel, bond, share, commodity interest, chose in action or other thing of value;

8. To hire, to discharge, and to compensate any attorney, accountant, expert witness or other assistant or assistants when the agent shall think such action to be desirable for the proper execution by him of any of the powers described in this section;

9. To pay, from funds in his control or for the account of the principal, any judgment against the principal or any settlement which may be made in connection with any transaction enumerated in this section, and to receive and conserve any moneys or other things of value paid in settlement of or as proceeds of one or more of the transactions enumerated in this section, and to receive and endorse checks and to deposit the same; and

10. In general, and in addition to all the specific acts in this section enumerated, to do any other act or acts, which the principal can do through an agent, in connection with any claim by or against the principal or with litigation to which the principal is or may become or be designated a party.

All powers described in this section 5-1502H of the general obligations law shall be exercisable equally with respect to any claim or litigation existing at the giving of the power of attorney or thereafter arising, and whether arising in the state of New York or elsewhere.

History: Add, L 1963, ch 576, § 1, eff Sept 27, 1964, with substance transferred from Gen Bus § 229; amd, L 2010, ch 340, § 15, eff Sept 12, 2010, deemed eff on and after Sept 1, 2009, provided, that any statutory short form power of attorney and any statutory gifts rider executed after Aug 31, 2009 shall remain valid as will any revocation of a prior power of attorney that was delivered to the agent before the effective date of this act.

§ 5-1502I. Construction—personal and family maintenance

In a statutory short form power of attorney, the language conferring general authority with respect to "personal and family maintenance" must be construed to mean that the principal authorizes the agent:

1. To do all acts necessary for maintaining the customary standard of living of the spouse and children, and other dependents of the principal, including by way of illustration and not by way of restriction, power to provide living quarters by purchase, lease or by other contract, or by payment of the operating costs, including interest, amortization payments, repairs and taxes, of premises owned by the principal and occupied by his family or dependents, to provide normal domestic help for the operation of the household, to provide usual vacations and usual travel expenses, to provide usual educational facilities, and to provide funds for all the current living costs of such spouse, children and other dependents, including, among other things, shelter, clothing, food and incidentals;

2. To provide, whenever necessary, medical, dental and surgical care, hospitalization and custodial care for the spouse, children and other dependents of the principal;

3. To continue whatever provision has been made by the principal, prior to the creation of the agency or thereafter, for his spouse, children and other dependents, with respect to automobiles, or other means of transportation, including by way of illustration but not by way of restriction, power to license, to insure and to replace any automobiles owned by the principal and customarily used by the spouse, children or other dependents of the principal;

4. To continue whatever charge accounts have been operated by the principal prior to the creation of the agency or thereafter, for the convenience of his spouse, children or other dependents, to open such new accounts as the agent shall think to be desirable for the accomplishment of any of the purposes enumerated in this section, and to pay the items charged on such accounts by any person authorized or permitted by the principal to make such charges prior to the creation of the agency;

5. To continue the discharge of any services or duties assumed by the principal, prior to the creation of the agency or thereafter, to any parent, relative or friend of the principal;

6. To supervise and to enforce, to defend or to settle any claim by or against the principal arising out of property damages or personal injuries suffered by or caused by the principal, or under such circumstances that the loss resulting therefrom will, or may fall on the principal;

7. To continue payments incidental to the membership or affiliation of the principal in any church, club, society, order or other organization or to continue contributions thereto;

8. To demand, to receive, to obtain by action, proceeding or otherwise any money or other thing of value to which the principal is or may become or may claim to be entitled as salary, wages, commission or other remuneration for services performed, or as a dividend or distribution upon any stock, or as interest or principal upon any indebtedness, or any periodic distribution of profits from any partnership or business in which the principal has or claims an interest, and to endorse, collect or otherwise realize upon any instrument for the payment so received;

9. To prepare, to execute and to file all tax, social security, unemployment insurance and information returns required by the laws of the United States, or of any state or subdivision

thereof, or of any foreign government, to prepare, to execute and to file all other papers and instruments which the agent shall think to be desirable or necessary for the safeguarding of the principal against excess or illegal taxation or against penalties imposed for claimed violation of any law or other governmental regulation, and to pay, to compromise, or to contest or to apply for refunds in connection with any taxes or assessments for which the principal is or may be liable;

10. To utilize any asset of the principal for the performance of the powers enumerated in this section, including by way of illustration and not by way of restriction, power to draw money by check or otherwise from any bank deposit of the principal, to sell any land, chattel, bond, share, commodity interest, chose in action or other asset of the principal, to borrow money and to pledge as security for such loan, any asset, including insurance, which belongs to the principal;

11. To execute, to acknowledge, to verify, to seal, to file and to deliver any application, consent, petition, notice, release, waiver, agreement or other instrument which the agent may think useful for the accomplishment of any of the purposes enumerated in this section;

12. To prosecute, to defend, to submit to alternative dispute resolution, to settle, and to propose or to accept a compromise with respect to, any claim existing in favor of, or against, the principal based on or involving any transaction enumerated in this section or to intervene in any action or proceeding relating thereto;

13. To hire, to discharge, and to compensate any attorney, accountant, expert witness or other assistant or assistants when the agent shall think such action to be desirable for the proper execution by him of any of the powers described in this section, and for the keeping of needed records thereof;

14. To continue gifts that the principal customarily made to individuals and charitable organizations prior to the creation of the agency, provided that in any one calendar year all such gifts shall not exceed five thousand dollars in the aggregate; and

15. In general, and in addition to all the specific acts in this section enumerated, to do any other act or acts, which the principal can do through an agent, for the welfare of the spouse, children or dependents of the principal or for the preservation and maintenance of the other personal relationships of the principal to parents, relatives, friends and organizations.

All powers described in this section 5-1502I of the general obligations law shall be exercisable equally whether the acts required for their execution shall relate to real or personal property owned by the principal at the giving of the power of attorney or thereafter acquired and whether such acts shall be performable in the state of New York or elsewhere.

History: Add, L 1963, ch 576, § 1, eff Sept 27, 1964, with substance transferred from Gen Bus § 230; amd, L 2008, ch 644, §§ 9, 10, as amd by L 2009, ch 4, eff Sept 1, 2009; L 2010, ch 340, § 16, eff Sept 12, 2010, deemed eff on and after Sept 1, 2010, provided, that any statutory short form power of attorney and any statutory gifts rider executed after Aug 31, 2009 shall remain valid as will any revocation of a prior power of attorney that was delivered to the agent before the effective date of this act; L 2020, ch 323, § 10, eff June 13, 2021.

§ 5-1502J. Construction—benefits from governmental programs or civil or military service

In a statutory short form power of attorney, the language conferring general authority with respect to "benefits from governmental programs or civil or military service," or in a statutory short form power of attorney properly executed in accordance with the laws in effect at the time of its execution, the language conferring authority with respect to "military service," must be construed to mean that the principal authorizes the agent:

1. To execute vouchers in the name of the principal for allowances and reimbursements payable by the United States, or a foreign government or by a state or subdivision of a state, to the principal, including but not limited to allowances and reimbursements for transportation of the principal and of the principal's spouse, children and other dependents, and for shipment of household effects, to receive, to indorse and to collect the proceeds of any check payable to the order of the principal drawn on the treasurer or other fiscal officer or depositary of the United States or a foreign government or of any state or subdivision thereof;

2. To take possession and to order the removal and shipment of property of the principal from a post, warehouse, depot, dock or other place of storage or safekeeping, either governmental or private, and execute and deliver a release, voucher, receipt, bill of lading, shipping ticket, certificate or other instrument for such purpose;

3. To enroll in, apply for, select, reject, change, amend, or discontinue a benefit or program on the principal's behalf;

4. To prepare, file and prosecute a claim of the principal to any benefit or assistance, financial or otherwise, to which the principal is, or claims to be, entitled, under a statute or governmental regulation, including any benefit or assistance which arises from or is based upon military service performed prior to or after the creation of the agency by the principal or by any person related by blood or by marriage to the principal, to execute any receipt or other instrument which the agent shall think to be desirable or necessary for the enforcement or for the collection of such claim;

5. To receive the financial proceeds of any claim of the type described in this section, conserve, invest, disburse or use anything so received for a lawful purpose;

6. To prosecute, defend, submit to alternative dispute resolution, settle, and propose or accept a compromise with respect to any benefit or assistance described in subdivision four of this section;

7. To communicate with any representative or employee of a government, governmental subdivision, agency, or instrumentality on behalf of the principal;

8. To hire, discharge, and compensate any attorney, accountant, expert witness, or other assistant or assistants when the agent shall think such action to be desirable for the proper execution of any of the powers described in this section; and

9. In general, and in addition to all the specific acts in this section enumerated, to do any other act or acts, which the principal can do through an agent, and which the agent shall think to be desirable or necessary, to assure to the principal, and to the dependents of the principal, the maximum possible benefit from governmental programs or from civil or military service performed prior to or after the creation of the agency by the principal or by any person related by blood or marriage to the principal.

All powers described in this section shall be exercisable equally with respect to any benefits from governmental programs or civil or military service existing at the giving of the power of attorney or thereafter accruing, and whether accruing in the state of New York or elsewhere.

History: Add, L 1963, ch 576, § 1, eff Sept 27, 1964, with substance transferred from Gen Bus § 231; amd, L 2008, ch 644, § 11, as amd by L 2009, ch 4, eff Sept 1, 2009.

§ 5-1502K. Construction—matters related to health care

In a statutory short form power of attorney, the language conferring general authority with respect to "matters related to health care," or in a statutory short form power of attorney properly executed in accordance with the laws in effect at the time of its execution, the language conferring authority with respect to "records, reports and statements," must be construed to mean that the principal authorizes the agent:

1. To be responsible for matters relating to the principal's health care, including, but not limited to, benefit entitlements and payment obligations, and in so doing, notwithstanding any law to the contrary, to receive from "health care providers" and "health plans," information, including, but not limited to, "protected health information" as defined in federal and state law, rules and regulations, in order to ascertain the benefits to which the principal is entitled and to determine the legitimacy and accuracy of charges for health care provided to the principal; to obtain for the principal the health care benefits to which the principal is entitled; to meet the principal's financial obligations, and pay bills due and owing, for health care provided to the principal; and to represent the principal, and to act as the principal's personal representative, with respect to matters pertaining to the principal's health care. The authority granted by this subdivision is limited to health care financial matters and shall not include authorization for the agent to make health care decisions for the principal;

2. To keep records of all cash received and disbursed for or on account of the principal, of all credits and debits to the account of the principal, and of all transactions affecting in any way the assets and liabilities of the principal;

3. To prepare, to execute and to file all tax, social security, unemployment insurance and information returns, required by the laws of the United States, of any state or of any subdivision thereof or of any foreign government, to prepare, to execute and to file all other papers and instruments which the agent shall think to be desirable or necessary for the safeguarding of the principal against excess or illegal taxation or against penalties imposed for claimed violation of any law or other governmental regulation;

4. To prepare, to execute and to file any record, report, statement, or other document to safeguard or promote the principal's interest, under a statute or governmental regulation;

5. To hire, to discharge, and to compensate any attorney, accountant, or other assistant or assistants when the agent shall think such action to be desirable for the proper execution by him of any of the powers described in this section; and

6. In general, and in addition to all the specific acts in this section enumerated, to do any other act or acts, which the principal can do through an agent, in connection with the preparation, execution, filing, storage or other utilization of any records, reports or statements of or concerning the principal's affairs.

All powers described in this section shall be exercisable equally with respect to any health care billing and payment matters, and records, reports or statements of or concerning the affairs of the principal existing at the giving of the power of attorney or thereafter arising, and whether arising in the state of New York or elsewhere.

Add, L 1963, ch 576, § 1, eff Sept 27, 1964, with substance transferred from Gen Bus § 232; amd, L 2008, ch 644, § 12, as amd by L 2009; , ch 4, eff Sept 1, 2009; L 2020, ch 323, § 11, eff June 13, 2021.

§ 5-1502L. Construction—retirement benefit transactions

In a statutory short form power of attorney, the language conferring general authority with respect to "retirement benefit transactions" must be construed to mean that the principal authorizes the agent:

1. To contribute to, withdraw from and deposit funds in any type of retirement benefit or plan (including, but not limited to, any tax qualified or nonqualified pension, profit sharing, stock bonus, employee savings and retirement plan, deferred compensation plan, individual retirement account, or any public pension fund or retirement system);

2. To make investment directions, to select and change payment options, and to exercise any other election for the principal with regard to any retirement benefit or plan in which the principal has an interest, provided, however, that the authority granted hereby shall not include the authority to add, delete, or otherwise change the designation of beneficiaries in effect for any such retirement benefit or plan, unless the authority to make such additions, deletions or changes is expressly stated otherwise in the "Modifications" section of a statutory short form power of attorney or in a non-statutory power of attorney signed and dated by the principal with the signature of the principal duly acknowledged in the manner prescribed for the acknowledgment of a conveyance of real property, and which is executed pursuant to the requirements of section 5-1501B of this title;

3. To make rollover contributions from any retirement benefit or plan to other retirement benefits or plans;

4. To prepare, execute and deliver any application, agreement, trust agreement, authorization, check or other instrument or document which may be required under the terms of any retirement benefit or plan in which the principal has an interest or by the administrator thereof, or which the agent deems useful for the accomplishment of any of the purposes enumerated in this section;

5. To represent the principal in any matter or thing relating to any interest that the principal has or may become entitled to under any retirement benefit or plan;

6. To prosecute, defend, submit to alternative dispute resolution, settle, and propose or accept a compromise with respect to any claim existing in favor of, or against, the principal based upon or involving any retirement benefit or plan and to intervene in any action or proceeding relating thereto;

7. To hire, discharge, and compensate any attorney, accountant, expert witness or other assistant or assistants when the agent deems such action to be desirable for the proper execution by the agent of the powers described in this section or for the keeping of required records thereof; and

8. In general, and in addition to all the specific acts in this section enumerated, to do any other act or acts, which the principal can do through an agent, with respect to any

retirement benefit or plan maintained by the principal or in which the principal has an interest or may thereafter have an interest.

All powers described in this section 5-1502L of the general obligations law shall be exercisable with respect to any retirement benefit or plan in which the principal has any interest, whether in the state of New York or elsewhere.

The powers explicitly authorized in the provisions of this section 5-1502L of the general obligations law shall not be construed to diminish any like powers authorized in any other section of title 15 of article 5 of the general obligations law. Accordingly, such powers as are authorized in any other section of title 15 of article 5 of the general obligations law shall be construed as if the provisions of this section do not exist.

> **History:** Add, L 1996, ch 499, § 2, eff Jan 1, 1997; amd, L 1996, ch 500, § 1, eff Jan 1, 1997; L 2008, ch 644, § 13, as amd by L 2009, ch 4, eff Sept 1, 2009; L 2010, ch 340, § 17, eff Sept 12, 2010, deemed eff on and after Sept 1, 2009, provided, that any statutory short form power of attorney and any statutory gifts rider executed after Aug 31, 2009 shall remain valid as will any revocation of a prior power of attorney that was delivered to the agent before the effective date of this act; L 2020, ch 323, § 12, eff June 13, 2021.

§ 5-1502M. Construction—tax matters

In a statutory short form power of attorney, the language conferring general authority with respect to "tax matters", must be construed to mean that the principal authorizes the agent:

1. To prepare, sign, and file federal, state, local, and foreign income, gift, payroll, federal insurance contributions act returns, and other tax returns, claims for refunds, requests for extension of time, petitions regarding tax matters, and any other tax-related documents, including receipts, offers, waivers, consents (including consents and agreements under United States Internal Revenue Code Section 2032A or cognate provisions of any successor statute), closing agreements, and any power of attorney required by the federal internal revenue service or other taxing authority with respect to a tax year upon which the statute of limitations has not run and with respect to the tax year in which the power of attorney was executed and with respect to any subsequent tax year;

2. To pay taxes due, collect refunds, post bonds, receive confidential information, and contest deficiencies determined by the United States Internal Revenue Service or other taxing authority;

3. To exercise any election available to the principal under federal, state, local, or foreign tax law; and

4. To represent the principal, or to designate another person to represent the principal, in all tax matters for all tax periods before the United States Internal Revenue Service and any other taxing authority.

The powers explicitly authorized in the provisions of this section shall not be construed to diminish any like powers authorized in any other section of this title, such as, but not limited to, those authorized in subdivision 9 of section 5-1502I of this title. Accordingly, such powers as are authorized in any other section of this title shall be construed as if the provisions of this section do not exist.

> **History:** Formerly GOL § 5-1502N, Add, L 1996, ch 499, § 2, eff Jan 1, 1997; renumbered and amd § 5-1502M, L 2008, ch 644, § 16, as amd by L 2009, ch 4, eff Sept 1, 2009.

§ 5-1502N. Construction—all other matters

In a statutory short form power of attorney, the language conferring general authority with respect to "all other matters" must be construed to mean that the principal authorizes the agent to act as an alter ego of the principal with respect to any and all possible matters and affairs which are not enumerated in sections 5-1502A to 5-1502M, inclusive, of this title, and which the principal can do through an agent; provided, however, that such authority shall not include authorization for the agent to designate a third party to act as agent for the principal or to make medical or other health care decisions for the principal, except as otherwise provided in subdivision one of section 5-1502K of this title.

History: Formerly GOL § 5-1502O, Add, L 1996, ch 499, § 2, eff Jan 1, 1997; renumbered and amd § 5–1502N, L 2008, ch 644, § 16, as amd by L 2009, ch 4, eff Sept 1, 2009.

§ 5-1503. Modifications of the statutory short form power of attorney

A power of attorney which satisfies the requirements of paragraphs (a), (b) and (c) of subdivision one of section 5-1501B and section 5-1513 of this title is not prevented from being a "statutory short form power of attorney", by the fact that it also contains additional language at the section labeled "modifications" which:

1. Eliminates from the statutory short form power of attorney one or more of the powers enumerated in one or more of the constructional sections of this title with respect to a subdivision of the statutory short form power of attorney, affirmatively chosen by the principal; or

2. Supplements one or more of the powers enumerated in one or more of the constructional sections in this title with respect to a subdivision of the statutory short form power of attorney, affirmatively chosen by the principal, by specifically listing additional powers of the agent; or

3. Makes some additional provision which is not inconsistent with the other provisions of the statutory short form power of attorney, including a provision revoking one or more powers of attorney previously executed by the principal.

History: Add, L 1963, ch 576, § 1, with substance transferred from Gen Bus § 234; amd, L 1994, ch 419, § 4; L 1994, ch 694, § 3; L 1996, ch 499, § 4, eff Jan 1, 1997; L 2008, ch 644, § 17, as amd by L 2009, ch 4, eff Sept 1, 2009; L 2010, ch 340, § 18, eff Sept 12, 2010, deemed eff on and after Sept 1, 2009, provided, that any statutory short form power of attorney and any statutory gifts rider executed after Aug 31, 2009 shall remain valid as will any revocation of a prior power of attorney that was delivered to the agent before the effective date of this act; L 2020, ch 323, § 13, eff June 13, 2021.

§ 5-1504. Acceptance of and reliance upon acknowledged and witnessed statutory short form power of attorney

1. (a) For purposes of this section, "acknowledged" means purportedly verified before a notary public or other individual authorized to take acknowledgements. For purposes of this section, "witnessed" means purportedly witnessed by two persons who are not named in the instrument as agents or as permissible recipients of gifts.

(b) A person that in good faith accepts an acknowledged and witnessed power of attorney without actual knowledge that the signature is not genuine may rely upon the presumption that the signature is genuine.

(c) A person that in good faith accepts an acknowledged and witnessed power of attorney without actual knowledge that the power of attorney is void, invalid, or terminated, that the purported agent's authority is void, invalid, or terminated, or that the agent is exceeding or improperly exercising the agent's authority may rely upon the power of attorney as if the power of attorney were genuine, valid and still in effect, the agent's authority were genuine, valid and still in effect, and the agent had not exceeded and had properly exercised the authority.

(d) A person that is asked to accept an acknowledged and witnessed power of attorney may request, and rely upon, without further investigation:

(1) an agent's certification under penalty of perjury of any factual matter concerning the principal, agent or power of attorney; and

(2) an opinion of counsel as to any matter of law concerning the power of attorney if the person making the request provides in a writing or other record the reason for the request.

(e) An opinion of counsel requested under this section must be provided at the principal's expense unless the request is made more than ten business days after the power of attorney is presented for acceptance.

(f) For purposes of this section, a person that conducts activities through employees is without actual knowledge of a fact relating to a power of attorney, a principal, or an agent if the employee conducting the transaction involving the power of attorney is without actual knowledge of the fact after making reasonable inquiry with respect thereto.

2. No third party located or doing business in this state shall refuse, without reasonable cause, to honor a statutory short form power of attorney properly executed in accordance with section 5-1501B of this title, or a statutory short form power of attorney properly executed in accordance with the laws in effect at the time of its execution.

(a) Reasonable cause under this subdivision shall include, but not be limited to:

(1) the refusal by the agent to provide an original power of attorney or a copy certified by an attorney pursuant to section twenty-one hundred five of the civil practice law and rules, or by a court or other government entity;

(2) the third party's good faith referral of the principal and the agent or a person acting for or with the agent to the local adult protective services unit;

(3) actual knowledge of a report having been made by any person to the local adult protective services unit alleging physical or financial abuse, neglect, exploitation or abandonment of the principal by the agent or a person acting for or with the agent;

(4) actual knowledge of the principal's death or a reasonable basis for believing the principal has died;

(5) actual knowledge of the incapacity of the principal or a reasonable basis for believing that the principal is incapacitated where the power of attorney tendered is a nondurable power of attorney;

(6) actual knowledge or a reasonable basis for believing that the principal was incapacitated at the time the power of attorney was executed;

(7) actual knowledge or a reasonable basis for believing that the power of attorney was procured through fraud, duress or undue influence;

(8) actual notice, pursuant to subdivision five of this section, of the termination or revocation of the power of attorney;

(9) the refusal by a title insurance company to underwrite title insurance for a gift of real property made pursuant to a statutory short form power of attorney or non-statutory power of attorney that does not contain express instructions or purposes of the principal with respect to gifts in the modifications section of the statutory short form power of attorney or in the non-statutory power of attorney; or

(10) the refusal of a request for a certification or an opinion of counsel under paragraph (d) of subdivision one of this section.

(b) It shall be deemed unreasonable for a third party to refuse to honor a statutory short form power of attorney properly executed in accordance with section 5-1501B of this title or a statutory short form power of attorney properly executed in accordance with the laws in effect at the time of its execution, if the only reason for the refusal is any of the following:

(1) the power of attorney is not on a form prescribed by the third party to whom the power of attorney is presented.

(2) there has been a lapse of time since the execution of the power of attorney.

(3) on the face of the statutory short form power of attorney, there is a lapse of time between the date of acknowledgment of the signature of the principal and the date of acknowledgment of the signature of any agent.

3. (a) Not later than the tenth business day after presentation of an original or attorney certified copy of a statutory short form power of attorney properly executed in accordance with section 5-1501B of this title or in accordance with the laws in effect at the time of its execution to a third party for acceptance, such third party shall either (a) honor the statutory short form power of attorney, or (b) reject the statutory short form power of attorney in a writing that sets forth the reasons for such rejection, which writing shall be sent to the principal and the agent at the addresses on the power of attorney and such other addresses as provided by the principal or the agent, or (c) request the agent to execute an acknowledged affidavit pursuant to subdivision seven of this section stating that the power of attorney is in full force and effect if the statutory short form power of attorney was not submitted for acceptance together with such an acknowledged affidavit. Such reasons for rejection may include, but not be limited to non-conforming form, missing or wrong signature, invalid notarization, or unacceptable identification. In the event that the statutory short form power of attorney presented is not an original or attorney certified copy, as part of the initial rejection, such short form power of attorney may be rejected for such reason, provided, however, in explaining the reason for rejecting the short form power of attorney, the third party shall also identify such other provisions of the short form power of attorney, if any, that would otherwise constitute cause for rejection of the statutory short form power of attorney. If the third party initially rejects the statutory short form power of attorney in a writing that sets forth the reasons for such rejection, the third party shall within seven business days after receipt of a writing in response to the reasons for such rejection (i) honor the statutory short form power of attorney, or (ii) finally reject the statutory short form power of attorney in a writing that sets forth the reasons for such rejection. Such writing shall be sent to the address provided on the power of attorney, to the address of the agent, if any, and may also be sent to such other address as shall be provided on the account documents, or to the address of the attorney as provided in an opinion of counsel pursuant to this section. If the third party requests the agent to execute

such an acknowledged affidavit, the third party shall honor such statutory short form power of attorney within seven business days after receipt by the third party of an acknowledged affidavit which complies with the provisions of subdivision seven of this section, stating that the power of attorney is in full force and effect unless reasonable cause exists as described in paragraph (a) of subdivision two of this section. For the purposes of this subdivision, notice shall be considered delivered at the time such notice is mailed and the time requirements in which to honor or reject the statutory short form power of attorney or request the agent to execute an acknowledged affidavit shall not apply to the department of audit and control, a public retirement system of the state as defined in subdivision six of section one hundred fifty-two of the retirement and social security law, or the department of health, including social services districts, in the administration of the medical assistance "Medicaid" program pursuant to title XIX of the federal social security act or other public health insurance programs.

(b) Notice to the agent as required by paragraph (a) of this subdivision shall not be sent until after a determination is made by adult protective services if the reason for rejection is a reason set forth in subdivision two of this section and is otherwise prohibited by law or regulation.

4. (a) Once reasonably accepted, if a third party conducts a transaction in reliance on a properly executed statutory short form power of attorney, the third party shall be held harmless from liability for the transaction.

(b) Except as provided in subdivision five of this section, it shall be deemed unlawful for a third party to unreasonably refuse to honor a properly executed statutory short form power of attorney executed in accordance with section 5-1501B of this title or a statutory short form power of attorney properly executed in accordance with the laws in effect at the time of its execution. If a special proceeding as authorized by section 5-1510 of this title is brought to compel the third party to honor the statutory short form power of attorney, the court may award damages, including reasonable attorney's fees and costs, if the court finds that the third party acted unreasonably in refusing to honor the agent's authority under the statutory short form power of attorney. Such special proceeding shall be the exclusive remedy for a violation of this section.

5. In the absence of actual knowledge that the principal lacked capacity to execute a statutory short form power of attorney or that the statutory short form power of attorney was procured through fraud, duress or undue influence, no third party receiving and retaining a statutory short form power of attorney properly executed in accordance with section 5-1501B of this title, or a statutory short form power of attorney properly executed in accordance with the laws in effect at the time of its execution, or a complete photostatic copy of the properly executed original thereof, nor any officer, agent, attorney-in-fact or employee of such third party shall incur any liability by reason of acting upon the authority thereof unless the third party shall have received actual notice of the revocation or termination of such power of attorney.

If a principal maintains an account at a financial institution, the financial institution is deemed to have actual notice after it has had a reasonable opportunity to act on a written notice of the revocation or termination following its receipt of the same at its office where such account is located.

6. If the application of the provisions of subdivision two or four of this section shall be held invalid to any third party the application of such provisions to any third party other than those

to which it is held invalid, shall not be affected thereby.

7. When the power of attorney is presented to a third party, it shall not be deemed unreasonable for a third party to require the agent to execute an acknowledged affidavit pursuant to this subdivision stating that the power of attorney is in full force and effect. Such an affidavit is conclusive proof to the third party relying on the power of attorney that the power of attorney is valid and effective, and has not been terminated, revoked or modified, except as to any third party who had actual notice that the power of attorney had terminated, been revoked or been modified prior to the execution of the affidavit. Such affidavit shall state that:

(a) the agent does not have, at the time of the transaction, actual notice of the termination or revocation of the power of attorney, or notice of any facts indicating that the power of attorney has been terminated or revoked;

(b) the agent does not have, at the time of the transaction, actual notice that the power of attorney has been modified in any way that would affect the ability of the agent to authorize or engage in the transaction, or notice of any facts indicating that the power of attorney has been so modified;

(c) if the agent was named as a successor agent, the prior agent is no longer able or willing to serve; and

(d) if the agent has been the principal's spouse, the power of attorney expressly provides that divorce or annulment as defined in subparagraph two of paragraph (f) of section 5-1.4 of the estates, powers and trusts law does not terminate the agent's authority thereunder, or the agent does not have actual notice that the marriage has been terminated by divorce or annulment as defined in subparagraph two of paragraph (f) of section 5-1.4 of the estates, powers and trusts law at the time of the transaction.

8. Nothing in this section shall require the acceptance of a form that is not a statutory short form power of attorney.

9. A statutory short form power of attorney or a non-statutory power of attorney that meets the requirements of subdivision one of section 5-1501B of this title shall be accepted for recording so long as it has been signed by one agent named therein whose signature has been acknowledged. If two or more agents acting on behalf of the principal are required to act together, the power of attorney shall be accepted for recording as long as their signatures have been acknowledged. When a successor or co-agent authorized to act separately from any other agents presents a certified copy of a recorded statutory short form power of attorney or non-statutory power of attorney with the agent's signature acknowledged, the instrument shall be accepted for recording.

History: Add, L 1986, ch 215, § 2; amd, L 1991, ch 89, § 1; L 1996, ch 499, § 5, eff Jan 1, 1997; L 2008, ch 644, § 18, as amd by L 2009, ch 4, eff Sept 1, 2009; L 2010, ch 340, §§ 19–22, eff Sept 12, 2010, deemed eff on and after Sept 1, 2009, provided, that any statutory short form power of attorney and any statutory gifts rider executed after Aug 31, 2009 shall remain valid as will any revocation of a prior power of attorney that was delivered to the agent before the effective date of this act; L 2020, ch 323, § 14, eff June 13, 2021; L 2021, ch 84, § 2, eff June 13, 2021.

§ 5-1505. Standard of care; fiduciary duties; compelling disclosure of record

1. Standard of care. In dealing with property of the principal, an agent shall observe the

standard of care that would be observed by a prudent person dealing with property of another.

2. Fiduciary duties.

(a) An agent acting under a power of attorney has a fiduciary relationship with the principal. The fiduciary duties include but are not limited to each of the following obligations:

(1) To act according to any instructions from the principal or, where there are no instructions, in the best interest of the principal, and to avoid conflicts of interest

(2) To keep the principal's property separate and distinct from any other property owned or controlled by the agent, except for property that is jointly owned by the principal and agent at the time of the execution of the power of attorney, and property that becomes jointly owned after the execution of the power of attorney as the result of the agent's acquisition of an interest in the principal's property by reason of the agent's exercise of authority granted in the modifications section of a statutory short form power of attorney or in a non-statutory power of attorney. The agent may not make gifts of the principal's property to himself or herself without specific authorization in a power of attorney.

(3) To keep a record of all receipts, disbursements, and transactions entered into by the agent on behalf of the principal and to make such record and power of attorney available to the principal or to third parties at the request of the principal. The agent shall make such record and a copy of the power of attorney available within fifteen days of a written request by any of the following:

(i) a monitor;

(ii) a co-agent or successor agent acting under the power of attorney;

(iii) a government entity, or official thereof, investigating a report that the principal may be in need of protective or other services, or investigating a report of abuse or neglect;

(iv) a court evaluator appointed pursuant to section 81.09 of the mental hygiene law;

(v) a guardian ad litem appointed pursuant to section seventeen hundred fifty-four of the surrogate's court procedure act;

(vi) the guardian or conservator of the estate of the principal, if such record has not already been provided to the court evaluator or guardian ad litem; or

(vii) the personal representative of the estate of a deceased principal if such record has not already been provided to the guardian or conservator of the estate of the principal.

The failure of the agent to make the record available pursuant to this paragraph may result in a special proceeding under subdivision one of section 5-1510 of this title.

(b) The agent may be subject to liability for conduct or omissions which violate any fiduciary duty.

(c) The agent is not liable to third parties for any act pursuant to a power of attorney if the act was authorized at the time and the act did not violate subdivision one or two of this section.

3. Resignation.

(a) An agent who has signed the power of attorney may resign by giving written notice to the principal and the agent's co-agent, successor agent or the monitor, if one has been named, or the principal's guardian if one has been appointed. If no co-agent, successor agent, monitor or guardian is known to the agent and the principal is incapacitated or the agent has notice of any facts indicating the principal's incapacity, the agent may give written notice to a government entity having authority to protect the welfare of the principal, or may petition the court to approve the resignation.

(b) The principal may provide for alternative means for an agent's resignation in the power of attorney.

History: Add, L 2008, ch 644, § 19, as amd by L 2009, ch 4, eff Sept 1, 2009, which repealed and replaced former section 5-1505; amd, L 2010, ch 340, § 23, eff Sept 12, 2010, deemed eff on the Sept 1, 2009, provided, that any statutory short form power of attorney and any statutory gifts rider executed after Aug 31, 2009 shall remain valid as will any revocation of a prior power of attorney that was delivered to the agent before the effective date of this act; L 2020, ch 323, § 15, eff June 13, 2021.

§ 5-1506. Compensation

1. An agent is not entitled to receive compensation from the assets of the principal for responsibilities performed under a power of attorney unless the principal specifically provides for compensation in the power of attorney.

2. An agent shall be entitled to receive reimbursement from the assets of the principal for reasonable expenses actually incurred in connection with the performance of the agent's responsibilities.

History: Add, L 2008, ch 644, § 19, as amd by L 2009, ch 4, eff Sept 1, 2009, which repealed former section 5-1506.

§ 5-1507. Signature of agent

1. (a) In any transaction where the agent is acting pursuant to a power of attorney and where the hand-written signature of the agent or principal is required, the agent shall disclose the principal and agent relationship by:

(1) signing "(name of agent) as agent for (name of principal)"; or

(2) signing "(name of principal) by (name of agent), as agent"; or

(3) any similar written disclosure of the principal and agent relationship.

(b) A third party shall incur no liability for accepting a signature that does not meet the requirements of this subdivision.

2. When the agent engages in a transaction on behalf of the principal, the agent is attesting that:

(a) the agent has actual authority to engage in the transaction;

(b) the agent does not have, at the time of the transaction, actual notice of the termination or revocation of the power of attorney, or notice of any facts indicating that the power of attorney has been terminated or revoked;

(c) if the power of attorney is one which terminates upon the principal's incapacity, the agent does not have, at the time of the transaction actual notice of the principal's incapacity, or notice of any facts indicating the principal's incapacity.

(d) the agent does not have, at the time of the transaction, actual notice that the power of attorney has been modified in any way that would affect the ability of the agent to engage in the transaction, or notice of any facts indicating that the power of attorney has been so modified.

3. The attestation of the agent pursuant to subdivision two of this section is not effective as to any third party who had actual notice that the power of attorney had terminated or been revoked prior to the transaction.

History: Add, L 2008, ch 644, § 19, as amd by L 2009, ch 4, eff Sept 1, 2009.

§ 5-1508. Co-agents and successor agents

1. A principal may designate two or more persons to act as co-agents. Unless the principal provides otherwise in the power of attorney, the co-agents must act jointly. However, if prompt action is required to accomplish a purpose of the power of attorney and to avoid irreparable injury to the principal's interest and a co-agent is unavailable because of absence, illness or other temporary incapacity, the other co-agent or co-agents may act for the principal. Unless the principal provides otherwise in the power of attorney, if a vacancy occurs because of the death, resignation or incapacity of a co-agent, the remaining agent or agents may act for the principal.

2. A principal may designate one or more successor agents to serve, if any initial or predecessor agent resigns, dies, becomes incapacitated, is not qualified to serve or declines to serve. Unless the principal provides otherwise in the power of attorney, a successor agent has the same authority as that granted to an initial agent. A principal may provide for specific succession rules.

3. A co-agent or a successor agent acting under a power of attorney shall have the authority to request, receive and seek to compel a co-agent or predecessor agent to provide a record of all receipts, disbursements and transactions entered into by the agent on behalf of the principal.

4. Any person, other than an estate or a trust, may act as an agent, co-agent or successor agent under a power of attorney.

History: Add, L 2008, ch 644, § 19, as amd by L 2009, ch 4, eff Sept 1, 2009; amd, L 2010, ch 340, §§ 24, 25, eff Sept 12, 2010, deemed eff on and after Sept 1, 2009, provided, that any statutory short form power of attorney and any statutory gifts rider executed after Aug 31, 2009 shall remain valid as will any revocation of a prior power of attorney that was delivered to the agent before the effective date of this act.

§ 5-1509. Appointment of monitor

A principal may appoint a monitor or monitors in the power of attorney who shall have the authority to request, receive and compel the agent to provide a record of all receipts, disbursements and transactions entered into by the agent on behalf of the principal, to request and receive such records held by third parties, and to request and receive a copy of the power of attorney. Nothing in this title shall be construed to impose a fiduciary duty on the monitor.

History: Add, L 2008, ch 644, § 19, as amd by L 2009, ch 4, eff Sept 1, 2009.

§ 5-1510. Special proceedings

1. If the agent has failed to make available a copy of the power of attorney and/or a record of all receipts, disbursements, and transactions entered into by the agent on behalf of a principal to a person who may request such record pursuant to subparagraph three of paragraph (a) of subdivision two of section 5-1505 of this title, that person may commence a special proceeding to compel the agent to produce a copy of the power of attorney and such record.

2. A special proceeding may be commenced pursuant to this section for any of the following additional purposes:

(a) to determine whether the power of attorney is valid;

(b) to determine whether the principal had capacity at the time the power of attorney was executed;

(c) to determine whether the power of attorney was procured through duress, fraud or undue influence;

(d) to determine whether the agent is entitled to receive compensation or whether the compensation received by the agent is reasonable for the responsibilities performed;

(e) to approve the record of all receipts, disbursements and transactions entered into by the agent on behalf of the principal;

(f) to remove the agent upon the grounds that the agent has violated, or is unfit, unable, or unwilling to perform, the fiduciary duties under the power of attorney;

(g) to determine how multiple agents must act;

(h) to construe any provision of a power of attorney; or

(i) to compel acceptance of the power of attorney.

A special proceeding may also be commenced by an agent who wishes to obtain court approval of his or her resignation.

3. A special proceeding may be commenced pursuant to subdivision two of this section by any person identified in subparagraph three of paragraph (a) of subdivision two of section 5-1505 of this title, the agent, the spouse, child or parent of the principal, the principal's successor in interest, or any third party who may be required to accept a power of attorney.

4. If a power of attorney is suspended or revoked under this section, or the agent is removed by the court, the court may require the agent to provide a record of all receipts, disbursements and transactions entered into by the agent on behalf of the principal and to deliver any property belonging to the principal and copies of records concerning the principal's property and affairs to a successor agent, a government entity or the principal's legal representative.

History: Add, L 2008, ch 644, § 19, as amd by L 2009, ch 4, eff Sept 1, 2009; L 2020, ch 323, § 16, eff June 13, 2021.

§ 5-1511. Termination or revocation of power of attorney; notice

1. A power of attorney terminates when:

(a) the principal dies;

(b) the principal becomes incapacitated, if the power of attorney is not durable;

(c) the principal revokes the power of attorney;

(d) the principal revokes the agent's authority and there is no co-agent or successor agent, or no co-agent or successor agent who is willing or able to serve;

(e) the agent dies, becomes incapacitated or resigns and there is no co-agent or successor agent or no co-agent or successor agent who is willing or able to serve;

(f) the authority of the agent terminates and there is no co-agent or successor agent or no co-agent or successor agent who is willing or able to serve;

(g) the purpose of the power of attorney is accomplished; or

(h) a court order revokes the power of attorney as provided in section 5-1510 of this title or in section 81.29 of the mental hygiene law.

2. An agent's authority terminates when:

(a) the principal revokes the agent's authority;

(b) the agent dies, becomes incapacitated or resigns;

(c) the agent's marriage to the principal is terminated by divorce or annulment, as defined in subparagraph two of paragraph (f) of section 5-1.4 of the estates, powers and trusts law, unless the power of attorney expressly provides otherwise. If the authority of an agent is revoked solely by this subdivision, it shall be revived by the principal's remarriage to the former spouse; or

(d) the power of attorney terminates.

3. A principal may revoke a power of attorney:

(a) in accordance with the terms of the power of attorney; or

(b) by delivering a revocation of the power of attorney to the agent in person or by sending a signed and dated revocation by mail, courier, electronic transmission or facsimile to the agent's last known address. The agent must comply with the principal's revocation notwithstanding the actual or perceived incapacity of the principal unless the principal is subject to a guardianship under article eighty-one of the mental hygiene law.

4. Where a power of attorney has been recorded pursuant to section two hundred ninety-four of the real property law, the principal shall also record the revocation in the office in which the power of attorney is recorded pursuant to section three hundred twenty-six of the real property law, provided the revocation complies with section three hundred seven of the state technology law.

5. (a) Termination of an agent's authority or of the power of attorney is not effective as to any third party who has not received actual notice of the termination and acts in good faith under the power of attorney. Any action so taken, unless otherwise invalid or unenforceable, shall bind the principal and the principal's successors in interest. A financial institution is deemed to have actual notice after it has had a reasonable opportunity to act

on a written notice of the revocation or termination following receipt of the same at its office where an account is located.

(b) Termination of an agent's authority or of the power of attorney is not effective as to the agent until the agent has received a revocation as required by subdivision three of this section. An agent is deemed to have received a revocation when it has been delivered to the agent in person, or within a reasonable time after it has been sent by mail, courier, electronic transmission or facsimile in accordance with subdivision three of this section.

6. The execution of a power of attorney does not revoke any power of attorney previously executed by the principal.

History: Add, L 2008, ch 644, § 19, as amd by L 2009, ch 4, eff Sept 1, 2009; amd, L 2010, ch 340, § 26, eff Sept 12, 2010, deemed eff on and after Sept 1, 2009, provided, that any statutory short form power of attorney and any statutory gifts rider executed after Aug 31, 2009 shall remain valid as will any revocation of a prior power of attorney that was delivered to the agent before the effective date of this act.

§ 5-1512. Powers of attorney executed in other jurisdictions

Notwithstanding the provisions of section 5-1501B of this title, a power of attorney executed in another state or jurisdiction in compliance with the law of that state or jurisdiction or the law of this state is valid in this state, regardless of whether the principal is a domiciliary of this state. A power of attorney that complies with section 5-1501B of this title and is executed in another state or jurisdiction by a domiciliary of this state is valid in this state. A power of attorney executed in this state by a domiciliary of another state or jurisdiction in compliance with the law of that state or jurisdiction or the law of this state is valid in this state.

History: Add, L 2008, ch 644, § 19, as amd by L 2009, ch 4, eff Sept 1, 2009; amd, L 2010, ch 340, § 27, eff Sept 12, 2010, deemed eff on and after Sept 1, 2009, provided, that any statutory short form power of attorney and any statutory gifts rider executed after Aug 31, 2009 shall remain valid as will any revocation of a prior power of attorney that was delivered to the agent before the effective date of this act.

§ 5-1513. Statutory short form power of attorney

1. The use of the following form, or one which substantially conforms to the following form, in the creation of a power of attorney is lawful, and, when used, and executed in accordance with subdivision one of section 5-1501B of this title, it shall be construed as a statutory short form power of attorney in accordance with the provisions of this title; provided however, that any section indicated as "Optional" which is not used may be omitted and replaced by the words "Intentionally Omitted":

"POWER OF ATTORNEY

NEW YORK STATUTORY SHORT FORM

(a) CAUTION TO THE PRINCIPAL: Your Power of Attorney is an important document. As the "principal," you give the person whom you choose (your "agent") authority to spend your money and sell or dispose of your property during your lifetime without telling you. You do not lose your authority to act even though you have given your agent similar authority.

When your agent exercises this authority, he or she must act according to any instructions you have provided or, where there are no specific instructions, in your best interest. "Important Information for the Agent" at the end of this document describes your agent's responsibilities.

Your agent can act on your behalf only after signing the Power of Attorney before a notary public.

You can request information from your agent at any time. If you are revoking a prior Power of Attorney, you should provide written notice of the revocation to your prior agent(s) and to any third parties who may have acted upon it, including the financial institutions where your accounts are located.

You can revoke or terminate your Power of Attorney at any time for any reason as long as you are of sound mind. If you are no longer of sound mind, a court can remove an agent for acting improperly.

Your agent cannot make health care decisions for you. You may execute a "Health Care Proxy" to do this.

The law governing Powers of Attorney is contained in the New York General Obligations Law, Article 5, Title 15. This law is available at a law library, or online through the New York State Senate or Assembly websites, www.nysenate.gov or www.nyassembly.gov.

If there is anything about this document that you do not understand, you should ask a lawyer of your own choosing to explain it to you.

(b) DESIGNATION OF AGENT(S)

I, _____, hereby appoint:

name and address of principal

_____ as my agent(s)

name(s) and address(es) of agent(s)

If you designate more than one agent above and you do not initial the statement below, they must act together.

( ) My agents may act SEPARATELY.

(c) DESIGNATION OF SUCCESSOR AGENT(S): (OPTIONAL)

If any agent designated above is unable or unwilling to serve, I appoint as my successor agent(s):

_____

name(s) and address(es) of successor agent(s)

If you do not initial the statement below, successor agents designated above must act together.

( ) My successor agents may act SEPARATELY.

You may provide for specific succession rules in this section. Insert specific succession provisions here:

(d) This POWER OF ATTORNEY shall not be affected by my subsequent incapacity unless I have stated otherwise below, under "Modifications".

(e) This POWER OF ATTORNEY DOES NOT REVOKE any Powers of Attorney previously executed by me unless I have stated otherwise below, under "Modifications."

(f) GRANT OF AUTHORITY:

To grant your agent some or all of the authority below, either

(1) Initial the bracket at each authority you grant, or

(2) Write or type the letters for each authority you grant on the blank line at (P), and initial the bracket at (P). If you initial (P), you do not need to initial the other lines.

I grant authority to my agent(s) with respect to the following subjects as defined in sections 5-1502A through 5-1502N of the New York General Obligations Law:

( ) (A) real estate transactions;

( ) (B) chattel and goods transactions;

( ) (C) bond, share, and commodity transactions;

( ) (D) banking transactions;

( ) (E) business operating transactions;

( ) (F) insurance transactions;

( ) (G) estate transactions;

( ) (H) claims and litigation;

( ) (I) personal and family maintenance. If you grant your agent this authority, it will allow the agent to make gifts that you customarily have made to individuals, including the agent, and charitable organizations. The total amount of all such gifts in any one calendar year cannot exceed five thousand dollars;

( ) (J) benefits from governmental programs or civil or military service;

( ) (K) financial matters related to health care; records, reports, and statements;

( ) (L) retirement benefit transactions;

( ) (M) tax matters;

( ) (N) all other matters;

( ) (O) full and unqualified authority to my agent(s) to delegate any or all of the foregoing powers to any person or persons whom my agent(s) select;

( ) (P) EACH of the matters identified by the following letters _____.

You need not initial the other lines if you initial line (P).

(g) CERTAIN GIFT TRANSACTIONS: (OPTIONAL)

In order to authorize your agent to make gifts in excess of an annual total of $5,000 for all gifts described in (I) of the grant of authority section of this document (under personal and family maintenance), and/or to make changes to interest in your property, you must expressly grant that authorization in the Modifications section below. If you wish to authorize your agent to make gifts to himself or herself, you must expressly grant such authorization in the Modifications section below. Granting such authority to your agent gives your agent the authority to take actions which could significantly reduce your property and/or change how your property is distributed at your death. Your choice to grant such authority should be discussed with a lawyer.

( ) I grant my agent authority to make gifts in accordance with the terms and conditions of the Modifications that supplement this Statutory Power of Attorney.

(h) MODIFICATIONS: (OPTIONAL)

In this section, you may make additional provisions, including, but not limited to, language to limit or supplement authority granted to your agent, language to grant your agent the specific authority to make gifts to himself or herself, and/or language to grant your agent the specific authority to make other gift transactions and/or changes to interests in your property. Your agent is entitled to be reimbursed from your assets for reasonable expenses incurred on your behalf. In this section, you may make additional provisions if you ALSO wish your agent(s) to be compensated from your assets for services rendered on your behalf, and you may define "reasonable compensation.

(i) DESIGNATION OF MONITOR(S): (OPTIONAL)

If you wish to appoint monitor(s), initial and fill in the section below:

(   ) I wish to designate _____, whose address(es) is (are) _____, as monitor(s). Upon the request of the monitor(s), my agent(s) must provide the monitor(s) with a copy of the power of attorney and a record of all transactions done or made on my behalf. Third parties holding records of such transactions shall provide the records to the monitor(s) upon request.

(j) COMPENSATION OF AGENT(S): (OPTIONAL)

Your agent is entitled to be reimbursed from your assets for reasonable expenses incurred on your behalf. If you ALSO wish your agent(s) to be compensated from your assets for services rendered on your behalf, and/or you wish to define "reasonable compensation", you may do so above, under "Modifications".

(k) ACCEPTANCE BY THIRD PARTIES: I agree to indemnify the third party for any claims that may arise against the third party because of reliance on this Power of Attorney. I understand that any termination of this Power of Attorney, whether the result of my revocation of the Power of Attorney or otherwise, is not effective as to a third party until the third party has actual notice or knowledge of the termination.

(l) TERMINATION: This Power of Attorney continues until I revoke it or it is terminated by my death or other event described in section 5-1511 of the General Obligations Law.

Section 5-1511 of the General Obligations Law describes the manner in which you may revoke your Power of Attorney, and the events which terminate the Power of Attorney.

(m) SIGNATURE AND ACKNOWLEDGMENT:

In Witness Whereof I have hereunto signed my name on _____, 20_____.

PRINCIPAL signs here: ==> _____

(acknowledgment)

(n) SIGNATURES OF WITNESSES:

By signing as a witness, I acknowledge that the principal signed the Power of Attorney in my presence and in the presence of the other witness, or that the principal acknowledged to me that the principal's signature was affixed by him or her or at his or her direction. I also acknowledge that the principal has stated that this Power of Attorney reflects his or her wishes and that he or she has signed it voluntarily. I am not named herein as an agent or as a permissible recipient of gifts.

Signature of Witness 1	Signature of Witness 2
Date	Date
Print name	Print name
Address	Address
City, State, Zip Code	City, State, Zip Code

(o) IMPORTANT INFORMATION FOR THE AGENT:

When you accept the authority granted under this Power of Attorney, a special legal relationship is created between you and the principal. This relationship imposes on you legal responsibilities that continue until you resign or the Power of Attorney is terminated or revoked. You must:

(1) act according to any instructions from the principal, or, where there are no instructions, in the principal's best interest;

(2) avoid conflicts that would impair your ability to act in the principal's best interest;

(3) keep the principal's property separate and distinct from any assets you own or control, unless otherwise permitted by law;

(4) keep a record of all transactions conducted for the principal or keep all receipts of payments and transactions conducted for the principal; and

(5) disclose your identity as an agent whenever you act for the principal by writing or printing the principal's name and signing your own name as "agent" in either of the following manners: (Principal's Name) by (Your Signature) as Agent, or (your signature) as Agent for (Principal's Name).

You may not use the principal's assets to benefit yourself or anyone else or make gifts to yourself or anyone else unless the principal has specifically granted you that authority in the modifications section of this document or a Non-Statutory Power of Attorney. If you have that authority, you must act according to any instructions of the principal or, where there are no such instructions, in the principal's best interest. You may resign by giving written notice to the principal and to any co-agent, successor agent, monitor if one has been named in this document, or the principal's guardian if one has been appointed. If there is anything about this document or your responsibilities that you do not understand, you should seek legal advice.

Liability of agent:

The meaning of the authority given to you is defined in New York's General Obligations Law, Article 5, Title 15. If it is found that you have violated the law or acted outside the authority granted to you in the Power of Attorney, you may be liable under the law for your violation.

(p) AGENT'S SIGNATURE AND ACKNOWLEDGMENT OF APPOINTMENT:

It is not required that the principal and the agent(s) sign at the same time, nor that multiple agents sign at the same time.

I/we, _____, have read the foregoing Power of Attorney. I am/we are the person(s) identified therein as agent(s) for the principal named therein.

I/we acknowledge my/our legal responsibilities.

In Witness Whereof I have hereunto signed my name on _____, 20_____.

Agent(s) sign(s) here:==> _____

(acknowledgment(s))

(q) SUCCESSOR AGENT'S SIGNATURE AND ACKNOWLEDGMENT OF APPOINTMENT:

It is not required that the principal and the SUCCESSOR agent(s), if any, sign at the same time, nor that multiple SUCCESSOR agents sign at the same time. Furthermore, successor agents can not use this power of attorney unless the agent(s) designated above is/are unable or unwilling to serve.

I/we, _____, have read the foregoing Power of Attorney. I am/we are the person(s) identified therein as SUCCESSOR agent(s) for the principal named therein.

In Witness Whereof I have hereunto signed my name on _____, 20_____.

Successor Agent(s) sign(s) here: ==> _____

(acknowledgment(s))"

History: Add, L 2008, ch 644, § 19, as amd by L 2009, ch 4, eff Sept 1, 2009; amd, L 2010, ch 340, § 28, eff Sept 12, 2010, deemed eff on and after Sept 1, 2009, provided, that any statutory short form power of attorney and any statutory gifts rider executed after Aug 31, 2009 shall remain valid as will any revocation of a prior power of attorney that was delivered to the agent before the effective date of this act; L 2020, ch 323, § 17, eff June 13, 2021; L 2021, ch 84, § 3, eff June 13, 2020.

MENTAL HYGIENE LAW

Table of Contents

ARTICLE 81
PROCEEDINGS FOR APPOINTMENT OF A GUARDIAN FOR PERSONAL NEEDS OR PROPERTY MANAGEMENT

SUMMARY OF ARTICLE

MHL-3

§ 81.01. Legislative findings and purpose

The legislature hereby finds that the needs of persons with incapacities are as diverse and complex as they are unique to the individual. The current system of conservatorship and committee does not provide the necessary flexibility to meet these needs. Conservatorship which traditionally compromises a person's rights only with respect to property frequently is insufficient to provide necessary relief. On the other hand, a committee, with its judicial finding of incompetence and the accompanying stigma and loss of civil rights, traditionally involves a deprivation that is often excessive and unnecessary. Moreover, certain persons require some form of assistance in meeting their personal and property management needs but do not require either of these drastic remedies. The legislature finds that it is desirable for and beneficial to persons with incapacities to make available to them the least restrictive form of intervention which assists them in meeting their needs but, at the same time, permits them to exercise the independence and self-determination of which they are capable. The legislature declares that it is the purpose of this act to promote the public welfare by establishing a guardianship system which is appropriate to satisfy either personal or property management needs of an incapacitated person in a manner tailored to the individual needs of that person, which takes in account the personal wishes, preferences and desires of the person, and which affords the person the greatest amount of independence and self-determination and participation in all the decisions affecting such person's life.

History: Add, L 1992, ch 698, § 3, eff April 1, 1993.

§ 81.02. Power to appoint a guardian of the person and/or property; standard for appointment

(a) The court may appoint a guardian for a person if the court determines:

1. that the appointment is necessary to provide for the personal needs of that person, including food, clothing, shelter, health care, or safety and/or to manage the property and financial affairs of that person; and

2. that the person agrees to the appointment, or that the person is incapacitated as defined in subdivision (b) of this section. In deciding whether the appointment is necessary, the court shall consider the report of the court evaluator, as required in paragraph five of subdivision (c) of section 81.09 of this article, and the sufficiency and reliability of available resources, as defined in subdivision (e) of section 81.03 of this article, to provide for personal needs or property management without the appointment of a guardian. Any guardian appointed under this article shall be granted only those powers which are necessary to provide for personal needs and/or property management of the incapacitated person in such a manner as appropriate to the individual and which shall constitute the least restrictive form of intervention, as defined in subdivision (d) of section 81.03 of this article.

(b) The determination of incapacity shall be based on clear and convincing evidence and shall consist of a determination that a person is likely to suffer harm because:

1. the person is unable to provide for personal needs and/or property management; and

2. the person cannot adequately understand and appreciate the nature and consequences of such inability.

(c) In reaching its determination, the court shall give primary consideration to the functional level and functional limitations of the person. Such consideration shall include an assessment of that person's:

1. management of the activities of daily living, as defined in subdivision (h) of section 81.03 of this article;

2. understanding and appreciation of the nature and consequences of any inability to manage the activities of daily living;

3. preferences, wishes, and values with regard to managing the activities of daily living; and

4. the nature and extent of the person's property and financial affairs and his or her ability to manage them.

It shall also include an assessment of (i) the extent of the demands placed on the person by that person's personal needs and by the nature and extent of that person's property and financial affairs; (ii) any physical illness and the prognosis of such illness; (iii) any mental disability, as that term is defined in section 1.03 of this chapter, alcoholism or substance dependence as those terms are defined in section 19.03 of this chapter, and the prognosis of such disability, alcoholism or substance dependence; and (iv) any medications with which the person is being treated and their effect on the person's behavior, cognition and judgment.

(d) In addition, the court shall consider all other relevant facts and circumstances regarding the person's:

1. functional level; and

2. understanding and appreciation of the nature and consequences of his or her functional limitations.

History: Add, L 1992, ch 698, § 3, eff April 1, 1993.

§ 81.03. Definitions

When used in this article,

(a) "guardian" means a person who is eighteen years of age or older, a corporation, or a public agency, including a local department of social services, appointed in accordance with terms of this article by the supreme court, the surrogate's court, or the county court to act on behalf of an incapacitated person in providing for personal needs and/or for property management.

(b) "functional level" means the ability to provide for personal needs and/or the ability with respect to property management.

(c) "functional limitations" means behavior or conditions of a person which impair the ability to provide for personal needs and/or property management.

(d) "least restrictive form of intervention" means that the powers granted by the court to the guardian with respect to the incapacitated person represent only those powers which are necessary to provide for that person's personal needs and/or property management and which are consistent with affording that person the greatest amount of independence and self-determination in light of that person's understanding and appreciation of the nature and consequences of his or her functional limitations.

(e) "available resources" means resources such as, but not limited to, visiting nurses, homemakers, home health aides, adult day care and multipurpose senior citizen centers, powers of attorney, health care proxies, trusts, representative and protective payees, and residential care facilities.

(f) "personal needs" means needs such as, but not limited to, food, clothing, shelter, health care, and safety.

(g) "property management" means taking actions to obtain, administer, protect, and dispose of real and personal property, intangible property, business property, benefits, and income and to deal with financial affairs.

(h) "activities of daily living" means activities such as, but not limited to, mobility, eating, toileting, dressing, grooming, housekeeping, cooking, shopping, money management, banking, driving or using public transportation, and other activities related to personal needs and to property management.

(i) "major medical or dental treatment" means a medical, surgical or diagnostic intervention or procedure where a general anesthetic is used or which involves any significant risk or any significant invasion of bodily integrity requiring an incision or producing substantial pain, discomfort, debilitation, or having a significant recovery period, or which involves the administration of psychotropic medication or electroconvulsive therapy; it does not include any routine diagnosis or treatment such as the administration of medications other than chemotherapy for non-psychiatric conditions or nutrition or the extraction of bodily fluids for analysis; dental care performed with a local anesthetic; and any procedures which are provided under emergency circumstances, pursuant to section two thousand five hundred four of the public health law.

(j) "life sustaining treatment" means medical treatment which is sustaining life functions and without which, according to reasonable medical judgment, the patient will die within a relatively short time period.

(k) "facility" means a facility, hospital, or school, or an alcoholism facility in this state as such terms are defined in section 1.03 of this chapter, a substance abuse program as such term is defined in article nineteen of this chapter, an adult care facility as such term is defined in section two of the social services law, or a residential health care facility or a general hospital as such terms are defined in section two thousand eight hundred one of the public health law.

(l) "mental hygiene facility" means a facility, hospital, or school, or an alcoholism facility in this state as such terms are defined in section 1.03 of this chapter.

History: Add, L 1992, ch 698, § 3, eff April 1, 1993; amd, L 2004, ch 438, § 1, eff Dec 13, 2004.

§ 81.04. Jurisdiction

(a) If after a hearing or trial in accordance with the provisions of this article it is determined that relief under this article is necessary, the supreme court, and the county courts outside the city of New York, shall have the power to provide the relief set forth in this article:

1. for a resident of the state;

2. for a nonresident of the state present in the state;

3. for a nonresident of the state pursuant to section 81.18 of this article.

(b) Notwithstanding the provisions of subdivision (a) of this section, when it appears in any proceeding in the surrogate's court that a person interested in an estate is entitled to money or property as a beneficiary of the estate, or entitled to the proceeds of any action as provided in section 5-4.1 of the estates, powers and trusts law, or to the proceeds of a settlement of a cause of action brought on behalf of an infant for personal injuries, and that the interested person is a resident of, is physically present, or has any property in, the county in which the proceeding is pending and is allegedly incapacitated with respect to property management under the provisions of this article, and the surrogate's court is satisfied after a hearing or trial in accordance with the provisions of this article that the interested person is incapacitated with respect to property management, the surrogate's court shall have the power to order relief for that person with respect to property management in accordance with the provisions of this article.

History: Add, L 1992, ch 698, § 3, eff April 1, 1993; amd, L 2004, ch 438, § 2, eff Dec 13, 2004.

§ 81.05. Venue

(a) A proceeding under this article shall be brought in the supreme court within the judicial district, or in the county court of the county in which the person alleged to be incapacitated resides, or is physically present, or in the surrogate's court having jurisdiction pursuant to subdivision (b) of section 81.04 of this article. If the person alleged to be incapacitated is being cared for as a resident in a facility, the residence of that person shall be deemed to be in the county where the facility is located and the proceeding shall be brought in that county, subject to application by an interested party for a change in venue to another county because of the inconvenience of the parties or witnesses or the condition of the person alleged to be incapacitated. If the person alleged to be incapacitated is not present in the state, or the residence of such person cannot be ascertained, the residence shall be deemed to be in the county in which all or some of such person's property is situated.

(b) After the appointment of a guardian, temporary guardian, special guardian, standby guardian, or alternate standby guardians, any proceeding to modify a prior order shall be brought in the supreme court, county court, or surrogate's court which granted the prior order. If, at the time of the application to modify a prior order, the incapacitated person is being cared for as a resident in a facility, the proceeding shall be brought in the county where the facility is located, subject to application by an interested party for a change in venue to the court which granted the prior order because of the inconvenience of the parties or witnesses or the condition of the incapacitated person.

History: Add, L 1992, ch 698, § 3, eff April 1, 1993; amd, L 2004, ch 438, § 3, eff Dec 13, 2004.

§ 81.06. Who may commence a proceeding

(a) A proceeding under this article shall be commenced by the filing of the petition with the court by:

1. the person alleged to be incapacitated;

2. a presumptive distributee of the person alleged to be incapacitated, as that term is defined in subdivision forty-two of section one hundred three of the surrogate's court procedure act;

3. an executor or administrator of an estate when the alleged incapacitated person is or may be the beneficiary of that estate;

4. a trustee of a trust when the alleged incapacitated person is or may be the grantor or a beneficiary of that trust;

5. the person with whom the person alleged to be incapacitated resides;

6. a person otherwise concerned with the welfare of the person alleged to be incapacitated. For purposes of this section a person otherwise concerned with the welfare of the person alleged to be incapacitated may include a corporation, or a public agency, including the department of social services in the county where the person alleged to be incapacitated resides regardless of whether the person alleged to be incapacitated is a recipient of public assistance;

7. the chief executive officer, or the designee of the chief executive officer, of a facility in which the person alleged to be incapacitated is a patient or resident.

History: Add, L 1992, ch 698, § 3, eff April 1, 1993; amd, L 2004, ch 438, § 4, eff Dec 13, 2004.

§ 81.07. Notice

(a) Proceeding. A proceeding under this article shall be commenced upon the filing of the petition.

(b) Order to show cause. Upon the filing of the petition, the court shall:

1. set the date on which the order to show cause is heard no more than twenty-eight days from the date of the signing of the order to show cause. The court may for good cause shown set a date less than twenty-eight days from the date of the signing of the order to show cause. The date of the hearing may be adjourned only for good cause shown;

2. include in the order to show cause the name, address, and telephone number of the person appointed as court evaluator in accordance with section 81.09 of this article;

3. require the order to show cause to be served together with a copy of the petition and any supporting papers upon the alleged incapacitated person, the court evaluator, and counsel for the alleged incapacitated person in the form and manner prescribed in this section; the court shall not require that supporting papers contain medical information; and

4. require notice of the proceeding together with a copy of the order to show cause to be given to the persons identified in paragraph one of subdivision (e) of this section and in the form and manner prescribed in this section.

(c) Form of the order to show cause. The order to show cause shall be written in large type, in plain language, and in a language other than English if necessary to inform the person alleged to be incapacitated of his or her rights, and shall include the following information:

1. date, time, and place of the hearing of the petition;

2. a clear and easily readable statement of the rights of the person alleged to be incapacitated that are set forth in section 81.11 of this article;

3. the name, address, and telephone number of the person appointed as court evaluator pursuant to section 81.09 of this article;

4. the name, address, and telephone number of the attorney if one has been appointed for the person alleged to be incapacitated pursuant to section 81.10 of this article; and

5. a list of the powers which the guardian would have the authority to exercise on behalf of the person alleged to be incapacitated if the relief sought in the petition is granted.

(d) Legend. The order to show cause shall also include on its face the following legend in twelve point or larger bold face double spaced type:

IMPORTANT

An application has been filed in court by _____ who believes you may be unable to take care of your personal needs or financial affairs. _____ is asking that someone be appointed to make decisions for you. With this paper is a copy of the application to the court showing why _____ believes you may be unable to take care of your personal needs or financial affairs. Before the court makes the appointment of someone to make decisions for you the court holds a hearing at which you are entitled to be present and to tell the judge if you do not want anyone appointed. This paper tells you when the court hearing will take place. If you do not appear in court, your rights may be seriously affected.

You have the right to demand a trial by jury. You must tell the court if you wish to have a trial by jury. If you do not tell the court, the hearing will be conducted without a jury. The name and address, and telephone number of the clerk of the court are:

The court has appointed a court evaluator to explain this proceeding to you and to investigate the claims made in the application. The court may give the court evaluator permission to inspect your medical, psychological, or psychiatric records. You have the right to tell the judge if you do not want the court evaluator to be given that permission. The court evaluator's name, address, and telephone number are:

You are entitled to have a lawyer of your choice represent you. If you want the court to appoint a lawyer to help you and represent you, the court will appoint a lawyer for you. You will be required to pay that lawyer unless you do not have the money to do so.

(e) Service of the order to show cause.

1. The persons entitled to service of the order to show cause shall include:

(i) the person alleged to be incapacitated; and

(ii) the attorney for the person alleged to be incapacitated, if known to the petitioner; and

(iii) the court evaluator.

2. Manner of service.

(i) the order to show cause and a copy of the petition shall be personally delivered to the person alleged to be incapacitated not less than fourteen days prior to the hearing date of the order to show cause. However, the court may direct that the order to show cause and a copy of the petition be served on the person alleged to be incapacitated in a manner other than personal delivery when the petitioner demonstrates to the court's satisfaction that the person alleged to be incapacitated has refused to accept service.

(ii) the order to show cause and a copy of the petition shall be served upon the court evaluator and the attorney for the alleged incapacitated person, if there is one, by facsimile, provided that a facsimile telephone number is designated by the attorney for that purpose, or by delivering the papers personally or by overnight delivery service to the office of the court evaluator and the attorney for the alleged incapacitated person, if there is one, within three business days following the appointment of the court evaluator and the appointment of the attorney or the appearance of an attorney retained by the alleged incapacitated person.

3. The court may direct that the order to show cause be served within a time period less than the period required in paragraph two of this subdivision for good cause shown.

(f) Form of the notice of the proceeding. The notice of the proceeding shall substantially set forth:

1. The name and address of the alleged incapacitated person to whom the guardianship proceeding relates;

2. The name and address of the petitioner;

3. The names of all persons to be given notice of the proceeding;

4. The time when and the place where the order to show cause shall be heard;

5. The object of the proceeding and the relief sought in the petition;

6. The name, address and telephone number of the petitioner's attorney.

(g) Notice of the proceeding.

1. Persons entitled to notice of the proceeding shall include:

(i) the following persons, other than the petitioner, who are known to the petitioner or whose existence and address can be ascertained by the petitioner with reasonably diligent efforts: the spouse of the person alleged to be incapacitated, if any; the parents of the person alleged to be incapacitated, if living; the adult children of the person alleged to be incapacitated, if any; the adult siblings of the person alleged to be incapacitated, if any; the person or persons with whom person alleged to be incapacitated resides; and

(ii) in the event no person listed in subparagraph (i) of this paragraph is given notice, then notice shall be given to at least one and not more than three of the living relatives of the person alleged to be incapacitated in the nearest degree of kinship who are known to the petitioner or whose existence and address can be ascertained by the petitioner with reasonably diligent efforts; and

(iii) any person or persons designated by the alleged incapacitated person with authority pursuant to sections 5-1501, 5-1505, and 5-1506 of the general obligations law, or sections two thousand nine hundred five and two thousand nine hundred eighty-one of the public health law, if known to the petitioner; and

(iv) if known to the petitioner, any person, whether or not a relative of the person alleged to be incapacitated, or organization that has demonstrated a genuine interest in promoting the best interests of the person alleged to be incapacitated such as by having a personal relationship with the person, regularly visiting the person, or regularly communicating with the person; and

(v) if it is known to the petitioner that the person alleged to be incapacitated receives public assistance or protective services under article nine-B of the social services law, the local department of social services; and

(vi) if the person alleged to be incapacitated resides in a facility, the chief executive officer in charge of the facility; and

(vii) if the person alleged to be incapacitated resides in a mental hygiene facility, the mental hygiene legal service of the judicial department in which the residence is located; and

(viii) such other persons as the court may direct based on the recommendation of the court evaluator in accordance with subparagraph (xvii) of paragraph five of subdivision (c) of section 81.09 of this article.

2. Notice of the proceeding together with a copy of the order to show cause shall be mailed to the persons identified in paragraph one of this subdivision not less than fourteen days prior to the hearing date in the order to show cause.

3. The court may direct that the notice of proceeding be mailed within a time period less than the period required in paragraph two of this subdivision for good cause shown.

History: Add, L 1992, ch 698, § 3, eff April 1, 1993; amd, L 1993, ch 32, §§ 1, 2, eff April 1, 1993; L 2004, ch 438, § 5, eff Dec 13, 2004.

§ 81.08. Petition

(a) The petition shall be verified under oath and shall include the following information:

1. the name, age, address, and telephone number of the person alleged to be incapacitated;

2. the name, address, and telephone number of the person or persons with whom the person alleged to be incapacitated resides, if any, and the name, address and telephone number of any persons that the petitioner intends to serve with the order to show cause and the nature of their relationship to the alleged incapacitated person;

3. a description of the alleged incapacitated person's functional level including that person's ability to manage the activities of daily living, behavior, and understanding and appreciation of the nature and consequences of any inability to manage the activities of daily living;

4. if powers are sought with respect to the personal needs of the alleged incapacitated person, specific factual allegations as to the personal actions or other actual occurrences involving the person alleged to be incapacitated which are claimed to demonstrate that the

person is likely to suffer harm because he or she cannot adequately understand and appreciate the nature and consequences of his or her inability to provide for personal needs;

5. if powers are sought with respect to property management for the alleged incapacitated person, specific factual allegations as to the financial transactions or other actual occurrences involving the person alleged to be incapacitated which are claimed to demonstrate that the person is likely to suffer harm because he or she cannot adequately understand and appreciate the nature and consequences of his or her inability to provide for property management; if powers are sought to transfer a part of the alleged incapacitated person's property or assets to or for the benefit of another person, including the petitioner or guardian, the petition shall include the information required by subdivision (b) of section 81.21 of this article;

6. the particular powers being sought and their relationship to the functional level and needs of the person alleged to be incapacitated;

7. the duration of the powers being sought;

8. the approximate value and description of the financial resources of the person alleged to be incapacitated and whether, to the best of the petitioner's knowledge, the person is a recipient of public assistance;

9. the nature and amount of any claim, debt, or obligations of the person alleged to be incapacitated, to the best of the petitioner's knowledge;

10. the names, addresses, and telephone numbers of presumptive distributees of the person alleged to be incapacitated as that term is defined in subdivision forty-two of section one hundred three of the surrogate's court procedure act unless they are unknown and cannot be reasonably ascertained;

11. the name, address, and telephone number of the petitioner;

12. the name, address, and telephone number of the person or persons, if any, proposed as guardian and standby guardian, the relationship of the proposed guardian or standby guardian to the person alleged to be incapacitated, and the reasons why the proposed guardian or standby guardian is suitable to exercise the powers necessary to assist the person alleged to be incapacitated;

13. any relief sought pursuant to section 81.23 of this article;

14. the available resources, if any, that have been considered by the petitioner and the petitioner's opinion as to their sufficiency and reliability;

15. any other information which in the petitioner's opinion will assist the court evaluator in completing the investigation and report in accordance with section 81.09 of this article.

History: Add, L 1992, ch 698, § 3, eff April 1, 1993; amd, L 2004, ch 438, §§ 6, 7, eff Dec 13, 2004.

§ 81.09. Appointment of court evaluator

(a) At the time of the issuance of the order to show cause, the court shall appoint a court evaluator.

(b) 1. the court may appoint as court evaluator any person including, but not limited to, the mental hygiene legal service in the judicial department where the person resides, a not-for-profit corporation, an attorney-at-law, physician, psychologist, accountant, social worker, or nurse, with knowledge of property management, personal care skills, the problems associated with disabilities, and the private and public resources available for the type of limitations the person is alleged to have. The name of the court evaluator shall be drawn from a list maintained by the office of court administration;

2. if the court appoints the mental hygiene legal service as the evaluator and upon investigation in accordance with section 81.10 of this article it appears to the mental hygiene legal service that the mental hygiene legal service represents the person alleged to be incapacitated as counsel, or that counsel should otherwise be appointed in accordance with section 81.10 of this article for the person alleged to be incapacitated, the mental hygiene legal service shall so report to the court. The mental hygiene legal service shall be relieved of its appointment as court evaluator whenever the mental hygiene legal service represents as counsel, or is assigned to represent as counsel, the person alleged to be incapacitated.

(c) The duties of the court evaluator shall include the following:

1. meeting, interviewing, and consulting with the person alleged to be incapacitated regarding the proceeding.

2. determining whether the alleged incapacitated person understands English or only another language, and explaining to the person alleged to be incapacitated, in a manner which the person can reasonably be expected to understand, the nature and possible consequences of the proceeding, the general powers and duties of a guardian, available resources, and the rights to which the person is entitled, including the right to counsel.

3. determining whether the person alleged to be incapacitated wishes legal counsel of his or her own choice to be appointed and otherwise evaluating whether legal counsel should be appointed in accordance with section 81.10 of this article.

4. interviewing the petitioner, or, if the petitioner is a facility or government agency, a person within the facility or agency fully familiar with the person's condition, affairs and situation.

5. investigating and making a written report and recommendations to the court; the report and recommendations shall include the court evaluator's personal observations as to the person alleged to be incapacitated and his or her condition, affairs and situation, as well as information in response to the following questions:

(i) does the person alleged to be incapacitated agree to the appointment of the proposed guardian and to the powers proposed for the guardian;

(ii) does the person wish legal counsel of his or her own choice to be appointed or is the appointment of counsel in accordance with section 81.10 of this article otherwise appropriate;

(iii) can the person alleged to be incapacitated come to the courthouse for the hearing;

(iv) if the person alleged to be incapacitated cannot come to the courthouse, is the person completely unable to participate in the hearing;

(v) if the person alleged to be incapacitated cannot come to the courthouse, would any meaningful participation result from the person's presence at the hearing;

(vi) are available resources sufficient and reliable to provide for personal needs or property management without the appointment of a guardian;

(vii) how is the person alleged to be incapacitated functioning with respect to the activities of daily living and what is the prognosis and reversibility of any physical and mental disabilities, alcoholism or substance dependence? The response to this question shall be based on the evaluator's own assessment of the person alleged to be incapacitated to the extent possible, and where necessary, on the examination of assessments by third parties, including records of medical, psychological and/or psychiatric examinations obtained pursuant to subdivision (d) of this section. As part of this review, the court evaluator shall consider the diagnostic and assessment procedures used to determine the prognosis and reversibility of any disability and the necessity, efficacy, and dose of each prescribed medication;

(viii) what is the person's understanding and appreciation of the nature and consequences of any inability to manage the activities of daily living;

(ix) what is the approximate value and nature of the financial resources of the person alleged to be incapacitated;

(x) what are the person's preferences, wishes, and values with regard to managing the activities of daily living;

(xi) has the person alleged to be incapacitated made any appointment or delegation pursuant to section 5-1501, 5-1505, or 5-1506 of the general obligations law, section two thousand nine hundred sixty-five or two thousand nine hundred eighty-one of the public health law, or a living will;

(xii) what would be the least restrictive form of intervention consistent with the person's functional level and the powers proposed for the guardian;

(xiii) what assistance is necessary for those who are financially dependent upon the person alleged to be incapacitated;

(xiv) is the choice of proposed guardian appropriate, including a guardian nominated by the allegedly incapacitated person pursuant to section 81.17 or subdivision (c) of section 81.19 of this article; and what steps has the proposed guardian taken or does the proposed guardian intend to take to identify and meet the current and emerging needs of the person alleged to be incapacitated unless that information has been provided to the court by the local department of social services when the proposed guardian is a community guardian program operating pursuant to the provisions of title three of article nine-B of the social services law;

(xv) what potential conflicts of interest, if any, exist between or among family members and/or other interested parties regarding the proposed guardian or the proposed relief;

(xvi) what potential conflicts of interest, if any, exist involving the person alleged to be incapacitated, the petitioner, and the proposed guardian; and

(xvii) are there any additional persons who should be given notice and an opportunity to be heard.

In addition, the report and recommendations shall include any information required under subdivision (e) of this section, and any additional information required by the court.

6. interviewing or consulting with professionals having specialized knowledge in the area of the person's alleged incapacity including but not limited to developmental disabilities, alcohol and substance abuse, and geriatrics.

7. retaining an independent medical expert where the court finds it is appropriate, the cost of which is to be charged to the estate of the allegedly incapacitated person unless the person is indigent.

8. conducting any other investigations or making recommendations with respect to other subjects as the court deems appropriate.

9. attending all court proceedings and conferences.

(d) The court evaluator may apply to the court for permission to inspect records of medical, psychological and/or psychiatric examinations of the person alleged to be incapacitated; except as otherwise provided by federal or state law, if the court determines that such records are likely to contain information which will assist the court evaluator in completing his or her report to the court, the court may order the disclosure of such records to the court evaluator, notwithstanding the physician/patient privilege, the psychologist/patient privilege, or the social worker/client privilege as set forth in sections four thousand five hundred four, four thousand five hundred seven, and four thousand five hundred eight of the civil practice law and rules; if the court orders that such records be disclosed to the court evaluator, the court may, upon the court's own motion, at the request of the court evaluator, or upon the application of counsel for the person alleged to be incapacitated, or the petitioner, also direct such further disclosure of such records as the court deems proper.

(e) The court evaluator shall have the authority to take the steps necessary to preserve the property of the person alleged to be incapacitated pending the hearing in the event the property is in danger of waste, misappropriation, or loss; if the court evaluator exercises authority under this subdivision, the court evaluator shall immediately advise the court of the actions taken and include in his or her report to the court an explanation of the actions the court evaluator has taken and the reasons for such actions.

(f) When judgment grants a petition, the court may award a reasonable compensation to a court evaluator, including the mental hygiene legal service, payable by the estate of the allegedly incapacitated person. When a judgment denies or dismisses a petition, the court may award a reasonable allowance to a court evaluator, including the mental hygiene legal service, payable by the petitioner or by the person alleged to be incapacitated, or both in such proportions as the court may deem just. When the person alleged to be incapacitated dies before the determination is made in the proceeding, the court may award a reasonable allowance to a court evaluator, payable by the petitioner or by the estate of the decedent, or by both in such proportions as the court may deem just.

History: Add, L 1992, ch 698, § 3, eff April 1, 1993; amd, L 1993, ch 32, §§ 3, 4, eff April

1, 1993.; L 2004, ch 438, § 8, eff Dec 13, 2004; L 2011, ch 37, § 71, eff June 1, 2011.

§ 81.10.   Counsel

(a) Any person for whom relief under this article is sought shall have the right to choose and engage legal counsel of the person's choice. In such event, any attorney appointed pursuant to this section shall continue his or her duties until the court has determined that retained counsel has been chosen freely and independently by the alleged incapacitated person.

(b) If the person alleged to be incapacitated is not represented by counsel at the time of the issuance of the order to show cause, the court evaluator shall assist the court in accordance with subdivision (c) of section 81.09 of this article in determining whether counsel should be appointed.

(c) The court shall appoint counsel in any of the following circumstances unless the court is satisfied that the alleged incapacitated person is represented by counsel of his or her own choosing:

1. the person alleged to be incapacitated requests counsel;

2. the person alleged to be incapacitated wishes to contest the petition;

3. the person alleged to be incapacitated does not consent to the authority requested in the petition to move the person alleged to be incapacitated from where that person presently resides to a nursing home or other residential facility as those terms are defined in section two thousand eight hundred one of the public health law, or other similar facility;

4. if the petition alleges that the person is in need of major medical or dental treatment and the person alleged to be incapacitated does not consent;

5. the petition requests the appointment of a temporary guardian pursuant to section 81.23 of this article;

6. the court determines that a possible conflict may exist between the court evaluator's role and the advocacy needs of the person alleged to be incapacitated;

7. if at any time the court determines that appointment of counsel would be helpful to the resolution of the matter.

(d) If the person refuses the assistance of counsel, the court may, nevertheless, appoint counsel if the court is not satisfied that the person is capable of making an informed decision regarding the appointment of counsel.

(e) The court may appoint as counsel the mental hygiene legal service in the judicial department where the residence is located.

(f) The court shall determine the reasonable compensation for the mental hygiene legal service or any attorney appointed pursuant to this section. The person alleged to be incapacitated shall be liable for such compensation unless the court is satisfied that the person is indigent. If the petition is dismissed, the court may in its discretion direct that petitioner pay such compensation for the person alleged to be incapacitated. When the person alleged to be incapacitated dies before the determination is made in the proceeding, the court may award reasonable compensation to the mental hygiene legal service or any attorney appointed pursuant to this section, payable by the petitioner or the estate of the decedent or by both in such proportions as the court may deem just.

(g) If the court appoints counsel under this section, the court may dispense with the appointment of a court evaluator or may vacate or suspend the appointment of a previously appointed court evaluator.

> **History:** Add, L 1992, ch 698, § 3, eff April 1, 1993; amd, L 1993, ch 32, § 5, eff April 1, 1993; L 2004, ch 438, § 9, eff Dec 13, 2004.

§ 81.11. Hearing

(a) A determination that the appointment of a guardian is necessary for a person alleged to be incapacitated shall be made only after a hearing.

(b) In a proceeding brought pursuant to this article any party to the proceeding shall have the right to:

1. present evidence;

2. call witnesses, including expert witnesses;

3. cross examine witnesses, including witnesses called by the court;

4. be represented by counsel of his or her choice.

(c) The hearing must be conducted in the presence of the person alleged to be incapacitated, either at the courthouse or where the person alleged to be incapacitated resides, so as to permit the court to obtain its own impression of the person's capacity. If the person alleged to be incapacitated physically cannot come or be brought to the courthouse, the hearing must be conducted where the person alleged to be incapacitated resides unless:

1. the person is not present in the state; or

2. all the information before the court clearly establishes that (i) the person alleged to be incapacitated is completely unable to participate in the hearing or (ii) no meaningful participation will result from the person's presence at the hearing.

(d) If the hearing is conducted without the presence of the person alleged to be incapacitated and the court appoints a guardian, the order of appointment shall set forth the factual basis for conducting the hearing without the presence of the person for whom the appointment is made.

(e) If the hearing is conducted in the presence of the person alleged to be incapacitated and the person is not represented by counsel, the court shall explain to that person, on the record, the purpose and possible consequences of the proceeding, the right to be represented by counsel and the fact that the court will appoint an attorney to represent the person alleged to be incapacitated if the person wishes to be represented by counsel, and shall inquire of the person whether he or she wishes to have an attorney appointed. If the person refuses the assistance of counsel, the court may nevertheless appoint counsel if the court is not satisfied that the person is capable of making an informed decision regarding the appointment of counsel.

(f) If on or before the return date designated in the order to show cause the alleged incapacitated person or counsel for the alleged incapacitated person raises issues of fact regarding the need for an appointment under this article and demands a jury trial of such issues, the court shall order a trial by jury thereof. Failure to make such a demand shall be deemed a waiver of the right to trial by jury.

> **History:** Add, L 1992, ch 698, § 3, eff April 1, 1993; amd, L 2004, ch 438, § 10, eff Dec 13, 2004.

§ 81.12.   Burden and quantum of proof

(a) A determination that a person is incapacitated under the provisions of this article must be based on clear and convincing evidence. The burden of proof shall be on the petitioner.

(b) The court may, for good cause shown, waive the rules of evidence. The report of the court evaluator may be admitted in evidence if the court evaluator testifies and is subject to cross examination; provided, however, that if the court determines that information contained in the report is, in the particular circumstance of the case, not sufficiently reliable, the court shall require that the person who provided the information testify and be subject to cross examination.

> **History:** Add, L 1992, ch 698, § 3, eff April 1, 1993.

§ 81.13.   Timing of hearing

Unless the court, for good cause shown, orders otherwise, a proceeding under this article is entitled to a preference over all other causes in the court. Unless the court, for good cause shown, orders otherwise, the hearing or trial shall be conducted within the time set forth in subdivision (b) of section 81.07 of this article. A decision shall be rendered within seven days after the hearing, unless for good cause shown, the court extends the time period for rendering the decision. In the event the time period is extended, the court shall set forth the factual basis for the extension. The commission shall be issued to the guardian within fifteen days after the decision is rendered.

> **History:** Add, L 1992, ch 698, § 3, eff April 1, 1993; amd, L 1993, ch 32, § 6, eff April 1, 1993; L 2004, ch 438, § 11, eff Dec 13, 2004.

§ 81.14.   Record of the proceedings

(a) A record of the proceedings shall be made in all cases.

(b) The court shall not enter an order sealing the court records in a proceeding under this article, either in whole or in part, except upon a written finding of good cause, which shall specify the grounds thereof. In determining whether good cause has been shown, the court shall consider the interest of the public, the orderly and sound administration of justice, the nature of the proceedings, and the privacy of the person alleged to be incapacitated. Where it appears necessary or desirable, the court may prescribe appropriate notice and opportunity to be heard. Court records shall include all documents and records of any nature filed with the clerk in connection with the proceeding. Documents obtained through disclosure and not filed with the clerk shall remain subject to protective orders under the civil practice law and rules.

(c) The court shall not exclude a person or persons or the general public from a proceeding under this article except upon written findings of good cause shown. In determining whether good cause has been shown, the court shall consider the interest of the public, the orderly and sound administration of justice, the nature of the proceedings, and the privacy of the person alleged to be incapacitated.

(d) At the time of the commencement of the hearing, the court shall inform the allegedly incapacitated person of his or her right to request for good cause that the court records be sealed and that a person, persons, or the general public be excluded from the hearing.

History: Add, L 1992, ch 698, § 3, eff April 1, 1993.

§ 81.15. Findings

(a) Where the court determines that the person agrees to the appointment and that the appointment is necessary, the court shall make the following findings on the record:

1. the person's agreement to the appointment;

2. the person's functional limitations which impair the person's ability to provide for personal needs or property management;

3. the necessity of the appointment of a guardian as a means of providing for personal needs and/or property management for the person;

4. the specific powers of the guardian which constitute the least restrictive form of intervention consistent with the person's functional limitations; and

5. the duration of the appointment.

(b) Where the petition requests the appointment of a guardian to provide for the personal needs for a person alleged to be incapacitated and the court determines that such person is incapacitated and that the appointment is necessary, the court shall make the following findings on the record:

1. the person's functional limitations which impair the person's ability to provide for personal needs;

2. the person's lack of understanding and appreciation of the nature and consequences of his or her functional limitations;

3. the likelihood that the person will suffer harm because of the person's functional limitations and inability to adequately understand and appreciate the nature and consequences of such functional limitations;

4. the necessity of the appointment of a guardian to prevent such harm;

5. the specific powers of the guardian which constitute the least restrictive form of intervention consistent with the findings of this subdivision;

6. the duration of the appointment; and

7. whether the incapacitated person should receive copies of the initial and annual report.

(c) Where the petition requests the appointment of a guardian for property management for the person alleged to be incapacitated, and the court determines that the person is incapacitated and that the appointment of a guardian is necessary, the court shall make the following findings on the record:

1. the type and amount of the property and financial resources of the person alleged to be incapacitated;

2. the person's functional limitations which impair the person's ability with respect to

property management;

3. the person's lack of understanding and appreciation of the nature and consequences of his or her functional limitations;

4. the likelihood that the person will suffer harm because of the person's functional limitations and inability to adequately understand and appreciate the nature and consequences of such functional limitations;

5. any additional findings that are required under section 81.21 of this article;

6. the necessity of the appointment of a guardian to prevent such harm;

7. if so, the specific powers of the guardian which constitute the least restrictive form of intervention consistent with the person's functional limitations and the likelihood of harm because of the person's inability to adequately understand and appreciate the nature and consequences of such functional limitations;

8. the duration of the appointment; and

9. whether the incapacitated person should receive copies of the initial and annual report.

History: Add, L 1992, ch 698, § 3, eff April 1, 1993; amd, L 2004, ch 438, §§ 12, 13, eff Dec 13, 2004.

§ 81.16.   Dispositional alternatives

(a) Dismissal of the petition.

If the person alleged to be incapacitated under this article is found not to be incapacitated, the court shall dismiss the petition.

(b) Protective arrangements and single transactions. If the person alleged to be incapacitated is found to be incapacitated, the court without appointing a guardian, may authorize, direct, or ratify any transaction or series of transactions necessary to achieve any security, service, or care arrangement meeting the foreseeable needs of the incapacitated person, or may authorize, direct, or ratify any contract, trust, or other transaction relating to the incapacitated person's property and financial affairs if the court determines that the transaction is necessary as a means of providing for personal needs and/or property management for the alleged incapacitated person. Before approving a protective arrangement or other transaction under this subdivision, the court shall consider the interests of dependents and creditors of the incapacitated person, and in view of the person's functional level, whether the person needs the continuing protection of a guardian. The court may appoint a special guardian to assist in the accomplishment of any protective arrangement or other transaction authorized under this subdivision. The special guardian shall have the authority conferred by the order of appointment, shall report to the court on all matters done pursuant to the order of appointment and shall serve until discharged by order of the court. The court may approve a reasonable compensation for the special guardian; however, if the court finds that the special guardian has failed to discharge his or her duties satisfactorily in any respect, the court may deny or reduce the amount of compensation or remove the special guardian.

(c) Appointing a guardian.

1. If the person alleged to be incapacitated is found to have agreed to the appointment

of a guardian and the court determines that the appointment of a guardian is necessary, the order of the court shall be designed to accomplish the least restrictive form of intervention by appointing a guardian with powers limited to those which the court has found necessary to assist the person in providing for personal needs and/or property management.

2. If the person alleged to be incapacitated is found to be incapacitated and the court determines that the appointment of a guardian is necessary, the order of the court shall be designed to accomplish the least restrictive form of intervention by appointing a guardian with powers limited to those which the court has found necessary to assist the incapacitated person in providing for personal needs and/or property management.

3. The order of appointment shall identify all persons entitled to notice of all further proceedings.

4. The order of appointment shall identify the persons entitled to receive notice of the incapacitated person's death, the intended disposition of the remains of the decedent, funeral arrangements and final resting place when that information is known or can be reasonably ascertained by the guardian.

5. The order of appointment may identify the person or persons entitled to notice of the incapacitated person's transfer to a medical facility.

6. The order of appointment may identify the persons entitled to visit the incapacitated person, if they so choose. However, the identification of such persons in the order shall in no way limit the persons entitled to visit the incapacitated person.

(d) The court shall direct that a judgment be entered determining the rights of the parties.

(e) The order and judgment must be entered and served within ten days of the signing of the order. A copy of the order and judgment shall be personally served upon and explained to the person who is the subject of the proceedings in a manner which the person can reasonably be expected to understand by the court evaluator, or by counsel for the person, or by the guardian.

(f) When a petition is granted, or where the court otherwise deems it appropriate, the court may award reasonable compensation for the attorney for the petitioner, including the attorney general and the attorney for a local department of social services.

History: Add, L 1992, ch 698, § 3, eff April 1, 1993; amd, L 1993, ch 32, § 7, eff April 1, 1993; L 2004, ch 438, § 14, eff Dec 13, 2004; L 2016, ch 98, § 2, eff July 21, 2016.

§ 81.17. Nomination of guardian

In the petition, or in a written instrument duly executed, acknowledged, and filed in the proceeding before the appointment of a guardian, the person alleged to be incapacitated may nominate a guardian.

History: Add, L 1992, ch 698, § 3, eff April 1, 1993.

§ 81.18. Foreign guardian for a person not present in the state

Where the person alleged to be incapacitated is not present in the state and a guardian, by whatever name designated, has been duly appointed pursuant to the laws of any other country where the person alleged to be incapacitated resides to assist such person in property management, the court in its discretion, may make an order appointing the foreign guardian as a guardian under this article with powers with respect to property management within this state on the foreign guardian's giving such security as the court deems proper. In its discretion, the court may utilize the provisions of article eighty-three of this title.

History: Add, L 1992, ch 698, § 3, eff April 1, 1993; amd, L 2004, ch 438, § 15, eff Dec 13, 2004; L 2013, ch 427, § 3, eff April 21, 2014.

§ 81.19. Eligibility as guardian

(a) 1. Any individual over eighteen years of age, or any parent under eighteen years of age, who is found by the court to be suitable to exercise the powers necessary to assist the incapacitated person may be appointed as guardian, including but not limited to a spouse, adult child, parent, or sibling.

2. A not-for-profit corporation organized to act in such capacity, a social services official, or public agency authorized to act in such capacity which has a concern for the incapacitated person, and any community guardian program operating pursuant to the provisions of title three of article nine-B of the social services law which is found by the court to be suitable to perform the duties necessary to assist the incapacitated person may be appointed as guardian, provided that a community guardian program shall be appointed as guardian only where a special proceeding for the appointment of a guardian under this article has been commenced by a social services official with whom such program was contracted.

3. A corporation except that no corporation (other than as provided in paragraph two of this subdivision) may be authorized to exercise the powers necessary to assist the incapacitated person with personal needs.

(b) The court shall appoint a person nominated as the guardian in accordance with the provisions of section 81.17 of this article unless the court determines the nominee is unfit or the alleged incapacitated person indicates that he or she no longer wishes the nominee to be appointed.

(c) In the absence of a nomination in accordance with section 81.17 of this article, the court shall appoint a person nominated by the person alleged to be incapacitated orally or by conduct during the hearing or trial unless the court determines for good cause that such appointment is not appropriate.

(d) In making any appointment under this article the court shall consider:

1. any appointment or delegation made by the person alleged to be incapacitated in accordance with the provisions of section 5-1501, 5-1601 or 5-1602 of the general obligations law and sections two thousand nine hundred sixty-five and two thousand nine hundred eighty-one of the public health law;

2. the social relationship between the incapacitated person and the person, if any, proposed as guardian, and the social relationship between the incapacitated person and other persons concerned with the welfare of the incapacitated person;

3. the care and services being provided to the incapacitated person at the time of the proceeding;

4. the powers which the guardian will exercise;

5. the educational, professional and business experience relevant to the nature of the services sought to be provided;

6. the nature of the financial resources involved;

7. the unique requirements of the incapacitated person; and

8. any conflicts of interest between the person proposed as guardian and the incapacitated person.

(e) Unless the court finds that no other person or corporation is available or willing to act as guardian, or to provide needed services for the incapacitated person, the following persons or corporations may not serve as guardian:

1. one whose only interest in the person alleged to be incapacitated is that of a creditor;

2. one, other than a relative, who is a provider, or the employee of a provider, of health care, day care, educational, or residential services to the incapacitated person, whether direct or indirect.

(f) Mental hygiene legal service may not serve as a guardian.

(g) 1. In making an appointment or considering a revocation of an appointment under this article, the court also may obtain and consider, and may authorize a court evaluator to review the same and report to the court concerning, any of the following information regarding the guardian or proposed guardian, and, if the incapacitated person resides or will reside with such guardian or proposed guardian, any person eighteen years or older residing in the guardian or proposed guardian's household:

(i) a criminal history record check of such person or persons; and in furtherance thereof, the court shall be authorized to: (1) obtain a set of such person's fingerprints; (2) direct that the division of criminal justice services promptly provide to the court a criminal history record, if any, with respect to such person or a statement that such person has no criminal record; and (3) direct the submission of such person's fingerprints by the division of criminal justice services to the federal bureau of investigation for purposes of a nationwide criminal history record check pursuant to and consistent with public law 92-544 to determine if such person has a criminal history in any state or federal jurisdiction;

(ii) reports for such person or persons from the sex offender registry established and maintained pursuant to section one hundred sixty-eight-b of the correction law;

(iii) indicated reports for such person or persons from the statewide central register of child abuse and maltreatment established and maintained pursuant to section four hundred twenty-two of the social services law, upon a finding by the court, pursuant to paragraph e of subdivision four of such section, that such information is necessary for the court to determine whether to make or continue an appointment pursuant to this article;

(iv) reports for such person or person from the statewide computerized registry of orders of protection established and maintained pursuant to section two hundred twenty-one-a of the executive law; and

(v) related decisions in court proceedings initiated pursuant to article ten of the family court act and related warrants issued under the family court act.

2. The court shall obtain and consider records and reports specified in paragraph one of

this subdivision between the time the judge executes the order to show cause and the hearing date of the order to show cause if a guardian or guardians are proposed in the petition or, as soon as a guardian or guardians are proposed by a party to the proceeding or nominated by the person alleged to be incapacitated, during a proceeding under this article.

3. Upon consideration of all factors bearing on the best interests of the incapacitated person including consideration of all relevant factors in section seven hundred fifty-three of the correction law, the records and reports specified in paragraph one of this subdivision, and the court evaluator's report thereon, and after notifying counsel involved in the proceeding, or in the event of a self-represented party notifying such party, the court may appoint, refuse to appoint or revoke the appointment of any person as guardian pursuant to this article.

4. Where the court requests a criminal history record for a person pursuant to this section, the court shall provide the subject of the request with a copy of his or her criminal history record, if any, a reasonable time before consideration of such record under this subdivision and inform such person of his or her right to seek correction of any incorrect information contained in such record pursuant to regulations and procedures established by the division of criminal justice services.

History: Add, L 1992, ch 698, § 3, eff April 1, 1993; amd, L 1993, ch 32, §§ 8, 9, eff April 1, 1993; L 2012, ch 475, § 2, eff April 1, 2013.

§ 81.20.   Duties of guardian

(a) Duties of guardian generally.

1. a guardian shall exercise only those powers that the guardian is authorized to exercise by court order;

2. a guardian shall exercise the utmost care and diligence when acting on behalf of the incapacitated person;

3. a guardian shall exhibit the utmost degree of trust, loyalty and fidelity in relation to the incapacitated person;

4. a guardian shall file an initial and annual reports in accordance with sections 81.30 and 81.31 of this article;

5. a guardian shall visit the incapacitated person not less than four times a year or more frequently as specified in the court order;

6. a guardian who is given authority with respect to property management for the incapacitated person shall:

(i) afford the incapacitated person the greatest amount of independence and self-determination with respect to property management in light of that person's functional level, understanding and appreciation of his or her functional limitations, and personal wishes, preferences and desires with regard to managing the activities of daily living;

(ii) preserve, protect, and account for such property and financial resources faithfully;

(iii) determine whether the incapacitated person has executed a will, determine the location of any will, and the appropriate persons to be notified in the event of the death of the incapacitated person and, in the event of the death of the incapacitated person, notify those persons;

(iv) use the property and financial resources and income available therefrom to maintain and support the incapacitated person, and to maintain and support those persons dependent upon the incapacitated person;

(v) at the termination of the appointment, deliver such property to the person legally entitled to it;

(vi) file with the recording officer of the county wherein the incapacitated person is possessed of real property, an acknowledged statement to be recorded and indexed under the name of the incapacitated person identifying the real property possessed by the incapacitated person, and the tax map numbers of the property, and stating the date of adjudication of incapacity of the person regarding property management, and the name, address, and telephone number of the guardian and the guardian's surety; and

(vii) perform all other duties required by law.

7. a guardian who is given authority relating to the personal needs of the incapacitated person shall afford the incapacitated person the greatest amount of independence and self-determination with respect to personal needs in light of that person's functional level, understanding and appreciation of that person's functional limitations, and personal wishes, preferences and desires with regard to managing the activities of daily living.

History: Add, L 1992, ch 698, § 3, eff April 1, 1993.

§ 81.21. Powers of guardian; property management

(a) Consistent with the functional limitations of the incapacitated person, that person's understanding and appreciation of the harm that he or she is likely to suffer as the result of the inability to manage property and financial affairs, and that person's personal wishes, preferences, and desires with regard to managing the activities of daily living, and the least restrictive form of intervention, the court may authorize the guardian to exercise those powers necessary and sufficient to manage the property and financial affairs of the incapacitated person; to provide for the maintenance and support of the incapacitated person, and those persons depending upon the incapacitated person; to transfer a part of the incapacitated person's assets to or for the benefit of another person on the ground that the incapacitated person would have made the transfer if he or she had the capacity to act.

Transfers made pursuant to this article may be in any form that the incapacitated person could have employed if he or she had the requisite capacity, except in the form of a will or codicil.

Those powers which may be granted include, but are not limited to, the power to:

1. make gifts;

2. provide support for persons dependent upon the incapacitated person for support, whether or not the incapacitated person is legally obligated to provide that support;

3. convey or release contingent and expectant interests in property, including marital property rights and any right of survivorship incidental to joint tenancy or tenancy by the

entirety;

4. exercise or release powers held by the incapacitated person as trustee, personal representative, guardian for minor, guardian, or donee of a power of appointment;

5. enter into contracts;

6. create revocable or irrevocable trusts of property of the estate which may extend beyond the incapacity or life of the incapacitated person;

7. exercise options of the incapacitated person to purchase securities or other property;

8. exercise rights to elect options and change beneficiaries under insurance and annuity policies and to surrender the policies for their cash value;

9. exercise any right to an elective share in the estate of the incapacitated person's deceased spouse;

10. renounce or disclaim any interest by testate or intestate succession or by inter vivos transfer consistent with paragraph (d) of section 2-1.11 of the estates, powers and trusts law;

11. authorize access to or release of confidential records;

12. apply for government and private benefits;

13. marshall assets;

14. pay the funeral expenses of the incapacitated person;

15. pay such bills as may be reasonably necessary to maintain the incapacitated person;

16. invest funds of the incapacitated person as permitted by section 11-2.3 of the estates, powers and trusts law;

17. lease the primary residence for up to three years;

18. retain an accountant;

19. pay bills after the death of the incapacitated person provided the authority existed to pay such bills prior to death until a temporary administrator or executor is appointed; and

20. defend or maintain any judicial action or proceeding to a conclusion until an executor or administrator is appointed.

The guardian may also be granted any power pursuant to this subdivision granted to committees and conservators and guardians by other statutes subject to the limitations, conditions, and responsibilities of the exercise thereof unless the granting of such power is inconsistent with the provisions of this article.

(b) If the petitioner or the guardian seeks the authority to exercise a power which involves the transfer of a part of the incapacitated person's assets to or for the benefit of another person, including the petitioner or guardian, the petition shall include the following information:

1. whether any prior proceeding has at any time been commenced by any person seeking such power with respect to the property of the incapacitated person and, if so, a description

of the nature of such application and the disposition made of such application;

2. the amount and nature of the financial obligations of the incapacitated person including funds presently and prospectively required to provide for the incapacitated person's own maintenance, support, and well-being and to provide for other persons dependent upon the incapacitated person for support, whether or not the incapacitated person is legally obligated to provide that support; a copy of any court order or written agreement setting forth support obligations of the incapacitated person shall be attached to the petition if available to the petitioner or guardian;

3. the property of the incapacitated person that is the subject of the present application;

4. the proposed disposition of such property and the reasons why such disposition should be made;

5. whether the incapacitated person has sufficient capacity to make the proposed disposition; if the incapacitated person has such capacity, his or her written consent shall be attached to the petition;

6. whether the incapacitated person has previously executed a will or similar instrument and if so, the terms of the most recently executed will together with a statement as to how the terms of the will became known to the petitioner or guardian; for purposes of this article, the term "will" shall have the meaning specified in section 1-2.19 of the estates, powers and trusts law and "similar instrument" shall include a revocable or irrevocable trust:

(i) if the petitioner or guardian can, with reasonable diligence, obtain a copy, a copy of the most recently executed will or similar instrument shall be attached to the petition; in such case, the petition shall contain a statement as to how the copy was secured and the basis for the petitioner or guardian's belief that such copy is a copy of the incapacitated person's most recently executed will or similar instrument.

(ii) if the petitioner or guardian is unable to obtain a copy of the most recently executed will or similar instrument, or if the petitioner or guardian is unable to determine whether the incapacitated person has previously executed a will or similar instrument, what efforts were made by the petitioner or guardian to ascertain such information.

(iii) if a copy of the most recently executed will or similar instrument is not otherwise available, the court may direct an attorney or other person who has the original will or similar instrument in his or her possession to turn a photocopy over to the court for its examination, in camera. A photocopy of the will or similar instrument shall then be turned over by the court to the parties in such proceeding unless the court finds that to do so would be contrary to the best interests of the incapacitated person;

7. a description of any significant gifts or patterns of gifts made by the incapacitated person;

8. the names, post-office addresses and relationships of the presumptive distributees of the incapacitated person as that term is defined in subdivision forty-two of section one hundred three of the surrogate's court procedure act and of the beneficiaries under the most recent will or similar instrument executed by the incapacitated person.

(c) Notice of a petition seeking relief under this section shall be served upon:

(i) the persons entitled to notice in accordance with paragraph one of subdivision (e) of section 81.07 of this article;

(ii) if known to the petitioner or guardian, the presumptive distributees of the incapacitated person as that term is defined in subdivision forty-two of section one hundred three of the surrogate's court procedure act unless the court dispenses with such notice; and

(iii) if known to the petitioner or guardian, any person designated in the most recent will or similar instrument of the incapacitated person as beneficiary whose rights or interests would be adversely affected by the relief requested in the petition unless the court dispenses with such notice.

(d) In determining whether to approve the application, the court shall consider:

1. whether the incapacitated person has sufficient capacity to make the proposed disposition himself or herself, and, if so, whether he or she has consented to the proposed disposition;

2. whether the disability of the incapacitated person is likely to be of sufficiently short duration such that he or she should make the determination with respect to the proposed disposition when no longer disabled;

3. whether the needs of the incapacitated person and his or her dependents or other persons depending upon the incapacitated person for support can be met from the remainder of the assets of the incapacitated person after the transfer is made;

4. whether the donees or beneficiaries of the proposed disposition are the natural objects of the bounty of the incapacitated person and whether the proposed disposition is consistent with any known testamentary plan or pattern of gifts he or she has made;

5. whether the proposed disposition will produce estate, gift, income or other tax savings which will significantly benefit the incapacitated person or his or her dependents or other persons for whom the incapacitated person would be concerned; and

6. such other factors as the court deems relevant.

(e) The court may grant the application if satisfied by clear and convincing evidence of the following and shall make a record of these findings:

1. the incapacitated person lacks the requisite mental capacity to perform the act or acts for which approval has been sought and is not likely to regain such capacity within a reasonable period of time or, if the incapacitated person has the requisite capacity, that he or she consents to the proposed disposition;

2. a competent, reasonable individual in the position of the incapacitated person would be likely to perform the act or acts under the same circumstances; and

3. the incapacitated person has not manifested an intention inconsistent with the performance of the act or acts for which approval has been sought at some earlier time when he or she had the requisite capacity or, if such intention was manifested, the particular person would be likely to have changed such intention under the circumstances

existing at the time of the filing of the petition.

(f) Nothing in this article imposes any duty on the guardian to commence a special proceeding pursuant to this article seeking to transfer a part of the assets of the incapacitated person to or for the benefit of another person and the guardian shall not be liable or accountable to any person for having failed to commence a special proceeding pursuant to this article seeking to transfer a part of the assets of the incapacitated person to or for the benefit of another person.

> **History:** Add, L 1992, ch 698, § 3, eff April 1, 1993; amd, L 1993, ch 32, §§ 10, 11, eff April 1, 1993; L 2004, ch 438, § 16, eff Dec 13, 2004; L 2010, ch 27, § 3, eff Jan 1, 2011; L 2015, ch 243, § 1, eff Sept 25, 2015.

§ 81.22. Powers of guardian; personal needs

(a) Consistent with the functional limitations of the incapacitated person, that person's understanding and appreciation of the harm that he or she is likely to suffer as the result of the inability to provide for personal needs, and that person's personal wishes, preferences, and desires with regard to managing the activities of daily living, and the least restrictive form of intervention, the court may grant to the guardian powers necessary and sufficient to provide for the personal needs of the incapacitated person. Those powers which may be granted include, but are not limited to, the power to:

1. determine who shall provide personal care or assistance;

2. make decisions regarding social environment and other social aspects of the life of the incapacitated person;

3. determine whether the incapacitated person should travel;

4. determine whether the incapacitated person should possess a license to drive;

5. authorize access to or release of confidential records;

6. make decisions regarding education;

7. apply for government and private benefits;

8. (i) for decisions in hospitals as defined by subdivision eighteen of section twenty-nine hundred ninety-four-a of the public health law, act as the patient's surrogate pursuant to and subject to article twenty-nine-CC of the public health law, and (ii) in all other circumstances, to consent to or refuse generally accepted routine or major medical or dental treatment, subject to the decision-making standard in subdivision four of section twenty-nine hundred ninety-four-d of the public health law;

9. choose the place of abode; the choice of abode must be consistent with the findings under section 81.15 of this article, the existence of and availability of family, friends and social services in the community, the care, comfort and maintenance, and where appropriate, rehabilitation of the incapacitated person, the needs of those with whom the incapacitated person resides; placement of the incapacitated person in a nursing home or residential care facility as those terms are defined in section two thousand eight hundred one of the public health law, or other similar facility shall not be authorized without the consent of the incapacitated person so long as it is reasonable under the circumstances to maintain the incapacitated person in the community, preferably in the home of the incapacitated person.

(b) No guardian may:

1. consent to the voluntary formal or informal admission of the incapacitated person to a mental hygiene facility under article nine or fifteen of this chapter or to a chemical dependence facility under article twenty-two of this chapter;

2. revoke any appointment or delegation made by the incapacitated person pursuant to sections 5-1501, 5-1601 and 5-1602 of the general obligations law, sections two thousand nine hundred sixty-five and two thousand nine hundred eighty-one of the public health law, or any living will.

> **History:** Add, L 1992, ch 698, § 3, eff April 1, 1993; amd, L 1993, ch 32, § 12, eff April 1, 1993; L 1999, ch 558, § 37, eff Oct 5, 1999, provided, however, that nothing contained in this act shall be deemed to affect the application, qualification, expiration, reversion or repeal of any provision of law amended by any section of this act and the provisions of this act shall be applied or qualified or shall expire or revert or be deemed repealed in the same manner, to the same extent and on the same date as the case may be as otherwise provided by law; L 2004, ch 438, § 17, eff Dec 13, 2004; L 2010, ch 8, § 25, eff June 1, 2010.

§ 81.23. Provisional remedies

(a) Temporary guardian.

1. At the commencement of the proceeding or at any subsequent stage of the proceeding prior to the appointment of a guardian, the court may, upon showing of danger in the reasonably foreseeable future to the health and well being of the alleged incapacitated person, or danger of waste, misappropriation, or loss of the property of the alleged incapacitated person, appoint a temporary guardian for a period not to extend beyond the date of the issuance of the commission to a guardian appointed pursuant to this article. The powers and duties of the temporary guardian shall be specifically enumerated in the order of appointment and are limited in the same manner as are the powers of a guardian appointed pursuant to this article. Prior to the expiration of the term of appointment, the temporary guardian shall report to the court all actions taken pursuant to the order appointment. The court may approve a reasonable compensation for the temporary guardian; however, if the court finds that the temporary guardian has failed to discharge his or her duties satisfactorily in any respect, the court may deny or reduce the amount of compensation or remove the temporary guardian.

2. Notice of the appointment of the temporary guardian shall be given to the person alleged to be incapacitated and to any person having custody or control over the person or property of the person alleged to be incapacitated in such manner as the court may prescribe.

3. The authority and responsibility of a temporary guardian begins upon the issuance of the commission of temporary guardianship.

4. The court may require the temporary guardian to file a bond in accordance with section 81.25 of this article.

(b) Injunction and temporary restraining order.

1. The court may, at any time prior to or after the appointment of a guardian or at the time of the appointment of a guardian with or without security, enjoin any person, other than the incapacitated person or the person alleged to be incapacitated from selling, assigning, or from disposing of property or confessing judgment which may become a lien

on property or receiving or arranging for another person to receive property from the incapacitated person or the person alleged to be incapacitated or doing or suffering to be done any act or omission endangering the health, safety or welfare of the incapacitated person or the person alleged to be incapacitated when an application under this article seeks such an injunction and it satisfactorily appears from the application, affidavits, and other proofs that a person has done, has suffered to be done or omitted to do, or threatens to do or is about to do an act that endangers the health, safety or welfare of the incapacitated person or the person alleged to be incapacitated or has acquired or is about to acquire any property from the incapacitated person or person alleged to be incapacitated during the time of that person's incapacity or alleged incapacity without adequate consideration. Such order shall be made upon an order to show cause or upon the initiative of the court and may, upon the application for the appointment of a guardian, in the discretion of the court, be continued for ten days after the appointment of a guardian. Notice of any injunction shall be given to any person enjoined, to the incapacitated person or the person alleged to be incapacitated, and to any person having custody or control over the person or property of the incapacitated person or the person alleged to be incapacitated in such manner as the court may prescribe.

2. A temporary restraining order may be granted with or without security when an application seeks an injunction under paragraph one of this subdivision and where the court is satisfied that in the absence of such restraining order, the property of the incapacitated person or person alleged to be incapacitated would be dissipated to that person's detriment or that the health, safety or welfare of the incapacitated person or the person alleged to be incapacitated would be endangered. Notice of the temporary restraining order shall be given to any person restrained, to the incapacitated person or the person alleged to be incapacitated, and to any person having custody or control over the person or property of the incapacitated person or person alleged to be incapacitated in such manner as the court may prescribe. Such temporary restraining order shall neither be vacated nor modified except upon notice to the petitioner and to each person required to receive notice of the petition pursuant to paragraph one of subdivision (g) of section 81.07 of this article.

3. When the court is satisfied that the interest of the incapacitated person or person alleged to be incapacitated would be appropriately served, the court may provide in a temporary restraining order that such temporary restraining order shall have the effect of:

(i) a restraining notice when served in a manner and upon such persons as the court in its discretion shall deem appropriate;

(ii) conferring information subpoena power upon the attorney for the petitioner when the court in its discretion shall deem appropriate.

4. Where such a temporary restraining order provides for a restraining notice a person having custody or control over the person or property of the incapacitated person or the person alleged to be incapacitated is forbidden to make or suffer any sale, assignment, transfer or interference with any property of the incapacitated person or the person alleged to be incapacitated except pursuant to the order of the court.

5. Where such a temporary restraining order provides the petitioner's attorney with information subpoena power, service of a copy of the order together with an information subpoena shall require any person so subpoenaed to provide petitioner's attorney with any

information concerning the financial affairs of the incapacitated person or the person alleged to be incapacitated.

History: Add, L 1992, ch 698, § 3, eff April 1, 1993; amd, L 2004, ch 438, § 18, eff Dec 13, 2004.

§ 81.24. Notice of pendency

The petitioner shall, prior to judgment, file a notice of pendency if real property or any interest therein is or may be affected by the proceeding.

History: Add, L 1992, ch 698, § 3, eff April 1, 1993.

§ 81.25. Filing of bond by guardian

(a) Before the guardian, or special guardian appointed under this article, or a trustee of a trust created pursuant to this article, enters upon the execution of his or her duties, the court may require or dispense with the filing of a bond.

(b) The court may require or dispense with the filing of a bond by the temporary guardian. If the temporary guardian is required to file a bond, such bond must be filed within ten days after the issuance of the temporary guardian's commission.

(c) If the value of the estate of the person for whom a guardian, special guardian, temporary guardian, or trustee is appointed is so great or for other sufficient reason the court deems it inexpedient to require security in the full amount prescribed by law it may direct that all or part of the assets of the estate be delivered subject to the further order of the court to the county treasurer, or other proper fiscal officer, the clerk of the court or a trust company, bank or safe deposit company or otherwise restrict the authority of the guardian or trustee. The court may thereupon fix the amount of the bond taking into consideration the value of the remainder only of the estate. The assets so deposited shall not be withdrawn from the custody of the depositary and no person other than the proper fiscal officer of such county or depository shall receive or collect any principal or income or other benefits derived from such assets without order of the court.

(d) Notwithstanding any other provision of this section, any community guardian program operating pursuant to the provisions of title three of article nine-B of the social services law, appointed as guardian pursuant to subdivision (a) of section 81.19 of this article, may file with the clerk of the court before the thirty-first day of January of each year, a consolidated undertaking up to the amount of one million five hundred thousand dollars, in lieu of filing individual undertakings for each incapacitated person for whom it serves as guardian, as required by subdivision (a) of this section. To the extent of the aggregate value of such consolidated undertaking, the community guardian program will certify to the clerk of the court faithful discharge of the trust imposed upon it, obey all directions of the court in regard to the trust, and make and render a true account of all properties received by it and the application thereof and of its acts in the administration of its trust whenever so required to do by the court. At such time as the aggregate amount of the individual bonds, fixed by the court pursuant to subdivision (a) of this section for persons for whom the community guardian program is appointed guardian, shall exceed the consolidated bond filed by such program, the program shall before entering upon the execution of its duties, file with the clerk of the court individual undertakings, in the amounts fixed by the court, that it will faithfully discharge the trust imposed upon it.

(e) If the court requires the filing of a bond, the guardian or special or temporary guardian, or trustee, appointed under this article shall file with the clerk of the court by which such guardian was appointed a bond that he or she will faithfully discharge the powers granted by the court to the guardian or special or temporary guardian, or trustee, obey all directions of the court in regard to the powers, and make and render a true account of all properties received by him or her and the application thereof and a true report of his or her acts in the administration of his or her powers, whenever so required to do by the court. The amount of the bond shall be fixed by the court. If the guardian, special or temporary guardian, or trustee, receives after-acquired property not covered by the bond, such guardian, special or temporary guardian, or trustee, shall immediately have such acquisition approved by the court and file a further bond.

> **History:** Add, L 1992, ch 698, § 3, eff April 1, 1993; amd, L 2004, ch 438, § 19, eff Dec 13, 2004.

§ 81.26. Designation of clerk to receive process

No commission shall issue nor shall any order which in itself constitutes a commission become effective until an instrument executed and acknowledged by the guardian has been filed with the clerk of the court designating the clerk and the clerk's successor in office as a person on whom service of any process may be made in like manner and with like effect as if it were served personally upon the guardian whenever the guardian cannot, with due diligence, be served within the state.

> **History:** Add, L 1992, ch 698, § 3, eff April 1, 1993.

§ 81.27. Commission to guardian

Within five days after the guardian has filed a designation under section 81.26 of this article, and has filed a bond in accordance with the provisions of section 81.25 of this article unless the court has waived the filing of the bond or unless the guardian's appointment is pursuant to section 81.23 of this article, the clerk of the court shall issue a commission which shall state:

    1. the title of the proceeding and the name, address, and telephone number of the incapacitated person; and

    2. the name, address, and telephone number of the guardian and the specific powers of such guardian; and

    3. the date when the appointment of the guardian was ordered by the court; and

    4. the date on which the appointment terminates if one has been ordered by the court.

> **History:** Add, L 1992, ch 698, § 3, eff April 1, 1993.

§ 81.28. Compensation of guardian

(a) The court shall establish, and may from time to time modify, a plan for the reasonable compensation of the guardian or guardians. The plan for compensation of such guardian must take into account the specific authority of the guardian or guardians to provide for the personal needs and/or property management for the incapacitated person, and the services provided to the incapacitated person by such guardian.

(b) If the court finds that the guardian has failed to discharge his or her duties satisfactorily in any respect, the court may deny or reduce the compensation which would otherwise be allowed.

History: Add, L 1992, ch 698, § 3, eff April 1, 1993; amd, L 2004, ch 438, § 20, eff Dec 13, 2004.

§ 81.29. Effect of the appointment on the incapacitated person

(a) An incapacitated person for whom a guardian has been appointed retains all powers and rights except those powers and rights which the guardian is granted.

(b) Subject to subdivision (a) of this section, the appointment of a guardian shall not be conclusive evidence that the person lacks capacity for any other purpose, including the capacity to dispose of property by will.

(c) The title to all property of the incapacitated person shall be in such person and not in the guardian. The property shall be subject to the possession of the guardian and to the control of the court for the purposes of administration, sale or other disposition only to the extent directed by the court order appointing the guardian.

(d) If the court determines that the person is incapacitated and appoints a guardian, the court may modify, amend, or revoke any previously executed appointment, power, or delegation under section 5-1501, 5-1505, or 5-1506 of the general obligations law or section two thousand nine hundred sixty-five of the public health law, or section two thousand nine hundred eighty-one of the public health law notwithstanding section two thousand nine hundred ninety-two of the public health law, or any contract, conveyance, or disposition during lifetime or to take effect upon death, made by the incapacitated person prior to the appointment of the guardian if the court finds that the previously executed appointment, power, delegation, contract, conveyance, or disposition during lifetime or to take effect upon death, was made while the person was incapacitated or if the court determines that there has been a breach of fiduciary duty by the previously appointed agent. In such event, the court shall require that the agent account to the guardian. The court shall not, however, invalidate or revoke a will or a codicil of an incapacitated person during the lifetime of such person.

History: Add, L 1992, ch 698, § 3, eff April 1, 1993; amd, L 2004, ch 438, § 21, eff Dec 13, 2004; L 2008, ch 176, § 1, eff July 7, 2008; L 2010, ch 8, § 26, eff June 1, 2010.

§ 81.30. Initial report

(a) No later than ninety days after the issuance of the commission to the guardian, the guardian shall file with the court that appointed the guardian a report in a form prescribed by the court stating what steps the guardian has taken to fulfill his or her responsibilities. Proof of completion of the guardian education requirements under section 81.39 of this article must be filed with the initial report.

(b) To the extent that the guardian has been granted powers with respect to property management, the initial report shall contain a verified and complete inventory of the property and financial resources over which the guardian has control, the location of any will executed by the incapacitated person, the guardian's plan, consistent with the court's order of appointment, for the management of such property and financial resources, and any need for any change in the powers authorized by the court.

(c) To the extent that the guardian has been granted powers regarding personal needs, the initial report shall contain a report of the guardian's personal visits with the incapacitated person, and the steps the guardian has taken, consistent with the court's order, to provide for the personal needs of that person, the guardian's plan, consistent with the court's order of appointment, for providing for the personal needs of the incapacitated person, a copy of any directives in accordance with sections two thousand nine hundred sixty-five and two thousand nine hundred eighty-one of the public health law, any living will, and any other advance directive, and any necessary change in the powers authorized by the court. The plan for providing for the personal needs of the incapacitated person shall include the following information:

1. the medical, dental, mental health, or related services that are to be provided for the welfare of the incapacitated person;

2. the social and personal services that are to be provided for the welfare of the incapacitated person;

3. any physical, dental, and mental health examinations necessary to determine the medical, dental, and mental health treatment needs; and

4. the application of health and accident insurance and any other private or government benefits to which the incapacitated person may be entitled to meet any part of the costs of medical, dental, mental health, or related services provided to the incapacitated person.

(d) If the initial report sets forth any reasons for a change in the powers authorized by the court, the guardian shall make an application within ten days of the filing of the report on notice to the persons entitled to such notice in accordance with paragraph one of subdivision (d) of section 81.07 of this article for such relief. If the initial report sets forth any reasons for a change in the powers authorized by the court and the guardian fails to act under this subdivision, any person entitled to commence a proceeding under this article may petition the court for a change in such powers on notice to the guardian and the persons entitled to such notice in accordance with paragraph one of subdivision (d) of section 81.07 of this article for such relief.

(e) The guardian shall send a copy of the initial report to the incapacitated person by mail unless the court orders otherwise pursuant to paragraph seven of subdivision (b) and paragraph nine of subdivision (c) of section 81.15 of this article.

(f) The guardian shall send a copy of the initial report to the court evaluator and counsel for the incapacitated person at the time of the guardianship proceeding unless the court orders otherwise pursuant to paragraph seven of subdivision (b) and paragraph nine of subdivision (c) of section 81.15 of this article.

(g) The guardian shall send a copy of the initial report to the court examiner.

(h) If the incapacitated person resides in a facility, the guardian shall send a duplicate of such report to the chief executive officer of that facility.

(i) If the incapacitated person resides in a mental hygiene facility, the guardian shall send a duplicate of such report to the mental hygiene legal service of the judicial department in which the residence is located.

> **History:** Add, L 1992, ch 698, § 3, eff April 1, 1993; amd, L 2004, ch 438, § 22, eff Dec 13, 2004.

§ 81.31. Annual report

(a) Filing of annual report. Every guardian shall file a report annually in the month of May, or at any other time upon motion or order of the court.

(b) The report shall be in a form prescribed by the court and shall include the following information:

1. the present address and telephone number of the guardian.

2. the present address, and telephone number of the incapacitated person; if the place of residence of the incapacitated person is not his or her personal home, the name, address, and telephone number of the facility or place at which the person resides and the name of the chief executive officer of the facility or person otherwise responsible for the person's care.

3. any major changes in the physical or mental condition of the incapacitated person and any substantial change in medication.

4. the date that the incapacitated person was last examined or otherwise seen by a physician and the purpose of that visit.

5. a statement by a physician, psychologist, nurse clinician, or social worker, or other person that has evaluated or examined the incapacitated person within the three months prior to the filing of the report regarding an evaluation of the incapacitated person's condition and the current functional level of the incapacitated person.

6. to the extent the guardian is charged with providing for the personal needs of the incapacitated person:

(i) a statement of whether the current residential setting is best suited to the current needs of the incapacitated person;

(ii) a resume of any professional medical treatment given to the ward in the preceding year;

(iii) the plan for medical, dental, and mental health treatment, and related services in the coming year;

(iv) information concerning the social condition of the incapacitated person, including: the social and personal services currently utilized by the incapacitated person; the social skills of the incapacitated person; and the social needs of the incapacitated person.

7. to the extent the guardian is charged with property management, information required by the provisions of the surrogate's court procedure act prescribing the form of papers to be filed upon the annual accounting of a general guardian of an infant's property.

8. where the guardian has used or employed the services of the incapacitated person or where moneys have been earned by or received on behalf of such incapacitated person an accounting of any moneys earned or derived from such services.

9. a resume of any other activities performed by the guardian on behalf of the incapacitated person.

10. facts indicating the need to terminate the appointment of the guardian, or for any alteration in the powers of the guardian and what specific authority is requested or what specific authority of the guardian will be affected.

11. any other information which the guardian may be required to file by the order of

appointment.

(c) The guardian shall send a copy of the annual report to the incapacitated person by mail unless the court orders otherwise pursuant to paragraph seven of subdivision (b) and paragraph nine of subdivision (c) of section 81.15 of this article, shall send a copy of the annual report to the court examiner, and shall file a copy of the annual report as provided herein. If the incapacitated person resides in a facility, the guardian shall send a duplicate of such report to the chief executive officer of that facility. If the incapacitated person resides in a mental hygiene facility, the guardian shall send a duplicate of such report to the mental hygiene legal service of the judicial department in which the residence is located. If mental hygiene legal service was appointed as court evaluator or as counsel for the incapacitated person at the time of the guardianship proceeding, the guardian shall send a duplicate of such report to the mental hygiene legal service of the judicial department where venue of the guardianship proceeding was located if so ordered by the court.

(d) The report shall be filed in the office of the clerk of the court which appointed the guardian.

(e) If the annual report sets forth any reasons for a change in the powers authorized by the court, the guardian shall make an application within ten days of the filing of the report on notice to the persons entitled to such notice in accordance with paragraph three of subdivision (c) of section 81.16 of this article for such relief. If the annual report sets forth any reasons for a change in the powers authorized by the court, and the guardian fails to act in accordance with this subdivision, any person entitled to commence a proceeding under this article may petition the court for a change in such powers on notice to the guardian and the persons entitled to such notice in accordance with paragraph three of subdivision (c) of section 81.16 of this article for such relief.

History: Add, L 1992, ch 698, § 3, eff April 1, 1993; amd, L 2004, ch 438, § 23, eff Dec 13, 2004.

§ 81.32.   Examination of initial and annual reports

(a) Examination of reports generally.

1. Initial report. Within thirty days of the filing of the initial report, the initial report filed by a guardian under this article shall be examined.

2. Annual examination. Within thirty days after the filing of the annual report of the preceding year, the annual reports filed by guardians under this article shall be examined to determine the condition and care of the incapacitated person, the finances of the incapacitated person, and the manner in which the guardian has carried out his or her duties and exercised his or her powers.

(b) Examiners. The presiding justice of the appellate division in each department, or a justice of the supreme court or a special referee designated by a majority of the justices of the appellate division in each department at the request of the presiding justice, shall examine, or cause to be examined by persons designated by the presiding justice or the justices as examiners, all such reports.

(c) Failure to report.

1. If a guardian fails to file his or her initial or annual report, the person authorized to examine the report shall demand that the guardian file the report within fifteen days after

the service of the demand upon him or her. A copy of the demand shall be served upon the guardian or his or her resident agent by certified mail.

2. Upon failure to comply with such demand, the court, may upon the motion of the court examiner, enter an order requiring compliance with the demand and may deny or reduce the amount of the compensation of the guardian, or remove the guardian pursuant to section 81.35 of this article absent a showing that the guardian has acted in good faith.

(d) Incomplete report.

1. If the person authorized to examine the report is of the opinion that a more complete or satisfactory report should be filed, the person authorized to examine the report shall demand that the guardian file a revised report or proof of any item in the report. A copy of the demand shall be served upon the guardian or his or her resident agent by certified mail.

2. Upon failure to comply with such demand, the court, may upon the motion of the court examiner, enter an order requiring compliance with the demand and may deny or reduce the amount of the compensation of the guardian, or remove the guardian pursuant to section 81.35 of this article absent a showing that the guardian has acted in good faith.

(e) Duty of examiners. The person examining the report may examine the guardian and other witnesses under oath and reduce their testimony to writing. The person examining the report, on five days notice to the guardian, shall file a report in the form and manner prescribed by the order appointing the examiner.

(f) Expenses of examination. The expenses of the examination shall be payable out of the estate of the incapacitated person examined if the estate amounts to five thousand dollars or more, or, if the estate amounts to less than this sum, by the county treasurer of the county or, within the city of New York by the comptroller of the city of New York, out of any court funds in his or her hands.

> **History:** Add, L 1992, ch 698, § 3, eff April 1, 1993; amd, L 1993, ch 32, §§ 13–15, eff April 1, 1993.

§ 81.33. Intermediate and final report

(a) A guardian may move in the court of his or her appointment for an order permitting him or her to render an intermediate report to the date of the filing thereof in a form prescribed by the court which shall include the same information as is required under section 81.31 of this article provided, however, that if the incapacitated person has died the report need not include information otherwise required in paragraphs five and six of subdivision (b) of section 81.31 of this article. The court may order the report to be filed with the clerk of the court on or before a fixed date.

(b) When a guardian dies or is removed, suspended, discharged pursuant to the provisions of this article, or allowed to resign, the court shall order a final report in a form prescribed by the court which shall include the same information as is required under section 81.31 of this article provided, however, that if the incapacitated person has died the report need not include information otherwise required in paragraphs five and six of subdivision (b) of section 81.31 of this article. When such a report has been made in the course of a proceeding to remove a guardian, the court may dispense with a further report.

(c) Notice of the filing of a report under this section shall be served upon the persons entitled to notice pursuant to paragraph three of subdivision (c) of section 81.16 of this article. If the incapacitated person is deceased, notice shall also be served upon his or her executor or administrator, if any.

(d) The court may appoint counsel for the incapacitated person, if living, for the protection of such person's rights and interests with regard to such report. The court may appoint a referee to hear the matter and report to the court.

(e) Upon the motion for a confirmation of the report of the referee, or if the report is made before the court, upon the court's determination, the report shall be judicially approved and filed. The compensation of the referee and of counsel shall be fixed by the court and shall be payable out of the estate of the incapacitated person unless it is determined that the incapacitated person is indigent.

(f) If the incapacitated person resides in a facility, a copy of a report under this section shall be served upon the chief executive officer in charge of that facility and upon the mental hygiene legal service of the judicial department in which the residence is located.

> **History:** Add, L 1992, ch 698, § 3, eff April 1, 1993; amd, L 2004, ch 438, § 24, eff Dec 13, 2004.

§ 81.34. Decree on filing instruments approving accounts

(a) The guardian or the personal representative of the guardian may present to the court a petition showing the names and addresses of all persons entitled to receive notice pursuant to paragraph three of subdivision (c) of section 81.16 of this article and the personal representative of the estate showing that, to the extent the guardian is responsible for the property of the incapacitated person, all taxes have been paid or that no taxes are due and that the petitioner has fully reported and has made full disclosure in writing of all the guardian's actions affecting the property of the incapacitated person to all persons interested and seeking a decree releasing and discharging the petitioner. Upon the death of the incapacitated person, the guardian is authorized to pay the funeral expenses of the incapacitated person and, in the absence of a duly appointed personal representative of the estate, pay estimated estate and income tax charges, as well as other charges of emergent nature.

(b) The petitioner shall also show that the incapacitated person has died or that the guardian has died, or has been removed, suspended, or discharged pursuant to the provisions of this article, or allowed to resign.

(c) The petitioner shall also file with the petition acknowledged instruments executed by all persons interested or in the case of an infant, or incapacitated person whose claim has been paid, by the guardian, or guardian receiving payment, approving the report of the petitioner and releasing and discharging the petitioner.

(d) The court may thereupon make a decree releasing and discharging the petitioner and the sureties on his or her bond, if any, from any further liability to the persons interested.

> **History:** Add, L 1992, ch 698, § 3, eff April 1, 1993; amd, L 2008, ch 175, § 1, eff Jan 3, 2009, however, that effective immediately, the addition, amendment and/or repeal of any rule or regulation necessary for the implementation of this act on its effective date are authorized and directed to be made and completed on or before such effective date.

§ 81.35. Removal of guardian

Upon motion, the court appointing a guardian may remove such guardian when the guardian fails to comply with an order, is guilty of misconduct, or for any other cause which to the court shall appear just. Notice of motion shall be served on the guardian and persons entitled to receive notice pursuant to paragraph three of subdivision (c) of section 81.16 of this article. The motion may be made by the person examining initial and annual reports pursuant to section 81.32 of this article, or by any person entitled to commence a proceeding under this article, including the incapacitated person. The court may fix the compensation of any attorney or person prosecuting the motion. It may compel the guardian to pay personally the costs of the motion if granted.

History: Add, L 1992, ch 698, § 3, eff April 1, 1993.

§ 81.36.   Discharge or modification of powers of guardian

(a) The court appointing the guardian shall discharge such guardian, or modify the powers of the guardian where appropriate, if it appears to the satisfaction of the court that:

1. the incapacitated person has become able to exercise some or all of the powers necessary to provide for personal needs or property management which the guardian is authorized to exercise;

2. the incapacitated person has become unable to exercise powers necessary to provide for personal needs or property management which the guardian is not authorized to exercise;

3. the incapacitated person has died; or

4. for some other reason, the appointment of the guardian is no longer necessary for the incapacitated person, or the powers of the guardian should be modified based upon changes in the circumstances of the incapacitated person.

(b) The application for relief under this section may be made by the guardian, the incapacitated person, or any person entitled to commence a proceeding under this article.

(c) There shall be a hearing on notice to the persons entitled to notice pursuant to paragraph three of subdivision (c) of section 81.16 of this article. The court may for good cause shown dispense with the hearing provided that an order of modification increasing the powers of the guardian shall set forth the factual basis for dispensing with the hearing. If the incapacitated person or his or her counsel raises an issue of fact as to the ability of the incapacitated person to provide for his or her personal needs or property management and demands a jury trial of such issue, the court shall order a trial by jury thereof.

(d) To the extent that relief sought under this section would terminate the guardianship or restore certain powers to the incapacitated person, the burden of proof shall be on the person objecting to such relief. To the extent that relief sought under this section would further limit the powers of the incapacitated person, the burden shall be on the person seeking such relief.

(e) If the guardian is discharged because the incapacitated person becomes fully able to care for his or her property, the court shall order that there be restored to such person the property remaining in the hands of the guardian. If the incapacitated person dies, the guardian shall provide for such person's burial or other disposition the cost of which shall be borne by the estate of the incapacitated person.

History: Add, L 1992, ch 698, § 3, eff April 1, 1993; amd, L 2004, ch 438, §§ 25, 26, eff Dec 13, 2004.

§ 81.37.   Resignation or suspension of powers of guardian

(a) The court appointing a guardian may allow the guardian to resign or may suspend the powers of the guardian.

(b) Where a guardian is engaged in war service as defined in section seven hundred seventeen of the surrogate's court procedure act, the court, upon motion by the guardian or any other person and upon such notice as the court may direct, may suspend the powers of the guardian until further order of the court. If the suspension will leave no other person acting as guardian, the motion shall seek the appointment of a successor. When the suspended guardian becomes able to serve, he or she may be reinstated by the court upon motion and such notice as the court may direct. If the suspended guardian is reinstated, the court shall thereupon discharge his or her successor, who may be required to account, and make any other order as justice requires.

> **History:** Add, L 1992, ch 698, § 3, eff April 1, 1993.

§ 81.38.   Vacancy in office

(a) Interim guardian. A vacancy created by the death, removal, discharge, resignation, or suspension of a guardian shall be filled by the court. Upon the application of any person entitled to commence a proceeding under this article, the court shall appoint an interim guardian who shall serve for a period of ninety days or until a final accounting is filed and a successor guardian is appointed by the court. The powers and duties of the interim guardian shall be specifically enumerated in the order of appointment. The court may require service of the order to show cause seeking the appointment of an interim guardian on any persons it deems appropriate.

(b) Standby guardian. At the time of the appointment of the guardian, the court may in its discretion appoint a standby guardian to act in the event that the guardian shall resign, die, be removed, discharged, suspended, or become incapacitated. The court may also appoint an alternate and/or successive alternates to the standby guardian, to act if the standby guardian shall resign, die, be removed, discharged, suspended, or become incapacitated. Such standby guardian, or the alternate in the event of the standby guardian's resignation, death, removal, discharge, suspension or adjudication of incapacity, shall without further proceedings be empowered to immediately assume the duties of office immediately upon resignation, death, removal, discharge, suspension or adjudication of incapacity, of the guardian or the standby guardian as set forth in the order of appointment, subject only to the confirmation of appointment by the court sixty days following the assumption of the duties of the office. Before confirming the appointment of a standby guardian, the court may conduct a hearing in accordance with the provisions set forth in section 81.11 of this article upon petition of any person entitled to commence a proceeding under this article.

> **History:** Add, L 1992, ch 698, § 3, eff April 1, 1993.

§ 81.39.   Guardian education requirements

(a) Each incapacitated person is entitled to a guardian whom the court finds to be sufficiently capable of performing the duties and exercising the powers of a guardian necessary to protect the incapacitated person.

(b) Each person appointed by the court to be a guardian must complete a training program approved by the chief administrator which covers:

1. the legal duties and responsibilities of the guardian;

2. the rights of the incapacitated person;

3. the available resources to aid the incapacitated person;

4. an orientation to medical terminology, particularly that related to the diagnostic and assessment procedures used to characterize the extent and reversibility of any impairment;

5. the preparation of annual reports, including financial accounting for the property and financial resources of the incapacitated person.

(c) The court may, in its discretion, waive some or all of the requirements of this section or impose additional requirements. In doing so, the court shall consider the experience and education of the guardian with respect to the training requirements of this section, the duties and powers assigned to the guardian, and the needs of the incapacitated person.

History: Add, L 1992, ch 698, § 3, eff April 1, 1993.

§ 81.40.   Court evaluator education requirements

(a) Each incapacitated person is entitled to a court evaluator whom the court finds to be sufficiently capable of performing the duties of a court evaluator necessary to ensure that all the relevant information regarding a petition for the appointment of a guardian comes before the court and to assist the court in reaching a decision regarding the appointment of a guardian.

(b) Each person appointed by the court to be an evaluator must complete a training program approved by the chief administrator which covers:

1. the legal duties and responsibilities of the court evaluator;

2. the rights of the incapacitated person with emphasis on the due process rights to aid the court evaluator in determining his or her recommendation regarding the appointment of counsel and the conduct of the hearing;

3. the available resources to aid the incapacitated person;

4. an orientation to medical terminology, particularly that related to the diagnostic and assessment procedures used to characterize the extent and reversibility of any impairment;

5. entitlements;

6. psychological and social concerns relating to the disabled and frail older adults.

(c) The court may, in its discretion, waive some or all of the requirements of this section or impose additional requirements. In doing so, the court shall consider the experience and education of the court evaluator with respect to the training requirements of this section.

History: Add, L 1992, ch 698, § 3, eff April 1, 1993.

§ 81.41.   Court examiner education requirements

(a) Each incapacitated person is entitled to a thorough examination of all reports required to be filed by the guardian.

(b) Each person appointed pursuant to section 81.32 of this article must complete a training program approved by the chief administrator which covers the legal duties and responsibilities of the examiner and of guardians.

(c) The court may, in its discretion, waive some or all of the requirements of this section or impose additional requirements. In so doing, the court shall consider the experience and education of the court examiner with respect to the training requirements of this section.

History: Add, L 1992, ch 698, § 3, eff April 1, 1993.

§ 81.42.   Compliance

(a) A motion to dismiss based on the alleged failure to comply with any of the provisions of this article, other than subparagraph (i) of paragraph one of subdivision (d) of section 81.07 of this article, must be determined without regard to technical mistakes, deficiencies, and omissions that do not result in actual prejudice that affects the integrity of the proceeding.

(b) A judgment or order made pursuant to this article, unless reversed on appeal, releases the guardian and the sureties from all claims of the incapacitated person and/or any person affected thereby based on any act or omission directly authorized, approved or confirmed in the judgment or order. This section does not apply where the judgment or order is obtained by fraud or conspiracy or by misrepresentation contained in the notice, petition, account, or in the judgment or order as to any material fact. For purposes of this subdivision, misrepresentation of a material fact includes but is not limited to the omission of a material fact.

History: Add, L 1992, ch 698, § 3, eff April 1, 1993.

§ 81.43.   Proceedings to discover property withheld

(a) To the extent that it is consistent with the authority otherwise granted by the court a guardian may commence a proceeding in the court which appointed the guardian to discover property withheld. The petition shall contain knowledge, or information and belief of any facts tending to show that any interest in real property or money or other personal property, or the proceeds or value thereof, which should be delivered and paid to the guardian, is in the possession, under the control, or within the knowledge or information of respondent who withholds the same from the guardian, whether such possession or control was obtained before or after the appointment of the guardian, or that the respondent refuses to disclose knowledge or information which such person may have concerning the same or which will aid the guardian in making discovery of such property. The petition shall request that respondent be ordered to attend an inquiry and be examined accordingly and deliver property of the incapacitated person if it is within his or her control. The petition may be accompanied by an affidavit or other written evidence, tending to support the allegations thereof. If the court is satisfied on the papers so presented that there are reasonable grounds for the inquiry, it must make an order accordingly, which may be returnable forthwith, or at a future time fixed by the court, and may be served at any time before the hearing. If it shall appear from the petition or from the answer interposed thereto, or in the course of the inquiry made pursuant to the order that a person other than the respondent in the proceeding claims an interest in the property or the proceeds or the value thereof, the court may by the original order or by supplemental order, direct such additional party to attend and be examined in the proceeding in respect of his or her adverse claim, and deliver the property if in his or her control or the proceeds or value thereof. Service of such an order must be made by delivery of a certified copy thereof to the person or persons named therein and the payment or tender, to each of the sum required by law to be paid or tendered to a witness who is subpoenaed to attend a trial in such court.

(b) If the person directed to appear submits an answer denying any knowledge concerning or the possession of any property which belongs to the incapacitated person or should be delivered to the guardian, or shall make default in answer, he or she shall be sworn to answer truly all questions put to him or her regarding the inquiry requested in the petition. Any claim of title to or right to the possession of any property of the incapacitated person must be made by verified answer in writing. If such answer is interposed, the issues raised thereby shall be tried according to the usual practice of the court as a litigated issue but the interposition of such answer shall not limit the right of the guardian to proceed with the inquiry in respect of property not so claimed by the verified answer. If possession of the property is denied, proof on that issue may be presented to the court by either party. The court may in an appropriate case make interim decrees directing the delivery of property not claimed by verified answer and may continue the proceeding for determination of any litigated issue. If it appears that the guardian is entitled to the possession of the property, the decree shall direct delivery thereof to the guardian or if the property shall have been diverted or disposed of, the decree may direct payment of the proceeds or the value of such property or may impress a trust upon said proceeds or make any determination which a court of equity might decree in following trust property funds. In any case in which a verified answer is served and the court after a trial or hearing determines the issue, the court may in its discretion award costs not exceeding fifty dollars and disbursements to be paid by the unsuccessful party.

History: Formerly added as § 81.44, L 1993, ch 32, § 16, eff April 1, 1993; renumbered § 81.43, L 2004, ch 438, § 27, eff Dec 13, 2004.

§ 81.44. Proceedings upon the death of an incapacitated person.

(a) When used in this section:

1. "Statement of death" means a statement, in writing and acknowledged, containing the caption and index number of the guardianship proceeding, and the name and address of the last residence of the deceased incapacitated person, the date and place of death, and the names and last known addresses of all persons entitled to notice of further guardianship proceedings pursuant to paragraph three of subdivision (c) of section 81.16 of this article including the nominated and/or appointed personal representative, if any, of the deceased incapacitated person's estate.

2. "Personal representative" means a fiduciary as defined by subdivision twenty-one of section 103 of the surrogate's court procedure act to whom letters have been issued and who is authorized to marshal the assets of the decedent's estate.

3. "Public administrator" means a public administrator within or without the city of New York, as established by articles eleven and twelve of the surrogate's court procedure act, or the chief fiscal officer of a county eligible to be appointed an administrator, pursuant to section twelve hundred nineteen of the surrogate's court procedure act. The role of the public administrator under this section is that of a stake holder or escrowee only, and the public administrator shall not, by virtue of this section, have a substantive role in administering the estate.

4. "Statement of assets and notice of claim" means a written statement under oath containing the caption and index number of the guardianship proceeding, the name and address of the incapacitated person at the time of death, a description of the nature and approximate value of guardianship property at the time of the incapacitated person's death; with the approximate amount of any claims, debts or liens against the guardianship

property, including but not limited to medicaid liens, tax liens and administrative costs, with an itemization and approximate amount of such costs and claims or liens.

(b) Unless otherwise directed by the court, all papers required to be served by this section shall be served by regular mail and by certified mail return receipt requested.

(c) Within twenty days of the death of an incapacitated person, the guardian shall:

1. serve a copy of the statement of death upon the court examiner, the duly appointed personal representative of the decedent's estate, or, if no personal representative has been appointed, then upon the personal representative named in the decedent's will or any trust instrument, if known, upon the local department of social services and upon the public administrator of the chief fiscal officer of the county in which the guardian was appointed, and

2. file the original statement of death together with proof of service upon the personal representative and/or public administrator or chief fiscal officer, as the case may be, with the court which issued letters of guardianship.

(d) Within one hundred fifty days of the death of the incapacitated person, the guardian shall serve upon the personal representative of the decedent's estate or where there is no personal representative, upon the public administrator or chief fiscal officer, a statement of assets and notice of claim, and, except for property retained to secure any known claim, lien or administrative costs of the guardianship pursuant to subdivision (e) of this section, shall deliver all guardianship property to:

1. the duly appointed personal representative of the deceased incapacitated person's estate, or

2. the public administrator or chief fiscal officer given notice of the filing of the statement of death, where there is no personal representative.

3. any dispute as to the size of the property retained shall be determined by the surrogate court having jurisdiction of the estate.

(e) Unless otherwise ordered by the court upon motion by the guardian on notice to the person or entity to whom guardianship property is deliverable, and the court examiner, the guardian may retain, pending the settlement of the guardian's final account, guardianship property equal in value to the claim for administrative costs, liens and debts.

(f) Within one hundred fifty days of the incapacitated person's death, the guardian shall file his or her final report with the clerk of the court of the county in which annual reports are filed, and thereupon proceed to judicially settle the final report upon such notice as required by subdivision (c) of section 81.33 of this article, including notice to the person or entity to whom the guardianship property was delivered. There shall be no extension of the time to file a final report except by order of the court.

(g) Upon failure of the guardian to comply with subdivisions (d) or (f) of this section, any person entitled to notice of this proceeding may file a petition to compel the guardian to account, to suspend and/or remove the guardian, and to take and state the guardian's account.

History: Add, L 2008, ch 175, § 2, eff Jan 3, 2009, provided, however, that effective immediately, the addition, amendment and/or repeal of any rule or regulation necessary for the implementation of this act on its effective date are authorized and directed to be made and completed on or before such effective date; amd, L 2011, ch 97, § 1 (Part C, Subpart G), eff Sept 22, 2011.

ARTICLE 83
UNIFORM GUARDIANSHIP AND PROTECTIVE PROCEEDINGS JURISDICTION ACT

SUMMARY OF ARTICLE

§ 83.01. Short title

This article shall be known and may be cited as the "uniform adult guardianship and protective proceedings jurisdiction act".

History: Add, L 2013, ch 427, § 1, eff April 21, 2014.

§ 83.03. Definitions

For purposes of this article, the following definitions shall apply:

(a) "Adult" means an individual who has attained eighteen years of age.

(b) "Emergency" means a circumstance that likely will result in substantial harm to a respondent's health, safety or welfare, and for which the appointment of a guardian is necessary because no other person has authority and is willing to act on the respondent's behalf.

(c) "Guardian of the property" means a person appointed by the court to administer the property of an adult, including a person appointed under article eighty-one of this title and article seventeen-A of the surrogate's court procedure act, and including a conservator appointed by a court in another state.

(d) "Guardian of the person" means a person appointed by the court to make decisions regarding the person of an adult, including a person appointed under article eighty-one of this title and article seventeen-A of the surrogate's court procedure act.

(e) "Home state" means the state in which the respondent was physically present, including any period of temporary absence, for at least six consecutive months immediately before the filing of a petition for a protective order or the appointment of a guardian of the person; or if none, the state in which the respondent was physically present, including any period of temporary absence, for at least six consecutive months ending within the six months prior to the filing of the petition.

(f) "Party" means the respondent, petitioner, guardian of the person, conservator guardian of the property, or any other person allowed by the court to participate in a guardianship proceeding for the appointment of a guardian of the person or a protective proceeding.

(g) "Person", except in the term incapacitated person for whom a guardian of the person has been appointed or protected person, means an individual, corporation, business trust, estate, trust, partnership, limited liability company, association, joint venture, public corporation, government or governmental subdivision, agency or instrumentality, or any other legal or commercial entity.

(h) "Protected person" means an adult for whom a protective order has been issued.

(i) "Protective order" means an order appointing a conservator guardian of the property or other order related to management of an adult's property.

(j) "Protective proceeding" means a judicial proceeding in which a protective order is sought or has been issued.

(k) "Record" means information that is inscribed on a tangible medium or that is stored in an electronic or other medium and is retrievable in perceivable form.

(l) "Respondent" means an adult for whom a protective order or the appointment of a guardian of the person is sought.

(m) "Significant-connection state" means a state, other than the home state, with which a respondent has a significant connection other than mere physical presence and in which substantial evidence concerning the respondent is available.

(n) "State" means a state of the United States, the District of Columbia, Puerto Rico, the United States Virgin Islands, a federally recognized Indian tribe, or any territory or insular possession subject to the jurisdiction of the United States.

History: Add, L 2013, ch 427, § 1, eff April 21, 2014; amd, L 2015, ch 458, § 1, eff Nov 20, 2015.

§ 83.05. International application of this article

A court of this state may treat a foreign country as if it were a state for the purpose of applying sections 83.01 through 83.37 of this article.

History: Add, L 2013, ch 427, § 1, eff April 21, 2014.

§ 83.07. Communication between courts

(a) A court of this state may communicate with a court in another state concerning a proceeding arising under this article. The court may allow the parties to participate in the communication.

(b) If the parties are not allowed to participate in the communication, the court shall give all parties the opportunity to present facts and legal arguments before the court issues an order establishing jurisdiction.

(c) Except as otherwise provided in subdivision (d) of this section, the court shall make a record of any communication under this section and promptly inform the parties of the communication and grant them access to the record.

(d) Courts may communicate concerning schedules, calendars, court records and other administrative matters without making a record.

    History: Add, L 2013, ch 427, § 1, eff April 21, 2014.

§ 83.09. Cooperation between courts

(a) In a proceeding for the appointment of a guardian of the person or protective proceeding in this state, a court of this state may request the appropriate court of another state to do any of the following:

    1. hold an evidentiary hearing;

    2. order a person in that state to produce evidence or give testimony pursuant to procedures of that state;

    3. order that an evaluation or assessment be made of the respondent;

    4. order any appropriate investigation of a person involved in a proceeding;

    5. forward to the court of this state a certified copy of the transcript or other record of a hearing under paragraph one of this subdivision or any other proceeding, any evidence otherwise produced under paragraph two of this subdivision, and any evaluation or assessment prepared in compliance with an order under paragraph three or four of this subdivision;

    6. issue any order necessary to assure the appearance in the proceeding of a person whose presence is necessary for the court to make a determination, including the respondent or the person subject to a guardianship of the person or protected person; and

    7. issue an order authorizing the release of medical, financial, criminal, or other relevant information in that state, including protected health information.

(b) The court may receive any evidence produced pursuant to subdivision (a) of this section in the same manner that it would admit into evidence the report of a court evaluator after the court evaluator had been subject to cross examination;

(c) If a court of another state in which a guardianship or protective proceeding is pending requests assistance of the kind provided in subdivision (a) of this section, a court of this state has jurisdiction for the limited purpose of granting the request or making reasonable efforts to comply with the request.

    History: Add, L 2013, ch 427, § 1, eff April 21, 2014.

§ 83.11. Taking testimony in another state

(a) In a proceeding for the appointment of a guardian of the person or protective proceeding, in addition to other procedures that may be available, testimony of a witness who is located in another state may be offered by deposition or other means allowable in this state for testimony taken in another state. The court on its own motion may order that the testimony of a witness be taken in another state and may prescribe the manner in which and the terms upon which the testimony is to be taken.

(b) In a proceeding for the appointment of a guardian of the person or protective proceeding, a court in this state may permit a witness located in another state to be deposed or to testify by telephone or audiovisual or other electronic means. A court of this state shall cooperate with the court of the other state in designating an appropriate location for the deposition or testimony.

(c) Documentary evidence transmitted from another state to a court of this state by technological means that do not produce an original writing may not be excluded from evidence on an objection based on the best evidence rule.

History: Add, L 2013, ch 427, § 1, eff April 21, 2014.

§ 83.13. Significant connection factors

In determining under section 83.17 and subdivision (e) of section 83.31 of this article whether a respondent has a significant connection with a particular state, the court shall consider:

(a) the location of the respondent's family and other persons required to be notified of the proceeding;

(b) the length of time the respondent at any time was physically present in the state and the duration of any absence;

(c) the location of the respondent's property; and

(d) the extent to which the respondent has ties to the state such as voting registration, state or local tax return filing, vehicle registration, driver's license, social relationship, and receipt of services.

History: Add, L 2013, ch 427, § 1, eff April 21, 2014.

§ 83.15. Exclusive basis

Subject to section 81.18 of this title, this article provides the exclusive jurisdictional basis for a court of this state to appoint a guardian of the person or issue a protective order for an adult.

History: Add, L 2013, ch 427, § 1, eff April 21, 2014.

§ 83.17. Jurisdiction

A court of this state has jurisdiction to appoint a guardian of the person or issue a protective order for a respondent if:

(a) the state is the respondent's home state;

(b) on the date the petition is filed, this state is a significant-connection state and:

1. the respondent does not have a home state or a court of the respondent's home state

has declined to exercise jurisdiction because this state is a more appropriate forum; or

2. the respondent has a home state, a petition for an appointment or order is not pending in a court of that state or another significant connection state, and before the court makes the appointment or issues the order:

(i) a petition for an appointment or order is not filed in the respondent's home state;

(ii) an objection to the court's jurisdiction is not filed by a person required to be notified of the proceeding; and

(iii) the court in this state concludes that it is an appropriate forum under the factors set forth in section 83.23 of this article;

(c) this state does not have jurisdiction under either subdivision (a) or (b) of this section, the respondent's home state and all significant-connection states have declined to exercise jurisdiction because this state is the more appropriate forum, and jurisdiction in this state is consistent with the constitutions of this state and the United States; or

(d) the requirements for special jurisdiction under section 83.19 of this article are met.

History: Add, L 2013, ch 427, § 1, eff April 21, 2014.

§ 83.19. Special jurisdiction

(a) A court of this state lacking jurisdiction under section 83.17 of this article has special jurisdiction to do any of the following:

1. appoint a guardian of the person in an emergency for a term not exceeding ninety days for a respondent who is physically present in this state;

2. issue a protective order with respect to a real or tangible personal property located in this state; and

3. appoint a guardian of the person or a guardian of the property for a person subject to a guardianship of the person or protected person for whom a provision order to transfer the proceeding from another state has been issued under procedures similar to section 83.31 of this article.

(b) If a petition for the appointment of a guardian of the person in an emergency is brought in this state and this state was not the respondent's home state on the date the petition was filed, the court shall dismiss the proceeding at the request of the court of the home state, if any, whether dismissal is requested before or after the emergency appointment.

History: Add, L 2013, ch 427, § 1, eff April 21, 2014.

§ 83.21. Exclusive and continuing jurisdiction

Except as otherwise provided in section 83.19 of this article, a court that has appointed a guardian of the person or issued a protective order consistent with this article has exclusive and continuing jurisdiction over the proceedings until it is terminated by the court or the appointment or order expires by its own terms.

History: Add, L 2013, ch 427, § 1, eff April 21, 2014.

§ 83.23. Appropriate forum

(a) A court of this state having jurisdiction under section 83.17 of this article to appoint a guardian of the person or issue a protective order may decline to exercise its jurisdiction if it determines at any time that a court of another state is a more appropriate forum.

(b) If a court of this state declines to exercise its jurisdiction under subdivision (a) of this section, it shall either dismiss or stay the proceeding. The court may impose any condition the court considers just and proper, including the condition that a petition for the appointment of a guardian of the person or issuance of a protective order be filed promptly in another state.

(c) In determining whether it is an appropriate forum, the court shall consider all relevant factors, including:

1. any expressed preference of the respondent;

2. whether abuse, neglect or exploitation of the respondent has occurred or is likely to occur, and which state could best protect the respondent from the abuse, neglect or exploitation;

3. the length of time the respondent was physically present in or was a legal resident of this or another state;

4. the distance of the respondent from the court in each state;

5. the financial circumstances of the respondent's estate;

6. the nature and location of the evidence;

7. the ability of the court in each state to decide the issue expeditiously and the procedures necessary to present evidence;

8. the familiarity of the court of each state with the facts and issues in the proceeding; and

9. if an appointment were made, the court's ability to monitor the conduct of the guardian or conservator.

History: Add, L 2013, ch 427, § 1, eff April 21, 2014.

§ 83.25. Jurisdiction declined by reason of conduct

(a) If at any time a court of this state determines that it acquired jurisdiction to appoint a guardian of the person or issue a protective order because of unjustifiable conduct, the court may:

1. decline to exercise jurisdiction;

2. exercise jurisdiction for the limited purpose of fashioning an appropriate remedy to ensure the health, safety and welfare of the respondent, or the protection of the respondent's property or prevent a repetition of the unjustifiable conduct, including staying the proceeding until a petition for the appointment of a guardian of the person or issuance of a protective order is filed in a court of another state having jurisdiction; or

3. continue to exercise jurisdiction after considering:

(i) the extent to which the respondent and all persons required to be notified of the proceedings have acquiesced in the exercise of the court's jurisdiction;

(ii) whether it is a more appropriate forum than the court of any other state under the factors set forth in subdivision (c) of section 83.23 of this article; and

(iii) whether the court of any other state would have jurisdiction under factual circumstances in substantial conformity with the jurisdictional standards of section 83.17 of this article.

(b) If a court of this state determines that it acquired jurisdiction to appoint a guardian of the person or issue a protective order because a party seeking to invoke its jurisdiction engaged in unjustifiable conduct, it may assess against that party necessary and reasonable expenses, including attorney's fees, investigative fees, court costs, communication expenses, witness fees and expenses, and travel expenses. The court may not assess fees, costs or expenses of any kind against this state or a governmental subdivision, agency or instrumentality of this state unless authorized by law other than this article.

History: Add, L 2013, ch 427, § 1, eff April 21, 2014.

§ 83.27. Notice of proceeding

If a petition for the appointment of a guardian of the person or issuance of a protective order is brought in this state and this state was not the respondent's home state on the date the petition was filed, in addition to complying with the notice requirements of this state, notice of the petition must be given to those persons who would be entitled to notice of the petition if a proceeding were brought in the respondent's home state. The notice must be given in the same manner as notice is required to be given in this state.

History: Add, L 2013, ch 427, § 1, eff April 21, 2014.

§ 83.29. Proceedings in more than one state

Except for a petition for the appointment of a guardian of the person in an emergency or issuance of a protective order limited to property located in this state under paragraph one or two of subdivision (a) of section 83.19 of this article, if a petition for the appointment of a guardian of the person or issuance of a protective order is filed in this state and in another state and neither petition has been dismissed or withdrawn, the following rules apply:

(a) If the court in this state has jurisdiction under section 83.17 of this article, it may proceed with the case unless a court in another state acquires jurisdiction under provisions similar to such section before the appointment or issuance of the order.

(b) If the court in this state does not have jurisdiction under section 83.17 of this article, whether at the time the petition is filed or at any time before the appointment or issuance of the order, the court shall stay the proceeding and communicate with the court in the other state. If the court in the other state has jurisdiction, the court in this state shall dismiss the petition unless the court in the other state determines that the court in this state is a more appropriate forum.

History: Add, L 2013, ch 427, § 1, eff April 21, 2014.

§ 83.31. Transfer of guardianship or conservatorship to another state

(a) A guardian of the person or a guardian of the property appointed in this state may petition the court to transfer the guardianship to another state.

(b) Notice of a petition under subdivision (a) of this section must be given to the persons that would be entitled to notice of a petition in this state for the appointment of a guardian of the person or a guardian of the property.

(c) On the court's own motion or on request of the guardian of the person, the guardian of the property, the person subject to the guardianship of the person, or the protected person, or other person required to be notified of the petition, the court shall hold a hearing on a petition filed pursuant to subdivision (a) of this section.

(d) The court shall issue an order provisionally granting a petition to transfer a guardianship of the person and shall direct the guardian of the person to petition for guardianship of the person in the other state if the court is satisfied that the guardianship of the person will be accepted by the court in the other state and the court finds that:

1. the person subject to the guardianship of the person is physically present in or is reasonably expected to move permanently to the other state;

2. an objection to the transfer has not been made or, if an objection has been made, the objector has not established that the transfer would be contrary to the interests of the person subject to the guardianship of the person; and

3. plans for care and services for the person subject to the guardianship of the person in the other state are reasonable and sufficient.

(e) The court shall issue a provisional order granting a petition to transfer a guardianship of the property and shall direct the guardian of the property to petition for guardianship of the property in the other state if the court is satisfied that the guardianship of the property will be accepted by the court of the other state and the court finds that:

1. the protected person is physically present in or is reasonably expected to move permanently to the other state, or the protected person has a significant connection to the other state considering the factors in section 83.13 of this article;

2. an objection to the transfer has not been made or, if an objection has been made, the objector has not established that the transfer would be contrary to the interests of the protected person; and

3. adequate arrangements will be made for management of the protected person's property.

(f) The court shall issue a final order confirming the transfer and terminating the guardianship of the person or property upon its receipt of:

1. a provisional order accepting the proceeding from the court to which the proceeding is to be transferred which is issued under provisions similar to section 83.33 of this article; and

2. the documents required to terminate a guardianship of the person or property in this state.

History: Add, L 2013, ch 427, § 1, eff April 21, 2014.

§ 83.33. Accepting guardianship or conservatorship transferred from another state

(a) To confirm transfer of a guardianship of the person or guardianship of the property transferred to this state under provisions similar to section 83.31 of this article, the guardian of the person or guardian of the property must petition the court in this state pursuant to article eighty-one of this title or article seventeen-A of the surrogate's court procedure act to accept the guardianship of the person or guardianship of the property. The petition must include a certified copy of the other state's provisional order of transfer.

(b) Notice of a petition under subdivision (a) of this section must be given to those persons that would be entitled to notice if the petition were a petition for the appointment of a guardian of the person or issuance of a protective order in both the transferring state and this state. The notice must be given in the same manner as notice is required to be given in this state.

(c) On the court's own motion or on request of the guardian of the person or guardian of the property, the person subject to the guardianship of the person or protected person, or other person required to be notified of the proceeding, the court shall hold a hearing on a petition filed pursuant to subdivision (a) of this section.

(d) The court shall issue an order provisionally granting a petition filed under subdivision (a) of this section unless:

1. an objection is made and the objector establishes that transfer of the proceeding would be contrary to the interests of the incapacitated or protected person; or

2. the guardian of the person or guardian of the property is ineligible for appointment in this state.

(e) The court shall issue a final order accepting the proceeding and appointing the guardian of the person or guardian of the property as guardian of the person or guardian of the property in this state upon its receipt from the court from which the proceeding is being transferred of a final order issued under provisions similar to section 83.31 of this article transferring the proceeding to this state.

(f) Not later than ninety days after issuance of a final order accepting transfer of a guardianship of the person or guardianship of the property, the court shall determine whether the guardianship of the person or guardianship of the property needs to be modified to conform to the law of this state.

(g) In granting a petition under this section, the court shall recognize a guardianship order from the other state, including the determination of incapacity and the appointment of the guardian of the person or guardian of the property.

(h) The denial by a court of this state of a petition to accept a guardianship of the person or guardianship of the property transferred from another state does not affect the ability of the guardian of the person or guardian of the property to seek appointment as guardian of the person or guardian of the property in this state under article eighty-one of this title or article seventeen-A of the surrogate's court procedure act if the court has jurisdiction to make an appointment other than by reason of the provisional order of transfer.

History: Add, L 2013, ch 427, § 1, eff April 21, 2014.

§ 83.35. Registration of orders appointing a guardian of the person

If a guardian of the person by whatever name designated has been appointed in another state and a petition for the appointment of a guardian of the person is not pending in this state, the guardian of the person appointed in the other state, after giving notice to the appointing court of an intent to register, may register the guardianship of the person order in this state by filing as a foreign judgment in a court, in any appropriate county of this state, certified copies of the order and letters of office.

History: Add, L 2013, ch 427, § 1, eff April 21, 2014.

§ 83.37. Registration of protective orders

If a guardian of the property has been appointed in another state and a petition for a protective order is not pending in this state, the guardian of the property appointed in the other state, after giving notice to the appointing court of an intent to register, may register the protective order in this state by filing as a foreign judgment in a court of this state, in any county in which property belonging to the protected person is located, certified copies of the order and letters of office and of any bond. Thereafter, said guardian of the property shall comply with the requirements of subparagraph (vi) of paragraph six of subdivision (a) of section 81.20 of this title with regard to any real property of the protected person in this state.

History: Add, L 2013, ch 427, § 1, eff April 21, 2014.

§ 83.39. Effect of registration

(a) Upon registration of an order appointing a guardian of the person or protective order from another state, the guardian of the person or guardian of the property may exercise in this state all powers authorized in the order of appointment or protective order except as prohibited under the laws of this state and, if the guardian of the person or guardian of the property is not a resident of this state, subject to any conditions imposed upon nonresident parties.

(b) A court of this state may grant any relief available under this article and other law of this state to enforce a registered order.

(c) Notwithstanding any provision of law to the contrary, upon registration of an order appointing a guardian of the person or protective order from another state, the guardian of the person or guardian of the property, if so authorized in the order of appointment or protective order, may commence and defend actions and proceedings in this state.

(d) Upon registration of a protective order from another state, the guardian of the property, if so authorized in the protective order, may petition the court pursuant to article seventeen of the real property actions and proceedings law, for permission to dispose of the real property, or an interest in the real property, of the protected person.

History: Add, L 2013, ch 427, § 1, eff April 21, 2014; amd, L 2015, ch 458, § 2, eff Nov 20, 2015.

§ 83.41. Uniformity of application and construction

In applying and construing this article, consideration must be given to the need to promote uniformity of the law with respect to its subject matter among states that enact it.

History: Add, L 2013, ch 427, § 1, eff April 21, 2014.

§ 83.43. Relation to electronic signatures in global and national commerce act

This article modifies, limits and supersedes the federal Electronic Signatures in Global and National Commerce Act, 15 U.S.C. Section 7001, et seq., but does not modify, limit or supersede Section 101(c) of such act, 15 U.S.C. Section 7001 (c), or authorize electronic delivery of any of the notices described in Section 103(b) of such act, 15 U.S.C. Section 7003(b).

History: Add, L 2013, ch 427, § 1, eff April 21, 2014.

§ 83.45. Transitional provision

(a) This article applies to proceedings begun on or after this article's effective date.

(b) Sections 83.01 through 83.05 and sections 83.31 through 83.43 of this article apply to proceedings begun before this article's effective date, regardless of whether a guardianship or protective order has been issued.

History: Add, L 2013, ch 427, § 1, eff April 21, 2014.

PUBLIC HEALTH LAW

Table of Contents

PHL

ARTICLE 25-B   GESTATIONAL SURROGACY

SUMMARY OF ARTICLE

§ 2599-cc.   Gestational surrogacy

§ 2599-cc. Gestational surrogacy

1. The commissioner shall promulgate regulations on the practice of gestational surrogacy. Such regulations shall include, but not be limited to:

(a) guidelines and procedures for obtaining fully informed consent from potential persons acting as surrogates, including but not limited to a full disclosure of any known or potential health risks and mental health impacts associated with acting as a surrogate;

(b) the development and distribution, in printed form and on the department's website, of informational material relating to gestational surrogacy;

(c) the establishment of a voluntary central tracking registry of persons acting as surrogates, as reported by surrogacy programs licensed by the department pursuant to article forty-four of the general business law upon the affirmative consent of a person acting as surrogate. Such registry shall provide a means for gathering and maintaining accurate information on the:

(i) number of times a person has acted as a surrogate;

(ii) health information of the person acting as surrogate; and

(iii) other information deemed appropriate by the commissioner;

(d) the development of guidelines, procedures or protocols, in consultation with the American college of obstetricians and gynecologists and the American society for reproductive medicine, to assist physicians in screening potential surrogates for their ability to serve as a surrogate as required under subdivision four of section 581-402 of the family court act including taking into consideration the potential surrogates family medical history and complications from prior pregnancies and known health conditions that may pose a risk to the potential surrogate during pregnancy; and

(e) the development of guidance to reduce conflicts of interest among physicians providing health care services to the surrogate.

2. All such regulations shall maintain the anonymity of the person acting as surrogate and any resulting offspring and govern access to information maintained by the registry. Such registry shall comply with all state and federal laws and regulations related to maintaining the privacy and confidentiality of records contained with the registry.

History: Add, L 2020, c 56, Pt L, § 12, eff Feb 15, 2020.

2020 Amendment

2020 N.Y. Laws 56, § 12, effective February 15, 2020, added the article consisting of section 2599-cc.

ORDERS NOT TO RESUSCITATE FOR RESIDENTS OF MENTAL HYGIENE FACILITIES*

SUMMARY OF ARTICLE

§ 2960. Legislative findings and purpose

The legislature finds that, although cardiopulmonary resuscitation has proved invaluable in the prevention of sudden, unexpected death, it is appropriate for an attending practitioner, in certain circumstances, to issue an order not to attempt cardiopulmonary resuscitation of a patient where appropriate consent has been obtained. The legislature further finds that there is a need to clarify and establish the rights and obligations of patients, their families, and health care providers regarding cardiopulmonary resuscitation and the issuance of orders not to resuscitate.

> **History:** Add, L 1987, ch 818, § 1, eff April 1, 1988; amd, L 2017, ch 430, § 1, eff May 28, 2018; L 2019, ch 708, § 1, eff June 17, 2020.

§ 2961. Definitions

---

* Amd L 2010, ch 8, eff June 1, 2010.

The following words or phrases, as used in this article, shall have the following meanings unless the context otherwise requires:

1. "Adult" means any person who is eighteen years of age or older, or is the parent of a child, or has married.

2. "Attending practitioner" means the physician, nurse practitioner, or physician assistant, licensed or certified pursuant to title eight of the education law, selected by or assigned to a patient in a hospital who has primary responsibility for the treatment and care of the patient. Where more than one physician, nurse practitioner, or physician assistant shares such responsibility, any such physician, nurse practitioner, or physician assistant may act as the attending practitioner pursuant to this article.

3. "Capacity" means the ability to understand and appreciate the nature and consequences of an order not to resuscitate, including the benefits and disadvantages of such an order, and to reach an informed decision regarding the order.

4. "Cardiopulmonary resuscitation" means measures to restore cardiac function or to support ventilation in the event of a cardiac or respiratory arrest. Cardiopulmonary resuscitation shall not include measures to improve ventilation and cardiac functions in the absence of an arrest.

5. "Close friend" means any person, eighteen years of age or older, who is a close friend of the patient, or relative of the patient (other than a spouse, adult child, parent, brother or sister) who has maintained such regular contact with the patient as to be familiar with the patient's activities, health, and religious or moral beliefs and who presents a signed statement to that effect to the attending practitioner.

5-a. "Correctional facilities medical care personnel" means personnel engaged in providing health care at correctional facilities, as that term is defined in subdivision four of section two of the correction law.

6. "Developmental disability" means a developmental disability as defined in subdivision twenty-two of section 1.03 of the mental hygiene law.

6-a. "Domestic partner" means a person who, with respect to another person:

(a) is formally a party in a domestic partnership or similar relationship with the other person, entered into pursuant to the laws of the United States or of any state, local or foreign jurisdiction, or registered as the domestic partner of the other person with any registry maintained by the employer of either party or any state, municipality, or foreign jurisdiction; or

(b) is formally recognized as a beneficiary or covered person under the other person's employment benefits or health insurance; or

(c) is dependent or mutually interdependent on the other person for support, as evidenced by the totality of the circumstances indicating a mutual intent to be domestic partners including but not limited to: common ownership or joint leasing of real or personal property; common householding, shared income or shared expenses; children in common; signs of intent to marry or become domestic partners under paragraph (a) or (b) of this subdivision; or the length of the personal relationship of the persons.

Each party to a domestic partnership shall be considered to be the domestic partner of the other party. "Domestic partner" shall not include a person who is related to the other person by blood in a manner that would bar marriage to the other person in New York state. "Domestic partner" also shall not include any person who is less than eighteen years of age or who is the adopted child of the other person or who is related by blood in a manner that would bar marriage in New York state to a person who is the lawful spouse of the other person.

7. [Repealed]

8. "Health care agent" means a health care agent of the patient designated pursuant to article twenty-nine-C of this chapter.

9. "Hospital" means a hospital as defined in subdivision ten of section 1.03 of the mental hygiene law or a school named in section 13.17 of the mental hygiene law.

10. [Repealed]

11. "Hospitalization" means the period during which a person is a patient in, or a resident of, a hospital.

12. "Medically futile" means that cardiopulmonary resuscitation will be unsuccessful in restoring cardiac and respiratory function or that the patient will experience repeated arrest in a short time period before death occurs.

13. [Repealed]

14. "Mental illness" means a mental illness as defined in subdivision twenty of section 1.03 of the mental hygiene law, provided, however, that mental illness shall not include dementia, such as Alzheimer's disease or other disorders related to dementia.

15. "Minor" means any person who is not an adult.

16. "Nurse practitioner" means a nurse practitioner certified pursuant to section sixty-nine hundred ten of the education law who is practicing in accordance with subdivision three of section sixty-nine hundred two of the education law.

17. "Order not to resuscitate" means an order not to attempt cardiopulmonary resuscitation in the event a patient suffers cardiac or respiratory arrest.

18. "Parent" means a parent who has custody of the minor.

19. "Patient" means a person admitted to a hospital.

20. "Reasonably available" means that a person to be contacted can be contacted with diligent efforts by an attending practitioner or another person acting on behalf of the attending practitioner or the hospital.

21. "Surrogate" means the person selected to make a decision regarding resuscitation on behalf of another person pursuant to section twenty-nine hundred sixty-five of this article.

22. "Surrogate list" means the list set forth in subdivision two of section twenty-nine hundred sixty-five of this article.

23. "Terminal condition" means an illness or injury from which there is no recovery, and which reasonably can be expected to cause death within one year.

History: Add, L 1987, ch 818, § 1, eff April 1, 1988; amd, L 1991, ch 370, § 1, eff July

15, 1991; L 1993, ch 577, §§ 1, 2, eff July 28, 1993; L 2010, ch 8, §§ 5–7, eff June 1, 2010; L 2017, ch 430, § 2, eff May 28, 2018; L 2019, ch 708, § 2, eff June 17, 2020.

§ 2962. Presumption in favor of resuscitation; lawfulness of order; effectiveness of order; duty to provide information; no duty to expand equipment

1. Every person admitted to a hospital shall be presumed to consent to the administration of cardiopulmonary resuscitation in the event of cardiac or respiratory arrest, unless there is consent to the issuance of an order not to resuscitate as provided in this article.

2. It shall be lawful for the attending practitioner to issue an order not to resuscitate a patient, provided that the order has been issued pursuant to the requirements of this article. The order shall be included in writing in the patient's chart. An order not to resuscitate shall be effective upon issuance.

3. Before obtaining, pursuant to this article, the consent of the patient, or of the surrogate of the patient, or parent or legal guardian of the minor patient, to an order not to resuscitate, the attending practitioner shall provide to the person giving consent information about the patient's diagnosis and prognosis, the reasonably foreseeable risks and benefits of cardiopulmonary resuscitation for the patient, and the consequences of an order not to resuscitate.

4. Nothing in this article shall require a hospital to expand its existing equipment and facilities to provide cardiopulmonary resuscitation.

5. (a) The provisions of article twenty-nine-C of this chapter, governing health care proxies and agents, take precedence over conflicting provisions of this article.

   (b) When a patient who has a health care agent lacks capacity, the agent shall have the rights and authority that a patient with capacity would have under this article, subject to the terms of the health care proxy and article twenty-nine-C of this chapter.

   History: Add, L 1987, ch 818, § 1, eff April 1, 1988; amd, L 1991, ch 370, § 2, eff July 15, 1991; L 2017, ch 430, § 3, eff May 28, 2018; L 2019, ch 708, § 4, eff June 17, 2020.

§ 2963. Determination of capacity to make a decision regarding cardiopulmonary resuscitation

1. Every adult shall be presumed to have the capacity to make a decision regarding cardiopulmonary resuscitation unless determined otherwise pursuant to this section or pursuant to a court order or unless a guardian is authorized to decide about health care for the adult pursuant to article eighty-one of the mental hygiene law or article seventeen-A of the surrogate's court procedure act. The attending practitioner shall not rely on the presumption stated in this subdivision if clinical indicia of incapacity are present.

2. A determination that an adult patient lacks capacity shall be made by the attending practitioner to a reasonable degree of medical certainty. The determination shall be made in writing and shall contain such attending practitioner's opinion regarding the cause and nature of the patient's incapacity as well as its extent and probable duration. The determination shall be included in the patient's medical chart.

3. (a) At least one other physician, selected by a person authorized by the hospital to make such selection, must concur in the determination that an adult lacks capacity. The concurring determination shall be made in writing after personal examination of the patient and shall contain the physician's opinion regarding the cause and nature of the

patient's incapacity as well as its extent and probable duration. Each concurring determination shall be included in the patient's medical chart.

(b) If the attending practitioner determines that a patient lacks capacity because of mental illness, the concurring determination required by paragraph (a) of this subdivision shall be provided by a physician licensed to practice medicine in New York state, who is a diplomate or eligible to be certified by the American Board of Psychiatry and Neurology or who is certified by the American Osteopathic Board of Neurology and Psychiatry or is eligible to be certified by that board.

(c) If the attending practitioner determines that a patient lacks capacity because of a developmental disability, the concurring determination required by paragraph (a) of this subdivision shall be provided by a physician or psychologist employed by a developmental disabilities services office named in section 13.17 of the mental hygiene law, or who has been employed for a minimum of two years to render care and service in a facility operated or licensed by the office for people with developmental disabilities, or who has been approved by the commissioner of developmental disabilities in accordance with regulations promulgated by such commissioner. Such regulations shall require that a physician or psychologist possess specialized training or three years experience in treating developmental disabilities.

4. Notice of a determination that the patient lacks capacity shall promptly be given (a) to the patient, where there is any indication of the patient's ability to comprehend such notice, together with a copy of a statement prepared in accordance with section twenty-nine hundred seventy-eight of this article, and (b) to the person on the surrogate list highest in order of priority listed, when persons in prior subparagraphs are not reasonably available. Nothing in this subdivision shall preclude or require notice to more than one person on the surrogate list.

5. A determination that a patient lacks capacity to make a decision regarding an order not to resuscitate pursuant to this section shall not be construed as a finding that the patient lacks capacity for any other purpose.

History: Add, L 1987, ch 818, § 1, eff April 1, 1988; amd, L 1994, ch 23, § 1, eff March 28, 1994; L 2010, ch 8, § 8, eff June 1, 2010; L 2012, ch 56, § 5 (Part J), eff March 30, 2012; L 2017, ch 430, § 4, eff May 28, 2018; L 2019, ch 708, § 5, eff June 17, 2020 .

§ 2964. Decision-making by an adult with capacity

1. (a) The consent of an adult with capacity must be obtained prior to issuing an order not to resuscitate, except as provided in subdivision three of this section.

(b) If the adult has capacity at the time the order is to be issued, the consent must be obtained at or about such time, notwithstanding any prior oral or written consent.

2. (a) During hospitalization, an adult with capacity may express a decision consenting to an order not to resuscitate orally in the presence of at least two witnesses eighteen years of age or older, one of whom is a physician, nurse practitioner, or physician assistant affiliated with the hospital in which the patient is being treated. Any such decision shall be recorded in the patient's medical chart.

(b) Prior to or during hospitalization, an adult with capacity may express a decision consenting to an order not to resuscitate in writing, dated and signed in the presence of at least two witnesses eighteen years of age or older who shall sign the decision.

(c) An attending practitioner who is provided with or informed of a decision pursuant to this subdivision shall record or include the decision in the patient's medical chart if the decision has not been recorded or included, and either:

(i) promptly issue an order not to resuscitate the patient or issue an order at such time as the conditions, if any, specified in the decision are met, and inform the hospital staff responsible for the patient's care of the order; or

(ii) promptly make his or her objection to the issuance of such an order and the reasons therefor known to the patient and either make all reasonable efforts to arrange for the transfer of the patient to another physician, nurse practitioner or physician assistant, if necessary, or promptly submit the matter to the dispute mediation system.

(d) Prior to issuing an order not to resuscitate a patient who has expressed a decision consenting to an order not to resuscitate under specified medical conditions, the attending practitioner must make a determination, to a reasonable degree of medical certainty, that such conditions exist, and include the determination in the patient's medical chart.

3. If the patient is in or is transferred from a correctional facility, notice of the patient's consent to an order not to resuscitate shall be given to the facility director and reasonable efforts shall be made to provide notice to an individual designated by the patient to receive such notification prior to the issuance of the order not to resuscitate. Notification to the facility director or the individual designated by the patient shall not unreasonably delay issuance of an order not to resuscitate.

History: Add, L 1987, ch 818, § 1, eff April 1, 1988; amd, L 1991, ch 370, § 3, eff July 15, 1991; L 1993, ch 577, § 3, eff July 28, 1993; L 2010, ch 8, § 9, eff June 1, 2010; L 2017, ch 430, §§ 5, 6, eff May 2, 2018; L 2019, ch 708, § 6, eff June 17, 2020.

§ 2965. Surrogate decision-making

1. (a) The consent of a surrogate or health care agent acting on behalf of an adult patient who lacks capacity or on behalf of an adult patient for whom consent by a surrogate or health care agent is authorized by subdivision three of section twenty-nine hundred sixty-four of this article must be obtained prior to issuing an order not to resuscitate the patient, except as provided in paragraph (b) of this subdivision or section twenty-nine hundred sixty-six of this article.

(b) The consent of a surrogate or health care agent shall not be required where the adult had, prior to losing capacity, consented to an order not to resuscitate pursuant to subdivision two of section twenty-nine hundred sixty-four of this article.

(c) A decision regarding cardiopulmonary resuscitation by a health care agent on a principal's behalf is governed by article twenty-nine-C of this chapter and shall have priority over decisions by any other person, except the patient or as otherwise provided in the health care proxy.

2. (a) One person from the following list, to be chosen in order of priority listed, when persons in the prior subparagraphs are not reasonably available, willing to make a decision regarding issuance of an order not to resuscitate, and competent to make a decision regarding issuance of an order not to resuscitate, shall have the authority to act as surrogate on behalf of the patient. However, such person may designate any other person on the list to be surrogate, provided no one in a higher class than the person designated objects:

(i) a guardian authorized to decide about health care pursuant to article eighty-one of the mental hygiene law or a guardian of a person appointed under article seventeen-A of the surrogate's court procedure act, provided that this paragraph shall not be construed to require the appointment of a guardian for the purpose of making the resuscitation decision;

(ii) the spouse, if not legally separated from the patient, or the domestic partner;

(iii) a son or daughter eighteen years of age or older;

(iv) a parent;

(v) a brother or sister eighteen years of age or older; and

(vi) a close friend.

(b) After the surrogate has been identified, the name of such person shall be included in the patient's medical chart.

3. (a) The surrogate shall make a decision regarding cardiopulmonary resuscitation on the basis of the adult patient's wishes including a consideration of the patient's religious and moral beliefs, or, if the patient's wishes are unknown and cannot be ascertained, on the basis of the patient's best interests.

(b) Notwithstanding any law to the contrary, the surrogate shall have the same right as the patient to receive medical information and medical records.

(c) A surrogate may consent to an order not to resuscitate on behalf of an adult patient only if there has been a determination by an attending practitioner with the concurrence of another physician, nurse practitioner or physician assistant selected by a person authorized by the hospital to make such selection, given after personal examination of the patient that, to a reasonable degree of medical certainty:

(i) the patient has a terminal condition; or

(ii) the patient is permanently unconscious; or

(iii) resuscitation would be medically futile; or

(iv) resuscitation would impose an extraordinary burden on the patient in light of the patient's medical condition and the expected outcome of resuscitation for the patient.

Each determination shall be included in the patient's medical chart.

4. (a) A surrogate shall express a decision consenting to an order not to resuscitate either (i) in writing, dated, and signed in the presence of one witness eighteen years of age or older who shall sign the decision, or (ii) orally, to two persons eighteen years of age or older, one of whom is a physician, nurse practitioner or physician assistant affiliated with the hospital in which the patient is being treated. Any such decision shall be recorded in the patient's medical chart.

(b) The attending practitioner who is provided with the decision of a surrogate shall include the decision in the patient's medical chart and, if the surrogate has consented to the issuance of an order not to resuscitate, shall either:

(i) promptly issue an order not to resuscitate the patient and inform the hospital staff responsible for the patient's care of the order; or

(ii) promptly make the attending practitioner's objection to the issuance of such an order known to the surrogate and either make all reasonable efforts to arrange for the transfer of the patient to another physician, nurse practitioner or physician assistant, if necessary, or promptly refer the matter to the dispute mediation system.

(c) If the attending practitioner has actual notice of opposition to a surrogate's consent to an order not to resuscitate by any person on the surrogate list, the physician, nurse practitioner or physician assistant shall submit the matter to the dispute mediation system and such order shall not be issued or shall be revoked in accordance with the provisions of subdivision three of section twenty-nine hundred seventy-two of this article.

History: Add, L 1987, ch 818, § 1, eff April 1, 1988; amd, L 1991, ch 370, §§ 4–7, eff July 15, 1991; L 2010, ch 8, §§ 10–12, eff June 1, 2010; L 2017, ch 430, § 7, eff May 28, 2018; L 2019, ch 708, § 7, eff June 17, 2020 .

§ 2966. Decision-making on behalf of an adult patient without capacity for whom no surrogate is available

1. If no surrogate is reasonably available, willing to make a decision regarding issuance of an order not to resuscitate, and competent to make a decision regarding issuance of an order not to resuscitate on behalf of an adult patient who lacks capacity and who had not previously expressed a decision regarding cardiopulmonary resuscitation, an attending practitioner (a) may issue an order not to resuscitate the patient, provided that the attending practitioner determines, in writing, that, to a reasonable degree of medical certainty, resuscitation would be medically futile, and another physician, nurse practitioner or physician assistant selected by a person authorized by the hospital to make such selection, after personal examination of the patient, reviews and concurs in writing with such determination, or, (b) shall issue an order not to resuscitate the patient, provided that, pursuant to subdivision one of section twenty-nine hundred seventy-six of this article, a court has granted a judgment directing the issuance of such an order.

2. Notwithstanding any other provision of this section, where a decision to consent to an order not to resuscitate has been made, notice of the decision shall be given to the patient where there is any indication of the patient's ability to comprehend such notice. If the patient objects, an order not to resuscitate shall not be issued.

History: Add, L 1987, ch 818, § 1, eff April 1, 1988; amd, L 2010, ch 8, §§ 13, 14, eff June 1, 2010; L 2017, ch 430, § 8, eff May 28, 2018; L 2019, ch 708, § 8, eff June 17, 2020.

§ 2967. Decision-making on behalf of a minor patient

1. An attending practitioner, in consultation with a minor's parent or legal guardian, shall determine whether a minor has the capacity to make a decision regarding resuscitation.

2. (a) The consent of a minor's parent or legal guardian and the consent of the minor, if the minor has capacity, must be obtained prior to issuing an order not to resuscitate the minor.

(b) Where the attending practitioner has reason to believe that there is another parent or a non-custodial parent who has not been informed of a decision to issue an order not to resuscitate the minor, the attending practitioner, or someone acting on behalf of the practitioner, shall make reasonable efforts to determine if the uninformed parent or non-custodial parent has maintained substantial and continuous contact with the minor and, if so, shall make diligent efforts to notify that parent or non-custodial parent of the decision prior to issuing the order.

3. A parent or legal guardian may consent to an order not to resuscitate on behalf of a minor only if there has been a written determination by the attending practitioner, with the written concurrence of another physician, nurse practitioner or physician assistant selected by a person authorized by the hospital to make such selections given after personal examination of the patient, that, to a reasonable degree of medical certainty, the minor suffers from one of the medical conditions set forth in paragraph (c) of subdivision three of section twenty-nine hundred sixty-five of this article. Each determination shall be included in the patient's medical chart.

4. (a) A parent or legal guardian of a minor, in making a decision regarding cardiopulmonary resuscitation, shall consider the minor patient's wishes, including a consideration of the minor patient's religious and moral beliefs, and shall express a decision consenting to issuance of an order not to resuscitate either (i) in writing, dated and signed in the presence of one witness eighteen years of age or older who shall sign the decision, or (ii) orally, to two persons eighteen years of age or older, one of whom is a physician, nurse practitioner or physician assistant affiliated with the hospital in which the patient is being treated. Any such decision shall be recorded in the patient's medical chart.

(b) The attending practitioner who is provided with the decision of a minor's parent or legal guardian, expressed pursuant to this subdivision, and of the minor if the minor has capacity, shall include such decision or decisions in the minor's medical chart and shall comply with the provisions of paragraph (b) of subdivision four of section twenty-nine hundred sixty-five of this article.

(c) If the attending practitioner has actual notice of the opposition of a parent or non-custodial parent to consent by another parent to an order not to resuscitate a minor, the physician, nurse practitioner or physician assistant shall submit the matter to the dispute mediation system and such order shall not be issued or shall be revoked in accordance with the provisions of subdivision three of section twenty-nine hundred seventy-two of this article.

History: Add, L 1987, ch 818, § 1, eff April 1, 1988; amd, L 1991, ch 370, §§ 9–11, eff July 15, 1991; L 2010, ch 8, § 15, eff June 1, 2010; L 2017, ch 430, § 9, eff May 28, 2018; L 2019, ch 708, § 9, eff June 17, 2020.

§ 2968. Effect of order not to resuscitate on other treatment

Consent to the issuance of an order not to resuscitate shall not constitute consent to withhold or withdraw medical treatment other than cardiopulmonary resuscitation.

History: Add, L 1987, ch 818, § 1, eff April 1, 1988.

§ 2969. Revocation of consent to order not to resuscitate

1. A person may, at any time, revoke his or her consent to an order not to resuscitate himself or herself by making either a written or an oral declaration to a physician or member of the nursing staff at the hospital where he or she is being treated, or by any other act evidencing a specific intent to revoke such consent.

2. Any surrogate, parent, or legal guardian may at any time revoke his or her consent to an order not to resuscitate a patient by (a) notifying a physician or member of the nursing staff of the revocation of consent in writing, dated and signed, or (b) orally notifying the attending

practitioner in the presence of a witness eighteen years of age or older.

3. Any physician, nurse practitioner or physician assistant who is informed of or provided with a revocation of consent pursuant to this section shall immediately include the revocation in the patient's chart, cancel the order, and notify the hospital staff responsible for the patient's care of the revocation and cancellation. Any member of the nursing staff, other than a nurse practitioner or physician assistant, who is informed of or provided with a revocation of consent pursuant to this section shall immediately notify a physician, nurse practitioner or physician assistant of such revocation.

> **History:** Add, L 1987, ch 818, § 1, eff April 1, 1988; amd, L 1991, ch 370, § 12, eff July 15, 1991; L 2017, ch 430, § 10, eff May 28, 2018; L 2019, ch 708, § 10, eff June 17, 2020.

§ 2970. Physician, nurse practitioner and physician assistant review of the order not to resuscitate

1. For each patient for whom an order not to resuscitate has been issued, the attending practitioner shall review the patient's chart to determine if the order is still appropriate in light of the patient's condition and shall indicate on the patient's chart that the order has been reviewed each time the patient is required to be seen by a physician but at least every sixty days.

Failure to comply with this subdivision shall not render an order not to resuscitate ineffective.

2. (a) If the attending practitioner determines at any time that an order not to resuscitate is no longer appropriate because the patient's medical condition has improved, the physician, nurse practitioner or physician assistant shall immediately notify the person who consented to the order. Except as provided in paragraph (b) of this subdivision, if such person declines to revoke consent to the order, the physician, nurse practitioner or physician assistant shall promptly (i) make reasonable efforts to arrange for the transfer of the patient to another physician or (ii) submit the matter to the dispute mediation system.

(b) If the order not to resuscitate was entered upon the consent of a surrogate, parent, or legal guardian and the attending practitioner who issued the order, or, if unavailable, another attending practitioner at any time determines that the patient does not suffer from one of the medical conditions set forth in paragraph (c) of subdivision three of section twenty-nine hundred sixty-five of this article, the attending practitioner shall immediately include such determination in the patient's chart, cancel the order, and notify the person who consented to the order and all hospital staff responsible for the patient's care of the cancellation.

(c) If an order not to resuscitate was entered upon the consent of a surrogate and the patient at any time gains or regains capacity, the attending practitioner who issued the order, or, if unavailable, another attending practitioner shall immediately cancel the order and notify the person who consented to the order and all hospital staff directly responsible for the patient's care of the cancellation.

> **History:** Add, L 1987, ch 818, § 1, eff April 1, 1988; amd, L 1991, ch 370, §12, eff July 15, 1991; L 2017, ch 430, § 11, eff May 28, 2018; L 2019, ch 708, § 11, eff June 17, 2020.

§ 2971. Interinstitutional transfers

If a patient for whom an order not to resuscitate has been issued is transferred from a hospital to a different hospital the order shall remain effective, unless revoked pursuant to this article, until the attending practitioner first examines the transferred patient, whereupon the attending practitioner must either:

1. Issue an order continuing the prior order not to resuscitate. Such order may be issued without obtaining further consent from the patient, surrogate or parent pursuant to this article; or

2. Cancel the order not to resuscitate, provided the attending practitioner immediately notifies the person who consented to the order and the hospital staff directly responsible for the patient's care of the cancellation. Such cancellation does not preclude the entry of a new order pursuant to this article.

3. For purposes of this section, an order not to resuscitate issued by a general hospital as defined in subdivision ten of section twenty-eight hundred one of this chapter, or by a residential health care facility as defined in subdivision three of section twenty-eight hundred one of this chapter, shall be deemed a hospital order not to resuscitate.

History: Add, L 1987, ch 818, § 1, eff April 1, 1988; amd, L 1991, ch 370, § 15, eff July 15, 1991; L 2010, ch 8, § 17, eff June 1, 2010; L 2017, ch 430, § 12, eff May 28, 2018; L 2019, ch 708, § 12, eff June 17, 2020.

§ 2972. Dispute mediation system

1. (a) Each hospital shall establish a mediation system for the purpose of mediating disputes regarding the issuance of orders not to resuscitate.

(b) The dispute mediation system shall be described in writing and adopted by the hospital's governing authority. It may utilize existing hospital resources, such as a patient advocate's office or hospital chaplain's office, or it may utilize a body created specifically for this purpose, but, in the event a dispute involves a patient deemed to lack capacity pursuant to (i) paragraph (b) of subdivision three of section twenty-nine hundred sixty-three of this article, the system must include a physician, nurse practitioner or physician assistant eligible to provide a concurring determination pursuant to such subdivision, or a family member or guardian of the person of a person with a mental illness of the same or similar nature, or (ii) paragraph (c) of subdivision three of section twenty-nine hundred sixty-three of this article, the system must include a physician, nurse practitioner or physician assistant eligible to provide a concurring determination pursuant to such subdivision, or a family member or guardian of the person of a person with a developmental disability of the same or similar nature.

2. The dispute mediation system shall be authorized to mediate any dispute, including disputes regarding the determination of the patient's capacity, arising under this article between the patient and an attending physician, attending nurse practitioner or the hospital that is caring for the patient and, if the patient is a minor, the patient's parent, or among an attending physician, an attending nurse practitioner, a parent, non-custodial parent, or legal guardian of a minor patient, any person on the surrogate list, and the hospital that is caring for the patient.

3. After a dispute regarding the issuance of an order not to resuscitate has been submitted to the dispute mediation system, an order not to resuscitate shall not be issued or shall be revoked and may not be reissued until (a) the dispute has been resolved or the system has

concluded its effort to resolve the dispute or (b) seventy-two hours have elapsed from the time of the submission of the dispute, whichever shall occur first. Persons participating in the dispute mediation system shall be informed of their right to judicial review.

4. If a dispute between a patient who expressed a decision rejecting cardiopulmonary resuscitation and an attending practitioner or the hospital that is caring for the patient is submitted to the dispute mediation system, and either:

(a) the dispute mediation system has concluded its efforts to resolve the dispute, or

(b) seventy-two hours have elapsed from the time of submission without resolution of the dispute, whichever shall occur first, the attending practitioner shall either: (i) promptly issue an order not to resuscitate the patient or issue the order at such time as the conditions, if any, specified in the decision are met, and inform the hospital staff responsible for the patient's care of the order; or (ii) promptly arrange for the transfer of the patient to another physician, nurse practitioner, physician assistant or hospital.

5. Persons appointed pursuant to this section to participate in the dispute mediation system shall not have authority to determine whether a do not resuscitate order shall be issued.

History: Add, L 1987, ch 818, § 1, eff April 1, 1988; amd, L 1991, ch 370, § 16, eff July 15, 1991; L 2010, ch 8, § 18, eff June 1, 2010; L 2017, ch 430, § 13, eff May 28, 2018; L 2019, ch 708, § 13, eff June 17, 2020.

§ 2973. Judicial review

1. The patient, an attending practitioner, a parent, non-custodial parent, or legal guardian of a minor patient, any person on the surrogate list, the hospital that is caring for the patient and the facility director, may commence a special proceeding pursuant to article four of the civil practice law and rules, in a court of competent jurisdiction, with respect to any dispute arising under this article, except that the decision of a patient not to consent to issuance of an order not to resuscitate may not be subjected to judicial review. In any proceeding brought pursuant to this subdivision challenging a decision regarding issuance of an order not to resuscitate on the ground that the decision is contrary to the patient's wishes or best interests, the person or entity challenging the decision must show, by clear and convincing evidence, that the decision is contrary to the patient's wishes including consideration of the patient's religious and moral beliefs, or, in the absence of evidence of the patient's wishes, that the decision is contrary to the patient's best interests. In any other proceeding brought pursuant to this subdivision, the court shall make its determination based upon the applicable substantive standards and procedures set forth in this article.

2. In any proceeding brought pursuant to this section, the court may issue an order, pursuant to the standards applicable to the issuance of a temporary restraining order according to section six thousand three hundred thirteen of the civil practice law and rules, which shall suspend the order not to resuscitate to permit review of the matter by the court.

3. Where a person or entity may invoke the dispute mediation system, no such proceeding shall be commenced until the dispute mediation system has concluded its efforts to resolve the dispute or seventy-two hours have elapsed from the submission of the dispute to the dispute mediation system, whichever shall occur first, provided, however, that the patient may commence an action for relief with respect to any dispute under this article at any time and provided further that the department of health or any other duly authorized state agency may commence an action or proceeding to enjoin a violation of this article at any time.

History: Add, L 1987, ch 818, § 1, eff April 1, 1988; amd, L 1993, ch 577, § 4, eff July 28, 1993; L 2010, ch 8, § 19, eff June 1, 2010; L 2017, ch 430, § 14, eff May 28, 2018; L 2019, ch 708, § 14, eff June 17, 2020.

§ 2974. Immunity

1. No physician, health care professional, nurse's aide, hospital or person employed by or under contract with the hospital shall be subject to criminal prosecution, civil liability, or be deemed to have engaged in unprofessional conduct for carrying out in good faith pursuant to this article a decision regarding cardiopulmonary resuscitation by or on behalf of a patient or for those actions taken in compliance with the standards and procedures set forth in this article.

2. No physician, health care professional, nurse's aide, hospital, or person employed by or under contract with the hospital shall be subjected to criminal prosecution, civil liability, or be deemed to have engaged in unprofessional conduct for providing cardiopulmonary resuscitation to a patient for whom an order not to resuscitate has been issued, provided such physician or person;

(a) reasonably and in good faith was unaware of the issuance of an order not to resuscitate; or

(b) reasonably and in good faith believed that consent to the order not to resuscitate had been revoked or cancelled.

3. No person shall be subject to criminal prosecution or civil liability for consenting or declining to consent in good faith, on behalf of a patient, to the issuance of an order not to resuscitate pursuant to this article.

4. No person shall be subject to criminal prosecution or civil liability or be deemed to have engaged in unprofessional conduct for acts performed in good faith as a mediator in the dispute mediation system established by this article.

History: Add, L 1987, ch 818, § 1, eff April 1, 1988.

§ 2975. Effect of order not to resuscitate on insurance and health care services

1. No policy of life insurance shall be legally impaired, modified, or invalidated in any manner by the issuance of an order not to resuscitate notwithstanding any term of the policy to the contrary.

2. A person may not prohibit or require the issuance of an order not to resuscitate for an individual as a condition for such individual's being insured or for receiving health care services.

History: Add, L 1987, ch 818, § 1, eff April 1, 1988.

§ 2976. Judicially approved order not to resuscitate

1. If no surrogate is reasonably available, willing to make a decision regarding issuance of an order not to resuscitate, and competent to make a decision regarding issuance of an order not to resuscitate on behalf of an adult patient who lacks capacity and who had not previously expressed a decision regarding cardiopulmonary resuscitation pursuant to this article, an attending practitioner or hospital may commence a special proceeding pursuant to article four of the civil practice law and rules, in a court of competent jurisdiction, for a judgment directing the physician, nurse practitioner or physician assistant to issue an order not to

resuscitate where the patient has a terminal condition, is permanently unconscious, or resuscitation would impose an extraordinary burden on the patient in light of the patient's medical condition and the expected outcome of resuscitation for the patient, and issuance of an order not to resuscitate is consistent with the patient's wishes including a consideration of the patient's religious and moral beliefs or, in the absence of evidence of the patient's wishes, the patient's best interests.

2. Nothing in this article shall be construed to preclude a court of competent jurisdiction from approving the issuance of an order not to resuscitate under circumstances other than those under which such an order may be issued pursuant to this article.

History: Add, L 1987, ch 818, § 1, eff April 1, 1988; amd, L 2017, ch 430, § 15, eff May 28, 2018; L 2019, ch 708, § 16, eff June 17, 2020.

§ 2977. [Repealed]

§ 2978. Regulations

The commissioners of mental health and the office for people with developmental disabilities shall establish such regulations as may be necessary for implementation of this article with respect to those persons in mental hygiene facilities.

History: Formerly § 2977, add, L 1987, ch 818, § 1; renumbered § 2978, L 1991, ch 370, § 17, eff July 15, 1991; L 2010, ch 8, § 21, eff June 1, 2010; L 2019, ch 672, § 22, eff Dec 16, 2019.

§ 2979. Rights to be publicized

1. The commissioners of mental health and the office for people with developmental disabilities shall prepare a statement summarizing the rights, duties, and requirements of this article and shall require that a copy of such statement:

(a) be furnished by the hospital to patients or to persons on the surrogate list known to the hospital at or prior to the time of admission to the hospital, and at the time of the first decision made pursuant to sections twenty-nine hundred sixty-four, twenty-nine hundred sixty-five, twenty-nine hundred sixty-six, or twenty-nine hundred sixty-seven of this article or as soon thereafter as practicable and to each member of the hospital's staff involved in the provision of medical care; and

(b) is posted in a public place in each hospital.

2. The statement of rights required by this section may be included in any other statement of patient's rights required by other provisions of this chapter.

History: Formerly § 2978, add, L 1987, ch 818, § 1; renumbered § 2979, L 1991, ch 370, § 17, eff July 15, 1991; L 2010, ch 8, § 22, eff June 1, 2010; L 2019, ch 672, § 23, eff Dec 16, 2019.

ARTICLE 29-C
HEALTH CARE AGENTS AND PROXIES
SUMMARY OF ARTICLE

§ 2980. **Definitions**

The following words or phrases, used in this article, shall have the following meanings, unless the context otherwise requires:

1. "Adult" means any person who is eighteen years of age or older, or is the parent of a child, or has married.

2. "Attending practitioner" means the physician, physician assistant, or nurse practitioner, licensed or certified pursuant to title eight of the education law, selected by or assigned to a patient, who has primary responsibility for the treatment and care of the patient. Where more than one physician, physician assistant, or nurse practitioner shares such responsibility, or where a physician, physician assistant, or nurse practitioner is acting on the attending practitioner's behalf, any such physician, nurse practitioner, or physician assistant may act as the attending practitioner pursuant to this article.

2-a. "Nurse practitioner" means a nurse practitioner certified under section sixty-nine hundred ten of the education law, practicing within his or her scope of practice.

2-b. "Psychiatric nurse practitioner" means a nurse practitioner certified by the department of education as a psychiatric nurse practitioner.

3. "Capacity to make health care decisions" means the ability to understand and appreciate the nature and consequences of health care decisions, including the benefits and risks of and alternatives to any proposed health care, and to reach an informed decision.

4. "Health care" means any treatment, service or procedure to diagnose or treat an individual's physical or mental condition.

5. "Health care agent" or "agent" means an adult to whom authority to make health care

PHL-19

decisions is delegated under a health care proxy.

6. "Health care decision" means any decision to consent or refuse to consent to health care.

7. "Health care provider" means an individual or facility licensed, certified, or otherwise authorized or permitted by law to administer health care in the ordinary course of business or professional practice.

8. "Health care proxy" means a document delegating the authority to make health care decisions, executed in accordance with the requirements of this article.

9. "Hospital" means a general hospital as defined in subdivision ten of section two thousand eight hundred one of this chapter and a residential health care facility as defined in subdivision three of section two thousand eight hundred one of this chapter, and a mental hygiene facility as defined in subdivision ten of this section and a hospice as defined in subdivision one of section four thousand two of this chapter.

9-a. "Life-sustaining treatment" means any medical treatment or procedure without which the patient will die within a relatively short time, as determined by an attending practitioner to a reasonable degree of medical certainty. For purposes of this article, cardiopulmonary resuscitation is presumed to be a life sustaining treatment without the necessity of a determination by an attending practitioner.

10. "Mental hygiene facility" means a residential facility, excluding family care homes, operated or licensed by the office of mental health or the office for people with developmental disabilities.

11. "Mental illness" means a mental illness as defined in subdivision twenty of section 1.03 of the mental hygiene law, provided, however, that mental illness shall not include dementia, such as alzheimer's disease or other disorders related to dementia.

12. "Principal" means a person who has executed a health care proxy.

13. "Reasonably available" means that a person to be contacted can be contacted with diligent efforts by an attending practitioner or another person acting on behalf of the attending practitioner or the hospital.

14. "Residential health care facility" means a residential health care facility as defined in subdivision three of section two thousand eight hundred one of this chapter.

15. "Qualified psychiatrist" means, for the purposes of this article, a physician licensed to practice medicine in New York state who: (a) is a diplomate of the American Board of Psychiatry and Neurology or is eligible to be certified by that board; or (b) is certified by the American Osteopathic Board of Neurology and Psychiatry or is eligible to be certified by that board.

History: Add, L 1990, ch 752, § 2, eff Jan 18, 1991; amd, L 1994, ch 23, §§ 2, 3, eff March 28, 1994; L 2010, ch 8, § 24, eff June 1, 2010; L 2018, ch 342, § 1, eff Feb 3, 2019; L 2019, ch 672, § 44, eff Dec 16, 2019; L 2019, ch 708, § 16, eff June 17, 2020.

§ 2981. Appointment of health care agent; health care proxy

1. Authority to appoint agent; presumption of competence.

(a) A competent adult may appoint a health care agent in accordance with the terms of this article.

(b) For the purposes of this section, every adult shall be presumed competent to appoint a health care agent unless such person has been adjudged incompetent or otherwise adjudged not competent to appoint a health care agent, or unless a committee or guardian of the person has been appointed for the adult pursuant to article seventy-eight of the mental hygiene law or article seventeen-A of the surrogate's court procedure act.

2. Health care proxy; execution; witnesses.

(a) A competent adult may appoint a health care agent by a health care proxy, signed and dated by the adult in the presence of two adult witnesses who shall also sign the proxy. Another person may sign and date the health care proxy for the adult if the adult is unable to do so, at the adult's direction and in the adult's presence, and in the presence of two adult witnesses who shall sign the proxy. The witnesses shall state that the principal appeared to execute the proxy willingly and free from duress. The person appointed as agent shall not act as witness to execution of the health care proxy.

(b) For persons who reside in a mental hygiene facility operated or licensed by the office of mental health, at least one witness shall be an individual who is not affiliated with the facility and, if the mental hygiene facility is also a hospital as defined in subdivision ten of section 1.03 of the mental hygiene law, at least one witness shall be a qualified psychiatrist or psychiatric nurse practitioner.

(c) For persons who reside in a mental hygiene facility operated or licensed by the office for people with developmental disabilities, at least one witness shall be an individual who is not affiliated with the facility and at least one witness shall be a physician, nurse practitioner, physician assistant or clinical psychologist who either is employed by a developmental disabilities services office named in section 13.17 of the mental hygiene law or who has been employed for a minimum of two years to render care and service in a facility operated or licensed by the office for people with developmental disabilities, or has been approved by the commissioner of developmental disabilities in accordance with regulations approved by the commissioner. Such regulations shall require that a physician, nurse practitioner, physician assistant, or clinical psychologist possess specialized training or three years experience in treating developmental disabilities.

3. Restrictions on who may be and limitations on a health care agent.

(a) An operator, administrator or employee of a hospital may not be appointed as a health care agent by any person who, at the time of the appointment, is a patient or resident of, or has applied for admission to, such hospital.

(b) The restriction in paragraph (a) of this subdivision shall not apply to:

(i) an operator, administrator or employee of a hospital who is related to the principal by blood, marriage or adoption; or

(ii) a physician, physician assistant, or nurse practitioner, subject to the limitation set forth in paragraph (c) of this subdivision, except that no physician or nurse practitioner affiliated with a mental hygiene facility or a psychiatric unit of a general hospital may serve as agent for a principal residing in or being treated by such facility or unit unless the physician is related to the principal by blood, marriage or adoption.

(c) If a physician, physician assistant, or nurse practitioner is appointed agent, the physician, physician assistant, or nurse practitioner shall not act as the patient's attending practitioner after the authority under the health care proxy commences, unless the physician, physician assistant, or nurse practitioner declines the appointment as agent at or before such time.

(d) No person who is not the spouse, child, parent, brother, sister or grandparent of the principal, or is the issue of, or married to, such person, shall be appointed as a health care agent if, at the time of appointment, he or she is presently appointed health care agent for ten principals.

4. Commencement of agent's authority. The agent's authority shall commence upon a determination, made pursuant to subdivision one of section two thousand nine hundred eighty-three of this article, that the principal lacks capacity to make health care decisions.

5. Contents and form of health care proxy.

(a) The health care proxy shall:

(i) identify the principal and agent; and

(ii) indicate that the principal intends the agent to have authority to make health care decisions on the principal's behalf.

(b) The health care proxy may include the principal's wishes or instructions about health care decisions, and limitations upon the agent's authority.

(c) The health care proxy may provide that it expires upon a specified date or upon the occurrence of a certain condition. If no such date or condition is set forth in the proxy, the proxy shall remain in effect until revoked. If, prior to the expiration of a proxy, the authority of the agent has commenced, the proxy shall not expire while the principal lacks capacity.

(d) A health care proxy may, but need not, be in the following form:

Health Care Proxy

I (name of principal) hereby appoint (name, home address and telephone number of agent) as my health care agent to make any and all health care decisions for me, except to the extent I state otherwise.

This health care proxy shall take effect in the event I become unable to make my own health care decisions.

NOTE: Although not necessary, and neither encouraged nor discouraged, you may wish to state instructions or wishes, and limit your agent's authority. Unless your agent knows your wishes about artificial nutrition and hydration, your agent will not have authority to decide about artificial nutrition and hydration. If you choose to state instructions, wishes, or limits, please do so below:

_____

_____

_____

I direct my agent to make health care decisions in accordance with my wishes and instructions as stated above or as otherwise known to him or her. I also direct my agent to abide by any limitations on his or her authority as stated above or as otherwise known to him or her.

In the event the person I appoint above is unable, unwilling or unavailable to act as my health care agent, I hereby appoint (name, home address and telephone number of alternate agent) as my health care agent.

I understand that, unless I revoke it, this proxy will remain in effect indefinitely or until the date or occurrence of the condition I have stated below:

(Please complete the following if you do NOT want this health care proxy to be in effect indefinitely):

This proxy shall expire: (Specify date or condition)

Signature:

Address:

Date:

I declare that the person who signed or asked another to sign this document is personally known to me and appears to be of sound mind and acting willingly and free from duress. He or she signed (or asked another to sign for him or her) this document in my presence and that person signed in my presence. I am not the person appointed as agent by this document.

Witness:

Address:

Witness:

Address:

(e) The health care proxy shall not be executed on a form or other writing that also includes the execution of a power of attorney, provided, however, that nothing in this paragraph shall invalidate a delegation of the authority to make health care decisions executed prior to the enactment of this article.

(f) A health care proxy may include the principal's wishes or instructions regarding organ and tissue donation and may limit the health care agent's authority to consent to organ or tissue donation or designate another person to do so, under article forty-three of this chapter. Failure to state wishes or instructions shall not be construed to imply a wish not to donate.

6. Alternate agent.

(a) A competent adult may designate an alternate agent in the health care proxy to serve in place of the agent when:

(i) the attending practitioner has determined in a writing signed by the physician, physician assistant, or nurse practitioner (A) that the person appointed as agent is not reasonably available, willing and competent to serve as agent, and (B) that such person is not expected to become reasonably available, willing and competent to make a timely decision given the patient's medical circumstances;

(ii) the agent is disqualified from acting on the principal's behalf pursuant to subdivision three of this section or subdivision two of section two thousand nine hundred ninety-two of this article, or

(iii) under conditions set forth in the proxy.

(b) If, after an alternate agent's authority commences, the person appointed as agent becomes available, willing and competent to serve as agent:

(i) the authority of the alternate agent shall cease and the authority of the agent shall commence; and

(ii) the attending practitioner shall record the change in agent and the reasons therefor in the principal's medical record.

History: Add, L 1990, ch 752, § 2, eff Jan 18, 1991; amd, L 1994, ch 23, § 4, eff March 28, 1994; L 2000, ch 540, § 1, eff Oct 4, 200; L 2009, ch 348, § 3, eff Oct 25, 2009; L 2012, ch 56, § 6 (Part J), eff March 30, 2012; L 2018, ch 342, § 2, eff Feb 3, 2019; L 2019, ch 708, § 18, eff June 17, 2020.

§ 2982. Rights and duties of agent

1. Scope of authority. Subject to any express limitations in the health care proxy, an agent shall have the authority to make any and all health care decisions on the principal's behalf that the principal could make. Such authority shall be subject to the provisions of section twenty-nine hundred eighty-nine of this article.

2. Decision-making standard. After consultation with a licensed physician, registered nurse, licensed psychologist, licensed master social worker, or a licensed clinical social worker, the agent shall make health care decisions: (a) in accordance with the principal's wishes, including the principal's religious and moral beliefs; or (b) if the principal's wishes are not reasonably known and cannot with reasonable diligence be ascertained, in accordance with the principal's best interests; provided, however, that if the principal's wishes regarding the administration of artificial nutrition and hydration are not reasonably known and cannot with reasonable diligence be ascertained, the agent shall not have the authority to make decisions regarding these measures.

3. Right to receive information. Notwithstanding any law to the contrary, the agent shall have the right to receive medical information and medical and clinical records necessary to make informed decisions regarding the principal's health care.

4. Priority over other surrogates. Health care decisions by an agent on a principal's behalf pursuant to this article shall have priority over decisions by any other person, except as otherwise provided in the health care proxy or in subdivision five of section two thousand nine hundred eighty-three of this article.

History: Add, L 1990, ch 752, § 2, eff Jan 18, 1991; amd, L 1991, ch 370, § 18, eff July 15, 1991; L 2004, ch 230, § 27, eff July 27, 2004.

§ 2983. Determination of lack of capacity to make health care decisions for the purpose of empowering agent

1. Determination by attending practitioner.

(a) A determination that a principal lacks capacity to make health care decisions shall be made by the attending practitioner to a reasonable degree of medical certainty. The determination shall be made in writing and shall contain such attending practitioner's opinion regarding the cause and nature of the principal's incapacity as well as its extent and probable duration. The determination shall be included in the patient's medical record. For a decision to withdraw or withhold life-sustaining treatment, the attending practitioner who makes the determination that a principal lacks capacity to make health care decisions must consult with another physician, physician assistant, or nurse practitioner to confirm such determination. Such consultation shall also be included within the patient's medical record.

(b) If an attending practitioner of a patient in a general hospital or mental hygiene facility determines that a patient lacks capacity because of mental illness, the attending practitioner who makes the determination must be, or must consult, for the purpose of confirming the determination, with a qualified psychiatrist. A record of such consultation shall be included in the patient's medical record.

(c) If the attending practitioner determines that a patient lacks capacity because of a developmental disability, the attending practitioner who makes the determination must be, or must consult, for the purpose of confirming the determination, with a physician, nurse practitioner, physician assistant, or clinical psychologist who either is employed by a developmental disabilities services office named in section 13.17 of the mental hygiene law, or who has been employed for a minimum of two years to render care and service in a facility operated or licensed by the office for people with developmental disabilities, or has been approved by the commissioner of developmental disabilities in accordance with regulations promulgated by such commissioner. Such regulations shall require that a physician, nurse practitioner, physician assistant, or clinical psychologist possess specialized training or three years experience in treating developmental disabilities. A record of such consultation shall be included in the patient's medical record.

(d) A physician, physician assistant, or nurse practitioner who has been appointed as a patient's agent shall not make the determination of the patient's capacity to make health care decisions.

2. Request for a determination. If requested by the agent, an attending practitioner shall make a determination regarding the principal's capacity to make health care decisions for the purposes of this article.

3. Notice of determination. Notice of a determination that a principal lacks capacity to make health care decisions shall promptly be given: (a) to the principal, orally and in writing, where there is any indication of the principal's ability to comprehend such notice; (b) to the agent; (c) if the principal is in or is transferred from a mental hygiene facility, to the facility director; and (d) to the conservator for, or committee of, the principal

4. Limited purpose of determination. A determination made pursuant to this section that a principal lacks capacity to make health care decisions shall not be construed as a finding that the patient lacks capacity for any other purpose.

5. Priority of principal's decision. Notwithstanding a determination pursuant to this section that the principal lacks capacity to make health care decisions, where a principal objects to the determination of incapacity or to a health care decision made by an agent, the principal's objection or decision shall prevail unless the principal is determined by a court of competent jurisdiction to lack capacity to make health care decisions.

6. Confirmation of lack of capacity.

(a) The attending practitioner shall confirm the principal's continued incapacity before complying with an agent's health care decisions, other than those decisions made at or about the time of the initial determination made pursuant to subdivision one of this section. The confirmation shall be stated in writing and shall be included in the principal's medical record.

(b) The notice requirements set forth in subdivision three of this section shall not apply to the confirmation required by this subdivision.

7. Effect of recovery of capacity. In the event the attending practitioner determines that the principal has regained capacity, the authority of the agent shall cease, but shall recommence if the principal subsequently loses capacity as determined pursuant to this section.

History: Add, L 1990, ch 752, § 2, eff Jan 18, 1991; amd, L 1994, ch 23, § 5, eff March 28, 1994; L 2012, ch 56, § 7 (Part J), eff March 30, 2012; L 2018, ch 342, § 3, eff Feb 3, 2019; L 2019, ch 708, § 19, eff June 17, 2020.

§ 2984. Provider's obligations

1. A health care provider who is provided with a health care proxy shall arrange for the proxy or a copy thereof to be inserted in the principal's medical record if the health care proxy has not been included in such record.

2. A health care provider shall comply with health care decisions made by an agent in good faith under a health care proxy to the same extent as if such decisions had been made by the principal, subject to any limitations in the health care proxy and pursuant to the provisions of subdivision five of section two thousand nine hundred eighty-three of this article.

3. Notwithstanding subdivision two of this section, nothing in this article shall be construed to require a private hospital to honor an agent's health care decision that the hospital would not honor if the decision had been made by the principal because the decision is contrary to a formally adopted policy of the hospital that is expressly based on religious beliefs or sincerely held moral convictions central to the facility's operating principles and the hospital would be permitted by law to refuse to honor the decision if made by the principal, provided:

(a) the hospital has informed the patient or the health care agent of such policy prior to or upon admission, if reasonably possible; and

(b) the patient is transferred promptly to another hospital that is reasonably accessible under the circumstances and is willing to honor the agent's decision and pending transfer the hospital complies with subdivision five of this section. If the agent is unable or unwilling to arrange such a transfer, the hospital may intervene to facilitate such a transfer. If such a transfer is not effected, the hospital shall seek judicial relief in accordance with section twenty-nine hundred ninety-two of this article or honor the agent's decision.

4. Notwithstanding subdivision two of this section, nothing in this article shall be construed to require an individual as a health care provider to honor an agent's health care decision that the individual would not honor if the decision had been made by the principal because the decision is contrary to the individual's religious beliefs or sincerely held moral convictions, provided the individual health care provider promptly informs the health care agent and the hospital of his or her refusal to honor the agent's decision. In such event, the hospital shall promptly transfer responsibility for the patient to another individual health care provider willing to honor the agent's decision. The individual health care provider shall cooperate in

facilitating such transfer of the patient and comply with subdivision five of this section.

5. Notwithstanding the provisions of this section or subdivision two of section twenty-nine hundred eighty-nine of this article, if an agent directs the provision of life-sustaining treatment, the denial of which in reasonable medical judgment would be likely to result in the death of the patient, a hospital or individual health care provider that does not wish to provide such treatment shall nonetheless comply with the agent's decision pending either transfer of the patient to a willing hospital or individual health care provider, or judicial review in accordance with section twenty-nine hundred ninety-two of this article.

> **History:** Add, L 1990, ch 752, § 2, eff Jan 18, 1991; amd, L 2010, ch 8, § 23, eff June 1, 2010.

§ 2985. Revocation

1. Means of revoking proxy.

(a) A competent adult may revoke a health care proxy by notifying the agent or a health care provider orally or in writing or by any other act evidencing a specific intent to revoke the proxy.

(b) For the purposes of this section, every adult shall be presumed competent unless determined otherwise pursuant to court order.

(c) A health care proxy shall also be revoked upon execution by the principal of a subsequent health care proxy.

(d) The creation by the principal of written wishes or instructions about health care, or limitations upon the agent's authority, shall not revoke a health care proxy unless such wishes, instructions or limitations expressly provide otherwise. Such wishes, instructions or limitations shall constitute evidence of the principal's wishes for purposes of subdivision two of section two thousand nine hundred eighty-two of this article.

(e) The appointment of the principal's spouse as health care agent shall be revoked upon the divorce or legal separation of the principal and spouse, unless the principal specifies otherwise.

2. Duty to record revocation.

(a) A physician, physician assistant, or nurse practitioner who is informed of or provided with a revocation of a health care proxy shall immediately (i) record the revocation in the principal's medical record and (ii) notify the agent and the medical staff responsible for the principal's care of the revocation.

(b) Any member of the staff of a health care provider informed of or provided with a revocation of a health care proxy pursuant to this section shall immediately notify a physician, physician assistant, or nurse practitioner of such revocation.

> **History:** Add, L 1990, ch 752, § 2, eff Jan 18, 1991; L 2018, ch 342, § 4, eff Feb 3, 2019; L 2019, ch 708, § 20, eff June 17, 2020.

§ 2986. Immunity

1. Provider immunity. No health care provider or employee thereof shall be subjected to criminal or civil liability, or be deemed to have engaged in unprofessional conduct, for honoring in good faith a health care decision by an agent, or for other actions taken in good

faith pursuant to this article.

2. Agent immunity. No person acting as agent pursuant to a health care proxy shall be subjected to criminal or civil liability for making health care decision in good faith pursuant to this article.

History: Add, L 1990, ch 752, § 2, eff Jan 18, 1991.

§ 2987. Liability for health care costs

Liability for the cost of health care provided pursuant to an agent's decision shall be the same as if the health care were provided pursuant to the principal's decision.

History: Add, L 1990, ch 752, § 2, eff Jan 18, 1991.

§ 2988. Requiring or prohibiting execution of proxy

No person may require or prohibit the execution of a health care proxy by an individual as a condition for providing health care services or insurance to such individual.

History: Add, L 1990, ch 752, § 2, eff Jan 18, 1991.

§ 2989. Effect on other rights

1. A competent adult's failure to appoint a health care agent or to provide the agent with specific health care instructions pursuant to this article shall create no presumptions regarding the adult's wishes about health care.

2. Nothing in this article creates, expands, diminishes, impairs or supersedes any authority that a principal may have under law to make or express decisions, wishes or instructions regarding health care, including decisions about life sustaining treatment, whether or not expressed in a health care proxy.

3. This article is not intended to permit or promote suicide, assisted suicide, or euthanasia; accordingly, nothing herein shall be construed to permit an agent to consent to any act or omission to which the principal could not consent under law.

History: Add, L 1990, ch 752, § 2, eff Jan 18, 1991.

§ 2990. Proxies executed in other states

A health care proxy or similar instrument executed in another state or jurisdiction in compliance with the law of that state or jurisdiction shall be considered validly executed for purposes of this article.

History: Add, L 1990, ch 752, § 2, eff Jan 18, 1991.

§ 2991. Creation and use of proxies in residential health care and mental hygiene facilities

1. Residential health care facilities and mental hygiene facilities shall establish procedures:

(a) to provide information to adult residents about their right to create a health care proxy under this article;

(b) to educate adult residents about the authority delegated under a health care proxy, what a proxy may include or omit, and how a proxy is created and revoked;

(c) to help ensure that each resident who creates a proxy while residing at the facility does so voluntarily.

2. Such procedures shall be established in accordance with regulations issued by the commissioners of health, mental health, and the office for people with developmental disabilities for facilities subject to their respective regulatory authorities.

History: Add, L 1990, ch 752, § 2, eff Jan 18, 1991; L 2019, ch 672, § 25, eff Dec 16, 2019.

§ 2992. Special proceeding authorized

The health care provider, the conservator for, or committee of the principal, members of the principal's family, a close friend of the principal as defined in subdivision five of section two thousand nine hundred sixty-one of this chapter, or the commissioner of health, mental health, or developmental disabilities may commence a special proceeding pursuant to article four of the civil practice law and rules, in a court of competent jurisdiction, with respect to any dispute arising under this article, including, but not limited to, a proceeding to:

1. determine the validity of the health care proxy;

2. have the agent removed on the ground that the agent (a) is not reasonably available, willing and competent to fulfill his or her obligations under this article; (b) is acting in bad faith; or (c) is the subject of an order of protection protecting the principal or has been arrested or charged for a criminal act that allegedly caused the principal's lack of capacity or substantially injured or impaired the health status of the principal, provided that the application of this provision in a particular case may be waived or modified in the interest of justice; or

3. override the agent's decision about health care treatment on the grounds that: (a) the decision was made in bad faith or (b) the decision is not in accordance with the standards set forth in subdivision one or two of section two thousand nine hundred eighty-two of this article.

History: Add, L 1990, ch 752, § 2, eff Jan 18, 1991; amd, L 2014, ch 93, § 1, eff July 22, 2014.

§ 2993. Regulations

The commissioner of health, in consultation with the commissioners of the office of mental health and the office for people with developmental disabilities, shall establish such regulations as may be necessary for the implementation of this article, subject to the provisions of subdivision two of section two thousand nine hundred ninety-one of this article.

History: Add, L 1990, ch 752, § 2, eff Jan 18, 1991; L 2019, ch 672, § 26, eff Dec 16, 2019.

§ 2994. Rights to be publicized

The commissioner of health shall prepare a statement summarizing the rights, duties and requirements of this article and shall require that a copy of such statement:

1. Be furnished to patients or their families at or prior to the time of admission to a hospital, and to each member of the hospital's staff; and

2. Be posted in a public place in each hospital.

The statement of rights required by this section may be included in any other statement of patients' rights required by other provisions of this chapter.

History: Add, L 1990, ch 752, § 2, eff Jan 18, 1991.

ARTICLE 29-CC
FAMILY HEALTH CARE DECISIONS ACT
SUMMARY OF ARTICLE

§ 2994-a. Definitions

The following words or phrases, used in this article, shall have the following meanings, unless the context otherwise requires:

1. "Adult" means any person who is eighteen years of age or older or has married.

2. "Attending practitioner" means a physician, nurse practitioner or physician assistant, selected by or assigned to a patient pursuant to hospital policy, who has primary responsibility for the treatment and care of the patient. Where more than one physician, nurse practitioner or physician assistant shares such responsibility, or where a physician, nurse practitioner or physician assistant is acting on the attending practitioner's behalf, any such physician, nurse practitioner or physician assistant may act as an attending practitioner pursuant to this article.

2-a "Attending nurse practitioner" means a nurse practitioner, selected by or assigned to a patient pursuant to hospital policy, who has primary responsibility for the treatment and care of the patient. Where more than one physician and/or nurse practitioner shares such responsibility, or where a physician or nurse practitioner is acting on the attending physician's or attending nurse practitioner's behalf, any such physician or nurse practitioner may act as an attending physician or attending nurse practitioner pursuant to this article.

3. "Cardiopulmonary resuscitation" means measures, as specified in regulations promulgated by the commissioner, to restore cardiac function or to support ventilation in the event of a cardiac or respiratory arrest. Cardiopulmonary resuscitation shall not include measures to improve ventilation and cardiac function in the absence of an arrest.

4. "Close friend" means any person, eighteen years of age or older, who is a close friend of the patient, or a relative of the patient (other than a spouse, adult child, parent, brother or sister), who has maintained such regular contact with the patient as to be familiar with the patient's activities, health, and religious or moral beliefs, and who presents a signed statement to that effect to the attending practitioner.

5. "Decision-making capacity" means the ability to understand and appreciate the nature and consequences of proposed health care, including the benefits and risks of and alternatives to proposed health care, and to reach an informed decision.

5-a. "Decisions regarding hospice care" means the decision to enroll or disenroll in hospice, and consent to the hospice plan of care and modifications to that plan.

6. "Developmental disability" means a developmental disability as defined in subdivision twenty-two of section 1.03 of the mental hygiene law.

7. "Domestic partner" means a person who, with respect to another person:

(a) is formally a party in a domestic partnership or similar relationship with the other person, entered into pursuant to the laws of the United States or of any state, local or foreign jurisdiction, or registered as the domestic partner of the other person with any registry maintained by the employer of either party or any state, municipality, or foreign jurisdiction; or

(b) is formally recognized as a beneficiary or covered person under the other person's employment benefits or health insurance; or

(c) is dependent or mutually interdependent on the other person for support, as evidenced by the totality of the circumstances indicating a mutual intent to be domestic partners including but not limited to: common ownership or joint leasing of real or personal property; common householding, shared income or shared expenses; children in common; signs of intent to marry or become domestic partners under paragraph (a) or (b) of this subdivision; or the length of the personal relationship of the persons.

Each party to a domestic partnership shall be considered to be the domestic partner of the other party. "Domestic partner" shall not include a person who is related to the other person by blood in a manner that would bar marriage to the other person in New York state. "Domestic partner" also shall not include any person who is less than eighteen years of age or who is the adopted child of the other person or who is related by blood in a manner that would bar marriage in New York state to a person who is the lawful spouse of the other person.

8. "Emancipated minor patient" means a minor patient who is the parent of a child, or who is sixteen years of age or older and living independently from his or her parents or guardian.

9. "Ethics review committee" means the interdisciplinary committee established in

accordance with the requirements of section twenty-nine hundred ninety-four-m of this article.

10. "General hospital" means a general hospital as defined in subdivision ten of section twenty-eight hundred one of this chapter excluding a ward, wing, unit or other part of a general hospital operated for the purpose of providing services for persons with mental illness pursuant to an operating certificate issued by the commissioner of mental health.

11. "Guardian of a minor" or "guardian" means a health care guardian or a legal guardian of the person of a minor.

12. "Health care" means any treatment, service, or procedure to diagnose or treat an individual's physical or mental condition. Providing nutrition or hydration orally, without reliance on medical treatment, is not health care under this article and is not subject to this article.

13. "Health care agent" means a health care agent designated by an adult pursuant to article twenty-nine-C of this chapter.

14. "Health care decision" means any decision to consent or refuse to consent to health care.

15. "Health care guardian" means an individual appointed by a court, pursuant to subdivision four of section twenty-nine hundred ninety-four-r of this article, as the guardian of a minor patient solely for the purpose of deciding about life-sustaining treatment pursuant to this article.

16. "Health care provider" means an individual or facility licensed, certified, or otherwise authorized or permitted by law to administer health care in the ordinary course of business or professional practice.

17. "Health or social service practitioner" means a registered professional nurse, nurse practitioner, physician, physician assistant, psychologist or licensed clinical social worker, licensed or certified pursuant to the education law acting within his or her scope of practice.

17-a. "Hospice" means a hospice as defined in article forty of this chapter, without regard to where the hospice care is provided.

18. "Hospital" means a general hospital, a residential health care facility, or hospice.

19. "Life-sustaining treatment" means any medical treatment or procedure without which the patient will die within a relatively short time, as determined by an attending physician to a reasonable degree of medical certainty. For the purpose of this article, cardiopulmonary resuscitation is presumed to be life-sustaining treatment without the necessity of a determination by an attending physician.

20. "Mental hygiene facility" means a facility operated or licensed by the office of mental health or the office for people with developmental disabilities as defined in subdivision six of section 1.03 of the mental hygiene law.

21. "Mental illness" means a mental illness as defined in subdivision twenty of section 1.03 of the mental hygiene law, and does not include dementia, such as Alzheimer's disease, or other disorders related to dementia.

22. "Minor" means any person who is not an adult.

22-a "Nurse practitioner" means a nurse practitioner certified pursuant to section sixty-nine hundred ten of the education law who is practicing in accordance with subdivision three of section sixty-nine hundred two of the education law.

23. "Order not to resuscitate" means an order not to attempt cardiopulmonary resuscitation in the event a patient suffers cardiac or respiratory arrest.

24. "Parent", for the purpose of a health care decision about a minor patient, means a parent who has custody of, or who has maintained substantial and continuous contact with, the minor patient.

25. "Patient" means a person admitted to a hospital.

26. "Person connected with the case" means the patient, any person on the surrogate list, a parent or guardian of a minor patient, the hospital administrator, an attending physician, any other health or social services practitioner who is or has been directly involved in the patient's care, and any duly authorized state agency, including the facility director or regional director for a patient transferred from a mental hygiene facility and the facility director for a patient transferred from a correctional facility.

27. "Reasonably available" means that a person to be contacted can be contacted with diligent efforts by an attending physician, another person acting on behalf of an attending physician, or the hospital.

28. "Residential health care facility" means a residential health care facility as defined in subdivision three of section twenty-eight hundred one of this chapter.

29. "Surrogate" means the person selected to make a health care decision on behalf of a patient pursuant to section twenty-nine hundred ninety-four-d of this article.

30. "Surrogate list" means the list set forth in subdivision one of section twenty-nine hundred ninety-four-d of this article.

History: Add, L 2010, ch 8, § 2, eff June 1, 2010; amd, L 2011, ch 167, § 1, eff Sept 18, 2011; L 2017, ch 430, § 16, eff May 28, 2018; L 2019, ch 672, § 27, eff Dec 16, 2019; L 2019, ch 708, § 21, eff June 17, 2020.

§ 2994-b. Applicability; priority of certain other surrogate decision-making laws and regulations

1. This article shall apply to health care decisions regarding health care provided in a hospital, and to decisions regarding hospice care without regard to where the decision is made or where the care is provided, for a patient who lacks decision-making capacity, except as limited by this section.

2. Prior to seeking or relying upon a health care decision by a surrogate for a patient under this article, the attending practitioner shall make reasonable efforts to determine whether the patient has a health care agent appointed pursuant to article twenty-nine-C of this chapter. If so, health care decisions for the patient shall be governed by such article, and shall have priority over decisions by any other person except the patient or as otherwise provided in the health care proxy.

3. Prior to seeking or relying upon a health care decision by a surrogate for a patient under

this article, if the attending practitioner has reason to believe that the patient has a history of receiving services for mental retardation or a developmental disability; it reasonably appears to the attending practitioner that the patient has mental retardation or a developmental disability; or the practitioner has reason to believe that the patient has been transferred from a mental hygiene facility operated or licensed by the office of mental health, then such physician, nurse practitioner or physician assistant shall make reasonable efforts to determine whether paragraphs (a), (b) or (c) of this subdivision are applicable:

(a) If the patient has a guardian appointed by a court pursuant to article seventeen-A of the surrogate's court procedure act, health care decisions for the patient shall be governed by section seventeen hundred fifty-b of the surrogate's court procedure act and not by this article.

(b) If a patient does not have a guardian appointed by a court pursuant to article seventeen-A of the surrogate's court procedure act but falls within the class of persons described in paragraph (a) of subdivision one of section seventeen hundred fifty-b of such act, decisions to withdraw or withhold life-sustaining treatment for the patient shall be governed by section seventeen hundred fifty-b of the surrogate's court procedure act and not by this article.

(c) If a health care decision for a patient cannot be made under paragraphs (a) or (b) of this subdivision, but consent for the decision may be provided pursuant to the mental hygiene law or regulations of the office of mental health or the office for people with developmental disabilities, then the decision shall be governed by such statute or regulations and not by this article.

4. If, after reasonable efforts, it is determined that a health care decision for the patient cannot be made pursuant to subdivision two or three of this section, then the health care decision shall be made pursuant to this article.

History: Add, L 2010, ch 8, § 2, eff June 1, 2010; amd, L 2011, ch 167, § 2, eff Sept 18, 2011; L 2017, ch 430, § 17, eff May 28, 2018; L 2019, ch 708, § 22, eff June 17, 2020.

§ 2994-c. Determination of incapacity

1. Presumption of capacity. For purposes of this article, every adult shall be presumed to have decision-making capacity unless determined otherwise pursuant to this section or pursuant to court order, or unless a guardian is authorized to decide about health care for the adult pursuant to article eighty-one of the mental hygiene law.

2. Initial determination by attending practitioner. An attending practitioner shall make an initial determination that an adult patient lacks decision-making capacity to a reasonable degree of medical certainty. Such determination shall include an assessment of the cause and extent of the patient's incapacity and the likelihood that the patient will regain decision-making capacity.

3. Concurring determinations.

(a) An initial determination that a patient lacks decision-making capacity shall be subject to a concurring determination, independently made, where required by this subdivision. A concurring determination shall include an assessment of the cause and extent of the patient's incapacity and the likelihood that the patient will regain decision-making capacity, and shall be included in the patient's medical record. Hospitals shall adopt written policies identifying the training and credentials of health or social services practitioners qualified to provide concurring determinations of incapacity.

(b) (i) In a residential health care facility, a health or social services practitioner employed by or otherwise formally affiliated with the facility must independently determine whether an adult patient lacks decision-making capacity.

(ii) In a general hospital a health or social services practitioner employed by or otherwise formally affiliated with the facility must independently determine whether an adult patient lacks decision-making capacity if the surrogate's decision concerns the withdrawal or withholding of life-sustaining treatment.

(iii) With respect to decisions regarding hospice care for a patient in a general hospital or residential health care facility, the health or social services practitioner must be employed by or otherwise formally affiliated with the general hospital or residential health care facility.

(c) (i) If the attending practitioner makes an initial determination that a patient lacks decision-making capacity because of mental illness, either such physician must have the following qualifications, or another physician with the following qualifications must independently determine whether the patient lacks decision-making capacity: a physician licensed to practice medicine in New York state, who is a diplomate or eligible to be certified by the American Board of Psychiatry and Neurology or who is certified by the American Osteopathic Board of Neurology and Psychiatry or is eligible to be certified by that board. A record of such consultation shall be included in the patient's medical record.

(ii) If the attending practitioner makes an initial determination that a patient lacks decision-making capacity because of a developmental disability, either such physician, nurse practitioner or physician assistant must have the following qualifications, or another professional with the following qualifications must independently determine whether the patient lacks decision-making capacity: a physician or clinical psychologist who either is employed by a developmental disabilities services office named in section 13.17 of the mental hygiene law, or who has been employed for a minimum of two years to render care and service in a facility operated or licensed by the office for people with developmental disabilities, or has been approved by the commissioner of developmental disabilities in accordance with regulations promulgated by such commissioner. Such regulations shall require that a physician or clinical psychologist possess specialized training or three years experience in treating developmental disabilities. A record of such consultation shall be included in the patient's medical record.

(d) If an attending practitioner has determined that the patient lacks decision-making capacity and if the health or social services practitioner consulted for a concurring determination disagrees with the attending practitioner's determination, the matter shall be referred to the ethics review committee if it cannot otherwise be resolved.

4. Informing the patient and surrogate. Notice of a determination that a surrogate will make health care decisions because the adult patient has been determined to lack decision-making capacity shall promptly be given:

(a) to the patient, where there is any indication of the patient's ability to comprehend the information;

(b) to at least one person on the surrogate list highest in order of priority listed when persons in prior classes are not reasonably available pursuant to subdivision one of section twenty-nine hundred ninety-four-d of this article;

(c) if the patient was transferred from a mental hygiene facility, to the director of the mental hygiene facility and to the mental hygiene legal service under article forty-seven of the mental hygiene law.

5. Limited purpose of determination. A determination made pursuant to this section that an adult patient lacks decision-making capacity shall not be construed as a finding that the patient lacks capacity for any other purpose.

6. Priority of patient's decision. Notwithstanding a determination pursuant to this section that an adult patient lacks decision-making capacity, if the patient objects to the determination of incapacity, or to the choice of a surrogate or to a health care decision made by a surrogate or made pursuant to section twenty-nine hundred ninety-four-g of this article, the patient's objection or decision shall prevail unless: (a) a court of competent jurisdiction has determined that the patient lacks decision-making capacity or the patient is or has been adjudged incompetent for all purposes and, in the case of a patient's objection to treatment, makes any other finding required by law to authorize the treatment, or (b) another legal basis exists for overriding the patient's decision.

7. Confirmation of continued lack of decision-making capacity. An attending practitioner shall confirm the adult patient's continued lack of decision-making capacity before complying with health care decisions made pursuant to this article, other than those decisions made at or about the time of the initial determination. A concurring determination of the patient's continued lack of decision-making capacity shall be required if the subsequent health care decision concerns the withholding or withdrawal of life-sustaining treatment. Health care providers shall not be required to inform the patient or surrogate of the confirmation.

History: Add, L 2010, ch 8, § 2, eff June 1, 2010; amd, L 2011, ch 167, § 3, eff Sept 18, 2011; L 2012, ch 56, § 8 (Part J), eff March 30, 2012; L 2017, ch 430, § 18, eff May 28, 2018; L 2019, ch 708, § 23, eff June 17, 2020.

§ 2994-d. Health care decisions for adult patients by surrogates

1. Identifying the surrogate. One person from the following list from the class highest in priority when persons in prior classes are not reasonably available, willing, and competent to act, shall be the surrogate for an adult patient who lacks decision-making capacity. However, such person may designate any other person on the list to be surrogate, provided no one in a class higher in priority than the person designated objects:

(a) A guardian authorized to decide about health care pursuant to article eighty-one of the mental hygiene law;

(b) The spouse, if not legally separated from the patient, or the domestic partner;

(c) A son or daughter eighteen years of age or older;

(d) A parent;

(e) A brother or sister eighteen years of age or older;

(f) A close friend.

2. Restrictions on who may be a surrogate. An operator, administrator, or employee of a hospital or a mental hygiene facility from which the patient was transferred, or a physician, nurse practitioner or physician assistant who has privileges at the hospital or a health care provider under contract with the hospital may not serve as the surrogate for any adult who is a patient of such hospital, unless such individual is related to the patient by blood, marriage, domestic partnership, or adoption, or is a close friend of the patient whose friendship with the patient preceded the patient's admission to the facility. If a physician, nurse practitioner or physician assistant serves as surrogate, the physician, nurse practitioner or physician assistant shall not act as the patient's attending practitioner after his or her authority as surrogate begins.

3. Authority and duties of surrogate.

(a) Scope of surrogate's authority.

(i) Subject to the standards and limitations of this article, the surrogate shall have the authority to make any and all health care decisions on the adult patient's behalf that the patient could make.

(ii) Nothing in this article shall obligate health care providers to seek the consent of a surrogate if an adult patient has already made a decision about the proposed health care, expressed orally or in writing or, with respect to a decision to withdraw or withhold life-sustaining treatment expressed either orally during hospitalization in the presence of two witnesses eighteen years of age or older, at least one of whom is a health or social services practitioner affiliated with the hospital, or in writing. If an attending practitioner relies on the patient's prior decision, the physician, nurse practitioner or physician assistant shall record the prior decision in the patient's medical record. If a surrogate has already been designated for the patient, the attending practitioner shall make reasonable efforts to notify the surrogate prior to implementing the decision; provided that in the case of a decision to withdraw or withhold life-sustaining treatment, the attending practitioner shall make diligent efforts to notify the surrogate and, if unable to notify the surrogate, shall document the efforts that were made to do so.

(b) Commencement of surrogate's authority. The surrogate's authority shall commence upon a determination, made pursuant to section twenty-nine hundred ninety-four-c of this article, that the adult patient lacks decision-making capacity and upon identification of a surrogate pursuant to subdivision one of this section. In the event an attending practitioner determines that the patient has regained decision-making capacity, the authority of the surrogate shall cease.

(c) Right and duty to be informed. Notwithstanding any law to the contrary, the surrogate shall have the right to receive medical information and medical records necessary to make informed decisions about the patient's health care. Health care providers shall provide and the surrogate shall seek information necessary to make an informed decision, including information about the patient's diagnosis, prognosis, the nature and consequences of proposed health care, and the benefits and risks of and alternatives to proposed health care.

4. Decision-making standards.

(a) The surrogate shall make health care decisions:

(i) in accordance with the patient's wishes, including the patient's religious and moral beliefs; or

(ii) if the patient's wishes are not reasonably known and cannot with reasonable diligence be ascertained, in accordance with the patient's best interests. An assessment of the patient's best interests shall include: consideration of the dignity and uniqueness of every person; the possibility and extent of preserving the patient's life; the preservation, improvement or restoration of the patient's health or functioning; the relief of the patient's suffering; and any medical condition and such other concerns and values as a reasonable person in the patient's circumstances would wish to consider.

(b) In all cases, the surrogate's assessment of the patient's wishes and best interests shall be patient-centered; health care decisions shall be made on an individualized basis for each patient, and shall be consistent with the values of the patient, including the patient's religious and moral beliefs, to the extent reasonably possible.

5. Decisions to withhold or withdraw life-sustaining treatment. In addition to the standards set forth in subdivision four of this section, decisions by surrogates to withhold or withdraw life-sustaining treatment (including decisions to accept a hospice plan of care that provides for the withdrawal or withholding of life-sustaining treatment) shall be authorized only if the following conditions are satisfied, as applicable:

(a) (i) Treatment would be an extraordinary burden to the patient and an attending practitioner determines, with the independent concurrence of another physician, nurse practitioner or physician assistant, that, to a reasonable degree of medical certainty and in accord with accepted medical standards, (A) the patient has an illness or injury which can be expected to cause death within six months, whether or not treatment is provided; or (B) the patient is permanently unconscious; or

(ii) The provision of treatment would involve such pain, suffering or other burden that it would reasonably be deemed inhumane or extraordinarily burdensome under the circumstances and the patient has an irreversible or incurable condition, as determined by an attending practitioner with the independent concurrence of another physician, nurse practitioner or physician assistant to a reasonable degree of medical certainty and in accord with accepted medical standards.

(b) In a residential health care facility, a surrogate shall have the authority to refuse life-sustaining treatment under subparagraph (ii) of paragraph (a) of this subdivision only if the ethics review committee, including at least one physician, nurse practitioner or physician assistant who is not directly responsible for the patient's care, or a court of competent jurisdiction, reviews the decision and determines that it meets the standards set forth in this article. This requirement shall not apply to a decision to withhold cardiopulmonary resuscitation.

(c) In a general hospital, if the attending practitioner objects to a surrogate's decision, under subparagraph (ii) of paragraph (a) of this subdivision, to withdraw or withhold nutrition and hydration provided by means of medical treatment, the decision shall not be implemented until the ethics review committee, including at least one physician, nurse practitioner or physician assistant who is not directly responsible for the patient's care, or a court of competent jurisdiction, reviews the decision and determines that it meets the standards set forth in this subdivision and subdivision four of this section.

(d) Providing nutrition and hydration orally, without reliance on medical treatment, is not health care under this article and is not subject to this article.

(e) Expression of decisions. The surrogate shall express a decision to withdraw or withhold life-sustaining treatment either orally to an attending practitioner or in writing.

History: Add, L 2010, ch 8, § 2, eff June 1, 2010; amd, L 2011, ch 167, § 4, eff Sept 18, 2011; L 2017, ch 430, § 19, eff May 28, 2018; L 2019, ch 708, § 24, eff June 17, 2020.

§ 2994-e. Decisions about life-sustaining treatment for minor patients

1. Authority of parent or guardian. The parent or guardian of a minor patient shall have the authority to make decisions about life-sustaining treatment, including decisions to withhold or withdraw such treatment, subject to the provisions of this section and subdivision five of section twenty-nine hundred ninety-four-d of this article.

2. Decision-making standards and procedures for minor patient.

(a) The parent or guardian of a minor patient shall make decisions in accordance with the minor's best interests, consistent with the standards set forth in subdivision four of section twenty-nine hundred ninety-four-d of this article, taking into account the minor's wishes as appropriate under the circumstances.

(b) An attending practitioner, in consultation with a minor's parent or guardian, shall determine whether a minor patient has decision-making capacity for a decision to withhold or withdraw life-sustaining treatment. If the minor has such capacity, a parent's or guardian's decision to withhold or withdraw life-sustaining treatment for the minor may not be implemented without the minor's consent.

(c) Where a parent or guardian of a minor patient has made a decision to withhold or withdraw life-sustaining treatment and an attending practitioner has reason to believe that the minor patient has a parent or guardian who has not been informed of the decision, including a non-custodial parent or guardian, an attending practitioner or someone acting on his or her behalf, shall make reasonable efforts to determine if the uninformed parent or guardian has maintained substantial and continuous contact with the minor and, if so, shall make diligent efforts to notify that parent or guardian prior to implementing the decision.

3. Decision-making standards and procedures for emancipated minor patient.

(a) If an attending practitioner determines that a patient is an emancipated minor patient with decision-making capacity, the patient shall have the authority to decide about life-sustaining treatment. Such authority shall include a decision to withhold or withdraw life-sustaining treatment if an attending practitioner and the ethics review committee determine that the decision accords with the standards for surrogate decisions for adults, and the ethics review committee approves the decision.

(b) If the hospital can with reasonable efforts ascertain the identity of the parents or guardian of an emancipated minor patient, the hospital shall notify such persons prior to withholding or withdrawing life-sustaining treatment pursuant to this subdivision.

History: Add, L 2010, ch 8, § 2, eff June 1, 2010; amd, L 2017, ch 430, § 20, eff May 28, 2018; L 2019, ch 708, § 25, eff June 17, 2020.

§ 2994-f. Obligations of attending practitioner

1. An attending practitioner informed of a decision to withdraw or withhold life-sustaining treatment made pursuant to the standards of this article shall record the decision in the patient's medical record, review the medical basis for the decision, and shall either: (a) implement the decision, or (b) promptly make his or her objection to the decision and the reasons for the objection known to the decision-maker, and either make all reasonable efforts to arrange for the transfer of the patient to another physician, nurse practitioner or physician assistant, if necessary, or promptly refer the matter to the ethics review committee.

2. If an attending practitioner has actual notice of the following objections or disagreements, he or she shall promptly refer the matter to the ethics review committee if the objection or disagreement cannot otherwise be resolved:

(a) A health or social services practitioner consulted for a concurring determination that an adult patient lacks decision-making capacity disagrees with the attending practitioner's determination; or

(b) Any person on the surrogate list objects to the designation of the surrogate pursuant to subdivision one of section twenty-nine hundred ninety-four-d of this article; or

(c) Any person on the surrogate list objects to a surrogate's decision; or

(d) A parent or guardian of a minor patient objects to the decision by another parent or guardian of the minor; or

(e) A minor patient refuses life-sustaining treatment, and the minor's parent or guardian wishes the treatment to be provided, or the minor patient objects to an attending practitioner's determination about decision-making capacity or recommendation about life-sustaining treatment.

3. Notwithstanding the provisions of this section or subdivision one of section twenty-nine hundred ninety-four-q of this article, if a surrogate directs the provision of life-sustaining treatment, the denial of which in reasonable medical judgment would be likely to result in the death of the patient, a hospital or individual health care provider that does not wish to provide such treatment shall nonetheless comply with the surrogate's decision pending either transfer of the patient to a willing hospital or individual health care provider, or judicial review in accordance with section twenty-nine hundred ninety-four-r of this article.

History: Add, L 2010, ch 8, § 2, eff June 1, 2010; amd, L 2017, ch 430, § 21, eff May 28, 2018; L 2019, ch 708, § 26, eff June 17, 2020.

§ 2994-g. Health care decisions for adult patients without surrogates

1. Identifying adult patients without surrogates. Within a reasonable time after admission as an inpatient to the hospital of each adult patient, the hospital shall make reasonable efforts to determine if the patient has appointed a health care agent or has a guardian, or if at least one individual is available to serve as the patient's surrogate in the event the patient lacks or loses decision-making capacity. With respect to a patient who lacks capacity, if no such health care agent, guardian or potential surrogate is identified, the hospital shall identify, to the extent reasonably possible, the patient's wishes and preferences, including the patient's religious and moral beliefs, about pending health care decisions, and shall record its findings in the patient's medical record.

2. Decision-making standards and procedures.

(a) The procedures specified in this and the following subdivisions of this section apply to health care decisions for adult patients who would qualify for surrogate decision-making under this article but for whom no surrogate is reasonably available, willing or competent to act.

(b) Any health care decision made pursuant to this section shall be made in accordance with the standards set forth in subdivision four of section twenty-nine hundred ninety-four-d of this article and shall not be based on the financial interests of the hospital or any other health care provider. The specific procedures to be followed depend on whether the decision involves routine medical treatment, major medical treatment, or the withholding or withdrawal of life-sustaining treatment, and the location where the treatment is provided.

3. Routine medical treatment.

(a) For purposes of this subdivision, "routine medical treatment" means any treatment, service, or procedure to diagnose or treat an individual's physical or mental condition, such as the administration of medication, the extraction of bodily fluids for analysis, or dental care performed with a local anesthetic, for which health care providers ordinarily do not seek specific consent from the patient or authorized representative. It shall not include the long-term provision of treatment such as ventilator support or a nasogastric tube but shall include such treatment when provided as part of post-operative care or in response to an acute illness and recovery is reasonably expected within one month or less.

(b) An attending practitioner shall be authorized to decide about routine medical treatment for an adult patient who has been determined to lack decision-making capacity pursuant to section twenty-nine hundred ninety-four-c of this article. Nothing in this subdivision shall require health care providers to obtain specific consent for treatment where specific consent is not otherwise required by law.

4. Major medical treatment.

(a) For purposes of this subdivision, "major medical treatment" means any treatment, service or procedure to diagnose or treat an individual's physical or mental condition: (i) where general anesthetic is used; or (ii) which involves any significant risk; or (iii) which involves any significant invasion of bodily integrity requiring an incision, producing substantial pain, discomfort, debilitation or having a significant recovery period; or (iv) which involves the use of physical restraints, as specified in regulations promulgated by the commissioner, except in an emergency; or (v) which involves the use of psychoactive medications, except when provided as part of post-operative care or in response to an acute illness and treatment is reasonably expected to be administered over a period of forty-eight hours or less, or when provided in an emergency.

(b) A decision to provide major medical treatment, made in accordance with the following requirements, shall be authorized for an adult patient who has been determined to lack decision-making capacity pursuant to section twenty-nine hundred ninety-four-c of this article.

(i) An attending practitioner shall make a recommendation in consultation with hospital staff directly responsible for the patient's care.

(ii) In a general hospital, at least one other physician, nurse practitioner or physician assistant designated by the hospital must independently determine that he or she concurs that the recommendation is appropriate.

(iii) In a residential health care facility, and for a hospice patient not in a general hospital, the medical director of the facility or hospice, or a physician, nurse practitioner or physician assistant designated by the medical director, must independently determine that he or she concurs that the recommendation is appropriate; provided that if the medical director is the patient's attending practitioner, a different physician, nurse practitioner or physician assistant designated by the residential health care facility or hospice must make this independent determination. Any health or social services practitioner employed by or otherwise formally affiliated with the facility or hospice may provide a second opinion for decisions about physical restraints made pursuant to this subdivision.

5. Decisions to withhold or withdraw life-sustaining treatment.

(a) A court of competent jurisdiction may make a decision to withhold or withdraw life-sustaining treatment for an adult patient who has been determined to lack decision-making capacity pursuant to section twenty-nine hundred ninety-four-c of this article if the court finds that the decision accords with standards for decisions for adults set forth in subdivisions four and five of section twenty-nine hundred ninety-four-d of this article.

(b) If the attending practitioner, with independent concurrence of a second physician, nurse practitioner or physician assistant designated by the hospital, determines to a reasonable degree of medical certainty that:

(i) life-sustaining treatment offers the patient no medical benefit because the patient will die imminently, even if the treatment is provided; and

(ii) the provision of life-sustaining treatment would violate accepted medical standards, then such treatment may be withdrawn or withheld from an adult patient who has been determined to lack decision-making capacity pursuant to section twenty-nine hundred ninety-four-c of this article, without judicial approval. This paragraph shall not apply to any treatment necessary to alleviate pain or discomfort.

5-a. Decisions regarding hospice care. An attending practitioner shall be authorized to make decisions regarding hospice care and execute appropriate documents for such decisions (including a hospice election form) for an adult patient under this section who is hospice eligible in accordance with the following requirements.

(a) The attending practitioner shall make decisions under this section in consultation with staff directly responsible for the patient's care, and shall base his or her decisions on the standards for surrogate decisions set forth in subdivisions four and five of section twenty-nine hundred ninety-four-d of this article;

(b) There is a concurring opinion as follows:

(i) in a general hospital, at least one other physician, nurse practitioner or physician assistant designated by the hospital must independently determine that he or she concurs that the recommendation is consistent with such standards for surrogate decisions;

(ii) in a residential health care facility, the medical director of the facility, or a physician, nurse practitioner or physician assistant designated by the medical director, must independently determine that he or she concurs that the recommendation is consistent with such standards for surrogate decisions; provided that if the medical director is the patient's attending practitioner, a different physician, nurse practitioner or physician assistant designated by the residential health care facility must make this independent determination; or

(iii) in settings other than a general hospital or residential health care facility, the medical director of the hospice, or a physician designated by the medical director, must independently determine that he or she concurs that the recommendation is medically appropriate and consistent with such standards for surrogate decisions; provided that if the medical director is the patient's attending physician, a different physician designated by the hospice must make this independent determination; and

(c) The ethics review committee of the general hospital, residential health care facility or hospice, as applicable, including at least one physician, nurse practitioner or physician assistant who is not the patient's attending practitioner, or a court of competent jurisdiction, must review the decision and determine that it is consistent with such standards for surrogate decisions. This requirement shall not apply to decisions about routine medical treatment. Such decisions shall be governed by subdivision three of this section.

6. Physician, nurse practitioner or physician assistant objection. If a physician, nurse practitioner or physician assistant consulted for a concurring opinion objects to an attending practitioner's recommendation or determination made pursuant to this section, or a member of the hospital staff directly responsible for the patient's care objects to an attending practitioner's recommendation about major medical treatment or treatment without medical benefit, the matter shall be referred to the ethics review committee if it cannot be otherwise resolved.

History: Add, L 2010, ch 8, § 2, eff June 1, 2010; amd, L 2011, ch 167, §§ 5, 6, eff Sept 18, 2011; L 2015, ch 107, §§ 1, 2, eff Aug 13, 2015; L 2017, ch 430, § 22, eff May 28, 2018; L 2019, ch 622, § 1, eff Dec 12, 2019; L 2019, ch 708, § 27, eff June 17, 2020 .

§ 2994-i. Specific policies for orders not to resuscitate

An order not to resuscitate shall be written in the patient's medical record. Consent to an order not to resuscitate shall not constitute consent to withhold or withdraw treatment other than cardiopulmonary resuscitation.

History: Add, L 2010, ch 8, § 2, eff June 1, 2010.

§ 2994-j. Revocation of consent

1. A patient, surrogate, or parent or guardian of a minor patient may at any time revoke his or her consent to withhold or withdraw life-sustaining treatment by informing an attending practitioner or a member of the medical or nursing staff of the revocation.

2. An attending practitioner informed of a revocation of consent made pursuant to this section shall immediately:

(a) record the revocation in the patient's medical record;

(b) cancel any orders implementing the decision to withhold or withdraw treatment; and

(c) notify the hospital staff directly responsible for the patient's care of the revocation and any cancellations.

3. Any member of the medical or nursing staff, other than a nurse practitioner or physician assistant, informed of a revocation made pursuant to this section shall immediately notify an attending practitioner of the revocation.

History: Add, L 2010, ch 8, § 2, eff June 1, 2010; amd, L 2017, ch 430, § 23, eff May 28, 2018; L 2019, ch 708, § 28, eff June 17, 2020.

§ 2994-k. Implementation and review of decisions

1. Hospitals shall adopt written policies requiring implementation and regular review of decisions to withhold or withdraw life-sustaining treatment in accordance with accepted medical standards. Hospitals shall also develop policies in accord with accepted medical standards regarding documentation of clinical determinations and decisions by surrogates and health care providers pursuant to this article.

2. If a decision to withhold or withdraw life-sustaining treatment has been made pursuant to this article, and an attending practitioner determines at any time that the decision is no longer appropriate or authorized because the patient has regained decision-making capacity or because the patient's condition has otherwise improved, the physician, nurse practitioner or physician assistant shall immediately:

(a) include such determination in the patient's medical record;

(b) cancel any orders or plans of care implementing the decision to withhold or withdraw life-sustaining treatment;

(c) notify the person who made the decision to withhold or withdraw treatment, or, if that person is not reasonably available, to at least one person on the surrogate list highest in order of priority listed when persons in prior classes are not reasonably available pursuant to subdivision one of section twenty-nine hundred ninety-four-d of this article; and

(d) notify the hospital staff directly responsible for the patient's care of any cancelled orders or plans of care.

History: Add, L 2010, ch 8, § 2, eff June 1, 2010; amd, L 2017, ch 430, § 24, eff May 28, 2018; L 2019, ch 708, § 29, eff June 17, 2020 .

§ 2994-l. Interinstitutional transfers

If a patient with an order to withhold or withdraw life-sustaining treatment is transferred from a mental hygiene facility to a hospital or from a hospital to a different hospital, any such order or plan shall remain effective until an attending practitioner first examines the transferred patient, whereupon an attending practitioner must either:

1. Issue appropriate orders to continue the prior order or plan. Such orders may be issued without obtaining another consent to withhold or withdraw life-sustaining treatment pursuant to this article; or

2. Cancel such order, if the attending practitioner determines that the order is no longer appropriate or authorized. Before canceling the order the attending practitioner shall make reasonable efforts to notify the person who made the decision to withhold or withdraw treatment and the hospital staff directly responsible for the patient's care of any such

cancellation. If such notice cannot reasonably be made prior to canceling the order or plan, the attending practitioner shall make such notice as soon as reasonably practicable after cancellation.

History: Add, L 2010, ch 8, § 2, eff June 1, 2010; amd L 2017, ch 430, § 25, eff May 28, 2018; L 2019, ch 708, § 30, eff June 17, 2020.

§ 2994-m. Ethics review committees

1. Establishment of an ethics review committee, written policy. Each hospital shall establish at least one ethics review committee or participate in an ethics review committee that serves more than one hospital, and shall adopt a written policy governing committee functions, composition, and procedure, in accordance with the requirements of this article. A hospital may designate an existing committee, or subcommittee thereof, to carry out the functions of the ethics review committee provided the requirements of this section are satisfied.

2. Functions of the ethics review committee.

(a) The ethics review committee shall consider and respond to any health care matter presented to it by a person connected with the case.

(b) The ethics review committee response to a health care matter may include:

(i) providing advice on the ethical aspects of proposed health care;

(ii) making a recommendation about proposed health care; or

(iii) providing assistance in resolving disputes about proposed health care.

(c) Recommendations and advice by the ethics review committee shall be advisory and nonbinding, except as specified in subdivision five of section twenty-nine hundred ninety-four-d of this article and subdivision three of section twenty-nine hundred ninety-four-e of this article.

3. Committee membership. The membership of ethics review committees must be interdisciplinary and must include at least five members who have demonstrated an interest in or commitment to patient's rights or to the medical, public health, or social needs of those who are ill. At least three ethics review committee members must be health or social services practitioners, at least one of whom must be a registered nurse and one of whom must be a physician, nurse practitioner or physician assistant. At least one member must be a person without any governance, employment or contractual relationship with the hospital. In a residential health care facility the facility must offer the residents' council of the facility (or of another facility that participates in the committee) the opportunity to appoint up to two persons to the ethics review committee, none of whom may be a resident of or a family member of a resident of such facility, and both of whom shall be persons who have expertise in or a demonstrated commitment to patient rights or to the care and treatment of the elderly or nursing home residents through professional or community activities, other than activities performed as a health care provider.

4. Procedures for ethics review committee.

(a) These procedures are required only when: (i) the ethics review committee is convened to review a decision by a surrogate to withhold or withdraw life-sustaining treatment for: (A) a patient in a residential health care facility pursuant to paragraph (b) of subdivision five of section twenty-nine hundred ninety-four-d of this article; (B) a patient in a general hospital pursuant to paragraph (c) of subdivision five of section twenty-nine hundred ninety-four-d of this article; or (C) an emancipated minor patient pursuant to subdivision three of section twenty-nine hundred ninety-four-e of this article; or (ii) when a person connected with the case requests the ethics review committee to provide assistance in resolving a dispute about proposed care. Nothing in this section shall bar health care providers from first striving to resolve disputes through less formal means, including the informal solicitation of ethical advice from any source.

(b) (i) A person connected with the case may not participate as an ethics review committee member in the consideration of that case.

(ii) The ethics review committee shall respond promptly, as required by the circumstances, to any request for assistance in resolving a dispute or consideration of a decision to withhold or withdraw life-sustaining treatment pursuant to paragraphs (b) and (c) of subdivision five of section twenty-nine hundred ninety-four-d of this article made by a person connected with the case. The committee shall permit persons connected with the case to present their views to the committee, and to have the option of being accompanied by an advisor when participating in a committee meeting.

(iii) The ethics review committee shall promptly provide the patient, where there is any indication of the patient's ability to comprehend the information, the surrogate, other persons on the surrogate list directly involved in the decision or dispute regarding the patient's care, any parent or guardian of a minor patient directly involved in the decision or dispute regarding the minor patient's care, an attending practitioner, the hospital, and other persons the committee deems appropriate, with the following:

(A) notice of any pending case consideration concerning the patient, including, for patients, persons on the surrogate list, parents and guardians, information about the ethics review committee's procedures, composition and function; and

(B) the committee's response to the case, including a written statement of the reasons for approving or disapproving the withholding or withdrawal of life-sustaining treatment for decisions considered pursuant to subparagraph (ii) of paragraph (a) of subdivision five of section twenty-nine hundred ninety-four-d of this article. The committee's response to the case shall be included in the patient's medical record.

(iv) Following ethics review committee consideration of a case concerning the withdrawal or withholding of life-sustaining treatment, treatment shall not be withdrawn or withheld until the persons identified in subparagraph (iii) of this paragraph have been informed of the committee's response to the case.

(c) When an ethics review committee is convened to review decisions regarding hospice care for a patient in a general hospital or residential health care facility, the responsibilities of this section shall be carried out by the ethics review committee of the general hospital or residential health care facility, provided that such committee shall invite a representative from hospice to participate.

5. Access to medical records and information; patient confidentiality. Ethics review committee members and consultants shall have access to medical information and medical records necessary to perform their function under this article. Any such information or records

disclosed to committee members, consultants, or others shall be kept confidential except to the extent necessary to accomplish the purposes of this article or as otherwise provided by law.

6. Ethics review committee confidentiality. Notwithstanding any other provisions of law, the proceedings and records of an ethics review committee shall be kept confidential and shall not be released by committee members, committee consultants, or other persons privy to such proceedings and records; the proceedings and records of an ethics review committee shall not be subject to disclosure or inspection in any manner, including under article six of the public officers law or article thirty-one of the civil practice law and rules; and, no person shall testify as to the proceedings or records of an ethics review committee, nor shall such proceedings and records otherwise be admissible as evidence in any action or proceeding of any kind in any court or before any other tribunal, board, agency or person, except that:

(a) Ethics review committee proceedings and records, in cases where a committee approves or disapproves of the withholding or withdrawal of life-sustaining treatment pursuant to subdivision five of section twenty-nine hundred ninety-four-d of this article, or subdivision three of section twenty-nine hundred ninety-four-e of this article, may be obtained by or released to the department;

(b) Nothing in this subdivision shall prohibit the patient, the surrogate, other persons on the surrogate list, or a parent or guardian of a minor patient from voluntarily disclosing, releasing or testifying about committee proceedings or records; and

(c) Nothing in this subdivision shall prohibit the justice center for the protection of people with special needs or any agency or person within or under contract with the justice center which provides protection and advocacy services from requiring any information, report or record from a hospital in accordance with the provisions of section five hundred fifty-eight of the executive law.

History: Add, L 2010, ch 8, § 2, eff June 1, 2010; amd, L 2011, ch 167, § 7, eff Sept 18, 2011; L 2012, ch 501, § 7 (Part A), eff June 30, 2013; L 2017, ch 430, § 26, eff May 28, 2018; L 2019, ch 708, § 31, eff June 17, 2020.

§ 2994-n. Conscience objections

1. Private hospitals. Nothing in this article shall be construed to require a private hospital to honor a health care decision made pursuant to this article if:

(a) The decision is contrary to a formally adopted policy of the hospital that is expressly based on sincerely held religious beliefs or sincerely held moral convictions central to the facility's operating principles;

(b) The hospital has informed the patient, family, or surrogate of such policy prior to or upon admission, if reasonably possible; and

(c) The patient is transferred promptly to another hospital that is reasonably accessible under the circumstances and willing to honor the decision and pending transfer the hospital complies with subdivision three of section twenty-nine hundred ninety-four-f of this article. If the patient's family or surrogate is unable or unwilling to arrange such a transfer, the hospital may intervene to facilitate such a transfer. If such a transfer is not effected, the hospital shall seek judicial relief in accordance with section twenty-nine hundred ninety-four-r of this article or honor the decision.

2. Individual health care providers. Nothing in this article shall be construed to require an individual as a health care provider to honor a health care decision made pursuant to this article if:

(a) the decision is contrary to the individual's sincerely held religious beliefs or sincerely held moral conviction; and

(b) the individual health care provider promptly informs the person who made the decision and the hospital of his or her refusal to honor the decision. In such event, the hospital shall promptly transfer responsibility for the patient to another individual health care provider willing to honor the decision. The individual health care provider shall cooperate in facilitating such transfer and comply with subdivision three of section twenty-nine hundred ninety-four-f of this article.

History: Add, L 2010, ch 8, § 2, eff June 1, 2010.

§ 2994-o. Immunity

1. Ethics review committee. No person shall be subject to criminal or civil liability, or be deemed to have engaged in unprofessional conduct, for acts performed reasonably and in good faith pursuant to this article as a member of or as a consultant to an ethics review committee or as a participant in an ethics review committee meeting.

2. Providers. No health care provider or employee thereof shall be subjected to criminal or civil liability, or be deemed to have engaged in unprofessional conduct, for honoring reasonably and in good faith a health care decision made pursuant to this article or for other actions taken reasonably and in good faith pursuant to this article.

3. Surrogates and guardians. No person shall be subjected to criminal or civil liability for making a health care decision reasonably and in good faith pursuant to this article or for other actions taken reasonably and in good faith pursuant to this article.

History: Add, L 2010, ch 8, § 2, eff June 1, 2010.

§ 2994-p. Liability for health care costs

Liability for the cost of health care provided to an adult patient pursuant to this article shall be the same as if the health care were provided pursuant to the patient's decision. No person shall become liable for the cost of health care for a minor solely by virtue of making a decision as a guardian of a minor pursuant to this article.

History: Add, L 2010, ch 8, § 2, eff June 1, 2010.

§ 2994-q. Effect on other rights

1. Nothing in this article creates, expands, diminishes, impairs, or supersedes any authority that an individual may have under law to make or express decisions, wishes, or instructions regarding health care on his or her own behalf, including decisions about life-sustaining treatment.

2. Nothing in this article shall affect existing law concerning implied consent to health care in an emergency.

3. Nothing in this article is intended to permit or promote suicide, assisted suicide, or euthanasia.

4. This article shall not affect existing law with respect to sterilization.

PHL

5. Nothing in this article diminishes the duty of parents and legal guardians under existing law to consent to treatment for minors.

History: Add, L 2010, ch 8, § 2, eff June 1, 2010.

§ 2994-r. Special proceeding authorized; court orders; health care guardian for minor patient

1. Special proceeding. Any person connected with the case and any member of the hospital ethics review committee may commence a special proceeding pursuant to article four of the civil practice law and rules in a court of competent jurisdiction with respect to any matter arising under this article.

2. Court orders designating surrogate. A court of competent jurisdiction may designate any individual from the surrogate list to act as surrogate, regardless of that individual's priority on the list, if the court determines that such appointment would best accord with the patient's wishes or, if the patient's wishes are not reasonably known, with the patient's best interests. The court may remove a surrogate on the ground that the surrogate: (a) is not reasonably available, willing and competent to fulfill his or her obligations under this article; (b) is acting in bad faith; or (c) is the subject of an order of protection protecting the patient or has been arrested or charged for a criminal act that allegedly caused the patient's lack of capacity or substantially injured or impaired the health status of the patient, provided that the application of this provision in a particular case may be waived or modified in the interest of justice. Unless otherwise determined by a court, no surrogate decision made prior to an order designating a surrogate shall be deemed to have been invalid because of the issuance of a designating order.

3. Court orders to withhold or withdraw life-sustaining treatment. A court of competent jurisdiction may authorize the withholding or withdrawal of life-sustaining treatment from a person if the court determines that the person lacks decision-making capacity, and withdrawing or withholding the treatment would accord with the standards set forth in subdivision five of section twenty-nine hundred ninety-four-d of this article.

4. Health care guardian for a minor patient.

(a) No appointment shall be made pursuant to this subdivision if a parent or legal guardian of the person is available, willing, and competent to decide about treatment for the minor.

(b) The following persons may commence a special proceeding in a court of competent jurisdiction to seek appointment as the health care guardian of a minor patient solely for the purpose of deciding about life-sustaining treatment pursuant to this article:

(i) the hospital administrator;

(ii) an attending practitioner;

(iii) the local commissioner of social services or the local commissioner of health, authorized to make medical treatment decisions for the minor pursuant to section three hundred eighty-three-b of the social services law; or

(iv) an individual, eighteen years of age or older, who has assumed care of the minor for a substantial and continuous period of time.

(c) Notice of the proceeding shall be given to the persons identified in section seventeen hundred five of the surrogate's court procedure act.

(d) Notwithstanding any other provision of law, seeking appointment or being appointed as a health care guardian shall not otherwise affect the legal status or rights of the individual seeking or obtaining such appointment.

History: Add, L 2010, ch 8, § 2, eff June 1, 2010; amd, L 2014, ch 93, § 2, eff July 22, 2014; L 2017, ch 430, § 27, eff May 28, 2018; L 2019, ch 708, § 32, eff June 17, 2020.

§ 2994-s. Remedy

1. Any hospital, attending practitioner that refuses to honor a health care decision by a surrogate made pursuant to this article and in accord with the standards set forth in this article shall not be entitled to compensation for treatment, services, or procedures refused by the surrogate, except that this subdivision shall not apply:

(a) when a hospital, physician, nurse practitioner or physician assistant exercises the rights granted by section twenty-nine hundred ninety-four-n of this article, provided that the physician, nurse practitioner, physician assistant or hospital promptly fulfills the obligations set forth in section twenty-nine hundred ninety-four-n of this article;

(b) while a matter is under consideration by the ethics review committee, provided that the matter is promptly referred to and considered by the committee;

(c) in the event of a dispute between individuals on the surrogate list; or

(d) if the physician, nurse practitioner, physician assistant or hospital prevails in any litigation concerning the surrogate's decision to refuse the treatment, services or procedure. Nothing in this section shall determine or affect how disputes among individuals on the surrogate list are resolved.

2. The remedy provided in this section is in addition to and cumulative with any other remedies available at law or in equity or by administrative proceedings to a patient, a health care agent appointed pursuant to article twenty-nine-C of this chapter, or a person authorized to make health care decisions pursuant to this article, including injunctive and declaratory relief, and any other provisions of this chapter governing fines, penalties, or forfeitures.

History: Add, L 2010, ch 8, § 2, eff June 1, 2010; amd, L 2017, ch 430, § 28, eff May 28, 2018; L 2019, ch 708, § 33, eff June 17, 2020.

§ 2994-t. Regulations

1. The commissioner shall establish such regulations as may be necessary to implement this article.

2. The commissioner, in consultation with the commissioners of the office of mental health and the office for people with developmental disabilities, shall promulgate regulations identifying the credentials of health care professionals qualified to provide an independent determination, pursuant to subdivision three of section twenty-nine hundred ninety-four-c of this article, that a patient lacks decision-making capacity because of mental illness or developmental disability.

History: Add, L 2010, ch 8, § 2, eff June 1, 2010; L 2019, ch 672, § 28, eff Dec 16, 2019.

§ 2994-u. Rights to be publicized

The commissioner shall prepare a statement summarizing the rights, duties, and requirements of this article and shall require that a copy of such statement be furnished to patients or to persons on the surrogate list known to the hospital, or to the parents or guardians of minor patients, at or prior to admission to the hospital, or within a reasonable time thereafter, and to each member of the hospital's staff directly involved with patient care.

History: Add, L 2010, ch 8, § 2, eff June 1, 2010.

ARTICLE 29-CCC
NONHOSPITAL ORDERS NOT TO RESUSCITATE
SUMMARY OF ARTICLE

§ 2994-aa. Definitions

1. "Adult" means any person who is eighteen years of age or older, or is the parent of a child or has married.

2. "Attending practitioner" means the physician, nurse practitioner or physician assistant who has primary responsibility for the treatment and care of the patient. Where more than one physician, nurse practitioner or physician assistant shares such responsibility, any such physician, nurse practitioner or physician assistant may act as the attending practitioner pursuant to this article.

2-a. "Attending nurse practitioner" means the nurse practitioner who has primary responsibility for the treatment and care of the patient. Where more than one physician and/or nurse practitioner shares such responsibility, any such physician or nurse practitioner may act as the attending physician or attending nurse practitioner pursuant to this article.

3. "Capacity" means the ability to understand and appreciate the nature and consequences of a nonhospital order not to resuscitate, including the benefits and disadvantages of such an order, and to reach an informed decision regarding the order.

4. "Cardiopulmonary resuscitation" means measures, as specified in regulations promulgated by the commissioner, to restore cardiac function or to support ventilation in the event of a cardiac or respiratory arrest. Such term shall not include measures to improve ventilation and cardiac function in the absence of an arrest.

5. "Emergency medical services personnel" means the personnel of a service or agency engaged in providing initial emergency medical assistance, including but not limited to first responders, emergency medical technicians, advanced emergency medical technicians and personnel engaged in providing health care at correctional facilities, as that term is defined in subdivision four of section two of the correction law.

6. "Health care agent" means a health care agent of the patient designated pursuant to article twenty-nine-C of this chapter.

7. "Health or social services practitioner" means a registered professional nurse, nurse practitioner, physician, physician assistant, psychologist or certified, licensed master social worker or licensed clinical social worker, licensed or certified pursuant to the education law, acting within his or her scope of practice.

8. "Home care services agency" means an entity certified, licensed or exempt under article thirty-six of this chapter.

9. "Hospice" means a hospice as defined in article forty of this chapter.

10. "Hospital" means a general hospital as defined in subdivision ten of section twenty-eight hundred one of this chapter and a residential health care facility as defined in subdivision three of section twenty-eight hundred one of this chapter or a hospital as defined in subdivision ten of section 1.03 of the mental hygiene law or a developmental disabilities services office named in section 13.17 of the mental hygiene law.

11. "Hospital emergency services personnel" means the personnel of the emergency service of a general hospital, as defined in subdivision ten of section twenty-eight hundred one of this chapter, including but not limited to emergency services attending physicians, emergency services registered professional nurses, and registered professional nurses, nursing staff and registered physician assistants assigned to the general hospital's emergency service.

12. "Mental hygiene facility" means a residential facility operated or licensed by the office of mental health or the office for people with developmental disabilities.

13. "Nonhospital order not to resuscitate" means an order that directs emergency medical services personnel, hospice personnel and hospital emergency services personnel not to attempt cardiopulmonary resuscitation in the event a patient suffers cardiac or respiratory arrest.

13-a. "Nurse practitioner" means a nurse practitioner certified pursuant to section sixty-nine hundred ten of the education law who is practicing in accordance with subdivision three of section sixty-nine hundred two of the education law.

14. "Patient" means a person who has been or who may be issued a nonhospital order not to resuscitate.

15. "Surrogate" means a person authorized to make a health care decision on behalf of a patient pursuant to article twenty-nine-CC of this chapter.

History: Add, L 2010, ch 8, § 2, eff June 1, 2010; amd, L 2011, ch 167, § 8, eff Sept 18, 2011; L 2012, ch 56, § 9 (Part J), eff March 30, 2012; L 2017, ch 430, § 29, eff May 28, 2018; L 2019, ch 672, § 29, eff Dec 16, 2019; L 2019, ch 708, § 34, eff June 17, 2020.

§ 2994-bb. General provisions

1. (a) Emergency medical services personnel, home care services agency personnel, hospice personnel, and hospital emergency services personnel shall honor nonhospital orders not to resuscitate, except as provided in section twenty-nine hundred ninety-four-ee of this article.

(b) A nonhospital order not to resuscitate shall not constitute an order to withhold or withdraw treatment other than cardiopulmonary resuscitation.

2. A nonhospital order not to resuscitate may be issued during hospitalization to take effect after hospitalization, or may be issued for a person who is not a patient in, or a resident of, a hospital.

History: Add, L 2010, ch 8, § 2, eff June 1, 2010.

§ 2994-cc. Consent to a nonhospital order not to resuscitate

1. An adult with decision-making capacity, a health care agent, or a surrogate may consent to a nonhospital order not to resuscitate orally to the attending practitioner or in writing. If

a patient consents to a nonhospital order not to resuscitate while in a correctional facility, notice of the patient's consent shall be given to the facility director and reasonable efforts shall be made to notify an individual designated by the patient to receive such notice prior to the issuance of the nonhospital order not to resuscitate. Notification to the facility director or the individual designated by the patient shall not delay issuance of a nonhospital order not to resuscitate.

2. Consent by a health care agent shall be governed by article twenty-nine-C of this chapter.

3. Consent by a surrogate shall be governed by article twenty-nine-CC of this chapter, except that: (a) a second determination of capacity shall be made by a health or social services practitioner; and (b) the authority of the ethics review committee set forth in article twenty-nine-CC of this chapter shall apply only to nonhospital orders issued in a hospital.

4. (a) When the concurrence of a second physician, nurse practitioner or physician assistant is sought to fulfill the requirements for the issuance of a nonhospital order not to resuscitate for patients in a correctional facility, such second physician, nurse practitioner or physician assistant shall be selected by the chief medical officer of the department of corrections and community supervision or his or her designee.

(b) When the concurrence of a second physician, nurse practitioner or physician assistant is sought to fulfill the requirements for the issuance of a nonhospital order not to resuscitate for hospice and home care patients, such second physician, nurse practitioner or physician assistant shall be selected by the hospice medical director or hospice nurse coordinator designated by the medical director or by the home care services agency director of patient care services, as appropriate to the patient.

5. Consent by a patient or a surrogate for a patient in a mental hygiene facility shall be governed by article twenty-nine-B of this chapter.

History: Add, L 2010, ch 8, § 2, eff June 1, 2010; amd, L 2011, ch 62, § 131 (Part C, Subpart B), eff March 31, 2011; L 2017, ch 430, § 30, eff May 28, 2018; L 2019, ch 708, § 35, eff June 17, 2020.

§ 2994-dd. Managing a nonhospital order not to resuscitate

1. The attending practitioner shall record the issuance of a nonhospital order not to resuscitate in the patient's medical record.

2. A nonhospital order not to resuscitate shall be issued upon a standard form prescribed by the commissioner. The commissioner shall also develop a standard bracelet that may be worn by a patient with a nonhospital order not to resuscitate to identify that status; provided, however, that no person may require a patient to wear such a bracelet and that no person may require a patient to wear such a bracelet as a condition for honoring a nonhospital order not to resuscitate or for providing health care services.

3. An attending practitioner who has issued a nonhospital order not to resuscitate, and who transfers care of the patient to another physician, nurse practitioner or physician assistant, shall inform the physician, nurse practitioner or physician assistant of the order.

4. For each patient for whom a nonhospital order not to resuscitate has been issued, the attending practitioner shall review whether the order is still appropriate in light of the patient's condition each time he or she examines the patient, whether in the hospital or elsewhere, but at least every ninety days, provided that the review need not occur more than once every

seven days. The attending practitioner shall record the review in the patient's medical record provided, however, that a physician assistant or a registered nurse, other than the attending nurse practitioner, who provides direct care to the patient may record the review in the medical record at the direction of the physician. In such case, the attending practitioner shall include a confirmation of the review in the patient's medical record within fourteen days of such review. Failure to comply with this subdivision shall not render a nonhospital order not to resuscitate ineffective.

5. A person who has consented to a nonhospital order not to resuscitate may at any time revoke his or her consent to the order by any act evidencing a specific intent to revoke such consent. Any health care professional, other than the attending practitioner, informed of a revocation of consent to a nonhospital order not to resuscitate shall notify the attending practitioner of the revocation. An attending practitioner who is informed that a nonhospital order not to resuscitate has been revoked shall record the revocation in the patient's medical record, cancel the order and make diligent efforts to retrieve the form issuing the order, and the standard bracelet, if any.

6. The commissioner may authorize the use of one or more alternative forms for issuing a nonhospital order not to resuscitate (in place of the standard form prescribed by the commissioner under subdivision two of this section). Such alternative form or forms may also be used to issue a non-hospital do not intubate order. Any such alternative forms intended for use for persons with developmental disabilities or persons with mental illness who are incapable of making their own health care decisions or who have a guardian of the person appointed pursuant to article eighty-one of the mental hygiene law or article seventeen-A of the surrogate's court procedure act must also be approved by the commissioner of developmental disabilities or the commissioner of mental health, as appropriate. An alternative form under this subdivision shall otherwise conform with applicable federal and state law. This subdivision does not limit, restrict or impair the use of an alternative form for issuing an order not to resuscitate in a general hospital or residential health care facility under article twenty-eight of this chapter or a hospital under subdivision ten of section 1.03 of the mental hygiene law.

> **History:** Add, L 2010, ch 8, § 2, eff June 1, 2010; amd, L 2012, ch 56, § 10 (Part J), eff March 30, 2012; L 2017, ch 430, § 31, eff May 28, 2018; L 2019, ch 708, § 36, eff June 17, 2020.

§ 2994-ee. Obligation to honor a nonhospital order not to resuscitate

Emergency medical services personnel, home care services agency personnel, hospice personnel, or hospital emergency services personnel who are provided with a nonhospital order not to resuscitate, or who identify the standard bracelet on the patient's body, shall comply with the terms of such order; provided, however, that:

1. Emergency medical services personnel, home care services agency personnel, hospice personnel, or hospital emergency services personnel may disregard the order if:

(a) They believe in good faith that consent to the order has been revoked, or that the order has been cancelled; or

(b) Family members or others on the scene, excluding such personnel, object to the order and physical confrontation appears likely; and

2. Hospital emergency services physicians and hospital emergency services nurse

practitioners and physician assistants may direct that the order be disregarded if other significant and exceptional medical circumstances warrant disregarding the order.

History: Add, L 2010, ch 8, § 2, eff June 1, 2010; amd, L 2017, ch 430, § 31, eff May 28, 2018; L 2019, ch 708, § 37, eff June 17, 2020.

§ 2994-ff. Interinstitutional transfer

If a patient with a nonhospital order not to resuscitate is admitted to a hospital, the order shall be treated as an order not to resuscitate for a patient transferred from another hospital, and shall be governed by article twenty-nine-CC of this chapter, except that any such order for a patient admitted to a mental hygiene facility shall be governed by article twenty-nine-B of this chapter.

History: Add, L 2010, ch 8, § 2, eff June 1, 2010.

§ 2994-gg. Immunity

No person shall be subjected to criminal prosecution or civil liability, or be deemed to have engaged in unprofessional conduct, for honoring reasonably and in good faith pursuant to this section a nonhospital order not to resuscitate, for disregarding a nonhospital order pursuant to section twenty-nine hundred ninety-four-ee of this article, or for other actions taken reasonably and in good faith pursuant to this section.

History: Add, L 2010, ch 8, § 2, eff June 1, 2010.

ARTICLE 42
CADAVERS
TITLE I   DISPOSITION

§ 4200. Cadavers; duty of burial

1. Except in the cases in which a right to dissect it is expressly conferred by law, every body of a deceased person, within this state, shall be decently buried or incinerated within a reasonable time after death.

2. The provisions of this section shall not impair the right to carry the body of a deceased person through this state, or to remove from this state the body of a person who has died within it, for the purpose of burying the same elsewhere.

> **History:** Add, L 1953, ch 879, § 1, eff June 1, 1954, with substance derived from Penal Law §§ 2211, 2212.

§ 4201. Disposition of remains; responsibility therefor

1. As used in this section, the following terms shall have the following meanings, unless the context otherwise requires:

(a) "Cremation" means the incineration of human remains.

(b) "Disposition" means the care, disposal, transportation, burial, cremation or embalming of the body of a deceased person, and associated measures.

(c) "Domestic partner" means a person who, with respect to another person:

(i) is formally a party in a domestic partnership or similar relationship with the other person, entered into pursuant to the laws of the United States or any state, local or foreign jurisdiction, or registered as the domestic partner of the person with any registry maintained by the employer of either party or any state, municipality, or foreign jurisdiction; or

(ii) is formally recognized as a beneficiary or covered person under the other person's employment benefits or health insurance; or

(iii) is dependent or mutually interdependent on the other person for support, as evidenced by the totality of the circumstances indicating a mutual intent to be domestic partners including but not limited to: common ownership or joint leasing of real or personal property; common householding, shared income or shared expenses; children in common; signs of intent to marry or become domestic partners under subparagraph (i) or (ii) of this paragraph; or the length of the personal relationship of the persons.

Each party to a domestic partnership shall be considered to be the domestic partner of the other party. "Domestic partner" shall not include a person who is related to the other person by blood in a manner that would bar marriage to the other person in New York state. "Domestic partner" shall also not include any person who is less than eighteen years of age or who is the adopted child of the other person or who is related by blood in a manner that would bar marriage in New York state to a person who is the lawful spouse of the other person.

(d) "Person" means a natural person eighteen years of age or older.

2. (a) The following persons in descending priority shall have the right to control the disposition of the remains of such decedent:

(i) the person designated in a written instrument executed pursuant to the provisions of this section;

(ii) the decedent's surviving spouse;

(ii-a) the decedent's surviving domestic partner;

(iii) any of the decedent's surviving children eighteen years of age or older;

(iv) either of the decedent's surviving parents;

(v) any of the decedent's surviving siblings eighteen years of age or older;

(vi) a guardian appointed pursuant to article seventeen or seventeen-A of the surrogate's court procedure act or article eighty-one of the mental hygiene law;

(vii) any person eighteen years of age or older who would be entitled to share in the estate of the decedent as specified in section 4-1.1 of the estates, powers and trusts law, with the person closest in relationship having the highest priority;

(viii) a duly appointed fiduciary of the estate of the decedent;

(ix) a close friend or relative who is reasonably familiar with the decedent's wishes, including the decedent's religious or moral beliefs, when no one higher on this list is reasonably available, willing, or competent to act, provided that such person has executed a written statement pursuant to subdivision seven of this section; or

(x) a chief fiscal officer of a county or a public administrator appointed pursuant to article twelve or thirteen of the surrogate's court procedure act, or any other person acting on behalf of the decedent, provided that such person has executed a written statement pursuant to subdivision seven of this section.

(b) If a person designated to control the disposition of a decedent's remains, pursuant to this subdivision, is not reasonably available, unwilling or not competent to serve, and such person is not expected to become reasonably available, willing or competent, then those persons of equal priority and, if there be none, those persons of the next succeeding priority shall have the right to control the disposition of the decedent's remains.

(c) The person in control of disposition, pursuant to this section, shall faithfully carry out the directions of the decedent to the extent lawful and practicable, including consideration of the financial capacity of the decedent's estate and other resources made available for disposition of the remains. The person in control of disposition shall also dispose of the decedent in a manner appropriate to the moral and individual beliefs and wishes of the decedent provided that such beliefs and wishes do not conflict with the directions of the decedent. The person in control of disposition may seek to recover any costs related to the disposition from the fiduciary of the decedent's estate in accordance with section eighteen hundred eleven of the surrogate's court procedure act.

(d) No funeral director, undertaker, embalmer or no person with an interest in, or who is an employee of any funeral firm, cemetery organization or business operating a crematory, columbarium or any other business, who also controls the disposition of remains in accordance with this section, shall receive compensation or otherwise receive financial benefit for disposing of the remains of a decedent.

(e) No person who: (1) at the time of the decedent's death, was the subject of an order of protection protecting the decedent; or (2) has been arrested or charged with any crime set forth in article one hundred twenty-five of the penal law as a result of any action allegedly causally related to the death of the decedent shall have the right to control the disposition of the remains of the decedent. However, the application of this paragraph in a particular case may be waived or modified in the interest of justice by order of (i) the court that issued the order of protection or in which the criminal action against the person is pending, or a superior court in which an action or proceeding under the domestic relations law or the family court act between the person and the decedent was pending at the time of the decedent's death, or (ii) if proceeding in that court would cause inappropriate delay, a court in a special proceeding.

3. The written instrument referred to in paragraph (a) of subdivision two of this section may be in substantially the following form, and must be signed and dated by the decedent and the agent and properly witnessed:

APPOINTMENT OF AGENT TO CONTROL DISPOSITION OF RE-MAINS

I, _____

(Your name and address)

being of sound mind, willfully and voluntarily make known my desire that, upon my death, the disposition of my remains shall be controlled by

_____ .

(name of agent)

With respect to that subject only, I hereby appoint such person as my agent with respect to the disposition of my remains.

SPECIAL DIRECTIONS:

Set forth below are any special directions limiting the power granted to my agent as well as any instructions or wishes desired to be followed in the disposition of my remains:

_____

_____

_____

_____

Indicate below if you have entered into a pre-funded pre-need agreement subject to section four hundred fifty-three of the general business law for funeral merchandise or service in advance of need:

[   ] No, I have not entered into a pre-funded pre-need agreement subject to section four hundred fifty-three of the general business law.

[   ] Yes, I have entered into a pre-funded pre-need agreement subject to section four hundred fifty-three of the general business law.

_____

(Name of funeral firm with which you entered into a pre-funded pre-need funeral agreement to provide merchandise and/or services)

AGENT:

Name: _____

Address: _____

Telephone Number: _____

SUCCESSORS:

If my agent dies, resigns, or is unable to act, I hereby appoint the following persons (each to act alone and successively, in the order named) to serve as my agent to control the disposition of my remains as authorized by this document:

    1. First Successor

       Name: _____

       Address: _____

       Telephone Number: _____

    2. Second Successor

       Name: _____

       Address: _____

       Telephone Number: _____

DURATION:

This appointment becomes effective upon my death.

PRIOR APPOINTMENT REVOKED:

I hereby revoke any prior appointment of any person to control the disposition of my remains.

Signed this _____ day of _____, _____.

_____

(Signature of person making the appointment)

Statement by witness (must be 18 or older)

I declare that the person who executed this document is personally known to me and appears to be of sound mind and acting of his or her free will. He or she signed (or asked another to sign for him or her) this document in my presence.

    Witness 1: _____

           (signature)

    Address: _____

    Witness 2: _____

           (signature)

    Address: _____

ACCEPTANCE AND ASSUMPTION BY AGENT:

1. I have no reason to believe there has been a revocation of this appointment to control disposition of remains.

2. I hereby accept this appointment.

Signed this _____ day of _____, _____.

_____

(Signature of Agent)

4. (a) In the absence of a written instrument made pursuant to subdivision three of this section, the designation of a person for the disposition of one's remains or directions for the disposition of one's remains in a will executed pursuant to the laws of the state of New York prior to the effective date of this section, or otherwise executed pursuant to the laws of a jurisdiction outside the state of New York, shall be: (i) considered reflective of the intent of the decedent with respect to the disposition of the decedent's remains; and (ii) superseded by a written instrument subsequently executed pursuant to subdivision three of this section, or by any other subsequent act by the decedent evidencing a specific intent to supersede the designation or direction in such a will with respect to the disposition of the decedent's remains. All actions taken reasonably and in good faith based upon such authorizations and directions regarding the disposition of one's remains in such a will shall be deemed valid regardless of whether such a will is later probated or subsequently declared invalid.

(b) In the absence of a written instrument made pursuant to subdivision three of this section, the designation of a person for the disposition of one's remains or directions for the disposition of one's remains in a will executed pursuant to the laws of the state of New York on or after the effective date of this section, shall be considered a reflection of the intent of the decedent with respect to the disposition of the decedent's remains, provided that the person who represents that he or she is entitled to control the disposition of remains of the decedent has complied with subdivision five and paragraph (a) of subdivision seven of this section and signed a written statement in accordance with paragraph (b) of subdivision seven of this section.

4-a. A written instrument under this section may limit the disposition of remains agent's authority to consent to organ or tissue donation or designate another person to do so, under article forty-three of this chapter. Failure to state wishes or instructions shall not be construed to imply a wish not to donate.

5. A written instrument executed under this section shall be revoked upon the execution by the decedent of a subsequent written instrument, or by any other subsequent act by the decedent evidencing a specific intent to revoke the prior written instrument and directions on disposition and agent designations in a will made pursuant to subdivision three of this section shall be superseded by a subsequently executed will or written instrument made pursuant to this section, or by any other subsequent act of the decedent evidencing a specific intent to supersede the direction or designation. The designation of the decedent's spouse or domestic partner as an agent in control of disposition of remains shall be revoked upon the divorce or legal separation of the decedent and spouse, or termination of the domestic partnership, unless the decedent specified in writing otherwise.

6. A person acting reasonably and in good faith, shall not be subject to any civil liability for:

(a) representing himself or herself to be the person in control of a decedent's disposition;

(b) disposing of a decedent's remains if done with the reasonable belief that such disposal is consistent with this section; or

(c) identifying a decedent.

7. No cemetery organization, business operating a crematory or columbarium, funeral director, undertaker, embalmer, or funeral firm shall be held liable for actions taken reasonably and in good faith to carry out the written directions of a decedent as stated in a will or in a written instrument executed pursuant to this section. No cemetery organization, business operating a crematory or columbarium, funeral director, undertaker, embalmer or funeral firm shall be held liable for actions taken reasonably and in good faith to carry out the directions of a person who represents that he or she is entitled to control of the disposition of remains, provided that such action is taken only after requesting and receiving written statement that such person:

(a) is the designated agent of the decedent designated in a will or written instrument executed pursuant to this section; or

(b) that he or she has no knowledge that the decedent executed a written instrument pursuant to this section or a will containing directions for the disposition of his or her remains and that such person is the person having priority under subdivision two of this section.

8. Every dispute relating to the disposition of the remains of a decedent shall be resolved by a court of competent jurisdiction pursuant to a special proceeding under article four of the civil practice law and rules. No person providing services relating to the disposition of the remains of a decedent shall be held liable for refusal to provide such services, when control of the disposition of such remains is contested, until such person receives a court order or other form of notification signed by all parties or their legal representatives to the dispute establishing such control.

9. This section does not supersede, alter or abridge any provision of section four hundred fifty-three of the general business law. In the event of a conflict or ambiguity, the provisions of section four hundred fifty-three of the general business law shall govern.

10. This section does not supersede, alter or abridge any provision of article forty-three of this chapter including, but not limited to, the persons authorized to execute an anatomical gift pursuant to section forty-three hundred one of this chapter.

11. This section does not diminish the enforceability of a contract or agreement in which a person controlling the disposition of the remains of a decedent agrees to pay for goods or services in connection with the disposition of such remains.

History: Add, L 2005, ch 768, § 1, eff Aug 2, 2006; amd, L 2006, ch 76, § 1, eff Aug 2, 2006; L 2007, ch 401, § 1, eff Aug 1, 2007, deemed eff on and after Aug 2, 2006; L 2009, ch 348, § 4, eff Oct 25, 2009; L 2012, ch 491, § 1 (Part B), eff Nov 24, 2012

§ 4202. Cremated remains; disposition

1. Every body delivered to a cemetery for cremation shall be accompanied by a statement

from a physician, coroner, or medical examiner certifying that such body does not contain a battery or power cell. The person in charge of a cemetery may refuse to cremate a body unless accompanied by such statement.

2. Cremated remains means human remains after incineration in a crematory.

3. An institution authorized by article forty-two or forty-three of this chapter to receive unclaimed cadavers or anatomical gifts, notwithstanding any other provision of law, may prepare or preserve cadavers in its lawful possession for purposes of research, study or anatomical instruction and may cremate the cadavers or dissected remains of such cadavers after the completion of such research, study or anatomical instruction thereon; provided, however, that cremation shall be performed only in a retort used exclusively for such purpose. For the purposes of the provisions of this subdivision, such institution shall not be subject to article fifteen of the not-for-profit corporation law.

4. At the time of the arrangement for a funeral performed by any undertaker or funeral director, the person contracting for funeral services shall designate his intentions with respect to the disposition of the remains of the deceased in a signed declaration of intent on a form as designated by the department which shall be provided by and retained by the undertaker. Every undertaker, administrator, executor, authorized representative of a deceased person, corporation, company or association, or other person having in his or its lawful possession cremated remains, except such remains committed to his or its care for permanent interment, which remains shall not have been claimed by a relative or friend of the deceased person within one hundred twenty days from the date of cremation, may dispose of such remains by placement in a tomb, mausoleum, crypt, niche in a columbarium, burial in a cemetery, or scattering of the remains at sea or by otherwise disposing of such remains as provided by rule of the department. A record of such disposition shall be made and kept by the person making such disposition. Upon disposing of such remains in the manner prescribed above, such person shall be discharged from any legal obligation or liability in relation to such remains.

History: Add, L 1968, ch 665, § 1, eff Sept 1, 1968; renumbered sub 3, L 1981, ch 903, § 1, eff Jan 1, 1982; L 1980, ch 617, § 2; L 1981, ch 903, § 1, eff Jan 1, 1982; L 1987, ch 91, § 1, eff Sept 26, 1987.

§ 4203. Cremated remains of a veteran; disposition

1. As used in this section, the following terms shall have the following meanings:

(a) "veteran" means a deceased person who:

(i) served in the active military or naval service of the United States; or

(ii) served in active duty in a force of any organized state militia in a full-time status; or

(iii) served in the reserve armed forces of the United States in active duty; or

(iv) was a recipient of the armed forces expeditionary medal, navy expeditionary medal, marine corps expeditionary medal or global war on terrorism expeditionary medal; and

(v) was released from such service otherwise than by dishonorable discharge.

(b) "veterans' service organization" means an association, corporation or other entity that qualifies under section 501(c)(3) or section 501(c)(19) of the Internal Revenue Code as a tax-exempt organization that has been organized for the benefit of veterans and recognized or chartered by the United States Congress, including, but not limited to the Disabled American Veterans, the Veterans of Foreign Wars, the American Legion and the Vietnam Veterans of America. The term also includes a member or employee of an eligible non-profit veterans' corporation, association or entity, such as the Missing In America Veteran Recovery Program, that specifically assists in facilitating the identification and internment of unclaimed remains of American veterans.

(c) "national cemetery" means any cemetery under the control of the United States department of veterans' affairs national cemetery administration.

(d) "interment" shall have the meaning set forth in paragraph (g) of section fifteen hundred two of the not-for-profit corporation law.

(e) "disposition" means disposal of cremated remains by placement in a tomb, mausoleum, crypt, niche in a columbarium or burial in a cemetery. Provided, however, for the purpose of this section the term "disposition" shall not include the scattering of cremated remains.

(f) "local veterans' service agencies" shall have the meaning set forth in section three hundred fifty-seven of the executive law.

2. A funeral director, undertaker or funeral firm which has held in its possession cremated remains for more than one hundred twenty days from the date of cremation may, in accordance with the provisions of this section, determine if such cremated remains are those of a veteran, and if so, may dispose of such remains as provided in this section.

3. (a) Notwithstanding any law or regulation to the contrary, nothing in this section shall prevent a funeral director, undertaker or funeral firm from sharing information with the United States department of veterans affairs (VA), a local veterans' service agency, a veterans' service organization, a national cemetery, or county veterans cemetery for the purpose of determining whether the cremated remains are those of a veteran.

(b) A funeral director, undertaker, or funeral firm shall be discharged from any legal obligations or liability with regard to releasing or sharing information to the United States department of veterans affairs, the local veterans' service agencies, veterans' service organizations, a national cemetery, or county veterans cemetery pursuant to this section.

4. (a) Should a funeral director, undertaker or funeral firm ascertain the cremated remains in its possession are those of a veteran, and they have not been instructed by the person in control of the disposition of the decedent to arrange for the final disposal or delivery of the cremated remains, the funeral director, undertaker or funeral firm may dispose of the cremated remains or relinquish possession of the cremated remains to a veterans' service organization.

(b) The method of disposition shall be made pursuant to section forty-two hundred two of this title in a national cemetery, a county veterans cemetery, a section of a cemetery corporation where veterans are memorialized by a veteran's marker if eligible, a veterans' section of a cemetery corporation or a veterans' cemetery if the deceased veteran is eligible for interment in such a manner.

5. The funeral director, undertaker, funeral firm or veterans' service organization notwith-standing any law to the contrary, upon:

(a) disposing of cremated remains in accordance with the provisions of this section, shall be held harmless for any costs or damages, except if there is gross negligence or willful misconduct; and

(b) shall be discharged from any legal obligation or liability concerning the cremated remains.

6. The estate of the decedent shall be responsible for reimbursing a funeral director, undertaker, funeral firm or veterans' service organization for all reasonable expenses incurred in relation to the disposition of such cremated remains.

7. A funeral director, undertaker or funeral firm shall establish and maintain a record identifying the veterans' service organization receiving the cremated remains and the site designated for final disposition of the cremated remains.

8. Nothing in this section shall require a funeral director, undertaker or funeral firm to determine or seek others to determine that an individual's cremated remains are those of a veteran if the funeral director, undertaker or funeral firm was informed by the person in control of disposition that such individual was not a veteran, or to relinquish possession of such cremated remains to a veterans' service organization if the funeral director, undertaker or funeral firm was instructed by such person in control, or had a reasonable belief, that the decedent did not desire any funeral or burial-related services or ceremonies recognizing such decedent's service as a veteran.

History: Add, L 2010, ch 444, § 2, eff Nov 11, 2010.

PHL

ARTICLE 43
ANATOMICAL GIFTS
SUMMARY OF ARTICLE

§ 4300. Definitions

As used in this section, the following terms shall have the following meanings:

1. "Anatomical gift" or "gift" means a donation of a whole body or part of a human body, to take effect after the donor's death, for the purpose of transplantation, therapy, research or education.

2. "Decedent" means a deceased individual of any age whose body or part is or may be the source of an anatomical gift. The term includes a stillborn infant and, subject to restrictions imposed by law other than this article, a fetus.

3. "Disinterested witness" means a witness other than the spouse, domestic partner, child, parent, sibling, grandchild, grandparent, or guardian of the individual who makes, amends, revokes, or refuses to make an anatomical gift, or a close friend, or another adult who is related to the decedent by blood, marriage, or adoption.

4. "Document of gift" means an organ donor card, whole body donor card, driver's license authorization to make an anatomical gift, pursuant to paragraph (a) of subdivision one of section five hundred four of the vehicle and traffic law, authorization to make an anatomical gift pursuant to any of the methods in subdivision five of section forty-three hundred ten of this article, or any other written authorization for an anatomical gift. The term "document of gift" includes a statement on a driver's license, identification card, enrollment in a donor registry, or any other anatomical gift document valid pursuant to the laws of this or any other state or of any document of gift valid pursuant to the laws of any other country appearing on a list of countries maintained by the commissioner for such purpose and published on the department's website.

5. "Domestic partner" has the same meaning as described in subdivision seven of section twenty-nine hundred ninety-four-a of this chapter.

6. "Donee" means an individual or entity authorized to accept an anatomical gift pursuant to section forty-three hundred two of this article.

7. "Donor" means an individual whose body or part is the subject of an anatomical gift.

8. "Eye bank" means a person that is licensed, accredited, or regulated under federal or state law to engage in the recovery, screening, testing, processing, storage, or distribution of human eyes or portions of human eyes.

9. "Guardian" means a person appointed by a court to make decisions regarding the support, care, education, health, or welfare of an individual. The term does not include a guardian ad litem.

10. "Hospital" means a hospital licensed, accredited, or approved under the laws of any state and includes a hospital operated by the United States Government, a state, or a subdivision thereof, although not required to be licensed under state laws.

11. "Non-transplant anatomic bank" means any person or facility that solicits, retrieves, performs donor selection and/or testing, preserves, transport, allocates, distributes, acquires, processes, stores, or arranges for the storage of non-transplant anatomic parts, including whole bodies, body segments, organs, or tissues from living or deceased donors, for education and/or research purposes specifically authorized by section forty-three hundred two of this article. The following shall not constitute a non-transplant anatomic bank:

(a) Any person or entity that stores non-transplant anatomic parts, except whole bodies and body segments, solely for purposes of research and/or education conducted by such person; provided the person or entity maintains on its premises a properly executed anatomical gift consent document, and

(i) such person or entity is a legal donee pursuant to section forty-three hundred two of this article and obtains all organs/tissues from a tissue bank or non-transplant anatomic bank licensed by the department; or

(ii) is a general hospital conducting pathology services or research on non-transplant anatomic parts including whole bodies, recovered from within the facility from a living or deceased source;

(b) Any person or entity whose activities within the state of New York are limited to distribution of non-transplant anatomic parts to a tissue bank or non-transplant anatomic bank licensed by the department;

(c) Any person or entity that uses prepared slides and/or human-derived stem cell lines for purposes of education and/or research; and

(d) An employee of the federal government, provided an anatomical gift consent document has been executed in accordance with section forty-three hundred one of this article.

12. "Organ" shall have the same definition as in article forty-three-B of this chapter, but shall not be applied to heart valves for the purposes of this article.

13. "Organ procurement organization" means a person designated by the secretary of the United States Department of Health and Human Services as an organ procurement organization.

14. "Parent" means a parent whose parental rights have not been terminated.

15. "Part" of a body means and includes organs, tissues, eyes, bones, arteries, blood, other fluids and other portions of a human body, and "part" includes "parts". The term does not include the whole body.

16. "Person" means an individual, corporation, government or governmental subdivision or agency, business trust, estate, trust, partnership or association, or any other legal entity.

17. "Physician" or "surgeon" means a physician or surgeon licensed or authorized to practice under the laws of any state.

18. "Prospective donor" means an individual who is dead or near death and has been determined by a procurement organization to have a part that could be medically suitable for transplantation, therapy, research, or education. The term does not include an individual who has made a refusal.

19. "Procurement organization" means an eye bank, organ procurement organization, or tissue bank.

20. "Reasonably available" means able to be contacted by a procurement organization without undue effort and willing and able to act in a timely manner consistent with existing medical criteria necessary for the making of an anatomical gift.

21. "Record" means information that is inscribed on a tangible medium or that is stored in an electronic or other medium and is retrievable in perceivable form.

22. "Refusal" means a record created under section forty-three hundred five of this article that expressly states an intent to bar other persons from making an anatomical gift.

23. "State" includes any state, district, commonwealth, territory, insular possession, and any other area subject to the legislative authority of the United States of America.

24. "Tissue bank" means a person that is licensed, accredited, or regulated under federal or state law to solicit, retrieve, perform donor selection and/or testing, preserve, transport, allocate, distribute, acquire, process, store or arrange for the storage of human tissues for transplantation, transfer, therapy, artificial insemination or implantation, including autogeneic procedures.

25. "Whole body" means the intact corporeal remains of an individual after the time of death.

26. "Whole body donor card" means a card or other writing indicating the donor's authorization to make an anatomical gift of a whole body to a non-transplant anatomic bank or other donee for purposes of education or research.

History: Add, L 1970, ch 466, § 1, eff May 5, 1970; amd L 2019, ch 742, pt A, § 1, eff Dec 26, 2019; L 2020, c 45, § 2, eff Dec 26, 2019.

2020 Amendment

2020 N.Y. Laws 45, § 2, effective December 26, 2019, amended subdivision 4 to include possible donations from countries outside of the US that follow NYS-acceptable standards; repealed subdivision 11, "Human-paired organ donation" and renumbered former subdivision 12 as 11; added new subdivision 12, defining "Organ".

§ 4301. Persons who may execute an anatomical gift

1. (a) Any individual of sound mind and eighteen years of age or more may make an anatomical gift to take effect upon their death for any purpose specified in section forty-three hundred two of this article, limit an anatomical gift to one or more of those purposes, or refuse to make an anatomical gift. In any case where the donor has a properly executed document of gift authorization for donation shall not be rescinded or amended by any other person except upon a showing that the donor revoked the authorization pursuant to section forty-three hundred five of this article.

(b) Any person who is sixteen or seventeen years of age and of sound mind may make an anatomical gift to take effect upon their death for any purpose specified in section forty-three hundred two of this article, limit an anatomical gift to one or more of those purposes, or refuse to make an anatomical gift. In any case where the donor has a properly executed document of gift, notice of such gift shall be provided to the donor's parents or guardians, and authorization for donation may be rescinded or amended by an objection by a parent or guardian of the donor at the time of death and prior to the recovery of any organ or tissue if the donor is less than eighteen years of age. An anatomical gift made by an individual more than sixteen years of age but less than eighteen shall otherwise not be rescinded, except upon a showing that the donor revoked the authorization pursuant to section forty-three hundred five of this article. Upon the donor reaching the age of eighteen, the donor's consent to donate his or her organs or tissue shall be regarded as consent for authorization to make an anatomical gift pursuant to paragraph (a) of this subdivision.

(c) In the absence of an express, contrary indication by the donor, an anatomical gift of a part is neither a refusal to give other parts nor a limitation on an individual's ability to make an anatomical gift under subdivision two of this section.

2. (a) In the absence of a gift made by the donor under subdivision one of this section, and in the absence of actual notice of contrary indications by the decedent, including religious or moral objections, an anatomical gift of the decedent's body may be made by any member of the following classes of persons who is reasonably available, in the order of priority listed, for any purpose specified in section forty-three hundred two of this article:

(i) the person designated as the decedent's health care agent under article twenty-nine-C of this chapter, subject to any written statement in the health care proxy form,

(ii) the person designated as the decedent's agent in a written instrument under article forty-two of this chapter, subject to any written statement in the written instrument,

(iii) the spouse, if not legally separated from the patient, or the domestic partner,

(iv) a son or daughter eighteen years of age or older,

(v) either parent,

(vi) a brother or sister eighteen years of age or older,

(vii) an adult grandchild of the decedent,

(viii) a grandparent of the decedent,

(ix) a guardian of the person of the decedent at the time of his or her death, or

(x) any other person authorized or under the obligation to dispose of the body.

(b) If there is more than one member of a class listed in subparagraph (iv), (vi), (vii), or (viii) of paragraph (a) of this subdivision entitled to make an anatomical gift, an anatomical gift may be made by a member of the class unless that member or person knows of an objection by another member of the class. If an objection is known, the gift may be made only by a majority of the members of the class who are reasonably available.

3. An anatomical gift may not be made by a person listed in subdivision two of this section if:

(a) a person in a prior class is reasonably available;

(b) the person proposing to make an anatomical gift knows of a refusal or contrary indications by the decedent, including that an anatomical gift is contrary to the decedent's religious or moral beliefs.

4. Any gift by a person designated in subdivision two of this section shall be by a document signed by him or her or made by his or her telegraphic, recorded telephonic, or other recorded message. Where a gift is made under this subdivision, either: (a) the authorizing party shall indicate in the document or message that he or she has no actual notice of contrary indications by the decedent and no reason to believe that an anatomical gift is contrary to the decedent's religious or moral beliefs; or (b) an agent of the organ procurement organization or of the donee shall make reasonable efforts to inquire of the authorizing party or otherwise determine that the authorizing party has no actual notice of contrary indications by the decedent and no reason to believe that an anatomical gift is contrary to the decedent's religious or moral beliefs.

5. The donee shall not accept the gift under the following circumstances:

(a) the donee has actual notice of contrary indication by the decedent;

(b) where an anatomical gift is not properly made pursuant to this section; or

(c) the donee has reason to believe that an anatomical gift is contrary to the decedent's religious or moral beliefs.

6. A gift of all or part of a body authorizes any examination necessary to assure medical acceptability of gift for the purposes intended.

7. The rights of the donee created by the gift are paramount to the rights of others except as provided by section forty-three hundred eight of this article.

8. The person who documents the making, amending or revoking of an anatomical gift, acting reasonably and in good faith in accordance with this article, may accept an anatomical gift under this article made by a person who represents that he or she is entitled to consent to the donation.

History: Add, L 1970, ch 466, § 1; so designated sub 7 and amd, L 2009, ch 348, § 1, eff Oct 25, 2009; L 1974, ch 894, § 5; L 1986, ch 786, § 1, eff Aug 2, 1986; L 1990, ch 589, § 2, eff July 18, 1990; L 1994, ch 62, § 1, eff May 18, 1994; L 2006, ch 639, § 1, eff Feb 12, 2007; L 2009, ch 348, § 1, eff Oct 25, 2009; L 2016, ch 248, § 1, eff Feb 14, 2017; L 2019, ch 742, pt B, § 1, eff June 23, 2020; L 2020, c 45, § 3, eff June 23, 2020.

2020 Amendment

2020 N.Y. Laws 45, § 3, effective June 23, 2020, amended subdivision 4 to remove a reference to a "federally designated" organ procurement organization.

§ 4302. Uses and dispositions of anatomical gifts

1. All anatomical gifts made under this article may be made to the following persons named in the document of gift:

(a) a hospital; accredited medical school, dental school, college or university; organ procurement organization; non-transplant anatomic bank; or other appropriate person, for research or education;

(b) subject to the provisions of subdivision two of this section, an individual designated by the person making the anatomical gift if the individual is the recipient of that part; if an anatomical gift to an individual under this paragraph cannot be transplanted into the individual, the part passes in accordance with subdivision six of this section in the absence of an express, contrary indication by the authorizing party making the anatomical gift; or

(c) an eye bank or tissue bank.

2. If an anatomical gift of one or more specific parts or of all parts is made in a document of gift that does not name a person described in subdivision one of this section, but identifies the purpose for which an anatomical gift may be used, the following rules apply:

(a) If the part is an eye and the gift is for the purpose of transplantation or therapy, the gift passes to the appropriate eye bank.

(b) If the part is tissue and the gift is for the purpose of transplantation or therapy, the gift passes to the appropriate tissue bank.

(c) If the part is an organ and the gift is for the purpose of transplantation or therapy, the gift passes to the appropriate organ procurement organization as custodian of the organ.

(d) If the part is an organ, eye, or tissue and the gift is for the purpose of research or education, the gift passes to the appropriate procurement organization.

3. For the purposes of subdivision two of this section, if there is more than one purpose of an anatomical gift set forth in the document of gift but the purposes are not set forth in any priority, the gift must be used for transplantation or therapy, if suitable. If the gift cannot be used for transplantation or therapy, the gift may be used for research or education.

4. If an anatomical gift of one or more specific parts is made in a document of gift that does not name a person described in subdivision one of this section and does not identify the purpose of the gift, the gift may be used only for transplantation or therapy, and the gift passes in accordance with subdivision six of this section.

5. If a document of gift specifies only a general intent to make an anatomical gift by words such as "donor", "organ donor" or "body donor", or a statement of similar import, the gift may be used only for transplantation or therapy, and the gift passes in accordance with subdivision six of this section.

6. For purposes of subdivisions four, five and paragraph (b) of subdivision one of this section, the following rules apply:

(a) If the part is an eye, the gift passes to the appropriate eye bank.

(b) If the part is tissue, the gift passes to the appropriate tissue bank.

(c) If the part is an organ, the gift passes to the appropriate organ procurement organization as custodian of the organ.

7. An anatomical gift of an organ for transplantation or therapy, other than an anatomical gift under paragraph (b) of subdivision one of this section, passes to the organ procurement organization as custodian of the organ.

8. If a prospective donor has been referred to a procurement organization or tissue bank pursuant to state or federal law, and the procurement organization has determined that the gift is medically unsuitable for transplant, or to the extent that a non-transplant anatomical gift may still be honored after a gift has been made pursuant to a superseding document of gift, then the procurement organization shall make reasonable efforts to determine whether the donor has previously made a gift of his or her body or parts for education or research, and the procurement organization informed of such gift shall notify the non-transplant anatomic bank of the gift consistent with the donor's intent.

9. If an anatomical gift does not pass pursuant to subdivisions one, two, three, four, five, six or seven of this section or the decedent's body or part is not used for transplantation, therapy, research, or education, custody of the body or part passes to the person under obligation to dispose of the body or part.

10. A person may not accept an anatomical gift if the person knows that the gift was not effectively made under section forty-three hundred one or forty-three hundred five of this article or if the person knows that the decedent made a refusal under section forty-three hundred one of this article that was not revoked. For purposes of this subdivision, if a person knows that an anatomical gift was made on a document of gift, the person is deemed to know of any amendment or revocation of the gift or any refusal to make an anatomical gift on the same document of gift.

11. Except as otherwise provided in paragraph (b) of subdivision one of this section, nothing in this section affects the allocation of organs for transplantation or therapy.

History: Add, L 1970, ch 466, § 1, eff May 5, 1970; amd, L 1990, ch 589, § 3, eff July 18, 1990; L 2019, ch 742, pt C, § 1, eff June 23, 2020; L 2020, c 45, § 6, eff June 23, 2020.

2020 Amendment

2020 N.Y. Laws 45, § 6, effective June 23, 2020, amended subdivision 5 to remove a reference to "symbol"; amended subdivision 8 to change "potential donor" to "prospective donor".

§ 4303. Manner of executing anatomical gifts

1. A gift of all or part of the body under this article may be made by will. The gift becomes effective upon the death of the testator without waiting for probate. If the will is not probated, or if it is declared invalid for testamentary purposes, the gift, to the extent that it has been acted upon in good faith, is nevertheless valid and effective.

2. A gift of all or part of the body under this article may also be made by document other than a will. The gift becomes effective upon the death of the donor. The document, which may be a card designed to be carried on the person, must be signed by the donor. Delivery of the document of gift during the donor's lifetime is not necessary to make the gift valid.

3. The gift may be made either to a specified donee or without specifying a donee. If the latter, the gift may be accepted by and utilized under the direction of the attending physician upon or following death. If the gift is made to a specified donee who is not available at the time and place of death, the attending physician upon or following death, in the absence of any expressed indication that the donor desired otherwise, may accept the gift as donee. The physician who becomes a donee under this subdivision shall not participate in the procedures for removing or transplanting a part.

4. Subject to the prohibitions in subdivision two of section four thousand three hundred six

the donor may designate in his will, card or other document of gift the surgeon or physician to carry out the appropriate procedures. In the absence of a designation, or if the designee is not available, the donee or other person authorized to accept the gift may employ or authorize any surgeon or physician for the purpose.

History: Add, L 1970, ch 466, § 1, eff May 5, 1970; amd, L 2005, ch 196, § 1, eff July 12, 2005; L 2012, ch 465, § 3, eff Oct 3, 2013; L 2019, ch 742, pt B, § 3-a, eff June 23, 2020.

§ 4304. Delivery of document of gift

If the gift is made by the donor to a specified donee, the will, card or other document or a copy of the executed document, may be delivered to him or her to expedite the appropriate procedures immediately after death; however delivery is not necessary to the validity of the gift. On request of an interested party upon or after the donor's death, the person in possession shall produce the document for examination.

History: Add, L 1970, ch 466, § 1, eff May 5, 1970; amd, L 2019, ch 742, pt D, § 1, eff Dec 26, 2019; L 2020, c 45, § 7, eff June 23, 2020.

2020 Amendment

2020 N.Y. Laws 45, § 7, effective June 23, 2020, amended the section to add the words "of the executed document".

§ 4305. Amendments or revocation of the gift

1. An individual who has created a document of gift may only amend or revoke his or her gift by:

(a) a record signed, subsequently to the creation of the document of gift by:

(i) such individual;

(ii) another person authorized to make the anatomical gift on behalf of such individual; or

(ii) another person acting at the direction of such individual or other person authorized to make the anatomical gift if such individual is unable to sign; or

(b) an oral statement of revocation, subsequent to the creation of the gift, made by such individual in the presence of two persons, at least one of whom is a disinterested witness; or

(c) a later-executed document of gift made by such individual that amends or revokes a previous anatomical gift or portion of an anatomical gift either expressly or by inconsistency; or

(d) a statement during a terminal illness or injury addressed to an attending physician and communicated to the donee made by such individual; or

(e) a signed card or document, found on such individual's person or in such individual's effects; or

(f) such individual's will, created subsequently to the creation of the document of gift, whether or not the will is admitted to probate or invalidated after such individual's death.

2. (a) Subject to paragraphs (b) and (c) of this subdivision, a person authorized to make an anatomical gift on behalf of another individual pursuant to subdivision two of section

forty-three hundred one of this article may revoke or amend such gift by:

(i) a record signed by that individual; or

(ii) an oral statement of revocation, subsequent to the creation of the document of gift, made by that individual in the presence of two persons, at least one of whom is a disinterested witness; or

(iii) a later-executed document of gift that amends or revokes a previous anatomical gift or portion of an anatomical gift made by that individual, either expressly or by inconsistency.

(b) If more than one member of a class listed in subparagraph (iv), (vi), (vii), or (viii) of paragraph (a) of subdivision two of section forty-three hundred one of this article is reasonably available, a gift made pursuant to subdivision two of section forty-three hundred one of this article shall be amended or revoked only if a majority of the reasonably available members agree.

(c) An amendment or revocation is effective only if, before an incision has been made to remove a part from the donor's body or before invasive procedures have begun to prepare the recipient, the procurement organization, transplant hospital, or physician or technician knows of the revocation.

3. Any document of gift may be revoked in the manner set out in subdivision one or two of this section or by destruction, cancellation, or mutilation of the document and all executed copies thereof.

4. Any gift made by a will may be revoked or amended in the manner provided for revocation or amendment of wills or as provided in subdivision one of this section.

5. In the absence of contrary indications by the donor, a revocation or amendment of an anatomical gift is not a refusal to make another anatomical gift not otherwise prohibited by the revocation or amendment, either by the prospective donor or another person specified in subdivision two of section forty-three hundred one of this article.

History: Add, L 1970, ch 466, § 1, eff May 5, 1970; amd, L 2019, ch 742, pt B, § 2, eff June 23, 2020; L 2020, c 45, § 4, eff June 23, 2020.

2020 Amendment

2020 N.Y. Laws 45, § 4, effective June 23, 2020, amended the section extensively to change "donor" to "individual" and clarify other provisions for amending or revoking an anatomical gift.

§ 4306. Rights and duties at death

1. The donee may accept or reject the gift. If the donee accepts a gift of the entire body, the donee may, subject to the terms of the gift, authorize embalming and the use of the body in funeral services. If the gift is of a part of the body, the donee upon the death of the donor and prior to embalming, may cause the part to be removed without unnecessary mutilation. After removal of the part, custody of the remainder of the body vests in the surviving spouse, next of kin, or other persons under obligation to dispose of the body.

2. When a donor is determined dead based on irreversible cessation of circulatory and respiratory functions, the time of death shall be certified by a physician. Such physician may not participate in the procedure to remove or transplant the body part. In all other cases the

time of death shall be certified by the physician who attends the donor at his death and one other physician, neither of whom shall participate in the procedure for removing or transplanting the part.

3. (a) (i) A person who acts in good faith in accord with the terms of this article or with the anatomical gift laws of another state, is not liable for damages in any civil action or subject to prosecution in any criminal proceeding for his or her act.

(ii) A person who acts in good faith in accord with the anatomical gift laws of another country is not liable for damages in any civil action or subject to prosecution in any criminal proceeding for his or her act provided that:

(A) such country has anatomical gift laws similar in requirements and effects to the anatomical gift laws of this state;

(B) such country appears on a list of such countries promulgated as a regulation by the department for such purpose; and

(C) such country appeared on such list at the time of such act.

(b) A person who documents the making, amending or revoking of an anatomical gift, acting reasonably and in good faith in accordance with this article, may accept an anatomical gift under this article made by a person who represents that the person is an authorized person under section forty-three hundred one of this article and is entitled to consent to the donation.

(c) An entity under section forty-three hundred two or forty-three hundred ten of this article or a health care professional, or an agent or employee thereof, who or which documents, records, recovers, procures, obtains, or utilizes an organ or tissue in reasonable and good faith reliance on information provided to or contained in the New York state donate life registry shall not be liable in any civil or criminal action or proceeding for action based on such reliance.

4. Any employee or agent of an organ procurement organization, eye bank or tissue bank acting pursuant to this article shall be held to the same standard of confidentiality as that imposed on employees of a hospital.

History: Add, L 1970, ch 466, § 1, eff May 5, 1970; amd, L 1990, ch 589, § 4, eff July 18, 1990,6, eff July 18, 1990; L 2019, ch 742, pt E, § 1, eff Dec 26, 2019, applying only to acts occurring on or after such effective date; L 2020, c 45, § 8, eff June 23, 2020.

2020 Amendment

2020 N.Y. Laws 45, § 8, effective June 23, 2020, amended subdivision 1 to replace "he or she" with "the donee"; amended subdivision 3 to add new subparagraph (ii) to clarify that a person acting in good in accordance with anatomical gift laws in other countries will not be liable for damages under certain circumstances; amended subdivision 4 to remove a reference to a "federally designated" organ procurement organization.

§ 4306-a. Advanced directives and health care proxies

1. If a prospective donor in a hospital has a declaration or advance health care directive and terms of the declaration, directive or proxy document concerning life-sustaining treatment are in conflict with the express or implied terms of a potential anatomical gift with regard to the administration of measures necessary to ensure the medical suitability of a part for

transplantation or therapy, the prospective donor's attending physician and the prospective donor shall confer to resolve the conflict. For purposes of this section, an advance directive shall mean a written or oral instruction by the adult patient relating to the provision of health care to the patient when an adult becomes incapacitated, including but not limited to a health care proxy, a consent to the issuance of an order not to resuscitate or other orders for life-sustaining treatment recorded in a patient's medical record, or a legally-recognized statement of wishes or beliefs.

2. If such prospective donor is incapable of resolving the conflict, and the patient in such declaration, directive, or proxy document did not expressly reject being a donor, then the health care proxy acting under the prospective donor's declaration, directive, or proxy or, if none, a surrogate authorized to make health care decisions on behalf of the patient, in accordance with the provisions of article twenty-nine-CC of this chapter, shall act for the patient to resolve the conflict.

3. Such conflict must be resolved expeditiously. Information relevant to the resolution of the conflict may be obtained from the appropriate procurement organization and any other person authorized to make an anatomical gift for the prospective donor described in subdivision two of section forty-three hundred one of this article. Before resolution of the conflict, measures necessary to ensure the medical suitability of the part may not be withheld or withdrawn from the patient if withholding or withdrawing the measures is not contraindicated by appropriate end-of-life care.

History: Add, L 2019, ch 742, pt F, § 1, eff June 23, 2020; amd, L 2020, c 45, § 9, eff June 23, 2020.

2020 Amendment

2020 N.Y. Laws 45, § 9, effective June 23, 2020, amended subdivision 1 to define "advance directive".

§ 4306-b. Withdrawal of life-sustaining treatment

This section applies in cases where a prospective donor who has made an anatomical gift or whose donation status has not been ascertained is in a hospital. The hospital shall not withdraw any measures that are necessary to maintain the medical suitability of the part until the procurement organization has had the opportunity to advise the applicable persons as set forth in section forty-three hundred one of this article of the option to make an anatomical gift, has documented or acted upon that decision, or has ascertained that the individual expressed a contrary intent. The procurement organization shall act expeditiously with respect to its responsibilities under this section.

History: Add, L 2019, ch 742, pt F, § 2, eff June 23, 2020.

§ 4307. Prohibition of sales and purchases of human organs

1. It shall be unlawful for any person to knowingly acquire, receive, or otherwise transfer for valuable consideration any part for use in human transplantation. The term "valuable consideration" does not include the reasonable payments associated with the removal, transportation, implantation, processing, preservation, quality control, and storage of a part or the expenses of travel, housing, and lost wages incurred by the donor of a human part in connection with the donation of the part or living donation. Any person who violates this section shall be guilty of a class E felony.

2. For the purposes of this section, the donation of a kidney or other organ from a live donor for transplantation into an individual conditioned upon the donation and transplantation of a

similar organ into an individual specified by the donor shall not, in and of itself, be considered to be "valuable consideration" provided that such donation and transplant are performed in accordance with other applicable laws, rules and regulations, including any specific rules and regulations the commissioner may adopt, with the advice and consent of the transplant council, with respect to such conditional donations. No individual may make a donation conditioned upon the race, color, creed, national origin or religious affiliation of the recipient, and no hospital, organ procurement organization, tissue bank, physician or other professional may participate in the performance of any procedure or otherwise facilitate the donation and/or transfer of organs and/or tissue conditioned on such factors.

> **History:** Add, L 1985, ch 122, § 1, eff May 28, 1985; amd, L 2006, ch 346, § 4, eff Nov 1, 2006; L 2009, ch 362, § 1, eff Aug 26, 2009; L 2019, ch 742, pt G, § 1, eff Dec 26, 2019; L 2020, c 45, § 10, eff June 23, 2020.

2020 Amendment

2020 N.Y. Laws 45, § 10, effective June 23, 2020, amended subdivision 1 to replace references to "organ" with "part".

§ 4308. Prohibition on charging a fee to a donor's estate

Notwithstanding any other provision of law, no physician, hospital or other health care provider may charge the donor's estate, family or insurer for any cost incurred in testing or removing a human organ or tissue from a donor and such charge shall be void and unenforceable.

> **History:** Add, L 1994, ch 323, § 1, eff Aug 19, 1994.

§ 4309. Application

The provisions of this article shall not be deemed to supersede or affect the provisions of the public health law relating to the functions, powers and duties of coroners, coroner's physicians or medical examiners.

> **History:** Formerly § 4307, add, L 1970, ch 466; renumbered § 4308, L 1985, ch 122, § 1; renumbered § 4309, L 1994, ch 323, § 1, eff Aug 19, 1994.

§ 4310. New York state donate life registry for organ, eye and tissue donations

1. The department shall establish an organ, eye, and tissue donor registry, which shall be called and be referred to as the "donate life registry", which shall provide a means to make and register a gift of organs, eyes and tissues to take place after death pursuant to this article. The donate life registry shall contain a listing of all donors who have declared their consent to make an anatomical gift.

2. The commissioner may enter into a multi-year contract for the operation and promotion of the donate life registry subject to such terms and conditions as may be contained within such contract with a not-for-profit organization that has experience working with organ, eye and tissue procurement organizations, has expertise in conducting organ, eye and tissue donor promotional campaigns, and is affiliated with the organ, eye and tissue donation community throughout the state. The contractor may subcontract as needed for the effective performance of the contract. All such subcontractors and the terms of such subcontracts shall be subject to approval by the commissioner. Any applicable state agency, including, but not limited to, the department, the department of motor vehicles and the board of elections, shall cooperate in the collection and transfer of registrant data to the donate life registry.

3. The duties of the contractor shall include, but not be limited to, the following:

(a) the development, implementation and maintenance of the donate life registry that includes online, mailed and other forms of organ, eye and tissue donor registration, verification, amendment and revocation;

(b) preparation and submission of a plan to encourage organ, eye and tissue donation through education and marketing efforts and other recommendations that would streamline and enhance the cost-effective operation of the donate life registry;

(c) provision of written or electronic notification of registration in the donate life registry to an individual enrolling in the donate life registry; and

(d) preparation and submission of an annual written report to the department. Such report shall include:

(i) a performance matrix including the number of registrants on the donate life registry and an analysis of the registration rates, including but not limited to, location, method of registration, demographic, and state comparisons;

(ii) the characteristics of registrants as determined from the donate life registry information;

(iii) the annual dollar amount of voluntary contributions received by the contractor for the purposes of maintaining the donate life registry and/or educational and promotional campaigns and initiatives;

(iv) a description of the promotional campaigns and initiatives implemented during the year; and

(v) accounting statements of expenditures for the purposes of maintaining the donate life registry and promotional campaigns and initiatives.

4. (a) For the period April first, two thousand fourteen through March thirty-first, two thousand fifteen, payments to the contractor shall be paid by the department.

(b) For the period beginning April first, two thousand fifteen and thereafter, payments to the contractor shall be paid by the department from funds available for these purposes, including, but not limited to, the funds deposited into the life pass it on trust fund pursuant to section ninety-five-d of the state finance law.

(c) In addition, the contractor may receive and use voluntary contributions.

5. (a) Such organ, eye and tissue registration of consent to make an anatomical gift can be made through: (i) indication made on the application or renewal form of a driver's license, (ii) indication made on a non-driver identification card application or renewal form, (iii) indication made on a voter registration form pursuant to subdivision five of section 5-210 of the election law, (iv) indication made on the application for health care coverage offered through the state health benefit exchange, (v) enrollment through the donate life registry website, (vi) paper enrollment submitted to the donate life registry, (vii) indication made on the application or renewal form of a hunting, fishing or trapping license issued pursuant to title seven of article eleven of the environmental conservation law, or (viii) through any other method identified by the commissioner. The department shall establish a means by which to register the consent given by individuals who are sixteen or seventeen years of age in the donate life registry, and shall make registration available by any of the methods

provided in subparagraphs (i), (ii), (iii), (iv), (v), (vi) and (vii) of this paragraph.

(b) (i) Where required by law for registration forms described in subparagraphs (i), (ii) and (iv) of paragraph (a) of this subdivision, the commissioner shall ensure that space is provided on any registration form so that the applicant shall register or decline registration in the donate life registry for organ, eye and tissue donations under this section and that the following is stated on the form in clear and conspicuous type:

"You must fill out the following section: Would you like to be added to the Donate Life Registry? Check box for 'yes' or 'skip this question'."

(ii) The commissioner shall not maintain records of any person who checks "skip this question". Except where the application is made in person or electronically, failure to check a box shall not impair the validity of an application, and failure to check "yes" or checking "skip this question" shall not be construed to imply a wish not to donate. In the case of an applicant under eighteen years of age, checking "yes" shall not constitute consent to make an anatomical gift or registration in the donate life registry, except as otherwise provided pursuant to the provisions of paragraph (b) of subdivision one of section forty-three hundred one of this article. Where an applicant has previously consented to make an anatomical gift or registered in the donate life registry, checking "skip this question" or failing to check a box shall not impair that consent or registration.

(c) Enrollment or amendment or revocation through the donate life registry website through any of the means listed in this subdivision may be signed by electronic signature, in accordance with the provisions of article three of the state technology law, supported by the use of suitable mechanisms including unique identifiers to provide confidence in the identity of the person providing the electronic signature. The registration shall take effect upon the provision of written or electronic notice of the registration to the individual enrolling in the donate life registry.

(d) Amendments or revocations from the donate life registry shall be made by the following, subject to the requirements of the commissioner:

(i) registrants submitting an amendment or revocation in writing to the donate life registry; or

(ii) registrants submitting an amendment or revocation electronically through the donate life registry website.

(e) Removal from the donate life registry shall not be deemed a refusal of any other or future anatomical gift.

(f) The donate life registry shall provide individuals enrolled the opportunity to specify which organs, eyes and tissues they want to donate and if the donation may be used for transplantation, research, or both.

6. An individual registered in the donate life registry before July twenty-third, two thousand eight shall be deemed to have expressed intent to donate, until and unless he or she files an amendment to his or her registration or a new registration expressing consent to donate.

7. (a) The donate life registry shall be maintained in a manner that allows immediate access

to organ, eye and tissue donation records twenty-four hours a day, seven days a week to the contractor, the department, federally designated organ procurement organizations, licensed eye and tissue banks, and such other entities which may be approved by the department for access. Access shall be available to registrants to confirm the accuracy and validity of their registration and to amend or revoke their registration, subject to reasonable procedures to verify identity.

(b) Access to the donate life registry shall have security measures set forth in the contract to protect the integrity of the identifiable data in the donate life registry, which may only be accessed by the parties described in paragraph (a) of this subdivision and only for the purposes of determining donor status at or near the time of death of an individual, by the department for any purpose, by the contractor only for purposes of quality assessment and improvement, technical support and donor services, or by individual registrants for the purposes of confirming the accuracy and validity of their registration or making, amending or revoking their registration.

(c) De-identified information may be accessed by the entities listed in paragraph (a) of this subdivision or their designees for purposes of analysis, promotion, education, quality improvement and technical support for the donate life registry. The information contained in the registry shall not be released to any person except as expressly authorized by this section, solely for the purposes so authorized.

8. The commissioner is authorized to promulgate rules and regulations necessary to implement the provisions of this section.

9. An interagency work group, composed of the commissioner, the commissioner of the department of motor vehicles, a chair of the board of elections, or their designees, and such other individuals as may be designated by the commissioner, shall be established to meet with the contractor annually and as needed to review the status of the donate life registry, to examine the steps that might be taken by state agencies to enhance its performance and to make recommendations to the contractor.

Add, L 2004, ch 454, § 1, eff Sept 14, 2004; amd, L 2006, ch 639, § 2, eff Feb 12, 2007; L 2006, ch 640, § 1, eff Oct 15, 2006; L 2008, ch 362, § 2, eff Jan 1, 2009; L 2010, ch 161, § 1, eff July 7, 2010; L 2012, ch 158, § 1, eff July 18, 2012; L 2012, ch 465, § 2, eff Oct 3, 2013; L 2014, ch 60, § 27 (Part A), eff March 31, 2014; L 2015, ch 405, §1, eff Oct 26, 2015; L 2016, ch 248, § 2, eff Feb 14, 2017; L 2017 ch 332, § 1, eff Oct 16, 2017; L 2020, c 149, § 1, eff Aug 24, 2021.

2020 Amendment

2020 N.Y. Laws 45, § 1, effective August 24, 2021, amended subdivision 5(a) to allow for registration as an organ donor on an application for a hunting, fishing, or trapping license.

DOMESTIC RELATIONS LAW

Table of Contents

SECTIONS

DRL

ARTICLE 2
MARRIAGES
SUMMARY OF ARTICLE

§ 5. Incestuous and void marriages

A marriage is incestuous and void whether the relatives are legitimate or illegitimate between either:

1. An ancestor and a descendant;

2. A brother and sister of either the whole or the half blood;

3. An uncle and niece or an aunt and nephew.

If a marriage prohibited by the foregoing provisions of this section be solemnized it shall be void, and the parties thereto shall each be fined not less than fifty nor more than one hundred dollars and may, in the discretion of the court in addition to said fine, be imprisoned for a term not exceeding six months. Any person who shall knowingly and wilfully solemnize such marriage, or procure or aid in the solemnization of the same, shall be deemed guilty of a misdemeanor and shall be fined or imprisoned in like manner.

> Add, L 1909, ch 19, eff Feb 17, 1909.

§ 6. Void marriages

A marriage is absolutely void if contracted by a person whose husband or wife by a former marriage is living, unless either:

1. Such former marriage has been annulled or has been dissolved for a cause other than the adultery of such person; provided, that if such former marriage has been dissolved for the cause of the adultery of such person, he or she may marry again in the cases provided for in section eight of this chapter and such subsequent marriage shall be valid;

2. [Repealed]

3. Such former marriage has been dissolved pursuant to section seven-a*of this chapter.

> Add, L 1909, ch 19; amd, L 1915, ch 266, § 1; L 1922, ch 279, § 1; L 1950, ch 144, § 3, eff March 22, 1950; L 1967, ch 680, § 20; L 1981, ch 118, § 2, eff July 17, 1981.

§ 7. Voidable marriages

A marriage is void from the time its nullity is declared by a court of competent jurisdiction if either party thereto:

1. Is under the age of legal consent, which is eighteen years, provided that such nonage shall not of itself constitute an absolute right to the annulment of such marriage, but such annulment shall be in the discretion of the court which shall take into consideration all the facts and circumstances surrounding such marriage;

---

* Repealed, L 1962, ch 313, § 2; see now Domestic Relations Law §§ 220, 221.

2. Is incapable of consenting to a marriage for want of understanding;

3. Is incapable of entering into the married state from physical cause;

4. Consent to such marriage by reason of force, duress or fraud;

5. Has been incurably mentally ill for a period of five years or more.

Add, L 1909, ch 19; amd, L 1922, ch 279, § 2; L 1922, ch 313, § 1; L 1924, ch 165, § 1; L 1928, ch 589, § 1; L 1929, ch 537, § 1; L 1945, ch 686, § 1; L 1948, ch 362, § 1; L 1958, ch 804, § 1; L 1962, ch 313, § 1, eff Sept 1, 1963; L 1978, ch 550, § 14, eff July 24, 1978.

§ 8. Marriage after divorce

Whenever, and whether prior or subsequent to September first, nineteen hundred sixty-seven, a marriage has been dissolved by divorce, either party may marry again.

Add, L 1909, ch 19; amd, L 1915, ch 266, § 1; L 1919, ch 265, § 1; L 1966, ch 254, § 1, eff Sept 1, 1967; L 1968, ch 584, eff June 16, 1968.

§ 109. Definitions

When used in this article, unless the context or subject matter manifestly requires a different interpretation:

1. "Adoptive parent" or "adopter" shall mean a person adopting and "adoptive child" or "adoptee" shall mean a person adopted.

2. "Judge" shall mean a judge of the family court of any county in the state.

3. "Surrogate" shall mean the surrogate of any county in the state and any other judicial officer while acting in the capacity of surrogate.

4. "Authorized agency" shall mean an authorized agency as defined in the social services law and, for the purpose of this article, shall include such corporations incorporated or organized under the laws of this state as may be specifically authorized by their certificates of incorporation to receive children for purposes of adoption.

5. "Private placement adoption" shall mean any adoption other than that of a minor who has been placed for adoption by an authorized agency.

6. "Lawful custody" shall mean a custody (a) specifically authorized by statute or (b) pursuant to judgment, decree or order of a court or (c) otherwise authorized by law.

7. "A child who has been surrendered to an authorized agency for the purpose of adoption" shall mean a child who has been surrendered to such an agency pursuant to the provisions of section three hundred eighty-three-c or three hundred eighty-four of the social services law.

Add, L 1938, ch 606, § 1; amd, L 1941, ch 13, § 2; L 1960, ch 717, § 2; L 1961, ch 147, § 1, eff Sept 1, 1961; L 1962, ch 689, § 16, eff Sept 1, 1962; L 1962, ch 947, § 2; L 1970, ch 570, § 1, eff Sept 1, 1970; L 1976, ch 666, § 8; L 1989, ch 751, § 1, eff Jan 1, 1990; L 1991, ch 48, § 1, eff April 12, 1991.

§ 110. Who may adopt; effect of article

An adult unmarried person, an adult married couple together, or any two unmarried adult intimate partners together may adopt another person. An adult married person who is living separate and apart from his or her spouse pursuant to a decree or judgment of separation or pursuant to a written agreement of separation subscribed by the parties thereto and acknowledged or proved in the form required to entitle a deed to be recorded or an adult

DRL

married person who has been living separate and apart from his or her spouse for at least three years prior to commencing an adoption proceeding may adopt another person; provided, however, that the person so adopted shall not be deemed the child or step-child of the non-adopting spouse for the purposes of inheritance or support rights or obligations or for any other purposes. An adult or minor married couple together may adopt a child of either of them born in or out of wedlock and an adult or minor spouse may adopt such a child of the other spouse. No person shall hereafter be adopted except in pursuance of this article, and in conformity with section three hundred seventy-three of the social services law.

An adult married person who has executed a legally enforceable separation agreement or is a party to a marriage in which a valid decree of separation has been entered or has been living separate and apart from his or her spouse for at least three years prior to commencing an adoption proceeding and who becomes or has been the custodian of a child placed in their care as a result of court ordered foster care may apply to such authorized agency for placement of said child with them for the purpose of adoption. Final determination of the propriety of said adoption of such foster child, however, shall be within the sole discretion of the court, as otherwise provided herein.

Adoption is the legal proceeding whereby a person takes another person into the relation of child and thereby acquires the rights and incurs the responsibilities of parent in respect of such other person.

A proceeding conducted in pursuance of this article shall constitute a judicial proceeding. An order of adoption or abrogation made therein by a surrogate or by a judge shall have the force and effect of and shall be entitled to all the presumptions attaching to a judgment rendered by a court of general jurisdiction in a common law action.

No adoption heretofore lawfully made shall be abrogated by the enactment of this article. All such adoptions shall have the effect of lawful adoptions hereunder.

Nothing in this article in regard to a minor adopted pursuant hereto inheriting from the adoptive parent applies to any will, devise or trust made or created before June twenty-fifth, eighteen hundred seventy-three, nor alters, changes or interferes with such will, devise or trust. As to any such will, devise or trust a minor adopted before that date is not an heir so as to alter estates or trusts or devises in wills so made or created. Nothing in this article in regard to an adult adopted pursuant hereto inheriting from the adoptive parent applies to any will, devise or trust made or created before April twenty-second, nineteen hundred fifteen, nor alters, changes or interferes with such will, devise or trust. As to any such will, devise or trust an adult so adopted is not an heir so as to alter estates or trusts or devises in wills so made or created.

It shall be unlawful to preclude a prospective adoptive parent or parents solely on the basis that the adoptor or adopters has had, or has cancer, or any other disease. Nothing herein shall prevent the rejection of a prospective applicant based upon his or her poor health or limited life expectancy.

A petition to adopt, pursuant to the terms of this article, where the petitioner's parentage is legally-recognized under New York State law shall not be denied solely on the basis that the petitioner's parentage is already legally-recognized.

Add, L 1938, ch 606, § 1; amd, L 1943, ch 186, § 1; L 1951, ch 211, § 1; L 1961, ch 147, § 1; L 1970, ch 570, § 2, eff Sept 1, 1970; L 1984, ch 218, § 1; L 1984, ch 745, § 4; L 1991, ch 254, § 1, eff July 1, 1991; L 1999, ch 522, § 2, eff Sept 28, 1999; L 2010, ch 509, § 1, eff Sept 17, 2010; L 2019, ch 258, § 1, eff Sept 16, 2019.

§ 111. Whose consent required

1. Subject to the limitations hereinafter set forth consent to adoption shall be required as follows:

(a) Of the adoptive child, if over fourteen years of age, unless the judge or surrogate in his discretion dispenses with such consent;

(b) Of the parents or surviving parent, whether adult or infant, of a child conceived or born in wedlock;

(c) Of the mother, whether adult or infant, of a child born out of wedlock;

(d) Of the father, whether adult or infant, of a child born out-of-wedlock and placed with the adoptive parents more than six months after birth, but only if such father shall have maintained substantial and continuous or repeated contact with the child as manifested by: (i) the payment by the father toward the support of the child of a fair and reasonable sum, according to the father's means, and either (ii) the father's visiting the child at least monthly when physically and financially able to do so and not prevented from doing so by the person or authorized agency having lawful custody of the child, or (iii) the father's regular communication with the child or with the person or agency having the care or custody of the child, when physically and financially unable to visit the child or prevented from doing so by the person or authorized agency having lawful custody of the child. The subjective intent of the father, whether expressed or otherwise, unsupported by evidence of acts specified in this paragraph manifesting such intent, shall not preclude a determination that the father failed to maintain substantial and continuous or repeated contact with the child. In making such a determination, the court shall not require a showing of diligent efforts by any person or agency to encourage the father to perform the acts specified in this paragraph. A father, whether adult or infant, of a child born out-of-wedlock, who openly lived with the child for a period of six months within the one year period immediately preceding the placement of the child for adoption and who during such period openly held himself out to be the father of such child shall be deemed to have maintained substantial and continuous contact with the child for the purpose of this subdivision.

(e) Of the father, whether adult or infant, of a child born out-of-wedlock who is under the age of six months at the time he is placed for adoption, but only if: (i) such father openly lived with the child or the child's mother for a continuous period of six months immediately preceding the placement of the child for adoption; and (ii) such father openly held himself out to be the father of such child during such period; and (iii) such father paid a fair and reasonable sum, in accordance with his means, for the medical, hospital and nursing expenses incurred in connection with the mother's pregnancy or with the birth of the child.

(f) Of any person or authorized agency having lawful custody of the adoptive child.

2. The consent shall not be required of a parent or of any other person having custody of the child: (a)

who evinces an intent to forego his or her parental or custodial rights and obligations as manifested by his or her failure for a period of six months to visit the child and communicate with the child or person having legal custody of the child, although able to do so; or

(b) who has surrendered the child to an authorized agency under the provisions of section three hundred eighty-three-c or three hundred eighty-four of the social services law; or

(c) for whose child a guardian has been appointed under the provisions of section three hundred eighty-four-b of the social services law; or

(d) who, by reason of mental illness or intellectual disability, as defined in subdivision six of section three hundred eighty-four-b of the social services law, is presently and for the foreseeable future unable to provide proper care for the child. The determination as to whether a parent is mentally ill or intellectually disabled shall be made in accordance with the criteria and procedures set forth in subdivision six of section three hundred eighty-four-b of the social services law; or

(e) who has executed an instrument, which shall be irrevocable, denying the paternity of the child, such instrument having been executed after conception and acknowledged or proved in the manner required to permit the recording of a deed.

3. (a) Notice of the proposed adoption shall be given to a person whose consent to adoption is required pursuant to subdivision one and who has not already provided such consent.

(b) Notice and an opportunity to be heard upon the proposed adoption may be afforded to a parent whose consent to adoption may not be required pursuant to subdivision two, if the judge or surrogate so orders.

(c) Notice under this subdivision shall be given in such manner as the judge or surrogate may direct.

(d) Notwithstanding any other provision of law, neither the notice of a proposed adoption nor any process in such proceeding shall be required to contain the name of the person or persons seeking to adopt the child.

4. Where the adoptive child is over the age of eighteen years the consents specified in paragraphs (b), (c) and (d) of subdivision one of this section shall not be required, and the judge or surrogate in his discretion may direct that the consent specified in paragraph (f) of subdivision one of this section shall not be required if in his opinion the best interests of the adoptive child will be promoted by the adoption and such consent cannot for any reason be obtained.

5. An adoptive child who has once been lawfully adopted may be readopted directly from such child's adoptive parents in the same manner as from its birth parents. In such case the consent of such birth parents shall not be required but the judge or surrogate in his discretion may require that notice be given to the birth parents in such manner as he may prescribe.

6. For the purposes of paragraph (a) of subdivision two:

(a) In the absence of evidence to the contrary, the ability to visit and communicate with a child or person having custody of the child shall be presumed.

(b) Evidence of insubstantial or infrequent visits or communication by the parent or other person having custody of the child shall not, of itself, be sufficient as a matter of law to preclude a finding that the consent of such parent or person to the child's adoption shall not be required.

(c) The subjective intent of the parent or other person having custody of the child, whether expressed or otherwise, unsupported by evidence of acts specified in paragraph (a) of subdivision two manifesting such intent, shall not preclude a determination that the consent of such parent or other person to the child's adoption shall not be required.

(d) Payment by a parent toward the support of the child of a fair and reasonable sum, according to the parent's means, shall be deemed a substantial communication by such parent with the child or person having legal custody of the child.

Add, L 1938, ch 606, § 1; amd, L 1941, ch 13, § 2; L 1942, ch 118, § 1; L 1945, ch 531, § 1; L 1959, ch 168, § 1; L 1959, ch 448, § 1; L 1961, ch 147, § 1; L 1962, ch 689, § 17; L 1970, ch 570, § 3; L 1973, ch 195 § 16; L 1974, ch 842, § 1; L 1974, ch 920, § 6; L 1975, ch 246, § 1; L 1975, ch 704, § 3; L 1976, ch 666, § 9, eff Jan 1, 1977; L 1980, ch 575, §§ 1–3, eff July 26, 1980; L 1983, ch 152, § 1, eff May 31, 1983; L 1983, ch 911, § 4, eff Jan 1, 1984; L 1985, ch 918, §§ 1, 2, eff Dec 20, 1985; L 1991, ch 48, § 2, eff April 12, 1991; L 1997, ch 375, § 1, eff Aug 5, 1997; L 2008, ch 305, § 3, eff July 21, 2008; L 2016, ch 37, §1, eff May 25, 2016.

§ 111-a. Notice in certain proceedings to fathers of children born out-of-wedlock

1. Notwithstanding any inconsistent provisions of this or any other law, and in addition to the notice requirements of any law pertaining to persons other than those specified in subdivision two of this section, notice as provided herein shall be given to the persons specified in subdivision two of this section of any adoption proceeding initiated pursuant to this article or of any proceeding initiated pursuant to section one hundred fifteen-b of this article relating to the revocation of an adoption consent, when such proceeding involves a child born out-of-wedlock provided, however, that such notice shall not be required to be given to any person who previously has been given notice of any proceeding involving the child, pursuant to section three hundred eighty-four-c of the social services law, and provided further that notice in an adoption proceeding, pursuant to this section shall not be required to be given to any person who has previously received notice of any proceeding pursuant to section one hundred fifteen-b of this article. In addition to such other requirements as may be applicable to the petition in any proceeding in which notice must be given pursuant to this section, the petition shall set forth the names and last known addresses of all persons required to be given notice of the proceeding, pursuant to this section, and there shall be shown by the petition or by affidavit or other proof satisfactory to the court that there are no persons other than those set forth in the petition who are entitled to notice. For the purpose of determining persons entitled to notice of adoption proceedings initiated pursuant to this article, persons specified in subdivision two of this section shall not include any person who has been convicted of one or more of the following sexual offenses in this state or convicted of one or more offenses in another jurisdiction which, if committed in this state, would constitute one or more of the following offenses, when the child who is the subject of the proceeding was conceived as a result: (A) rape in first or second degree; (B) course of sexual conduct against a child in the first degree; (C) predatory sexual assault; or (D) predatory sexual assault against a child.

2. Persons entitled to notice, pursuant to subdivision one of this section, shall include:

(a) any person adjudicated by a court in this state to be the father of the child;

(b) any person adjudicated by a court of another state or territory of the United States to be the father of the child, when a certified copy of the court order has been filed with the putative father registry, pursuant to section three hundred seventy-two-c of the social services law;

(c) any person who has timely filed an unrevoked notice of intent to claim paternity of the child, pursuant to section three hundred seventy-two-c of the social services law;

(d) any person who is recorded on the child's birth certificate as the child's father;

(e) any person who is openly living with the child and the child's mother at the time the proceeding is initiated and who is holding himself out to be the child's father;

(f) any person who has been identified as the child's father by the mother in written, sworn statement;

(g) any person who was married to the child's mother within six months subsequent to the birth of the child and prior to the execution of a surrender instrument or the initiation of a proceeding pursuant to section three hundred eighty-four-b of the social services law; and

(h) any person who has filed with the putative father registry an instrument acknowledging paternity of the child, pursuant to section 4-1.2 of the estates, powers and trusts law.

3. The provisions of this section shall not apply to persons entitled to notice pursuant to section one hundred eleven.

The sole purpose of notice under this section shall be to enable the person served pursuant to subdivision two to present evidence to the court relevant to the best interests of the child.

4. Notice under this section shall be given at least twenty days prior to the proceeding by delivery of a copy of the petition and notice to the person. Upon a showing to the court, by affidavit or otherwise, on or before the date of the proceeding or within such further time as the court may allow, that personal service cannot be effected at the person's last known address with reasonable effort, notice may be given, without prior court order therefor, at least twenty days prior to the proceeding by registered or certified mail directed to the person's last known address or, where the person has filed a notice of intent to claim paternity pursuant to section three hundred seventy-two-c of the social services law, to the address last entered therein. Notice by publication shall not be required to be given to a person entitled to notice pursuant to the provisions of this section.

5. A person may waive his right to notice under this section by written instrument subscribed by him and acknowledged or proved in the manner required for the execution of a surrender instrument pursuant to section three hundred eighty-four of the social services law.

6. The notice given to persons pursuant to this section shall inform them of the time, date, place and purpose of the proceeding and shall also apprise such persons that their failure to appear shall constitute a denial of their interest in the child which denial may result, without further notice, in the adoption or other disposition of the custody of the child.

7. No order of adoption and no order of the court pursuant to section one hundred fifteen-b shall be vacated, annulled or reversed upon the application of any person who was properly

served with notice in accordance with this section but failed to appear, or who waived notice pursuant to subdivision five. Nor shall any order of adoption be vacated, annulled or reversed upon the application of any person who was properly served with notice in accordance with this section in any previous proceeding pursuant to section one hundred fifteen-b in which the court determined that the best interests of the child would be served by adoption of the child by the adoptive parents.

Add, L 1976, ch 665, § 3, eff Jan 1, 1977; amd, L 1977, ch 862, §§ 7–9, eff Oct. 10, 1977; L 1980, ch 575, §§ 4–6, eff July 26, 1980; L 1993, ch 353, § 1, eff July 21, 1993; L 2013, ch 371, § 2, eff Sept 27, 2013.

§ 111-b. Determination of issue of paternity by surrogate; limitations

1. In the course of an adoption proceeding conducted pursuant to this article the surrogate shall have jurisdiction to determine any issue of paternity arising in the course of the same proceeding and to make findings and issue an order thereon.

2. Such determination shall be made substantially in accordance with the relevant and otherwise consistent provisions of the family court act except that the surrogate shall have no power to grant any relief relating to support of the child as an incident thereto.

3. A judge of the family court shall continue to exercise all of the powers relating to adoption and declaration of paternity conferred upon the family court by law.

Add, L 1980, ch 575, § 7, eff July 26, 1980.

§ 111-c. Adoption order from foreign country or foreign jurisdiction

1. A final judgment of adoption granted by a judicial, administrative or executive body of a jurisdiction or country other than the United States shall have the same force and effect in this state as that given to a judgment of adoption entered by a court of competent jurisdiction of New York state, without additional proceedings or documentation provided:

(a) either adopting parent is a resident of this state; and

(b) the validity of the foreign adoption has been verified by the granting of an IR-3, IH-3, or a successor immigrant visa, for the child by the United States Citizenship and Immigration Services.

2. Notwithstanding any other provision of law or rule or regulation to the contrary, an adoptive parent referred to in subdivision one of this section shall not be required to petition a court in this state for adoption of the child provided the conditions of paragraphs (a) and (b) of subdivision one of this section are met. The foreign adoption shall be considered "final" under the laws of New York state upon the satisfaction of paragraphs (a) and (b) of subdivision one of this section.

3. Either adoptive parent or a guardian or a guardian ad litem may register the order in this state with the judge or surrogate of the county in which the adoptive parent or parents reside. A petition for registration of a foreign adoption order may be combined with a petition for a name change. If the court finds that the foreign adoption order meets the requirements of subdivision one of this section, the court shall issue a finding as to aspects of the foreign adoption, to wit, the names of the adoptive parents, the name or names and reported birth date of the adoptive child, the country of the adoptive child's birth, the country and the date of the foreign adoption, the state residency of the adoptive parent or parents and adoptive child, and a finding as to the date and issuance of an IR-3, IH-3, or a successor immigrant visa; and, the

court shall issue an order of adoption to the party who has petitioned for such an order.

4. The judge or surrogate is hereby directed to expedite the issuance of an order of adoption pursuant to the provisions of subdivision three of this section in order to ensure minimal expense of time and money to the petitioning parties in attaining such order of adoption.

Add, L 2008, ch 329, § 1, eff Oct 19, 2008; amd, L 2012, ch 395, §§ 1, 2, eff Aug 17, 2012.

§ 111-d. Consideration of blindness during adoption proceedings. [Effective January 6, 2022]

1. The court may not deny or decide a petition for adoption solely on the basis that the petitioner is blind. The blindness of the petitioner shall be considered relevant only to the extent that the court finds, based on evidence in the record, that the blindness affects the best interests of the child whose adoption is the subject of the petition.

2. As used in this section, "blind" or "blindness" means:

a. vision that is 20/200 or less in the best corrected eye; or

b. vision that subtends an angle of not greater than twenty degrees in the best corrected eye.

Added, L 2021, ch 442, § 4, effective January 6, 2022.

TITLE II   ADOPTION FROM AN AUTHORIZED AGENCY

§ 112. General provisions relating to adoption from authorized agencies

In an adoption from an authorized agency the following requirements shall be observed:

1. The adoptive parents or parent and the adoptive child must appear for examination before a judge or surrogate of the county specified in section one hundred thirteen of this title. The judge or surrogate, however, may in his discretion dispense with the personal appearance of the adoptive child or of an adoptive parent who is on active duty in the armed forces of the United States.

2. The adoptive parents or parent and the adoptive child if over eighteen years of age must present to such judge or surrogate (a) a petition stating the names and place of residence of the petitioners; whether they are of full age; whether they are married or unmarried and, if married, whether they are living together as husband and wife; the first name, date and place of birth of the adoptive child as nearly as the same can be ascertained; a statement on information and belief that there will be annexed to the petition a schedule verified by a duly constituted official of the authorized agency as required by this section; the religious faith of the petitioners; the religious faith of the adoptive child

and his or her parents as nearly as the same can be ascertained; the manner in which the adoptive parents obtained the adoptive child; whether the child was placed or brought into the state of New York from out of state for the purpose of adoption, whether the placement was subject to the provisions of section three hundred seventy-four-a of the social services law and if the placement was subject to the provisions of such section, whether the provisions of such section were complied with; the period of time during which the adoptive child has resided with the adoptive parents; the occupation and approximate income of the petitioners, including support and maintenance, if any, to be received on behalf of the adoptive child from a commissioner of social services, pursuant to the social services law, and the new name, if any, by which the adoptive child is to be known; whether the adoptive parent or parents has or have knowledge that an adoptive parent is the subject of an indicated report, as such terms are defined in section four hundred twelve of the social services law, filed with the statewide central register of child abuse and maltreatment pursuant to title six of article six of the social services law, or has been the subject of or the respondent in a child protective proceeding commenced under article ten of the family court act, which proceeding resulted in an order finding that the child is an abused or neglected child; that no previous application has been made to any court or judge for the relief sought or if so made, the disposition of it and a statement as to whether the adoptive child had been previously adopted, all of which statements shall be taken prima facie as true; (b) an agreement on the part of the adoptive parents or parent to adopt and treat the adoptive child as their or his or her own lawful child; (c) the consents required by section one hundred eleven of this article.

2-a. In the petition provided for in subdivision two of this section, the adoptive parents or parent and the adoptive child if over eighteen years of age shall present to the judge or surrogate as nearly as can be ascertained the heritage of the parents, which shall include nationality, ethnic background and race; education, which shall be the number of years of school completed by the parents at the time of the birth of the adoptive child; general physical appearance of the parents at the time of the birth of the adoptive child, which shall include height, weight, color of hair, eyes, skin; occupation of the parents at the time of the birth of the adoptive child; health and medical history of the parents at the time of the birth of the adoptive child, including all available information setting forth conditions or diseases believed to be hereditary, any drugs or medication taken during the pregnancy by the child's mother; and any other information which may be a factor influencing the child's present or future health, talents, hobbies and special interests of parents. The petition shall also include the names and current addresses of the biological parents, if known.

3. The authorized agency must present to such judge or surrogate a schedule to be annexed to the petition which shall be verified by a duly constituted official of the authorized agency having custody of the adoptive child or actually placing the child for adoption and shall contain (1) the full name of the child, (2) the manner in which the authorized agency obtained custody of the adoptive child, (3) the facts, if any, which render unnecessary the consent of either or both of the parents of the adoptive child, (4) a statement whether either parent had ever requested the agency to return the child to the parent, within thirty days of the execution and delivery of an instrument of surrender to an authorized agency and, if so, all facts relating thereto. If a request for return of the child to a parent be made after the presentation to the court of the petition and schedule, the authorized agency shall promptly report to the court in writing the facts relating thereto and (5) all available information comprising the child's medical history. If the child was

DRL

placed into the state of New York for the purpose of adoption and such placement was subject to the provisions of section three hundred seventy-four-a of the social services law, the authorized agency shall attach to the petition a copy of the document, signed by New York's administrator of the interstate compact for the placement of children or his designee, which informs the agency or person who placed the child into the state that such placement complied with the provisions of the compact.

4. None of the papers in the proceeding shall state the surname of the child in the title and no petition, agreement, consent, affidavit, nor any other document which is required to be signed by the adoptive parents shall contain the surname of the adoptive child.

5. The petition must be verified, the agreement and consents executed and acknowledged and the proof given by the respective persons before such judge or surrogate; but where the verification, agreement or necessary consent is duly acknowledged or proved and certified in form sufficient to entitle a conveyance to be recorded in this state, (except that when executed and acknowledged within the state of New York, no certificate of the county clerk shall be required), such judge or surrogate may grant the order of adoption without the personal appearance of such persons or parties or any of them for good cause shown, which reason shall be recited in the order of adoption.

6. Where the adoptive child is less than eighteen years of age, no order of adoption shall be made until such child has resided with the adoptive parents for at least three months unless the judge or surrogate in his discretion shall dispense with such period of residence and shall recite in the order the reason for such action. When the adoptive parents are the foster parents in whose home the adoptive child has been placed out or boarded out for a period in excess of three months, such period shall be deemed to constitute the required period of residence.

7. Before making an order of adoption the judge or surrogate shall inquire of the department of social services and the department shall inform the court whether an adoptive parent is the subject of an indicated report, as such terms are defined in section four hundred twelve of the social services law, filed with the statewide central register of child abuse and maltreatment pursuant to title six of article six of the social services law and shall cause to be made an investigation by a disinterested person or by an authorized agency specifically designated by the judge or surrogate to examine into the allegations set forth in the petition and to ascertain such other facts relating to the adoptive child and adoptive parents as will give such judge or surrogate adequate basis for determining the propriety of approving the adoption. A written report of such investigation shall be submitted before the order of adoption is made. As used in this subdivision, "disinterested person" includes the probation service of the family court. Such an inquiry shall not be required if the findings of such an inquiry made within the past twelve months is available to the judge or surrogate.

7-a. Any order subject to the provisions of this section shall include an adoption information registry birth parent registration consent form, stating whether or not such biological parent or parents whose consent is subject to the provisions of this section, consents to the receipt of identifying information by the child to be adopted upon registration with the adoption information registry established by section forty-one hundred thirty-eight-c of the public health law and upon the adoptee reaching the age of eighteen. If such consent is made, it shall be revocable by either of the biological parents at any time. The revocation of the consent by one of the parents shall revoke the consent of both parents. The failure of a biological parent to complete the consent form shall have no effect on the finality of the consent to adoption. A copy of the form required by this subdivision, shall be forwarded to the state adoption information registry for inclusion in the records maintained by such registry. Any fees authorized to be charged by the state adoption registry for filing documentation with such registry shall be waived for the form required by this subdivision.

8. Rules of court shall permit the filing of a petition for adoption of a child whose custody and guardianship has not yet been committed to an authorized agency where a proceeding to terminate parental rights is pending. Such adoption petition shall be filed in the court where the termination of parental rights proceeding is pending. The clerk of such court shall accept the adoption petition for filing and processing and shall request such inquiries of the department of social services as are required by subdivision seven of this section, provided, however, that the petition, supporting documents and the fact of their filing shall not be provided to the judge before whom the petition for termination of parental rights is pending until such time as fact-finding is concluded under such petition.

Add, L 1938, ch 606, § 1; amd, L 1943, ch 610, § 1; L 1945, ch 98, § 1; L 1945, ch 231, § 1; L 1946, ch 287, § 1; L 1961, ch 147, § 1, eff Sept 1, 1961; L 1962, ch 689, § 18; L 1962, ch 690, § 2; L 1967, ch 740, § 1; L 1968, ch 320, § 2; L 1968, ch 1038, §§ 1–3, eff Sept 1, 1968; L 1970, ch 570, § 4, eff Sept 1, 1970; L 1973, ch 613, § 1; L 1974, ch 1011, § 1; L 1975, ch 424, § 1; L 1976, ch 666, § 10; L 1985, ch 531, §§ 1, 2, eff Oct 22, 1985; L 1989, ch 707, §§ 1, 2; L 1989, ch 751, §§ 2, 3, eff Jan 1, 1990; L 1991, ch 164, §§ 3, 4, eff Jan 1, 1992; L 1991, ch 588, § 8, eff Sept 30, 1991; L 1996, ch 309, § 275, eff July 13, 1996; L 2008, ch 435, § 1, eff Nov 3, 2008.

§ 112-a. Expedited calendaring of adoption proceedings

1. The adoption proceeding shall be deemed filed upon receipt by the clerk of the court of all the documents required in subdivisions two, two-a, three, five and seven of section one hundred twelve of this title, and by rules of the court, together with an affidavit of readiness from the petitioner's attorney. The affidavit of readiness shall attest that the petitioner has prepared a petition for the adoption of the child and has collected documentation as required by such rules and subdivisions two, two-a, three and five of section one hundred twelve of this title.

2. Upon the filing of the documents required by subdivision one of this section, the court, pursuant to rules promulgated by the chief administrator of the court, shall schedule the proceeding for a review, to take place within time frames established by such rules, to determine if there is adequate basis for approving the adoption.

(a) If such basis is found, the appearance of the adoptive parents and child before the court for approval of the adoption shall be calendared pursuant to such rules.

(b) If, upon the court's review, the court finds that there is not an adequate basis for approval of the adoption, the court shall direct such further hearings, submissions or appearances as may be required, and the proceedings shall be adjourned as required for such purposes.

3. The chief administrator of the court shall establish by rule time frames for the calendaring and disposition of adoption proceedings and shall report by the thirty-first day of December of each year to the governor and the temporary president of the senate, speaker of

the assembly, and chairpersons of the judiciary and children and families committees on the implementation of such rules and their impact upon adoptions from authorized agencies.

Add, L 1993, ch 294, § 3, eff Sept 19, 1993; amd, L 2005, ch 524, § 14, eff Nov 14, 2005.

§ 112-b. Post-adoption contact agreements; judicial approval; enforcement

1. Nothing in this section shall be construed to prohibit the parties to a proceeding under this chapter from entering into an agreement regarding communication with or contact between an adoptive child, adoptive parent or parents and a birth parent or parents and/or the adoptive child's biological siblings or half-siblings.

2. Agreements regarding communication or contact between an adoptive child, adoptive parent or parents, and a birth parent or parents and/or biological siblings or half-siblings of an adoptive child shall not be legally enforceable unless the terms of the agreement are incorporated into a written court order entered in accordance with the provisions of this section. The court shall not incorporate an agreement regarding communication or contact into an order unless the terms and conditions of the agreement have been set forth in writing and consented to in writing by the parties to the agreement, including the attorney representing the adoptive child. The court shall not enter a proposed order unless the court that approved the surrender of the child determined and stated in its order that the communication with or contact between the adoptive child, the prospective adoptive parent or parents and a birth parent or parents and/or biological siblings or half-siblings, as agreed upon and as set forth in the agreement, would be in the adoptive child's best interests. Notwithstanding any other provision of law, a copy of the order entered pursuant to this section incorporating the post-adoption contact agreement shall be given to all parties who have agreed to the terms and conditions of such order.

3. Failure to comply with the terms and conditions of an approved order regarding communication or contact that has been entered by the court pursuant to this section shall not be grounds for setting aside an adoption decree or revocation of written consent to an adoption after that consent has been approved by the court as provided in this section.

4. An order incorporating an agreement regarding communication or contact entered under this section may be enforced by any party to the agreement or the attorney for the child by filing a petition in the family court in the county where the adoption was approved. Such petition shall have annexed to it a copy of the order approving the agreement regarding communication or contact. The court shall not enforce an order under this section unless it finds that the enforcement is in the child's best interests.

5. If a birth parent has surrendered a child to an authorized agency pursuant to the provisions of section three hundred eighty-three-c or section three hundred eighty-four of the social services law, and if the court before whom the surrender instrument was presented for approval approved an agreement providing for communication or contact pursuant to paragraph (a) of subdivision two of section three hundred eighty-three-c or paragraph (a) of subdivision two of section three hundred eighty-four of the social services law, a copy of the surrender instrument and of the approved agreement shall be annexed to the petition of adoption. The court shall issue an order incorporating the terms and conditions of the approved agreement into the order of adoption. Notwithstanding any other provision of law, a copy of any order entered pursuant to this subdivision shall be given to the parties who approved such agreement.

6. If a surrender instrument executed by a birth parent pursuant to section three hundred eighty-three-c or three hundred eighty-four of the social services law contains terms and conditions that provide for communication with or contact between a child and a birth parent or parents, such terms and conditions shall not be legally enforceable after any adoption approved by a court pursuant to this article unless the court has entered an order pursuant to this section incorporating those terms and conditions into a court ordered adoption agreement.

Add, L 2005, ch 3, § 63 (Part A), eff Dec 21, 2005; amd, L 2006, ch 437, § 17, eff July 26, 2006; L 2010, ch 41, § 4, eff April 14, 2010.

§ 113. Special provisions relating to adoption from authorized agencies

1. An authorized agency may consent to the adoption of a minor whose custody and guardianship has been transferred to such agency. An authorized agency may also consent to the adoption of a minor whose care and custody has been transferred to such agency pursuant to section one thousand fifty-five of the family court act or section three hundred eighty-four-a of the social services law, where such child's parents are both deceased, or where one parent is deceased and the other parent is not a person entitled to notice pursuant to sections one hundred eleven and one hundred eleven-a of this chapter.

2. In accordance with subparagraph three of paragraph (g) of subdivision six of section three hundred ninety-eight of the social services law, an authorized agency may submit a written request to a social services district with a population of more than two million for approval to consent to the adoption of a child whose custody and guardianship, or of a child where such child's parents are both deceased, or where one parent is deceased and the other parent is not entitled to notice pursuant to sections one hundred eleven and one hundred eleven-a of this chapter, and whose care and custody, has been transferred to a social services official and who has been placed by the social services official with the authorized agency. If the request is not disapproved by the social services district within sixty days after its submission, it shall be deemed approved, and the authorized agency may give all necessary consent to the adoption of the child. Nothing herein shall result in the transfer of care and custody or custody and guardianship of the child from the social services official to the authorized agency.

3. (a) The agreement of adoption shall be executed by such authorized agency.

(b) (i) If the adoption petition is filed pursuant to subdivision eight of section one hundred twelve of this article or subdivision ten of section three hundred eighty-three-c or subdivision eleven of section three hundred eighty-four-b of the social services law, the petition shall be filed in the county where the termination of parental rights proceeding or judicial surrender proceeding, as applicable, is pending and shall be assigned, wherever practicable, to the same judge.

(ii) In any other agency adoption proceeding, the petition shall be filed in the same court and, wherever practicable, shall be assigned to the same judge of the county in which parental rights had been terminated, a judicial surrender had been approved or the most recent proceeding under article ten or ten-A of the family court act or section three hundred fifty-eight-a of the social services law had been heard, whichever occurred last, or in the county where the adoptive parents reside or, if such adoptive parents do not reside in this state, in the county where such authorized agency has its principal office. The following procedures shall be applicable in cases where the child is under the jurisdiction of a family court, but where the adoption petition has been filed in a court other than the court that presided over the termination of parental rights, surrender or most recent proceeding under article ten or ten-A of the family court act or section three hundred fifty-eight-a of the social services law, whichever occurred last:

(A) Before hearing such an adoption proceeding, the court in which the adoption petition was filed shall ascertain whether the child is under the jurisdiction of a family court as a result of a placement under article ten or ten-A of the family court act or section three hundred fifty-eight-a of the social services law, a surrender under section three hundred eighty-three-c or three hundred eighty-four of the social services law or an order committing guardianship and custody under article six of the family court act or section three hundred eighty-four-b of the social services law, and, if so, which court exercised jurisdiction over the most recent permanency or other proceeding involving the child.

(B) If the court determines that the child is under the jurisdiction of a different family court, the court in which the adoption petition was filed shall stay its proceeding for not more than thirty days and shall communicate with the family court judge who exercised jurisdiction over the most recent permanency or other proceeding involving the child. The communication shall be recorded or summarized on the record by the court in which the adoption petition was filed. Both courts shall notify the parties and the attorney for the child, if any, in their respective proceedings and shall give them an opportunity to present facts and legal argument or to participate in the communication prior to the issuance of a decision on jurisdiction.

(C) The family court judge who exercised jurisdiction over the most recent permanency or other proceeding involving the child shall determine whether he or she should assume or decline jurisdiction over the adoption proceeding. In making its determination, the family court judge shall consider, among other factors: the relative familiarity of each court with the facts and circumstances regarding permanency planning for, and the needs and best interests of, the child; the ability of the attorney for the child to continue such representation in the adoption proceeding, if appropriate; the convenience of each court to the residence of the prospective adoptive parent or parents; and the relative ability of each court to hear and determine the adoption petition expeditiously. The court in which the adoption petition was filed shall issue an order incorporating this determination of jurisdiction within thirty days of the filing of the adoption petition.

(D) If the family court that exercised jurisdiction over the most recent permanency or other proceeding determines that it should exercise jurisdiction over the adoption petition, the order of the court in which the adoption petition was filed shall direct the transfer of the proceeding forthwith but in no event more than thirty-five days after the filing of the petition. The petition shall be assigned, wherever practicable, to the family court judge who heard the most recent permanency or other proceeding involving the child.

(E) If the family court that exercised jurisdiction over the permanency or other proceeding involving the child declines to exercise jurisdiction over the adoption petition, the court in which the adoption petition was filed shall issue an order incorporating that determination and shall proceed forthwith.

(iii) Neither such authorized agency nor any officer or agent thereof need appear before the judge or surrogate. The judge or surrogate in his or her discretion may accept the report of an authorized agency verified by one of its officers or agents as the report of investigation hereinbefore required. In making orders of adoption the judge or surrogate when practicable must give custody only to persons of the same religious faith as that of the adoptive child in accordance with article six of the social services law.

Add, L 1938, ch 606, § 1, with substance transferred from former § 115; amd, L 1941, ch 13, § 2; L 1961, ch 147, § 1; L 1970, ch 570, § 5; L 1993, ch 108, § 1; L 1995, ch 83, § 251, eff July 1, 1995; L 1996, ch 607, § 2, eff Sept 4, 1996; L 1997, ch 375, § 2; L 1998, ch 531, § 1, 2006, ch 185, § 7, eff Oct 24, 2006; L 2010, ch 41, § 5, eff April 14, 2010.

§ 113-a. Effect of death of potential adoptive parent

Notwithstanding any other provision of law to the contrary, when a petition for adoption by two persons has been duly filed, and one of the petitioners dies before the adoption is complete, it shall be treated as a change of circumstance. This change may be reviewed to assure that the adoption is in the best interest of the child. The death of one of the adoptive parents shall not, by itself, invalidate a certification nor shall the death of one of the adoptive parents cause a new petition for adoption to be filed. The deceased adoptive parent shall be considered one of the legal parents, unless the surviving adoptive parent requests otherwise.

Add, L 2008, ch 160, § 1, eff July 7, 2008.

§ 114. Order of adoption

1. If satisfied that the best interests of the adoptive child will be promoted thereby, the judge or surrogate shall make an order approving the adoption and directing that the adoptive child shall thenceforth be regarded and treated in all respects as the child of the adoptive parents or parent. In determining whether the best interests of the adoptive child will be promoted by the adoption, the judge or surrogate shall give due consideration to any assurance by a local commissioner of social services that he or she will provide necessary support and maintenance for the adoptive child pursuant to the social services law. Such order shall contain the full name, date and place of birth and reference to the schedule annexed to the petition containing the medical history of the child in the body thereof and shall direct that the child's medical history, heritage of the birth parents, which shall include nationality, ethnic background and race; education, which shall be the number of years of school completed by the birth parents at the time of the birth and also at the time of surrender of the adoptive child; general physical appearance of the birth parents at the time of the birth and also at the time of surrender of the adoptive child, which shall include height, weight, color of hair, eyes, skin; occupation of the birth parents at the time of the birth and also at the time of surrender of the adoptive child; health and medical history of the birth parents at the time of the birth and also at the time of surrender of the adoptive child, including all available information setting forth conditions or diseases believed to be hereditary, any drugs or medication taken during the pregnancy by the child's mother; and any other information which may be a factor influencing the child's present or future health, including the talents, hobbies and special interests of the birth parents as contained in the petition, be furnished to the adoptive parents, the commissioner and the appropriate local registrar of vital statistics. If the judge or surrogate is also satisfied that there is no reasonable objection to the change of name proposed, the order shall direct that the name of the adoptive child be changed to the

DRL

name stated in the agreement of adoption and that henceforth he or she shall be known by that name. All such orders made by a family court judge of Westchester county since September first, nineteen hundred sixty-two, and on file in the office of the county clerk of such county shall be transferred to the clerk of the family court of such county. Such order and all the papers in the proceeding shall be filed in the office of the court granting the adoption and the order shall be entered in books which shall be kept under seal and which shall be indexed by the name of the adoptive parents and by the full original name of the child. Such order, including orders heretofore entered, shall be subject to inspection and examination only as hereinafter provided. Notwithstanding the fact that adoption records shall be sealed and secret, they may be microfilmed and processed pursuant to an order of the court, provided that such order provides that the confidentiality of such records be maintained. If the confidentiality is violated, the person or company violating it can be found guilty of contempt of court. The fact that the adoptive child was born out of wedlock shall in no case appear in such order. The written report of the investigation together with all other papers pertaining to the adoption shall be kept by the judge or surrogate as a permanent record of his or her court and such papers must be sealed by him or her and withheld from inspection. No certified copy of the order of adoption shall issue unless authorized by court order, except that certified copies may issue to the agency or agencies in the proceeding prior to the sealing of the papers. Before the record is sealed, such order may be granted upon written ex parte application on good cause shown and upon such conditions as the court may impose. After the record is sealed, such order may be granted only upon notice as hereinafter provided for disclosure or access and inspection of records. The clerk upon request of a person or agency entitled thereto shall issue certificates of adoption which shall contain only the new name of the child and the date and place of birth of the child, the name of the adoptive parents and the date when and court where the adoption was granted, which certificate as to the facts recited therein shall have the same force and effect as a certified copy of an order of adoption. For the purposes of this subdivision, the term "commissioner" shall mean the state commissioner of health and, with respect to an adoptive child born in the city of New York, the commissioner of health and mental hygiene of the city of New York.

2. No person, including the attorney for the adoptive parents shall disclose the surname of the child directly or indirectly to the adoptive parents except upon order of the court. No person shall be allowed access to such sealed records and order and any index thereof except upon an order of a judge or surrogate of the court in which the order was made or of a justice of the supreme court. No order for disclosure or access and inspection shall be granted except on good cause shown and on due notice to the adoptive parents and to such additional persons as the court may direct. Nothing contained herein shall be deemed to require the state commissioner of health or his designee to secure a court order authorizing disclosure of information contained in adoption or birth records requested pursuant to the authority of section forty-one hundred thirty-eight-c or section forty-one hundred thirty-eight-d of the public health law; upon the receipt of such request for information, the court shall transmit the information authorized to be released thereunder to the state commissioner of health or his designee.

3. In like manner as a court of general jurisdiction exercises such powers, a judge or surrogate of a court in which the order of adoption was made may open, vacate or set aside such order of adoption for fraud, newly discovered evidence or other sufficient cause.

4. Good cause for disclosure or access to and inspection of sealed adoption records and

orders and any index thereof, hereinafter the "adoption records", under this section may be established on medical grounds as provided herein. Certification from a physician licensed to practice medicine in the state of New York that relief under this subdivision is required to address a serious physical or mental illness shall be prima facie evidence of good cause. Such certification shall indentify* the information required to address such illness. Except where there is an immediate medical need for the information sought, in which case the court may grant access to the adoption records directly to the petitioner, the court hearing petition under the subdivision shall appoint a guardian ad litem or other disinterested person, who shall have access to the adoption records for the purpose of obtaining the medical information sought from those records or, where the records are insufficient for such purpose, through contacting the biological parents. The guardian or other disinterested person shall offer a biological parent the option of disclosing the medical information sought by the petitioner pursuant to this subdivision, as well as the option of granting consent to examine the parent's medical records. If the guardian or other disinterested person appointed does not obtain the medical information sought by the petitioner, such guardian or disinterested person shall make a report of his or her efforts to obtain such information to the court. Where further efforts to obtain such information are appropriate, the court may in its discretion authorize direct disclosure or access to and inspection of the adoption records by the petitioner.

Add, L 1938, ch 606, § 1; amd, L 1943, ch 591, § 1; L 1944, ch 29, § 1; L 1944, ch 255, § 1; L 1945, ch 220, § 1; L 1950, ch 559, § 1; L 1951, ch 256, § 1; L 1954, ch 633, § 1; L 1959, ch 499, § 1; L 1960, ch 218, § 1; L 1961, ch 147, § 1; L 1962, ch 689, § 19; L 1968, ch 320, § 3; L 1968, ch 365, § 1; L 1968, ch 1038, § 4; L 1970, ch 570, § 6; L 1974, ch 261, § 1; L 1974, ch 1011, § 2; L 1976, ch 666, § 11; L 1985, ch 37, § 2; L 1989, ch 751, § 4, eff Jan 1, 1990; L 1992, ch 559, § 11; L 1994, ch 601, § 1, eff Oct 24, 1994; L 2019, ch 491, § 9, eff Jan 15, 2020.

TITLE III   PRIVATE-PLACEMENT ADOPTION

§ 115. General provisions relating to private-placement adoptions

1. (a) Except as otherwise provided in this title, private-placement adoptions shall be effected in the same manner as provided in sections one hundred twelve and one hundred fourteen of title two of this article.

(b) A person or persons seeking to commence a private-placement adoption shall, prior to the submission of a petition for such adoption and prior to any transfer of physical custody of an adoptive child, be certified as a qualified adoptive parent or parents by a court of competent jurisdiction pursuant to section one hundred fifteen-d of this title. The provisions of such section may be waived upon the court's own motion or upon the

---

* So in original. Should be "identify".

application of any party for good cause shown.

(c) A non-resident person or persons seeking to commence a private-placement adoption of a child present within the state at the time of placement shall, prior to any transfer of physical custody of an adoptive child, make application for certification as a qualified adoptive parent or parents by a court of competent jurisdiction pursuant to section one hundred fifteen-d of this title. Upon application of such person or persons, the court of the county to which the certification petition is properly filed may take or retain jurisdiction of the adoption proceeding. The provisions of this paragraph may be waived upon the court's own motion or upon the application of any party for good cause shown.

2. The proceeding shall be instituted in the county where the adoptive parents reside or, if such adoptive parents do not reside in this state, in the county where the adoptive child resides.

3. The adoptive parents or parent, the adoptive child and all persons whose consent is required by section one hundred eleven of this article must appear for examination before the judge or surrogate of the court where the adoption proceedings are instituted. The judge or surrogate may dispense with the personal appearance of the adoptive child or of an adoptive parent who is on active duty in the armed forces of the United States.

4. The agreement of adoption shall be executed by the adoptive parents or parent.

5. Where the petition alleges that either or both of the birth parents of the child have been deprived of civil rights or are mentally ill or mentally retarded, proof shall be submitted that such disability exists at the time of the proposed adoption.

6. The adoptive parent or parents shall also present in an affidavit a description of any change of circumstances since their certification as a qualified adoptive parent or parents, pursuant to section one hundred fifteen-d of this title, which may be relevant and material to such certification.

7. Where the adoptive child is to be adopted upon the consent of some person other than his father or mother, there shall also be presented the affidavit of such person showing how he or she obtained lawful custody of the child.

8. The adoptive parent or parents shall also present an affidavit describing all fees, compensation and other remunerations paid by such parent or parents on account of or incidental to the birth or care of the adoptive child, the pregnancy or care of the adoptive child's mother or the placement or adoption of the child and on account of or incidental to assistance in arrangements for such placement or adoption. The attorney representing the adoptive parents shall also present an affidavit describing all fees, compensation and other remuneration received by him on account of or incidental to the placement or adoption of the child or assistance in arrangements for such placement or adoption.

9. The petition must be verified, the agreement and consents executed and acknowledged, the proof given and the affidavit sworn to by the respective persons before such judge or surrogate; but where the verification, agreement or consent of an adoptive parent, birth parent or person whose consent is necessary to the adoption is duly acknowledged or proved and certified in form sufficient to entitle a conveyance to be recorded in this state, (except that when executed and acknowledged within the state of New York, no certificate of the county clerk shall be required), such judge or surrogate may grant the order of adoption without the

personal appearance of such adoptive parent, birth parent or person. The judge or surrogate may, in his discretion, dispense with the requirement that the adoptive child appear for examination or join in the petition, where otherwise required. In any adoption proceeding where the judge or surrogate shall dispense with the personal appearance of such adoptive parent, birth parent, person whose consent is necessary to the adoption, or adoptive child, the reason therefor must be for good cause shown, and shall be recited in the order of adoption.

10. In all cases where the consents of the persons mentioned in subdivision two, three and four of section one hundred eleven of this article are not required or where the adoptive child is an adult notice of such application shall be served upon such persons as the judge or surrogate may direct.

11. The provisions of title two prohibiting the surname of the child from appearing in the papers, prohibiting disclosure of the surname of the child to the adoptive parents, and requiring a separate application for issuance of a certified copy of an order of adoption prior to the sealing of the papers, requiring the filing of a verified schedule, shall not apply to private-placement adoptions; provided, however, that the facts required to be stated in the verified schedule in an agency adoption shall be set forth in the petition.

12. (a) If the child who is being adopted was placed or brought into New York for the purpose of adoption from a state which is a party to the interstate compact on the placement of children and the provisions of the compact applied to such placements, the petition must contain a statement that the provisions of section three hundred seventy-four-a of the social services law were complied with and where applicable, that the provisions of section three hundred eighty-two of such law were also complied with.

(b) If the child who is being adopted was placed or brought into New York for the purpose of adoption from a state which is not a party to the interstate compact on the placement of children, the petition, where applicable, must contain a statement that the provisions of section three hundred eighty-two of the social services law were complied with.

13. If the placement of a child into the state of New York is subject to the provisions of sections three hundred seventy-four-a and/or three hundred eighty-two of the social services law, there shall be attached to the petition a copy of the document signed by New York's administrator of the interstate compact on the placement of children or his designee which informs the agency or person who placed the child into the state that such placement complied with the provisions of the compact and/or a copy of the license which is issued pursuant to the provisions of section three hundred eighty-two of the social services law to the person, institution, corporation or agency which placed or brought the child into this state.

Add, L 1961, ch 147, § 1; amd, L 1968, ch 1038; L 1970, ch 570, § 7, eff Sept 1, 1970; L 1976, ch 666, § 12; L 1981, ch 283, § 2; L 1985, ch 531, § 3; L 1989, ch 700, §§ 1, 2, eff Nov 1, 1989; L 1992, ch 704, § 3, eff July 31, 1992; L 2008, ch 305, §§ 4, 5, eff July 21, 2008.

§ 115-a. Special provisions relating to children to be brought into the state for private-placement adoption

1. In the case of a child whose admission to the United States as an eligible orphan with non-quota immigrant status pursuant to the federal immigration and nationality act is sought for the purpose of adoption in the state of New York, the following pre-adoption requirements shall be observed:

(a) The adoptive parents or parent must present to a judge or surrogate having jurisdiction of adoption proceedings, in the county of residence of such adoptive parents or parent, a verified written application containing the information set forth in subdivision two of this section, in such form as the judge or surrogate may prescribe for an order of pre-adoption investigation, to determine whether the adoption may be in the best interests of the child.

(b) The adoptive parents or parent must appear for examination before the judge or surrogate of the court where the pre-adoption proceedings are instituted.

(c) The application must be accompanied by duly authenticated documentary evidence: (1) that the child is an alien under the age of sixteen and (2) that he is an orphan because of the death or disappearance of both parents, or because of abandonment, or desertion by, or separation or loss from, both parents, or who has only one parent due to the death or disappearance of, abandonment, or desertion by, or separation or loss from the other parent, and the remaining parent is incapable of providing care for such orphan and has in writing irrevocably released him for emigration and adoption, and has consented to the proposed adoption. In all cases where the orphan has no remaining parent under the circumstances set forth above, documentary evidence must be presented that the person, public authority or duly constituted agency having lawful custody of the orphan at the time of the making of the application, hereunder, has in writing irrevocably released him for immigration and adoption and has consented to the proposed adoption and (3) that the adoptive parents agree to adopt and treat the adoptive child as their or his or her own lawful child.

(d) In addition thereto such additional releases and consents as the court may in its sound discretion require.

2. The verified written application shall contain the following information: the names and place of residence of the adoptive parent or parents; whether they are of full age; whether they are married or unmarried and, if married, whether they are living together as husband and wife; the name, date and place of birth of the adoptive child as nearly as the same can be ascertained; the religious faith of the adoptive parent or parents; the religious faith of the adoptive child and his parents as nearly as the same can be ascertained; the medical history of the adoptive child as nearly as the same can be ascertained; the occupation and approximate income of the adoptive parent or parents, and the name by which the adoptive child is to be known; that no previous application has been made to any court or judge for the relief sought or if so made, the disposition of it and a statement as to whether the adoptive child has been previously adopted, if such fact is known to the adoptive parent or parents; the facts which establish that the child is an eligible orphan who would be entitled to enter the United States with non-quota immigrant status for the purpose of adoption in New York state, pursuant to the provisions in the federal immigration and nationality act, in such case made; the circumstances whereby, and names and addresses of the intermediaries, if any, through whom the adoptive parent or parents learned of the existence and eligibility of the child and the names and addresses of the person or persons, public authority or duly constituted agency in the land of the child's residence executing the written release of the child for emigration and adoption, and the consent to such adoption, the circumstances under which the release and consent were obtained, insofar as they are known to the adoptive parent or parents.

2-a. The verified written application shall contain the following information: the heritage of the parents as nearly as the same can be ascertained, which shall include nationality, ethnic background and race; education, which shall be the number of years of school completed by the parents at the time of the birth of the adoptive child; general physical appearance of the parents at the time of the birth of the adoptive child, which shall include height, weight, color of hair, eyes, skin; occupation of the parents at the time of the birth of the adoptive child; health and medical history of the parents at the time of the birth of the adoptive child, including all available information setting forth conditions or diseases believed to be hereditary, any drugs or medication taken during the pregnancy by the child's mother; and any other information which may be a factor influencing the child's present or future health, talents, hobbies and special interests of parents.

3. Upon receiving the verified written application, required documentary evidence, agreement and consents, the judge or surrogate, upon finding that the applicable provisions of section one hundred fifteen-a have been complied with and that it appears that the proposed adoption may be in the best interests of the child, shall issue an order of pre-adoption investigation hereunder. The order of pre-adoption investigation shall require that the report of such investigation be made by a disinterested person who in the opinion of the judge or surrogate is qualified by training and experience, or by an authorized agency specifically designated by him to examine into the statements set forth in the application. The investigator shall make a written report of his investigation into the truth and accuracy of the statements in the application and where applicable, into the validity of the documentary evidence, submitted with the application, and he shall ascertain as fully as possible, and incorporate in his report the various factors which may bear upon the determination of the application for adoption including, but not limited to, the following information:

(a) the marital and family status, and history, of adoptive parents;

(b) the physical and mental health of the adoptive parents;

(c) the property owned by and the income of the adoptive parents;

(d) the compensation paid or agreed upon with respect to the placement of the child for adoption;

(e) whether either adoptive parent has ever been respondent in any proceeding concerning allegedly neglected, abandoned or delinquent children;

(f) the desirability of bringing the child into New York state for private-placement adoption;

(g) any other facts relating the familial, social, religious, emotional and financial circumstances of the adoptive parents which may be relevant to a determination of suitability of the adoption.

The written report of pre-adoption investigation shall be submitted to the judge or surrogate within thirty days after the same is directed to be made, unless for good cause shown the judge or surrogate shall grant a reasonable extension of such period. The report shall be filed with the judge or surrogate, in any event, before the court shall issue its pre-adoption certificate that it appears that the adoption is in the best interests of the child.

4. On the return of the pre-adoption investigation order the judge or surrogate shall examine the written report of the pre-adoption investigation, and shall determine upon the basis of such written report and such further proof, if any, as he may deem necessary, whether

to issue a pre-adoption certificate as provided for in this subdivision.

If the court is satisfied that the adoption may be in the best interests of the child, and that there has been compliance with all requirements hereof and is satisfied that the moral and temporal interests of the child will be promoted by the adoption, the judge or surrogate shall issue an original certificate under seal of the court and two certified copies thereof, setting forth the fact that a pre-adoption investigation has been conducted, and reciting the documents and papers submitted therewith and stating that in the opinion of the court there is compliance with all applicable laws and that it appears from such investigation that the moral and temporal interests of the child will be promoted by the proposed adoption. The original certificate shall be filed with the clerk of the court, one certified copy with the state commissioner of social services, and the adoptive parents shall receive the second certified copy. The fact that the adoptive child was born out of wedlock shall in no case appear in such certificate. The written report of pre-adoption investigation together with all other papers pertaining to the pre-adoption investigation and the original certificate shall be kept by the court as a permanent record and such papers must be sealed by the judge and withheld from inspection. No person shall be allowed access to such sealed records and original certificate and any index thereof except upon an order of the court in which the pre-adoption certificate was made or an order of a justice of the supreme court. No order for access and inspection shall be granted except on due notice to the adoptive parents and on good cause shown. In like manner as a court of general jurisdiction exercises such powers, the court in which the pre-adoption certificate was made may open, vacate or set aside such certificate for fraud, newly discovered evidence or other sufficient cause.

5. The private-placement adoption of children who have been brought into the United States and the state for such purpose and placed with the adoptive parent or parents, shall be effected after issuance of the pre-adoption certificate, in the manner provided by this title, excepting that (a) the petition shall also recite the pre-adoption proceedings, and (b) the court may in its discretion for good cause shown, waive a subsequent investigation. In such case the order of adoption shall recite the reason for such action.

6. In any case where there has been a failure to comply with the requirements of this section, if applicable, no order of adoption shall be made until one year after the court shall have received the petition to adopt. The court may shorten such waiting period for good cause shown, and, in such case the order of adoption shall recite the reason for such action.

7. The provisions of this section, shall not be applicable to the adoption of children placed out or to be placed out for adoption by an authorized agency as defined in section three hundred seventy-one of the social services law.

8. Notwithstanding any provision of law to the contrary, where a child is placed with a couple or individual in New York state for the purpose of adoption, and where said adoption has theretofore been finalized in the country of birth, outside the United States, the couple or person may petition the court in their county of residence in New York state, for the readoption of said child in accordance with the provisions of this chapter, providing for adoptions originally commenced in this state. In any proceeding for readoption, proof of finalization of an adoption outside the United States shall be prima facie evidence of the consent of those parties required to give consent to an adoption pursuant to section one hundred eleven of this article.

Add, L 1962, ch 527, § 1; amd, L 1965, ch 251, § 1; L 1970, ch 570, § 8, eff Sept 1, 1970; L 1974, ch 1011, § 3; L 1975, ch 605, § 1, eff Aug 31, 1975; L 1979, ch 368, § 3, eff Nov 1,

1979; L 1983, ch 79, § 1, eff May 10, 1983; L 1989, ch 148, § 1, eff June 17, 1989; L 1989, ch 751, § 5, eff Jan 1, 1990; L 1990, ch 547, § 1, eff July 18, 1990.

§ 115-b. Special provisions relating to consents in private-placement adoptions

1. A duly executed and acknowledged consent to a private-placement adoption shall state that no action or proceeding may be maintained by the consenting parent for the custody of the child to be adopted except as provided in this section. Notwithstanding any other section of law, a consent to adoption executed by a person who is in foster care shall only be executed before a judge of the family court.

2. Judicial consents.

(a) A consent to a private placement adoption may be executed or acknowledged before any judge or surrogate in this state having jurisdiction over adoption proceedings. Such consent shall state that it is irrevocable upon such execution or acknowledgement. A consent executed or acknowledged before a court in another state shall satisfy the requirements of this section if it is executed by a resident of the other state before a court of record which has jurisdiction over adoption proceedings in that state, and a certified copy of the transcript of that proceeding, showing compliance with paragraph (b) of this subdivision, is filed as part of the adoption proceeding in this state.

(b) At the time that a parent appears before a judge or surrogate to execute or acknowledge a consent to adoption, the judge or surrogate shall inform such parent of the consequences of such act pursuant to the provisions of this section, including informing such parent of the right to be represented by legal counsel of the parent's own choosing; of the right to obtain supportive counseling and of any rights the parent may have pursuant to section two hundred sixty-two of the family court act, section four hundred seven of the surrogate's court procedure act, or section thirty-five of the judiciary law. The judge or surrogate shall give such parent a copy of such consent upon the execution thereof.

3. Extrajudicial consents.

(a) Whenever a consent is not executed or acknowledged before a judge or surrogate pursuant to subdivision two of this section such consent shall become irrevocable forty-five days after the execution of the consent unless written notice of revocation thereof is received by the court in which the adoption proceeding is to be commenced within said forty-five days.

(b) Notwithstanding that such written notice is received within said forty-five days, the notice of revocation shall be given effect only if the adoptive parents fail to oppose such revocation, as provided in subdivision six of this section, or, if they oppose such revocation and the court as provided in subdivision six of this section has determined that the best interests of the child will be served by giving force and effect to such revocation.

4. (a) In any case where a consent is not executed or acknowledged before a judge or surrogate pursuant to subdivision two of this section, the consent shall state, in conspicuous print of at least eighteen point type:

(i) the name and address of the court in which the adoption proceeding has been or is to be commenced; and

(ii) that the consent may be revoked within forty-five days of the execution of the document and where the consent is not revoked within said forty-five days no proceeding may be maintained by the parent for the return of the custody of the child; and

(iii) that such revocation must be in writing and received by the court where the adoption proceeding is to be commenced within forty-five days of the execution of said consent; and

(iv) that, if the adoptive parents contest the revocation, timely notice of the revocation will not necessarily result in the return of the child to the parent's custody, and that the rights of the parent to custody of the child shall not be superior to those of the adoptive parents but that a hearing will be required before a judge pursuant to the provisions of this section to determine: (1) whether the notice of revocation was timely and properly given; and if necessary, (2) whether the best interests of the child will be served by: (A) returning custody of the child to the parent; or (B) by continuing the adoption proceeding commenced by the adoptive parents; or (C) by disposition other than adoption by the adoptive parents; or (D) by placement of the child with an authorized agency, and if any such determination is made, the court shall make such disposition of the custody of the child as will best serve the interests of the child; and

(v) that the parent has the right to legal representation of the parent's own choosing; the right to obtain supportive counseling and may have the right to have the court appoint an attorney pursuant to section two hundred sixty-two of the family court act, section four hundred seven of the surrogate's court procedure act, or section thirty-five of the judiciary law.

(b) Such consent shall be executed or acknowledged before a notary public or other officer authorized to take proof of deeds.

(c) A copy of such consent shall be given to such parent upon the execution thereof. The consent shall include the following statement: "I, (name of consenting parent), this day of   ,   , have received a copy of this consent. (Signature of consenting parent)". Such consenting parent shall so acknowledge the delivery and the date of the delivery in writing on the consent.

(d) The adoptive parent may commence the adoption proceeding in a court of competent jurisdiction other than the court named in the consent provided that such commencement is initiated more than forty-five days after the consent is executed. Such commencement shall not revive, extend or toll the period for revocation of a consent pursuant to this section.

5. For the purposes of commencing an adoption proceeding, the clerk of a court of competent jurisdiction shall accept an adoption petition for filing which is complete on its face and shall not require any supplementary documentation as a condition of filing. Nothing in this section shall compel a court to hear an adoption petition until all documents necessary to the adoption proceeding have been filed to the satisfaction of the court.

6. (a) A parent may revoke his consent to adoption only by giving notice, in writing, of such revocation, no later than forty-five days after the execution of the consent, or twenty days after the receipt of a notice of denial, withdrawal or removal pursuant to paragraph (a) of subdivision four of section seventeen hundred twenty-five of the surrogate's court procedure act, whichever is later, to the court in which the adoption proceeding has been

or is to be commenced. Such notice shall set forth the name and address of the court in which the adoption proceeding is to be commenced, the address of the parent and may, in addition, set forth the name and address of the attorney for the parent.

(b) If, within forty-five days of the execution of the consent, the court has received such notice of revocation, the court shall promptly notify the adoptive parents and their attorney, by certified mail, of the receipt by the court of such notice of revocation.

(i) Such notice to the adoptive parents shall set forth that if within fifteen days from the date of such notice the court has not received from the adoptive parents or their attorneys notice, in writing, of their intention to oppose such revocation by the parents, the adoption proceeding will be dismissed and that, in case of such dismissal, the court will send to the parents, the adoptive parents and their respective attorneys the notice of dismissal, as provided in paragraph (c) of this subdivision.

(ii) Such notice to the adoptive parents shall further set forth that if, within fifteen days from the date of such notice, the court shall receive from the adoptive parents notice, in writing, of their intention to oppose such revocation by the parents, the court will, upon notice to the parents, the adoptive parents and their respective attorneys, proceed, as provided in paragraph (d) of this subdivision, to a determination of whether such notice of revocation by the parents shall be given force and effect and to a determination of what disposition shall be made of the custody of the child.

(c) If the adoption proceeding is dismissed pursuant to the provisions of paragraph (b) of this subdivision,

(i) Written notice of such dismissal shall forthwith be sent to the parent, the adoptive parents and their respective attorneys.

(ii) Such notice of dismissal shall set forth the name and address of the parent, the name and address of the attorney for the parent, if any, the name and address of the attorney for the adoptive parents.

(iii) Such notice of dismissal shall further set forth that if the child is not returned to the custody of the parent within ten days from the date of such notice of dismissal, the court will forthwith upon request, in writing, by the parent or by the attorney for the parent, furnish to said parent or attorney so requesting, the names and address of the adoptive parents.

(iv) Such notice of dismissal shall further state that, in the event the custody of the child is not returned to the parent by the adoptive parents upon request therefor, a proceeding to obtain custody may be instituted by the parent in the Supreme Court or the Family Court.

(d) If, pursuant to the provisions of paragraph (b) of this subdivision, the adoptive parents give timely and proper notice of their intention to oppose the revocation of the parent's consent:

(i) The court shall promptly notify, in writing, the parent, the adoptive parents, their respective attorneys, and the attorney for the child appointed pursuant to section two hundred forty-nine of the family court act or a guardian ad litem appointed pursuant to section four hundred three-a of the surrogate's court procedure act, that the court will, upon the date specified in such notice by the court, or as soon thereafter as the parties may be heard pursuant to this paragraph, hear and determine whether revocation of the consent of the parent was timely and properly given and whether the adoptive parent's notice of intent to oppose such revocation was timely and properly given and if necessary, hear and determine what disposition should be made with respect to the custody of the child.

(ii) The court shall, upon the date specified, take proof as to whether the best interests of the child will be served by returning custody of the child to the parents, or by the adoption of the child by the adoptive parents, or by placement of the child with an authorized agency for foster care with or without authority to consent to the adoption of the child, or by other disposition of the custody of the child.

(iii) If the court determines that the best interests of the child will be served by returning custody of the child to the parent or by placement of the child with an authorized agency or by disposition other than adoption by the adoptive parents, the revocation of consent shall be given force and effect and the court shall make such disposition of the custody of the child as will best serve the interests of the child.

(iv) If the court determines that the best interests of the child will be served by adoption of the child by the adoptive parents, the court shall enter an order denying any force or effect to the notice of revocation of consent and shall dispose of the custody of the child as if no such notice of revocation had been given by the parent.

(v) In such proceeding the parent or parents who consented to such adoption shall have no right to the custody of the child superior to that of the adoptive parents, notwithstanding that the parent or parents who consented to the adoption are fit, competent and able to duly maintain, support and educate the child. The custody of such child shall be awarded solely on the basis of the best interests of the child, and there shall be no presumption that such interests will be promoted by any particular custodial disposition.

7. Nothing contained in this section shall limit or affect the power and authority of the court in an adoption proceeding, pursuant to the provisions of section one hundred sixteen of this title, to remove the child from the home of the adoptive parents, upon the ground that the welfare of the child requires such action, and thereupon to return the child to a birth parent or place the child with an authorized agency, or, in the case of a surrogate, transfer the child to the family court; nor shall this section bar actions or proceedings brought on the ground of fraud, duress or coercion in the execution or inducement of an adoption consent.

8. Notwithstanding any other provision of this section, a parent having custody of a child whose adoption is sought by his or her spouse need only consent that his or her child be adopted by a named stepfather or stepmother.

9. Any consent to adoption subject to the provisions of this section shall include an adoption information registry birth parent registration consent form, stating whether or not such biological parent or parents whose consent is subject to the provisions of this section, consents to the receipt of identifying information by the child to be adopted upon registration with the adoption information registry established by section forty-one hundred thirty-eight-c of the public health law and upon the adoptee reaching the age of eighteen. If such consent is made, it shall be revocable by either of the biological parents at any time. The revocation of the consent by one of the parents shall revoke the consent of both parents. The failure of

a biological parent to complete the consent form shall have no effect on the finality of the consent to adoption. A copy of the form required by this subdivision, shall be forwarded to the state adoption information registry for inclusion in the records maintained by such registry. Any fees authorized to be charged by the state adoption registry for filing documentation with such registry shall be waived for the form required by this subdivision.

> Add, L 1972, ch 639, § 3, eff Aug 28, 1972; amd, L 1973, ch 1035, §§ 1–3; L 1983, ch 218, § 1; L 1986, ch 817, § 1, eff Sept 1, 1986; L 1988, ch 557, § 1, eff Oct 1, 1988; L 1989, ch 722, § 1, eff Oct 1, 1989; L 1994, ch 371, § 1; L 1994, ch 601, § 2, eff Oct 24, 1994; L 2002, ch 312, § 1, eff Aug 6, 2002; L 2007, ch 680, § 1, eff April 28, 2008; L 2008, ch 435, § 2, eff Nov 3, 2008; L 2010, ch 41, § 6, eff April 14, 2010.

§ 115-c. Temporary guardianship by adoptive parent

In any case where physical custody of a child is transferred from the child's parent or guardian to another person or persons for the purposes of adoption and a consent to the adoption of such child has been executed pursuant to section one hundred fifteen-b of this title, the adoptive parent or parents shall, within ten court days of taking physical custody, either file a petition for adoption with a court of competent jurisdiction or file an application for temporary guardianship of the person of the child pursuant to this section with the court in which the adoption will be filed, pursuant to section seventeen hundred twenty-five of the surrogate's court procedure act or section six hundred sixty-one of the family court act except as otherwise provided herein. Such application shall include an affidavit by the adoptive parent or parents describing any change of circumstances since their certification as a qualified adoptive parent or parents, pursuant to section one hundred fifteen-d of this title, which may be material to such certification. Such a petition for adoption shall also be deemed an application for temporary guardianship, where no prior application for an order for temporary guardianship has been filed.

In any case where the adoptive parent or parents take physical custody of an adoptive child and requirements for certification as a qualified adoptive parent or parents have been waived, pursuant to section one hundred fifteen-d of this title, an application for temporary guardianship or petition for adoption for such child shall be filed with the court not later than five court days from obtaining physical custody of such child. Such time period may be extended upon motion of any person or upon the court's own motion for good cause shown.

> Add, L 1988, ch 557, § 2; amd, L 1989, ch 700, § 3, eff Nov 1, 1989.

§ 115-d. Petition for certification

1. Except as provided for in subdivision eight of this section, a person or persons petitioning for certification as a qualified adoptive parent or parents shall upon a form, promulgated by the chief administrator of the courts, provide to the court:

(a) the applicant's name or applicants' names, residential address and telephone number;

(b) a statement by the applicant or applicants that they are seeking certification by the court as a person or persons qualified to take physical custody of an infant prior to or contemporaneous with the filing of a private-placement adoption petition;

(c) a statement by the applicant or applicants as to whether such applicant or applicants have been the subject of an indicated report of child abuse or maltreatment, pursuant to title six of article six of the social services law; and

(d) a statement that a pre-placement investigation will be undertaken by a disinterested person, as such term is defined in subdivision four of this section, and that a written report of such investigation will be furnished directly to the court by such disinterested person with a copy of such report to be delivered simultaneously to the applicant or applicants. Such disinterested person shall certify to the court that he or she is a disinterested person and has no interest in the outcome of the party's or parties' application. Such disinterested person shall further disclose to the court any fee paid or to be paid to such person for services rendered in connection with the pre-placement investigation.

Such petition shall also require information regarding:

(i) the marital and family status and history of the adoptive parent or parents;

(ii) the physical and mental health of the adoptive parent or parents;

(iii) the property owned by and the income of adoptive parent or parents;

(iv) whether the adoptive parent or either of the adoptive parents has ever been a respondent in any proceeding concerning allegedly abused, neglected, abandoned or delinquent children; and

(v) whether the applicant or applicants have made any prior application for certification as a qualified adoptive parent or parents and, if so, the disposition of such application for certification.

2. In any case where the applicant or applicants do not intend to cause a pre-placement investigation to be undertaken pursuant to the provisions of paragraph (d) of subdivision one of this section, such applicant or applicants shall request the court to appoint a disinterested person to conduct such pre-placement investigation. The investigative written report shall be submitted to the judge or surrogate within thirty days, unless for good cause shown the judge or surrogate shall grant a reasonable extension of such period.

3. Such applicant or applicants shall be financially responsible for the costs of any pre-placement investigation conducted pursuant to subdivision one or two of this section.

3-a. (a) The court shall submit fingerprint cards and order a report from the division of criminal justice services setting forth any existing criminal history record of the applicant for certification as a qualified adoptive parent.

(b) Notwithstanding any other provision of law to the contrary, a petition for certification as a qualified adoptive parent shall be denied where a criminal history record of the applicant reveals a conviction for (i) a felony conviction at any time involving: (1) child abuse or neglect; (2) spousal abuse; (3) a crime against a child, including child pornography; or (4) a crime involving violence, including rape, sexual assault, or homicide, other than a crime involving physical assault or battery; or (ii) a felony conviction within the past five years for physical assault, battery, or a drug-related offense.

(c) For the purposes of this subdivision, "spousal abuse" is an offense defined in section 120.05, 120.10, 121.12, or 121.13 of the penal law where the victim of such offense was the defendant's spouse; provided, however, spousal abuse shall not include a crime in which the applicant was the defendant, and the court finds in accordance with this subdivision that he or she was the victim of physical, sexual or psychological abuse by the victim of such offense and such abuse was a factor in causing the applicant to commit such offense.

4. A pre-placement investigation conducted pursuant to the provisions of this section shall be made by a disinterested person who in the opinion of the judge or surrogate is qualified by training and experience to examine into the allegations set forth in the application and any other factors which may be relevant to the suitability of the applicant or applicants as a qualified adoptive parent or parents. For the purposes of this section, a disinterested person shall also include a licensed master social worker, licensed clinical social worker, the probation service of the family court or an authorized agency specifically designated by the court to conduct pre-placement investigations.

5. Such disinterested person shall file with the court a written report of his or her investigation into the truth and accuracy of the allegations set forth in the application and his or her investigation of the various factors which may be relevant to the suitability of the applicant or applicants as qualified adoptive parents. Such investigation shall include, but not be limited to, a personal interview and visit at the applicant's or applicants' home and an investigation of any other facts relating to the familial, social, religious, emotional and financial circumstances of the adoptive parent or parents which may be relevant to certification as a qualified adoptive parent or parents.

6. Certification and provisional certification. If after consideration of the report submitted by the disinterested person, and all other relevant and material factors, the court grants the application, the applicant or applicants may accept physical custody of a child for the purposes of adoption, either prior to or contemporaneous with the filing of an adoption petition. The order granting the petition shall be valid for a period not to exceed eighteen months and shall be accepted as proof of certification by any court of competent jurisdiction within the state. The court may in its discretion grant a conditional order of certification upon satisfactory completion and submission of a petition wherein the prospective adoptive parent or parents indicate no prior criminal convictions or founded findings of child abuse or neglect, and after completion of a disinterested person investigation provided for in this section, pending completion of any further reports, investigations or inquiries ordered by the court or required by any other statute or court rule. A conditional order of certification shall be valid and remain in force and effect until replaced by an order of certification or by an order denying the petition, whichever shall first occur, but in no event shall such provisional certification continue beyond one hundred eighty days from the date of original issuance. If the court denies the petition, the reasons for such denial shall be stated on the record or in the order.

7. Nothing in this section shall be deemed to waive, limit or restrict the provisions of any other law requiring any inquiry, disinterested person investigation or court review of any persons seeking to adopt a child under any provision of law.

8. The provisions of this section shall not apply to petitions brought by a step-parent for the adoption of a step-child where the step-child has resided with the birth parent and the step-parent for a continuous period of at least one year.

9. Extension of certification. When a petition for adoption is filed by a qualified parent or parents previously certified and the balance of the time period remaining under such certification in accordance with subdivision six of this section is less than one year, the court may on its own motion or on the motion of the petitioners extend the time period of the original certification to a date eighteen months from the date of filing of the adoption petition. When a petition for adoption is filed by a qualified parent or parents who have previously

been certified by an order which has expired within a year preceding the date of the adoption petition, the court may extend the termination date of the earlier certification until eighteen months from the filing of such petition, provided the petitioner apply for such extension and set forth any change of circumstances of the qualified parent or parents since issuance and expiration of the last certification which may be relevant and material to the extension of such certification and affix thereto written verification of any such changed circumstance or lack thereof by a disinterested person as defined in subdivision four of this section. Except as is provided for by this subdivision, the court shall not extend a previously expired order of certification. Any further certification shall require the filing of a new petition for certification in accordance with subdivision six of this section.

In any instance when the court determines whether to extend a certification under this subdivision, the court, in its discretion, may order each or any of (a) a report from the statewide central registry of child abuse and maltreatment to determine whether the child or the petitioner is or has been the subject of or another person named in an indicated report, as such terms are defined in section four hundred twelve of the social services law, filed with such register, (b) a report from the division of criminal justice services setting forth any criminal record of such petitioner or petitioners, and (c) an additional pre-placement investigation to be undertaken by a disinterested person. Nothing herein shall be deemed to require that the court enter such an order.

Add, L 1989, ch 700, § 4, eff Nov 1, 1989; amd, L 1990, ch 508, §§ 1, 2; L 1992, ch 704, §§ 1, 2, eff July 31, 1992; L 1994, ch 601, § 10, eff Oct 24, 1994; L 1999, ch 7, § 54, eff Feb 11, 1999; L 2000, ch 145, § 18; L 2002, ch 312, § 2, eff Aug 6, 2002; L 2004, ch 230, § 3, eff July 27, 2004; L 2008, ch 623, § 2, eff Oct 1, 2008; L 2010, ch 405, § 5, eff Nov 11, 2010.

§ 115-e. Effect of death of potential adoptive parent

Notwithstanding any other provision of law to the contrary, when a petition for adoption by two persons has been duly filed, and one of the petitioners dies before the adoption is complete, it shall be treated as a change of circumstance. This change may be reviewed to assure that the adoption is in the best interest of the child. The death of one of the adoptive parents shall not, by itself, invalidate a certification nor shall the death of one of the adoptive parents cause a new petition for adoption to be filed. The deceased adoptive parent shall be considered one of the legal parents, unless the surviving adoptive parent requests otherwise.

Add, L 2008, ch 160, § 2, eff July 7, 2008.

§ 116. Orders of investigation and order of adoption

1. When the adoptive child is less than eighteen years of age, no order of adoption shall be made until three months after the court shall have received the petition to adopt, except where the spouse of the adoptive parent is the birth parent of the child and the child has resided with the birth parent and adoptive parent for more than three months, such waiting period shall not be required. The judge or surrogate may shorten such waiting period for good cause shown, and, in such case the order of adoption shall recite the reason for such action. The three months residence period specified in section one hundred twelve of title two of this article and the three months waiting period provided in this subdivision may run concurrently in whole or in part.

2. Stage one of private-placement adoption. At the time of receiving the petition, agreement and consents, the judge or surrogate, upon finding that the applicable provisions of this title have been complied with and that it appears that the adoption may be in the best interests of

the child, shall issue an order of investigation hereunder. The order of investigation shall require that the report of such investigation be made in accordance with subdivision three of this section, and may require or authorize further investigations from time to time until the granting of the order of adoption. Such order shall direct that such investigation shall not unnecessarily duplicate any previous investigations which have been made of the petitioner or petitioners pursuant to section one hundred fifteen-d of this title. Should such investigation give apparent cause, the judge or surrogate shall require the petitioner or petitioners to show cause why the child should not be removed from the home, upon due notice to all persons whose consent is required for the adoption, and in any case where the consent of the birth mother would not otherwise be required, the judge or surrogate may in his discretion require that she be given due notice. On the return date the judge or surrogate shall take proof of the facts shown by any such investigation. If the court is satisfied that the welfare of the child requires that it be removed from the home, the judge or surrogate shall by order remove the child from the home of the petitioner or petitioners and return the child to a birth parent or place the child with an appropriate authorized agency, or, in the case of a surrogate, transfer the child to the family court. The judge or surrogate may also require that notice be given to an appropriate authorized agency.

3. The judge or surrogate shall cause to be made an investigation by a disinterested person who in the opinion of the judge or surrogate is qualified by training and experience, or by an authorized agency specifically designated by him to examine into the allegations set forth in the petition. A post-placement investigation conducted pursuant to the provisions of this section shall be made by a disinterested person who in the opinion of the judge or surrogate is qualified by training and experience to perform post-placement investigations. Such disinterested person shall certify to the court that he or she is a disinterested person and has no interest in the outcome of petitioner's or petitioners' application. Such disinterested person shall further disclose to the court any fee paid or to be paid to such person for services rendered in connection with the post-placement investigation. The investigator shall make a written report of his investigation into the truth and accuracy of the allegations of the petition, and, where applicable, into the statements contained in the affidavit required by section one hundred fifteen of this title, and he shall ascertain as fully as possible, and incorporate in his report the various factors which may bear upon the determination of the application for adoption including, but not limited to, the following information:

(a) the marital and family status, and history, of the adoptive parents and adoptive child;

(b) the physical and mental health of the adoptive parents and adoptive child;

(c) the property owned by and the income of the adoptive parents;

(d) the compensation paid or agreed upon with respect to the placement of the child for adoption;

(e) whether either adoptive parent has ever been respondent in any proceeding concerning allegedly abused, neglected, abandoned or delinquent children;

(f) any other facts relating to the familial, social, religious, emotional and financial circumstances of the adoptive parents which may be relevant to a determination of adoption.

The written report of investigation shall be submitted to the judge or surrogate within thirty days after the same is directed to be made, unless for good cause shown the judge or surrogate shall grant a reasonable extension of such period. The report shall be filed with the judge or surrogate, in any event, before the final order of adoption is granted.

4. Stage two of private-placement adoption. If the judge or surrogate has found that there has been compliance with all the requirements hereof and is satisfied that the best interests of the child will be promoted by granting an order of adoption, the provisions of section one hundred fourteen of title two of this article shall apply.

5. As used in this section, "disinterested person" includes the probation service of the family court, a licensed master social worker, licensed clinical social worker, or an authorized agency specifically designated by the court to conduct pre-placement investigations.

> Add, L 1961, ch 147, § 1, eff Sept 1, 1961; amd, L 1962, ch 690, §§ 3, 4; L 1964, ch 569, § 1; L 1970, ch 570, § 9, eff Sept 1, 1970; L 1976, ch 666, § 13, eff Jan 1, 1977; L 1989, ch 700, §§ 5, 6, eff Nov 1, 1989; L 1997, ch 375, § 3; L 1999, ch 81, § 1; L 2000, ch 423, § 1, eff Sept 20, 2000; L 2002, ch 312, § 3, eff Aug 6, 2002; L 2004, ch 230, § 4, eff July 27, 2004.

TITLE IV   EFFECT OF ADOPTION FROM AN AUTHORIZED AGENCY, OF PRIVATE-PLACEMENT ADOPTION, AND ABROGATIONS THEREOF

§ 117.   **Effect of adoption**

§ 117. Effect of adoption

1. (a) After the making of an order of adoption the birth parents of the adoptive child shall be relieved of all parental duties toward and of all responsibilities for and shall have no rights over such adoptive child or to his property by descent or succession, except as hereinafter stated.

(b) The rights of an adoptive child to inheritance and succession from and through his birth parents shall terminate upon the making of the order of adoption except as hereinafter provided.

(c) The adoptive parents or parent and the adoptive child shall sustain toward each other the legal relation of parent and child and shall have all the rights and be subject to all the duties of that relation including the rights of inheritance from and through each other and the birth and adopted kindred of the adoptive parents or parent.

(d) When a birth or adoptive parent, having lawful custody of a child, marries or remarries and consents that the stepparent may adopt such child, such consent shall not relieve the parent so consenting of any parental duty toward such child nor shall such consent or the order of adoption affect the rights of such consenting spouse and such adoptive child to inherit from and through each other and the birth and adopted kindred of such consenting spouse.

(e) Notwithstanding the provisions of paragraphs (a), (b) and (d) of this subdivision, as to estates of persons dying after the thirty-first day of August, nineteen hundred eighty-seven, if:

(1) the decedent is the adoptive child's birth grandparent or is a descendant of such grandparent, and

(2) an adoptive parent (i) is married to the child's birth parent, (ii) is the child's birth grandparent, or (iii) is descended from such grandparent,

the rights of an adoptive child to inheritance and succession from and through either birth parent shall not terminate upon the making of the order of adoption.

However, an adoptive child who is related to the decedent both by birth relationship and by adoption shall be entitled to inherit only under the birth relationship unless the decedent is also the adoptive parent, in which case the adoptive child shall then be entitled to inherit pursuant to the adoptive relationship only.

(f) The right of inheritance of an adoptive child extends to the distributees of such child and such distributees shall be the same as if he were the birth child of the adoptive parent.

(g) Adoptive children and birth children shall have all the rights of fraternal relationship including the right of inheritance from each other. Such right of inheritance extends to the distributees of such adoptive children and birth children and such distributees shall be the same as if each such child were the birth child of the adoptive parents.

(h) The consent of the parent of a child to the adoption of such child by his or her spouse shall operate to vest in the adopting spouse only the rights as distributee of a birth parent and shall leave otherwise unaffected the rights as distributee of the consenting spouse.

(i) This subdivision shall apply only to the intestate descent and distribution of real and personal property.

2. (a) Except as hereinafter stated, after the making of an order of adoption, adopted children and their issue thereafter are strangers to any birth relatives for the purpose of the interpretation or construction of a disposition in any instrument, whether executed before or after the order of adoption, which does not express a contrary intention or does not expressly include the individual by name or by some classification not based on a parent-child or family relationship.

(b) As to the wills of persons executed after the thirty-first day of August, nineteen hundred eighty-six, or to lifetime instruments executed after such date whether executed before or after the order of adoption, a designation of a class of persons described in section 2-1.3 of the estates, powers and trusts law shall, unless the will or instrument expresses a contrary intention, be deemed to include an adoptive child who was a member of such class in his or her birth relationship prior to adoption, and the issue of such child, only if:

(1) an adoptive parent (i) is married to the child's birth parent, (ii) is the child's birth grandparent, or (iii) is a descendant of such grandparent, and

(2) the testator or creator is the child's birth grandparent or a descendant of such grandparent.

(c) A person who, by reason of this subdivision, would be a member of the designated class, or a member of two or more designated classes pursuant to a single instrument, both by birth relationship and by adoption shall be entitled to benefit only under the birth relationship, unless the testator or creator is the adoptive parent, in which case the person shall then be entitled to benefit only under the adoptive relationship.

(d) The provisions of this subdivision shall not impair or defeat any rights which have vested on or before the thirty-first day of August, nineteen hundred eighty-six, or which have vested prior to the adoption regardless of when the adoption occurred.

3. The provisions of law affected by the provisions of this section in force prior to March first, nineteen hundred sixty-four shall apply to the estates or wills of persons dying prior thereto and to lifetime instruments theretofore executed which on said date were not subject to grantor's power to revoke or amend.

> Formerly § 115, add, L 1938, ch 606, § 1; amd, L 1940, ch 442, § 1; L 1961, ch 147, § 1; L 1963, ch 406, § 1; L 1966, ch 14, § 1, eff March 8, 1966, deemed eff from and after March 1, 1964; L 1970, ch 570, § 10; L 1986, ch 408, § 1; L 1987, ch 499, § 1, eff Sept 1, 1987; L 2002, ch 312, § 4, eff Aug 6, 2002.

NEW YORK SURROGATES' COURTS COUNTY DIRECTORY

COUNTY SURROGATE'S COURTS

Albany County

Surrogate's Court

16 Eagle Street, Room 123
Albany, New York 12207
(518) 285-8585
Fax: (518) 285-8237
For the most current information regarding operating procedures, see
http://ww2.nycourts.gov/courts/3jd/albany/3JD-Albany%20Surrogate%20Court.shtml

Allegany County

Surrogate's Court

7 Court Street
Belmont, New York 14813
(585) 449-3464
Fax: (585) 449-3471
For the most current information regarding operating procedures, see
http://ww2.nycourts.gov/courts/8jd/Allegany/index.shtml

Bronx County

Surrogate's Court

851 Grand Concourse
Bronx, New York 10451
(718) 618–2300
Fax: (718) 537-5158
For the most current information regarding operating procedures, see
http://ww2.nycourts.gov/COURTS/12jd/BRONX/Surrogates/index.shtml

Broome County

Surrogate's Court

92 Court Street
Binghamton, New York 13901-3301
(607) 240-5789
For the most current information regarding operating procedures, see
http://ww2.nycourts.gov/courts/6jd/broome/surrogate.shtml

DIR-1

Cattaraugus County

Surrogate's Court

303 Court Street
Little Valley, New York 14755
(716) 379-6638
Fax: (716) 938-6413
For the most current information regarding operating procedures, see
http://ww2.nycourts.gov/courts/8jd/Cattaraugus/index.shtml

Cayuga County

Surrogate's Court

152 Genesee Street
Auburn, New York 13021
(315) 237-6210
Fax: (315) 237-6211
For the most current information regarding operating procedures, see
http://ww2.nycourts.gov/courts/7jd/cayuga/Surrogate/index.shtml

Chautauqua County

Surrogate's Court

P.O. Box C
3 North Erie Street
Mayville, New York 14757
(716) 753-4339
Fax: (716) 753-4600
For the most current information regarding operating procedures, see
http://ww2.nycourts.gov/courts/8jd/Chautauqua/surrogates.shtml

Chemung County

Surrogate's Court

Hazlett Building
203–205 Lake Street
P.O. Box 588
Elmira, New York 14902–0588
(607) 873-9440
Fax: (646) 963-6606
For the most current information regarding operating procedures, see
http://ww2.nycourts.gov/courts/6jd/chemung/Surrogate.shtml

Chenango County

Surrogate's Court

13 Eaton Avenue

Norwich, New York 13815
(607) 337-1827 or (607) 337-1822
Fax: (646) 963-6603
For the most current information regarding operating procedures, see
http://ww2.nycourts.gov/courts/6jd/chenango/Surrogate.shtml

Clinton County

Surrogate's Court

Clinton County Office Building
137 Margaret Street
Plattsburgh, New York 12901
(518) 536-3830
For the most current information regarding operating procedures, see
http://ww2.nycourts.gov/courts/4jd/Clinton/index.shtml

Columbia County

Surrogate's Court

401 Union Street
Hudson, NY 12534
(518) 267-3150
Fax: (518) 267-3126
For the most current information regarding operating procedures, see
http://ww2.nycourts.gov/courts/3jd/columbia/3JD-
Columbia%20Multi%20Courts.shtml

Cortland County

Surrogate's Court

46 Greenbush Street, Suite 303
Cortland, New York 13045–2725
(607) 218-3335
Fax: (212) 457-2661 (Chief Clerk)
For the most current information regarding operating procedures, see
http://ww2.nycourts.gov/courts/6jd/cortland/surrogate.shtml

Delaware County

Surrogate's Court

Delaware County Courthouse
3 Court Street
Delhi, New York 13753
(607) 376-5405
Fax: (646) 963-6403
For the most current information regarding operating procedures, see

Sur Ct Directory

http://ww2.nycourts.gov/courts/6jd/delaware/surrogate.shtml

Dutchess County

Surrogate's Court

10 Market Street
Poughkeepsie, New York 12601
(845) 431-1770
Fax: (845) 476-3659
For the most current information regarding operating procedures, see
http://ww2.nycourts.gov/COURTS/9jd/Dutchess/dutchesssurrogate.shtml

Erie County

Surrogate's Court

92 Franklin Street
Buffalo, New York 14202
(716) 845-2560
Fax: (716) 845-7565
For the most current information regarding operating procedures, see
http://ww2.nycourts.gov/courts/8jd/erie/surrogates/index.shtml

Essex County

Surrogate's Court

P.O. Box 217
7559 Court Street
Elizabethtown, New York 12932
(518) 873-3384
Fax: (518) 451-8740
For the most current information regarding operating procedures, see
http://ww2.nycourts.gov/courts/4jd/Essex/index.shtml

Franklin County

Surrogate's Court

355 West Main Street
Malone, New York 12953
(518) 353-7350
Email: FranklinSurrogate@nycourts.gov
For the most current information regarding operating procedures, see
http://ww2.nycourts.gov/courts/4jd/Franklin/index.shtml

Fulton County

Surrogate's Court

223 West Main Street

Johnstown, New York 12095
(518) 706-3280
Email: FultonSurrogate@nycourts.gov
For the most current information regarding operating procedures, see
http://ww2.nycourts.gov/courts/4jd/Fulton/index.shtml

Genesee County

Surrogate's Court

Courts Facility Building
1 West Main Street
Batavia, New York 14020
(585) 201-5733
Fax: (585) 344-8517
For the most current information regarding operating procedures, see
http://ww2.nycourts.gov/courts/8jd/Genesee/index.shtml

Greene County

Surrogate's Court

320 Main Street
Catskill, New York 12414
(518) 625-3150
For the most current information regarding operating procedures, see
http://ww2.nycourts.gov/courts/3jd/greene/3JD-
Greene%20Multi%20Courts.shtml

Hamilton County

Surrogate's Court
mailing address:
139 White Birch Lane
P.O. Box 780
Indian Lake, New York 12842-0780
(518) 648-5411 (Indian Lake)
Fax: (518) 453-8687
(518) 548-3211 (Lake Pleasant)
Fax: (518) 453-8687
For the most current information regarding operating procedures, see
http://ww2.nycourts.gov/courts/4jd/Hamilton/index.shtml

Herkimer County

Surrogate's Court

Herkimer County Office and Courts Facility
301 North Washington Street
Herkimer, New York 13350

Sur Ct Directory

(315) 619-3400
Fax: (315) 266-4696
For the most current information regarding operating procedures, see
http://ww2.nycourts.gov/courts/5jd/herkimer/surrogate/index.shtml

Jefferson County

Surrogate's Court

Jefferson County Court Complex
163 Arsenal Street
Watertown, New York 13601
(315) 785-3019
Fax: (315) 266-4771
For the most current information regarding operating procedures, see
http://ww2.nycourts.gov/courts/5jd/jefferson/surrogate/index.shtml

Kings County

Surrogate's Court

2 Johnson Street
Brooklyn, New York 11201
(347) 404-9700
For the most current information regarding operating procedures, see
http://www.nycourts.gov/courts/nyc/surrogates/index.shtml

Lewis County

Surrogate's Court

7660 North State Street, Second Floor
Lowville, New York 13367
(315) 376-5344
Fax: (315) 671-6082
For the most current information regarding operating procedures, see
http://ww2.nycourts.gov/courts/5jd/lewis/surrogate/index.shtml

Livingston County

Surrogate's Court

2 Court Street
Geneseo, New York 14454
(585) 371-3921
Fax: (585) 371-3936
For the most current information regarding operating procedures, see
http://ww2.nycourts.gov/courts/7jd/livingston/Surrogate/index.shtml

Madison County

Surrogate's Court

138 North Court Street

P.O. Box 607
Madison County Courthouse
Wampsville, New York 13163
(315) 231-5321
Fax: (646) 963-6594
For the most current information regarding operating procedures, see
http://ww2.nycourts.gov/courts/6jd/madison/surrogate.shtml

Monroe County

Surrogate's Court

Hall of Justice
5th Floor Room 541
99 Exchange Boulevard
Rochester, New York 14614
(585) 371-3310
Fax: (585) 371-3313
For the most current information regarding operating procedures, see
http://ww2.nycourts.gov/courts/7jd/monroe/Surrogate/index.shtml

Montgomery County

58 Broadway
P.O. Box 1500
Fonda, New York 12068
(518) 853-8108
Fax: (518) 853-8230
For the most current information regarding operating procedures, see
http://ww2.nycourts.gov/courts/4jd/Montgomery/index.shtml

Nassau County

Surrogate's Court

262 Old Country Road
Mineola, New York 11501
(516) 493-3800
For the most current information regarding operating procedures, see
http://ww2.nycourts.gov/COURTS/10JD/nassau/surrogates.shtml

New York County

Surrogate's Court

31 Chambers Street
New York, New York 10007
(646) 386-5000
Fax: (212) 374-3250
For the most current information regarding operating procedures, see

http://ww2.nycourts.gov/courts/1jd/surrogates/index.shtml

Niagara County

Surrogate's Court

175 Hawley Street
Lockport, New York 14094
(716) 280-6460
Fax: (716) 280-6480
For the most current information regarding operating procedures, see
http://ww2.nycourts.gov/courts/8jd/Niagara/index.shtml

Oneida County

Surrogate's Court

Oneida County Office Building
800 Park Avenue, 8th Floor
Utica, New York 13501
(315) 266-4550
Rome Office: (315) 266-4309
Fax: (315) 266-4703
For the most current information regarding operating procedures, see
http://ww2.nycourts.gov/courts/5jd/oneida/surrogate/index.shtml

Onondaga County

Surrogate's Court

Onondaga County Courthouse
401 Montgomery Street
Syracuse, New York 13202
(315) 671-2100
Fax: (315) 671-1162
For the most current information regarding operating procedures, see
http://ww2.nycourts.gov/courts/5jd/onondaga/surrogate/index.shtml

Ontario County

Surrogate's Court

27 North Main Street
Canandaigua, New York 14424
(585) 412-5301
Fax: (585) 412-5331
For the most current information regarding operating procedures, see
http://ww2.nycourts.gov/courts/7jd/ontario/Surrogate/index.shtml

Orange County

Surrogate's Court

30 Park Place

Goshen, New York 10924
(845) 476-3655
Fax: (845) 291-2196
For the most current information regarding operating procedures, see
http://ww2.nycourts.gov/courts/9jd/orange/orangesurrogate.shtml

Orleans County

Surrogate's Court

1 South Main Street, Suite 3
Albion, New York 14411-1497
(585) 283-6658
Fax: (585) 589-0632
For the most current information regarding operating procedures, see
http://ww2.nycourts.gov/courts/8jd/Orleans/index.shtml

Oswego County

Surrogate's Court

Oswego County Courthouse
25 East Oneida Street
Oswego, New York 13126
(315) 207-7566
Fax: (315) 266-4784
For the most current information regarding operating procedures, see
http://ww2.nycourts.gov/courts/5jd/oswego/surrogate/index.shtml

Otsego County

Surrogate's Court

197 Main Street
Cooperstown, New York 13326
(607) 322-3150
Fax: (607) 240-5966
For the most current information regarding operating procedures, see
http://ww2.nycourts.gov/courts/6jd/otsego/surrogate/index.shtml

Putnam County

Surrogate's Court

Historic Courthouse
44 Gleneida Avenue
Carmel, New York 10512
(845) 208-7860
Fax: (845) 431-1936
For the most current information regarding operating procedures, see

http://ww2.nycourts.gov/COURTS/9jd/Putnam/putnamsurrogate.shtml

Queens County

Surrogate's Court

88-11 Sutphin Boulevard
Queens County Courthouse
Jamaica, New York 11435
(718) 298-0400/0500
For the most current information regarding operating procedures, see
http://ww2.nycourts.gov/courts/11jd/surrogates/index.shtml

Rensselaer County

Surrogate's Court

80 Second Street
Troy, New York 12180
(518) 285-6100
Fax: (518) 285-5091
For the most current information regarding operating procedures, see
http://ww2.nycourts.gov/courts/3jd/rensselaer/3JD-
Rensselaer%20Surrogate%20Court.shtml

Richmond County

Surrogate's Court

18 Richmond Terrace
Staten Island, New York 10301
(718) 675-8500
For the most current information regarding operating procedures, see
http://ww2.nycourts.gov/courts/13jd/surrogates/index.shtml

Rockland County

Surrogate's Court

1 South Main Street
New City, New York 10956
(845) 483-8260
Fax: (914) 358-8067
For the most current information regarding operating procedures, see
http://ww2.nycourts.gov/COURTS/9jd/Rockland/rocklandsurrogate.shtml

St. Lawrence County

Surrogate's Court

48 Court Street
Canton, New York 13617

(315) 379-2217
Fax: (315) 379-2372
For the most current information regarding operating procedures, see
http://ww2.nycourts.gov/courts/4jd/StLawrence/index.shtml

Saratoga County

Surrogate's Court

Municipal Center
30 McMaster Street, Building Three
Ballston Spa, New York 12020
(518) 451-8830
Fax: (518) 453-8693
For the most current information regarding operating procedures, see
http://ww2.nycourts.gov/courts/4jd/Saratoga/index.shtml

Schenectady County

Surrogate's Court

Schenectady County Judicial Building
612 State Street
Schenectady, New York 12305
(518) 285-8455
Fax: (518) 451-8732
For the most current information regarding operating procedures, see
http://ww2.nycourts.gov/courts/4jd/Schenectady/index.shtml

Schoharie County

Surrogate's Court

290 Main Street
Schoharie, New York 12157
(518) 295-8383
Fax: (518) 295-8451
For the most current information regarding operating procedures, see
http://ww2.nycourts.gov/courts/3jd/schoharie/3JD-
Schoharie%20Multi%20Courts.shtml

Schuyler County

Surrogate's Court

105 Ninth Street, Unit 35
Watkins Glen, New York 14891
(607) 228-3351
Fax: (646) 963-6590
For the most current information regarding operating procedures, see

Sur Ct Directory

http://ww2.nycourts.gov/courts/6jd/schuyler/surrogate/index.shtml

Seneca County

Surrogate's Court

48 West Williams Street
Waterloo, New York 13165
(315) 835-6232
Fax: (315) 835-6234
For the most current information regarding operating procedures, see
http://ww2.nycourts.gov/courts/7jd/Seneca/Surrogate/index.shtml

Steuben County

Surrogate's Court

3 East Pulteney Square
Bath, New York 14810
(607) 622-8221
Fax: (607) 622-8243
For the most current information regarding operating procedures, see
http://ww2.nycourts.gov/courts/7jd/Steuben/Surrogate/index.shtml

Suffolk County

Surrogate's Court

County Center Building
320 Center Drive
Riverhead, New York 11901
(631) 852-1745
For the most current information regarding operating procedures, see
http://ww2.nycourts.gov/COURTS/10jd/suffolk/surrogates.shtml

Sullivan County

Surrogate's Court

Sullivan County Government Center
100 North Street
Monticello, New York 12701
(845) 791-3500
Fax: (845) 481-9337
For the most current information regarding operating procedures, see
http://ww2.nycourts.gov/COURTS/3jd/sullivan/3JD-
Sullivan%20Surrogate%20Court.shtml

Tioga County

Surrogate's Court

Court Annex Building

20 Court Street
P.O. Box 10
Owego, New York 13827
(607) 689-6099
Fax: (646) 963-6398
For the most current information regarding operating procedures, see
http://ww2.nycourts.gov/COURTS/6jd/tioga/surrogate/index.shtml

Tompkins County

Surrogate's Court

320 North Tioga Street
Ithaca, New York 14850
Mailing Address:
P.O. Box 70
Ithaca, New York 14851-0070
(607) 216-6655
Fax: (212) 457-2952
For the most current information regarding operating procedures, see
http://ww2.nycourts.gov/courts/6jd/tompkins/surrogate/index.shtml

Ulster County

Surrogate's Court

240 Fair Street
Kingston, New York 12401
(845) 481-9338
Fax: (845) 483-8427
For the most current information regarding operating procedures, see
http://ww2.nycourts.gov/courts/3jd/ulster/3JD-
Ulster%20Surrogate%20Court.shtml

Warren County

Surrogate's Court

Warren County Municipal Center
1340 State Route 9
Lake George, New York 12845
(518) 480-6360
Email:WarrenSurrogate@nycourts.gov
For the most current information regarding operating procedures, see
http://ww2.nycourts.gov/courts/4jd/warren/index.shtml

Washington County

Surrogate's Court

383 Broadway

Fort Edward, New York 12828-1015
(518) 746-2545
Fax: (518) 285-4389
For the most current information regarding operating procedures, see
http://ww2.nycourts.gov/courts/4jd/Washington/index.shtml

Wayne County

Surrogate's Court

Hall of Justice
54 Broad Street
Lyons, New York 14489
(315) 665-8119
Fax: (315) 665-8110
For the most current information regarding operating procedures, see
http://ww2.nycourts.gov/courts/7jd/Wayne/Surrogate/index.shtml

Westchester County

Surrogate's Court

111 Dr. Martin Luther King Jr. Boulevard
19th Floor
White Plains, New York 10601
(914) 824-5656
Fax: (914) 358-8042
For the most current information regarding operating procedures, see
http://ww2.nycourts.gov/COURTS/9jd/westchester/
westchestersurrogate.shtml

Wyoming County

Surrogate's Court

147 North Main Street
Warsaw, New York 14569
(585) 228-3217
Fax: (585) 228-3230
For the most current information regarding operating procedures, see
http://ww2.nycourts.gov/courts/8jd/Wyoming/index.shtml

Yates County

Surrogate's Court

415 Liberty Street
Penn Yan, New York 14527
(315) 835-6321
Fax: (315) 835-6322

For the most current information regarding operating procedures, see
http://ww2.nycourts.gov/courts/7jd/Yates/Surrogate/index.shtml

For the most current information regarding operating procedures, see https://www.nvcourts.gov/County/ValleySubrogate_index.shtml

INDEX

[References are to SCPA and EPTL; if number contains dash (-), it refers to EPTL. Other references are preceded by the following abbreviations: Form–Official Forms; R–Court Rules; Tax L.–New York State Tax Law; MHL–Mental Hygiene Law; GOL–General Obligations Law; Pub. Health L.–Public Health Law.]

I-1

[References are to SCPA and EPTL; if number contains dash (-), it refers to EPTL. Other references are preceded by the following abbreviations: Form–Official Forms; R–Court Rules; Tax L.–New York State Tax Law; MHL–Mental Hygiene Law; GOL–General Obligations Law; Pub. Health L.–Public Health Law.]

ACCOUNTINGS—Cont.
Nonjudicial settlement—Cont.
   Release and discharge, fiduciary's petition
    for—Cont.
     Instruments approving accounts, filing
      with, requirement . . . 2203
Objections to accountings
   Generally . . . 1807; 1808
   Affirmative defense, time for fiduciary reply
    asserting . . . 1808
   Collusion, judgment against fiduciary on
    claim obtained . . . 1807
   Compounding claim or debt as grounds for
    . . . 1813
   Copy of objections, service of . . . 1807
   Court fee for filing . . . 2402
   Dismissal of unpaid claim or imposition of
    surcharge . . . 1807
   Fiduciary's reply asserting affirmative de-
    fense, time for . . . 1808
   Fraud
    Fraudulent compromise . . . 1813
    Judgment against fiduciary on claim ob-
     tained . . . 1807
    Payment of claim, in . . . 1807
   Grounds for . . . 1807; 1808
   Imposition of surcharge against fiduciary
    . . . 1807
   Improper allowance of claim as grounds
    . . . 1807
   Negligent payment of claim as grounds
    . . . 1807
   Order sustaining objection . . . 1807
   Real property disposition; petition for authori-
    zation in settlement proceeding . . . 1906
   Rejection of claim as grounds . . . 1808
   Voluntary accountings, objections to
    . . . 2211
Profit and loss, accounting for . . . 2212
Public administrator's accounts, requirements as
   to . . . 1123; 1213
Real property disposition
   Court authorization
    Generally . . . 1904; 1906
    Application for . . . 1904; 1906
    Notice requirements . . . 1904
    Objections to . . . 1906
    Proceeds of disposition, filing supplemen-
     tal account for . . . 1914
   Order for disposition during settlement
    Adjournment of settlement proceedings
     . . . 1907; 1914
    Decree for payment and distribution
     . . . 2215

ACCOUNTINGS—Cont.
Real property disposition—Cont.
   Order for disposition during settlement—
    Cont.
    Resumption and completion of adjourned
     settlement proceedings . . . 1914
    Stay of proceedings in creditor's action
     . . . 12-2.3
    Supplemental account, fiduciary filing
     . . . 1914
Rejected claims . . . 1808
Representation, requirements for . . . 315; R
   207.18
Sales contract for real property made by dece-
   dent, completion by fiduciary of . . . 1921
Time limits for administration . . . R 207.42
Trustees' accounts (See TRUSTEES, subhead:
   Accounting by)
Trustees, by (See TRUSTEES)
Voluntary accountings
   Citation of attorney general . . . 2210
   Court's function . . . 2211
   Examination of fiduciary, right of parties to
    . . . 2211
   Guardians, time for accountings by . . . 2208
   Objections to account . . . 2211
   Petition for
    Generally . . . R 207.40(a)
    Fees of court . . . 2402
    Filing, eligibility for . . . 2208
   Service of process . . . 2210
   Time for . . . 2208
   Waiver of service of process requirement
    . . . 2210
Will construction issued, effect of . . . 1420
Wrongful death action judgment or compromise,
   proceeds of . . . 2204

ACCUMULATION OF TRUST INCOME
Charitable trusts (See CHARITABLE TRUSTS)
Directions for accumulations
   Statute authorization . . . 9-2.1(a)
   Undistributed income . . . 9-2.3
Education of trust beneficiary, accumulations
   used for . . . 9-2.2
Powers of appointment . . . 10-8.4
Support of trust beneficiary, used for . . . 9-2.2
Time limit on accumulations
   Employer-created trusts for employee benefit
    plans . . . 9-2.1(d)
   Rule against perpetuities governing . . . 9-
    2.1(b), (c), (d)
   Self-employed individuals' retirement trust
    income, exceptions . . . 9-1.7

[References are to SCPA and EPTL; if number contains dash (-), it refers to EPTL. Other references are preceded by the following abbreviations: Form–Official Forms; R–Court Rules; Tax L.–New York State Tax Law; MHL–Mental Hygiene Law; GOL–General Obligations Law; Pub. Health L.–Public Health Law.]

[References are to SCPA and EPTL; if number contains dash (-), it refers to EPTL. Other references are preceded by the following abbreviations: Form–Official Forms; R–Court Rules; Tax L.–New York State Tax Law; MHL–Mental Hygiene Law; GOL–General Obligations Law; Pub. Health L.–Public Health Law.]

ADMINISTRATORS (See also EXECUTORS; FIDUCIARIES (GENERALLY))—Cont.
Proceeding Checklist . . . A-CHKLST
Public administrators (See PUBLIC ADMINIS-TRATORS)
Small estates, voluntary administrators of (See SMALL ESTATES)
Testamentary trustee and, proceeding when . . . 1505
Trustee-administrators . . . 720; 1505
Vacancy in office as grounds for appointment of administrator *de bonis non* . . . 1007
Value of estate
  Bonding requirement, effect on . . . 801
  Notification of court subsequent to letters, rules for . . . 725
Voluntary administrator of small estate (See SMALL ESTATES)
With will annexed (See ADMINISTRATORS C.T.A. *(CUM TESTAMENTO ANNEXO)*)
Wrongful death action
  Application to compromise action . . . 5-4.6(a)
  Attorney's continued service . . . 5-4.6(a)(3)
  Filing fee . . . 5-4.6(c)
  Guardians *ad litem*, appointment of . . . 5-4.6(b)
  Letters of administration . . . 5-4.6(f)
  Payable expenses . . . 5-4.6(a)(1); 5-4.6(a)(2)
  Petition for compromise, right to . . . 5-4.6(e)
  Prosecution for benefit of distributees . . . 5-4.1
  Written approval of compromise . . . 5-4.6(d)

ADMINISTRATORS C.T.A. *(CUM TESTAMENTO ANNEXO)*
Ancillary administrators c.t.a. (See FOREIGN ESTATES)
Bonding requirement
  Generally . . . 801
  Dispensing with, consents required for
    Generally . . . 805
    Official form . . . Form CTA-3
Citation
  Official form . . . Form CTA-2
  Waiver; official form . . . Form CTA-3
Consent to letters; official form . . . Form CTA-3
Defined . . . 103(3)
Fiduciary, status as . . . 11-1.1(a); 103(3)

ADMINISTRATORS C.T.A. *(CUM TESTAMENTO ANNEXO)*—Cont.
Letters of administration
  Generally . . . 1418
  Ancillary letters on foreign will, right to receive . . . 1604
  Beneficiaries entitled to letters . . . 1604
  Bonding requirement (See subhead: Bonding requirement)
  Citation
    Official form . . . Form CTA-2
    Waiver; official form . . . Form CTA-3
  Consent; official form . . . Form CTA-3
  Issuance of, petition for . . . 1419
  Lack of debt, affidavit of . . . Form P-12
  Petition; official form . . . Form CTA-1
  Renunciation; official form . . . Form CTA-3; Form P-11
  Verification, oath and designation; official form . . . Form CTA-1; Form P-1
Oath and designation; official form . . . Form CTA-1; Form P-1
Petition; official form . . . Form CTA-1
Powers, duties and limitations . . . 11-1.1
Proceeding Checklist . . . Acta-CHKLST
Renunciation of letters; official form . . . Form CTA-3
Value of estate as affecting bonding requirement . . . 801
Verification, oath and designation; official form . . . Form CTA-1; Form P-1

ADMINISTRATORS D.B.N. *(DE BONIS NON)*
Bonding requirements
  Generally . . . 801
  Amount of bond . . . 801; 1007
Citation
  Affidavit of service; official form . . . Form ADM/DBN-8
  Official form . . . Form ADM/DBN-2
  Waiver; official form . . . Form ADM/DBN-3
Consent to appointment; official form
  Corporation . . . Form ADM/DBN-4
  Individual . . . Form ADM/DBN-3
Consul general, notice to; official form . . . Form ADM/DBN-7
Defined . . . 103(4)
Fiduciary, status as . . . 11-1.1(a); 103(4)
Letters of administration
  Generally . . . 1007
  Citation (See subhead: Citation)

[References are to SCPA and EPTL; if number contains dash (-), it refers to EPTL. Other references are preceded by the following abbreviations: Form–Official Forms; R–Court Rules; Tax L.–New York State Tax Law; MHL–Mental Hygiene Law; GOL–General Obligations Law; Pub. Health L.–Public Health Law.]

[References are to SCPA and EPTL; if number contains dash (-), it refers to EPTL. Other references are preceded by the following abbreviations: Form–Official Forms; R–Court Rules; Tax L.–New York State Tax Law; MHL–Mental Hygiene Law; GOL–General Obligations Law; Pub. Health L.–Public Health Law.]

[References are to SCPA and EPTL; if number contains dash (-), it refers to EPTL. Other references are preceded by the following abbreviations: Form–Official Forms; R–Court Rules; Tax L.–New York State Tax Law; MHL–Mental Hygiene Law; GOL–General Obligations Law; Pub. Health L.–Public Health Law.]

[References are to SCPA and EPTL; if number contains dash (-), it refers to EPTL. Other references are preceded by the following abbreviations: Form–Official Forms; R–Court Rules; Tax L.–New York State Tax Law; MHL–Mental Hygiene Law; GOL–General Obligations Law; Pub. Health L.–Public Health Law.]

[References are to SCPA and EPTL; if number contains dash (-), it refers to EPTL. Other references are preceded by the following abbreviations: Form–Official Forms; R–Court Rules; Tax L.–New York State Tax Law; MHL–Mental Hygiene Law; GOL–General Obligations Law; Pub. Health L.–Public Health Law.]

AFTERBORN CHILDREN—Cont.

Share of parents' estate, right to
Character of after-born child's share . . . 5-3.2
Enforcement of right
Action in supreme court after distribution of estate . . . 5-3.4
Interests liable . . . 5-3.2
Revocatory effect on will . . . 5-3.2
Extent of share in estate . . . 5-3.2
Fiduciary's powers with respect to estate property, effect on . . . 11-1.1(b)(5)(E)
Provision for children living at time of execution of will as condition to . . . 5-3.2
Will as condition to . . . 5-3.2

ALIENS

Beneficiaries, deposit of money or property due in court for benefit of . . . 2218
Consul
Public administrator's application for letters, notice of . . . 1119
Representation by . . . 1120
Uniform Rules for Surrogate's Court . . . R 207.21
Estates of; public administrator's application for letters . . . 1119
Incompetent alien, representation of . . . 1120
Infant alien, representation of . . . 1120
Nonresident aliens (See NONRESIDENT ALIENS)
Public administrator, actions by or against . . . 1120
Representation by consul for . . . 401; 1120
Termination of consul authority . . . 401
Uniform Rules for Surrogate's Court . . . R 207.21

ALLOWANCES, COSTS AND (See COSTS AND ALLOWANCES)

ANATOMICAL GIFTS

Advanced heath care directives, conflicts with . . . Pub. Health L. 4306-a
Amendments or revocation of
Attending physician as witness to . . . Pub. Health L. 4305(1)(d)
Destruction of documentation . . . Pub. Health L. 4305(3)
Later-executed document . . . Pub. Health L. 4305(1)(c)
Oral statement . . . Pub. Health L. 4305(1)(b)
Person authorized to make decision on behalf of another . . . Pub. Health L. 4305(2)

ANATOMICAL GIFTS—Cont.

Amendments or revocation of—Cont.
Post-death discovery of written document . . . Pub. Health L. 4305(1)(e)
Signed card or document . . . Pub. Health L. 4305(1)(e)
Subsequent gifts . . . Pub. Health L. 4305(5)
Will . . . Pub. Health L. 4305(1)(f); Pub. Health L. 4305(4)
Written statement . . . Pub. Health L. 4305(1)(a)
Application . . . Pub. Health L. 4309
Definitions
Anatomical gift . . . Pub. Health L. 4300(1)
Decedent . . . Pub. Health L. 4300(2)
Designated requestor . . . R 405.25(a)(1)
Disinterested witness . . . Pub. Health L. 4300(3)
Document of gift . . . Pub. Health L. 4300(4)
Domestic partner . . . Pub. Health L. 4300(5)
Donee . . . Pub. Health L. 4300(6)
Donor . . . Pub. Health L. 4300(7)
Eye bank . . . Pub. Health L. 4300(8)
Gift . . . Pub. Health L. 4300(1)
Guardian . . . Pub. Health L. 4300(9)
Hospital . . . Pub. Health L. 4300(10)
Non-transplant anatomic bank . . . Pub. Health L. 4300(11)
Organ . . . Pub. Health L. 4300(12)
Organ procurement organization . . . Pub. Health L. 4300(13)
Organ procurement organization (OPO) . . . R 405.25(a)(3)
Parent . . . Pub. Health L. 4300(14)
Part . . . Pub. Health L. 4300(15)
Person . . . Pub. Health L. 4300(16)
Physician or surgeon . . . Pub. Health L. 4300(17)
Procurement organization . . . Pub. Health L. 4300(19)
Prospective donor . . . Pub. Health L. 4300(18)
Reasonably available . . . Pub. Health L. 4300(20)
Record . . . Pub. Health L. 4300(21)
Refusal . . . Pub. Health L. 4300(22)
State . . . Pub. Health L. 4300(23)
Suitability . . . R 405.25(a)(2)
Tissue bank . . . Pub. Health L. 4300(24); R 405.25(a)(4)
Whole body . . . Pub. Health L. 4300(25)

ANATOMICAL GIFTS—Cont.

Definitions—Cont.

Whole body donor card . . . Pub. Health L. 4300(26)

Delivery of document of gift . . . Pub. Health L. 4304

Disposition of gifts . . . Pub. Health L. 4302

Donate life registry . . . Pub. Health L. 4310

Donation prohibited; conditions . . . R 405.25(d)

Donor

Age of donor . . . Pub. Health L. 4301(1)

Defined . . . Pub. Health L. 4300(7)

Documentation and acceptance of gift . . . Pub. Health L. 4301(8)

Domestic partner of . . . Pub. Health L. 4301(2); Pub. Health L. 4301(4)

Donee rejection of gift, circumstances surrounding . . . Pub. Health L. 4301(5)

Medical acceptability, examination determining . . . Pub. Health L. 4301(6)

Persons who may execute anatomical gift on behalf of decedent . . . Pub. Health L. 4301(2); Pub. Health L. 4301(4)

Reasonably available, persons who may execute anatomical gift are . . . Pub. Health L. 4301(3)

Rights of donee . . . Pub. Health L. 4301(7)

Execution of

Documentation of gift . . . Pub. Health L. 4303(5)

Non-will documentation . . . Pub. Health L. 4303(2)

Physician or surgeon as designate . . . Pub. Health L. 4303(4)

Unspecified donee . . . Pub. Health L. 4303(3)

Will . . . Pub. Health L. 4303(1)

Family consultation . . . R 405.25(e)

Fee to donor's estate, prohibition on charging . . . Pub. Health L. 4308

Heath care proxies, conflicts with . . . Pub. Health L. 4306-a

Hospital administrators, duties of

Eye bank or tissue bank

Commissioner regulations . . . Pub. Health L. 4351(12); Pub. Health L. 4351(13)

Confidentiality . . . Pub. Health L. 4351(8)

Defined . . . Pub. Health L. 4300(8)

Designated requestor defined . . . Pub. Health L. 4351(7)

ANATOMICAL GIFTS—Cont.

Hospital administrators, duties of—Cont.

Eye bank or tissue bank—Cont.

Documentation and acceptance of gift . . . Pub. Health L. 4351(9)

Domestic partner of donor . . . Pub. Health L. 4351(4); Pub. Health L. 4351(6)

Inappropriateness of . . . Pub. Health L. 4351(3)

Legal responsibility . . . Pub. Health L. 4351(10)

Medical screening . . . Pub. Health L. 4351(2)

Reasonably available, persons who may execute anatomical gift are . . . Pub. Health L. 4351(5)

Suitability of candidate . . . Pub. Health L. 4351(4)

Organ procurement organization, contact of . . . Pub. Health L. 4351(1)(a)-(d)

Life-sustaining treatment, withdrawal of . . . Pub. Health L. 4306-b

Patient suitability

Authorized persons, request of . . . R 405.25(c)(1)

Consent or refusal . . . R 405.25(c)(2)

Disposal of body . . . R 405.25(c)(3)

Revocation of (See subhead: Amendments or revocation of)

Donate life registry, revocations from . . . Pub. Health L. 4310

Rights and duties at death

Acceptance or rejection of gift by donee . . . Pub. Health L. 4306(1)

Civil actions, not liable for . . . Pub. Health L. 4306(3)

Employee or agent of organ procurement organization . . . Pub. Health L. 4306(4)

Transplantation, limits to physician's involvement in . . . Pub. Health L. 4306(2)

Sales and purchases of human organs, prohibition of . . . Pub. Health L. 4307

Uses and disposition of gifts . . . Pub. Health L. 4302

Withdrawal of life-sustaining treatment . . . Pub. Health L. 4306-b

Written policies and procedures, establishment of

Designated requestor's consent . . . R 405.25(b)(2)

Hospital methods . . . R 405.25(b)(5)

Medical record notification, documentation of . . . R 405.25(b)(3)

Index

[References are to SCPA and EPTL; if number contains dash (-), it refers to EPTL. Other references are preceded by the following abbreviations: Form–Official Forms; R–Court Rules; Tax L.–New York State Tax Law; MHL–Mental Hygiene Law; GOL–General Obligations Law; Pub. Health L.–Public Health Law.]

ANATOMICAL GIFTS—Cont.

Written policies and procedures, establishment of—Cont.

Notification of procurement, protocol for . . . R 405.25(b)(1)

Potential donors, monitoring of . . . R 405.25(b)(4)

ANCILLARY LETTERS (See FOREIGN ESTATES)

ANNUITIES

Beneficiary's right to take capital sum earmarked for purchase of . . . 3-3.9

Employees' trust; payments received by beneficiary . . . R 360.7(a)(1)

Exemptions to waivers for payments . . . R 360.7(a)(2)

Gifts to minors; prior to January 1, 1997

Contract defined . . . 7-4.1(k)

Custodian's rights and duties as to . . . 7-4.3(j)(1), (2)

Method of making . . . 7-4.1(a)(4)

Possession and control, transfer to custodian or successor custodian, method and effect . . . 7-4, 6(b)(1), (2)

Lifetime trust established to receive proceeds, testamentary disposition to . . . 3-3.7

Payments as income and principal . . . 11-A-4.9

Structured settlement paying funds on installment basis . . . 2220

Surviving spouse's right of election, subject for . . . 5-1.1(a)(1)(G), (c)(1)(I)

Testamentary trust income or principal, allocation of . . . 11-2.1(c)(2)

ANNULMENT OF MARRIAGE (See also DIVORCE)

Incestuous marriages . . . 5

Registration of security, revocation of . . . 5-1.4(c)

Surviving spouse status, disqualification for . . . 5-1.2

Voidable marriages . . . 8

Void marriages . . . 5; 6

Will executed prior to, provisions for former spouse, revocation by annulment . . . 5-1.4

ANTENUPTIAL AGREEMENTS

Surviving spouse's right to intestate share of testator's estate, effect on; will executed prior to Sept. 1, 1930 . . . 5-1.3

ANTI-LAPSE STATUTES (See also LAPSE OF DISPOSITION)

Adopted children . . . 3-3.3

Dispositions to issue or brothers or sisters of testator . . . 3-3.3

Nonmarital children; anti-lapse provisions for class dispositions . . . 3-3.3

APPEALS (GENERALLY)

Civil Practice Law and Rules

Applicability, generally . . . 2701

Remittitur from appellate court, proceedings on . . . 2702

Costs of appeal, award of

Generally . . . 2304

Fiduciary, award of fees and expenses of . . . 2302

Directed verdict motion, failure to return verdict on appeal as denial of . . . 2701

Estate or transfer tax determination, appeal from; pre-May 25, 1990 . . . 2008

Final determination, reservation of award of costs pending, court's power to direct . . . 2301

Letters, effect of appeal on decree granting . . . 703

Period for, expiration, reservation of award of costs pending, court's power to direct . . . 2301

Remittitur from appellate court . . . 2702

APPEARANCE OF PARTIES

Generally . . . 401

Incompetent persons (See INCOMPETENT PERSONS)

Uniform rules for Surrogate's Court (See UNIFORM RULES FOR SURROGATE'S COURT)

APPOINTIVE PROPERTY (See POWERS OF APPOINTMENT)

APPRAISERS

Estate tax, determination by

Grounds for; pre-May 25, 1990 . . . 2005

No necessity for, determination by court; pre-May 25, 1990 . . . 2004

Fee payment, procedure for . . . 2305

ARMED SERVICES

Fiduciary or fiduciary-nominee powers suspended for period of (See WAR SERVICE)

Government benefits due decedent-members, collection of . . . 2402

Holographic will of member . . . 3-2.2

Nuncupative will of member . . . 3-2.2

[References are to SCPA and EPTL; if number contains dash (-), it refers to EPTL. Other references are preceded by the following abbreviations: Form–Official Forms; R–Court Rules; Tax L.–New York State Tax Law; MHL–Mental Hygiene Law; GOL–General Obligations Law; Pub. Health L.–Public Health Law.]

[References are to SCPA and EPTL; if number contains dash (-), it refers to EPTL. Other references are preceded by the following abbreviations: Form–Official Forms; R–Court Rules; Tax L.–New York State Tax Law; MHL–Mental Hygiene Law; GOL–General Obligations Law; Pub. Health L.–Public Health Law.]

[References are to SCPA and EPTL; if number contains dash (-), it refers to EPTL. Other references are preceded by the following abbreviations: Form–Official Forms; R–Court Rules; Tax L.–New York State Tax Law; MHL–Mental Hygiene Law; GOL–General Obligations Law; Pub. Health L.–Public Health Law.]

[References are to SCPA and EPTL; if number contains dash (-), it refers to EPTL. Other references are preceded by the following abbreviations: Form–Official Forms; R–Court Rules; Tax L.–New York State Tax Law; MHL–Mental Hygiene Law; GOL–General Obligations Law; Pub. Health L.–Public Health Law.]

BONDING REQUIREMENTS—Cont.

Sureties on bond—Cont.

Instrument filed . . . 802

Liability for assets received in another fiduciary capacity . . . 808

New surety requirement . . . 803

Trust companies

Generally . . . 708

Co-fiduciary, deposit of assets with . . . 804

BONDS (GENERALLY)

Powers of attorney, statutory short form . . . GOL 5-1502C

BROTHERS AND SISTERS OF DECEDENT

"Debt" owed decedent; payment without administration . . . 1310

Estate tax deduction or exemption based on relationship to decedent, apportionment of . . . 2-1.8(c)(2)

Letters of administration . . . 1001

Testamentary beneficiaries, death during lifetime of testator, no grounds for lapse of disposition . . . 3-3.3

Voluntary administrator of small estate, eligibility to serve as . . . 1303

BURIAL PLOTS (See also CEMETERIES)

Deed in decedent's safe deposit box; delivery to clerk of court of . . . 2003

Funeral expense, as . . . 103(22)

Perpetual care of decedent's lot as funeral expense . . . 104

BUSINESS OF DECEDENT

Continuation of business (See CONTINUATION OF BUSINESS)

Discontinuance and winding up, petition by creditor or interested person for . . . 2108

Powers of attorney, statutory short form . . . GOL 5-1502E

C

CADAVERS

Burial, duty of . . . Pub. Health L. 4200

Disposition of remains – responsibility

Agent, appointment of – form . . . Pub. Health L. 4201(3)

Civil liabilities, not subject to . . . Pub. Health L. 4201(6)(a)-(c)

Control of remains . . . Pub. Health L. 4201(2)(a)(i)-(x)

"Cremation" defined . . . Pub. Health L. 4201(1)(a)

CADAVERS—Cont.

Disposition of remains – responsibility—Cont.

Decedent, wishes of . . . Pub. Health L. 4201(2)(c)

Designate unavailable . . . Pub. Health L. 4201(2)(b)

"Disposition" defined . . . Pub. Health L. 4201(1)(b)

Disputes, resolution of . . . Pub. Health L. 4201(8)

"Domestic partner"

Generally . . . Pub. Health L. 4201(1)(c)

Common household . . . Pub. Health L. 4201(1)(c)(iii)

Employment benefits, recognized as beneficiary of . . . Pub. Health L. 4201(1)(c)(ii)

Jurisdiction . . . Pub. Health L. 4201(1)(c)(i)

Funeral directors

Compensation . . . Pub. Health L. 4201(2)(d)

Liability . . . Pub. Health L. 4201(7)(a), (b)

"Person" defined . . . Pub. Health L. 4201(1)(d)

Written instrument

Absence of . . . Pub. Health L. 4201(4)(a); Pub. Health L. 4201(4)(b)

Limiting authority of remains agent . . . Pub. Health L. 4201(4-a)

Revocation of . . . Pub. Health L. 4201(5)

CARDIOPULMONARY RESUSCITATION

Defined . . . R 405.43(b)(4)

Orders not to resuscitate (See DO-NOT-RESUSCITATE ORDERS)

CASUALTY INSURANCE

Estate or trust property, insurance on, purchase and maintenance, power of fiduciary . . . 11-1.1.(b)(4)

CEMETERIES (See also BURIAL PLOTS)

Cemetery corporations, registration and reporting requirement for . . . 8-1.4(b)

Charitable trust for

Authorization . . . 8-1.2

Bank, deposit with . . . 8-1.6

"Charitable purposes" defined . . . 8-1.5

Deposit of money in trust by owner in private unincorporated cemetery . . . 8-1.6

Dispositions for . . . 8-1.5

Rules governing . . . 8-1.3

[References are to SCPA and EPTL; if number contains dash (-), it refers to EPTL. Other references are preceded by the following abbreviations: Form–Official Forms; R–Court Rules; Tax L.–New York State Tax Law; MHL–Mental Hygiene Law; GOL–General Obligations Law; Pub. Health L.–Public Health Law.]

[References are to SCPA and EPTL; if number contains dash (-), it refers to EPTL. Other references are preceded by the following abbreviations: Form–Official Forms; R–Court Rules; Tax L.–New York State Tax Law; MHL–Mental Hygiene Law; GOL–General Obligations Law; Pub. Health L.–Public Health Law.]

CHARITABLE TRUSTS—Cont.

Investigation of trustees by attorney general—Cont.

  Witnesses . . . 8-1.4(j)

Jurisdiction of court

  Supreme court . . . 8-1.1(g)

  Surrogate's court . . . 8-1.1(g); 209

Lead trusts, registration of

  Generally . . . R 92.4(a)

  Annual reports, Attorney General filing . . . R 92.4(b)

  Final reports, Attorney General filing . . . R 92.4(c)

Library, for . . . 8-1.3(a), (b)

Literary institutions (See LITERARY INSTITUTIONS)

Municipal corporations . . . 8-1.2(c)

Museums, for . . . 8-1.3(b) *et seq.*

Observatories . . . 8-1.2

Parks . . . 8-1.2

Principal of . . . 7-1.11(b)

Private foundation . . . 8-1.8

Property subject to

  Administration and use, trustee's petition for . . . 8-1.4(e)

  Disposition or distribution of, trustee's petition for . . . 8-1.4(e)

  Real property (See subhead: Real property)

  Title to property, vesting of . . . 8-1.1(a)

Real property

  Absentees, representation of . . . 8-1.1(h)

  Incompetents, representation of . . . 8-1.1(h)

  Lessee, rights of . . . 8-1.1(i)

  Minors, representation of . . . 8-1.1(h)

  Mortgagee, rights of . . . 8-1.1(i)

  Notice requirements . . . 8-1.1(h)

  Purchaser, rights of . . . 8-1.1(i)

  Sale, mortgage or lease, grounds for . . . 8-1.1(g), (h), (i)

Registration of trustees

  Exceptions . . . 8-1.4(b)

  Instrument granting title . . . 8-1.4(d)

  Noncompliance, effect of . . . 8-1.4(m)

  Register of trustees

    Establishment and maintenance, duty of attorney general . . . 8-1.4(c)

    Public inspection, availability for . . . 8-1.4(l)

Remainder trusts; registration with notice of termination

  Generally . . . R 92.3(a)

  Final report, Attorney General filing . . . R 92.3(c)

  Periodic reports . . . R 92.3(b)

CHARITABLE TRUSTS—Cont.

Reporting by trustees

  Account requirement, compliance with . . . 8-1.4; 8-1.4(h)

  Contents, requirements for . . . 8-1.4(f)

  Exceptions . . . 8-1.4(b)

  Fees for filing; schedule . . . 8-1.4(p)

  Noncompliance, effect of . . . 8-1.4(m)

  Public inspection, availability for . . . 8-1.4(l)

  Rules and regulations . . . 8-1.4(h)

  State welfare department, report to . . . 8-1.4(f)(2)

  Suspension of requirement . . . 8-1.4(h)

  Time for filing . . . 8-1.4(f); 8-1.4(g)

Subscriptions to voluntary association or committee . . . 8-1.1(j); 8-1.1(j), (k), (l)

Supervision by attorney general

  Generally . . . 8-1.4

  Investigation of trustees (See subhead: Investigation of trustees by attorney general)

  Registration of trustees (See subhead: Registration of trustees)

  Reporting by trustees (See subhead: Reporting by trustees)

Tax-exempt status . . . 8-1.4(o)

Trustees

  Accounting by (See subhead: Accounting by trustees)

  Commissions . . . 2308

  Defined, supervision by attorney general . . . 8-1.4(a)

  Investigation by attorney general (See subhead: Investigation of trustees by attorney general)

  Petitions filed by, notice requirements . . . 8-1.4(e)

  Registration requirements (See subhead: Registration of trustees)

  Reporting requirements (See subhead: Reporting by trustees)

  Status as . . . 8-1.4(a)

  Title to property, vesting in named trustees . . . 8-1.1(a)

Trust governance . . . 8-1.9

Will, creation by

  Incorporation by reference . . . 8-1.1(b)

  Probate notice requirements . . . 8-1.4(e)

  Surrogate's court jurisdiction . . . 8-1.1(c)

CHATTELS (See PERSONAL PROPERTY)

CHIEF FISCAL OFFICER OF COUNTY

Administrator, service as

  Generally . . . 1219

[References are to SCPA and EPTL; if number contains dash (-), it refers to EPTL. Other references are preceded by the following abbreviations: Form–Official Forms; R–Court Rules; Tax L.–New York State Tax Law; MHL–Mental Hygiene Law; GOL–General Obligations Law; Pub. Health L.–Public Health Law.]

[References are to SCPA and EPTL; if number contains dash (-), it refers to EPTL. Other references are preceded by the following abbreviations: Form–Official Forms; R–Court Rules; Tax L.–New York State Tax Law; MHL–Mental Hygiene Law; GOL–General Obligations Law; Pub. Health L.–Public Health Law.]

[References are to SCPA and EPTL; if number contains dash (-), it refers to EPTL. Other references are preceded by the following abbreviations: Form–Official Forms; R–Court Rules; Tax L.–New York State Tax Law; MHL–Mental Hygiene Law; GOL–General Obligations Law; Pub. Health L.–Public Health Law.]

CLAIMS AGAINST ESTATES—Cont.
Rejection of claim by fiduciary—Cont.
  Limitations period . . . 1810
  Notice to claimant, requirements
    Generally . . . 1806
    Absence of written notice prior to filing of account, treatment as allowance . . . 1806
    Reason for rejection, inclusion in notice . . . 1806
    Service of notice, time for . . . 1808
  Real property; limitations period . . . 1906
  Retention of property to satisfy rejected claims . . . 2217
  Validity of rejected claims, trial and determination . . . 1808
Settlement of (See COMPROMISE OF CLAIMS)
Surviving spouse's right of election, no effect on claims . . . 5-1.1
$10,000 or 25% or more of estimated gross probate estate, claims in excess of . . . 1809
Validity of
  Allowance of claim by fiduciary, establishment through . . . 1807; 1906
  Objection to proceeding of court approval of real property disposition . . . 1906
  Real property disposition, objection to claims in . . . 1906
  Rejected claims . . . 1808
  Specific claim . . . 1809

CLASS MEMBERS
Citation, designation in; members of class exceeding 50 persons, method . . . 306
Petition, designation in, method . . . 304

CLERKS OF SURROGATE'S COURTS
Agent of fiduciary for receipt of process
  Designation as acknowledged instrument filed with surrogate . . . 708
  Service on clerk as personal service on fiduciary . . . 308
Appointment by surrogate
  Generally . . . 2605
  Commissioner of taxation and finance, recommendations to . . . Tax L. 983
  New York City . . . 2606
Bonding requirements
  Generally . . . 2605
  Bonds of fiduciaries, approval by . . . 802
  New York City . . . 2606

CLERKS OF SURROGATE'S COURTS—Cont.
Chief and deputy clerks
  Appointment and removal of . . . 2605; 2606
  Compensation of . . . 2606
  Deputy chief clerk . . . 2605; 2606; 2609
  New York City, counties within . . . 2606
  Powers and duties . . . 2605; 2606
County clerk (See COUNTY CLERKS)
Decrees and orders of court
  Docketing . . . 603
  Signing, delegating authority of . . . 2609
  Transcripts of . . . 603
Deputy chief clerk (See subhead: Chief and deputy clerks)
Guardian's accounts, annual examination of . . . 1721
Letters granted by court
  Certificate of letters, facsimile of chief clerk's signature on . . . 2609
  Signing of . . . 701
Oaths of office
  Administration of . . . 2609
  Taking by clerks . . . 2605; 2606
Personnel of Surrogate's Court (See subhead: Chief and deputy clerks)
Powers and duties . . . 2605; 2606; 2609
Public administrators, clerk's duty in absence of; counties outside New York City . . . 1205
Recordkeeping duties
  Generally . . . 2501; 2502
  Infant's property deposited under joint control, receipts and withdrawals . . . 1719
  Small estates settled without administration . . . 1304
Removal of . . . 2606
Safe deposit box contents delivered to . . . 2003
Submission of papers to
  Generally . . . R 207.5
  Form, label, file number . . . R 207.4
Temporary chief clerk of court, designation of . . . 2605; 2606
Testimony of witnesses, clerk taking
  Authorization, testimony of attesting or material witnesses in uncontested proceeding unable to attend . . . 507
  Delegation of authority to clerk, discretion of surrogate . . . 2609
  Travel expenses of clerk, reimbursement for . . . 2608

CODICILS
Definition . . . 1-2.1

Index

[References are to SCPA and EPTL; if number contains dash (-), it refers to EPTL. Other references are preceded by the following abbreviations: Form–Official Forms; R–Court Rules; Tax L.–New York State Tax Law; MHL–Mental Hygiene Law; GOL–General Obligations Law; Pub. Health L.–Public Health Law.]

CODICILS—Cont.
Revocation . . . 3-4.1

CO-FIDUCIARIES (See FIDUCIARIES (GENERALLY))

COMMISSIONER OF RECORDS
Generally . . . 2610
Records of court (See RECORDS AND RECORDATION OF SURROGATE'S COURT)

COMMISSIONS
Advance payment of . . . 2311
Computation of . . . 2307
Corporate executor . . . 2307
Executor, corporate . . . 2307
Multiple fiduciaries, apportionment among . . . 2307
Payment on account, proceeding for . . . 2310
Pre-July 1, 1956, fiduciary entitled to commission of principal and income . . . 2307
Real property management, allowance for . . . 2307
Real property sale proceeds, awarded from . . . 2302; 2307
Retention of . . . 1106
September eleventh victim compensation fund of 2001, on awards from . . . 205; 2307
Trustees (See TRUSTEES)
Value of estate determining . . . 2307

COMMITTEE OF INCOMPETENT (See INCOMPETENT PERSONS)

COMMON DISASTER (See SIMULTANEOUS DEATH)

COMMUNITY PROPERTY
Application of the part . . . 6-6.1
Death, disposition at
  Generally . . . 6-6.1 *et seq.*
  Applicability of part . . . 6-6.1
  Construction of part . . . 6-6.6
  Effect of part . . . 6-6.6
  Lender taking security interest in property . . . 6-6.5(b)
  Purchaser for value, interest in property, where taken . . . 6-6.5(a)
  Real property; rents, issues or income of . . . 6-6.2
  Rebuttable presumption arising . . . 6-6.2
  Sale or creation of security interest; treatment of proceeds of . . . 6-6.5
  Title, perfection of . . . 6-6.4
Disposition at death (See subhead: Death, disposition at)

COMMUNITY PROPERTY—Cont.
Perfection of title to . . . 6-6.4
Surviving spouse's rights (See subhead: Death, disposition at)

COMPENSATION
Deferred compensation as income and principal . . . 11-A-4.9
Fiduciaries, of (See COMMISSIONS)
Powers of attorney, persons acting under (See POWERS OF ATTORNEY, subhead: Compensation of persons acting under)

COMPROMISE OF CLAIMS
Application of fiduciary, on . . . 1813
Court's authorization, procedure for obtaining . . . 1813
Disabled persons . . . 2106
Fiduciary's power, restriction by letters . . . 702
Fraudulent compromise . . . 1813
Incompetent persons . . . 2106
Infant's claims . . . 1813
Personal injuries . . . R 207.38
Supreme court action . . . 13-1.4
Wrongful death . . . R 207.38

COMPTROLLER OF STATE
Funds due unknown legatees, distributees or creditors
  Generally . . . 2223
  Payment to comptroller by fiduciary . . . 2222
Letters issued to chief fiscal officer of county, transmittal of copy to . . . 723
Public administrators outside New York City remitting payment of balance of assets remaining after settlement of account to . . . 1213

COMPULSORY ACCOUNTING (See ACCOUNTINGS)

CONDEMNATION OF PROPERTY IN DECEDENTS' ESTATES
Testamentary trust property; courts' authority over trustee release of claims against state for compensation or damages
  Conclusive effect of court's decree . . . 1508
  Procedure for obtaining
    Generally . . . 1508
    Filing fees . . . 2402

[References are to SCPA and EPTL; if number contains dash (-), it refers to EPTL. Other references are preceded by the following abbreviations: Form–Official Forms; R–Court Rules; Tax L.–New York State Tax Law; MHL–Mental Hygiene Law; GOL–General Obligations Law; Pub. Health L.–Public Health Law.]

CONSERVATORS (See GUARDIANS FOR INCOMPETENTS)

CONSOLIDATION OF PROCEEDINGS
Generally . . . 501

CONSTITUTION OF STATE
Jurisdiction of Surrogate's Court, grant of as exercise of legislative power conferred by constitution . . . 201

CONSTRUCTION OF WILL (See WILLS (GENERALLY))

CONSULAR OFFICIALS
Nonresident aliens, representation of (See ALIENS)

CONTEMPT PROCEEDINGS
Creditor's proceeding to obtain information concerning trust beneficiary . . . 7-3.5(e)
Orders or decrees of Surrogate's Court, enforcement by contempt proceeding
　Bond of respondent, actions on, no bar to . . . 606
　Denial of contempt citation, grounds for . . . 606
　Fees of court on filing petition . . . 2402
　Grounds for . . . 606
　Money payment, order for, applicability . . . 606
　Performance of act, order requiring, applicability . . . 606
　Petition for, contents, requirement . . . 607
　Procedure . . . 607
　Proceeding decree issued in, continuance . . . 606
　Show-cause order, issuance and service requirements . . . 607
　Warrant of commitment, issuance . . . 607
Public administrators' subpoenas, effect of non-compliance with . . . 1114; 1216

CONTEST OF WILL (See PROBATE PROCEEDINGS; WILLS (GENERALLY))

CONTINUATION OF BUSINESS
Answer by respondent . . . 2108
Corporate form, continued in other than . . . 2108
Decree for proceeding by fiduciary . . . 2108
Filing fee . . . 2402
Funds collected from business segregated from assets of estate . . . 2108
Liability of assets of business . . . 2108
Proceeding by fiduciary for . . . 2108; 2402

CONTINUATION OF BUSINESS—Cont.
Professional exemption . . . 2108
Unincorporated form . . . 2108

CONTRIBUTORY NEGLIGENCE
Personal injury action joined with wrongful death action, defense to . . . 11-3.2(b)

CORPORATE BONDS (See also STOCKS AND SECURITIES)
Calls, assessments and other charges, payment of, power of fiduciaries . . . 11-1.1
Trust funds, investment in, power of fiduciaries . . . 11-2.2
Trust property
　Generally . . . 11-2.1(f)(1)
　Discount bonds, increment in value of . . . 11-2.1(f)(2)

CORPORATIONS
Appearance by attorney, requirement . . . 401
Bonds of (See CORPORATE BONDS)
Commission for corporate executor . . . 2307
Distributions to trust estate, allocation between principal and income
　Accrual of distribution, date of . . . 11-2.1(e)(11)
　Cash dividends . . . 11-2.1(e)(9)(A)
　Character of distribution, distributing corporation's statement, reliance on . . . 11-2.1(e)(10)
　Discretionary power of trustee under instrument creating trust . . . 11-2.1(e)(1)
　Guaranteed dividends settled on liquidation . . . 11-2.1(e)(9)(D)
　Lifetime trusts . . . 11-2.1(d), (e)
　Liquidating distributions . . . 11-2.1(e)(6), (9)(D)
　Merger or consolidation, shares issued by successor corporation . . . 11-2.1(e)(5)
　Option to receive distribution in cash or stock . . . 11-2.1(e)(8), (9)(F)
　Other corporation's shares, securities or obligations, distribution of or proceeds of . . . 11-2.1(e)(9)(C)
　Preferred dividends settled on liquidation . . . 11-2.1(e)(9)(D)
　Real estate investment trust distributions . . . 11-2.1(e)(7), (9)(E)
　Redemption, shares issued for redeemed shares . . . 11-2.1(e)(5)
　Regulated investment company distribution . . . 11-2.1(e)(7), (9)(E)
　Reorganization shares issued by successor corporation . . . 11-2.1(e)(5)

Index

[References are to SCPA and EPTL; if number contains dash (-), it refers to EPTL. Other references are preceded by the following abbreviations: Form–Official Forms; R–Court Rules; Tax L.–New York State Tax Law; MHL–Mental Hygiene Law; GOL–General Obligations Law; Pub. Health L.–Public Health Law.]

CORPORATIONS—Cont.

Distributions to trust estate, allocation between principal and income—Cont.

Rights . . . 11-2.1(e)(4)

Source of distributions, distributing corporation's statement, reliance on . . . 11-2.1(e)(10)

Stock dividends and splits . . . 11-2.1(e)(2), (3), (9)(B)

Trusts covered, date of creation as determining . . . 11-2.1(e)(13)

Uncertainty of trustee concerning proper allocation, treatment of shares as principal . . . 11-2.1(e)(12)

Executor, commission for corporate . . . 2307

Letters of administration, grant to corporation authorized to act as fiduciary

Generally . . . 1001

Consent of beneficiaries . . . 1418

Letters of administration with will annexed, sole or residuary legatee-corporation's right to . . . 1418

Liquidation of, distributions to trust estate on, allocation between principal and income . . . 11-2.1(e)(6), (9)(D)

Merger or consolidation, shares issued by successor to trust estate, allocation between principal and income . . . 11-2.1(e)(5)

National securities exchange

Defined . . . 9-1.8(b)

Trust created by for members of, no violation of rule against perpetuities . . . 9-1.8(a)

Person as corporation . . . 1-2.12

Reorganization, shares issued by successor to trust estate, allocation between principal and income . . . 11-2.1(e)(5)

Stock of (See STOCKS AND SECURITIES)

Successor letters testamentary and waiver of process, renunciation of . . . Form P-16; Form SLT-3

COSTS AND ALLOWANCES

Accounts of fiduciaries, judicial settlement, award of attorneys' fees and expenses to fiduciary, power of court . . . 2302

Amount of

Decree or order, inclusion in . . . 2301

Fixing amount, power of court

Generally . . . 2301

Dollar limits specified . . . 2302

Appeals, award of costs of (See APPEALS (GENERALLY))

Attorneys' fees (See ATTORNEYS' FEES)

COSTS AND ALLOWANCES—Cont.

Award of

Any party, award to on motion, dollar limitation . . . 2302

Appeals, costs of (See APPEALS (GENERALLY), subhead: Costs of appeal, award of)

Contested proceedings, award in decree . . . 2302

Discretion of court . . . 2301

Motion, award to any party on, dollar limitation . . . 2302

Reservation pending expiration of period for appeal or final determination of appeal, court's power to direct . . . 2301

Uncontested proceedings, award in decree for attorneys' fees to petitioner or party, dollar limitation on . . . 2302

Construction of will, proceeding for or appeal in proceeding; award of costs in, power of court . . . 2302; 2304

Court personnel, expenses for travel required for legal purposes . . . 2404

Payment of . . . 2301; 2304

Real property disposition, proceeding for (See REAL PROPERTY DISPOSITIONS)

Security for costs, furnishing of . . . 2303

Trustee, review of reasonableness of costs of delegation by . . . 2115

COUNSEL FEES (See ATTORNEYS' FEES)

COUNTIES

Board of supervisors

Appropriations by for Surrogate's Court personnel . . . 2605

Public administrators, supervisors' functions with respect to; certain counties outside New York City

Bond, fixing amount of . . . 1203

Salary, fixing amount of . . . 1207

Staff and offices, provision for . . . 1206

Clerks (See COUNTY CLERKS)

Court (See COUNTY COURTS)

Guardian's account, defect in . . . 1722

New York City, appointment and removal of personnel by Surrogate's Court in counties within . . . 2606

Obligations and securities of counties within and outside state, investment in, power of fiduciary . . . 11-2.2

Records of Surrogate's Court, expense of keeping, charge against county . . . 2501

Temporary court reporter, compensation of, charge against county . . . 2607

[References are to SCPA and EPTL; if number contains dash (-), it refers to EPTL. Other references are preceded by the following abbreviations: Form–Official Forms; R–Court Rules; Tax L.–New York State Tax Law; MHL–Mental Hygiene Law; GOL–General Obligations Law; Pub. Health L.–Public Health Law.]

[References are to SCPA and EPTL; if number contains dash (-), it refers to EPTL. Other references are preceded by the following abbreviations: Form–Official Forms; R–Court Rules; Tax L.–New York State Tax Law; MHL–Mental Hygiene Law; GOL–General Obligations Law; Pub. Health L.–Public Health Law.]

COURTS—Cont.
Disqualification of judge . . . 2604
Referees, appointment of personnel as
 . . . 506(6)
Terms . . . R 207.2

CPLR (GENERALLY) (See CIVIL PRACTICE LAW AND RULES (CPLR))

CREDITORS OF DECEDENT (See also DEBTS OWED DECEDENT)
Generally . . . 103(11)
Accounting by decedent's fiduciary, petition for, right to file
 Generally . . . 2205
 Temporary administrator, accounting by
 . . . 908
Action to enforce debt of decedent against distributees or testamentary beneficiaries (See DEBTS OF DECEDENT)
Acts or property dispositions by decedent in fraud of creditors' rights
 Disaffirmance of . . . 13-3.6
 Employee benefit plan beneficiaries, rights of, limitation on . . . 13-3.2
 Insurance policy beneficiaries, rights of, limitation on . . . 13-3.2
 Setting aside of, action by insolvent decedent's creditor . . . 13-3.6
 United States savings bonds, nontransferable, payees' rights, limitation on . . . 13-3.1
Administrator's qualification within specific time period, petition for, right to file . . . 1006
Assignee for benefit of creditors (See ASSIGNEE FOR BENEFIT OF CREDITORS)
Bond of administrator, temporary administrator or administrator c.t.a., amount of, determination by amount of creditors' claims . . . 805
Business of decedent, discontinuance and winding up, petition for, right to file . . . 2108
Claims against decedents' estates, presentation and processing (See CLAIMS AGAINST ESTATES)
Decedent as "creditor," payment of certain debts without administration, small estates
 . . . 1310
Defined
 Generally . . . 103(11)
 SCPA § 1310, for purposes of . . . 1310
Executor's qualification within specific time period, petition for, right to file . . . 1416
Fraud on (See subhead: Acts or property dispositions by decedent in fraud of creditors' rights)
Letters of administration, petition for
 Filing of, creditor's right . . . 1002

CREDITORS OF DECEDENT (See also DEBTS OWED DECEDENT)—Cont.
Letters of administration, petition for—Cont.
 Service of process on creditors, requirement
 . . . 1003
 Temporary letters, right to file . . . 902
Miscellaneous proceedings, authorization for commencement of . . . 2101
Non-domiciliary decedent's creditors
 Absence of domiciliary creditors, grounds for issuance of ancillary letters without bond
 . . . 1608
 Petition for ancillary probate or ancillary letters, right to file . . . 1609
 Service of process on, requirement; petition for ancillary probate or ancillary letters
 . . . 1609
Notice to directing filing of claims against estate (See CLAIMS AGAINST ESTATES)
Persons interested, no status as . . . 103(39)
Powers of appointment, donee's creditors, rights in appointive property . . . 10-7.1 *et seq.*
Probate of will, right to file petition for
 . . . 1403
Property disposition to one person for consideration paid by another . . . 7-1.3
Real property of decedent
 Disposition of
 Proceeding for, service of process on creditor's requirement . . . 1904
 Purchase of property by creditor, credit on bid for amount of debt . . . 1915
 Execution against, leave of court for
 . . . 1812
Real property trust for benefit of, duration
 . . . 7-1.8
Revocation of letters for disqualification or misconduct, petition for . . . 711
Service of process on
 Domiciliary creditors of non-domiciliary, service on, requirement; petition for ancillary probate or ancillary letters . . . 1609
 Letters of administration, petition for, service on creditors, requirement . . . 1003
 More than 25 creditors, method . . . 307
 Public administrators' power . . . 1123; 1214
 Real property of decedent, proceeding for disposition of . . . 1904
Surviving spouse's right of election to take against will, no effect on creditors' rights
 . . . 5-1.1
Trustee's creditors, protection of, reliance on trustee's apparent ownership of property
 . . . 7-3.2

CREDITORS OF DECEDENT (See also DEBTS OWED DECEDENT)—Cont.

Trusts
Beneficiaries of, persons furnishing "necessaries" to, rights to obtain information on beneficiaries . . . 7-3.5
Creator's creditors, disposition in trust as void against . . . 7-3.1
Income of as subject to creditors' claims . . . 7-3.4
Unknown name or whereabouts, payment of amount due into court . . . 2223
Voluntary administrator's liability to . . . 1308

CREDIT UNIONS

Gifts to minors; financial institution, status as . . . 7-4.8
Money payable to decedent's estate or designated beneficiary . . . 1310
Small estate funds deposited in estate account; duty of voluntary administrator . . . 1307

CREMATION (See CREMATORIES)

CREMATORIES

Charitable trusts for
Authorization of . . . 8-1.3(a)
Rules governing trust disposition . . . 8-1.3(b) *et seq.*
Disposition of remains
Generally . . . Pub. Health L. 4202(1)
Cadavers, preservation of . . . Pub. Health L. 4202(3)
Cremated remains defined . . . Pub. Health L. 4202(2)
Funeral services . . . Pub. Health L. 4202(4)
Veterans . . . Pub. Health L. 4203

CURATOR

Fiduciary, status as . . . 1-2.7
Guardian of minor, status as; gifts to minors . . . 7-4.9
Legal representative, status as; gifts to minors . . . 7-4.9
"Personal representative," no status as . . . 1-2.13

CURTESY

Real property in decedents' estate; disposition to pay estate obligations or distributive shares
Generally . . . 1918
Purchase contract held by decedent, sale of part interest in . . . 1917

CUSTODIANS OF GIFTS TO MINORS (See GIFTS TO MINORS)

CUSTODY PROCEEDINGS

Indigent parent, assignment of counsel for . . . 407
Native American child, verification of status of . . . R 207.59
Uniform Rules for Surrogate's Court (See UNIFORM RULES FOR SURROGATE'S COURT)

CY PRES DOCTRINE

Charitable dispositions . . . 8-1.1

D

DAMAGES

Wrongful death (See WRONGFUL DEATH ACTIONS)

DEATH

Community property (See COMMUNITY PROPERTY)
Intestate's death, establishment in proceeding for letters of administration . . . 1004
Presumption from 5-year absence . . . 2-1.7(a)
Simultaneous death, disposition of property where . . . 2-1.6(b)
Transfer-on-Death Security Registration Act (See TRANSFER-ON-DEATH SECURITY REGISTRATION ACT)

DEATH ACTIONS (See WRONGFUL DEATH ACTIONS)

DEATH BENEFITS

Certification of checks
Notification of State Tax Commission . . . R 360.8(c)
Remaining balances; form . . . R 360.8(d)
Without estate tax waiver . . . R 360.8(a), (b)
Employee benefits
Generally . . . 1310
Beneficiaries, designation of
Generally . . . 1310
Requirements . . . 13-3.2(d)
Revocability, no effect on beneficiaries' rights . . . 13-3.2(b)
Beneficiaries, rights of . . . 13-3.2(a)
Benefits payable as "debt" owed decedent; payment of certain debts without administration; small estates . . . 1310

[References are to SCPA and EPTL; if number contains dash (-), it refers to EPTL. Other references are preceded by the following abbreviations: Form–Official Forms; R–Court Rules; Tax L.–New York State Tax Law; MHL–Mental Hygiene Law; GOL–General Obligations Law; Pub. Health L.–Public Health Law.]

DEATH BENEFITS—Cont.

Employee benefits—Cont.

Pension or profit-sharing plans

Coverage after June 30, 1978 . . . R 360.5(a)(1)

Coverage before July 1, 1978 . . . R 360.5(a)(2)

Notice of payment of death benefit; form . . . R 360.5(c)

Surviving spouse, payment to . . . R 360.5(a)(3)

Value of interest, computation of . . . R 360.5(b)

Persons entitled to receive benefits

Defined . . . 13-3.2(c)

Rights of . . . 13-3.2(a)

Trust created by employer

Accumulation of income, time limit on, exception to . . . 9-2.1(d)

Rule against perpetuities, no violation of . . . 9-1.6

Trust established to receive benefits payable under plan, testamentary disposition to trustee, rules governing . . . 3-3.7

DEATH CERTIFICATE

Filing requirements

Uniform Rules for Surrogate's Court . . . R 207.15

Voluntary administrator of small estates; settlement without administration . . . 1304

Omission or redaction of confidential personal information in . . . R 207.64

DEATH TAXES (See ESTATE TAX (GENERALLY); ESTATE TAX, STATE)

DEBTS (GENERALLY)

Continuation of business, fiduciary action for . . . 2108

Debtor defined . . . 1310

Defined . . . 1310

Gifts to minors, transfers by obligors as . . . 7-6.7

Non-domiciliary infant's debts to domiciliary

Allegation in foreign guardian's petition for ancillary letters of guardianship . . . 1716

Condition to issuance of ancillary letters of guardianship to foreign guardian . . . 1717

Furnishing of security for . . . 1716; 1717

Payment of . . . 1716; 1717

Small estates, payment of certain debts without administration, . . . 1310

DEBTS OF DECEDENT

Action on debt

Commencement of; effect on order of payment of debts . . . 1811

Enforcement action (See subhead: Enforcement action by creditors)

Judgment obtained

Execution against real property of decedent, leave of court for . . . 1812

Order of payment of debts, effect on . . . 1811

Pendency at time of final accounting . . . 2217

Temporary administrator, action against . . . 905

Adjustment of, letters limited to . . . 702

Assets of estate chargeable with . . . 13-1.3

Assumption by personal representative, writing requirement . . . 13-2.1

Bill payment, priority of . . . 1811

Bonds; priority of payment . . . 1811

Claims against estates (See CLAIMS AGAINST ESTATES)

Claims for (See CLAIMS AGAINST ESTATES)

Compromise or compounding of debts by fiduciary . . . 1813

Contract by personal representative to assume debt, writing requirement . . . 13-2.1

Creditors of decedent (See CREDITORS OF DECEDENT)

Decrees entered against decedent; priority of payment . . . 1811

Discharge of, letters limited to . . . 702

Distributees' liability for

Conditions to . . . 12-1.1(b)

Enforcement action against distributees (See subhead: Enforcement action by creditors)

Extent of . . . 12-1.1(a); 12-1.3(a)

Order of liability . . . 12-1.2

Dividends payable to secured creditors of insolvent estate; priority of payment . . . 1811

Enforcement action by creditors

Contribution

Judgment debtor's right to . . . 12-1.3(b)(2)

Persons liable for, impleader, right of defendant . . . 12-2.2

Failure to present claim to decedent's personal representative, no bar to action . . . 12-2.1

Indemnity

Judgment debtor's right to . . . 12-1.3(b)(1)

[References are to SCPA and EPTL; if number contains dash (-), it refers to EPTL. Other references are preceded by the following abbreviations: Form–Official Forms; R–Court Rules; Tax L.–New York State Tax Law; MHL–Mental Hygiene Law; GOL–General Obligations Law; Pub. Health L.–Public Health Law.]

DEBTS OF DECEDENT—Cont.
Enforcement action by creditors—Cont.
   Indemnity—Cont.
      Persons liable for, impleader, right of defendant . . . 12-2.2
   Joint or several action . . . 12-2.2
   Judgment obtained
      Bona fide purchaser from distributee or beneficiary, title of, effect on . . . 12-2.5
      Contribution, judgment debtor's right to . . . 12-1.3(b)(2)
      Effect . . . 12-2.4
      Indemnity, judgment debtor's right to . . . 12-1.3(b)(1)
Fiduciary, debt allegedly owed to
   Contested claims, method of settlement . . . 1805
   Payment
      Priority of payment . . . 1811
      Proof and allowance by court as condition to . . . 1805
      Petition for permission to pay . . . 1805
      Statute of limitations period, cases for suspension of . . . 1805
Judgments and decrees entered against decedent; priority of payment . . . 1811
Life insurance proceeds received by trustee, chargeability against, extent . . . 13-3.3
Matured debt; priority of payment . . . 1811
Non-domiciliary-decedent's debts to domiciliary, payment by ancillary fiduciary on direction of court . . . 1610
Notes; priority of payment . . . 1811
Order of liability . . . 12-1.2
Payment of
   Estate's duration or vesting contingent on . . . 9-1.3(d)
   Priority of payment . . . 1811
   Voluntary administrator's duty as to . . . 1307
Priority of payment . . . 1811
Real property taxes; priority of payment . . . 1811
Rents due or accruing on leases held by decedent; priority of payment . . . 1811
Satisfaction of
   Generally . . . 2217
   Real property disposition as method (See REAL PROPERTY DISPOSITIONS)
Sealed instruments; priority of payment . . . 1811
Secured debt; priority of payment . . . 1811
Securities payable to beneficiary . . . 1310

DEBTS OF DECEDENT—Cont.
Settlement of . . . 702
State law, debts entitled to preference under . . . 1811
Testamentary beneficiaries, liability for
   Condition to . . . 12-1.1(b)
   Enforcement action against testamentary beneficiaries (See subhead: Enforcement action by creditors)
   Extent of . . . 12-1.1(a); 12-1.3(a)
   Order of liability . . . 12-1.2
Trusts
   Life insurance proceeds received by trustee, chargeability of debts against, extent . . . 13-3.3
   Principal of trust, debts as charge against . . . 11-2.1(d)
Unliquidated demands and accounts; priority of payment . . . 1811
Unmatured debt, payment of
   Claim disputed or rejected . . . 2217
   Creditor's refusal to accept payment with rebate of legal interest . . . 2217
   Priority of payment . . . 1811
   Real property disposition, proceeds of, reservation of sufficient funds for payment . . . 1916

DEBTS OWED DECEDENT (See also DEBTS (GENERALLY))
Compromise or compounding of by fiduciary . . . 1813
"Debt," defined . . . 1310
Discharge or disposition of claim by will . . . 13-1.2
Executor, debts owed by . . . 13-1.2
Mortgages, debts secured by, classification as personal property . . . 13-1.1(a)(7)
Non-domiciliary decedent, debt owed to by domiciliary . . . 208
Payment, factors affecting . . . 1310
Personal property in decedent's estate, classification of certain debts as . . . 13-1.1
Real property sales contracts, money unpaid on, classification as personal property . . . 13-1.1(a)(7)
Rents accrued at time of decedent's death, classification as personal property . . . 13-1.1(a)(6)
Small estates, settlement without court administration (See also SMALL ESTATES)
   Discharge of debtor . . . 1305
   Eligibility to receive money . . . 1310

[References are to SCPA and EPTL; if number contains dash (-), it refers to EPTL. Other references are preceded by the following abbreviations: Form–Official Forms; R–Court Rules; Tax L.–New York State Tax Law; MHL–Mental Hygiene Law; GOL–General Obligations Law; Pub. Health L.–Public Health Law.]

[References are to SCPA and EPTL; if number contains dash (-), it refers to EPTL. Other references are preceded by the following abbreviations: Form–Official Forms; R–Court Rules; Tax L.–New York State Tax Law; MHL–Mental Hygiene Law; GOL–General Obligations Law; Pub. Health L.–Public Health Law.]

Index

[References are to SCPA and EPTL; if number contains dash (-), it refers to EPTL. Other references are preceded by the following abbreviations: Form–Official Forms; R–Court Rules; Tax L.–New York State Tax Law; MHL–Mental Hygiene Law; GOL–General Obligations Law; Pub. Health L.–Public Health Law.]

[References are to SCPA and EPTL; if number contains dash (-), it refers to EPTL. Other references are preceded by the following abbreviations: Form–Official Forms; R–Court Rules; Tax L.–New York State Tax Law; MHL–Mental Hygiene Law; GOL–General Obligations Law; Pub. Health L.–Public Health Law.]

DISABILITY, PERSONS UNDER—Cont.
Committee of
    Construction-of-will action, appeals in
        . . . 2304
    Contested probate proceeding . . . 2302
Controversies between claimants to estate affect-
    ing, compromise of, Surrogate's Court ap-
    proval, procedure . . . 2106
Defined . . . 103(40)
Guardians *ad litem,* qualifications and duties of
    . . . 404
Guardians for personal needs and property man-
    agement under Mental Hygiene Law (See
    GUARDIANS UNDER ARTICLE 81)
Incapacitated person, death of
    Administrative costs, liens and debts
        . . . MHL 81.44(e)
    Definitions
        Notice of claim . . . MHL 81.44(a)(4)
        Personal representative . . . MHL
            81.44(a)(2)
        Public administrator . . . MHL
            81.44(a)(3)
        Statement of assets . . . MHL 81.44(a)(4)
        Statement of death . . . MHL 81.44(a)(1)
    Final report, filing of . . . MHL 81.44(f)
    Guardian duties . . . MHL 81.44(c)
    Property to guardian, delivery of . . . MHL
        81.44(d)
    Removal of guardian, petition for . . . MHL
        81.44(g)
    Service of notice – certified mail . . . MHL
        81.44(b)
Infants
    Generally (See INFANTS)
    Guardians (See GUARDIANS OF INFANTS)
Intellectually disabled persons (See DEVELOP-
    MENTALLY DISABLED PERSONS)
Mental Hygiene Law Article 81, guardians ap-
    pointed under (See GUARDIANS UNDER
    ARTICLE 81)
Payment to
    Fiduciary powers . . . 11-1.1(b)(19)
    Shares of stock . . . 7-5.3; 2220
Prisoners as . . . 103(40)
Supplemental needs trusts established for
    . . . 7-1.12

DISCLAIMER (See TESTAMENTARY DISPO-
    SITIONS)

DISCOVERY
Against fiduciary
    Generally . . . 2102

DISCOVERY—Cont.
Against fiduciary—Cont.
    Court order to supply information, effect of
        noncompliance with . . . 719
By fiduciary
    Generally . . . 2103
    Delivery of property of fiduciary, direction
        for, power of court . . . 2104
    Disposition of property, petitioner entitled to
        payment of proceeds . . . 2104
    Examination of respondent . . . 2104
    Interim decree, grounds for . . . 2104
    Order, service of . . . 2103
    Person other than respondent claiming interest
        in property . . . 2103
    Possession of property denied, effect of
        . . . 2104
    Title, claim of . . . 2104

DISPOSITION (See also specific subject head-
    ings, e.g., REAL PROPERTY DISPOSI-
    TIONS; TESTAMENTARY DISPOSITIONS)
Defined . . . 1-2.4
Pecuniary disposition defined . . . 2-1.9

**DISQUALIFICATION OF SURVIVING
    SPOUSE**
Annulment of marriage . . . 5-1.2
Intestate succession
    Generally . . . 4-1.5
    Distribution of estate, effect on . . . 4-1.4(b);
        4-1.4(c)
    Grounds for . . . 5-1.2
Right of election (See RIGHT OF ELECTION)

DISTRIBUTEES
Defined . . . 1-2.5; 103(14)
Determination of . . . 2225
Incarcerated individual or prisoner, notice of
    legacy or distributive share payable to
    . . . 2222-a
Intestate succession (See INTESTATE SUCCES-
    SION)
Petition statement of relationship of parties
    . . . R 207.16(b)
Presumptive distributee defined . . . 103(42)

DISTRIBUTION OF ESTATE
Advancement, adjustments for (See ADVANCE-
    MENTS)
Decree for . . . 2215
Time limits . . . R 207.42

[References are to SCPA and EPTL; if number contains dash (-), it refers to EPTL. Other references are preceded by the following abbreviations: Form–Official Forms; R–Court Rules; Tax L.–New York State Tax Law; MHL–Mental Hygiene Law; GOL–General Obligations Law; Pub. Health L.–Public Health Law.]

DIVIDENDS (See CORPORATIONS, subhead: Distributions to trust estate, allocation between principal and income)

DIVORCE (See also ANNULMENT OF MAR-RIAGE)

Decree, copy of . . . R 207.50

Marriage after . . . 8

Registration of security, revocation of . . . 5-1.4(c)

Remarriage to testator, restoration of rights to former spouse . . . 5-1.4(a)

Will executed prior to, provision in for former spouse, revocation . . . 5-1.4

DOMICILE

Defined . . . 103(15)

DOMICILIARY (See also NONDOMICILI-ARY)

Defined . . . 103(16)

Jurisdiction of Surrogate's Court over estate of, effect . . . 205

DONATE LIFE REGISTRY

Generally . . . Pub. Health L. 4310

DO-NOT-RESUSCITATE ORDERS

Attending physician's opinion of capacity

  Certification of concurring physician . . . Pub. Health L. 2963(3)(b)

  Developmental disability, lack of patient's capacity due to . . . Pub. Health L. 2963(3)(c)

  Initial determination . . . Pub. Health L. 2963(2)

  Mental illness, lack of patient's capacity due to . . . Pub. Health L. 2963(3)(b)

  Secondary physician, concurring opinion of . . . Pub. Health L. 2963(3)(a)

  Specialized training of physician . . . Pub. Health L. 2963(3)(c)

Child patients (See subhead: Minor patients, decision-making on behalf of)

Commissioner of health

  Publication of rights . . . Pub. Health L. 2979

  Regulations . . . Pub. Health L. 2978

Criminal prosecution, protection from . . . Pub. Health L. 2974

Definitions . . . Pub. Health L. 2961

Dispute mediation system

  Authority to settle dispute . . . Pub. Health L. 2972(5)

  Governed by . . . Pub. Health L. 2972(1)(b)

DO-NOT-RESUSCITATE ORDERS—Cont.

Dispute mediation system—Cont.

  Order in dispute, effect on . . . Pub. Health L. 2972(3); Pub. Health L. 2972(4)(b)

  Purpose of . . . Pub. Health L. 2972(1)(a)

  Usage, capacity of . . . Pub. Health L. 2972(2)

Execution of patient's decision

  Correctional facility, patient in or transferred from . . . Pub. Health L. 2964(3)

  Obtainment of consent . . . Pub. Health L. 2964(1)(a); Pub. Health L. 2964(1)(b)

  Patient's medical chart

    Physician's evidence supporting order . . . Pub. Health L. 2964(2)(d)

    Proceed with order, decision to . . . Pub. Health L. 2964(2)(c)(i)

    Secondary physician, transfer of patient to . . . Pub. Health L. 2964(2)(c)(ii)

    Witnesses; number required . . . Pub. Health L. 2964(2)(a)

    Written requests . . . Pub. Health L. 2964(2)(b)

Expansion of existing equipment, hospital obligation . . . Pub. Health L. 2962(4)

Foreseeable risks, physician's obligation to provide information regarding . . . Pub. Health L. 2962(3)

Health care agents

  Authority of . . . Pub. Health L. 2962(5)(b)

  Conflicting provisions, Article 29C's precedence over . . . Pub. Health L. 2962(5)(a)

Immunity from criminal prosecution and civil liability . . . Pub. Health L. 2974; Pub. Health L. 2994-gg

Insurance and health care services, effect on . . . Pub. Health L. 2975

Interinstitutional transfers

  Cancellation of prior order upon notification . . . Pub. Health L. 2971(2)

  Continuance of prior order . . . Pub. Health L. 2971(1)

  Hospital do not resuscitate orders . . . Pub. Health L. 2971(3)

  Nonhospital do not resuscitate orders . . . Pub. Health L. 2994-ff

Judicially approved orders . . . Pub. Health L. 2976

Judicial review . . . Pub. Health L. 2973

Lawfulness of order . . . Pub. Health L. 2962(2)

Legislative findings . . . Pub. Health L. 2960

Medical facilities (See MEDICAL FACILITIES)

[References are to SCPA and EPTL; if number contains dash (-), it refers to EPTL. Other references are preceded by the following abbreviations: Form–Official Forms; R–Court Rules; Tax L.–New York State Tax Law; MHL–Mental Hygiene Law; GOL–General Obligations Law; Pub. Health L.–Public Health Law.]

[References are to SCPA and EPTL; if number contains dash (-), it refers to EPTL. Other references are preceded by the following abbreviations: Form–Official Forms; R–Court Rules; Tax L.–New York State Tax Law; MHL–Mental Hygiene Law; GOL–General Obligations Law; Pub. Health L.–Public Health Law.]

DO-NOT-RESUSCITATE ORDERS—Cont.
Surrogate decision-making—Cont.
Persons responsible . . . Pub. Health L. 2965(2)(a)
Requirements . . . Pub. Health L. 2965(1)(b)
Written consent . . . Pub. Health L. 2965(4)(a)

DOWER
Real property in decedents' estates . . . 1918

E

EDUCATIONAL INSTITUTIONS
Generally . . . 8-1.2
Inter vivos gifts
Alteration, amendment or modification of gift . . . 8-1.3(e)
Authorization . . . 8-1.3(a)
Buildings, power of creator as to . . . 8-1.3(b)(6)
Control of trust property by creator or surviving spouse . . . 8-1.3(e)
Creator of trust, powers and rights of . . . 8-1.3(b), (d), (e)
Income from trust property, right to . . . 8-1.3(g)
Legality of gift . . . 8-1.3(g)
Management of property, rules for . . . 8-1.3(b)(4)
Name of institution . . . 8-1.3(b)(2)
Nature of institution . . . 8-1.3(b)(1)
Possession of trust property, right to . . . 8-1.3(g)
Purpose of institution . . . 8-1.3(b)(1)
Title to trust property . . . 8-1.3(g)
Trustees, accounting requirements of
Generally . . . 8-1.3(b)(3)
Capacity to sue or defend on behalf of institution . . . 8-1.3(c)
Creator as trustee during his lifetime . . . 8-1.3(d)
Powers and duties of . . . 8-1.3(b)(3)
Successor trustee, appointment of . . . 8-1.3(b)(5)
Surviving spouse of creator as trustee during lifetime . . . 8-1.3(d)
Trust instrument . . . 8-1.3(f)

ELECTIVE SHARE OF SURVIVING SPOUSE (See RIGHT OF ELECTION)

ELECTRONIC FILING
Authorized program in use of electronic means . . . 107

ELECTRONIC FILING—Cont.
Uniform Rules for Surrogate's Court (See UNIFORM RULES FOR SURROGATE'S COURT, subhead: Electronic filing)

EMERGENCY MEDICAL SERVICES
Nonhospital orders not to resuscitate
DNR bracelet
Description of . . . R 800.90(b)
Right to sell . . . R 800.90(c)
"Emergency medical services personnel" defined . . . R 405.43(b)(7)
Issuance of . . . R 800.90(a)

EMINENT DOMAIN (See also CONDEMNATION OF PROPERTY IN DECEDENTS' ESTATES)
Trust property taken under, proceeds from as principal of trust . . . 11-2.1

EMPLOYEE BENEFITS
Death benefits (See DEATH BENEFITS)

EPTL
Definitions for purposes of . . . 1-2.1 to 1-2.18
Estates, Powers and Trusts Law cited as EPTL . . . 1-1.1
References, method of citing . . . 1-1.2
Sections of, method of citing . . . 1-1.1
Words, rules governing use of . . . 1-1.3

ESTATES (GENERALLY)
Absentees (See ABSENTEES)
Classification of
Number of owners as basis . . . 6-2.1
Time of enjoyment and creation as basis . . . 6-3.1
Compromise of controversies, application for . . . 2106
Decedents' estates (See DECEDENTS' ESTATES)
Defined . . . 1-2.6; 103(19)
Digital assets, administration of (See DIGITAL ASSETS, ADMINISTRATION OF)
Persons interested in . . . 315
Small estates (See SMALL ESTATES)

ESTATES IN POSSESSION
Defined . . . 6-4.1

ESTATES IN PROPERTY (GENERALLY)
Classification of, duration as basis . . . 6-1.1
Definitions . . . 6-4.1 *et seq.*
"Estate," defined . . . 1-2.6

ESTATE TAX (GENERALLY)
Abatement, order of . . . 13-1.3

[References are to SCPA and EPTL; if number contains dash (-), it refers to EPTL. Other references are preceded by the following abbreviations: Form–Official Forms; R–Court Rules; Tax L.–New York State Tax Law; MHL–Mental Hygiene Law; GOL–General Obligations Law; Pub. Health L.–Public Health Law.]

[References are to SCPA and EPTL; if number contains dash (-), it refers to EPTL. Other references are preceded by the following abbreviations: Form–Official Forms; R–Court Rules; Tax L.–New York State Tax Law; MHL–Mental Hygiene Law; GOL–General Obligations Law; Pub. Health L.–Public Health Law.]

[References are to SCPA and EPTL; if number contains dash (-), it refers to EPTL. Other references are preceded by the following abbreviations: Form–Official Forms; R–Court Rules; Tax L.–New York State Tax Law; MHL–Mental Hygiene Law; GOL–General Obligations Law; Pub. Health L.–Public Health Law.]

[References are to SCPA and EPTL; if number contains dash (-), it refers to EPTL. Other references are preceded by the following abbreviations: Form–Official Forms; R–Court Rules; Tax L.–New York State Tax Law; MHL–Mental Hygiene Law; GOL–General Obligations Law; Pub. Health L.–Public Health Law.]

ESTATE TAX, STATE—Cont.

Returns by executor—Cont.

Federal return, requirements for . . . . Tax L. 977(b)

Filing of . . . R 207.43

Identifying numbers, requirements for . . . Tax L. 977(c)

Joint fiduciaries . . . Tax L. 971

Nonresidents . . . Tax L. 971

Place for filing . . . Tax L. 972(b)

Residents . . . Tax L. 971

Secrecy requirements (See subhead: Secrecy requirement, penalties for violation of)

Signing of returns and other documents

Generally . . . Tax L. 973(a)

Certifications . . . Tax L. 973(c)

Signature filing with Surrogate's Court . . . Tax L. 973(b)

Simultaneous filing with Surrogate's Court . . . Tax L. 972(c)

Tax as debt . . . Tax L. 971

Time for filing . . . Tax L. 972(a)

Searches and certificates, fees for . . . R 362.1(a), (b)

Secrecy requirement, penalties for violation of

Generally . . . Tax L. 994(a)

Filing of returns . . . Tax L. 994(d)

Investigations by committees of U.S. Congress, cooperation with . . . Tax L. 994(b-1)

Other jurisdictions, cooperation with . . . Tax L. 994(b)

Payments to depository banks . . . Tax L. 994(d)

Procedure and preservation of returns . . . Tax L. 994(c)

U.S. Congress investigations, cooperation with . . . Tax L. 994(b-1)

Surrogates, administrative expenses for . . . Tax L. 983

Surviving spouse not United States citizen, disposition to . . . Tax L. 951

Tangible personal property

Defined . . . Tax L. 951-a(c)

Resident's gross estate reduced by value of property outside state . . . Tax L. 954

Tangible personal property defined . . . Tax L. 951-a(c)

Taxable estate defined . . . Tax L. 953

Taxpayer defined . . . Tax L. 951-a(e)

Victims of Terrorism Tax Relief Act of 2001, federal . . . Tax L. 951

EXECUTION OF WILLS (See WILLS (GENERALLY))

EXECUTORS (See also ADMINISTRATORS; FIDUCIARIES (GENERALLY))

Accounting by

Generally . . . Form No.12

Trusts . . . Form No.14

Attorney-executor, compensation of . . . 2307-a

Bonding requirements

Absence of . . . 710

Amount of bond . . . 801

Degree of responsibility required of fiduciary, absence of . . . 710

Domiciliary becoming non-domiciliary after issuance of letters, objection based on . . . 710

Exemption, estate less than $3,000 . . . 801

Non-domiciliary status, objection to grant of letters based on . . . 710

Removal of estate property as grounds . . . 710

Trustee-executor . . . 806

Value of estate . . . 801

Compensation of

Generally . . . 2302; 2307

Corporation as executor . . . 2307

Multiple executors . . . 2307

Corporation as, commission for . . . 2307

Costs of actions, award of, right to

Construction-of-will action, appeals in . . . 2304

Contested probate proceeding . . . 2302

Debts owed to testator . . . 13-1.2

Deeds, mortgages or leases executed by less than all qualifying executors . . . 11-1.4

Defined . . . 103(20)

Degree of responsibility required of fiduciary, absence of

Grounds for suspension, modification or revocation of letters . . . 711; 719

Objection to grant of letters based on, grounds for furnishing of bond as condition to obtaining letters . . . 710

Digital assets, administration of (See DIGITAL ASSETS, ADMINISTRATION OF)

Estate tax, state (See ESTATE TAX, STATE)

In-kind distributions by, transfer in trust of pecuniary amount . . . 2-1.9

Joint income tax return to be filed by, joinder in, power of other fiduciary . . . 11-1.1

Less than all qualifying executors, powers of . . . 11-1.4

[References are to SCPA and EPTL; if number contains dash (-), it refers to EPTL. Other references are preceded by the following abbreviations: Form–Official Forms; R–Court Rules; Tax L.–New York State Tax Law; MHL–Mental Hygiene Law; GOL–General Obligations Law; Pub. Health L.–Public Health Law.]

EXECUTORS (See also ADMINISTRATORS; FIDUCIARIES (GENERALLY))—Cont.

Letters testamentary, issuance to (See LETTERS TESTAMENTARY)

Liability of personal representative

Generally . . . 11-4.7

Nonliability for actions of predecessor executor . . . 1506

Multiple executors, compensation of . . . 2307

Oath and designation; official form . . . Form P-1

Powers

Generally . . . 11-1.1

In-kind distributions, making of . . . 2-1.9(b)

Limitations on . . . 11-1.7

Prior to probate . . . 11-1.3

Preliminary executor defined . . . 103(41)

Qualification of nominee within specified time period, court order for . . . 1416

Renunciation

Court order for qualification . . . 1416

Method . . . 1417

Official form . . . Form P-10

Retraction of . . . 1417

Successor executors . . . 801

Testamentary trustee and, proceeding when same person both . . . 1505

Trustee-executor

Bonding requirement

Generally . . . 806

Amount of bond . . . 801

Testamentary trustee and, proceeding when same person both . . . 720; 1505

Value of estate as effecting bonding requirement as to . . . 801

Verification, oath and designation; official form . . . Form P-1

War service, executors engaged in (See WAR SERVICE)

EXEMPTION FOR BENEFIT OF FAMILY (See FAMILY RIGHTS)

EXPENSES OF ADMINISTRATION (See ADMINISTRATION EXPENSES)

F

FAMILY EXEMPTION (See FAMILY RIGHTS)

FAMILY OF DECEDENT

Brothers and sisters of decedent (See BROTHERS AND SISTERS OF DECEDENT)

FAMILY OF DECEDENT—Cont.

Estate tax deduction or exemption based on relationship to decedent, apportionment . . . 2-1.8(c)(2)

Exemptions, property items excluded from estate assets for surviving spouse and decedent's minor children . . . 5-3.1

Issue of decedent (See ISSUE)

Parent of decedent (See PARENTS OF DECEDENT)

Property items excluded from estate assets, set aside for surviving spouse and decedent's minor children . . . 5-3.1

Rights of (See FAMILY RIGHTS)

Surviving spouse (See SURVIVING SPOUSE)

FAMILY RIGHTS (See also specific members of family)

Afterborn child (See AFTERBORN CHILDREN, subhead: Share of parents' estate, right to)

Charitable dispositions, limitations on; repealed . . . 5-3.3

Children; exemptions for benefit of minor children . . . 5-3.1

Exemption for benefit of family . . . 5-3.1

Revocatory effect of certain events after will execution . . . 5-3.2

Spouse (See SURVIVING SPOUSE)

Wrongful death of decedent, action for

Burden of proof . . . 5-4.2

Contributory negligence, trial and burden of proof for . . . 5-4.2

Damages recovered

Amount of . . . 5-4.3

Distribution of . . . 5-4.4

Personal representative, action by . . . 5-4.1

FAMILY TREE

Official form . . . Form FT-1

FEDERAL AIR TRANSPORTATION SAFETY AND SYSTEM STABILIZATION ACT

September eleventh victim compensation fund of 2001; liability of personal representative of decedent . . . 11-4.7(e)

FEES (GENERALLY)

Attorneys' fees (See ATTORNEYS' FEES)

Banks, to . . . 11-2.1(6)

Commissions (See COMMISSIONS)

Court, of (See COURT FEES)

Gifts to minors, custodians of . . . 7-6.15(b)

Registered investment advisers, to . . . 11-2.1(6)

[References are to SCPA and EPTL; if number contains dash (-), it refers to EPTL. Other references are preceded by the following abbreviations: Form–Official Forms; R–Court Rules; Tax L.–New York State Tax Law; MHL–Mental Hygiene Law; GOL–General Obligations Law; Pub. Health L.–Public Health Law.]

[References are to SCPA and EPTL; if number contains dash (-), it refers to EPTL. Other references are preceded by the following abbreviations: Form–Official Forms; R–Court Rules; Tax L.–New York State Tax Law; MHL–Mental Hygiene Law; GOL–General Obligations Law; Pub. Health L.–Public Health Law.]

FIDUCIARIES (GENERALLY)—Cont.

Donee of power during minority, status as . . . 103(21)

Estate tax, power in (See ESTATE TAX (GENERALLY))

Execution on judgment

Assets of estate insufficient to pay claims . . . 11-4.6(b), (c)

Bond for repayment of sum collected or ratable part . . . 11-4.6(c)

Exception . . . 11-4.6(a)

Money judgment against fiduciary in representative capacity . . . 11-4.6(a) *et seq.*

Order of court, contents . . . 11-4.6(b)

Predecessor obtaining in name of fiduciary . . . 11-4.6(d)

Procedure for obtaining leave of court . . . 11-4.6(b)

Falsification of facts to obtain letters . . . 711; 719

Felony conviction of . . . 719

Foreign fiduciaries

Action within state by . . . 13-3.5

Delivery of property to . . . 13-3.3

Payment to

Court order absent, effect of . . . 13-3.4

Court order directing . . . 2221

Delivery of property or . . . 13-3.3

Fraudulent acts by personal representatives, disaffirmance of . . . 13-3.6

Gifts to minors by; on or after January 1, 1997 (See UNIFORM TRANSFERS TO MINORS ACT (UTMA))

Immunity, limitations on . . . 11-1.7

Incompetent person, fiduciary as

Committee of incompetent fiduciary

Accounting for (See ACCOUNTINGS)

Compensation for services rendered to estate . . . 2207

Delivery of estate property by, court's power to order . . . 2214

Powers and rights of incompetent fiduciary . . . 2207

Insanity . . . 719

Suspension, modification or revocation of letters . . . 719

Ineligibility to serve as grounds for petition for suspension, modification or revocation of letters . . . 711

Information on estate assets or affairs, discovery as to, actions by or against fiduciary (See DISCOVERY)

Insanity as grounds for suspension, modification or revocation of letters . . . 719

FIDUCIARIES (GENERALLY)—Cont.

Investment of trust funds (See FIDUCIARIES' POWERS)

Joinder

Authorization . . . 11-4.2

Costs, personal liability for, separate docketing and execution . . . 11-4.3

Judgment for plaintiff

Personal and representative liability of fiduciary . . . 11-4.2

Personal judgment, separate docketing and execution . . . 11-4.3

Joint fiduciaries . . . 1001

Liability of

Generally . . . 808

Assets received in another fiduciary capacity, liability for . . . 808

Disaffirmance of; writing . . . 10-10.7

Minority fiduciary when three or more appointed . . . 11-1.1

Name or whereabouts of heir unknown, payment of funds into court as discharge of liability . . . 2224

Personal representative . . . 11-4.7

Reasonable care, diligence and prudence, release from as contrary to public policy . . . 11-1.7

Sale of property, compliance with court's authorization of as relief from liability . . . 2107

Transmission of property authorized, will subject to contest of probate in testator's domicile . . . 1603

Misconduct as grounds for suspension, modification or revocation of letters . . . 711; 719

Multiple fiduciaries

Accounting by one co-fiduciary, other co-fiduciary's power to compel . . . 2205

Action against, service of process required on one only . . . 11-4.4

Compensation of . . . 2307

Death of fiduciaries . . . 706

Revocation of letters . . . 706

Survivor to administer property of estate, no appointment of successor trustee for decedent trustee . . . 11-1.1

Nonappearance on return of process without valid excuse . . . 719

Non-domiciliary fiduciary . . . 710

Nonresident alien fiduciary . . . 2218

Oath of office . . . 708

Order permitting judgment creditor to issue execution against fiduciary . . . 602

[References are to SCPA and EPTL; if number contains dash (-), it refers to EPTL. Other references are preceded by the following abbreviations: Form–Official Forms; R–Court Rules; Tax L.–New York State Tax Law; MHL–Mental Hygiene Law; GOL–General Obligations Law; Pub. Health L.–Public Health Law.]

[References are to SCPA and EPTL; if number contains dash (-), it refers to EPTL. Other references are preceded by the following abbreviations: Form–Official Forms; R–Court Rules; Tax L.–New York State Tax Law; MHL–Mental Hygiene Law; GOL–General Obligations Law; Pub. Health L.–Public Health Law.]

FOREIGN ESTATES

Absentees, ancillary administration of . . . 1611

Ancillary administration
  Absentees . . . 1611
  Application of . . . 1616
  Domiciliary administration as condition to
    . . . 1601
  Letters (See subhead: Ancillary letters)
  Purpose of . . . 1601

Ancillary administrators
  Checklist . . . ANCA-CHK
  Conflicting or plural designations . . . 1608
  Defined . . . 103(5)
  Designation by domiciliary executor or ad-
    ministrator . . . 1608
  Fiduciaries (See subhead: Ancillary fiducia-
    ries)
  Fiduciary, status as . . . 103(5)
  Letters (See subhead: Ancillary letters)

Ancillary administrators c.t.a.
  Conflicting or plural designations, court's
    power to resolve . . . 1608
  Defined . . . 103(6)
  Designation by domiciliary executor or ad-
    ministrator . . . 1608
  Fiduciary, status as . . . 103(6)

Ancillary fiduciaries
  Bonding requirements . . . 1608
  Corporate banking institution, eligibility to
    serve . . . 1608
  Persons eligible to serve, rules governing
    . . . 1608
  Powers and duties . . . 1610
  Prior adjudication for or against domiciliary
    fiduciary, binding effect on . . . 1612
  Qualification requirements for . . . 1608

Ancillary letters
  Citation . . . Form AA-2
  Domiciliary letters, issuance and revocation
    of . . . 719
  Eligibility to receive, priority of . . . 1604;
    1607
  Issuance, grounds and procedure for
    . . . 1607
  Notice of application
    Generally . . . 1608; Form AA-3
    Affidavit of mailing . . . Form AA-3
  Petition . . . 1609; Form AA-1
  Verification, consent and designation
    . . . Form AA-1

Ancillary probate
  Checklist . . . ANCP-CHK
  Citation . . . Form AP-2

FOREIGN ESTATES—Cont.

Ancillary probate—Cont.
  Contest of will
    Domiciliary jurisdiction . . . 1603
    Effect of admission to . . . 1603
    Grounds for . . . 1602
  Court fees . . . 2402
  Domiciliary probate as basis for . . . 1602
  Notice of application
    Generally . . . 1616; Form AP-3
    Affidavit of mailing . . . Form AP-3
  Petition . . . 1609; Form AP-1
  Verification, consent and designation
    . . . Form AP-1

Claims against . . . 1608

Debts of decedent, payment of . . . 1610

Domiciliary fiduciary, prior judgments for or
  against . . . 1612

Foreign will
  Authentication method . . . 1614
  Effect . . . 3-5.1
  Interpretation . . . 3-5.1
  Original probate (See subhead: Original pro-
    bate of foreign will)
  Proof, determination of
    Generally . . . 1424
    Original probate purposes . . . 1606
    Record in court under former law
      . . . 1615
  Recording or filing authenticated copy of,
    court fees for . . . 2402
  Validity . . . 3-5.1

Law governing . . . 1613

Original probate of foreign will
  Authorization . . . 1605
  Denial in testator's domicile . . . 1605
  Domiciliary probate as bar . . . 1605
  Proof, determination of . . . 1606

Remaining assets, disposition of . . . 1610

FOREIGN NATIONS

Enemy nations, service of process on persons in
  . . . 307

National of, service of process on (See NON-
  RESIDENT ALIENS)

FOREIGN WILLS (See FOREIGN ESTATES)

FRAUD

Accounting by fiduciaries, objections to (See
  ACCOUNTINGS, subhead: Objections to accountings)

[References are to SCPA and EPTL; if number contains dash (-), it refers to EPTL. Other references are preceded by the following abbreviations: Form–Official Forms; R–Court Rules; Tax L.–New York State Tax Law; MHL–Mental Hygiene Law; GOL–General Obligations Law; Pub. Health L.–Public Health Law.]

FUNERAL EXPENSES

Assets of estate chargeable with reasonable funeral expenses . . . 13-1.3(a)(1)

Burial plots, perpetual care of . . . 103(22)

Church expenses . . . 103(22)

Definition of funeral expense . . . 103(22)

Distributees of estate, liability for . . . 12-1.1

Nonpayment effect on accounting by fiduciary . . . 2213

Payment of

    Fiduciary, commencement of proceedings to require payment of funeral expenses . . . 2102

    Infant's property used to pay for parent's funeral expenses . . . 1713

    Priority of payment . . . 1811

    Probate, payment prior to, permissibility . . . 11-1.3

    Public administrator's authority to pay . . . 1212

    Real property in estate; disposition for payment . . . 1902

    Temporary administrator appointed, direction for payment, power of court . . . 908

Principal of estate, funeral expenses charged against . . . 11-2.1(d)(1)

Social security funds, use of . . . 1311

Unemployment insurance funds, use of . . . 1311

Workmen's compensation funds, use of . . . 1311

Wrongful death, damages for, funeral expenses included in . . . 5-4.3

FUTURE INTERESTS

Alienability of . . . 6-5.1

Alternative future interests defined . . . 6-5.3

Classification . . . 6-3.2

Condition precedent, future estate subject to . . . 6-4.10

Contingency, improbability of, no effect on validity of future estate . . . 6-5.5

Creation of

    Limitations on . . . 6-3.3

    When created . . . 6-3.4

Defeat of future estate . . . 6-5.10

Defined . . . 6-4.2

Indefeasibly vested future estate . . . 6-4.7

Persons interested in the estate . . . 315

Possibility of reverter defined . . . 6-4.5

Posthumous children right to take . . . 6-5.7

Powers of appointment unexecuted preventing vesting of estate . . . 6-5.2

FUTURE INTERESTS—Cont.

Precedent estates

    Destruction of as no defeat of future estate . . . 6-5.10

    Principal of, application to income beneficiary, allowability . . . 7-1.6

Reacquisition of . . . 6-4.6

Remainders

    Cross remainders, implication of between tenants in common, limitation in will or deed as causing . . . 6-5.4

    Distributees, meaning of . . . 6-5.6

    Heirs, meaning of . . . 6-5.6

    Indestructibility of . . . 6-5.11

    Issue, meaning of . . . 6-5.6

    Life tenant, heirs or distributees right to take remainder as purchasers . . . 6-5.8

    Limitation to heirs or distributees of creator, taking as purchasers . . . 6-5.9

    Rents and profits accruing, treatment of . . . 6-5.12

    Renunciation . . . 3-3.10

    Representation of persons with, proceedings for . . . 315

    Reversions of, defined . . . 6-4.4

    Rules governing . . . 6-5.1

    Validity of future estate, no effect of improbable contingency upon . . . 6-5.5

    Vested subject to complete defeasance defined . . . 6-4.9

    Vested subject to open, defined . . . 6-4.8

G

GENERAL DISPOSITIONS

Abatement of . . . 13-1.3

Defined . . . 1-2.8

Demonstrative disposition, treatment as general disposition for abatement purposes . . . 13-1.3

GENERATION-SKIPPING TRANSFER TAX

Generally . . . Tax L. 951

Construction of wills and trusts referring to . . . 2-1.13

GENETIC CHILDREN

Intestate succession . . . 4-1.3

Testamentary dispositions . . . 11-1.5(a) *et seq.*

GESTATIONAL SURROGACY

Regulations . . . Pub. Health L. 2599-cc

GIFTS *CAUSA MORTIS*

Testamentary substitute . . . 5-1.1(b)

[References are to SCPA and EPTL; if number contains dash (-), it refers to EPTL. Other references are preceded by the following abbreviations: Form–Official Forms; R–Court Rules; Tax L.–New York State Tax Law; MHL–Mental Hygiene Law; GOL–General Obligations Law; Pub. Health L.–Public Health Law.]

[References are to SCPA and EPTL; if number contains dash (-), it refers to EPTL. Other references are preceded by the following abbreviations: Form–Official Forms; R–Court Rules; Tax L.–New York State Tax Law; MHL–Mental Hygiene Law; GOL–General Obligations Law; Pub. Health L.–Public Health Law.]

[References are to SCPA and EPTL; if number contains dash (-), it refers to EPTL. Other references are preceded by the following abbreviations: Form–Official Forms; R–Court Rules; Tax L.–New York State Tax Law; MHL–Mental Hygiene Law; GOL–General Obligations Law; Pub. Health L.–Public Health Law.]

GUARDIANS, APPOINTMENT OF—Cont.

Judicial appointments—Cont.
Disqualification . . . R 36.2(c)
Lists, use of . . . R 36.2(b)
Not applicable . . . R 36.1(b)
Notice of . . . R 36.4(b)
Procedure
  Application for appointment . . . R 36.3(a)
  Lists, establishment of and removal from . . . R 36.3(c); R 36.3(e)
  Qualifications . . . R 36.3(b)
  Reregistration . . . R 36.3(d)
Publication of . . . R 36.5
Minors (See GUARDIANS OF INFANTS)
Notice . . . Form UCS 830.1
Petitions for
  Person and property/property only, guardian of . . . Form G-2B
  Person only, guardian of . . . Form G-2A
Physician, examining
  Affidavit (certification) of . . . Form GMD-2A
  Affirmation (certification) of . . . Form GMD-2B
Psychologist, affidavit (certification) of examining . . . Form GMD-2A
Renunciation of appointment . . . Form GMD-3
Selection process . . . R 36.0
Supreme court appointing . . . 1709
UAGPPJA (See UNIFORM ADULT GUARDIANSHIP AND PROTECTIVE PROCEEDINGS JURISDICTION ACT)
Waiver of process . . . Form GMD-3

GUARDIANS FOR INCOMPETENTS

Accountability of conservator of legal life tenant . . . 2202
Accounting proceeding for lifetime trust . . . 2402(4)
Account of conservator, petition for termination of . . . 1727
Appearance by conservator for conservatee
  Generally . . . 402
  Binding notice of proceeding . . . 406
Appointment, notice of . . . Form UCS 830.1
Conservatees
  Beneficiary of estate, as, payments . . . 2220
  Conservator appearing for
    Generally . . . 401 *et seq.*
    Binding notice of proceeding . . . 406
  Conveyance of property of . . . 3-4.4
  Death of . . . 3-4.4
  Disability, as person under . . . 2220

GUARDIANS FOR INCOMPETENTS—Cont.

Conservatees—Cont.
Disposition to, renunciation of . . . 2-1.11
Distributee, as (See subhead: Distributee, conservatee as)
Fiduciary, applicability of part to . . . 2207
Injuries to . . . 2220
Legal life tenant, as; conservator's accountability . . . 2202
Life insurance proceeds, use of . . . 9-2.2
Money payable to, payments to conservator . . . 2220
Payments to
  Fiduciary powers . . . 11-1.1(b)(19)
  Injury of conservatee, to conservator upon . . . 2220
  Maximum amount by conservator without court order . . . 11-1.1(b)(19)
  Shares of stock . . . 7-5.3; 2220
Conservators
Defined . . . 11-2.2
Fees payable upon filing for proceedings . . . 2402(4)
Proceedings, filing fees payable upon filing for . . . 7-4.6
Death of conservatee, effect of . . . 3-4.4
Distributee, conservatee as
Generally . . . 1001
Letters of administration
  Generally . . . 1001(2), (6), (7); 1303; 1418
  Aliens . . . 1003(2)
  Granting of . . . 1003(2)
  Prior or equal right, renunciation or exclusion of persons having . . . 1419
Gifts to minors . . . 7-4.1
Guardians for personal needs and property management under Mental Hygiene Law (See GUARDIANS UNDER ARTICLE 81)
Injuries to conservatee, payments to conservator . . . 2220
Instruments settling accounts in part or in whole, recording or filing . . . 2202
Lack of conservator, treatment of money payable to person under substantial impairment . . . 2220
Legal representative, status as; gifts to minors . . . 7-4.1
Mental Hygiene Law Article 81, guardians appointed under (See GUARDIANS UNDER ARTICLE 81)
Money payable to conservatee, payment to conservator . . . 11-1.1(b)(19); 2220

Index

[References are to SCPA and EPTL; if number contains dash (-), it refers to EPTL. Other references are preceded by the following abbreviations: Form–Official Forms; R–Court Rules; Tax L.–New York State Tax Law; MHL–Mental Hygiene Law; GOL–General Obligations Law; Pub. Health L.–Public Health Law.]

GUARDIANS UNDER ARTICLE 81—Cont.

UAGPPJA (See UNIFORM ADULT GUARDIANSHIP AND PROTECTIVE PROCEEDINGS JURISDICTION ACT)

Vacancy in office . . . MHL 81.38

Venue . . . MHL 81.05

H

HEALTH CARE AGENTS AND PROXIES

Adult defined . . . Pub. Health L. 2980(1)

Alternate agents, designation of

    Authority of agent . . . Pub. Health L. 2981(6)(b)(i)

    Conditions set forth in proxy . . . Pub. Health L. 2981(6)(a)(iii)

    Disqualification of agent . . . Pub. Health L. 2981(6)(a)(ii)

    Original appointee, unavailability of . . . Pub. Health L. 2981(6)(a)(i)

    Record of change . . . Pub. Health L. 2981(6)(b)(ii)

Anatomical gifts, conflicts with terms of . . . Pub. Health L. 4306-a

Appointment of . . . Pub. Health L. 2981(1)(a)

Attending practitioner defined . . . Pub. Health L. 2980(2)

Authority, commencement of . . . Pub. Health L. 2981(4)

"Capacity to make health care decisions" defined . . . Pub. Health L. 2980(3)

Commissioner of health

    Publication of rights . . . Pub. Health L. 2994-u

    Regulations . . . Pub. Health L. 2993; Pub. Health L. 2994-t

Definitions . . . Pub. Health L. 2980; Pub. Health L. 2994-a; R 400.21(b)(2); R 400.21(b)(4); R 700.5(b)(2); R 700.5(b)(4)

Dispute proceedings

    Overridden agent decision . . . Pub. Health L. 2992(3)

    Removal of agent . . . Pub. Health L. 2992(2)

    Validity of proxy, determination of . . . Pub. Health L. 2992(1)

Ethics review committees

    Generally . . . Pub. Health L. 2994-m

    Immunity of participants . . . Pub. Health L. 2994-o(1)

    Referral of matters to, requirement of . . . Pub. Health L. 2994-f

Health care agent defined . . . Pub. Health L. 2980(5)

HEALTH CARE AGENTS AND PROXIES—Cont.

Health care decision defined . . . Pub. Health L. 2980(6)

Health care defined . . . Pub. Health L. 2980(4)

Health care provider defined . . . Pub. Health L. 2980(7)

Health care proxy defined . . . Pub. Health L. 2980(8)

Hospital defined . . . Pub. Health L. 2980(9)

Immunity

    Agent . . . Pub. Health L. 2986(2); Pub. Health L. 2994-o(3)

    Ethics review committee members . . . Pub. Health L. 2994-o(1)

    Provider . . . Pub. Health L. 2986(1); Pub. Health L. 2994-o(2)

Liability for health care costs . . . Pub. Health L. 2987

Life-sustaining treatment

    Court orders to withhold or withdraw . . . Pub. Health L. 2994-r(3)

    Hospital implementation and review of decisions to withhold or withdraw . . . Pub. Health L. 2994-k

    Interinstitutional transfers, effect of . . . Pub. Health L. 2994-l

    Minor patients . . . Pub. Health L. 2994-e; Pub. Health L. 2994-r(4)

    Orders not to resuscitate not consent to fully withhold . . . Pub. Health L. 2994-i

    Revocation of consent to withhold . . . Pub. Health L. 2994-j

Life-sustaining treatment defined . . . Pub. Health L. 2980(9-a)

Mental hygiene facilities, use of proxies in

    Generally . . . Pub. Health L. 2991(1)

    Rights of residents, information regarding . . . Pub. Health L. 2991(1)

Mental hygiene facility defined . . . Pub. Health L. 2980(10)

Mental illness defined . . . Pub. Health L. 2980(11)

Nurse practitioner defined . . . Pub. Health L. 2980(2-a)

Nurses

    Nurse practitioner defined . . . Pub. Health L. 2980(2-a)

    Psychiatric nurse practitioner defined . . . Pub. Health L. 2980(2-b)

Other states or jurisdictions . . . Pub. Health L. 2990

[References are to SCPA and EPTL; if number contains dash (-), it refers to EPTL. Other references are preceded by the following abbreviations: Form–Official Forms; R–Court Rules; Tax L.–New York State Tax Law; MHL–Mental Hygiene Law; GOL–General Obligations Law; Pub. Health L.–Public Health Law.]

HEALTH CARE AGENTS AND PROXIES— Cont.

Powers of attorney regarding health care related matters, statutory short form . . . GOL 5-1502K

Presumed competency of . . . Pub. Health L. 2981(1)(b); Pub. Health L. 2994-c(1)

Principal defined . . . Pub. Health L. 2980(12)

Principal's incapacity to make decisions, determination of

Concurring determinations . . . Pub. Health L. 2994-c(3)

Confirmation of lack of capacity . . . Pub. Health L. 2983(6); Pub. Health L. 2994-c(7)

Developmental disability as determined by physician . . . Pub. Health L. 2983(1)(c)

Limited purpose of . . . Pub. Health L. 2983(4); Pub. Health L. 2994-c(5)

Mental hygiene facility patients . . . Pub. Health L. 2983(1)(b)

Notice . . . Pub. Health L. 2983(3); Pub. Health L. 2994-c(4)

Objection of principal . . . Pub. Health L. 2983(5); Pub. Health L. 2994-c(6)

Physician's determination of . . . Pub. Health L. 2983(1)(a)

Practitioner's determination of . . . Pub. Health L. 2994-c(2)

Priority among surrogate decision-making laws and regulations . . . Pub. Health L. 2994-b

Recovery of capacity, effect of . . . Pub. Health L. 2983(7)

Request for . . . Pub. Health L. 2983(2)

Provider obligations

Agent's directives, compliance with . . . Pub. Health L. 2984(5)

Attending practitioner's obligations . . . Pub. Health L. 2994-f

Conscience objections . . . Pub. Health L. 2994-n

Decisions made in good faith, compliance with . . . Pub. Health L. 2984(2)

Medical record documentation . . . Pub. Health L. 2984(1)

Referral of matters to ethics review committee . . . Pub. Health L. 2994-f

Religious belief considerations . . . Pub. Health L. 2984(3); Pub. Health L. 2984(4)

Proxy contents

Execution of powers of attorney, distinction between . . . Pub. Health L. 2981(5)(e)

HEALTH CARE AGENTS AND PROXIES—Cont.

Proxy contents—Cont.

Expiration date . . . Pub. Health L. 2981(5)(c)

Health care decisions, instructions regarding . . . Pub. Health L. 2981(5)(b)

Intentions of agent . . . Pub. Health L. 2981(5)(a)(ii)

Organ donation . . . Pub. Health L. 2981(5)(f)

Principal and agent, identity of . . . Pub. Health L. 2981(5)(a)(i)

Sample form . . . Pub. Health L. 2981(5)(d)

Psychiatric nurse practitioner defined . . . Pub. Health L. 2980(2-b)

Qualified psychiatrist defined . . . Pub. Health L. 2980(15)

Reasonably available defined . . . Pub. Health L. 2980(13)

Remedies for failures to honor health care decisions . . . Pub. Health L. 2994-s

Requiring or prohibiting execution of proxy . . . Pub. Health L. 2988

Residential health care facility defined . . . Pub. Health L. 2980(14)

Restrictions on appointees

Generally . . . Pub. Health L. 2981(3)(a)

Attending physician or agent, role as . . . Pub. Health L. 2981(3)(c)

Blood relatives . . . Pub. Health L. 2981(3)(b)(i); Pub. Health L. 2981(3)(d)

Physicians related to patient . . . Pub. Health L. 2981(3)(b)(ii)

Revocation of proxy

Competency, presumption of . . . Pub. Health L. 2985(1)(b)

Documentation of . . . Pub. Health L. 2985(2)

Limitations of agent as expressed by principal . . . Pub. Health L. 2985(1)(d)

Marital status, changes in . . . Pub. Health L. 2985(1)(e)

Notification of agent . . . Pub. Health L. 2985(1)(a)

Subsequent health care proxies . . . Pub. Health L. 2985(1)(c)

Rights and duties

Effects on other rights . . . Pub. Health L. 2989; Pub. Health L. 2994-q

Liability for health care costs . . . Pub. Health L. 2994-p

Medical information, receipt of . . . Pub. Health L. 2982(3)

[References are to SCPA and EPTL; if number contains dash (-), it refers to EPTL. Other references are preceded by the following abbreviations: Form–Official Forms; R–Court Rules; Tax L.–New York State Tax Law; MHL–Mental Hygiene Law; GOL–General Obligations Law; Pub. Health L.–Public Health Law.]

HEALTH CARE AGENTS AND PROXIES—Cont.

Rights and duties—Cont.

No surrogate available, procedures when . . . Pub. Health L. 2994-g

Other surrogates, priority over . . . Pub. Health L. 2982(4)

Scope of authority . . . Pub. Health L. 2982(1); Pub. Health L. 2994-d(3)

Selection of surrogates

Court orders designating surrogate . . . Pub. Health L. 2994-r(2)

Persons qualified . . . Pub. Health L. 2994-d(1)

Restrictions on . . . Pub. Health L. 2994-d(2)

Standards for decision-making . . . Pub. Health L. 2982(2); Pub. Health L. 2994-d(4); Pub. Health L. 2994-d(5)

Special proceedings . . . Pub. Health L. 2994-r(1); Pub. Health L. 2994-r(4)

Witnesses

Affiliation of . . . Pub. Health L. 2981(2)(c)

Appointment of . . . Pub. Health L. 2981(2)(a)

Mental hygiene facility, residents of . . . Pub. Health L. 2981(2)(b)

HEALTH INSURANCE (See ACCIDENT AND HEALTH INSURANCE)

HEARINGS (See TRIALS AND HEARINGS (GENERALLY))

HEIRS AT LAW

Adopted children as

Generally . . . 2-1.3

Proceeding for . . . 307(2)(a)(iv)

Afterborn child . . . 2-1.3

Defined . . . 2-1.1

Remainders . . . 6-5.6

HOLOGRAPHIC WILLS

Generally . . . 3-2.2

Defined . . . 3-2.2

Invalidity . . . 3-2.2

Time for filing of proofs . . . 1404

HUSBAND AND WIFE

Definitions

Disposition or appointment of property . . . 5-1.4(f)(1)

Divorced individual . . . 5-1.4(f)(3)

Divorce or annulment . . . 5-1.4(f)(2)

Former spouse . . . 5-1.4(f)(4)

HUSBAND AND WIFE—Cont.

Definitions—Cont.

Governing instrument . . . 5-1.4(f)(5)

Revocable . . . 5-1.4(f)(6)

Divorce, revocatory effect of . . . 5-1.4(a)

Former spouse predeceased, provisions of . . . 5-1.4(b)(1)

Marital deduction (See MARITAL DEDUCTION)

Purchase of property from former spouse . . . 5-1.4(e)

Real property disposition as creation of tenancy by the entirety . . . 6-2.2

Remarriage to former spouse; revived provisions . . . 5-1.4(b)(2)

Severance of property . . . 5-1.4(c)

Support duty of . . . 5-1.2

Surviving spouse (See SURVIVING SPOUSE)

Voluntary administrator, spouse qualifying as . . . 1303

Written notice

Mailing of . . . 5-1.4(d)(2)

Payments owed . . . 5-1.4(d)(2)

Payor or third party liability . . . 5-1.4(d)(1)

Transfer of property . . . 5-1.4(d)(2)

I

ILLEGITIMATE CHILDREN (See NON-MARITAL CHILDREN)

INCAPACITATED PERSONS (See also DISABILITY, PERSONS UNDER; INCOMPETENT PERSONS)

Defined . . . 103(25); 1726

"Person under disability," status as . . . 103(25)

Petition, naming in . . . 304

INCOME (See PRINCIPAL AND INCOME)

INCOMPETENT PERSONS

Appearance of

Committee required . . . 401

Guardian representing . . . 402

Guardians *ad litem* representing . . . 402

Charitable dispositions, right to contest; repealed . . . 5-3.3

Committee of incompetent

Account of committee, petition for termination of . . . 1727

Appeals, costs of . . . 2304

Costs and expenses incurred, right to . . . 2302; 2304

Personal representative status . . . 1-2.13

[References are to SCPA and EPTL; if number contains dash (-), it refers to EPTL. Other references are preceded by the following abbreviations: Form–Official Forms; R–Court Rules; Tax L.–New York State Tax Law; MHL–Mental Hygiene Law; GOL–General Obligations Law; Pub. Health L.–Public Health Law.]

INCOMPETENT PERSONS—Cont.

Committee of incompetent—Cont.

Surviving spouse, right to make election for . . . 5-1.1(d)(4)(B)

Unsuccessful contestant, right to award of costs of . . . 2302

Voluntary administrator, qualifications for . . . 1303

Compromise of claims . . . 2106

Conservatorship (See GUARDIANS FOR IN-COMPETENTS)

Contest of will by . . . 3-3.5(b)(2)

Decedents' estates not exceeding $1,000 . . . 11-1.1(b)(19)

Defined

EPTL . . . 1-2.9

SCPA . . . 103(26)

Deposit of monies for account of

Notice to corporation counsel of pending proceeding . . . 1125

Public administrator as interested party . . . 1123; 1215

Service on administrator, sufficiency of . . . 1125

Disability, persons under (See DISABILITY, PERSONS UNDER)

Distributee of decedent's estate, payment to

Committee of incompetent, absence of, deposit of sum in court . . . 2220

Decree or order for, requirements . . . 2220

Persons to receive, decree or order authorizing . . . 2220

Renunciation of testamentary distribution on behalf of incompetent person . . . 3-3.10

Fiduciary adjudicated as (See FIDUCIARIES (GENERALLY))

Foreign fiduciary, share to . . . 2221

Guardians for personal needs and property management under Mental Hygiene Law (See GUARDIANS UNDER ARTICLE 81)

Infants

Generally (See INFANTS)

Guardians (See GUARDIANS OF INFANTS)

Intellectually disabled persons (See DEVELOPMENTALLY DISABLED PERSONS)

Intestate administration

Administrator, appointment of . . . 1001

Service of process to incompetent . . . 1003

Letters

Committee of incompetent, issuance of letters to . . . 1418

Eligibility to receive . . . 707; 1418

INCOMPETENT PERSONS—Cont.

Mental Hygiene Law Article 81, guardians appointed under (See GUARDIANS UNDER ARTICLE 81)

Non-domiciliary beneficiary as . . . 2221

Payment of legacies to (See FIDUCIARIES (GENERALLY))

Petition, naming in . . . 304

Property conveyance disposed by will during competency, effect of . . . 3-4.4

Renunciation of disposition to . . . 2-1.11

Service of process on . . . 307

Shares of stock to, payment of . . . 7-5.3; 2220

Social security payments for benefit of . . . 1311

Specific disposition by will while competent, conveyance of subject property by committee . . . 3-4.4

Unemployment insurance payments for benefit of . . . 1311

Workmen's compensation payments for benefit of . . . 1311

INFANTS

Adopted children (See ADOPTED CHILDREN)

Afterborn children (See AFTERBORN CHILDREN)

Appearance of (See GUARDIANS *AD LITEM*; GUARDIANS OF INFANTS)

Charitable dispositions . . . 5-3.3

Compromise of claims . . . 1813

Compromise of controversies, effect of . . . 2106

Compulsory accounting by fiduciary, power to petition for . . . 2205

Contest of will by . . . 3-3.5(b)(2)

Custody proceeding, assignment of counsel for indigent parent in . . . 407

Defined . . . 1-2.9-a; 103(27)

Deposit of monies for account of

Notice to corporation counsel of . . . 1125

Public administrator as interested party . . . 1123; 1215

Service on administrator, sufficiency of . . . 1125

Uniform Rules for Surrogate's Court . . . R 207.14

Disabled person, as . . . 103(40)

Disposition to, renunciation of . . . 2-1.11

Distributee of decedent's estate, payment of share to

Generally . . . 4-1.1

Decree or order for, requirements . . . 2220

[References are to SCPA and EPTL; if number contains dash (-), it refers to EPTL. Other references are preceded by the following abbreviations: Form–Official Forms; R–Court Rules; Tax L.–New York State Tax Law; MHL–Mental Hygiene Law; GOL–General Obligations Law; Pub. Health L.–Public Health Law.]

[References are to SCPA and EPTL; if number contains dash (-), it refers to EPTL. Other references are preceded by the following abbreviations: Form–Official Forms; R–Court Rules; Tax L.–New York State Tax Law; MHL–Mental Hygiene Law; GOL–General Obligations Law; Pub. Health L.–Public Health Law.]

INTESTATE SUCCESSION—Cont.

Distributees—Cont.

Remainders limited to (See FUTURE INTERESTS)

Renunciation of share . . . 2-1.11

Wrongful death actions on behalf of (See WRONGFUL DEATH ACTIONS)

Estate of intestate (See DECEDENTS' ESTATES)

Genetic children of decedent . . . 4-1.3

Grandparents of decedent, rights of . . . 4-1.1

Great-grandparents and issue, distribution to . . . 4-1.1(a)(7)

Half-blood relatives, rights of . . . 4-1.1(b)

Intended parent, rights of children conceived after death of . . . 4-1.3

Issue of decedent, rights of . . . 4-1.1

Joint tenant in certain instances, disqualification of . . . 4-1.6

Missing distributee

Generally . . . 9-1.3(d)

Returned distributee, liability to . . . 721; 2226

Testamentary beneficiaries, liability to . . . 721

Parents of decedent (See PARENTS OF DECEDENT)

Real property

Devised property, sale of . . . 1903

Distributees' petition for . . . 2113

Mortgage of property . . . 1903

Petition by distributees for right to . . . 2113

Sales by distributees . . . 3-3.8

Relatives of half blood, rights of . . . 4-1.1(b)

Renunciation of share . . . 2-1.11

Rules governing . . . 4-1.1 *et seq.*

Surviving spouse

Antenuptial agreement . . . 5-1.3(a)

Disqualification

Generally . . . 4-1.5

Distribution of estate, effect on . . . 4-1.4(b)

Grounds for . . . 5-1.2

Dower, intestate share in lieu of . . . 4-1.1(e)

Election after Aug. 31, 1966 . . . 5-1.1(c)(2)

Marriage after execution of will . . . 5-1.3 *et seq.*

Nonmarital child, rights of spouse of . . . 4-1.2(b)

Rights of . . . 4-1.1; 5-1.3

Rules . . . 5-1.1(c)(2)

Source of payment of intestate share to . . . 5-1.3(b)

Waiver of spousal rights . . . 5-1.3(c)

INTESTATE SUCCESSION—Cont.

Surviving spouse—Cont.

Wills executed prior to Sept. 1, 1930, rights under . . . 5-1.3(a)

ISSUE

Adopted children as . . . 1-2.10; 2-1.3

Afterborn children as . . . 2-1.3

Charitable dispositions, right to contest to; repealed . . . 5-3.3

Defined . . . 1-2.10

Dispositions to

Death of beneficiary during lifetime of testator

Class, disposition to . . . 3-3.3(a)(2)

Lapse of disposition . . . 3-3.3(a)(1), (2)

Per capita taking, grounds for . . . 2-1.2

Per stirpes taking, grounds for . . . 2-1.2

Representation, grounds to take by . . . 2-1.2

Nonmarital child . . . 4-1.2

Remainders . . . 6-5.6

J

JOINT BANK ACCOUNTS

Disqualification of joint tenant from distribution . . . 4-1.6

Right of election by spouse, subject to . . . 5-1.1(b)

Trust form . . . 7-5.6

JOINT TENANCY (See also INTERNEES' ESTATES; TENANCY BY THE ENTIRETY)

Cooperative apartment corporation shares as . . . 6-2.2

Defined . . . 6-2.1

Disqualification of joint tenant from distribution . . . 4-1.6

Temporary administrator of absentee's or internee's estate, power of . . . 903

JUDGES OF SURROGATE'S COURT (See SURROGATES)

JUDICIAL SETTLEMENT

Accounting by fiduciaries (See ACCOUNTINGS)

Account Proceeding Checklist . . . JUD-ACTG-CHK

Defined . . . 103(29)

JURISDICTION OF SURROGATE'S COURT (See also SURROGATES)

Constitution of State of New York granting legislative power to court . . . 201

Index

[References are to SCPA and EPTL; if number contains dash (-), it refers to EPTL. Other references are preceded by the following abbreviations: Form–Official Forms; R–Court Rules; Tax L.–New York State Tax Law; MHL–Mental Hygiene Law; GOL–General Obligations Law; Pub. Health L.–Public Health Law.]

JURISDICTION OF SURROGATE'S COURT (See also SURROGATES)—Cont.

Debts in favor of non-domiciliary against domiciliary . . . 208

Domiciliaries' estates, over . . . 205

Enumerated proceedings as not exclusive . . . 202

Establishment of, method . . . 204

Estate tax; pre-May 25, 1990 powers in determination of . . . 2002

General jurisdiction . . . 201

Incidental powers, specified powers . . . 209

In personam, when obtained . . . 211

Life insurance policy on life of non-domiciliary, as personal property in county of insurance company's office . . . 208

Lifetime trusts . . . 207

Multicounty venue

    Lifetime trusts . . . 207

    Non-domiciliary estate . . . 206

Non-domiciliary

    Personal jurisdiction over, grounds for . . . 210

    Predicate, jurisdictional . . . 206

Parties, personal jurisdiction over . . . 203

Persons and property, jurisdiction over as traditional bases for . . . 210

Presumption of jurisdiction . . . 204

Submission to, what constitutes . . . 210

Transfer of proceedings

    Domiciliaries' estates . . . 205

    Lifetime trusts . . . 207

    Non-domiciliaries' estates . . . 206

Trusts, jurisdiction over

    Generally . . . 1501

    Lifetime trusts . . . 1509

Victim of September eleventh 2001 terrorist attacks, over estate of . . . 205

Wrongful death action in favor of non-domiciliary against domiciliary . . . 208

JURY TRIAL

Advisory jury . . . 502

Court decision on issues not requiring . . . 505

Demand for

    Generally . . . 502

    Court fee for filing . . . 502; 2402

Entitlement to, grounds for . . . 502

Fee for, persons liable . . . 502; 2402

Issues withdrawn from jury . . . 503

Jurors, selection of . . . 504

Order for . . . 502; R 207.31

Pretrial conferences . . . 510

JURY TRIAL—Cont.

Right of in proceeding for probate of will . . . 502

Transfer of proceedings under Uniform Rules for Surrogate's Court . . . R 207.6

Verdicts, certification of . . . 502; 503

Waiver requirements . . . 502

Withdrawal of demand for jury trial without consent of other parties . . . 502

L

LAPSE OF DISPOSITION (See also ANTI-LAPSE STATUTES)

Death of beneficiary during lifetime of testator . . . 3-3.3(a)(1), (2)

Testamentary dispositions

    Brothers or sisters of testator . . . 3-3.3(a)(1)

    Death during lifetime of testator, no grounds for lapse of disposition . . . 3-3.3

LEGACIES (See TESTAMENTARY DISPOSITIONS)

LEGAL FEES (See ATTORNEYS' FEES)

LEGATEE

Abandoned property . . . 2223

Defined . . . 103(33)

Deposit in court for benefit of . . . 2218

Determination of . . . 2225

Incarcerated individual or prisoner, notice of legacy or distributive share payable to . . . 2222-a

Payout of share

    Generally . . . 2223; 2224

    Court order for . . . 2218

Unknown name or location . . . 2223; 2224

LETTERS (GENERALLY)

Ancillary letters (See FOREIGN ESTATES)

Appeal, modification of letters by . . . 703

Attestation of . . . 701

Authority of grantee, letters as conclusive evidence of . . . 703

Certificate of

    Court fee for . . . 2402

    Sufficient as evidence of existence of such letters . . . 703

Chief fiscal officer of county, letters issued to, copy of transmittal to comptroller . . . 723

Defined . . . 103(34)

Eligibility to receive letters

    Defined . . . 103(18)

    Exceptions . . . 707

[References are to SCPA and EPTL; if number contains dash (-), it refers to EPTL. Other references are preceded by the following abbreviations: Form–Official Forms; R–Court Rules; Tax L.–New York State Tax Law; MHL–Mental Hygiene Law; GOL–General Obligations Law; Pub. Health L.–Public Health Law.]

LETTERS OF ADMINISTRATION—Cont.
Notice of application for—Cont.
  Consul General, notice to . . . Form A-5
  Official form . . . Form A-3
Personal representative status . . . 1-2.13
Petition
  Contents, requirements . . . 1002
  Filing, eligibility for . . . 1002
  Notice requirements . . . 1005
  Official form . . . Form A-1
  Petitioner, grant to . . . 1001
Powers, duties and limitations . . . 11-1.1
Priorities in granting . . . 1001
Probate proceedings
  Court fees . . . 2402
  Failure to institute within reasonable time
   . . . 1001
  Failure to prosecute diligently . . . 1001;
   1003
  Service of process . . . 1003
Proceeding for
  Death of alleged decedent, proof required
   . . . 1004
  Decree granting letters . . . 1004
  Investment powers . . . 11-2.2
  Petition (See subhead: Petition)
  Public administrator, grant to . . . 1001
  Service of process . . . 1003
  Trust company, grant to, consents of all distributees as condition to . . . 1001
Public administrators (See PUBLIC ADMINISTRATORS)
Qualification within specific time period, requirement . . . 1006
Recordation requirements . . . 1615; 2503
Requirements as to . . . 1115; 1211
Resignation, trustee-administrator's petition for permission of court . . . 1505
Revocation of (See also LETTERS (GENERALLY), subhead: Suspension, modification or revocation)
  Administrator-trustee's letters . . . 720; 1505
  Subsequent discovery of will as grounds
   Direction for revocation, inclusion in probate order of . . . 1413
   Distributee's liability for property received, effect of revocation order on . . . 721
Successor administrators (See ADMINISTRATORS D.B.N. *(DE BONIS NON)*)
Temporary administrators (See TEMPORARY ADMINISTRATION OF ESTATES)
Trust company as fiduciary, issuance to
  Generally . . . 1001

LETTERS OF ADMINISTRATION—Cont.
Trust company as fiduciary, issuance to—Cont.
  Consent of beneficiaries, requirement
   . . . 1418

LETTERS TESTAMENTARY
Ancillary letters (See FOREIGN ESTATES)
Issuance of, time for . . . 1414
Preliminary letters, issuance of
  Generally . . . 1412
  Application; official form . . . Form P-2
  Time for . . . 1414
Recordation requirements . . . 2503
Revocation of
  Generally (See LETTERS (GENERALLY), subhead: Suspension, modification or revocation)
  Executor-trustee's letters (See EXECUTORS, subhead: Trustee-executor)
  Subsequent will admitted to probate as grounds
   Direction for revocation, inclusion in probate order of . . . 1413
   Liability of legatee or distributee for property received, effect of revocation order on . . . 721
Supplementary letters, issuance of . . . 1415

LIBRARIES, PUBLIC
Charitable trust for founding, endowing and maintaining, creation by *inter vivos* gift to trustee
  Authorization . . . 8-1.3(a)
  Rules governing trust disposition . . . 8-1.3(b) *et seq.*
Trust for, rules regulating . . . 8-1.3

LIENS
Estate tax, state (See ESTATE TAX, STATE)

LIFE ESTATES (See also LIFE TENANTS)
Estate tax, payment from principal of property, no apportionment with remainder . . . 2-1.8(b)
Heirs or distributees of life tenant, taking as purchasers . . . 6-5.8
Remainder interests (See REMAINDER INTERESTS IN PROPERTY)
Surviving spouse, established for, right to elect against . . . 5-1.1(a)(1)(G), (c)(1)(I)
Third person, disposition for, real or personal property . . . 6-1.3

LIFE INSURANCE
Conservatee's use of proceeds . . . 9-2.2

[References are to SCPA and EPTL; if number contains dash (-), it refers to EPTL. Other references are preceded by the following abbreviations: Form–Official Forms; R–Court Rules; Tax L.–New York State Tax Law; MHL–Mental Hygiene Law; GOL–General Obligations Law; Pub. Health L.–Public Health Law.]

[References are to SCPA and EPTL; if number contains dash (-), it refers to EPTL. Other references are preceded by the following abbreviations: Form–Official Forms; R–Court Rules; Tax L.–New York State Tax Law; MHL–Mental Hygiene Law; GOL–General Obligations Law; Pub. Health L.–Public Health Law.]

LIFETIME TRUSTS—Cont.

Persons with disabilities, supplemental needs trusts established for . . . 7-1.12

Principal

Bonds, disbursements as . . . 11-2.1(f)

Change in form of principal, status of profit from . . . 11-2.1(k)

Charges to be made against . . . 11-2.1(1)

Defined . . . 11-2.1(b)(2)

Depletable property, receipts as . . . 11-2.1(h)

Eminent domain, proceeds from property taken under . . . 11-2.1(b)(2)(B)

Income beneficiary, application to use of (See subhead: Income beneficiaries)

Ineffective disposition to one or more beneficiaries . . . 2-1.15

Insurance proceeds on property forming part of principal . . . 11-2.1(b)(2)(C)

Natural resources, royalties from disposition of . . . 11-2.1(h)

Powers of appointment, trustee's exercise of . . . 10-6.6

Stock distributions as . . . 11-2.1(e)

Process, grounds for removal of trustee in absence of . . . 719

Property includable in . . . 7-1.15

Purchase money resulting trust, abolition of . . . 7-1.3

Real property trusts

Benefit of creditors, duration . . . 7-1.8

Mortgage, sale, lease or exchange of . . . 1507

Surrogate's court jurisdiction over . . . 1501

Remaining interest of property in trust, fiduciary's power to acquire . . . 11-1.1(b)(2)

Removal order for trustee, effect of . . . 720

Revocation of trust

Generally . . . 7-1.17

Beneficially interested persons, consent requirements

Generally . . . 7-1.9(a)

Class dispositions as not creating beneficial interest in persons in class . . . 7-1.9(b)

Procedure for . . . 7-1.9

Recordation in county where instrument creating trust recorded, requirement . . . 7-1.9(a)

Unqualified power to revoke reserved by creator-donee of powers of appointment . . . 10-8.1

Will, by . . . 7-1.16

Situs of trust property . . . 1501

LIFETIME TRUSTS—Cont.

Supplemental needs trusts established for persons with disabilities . . . 7-1.12

Surviving spouse, created for, taking of elective share against, amount allowed . . . 5-1.1(a)(1)(B), (D), (E), (F)

Taxation of, principal of trust as reimbursement to creator of trust for

Generally . . . 7-1.11(a)

Future estate indefeasibly vested for public purposes . . . 7-1.11(b)

Testamentary disposition of trustee, rules governing . . . 3-3.7

Transferable certificates, trust with . . . 9-1.5

Transfer of income by beneficiary

$10,000, amount in excess of, permissibility . . . 7-1.5(b)(1)

Benefit of person for which beneficiary liable for support, transfer to, allowability . . . 7-1.5(d)

Conditions to . . . 7-1.5(b)(1)

Effective period of . . . 7-1.5(b)(2)

Exceptions . . . 7-1.5(a)

Instrument transferring

Affidavits to accompany, requirement . . . 7-1.5(b)(1)

Payment made pursuant to, trustee's liability . . . 7-1.5(b)(3)

Trustee of trust to receive . . . 7-1.5(b)(1)

Life insurance proceeds left with insurance company, inalienability of . . . 7-1.5(a)(2)

Priority of transferees . . . 7-1.5(b)(2)

Recipients, eligibility as . . . 7-1.5(b)(1)

Two or more transfers, parties eligible to receive . . . 7-1.5(c)

Writing requirement . . . 7-1.5(b)(1)

Trustees, dispositions to

Death of testator prior to effective date of act, effect of . . . 3-3.7(d)

Instruments

Amendment allowed, effect on validity of disposition where . . . 3-3.7(b)(1)

Formality of execution, requirements . . . 3-3.7(b)(3)

Requirements . . . 3-3.7(a)

Revocability, effect on validity of disposition of . . . 3-3.7(b)(1)

Property transferred under

Power over reserved by testator, effect on validity of disposition . . . 3-3.7(b)(2)

Vesting of in trustee . . . 3-3.7(c)

Purposes allowed . . . 3-3.7(a)

Revocation prior to death of testator, effect of . . . 3-3.7(e)

[References are to SCPA and EPTL; if number contains dash (-), it refers to EPTL. Other references are preceded by the following abbreviations: Form–Official Forms; R–Court Rules; Tax L.–New York State Tax Law; MHL–Mental Hygiene Law; GOL–General Obligations Law; Pub. Health L.–Public Health Law.]

LIFETIME TRUSTS—Cont.

Trustees, dispositions to—Cont.

Termination prior to death of testator, effect of . . . 3-3.7(e)

Two or more created by same instrument, power of trustee to hold as undivided whole . . . 11-1.1

Underproductive property in (See UNDERPRO-DUCTIVE PROPERTY)

Unincorporated associations, creation of trust for prior to incorporation, grounds . . . 3-1.3(b)(2)

War service by trustee . . . 718

Will of domiciliary, trust created by, applicability of SCPA . . . 1501

LIMITED LETTERS (See LETTERS (GENERALLY))

LITERARY INSTITUTIONS

Generally . . . 8-1.2; 8-1.2(b)

LOST OR DESTROYED WILLS (See WILLS (GENERALLY))

M

MAIL OR MAILING

Generally . . . 103(35)

Express mail . . . 103(35-a)

Registered or certified mail . . . 103(36)

Return receipt requested . . . 103(37)

Service of process (See SERVICE OF PROCESS)

Special mail service . . . 103(37-a)

MARITAL DEDUCTION

Generally . . . 2-1.12; 11-1.2

Bequest of maximum deductible share . . . 11-1.2

Construction of wills and trusts referring to . . . 2-1.13

Non-citizen surviving spouse . . . Tax L. 951

QTIP election . . . Tax L. 955

MARRIAGE (See also HUSBAND AND WIFE)

Annulment of marriage (See ANNULMENT OF MARRIAGE)

Community property (See COMMUNITY PROPERTY)

Developmentally disabled person's marriage, guardianship termination at . . . 1759

Divorce, after . . . 8

Incestuous marriages . . . 5

MARRIAGE (See also HUSBAND AND WIFE)—Cont.

Intellectually disabled person's marriage, guardianship termination at . . . 1759

Voidable marriages . . . 7

Void marriages . . . 5; 6

MEDICAL FACILITIES

Advance directives

"Adult" defined . . . R 400.21(b)(5)

Facility compliance . . . R 400.21(c)

"Health care agent" defined . . . R 400.21(b)(4)

"Health care proxy" defined . . . R 400.21(b)(2)

"Living will" defined . . . R 400.21(b)(3)

Nursing homes (See NURSING HOMES)

Publication of rights . . . R 400.21(e)

Responsibilities

Community education . . . R 400.21(d)(5)

Discrimination, safeguards against . . . R 400.21(d)(6)

Medical records, documentation of . . . R 400.21(d)(2)

Patient furnishings . . . R 400.21(d)(1)

Staff education, provisions for . . . R 400.21(d)(4)

Statement of purpose . . . R 400.21(a)

Do-not-resuscitate orders

"Adult" defined . . . R 405.43(b)(1)

"Attending physician" defined . . . R 405.43(b)(2)

"Capacity" defined . . . R 405.43(b)(3)

"Cardiopulmonary resuscitation" defined . . . R 405.43(b)(4)

"Close friend" defined . . . R 405.43(b)(5)

Decision-making capacity

Adult with capacity . . . R 405.43(e)

Determination of . . . R 405.43(d)

Minor patients . . . R 405.43(h)

Non-surrogate decision-making . . . R 405.43(g)

Surrogate decision-making . . . R 405.43(f)

"Developmental disability" defined . . . R 405.43(b)(6)

Dispute mediation system . . . R 405.43(m)

Duty to provide information . . . R 405.43(c)

"Emergency medical services personnel" defined . . . R 405.43(b)(7)

"Health care agent" defined . . . R 405.43(b)(8)

"Hospital" defined . . . R 405.43(b)(9)

[References are to SCPA and EPTL; if number contains dash (-), it refers to EPTL. Other references are preceded by the following abbreviations: Form–Official Forms; R–Court Rules; Tax L.–New York State Tax Law; MHL–Mental Hygiene Law; GOL–General Obligations Law; Pub. Health L.–Public Health Law.]

MEDICAL FACILITIES—Cont.

Do-not-resuscitate orders—Cont.

"Hospital emergency service personnel" defined . . . R 405.43(b)(11)

"Hospitalization" defined . . . R 405.43(b)(10)

Hospital provisions . . . R 405.43(r)

Immunity . . . R 405.43(o)

Interinstitutional transfer . . . R 405.43(l)

Judicial review

Generally . . . R 405.43(n)

Judicially approved order not to resuscitate . . . R 405.43(q)

Lawfulness and effectiveness of . . . R 405.43(c)

"Medically futile" defined . . . R 405.43(b)(12)

"Mental hygiene facility" defined . . . R 405.43(b)(13)

"Mental illness" defined . . . R 405.43(b)(14)

"Minor" defined . . . R 405.43(b)(15)

"Nonhospital order not to resuscitate" defined . . . R 405.43(b)(16)

"Order not to resuscitate" defined . . . R 405.43(b)(17)

Other treatments, effect of order on . . . R 405.43(i)

"Parent" defined . . . R 405.43(b)(18)

"Patient" defined . . . R 405.43(b)(19)

Physician's review of order . . . R 405.43(k)

Policies concerning . . . R 405.43(a)

Presumed consent of patient . . . R 405.43(c)

"Reasonably available" defined . . . R 405.43(b)(20)

Revocation of consent . . . R 405.43(j)

"Surrogate" defined . . . R 405.43(b)(21)

"Terminal condition" defined . . . R 405.43(b)(23)

MENTAL HYGIENE LAW

Guardians (See GUARDIANS UNDER ARTICLE 81)

MILITARY SERVICE BENEFITS

Powers of attorney, statutory short form . . . GOL 5-1502J

MINORS (See INFANTS)

MISSING PERSONS' ESTATES (See ABSENTEES)

MULTI-STATE JURISDICTIONAL DISPUTES (See UNIFORM ADULT GUARDIANSHIP AND PROTECTIVE PROCEEDINGS JURISDICTION ACT)

MUNICIPAL CORPORATIONS

Charitable trust, creation of, authorization for . . . 8-1.2

Investment power of fiduciaries . . . 11-2.2; 11-2.2(a)(1)(D)

Obligations and securities of, investment in . . . 11-2.2

N

NATURAL RESOURCES

Interest in natural resources as income and principal, receipts from . . . 11-A-4.11

Timber, receipts from sale of . . . 11-2.1(i); 11-A-4.12

Trust property, allocation of proceeds from

Effective date of . . . 11-2.1(h)(2)

Production payment proceeds . . . 11-2.1(h)(1)(B)

Rent on lease as receipt, status as income . . . 11-2.1(h)(1)(A)

Royalty proceeds, apportionment of with allowance for depletion . . . 11-2.1(h)(1)(B)

Specific properties, allocation of receipts . . . 11-2.1(j)

Timber, receipts from sale of . . . 11-2.1(i); 11-A-4.12

NEW YORK STATE ESTATE TAX (See ESTATE TAX, STATE)

NEW YORK UNIFORM DISPOSITION OF COMMUNITY PROPERTY ACT

General provisions . . . 6-6.1 *et seq.*

NEXT OF KIN (See also BROTHERS AND SISTERS OF DECEDENT; FAMILY OF DECEDENT; HEIRS AT LAW; PARENTS OF DECEDENT; SURVIVING SPOUSE)

Adopted children as . . . 2-1.3

Afterborn child as . . . 2-1.3

Defined . . . 2-1.1

NO CONTEST CLAUSES (See TESTAMENTARY DISPOSITIONS, subhead: *In terrorem* clauses)

NONDOMICILIARY

Ancillary proceedings on will held in state, effect . . . 1501

[References are to SCPA and EPTL; if number contains dash (-), it refers to EPTL. Other references are preceded by the following abbreviations: Form–Official Forms; R–Court Rules; Tax L.–New York State Tax Law; MHL–Mental Hygiene Law; GOL–General Obligations Law; Pub. Health L.–Public Health Law.]

NONDOMICILIARY—Cont.

Appearance by attorney; authority of attorney, proof of, court's power to require . . . 401

Contestants in probate proceedings, court's power to require furnishing of security for costs to . . . 2303

Decedent-beneficiary, distributive share of, delivery or payment to foreign fiduciary, court's power to direct . . . 2221

Decedents, additional proceedings in estates of (See ESTATE TAX, STATE, subhead: Non-domiciliary decedents, estates of)

Distributees, non-domiciliaries as . . . 1213

Estates of (See FOREIGN ESTATES)

Fiduciary, non-domiciliary named, effect on bond . . . 710

Incompetent-beneficiary, distributive share of, delivery or payment to foreign fiduciary, court's power to direct . . . 2221

Infant-beneficiary, distributive share of . . . 2221

Jurisdiction of Surrogate's Court over estate . . . 206

Original probate of will in county of this state, effect . . . 1501

Petitioners in any proceedings, furnishing of security for costs, court's power to require . . . 2303

Service of process on, value of estate as factor in . . . 307

Transfer of proceedings, surrogate court . . . 206

Trust created by, laws of state governing, provisions for, validity . . . 7-1.10

NONMARITAL CHILDREN

Distributees, wrongful death proceeds . . . 5-4.5

Father's intestate estate, inheritance from . . . 4-1.2

Inheritance rights of . . . 4-1.2

"Issue," status as; anti-lapse provisions for class dispositions . . . 3-3.3

Mother's intestate estate, inheritance rights in . . . 4-1.2

Paternity established by clear and convincing evidence; father openly acknowledges child as own . . . 4-1.2

NONRESIDENT ALIENS (See also ALIENS)

Letters

Eligibility to receive . . . 707; 1415

Executor-nominee, issuance of supplementary letters testamentary to . . . 1415

NONRESIDENT ALIENS (See also ALIENS)—Cont.

Service of process on

Consular official, service on

Completion of service . . . 308; 309

Court order for, authorization and grounds . . . 307

Public administrator, actions by and against . . . 1120

Time for service . . . 308

NOT-FOR-PROFIT CORPORATIONS

Administration of trust . . . 8-1.8

Charitable trusts (See CHARITABLE TRUSTS)

Guardian of intellectually disabled person, power to act as . . . 1760

Public inspection . . . 8-1.8

Trustee for charitable purposes, supervision of . . . 8-1.4

NOTICE (See also specific subject headings)

Consul General, to . . . Form A-5

Guardian, appointment of; notice of petition . . . Form GMD-8

Manner of giving, form of notice, time of giving . . . 313

Probate (See PROBATE PROCEEDINGS)

NUNCUPATIVE WILLS

Generally . . . 3-2.2

Defined . . . 3-2.2

Invalidity . . . 3-2.2

Probate of, proofs necessary . . . 1404

Time for filing of proofs . . . 1404

Witness to as beneficiary, validity of deposition . . . 3-3.2

NURSING HOMES

Advance directives

Alternate designates . . . R 400.21(7)(iii)

Health care proxy, adult understanding of . . . R 400.21(7)(i)

Voluntary creation of proxy . . . R 400.21(7)(ii)

O

OATHS

Administration by clerks in Surrogate's Court . . . 2609

Administrator *cum testamento annexo;* official form . . . Form CTA-1; Form P-1

Administrator *de bonis non;* official form . . . Form ADM/DBN-1

[References are to SCPA and EPTL; if number contains dash (-), it refers to EPTL. Other references are preceded by the following abbreviations: Form–Official Forms; R–Court Rules; Tax L.–New York State Tax Law; MHL–Mental Hygiene Law; GOL–General Obligations Law; Pub. Health L.–Public Health Law.]

OATHS—Cont.
Clerks of Surrogate's Courts (See CLERKS OF SURROGATE'S COURTS)
Fiduciaries, oath of office for . . . 708
Standby guardians . . . CSMD-6; Form GMD-4

OBJECTIONS
Accounting, to . . . 2211
Letters, objections to . . . 709
Probate, objections to (See PROBATE PRO-CEEDINGS)

OFFICERS OF SURROGATE'S COURT
Acts in compliance with pre-existing statutory requirements, validity of . . . 104
Clerks of court (See CLERKS OF SURRO-GATE'S COURTS)

OFFICIAL FORMS (See also specific subject headings)
Appendix . . . 106
Interim forms . . . R 207.52

OPTIONAL UNITRUST PROVISION
Current beneficiary's interest, commencement of
Assets subject to trust; dates specified
. . . 11-2.4(d)(1)(A)-(E)
New trust, determination of . . . 11-2.4(d)(2)
Definitions
Current beneficiary . . . 11-2.4(c)(1)
Net fair market value
Generally . . . 11-2.4(c)(5)
Determination of . . . 11-2.4(c)(7)
Exclusions . . . 11-2.4(c)(6)(A)-(D)
Short year . . . 11-2.4(c)(4)
Trust . . . 11-2.4(c)(9)
Trustee . . . 11-2.4(c)(8)
Valuation year
Current . . . 11-2.4(c)(2)
Prior . . . 11-2.4(c)(3)
Terms of trust . . . 11-2.4(a)
Trust applicability
Generally . . . 11-2.4(e)(1)
Court jurisdiction . . . 11-2.4(e)(2)(A); 11-2.4(e)(2)(B)
Governing instrument, provisions of . . . 11-2.4(e)(4)(A); 11-2.4(e)(4)(B)
Interested persons . . . 11-2.4(e)(3)
Relevance considered . . . 11-2.4(e)(5)(A)
Trust inapplicability . . . 11-2.4(f)
Unitrust amount
Assets held in trust . . . 11-2.4(b)(6)
Beneficiary distribution, reductions for
. . . 11-2.4(b)(3)
Calculation of . . . 11-2.4(b)(2)

OPTIONAL UNITRUST PROVISION—Cont.
Unitrust amount—Cont.
Defined . . . 11-2.4(b)(1)
Fair market value adjustments . . . 11-2.4(b)(4)
Prorated unitrust amount . . . 11-2.4(b)(5)
Undervaluation, correction of . . . 11-2.4(b)(7)

ORAL WILLS (See NUNCUPATIVE WILLS)

ORDERS AND DECREES (GENERALLY)
(See also specific proceedings)
Clerk of court, power to sign decrees . . . 2609
Decrees
Defined . . . 601
Distribution, decree of . . . 2215
Enforcement of
Generally . . . 601
Contempt proceedings, procedure for
. . . 607
Execution as method
Bond, effect upon action or proceeding on
. . . 606
Docketing of transcript prior to execution
as requirement . . . 605
No adherence to, contempt as remedy
. . . 606
Time for . . . 605
Evidence of assets by order or decree . . . 602
Modification of, Surrogate's Court . . . 209
Money payment, order or decree for, enforce-ability by contempt proceedings . . . 606
Opening of, Surrogate's Court . . . 209
Order defined . . . 601
Payment of monies pursuant to, instruments ac-knowledging . . . 604
Performance of act, order or decree directing, enforceability by contempt proceedings
. . . 606
Recordation requirements . . . 2503
Signing, power of Surrogate's Court . . . 209
Transcripts of
Generally . . . 603
Court fee for furnishing . . . 2402
Vacating of, power of Surrogate's Court
. . . 209

ORGAN DONATION (See ANATOMICAL GIFTS)

OUT-OF-WEDLOCK CHILDREN (See NON-MARITAL CHILDREN)

[References are to SCPA and EPTL; if number contains dash (-), it refers to EPTL. Other references are preceded by the following abbreviations: Form–Official Forms; R–Court Rules; Tax L.–New York State Tax Law; MHL–Mental Hygiene Law; GOL–General Obligations Law; Pub. Health L.–Public Health Law.]

P

PARENTS OF DECEDENT (See also FAMILY OF DECEDENT)
Intestate succession
  Disqualification to take intestate share
    Distribution of estate, effect on . . . 4-1.4(b)
    Grounds for . . . 4-1.4(a)
  Rights of parents
    Generally . . . 4-1.1
    Nonmarital child's parents . . . 4-1.2(b)
Letters of administration, right to as parents of intestate . . . 1001
Surviving spouse (See SURVIVING SPOUSE)

PASSIVE TRUSTS
Trustee of . . . 7-1.2

PATERNITY PROCEEDINGS (See NON-MARITAL CHILDREN)

PAYMENT OF LEGACIES
Fiduciaries (See FIDUCIARIES (GENER-ALLY))

PECUNIARY BEQUESTS (See TESTAMEN-TARY DISPOSITIONS)

PENSION PLANS
Beneficiaries of . . . 13-3.2

PER CAPITA
Defined . . . 1-2.11
Disposition made to "issue," per capita taking when equal degrees of consanguinity to decedent . . . 2-1.2

PERPETUITIES, RULE AGAINST (See RULE AGAINST PERPETUITIES)

PERSONAL INJURY ACTIONS
Punitive damages . . . 5-4.3; 11-3.2

PERSONAL PROPERTY (See also PROP-ERTY (GENERALLY))
Defined . . . 3-5.1
Interest as gift to minor; New York Uniform Gifts to Minors Act . . . 7-4.2
Inter vivos trusts . . . 1501
Powers of attorney, statutory short form . . . GOL 5-1502B
Tangible personal property defined . . . Tax L. 951-a(c)

PERSONAL PROPERTY IN DECEDENTS' ESTATES
Assets of decedent's estate as personal property . . . 13-1.1
Clothing of decedent, exclusion from gross estate for benefit of surviving spouse or minor children
  Generally . . . 5-3.1
  Community property, disposition at death of . . . 6-6.1 *et seq.*
Crops . . . 13-1.1
Debts of decedent
  Personal property in county of domiciliary decedent as . . . 208
  Personal property on deposit in care facility at time of death . . . 1310
Defined, choice-of-laws purposes . . . 3-5.1(a)(2)
Encumbrances on
  Assets of estate, chargeability against . . . 3-3.6(b)
  Personal representative's liability for . . . 3-3.6(a)
Estate for years, status as . . . 13-1.1
Guardian's power over . . . 1713
Intestate disposition, choice-of-laws rule . . . 3-5.1(b)(2)
Legacies, intrinsic validity of
  Non-domiciliary testator's election for disposition to be governed by New York law, effect . . . 3-5.1(h)
  Testator's change of domicile to jurisdiction in which legacy is invalid, effect . . . 3-5.1(d)
Life estate for third person as personal property . . . 6-1.3
Life insurance policy on life of non-domiciliary as personal property in county of insurance company's office . . . 208
Petition for appointment of administrator, estimated value of intestate's personal property as requirement . . . 1002
Power of voluntary administrator to enforce payment, delivery and transfer of property . . . 1306
Powers of appointment over, exercise by will, law governing exercise and disposition, choice-of-laws rule . . . 3-5.1(g)
Private sale of property valued at less than $1000
  Condition to sale; counties outside New York City . . . 1213
  Counties within New York City . . . 1123

[References are to SCPA and EPTL; if number contains dash (-), it refers to EPTL. Other references are preceded by the following abbreviations: Form–Official Forms; R–Court Rules; Tax L.–New York State Tax Law; MHL–Mental Hygiene Law; GOL–General Obligations Law; Pub. Health L.–Public Health Law.]

PLEADINGS—Cont.

Appearance, pleading made by . . . 401

Content of . . . 302

Objection to, time for service of . . . 302

Requirements for . . . 302

Service of, parties to be served . . . 302

Verification of . . . 303

POWER DURING MINORITY

Fiduciaries . . . 103(17)

Gifts to minors (See GIFTS TO MINORS)

Infants (See INFANTS, subhead: Donee of power during minority)

POWERS OF APPOINTMENT

Appointees

   Defined . . . 10-2.2; 10-2.2(c)

   Number of, reduction in or limitation on . . . 10-9.2(b)

Appointive property

   Creditors' rights in (See subhead: Creditors' rights in appointive property)

   Defined . . . 10-2.2(d)

   Real property, interest of donee and appointees, priority of . . . 10-5.4

   Release, total or partial . . . 10-9.2(a)

Classification of

   Duty to exercise . . . 10-3.4

   Time of exercise as basis . . . 10-3.3

   Type of power as basis . . . 10-3.2

Contract to appoint, donee's power

   Postponed power, donee of (See subhead: Postponed power)

   Presently exercisable power, donee of . . . 10-5.2

Creation

   Qualifications of donor . . . 10-4.1

   Rule against perpetuities . . . 10-8.1(a)(2); 10-8.3

Creditors' rights in appointive property

   Generally . . . 10-7.1 *et seq.*

   Defined . . . 10-2.2(d)

   General power, property subject to

      Condition precedent . . . 10-7.3

      Limitations on liability for claim . . . 10-7.4(a)

      Not presently exercisable power . . . 10-7.4(a)

      Postponed power . . . 10-7.2

      Presently exercisable power . . . 10-7.2

   Special power, property subject to . . . 10-7.1

Decanting statute . . . 10-6.6

Defined . . . 10-3.1(a)

POWERS OF APPOINTMENT—Cont.

Discretionary power

   Defined . . . 10-3.4(c)

   Imperative power (See subhead: Imperative power)

Donee of power

   Authority, extent of . . . 10-5.1

   Creditors' rights in appointive property . . . 10-7.1 *et seq.*

   Death without exercising power

      Exclusive power . . . 10-6.8(b)(1)

      Grounds for exercise by court . . . 10-6.8(a)(2)

      Defined . . . 10-2.2(b)

      Failure to designate . . . 10-6.8(a)(1)

      Incompetence of sole donee . . . 10-6.8(a)(3)

      Two or more donees . . . 10-6.7

Donor of power

   Defined . . . 10-2.2(a)

   Directions of, conformity to . . . 10-6.2

   Qualifications for creation of power . . . 10-4.1

Estate tax, state

   Pre-September 1, 1930, modification of limited powers

      Generally . . . Tax L. 957(a)

      Allowance of deductions . . . Tax L. 957(c)

      Definition . . . Tax L. 957(b)

   Property transfers with powers of appointment in decedent, tax liability for . . . Tax L. 975(d)

Exclusive power

   Defined . . . 10-3.2(d)

   Exercise of . . . 10-6.5(a)(1)

   Imperative power . . . 10-6.8(b)(1)

Exercise

   Accumulation of income . . . 10-8.4

   Additional formality directed by donor, conformity to . . . 10-6.2(a)(2)

   Choice-of-laws rules . . . 3-5.1(g)

   Consent

      Requirements for . . . 10-6.4

      Two or more persons, of . . . 10-6.4(b)(1)

   Deed, exercise by . . . 10-6.2(a)(3)

   Defective exercise (See subhead: Imperative power)

   Donor's directions, conformity to . . . 10-6.2

   Duty to exercise, classification of powers by . . . 10-3.4

   Effective exercise

      Generally . . . 10-6.1(a)

      Choice-of-laws rules . . . 3-5.1(g)

[References are to SCPA and EPTL; if number contains dash (-), it refers to EPTL. Other references are preceded by the following abbreviations: Form–Official Forms; R–Court Rules; Tax L.–New York State Tax Law; MHL–Mental Hygiene Law; GOL–General Obligations Law; Pub. Health L.–Public Health Law.]

[References are to SCPA and EPTL; if number contains dash (-), it refers to EPTL. Other references are preceded by the following abbreviations: Form–Official Forms; R–Court Rules; Tax L.–New York State Tax Law; MHL–Mental Hygiene Law; GOL–General Obligations Law; Pub. Health L.–Public Health Law.]

[References are to SCPA and EPTL; if number contains dash (-), it refers to EPTL. Other references are preceded by the following abbreviations: Form–Official Forms; R–Court Rules; Tax L.–New York State Tax Law; MHL–Mental Hygiene Law; GOL–General Obligations Law; Pub. Health L.–Public Health Law.]

POWERS OF ATTORNEY—Cont.
Statutory short form power—Cont.
Durable (See subhead: Durable statutory short form power)
Effective date . . . GOL 5-1501B
Form . . . GOL 5-1513
Health care related matters . . . GOL 5-1502K
Incapacity, not affected by . . . GOL 5-1501A
Modifications . . . GOL 5-1503
Stock transactions . . . GOL 5-1502C
Successor agents, designation of . . . GOL 5-1508
Tax matters . . . GOL 5-1502M
Termination of . . . GOL 5-1511
Writing requirement . . . 13-2.3

PRELIMINARY EXECUTOR (See LETTERS TESTAMENTARY, subhead: Preliminary letters, issuance of)

PRENUPTIAL AGREEMENTS (See ANTE-NUPTIAL AGREEMENTS)

PRESUMPTIONS
Conclusiveness of real property disposition . . . 1922
Death, of; absence for five years . . . 2-1.7
Rebuttable presumptions . . . 6-6.2

PRETRIAL CONFERENCES
Purpose of . . . 510
Uniform rules for . . . R 207.29(b)

PRINCIPAL AND INCOME
Distributions to trust estate (See CORPORA-TIONS, subhead: Distributions to trust estate, allocation between principal and income)
Distributions to trust, rules governing . . . 11-2.1(e)
Pre-July 1, 1956, fiduciary entitled to commission . . . 2307
Stocks and securities (See STOCKS AND SE-CURITIES)
Trustees (See TRUSTEES, subhead: Principal and income)
Uniform Principal and Income Act (See UNI-FORM PRINCIPAL AND INCOME ACT)

PRIORITY OF CREDITORS (See DEBTS OF DECEDENT)

PRISONERS
Notice of legacy or distributive share payable to incarcerated individual or prisoner . . . 2222-a
Temporary administration of internees' estate (See INTERNEES' ESTATES, subhead: Temporary administration of estate)

PROBATE PROCEEDINGS
Affidavit of attesting witness as proof
Generally . . . 1406
Official form . . . Form P-3
Ancillary probate (See FOREIGN ESTATES)
Attesting witnesses
Absence from state . . . 1405
Affidavits by
Generally . . . 1406
Official form . . . Form P-3
Allocation of expenses of . . . 1404
Commission for examination of . . . 1404
Dispensing with testimony of
Generally . . . 1405; 1406
Application; official form . . . Form P-8
Number required . . . 1404
Preliminary examination by testamentary beneficiary . . . 3-3.5(b)(3)(D)
Taking testimony outside jurisdiction . . . 1404
Attorney's fees . . . 2302
Charitable dispositions . . . 8-1.4
Checklist . . . P-CHKLST
Citation
Affidavit of service; official form . . . Form P-7
Objections to probate, upon filing of . . . 1411
Official form . . . Form P-5
Successor letters testamentary . . . Form SLT-5
Comparison, affidavit of; official form . . . Form P-13
Consent to probate; official form . . . Form P-4
Contested proceedings
Committee of incompetent . . . 2302
Costs and expenses . . . 1404; 2302
Guardians . . . 2302
Incompetent person, contest by . . . 3-3.5(b)(2)
Infant, contest by . . . 3-3.5(b)(2)
Minutes of trial furnished for appeals . . . 2302

[References are to SCPA and EPTL; if number contains dash (-), it refers to EPTL. Other references are preceded by the following abbreviations: Form–Official Forms; R–Court Rules; Tax L.–New York State Tax Law; MHL–Mental Hygiene Law; GOL–General Obligations Law; Pub. Health L.–Public Health Law.]

[References are to SCPA and EPTL; if number contains dash (-), it refers to EPTL. Other references are preceded by the following abbreviations: Form–Official Forms; R–Court Rules; Tax L.–New York State Tax Law; MHL–Mental Hygiene Law; GOL–General Obligations Law; Pub. Health L.–Public Health Law.]

PROBATE PROCEEDINGS—Cont.

Successor letters testamentary—Cont.

Renunciation of letters and waiver of process

Corporation . . . Form P-16; Form SLT-3

Individual . . . Form P-15; Form SLT-2

Supplementary letters testamentary . . . 1415

Unsuccessful party, award to . . . 2302

Verification, oath and designation; official form . . . Form P-1

Waiver of process; consent to probate

Official form . . . Form P-4

Renunciation of letters c.t.a., with . . . Form P-11

Wills (See WILLS (GENERALLY))

Witnesses (See subhead: Attesting witnesses)

Writing, proofs in . . . 1404

PROCESS (GENERALLY)

Adoption proceeding . . . 307(2)(a)(iv)

Defined . . . 103(43)

Issuance of, powers of chief clerk of Surrogate's Court . . . 2609

Letters of administration, application for, person required to be served . . . 1003

Public administrators' powers

New York City . . . 1123

Outside New York City . . . 1214

Return of

Place for . . . 305

Time for . . . 308

Service of process (See SERVICE OF PROCESS; SUBPOENAS)

Subpoenas (See SUBPOENAS)

Supplemental process, issuance and service to bring in additional parties, court's power to required . . . 312

Voluntary account . . . 2210

Waiver of process as method of appearance . . . 401

PROOF OF DEATH (See DEATH)

PROPERTY (GENERALLY) (See also REAL PROPERTY DISPOSITIONS)

Abandoned property (See ABANDONED PROPERTY)

Agreement to convey by testator, prior testamentary disposition made, effect . . . 3-4.2

Charitable trusts, property subject to (See CHARITABLE TRUSTS)

Claim on specific property, proceeding to compel delivery by fiduciary to claimant . . . 2105

Defined

EPTL . . . 1-2.15

SCPA . . . 103(44)

PROPERTY (GENERALLY) (See also REAL PROPERTY DISPOSITIONS)—Cont.

Encumbrances on decedent's property

Assets of estate, chargeability against . . . 3-3.6(b)

Personal representative's liability for . . . 3-3.6(a)

Estate tax, state (See ESTATE TAX, STATE, specific subheads, e.g., Tangible personal property)

Execution of power to sell, mortgage or lease by less than all qualifying executors, validity of . . . 11-1.4

Fiduciaries' power over estate of decedent

Overview . . . 11-1.1

Temporary administrator . . . 903

Guardian of infant, rights of (See GUARDIANS OF INFANTS)

Holding of property by fiduciary, property of fiduciary to be kept separate from, requirement . . . 11-1.6(a)

Insurance on property of estate or trust, power of fiduciary to maintain and enforce . . . 11-1.1(b)(4)

Intestate disposition, choice-of-laws rule . . . 3-5.1(b)(1)

Intestate succession (See INTESTATE SUCCESSION, subhead: Real property)

Investment and reinvestment of property of estate or trust, power of fiduciary . . . 11-1.1(b)(3)

Items of property excluded from estate assets, set aside for surviving spouse and decedent's minor children . . . 5-3.1

Joint tenancy (See JOINT TENANCY)

Leasing property of estate

Fiduciary's power in . . . 11-1.1(b)(5)(E)

Guardian's powers in . . . 1715

Power to lease in tenant for life

Assignability of power . . . 10-10.3

Mortgage, effect of . . . 10-10.4

Passing of in estate of tenant . . . 10-10.3

Release by tenant of person entitled to future estate as extinguishment . . . 10-10.3

Scope of power . . . 10-10.2

Term of power . . . 10-10.2

Temporary administrators' power, limitations on . . . 903

Term of lease . . . 11-1.1(b)(5)(C)

Trustee's power in . . . 1507

Leave to issue execution against decedent's real property . . . 1812

[References are to SCPA and EPTL; if number contains dash (-), it refers to EPTL. Other references are preceded by the following abbreviations: Form–Official Forms; R–Court Rules; Tax L.–New York State Tax Law; MHL–Mental Hygiene Law; GOL–General Obligations Law; Pub. Health L.–Public Health Law.]

[References are to SCPA and EPTL; if number contains dash (-), it refers to EPTL. Other references are preceded by the following abbreviations: Form–Official Forms; R–Court Rules; Tax L.–New York State Tax Law; MHL–Mental Hygiene Law; GOL–General Obligations Law; Pub. Health L.–Public Health Law.]

[References are to SCPA and EPTL; if number contains dash (-), it refers to EPTL. Other references are preceded by the following abbreviations: Form–Official Forms; R–Court Rules; Tax L.–New York State Tax Law; MHL–Mental Hygiene Law; GOL–General Obligations Law; Pub. Health L.–Public Health Law.]

PUBLIC ADMINISTRATORS—Cont.
Commissions—Cont.
  Deposits into New York City treasury; counties within New York City . . . 1107
  Rates within New York City . . . 1106
  Retention of
    Generally . . . 1106
    Erie County administrator, by . . . 1207
    Restriction on . . . 1105; 1207
Compensation
  Counties outside New York City, determination in . . . 1207
  Counties within New York City . . . 1105
Consular representative of decedent's country, notice to . . . 1119
Continuation of office . . . 1101
Corporation counsel of New York City, notice to . . . 1125
Counsel to
  Appointment of . . . 1108; 1206
  Compensation of; counties within New York City . . . 1108
Death of, effect of . . . 1111
Deaths and burials report requirements
  Boarding house, death in . . . 1113; 1209
  Burial of decedent having no known distributees, undertaker's report to administrator . . . 1113; 1209
  Hotel, death in . . . 1113; 1209
  Inquest, medical examiner's report of . . . 1113; 1209
  Rooming house, death in . . . 1112; 1209
Definitions . . . 1201
Deposit of estate funds by
  Documents of, requirements for; counties within New York City . . . 1107
  Insolvency or involuntary liquidation, priority of payment on . . . 1107; 1208
  Interest on funds, credit to respective estate, counties within New York City . . . 1107
  Place for deposit; counties within New York City . . . 1107
  Report to be filed on, court's power to compel; counties outside New York City . . . 1208
Deputy public administrators
  Annual salary of; counties within New York City . . . 1105
  Appointment of . . . 1103; 1206
  Assistant public administrator of Richmond County to be known as . . . 1103
  Court deputizing assistant or employee as; counties outside New York City . . . 1206

PUBLIC ADMINISTRATORS—Cont.
Deputy public administrators—Cont.
  Duties and powers; counties within New York City . . . 1103
  Removal of; counties within New York City . . . 1103
  Term of office . . . 1202
  Vacancy; counties within New York City . . . 1103
Discharge and release . . . 1115; 1205
Distribution of assets of estate without accounting, power of public administrator; counties within New York City . . . 1123
Employees of (See subheads: Assistants and employees; Deputy public administrators)
Expenses of
  Counties outside New York City . . . 1207
  Counties within New York City . . . 1106
Finally settled accounts, report requirements; counties within New York City . . . 1109
Funeral of decedent arranged prior to issuance of letters
  Counties outside New York City . . . 1212
  Counties within New York City . . . 1118
Infants, payment of legacy to; discretion of public administrator . . . 1123; 1213
Informatory account, filing of . . . 1123
Inquiries, power to institute . . . 1114; 1216
Intestate, power over property of
  Counties outside New York City . . . 1212
  Counties within New York City . . . 1112
Letters of administration
  Application for, power to file . . . 1116; 1210
  Application for, public administrator's power to file . . . 1116
  Certificate evidencing authority to act . . . 1115
  Grant to others, conditions for . . . 1121
  Requirements as to . . . 1115; 1211
  Statement to be filed upon commencement of action, content requirements; counties outside New York City . . . 1211
  Value of estate under $3000
    Generally . . . 1115; 1211
    Certificate evidencing authority to act . . . 1115
    Limit exceeded after commencement of administration, effect on . . . 1115; 1211
    Powers of public administrator in decedent's estate . . . 1115; 1211

[References are to SCPA and EPTL; if number contains dash (-), it refers to EPTL. Other references are preceded by the following abbreviations: Form–Official Forms; R–Court Rules; Tax L.–New York State Tax Law; MHL–Mental Hygiene Law; GOL–General Obligations Law; Pub. Health L.–Public Health Law.]

PUBLIC ADMINISTRATORS—Cont.

Liability of New York City for acts of administrators of counties within New York City . . . 1110

Necessary party, status as . . . 1123; 1125; 1215

Oaths . . . 1104; 1117

Office space, counties to supply . . . 1108; 1206

Perishable property of decedent, sale of . . . 1118; 1212

Personal property of decedent, sale of

    Authorization of . . . 1112

    Collection prior to issuance of letters, conditions to . . . 1118; 1212

    Property valued at less than $1000

        Counties outside New York City . . . 1213

        Counties within New York City . . . 1123

    Public sale

        Notice requirements . . . 1123; 1213

        Property valued at more than $1000 . . . 1123

    Time lapse before . . . 1118

Powers

    Counties outside New York City . . . 1219

    Counties within New York City . . . 1123

    Prior to issuance of letters . . . 1118; 1212

Probate of will, petition for

    Counsel fees and expenses for participation in probate proceedings . . . 2302

    Counties outside New York City . . . 1210

    Counties within New York City . . . 1116; 1123

    Grounds for court authorization . . . 1402

Property insufficient to require administration . . . 1126

Real property of decedent, powers over

    Authorization of . . . 1112

    Collection and management; conditions prior to issuance of letters . . . 1118; 1212

Records, destruction of; counties within New York City . . . 1127

Resignation or removal of . . . 1111

Salaries (See subhead: Compensation)

Securities marketable in decedents' estate, retention of . . . 1123; 1213

Service of process to non-domiciliaries of administrator's county

    Counties outside New York City . . . 1214

    Counties within New York City, requirements . . . 1123

Settlement of accounts of

    Balances remaining payable to certain persons, disposition of . . . 1123; 1213

PUBLIC ADMINISTRATORS—Cont.

Settlement of accounts of—Cont.

    Expenses and disbursements; counties outside New York City . . . 1207

    Finance Director of New York City, payment or delivery to; . . . 1123

    Procedure for obtaining; estates valued at less than $3,000; counties outside New York City . . . 1213

Staff of (See subhead: Assistants and employees)

Subpoena, power to issue . . . 1114; 1216

Successor of

    Appointment of . . . 1202

    Immediate succession to rights, duties and powers of predecessor . . . 1111; 1205

Superseded by distributee of decedent

    Account, settlement of after revocation of letters . . . 1217

    Delivery of assets to fiduciary, requirements for . . . 1122; 1217

    Letters, grant of to others, time for . . . 1121

Term of office . . . 1102

Unknown persons or unknown domiciles, funds deposited for account of . . . 1123; 1213

Vacancy in office of . . . 1202; 1205

PUBLICATION, SERVICE OF PROCESS BY (See SERVICE OF PROCESS)

PUNITIVE DAMAGES (See specific subject headings, e.g., WRONGFUL DEATH ACTIONS)

PURCHASE MONEY RESULTING TRUST

Abolition of . . . 7-1.3

Q

QTIP TRUSTS

Generally . . . Tax L. 955

Apportionment of . . . 2-1.8(d)(1)

R

REAL PROPERTY DISPOSITIONS (See also PROPERTY (GENERALLY))

Accounting by fiduciaries (See ACCOUNTINGS)

Administrative expenses

    Allowability . . . 1902

    Credit allowances at net on insufficient proceeds from sales . . . 1915

Assignment of decedent's rights, conveyance as . . . 1917

[References are to SCPA and EPTL; if number contains dash (-), it refers to EPTL. Other references are preceded by the following abbreviations: Form–Official Forms; R–Court Rules; Tax L.–New York State Tax Law; MHL–Mental Hygiene Law; GOL–General Obligations Law; Pub. Health L.–Public Health Law.]

REAL PROPERTY DISPOSITIONS (See also PROPERTY (GENERALLY))—Cont.

Beneficiaries, sales to . . . 1915
Bonds, fiduciary
   Administrator furnishing of additional
     . . . 805
   Failure to give, administrator . . . 719
   Required, court . . . 1910
Community property dispositions at spousal
   death . . . 6-6.1 *et seq.*
Conclusiveness of action, presumption of
   . . . 1922
Confirmation of prior lease without court ap-
   proval . . . 1901
Contract for disposition . . . 1907; 1911
Conveyance
   Binding effect of . . . 1913
   Property held under contract for purchase
     . . . 1917
   Vendee of sales contract made by decedent,
     made by . . . 1921
Court authorized
   Determination of best manner of disposition
     . . . 1907
   Purposes, accepted . . . 1901
   Subject to disposition, purposes deemed
     . . . 1902
Credit allowances for insufficient proceeds to
   cover decedent's expenses . . . 1915
Curtesy rights . . . 1918
Debts
   Payment of . . . 1902
   Provisions for . . . 1916
Defined . . . 1901
Delay of application . . . 1905
Denial of application for . . . 1905
Dower rights . . . 1918
Eminent domain, release of right to award for
   taking of property . . . 1901
Exchange as disposition . . . 1901
Fiduciary
   Accounting for disposed property . . . 1910
   Bonding (See subhead: Bonds, fiduciary)
   Commission awarded from proceeds
     . . . 2302
   Death, removal or disqualification . . . 1912
   Defined . . . 1901
   Expenses awarded from proceeds . . . 2302
   Final judicial settlement of accounts, post-
     ponement of sale until . . . 1909
   Report of proceedings . . . 1911
   Successor . . . 1912
   Supplemental accounting . . . 1914
Funeral expenses, payment of . . . 1902

REAL PROPERTY DISPOSITIONS (See also PROPERTY (GENERALLY))—Cont.

Interested parties
   Remainder, binding of . . . 1913
   Rights, court determination of . . . 1909
   Uniform Gifts to Minors Act . . . 7-4.2
Intestate share in, petition for . . . 2113
Lease
   Binding effect of . . . 1913
   Defined as disposition . . . 1901
Legacies, time limits on satisfaction of
   . . . 1903
Levy, property exempt from law of . . . 1903
Life tenants rights . . . 1918
Limitations . . . 1903
Mortgages
   Binding effect of . . . 1913
   Defined as disposition . . . 1901
   Payment of mortgage existing at time of de-
     cedent's death . . . 1902
   Surplus disposition to enforce . . . 1920
Partition actions . . . 1901
Personal property in decedents' estates (See
   PERSONAL PROPERTY IN DECEDENTS'
   ESTATES)
Petition
   Claims, objection to . . . 1906
   Content requirement . . . 1904
   Contract for disposition accompanying
     . . . 1907
   Conveyance of property to vendee of sales
     contract made by decedent, for . . . 1921
   Filing . . . 1904
Powers of attorney, statutory short form
   . . . GOL 5-1502A
Reimbursement of aggrieved parties, proper
   . . . 1919
Release, binding effect of . . . 1913
Rents
   Court directed application of . . . 1901
   Postponement of application, collection of
     rents during . . . 1905
Sale
   Confirmation requirement; contract for dispo-
     sition annexed to petition . . . 1911
   Credit allowances for insufficient proceeds to
     cover decedent's expenses . . . 1915
   Execution as basis for limitation on disposi-
     tion . . . 1903
   Order of, determining . . . 1908
   Public versus private, determination of
     . . . 1907
   Spouse or beneficiary, to . . . 1915
Spouse, transfers to . . . 1901

REAL PROPERTY DISPOSITIONS (See also PROPERTY (GENERALLY))—Cont.
Statute of limitations, defense arising under . . . 1906
Surplus
   Disposition of . . . 1920
   Distribution of . . . 1916
Taxes, payment of . . . 1902
Time limitations . . . 1903
Undetermined claims, fund provisions for . . . 1916
Unknown party entitled to estate or property interest, protection of . . . 1909
Unlawful transfers, civil penalties for . . . Tax L. 992(b)

RECEIVERS
Appointment, notice of . . . Form UCS 830.1
Interested party in estate, receiver classified as . . . 103(39)

RECORDING OF WILLS (See WILLS (GENERALLY))

RECORDS AND RECORDATION OF SURROGATE'S COURT
Certification of records or papers
   Generally . . . 2609
   Fee requirement . . . 2501
Clerk of court, responsibilities and duties (See CLERKS OF SURROGATE'S COURTS)
Commissioner of records (See COMMISSIONER OF RECORDS)
Copy of paper, accuracy of, processes for reproducing . . . 2501
Documents, recordation requirements . . . 2503
Expenses of record keeping, funds for
   Generally . . . 2501
   Conclusiveness of release executed pursuant to order . . . 1913
   "Disposition," status as . . . 1901
Filing requirements . . . 2501
Firearms inventory . . . 2509
General requirements . . . 2501
Indexing of record books, sufficiency of; requirements . . . 2502
Inspection of books and records, right to . . . 2501
Issue or seal papers or records, power of clerks and officers of court . . . 2609
Permanent records of court, minute book recording proceedings preserved as . . . 2501
Record book, method of maintaining . . . 2501; 2502

RECORDS AND RECORDATION OF SURROGATE'S COURT—Cont.
Rents, right to receive and apply, disposition as . . . 1901
Sale of, "disposition," status as . . . 1901
Sealed records and papers, court authorization for opening . . . 2501
Signing of papers or records, power of clerks and officers of court . . . 2609
Spouse, transfer to; status as disposition . . . 1901
System for maintaining, CPLR 9703 . . . 2501

REFEREES
Generally . . . 506
Court personnel as referees, appointment of . . . 506(6)

RELATIVES OF DECEDENT (See also NEXT OF KIN)
Adoption of surviving children by . . . 2-1.3
Aunts and uncles (See AUNTS AND UNCLES OF DECEDENT)
Brothers and sisters (See BROTHERS AND SISTERS OF DECEDENT)
Half-blood relatives, intestate succession rights of . . . 4-1.1(b)
Infants (See INFANTS)
Spouse (See HUSBAND AND WIFE)

REMAINDER INTERESTS IN PROPERTY
Charitable dispositions contested as invalid by issue or parent of testator; repealed . . . 5-3.3
Class remaindermen, representation of . . . 315
Contingent remaindermen not in being . . . 2106
Remainder, defined . . . 6-4.3
Remaindermen in future interests, representation of . . . 315
Representation of contingent remaindermen in future interests . . . 315
Service of process on, requirements . . . 315
Tenancy in common, creation of by will limitation, implication of cross remainders . . . 6-5.4

REMOVAL OF PROCEEDINGS (See TRANSFER OF PROCEEDINGS)

RENTS
Amounts due or accruing on leases held by decedent; priority of payment . . . 1811
Fiduciaries' power to collect rents from real property in decedent's estates . . . 11-1.1(b)(5)(A)(E)

[References are to SCPA and EPTL; if number contains dash (-), it refers to EPTL. Other references are preceded by the following abbreviations: Form–Official Forms; R–Court Rules; Tax L.–New York State Tax Law; MHL–Mental Hygiene Law; GOL–General Obligations Law; Pub. Health L.–Public Health Law.]

RENTS—Cont.
Part of decedent's estate, rent as, due but unpaid at death of testator, accrual of, allotment to income and principal . . . 11-2.1(c)(2)
Property rent as income and principal . . . 11-2.1(b)(1)(A); 11-A-4.5
Residuary beneficiaries entitlement to, property not specifically disposed of . . . 11-2.1(d)(3)(A)
Temporary administrator, power to receive rents from real property in decedent's estates . . . 903

RENUNCIATION (See TESTAMENTARY DISPOSITIONS)

REPEAL OF SURROGATE'S COURT ACT
Pending actions and proceedings at time of, applicability of SCPA . . . 2802
Prior actions to, inapplicability of SCPA . . . 2802
SCPA replacing . . . 2801; 2805

RESIDENCE
Defined . . . 103(15)

RESIDUARY DISPOSITIONS (See TESTA-MENTARY DISPOSITIONS)

RESIGNATION (See FIDUCIARIES (GENER-ALLY))

RESPONDENT
Defined . . . 103(45)

RESULTING TRUST
Purchase money resulting trust, abolition of . . . 7-1.3

RETIREMENT PLANS
Beneficiaries of . . . 13-3.2
Powers of attorney regarding benefits, statutory short form . . . GOL 5-1502L

"REVERSE" DISCOVERY
Against fiduciary
  Generally . . . 2102
  Court order to supply information, effect of noncompliance with . . . 719

REVERSIONS
Defined . . . 6-4.4

REVOCABLE TRUSTS (See LIFETIME TRUSTS)

RIGHT OF ELECTION
Generally . . . 5-1.1

RIGHT OF ELECTION—Cont.
Advancements, effect of . . . 2-1.5(e)
Annuity trust or unitrust . . . 5-1.1(a)(1)(G), (c)(1)(I)
Antenuptial agreement in writing, effect of . . . 5-1.3(a)
Bank deposits and dividends . . . 5-1.1(b)(1)(B), (C)
Cancellation of . . . 5-1.1(d)(6)
Change of . . . Tax L. 980
Death less than one hundred twenty hours after death of spouse . . . 2-1.6(b)
Disqualification as surviving spouse
  Abandonment of decedent as grounds . . . 5-1.2
  Revocation of status . . . 5-1.4(a), (b)
  Types of actions establishing . . . 5-1.2 *et seq.*
Executor named in will prior to probate, written notice served on . . . 5-1.1
Inter vivos dispositions as testamentary substitutes for purposes of . . . 5-1.1-A(b); 5-1.1(b), (1)
Intestate succession (See INTESTATE SUCCES-SION)
Out-of-state property included in estate . . . 5-1.1
Procedure for exercise of . . . 5-1.1-A(d); 5-1.1(e)
Property excluded from estate assets; set aside for surviving spouse and minor children . . . 5-1.2; 5-3.1
Recovery of designated portion of testator's estate from beneficiaries, right of surviving spouse, procedure . . . 5-1.3(b)
Release of . . . 5-1.1-A(e)
Remarriage to testator, restoration of rights to former spouse . . . 5-1.4(a)
Satisfaction of IRC terms . . . 5-1.1(c)(K)
Sept. 1, 1992, decedent dying on or after
  Generally . . . 5-1.1-A(a), (c)
  Inter vivos dispositions as testamentary sub-stitutes . . . 5-1.1-A(b)(1)
Testamentary substitute, *inter vivos* dispositions as . . . 5-1.1-A(b)
Time for filing . . . 5-1.1(d)(6)
Validity or effect of . . . 1421
Waiver of
  Generally . . . 5-1.1-A(e); 5-1.1(f)
  Intestate share of testator's estate, surviving spouse's right to . . . 5-1.3(c)
Wills executed after Aug. 31, 1930 and prior to Sept. 1, 1966 . . . 5-1.1(a)

[References are to SCPA and EPTL; if number contains dash (-), it refers to EPTL. Other references are preceded by the following abbreviations: Form–Official Forms; R–Court Rules; Tax L.–New York State Tax Law; MHL–Mental Hygiene Law; GOL–General Obligations Law; Pub. Health L.–Public Health Law.]

RIGHT OF ELECTION—Cont.
Wills executed after Aug. 31, 1966
   Generally . . . 5-1.1(c)
   Rules governing election under . . . 5-1.1(c)(1)

RULE AGAINST PERPETUITIES
Accumulations
   Generally . . . 9-2.1(b)
   Employers' trust for employees, from . . . 9-2.1
Age contingency, conditions for reduction of
   . . . 9-1.2
Childbearing capabilities . . . 9-1.3
Employers' trust for employees . . . 9-1.6
Intention of creator, assumption . . . 9-1.3
National securities exchange members, trust created for . . . 9-1.7
Powers of appointment
   Commencement of exercise of . . . 10-8.1
   Law governing exercise of . . . 10-8.2
Retirement plans . . . 9-2.1
Stated . . . 9-1.1
Vesting of estate, time for . . . 9-1.3
Violation of
   Foreign trust acquiring real property situated in this state, law determining validity
    . . . 9-1.4
   Transferable certificates, trust with, as violation . . . 9-1.5

S

SAFE DEPOSIT BOXES
Definition of company . . . 103(46)
Delivery of contents; nonresidents . . . R 360.3
Delivery of contents; residents
   Application for release . . . R 360.2(a)
   Copying of papers regarding burial . . . R 360.2(d)
   Will-search order
    Made . . . R 360.2(b)
    Not made . . . R 360.2(c)
Opening of
   Court fees for . . . 2402
   Order ex parte directing examination of contents of box . . . 2003
Order to examine . . . Form SD BOX-2
Petition to search . . . Form SD BOX; Form SD BOX-1
Small estates, discharge and release of company holding . . . 1305

SALE OF ESTATE PROPERTY (See PROPERTY (GENERALLY); REAL PROPERTY DISPOSITIONS)

SCPA
Construction of . . . 1312
Definitions for purposes of . . . 103
Electronic filing authorized, use of . . . 107
Provision of, method of citing . . . 101
Savings clause . . . 2804
Surrogate's Court Procedure Act cited as SCPA
   . . . 101

SECURITIES (See STOCKS AND SECURITIES)

SELF-PROVING AFFIDAVITS (See WILLS (GENERALLY))

SEPTEMBER ELEVENTH TERRORIST ATTACKS
Jurisdiction of surrogate's court over victim's estate . . . 205
Victims of Terrorism Tax Relief Act of 2001
   . . . Tax L. 951

SEPTEMBER ELEVENTH VICTIM COMPENSATION FUND OF 2001
Commissions for fiduciaries on awards from
   . . . 205; 2307
Personal representative of decedent, liability of
   . . . 11-4.7(e)
Workers' compensation law and . . . 11-4.7; 205

SERVICE OF PROCESS
Adoption proceedings, service in
   . . . 307(2)(a)(iv)
Agent designated to receive service, personal delivery to
   Completion of service, what constitutes
    . . . 309
   Court order for, authorization . . . 307
   Fiduciary, personal service on clerk of court as; time limit . . . 308
Beneficiary designated in will; probate requirement . . . 1403
Certified mail
   Completion of service . . . 309
   Court order for . . . 307
Citation (See CITATION)
Clerk of court, on
   Agent designated to receive service, as
    . . . 308
   Fiduciary status, personal service on
    . . . 308; 309

[References are to SCPA and EPTL; if number contains dash (-), it refers to EPTL. Other references are preceded by the following abbreviations: Form–Official Forms; R–Court Rules; Tax L.–New York State Tax Law; MHL–Mental Hygiene Law; GOL–General Obligations Law; Pub. Health L.–Public Health Law.]

SERVICE OF PROCESS—Cont.
Clerk of court, on—Cont.
  Grounds for . . . 708
  Personal service on fiduciary, status as
    . . . 309
Completion of service
  Generally . . . 309
  Time limits, commencement of period with
    completion . . . 308
Court order, by . . . 307
Creditors of decedent (See CREDITORS OF
  DECEDENT)
E-service . . . R 207.4-a(g); R 207.4-aa(c)
Fiduciaries (See FIDUCIARIES (GENER-
  ALLY))
Guardians *ad litem,* appointment of . . . 406
Incompetent persons, service on . . . 307;
  307(2)(a)(iv)
Infants, service on
  Generally . . . 307
  Completion of service . . . 309
Letters of administration . . . 1419
Mail
  Certified mail . . . 307; 309
  Completion of service . . . 309
  Court order for . . . 307
  Return receipt . . . 309
  Time of completion of service . . . 309
Nonresident alien, on (See NONRESIDENT
  ALIENS)
Other than natural persons, service on, methods
  . . . 307
Outside state, within United States, territories or
  possessions
  Authorization by law, requirement . . . 212
  Time limit on service . . . 308
Personal service
  Authorization of persons under CPLR 313
    . . . 310
  Completion of service . . . 309
Person under disability, designation of person to
  receive process for, court's power . . . 311
Place of service, extent of . . . 212
Probate proceedings (See PROBATE PRO-
  CEEDINGS)
Proof of service . . . 314
Public administrators . . . 310; 1123; 1214
Publication
  Completion of service, what constitutes
    . . . 309
  Court order for . . . 307; 307(2)(a)(iv)
  Return date for service . . . 308

SERVICE OF PROCESS—Cont.
Registered mail as method
  Completion of service, what constitutes
    . . . 309
  Court order for, authorization . . . 307
State, within
  Authorization . . . 212
  Time limit on service . . . 308
Substituted service
  Completion of service . . . 309
  Court order for . . . 307
Supplemental process to bring in additional par-
  ties, court's power to require . . . 312
Time limits on
  Clerk of court designated to receive service,
    personal service on fiduciary . . . 308
  Commencement of period, completion of,
    service as . . . 309
Unknown persons, service of, service on attor-
  ney general as method . . . 316

SEVERANCE OF ACTIONS
Generally . . . 501

SIGNIFICANT CONNECTION (See UNI-
  FORM ADULT GUARDIANSHIP AND PRO-
  TECTIVE PROCEEDINGS JURISDICTION
  ACT)

SIMULTANEOUS DEATH
Disposition of property where . . . 2-1.6(b)

SISTER OF DECEDENT (See BROTHERS
  AND SISTERS OF DECEDENT)

SMALL ESTATES
Accounting procedures . . . 1307
Bank, discharge and release of small estates by
  . . . 1305
Banks and banking (See BANKS AND BANK-
  ING)
Creditors of, defined . . . 1310
Debtor, discharge and release of small estates by
  . . . 1305; 1310
Debts payable to estate without administration
  . . . 1310
Defined . . . 1301(1)
Deposit of monies of, voluntary administrator's
  duty to make . . . 1307
Expenses of administration, payment of
  . . . 1307
Funeral expenses, estate paying . . . 1307
Letters not required for . . . 1115
Personal property of decedent
  Care facility, on deposit in . . . 1310

[References are to SCPA and EPTL; if number contains dash (-), it refers to EPTL. Other references are preceded by the following abbreviations: Form–Official Forms; R–Court Rules; Tax L.–New York State Tax Law; MHL–Mental Hygiene Law; GOL–General Obligations Law; Pub. Health L.–Public Health Law.]

[References are to SCPA and EPTL; if number contains dash (-), it refers to EPTL. Other references are preceded by the following abbreviations: Form–Official Forms; R–Court Rules; Tax L.–New York State Tax Law; MHL–Mental Hygiene Law; GOL–General Obligations Law; Pub. Health L.–Public Health Law.]

[References are to SCPA and EPTL; if number contains dash (-), it refers to EPTL. Other references are preceded by the following abbreviations: Form–Official Forms; R–Court Rules; Tax L.–New York State Tax Law; MHL–Mental Hygiene Law; GOL–General Obligations Law; Pub. Health L.–Public Health Law.]

TAXATION—Cont.

Income taxes—Cont.

Wrongful death actions . . . 5-4.3(1)

Marital deduction cases, recovery of gift taxes in . . . 2-1.12

Omission or redaction of confidential personal information in court submissions . . . R 207.64

Powers of attorney for tax matters, statutory short form . . . GOL 5-1502M

Proceedings for, court fees on filing for commencement of . . . 2402(3)

Real property

Priority of payment from decedent's estate . . . 1811

Transfer tax, disposition to pay . . . 1902

Reimbursement for taxes

Application of principal of trust to creator of trust as . . . 7-1.11(a), (b)

Future interests indefeasibly vested for exclusively public purposes . . . 7-1.11(b)

Temporary administrator, power to pay . . . 903

Wrongful death actions . . . 5-4.3(1)

TEMPORARY ADMINISTRATION OF ESTATES

Absentees allegedly deceased, of (See ABSENTEES)

Accounting by temporary administrator

Claims, payment of following . . . 908

Court's power in ordering . . . 908

Fiduciaries, as (See ACCOUNTINGS)

Filing of annual account, requirement . . . 910

Time for . . . 908

Actions by or against . . . 905

Appointment of (See subhead: Letters of temporary administration)

Bonding requirements

Generally (See FIDUCIARIES (GENERALLY))

Amount . . . 801

Dispensing with, consents required . . . 805

Exemptions . . . 801

Claims, payment of after issuance of letters, requirement . . . 906

General powers of temporary administrators . . . 903

Grounds for . . . 901

Interned person (See INTERNEES' ESTATES)

Letters of temporary administration

Petition for . . . 902

Revocation

Generally . . . 902

TEMPORARY ADMINISTRATION OF ESTATES—Cont.

Letters of temporary administration—Cont.

Revocation—Cont.

Alleged decedent's return (See ABSENTEES)

Direction for included in probate order . . . 1413

Distributee's liability for property received, effect of revocation order on . . . 721

Will subsequently admitted to probate as grounds . . . 721; 1413

Liability of temporary administrators . . . 903

Payment of claims after issuance of letters, requirement . . . 906

Real property, powers concerning . . . 903

Temporary administrator defined . . . 103(47)

TENANCY BY THE ENTIRETY (See also INTERNEES' ESTATES; JOINT TENANCY)

Absentee case, temporary administrator appointed, powers of . . . 903

Cooperative apartment corporation shares as . . . 6-2.1, 2.2

Creation of, real property disposition to husband and wife causing . . . 6-2.2

Internee case, temporary administrator appointed, powers of . . . 903

Parties not married, effect when . . . 6-2.2

TENANCY IN COMMON

Absentee case, powers of temporary administrator appointed in . . . 903

Cooperative apartment corporation shares as . . . 6-2.2

Creation of . . . 6-2.2

Cross remainders, implication of by will limitation . . . 6-5.4

Internee case, powers of temporary administrator appointed in . . . 903

TESTAMENTARY DISPOSITIONS

Abatement, order of (See ABATEMENT)

Ademption

Committee's conveyance of property made subject during competence . . . 3-4.4

Insurance proceeds from specific devise or legacy paid after death of testator . . . 3-4.5

Advance payments

Authorization; retention of sufficient assets to pay estate obligations as condition to . . . 11-1.5(a)

[References are to SCPA and EPTL; if number contains dash (-), it refers to EPTL. Other references are preceded by the following abbreviations: Form–Official Forms; R–Court Rules; Tax L.–New York State Tax Law; MHL–Mental Hygiene Law; GOL–General Obligations Law; Pub. Health L.–Public Health Law.]

TESTAMENTARY DISPOSITIONS—Cont.

Advance payments—Cont.

Beneficiary's action to compel payment . . . 2102

Direction in will, compliance with; fiduciary's right to require bond of recipient . . . 11-1.5(b)

Distribution of estate, adjustments for advance payments

Method . . . 2-1.5(c)

Property of testator, equitable adjustment from . . . 2-1.5(d)(1)

Valuation of advance payments . . . 2-1.5(d)(2)

Gift as, intention of testator, contemporaneous writing as required proof . . . 2-1.5(b)

Inclusion in estate for distribution purposes . . . 2-1.5(c)

Surviving spouse's elective share, effect on . . . 2-1.5(e)

Agreement to make disposition, writing requirement . . . 13-2.1

Attesting witness also beneficiary, grounds for voiding of disposition to . . . 3-3.2

Beneficiary's action to compel payment . . . 2102

Capacity to acquire and hold property, eligibility requirement for beneficiaries . . . 3-1.3(a)

Conditional dispositions

No-contest condition (See subhead: *In terrorem* clauses)

Validity, effect of failure to provide for alternative gift in event or nonoccurrence of condition . . . 3-3.5(a)

Conveyance of subject property

Agreement by testator to convey, no status as revocation of disposition . . . 3-4.2

Committee's conveyance of property . . . 3-4.4

Testator's conveyance of all or part of property, revocatory effect . . . 3-4.3

Demonstrative disposition

Defined . . . 1-2.3

General disposition, status as for abatement purposes . . . 13-1.3(c)

Specific disposition, status as for abatement purposes . . . 13-1.3(c)

Devises

Alteration

Choice-of-laws rule . . . 3-5.1(b)(1)

Non-domiciliary testator's election to have disposition governed by New York law, effect . . . 3-5.1(h)

Defined . . . 103(12)

TESTAMENTARY DISPOSITIONS—Cont.

Devises—Cont.

Devisee defined . . . 103(13)

Effect, choice-of-laws rule . . . 3-5.1(b)(1)

Interpretation, choice-of-laws rule . . . 3-5.1(b)(1)

Purchaser of subject property from distributee, title of, validity; limitations period on admission of will to probate . . . 3-3.8

Revocation, choice-of-laws rule . . . 3-5.1(b)(1)

Validity, choice-of-laws rule

Generally . . . 3-5.1(b)(1)

Non-domiciliary testator's election to have disposition governed by New York law, effect . . . 3-5.1(h)

Future interests as subject for . . . 6-5.1

General dispositions

Abatement, order of . . . 13-1.3(c)

"All property of testator," general disposition of, defined . . . 3-3.1

Defined . . . 1-2.8

Demonstrative disposition as; abatement purposes . . . 13-1.3(c)

Genetic children . . . 11-1.5(a) *et seq.*

In-kind distribution of (See IN-KIND DISTRIBUTIONS)

In terrorem clauses

Attesting witnesses . . . 3-3.5(b)(3)(D)

Construction of will or provision thereof . . . 3-3.5(b)(3)(E)

Disclosure of information relevant to alleged will or probate proceeding . . . 3-3.5(b)(3)(B)

Effectiveness, presence or absence of probable cause for contest as no factor . . . 3-3.5(b)

Forgery of will, effect of contest based on . . . 3-3.5(b)(1)

Incompetent persons, exemption for contest by . . . 3-3.5(b)(2)

Infants, exemption for contest by . . . 3-3.5(b)(2)

Jurisdiction of probate court, effect of objection to . . . 3-3.5(b)(3)(A)

Notice of probate proceeding, effect of refusal or failure to execute consent or waiver as to . . . 3-3.5(b)(3)(C)

Petition for probate, effect of nonjoinder in . . . 3-3.5(b)(3)(C)

Revocation of will by later will, effect of contest based on . . . 3-3.5(b)(1)

Joint tenants, disqualification as . . . 4-1.6

[References are to SCPA and EPTL; if number contains dash (-), it refers to EPTL. Other references are preceded by the following abbreviations: Form–Official Forms; R–Court Rules; Tax L.–New York State Tax Law; MHL–Mental Hygiene Law; GOL–General Obligations Law; Pub. Health L.–Public Health Law.]

TESTAMENTARY DISPOSITIONS—Cont.

Lapse of, ban on; dispositions to issue or brothers or sisters of testator . . . . 3-3.3(a)(1)

Legacies

  Alteration, choice-of-laws rule

    Generally . . . . 3-5.1(b)(2)

    Non-domiciliary testator's election to have law governed by New York law, effect . . . 3-5.1(h)

    Subsequent will or physical act to or on original will as . . . . 3-5.1(f)

  Payment by fiduciary (See subhead: Payment of legacies by fiduciary)

  Pecuniary legacy (See subhead: Pecuniary disposition)

  Revocation, choice-of-laws rule

    Generally . . . . 3-5.1(b)(2)

    Non-domiciliary testator's election to have disposition governed by New York law, effect . . . . 3-5.1(h)

    Subsequent will or physical act to or on original will as . . . . 3-5.1(f)

  Validity, choice-of-laws rule . . . . 3-5.1(b)(2)

Lifetime trust, dispositions to trustee

  Trust instrument, requirements . . . . 3-3.7(a)

  Validity . . . . 3-3.7(b)

Payment of legacies by fiduciary

  Advance payment by fiduciary (See subhead: Advance payments)

  Beneficiary's action to compel payment . . . 2102

  Foreign fiduciary, payment to 13-3.4; 2221

  Incompetent person, legacy of . . . 11-1.1(b)(19)

  Infant's legacy not exceeding $1,000, power of fiduciary . . . 11-1.1(b)(19)

  Preliminary executor's power, absence of . . . 1412

  Seven-month statutory period . . . 11-1.5; 11-A-2.1(3)

  Time for . . . . 11-1.5(a)

Pecuniary disposition

  Defined . . . . 2-1.9(a)(1)

  Fractional disposition . . . . 2-1.9(a)(2)

  In-kind distribution . . . . 2-1.9(b)(1), (2)

  Wills covered . . . . 2-1.9(c)

Per capita disposition, defined 1-2.11

Per stirpes disposition, defined 1-2.14

Powers of appointment, exercise of (See POWERS OF APPOINTMENT)

Property subject to

  Generally 3-1.2

TESTAMENTARY DISPOSITIONS—Cont.

Property subject to—Cont.

  Conveyance during lifetime of testator (See subhead: Conveyance of subject property)

  Future interests 6-5.1

Renunciation of

  Acceptance of property as bar to . . . 2-1.11(g)

  Deceased person, on behalf of . . . . 2-1.11(d)

  Disclaimer, validity of . . . 2-1.11(a)

  Disposition

    Defined . . . 2-1.11(b)

    Effective date . . . . 2-1.11(j)

  Effect . . . 2-1.11(e)

  Incompetent, on behalf of . . . 2-1.11(d)

  Infant, on behalf of . . . 2-1.11(d)

  Notice of . . . 2-1.11(c)

  Partial renunciation . . . 2-1.11(f)

  Procedure . . . 2-1.11(c)

  Revocation of renunciation . . . 2-1.11(h)

  Right to renounce . . . 2-1.11

  Successor letters testamentary and waiver of process

    Corporation . . . Form P-16; Form SLT-3

    Individual . . . Form P-15; Form SLT-2

  Time for . . . 2-1.11

  Unabridged rights of beneficiary . . . 2-1.11(i)

Residuary dispositions

  Abatement, order of . . . 13-1.3(c)

  Partly ineffective disposition to two or more residuary beneficiaries . . . 3-3.4

Revocation

  Agreement by testator to convey subject property, no status as revocation . . . 3-4.2

  Committee's conveyance of property made subject of specific disposition . . . 3-4.4

  Conveyance by testator of all or part of subject property as . . . 3-4.3

  Former spouse, dispositions to; divorce, annulment or other dissolution of marriage as revoking . . . 5-1.4

  Settlement or other act by testator affecting testator's interest in subject property as . . . 3-4.3

Seven-month period for payment of legacies by fiduciary . . . 11-1.5; 11-A-2.1(3)

Simultaneous death . . . 2-1.6(b)

Specific disposition

  Abatement, order of . . . 13-1.3(c)

  Committee's conveyance of property specifically disposed of by incompetent while competent, effect of . . . 3-4.4

  Defined . . . 1-2.17

[References are to SCPA and EPTL; if number contains dash (-), it refers to EPTL. Other references are preceded by the following abbreviations: Form–Official Forms; R–Court Rules; Tax L.–New York State Tax Law; MHL–Mental Hygiene Law; GOL–General Obligations Law; Pub. Health L.–Public Health Law.]

TESTAMENTARY DISPOSITIONS—Cont.

Specific disposition—Cont.

Delivery of subject property by fiduciary, beneficiary's action to compel . . . 2102

Demonstrative disposition as, abatement purposes . . . 13-1.3(c)

Encumbrances on subject property

Chargeability against property . . . . 3-3.6(b), (c)(1), (2)

No charge against assets of decedent's estate . . . 3-3.6(a)

Insurance proceeds from subject property paid after death of testator, no subject for ademption . . . 3-4.5

Sale or other disposition of property by preliminary executor; consent requirements . . . 1412

Successor letters testamentary (See PROBATE PROCEEDINGS, subhead: Successor letters testamentary)

Survival requirements . . . 2-1.6

Trustee of lifetime trust, dispositions to, rules governing . . . 3-3.7

Unincorporated associations, dispositions to, validity, prerequisites . . . 3-1.3(b)

Use, benefit and control . . . 2218

Waiver, right of election . . . 5-1.1(f)

Words of inheritance, no requirement to create fee . . . 2-1.4

TESTAMENTARY SUBSTITUTES (See RIGHT OF ELECTION)

TESTAMENTARY TRUSTEES

Account of, time for . . . 2208

Administrator-trustee

Letters of administration, revocation

Court order, effect on status as testamentary trustee . . . 720

Petition for, inclusion of prayer for removal in trustee capacity, authorization . . . 1505

Proceeding when testamentary trustee also executor . . . 1505

Resignation, petition for court permission to resign both capacities, authorization . . . 1505

Bonding requirement

Generally . . . 806

Amount of bond . . . 801(c)

Domiciliary's becoming non-domiciliary after issuance of letters, where objection based on . . . 710

TESTAMENTARY TRUSTEES—Cont.

Bonding requirement—Cont.

Failure to exercise fiduciary responsibility, where objection to grant of letters based on . . . 710

Non-domiciliary status, where objection to grant of letters based on . . . 710

Removal of estate property as grounds for . . . 710

Defined . . . 103(49)

Executor-trustee

Letters testamentary, revocation

Court order, effect on status as testamentary trustee . . . 720

Petition for, inclusion of prayer for removal in trustee capacity, authorization . . . 1505

Proceeding when testamentary trustee also executor . . . 1505

Resignation, petition for court permission to resign both capacities, authorization . . . 1505

Fiduciary, status as . . . 103(49)

Insolvency as grounds for suspension, modification or revocation of letters . . . 711; 719

Life insurance proceeds, trustee as beneficiary (See TRUSTEES, subhead: Life insurance proceeds, trustees as beneficiaries of)

Release of claims against state, appropriation of property by state as grounds for . . . 1508

Suspension or removal of . . . 714

Violation or threatened violation of trust as grounds for petition for suspension, modification or revocation of letters . . . 711; 719

War service, trustees in (See WAR SERVICE)

TESTAMENTARY TRUSTS

Administration expenses (See ADMINISTRATION EXPENSES)

Beneficiary of income from trust, termination of interest, income due to . . . 11-2.1(c)(4)

Bonds as part of . . . 11-2.1

Decanting of trusts . . . 10-6.6

Defined . . . 103(48)

Disposition by, renunciation of . . . 2-1.11

Expenses of settlement, principal of estate, to be charged against . . . 11-2.1(d)

Income of

Generally . . . 11-2.1(b)

Bonds issued at discount, accrued interest on as income . . . 11-2.1(f)

Charges to be made against . . . 11-2.1(l)

Corporate distributions as . . . 11-2.1(e)

[References are to SCPA and EPTL; if number contains dash (-), it refers to EPTL. Other references are preceded by the following abbreviations: Form–Official Forms; R–Court Rules; Tax L.–New York State Tax Law; MHL–Mental Hygiene Law; GOL–General Obligations Law; Pub. Health L.–Public Health Law.]

TESTAMENTARY TRUSTS—Cont.
Income of—Cont.
  Depletable property, receipts from, status as
    . . . 11-2.1(h)
  Income producing assets, receipts from
    . . . 11-2.1(c)(3)
  Interest paid on money lent, as income
    . . . 11-2.1(b)(1)(B)
  Natural resources, disposition of, receipts
    from as income . . . 11-2.1(h)
  Periodic payments not due at death of testator
    as income . . . 11-2.1(c)(2)
  Principal used in business, receipts from, sta-
    tus as . . . 11-2.1(g)
  Rents from property as . . . 11-2.1(b)(1)(A),
    (c)(2)
  Right to, when beneficiary entitled . . . 11-
    2.1(c)(1)
  Underproductive property, receipts from, sta-
    tus as . . . 11-2.1(k)
Joinder and representation of, persons interested
  in estate . . . 315
Non-domiciliary's will as creating, jurisdiction
  of Surrogate's Court over, determination of,
  factors in . . . 1501
Persons with disabilities, supplemental needs
  trusts established for . . . 7-1.12
Pets, for (See PETS, TRUSTS FOR)
Principal of
  Generally . . . 11-2.1(b)(2)
  Bonds, receipts from sale, redemption or
    other disposition . . . 11-2.1(f)(1)
  Change in form of principal, profit from, as
    principal . . . 11-2.1(b)(2)(H)
  Charges to be made against . . . 11-2.1(l)
  Depletable property, receipts from . . . 11-
    2.1(h)
  Eminent domain, property taken under, pro-
    ceeds from . . . 11-2.1(b)(2)(B)
  Expenses of settling estate to be charged
    against . . . 11-2.1(a)(1)
  Ineffective disposition to one or more benefi-
    ciaries . . . 2-1.15
  Insurance proceeds on property forming part
    of principal, as . . . 11-2.1(b)(2)(C)
  Natural resources, royalties from disposition
    of as principal . . . 11-2.1(h)
  Periodic payment not due at death of testator,
    portion accruing before death as principal
    . . . 11-2.1(c)(2)
  Powers of appointment, trustee's exercise of
    . . . 10-6.6
  Receipts due but not paid at death of testator
    . . . 11-2.1(c)(2)

TESTAMENTARY TRUSTS—Cont.
Principal of—Cont.
  Stock distributions as . . . 11-2.1(e)
  Residuary beneficiaries of, rent from property,
    entitlement to . . . 11-2.1(d)(3)(A)
  Supplemental needs trusts established for per-
    sons with disabilities . . . 7-1.12
  Surrogate's court's jurisdiction over, grounds for
    . . . 1501
  Underproductive property in (See UNDERPRO-
    DUCTIVE PROPERTY)

TITLE PERFECTION
Death; title passing to surviving spouse . . . 6-
  6.4

TOTTEN TRUSTS
Generally . . . Art. 7, Part 5
Application . . . 7-5.8
Definitions . . . 7-5.1
Effect of payment . . . 7-5.4
Joint depositors . . . 7-5.6
Multiple beneficiaries, proportions passing to
  . . . 7-5.7
Payment to beneficiary . . . 7-5.3
Right of election of spouse, subject to . . . 5-
  1.1(b)
Rights not affected . . . 7-5.5
Terms . . . 7-5.2

TRANSFER OF PROCEEDINGS
Any court, transferability from, bar to supreme
  court . . . 501
Domiciliaries' estates; Surrogate's Courts
  . . . 205
Lifetime trust proceedings; Surrogate's Courts
  . . . 207
Motion initiating transfer . . . 501
Non-domiciliaries' estates; Surrogate's Court
  . . . 206
Supreme court, transfer from . . . 501

**TRANSFER-ON-DEATH SECURITY REGIS-
  TRATION ACT**
Appearance of registration in beneficiary form
  . . . 13-4.5
Applicable law . . . 13-4.3
Application of . . . 13-4.12
Definitions . . . 13-4.1
Nontestamentary transfer . . . 13-4.9
Origin of registration . . . 13-4.4
Ownership
  Death of owner . . . 13-4.7
  Effect on . . . 13-4.6
Registering entity, protection of . . . 13-4.8

[References are to SCPA and EPTL; if number contains dash (-), it refers to EPTL. Other references are preceded by the following abbreviations: Form–Official Forms; R–Court Rules; Tax L.–New York State Tax Law; MHL–Mental Hygiene Law; GOL–General Obligations Law; Pub. Health L.–Public Health Law.]

TRUSTEES—Cont.
Successor trustee—Cont.
    Security to be given by . . . 7-2.3(b)(1)
    War service, trustee engaged in (See WAR SERVICE)
Testamentary trustees (See TESTAMENTARY TRUSTEES)
Three or more trustees . . . 10-10.7
Transfer of money or property to, misapplication of by trustee, liability of transferor . . . 7-3.3
Trusts, two or more created by same instrument, power of trustee to hold as an undivided whole . . . 11-1.1(b)(18)
Two or more trustees
    Commissions allowed to, value of principal of estate or income of estate as determining . . . 2308; 2309
    Distribution of principal or allocation of income, power conferred upon . . . 10-10.1
Verification, oath and designation; official form . . . Form P-1
Violation of trust as grounds for removal of . . . 7-2.6
War service, trustee engaged in (See WAR SERVICE)

TRUSTS
Administration of . . . 8-1.8
Charitable (See CHARITABLE TRUSTS)
Compromise of controversies, application for . . . 2106
Creator of
    Interest remaining in . . . 7-1.7
    Non-domiciliary creator, law of state governing trust provision . . . 7-1.10
    Principal of trust as reimbursement for taxes paid by . . . 7-1.11
Decanting of trusts . . . 10-6.6
Definition of trust for purposes of IRC of 1954 . . . 8-1.8
Division of trusts and establishment of separate trusts . . . 7-1.13
Establishment of . . . 7-1.4
Estates, powers and trust law, amendment to . . . 7-1.19
Gifts to minors by . . . 7-6.5
Income beneficiaries of, application of principal to . . . 7-1.6
Invasion of principal . . . 10-6.6
Lifetime trusts (See LIFETIME TRUSTS)
Merger of interests . . . 7-1.1
Persons with disabilities, supplemental needs trusts established for . . . 7-1.12
Pets, for (See PETS, TRUSTS FOR)

TRUSTS—Cont.
Private foundation . . . 8-1.8
Public inspection . . . 8-1.8
QTIP trusts, apportionment of . . . 2-1.8(d)(1)
Revocation of trust, procedure for . . . 7-1.9
Separate trusts, establishment of . . . 7-1.13
Supplemental needs trusts established for persons with disabilities . . . 7-1.12
Termination of uneconomical trust, application for
    Generally . . . 7-1.19(a)(1)
    Charitable deduction, elimination of . . . 7-1.19(c)
    Economic impracticability of . . . 7-1.19(a)(2)
    Notice . . . 7-1.19(b)
    Supplemental needs trust; not applicable to . . . 7-1.19(d)
Testamentary trusts (See TESTAMENTARY TRUSTS)
Transfer of income from by beneficiary . . . 7-1.5

U

UNBORN PERSONS
Remaindermen as, service of process to . . . 315

UNDERPRODUCTIVE PROPERTY
Defined . . . 11-2.1(k)(1)
Delayed income from transactions with respect to
    Computation of . . . 11-2.1(k)(2)
    Income beneficiaries' entitlement to
        Generally . . . 11-2.1(k)(1)
        Accrual date . . . 11-2.1(k)(3)
    Sum allocated as delayed income, method of computing . . . 11-2.1(k)
Dispositions
    Conversion into property which cannot be apportioned easily, income beneficiaries' entitlement to net income from . . . 11-2.1(k)(4)
    Net proceeds from, computation . . . 11-2.1(k)(1)

UNEMPLOYMENT INSURANCE
Generally . . . 1311

UNIFORM ADULT GUARDIANSHIP AND PROTECTIVE PROCEEDINGS JURISDICTION ACT
Appointment of guardian
    Definitions . . . MHL 83.03

[References are to SCPA and EPTL; if number contains dash (-), it refers to EPTL. Other references are preceded by the following abbreviations: Form–Official Forms; R–Court Rules; Tax L.–New York State Tax Law; MHL–Mental Hygiene Law; GOL–General Obligations Law; Pub. Health L.–Public Health Law.]

UNIFORM GIFTS TO MINORS ACT (UGMA) (See also UNIFORM TRANSFERS TO MINORS ACT (UTMA))—Cont.

Construction of statute
  Exclusivity of prescribed methods . . . 7-4.12(b)
  Expiration . . . 7-4.12(d)
  Personal property law, applicability to gifts under . . . 7-4.12(c)
  Purpose . . . 7-4.12(a)
"Court" defined . . . 7-4.1(d)
Custodial property
  Application by custodian, duty of third person in . . . 7-4.6
  Collection of . . . 7-4.4(a)
  Death of minor prior to age 21, effect of . . . 7-4.4(d)
  Defined . . . 7-4.1(e)(1) *et seq.*
  Delivery to minor on attainment of majority . . . 7-4.4(d)
  Education, use for . . . 7-4.4(c)
  Holding of, power of custodian . . . 7-4.4(a)
  Investment powers
    Generally . . . 7-4.4(a)
    Prudent-man rule . . . 7-4.4(e)
  Management of . . . 7-4.4
  Recordkeeping requirements . . . 7-4.4(h)
  Sale or other disposition
    Power of custodian . . . 7-4.4(f)
    Validity or propriety, duty of third persons to inquire into . . . 7-4.6
  Securities (See subhead: Securities, gift of)
  Segregation of . . . 7-4.4(g)
  Support, maintenance and education of minor, use for
    Court order for payment to minor over 14 on application of parent or guardian . . . 7-4.4(c)
    Discretionary power of custodian . . . 7-4.4(b)
    When expended . . . 7-4.4(k)
Custodians
  Accountings by
    Court's power to require . . . 7-4.8(b)
    Guardians *ad litem* for minor . . . 7-4.8(c)
    Petition for, eligibility to file . . . 7-4.8(a)
    Removed custodians . . . 7-4.8(b)
  Acts of, validity or propriety, inquiry into, no duty of third persons . . . 7-4.6
  Age of minor, payment dependent on . . . 7-4.4(d)

UNIFORM GIFTS TO MINORS ACT (UGMA) (See also UNIFORM TRANSFERS TO MINORS ACT (UTMA))—Cont.

Custodians—Cont.
  Bond, furnishing by or removal and designation of successor, petition for
    Filing, eligibility for . . . 7-4.7(e)
    Grant of order by court . . . 7-4.7(f)
  Compensation
    Liability, compensated custodian subject to . . . 7-4.5(f)
    No requirement, persons other than trustee, or guardian . . . 7-4.5(b)
    Requirement, trust company or guardian serving as custodian . . . 7-4.5(c)
  Death prior to minor's attainment of majority (See subhead: Successor custodian)
  Designation of, propriety, determination, liability of third persons . . . 7-4.6
  Designee's ineligibility to serve, guardian of minor as successor . . . 7-4.7(d)
  Duties of . . . 7-4.4
  Expenses, reimbursement for . . . 7-4.5(a)
  Guardian of minor as successor . . . 7-4.7(d)
  Incapacitation of . . . 7-4.7(d)
  Legal incapacity prior to minor's attainment of majority . . . 7-4.7(d)
  Liability of, compensated and uncompensated custodian distinguished . . . 7-4.5(e), (f)
  One custodian, restriction to . . . 7-4.2(b)
  Powers of . . . 7-4.4
  Prompt delivery of gift to, duty of donor . . . 7-4.2(c)
  Removal of or furnishing of bond by, petition for
    Filing, eligibility for . . . 7-4.7(e)
    Grant of order by court . . . 7-4.7(f)
    Successor custodian designated on grant of removal, giving of bond by, court's power to require . . . 7-4.7(g)
  Removed custodian, accounting by, requirement . . . 7-4.8(b)
  Resignation of, designation of successor custodian . . . 7-4.7
  Rights and immunities . . . 7-4.3(b)
  Successor custodian (See subhead: Successor custodian)
  Uncompensated custodians, liability, extent of . . . 7-4.5(e)
Effect of gift to minor . . . 7-4.3
Expiration of statute . . . 7-4.12(d)
"Financial institution" defined . . . 7-4.1(g)
Guardian (See GUARDIANS)

Index

[References are to SCPA and EPTL; if number contains dash (-), it refers to EPTL. Other references are preceded by the following abbreviations: Form–Official Forms; R–Court Rules; Tax L.–New York State Tax Law; MHL–Mental Hygiene Law; GOL–General Obligations Law; Pub. Health L.–Public Health Law.]

UNIFORM RULES FOR SURROGATE'S COURT—Cont.

Electronic filing—Cont.
  Mandatory program—Cont.
    Commencement of proceedings . . . R 207.4-aa(b)
    Exemption from requirement of electronic filing . . . R 207.4-aa(e)
    Filing and service of documents after commencement of proceedings . . . R 207.4-aa(c)
    Hard copies of documents, refusal to accept . . . R 207.4-aa(d)
Estate tax
  Filing of return . . . R 207.43
  Payment of . . . R 207.44
Family tree as proof of distributee . . . R 207.16; R 207.17; R 207.19
File number, clerk's . . . R 207.4
Filing of papers . . . R 207.4
Foreign consul, notification to as to alien's estate . . . R 207.21
Forms, use of local court's on interim basis . . . R 207.52
Guardians
  Affidavit as to interest in estate . . . R 207.51
  Annual accounts, reference to SCPA 1719, requirement . . . R 207.11(b)
  Settlement proceedings . . . R 207.11(c)
  Two or more infants, appointment for . . . R 207.11(a)
Guardians *ad litem*
  Allowances to . . . R 207.13(c)
  Appointment of . . . R 207.12
  Notice to . . . R 207.19(d)
  Objection to accounting, filing of . . . R 207.41
  Qualification of . . . R 207.13
Infants' fund . . . R 207.14
Jury trials
  Order for . . . R 207.31
  Transfer of proceedings . . . R 207.6
Kinship matters . . . R 207.16, R 207.17, R 207.19, R 207.25
Letters of administration . . . R 207.17
Local courts . . . R 207.52
Nonmarital children, statement as to . . . R 207.16(a)
Note of issue, filing of . . . R 207.29(a)
Oral argument . . . R 207.7(f), (g)
Personal injury action, compromise of claim for . . . R 207.38

UNIFORM RULES FOR SURROGATE'S COURT—Cont.

Petitions, content
  Nonmarital children . . . R 207.16(a)
  Relationship to decedent . . . R 207.16(b)
  SCPA 304 requirements . . . R 207.16(a)
Pleadings, demand for . . . R 207.10
Powers of appointment . . . R 207.19(e)
Powers of attorney, recording of . . . R 207.48
Pretrial conference . . . R 207.29(b)
Pretrial examination of witnesses in contested probate proceedings . . . R 207.27
Relationship of distributees to decedent, statement and proof of . . . R 207.16; R 207.17; R 207.19; R 207.25
Removal of papers . . . R 207.8
Rules . . . R 207.1(c)
SCPA, relation to . . . R 207.1(d)
Service of paper or notice . . . R 207.7
Settlement, notice of . . . R 207.37
Signature, submission of; orders, judgments and decrees . . . R 207.37
Special rules . . . R 207.1
Statement of issues . . . R 207.30
Submission of papers . . . R 207.5
Surviving spouse . . . R 207.50
Terms of court . . . R 207.2
Transfer of proceedings . . . R 207.6
Unknown distributees, affidavit as to . . . R 207.19(c)
Virtual representation, use of . . . R 207.18
Waiver . . . R 207.1(b)
Wills . . . R 207.19
Witnesses
  Examination of . . . R 207.28
  Notice required before taking deposition or testimony . . . R 207.19(d)
  Out of county witnesses . . . R 207.22
  Pretrial examination in contested probate proceedings . . . R 207.27
Wrongful death action, compromise of claim for . . . R 207.38

UNIFORM TRANSFERS TO MINORS ACT (UTMA) (See also UNIFORM GIFTS TO MINORS ACT (UGMA))
Accounting by custodian . . . 7-6.19
Age of minor
  Age 18 election . . . 7-6.21
  Termination of custodianship . . . 7-6.20(a), (b)
Application of statute . . . 7-6.23; 7-6.24
Construction of statute . . . 7-6.24

[References are to SCPA and EPTL; if number contains dash (-), it refers to EPTL. Other references are preceded by the following abbreviations: Form–Official Forms; R–Court Rules; Tax L.–New York State Tax Law; MHL–Mental Hygiene Law; GOL–General Obligations Law; Pub. Health L.–Public Health Law.]

UNIFORM TRANSFERS TO MINORS ACT (UTMA) (See also UNIFORM GIFTS TO MINORS ACT (UGMA))—Cont.

Custodial property
  Care of . . . 7-6.12
  Control, transfer of . . . 7-6.9(c)
  Creation of . . . 7-6.9(a)
  Delivery to minor, discretion in . . . 7-6.14
  Existing custodianships, effect of act upon . . . 7-6.22
  Form for effecting transfer . . . 7-6.9(b)
  Investment of . . . 7-6.12(c)
  Receipt for . . . 7-6.8
  Recordkeeping requirements . . . 7-6.12(e)
  Separate accounts, requirement for . . . 7-6.12(d)
Custodians
  Accountings . . . 7-6.19
  Bond . . . 7-6.15(c)
  Care of property . . . 7-6.12
  Compensation . . . 7-6.15(b)
  Death . . . 7-6.18
  Effective date of custodianship . . . 7-6.3(c)
  Expenses, reimbursement for . . . 7-6.15(a)
  Investments by . . . 7-6.12(c)
  Jurisdiction over . . . 7-6.2(b)
  Liability . . . 7-6.13(b); 7-6.19(a)
  Nomination . . . 7-6.3
  Personal representative, designation by . . . 7-6.5(c)
  Powers . . . 7-6.13
  Receipt from . . . 7-6.8
  Recordkeeping requirements . . . 7-6.12(e)
  Removal . . . 7-6.18
  Renunciation . . . 7-6.18
  Resignation . . . 7-6.18
  Separate accounts, maintenance of . . . 7-6.12(d)
  Single custodianship, requirement for . . . 7-6.10
  Substitute custodian, nomination of . . . 7-6.3(b)
  Successor custodian, designation of . . . 7-6.18
  Termination of custodianship . . . 7-6.20
  Trustee, designation by . . . 7-6.5(c)
Death of minor, termination of custodianship upon . . . 7-6.20(c)
Definitions under statute . . . 7-6.1
Existing custodianships, effect of act upon . . . 7-6.22
Fiduciaries, transfers by
  Designation of custodian . . . 7-6.5(c)
  Discretionary . . . 7-6.6

UNIFORM TRANSFERS TO MINORS ACT (UTMA) (See also UNIFORM GIFTS TO MINORS ACT (UGMA))—Cont.

Fiduciaries, transfers by—Cont.
  Trust instrument, authorized by . . . 7-6.5
Form for effecting transfer . . . 7-6.9(b)
Gift, transfers by . . . 7-6.4
Guardians, transfers by . . . 7-6.6(b), (c)
Incorporation of provisions of statute . . . 7-6.11(c)
Jurisdiction
  Custodian, over . . . 7-6.2(b)
  Other state, transactions in . . . 7-6.2(c)
Liability under
  Custodians . . . 7-6.13(b); 7-6.19(a)
  Third parties . . . 7-6.16; 7-6.17
Obligors, transfers by . . . 7-6.7
Powers of appointment, transfers by exercise of . . . 7-6.4
Receipt for . . . 7-6.8
Revocability of transfers . . . 7-6.11(b)
Scope . . . 7-6.2
Severability of parts of statute . . . 7-6.26
Termination of custodianship . . . 7-6.20
Title of act . . . 7-6.25
Trustees, transfers by
  Designation of custodian . . . 7-6.5(c)
  Discretionary . . . 7-6.6
  Trust instrument, authorized by . . . 7-6.5
Trust, transfers by . . . 7-6.5
Validity of transfers . . . 7-6.11(a)
Will, transfers by . . . 7-6.5

UNINCORPORATED ASSOCIATIONS

Testamentary disposition to
  Generally . . . 3-1.3(b)
  Charitable dispositions, limitations on . . . 3-1.3(b)(6)
  Court's power to effect intention of testator . . . 3-1.3(b)(1)
  Failure to incorporate within three-year period
    Rents, profits and other income from property accrued during period, effect on . . . 3-1.3(b)(3)
    Transfer of property to persons entitled thereto, duty of trustee . . . 3-1.3(b)(2)
  Incorporation within three-year period
    Rents, profits or other income accrued prior to incorporation, transfer to corporation, duty of trustee . . . 3-1.3(b)(3)
    Transfer of property to corporation, duty of trustee . . . 3-1.3(b)(2)
  Incorporation within three years after probate of will as prerequisite . . . 3-1.3(b)(2)

UNINCORPORATED ASSOCIATIONS—Cont.

Testamentary disposition to—Cont.

Trust for benefit of association during period for incorporation

Creation of . . . 3-1.3(b)(2)

Enforcement of trust, right of unincorporated association . . . 3-1.3(b)(5)

Income accumulations rule, no effect on validity . . . 3-1.3(b)(4)

Jurisdiction of Surrogate's Court over . . . 3-1.3(b)(2)

Renunciation of disposition during continuance of trust, effect of . . . 3-1.3(b)(5)

Rule against perpetuities; effect on validity . . . 3-1.3(b)(4)

Termination of trust, renunciation of disposition by association as grounds for . . . 3-1.3(b)(5)

Validity . . . 3-1.3(b)(4)

UNITED STATES

Obligations and securities of, fiduciaries' power to invest in . . . 11-2.2

Savings bonds of, non-transferable; no impairment of rights of payee . . . 13-3.1

UNKNOWN PERSONS

Abandoned property of . . . 2223

Citations, included in . . . 306

Court, payment of share to

Generally . . . 2223; 2224

Time for . . . 2223

Deposit of money to account of, proceeding to effect

Generally . . . 1123; 1215

Notice to corporation counsel of pending proceeding, requirements . . . 1125

Service on, sufficiency of . . . 1125

Distributee, as . . . 1213

Distribution of monies or property deposited for account of, authority of public administrator, procedure . . . 1123

Funds deposited for account of, recovery and distribution of amounts recovered, power of public administrator . . . 1123; 1213

Intestate administration, dispensing of service of process in unknown person cases . . . 1003

Legacy or distributive share payable to . . . 2222

Liability of fiduciary, discharge from . . . 2224

"Person under disability," status as . . . 103(40)

UNKNOWN PERSONS—Cont.

Petitions, description of unknown person included . . . 304

Probate proceedings, notice requirements for . . . 1409

Process, issuance of . . . 316

Public administrator, power over funds deposited for account of, recovery and distribution of amounts recovered . . . 1123; 1213

Remainderman, unknown person as, service of process to . . . 315

V

VALUATION OF ESTATE

Adjustment of fees when actual value differs from petition statement . . . 2402

Civil penalties for understatement of . . . Tax L. 992(a)

Court proceedings or documents involving estate, use . . . 2402(1), (2)

Notification of court subsequent to letters, administrator's rules . . . 725

Understatement of, civil penalties for . . . Tax L. 992(a)

VICTIMS OF TERRORISM TAX RELIEF ACT OF 2001

Generally . . . Tax L. 951

VOLUNTARY ADMINISTRATOR

Checklist . . . V-CHKLST

Small estates (See SMALL ESTATES, subhead: Voluntary administrator)

Validity of purchase . . . 3-3.8

W

WAIVER

Appearance by waiver of process . . . 401

Guardian appointment of; waiver of process . . . Form GMD-3

Spouse's election . . . 5-1.1(f)

Standby guardians, appointment of; waiver of process . . . Form SG-3

WAR SERVICE

Appointment of fiduciaries engaged in, prayer for . . . 717

Co-fiduciary with original nominee, appointment as . . . 718

Defined

EPTL . . . 7-2.5(b)

SCPA . . . 717

[References are to SCPA and EPTL; if number contains dash (-), it refers to EPTL. Other references are preceded by the following abbreviations: Form–Official Forms; R–Court Rules; Tax L.–New York State Tax Law; MHL–Mental Hygiene Law; GOL–General Obligations Law; Pub. Health L.–Public Health Law.]

[References are to SCPA and EPTL; if number contains dash (-), it refers to EPTL. Other references are preceded by the following abbreviations: Form–Official Forms; R–Court Rules; Tax L.–New York State Tax Law; MHL–Mental Hygiene Law; GOL–General Obligations Law; Pub. Health L.–Public Health Law.]

[References are to SCPA and EPTL; if number contains dash (-), it refers to EPTL. Other references are preceded by the following abbreviations: Form–Official Forms; R–Court Rules; Tax L.–New York State Tax Law; MHL–Mental Hygiene Law; GOL–General Obligations Law; Pub. Health L.–Public Health Law.]

WILLS (GENERALLY)—Cont.
Witnesses—Cont.
  Intestate share, receipt of by, provisions governing . . . 3-3.2
  Legacy or devise to
    Competency of witness to testify as to execution of will, effect on . . . 3-3.2(a)
    Validity of disposition, conditions to . . . 3-3.2(a)(1), (2)
    Void legacy or devise, disposition of . . . 3-3.2(a)(3)
  Number required . . . 3-2.1(a)(4)
  Persons signing for testator, no status as witness . . . 3-2.1(a)(1)(C)
  Signature to, requirements . . . 3-2.1
  Writing requirement . . . 3-2.1

WORKMEN'S COMPENSATION
Generally . . . 1311
September eleventh victim compensation fund of 2001 and . . . 11-4.7; 205

WRONGFUL DEATH ACTIONS
Account by administrator . . . Form WD-3
Administrators (See ADMINISTRATORS)
Amount of recovery, items to be included
  Generally . . . 5-4.3
  Income taxes, decedent's, consideration of . . . 5-4.3(1)
Attorney's affidavit . . . Form WD-4
Citation in
  Official form . . . Form WD-1
  Waiver of issue and service of . . . Forms WD-5, WD-6
Compromise of action by fiduciary . . . 2204
Compromise Settlement Proceeding Checklist . . . WDCS-CHK
Contributory negligence . . . 5-4.2

WRONGFUL DEATH ACTIONS—Cont.
Criminal actions against defendant . . . 5-4.1
Damages
  Amount of damages
    Income taxes of decedent . . . 5-4.3(1)
    Itemization . . . 5-4.3
  Distribution of . . . 5-4.4(a)
  Fiduciary of decedent, action by . . . 5-4.1; 5-4.3
  Pecuniary injuries . . . 5-4.4(a)(2)
  Punitive damages . . . 5-4.3
Family rights (See FAMILY RIGHTS)
Fiduciary of decedent
  Action by . . . 5-4.1
  Punitive damages . . . 5-4.3
  Refusal to bring action, distributee's right to appointment of administrator to prosecute action for benefit . . . 5-4.1
Insurance company's waiver and consent . . . Form WD-5
Judgment proceeds, fiduciary's petition for judicial settlement of account . . . 2204
Non-domiciliary leaving country during proceeding against domiciliary, jurisdiction in . . . 206
Personal injury action, consolidation with . . . 11-3.3
Personal property in county of domiciliary's residence, debt as, action in favor of non-domiciliary
  Generally . . . 5-4.4(a)
  Pecuniary injuries suffered by distributees . . . 5-4.4(a)(2)
Petition for . . . Form WD-2
Settlement of account, decree as to . . . Form WD-7
Waiver and consent forms . . . Forms WD-5, WD-6

Notes

Notes

Notes

Notes

Notes

Notes

Notes

Notes

Notes

Notes

Notes

Notes

Notes

Notes

Notes

Notes

Notes

Notes

Notes

Notes

Notes

Notes

Notes

Notes

Notes

Notes